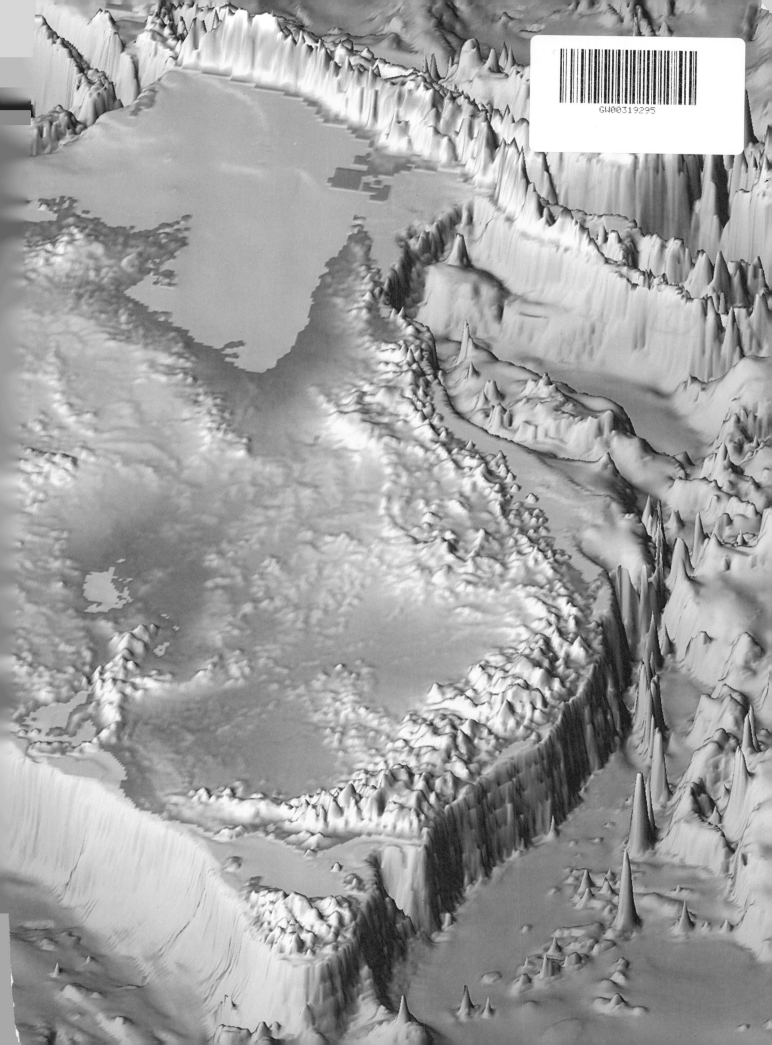

~ 2003 ~ to David & Sarah

Thanks for your friendship ~

AND you must use this book

All our love

Pino & Amanda ~ Sam

Hello to Will & Jack ~

Gregory's

The Essential
Touring Atlas

AUSTRALIA

Published in Australia by Gregory's Publishing Company
(A division of Universal Press Pty Ltd)
ABN 83 000 087 132

Marketed and distributed by Universal Press Pty Ltd
New South Wales: 1 Waterloo Road, Macquarie Park 2113
Ph: (02) 9857 3700 Fax: (02) 9888 9850

Queensland: 1 Manning Street, South Brisbane 4101
Ph: (07) 3844 1051 Fax: (07) 3844 4637

South Australia: Freecall: 1800 021 987

Victoria: 585 Burwood Road, Hawthorn 3122
Ph: (03) 9818 4455 Fax: (03) 9818 6123

Western Australia: 38a Walters Drive, Osborne Park 6017
Ph: (08) 9244 2488 Fax: (08) 9244 2554

International distribution
Ph: (61) 2 9857 3700 Fax: (61) 2 9888 9850

ISBN: 0 7319 15828

Publishing Manager: David Jackson

Production Manager: Harold Yates

DTP & Design Manager: Bronwynne Davis

Project Editor: Susan Page

Cover Design: Mike Moule

Internal Design: *Dizign*

DTP/Layout: Bronwynne Davis

Text Research and Writing: Kellie Firth, Justine Joffe, Germaine Leece, Grant Nichol, Greg Reid

Copy Editing: Jonathan Eagleton, Shelley Kenisburg, Grant Nichol, Greg Reid, Paul Ritchard

Cartographic Manager: Harold Yates

Cartographic Research: Ray Kerkin, Grant Nichol

Cartography: Steve Elliott, Frank Guerreiro, Robyn Hinchliffe, Harold Yates

Indexing: Glenda Browne

Front and Back End Papers: Laurie Whiddon, Map Illustrations

Photographic Researcher: Grant Nichol

Pre-Press: Graphic Skills (Sunshine Coast)

Printed by: Sing Cheong Printing Co. Ltd

Disclaimer

Stonehaven Bay on Hook Island, The Whitsundays, Queensland

CONTENTS

Australia

Queensland

216

South Australia

288

Western Australia

350

Northern Territory

408

Tasmania

444

MAP SYMBOLS

City

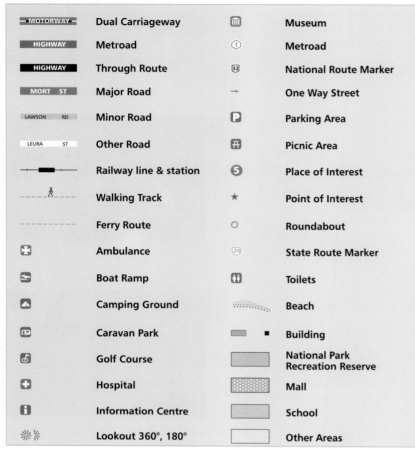

MOTORWAY	Dual Carriageway	🏛	Museum
HIGHWAY	Metroad	①	Metroad
HIGHWAY	Through Route	32	National Route Marker
MORT ST	Major Road	→	One Way Street
LAWSON RD	Minor Road	P	Parking Area
LEURA ST	Other Road	🎋	Picnic Area
	Railway line & station	⑤	Place of Interest
	Walking Track	★	Point of Interest
	Ferry Route	○	Roundabout
✚	Ambulance	20	State Route Marker
	Boat Ramp	⛨	Toilets
	Camping Ground		Beach
	Caravan Park	▭ ▪	Building
	Golf Course	▭	National Park Recreation Reserve
✚	Hospital	▦	Mall
i	Information Centre	▭	School
※※	Lookout 360°, 180°	▭	Other Areas

Suburban

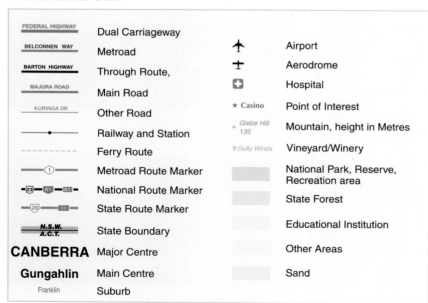

FEDERAL HIGHWAY	Dual Carriageway	✈	Airport
BELCONNEN WAY	Metroad	✚	Aerodrome
BARTON HIGHWAY	Through Route,	✚	Hospital
MAJURA ROAD	Main Road	★ Casino	Point of Interest
KURINGA DR	Other Road	+ Glebe Hill 135	Mountain, height in Metres
	Railway and Station	⚒ Gully Winds	Vineyard/Winery
	Ferry Route		National Park, Reserve, Recreation area
①—	Metroad Route Marker		
23 A1 A1	National Route Marker		State Forest
20 C1	State Route Marker		Educational Institution
N.S.W. A.C.T.	State Boundary		Other Areas
CANBERRA	Major Centre		Sand
Gungahlin	Main Centre		
Franklin	Suburb		

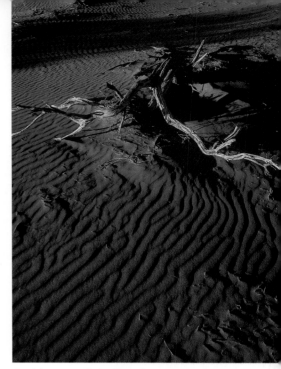

Sand-dune texture in the Gibson Desert, Western Australia

Sydney icons—the Opera House and Harbour Bridge New South Wales

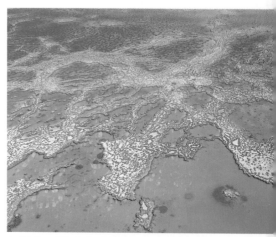

Aerial view of Hardy Reef, Great Barrier Reef, Queensland

KEY TO ATLAS

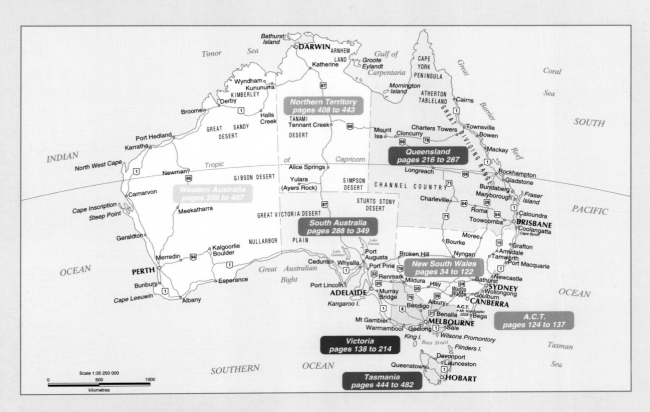

State and Regional

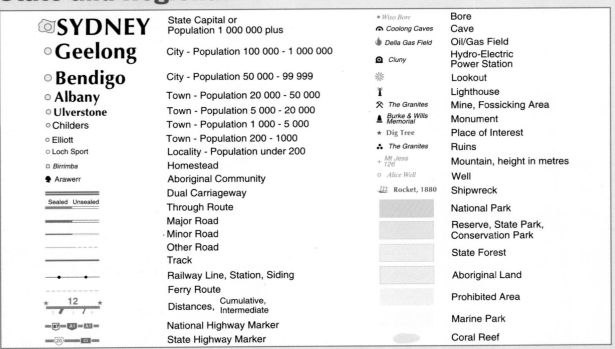

⊚ **SYDNEY**	State Capital or Population 1 000 000 plus
◎ **Geelong**	City - Population 100 000 - 1 000 000
◎ **Bendigo**	City - Population 50 000 - 99 999
◎ **Albany**	Town - Population 20 000 - 50 000
◎ Ulverstone	Town - Population 5 000 - 20 000
◎ Childers	Town - Population 1 000 - 5 000
◎ Elliott	Town - Population 200 - 1000
◦ Loch Sport	Locality - Population under 200
▫ Birrimba	Homestead
♣ Arawerr	Aboriginal Community
	Dual Carriageway
	Through Route
	Major Road
	Minor Road
	Other Road
	Track
	Railway Line, Station, Siding
	Ferry Route
★ 12 ★	Distances, Cumulative, Intermediate
87 A1 A1	National Highway Marker
20 C3	State Highway Marker

• Wiso Bore	Bore
⌒ Coolong Caves	Cave
◖ Della Gas Field	Oil/Gas Field
◙ Cluny	Hydro-Electric Power Station
❉	Lookout
⌁	Lighthouse
⚒ The Granites	Mine, Fossicking Area
▲ Burke & Wills Memorial	Monument
★ Dig Tree	Place of Interest
⁂ The Granites	Ruins
+ Mt Jess 126	Mountain, height in metres
◦ Alice Well	Well
⧟ Rocket, 1880	Shipwreck
	National Park
	Reserve, State Park, Conservation Park
	State Forest
	Aboriginal Land
	Prohibited Area
	Marine Park
	Coral Reef

CP = Conservation Park; CR = Conservation Reserve; NP = National Park, SF = State Forest; SP = State Park; SRA = State Recreation Area

INTERCITY DISTANCE CHART

Approximate Distance	Adelaide SA	Albany WA	Albury NSW	Alice Springs NT	Ayers Rock/Yulara NT	Bairnsdale VIC	Ballarat VIC	Bathurst NSW	Bega NSW	Bendigo VIC	Bordertown SA	Bourke NSW	Brisbane QLD	Broken Hill NSW	Broome WA	Bunbury WA	Cairns QLD	Canberra ACT	Carnarvon WA	Ceduna SA	Charleville QLD	Coober Pedy SA	Darwin NT	Dubbo NSW	Esperance WA
Adelaide SA		2642	932	1526	1570	1006	611	1183	1329	770	267	1129	2054	514	4242	2855	2964	1153	3556	769	1583	837	3018	1175	2168
Albany WA	2642		357	3558	3602	3648	3253	3664	3810	3251	2909	3366	4291	2751	2582	361	5201	3634	1292	1873	3820	2869	4375	3503	474
Albury NSW	932	357		2458	2502	310	372	443	426	297	665	847	1375	866	4905	3637	2650	346	4338	1551	918	1619	3662	531	2950
Alice Springs NT	1526	3558	2458		442	2532	2137	2548	2694	2135	1793	2250	3004	1635	2735	3771	2293	2518	4128	1685	2332	689	1492	2387	3084
Ayers Rock/Yulara NT	1570	3602	2502	442		2574	2181	2592	2738	2179	1837	2294	3219	1679	3177	3815	2735	2562	4516	1729	2748	733	1934	2431	3128
Bairnsdale VIC	1006	3648	310	2532	2574		395	878	326	432	739	1157	1691	1120	5215	3861	2960	450	4562	1775	1611	1843	3972	841	3174
Ballarat VIC	611	3253	372	2137	2181	395		815	721	121	344	995	1655	753	5436	3466	2830	718	4167	1380	1449	1448	4193	882	2779
Bathurst NSW	1183	3664	443	2548	2592	878	815		468	740	1093	574	1004	958	5015	3877	2325	274	4578	1791	1028	1859	3772	206	3190
Bega NSW	1329	3810	426	2694	2738	326	721	468		709	1065	965	1373	1292	5406	4023	2723	222	4724	1937	1419	2005	4163	604	3336
Bendigo VIC	770	3251	297	2135	2179	432	121	740	709		368	874	1534	697	4851	3464	2795	643	4165	1378	1328	1446	3627	761	2777
Bordertown SA	267	2909	665	1793	1837	739	344	1093	1065	368		1242	1929	781	4509	3122	3160	1011	3823	1036	1779	1104	3285	1085	2435
Bourke NSW	1129	3366	847	2250	2294	1157	995	574	965	874	1242		924	615	4441	3579	1835	743	4280	1493	454	1561	3198	368	2892
Brisbane QLD	2054	4291	1375	3004	3219	1691	1655	1004	1373	1534	1929	924		1540	4659	4504	1701	1223	5205	2418	754	2486	3416	844	3817
Broken Hill NSW	514	2751	866	1635	1679	1120	753	958	1292	697	781	615	1540		4351	2964	2450	1080	3665	878	1069	946	3127	752	2277
Broome WA	4242	2582	4905	2735	3177	5215	5436	5015	5406	4851	4509	4441	4659	4351		2538	3948	5184	1461	3569	3987	3405	1861	4809	912
Bunbury WA	2855	361	3637	3771	3815	3861	3466	3877	4023	3464	3122	3579	4504	2964	2538		5414	3847	1069	2086	4033	3082	4183	3716	687
Cairns QLD	2964	5201	2650	2293	2735	2960	2830	2325	2723	2795	3160	1835	1701	2450	3948	5414		2435	5429	3328	1381	2982	2705	2119	4727
Canberra ACT	1153	3634	346	2518	2562	450	718	274	222	643	1011	743	1223	1080	5184	3847	2435		4548	1761	1197	1829	3941	382	3160
Carnarvon WA	3556	1292	4338	4128	4516	4562	4167	4578	4724	4165	3823	4280	5205	3665	1461	1069	5429	4548		2787	4734	3783	3254	4417	1600
Ceduna SA	769	1873	1551	1685	1729	1775	1380	1791	1937	1378	1036	1493	2418	878	3569	2086	3328	1761	2787		1947	996	3177	1630	1399
Charleville QLD	1583	3820	918	2332	2748	1611	1449	1028	1419	1328	1779	454	754	1069	3987	4033	1381	1197	4734	1947		2015	2744	822	3346
Coober Pedy SA	837	2869	1619	689	733	1843	1448	1859	2005	1446	1104	1561	2486	946	3405	3082	2982	1829	3783	996	2015		2181	1698	2395
Darwin NT	3018	4375	3662	1492	1934	3972	4193	3772	4163	3627	3285	3198	3416	3127	1861	4183	2705	3941	3254	3177	2744	2181		3566	4307
Dubbo NSW	1175	3503	531	2387	2431	841	882	206	604	761	1085	368	844	752	4809	3716	2119	382	4417	1630	822	1698	3566		3029
Esperance WA	2168	474	2950	3084	3128	3174	2779	3190	3336	2777	2435	2892	3817	2277	912	687	4727	3160	1600	1399	3346	2395	4307	3029	
Eucla WA	1256	1386	2038	2172	2216	2262	1867	2278	2424	1865	1523	1980	2905	1365	3082	1599	3815	2248	2300	487	2434	1483	3664	2117	912
Geraldton WA	3083	819	3865	3999	404	4089	3694	4105	4251	3692	3350	3807	4732	3192	1934	596	5642	4075	473	2314	4261	3310	3727	3944	1319
Grafton NSW	1815	4079	1162	2963	3007	1334	1522	735	1034	1401	1725	813	339	1328	4901	4292	2048	884	4993	2206	997	2274	3658	640	3605
Horsham VIC	424	3066	508	1950	1994	582	187	951	908	211	157	1085	1745	609	4666	3279	3006	854	3980	1193	1539	1261	3442	972	2592
Kalgoorlie/Boulder WA	2153	799	2935	3069	3113	3159	2764	3175	3321	2762	2420	2877	3802	2262	2185	764	4712	3145	1161	1384	3331	2380	3978	3014	389
Katherine NT	2709	4066	3353	1183	1625	3663	3884	3463	3854	3318	2976	2889	3107	2818	1552	3874	2396	3632	2945	2868	2435	1872	309	3257	3998
Kununurra WA	3202	3554	3865	1695	2137	4175	4396	3975	4366	3830	3488	3401	3619	3330	1040	3362	2908	4144	2433	3380	2947	2384	821	3769	3486
Longreach QLD	2097	4334	1432	1818	2260	1671	1963	1542	1933	1842	2293	968	1186	1583	3473	4547	1053	1711	4954	2461	514	2507	2230	1336	3860
Mackay QLD	2475	4712	2009	2396	2838	2319	2341	1684	2082	2220	2588	1346	980	1961	4051	7925	729	1860	5532	2839	892	2907	2808	1478	4238
Meekatharra WA	2872	1116	3654	3788	3832	3837	3483	3894	4040	3481	3139	3596	4521	2981	1466	924	5344	3864	620	2103	4050	3099	3248	3733	1108
Melbourne VIC	723	3365	314	2249	2293	283	112	759	609	149	456	989	1658	837	4965	3578	2933	660	4279	1492	1443	1560	3741	814	2891
Mildura VIC	372	2849	571	1733	1777	821	454	811	957	398	411	877	1647	299	449	3062	2749	781	3763	976	1368	1044	3225	803	2375
Moree NSW	1548	3812	904	2696	2740	1214	1255	579	977	1134	1458	445	479	1061	4616	4025	1790	755	4726	1939	629	2007	3373	373	3338
Mt Gambier SA	435	3077	677	1961	2005	695	305	1120	1026	426	183	1300	1960	870	4677	3290	3135	1023	3991	1204	1754	1272	3453	1187	2603
Mt Isa QLD	2702	4734	2074	1176	1618	2313	2605	2184	2575	2484	2852	1610	1828	2225	2831	4947	1117	2353	4312	5861	1156	1865	1588	1978	4279
Newcastle NSW	1509	3884	693	2768	2812	865	1065	326	570	990	1358	749	818	1133	5099	4097	2339	415	4798	2011	1121	2079	3856	381	3410
Perth WA	2689	406	3471	3605	3649	3695	3300	3711	3857	3298	2956	3413	4338	2798	2372	182	5248	3681	903	1920	3867	2916	4017	3550	714
Port Augusta SA	305	2337	1087	1221	1265	1311	916	1327	1473	914	572	1029	1954	414	3937	2550	2864	1297	3251	464	1483	532	2713	1166	1863
Port Hedland WA	3744	1988	4526	3349	3791	4750	4355	4766	4912	4353	4011	4468	5205	3853	614	1796	4543	4736	867	2975	4533	3971	2407	4605	1980
Port Lincoln SA	642	2277	1424	1558	1602	1648	1253	1664	1810	1251	909	1366	2291	751	3973	2490	3201	1634	3191	404	1820	869	3050	1503	1803
Renmark SA	247	2724	696	1608	1652	940	573	1714	1082	517	279	1039	1772	424	4324	2937	2874	906	3638	857	1493	919	3100	928	2250
Rockhampton QLD	2268	4505	3255	3389	3433	1986	2027	1351	1749	1906	2230	1139	647	1754	4154	4718	1062	1527	5419	2632	780	2700	2911	1145	4031
Sydney NSW	1384	3865	562	2749	2793	734	934	201	418	859	1227	775	957	1159	5216	4078	2400	284	4779	1992	1229	2060	3973	407	3391
Tamworth NSW	1510	3774	866	2658	2702	1129	1217	430	813	1096	1420	584	574	1023	4879	3987	2062	704	4688	1901	901	1969	3636	335	3300
Tennant Creek NT	2040	4072	2736	514	956	2975	3267	2846	3237	2649	2307	2272	2490	2149	2221	4285	1779	3015	3614	2199	1818	1203	978	2640	3598
Toowoomba QLD	1894	4158	1250	3042	3086	1560	1601	3148	1314	1480	1786	791	125	1407	4534	4371	1702	1205	5072	2285	629	2353	3291	719	3684
Townsville QLD	2617	4854	2303	2067	2509	2613	2483	1978	2420	2362	2813	1488	1376	2103	3722	5067	347	2088	5203	2981	1034	3049	2479	1772	4380
Wagga Wagga NSW	936	3417	125	2301	2345	435	497	318	393	422	790	722	1250	863	5017	3630	2525	244	4331	1544	1176	1612	3793	406	2943
Warrnambool VIC	617	3259	544	2143	2187	513	171	986	839	292	365	1162	1826	850	4859	3472	3001	889	4173	1386	1621	922	3635	1053	2785
West Wyalong NSW	919	3400	278	2284	2328	588	626	264	501	505	829	572	1100	846	5000	3613	2375	271	4314	1527	1026	1595	3776	256	2926

Eucla WA	Geraldton WA	Grafton NSW	Horsham VIC	Kalgoorlie/Boulder WA	Katherine NT	Kununurra WA	Longreach QLD	Mackay QLD	Meekatharra WA	Melbourne VIC	Mildura VIC	Moree NSW	Mt Gambier SA	Mt Isa QLD	Newcastle NSW	Perth WA	Port Augusta SA	Port Hedland WA	Port Lincoln SA	Renmark SA	Rockhampton QLD	Sydney NSW	Tamworth NSW	Tennant Creek NT	Toowoomba QLD	Townsville QLD	Wagga Wagga NSW	Warrnambool VIC	West Wyalong NSW
1256	3083	1815	424	2153	2709	3202	2097	2475	2872	723	372	1548	435	2702	1509	2689	305	3744	642	247	2268	1384	1510	2040	1894	2617	936	617	919
1386	819	4079	3066	799	4066	3554	4334	4712	1116	3365	2849	3812	3077	4734	3884	406	2337	1988	2277	2724	4505	3865	3774	4072	4158	4854	3417	3259	3400
2038	3865	1162	508	2935	3353	3865	1432	2009	3654	314	571	904	677	2074	693	3471	1087	4526	1424	696	3255	562	866	2736	1250	2303	125	544	278
2172	3999	2963	1950	3069	1183	1695	1818	2396	3788	2249	1733	2696	1961	1176	2768	3605	1221	3349	1558	1608	3389	2749	2658	514	3042	2067	2301	2143	2284
2216	404	3007	1994	3113	1625	2137	2260	2838	3832	2293	1777	2740	2005	1618	2812	3649	1265	3791	1602	1652	3433	2793	2702	956	3086	2509	2345	2187	2328
2262	4089	1334	582	3159	3663	4175	1671	2319	3837	283	821	1214	695	2313	865	3695	1311	4750	1648	940	1986	734	1129	2975	1560	2613	435	513	588
1867	3694	1522	187	2764	3884	4396	1963	2341	3483	112	454	1255	305	2605	1065	3300	916	4355	1253	573	2027	934	1217	3267	1601	2483	497	171	626
2278	4105	735	951	3175	3463	3975	1542	1684	3894	759	811	579	1120	2184	326	3711	1327	4766	1664	1714	1351	201	430	2846	3148	1978	318	986	264
2424	4251	1034	908	3321	3854	4366	1933	2082	4040	609	957	977	1026	2575	570	3857	1473	4912	1810	1082	1749	418	813	3237	1314	2420	393	839	501
1865	3692	1401	211	2762	3318	3830	1842	2220	3481	149	398	1134	426	2484	990	3298	914	4353	1251	517	1906	859	1096	2649	1480	2362	422	292	505
1523	3350	1725	157	2420	2976	3488	2293	2588	3139	456	411	1458	183	2852	1358	2956	572	4011	909	279	2230	1227	1420	2307	1786	2813	790	365	829
1980	3807	813	1085	2877	2889	3401	968	1346	3596	989	877	445	1300	1610	749	3413	1029	4468	1366	1039	1139	775	584	2272	791	1488	722	1162	572
2905	4732	339	1745	3802	3107	3619	1186	980	4521	1658	1647	479	1960	1828	818	4338	1954	5205	2291	1772	647	957	574	2490	125	1376	1250	1826	1100
1365	3192	1328	609	2262	2818	3330	1583	1961	2981	837	299	1061	870	2225	1133	2798	414	3853	751	424	1754	1159	1023	2149	1407	2103	863	850	846
3082	1934	4901	4666	2185	1552	1040	3473	4051	1466	4965	449	4616	4677	2831	5099	2372	3937	614	3973	4324	4154	5216	4879	2221	4534	3722	5017	4859	5000
1599	596	4292	3279	764	3874	3362	4547	7925	924	3578	3062	4025	3290	4947	4097	182	2550	1796	2490	2937	4718	4078	3987	4285	4371	5067	3630	3472	3613
3815	5642	2048	3006	4712	2396	2908	1053	729	5344	2933	2749	2790	3135	1117	2339	5248	2864	4543	3201	2874	1062	2400	2062	1779	1702	347	2525	3001	2375
2248	4075	884	854	3145	3632	4144	1711	1860	3864	660	781	755	1023	2353	415	3681	1297	4736	1634	906	1527	284	704	3015	1205	2088	244	889	271
2300	473	4993	3980	1161	2945	2433	4954	5532	620	4279	3763	4726	3991	4312	4798	903	3251	867	3191	3638	5419	4779	4688	3614	5072	5203	4331	4173	431
487	2314	2206	1193	1384	2868	3380	2461	2839	2103	1492	976	1939	1204	5861	2011	1920	464	2975	404	857	2632	1992	1901	2199	2285	2981	1544	1386	1527
2434	4261	997	1539	3331	2435	2947	514	892	4050	1443	1368	629	1754	1156	1121	3867	1483	4533	1820	1493	780	1229	901	1818	629	1034	1176	1621	1026
1483	3310	2274	1261	2380	1872	2384	2507	2907	3099	1560	1044	2007	1272	1865	2079	2916	532	3971	869	919	2700	2060	1969	1203	2353	3049	1612	922	1595
3664	3727	3658	3442	3978	309	821	2230	2808	3248	3741	3225	3373	3453	1588	3856	4017	2713	2407	3050	3100	2911	3973	3636	978	3291	2479	3793	3635	3776
2117	3944	640	972	3014	3257	3769	1336	1478	3733	814	803	373	1187	1978	381	3550	1166	4605	1503	928	1145	407	335	2640	719	1772	406	1053	256
912	1319	3605	2592	389	3998	3486	3860	4238	1108	2891	2375	3338	2603	4279	3410	714	1863	1980	1803	2250	4031	3391	3300	3598	3684	4380	2943	2785	2926
1827		4520	3507	988	3128	2906	4775	5153	540	3806	3290	4253	3518	4697	4325	430	2778	1340	2718	3165	4946	4306	4215	4087	4599	5295	3858	3700	3841
2693	4520		1612	3590	3349	3861	1428	1319	4309	1476	1443	368	1827	2070	479	4126	1742	5447	2079	1568	986	618	305	2732	367	1701	1046	1693	896
1680	3507	1612		2577	3133	3645	2053	2431	3296	299	310	1345	261	2695	1201	3113	729	4168	1066	429	2117	1070	1307	2464	1691	2573	633	241	580
897	988	3590	2577		3669	3157	3845	4223	719	2876	2360	3323	2588	4264	3395	594	1848	1591	1788	2235	4016	3376	3285	3583	3669	4365	2928	2770	2911
3355	3418	3349	3133	3669		512	1921	2499	2948	3432	2916	3064	3144	1279	3547	3708	2404	2098	2741	2791	2602	3664	3327	669	2982	2170	3484	3326	3467
3867	2906	3861	3645	3157	512		2433	3011	2436	3944	3428	3576	3656	1791	4059	3196	2916	1586	3253	3303	3114	4176	3839	1181	3494	2682	3996	3838	3979
2948	4775	1428	2053	3845	1921	2433		793	4564	1957	1845	1143	2268	642	1626	4381	1997	4068	2334	2007	681	1743	1406	1304	1061	706	1690	2134	1540
3326	5153	1319	2431	4223	2499	3011	793		4942	2175	2223	1105	2624	1220	1764	4759	2375	4646	2712	2385	333	1882	973	382	1884	2512	1734	
1616	540	4309	3296	719	2948	2436	4564	4942		3595	3079	4042	3307	4227	4114	758	2567	872	2567	2954	4735	4095	4004	3617	5094	3647	3489	3630	
1979	3806	1478	299	2876	3432	3944	1957	2175	3595		538	1187	412	2599	1007	3412	1028	4467	1365	657	1959	876	1180	2763	1533	2477	439	230	558
1463	3290	1443	310	2360	2916	3428	1845	2223	3079	538		1176	571	2524	1137	2896	512	3951	849	125	1948	1012	1138	2247	1522	2365	564	551	547
2426	4253	368	1345	3323	3064	3576	1143	1105	4042	1187	1176		1560	1785	492	3859	1475	4914	1812	1301	772	610	272	2447	346	1443	779	1426	629
1691	3518	1827	261	2588	3144	3656	2268	2624	3307	412	571	1560		2910	1370	3124	740	4179	1077	462	2332	2268	1522	2475	1906	2788	802	182	795
3348	4697	2070	2695	4264	1279	1791	642	1220	4227	2599	2524	1785	2910		2268	4781	2397	3426	2734	2649	1323	2385	2048	662	1703	891	2332	2776	2182
2498	4325	479	1201	3395	3547	4059	1626	1764	4114	1007	1137	492	1370	2268		3931	1547	4986	1884	1262	1264	152	277	2930	778	1992	591	1236	590
1433	430	4126	3113	594	3708	3196	4381	4759	758	3412	2896	3859	3124	4781	3931		2384	1630	2324	2771	4552	3912	3821	4119	4205	4901	3464	3306	3447
951	2778	1742	729	1848	2404	2916	1997	2375	2567	1028	512	1475	740	2397	1547	2384		3439	337	387	2168	1528	1437	1735	1821	2517	1080	922	106
2488	1340	5447	4168	1591	2098	1586	4068	4646	872	4467	3951	4914	4179	3426	4986	1630	3439		3776	3826	5607	4976	4876	2767	5080	4317	4519	4361	4502
891	2718	2079	1066	1788	2741	3253	2334	2712	2507	1365	849	1821	1077	2734	1884	2324	337	3776		724	2505	1865	1774	2072	2158	2854	1417	1259	1400
1388	3165	1568	429	2235	2791	3303	2007	2954	657	125	1301	462	2649	1262	2771	387	3826	724		2073	1137	1263	2122	1647	2527	689	676	672	
3119	4946	986	2117	4016	2602	3114	681	333	4735	1959	1948	772	2332	1323	1264	4552	2168	5607	2505	2073		1382	1044	1985	640	715	1554	2198	1401
2479	4306	618	1070	3376	3664	4176	1743	1715	4095	876	1012	610	1239	2385	152	3912	1528	4967	1865	1137	1382		395	3263	896	2053	470	1105	465
2388	4215	305	1307	3285	3327	3839	1406	1377	4004	1180	1138	272	1522	2048	277	3821	1437	4876	1774	1263	1044	395		2710	501	1715	741	1388	591
2686	4087	2732	2464	3583	669	1181	1304	1882	3617	2763	2247	2447	2475	662	2930	4119	1735	2767	2072	2122	1985	3263	2710		2365	1553	2815	2657	2798
2772	4599	367	1691	3669	2982	3494	1061	973	4288	1533	1522	346	1906	1703	778	4205	1821	5080	2158	1647	640	896	501	2365		1355	1125	1772	975
3468	5295	1701	2573	4365	2170	2682	706	382	5094	2477	2365	1443	2788	891	1992	4901	2517	4317	2854	2527	715	2053	1715	1553	1355		2178	2654	2028
2031	3858	1046	633	2928	3484	3996	1690	1884	3647	439	564	779	802	2332	591	3464	1080	4519	1417	689	1554	470	741	2815	1125	2178		668	153
1873	3700	1693	241	2770	3326	3838	2134	2512	3489	230	551	1426	182	2776	1236	3306	922	4361	1259	676	2198	1105	1388	2657	1772	2654	668		661
2014	3841	896	580	2911	3467	3979	1540	1734	3630	558	547	629	795	2182	590	3447	1063	4502	1400	672	1401	465	591	2798	975	2028	153	661	

TOURING AUSTRALIA

Australia: The Land Down Under

◈ Area: 7 686 291 km²

◈ World's smallest continent and largest island

◈ World's lowest and flattest continent; average elevation is only 330m; Lake Eyre is 15m below sea level

◈ World records: Uluru (largest monolith); Great Barrier Reef (longest coral reef); Nullarbor Plain (largest flat bedrock surface); Simpson Desert (largest sand ridge desert); and Mount Augustus (largest exposed rocky outcrop)

◈ Sixth largest country in the world after the Russian Federation, Canada, China, USA and Brazil

◈ Fifth longest coastline in the world with the world's largest Exclusive Economic Marine Zone when offshore territories are included

◈ The Great Dividing Range is the fourth longest mountain range in the world

◈ About 39% of Australia lies within the tropical zone and 61% in the temperate zone

◈ Australia extends across 40° of longitude and almost 33° of latitude

◈ World's oldest fossilised life forms—cyanobacteria (about 3.8 billion years old) have been found in Western Australia

Geography: The Island Continent

The oldest rocks discovered in Australia, thought to be around 4 300 million years old, are also among the world's most ancient rocks. Australia is the world's sixth largest country, the largest island, and the world's smallest continent. Covering approximately 7 700 000km² of the earth's Southern Hemisphere, Australia is the only continent occupied by one nation alone, albeit multicultural. It is often difficult for visitors, as well as many Australians, to grasp just how huge the country is. Australia is approximately the same size as the European continent, excluding the former USSR, and around 2% smaller than the mainland area of the United States of America.

This very old and enormous area forms the earth's flattest and, apart from Antarctica, driest continent. In the east, a narrow, fertile coastal plain meets the **Great Dividing Range** which itself stretches almost the entire length of the country, from north Queensland to Victoria.

Red desert earth of Uluru-Kata Tjuta NP, Central Australia

The highest peak in Australia, **Mount Kosciuszko**, rises only 2228m above sea-level in the south of the Great Dividing Range. Relative to international standards, Mount Kosciuszko is but a foothill upon this seemingly endless plateau. West of the range, grassy plains supporting sheep and cattle gradually give way to the hot, dry Outback for which Australia is famous. The red dirt and central deserts of the continent stretch almost the entire way to the coastline of Western Australia. There are more than 665 national parks occupying around 410 000km² of the island continent and 14 unique sites have been declared World Heritage Areas.

The Australian environment is so diverse, ranging from the tropical rainforests and coral reefs of the north-east, to the harsh and inhospitable deserts and huge but mainly dry, salt lakes, (occasionally filled by inland flowing rivers in

Snow-laden tree near Mount Kosciuszko

flood) in the central west. The **Darling River** is the longest in Australia, stretching 2736km from southern Queensland to the junction of the **Murray River** in the south of New South Wales.

Australia's 37 000km coastline is washed by 3 oceans—the **Indian** in the west, the **Pacific** in the east, and the spectacular cliff-carving **Southern Ocean** in the south. Four seas lap Australia's shores—the **Timor** and **Arafura** seas on the northern shores, the **Coral Sea** surrounding the north-east coastline and the **Tasman Sea** bordering the south-east of the continent.

Climate

Australia's climate is as diverse and varied as its environment, due to the continent's size, location and the dominance of low plateaus and plains. It is the driest continent in the world (excluding Antarctica) with an average annual rainfall of 465mm. The seasons are the reverse of those in the Northern Hemisphere. The months of December and January are mid-summer months—it is always a hot Christmas in Australia; and,

depending on the area, the months of July and August bring wintry conditions, almost always perfect for skiing in the **Australian Alps**.

In the northern parts of Western Australia, Queensland and the Northern Territory, the weather is tropical and often conditions are monsoonal, depending on the season. Here, above the Tropic of Capricorn, there are really only 2 seasons: the Wet and the Dry. The Wet, November–April, is characterised by rainfall and hot, humid conditions. The Dry season, May–October, is often still hot, although in the desert areas and around Alice Springs, temperatures at night can be quite cold.

South of the Tropic of Capricorn, the climate becomes more temperate. Generally the seasons in Australia are not as defined as those in the Northern Hemisphere, except in highland regions. Any season is a good time to visit Australia depending of course on the places and activities you plan. It is possible to dive on the reefs off the northern coasts, even in winter, and a day later ski in the southern **Snowy Mountains**.

Statue of Capt James Cook in Hyde Park, Sydney

History

Before European settlement in 1788, the entire continent of Australia was inhabited by different **Aboriginal societies**. It is thought the Aborigines first crossed to the continent from Asia more than 60 000 years ago, when the sea level was much lower than it is today. Aboriginal histories and stories were not written down in the conventional sense; they were painted on bark, rocks, inside caves and sculpted on the ground and on trees, spoken and sung.

For a long time it was thought that **Capt James Cook** was the first European to discover Australia, in 1770. However, it is now known that **Macassan** sailors visited the northern shores of Australia long before that date, and that the Dutchman, **Willem Jansz**, landed here in 1601. The first Englishman to land was **William Dampier**, a pirate/buccaneer who went ashore in 1688, somewhere near the town in Western Australia that is named after him. Dampier recorded nothing good about the land or its inhabitants.

Agincourt Reef pontoon in the Great Barrier Reef, Coral Sea, Queensland

Goldrush architecture in Sturt St, Ballarat, Victoria

Cook, however, gave a more favourable report of the eastern coastline in 1770, and this was remembered when the harsh criminal laws in Britain resulted in overcrowded prisons.

A penal colony was created in 1788, when 11 tall ships of the **First Fleet** sailed into Botany Bay, in what is now New South Wales. The fleet brought only enough food to last 2 years, so until farms could be established, the threat of starvation loomed. By 1790, the **Second Fleet** had landed and a year later the arrival of the **Third Fleet** increased the population to 4000.

For the first 20 years the spread of settlement was slow. **Sydney** was established and there were small colonies at **Norfolk Island** and **Hobart**. Any expansion inland from Sydney was restricted until the formidable barrier of the **Blue Mountains** was crossed in 1813. Following this, a wave of exploration occurred. Explorers such as **Charles Sturt**, **Ludwig Leichhardt** and **Burke** and **Wills** have been noted in history for making journeys across often rugged and inhospitable terrain to open the way for European settlement.

When gold was discovered near **Ballarat** and then **Bendigo** in 1851, in what is now Victoria, miners from all over the world made their way to Australia. The **Goldrushes** of the 1850s and 1860s increased the population and opened up large areas of the country. Wealth from the mines helped to build inland towns, and when the rushes were over, many of the miners settled where they had found their fortunes and turned to farming, grazing and other pursuits.

Government

It was not until 1 January 1901 that the **Commonwealth of Australia** came into being. Rivalry between the cities of **Sydney** and **Melbourne** meant that neither would agree to the other having primacy—a new capital had to be created.

Today, the government of Australia sits in the nation's purpose-built capital, **Canberra**, in the **Australian Capital Territory**. The land on which the city is located was acquired in 1911 by the Commonwealth Government and lies 290km SW of Sydney. In 1927 Parliament House, now known as **Old Parliament House**, was completed, and used for the following 60 years. The new **Parliament House** was opened in 1988 and is the current seat of the **Federal Government**.

Australia's democratic political system is a complex 3-tiered structure of federal, state and local levels. The federal and state governments are modelled on the **British Westminster system** with elected parliamentary representatives. In the Federal Government there are 2 houses of parliament—the House of Representatives and the Senate. The **Prime Minister** is the national leader. Each of the 6 states and 2 territories has a **Premier** or **Chief Minister**, who is the leader of the party in power. Local regions are led by an elected mayor and council.

Australia's Parliament House, Canberra, with the forecourt mosaic designed by an Aboriginal artist

Aboriginal women in Arnhem Land,
Northern Territory

People

There are no accurate estimations of the **Aboriginal** population before European settlement. In 1788, there may have been more than 600 000 Aborigines living in Australia, but by 1830 only around 100 000 remained. The population was considerably reduced due to the introduction of diseases like measles and smallpox and dispossession of land. There was an ongoing decline in the Aboriginal population itself, and a continuing mistreatment of their communities following European settlement.

It is only in more recent years that there has been an acknowledgment of injustices, and an attempt at reconciliation, although many would argue that there is still a deficiency of understanding. The Sydney 2000 Olympic Games portrayed to the world a young nation in the first stages of unification, in the throes of compromise, understanding and acceptance.

In the years before WWII, the majority of the population was of English, Scottish and Irish descent; a mix of descendants of the convicts and free settlers. A variety of nationalities made up a minority of the population originally as refugees or as prospectors during the goldrushes of the 19th century. After WWII, a strong drive for immigration brought in more people from Britain and thousands of refugees from Italy, Greece, Yugoslavia, Germany and other parts of war-torn Europe. Since then, and especially after the Vietnam War in the 1960s and 1970s immigration from many countries has continued to play an integral, sometimes controversial part in the development of the Australian nation.

Today, Australia can truly be considered a diverse and **multicultural society**. It has also become one of the world's most urbanised countries, with more than 90% of the population living in the cities, which are located along the coast.

Economy

Australia has a prosperous Western-style capitalist economy. A land rich in natural resources, Australia is a major exporter of **minerals**, metals, **fossil fuels**, and **agricultural products**—despite around two-thirds of Australia being arid or semi-arid. Primary products account for more than 60% of exports.

Australia leads the world in **wool** production, and is a significant contributor to the world supplies of **cotton**, **wheat**, **dairy products**, **meat**, **sugar**, **fruit**, **fisheries' products** and **timber**.

While the Australian government is encouraging an increase in the export of manufactured goods, severe competition from international markets means that currently these exports account for approximately 14% of total GDP.

The **service industry** is now the largest, and fastest growing, segment of the economy. It includes property, finance, construction, trade, communication, education, tourism and business services. **Tourism** is currently the fastest growing sector of the Australian service industry.

The Australian **wine industry** is a relatively recent addition to the international export trade. Known for their good quality and distinctive flavour, Australian wines are increasingly popular and seem set for a prosperous future.

Migrant dancers at Sydney Opera House

AUSTRALIAN FLORA

Jewel beetle on eucalypt flower

of plant evolution and heritage. In the south-west of Western Australia, the wildflowers dominate, while in the north-east of the continent the 'green dinosaurs' (cycads and king ferns), inhabit some of the oldest rainforests in the world.

In 1788, the arrival of the First Fleet introduced various exotic plants and domestic animals that altered the natural botanical balance of the country forever. However, most of the native plants that existed then, can still be found today. More than 85% of the continent's species of plants, trees and wildflowers are uniquely Australian.

Eucalypts

The eucalypt, more commonly known as the **gum tree**, is perhaps the most dominant plant of the Australian landscape. There are close to 600 species of eucalypts found across the continent, thriving in environments ranging from coastal forests and woodlands, to the arid inland, and the mountainous sub-alpine terrain.

The term 'gum tree' is derived from particular eucalyptus trees

Floral Emblems

❖ **Commonwealth of Australia**
  Golden Wattle, *Acacia pycnantha*

❖ **Australian Capital Territory**
  Royal Bluebell,
  Wahlenbergia gloriosa

❖ **New South Wales**
  Waratah,
  Telopea speciosissima

❖ **Northern Territory**
  Sturt's Desert Rose,
  Gossypium sturtianum

❖ **Queensland**
  Cooktown Orchid,
  Dendrobium bigibbum

❖ **South Australia**
  Sturt's Desert Pea,
  Clianthus formosus

❖ **Tasmania**
  Tasmanian Blue Gum,
  Eucalyptus globulus

❖ **Victoria**
  Common Heath, *Epacris impressa*

❖ **Western Australia**
  Red and Green Kangaroo Paw,
  Anigozanthos manglesii

For thousands of years before European settlement, the Aboriginal people lived on the Australian continent in harmony with the native flora and fauna. Regular burning of plants was a practice of various Aboriginal tribes, and earned them the name **'firestick farmers'**. This practice is now thought to be at least partly responsible for the evolution of Australia's fire-resistant and regenerative native flora.

Australia is home to an exceptionally diverse group of flora. Regions range from tropical and subtropical rainforests and desert environments to sub-alpine areas. These, combined with the latitudinal spread of the country and the resulting variable climates, create a continent rich in diversity. With 2 of the most unique floristic provinces in the world, Australia provides scientists with vital records

Eucalypts at Lake Brewster, New South Wales

WATTLE

Australia's floral emblem is the **Golden Wattle**, *Acacia pycnantha*, which produces a profusion of rounded flowerheads in spring. Of the 1200 species of *Acacia*, Australia is home to 900, which are scattered throughout the continent. The green and gold of the wattles have become an internationally recognised representation of Australia and its flora.

It is thought that wattles have been growing in Australia for eons. Africa and South America are home to the majority of the other 300 species. These often short-lived plants have adapted over time to drought, poor soil and bushfire conditions, making them the perfect Australian symbol.

Wattles range in size from low ground mats and shrubs, to tall forest trees. Many wattles are cultivated for their attractive yellow

Acacia pustula, one of hundreds of Australian wattles

blossom, but others are used for timber, for example, blackwood, used for furniture making. Aborigines used wattle wood for tools and weapons, and the seeds and gum for food. Wattles are also valuable to native fauna. Possums like to nibble on the flowers, and the nectar and seeds are food for birds such as cockatoos and galahs. Wattle seed is also popular 'bush tucker' food today.

that leak a sticky, gum-like substance from the trunk. Although this is not a general characteristic of all eucalypts, 'gum tree' has become a generic term. Names have also been given to certain groups of trees because of their appearance or growth habits. Some examples include ash, blackbutt, bloodwood, box, ghost, ironbark, snow, ribbon, scribbly, and stringybark.

Wildflowers

Australia has a colourful and distinct array of wildflowers. There are 92 species of **banksias** ranging from small shrubs to trees. These plants were named after **Sir Joseph Banks**, botanist and noted naturalist on Capt James Cook's *Endeavour* voyage of discovery in 1770.

Sturt's Desert Pea, which is the floral emblem of South Australia, was named after **Charles Sturt**, who explored the Simpson and Sturt's Stony deserts in 1844–46. The state flower of New South Wales, the **waratah**, is an unusual and beautiful flower that has been a favourite of artists for years. The Kangaroo Paw, Western Australia's state flower, is noted for its velvety appearance and claw-like structure, hence its name. Other distinctly Australian flowers include **boronias, bottlebrushes, Christmas bushes, everlasting daisies** and **grevilleas**.

Both Western Australia and South Australia are famous for their beautiful array of wildflowers, and there are festivals all around the country, at different times of the year, in celebration of local unique flowering plants.

Waratah, *Telopea speciosissima*

AUSTRALIAN FAUNA

Australia's geographic isolation for millions of years is believed to be the main reason for the existence of so many species of fauna found nowhere else in the world. The unique wildlife crosses all animal families, from marsupials and reptiles, to fish and birds. Perhaps the best way to see the variety of wildlife is by visiting the many sanctuaries and zoos found across the continent.

Short-beaked echidna, *Tachyglossus aculeatus*

Fauna Emblems

◈ **Commonwealth of Australia**
Red Kangaroo, *Macropus rufus*, and Emu, *Dromaius novaehollandiae*

◈ **Australian Capital Territory**
Gang Gang Cockatoo, *Callocephalon fimbriatum*

◈ **New South Wales**
Platypus, *Ornithorhynchus anatinus*

◈ **Northern Territory**
Red Kangaroo, *Macropus rufus*

◈ **Queensland**
Koala, *Phascolarctos cinereus*

◈ **South Australia**
Southern Hairy-nosed Wombat, *Lasiorhinus latifrons*

◈ **Tasmania**
Tasmanian Devil, *Sarcophilus harrisii*

◈ **Victoria**
Leadbeater's Possum, *Gymnobelideus leadbeateri*

◈ **Western Australia**
Numbat, *Myrmecobius fasciatus*

Marsupials

Marsupials are defined as a group of mammals where the female has a pouch to carry her young. A large proportion (almost 50% or 141 species) of the mammals of Australia are marsupials and Australia has 52% of the world's marsupials.

The largest of them, the **kangaroo** (macropod), has become a wildlife symbol of the nation. It flies around the world on the tail of the national airline, Qantas, and it is depicted on the Australian Coat of Arms. There are 40 species of kangaroos bounding across the continent, varying in size from 30cm to 2m; they are well adapted to the hot and dry regions of Australia.

The **koala**, best known as a cute and cuddly 'bear', has a somewhat patchier distribution than the kangaroo. Koalas are found only on the eastern side of the continent, feeding off about 35 of the 600 species of eucalyptus trees found in Australia. Koalas are now a protected species. Perhaps the easiest way to see them is in the national parks, koala parks or zoos.

There are 3 species of **wombat** in Australia. The **common wombat** is found in woodlands and sclerophyll forests throughout the eastern part of the continent. The **southern hairy-nosed wombat** is found in isolated areas of the Nullarbor Plain, and in parts of South Australia. The rarest—the **northern hairy-nosed wombat**—is found in an isolated area of central Queensland. This wombat is nearly extinct—numbers are estimated at between 40 to 70 animals, making it one of the most endangered animals in the country.

There are many varieties of **possums** in Australia, but the most numerous is the **common brushtail possum**, which resides in the bush and suburbs over much of Australia.

Monotremes

Monotremes are relatively primitive animals. They are warm-blooded egg-layers who feed their young milk. Australia is home to 2 of the world's 3 monotremes.

These 2 unique Australian residents are the **echidna** and the **platypus**. The echidna, known commonly as the spiny anteater, can be found all over the continent. The platypus is a more confined resident than its spiky relation, and is found in the streams and rivers of eastern Australia. It is an unusual animal, with a soft, leathery, duck-like bill and clawed, webbed feet. In the past platypus were hunted by the fur industry but they are now fully protected.

Red kangaroo, *Macropus rufus*

DANGEROUS CREATURES

Australia is renowned for its array of dangerous creatures. However, the threat to visitors of encountering danger or harm is unlikely if common sense prevails.

Snakes

Australia has more poisonous snakes than any other country in the world, although few species will attack unless threatened. By far the most dangerous is the **inland taipan**—the most venomous terrestrial snake known. Its venom is 100 times more deadly than that of the infamous king cobra. Other varieties of snake are found throughout Australia—the more common are **brown snakes** found in the eastern half of the country. The **tiger snake**, **death adder** and **red-bellied black snake** all have potent venom and are capable of serious harm if you are bitten.

Spiders

There are 2000 spider species in Australia; 2 in particular are known to be deadly. The world's most poisonous spider, the **Sydney funnel-web** has caused 15 deaths in the last 60 years—antivenom is now available. The male is 6 times more venomous than his larger female counterpart. Interestingly, this is in contrast to the **redback spider**, the male of which is completely harmless. The female, however, caused 13 deaths prior to the development of the antivenom in 1956.

Marine creatures

Australia's most beautiful coral reefs and northern beaches are home to another group of dangerous creatures. Perhaps the most feared is the **box jellyfish**, or sea wasp. Encountered in the northern waters from October to May, it can kill a human in 4mins. Also found in northern waters, the highly venomous **stonefish** lurks in rockpools. Another creature—the tiny and misleadingly beautiful **blue-ringed octopus**—is found in rockpools off the east coast. The painless bite that has been known to cause death has no known antitoxin.

Found in the temperate and tropical waters around Australia, the **great white shark** can grow to 7m in length. Although it is aggressive when provoked, fatal shark attacks are relatively rare in Australia. It is thought that sharks commonly mistake swimmers and surfers for their food source—seals.

Saltwater crocodiles inhabit fresh and saltwater in the northern parts of the country and are internationally feared creatures. The 'saltie' can grow up to 6m long, and is the world's largest living reptile. Saltwater crocodiles are now a protected species in the wild and are farmed commercially for their meat and skin.

Saltwater crocodile, *Crocodylus porosus*

The Dingo

Another symbol of Australia is the 'native dog', the dingo, which is found all over the country except in Tasmania. However, dingoes are not considered native, as they were introduced from Asia some 3500–4000 years ago.

Reptiles

Australian reptiles include saltwater and freshwater crocodiles, sea and freshwater turtles, 172 snake species and more than 520 lizard species. They range from the common gecko, to the more exotic-looking **frilled lizard** and **thorny devil**. Other lizard types include **goannas** that can grow to 2m in length.

Birds

Australia has more than 777 bird species, of which 300 are unique to this country. Alongside the red kangaroo on the Coat of Arms is the large flightless **emu** which is found throughout Australia.

Australia's native birds are renowned for their variety, colourful plumage and interesting (and noisy) calls. The **kookaburra** is noted for its famous laugh-like call. Colourful **parrots** and **cockatoos**—the most common of which are the **galahs**—are famous for their wing-flapping and crest raising. The **rainbow lorikeet** can be found in abundant numbers in eastern Australia. **Budgerigars** are found over most of inland Australia. The **wedge-tailed eagle** is the largest bird of prey.

HAZARDS

Bushfires

Bushfires are a common Australian environmental hazard. In a continent as dry as Australia, fire, and the damage it can cause to life, property and wildlife, is a continual threat.

Fires can be inadvertent or malicious—the result of human carelessness or arson. Common causes of fire are lightning, discarded cigarette butts, broken glass on dry leaves, firecrackers, and smouldering BBQs left unattended. Experienced firefighters may conduct backburning in fire-prone areas, to reduce the fuel available to wildfires in the hotter months, but even these deliberate small fires can get out of control.

Hundreds of lives have been lost in bushfires in Australia, and several billion dollars worth of property has been destroyed. Major fire disasters such as those in Victoria (1983) and New South Wales (1994 and 2001–2002) demonstrated the brutal nature of bushfires fuelled by high temperatures, dry undergrowth and pushed by the wind.

Cyclones

Cyclones are large tropical storms accompanied by gale-force winds and heavy rain. They originate as low-pressure systems out at sea and often bring tidal surges, which result in low-level areas being flooded by the sea. Heavy rain can also cause rivers and creek banks to burst, creating further flooding. In the northern coastal zones of Australia, cyclones are a potential hazard in the summer months.

Flash Floods

These can occur without warning after periods of heavy rain in many regions of Australia. As a safety precaution, it is inadvisable to camp in dry river beds or near the banks of creeks or rivers.

Solar Radiation

The Australian sun is a well-known health hazard and Australia has the highest rate of skin cancer in the world. Skin cancer is caused by the ultraviolet (UV) light in the sun's beams. These UV rays operate not only in bright sunlight but even when days are overcast. It is imperative to use an effective sunscreen, wear a hat and protective clothing whenever you are outdoors.

Reptiles

Saltwater crocodiles are common in northern Australia and extreme caution should be exercised around both salt and fresh water locations. Freshwater crocodiles are far less dangerous, but have been known to bite humans. Australia has many species of venomous snakes, but very few will attack unless they feel threatened. *See* p.17.

Sharks

Several species of shark, considered dangerous to man, are commonly found around the Australian coastline and in river estuaries. To minimise the risk, avoid swimming in murky water, swimming at dusk or later, and wherever possible seek out beaches that are patrolled by lifeguards. *See* p.17 for further information on marine creatures.

Small creatures

Only a few of Australia's estimated 2000 species of spider are considered dangerous (*see* p.17). Centipedes and scorpions can deliver a painful sting. Paralysis ticks, found in coastal bushland in eastern Australia, are best removed with tweezers or by a medical practitioner. Blood-sucking leeches are prevalent in moist forests of eastern Australia (including Tasmania) and, like ticks, can be difficult to remove. Many species of wasps, bees, ants and flies can bite or sting, but are usually dangerous only to those with allergies. The persistent bushflies of Australia's Outback are a nuisance as they seek moisture from human sweat; midges and beach sandflies often bite. Mosquitoes are rarely carriers of malaria in Australia, but in certain areas may transmit diseases such as dengue fever and Ross River virus.

Poisonous plants

Aboriginal peoples have used Australian wild plants for food and medicinal purposes with skill and knowledge honed over thousands of years. Without such expert knowledge, such plants, which may contain toxins, should be treated with caution.

Cyclone Tracy

The most ferocious cyclone ever to hit modern Australia arrived on Christmas Day 1974. For 6 hours, winds of around 250km/hr tore the city of Darwin apart. Cyclone Tracy destroyed almost 90% of the city and killed 50 people in the process. Building laws have since been passed in the Northern Territory to regulate the minimum safety standards for all new buildings—if a cyclone happened again, the modern city is better placed to withstand the onslaught.

PLANNING A TRIP

Before any road trip, either short or long, it is important to be prepared. The following are a few tips to ensure a comfortable, safe, enjoyable and memorable trip.

Passes and permits

Passes and permits are necessary for travelling through certain parts of Outback Australia and should be organised well before you begin the journey. For information on permits to travel in Aboriginal land, see the section on Access to Aboriginal Land on p. 30.

If travelling into the desert parks of northern South Australia, you will need to obtain a **Desert Parks Pass**. It is issued by National Parks and Wildlife South Australia and replaces the usual daily camping permit required for entering the parks. Passes include detailed maps as well as information on first aid and survival skills. For information on the splendidly varied national parks of Australia, refer to the specific state/territory national parks section of this book.

What to take

As a good deal of your holiday may be spent driving in the car, make sure you take lots of comfortable, loose-fitting clothing. Even if travelling in summer, take at least one set of warm clothing because nights can still get cool in many inland parts of the continent. Soft luggage bags are ideal for packing, as they can be squashed into small, tight spaces.

Essential items that you should not forget when travelling in Australia include plenty of water, hats, walking shoes and good socks, sunscreen, sunglasses, insect re-pellent and a camera. It is also a good idea to have tissues, snacks,

and maps in the car within easy reach. Remember to take important documents with you, such as your driver's licence, vehicle registration, the details of your insurance policy, emergency contacts and medical prescriptions. It is also worthwhile making a note of any allergies you are aware of and your blood type.

Things to check before you leave

Vehicle and trailer/caravan

It is essential that your car is well maintained and just needs some minor fluid level checks before the trip. Keep in mind that a 2 or 3 day trip with a light load is a lot less taxing on the car than weeks of extensive touring fully laden. If you are going to be towing a trailer, the car will be working much harder than normal so car preparation needs to be even more thorough. See the section on *Car Preparation* (pp.20–21) for a suggested list of things to check if you are undertaking a big trip.

Home and contents

- Secure your home (all windows and doors) and belongings carefully.
- Cancel any regular deliveries—milk/newspaper.
- Organise someone to collect your mail and keep an eye on the house.
- Leave a light on in the house, or arrange a time switch to turn lights on and off regularly.
- Organise pet care.
- Organise someone to water the garden and mow the lawn.
- Leave contact details and a spare set of house keys with someone you trust.

Road sign at Travellers Village, South Australia–Western Australia border

Personal preparation

If you are going on a long trip it is most important that enjoyment and lack of stress are high priorities. If you don't know how to do the things listed below and they could be part of your trip, practice in a quiet location with a friend before you go, so that they will not be an issue when travelling.

- Changing a tyre—both the car and trailer.
- Basic car maintenance—courses are run by Evening Colleges and Motoring Organisations.
- Reversing a trailer into a tight spot.
- Using a GPS (Global Positioning System).

Fuel storage tips

- Carry extra fuel in metal jerry cans. Plastic containers might crack and break.
- Store extra fuel on the back of the 4WD or in a trailer.
- Do not pack fuel on the roof racks or inside the vehicle in case of fire or dangerous fumes.

CAR PREPARATION

Many of Australia's roads are now sealed or well-graded, so driving conditions are suitable for most cars. However, if venturing off the bitumen and into the rough is more your style, perhaps hiring or buying a 4WD is worth investigating. If you are planning to tow a caravan or trailer, it's best to stay on sealed roads, regardless of whether you are travelling in a 4WD or not.

Before You Leave Home ...

Make sure that your car has been checked by a qualified mechanic and that he/she knows that you are going on a long trip. If you are towing a caravan or trailer get that serviced as well—particularly the tyres, wheel bearings, suspension, brakes, coupling and lights.

Before and during the trip you need to check:

- There is anti-freeze coolant in the radiator
- Lubricant levels—engine, transmission etc
- Heater and demister work properly
- The battery and mountings
- Tyre condition and pressure (remember the spare!)
- Wheel balance and alignment

Pre-trip inspection by a qualified mechanic

- Wheel bearings
- Condition of windscreen wipers—blades and reservoir
- Brake system
- Exhaust system
- Cooling system—radiator, hoses and thermostat
- Engine drive belt
- Automatic transmission
- Air conditioning
- Lights, including high/low beam
- Filters—air, oil and fuel
- Suspension

Packing the car

Try not to overload your car or 4WD, as extra loads can cause suspension problems. It is a good idea to have heavy duty suspension fitted if you think you may need to carry unusual loads. Pack the heaviest items inside the car, in the boot or in the trailer. The weight of heavy items on the roof could easily throw the car off balance. When packing lighter items on a roof rack, make the load lower at the front and higher at the back. This reduces wind resistance when travelling.

Spare Keys

Spare keys are important. Most cars are now equipped with engine immobilisers and these rely on getting a coded electronic signal from the ignition key or remote unit. This is why it is so important to carry a spare key/remote unit with you on a trip. Without a spare, the car may have to be towed a long distance to an authorized dealer or you may have to wait until the spare keys can be sent from home.

Servicing the air filter

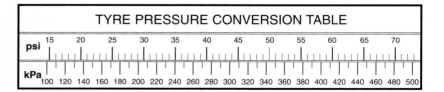

TYRE PRESSURE CONVERSION TABLE												
psi	15	20	25	30	35	40	45	50	55	60	65	70
kPa	100 120	140 160	180 200	220 240	260 280	300 320	340 360	380 400	420 440	460 480	500	

If carrying tools and equipment inside the car, make sure they are tightly secured. It is sensible to install a cargo barrier for this purpose. Emergency equipment, such as a fire extinguisher, should be easily accessible. Keep close at hand the things you may want or need during the journey.

Extras to take

It is always sensible to carry a spare set of car keys, a jack and tools wherever you go. The Tools and Spare Parts lists below are suggested for more remote areas and if packed carefully would take up very little room in the car. The lists are just a guide and may have to be adapted for different makes and models. Most cars use metric fasteners but it pays to check.

Tools and Equipment
- Set of ring/open end spanners
- Set of sockets
- Assorted screwdrivers
- Assorted pliers—combination, long nose and multi-grip

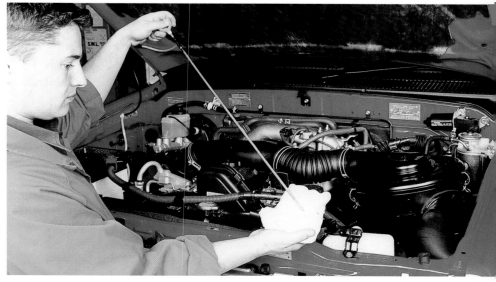
Checking the oil level

On the road near Dubbo, New South Wales

- Vise grips
- 30 cm and 15 cm adjustable spanners (shifters)
- Cold chisel and scraper
- Medium ball pein hammer
- Assorted files
- Feeler gauges
- Hacksaw/blade
- Epoxy fuel tank repair kit
- Radiator sealant
- Loctite Blue Max or equivalent gasket maker
- Rolls of cloth (Gaffer) and electrical tape
- Pump or siphon
- Hand drill and bits
- Plastic sheets (tarp) and blanket
- Collapsible water container
- Aerosol puncture repair
- Tyre pump—12 volt
- Puncture repair kit
- Tyre-pressure gauge
- Four-way wheel brace
- Jack with plywood base 30 cm × 30 cm × 3 cm for sand or mud
- Jumper leads—surge protected for late model vehicles
- Small spade and axe
- Snatchum strap or quality tow rope
- Heavy duty torch, spare globe and batteries
- Pocket knife
- WD40 or equivalent

- Fire extinguisher(s)
- Rags and some hand cleaner
- Folding red warning triangle

Spare Parts
- Radiator and heater hoses—with clamps
- Engine drive belt(s)
- Length of fuel hose—with clamps
- Length of 4mm wire and assorted connectors
- Assorted globes and fuses
- Distributor cap and rotor— if applicable
- High tension leads
- Spark plugs
- Set of points and condenser— if applicable
- Spare fuel, oil and air filters
- Engine and transmission oil
- Assorted nuts, bolts, washers and split pins

Spare Tyre

At least one spare wheel with air pressure slightly above normal should be carried at all times. In remote areas or if the car has a space-saver spare, consider taking an extra spare wheel if space permits.

MOTORING HINTS

Fuel economy

Fuel consumption is affected by both the condition of the car and the roads it will be travelling on. Here are some ways to help conserve petrol.

- Try to avoid delays such as peak-hour traffic or scheduled bridge closures.
- Try to distribute weight of passengers and baggage evenly.
- Drive as smoothly as possible.
- Ensure the tyres are properly inflated and that wheel alignment and balance are correct.
- Service and tune the vehicle regularly following the manufacturer's recommendations. The air cleaner, spark plugs and, on older cars, ignition timing are especially important.
- Avoid long periods of idling. When held up in traffic switch the engine off if it is safe to do so.
- Make sure you fully release the handbrake when driving.
- Avoid driving at high speeds.
- Only use air-conditioning when absolutely necessary.

Measuring fuel consumption

When covering long distances on remote roads, you need to keep a check on your car's fuel consumption. Here is a basic formula for working out fuel consumption.

Total Litres	÷	Total km / 100	=	Litres per 100km
60 Litres	÷	300km / 100	=	20 Litres per 100km

Driving in northern Australia

There are 2 distinct seasons in the north, the Wet (November–April) and the Dry (May–October). Generally, the Dry season consists of comfortable daytime temperatures of around 25°C and cool nights. It is the safest and best time of year to explore northern Australia by car. During the Wet season, it is quite common for roads to become impassable due to heavy monsoonal rainfall. Refer to *Travelling in the Outback* (pp.28–29) for other driving skills not covered here.

Night driving

Avoid planning long drives overnight. Road accidents are 3 times more likely to occur at night because depth perception, colour recognition and peripheral vision are compromised in the dark. Be aware that the risk of encountering kangaroos and wallabies on some roads is increased at night because it is cooler and they often feed on the grass at the edge of the road. Stock wandering onto roads is also a major hazard especially in unfenced parts of the country. If you do have to drive at night, here are some tips so that you can avoid problems.

- Prepare your car for night driving by specifically checking and cleaning the headlights, tail-lights, indicators and all windows, inside and out.
- Ensure your headlights are on when you are driving! Remember,

Driving on an icy road, Ben Lomond NP, Tasmania

being seen by other drivers is just as important as you seeing them.
- Always dim high-beam lights for oncoming cars and those in front of you as a safety measure and as a courtesy.
- If someone fails to do this for you, avoid the glare by watching the left edge of the road and using it as a guide.

Driving in alpine regions

Driving in alpine regions can be difficult, and, in the winter and snow season, dangerous. Here are some tips for driving in snowy and icy conditions.

- Don't put the handbrake on when parking unless the slope demands it.
- Use brakes as little as possible to avoid skidding.
- Control speed—on downhill sections, use low gear instead of brakes.
- Use higher gears when going up hills to avoid over-revving and slipping.
- When changing down gears, do so smoothly with engine speed the same as wheel speed.
- Always put lights on low beam and chains on tyres when travelling while it is snowing.

FUEL ECONOMY CALCULATOR

5	5.5	6	6.5	7	8	9	10	11	12	13	14	15	16	17	18	19	20	25	**L/100k**
55	50	45	40	35	30	25	20	19	18	17	16	15	14	13	12	11	10		**mpg**

AND DRIVING SKILLS

Driving in fog
- If there is near zero visibility, then pull off the road and wait for fog to lift.
- Always put headlights on, and if you feel the need, hazard lights as well.
- Try to avoid crossing roads or highways when visibility is reduced.
- Drive slowly and cautiously.

Driving in wet weather
- Always have properly inflated tyres with good tread.
- Slow down, especially when taking curves.
- Try to avoid the large puddles, they can cause aquaplaning.
- Steer and brake lightly.
- If you go into a skid, decelerate slowly and try to control the steering. Also try to remain calm!
- Try to drive in the tyre tracks left by other cars.

Beating fatigue
It is a well-known fact that driving in a fatigued state is highly danger-ous, and can be fatal. Fatigue happens more often on long drives and at night, but it can be felt at any time. Here are some tips to help combat driver fatigue.
- Have at least 8 hours of sleep the night before any trip.
- Start a long road trip in the morning when you are fresh.
- Try not to drive alone, take turns driving and keep talking to your fellow traveller.
- Keep the temperature cool or the windows open.
- Take frequent breaks—rest at least every 2 hours.
- When you stop, get out and walk around. Exercise combats fatigue.
- Have light meals and snacks (avoid eating heavy meals).

- Drink lots of water.
- Wear comfortable clothes and drive sitting upright with shoulders back.
- Wear sunglasses to fight glare.
- Don't use cruise control (stay involved in the driving).
- Keep the windscreen clean.
- Never drink and drive. It's illegal, stupid, and even one drink can induce fatigue.
- If you feel tired, even just a little, Stop and Rest, even if it means having a 20min snooze, or checking into a motel for the night. Arriving a day later is better than not arriving at all.

Survival hints
If you get stuck in the 'middle of nowhere', here are some tips for staying safe.
- Try not to panic—think of a course of action that will see you helped or rescued.
- Stay with your vehicle—it provides shelter, increasing chances of survival. If a search for you is underway, spotting a car is easier than a person.
- Conserve food and water—always carry enough food and water to keep you supplied for a few days (4ltrs of water per person per day).
- Stay in the shade—keep clothes on to protect against exposure.
- Prepare adequate signals—if in a remote area light a smoky fire to attract attention. Remember to be careful—you don't want to start a bushfire.

Surviving a bushfire
If you get caught in a bushfire, it is important that you don't keep driving through the dense smoke. Also note that there is little risk of the petrol tank exploding in a

bushfire. Here are some guidelines for your safety.
- Pull to the side of the road away from the leading edge of the fire and stop.
- Switch on the headlights.
- Stay in the car.
- Wind up windows and close the air vents.
- Crouch in the car and shelter your body.
- Stay there until the fire passes.

Surviving a flash flood
If your car is caught in a flash flood, remember that your life is more important than the car or its contents.
- Get out of the car and onto higher ground as quickly as possible.
- Swim or float with the current, not against it, if you cannot keep your footing.
- Look for an overhanging limb or embankment to help you reach the safety of higher ground.
- After the flood has passed, you may be able to retrieve your car and dry it out. It is unlikely to have travelled far.

Negotiating a developing flash flood, Northern Territory

DRIVING INFORMATION

Here are some useful tips on driving in Australia.

Travelling with pets

If you want to go on a driving holiday and take the family pet along, it is advisable to plan where you are going to stay before you leave. This is to ensure your pet will be welcomed wherever you go. Even if you plan on camping, check that the site you're choosing does not have restrictions on animals. Most national parks restrict domestic animals from entering.

Driving Licence

- Tourists can drive in Australia if they have a valid licence from their home country for the same class of vehicle.
- Drivers must always carry their licence with them.
- Tourists cannot drive on an international permit alone. It must always be accompanied by a valid overseas licence.

Motoring in the Charters Towers district, Queensland

Quarantine and fruit fly

The Australian countryside is relatively free of disease. There are, however, places where it will be necessary to dispose of certain materials before entering another region. State border regulations require that plant materials, sugarcane, banana plants and fruit are not carried from one state to another. If you plan to travel across the country, be sure to note the relevant quarantine laws for each state—particularly on fruit flies—spreading the pest is a chargeable offence.

Defensive driving

If you are planning a long trip, it might be wise to enrol in a defensive driving course, or at least read up on some driving skills. Defensive driving means that you are not only taking responsibility for yourself, your passengers and your actions, but you are also able to watch out for other motorists and minimise or avoid potentially dangerous situations. The keys to survival are awareness, anticipation and confidence in your defensive driving skills. Here are a few pointers to get you started.

- Be alert and do not assume that everyone else will drive perfectly on the road.
- Do not start the engine without being 100% sure that all passengers have their seat belts on and pets and luggage are secured.
- Do not be extreme by driving too fast, or too slow. Follow the speed limits and enjoy the drive.
- Only overtake other vehicles when it is completely safe to do so. Don't take unnecessary risks.
- Never cut in too quickly when overtaking another vehicle. Allow

Petrol

- In Australia, petrol is either lead replacement (super), regular unleaded or premium unleaded.
- It is sold by the litre and petrol prices are usually higher in country or remote areas.
- You can find petrol stations everywhere. Many are open 24hrs, 7 days—except in more remote areas.

at least 4–5 car lengths before you signal and pull in front of them.
- Always indicate your change of direction allowing plenty of time for other drivers to see you.
- If you have to pull over on the side of the road for any reason, allow a safe distance from the road and make sure you are clearly visible.
- Most importantly, have courtesy and respect for all other motorists, as well as the road rules.
- Always be 100% aware of what's going on around you.

Driving Laws

- Drive on the left hand side of the road.
- Maximum speed in some suburban areas and in most cities and towns is now 50km/hr.
- Country roads and highways have a limit of between 100 and 110km/hr, unless otherwise stated.
- It is illegal to drink and drive.
- It is illegal to not wear a seatbelt (all passengers).
- It is illegal to speed.
- Driving offences carry heavy fines and sometimes a jail sentence. Police patrol the highways in both marked and unmarked cars, and they carry out regular speed radar checks as well as conduct random breath tests.

BREAKDOWNS

Distances between towns in country Australia can be vast. If you are on a driving holiday around Australia, it is possible that your car will break down or get a flat tyre at some time during the journey. Here are some tips for how to deal with a breakdown.

General tips

- Your first concern should always be your personal safety and the safety of your passengers.
- If possible, try to get your car to a safe place, out of the way of passing traffic, before getting out to examine any damage to the vehicle.
- If the vehicle is undriveable, stay inside it and call for help. If you do not have a phone and you have to get out to flag down help, take care where you position yourself in relation to passing traffic.
- Put the hazard lights on to alert other motorists that there is a problem.

Breakdown on the Gunbarrel Hwy, Western Australia

Calling for assistance on a 2-way radio

Tips for breakdowns on highways/freeways/motorways

- At the first sign of car trouble, take your foot off the accelerator very gently.
- Do not apply the brakes suddenly or with great force.
- Use indicators as you move to the side of the road. Always alert other motorists to your movements.
- Once you are off the road, make your car as visible as possible. Turn on the hazard lights.
- Call for help on a mobile or emergency phone. If not possible, take care when trying to attract the help of a passing motorist.
- Always stand clear of the passing traffic.
- If you think you can walk to a source of help, lock your car, take valuables and take great care.

Help in the event of breakdowns

Wherever you are in Australia, you can call this emergency number for assistance—**13 11 11**

- Never attempt to cross a multi-lane highway, freeway or motor-way without extreme caution.

Dealing with a flat tyre

- At the first sign of trouble, hold the steering wheel firmly.
- Slowly decelerate.
- Signal all movement intentions to fellow motorists as you move off the road.
- Move your car off the road if you can—to avoid collisions and traffic hold ups.
- Brake very lightly until you come to a stop.
- Change the tyre if you feel you are a safe distance from the road and have the appropriate tools.
- If you are unable to do so, or your position is precarious, signal for help.
- After you have changed a tyre, and are in a centre where there is a qualified mechanic, get them to check the car to ensure no other damage has been caused to the wheel or car.
- Get the damaged tyre fixed as soon as possible.

ACCIDENT CHECKLIST

If you are involved in a road accident and not injured, it is worthwhile recording the facts while still at the scene. You will need a record of the accident if you are reporting it to the police, filling in your insurance claim, or taking any other action to cover your repair costs. Here is a checklist:

Details of accident
- Date, time and location of accident.
- Was the road wet or dry?
- Width of road.
- Was your car on the correct side of road?
- Estimated speed of both cars at time of impact.
- If accident occurred after sunset, was the site well lit?
- What lights were on, in cars involved?
- Sketch of accident scene.
- Names, addresses and phone numbers of witnesses.

Other car(s)
- Driver's name, licence number, address and phone number.
- Owner's name and address (if different from driver).
- Make, model and registration number.
- Extent of damage.
- Was car already damaged before this accident?
- Name of insurance company, policy number and type.
- Did other driver admit liability? Record exact words.

Injured persons
- Names and addresses of injured persons.
- Degree of injuries.

Damage to property
- Details of damage to property other than cars.
- Name and address of owner of damaged property.

Towing
- Name of tow-truck service.
- Destination of towed car.

Summoning help
Dial 000 to summon emergency help from Ambulance, Police or Fire Brigade. Instruct a bystander or passing motorist to contact the necessary emergency services, giving:
- The location—district, suburb etc.
- The name of the street and the nearest cross-street (suburban).
- The distance from a town or major landmark (country) in kilometres north, south, east or west.
- The nature of the accident—two cars, a pedestrian, a motor cycle etc.
- The number of people injured or trapped.
- Suspected nature of the injuries.
- Special hazards—electricity cables, fuel spilled, fire, railway crossing or any others.
- The time of the accident.
- Ensure that the message is understood and repeated by the person receiving it.

Police involvement
Police must be called to an accident if anyone is hurt or killed, if either of the drivers involved appear to be affected by alcohol or drugs or if a driver leaves the scene without exchanging details.

   If the police are called, record the names of attending officers and their police station.

   If the police are not called, the accident should be reported to the nearest local police station within 24 hrs.

Checking the vehicle after an accident
Where the vehicle has been involved in only a minor accident it may be quite possible to drive the vehicle. Use the following checks to determine the vehicle's roadworthiness. If any doubt exists do not take the risk, have the vehicle towed.
- Check the radiator and cooling system for damage or leaks. DO NOT remove the radiator cap if the engine is hot.
- Ensure there is clearance between the fan and the radiator.
- Inspect all wheels and tyres for damage.
- Turn the steering from lock to lock ensuring that there is adequate clearance between the mudguards and the tyres. At the same time check for suspension and steering damage.
- Check the fluid level in the brake master cylinder. If the fluid level is low, investigate the cause.
- Depress the brake pedal and hold it under pressure. The brake pedal must be hard and should not fall away.
- Check the engine oil for correct level on the dipstick.
- Check the battery for correct electrolyte level and the security of clamps and terminals.
- Ensure that no electrical wiring is caught between damaged components.
- Check lights and wipers for damage and correct operation.
- Ensure that the bonnet closes securely and will not open unexpectedly while travelling.

First Aid

It is a good idea to keep a first-aid kit in your car. You can buy commercially prepared first-aid kits from chemists and camping equipment shops. Alternatively, you can make up your own kit in a clean, waterproof container.

Recommended contents of a first aid kit

- Absorbent gauze
- Alcohol swabs
- Antihistamine (for bee stings)
- Antiseptic cream and swabs
- Aspirin or paracetamol
- Clinical thermometer
- Conforming bandages
- Cotton wool
- Crepe bandages
- Current first aid manual
- Eye bath
- Latex gloves
- Pen torch
- Safety pins
- Saline eyewash
- Scissors
- Sterile dressings
- Sticking plaster and assorted adhesive dressings
- Tongue depressor
- Travel-sickness tablets
- Triangular bandages
- Tweezers

First aid

Snake and spider bites

Try to identify the snake or spider—at no further threat to safety.

- Wrap the area bitten with an elastic bandage or you can use a strip of cloth if you don't have a bandage. This should slow the flow of venom in the bloodstream and most importantly, keep the venom localised.
- Do not apply a tourniquet. This can cause gangrene if it stops the flow of blood completely.

- Don't loosen the bandage once it is applied.
- Get the victim to a hospital so that antivenom can be administered.

Bleeding

Wipe away blood and/or remove clothing to find source of bleeding. Apply direct pressure to the source with a bandage, piece of material or your hand.

- If possible, elevate the affected area (site of bleeding).
- Apply a tourniquet, firm and not too tight, only if you can't stop the bleeding any other way.

Shock

A person is in shock if he or she exhibits some of these symptoms: is cold and clammy to the touch, has a fast but weak pulse, is breathing shallowly, has a thirst, is anxious and restless, and feels nauseous.

- First, cover the person to keep him or her warm.
- Raise the legs so that blood flows to the heart.
- Protect from external elements—wind, cold, rain.
- Moisten the person's lips.
- Do NOT give him/her alcohol.

Heat stroke

Suffering heat stroke is common in Outback areas after long exposure to sun and heat. Symptoms include feeling hot and flushed, a rapid pulse rate, dizziness, fatigue, irrational behaviour and cessation of sweating.

- Seek a cool and shady place and move the heat-stroke victim out of the sun.
- Apply ice packs or cold water to the skin.
- Ensure the head, neck and chest are cooled.

- Ensure the person drinks plenty of fluids.
- Ensure the person gets sufficient rest.

Confidently managing a first aid emergency

When travelling in Australia, with its vast distances, unpredictable and sometimes harsh climate, help may not be close at hand. Knowing what to do in the case of an emergency could save a life.

Before heading out on your next trip, it makes good sense to do a certified first-aid course, such as those run by St John Ambulance Australia. A fully stocked first-aid kit and copy of one of St John's authorised first-aid manuals, or remote area first-aid books could also be life-savers. First aid gives you the confidence to effectively deal with an emergency until medical attention arrives. Call 1300 360 455 for information on St John first-aid training, kits and manuals. Two guides that are especially recommended are the *Remote Area First Aid Field Guide* and *Emergency First Aid*, both available from St John Ambulance Australia.

General assistance after an accident

Injuries should only be treated by competent first aiders. Where possible:

- Keep the casualty comfortable by careful handling, support and reassurance.
- Gently support the injured parts and avoid overhandling.
- Pay particular attention to an unconscious casualty who has an airway problem, breathing difficulty or serious bleeding.
- Hand over immediately when qualified help arrives.

TRAVELLING IN THE

The Australian Outback is vast, and very different from the coastal cities and developed towns. Some of Australia's most spectacular scenery can be found in remote and isolated areas of the Outback. A multitude of shades of red earth contrast with the clear blue of the sky and a horizon that seems to go on forever. With its stark desert landscapes, the Outback is both a beautiful and formidable place. The roads in the Outback are generally unsealed, and there are often no people or pit stops for hundreds of kilometres. If you are considering driving in the Outback independently of a tour, there are some points you should note.

You can employ special driving techniques for avoiding problems on unsealed roads.

- Most Outback roads are unfenced. This means that any wildlife and livestock around can suddenly appear. It is quite common for kangaroos to bound in front of a car. If this happens, try not to panic or brake dangerously. Often a roo will cause less damage to you and your family than a rolled car will. Emus have been known to pace cars (run alongside them), and then dart out in front of the car when they get tired of the race!
- When overtaking, beware of soft or loose verges. The dust caused by the vehicle in front can mask turns, dips et cetera, so make absolutely sure you can see properly.
- Driving directly into the harsh sun can make visibility almost impossible. If you are travelling in a westerly direction, try to arrive at your destination by 4pm. If travelling in an easterly direction, do not start your journey until the sun has risen well above the horizon.

A typical Outback dirt road, South Australia

- Drive carefully and at a safe speed on dirt roads, as dust can mean reduced visibility of potholes and oncoming traffic.
- Avoid driving at night, as the ability to see livestock or wildlife crossing the road is hindered.
- Bulldust can be encountered on many Outback roads. It's a fine dust with the consistency of talcum powder that settles on the road, masking severe potholes or corrugations. Bulldust can also quickly clog the car's air cleaner and can permeate every component and cavity of the car, causing wear and deterioration. Drive with caution through bulldust and, if following another vehicle, always drop right back to allow the dust cloud to clear so the effect is minimised.
- Road trains are multi-trailer trucks that require special caution. The size of the rig means that the driver cannot brake or turn in a hurry and there is a huge amount of momentum. If one is coming towards you on a dirt road, pull

Road train on an Outback gravel road, Northern Territory

OUTBACK

well off to the side and wait until it has passed. Overtaking is often best avoided, especially on dirt roads. It's better to have a rest break than tangle with one of these monsters. If you absolutely must overtake make sure you get your vehicle in a position where the road-train driver can see you in the mirrors, then wait for a signal from the driver that it is safe to proceed.

- Driving through mud is difficult. To avoid getting bogged, use speed and power. Put the car into low, second or third gear and maintain a steady pace through the muddy terrain.
- On sand, keep the 4WD in a straight line—if you have to make a turn, do it by turning the wheel quickly, then back to the original position. Try to stick to existing tyre tracks. When driving down a dune, avoid braking, but don't go too fast, or too slow so that the wheels stop turning. If you get stuck in sand, lower the tyre

Driving near Red Lily Lagoon, Oenpelli, Arnhem Land

pressure, use floor mats to give support and traction, dig out excess sand in front of the tyres to help get moving again.
- When attempting to cross a creek, check the underlying surface, depth and flow of the water by first wading across. A 4WD should be able to manage water of about 60cm deep, but be careful of soft, sandy bottoms and strong currents. Drive slowly into the centre of the crossing, keep the wheels straight and do not change gear midstream. Remember to keep the engine running even if you have to stop the car midstream. Covering the radiator grille with a tarp and removing the fan belt might be advisable on some vehicles.
- Before setting out, know the conditions and distances of your journey, and leave the details of your trip with a family member or friend. If you know you are going to be driving through an isolated area, always notify the local authority of your intended destination and arrival time. This way they can help find you, if you become lost or break down.

- The featureless land of the Outback can make it difficult to know which direction you are travelling in. Always carry a compass—an orienteering compass is reliable, easy to use and inexpensive—and a topographical map. Make sure that the scale on the map is accurate and sufficient detail is given.
- If your vehicle has broken down, do not abandon it unless you are absolutely sure of where you are going and that you can get there safely. If it becomes necessary for others to search for you, remember it is easier to find a car than a person on foot. If you do decide to walk for help, always leave a note with details of who you are and where you are heading. Remember to take plenty of water and suitable clothing, and matches or lighter and a torch, which can be used for signalling, if necessary.
- Cover the risk of getting stranded or lost in a remote area by carrying enough food and plenty of water to keep you supplied for a few days—allow at least 4ltrs of water per person per day.

Fording a creek, Cape Tribulation, Queensland

ACCESS TO ABORIGINAL LAND

If you are planning to visit or travel through Aboriginal land, you must obtain a special permit. There are several types of permits, which vary considerably between different land councils in different states. A transit permit will allow you to drive through Aboriginal land but you may not stop or leave the designated road. An entry permit will allow you to enter a certain area for a specific reason and period of time. Public roads that cross Aboriginal land are generally exempt from permit requirements, with the exemption applicable only to the immediate road corridor.

Applying for a Permit

Permit applications are available on land council websites or at the offices listed below, and may be made by email, fax or in person. To avoid disappointment, please allow enough time for your application to be processed. Generally speaking, an application can be issued within 10 working days. However, in peak tourist seasons and in the event of an extended stay or deviation off the main road, it may take up to 4 weeks for a permit to be issued.

There is no charge for a transit permit, but there may be a levy or fee charged by the Aboriginal community for extended stays. For more detailed information about the permits, conditions, rules and safety regulations, it is essential that you contact one of the following offices well in advance of your intended travel.

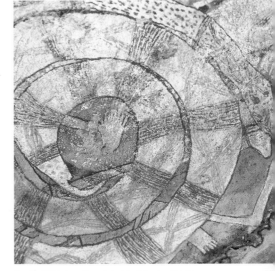

A coiled Rainbow Serpent—Aboriginal rock art, Umorrduk, Arnhem Land

Western Australia
Department of Indigenous Affairs
Level 1, 197 St George's Tce
Perth, WA 6850
P.O. Box 7770, Cloisters Sq,
Perth, WA 6850
Ph: (08) 9235 8000
Fax: (08) 9235 8088
www.dia.wa.gov.au

Northern Territory
Central Land Council
(for Alice Springs and Tennant Creek regions)
31–33 Stuart Hwy North
Alice Springs, NT 0871
P.O. Box 3321
Alice Springs, NT 0871
Ph: (08) 8951 6211, 8951 6320
Fax: (08) 8953 4345
www.clc.org.au
(permit applications closed between 12noon and 2pm)
Northern Land Council
(for Darwin, Jabiru, Katherine and Nhulunbuy regions)
9 Rowling St,
Casuarina, NT 0810
P.O. Box 42921

Casuarina, NT 0811
Ph: (08) 8920 5100
Fax: (08) 8945 2633
www.nlc.org.au
Tiwi Land Council
(for Bathurst and Melville Islands)
Unit 5, 3 Bishop St
Stuart Park, NT 0820
Ph: (08) 8981 4898
Fax: (08) 8981 4282

South Australia
Anangu Pitjantjatjara Yankunytjatjara Land Council
PMB Umuwa
via Alice Springs, NT 0872
Ph: (08) 8950 1511
Fax: (08) 8950 1510

Queensland
Queensland Aboriginal Co-ordinating Council
P.O. Box 6512, Cairns Mail Centre
Cairns, Qld 4870
Ph: (07) 4044 2999
Fax: (07) 4031 2534

NORTHERN LAND COUNCIL
ABORIGINAL LAND ACT
YOU ARE NOW ON ABORIGINAL LAND. TO ENTER ABORIGINAL LAND YOU ARE REQUIRED TO BE IN POSSESSION OF A WRITTEN PERMIT ISSUED BY TRADITIONAL ABORIGINAL OWNERS, THEIR DELEGATE OR THE NORTHERN LAND COUNCIL. PENALTY FOR ENTERING ABORIGINAL LAND WITHOUT A PERMIT IS $1000.00 (SECTION 4 OF THE ABORIGINAL LAND ACT). PLEASE PRESENT YOUR PERMIT ON REQUEST

Aboriginal land sign at Cahill's Crossing, East Alligator River

TRAVELLING WITH CHILDREN

A long drive and travelling with children does not have to be a difficult or uncomfortable experience. Here are some tips for making long car trips more enjoyable for your children—and even you!

- First, prepare the children's first-aid kit with basic ointments, creams, over-the-counter medications and importantly, any individual medications for personal conditions, for example, asthma sprays.
- Make sure you schedule enough time during the trip to make frequent stops. Try to have a 15min stop every 2hrs. Use parks, rest stops and picnic areas to let children run around and play.
- When you stop for lunch, try having a picnic outside rather than sitting in a restaurant, even if it means buying takeaway food to eat outside. You will all be much happier.
- Pack separate bags for your children and place them on top of other luggage, as this minimises inconvenience.
- If they are old enough, give them a map of the route and a highlighter, and let them follow the road. They will be much more interested in the journey and it will occupy some of their time.
- Entertain your younger children with stories—made up or true. Tell them yourself or get some audiobooks—the tapes can provide hours of fun and concentration.
- Play a variety of interactive games like 'I spy' and 'Guess what I am', that everyone can play. Variety is the antidote to boredom.

- Try to schedule your departure for early in the morning. Children will be more likely to sleep for a couple of hours at the start of the trip and wake up for a breakfast stop.
- Try to make children as comfortable as possible. Use car shades and sunglasses to stop the heat and glare. Take pillows to prop up their heads, and blankets for warmth and comfort.
- If your children are old enough, swap seats with them if they are bored or fighting with each other. Give everyone a turn in the front seat on really long trips.
- Make sure you have plenty of dry and salty snacks, and enough water for each person.
- Always pack tissues, face cleaners, a towel and a change of clothes.
- Try to dress your children in layers so they can be comfortable whatever the temperature is.

Avoiding travel sickness

Motion or travel sickness occurs because of a conflict between what the eyes and ears are taking in. The inner ear senses the car as moving, while the eyes (if they are focussed inside) do not. Therefore, the brain gets confused, and nausea results. If your children complain of feeling 'yucky' or 'sick', there are a few different things you can do.

- Suggest they look outside the car. You can do this by playing 'I spy…', or, if possible reposition the seats so they can see out.
- Limit reading and hand-held games.
- Give them some fresh air—open the window.
- Avoid any strong smelling food, and especially, smoke from cigarettes or cigars.
- Feed them dry biscuits—this often settles the stomach.
- Remember to drive smoothly.
- Stop for rests frequently.
- Inquire about over-the-counter medication and remedies from your chemist or doctor before you leave. There are also some very good herbal remedies available, which can be taken prior to setting off on your journey.

Family at Forest Glen Sanctuary on Queensland's Sunshine Coast

USEFUL CONTACTS

NEW SOUTH WALES

Tourism New South Wales
Sydney Visitors Centre
106 George St
The Rocks, NSW 2000
Ph: (02) 9255 1788
NSW Tourist Information,
Ph: 132 077
www.visitnsw.com.au

National Parks and Wildlife Information Centre
102 George St, The Rocks
Sydney, NSW 2000
Ph: 1300 361 967, (02) 9585 6444
www.npws.nsw.gov.au

ACT

Canberra Visitors Centre
330 Northbourne Ave
Dickson, ACT 2602
Ph: (02) 6205 0044
www.canberratourism.com.au

Environment ACT
Level 2, Macarthur House
12 Wattle St, Lyneham, ACT 2602
Ph: (02) 6207 9777, 6207 2900
www.environment.act.gov.au

4WD at Mount Hay, Blue Mountains, New South Wales

VICTORIA

Melbourne Visitor Centre
Federation Square
cnr Swanston and Flinders sts
Melbourne, VIC 3000
Ph: (03) 9658 9658
Victorian Tourism Information
Service, Ph: 132 842
www.visitvictoria.com

Parks Victoria
Level 10, 535 Bourke St, Melbourne,
VIC 3000
Ph: 13 19 63
www.parkweb.vic.gov.au

QUEENSLAND

Queensland Travel Centre
Tourism Queensland House
30 Makerston St
Brisbane, QLD 4000
Ph: 138 833
www.tq.com.au

Brisbane Visitor Information Centre
Queen St Mall
Brisbane, QLD 4000
Ph: (07) 3229 5918
www.brisbanetourism.com.au

Queensland Parks and Wildlife Service
PO Box 155, Albert St
Brisbane, QLD 4002
Ph: (07) 3227 8185
www.epa.qld.gov.au

SOUTH AUSTRALIA

South Australian Travel Centre
18 King William St
Adelaide, SA 5000
Ph: 1300 655 276
www.southaustralia.com

National Parks and Wildlife South Australia
GPO Box 1047
Adelaide, SA 5001
Ph: (08) 8204 1910
Desert Parks Hotline
Ph: 1800 816 078
www.parks.sa.gov.au

WESTERN AUSTRALIA

Perth Visitor Centre
Forrest Place
cnr Wellington St
Perth, WA 6000
Ph: 1300 361 351
www.westernaustralia.net

Camel sign, Central Australia

Western Australia Conservation and Land Management (CALM)
Hackett Drive, Crawley, WA 6009
Ph: (08) 9442 0300
www.calm.wa.gov.au

NORTHERN TERRITORY

Tourism Top End
Cnr Mitchell and Knuckey sts,
Darwin, NT 0800
Ph: (08) 8936 2499
www.ntholidays.com.au

Central Australia Tourism and Visitors Information Centre
Gregory Tce, Alice Springs, NT 0870
Ph: (08) 8952 5800

Northern Territory Parks and Wildlife Commission
Goyder Centre, 25 Chung Wah Tce,
Palmerston, NT 0830
Ph: (08) 8999 5511
www.nt.gov.au/paw

TASMANIA

Tasmanian Travel and Information Centre
20 Davey St, Hobart, TAS 7000
Ph: (03) 6230 8233, 1800 806 846
www.tourism.tas.gov.au

Tasmania Parks and Wildlife Service
GPO Box 44
Hobart, TAS 7001
Ph: 1300 368 550
www.parks.tas.gov.au

Please note that the contact address and phone number for local tourist information centres are shown at the end of each town in the A to Z section of this book. Contacts for Aboriginal Land Councils are shown on p.30.

MOTORING ORGANISATIONS

NSW
NRMA (National Roads and Motorists Association)
388 George St, Sydney 2000
Ph: 132 132
www.nrma.com.au

ACT
NRMA (National Roads and Motorists Association)
92 Northbourne Ave
Canberra 2601
Ph: 132 132
www.nrma.com.au

Victoria
RACV (Royal Automobile Club of Victoria)
360 Bourke St, Melbourne 3000
Ph: 131 955
www.racv.com.au

Queensland
RACQ (Royal Automobile Club of Queensland)
300 St Pauls Tce
Fortitude Valley 4006
Ph: (07) 3361 2468, 131 905
www.racq.com.au

Crocodile warning sign in Kakadu NP

South Australia
RAA (Royal Automobile Association)
41 Hindmarsh Sq
Adelaide 5000
Ph: (08) 8202 4600
www.raa.net

Northern Territory
AANT (Automobile Association Northern Territory)
AANT Building
79-81 Smith St
Darwin 0800
Ph: (08) 8981 3837

Western Australia
RACWA (Royal Automobile Club WA)
228 Adelaide Tce
Perth 6000
Ph: (08) 9421 4444
www.rac.com.au

Tasmania
RACT (Royal Automobile Club of Tasmania)
Cnr Patrick and Murray sts
Hobart 7000
Ph: (03) 6232 6300
www.ract.com.au

**Road Service Nationwide
Ph: 13 11 11**

EMERGENCIES
Nationwide, Ph: 000

Travellers at Mary Cairncross Park, Queensland, overlooking the Glass House Mountains

NEW SOUTH

From the Snowy Mountains to the beaches of the state, New South Wales certainly has something for everyone. Spend a few days skiing; explore the magnificent gorges and waterfalls of the Blue Mountains by foot; take a tour of the Hunter Valley, home to some of the best wineries in Australia; discover hidden rainforests; fish in some of the country's most secluded spots; sail or cruise the bays of Sydney Harbour; watch whales and dolphins off the coast, visit the country's oldest townships; or perhaps just let a saltwater wave wash you ashore on one of the state's golden beaches.

The oldest state in Australia, New South Wales is a prime example of the diversity of the continent's landscape and climate. Located in the south-east of the country, New South Wales is 7 times the size of Great Britain and the same size as California. It boasts the largest population of any state or territory in Australia with around 6.2 million people. The climate varies from subtropical temperatures in the north and along parts of the coast, to the dry, desert-like conditions of the far west, and to the snowfalls of the Southern Alps.

New South Wales: The Premier State

- ◈ Population: 6 200 000
- ◈ Total area: 800 642km^2
- ◈ % of Australia: 10%
- ◈ Coastline: 2137km
- ◈ Length of border: 4635km
- ◈ Floral emblem: Waratah
- ◈ Fauna emblem: Platypus

WALES

ℹ️ Tourist information

Tourism New South Wales
Sydney Visitors Centre
106 George St, The Rocks, NSW 2000
Ph: (02) 9255 1788
NSW Tourist Information, Ph: 132 077
www.visitnsw.com.au

Main ATTRACTIONS

◈ Blue Mountains

The spectacular World Heritage-listed blue-grey gorges and mountainous walking paths are home to some of the state's most amazing rock formations, native flora and fauna, and quaint townships.

◈ Central Coast

With around 1000ha of coastal hinterland, this area is more than just a playground of beaches, holiday retreats and waterways. Horse trails, walking tracks and cycle paths make the region easily accessible for the whole family.

◈ Hunter Valley

The Hunter is home to some of the country's most respected vineyards. In the Lower and Upper valley regions there are more than 90 wineries, ranging from small, family owned businesses, to larger companies with outstanding tourist facilities.

◈ Port Stephens

The magical beaches and waterways of this area make it an ideal recreational destination. Watersports, whale- and dolphin-watching, and fishing are popular activities.

◈ Snowy Mountains

Encompassing the state's largest national park, Kosciuszko, this alpine region boasts world-class ski resorts. Not only known for the powdery winter ski fields, the Snowy Mountain region has walking, camping, fishing and sightseeing opportunities to be enjoyed all year round.

◈ Southern Highlands

Not far from Sydney, the Southern Highlands are a paradise for garden, art, craft and antique lovers. Picturesque towns and local national parks make it the perfect destination for a daytrip or weekend away.

Throughout New South Wales, there are many reminders of a rich historical and cultural heritage. Aboriginal middens, rock art and 60 000 year-old artefacts at Lake Mungo, are amongst the lasting legacy of the first Australians.

European settlement, despite its relatively shorter history, has had a profound impact on the land. The relics of gold-mining towns, heritage-listed buildings and the present-day built environment are testament to the tremendous changes that have taken place since Capt Arthur Phillip raised the British flag at Sydney Cove in 1788.

The capital—Sydney—also has the largest population of any city in the country and is the business and financial capital of Australia. Since the 2000 Olympic Games, Sydney has cemented its reputation as a city with a uniquely welcoming and cosmopolitan atmosphere.

Photo above: The Three Sisters, Blue Mountains

THE PREMIER STATE

In 1770, Capt James Cook named the eastern half of the continent, New South Wales. When the First Fleet arrived in 1788, they landed at **Botany Bay**, but found it an unsuitable spot for settlement. Once Capt Arthur Phillip and his crew discovered the outstanding harbour further north with its reliable supply of fresh water, the convict colony was established at Sydney Cove. The oldest buildings in the country still stand in **The Rocks** today.

The goldrushes of the 1850s transformed the fledgling colony, increased population, stimulated industries and hastened the granting of responsible government in 1856. Today, mining and manufacturing are still major sectors of the state's economy with **Sydney**, **Newcastle** and **Wollongong-Port Kembla** being the largest industrial centres in Australia. Coal was first discovered in the Newcastle area in the 1790s, and today, New South Wales still produces two-thirds of Australia's coal from rich deposits in the **Hunter** and **Illawarra** regions. Silver, lead and zinc continue to be mined, particularly in **Broken Hill**—a major mineral provider since 1883.

Wheat, wool, beef, dairy and cotton farms contribute hugely to national and international markets. One-third of Australia's sheep are bred in New South Wales, carrying on the tradition established by Elizabeth and John Macarthur, who developed the merino breed. Along the northern coast of New South Wales, bananas and sugarcane are cultivated. Rice is an important crop in the **Murrumbidgee Irrigation Area**. Forestry resources are also important, especially in the north- and south-east of the state. With most of the population living within 50km of the coast, fisheries are well developed.

New South Wales can be divided into 4 geographic regions. The coastal strip, where Sydney is

Wheat crop in Central New South Wales

located, is dotted with sunny beaches, some of which are well-known surfing destinations. Most of the towns in the state are located near the coast. Further inland, the rugged mountains and plateaus of the **Great Dividing Range** display some of the most diverse landforms the state has to offer. The **Blue Mountains**, officially uncharted by Europeans until 1813, the **Snowy Mountains**, and the **New England Plateau**, are all well-known tourist destinations in this region. The grassy western slopes, ideal for sheep and cattle grazing and wheat and cotton growing, expand further inland giving way to the western plains that stretch over the remaining two-thirds of the state. Settlement in this region is sparse and drought is frequent, making extensive grazing of sheep and cattle the predominant activity.

Tall Ships in Port Jackson (Sydney Harbour), Australia Day

New South Wales

TOURISM REGION HIGHLIGHTS

New South Wales is Australia in microcosm, from the rugged beauty of the Outback to the alpine splendour of the Snowy Mountains, the lush subtropical rainforests of the north and south and the sparkling beaches of the coast.

A Sydney (pp.42-49)
AMP Tower Centrepoint; Bondi Beach; Darling Harbour; Parramatta; Richmond and Windsor; Royal Botanic Gardens; Royal NP; Sydney Harbour; Sydney Harbour Bridge; Sydney Opera House; Taronga Zoo; The Rocks

B Blue Mountains (pp.79-81)
Blue Mountains NP; Everglades Gardens; Hartley Historic Site; Jenolan Caves; Kanangra Walls; Katoomba; Mount Tomah Botanic Garden; Mount Wilson; Norman Lindsay Gallery; Three Sisters; Zig Zag Railway

C Capital Country
Berrima; Bradman Museum, Bowral; Braidwood; Bundanoon; Bungonia Gorge; Burrinjuck Dam; Canberra; Goulburn; Wombeyan Caves; Young

Rainforest, Mount Warning NP

D Central Coast (pp.70-71)
Australian Reptile Park; Bouddi NP; Old Sydney Town; Tuggerah Lakes

E Explorer Country
Abercrombie Caves; Age of Fishes Museum, Canowindra; Bathurst; Carcoar; Cowra Japanese Garden; Gulgong; Hill End and Sofala; Lachlan Historic Village, Forbes; Lake Burrendong; Mudgee Vineyards; Orange; Parkes Radio Telescope; Siding Spring Observatory; Warrumbungle NP; Wellington Caves; Western Plains Zoo, Dubbo

F Hunter (pp.58-59 and 90-91)
Barrington Tops NP; Lake Macquarie; Lower Hunter Wineries; Maitland and Morpeth; Newcastle; Port Stephens; Upper Hunter Wineries

G Illawarra (pp.106-107)
Fitzroy Falls; Jamberoo; Kiama Blowhole; Minnamurra Rainforest; Shellharbour; Wollongong

H The Living Outback
Broken Hill; Kinchega NP; Menindee Lakes; Mungo NP; Silverton; Sturt NP; White Cliffs Opal Mines

I Lord Howe Island

J The Murray
Albury; Corowa; Deniliquin; Ettamogah Pub; Holbrook; Jindera Pioneer Museum; Lake Hume; Lake Mulwala; Murray River; Tocumwal

K New England/North West
Armidale; Bald Rock NP; Ebor Falls; Inverell Pioneer Village; Lightning Ridge; Moree Hot Mineral Baths; Mount Kaputar NP; Oxley Rivers NP; Tamworth; Tenterfield

L North Coast NSW
Bellingen; Coffs Harbour; Dorrigo NP; Ellenborough Falls; Great Lakes; Kempsey and Macleay Valley; Myall Lakes; Nambucca Heads; Port Macquarie; Seal Rocks; Taree and Manning Valley; Timbertown; Trial Bay Gaol

M Northern Rivers/ Subtropical NSW
Ballina; Border Ranges NP; Byron Bay; Evans Head; Lismore; Mount Warning NP; Nightcap NP; Nimbin; Thursday Plantation; Tropical Fruit World; Tweed Heads

N Riverina
Cootamundra; Griffith Wineries; Gundagai; Khancoban; Narrandera; Tumut; Wagga Wagga; Willandra NP

O Snowy Mountains (pp.76-77)
Kosciuszko NP; Lake Jindabyne; Snowy Mountains Scheme; Thredbo/Blue Cow/Perisher Valley Ski Resorts; Yarrangobilly Caves

P South Coast
Batemans Bay; Bermagui; Central Tilba; Jervis Bay; Kangaroo Valley; Killer Whale Museum, Eden; Merimbula; Montague Island; Murramarang NP; Narooma; Naval Aviation Museum, Nowra; Sussex Inlet

NATIONAL PARKS

New South Wales embraces some of the most varied landscapes in Australia. There are more than 600 national parks and other protected areas in the state. They range in environments from coastal hinterland, to dry bush, to lush waterways and dense forests.

facts

- No. of parks/reserves: 600
- Area: 53 870km^2
- % of state: 6.73%
- World Heritage Areas: Central Eastern Australian Rainforest Reserves, Greater Blue Mountains Region, Lord Howe Island Group, Willandra Lakes Region

A Ben Boyd NP (Map 122, D6)

In the south-east of the state, Ben Boyd NP is separated by the town of **Eden** and **Twofold Bay**. This 103km^2 park is a haven of historic whaling sites, clear-water inlets and coastal forests. The coastline is well-known for the rock formations, flowering heaths, the banksia forest and specifically, the **Quoraburagen Pinnacles**. Visitors are welcome to camp, fish, BBQ, swim, dive and picnic.

B Blue Mountains NP
(Map 81, H2)

With the highest number of visitors of any national park in New South Wales, the World Heritage-listed Blue Mountains NP is a feast of lookouts, bushwalks, wildflowers and wildlife. Only 105km west of Sydney, the park has some of the most spectacular rock formations and gorges in the state. Within the 2482km^2 of bushland, the **Three Sisters** and the **Grose Valley** are popular spots. There are plenty of walking tracks, and camping, picnic and BBQ facilities. Well worth a visit are the cable cars at **Scenic World**, and the towns of **Katoomba**, **Leura** and **Blackheath** with look-outs for keen photographers. For the adventurous there is abseiling, rockclimbing and canyoning.

C Kosciuszko NP
(Map 77, C1)

The largest in the state, Kosciuszko NP, 6744km^2, is home to the continent's highest mountain peak, the New South Wales snowfields and the **Snowy River**. The park expands from the Victorian border across to the **Brindabella Range** west of Canberra. Visit from June to Sept for skiing, and anytime during spring/summer for bushwalking adventures, camping, horseriding, swimming, BBQs, picnicking and trout fishing. A major attraction is the **hydro-electric scheme** (est.1949) that has reshaped the mountains and added to the electricity generating capacity of eastern Australia.

D Mungo NP (Map 116, E5)

In outback New South Wales, Mungo NP, 278km^2, and Sturt NP, 3106km^2, can reach over 50^{0}C in summer. Therefore, they are best explored in the cooler months. Both national parks are of historic significance, and remote, semi-arid desert environments with 4WD

Thredbo River, Kosciuszko NP

New South Wales

access. **Lake Mungo**, now dry, is an archaeologist's dream, with bones, middens and artefacts dating back to the earliest human existence in Australia. The bones of the well-known Mungo Woman have been recently redated to 60 000 years old.

E Myall Lakes NP

(Map 95, D1)

The 442km^2 of Myall Lakes NP contains the largest coastal lake system in New South Wales and is a great spot for waterbird watching and watersports like sailing, wind-surfing, canoeing and waterskiing. Camping, BBQ, picnic and boat hire facilities are available.

F Sturt NP

(Map 111, C2)

Sturt NP, 3106km^2, is referred to as **'the living Outback'** and is home to red kangaroos, emus, goannas, bearded dragons and wedge-tailed eagles. The park has camping, BBQ, picnic and lookout facilities, with extensive walk and drive touring routes.

G Sydney Harbour NP

(Map 47, K6)

Set on perhaps the most beautiful harbour in Australia, Sydney Harbour NP is a landscape of natural bush-land, sandy beaches and sandstone cliffs. With the city as a backdrop,

Superb fairy wren, *Malurus cyaneus*, and nest

the park is divided into a number of sections around the harbour. There is easy access to most parts via public transport. Attractions include Middle Head, North Head, South Head and The Gap, the Manly Scenic Walkway, Nielsen Park, the Quarantine Station, the Harbour Islands and Fort Denison.

H Warrumbungle NP

(Map 118, D1)

The most popular national park of central New South Wales is Warrumbungle. Best visited in spring and autumn, the 232km^2 park boasts great walking tracks, rugged scenery and 4WD access. It lies on ancient volcanoes, which makes rockclimbing popular, although you need a permit to do so. BBQ, camping, picnic and lookout facilities make it a favourite destination for families.

I Wollemi NP (Map 119, F3)

The largest wilderness area in New South Wales, World Heritage-listed Wollemi NP is a rugged 4930km^2 landscape of canyons, undisturbed forests, plateaus and escarpments. Perhaps its most recent claim to fame was the 1994 discovery of the Wollemi Pine (*Wollemia nobilis*), 'the living fossil', which is only known to exist in the wild in this park at a secret location. Canoeing, bushwalking, camping, canyoning, 4WDing and swimming are all popular activities.

National Park Information

National Parks and Wildlife Information Centre
102 George St, The Rocks
Sydney, NSW 2000
Ph: 1300 361 967 or (02) 9585 6444
www.npws.nsw.gov.au

WINERIES

The first vines to be planted in Australia were from cuttings that arrived with Capt Arthur Phillip on the First Fleet of 1788. They were planted at **Farm Cove** in Sydney, but due to poor, sandy soil conditions they did not thrive.

Subsequently, vineyards sprang up in other areas around Sydney and the first commercial wine was produced at **Camden Park** in 1807. **Gregory Blaxland**, of the famous pioneering family, also made commercial wine from his vineyard at **Brush Farm**. Much of the credit for the establishment of an Australian wine industry goes to **James Busby**. Busby arrived in Sydney in 1824 and decided to try to change the drinking habits of colonial New South Wales. He established his vineyard at **Kirkton** in the **Hunter Valley** in 1825. Another New South Wales wine industry pioneer was **George Wyndham**, whose **Branxton** vineyard in the Hunter Valley, established in 1828, is the oldest continuously operating winery in Australia.

The New South Wales wine industry has grown to a point where there are now around 300 wineries, large and small, spread around the state. Today, New South Wales produces high quality wines and is firmly placed on the international wine map.

A Cowra

(p.64)

From modest beginnings in 1973, vine plantings in this area now total 2000ha, with over 30 vineyards between **Woodstock**, Cowra and **Canowindra**. Cowra chardonnays have won many awards, with verdelho, cabernet sauvignon, merlot and shiraz also gaining widespread recognition.

B Hastings River

(p.98)

There are several wineries in the subtropical region around **Port Macquarie**, pioneered in the 1980s by the Cassegrain family. The main wines produced are pinot noir, chardonnay, merlot, semillon, verdelho, and chambourcin a French red varietal, which is perfect with Mediterranean dishes.

C Hawkesbury/Nepean

(maps 46 and 48)

Several small wineries are to be found near Sydney, close to the Hawkesbury/Nepean river system. Locations include **Ebenezer** near Windsor, **Luddenham** and the **Camden** district where it all began. **Gledswood** at Catherine Field is situated on a historic property that produced wines in early colonial times. Classic grape varieties such as chardonnay, semillon, merlot and cabernet sauvignon are grown in the region.

D Lower Hunter Valley

(pp.58–59)

Although wine production began here in 1832, it was not until the 1960s that the industry really started to flourish. By 2001 there were more than 4000ha of vines and over 90 wineries with cellar doors open to the public. The region, centred around **Pokolbin**, near Cessnock, on the slopes of the Broken Back Range, produces around 5% of Australia's wine. Famous names such as **McWilliam**, **Lindeman**, **Wyndham**, **Tyrrell** and **McGuigan** have been joined by dozens of boutique winemakers. Despite 'unsuitable' soils and climate, Hunter wines are rich and full-flavoured, with the capacity to develop in the bottle over many years, and internationally acclaimed. Wines of note include chardonnay, verdelho, traminer, merlot, riesling, shiraz (hermitage) and the exceptional Hunter semillon.

Tyrrells winemaker taking wine samples from barrels for tasting

New South Wales

Vineyard in the Upper Hunter Valley

E Mudgee (p.88)

Like the Barossa Valley in South Australia, Mudgee's wine industry was inaugurated by German immigrants in the mid-19th century. Mudgee grapes are in high demand due to their rich flavours, especially the spectacularly flavoured shiraz and cabernet sauvignon. A Mudgee winery provided the first cuttings for Australia's famous chardonnays in the 1960s.

F Orange (p.95)

Wine grapevines were first planted here in 1983, and there are already about 50 vineyards in the area (including **Mount Panorama** at

nearby Bathurst). At 860m above sea level, these are the highest vineyards in New South Wales. Nutrient-rich volcanic soils, mild summers and cold winter nights assist in producing quality wine with intense flavour and colour.

G Riverina (pp.72 and 83)

The area around **Griffith** and **Leeton** in the **Murrumbidgee Irrigation Area** is the largest winemaking region in New South Wales and one of the largest in Australia. **J J McWilliam** planted the first vines here in 1912. Today, 100 000 tonnes of grapes are produced by 500 growers in an average year. Dry semillon wine is produced in the Riverina as well as shiraz, chardonnay, cabernet sauvignon, merlot and verdelho. The delicious dessert wine 'Riverina Gold' has won international recognition.

H Shoalhaven
(pp.53 and 96–97)

There are several wineries in the triangle formed by **Shoalhaven Heads**, **Berry** and **Bomaderry**,

including one at the historic **Coolangatta Village**. Verdelho and chambourcin have made their mark here, with Australia's first gold medallist for the latter emanating from this area.

I Tumbarumba (map 77)

The newest wine-producing region of New South Wales lies in the foothills of the **Snowy Mountains**. Contemporary viticulture methods are used to produce fine cool-climate wines, mainly pinot noir, chardonnay and sauvignon blanc, with smaller quantities of pinot meunier, cabernet sauvignon and merlot.

J Upper Hunter Valley
(pp.90–91)

The wineries scattered around **Denman** and **Muswellbrook** are generally smaller than those of the Lower Hunter with the notable exception of **Arrowfield** and **Rosemount**. Rosemount's rieslings and traminers first brought wide acclaim to the area in the 1970s. More recently, its chardonnays have won worldwide accolades. Other wine varieties include semillon, verdelho, chambourcin, pinot noir, shiraz and cabernet sauvignon.

K Young (Hilltops)
(p.109)

The vineyards around Young thrive on deep fertile soils. A local wheat and sheep farmer pioneered the first winery in 1969 and the success of his 1974 cabernet sauvignon encouraged others to plant vines. Riesling, sauvignon blanc and shiraz are also popular.

The **Pericoota region** (see L on map) around Moama, and the **New England region** (see M on map) between Tenterfield, Inverell and Quirindi are emerging new wine areas. Canberra District wineries are covered on page 127.

SYDNEY

A harbour ferry passes Sydney Opera House

main attractions

❖ **Chinatown**

The Dixon St area features many restaurants and authentic Chinese stores. Kam Fook, the biggest Chinese restaurant in the Southern Hemisphere is here.

❖ **Darling Harbour**

This is a waterside plaza with parks, shops, restaurants, nightclubs and museums.

❖ **Macquarie St**

This is an elegant street lined with many historic sandstone buildings such as Government House, the State Library of NSW, Parliament House and The Mint.

❖ **Queen Victoria Building**

The QVB is a beautifully restored heritage building next door to Sydney Town Hall.

❖ **Royal Botanic Gardens**

Covering 30ha, these lovely gardens display a variety of rare and exotic plant life.

❖ **Sydney Harbour Bridge**

The world's widest single span arch bridge links the city to the North Shore.

❖ **Sydney Opera House**

This has been regarded as one of the architectural wonders of the modern world since it opened in 1973.

❖ **The Rocks**

This historic area now has galleries, shops, restaurants and Sydney's oldest pubs and buildings. There is a tourist market of handicrafts on weekends.

Australia's most vibrant city, Sydney, is a flourishing cosmopolitan cultural and financial centre. Although Sydney is not Australia's capital, it is the nation's oldest and largest city, occupying 3700km² of the country. Sydney's urban sprawl is an immense natural playground bordered by the **Pacific Ocean** in the east, the **Blue Mountains** in the west and stunning national parks in both the north and south. With its temperate climate, it is possible to make the most of Sydney's striking surroundings in any season.

The major gateway to Australia, Sydney is undoubtedly a leading tourist destination in its own right. Featuring many prime tourist attractions, sightseeing in and around the city is easy. The CBD itself is a manageable size, with many people preferring to see the attractions on foot. Alternatively, the bright red **Sydney Explorer** bus takes in almost all of the major tourist attractions on its 20km route. No one should visit Sydney without taking a ferry ride or cruise on the magnificent **Sydney Harbour**. Cruises and regular harbour ferries all depart from **Circular Quay**.

ℹ Tourist information

Sydney Visitors Centre
106 George St, The Rocks, NSW 2000
Ph: (02) 9255 1788
NSW Tourist Information, Ph: 132 077
www.visitnsw.com.au

facts

❖ Population: 3 700 000
❖ Date founded: 26 January, 1788
❖ Tallest building: AMP Tower Centrepoint, 305m
❖ Oldest building: The Mint (1815)
❖ Average temp: 22.5°C (Jan), 13°C (June)

Places of Interest

AMP Tower Centrepoint (A) C4
Art Gallery of NSW (B) D3
Australian Museum (C) D4
Cadman's Cottage (D) C2
Chinatown (E) B5
Chinese Garden (F) B5
Circular Quay (G) C2
Customs House (H) C2
Darling Harbour (I) B5
Hyde Park (J) C4
Martin Place (K) C3
Museum of Contemporary Art (L) C2
Museum of Sydney (M) C3
National Maritime Museum (N) A4
Powerhouse Museum (O) A5
Queen Victoria Building (P) B4
Royal Botanic Gardens (Q) D3
Star City (R) A3
State Library of NSW (S) C3
Sydney Aquarium (T) B4
Sydney Harbour Bridge (U) C1
Sydney Observatory (V) B2
Sydney Opera House (W) D2
Sydney Town Hall (X) B4
The Rocks (Y) C2
Victoria Barracks (Z) E6

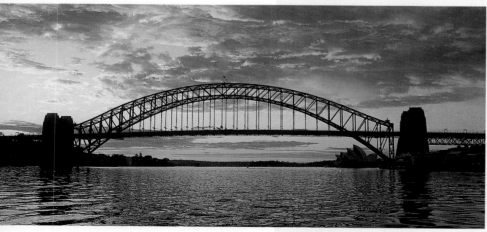

Sydney's famous Harbour Bridge at sunrise

New South Wales

Scale 1:15 000

0 500 Metres

Port Jackson

Goat Island

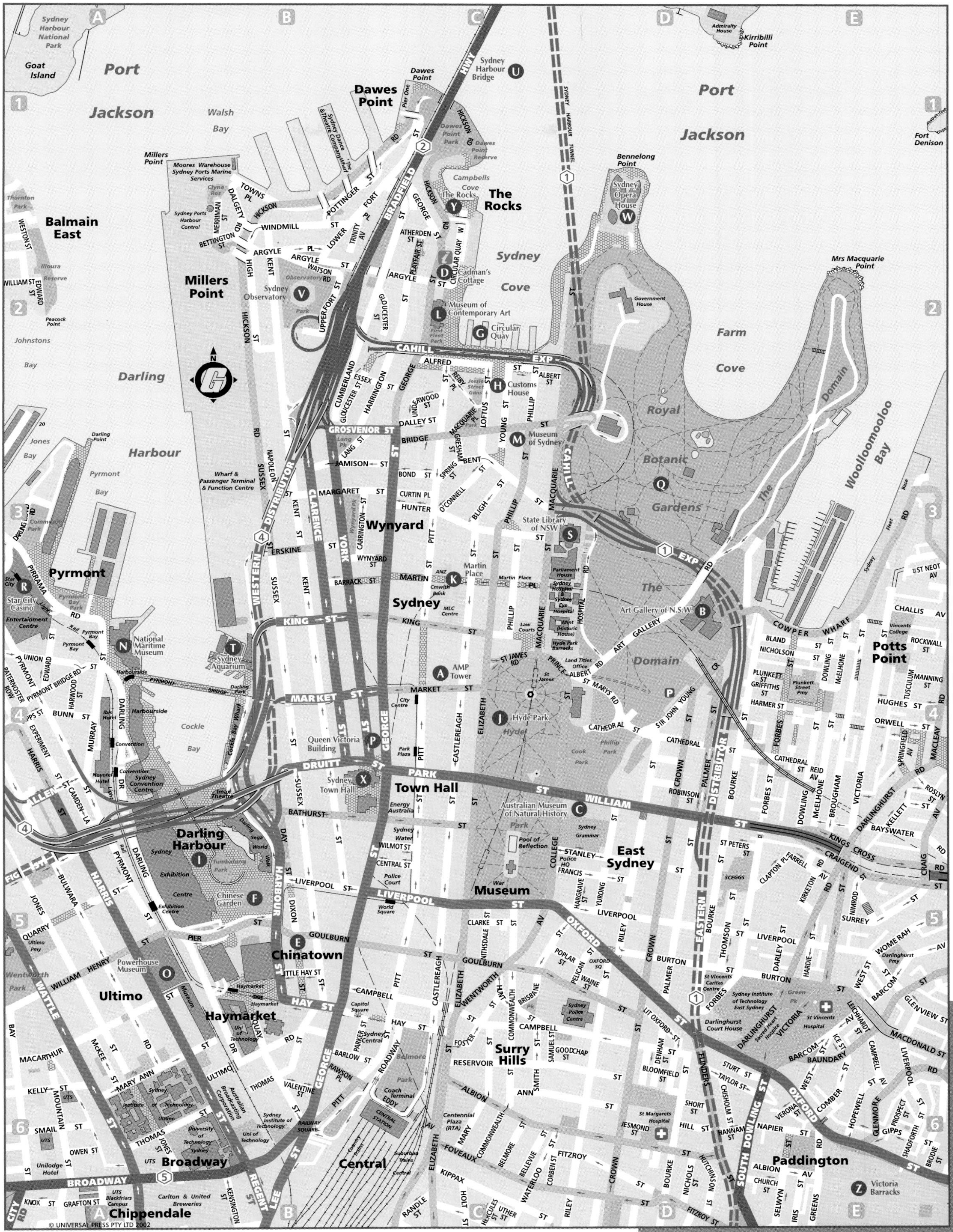

Sydney Harbour National Park

Walsh Bay

Admiralty House

Kirribilli Point

Dawes Point

Sydney Harbour Bridge

Millers Point

Moores Warehouse
Sydney Ports Marine Services

Clyne Res

Sydney Dance Company wharf & theatre

The Rocks

Campbells Cove

Bennelong Point

Fort Denison

Balmain East

Thornton Park

Illoura Reserve

Peacock Point

Johnstons Bay

Millers Point

Sydney Observatory

Dawes Point Park

Dawes Point Reserve

Cadman's Cottage

Museum of Contemporary Art

Circular Quay

Customs House

Sydney Cove

Sydney Opera House

Government House

Port Jackson

Mrs Macquarie Point

Darling Harbour

Darling Point

Wharf & Passenger Terminal & Function Centre

Royal Botanic Gardens

Farm Cove

The Domain

Woolloomooloo Bay

Jones Bay

Pyrmont Bay

Wynyard

Museum of Sydney

State Library of NSW

Pyrmont

Star City Casino

Entertainment Centre

National Maritime Museum

Pyrmont Bay

Darling Park

Sydney Aquarium

Sydney

Martin Place

ANZ

MLC Centre

Parliament House

Sydney Hospital Sydney Eye Hospital

Mint (Historic House)

Art Gallery of N.S.W.

The Domain

Potts Point

Cowper Wharf

Vincents College

Challis Av

Rockwall

AMP Tower

Law Courts

St James Rd

Hyde Park Barracks

Land Titles Office

Cockle Bay

Convention

Novotel Hotel

Sydney Convention Centre

Queen Victoria Building

City Centre

Park Plaza

Hyde Park

Hyde Park

St James

Cook Park

Phillip Park

Cathedral

Darling Harbour

Tumbalong Park

Sydney Town Hall

Town Hall

Energy Australia

Australian Museum of Natural History

Pool of Reflection

Sydney Grammar

East Sydney

Kings Cross

Exhibition Centre

World Square

Police Court

Museum

War Memorial

Ultimo

Powerhouse Museum

Chinese Garden

Chinatown

Haymarket

Haymarket

Capitol Square

Sydney Central

Sydney Police Centre

Surry Hills

St Vincents Caritas Centre

Sydney Institute of Technology East Sydney

Darlinghurst Court House

St Vincents Hospital

Sacred Heart Hospice

Broadway

University of Technology

UTS

Central Plaza (RTA)

Central

CENTRAL STATION

Coach Terminal EDDY

St Margarets Hospital

Centennial Plaza

Paddington

Victoria Barracks

Chippendale

UTS Blackfriars Campus

Carlton & United Breweries

© UNIVERSAL PRESS PTY LTD 2002

CBD & SUBURBS

Sydney's CBD stretches from **Sydney Cove**, in the north, to **Central Railway Station** in the south. The best way to explore the city is on foot and by public transport. Try to avoid taking a car into the city—not only is there a lot of traffic, but parking is scarce and what is available in the city's car parks is expensive.

Walking tour of the CBD

Arrive at **Circular Quay** via ferry, train or bus. Begin with a wander through **The Rocks**, perhaps stopping to browse in the shops and markets. On the way, take a look at **Cadman's Cottage**—built in 1816. The **Museum of Contemporary Art** is a nice place to observe Australia's modern art and perhaps there's even time for a coffee on the terrace that overlooks the Quay. Wander around to the **Sydney Opera House**, on the way taking a look at **Government House**, which sits at the opening to the **Royal Botanic Gardens**. Walking up Young St, past **Customs House** you will reach the **Museum of Sydney**. Inside, an interactive presentation brings Sydney's colonial heritage

to life. From here, venture along **Macquarie St**, past the **State Library**, **Parliament House**, **Sydney Hospital**, the **Mint** and **Hyde Park Barracks**. Once you reach **Hyde Park**, wander through to the **ANZAC War Memorial**, or perhaps visit the **Australian Museum** on William St. It is one of the top 5 natural history museums in the world, and is Australia's oldest. Take a detour to **Stanley St**, where some of the city's best cuisine is to be found, or walk back along College St, to see **St Mary's Cathedral**, which was finally resurrected after the 1865 fire that burnt it to the ground. The twin spires were completed in 2000. Walk through the **Domain** to the **Art Gallery of NSW**, to view some of the finest works of art in the country, including historic, contemporary and photographic works, as well as major overseas exhibitions.

For those who love to shop, don't miss getting a train to the **Queen Victoria Building**, or wander back down towards the Quay to find the **Pitt Street Mall** and the **Strand Arcade**. Perhaps visit the tallest building in the city, the **AMP Tower Centrepoint** for a panoramic view.

On the **Darling Harbour** side of the city (which can be reached by ferry, monorail or bus), take a stroll through **Chinatown**, and on the way, stop for an authentic Yum Cha experience. Worth a look on this side of town are the **Powerhouse Museum**, **Imax Theatre** and the **Chinese Garden**. Darling Harbour is also home to the **Sydney Aquarium**, **National Maritime Museum** and **Star City Casino**, as well as the variety of shops and the restaurants, clubs and bars of **Cockle Bay**.

Take a look at the well-regarded **Sydney Fish Markets** in Ultimo. Be tempted by some of the fresh produce available, and find a spot in the sun to enjoy your seafood experience.

For movie- and theatre-goers, there is an abundance of **cinemas** along George St, and **theatres** dotted throughout the city, all of which have a rich tradition of outstanding theatrical productions.

To the north

The beachside suburb of **Manly** is easily accessible by bus or ferry, and is a well-regarded surfing and tourist destination. Both the **Food and Wine Festival** (late May–early June) and **Jazz Festival** (end Sept) draw huge crowds every year—locals and visitors alike.

Another beachside suburb, **Palm Beach**, is a holiday playground for many Sydneysiders. Beaches lie on both sides of the northernmost point of the peninsula, bordering a golf course and recreation reserve.

Closer to the city, **Taronga Zoo** sits nestled in Bradley's Head, Mosman and enjoys amazing harbour and city views. It is regarded as one of the world's finest zoos.

In a more secluded part of the northern suburbs, **Berowra Waters** is known for its quiet waterfront setting. There are 4 restaurants and 2 marinas to enjoy, or a picnickers' paradise on the western bank next to a handy boat ramp.

To the south

The south of Sydney boasts the famous **Bondi Beach**. Wander the promenade with its restaurants and cafes, or perhaps join the Christmas and New Year's Eve celebrations.

AMP Tower Centrepoint, Sydney

New South Wales

FESTIVALS AND EVENTS

The city of Sydney is known for its party atmosphere so there is never a shortage of annual festivals and events. The **Sydney Festival** is held in January, soon after locals and visitors have feasted on the spectacular **New Year's Eve Harbour Bridge fireworks display**. The following few weeks are filled with free street theatre, concerts, exhibitions and events. Only 2 months later, the **Gay and Lesbian Mardi Gras** takes over the heart of the city with a world famous parade and all-night parties in celebration of gay pride. Soon after, on April 25th, the **ANZAC Day March** walks down the same streets in memory of our war heroes. The **City to Surf** is the most popular public sporting event in the city. Held in August, the 14km run starts from Hyde Park and finishes at Bondi Beach.

New Year's Eve fireworks display on Sydney Harbour Bridge

A most amazing sight is that of **Waverley Cemetery**, which is situated on a promontory of Sydney's south-east coastline and dominated by tall, white marble headstones.

Closer to the city centre is the bustling and colourful district of **Kings Cross**. Nestled together with the strip shows and sex shops are some of the city's best restaurants and night spots.

A visit to **Vaucluse** to see some of Sydney's most exclusive residences and the gothic mansion, **Vaucluse House**, could end with a lunchtime stop at **Watsons Bay**. This prime harbour position boasts the famous Doyles Wharf Restaurant and impressive scenic walks to **South Head**. Alternatively, picnic in shady **Nielsen Park**.

The **University of Sydney** in Camperdown is one of the most striking universities in Australia. Modelled on Cambridge and Oxford, Sydney Uni has a heritage worth discovering on one of the guided tours on offer.

To the north-west
This region is dominated by the mighty **Hawkesbury/Nepean** river system, which winds its way through recreational parks, picnic spots and holiday retreats.

The City of **Parramatta** contains 24 historic buildings as well as several memorials in and around **Parramatta Regional Park**.

While travelling up the Great Western Hwy towards Penrith and the Blue Mountains, **Wonderland Sydney** will be top of the children's

list of places to visit, with over 80 rides, food outlets and theme shows.

To the south-west
This is **Macarthur Country**, named after the early pioneers John and Elizabeth Macarthur who bred merino sheep and provided the foundation for Australia's wool industry. Today, it is a relatively urbanised region but has successfully preserved a few rural pockets and parts of its colonial heritage.

The historic centre of **Camden** boasts 3 reserves, which are perfect for picnicking, as well as many heritage-listed buildings.

Mount Annan Botanic Garden is the largest in Australia and will eventually include most of the country's 25 000 known plant species organised in themes.

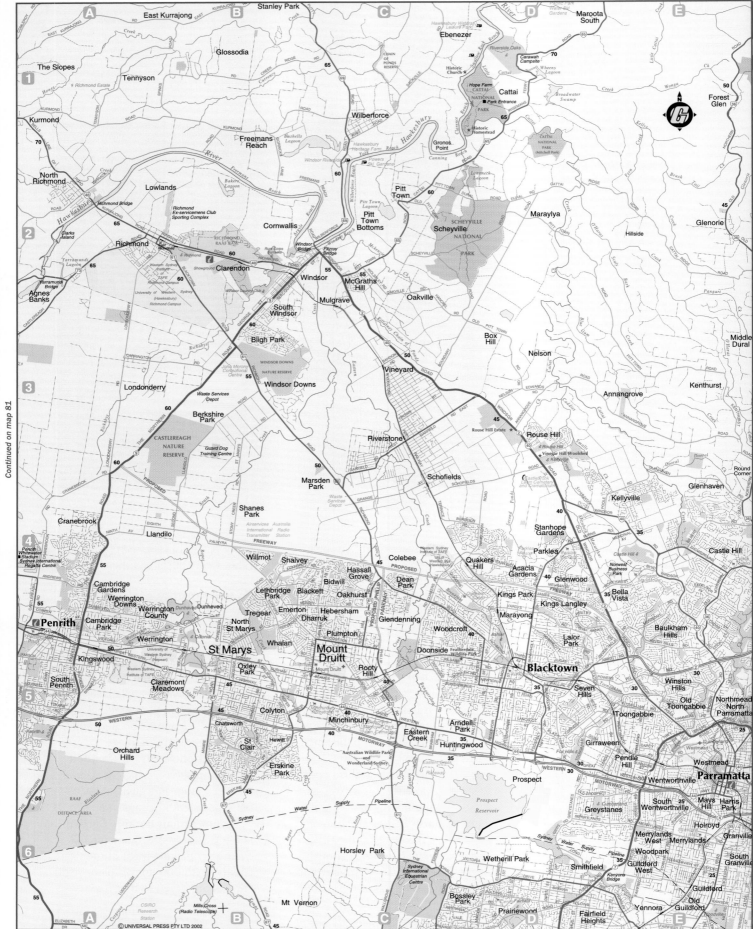

New South Wales

Continued on map 81

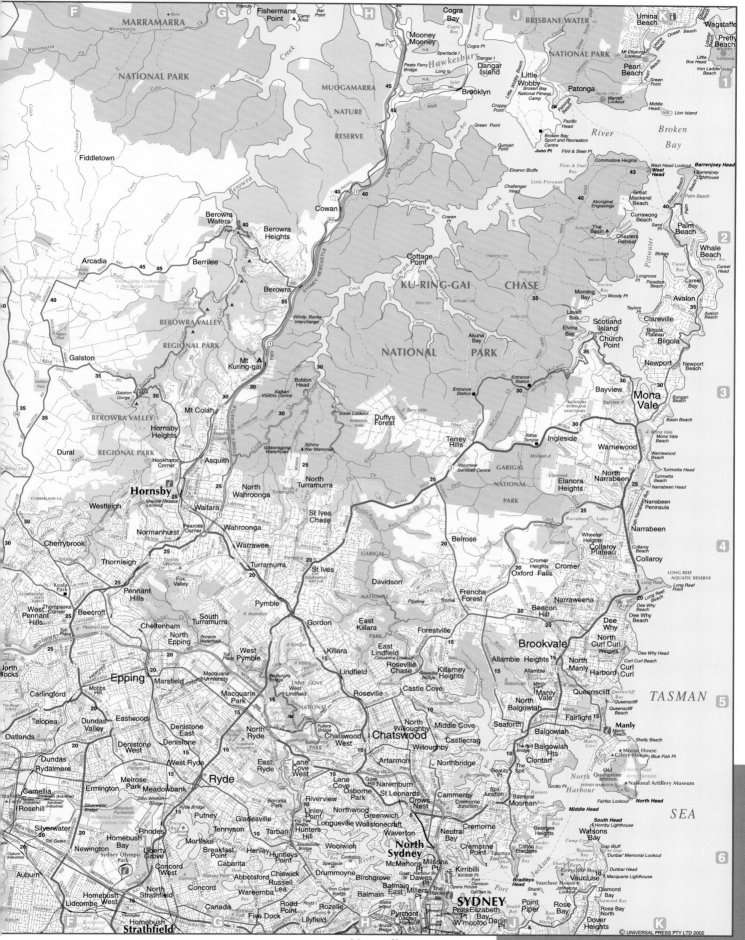

© UNIVERSAL PRESS PTY LTD 2002

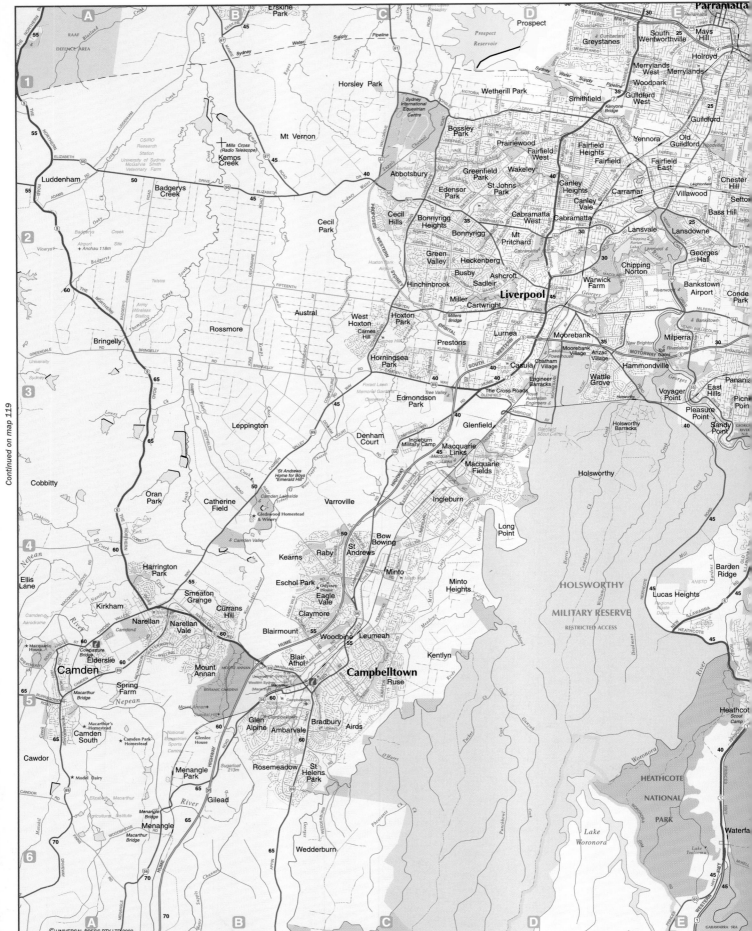

Continued on map 119

Continued on map 107

New South Wales

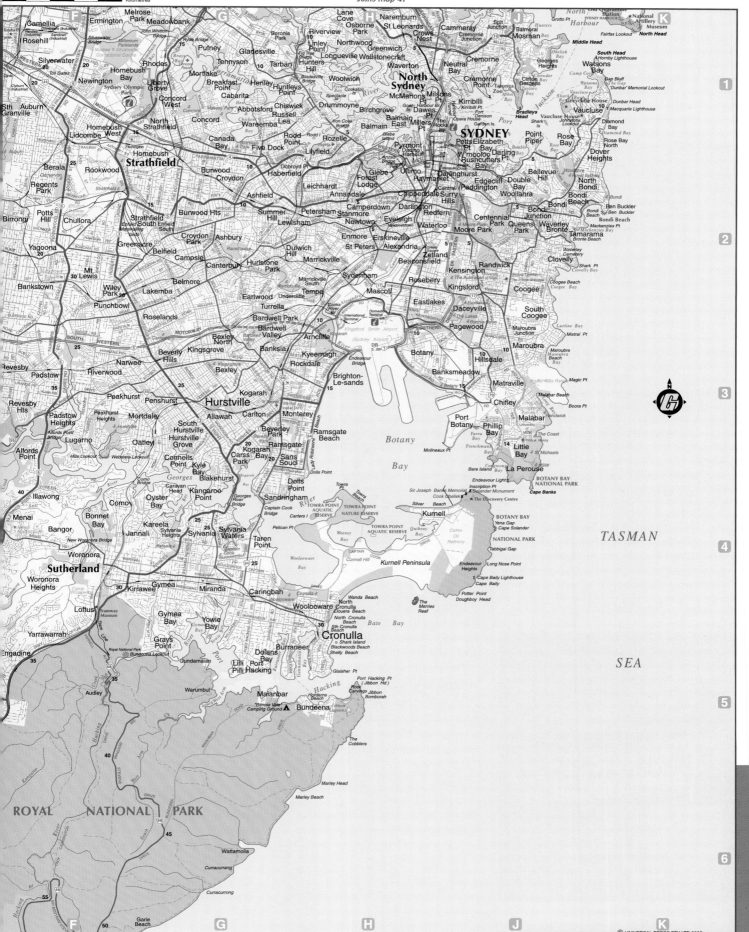

Continued on map 107

■ Albury   POP 45 000

Map 121, K4

Sometimes known as only Albury, the real city is a conjoining of 2, Albury-Wodonga, and lies 575km SW of Sydney on the **Murray River**. Albury lies within New South Wales, while Wodonga, is on the Victorian side. The region was discovered by Hume and Hovell during their 1824 exploration, and Albury grew as an important paddlesteamer port in the heyday of the river trade. Today, the city serves a region rich in crops, cattle, wine and scenery. It is also a convenient stopover for those driving between Sydney and Melbourne.

MAIN ATTRACTIONS: Points of interest include the many buildings dating from the late 1800s, such as the Turks Head Inn, which now houses **Albury Regional Museum**. The **Albury Botanic Gardens** were established on Bungambrawatha Creek over 100 years ago. The **Regional Arts Centre** features the locally made *Aurora Australis* tapestry, paintings, ceramics and photographs.

NEARBY ATTRACTIONS: **Ettamogah Sanctuary**, north of Albury, is the place to view native wildlife. Further on at **Table Top** is the eccentric **Ettamogah Pub**, a living replica of Ken Maynard's cartoon, published in *Australia Post* in 1959. Opposite is the **Table Top Winery**, which is open for tastings and sales. For those interested in military matters, **Bandiana Military Camp** covers a considerable area on the south-east outskirts of Wodonga. A hangar-type building houses the **RAA Ordnance Corps Museum**, which displays tanks, armoured vehicles, uniforms, weapons and other paraphernalia. In the warmer months, the paddlesteamer **PS *Cumberoona*** cruises the Murray River.

TOURIST INFO: Gateway Village, Lincoln Causeway, Hume Hwy, Wodonga, Ph: 1800 800 743

■ Armidale   POP 22 500

Map 115, F5

Nestled in the **New England Ranges**, 567km north of Sydney, is the main city of the Tablelands, Armidale. The city is renowned for its churches and as a seat of learning. The **University of New England** is located here as well

The Ettamogah Pub, north of Albury

New South Wales

as a TAFE college and some long-established private schools.

MAIN ATTRACTIONS: **The Heritage Tour** is a good way to see Armidale. The bus leaves the visitors centre at 10am weekdays, and 10.30am weekends and holidays for a 2hr guided tour exploring the city's history and heritage—the cost is a gold coin donation. The **Heritage Walk** is also worthwhile. Leaflets are available from the visitors centre and the walk includes 34 points of interest. Armidale's parks and gardens are especially attractive during spring and autumn. **The Apex Memorial Lookout** in **Drummond Park** provides a view of the whole city. There are many museums to visit, including the modern **Regional Art Museum** in Kentucky St. Exhibits include the collections of Howard Hinton, Chandler Coventry as well as works by other Australian artists. **Armidale and New England Folk Museum** is housed in the old School of Arts and Mechanics Institute (1863) and depicts the life and history of the city. Several rooms are furnished in period-style. The museum is located on the corner of Faulkner and Rusden sts and is open daily, 1pm–4pm.

NEARBY ATTRACTIONS: The old gold-mining town **Hillgrove** is located 27km to the east. Hillgrove was once home to 3000 residents. The 2 mines here produced over $1.6 million worth of gold. The **Hillgrove Rural Life and Industry Museum** is open Fri–Mon and holidays, 10am–5pm. Approximately 6km south is **Saumarez Homestead**, a house museum developed by the National Trust. The museum reflects the history of the New England pastoral properties. Surrounded by gardens and views of pastureland, the property is open daily from September to the June long weekend. Arrange to view inside the house with the information

Point Lookout, New England NP

centre. Within a 1hr drive of the city are 3 national parks: **New England, Cathedral Rock** and **Oxley Wild Rivers**. Oxley Wild Rivers NP contains **Dangars Gorge**, 23km south of Armidale and is well worth visiting. **Wollomombi Falls**, 40km east on Waterfall Way, is the second highest waterfall in Australia, with a drop of 220m.

TOURIST INFO: 82 Marsh St, Ph: (02) 6772 4655 or 1800 627 736

■ Ballina   POP 16 500

Map 84, D3

Ballina lies inside the breakwaters of the **Richmond River**. The area is the traditional home of the Bandjalung Aboriginal people. Capt Henry Rous named the Richmond River in 1828. Cedar-cutters were the first settlers in the area and the town was gazetted in 1856. Sugar and dairy farms were established in the 1860s and continue as major local industries, along with fishing and boat building. The tourism boom of the 1960s saw the town develop into a major attraction centred on its idyllic beaches, the

river and attractive hinterland. Ballina also has very good markets, cafes and restaurants.

MAIN ATTRACTIONS: The **Big Prawn Complex** on the Pacific Hwy is an instantly recognisable landmark and a sign of the town's busy fishing industry. It has an **Opal and Gem Museum** as well as arts and crafts and fresh seafood. Other attractions in Ballina include the **Naval and Maritime Museum** in Regatta Ave and the **Kerry Saxby Cycleway and Walkway**. River cruises, whale- and dolphin-watching cruises and parasailing are also popular as well as water-based recreational activities like fishing, surfing and swimming.

NEARBY ATTRACTIONS: On the Pacific Hwy, just north of Ballina are the **Bicentennial Gardens**, and **Thursday Plantation Tea Tree Centre**—a working tea-tree plantation. The **Macadamia Castle** at Knockrow and **Summerland House with no Steps**, located at **Alstonville**, west of Ballina, are popular family attractions.

TOURIST INFO: cnr Norton St and Las Balsas Plaza, Ph: (02) 6686 3484

■ Batemans Bay   POP 8500
Map 122, E3

Located at the mouth of the **Clyde River**, Batemans Bay is a fishing town and holiday destination—only 152km from **Canberra**, so it attracts many visitors from the capital. The town is also a service centre for the surrounding hinterland, which produces timber, dairy products and vegetables.

MAIN ATTRACTIONS: The beaches, rivers and lakes are prime attractions. Lunchtime river cruises, fishing charters and houseboat hire are all available. Boat ramps give boat owners easy access to the Clyde River or the ocean. The **Old Court House Museum** displays local history through collections of photographs and memorabilia.

NEARBY ATTRACTIONS: South of Batemans Bay is the old gold-mining region of Mogo. **Old Mogo Town** is a re-creation of a 19th-century gold town and is open daily. Visitors can see a blacksmith's shop and forge, an ore-crushing plant, tavern and Cobb & Co freight station. In the same area is **Mogo Zoo**. Open daily, 9am–5pm, the zoo specialises in Australian native animals and wild cats, successfully breeding snow leopards. The **Eurobodalla Nature and Botanic Gardens** are located approximately 7km south of Batemans Bay at **Deep Creek Dam**. The gardens are open Wednesdays, Sundays and school holidays and offer visitors the chance to enjoy the native flora. There are 2 national parks close to the town. **Budawang NP** in the hinterland is part of the eastern scarp of the **Southern Highlands**. It is small, rugged, remote and with no facilities. **Murramarang NP**, extending along the coast 20km to the north, is a more popular recreation area offering sandy beaches, surfing, rock and beach fishing, and gentle walks.

TOURIST INFO: Cnr Princes Hwy and Beach Rd, Ph: (02) 4472 6900

■ Bathurst   POP 30 053
Map 118, E4

Australia's oldest inland settlement, Bathurst, is a thriving rural area with education being the city's largest industry. The main campus of **Charles Sturt University**, 2 TAFE campuses, 4 private and 2 public high schools are all located here. It is also well-known for its car-racing circuit, Mount Panorama. In October the **Bathurst (Supertourers) Car Races** are held and in November it's the famous **Bathurst 1000 V8 Supercar Race**.

MAIN ATTRACTIONS: Ben Chifley, Prime Minister of Australia from 1945 to 1949, was born in Bathurst. Located at 10 Busby Street, **Chifley Home** is open to the public Tuesday to Saturday 2pm–4pm and Sunday, 10am–12 noon. Also worthwhile visiting is **Miss Triall's House and Garden**—a house museum recording 100 years of family life. Miss Ida Triall bequeathed her colonial Georgian house to the National Trust. The **National Motor Racing Museum**, located at Murray's Cnr, is where you can experience the excitement of past motor racing, with displays, videos, photographs and memorabilia. Visitors can arrange to drive the famous international **Mount Panorama Motor Racing Circuit**. There are many parks in Bathurst. **Machattie Park** was developed in the late 19th century and visitors can enjoy the bandstand, fountain, fern house and duck ponds. **Macquarie River Bicentennial Park** is a popular site for picnics. It offers covered tables, BBQs, children's play areas, lovely gardens and the **Heritage Wall**.

NEARBY ATTRACTIONS: The **Bathurst Goldfields**, a reconstruction of the historic gold-mining area, are located south-west of the city centre. The former goldfield, **Hill End**, still has many original buildings and has inspired paintings by John Olsen and Brett Whiteley. It is about 86km NW of Bathurst. **Abercrombie Caves**, 72km to the south, has camping areas and features the largest natural limestone bridge in the Southern Hemisphere.

TOURIST INFO: 28 William Street, Ph: (02) 6332 1444

Eastern grey kangaroo, *Macropus giganteus*, and joey at Pebbly Beach, Murramarang NP, north of Batemans Bay

New South Wales

Abercrombie Caves, south of Bathurst

■ Bega   POP 4300

Map 122, D5.

This picturesque town is located in prime dairy country, 431km south of Sydney, at the junction of the Princes and Snowy Mountains hwys linking Sydney, Canberra and Melbourne.

MAIN ATTRACTIONS: Lookouts around Bega include the **Dr George**, 8km to the NE, and **Bega Valley**, 2km north, and offer views of the **Bega River** winding around the town. The **Bega Co-operative Cheese Factory** is open daily 9am–5pm. Here visitors can watch the cheese-making process and sample the products. A Heritage Centre displays early cheese-making equipment and there is also a cafe and art gallery. The **Grevillea Estate Winery** is 5km west of Bega, on Buckajo Rd. Open for tastings, the winery also has a restaurant. Children can watch cows being milked on the **Rotolactor** and meet farm animals. Leaflets describing Bega's **historic walk** are available from the information centre. Stops include the **Court House** (1881), the **Old Bega Hospital Complex** (now a cultural centre)

and **Bega Family Museum**. The museum, a building that was once the Bega Family Hotel, displays pioneer memorabilia and local crafts. The museum is located on the corner of Bega and Auckland sts.

NEARBY ATTRACTIONS: In summer it is worthwhile visiting **Mumbulla Falls** with its many rockpools. The falls are located in the hills 15km NW of the town. **Tathra** is the closest beach to Bega. At one end of the beach is the mouth of the **Bega River**. The original **1860s wharf** still stands and the old cargo shed houses a maritime and history museum.

TOURIST INFO: 91 Gipps St, Ph: (02) 6492 2045

■ Berrima   POP 750

Map 107, A2

This historic town is located 14km south of Mittagong on the Hume Hwy. Still preserved as a village of the 1850s, Berrima offers the visitor many attractions.

MAIN ATTRACTIONS: A self-guided **walking tour** around the town is recommended. Leaflets describing the walk are available from the Court House. A guided walking tour

can also be booked a day ahead. Buildings of interest include **Berrima Court House**, built in 1838. This Court House held the first trial by jury in New South Wales and now houses the information centre, which is open daily 10am–4pm. Displays include a sentencing session of a 19th-century trial and a video history of the town and district. **Berrima Gaol**, built in 1839, is across the road and is now a medium security facility and rehabilitation centre. **Berrima Court House Museum** displays local memorabilia and items of historic interest. Now a member of the worldwide Booktown organisation, the **Petty Jury Bookshop**, located in the museum, specialises in Australian history and has copies of antique maps. It is open weekends and holidays from 10am to 4pm. **Holy Trinity** and **St Francis Xavier** churches are worthwhile visiting. **Berkelouw's Antiquarian Book Barn** is located on the Old Hume Hwy and stocks over 200 000 rare and second-hand books.

TOURIST INFO: Berrima Court House, Cnr Wilshire and Argyle St, Ph: (02) 4877 1505

■ Berry   POP 1600

Map 97, C1

Known as **'The Town of Trees'**, Berry is a picturesque town with beautiful deciduous trees, planted at the turn of the 19th century, lining its streets. Located on the Princes Hwy, 16km north of Nowra, Berry is popular as a weekend getaway and offers many B&B's, guesthouses and motels.

MAIN ATTRACTIONS: There are plenty of activities available in Berry; walking, horseriding, cycling and 4 local wineries are open for tastings and sales. Many of Berry's heritage buildings have been renovated and now house cafes, antique shops, nurseries, and art and craft galleries.

NEARBY ATTRACTIONS: Alexander Berry, the district's first and most prominent settler, constructed **Coolangatta Estate**, a private village in 1822. It has been beautifully restored and is now a resort open to the public. The old Coolangatta schoolhouse has become **Coolangatta Craft Centre**, featuring wood and folk art, hand-blown glass and pottery. It is open Wed–Mon, 9am–5pm and daily during school holidays.
TOURIST INFO: Cnr Princes Hwy and Pleasant Way, Nowra,
Ph: (02) 4421 0778

■ Blayney   POP 2700
Map 118, E4
This mid-19th century gold-mining town is a centre for the surrounding farming and grazing region of the picturesque **Belubula River Valley**. The goldrush of the 1850s and 60s sparked development in the district and gold is still mined at **Cadia Gold Mine**. The opening of another mine is planned for the future.
MAIN ATTRACTIONS: Many items associated with the development of Blayney are displayed at the **Viv Kable Museum** in the **Blayney Library**, Adelaide St. Here you can also carry out family and local history research. The town also has a number of art and craft outlets. There are 2 parks with picnic facilities: **Heritage Park** in Adelaide St and **Carrington Park** in Osman St. **Church Hill Lookout**, accessed through the industrial estate north of the town, gives a panoramic view of the surrounding Belubula Valley.
NEARBY ATTRACTIONS: Blayney is a good base for exploring the district's historic settlements. **Carcoar**, 14km SW, is in a pleasant valley setting. In 1863, it was the scene of the first recorded daylight bank robbery in New South Wales. The third oldest town west of the Blue Mountains, Carcoar has remained relatively untouched since the 19th century. Some of the historic buildings now

Local museum, Carcoar

house antique shops and tea-rooms. **Carcoar Dam** is a popular recreation area with camping facilities. From Carcoar Dam there are excellent views of the recently opened **Blayney Wind Farm**. **Millthorpe** is a National Trust-classified village, 11km NW, with bluestone churches and workers' cottages. Millthorpe's **Golden Memories Museum** displays more than 5000 items illustrating how people lived in the late 1800s.
TOURIST INFO : 97 Adelaide St,
Ph: (02) 6368 3534

■ Bourke   POP 4200
Map 113, F4
This far western **Darling River** town is the gateway to the real Outback and the main centre for an extensive pastoral district that produces more wool than anywhere else in New South Wales. In 1897, the construction of a lock and weir

on the Darling River meant that paddlesteamers were able to go further up the river and eventually, in 1964, there was sufficient water for irrigation, allowing crops such as citrus, grapes, lucerne and sorghum to be grown. In recent years cotton farming has become one of the main industries in the area.
MAIN ATTRACTIONS: Bourke has many historic buildings and places to see. **The Back O'Bourke Mud Map Tours'** booklet is available from the information centre and is an essential guide. There is also a Back O'Bourke 3hr minibus tour of the town. In season, there are tours of cotton farms. The paddle-vessel **PV Jandra**, is available for cruises on the Darling River. More details on these tours are available from the information centre. The **Old Railway Station** in Anson St has displays of Aboriginal artefacts and a selection of literature on local

New South Wales

history. The famous eye surgeon, Fred Hollows' grave and memorial is in the cemetery.

NEARBY ATTRACTIONS: There is a wildlife sanctuary and Aboriginal rock art painted by the Ngemba tribe at **Gunderbooka**, 74km south. **Mount Oxley** is the highest landmark in the area, 34km NE.

TOURIST INFO: Old Railway Station, Anson St, Ph: (02) 6872 1222

■ Bowral POP 5000

Map 107, B2

A popular town in the **Southern Highlands**, Bowral is well known for its country resorts, B&B's, and excellent cafes and restaurants. A highlight of the year is **Tulip Time**, an annual spring celebration with thousands of tulips and spring flowers blooming in both public and private gardens—some open to the public. The deciduous trees planted along the roadside highlight the change of the seasons and are another attraction for visitors.

MAIN ATTRACTIONS: The **Bradman Museum** in St Jude Street is a must-see for cricket fans. The museum highlights Sir Donald Bradman's achievements, displays cricket memorabilia, and documents the origins of the game and its growth in Australia, the history of the Ashes and the Bradman era. The museum is open daily 10am–5pm. There is a self-guided walk, which takes in a number of sites around Bowral associated with Sir Donald. Called the **Bradman Walk**, it begins at the museum. Many buildings and houses built in the late 19th century have been beautifully preserved. Buildings of interest include the **Court House, Municipal Chambers, St Jude's Church and Rectory. Merrigang, Wingecarribee** and **Bendooley sts** are particularly attractive streetscapes.

NEARBY ATTRACTIONS: Over the town **Mount Gibraltar** rises 863m above sea level. Picnic facilities are located on top of the mountain and there are views from 4 lookouts. Native flora and fauna can also be seen from the tracks in **Gibbergunyah Reserve**, accessed off Boronia St.

TOURIST INFO: 62–70 Main St, (Old Hume Hwy), Mittagong, Ph: (02) 4871 2888

■ Broken Hill POP 21 356

Map 116, B2

This city is located 1158km west of Sydney and operates on South Australian time. Broken Hill remains one of the world's great mining centres, despite its downsizing in recent years.

MAIN ATTRACTIONS: Broken Hill attracted many well-known Australian artists (the 'Brushmen of the Bush') during the 1970s. Showrooms and art galleries are now a feature of the city. **Pro Hart's Gallery** at 108 Wyman St displays his own work together with his private collection. The **City Art Gallery**, on the corner of Blende and Chloride sts, features European and Aboriginal art, and works by local artists. *The Big Picture* at **Silver City Mint and Art Centre** is the world's largest acrylic painting on canvas measuring 12m by 100m.

NEARBY ATTRACTIONS: The **Living Desert Reserve**, 6km from the city on Nine Mile Rd, displays the **Living Desert Sculptures**—12 works of art by international artists dedicated to renowned eye surgeon, Fred Hollows. **Delprats Underground Mine Tours** is near the **Line of Lode Miners' Memorial. Day Dream Mine** on the Silverton road, 33km NW, is a pioneers' mine, discovered in 1881, that offers underground tours. **Silverton**, known as **'Hollywood of the Outback'**, is popular with tourists. It is a virtual ghost town and was used as the setting for movies like *Mad Max*.

TOURIST INFO: Cnr Blende and Bromide sts, Ph: (08) 8087 6077

Palace Hotel, Broken Hill

MYALL LAKES

Myall Lakes is a system of shallow waterways stretching along the coast of the Tasman Sea, 236km north of Sydney. The tranquillity of this area is conserved in a very popular national park scattered with numerous camping retreats.

Myall Lakes NP contains the largest coastal lake system in New South Wales and is an important waterbird habitat. Walk through rainforest, hire a houseboat or take a 4WD along the beach. With an area of 442km^2, this popular park has something to offer everyone.

The western edges of the lakes can be accessed via numerous roads and trails leading from the **Pacific Hwy**. Access in the east is possible from **Mungo Brush Rd**, via **Hawks Nest** and by 4WD from a turnoff at **Bungwahl to Seal Rocks Road**. (map p.95)

Canoeing on the Myall Lakes

Part of the Great Lakes district, the Myall Lakes, which cover more than 100km^2, are ideal for watersports and boating. Boats can be hired from **Myall Shores** and from **Tea Gardens** and houseboats from **Bulahdelah**.

■ Brunswick Heads   POP 2000
Map 84, D1

Located at the mouth of the **Brunswick River**, approximately 20km north of **Byron Bay**, is the commercial fishing town of Brunswick Heads. With its surf beaches stretching for many kilometres, particularly good fishing and boating and its warm climate, Brunswick Heads is a very popular holiday town.

NEARBY ATTRACTIONS: Only 19km south of Brunswick Heads is **Cape Byron**, the easternmost point in Australia. **Ocean Shores** lies north of the Brunswick River and offers excellent coastal views from **Lions Lookout**. The hinterland is also very attractive and visitors can take advantage of the scenic drives and rainforest walks at **Minyon Falls**

and **Goonengerry**, behind **Mullumbimby**. The **Tyagarah Flora and Nature Reserve** is also worthwhile visiting and can be accessed by road and footbridge across the south arm of the Brunswick River.
TOURIST INFO : 80 Jonson St, Byron Bay, Ph: (02) 6680 9271 or (02) 6685 8050

■ Bulahdelah   POP 1200
Map 95, C1

Lying approximately halfway between Newcastle and Taree is the township of Bulahdelah. State forests and **Myall Lakes NP** are in close proximity, so those who enjoy bushwalking, horseriding, birdwatching, boating, canoeing, sailing, fishing and swimming will find the town a convenient base.
MAIN ATTRACTIONS: **Bulahdelah Mountain** is known locally as

Mount Alum because of its huge deposits of the substance used in medicine, dyeing and many other technical processes. **Bulahdelah Mountain Park**, approximately 2km down Meade St, offers picnic and BBQ facilities. There are also many walking trails throughout the rainforest leading to picnic areas with good views over Bulahdelah and the **Myall Valley** and through to the ocean beyond.
NEARBY ATTRACTIONS: There are over 500km of forest roads throughout the state forests and national parks in the district. Maps and leaflets are available from the information centre. **Wang Wauk Forest Drive** passes through some of the largest stands of flooded gum trees in New South Wales and leads to a flooded gum (*Eucalyptus grandis*) known as

New South Wales

The Grandis—the tallest tree in New South Wales. Access to this tree is via the Old Pacific Hwy, to the north of Bulahdelah, then right into Stoney Creek Rd. **O'Sullivans Gap Flora Reserve** is also located in the Wang Wauk Forest, offering bushwalking and picnic facilities.
TOURIST INFO : Cnr Pacific Hwy and Crawford St, Ph: (02) 4997 4981

Byron Bay POP 5200
Map 84, D1

One of Australia's most fashionable and popular holiday destinations, Byron Bay is renowned for its balmy climate and excellent surfing beaches—it is also a popular area for scuba diving. A whaling town in the 1950s, Byron Bay is now full of galleries, boutiques, cafes and 'new age' shops, reflecting the holiday atmosphere and alternative lifestyle of the town. It is such a popular tourist destination, in summer the locals are frequently outnumbered by the tourists.
MAIN ATTRACTIONS: **Cape Byron**, a rocky promontory 107m high, is the most easterly point in Australia. **Cape Byron Lighthouse** beams its light over 40km out to sea. A walking trail leads past the lighthouse to the tip of the Cape and the amazing coastal views. In July, humpback whales can be seen as they migrate up the coast and then seen again in September, **Whale Festival** time, when they make their return journey. Exclusive **Wategos Beach** is wholly north-facing and therefore very popular with surfers.
NEARBY ATTRACTIONS: **Bangalow**, south-west of Byron Bay, is an interesting little village offering antique, craft and coffee shops.
TOURIST INFO: 80 Jonson St, Ph: (02) 6680 9271

Canowindra POP 1720
Map 118, D5

Hot-air balloons floating silently overhead have earned this **Central West** town the title '**Balloon Capital of Australia'**. Canowindra lies in a natural basin on the **Belubula River**, 335km west of Sydney. The weather is almost always calm and conditions are usually ideal for balloon flights over the countryside.
MAIN ATTRACTIONS: There are 3 local balloon flight operators and many people travel to Canowindra for this experience alone. An interesting time to visit is during **Marti's Balloon Fiesta**, a special 4-day annual event, held late March/early April, attracting thousands of visitors. **Gaskill St**, Canowindra's main street, follows the route of an old bullock track. It is lined with early commercial buildings and is classified by the National Trust as a Heritage Conservation Area. There are many antique shops, a local memorabilia museum and a gallery offering quality crafts. One of the great fossil sites in Australia was discovered between Canowindra and **Gooloogong** in 1955. Approximately 3500 fossils, dating to 360 million years, have been recovered, many of them complete. Seven new species have been discovered, with more expected. The collection is displayed at the **Age of Fishes Museum**, in Gaskill St, open daily and most holidays, 10am–4pm.
NEARBY ATTRACTIONS: Canowindra lies in the Cabonne Shire, a rich agricultural district famous for the abundance and quality of its fresh produce. Many shops provide the opportunity to sample all kinds of locally grown food. Bushwalking, historic sites and highly regarded wineries dot the surrounding areas.
TOURIST INFO: Age of Fishes Museum, Gaskill St, Ph: (02) 6344 1008

Cape Byron Lighthouse

THE LOWER HUNTER

A scenic 2hr (180km) drive from Sydney, the Lower Hunter is one of Australia's premier wine-producing regions. The first vines were planted as far back as 1832 and medals for Hunter wines were won as early as 1882. Today, there are over 90 wineries, large and boutique, and many restaurants. Although only around 5% of Australia's wine comes from here, the Hunter is home to some of the most respected wineries, including **Draytons**, **Lindemans**, **Tyrrells** and **Tulloch**.

While the region is bursting with natural beauty, seams of high quality coal are found throughout the valley. Coal mining has been a pillar of the local economy, although the current focus is on wine tourism. **Maitland** is a main centre for the region and has a rich heritage, being one of colonial Australia's most important towns.

There is much to see and do in this region and while many may initially come to sample the fruits of the vine, it will not be just the wine that encourages their return.

main attractions

◈ Hunter Valley Gardens
These gardens are the site of a wine-theme village with a resort, restaurants and activities.

◈ Koolang Observatory
Nestled in bushland, this observatory offers viewings of the night sky.

◈ Morpeth
One of the most unspoilt heritage towns in New South Wales, the entire village of Morpeth has been classified by the National Trust.

◈ Pokolbin
Home to many wineries, both large and boutique, Pokolbin is home to the Hunter Valley Wine Society headquarters, a good starting point for a tour of the vineyards.

◈ Richmond Vale Railway and Mining Museum
This museum brings the era of steam locomotives alive.

◈ Rusa Park Zoo
See the only albino kangaroos in captivity, the white euro kangaroos, at Rusa Park Zoo.

◈ Wollombi
This quaint country village includes the Endeavour Museum, cafes and antiques.

Church of the Immaculate Conception (1897), Morpeth

 Tourist information

Hunter Wine and Visitors Centre
Main Rd, Pokolbin, NSW 2325
Ph: (02) 4990 4477
www.winecountry.com.au

Hunter Valley Harvest Festival
This is a perfect opportunity to experience wine-country culture and tradition at its best. After harvesting the crop (Feb–March), leading wineries toast their crop with banquets, lunches and dinners as well as more traditional activities like barrel tastings from February to April.

A wagon ride through the vines of the Lower Hunter Valley

New South Wales

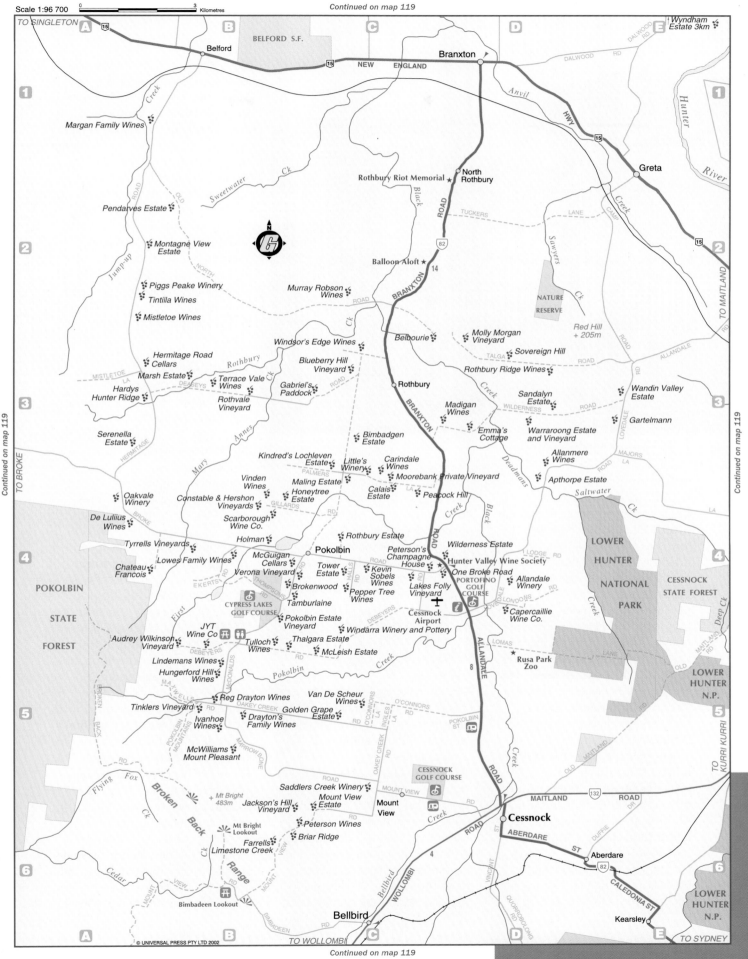

© UNIVERSAL PRESS PTY LTD 2002

The historic village of Wollombi, SW of Cessnock

■ Casino   POP 10 774

Map 115, H2

Casino is located on the **Richmond River** 733km north of Sydney. The town has about 20 parks attracting a variety of wildlife. While the surrounding land is rich in timber, Casino is primarily a beef-cattle town with a meatworks and tannery.

MAIN ATTRACTIONS: There are many historical buildings to be seen in Casino. The **public school**, built in 1861, and the **Court House** in 1882 are located in Walker St. The **Casino Folk Museum**, also in Walker St, exhibits mementos of pioneering days and a collection of early photographs. The museum is open Wednesdays and Sundays, 2.30pm to 4.30pm. There are numerous parks to enjoy in Casino with many located along the river. **Jabiru Geneebeinga Wetlands**, next to the golf course in **North Casino**, has an abundance of birdlife, including black swans, ducks, egrets and jabiru. Each

Sunday, a miniature railway operates through the wetlands area.

NEARBY ATTRACTIONS: Visitors can fossick for gold, labradorite, and smoky and clear quartz. Fishing for a variety of freshwater species is popular on the Richmond River and **Cooke's Weir**.

TOURIST INFO: Cnr Centre and Richmond sts, Ph: (02) 6662 3566

■ Cessnock   POP 18 000

Map 59, D6

Once a major coal-mining centre, this **Hunter Valley** town now attracts tourists who are visiting the wineries of the **Pokolbin** area just a short distance away.

MAIN ATTRACTIONS: Excellent food and wine are available throughout the region. There are also many antique shops, craft outlets and galleries worthwhile visiting. For thrill seekers there are skydiving flights and hot-air balloon flights available.

NEARBY ATTRACTIONS: The historic village of **Wollombi**, south-west of

Cessnock, has many old sandstone buildings. Tours to Aboriginal art sites in the Wollombi area can be organised through **Yarnteen Aboriginal Sites Tours**. A museum now occupies the **old Police Station** and is generally open weekends. **Broke** is another historic village. Here, there is an interesting pioneer cemetery and several buildings dating back to the 1840s. South of Cessnock are the **Watagan Mountains**, where the walking tracks lead to views and attractive picnic and BBQ areas. There are over 90 wineries in the Hunter Valley area and these can be explored either by driving to the vineyards, or organising coach, chauffeur-driven, bicycle, horse-drawn or 4WD tours.

TOURIST INFO: Hunter Wine Centre, Allandale Rd, Pokolbin, Ph: (02) 4990 4477

■ Cobar   POP 5500

Map 117, J1

Cobar is known for the mineral wealth—copper, zinc, lead and silver—extracted from its mines. The Great Cobar mine closed in 1919 but the opening up of new mining ventures in more recent times has seen Cobar become prosperous once again. Wool is also a major industry. The town is 723km NW of Sydney and is a rest stop on the way to **Broken Hill**.

MAIN ATTRACTIONS: Brochures on the self-guided **heritage walks** are available from the information centre. There are also heritage tours by bus. The **Great Western Hotel** in Marshall St has the longest iron-lace verandah in New South Wales. There is a **water recreation area** accessed off Knight Dr, where visitors can enjoy swimming, picnics, waterskiing and bird-watching in a relaxing setting.

NEARBY ATTRACTIONS: **Mount Drysdale**, a ghost mining town 30km north on the Kidman Way, was once home to 6000 people. Stone foundations are all that is left of the town, but the area has walk-in mines, Aboriginal waterholes and a ruined homestead to explore. The **Mount Grenfell Historic Site** has Aboriginal cave paintings and is located 40km west on the Barrier Hwy.

TOURIST INFO: Cobar Regional Museum, Barrier Hwy, Ph: (02) 6836 2448

■ Coffs Harbour   POP 22 700
Map 62, D3

A very attractive holiday destination, Coffs Harbour is an area of contrasts: beaches, high mountains, dense rainforest and banana plantations.

MAIN ATTRACTIONS: Long stretches of sand and surf have been drawing visitors to Coffs Harbour for decades. **Park**, **Jetty** and **Boambee beaches** edge the city, and to the north some hideaway beaches include **Moonee**, **Emerald** and **Sandy**. The **Big Banana** theme park is perhaps the most popular tourist attraction. Hard to miss with its huge concrete banana on the Pacific Hwy, north of town, it is open daily. There are plantation tours, hydroponics' exhibitions, a toboggan run, banana barn, food, souvenirs and a lookout; something for the whole family to enjoy. The **Pet Porpoise Pool** has performing dolphins and sea-lions, with daily shows at 10.30am and 2.15pm. There is also a native fauna sanctuary and a reef tank. **Muttonbird Island Nature Reserve** is an excellent spot to see whales and muttonbirds in season.

NEARBY ATTRACTIONS: **Coffs Harbour Zoo**, located 10min north of the city, allows visitors to hand-feed kangaroos and waterbirds, see a koala presentation, visit the animal nursery and walk through a rainforest aviary. **Bruxner Park Flora Reserve**, 9km NW of Coffs Harbour has a walking track through a mass of vines, ferns and orchids. The **Vincent Tree** (flooded gum) is a major attraction, and from **Sealy Lookout** there are panoramic views of the city, coastline and hills. **Dorrigo NP** is in the hinterland ranges and there are many rainforest walks, with a diversity of flora and fauna. **George's Goldmine** is located near **Coramba**, 40km NW of Coffs Harbour, and offers a guided tour into a tunnel mine and demonstrations of a working stamper battery. There are also picnic areas and food is available.

TOURIST INFO: Cnr Pacific Hwy and Marcia St, Ph: (02) 6652 1522

■ Condobolin   POP 3500
Map 118, A4

Located on the **Lachlan River**, Condobolin is near the geographic centre of New South Wales. It is the service centre for the surrounding pastoral district that produces wheat, wool, lambs, fruit and cotton.

MAIN ATTRACTIONS: The **Community Crafts Centre** in Denison St, once the old Commercial Hotel, is now a shop in what was the old bar. **Memorial Park**, beside the river bridge, is a shady picnic area. Visitors are welcome at Condobolin RSL in McDonnell St and for a game at the Golf Club off Orange St.

NEARBY ATTRACTIONS: A monument marks the burial place of an Aborigine, believed to have been a Lachlan chief, stands beside the road 40km west of Condobolin. Nearby are other **Aboriginal sites**, waterholes and grooved rocks. **Gum Bend Lake** is a small recreation area for swimming, sailing, windsurfing and limited-power boating. Located 4km west, it was created by diverting water from the Lachlan River. **Mount Tilga**, 8km north on Melrose Rd, is claimed to be the true geographic centre of the state. A dirt road travels halfway up the hill and there is a climb to the top for views of the western plains.

TOURIST INFO: Lachlan Shire Council Offices, 62-64 Molong St, Ph: (02) 6895 4444

■ Cooma   POP 7500
Map 122, C4

Being the gateway to the **Snowy Mountains** resorts and **Kosciuszko NP**, and located at the junction of 2 highways linking **Canberra**, the coast and the mountains, Cooma is a busy tourist centre. The town is also the administrative centre for the **Snowy Mountains Hydro-Electric Scheme**.

MAIN ATTRACTIONS: **Centennial Park** is particularly worthwhile visiting. There is the **International Avenue**

Pleasurecraft at Coffs Harbour boat harbour

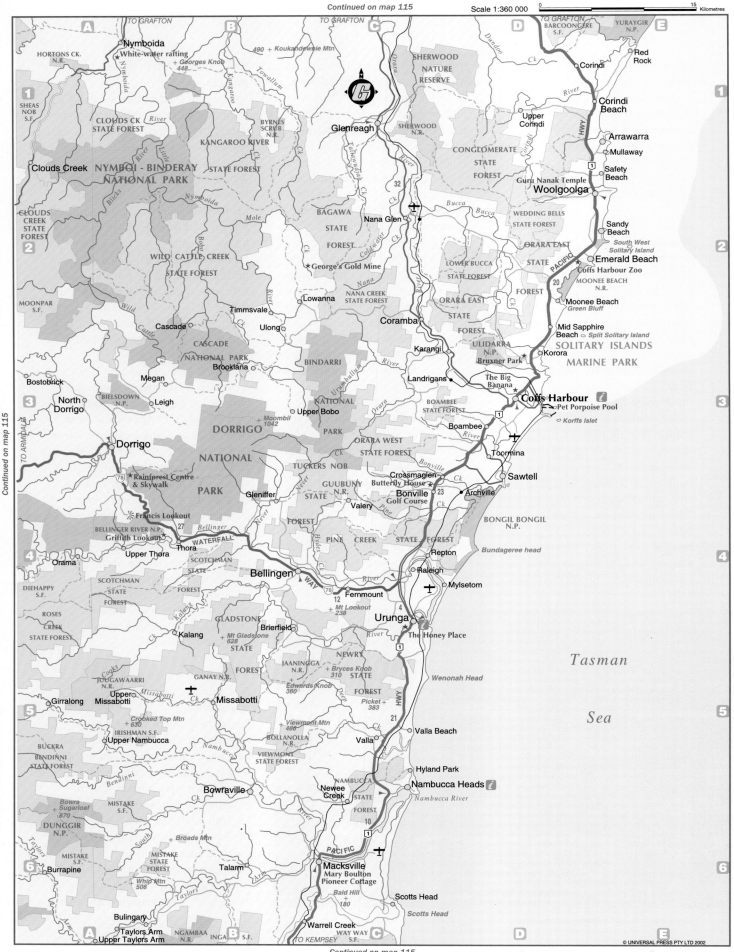

Scale 1:360 000

New South Wales

of Flags in honour of the people from 27 nations who worked on the Snowy River Scheme in the 1950s; a statue of Banjo Paterson's *Man From Snowy River*; and the **Monaro Time Walk**, a series of 40 mosaic murals depicting the history of the region. **Nannygoat Hill** is a reserve in the centre of Cooma with a 360° view of the Monaro district and the Snowy Mountains. **Mount Gladstone** also offers a panoramic view. Cooma's oldest street, Lambie St, has many buildings classified by the National Trust. These can be seen on the self-guided **Lambie Town Walk**—a 5km walk beginning at the visitors centre. Cooma's original Anglican Church, **Christ Church**, built in 1845, can be seen in Church Rd. **Cooma Gaol Museum** offers tours on weekdays at 11am and 1pm and should be booked through the information centre. Located in Vale St, the museum is open Mon–Sat, 10am–4pm.
NEARBY ATTRACTIONS: **Kosciuszko NP** surrounds much of the New South Wales section of the **Great Dividing Range**, west of Cooma. The park contains Australia's highest point, **Mount Kosciuszko**, rising to 2228m. The park is a popular summer destination with bushwalkers and campers.
TOURIST INFO: 119 Sharp St, Ph: (02) 6450 1742

■ Coonabarabran   POP 2970
Map 114, B6
Coonabarabran is an agricultural town located 455km NW of Sydney. The town started developing after an inn was built beside a crossing on the **Castlereagh River**. From the mid-1850s until the turn of the century, flour mills were important to the local economy. Today, timber and sheep are the other main agricultural activities.
MAIN ATTRACTIONS: At the Coonabarabran Information Centre, visitors can see the full skeleton of a **diprotodon**—the largest known marsupial ever to have lived. The fossilised bones were found in the area and are believed to be approximately 35 000 years old.

The **Crystal Kingdom**, on the Oxley Hwy, displays minerals from Australia and overseas. It is open daily from 8am to 5pm.
NEARBY ATTRACTIONS: Only 35km west of the town is the **Warrumbungle NP**. The rock formations are the result of volcanic activity over 13 million years ago. The Warrumbungle NP Visitors Centre has walking trail maps and camping information and is open daily from 8.30am to 4pm. North of Coonabarabran lies an area of wild forest and scrubland known as the **Pilliga Scrub**. Displays of wildflowers are common here between August and December and there is a series of small caves in the sandstone ridges and outcrops. **Pilliga Pottery and Bush Cafe**, located in the scrub, specialises in terracotta pots and ornamental figurines. Coonabarabran is known as the **'Astronomy Capital of Australia'**, with the area being home to the **Siding Spring Observatory**, which has the largest optical telescope in Australia, and at the **Skywatch Night and Day Observatory**, visitors can view the stars and play Astro Mini Golf.
TOURIST INFO: Newell Hwy, Ph: (02) 6842 1441 or 1800 242 881

■ Cootamundra   POP 7457
Map 122, A2
This crop-growing and grazing district 94km NE of **Wagga Wagga**, was the birthplace of Sir Donald Bradman. Famous for the wattle that bears its name, the time to visit Cootamundra is **Wattle Time**, July and August, to see the vivid colour displayed throughout the town.
MAIN ATTRACTIONS: The information centre has brochures describing walking tours around Cootamundra. These include the **Two-Foot Tour**, a 1–2hr walking tour of the town's main sites; and the **Captain's Walk**, which includes a walk through **Jubilee Park** to see the busts of 11 famous cricketers. **Bradman's**

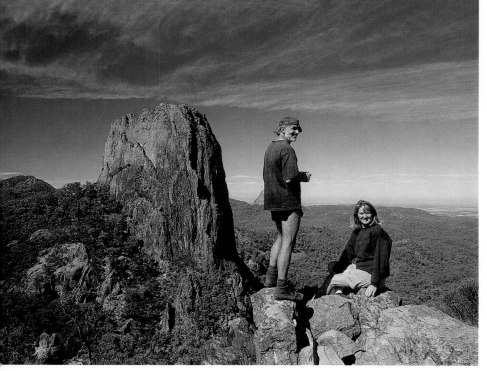
Bushwalkers on Crater Bluff, Warrumbungle NP, west of Coonabarabran

Birthplace is a stop on the Two-Foot Tour and was the nursing home where Sir Donald was born. It is now a museum furnished in period-style and with displays of Bradman cricketing memorabilia. Located at 89 Admas St, it is open weekends and public holidays, 9am–5pm. The focal point of the CBD is the **Bicentennial Post Office Plaza**, which incorporates the historic Post Office building and clocktower. The grand old Railway Station has been refurbished and is also a busy Countrylink rail and coach connection.

NEARBY ATTRACTIONS: For picnics and walks to get panoramic views, visitors shouldn't miss **Pioneer Park** which is a natural reserve on the southern outskirts of town. At **Harden**, 37km NE, there are wineries offering tastings and sales.
TOURIST INFO: Railway Station Complex, Hovell St, Ph: (02) 6942 4212

■ **Corowa** POP 5242
Map 121, J4
A rich wheat-growing district surrounds the New South Wales town of Corowa, located on the northern bank of the **Murray River**. The town was also the birthplace of Australia's Federation. On the other side of the river is the Victorian town of **Wahgunyah**, joined to Corowa by the **John Foord Bridge**.
MAIN ATTRACTIONS: Watersports are popular, including boating, waterskiing and fishing. Heritage buildings with iron-lace balconies, built in the heyday of the river trade, line Corowa's **Sanger St** and give the town its character. The historic **Court House** has an important place in Australian history. It was here during the 1893 Federation Conference Meeting that the decision was made to draw up a constitution for the new nation. The **Corowa Federation Museum** focuses on the full history of the Federation movement and also

Japanese Garden, Cowra

displays a collection of farming implements and machinery from the early part of the 20th century. A collection of works by the Australian artist **Tom Roberts** is housed here, along with sketches by Aboriginal artist **Tommy McRae**.
NEARBY ATTRACTIONS: The 17 wineries of the **Rutherglen** district are within a 15km radius of Corowa. Several wineries have restaurants attached. **All Saints Estate** is one of the most historic wineries in the district. The winery is located 5km SE at Wahgunyah.
TOURIST INFO: 88 Sanger St, Ph: (02) 6033 3221 or 1800 814 054

■ **Cowra** POP 9400
Map 118, D5
Located on the **Lachlan River**, 311km west of Sydney, Cowra is a busy country town. Part of a thriving farming district, much of the New South Wales asparagus crop, tomatoes and corn are processed at the local cannery. Cowra is also well-known for its **wineries**. A number of vineyards are open for wine tasting and cellar door sales.

MAIN ATTRACTIONS: Every October Cowra celebrates the **Cherry Blossom Festival**. Flowering cherry trees line Sakura Ave, a walkway linking the Japanese Garden to the POW camp and on to the Japanese Cemetery. The largest prisoner-of-war breakout of modern military history occurred on 5th August 1944, in Cowra. The remains of the prison camp and the site of the breakout are open to the public, as are the **Japanese** and **Australian War cemeteries**. The **Japanese Garden and Cultural Centre** was donated by the Japanese Government and is renowned as one of the biggest and best Japanese gardens in the world. The Cultural Centre displays Japanese art and pottery, a traditional open-air Tea House, cabana restaurant and bonsai house. The garden is open daily, 8.30am–5pm. There are many parks with picnic and BBQ facilities to enjoy, both alongside the Lachlan River and around the town.
NEARBY ATTRACTIONS: **Conimbla NP** is a small park in 2 sections, located west of Cowra. Spring is the best time to visit and see the wildflowers,

New South Wales

which are seen on 2 walks. Both walks commence from a car park adjacent to Barryrennie Rd. **Croote Cottage**, located at **Gooloogong** approximately 38km from Cowra, was built of pise by convicts in 1827, and in the past was the target of bushrangers. It has since been restored and can now be inspected by appointment.
TOURIST INFO: Olympic Park, Mid Western Hwy, Ph: (02) 6342 4333

■ Crescent Head   POP 1210
Map 115, H6
This small **North Coast** resort town lies 19km SE of Kempsey. National parks protect the coastline, both to the north and south. To the south, sandy beaches stretch all the way to **Port Macquarie**. The beaches of Crescent Head are excellent for swimming and fishing, and are also popular with hang gliders.
MAIN ATTRACTIONS: Facilities in the town include a country club with a 6-hole waterfront golf course, lawn and indoor bowls, tennis, indoor sports and swimming pool. **Killick Beach** is renowned as a board-riding and bodysurfing beach, whereas **Killick Creek** is sheltered and ideal for young children.
NEARBY ATTRACTIONS: **Hat Head NP** is full of birdlife, with the wetlands and lagoons providing breeding grounds for several species of waterbirds. Inland, the dry, open forest provides ideal nesting conditions for falcons and hawks. The national park also comprises a coastal strip of high dunes. The park is popular for fishing, swimming, bushwalking, camping and picnicking. Many visitors walk to **Korogoro Point** to spot whales (in season). Aboriginal sites can be found in the area between **Big Hill** and **Queens Head**. An unsealed road links Crescent Head with **Port Macquarie** and gives access to these sites.
TOURIST INFO: Pacific Hwy, South Kempsey, Ph: (02) 6563 1555

■ Crookwell   POP 2100
Map 122, C1
Situated high in the **Great Dividing Range**, 230km SW of Sydney, Crookwell is the centre of some of Australia's best agricultural and pastoral land. It is also the birth-place of the Australian potato industry (1828). High quality fine wool, lambs, beef, apples and pears are also produced and there are an abundance of trout streams, stunning gardens and a wind farm.
MAIN ATTRACTIONS: At the **Crookwell Weaving Mill and Gallery**, visitors can see professional weaver and tailor, Allan Craven demonstrate weaving from natural fibres, especially wool. Many items, including skirts, jackets, scarves and shawls are on display and some are for sale. **Linder's Sock Factory**, in the main street, is a great place to visit with socks at factory-direct prices.
NEARBY ATTRACTIONS: There are many historic villages in the area, which were once associated with gold and bushranging. These towns, all north of Crookwell, include **Roslyn**, **Tuena**, **Peelwood**, **Laggan**, **Bigga** and **Binda**. **Wombeyan Caves** is located 60km NE and there are 5 caves open to the public. The **Sheck Webster Lookout** at **Snowy Mount** 42km NW on the Bigga Rd, offers a scenic view of the surrounding countryside. For experienced walkers, the climb up **Decca Hill** (at **Grabine Lakeside SP**, 65km NW) provides views of **Wyangala Dam** and the surrounding country.
TOURIST INFO : 106 Goulburn St, Ph: (02) 4832 1988

■ Deniliquin   POP 8200
Map 121, G3
Situated on the **Edward River**, this southern **Riverina** town is surrounded by extensively irrigated farmland producing wheat, canola, barley, sheep, pigs and cattle. Wool and rice are the region's main products, with the rice processed at the **Deniliquin Mill**, the largest rice mill in the Southern Hemisphere.

Aerial view of Hat Head NP, near Crescent Head

MAIN ATTRACTIONS: The Mill's **SunRice Country Centre** explains the industry through an audiovisual presentation and afterwards there is the opportunity to taste the various rice products. SunRice Centre operates Mon–Fri, 9am–5pm. Public presentations are at 9.30am and 2.45pm daily. A brochure about the self-guided **historical and nature walk** is available at the information centre. On the Hay Road north of town is **Pioneer Tourist Park**. The park incorporates a garden centre; craft gallery; and a display of restored antique steam engines, petrol pumps and pioneer pumping equipment from the Snowy Mountains Scheme, Deniliquin and South Australia.

NEARBY ATTRACTIONS: The **Conargo Pub**, located 25km NE, has a gallery of photographs showing the history of merino wool in the area.

TOURIST INFO: Peppin Heritage Centre, George St, Ph: (02) 5881 4150

■ Dorrigo   POP 1300

Map 62, A3

This **North Coast** timber town lies 40km west of Coffs Harbour. Dorrigo is a relaxed and friendly town set amidst majestic scenery.

MAIN ATTRACTIONS: Dorrigo has 3 licensed clubs: the RSL and Bowling Club in Hickory St, and the Golf Club off Whiskey Creek Rd. All welcome visitors. Local artists display their work at the **Art Place**, an art gallery in Cudgery St. The **Art of the Country**, a craft gallery, is next door. **Don Dorrigo Museum** is run by the local historical society. Located in Myrtle St, it is open Tuesday, Friday, Sunday and all school holidays 11am–3pm. **Griffith Lookout** is probably the district's best view—looking over the mountains, out to sea and as far as **Kempsey** and **Armidale**. To reach it, turn off at the Waterfall Way, near Dorrigo Mountain Resort.

NEARBY ATTRACTIONS: **Dorrigo NP** is a World Heritage-listed rainforest park located a few kilometres south-east. At the **Rainforest Centre** visitors will find a shop, exhibition and cafe. Don't miss the **Skywalk**, a tree-top canopy walk and lookout platform hanging over the edge of the escarpment. There are 3 other national parks nearby; **New England**, **Guy Fawkes River** and **Cathedral Rock**.

TOURIST INFO: Hickory St, Ph: (02) 6657 2486

■ Dubbo   POP 36 000

Map 118, D2

Known as the **'Hub of the West'**, the rural city of Dubbo is a busy road, rail and air junction on the **Macquarie River**. The town is located halfway between Melbourne and Brisbane and just over 400km from Sydney. The surrounding areas support pigs, sheep, cattle stud farms and produce wheat, fodder, cotton, wool, fruit and vegetables.

MAIN ATTRACTIONS: **Dubbo Museum** is located at 232 Macquarie St and is open daily, 12pm–4.30pm. Displays include Aboriginal artefacts and early farm, home and commercial memorabilia. The **Dubbo Military Museum** on the Newell Hwy is open daily, 9am–5pm. There is a good display of WWII memorabilia, and a Jurassic Supermaze hands-on science exhibit. **Old Dubbo Gaol** is a major attraction in the heart of the city. Open daily, 9.30am–4.30pm, this sandstone gaol was built around 1871 and operated until 1966 when it was turned into a museum. The **Dubbo Regional Art Gallery** has a permanent collection of works based on the theme 'Animals in Art', and presents regular touring exhibitions. Located at 165 Darling St, the gallery is open daily 12pm–4.30pm.

NEARBY ATTRACTIONS: **Western Plains Zoo** is perhaps the best-known attraction in Dubbo. There are more than 800 exotic and native animals in open exhibits. You can walk, cycle or drive around the 6km of sealed road and walking trails. The National Trust property, **Dundullimal** is in the same area as the zoo. Guided audio tours describe the timber-slab farmhouse (1840), one of the earliest surviving squatter's homesteads in the country. The homestead is open daily, 9am–5pm.

TOURIST INFO: Cnr Macquarie and Erskine sts, Ph: (02) 6884 1422

Dangar Falls, 2km north of Dorrigo

New South Wales

Dungog   POP 2500

Map 119, H3

First settled in the 1820s, Dungog is 225km from Sydney. This rural township is the service centre for surrounding logging, dairying, beef cattle and deer-farming industries. Dungog is also on the main southern route into **Barrington Tops NP**. This World Heritage-listed park offers a diversity of landscapes, including subtropical rainforests with refreshing clear-water rivers, a mountainous plateau, and at approximately 1000m are spectacular **Antarctic beech forests**. There are many walking tracks to beautiful waterfalls and lookouts. Camping is permitted at a number of designated camping areas.
NEARBY ATTRACTIONS: **Chichester Dam** and **Chichester SF** lie 23km NE of the town. The dam, opened in 1985, has picnic areas and walking trails. **Telegherry Forest Park**, located 30km north, offers walking trails along the **Telegherry River** with picnic, swimming and camping spots. One of the first European settlements in Australia, **Clarence Town** historical village is 24km SE of Dungog.
TOURIST INFO: Cnr Dowling and Brown sts, Ph: (02) 4992 2212

Eden   POP 3500

Map 122, D6

Approximately 50km from the Victorian border, the fishing port of Eden is the southern gateway to the **South Coast**. A deepwater port and tourist centre with many attractions, Eden has a long history founded on the whaling industry, which flourished from 1818 until the 1930s.
MAIN ATTRACTIONS: Eden lies on the northern shore of **Twofold Bay**. The **Eden Killer Whale Museum**, in Imlay St, features a skeleton of 'Tom the killer whale', which assisted early whalers. Whale-watching (southern right, minke, humpback and killer), between September and November

is very popular; there are 2 viewing platforms along **Aslings Beach**.
NEARBY ATTRACTIONS: **Ben Boyd NP** is in 2 sections, covering the rocky coastline either side of Twofold Bay. The park offers scenic views, bushwalking, fishing, swimming and wreck diving. **Boyd's Tower**—a private lighthouse built with sandstone shipped from Sydney—is a highlight of the southern section of the park. **Davidson Whaling Station Historic Site** 30km SE on **Kiah Inlet** is another highlight.
TOURIST INFO: The Roundabout, Princes Hwy, Ph: (02) 6496 1953

Forbes   POP 10 138

Map 118, C4

The centre of a prosperous farming district, located on the **Lachlan River**, Forbes is a town of historic buildings, parks and gardens. This former gold-mining town is located near where bushranger **Ben Hall** was shot by police, in 1865.
MAIN ATTRACTIONS: **Forbes Historical Museum** in Cross St (open daily 3pm–5pm) was once a music hall. A large exhibit is devoted to the bushranging days of Ben Hall. **Gum Swamp Wildlife Sanctuary** is 4km SW of Forbes on the Newell Hwy. Here it is possible to view 60 to 70 species of birds within a few hours. **Lachlan Vintage Village** (open daily, 8am–5pm) re-creates the community as it was in the late 19th century, with an emphasis on life in the goldfields. **Ben Hall's cottage** and the home of **Henry Lawson** are features. The **cemetery**, located in Bogan Gate Rd, has the graves of Ben Hall, Kate Foster (Ned Kelly's sister), and Rebecca Shields (Capt Cook's niece). Also worthwhile is a self-guided walk of the town's historic buildings, most of which are in **Court** and **Lachlan sts**. An historic buildings walk leaflet available from the information centre.
TOURIST INFO: Railway Art and Craft Centre, Union St, Ph: (02) 6852 4155

Fishing fleet, Eden

Forster   POP 15 000

Map 119, K3

The twin towns of **Forster** and **Tuncurry** lie at the entrance to **Wallis Lake**, on either side of the **Wallamba River**. Part of the **Great Lakes** holiday region, Forster has long been popular for family holidays, as it is a comfortable 4hr drive from Sydney, and is renowned for its clean, clear beaches, waterways and fresh seafood.
MAIN ATTRACTIONS: Beach, estuary, lake and river fishing attract large numbers of visitors, especially in

the winter months. Local tourist brochures offer tips on where to catch bream, flathead, whiting and tailor. Alternatively, you can enjoy the fresh seafood from many of the local restaurants. The **Bicentennial Walk** links **Forster Main Beach** with **One Mile Beach**. An overall view of Forster-Tuncurry can be seen during this walk, from the **Scenic Platform** at **Bennetts Head**. **The Curtis Collection**—a museum exhibiting vintage to rare modern cars, horse-drawn vehicles, Cyclops toys and gramophones—is located only 3km south of town.

NEARBY ATTRACTIONS: **Booti Booti NP** covers the coastal strip between Forster to the north and **Pacific Palms** to the south. Many walking tracks lead to magnificent coastal views. Picnic areas are located around **Wallis Lake** where visitors can enjoy the many different watersports. At **Tiona**, 15km south, the open-air **Green Cathedral** is a consecrated church on the shores of Wallis Lake. Cabbage palms form the roof of the church and logs the seats, while the lake is a backdrop to the stone altar.

TOURIST INFO: Little St, Ph: (02) 6554 8799

■ Gilgandra POP 2822
Map 118, D2

This town is the centre of one of the best wheat-growing and wool-producing areas in New South Wales. Also produced are other cereal, oil seed and legume crops, lambs and cattle. Aquaculture is in the early stages of expansion. Located by the **Castlereagh River**, Gilgandra is 435km NW of Sydney.

MAIN ATTRACTIONS: Before 1966, when the town water supply was connected, Gilgandra was famous for its many windmills, used for pumping water to residents' homes. Most were removed when town water was connected, but as a reminder, some of the old windmills now form an **Avenue of Windmills** from **Coo-ee Park** along to the riverbank picnic area. The Gilgandra Visitors Centre houses the local **Historical Society Museum**, which has a special collection dedicated to the **Coo-ee March** (1915) from Gilgandra to Sydney. The aim was to recruit men along the route willing to fight in WW1. **Orana Cactus World** has a large collection of cacti, which has taken local grower Lester Meyers more than 40 years to accumulate.

It is open weekends or by appointment. The privately operated **Gilgandra Observatory** is a big attraction. Visitors are able to safely view sunspots and the stars through the 31cm-diameter telescope.

NEARBY ATTRACTIONS: Wildflowers and shrubs, including rare and ancient plants, grow in **Gilgandra Native Flora Reserve**. Located 14.5km NE, the reserve is off the Newell Hwy. The reserve is most spectacular during the spring-flowering period (August–Oct). Facilities include shelter, water, BBQs and toilets. Nearby, **Warrumbungle NP**, with its volcanic pipes, is an ideal place for bushwalkers, birdwatchers and nature lovers.

TOURIST INFO: Coo-ee March, Memorial Park, Newell Hwy, Ph: (02) 6847 2045

■ Glen Innes POP 6234
Map 115, F3

The historic town of Glen Innes is perched high in the **New England Range** and surrounded by rich, rolling countryside. In the past it was often the scene of bushranger activity. The surrounding area produces wool, sheep, beef, honey, timber and yields sapphires, tin and other minerals.

MAIN ATTRACTIONS: Glen Innes is also known for its beautiful parklands, restored heritage buildings, and as the home of the **Australian Standing Stones**. A **walking tour** brochure is available from the information centre. On the corner of McKenzie St and New England Hwy, is the **Cooramah Aboriginal Cultural Centre**. Visitors can see Aboriginal arts and crafts, historic artefacts and there is a restaurant with bush tucker. **Land of the Beardies History House** also houses quality pioneering and cultural displays.

NEARBY ATTRACTIONS: Fossicking for gemstones has attracted many visitors to the district. The information centre has details of what

Windmill, Gilgandra

New South Wales

to look for, and where to find gemstones in public fossicking areas and the equipment required. Popular places include **Emmaville**, 39km NW and **Torrington**, 66km NW. Fishing for trout, perch and cod is popular and at **Deepwater**, 40km north of Glen Innes, fishing safaris can be booked. World Heritage-listed **Washpool NP** is located 75km NE and is a rainforest wilderness.
TOURIST INFO: 152 Church St, Ph: (02) 6732 2397

■ Gloucester   POP 2682

Map 119, J2
This town lies in the sheltered valley of the **Gloucester River** and is surrounded by agricultural land ideal for beef and dairying. The main access road is the Bucketts Way, named after the unusual chain of hills known as **The Bucketts** that forms a backdrop to the town.
MAIN ATTRACTIONS: **Billabong Native Garden** in Denison St has a diverse range of flora and is an ideal spot for picnics and BBQs. Maps describing the town's **historic walk** are available from the information centre. Insights into local history can be found in the **Folk Museum**. Housed in the old Council Chambers in Church St, the museum is open Thursdays, Saturdays and on Tuesdays in school holidays, 10am–2pm.
NEARBY ATTRACTIONS: Gloucester is often considered the **'Base Camp of the Barringtons'**, making this World Heritage-listed national park worthwhile exploring from the town. The rivers and streams in the area provide some of the best canoeing in New South Wales. In the freshwater streams fish, including trout and perch abound. There are scenic drives and walks in the surrounding countryside and scattered throughout are picnic and camping spots, and a number of old timber and gold-mining settlements. In the 1870s, gold was discovered at nearby **Copeland** and the workings of

Waterfall on the Antarctic Beech Forest Walk, Barrington Tops NP, near Gloucester

the old **Mountain Maid Gold Mine** can be seen. There is a walking track from the car park.
TOURIST INFO: 27 Denison St, Ph: (02) 6558 1408

■ Gosford   POP 39 000

Map 71, B4
This regional centre for commerce and industry is a popular tourist destination. It has also become a commuter suburb of Sydney.
MAIN ATTRACTIONS: Gosford offers easy access to the sheltered waters of **Brisbane Water**, **Broken Bay** and the **Hawkesbury River**, all offering fishing and boating opportunities. Coastal beaches including **Pearl Beach** south of Woy Woy, and those stretching north from **MacMasters** to **Terrigal** are a major attraction.
NEARBY ATTRACTIONS: Covering a huge area south-east of Gosford, **Brisbane Water NP** offers opportunities for picnicking, fishing, bushwalking and photography. Many of the bushwalking tracks lead to lookouts with wonderful coastal views. The spring wildflowers are stunning and also

worth a visit is the **Bulgandry Aboriginal Engraving** site near **Kariong**. This collection is one of the best groups in the Sydney area. The **Australian Reptile Park and Wildlife Sanctuary** is located at **Somersby**, 15km SW of Gosford. **Old Sydney Town**, a reconstruction of an early pioneer settlement, is next door, and nearby **Somersby Falls** is an ideal place for a picnic
TOURIST INFO: 200 Mann St, Ph: (02) 4385 4430

■ Goulburn   POP 21 895

Map 122, D2
Claimed as Australia's first inland city, Goulburn is the major centre on the **Southern Tablelands**. The surrounding country is famous for wool production and there are several well-known studs in the area. Goulburn has 5 big wool stores and one of the largest livestock markets in New South Wales.
MAIN ATTRACTIONS: **Goulburn Regional Art Gallery**, in the Civic Centre, exhibits a wide range of arts and crafts. The gallery is open Tuesday

THE CENTRAL COAST

Close proximity to **Sydney** and easy accessibility via fast freeways has ensured the Central Coast's development as a prime holiday destination. Characterised by large, calm saltwater lagoons, connected to the ocean via a number of small waterways, with an array of excellent beaches on the coastline, this area is a haven for watersports. Swimming, fishing and surfing opportunities abound, charter cruises and hire boats are available on all major bodies of water, and it is also possible to rent a houseboat on **Lake Macquarie**, the region's largest lake.

Much of the Central Coast is covered by national parks, where bushwalking, camping and picnicking are popular pastimes. **Gosford** is the hub of the Central Coast, while a number of smaller townships such as **Patonga** and **Umina** offer seaside retreats.

main attractions

- ❖ Australian Reptile Park and Wildlife Sanctuary
- ❖ Bouddi NP
- ❖ Bulgandry Aboriginal Engraving site
- ❖ Calga Springs Sanctuary
- ❖ Forest of Tranquillity, Ourimbah
- ❖ Glenworth Valley horseriding
- ❖ Old Sydney Town
- ❖ Terrigal
- ❖ The Entrance
- ❖ The Fragrant Garden, Erina
- ❖ Watagan NP

ℹ Tourist information

Central Coast Tourism
200 Mann St, Gosford, NSW 2250
Rotary Park, Terrigal Dr, Terrigal, NSW 2260
Marine Pde, The Entrance, NSW 2261
Ph: (02) 4385 4430
www.cctourism.com.au

Bouddi NP, Central Coast

The Big Merino, Goulburn

to Friday, 10am–4pm; Saturday and public holidays, 1pm–4pm. **Belmore Park**, across the road from the information centre, is an attractive picnic area with gardens, large trees and a band rotunda. The **Big Merino** is a landmark on the southern outskirts of the town. It includes a wool exhibit, merino gift shop, licensed restaurant, tavern and service station. Other points of interest include the **Old Goulburn Brewery** complex. Situated on Bungonia Rd, it now operates as a hotel and function centre. Heritage buildings include Australia's oldest brewery, a steam-powered flour mill, a cooperage, a tobacco curing kiln, mews and workers' cottages. The complex is open daily from 11am and tours are available on Sundays.

NEARBY ATTRACTIONS: **Pelican Sheep Station** is located 10km from Goulburn on the **Braidwood Rd**. Visitors can see sheep-shearing demonstrations and there are tours, a souvenir shop and restaurant. TOURIST INFO: 201 Sloane St, Ph: (02) 4823 4492

■ **Grafton**   POP 17 110
Map 115, H3
The **Clarence River** almost encircles the city of Grafton, the commercial and cultural centre of the **Clarence Valley**. Beef cattle, timber and tourism are the mainstays of the district, while crops grown include maize, lucerne and sugarcane.
MAIN ATTRACTIONS: Known as the '**Jacaranda City**', Grafton is famous for its many attractive parks and

New South Wales

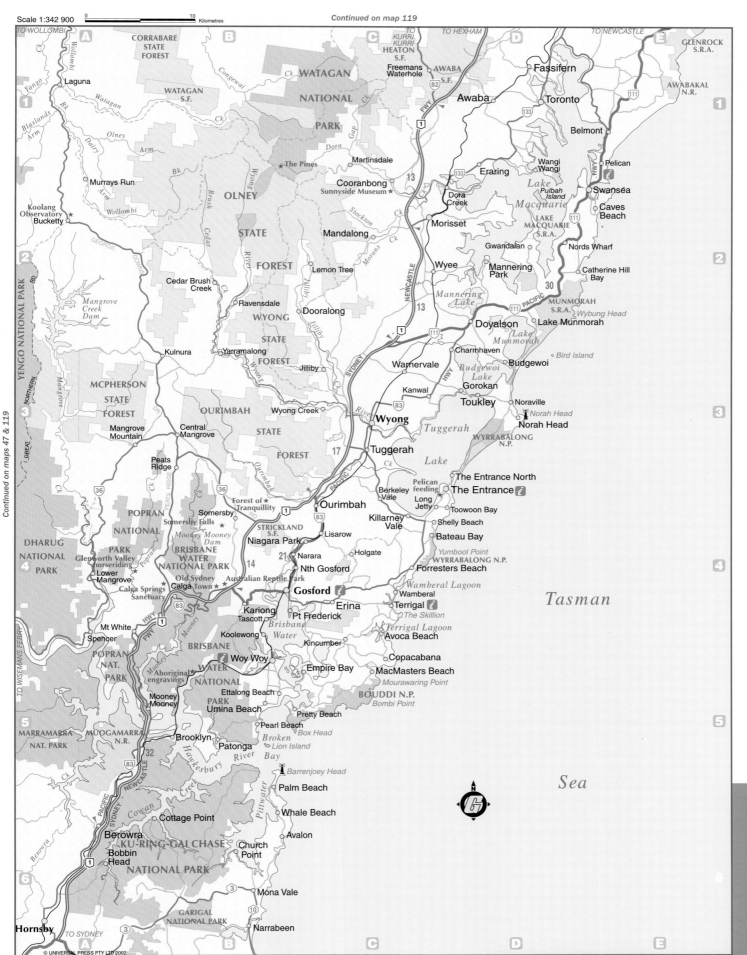

© UNIVERSAL PRESS PTY LTD 2002

Gibraltar Range NP, near Grafton

gardens and the broad streets lined with jacaranda trees. The **Jacaranda Festival** is held Oct–Nov when the trees bloom, and attract thousands of visitors. The parks remain worthwhile visiting at any time of the year, particularly **Market Square** in Prince St; **Memorial Park and Boulevard** at the river end of Prince St; and the **See Park Arboretum** in Pound St.

NEARBY ATTRACTIONS: Grafton is centrally located for scenic drives to the fishing town of **Maclean**, on the Clarence River; **Glen Innes**, in the New England Ranges; and **Iluka**, **Yamba**, **Wooli** and **Coffs Harbour** on the coast. The historic river port village of **Ulmarra** is just 13km NE and 4 major national parks— **Yuraygir** and **Bundjalung** on the coast and **Gibraltar Range** and **Washpool** in the ranges—are a worthwhile daytrip. The **Nymboida River** located 30km SW offers white-water rafting trips and visitors can also hire canoes.

TOURIST INFO: Cnr Pacific Hwy and Spring St, South Grafton, Ph: (02) 6642 4677

■ Grenfell   POP 1984
Map 118, C5

Grenfell is a charming little town situated at the foot of the **Weddin Mountains**, and 377km west of Sydney. The town's streets feature many buildings relatively unaltered since the 1880s. Grenfell was also the birthplace of Henry Lawson.

MAIN ATTRACTIONS: The **Henry Lawson Obelisk** marks the site where Lawson was born in 1867. His father was a miner from Mudgee who brought his family to Grenfell to prospect for gold. The **Grenfell Historical Museum** holds some unique cricket photographs as the Stan McCabe family have lived in the town for some time. The museum is located in Camp St and is open weekends, 2pm–4pm, or by appointment. The most interesting place to picnic is at **O'Brien's Lookout** on the Cowra Rd. This is the place where gold was first discovered and there are walking tracks past the old workings and machinery. **Grenfell Endemic Garden** displays local plants;

and **The Town Drive** takes in everything that is of interest in the town and a leaflet is available from the information centre.

NEARBY ATTRACTIONS: **Weddin Mountains NP** covers a range of hills 19km SW of Grenfell. This large, natural area provides sanctuary from the surrounding agricultural land for many indigenous plants and animals. **Ben Hall's Cave**, the park's most popular attraction, was used by Hall, Johnnie Gilbert, Frank Gardiner and other members of the bushranger gang as a shelter and a place to hide their spoils. There are walking trails and 2 lookouts in the park but no other facilities.

TOURIST INFO: Main St, Ph: (02) 6343 1612

■ Griffith   POP 15 000
Map 117, J6

Designed by Walter Burley Griffin, Griffith is the largest centre in the rich agricultural **Murrumbidgee Irrigation Area**. Famous for its citrus crops, Griffith is one of the largest wine and vegetable production areas in the country. More than 70% of New South Wales' wines are produced here.

MAIN ATTRACTIONS: The **Griffith Food and Wine Festival** is held every Easter to celebrate the harvest. There are champagne breakfasts, country music shows, wine tastings, banquets, wine auctions, a street procession and the **Venetian Carnival,** held on the main irrigation canal. **Griffith Regional Art Gallery** is housed in the old Soldiers Memorial Hall, a 1930s Art Deco building. The gallery has a growing collection of Australian-designed jewellery displayed in one gallery, while touring exhibitions from all over Australia are in another. The gallery is located in Banna Ave, and is open Tues–Sat, 10.30am–4.30pm.

NEARBY ATTRACTIONS: **Cocoparra NP** is 30km NE of Griffith and can be

New South Wales

reached via the Whitton Stock Route, the route taken by Cobb & Co coaches in the early days. The spring wildflowers are spectacular and wildlife is abundant. Good views of the surrounding countryside can be seen from the summits of **Mount Caley** and **Mount Brogden**. Many of the wineries in the area are open for tastings and sales.

TOURIST INFO: Cnr Banna and Jondaryan aves, Ph: (02) 6962 4145 or 1800 681 141

■ Gundagai   POP 2064
Map 122, A2

The centre of prosperous wool and meat-producing country on the **Murrumbidgee River**, 398km SW of Sydney, Gundagai is one of the best known country towns in Australia. Gold discoveries in the 19th century attracted thousands of prospectors, as well as the notorious bushrangers Ben Hall and Capt

Statues of Dad and Dave, north of Gundagai

Moonlite, to the district. Poems and songs, such as Jack O'Hagen's *Along the Road to Gundagai* have helped this town become part of Australian folklore.

MAIN ATTRACTIONS: ***Rusconi's Marble Masterpiece*** is on show at the tourist information centre. It is a unique miniature cathedral containing 20 948 pieces of Australian marble. Each piece was hand-cut and polished and it took 28 years to build. After the ***Dog on the Tuckerbox***, the Rusconi sculpture is the town's number 2 attraction with over 50 000 people visiting every year. The **Gabriel Gallery** displays a collection of photographs, letters and possessions of **Henry Lawson**. It is located in Sheridan St. Also here is the National Trust-classified **Court House**, built in 1859. Trials held here include that of bushranger Capt Moonlite. For panoramic views of the area, visit **Mount Parnassus Lookout** in Hanley St, and **Rotary Lookout** in Luke St.

NEARBY ATTRACTIONS: Local sculptor Frank Rusconi created the *Dog on the Tuckerbox* memorial, which is 9km from Gundagai. It was built as a monument to pioneer teamsters and their dogs. Nearby are the copper statues of **Dad and Dave**, popular characters from the writings of Steele Rudd.

TOURIST INFO: 249 Sheridan St, Ph: (02) 6944 0250 or 6944 0251

■ Gunnedah   POP 9500
Map 114, D5

Surrounded by rich agricultural land, this modern country town lies on gentle sloping terrain on the southern side of the **Namoi River**. The livestock industry is important to the town: **Gunnedah Saleyard** handles the largest cattle sales in New South Wales.

MAIN ATTRACTIONS: The Gunnedah district has one of the largest and healthiest koala populations west

of the **Great Dividing Range**. They can be seen in the trees around town. Standing in **Anzac Park** is the life-sized equestrian statue commemorating Gunnedah's link with the poet Dorothea Mackellar. The Gunnedah Visitors Information Centre contains the **Dorothea Mackellar wing**: a collection of memorabilia associated with her family. In front of the State Office Block in Abbott St stands a memorial to **Cumbo Gunnerah**, a legendary Aboriginal warrior of the Gunn-e-dar people, who died in the late 1700s and was immortalised in Ion Idriess' book, *The Red Chief*. In **Brock's Court**, opposite the Town Hall, stands Gunnedah's **Miner's Memorial Statue** built (and dedicated in Nov 2000) in remembrance of the 20 miners who lost their lives in mining accidents since 1911. Being 125% life-size, the statue depicts a miner erecting a prop, with a symbolic broken shaft at his feet.

NEARBY ATTRACTIONS: **Lake Keepit**, approximately 34km NE of town, offers watersports including boating, sailing, swimming, waterskiing and fishing. On the way to the village of **Mullaley**, approximately 40km SW, visitors will pass the 150° east meridian marking Eastern Standard Time.

TOURIST INFO: Anzac Park, South St, Ph: (02) 6740 2230

■ Hawks Nest   POP 2300
Map 95, C2

This small town is a coastal resort on the northern shores of **Port Stephens**. Popular as a quiet getaway, Hawks Nest is isolated from the bustle of **Nelson Bay**. Swimming, boating and fishing and many other watersports are available.

MAIN ATTRACTIONS: There are many picnic and BBQ facilities around the area, including several riverfront reserves from **Tea Gardens** around to **Winda Woppa**. Both **Jimmys** and **Bennetts beaches** have picnic tables and the **Lions Park** has headland and harbour views. **Koala Zone**, off Kingfisher Ave, gives visitors the opportunity to see a colony of koalas in their natural habitat. NEARBY ATTRACTIONS: Dolphin-watching cruises on Port Stephens are available, as are cruises up the river to **Myall Lakes NP**. This national park is a favourite destination with both campers and boaties. There are 4 lakes, spectacular headlands, long expanses of beaches and sand dunes. Watersports are popular on the lakes and canoes, sailboards, catamarans and powerboats can be hired at **Myall Shores**. At **Bulahdelah** houseboats can be hired. TOURIST INFO: Myall St, Tea Gardens, Ph: (02) 4997 0111

■ Hay   POP 3160
Map 121, F1
Almost surrounded by the **Murrumbidgee River**, Hay lies in the middle of flat saltbush plains, 726km SW of Sydney. The plains support merino flocks producing

Walls of China, Mungo NP, west of Hay

medium-fine wools. Although wool is the main industry, there is also dairying, and irrigation allows fruit and vegetable growing. Many world-famous sheep studs are located here, including **Mungadal**, **Uardry** and **Cedar Grove**.
MAIN ATTRACTIONS: The **Australian Shearers' Hall of Fame**, cnr Cobb and Sturt hwys, is a superb living museum showcasing shearing life in the Outback. **Hay Gaol Museum**, built in 1878, has been a penal institute, maternity hospital, asylum, POW camp and a security institute for girls. The building is now a local history museum in Church St. It is open 9am–5pm daily. The restored Railway Station now houses the **POW Internment Camp Interpretive Centre** The centre documents WWII internment of over 3000 prisoners-of-war in Hay.
NEARBY ATTRACTIONS: The Murrumbidgee River offers many excellent fishing spots and is popular in summer for waterskiing, canoeing and swimming. There are several river beaches close to town offering swimming and picnicking. Over 62 species of birds have been identified at **Hay Wetlands**, located off the Old Thelangerlin Rd on the north-west of town. Springtime is a lovely time to visit with many waterbirds, including swans and ducks, nesting and breeding.
TOURIST INFO: 407 Moppett St, Ph: (02) 6993 4045

■ Huskisson   POP 2200
Map 97, C4
A flourishing little tourist and fishing town lying in the curve of **Jervis Bay**, Huskisson is the main shopping and accommodation centre in the district. Around 24km SE of Nowra, Huskisson is a popular destination for families as it offers easy access to the clear waters of the bay and all facilities. Popular watersports include swimming, sailing, windsurfing, scuba diving and fishing.

MAIN ATTRACTIONS: Many visitors spend time on the beaches that line the shore of Jervis Bay. Regular dolphin-watching cruises leave from **Huskisson Wharf**. Anglers can hire boats or fish from the beach, rocks or riverbank. Those interested in the history of boat-building, should visit the **Lady Denman Heritage Complex** in Dent St. The *Lady Denman*, a Sydney Harbour ferry built at Huskisson and launched in 1911, is the centrepiece of the **Lady Denman Museum** within the complex. **Laddie Timbery's Aboriginal Art and Craft Centre** is also located in the complex. Local Koori artists make works on site. The award-winning complex also features a stand of spotted gum trees, freshwater and saltwater wetlands, the **Wirreecoo Walking Trail**, mangrove boardwalk and fish feeding in the harbour.
NEARBY ATTRACTIONS: **Jervis Bay NP** is located both north and south of the town and there are many walking tracks to explore. The **Botanic Gardens**, located in **Booderee NP**, showcases the unique plants of the area. The park is south of Huskisson. **Barry's Bush Tucker Tours** offers guided walks while explaining the Aboriginal history of the area.
TOURIST INFO: Cnr Princes Hwy and Pleasant Way, Nowra, Ph: (02) 4421 0778

■ Iluka   POP 1800
Map 115, J3
This small fishing and resort town lies 20km off the Pacific Hwy at the mouth of the **Clarence River**. A regular passenger ferry service links Iluka, on the north shore, to the larger resort of **Yamba** on the south side of the river mouth. Both towns have their own commercial fishing fleets and attract keen anglers for the beach, rock, estuary and deep-sea fishing opportunities.
MAIN ATTRACTIONS: The Iluka–Yamba passenger ferry offers river cruises to **Harwood Island** on Wednesdays

Fishing boat at dawn, Iluka

and Fridays. There are also BBQ cruises on Wednesday and Friday evenings. Immediately behind the town is the World Heritage-listed **Iluka Nature Reserve** containing a remnant of what was once an extensive coastal rainforest. The seaward end of the park emerges at **Iluka Bluff** picnic area, where the short walk reveals a wonderful view of Iluka township and the Clarence River estuary.

NEARBY ATTRACTIONS: The **Clarence Valley** has many sites significant to the Bundjalung Aboriginal people and 13 of these sites are covered on the **Lower Clarence Aboriginal Site Tourist Drive**. Brochures are available from the information centres at **Grafton** and **Maclean**. **Bundjalung NP** stretches north to **Evans Head** with 38km of unspoilt beaches perfect for surfing and fishing. **Wombah Coffee Plantation**, the world's southernmost coffee plantation, is located 4km from the Pacific Hwy on the Iluka Rd. It is open weekends and holidays,

10am–5pm. Tour guides explain the growing and processing of coffee.
TOURIST INFO: Ferry Park, Pacific Hwy, Ph: (02) 6645 4121

■ Inverell   POP 10 000
Map 114, E3
Known as the **Sapphire City**, Inverell is one of the world's leading suppliers of these lovely gems. This **New England** town is set on the **MacIntyre River** and is the centre of a diverse rural district.
MAIN ATTRACTIONS: Inverell's **Pioneer Village** contains an impressive collection of historic buildings relocated from the surrounding district. The museum realistically displays local history from 1840–1930. Original buildings include Paddy's Pub (1847), Grove Homestead (1840), Nullamanna Village Church (1901), Slaughter House Creek Bridge, a school, village hall, Railway Station and much more. The museum is open Tuesday to Saturday 10am–5pm; Sunday 10am–4pm; and Monday

by appointment. **The Town Walk**, and **Town and Country Drive** leaflets are available from the information centre.
NEARBY ATTRACTIONS: The **DeJon Sapphire Centre** is located 19km east on Glen Innes Rd. Here, visitors can see a working sapphire mine. **Green Valley Farm**, 36km SE, is home to **Smith's Mining and Natural History Museum**.
TOURIST INFO: Water Towers Complex, Campbell St, Ph: (02) 6728 8161

■ Jindabyne   POP 4750
Map 77, C5
The gateway to the alpine ski resorts, Jindabyne lies on the shores of the man-made **Lake Jindabyne**. The original township was beside the **Snowy River**. In 1962, to create **Lake Jindabyne**, the site of the old township was flooded to form a water storage area as part of the **Snowy Mountains Hydro-Electric Scheme**.
MAIN ATTRACTIONS: While being a good base for visiting the **ski resorts**, Jindabyne also attracts visitors during summer. Activities at this time of year include bushwalking, trout fishing, sailing, sailboarding, waterskiing, canoeing and swimming. There is also a walkway and cycleway around part of Lake Jindabyne's foreshore.
NEARBY ATTRACTIONS: **Kosciuszko NP** occupies most of the Snowy Mountains region; in fact it is the largest national park in New South Wales. The park has much to offer year-round, including horseriding, mountain-biking, trout fishing, canoeing and white-water rafting. At 2228m above sea level, **Mount Kosciuszko** is Australia's highest point. An accessible walking trail crosses the flattened top of the mountain providing stunning panoramic views.
TOURIST INFO: Snowy Region Visitor Information, Kosciuszko Rd, Ph: (02) 6450 5600

Part of the New South Wales section of the **Great Dividing Range**, the Snowy Mountains are approximately 160km long and 80km wide. Much of the rugged terrain is 900m or more above sea level, with the mountainous ridge rising to 2228m at **Mount Kosciuszko**, the highest point in Australia. Although the Snowy Mountains are situated in New South Wales, they are close to the **Australian Capital Territory** and their southern boundary extends to the Victorian border.

Kosciuszko NP occupies most of the Snowy Mountains region and at 6744km^2 is the largest national park in New South Wales.

Despite the mountain range's name, the Snowy Mountains lie below the line of permanent snow, so heavy snowfall will only be seen from June to October. During the winter months skiers, both local and international, flock to the many ski resorts dotting the mountains.

Summer also has much to offer visitors. Lower prices and fewer people make the area a perfect destination for a bushwalking, trout-fishing or mountain-biking holiday. The wildflowers and abundance of birdlife are particularly impressive during these months.

Snowfield resorts

Thredbo is a popular ski resort town, sandwiched in a small valley between Crackenback River and the road. **Charlotte Pass**, **Perisher Valley** and **Smiggin Holes** lie within the Kosciuszko NP's borders. All offer great skiing and visitors can easily travel between some of the resorts on the **Skitube**.

 Tourist information

Snowy Region Visitor Information
National Parks and Wildlife Service (NPWS)
Kosciuszko Rd, Jindabyne, NSW 2627
Ph: (02) 6450 5600
www.npws.nsw.gov.au

Skiing at Thredbo

main attractions

❖ **Jindabyne**

This town on the shores of Lake Jindabyne is the gateway to the alpine ski resorts.

❖ **Kosciuszko NP**

Vehicles in 2 sections of the park must carry chains between June 1 and October 10. Summer activities include trout fishing and bushwalking.

❖ **Mt Kosciuszko**

A walking trail crosses the flattened top, providing breathtaking views.

❖ **Yarrangobilly Caves**

This limestone cave system consists of about 60 caves, only 4 of which are open to the public. Walking trails, located by the edge of the rocky plateau next to the caves, offer panoramic views of Yarrangobilly Gorge.

Khancoban Dam in autumn, Snowy Mountains

New South Wales

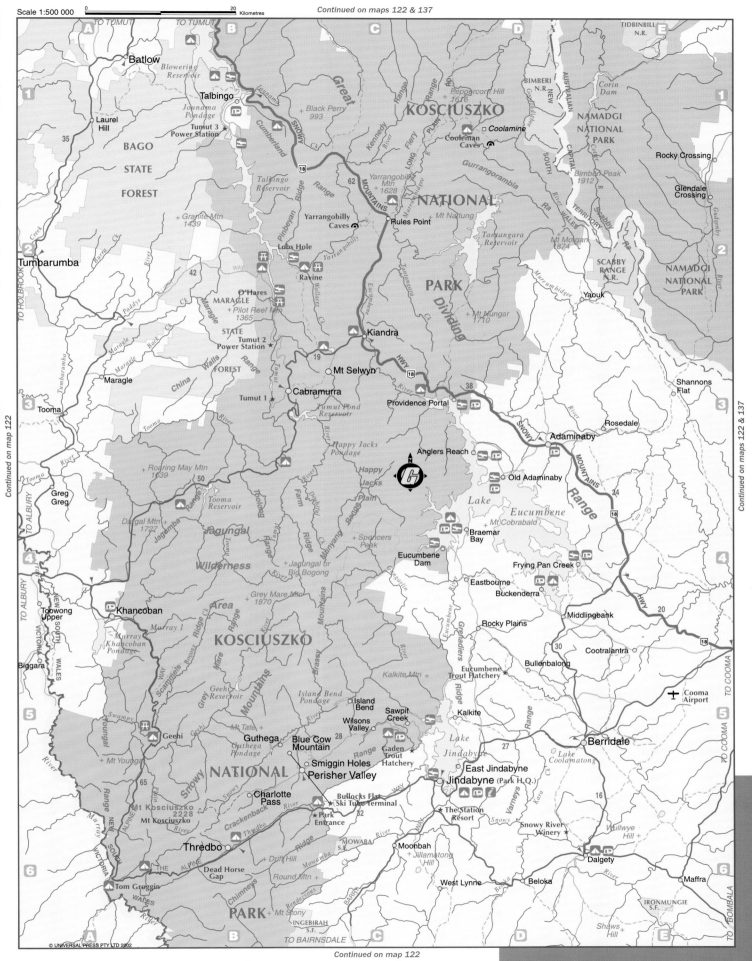

Kilometres

TO TUMUT
TO TUMUT

Batlow

Blowering Reservoir

Talbingo

Laurel Hill

Jounama Pondage

Tumut 3 Power Station

Black Perry 993

KOSCIUSZKO

Peppercorn Hill 1616

BIMBERI N.R.

TIDBINBILL N.R.

Corin Dam

NAMADGI NATIONAL PARK

BAGO STATE FOREST

Granite Mtn 1439

Yarrangobilly Caves

Coolamine

Cooleman Caves

Bimberi Peak 1912

Rocky Crossing

Yarrangobilly Mtn 1628

Rules Point

NATIONAL

Mt Nattung

Glendale Crossing

TO HOLBROOK

Tumbarumba

Lobs Hole

Ravine

Tantangara Reservoir

Mt Morgan 1874

SCABBY RANGE N.R.

NAMADGI NATIONAL PARK

O'Hares

MARAGLE

Pilot Reef Mtn 1365

STATE

Tumut 2 Power Station

Kiandra

PARK

Mt Nungar 1710

Yaouk

Shannons Flat

Maragle

Mt Selwyn

Dividing

Tooma

Tumut 1

Cabramurra

Providence Portal

38

Rosedale

Greg Greg

Tumut Pond Reservoir

Happy Jacks Pondage

Anglers Reach

Adaminaby

Roaring May Mtn 1039

Happy Jacks Plain

Old Adaminaby

24

Tooma Reservoir

Dargal Mtn 1727

Jagungal Wilderness

Jagungal or Big Bogong

Spencers Peak

Lake Eucumbene

Mt Cobrabald

Braemar Bay

Eucumbene Dam

Frying Pan Creek

Khancoban

Grey Mare Mtn 1870

Area

Toowong Upper

Murray 1

Murray Khancoban Pondage

KOSCIUSZKO

Eastbourne

Buckenderra

Middlingbank

20

Biggara

Geehi Reservoir

Kalkite Mtn

Rocky Plains

30

Cootralantra

Eucumbene Trout Hatchery

Bullenbalong

Island Bend Pondage

Island Bend

Sawpit Creek

Kalkite

Cooma Airport

Geehi

Mt Tate

Wilsons Valley

Lake Jindabyne

28

Guthega Pondage

Guthega

Blue Cow Mountain

Gaden Trout Hatchery

Berridale

27

Lake Coolamatong

Mt Younger

Smiggin Holes

Perisher Valley

NATIONAL

Jindabyne (Park H.Q.)

East Jindabyne

Charlotte Pass

Bullocks Flat Ski Tube Terminal

32

The Station Resort

Snowy River Winery

16

Mt Kosciuszko 2228

Park Entrance

Wullwye Hill

Mt Kosciuszko

Thredbo

Moonbah

Dalgety

Dead Horse Gap

Jillamatong Hill

Maffra

Tom Groggin

Round Mtn

Mt Stony

West Lynne

Beloka

IRONMUNGIE S.F.

PARK

INGEBIRAH S.F.

Shaws Hill

TO BAIRNSDALE

TO COOMA

TO BOMBALA

© UNIVERSAL PRESS PTY LTD 2002

Continued on map 122

Continued on maps 122 & 137

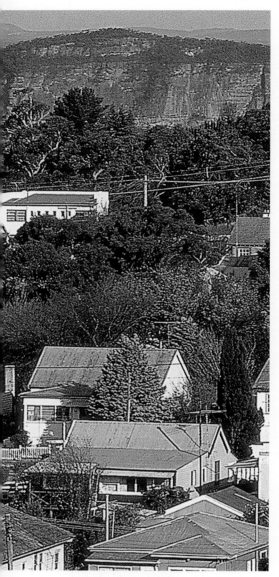
Katoomba, Blue Mountains

■ Junee   POP 5000

Map 122, A2

An agricultural and grazing town, Junee is also an important rail centre for southern New South Wales. The railway track runs through the middle of the CBD and the station, built in 1883, is an impressive Renaissance-style building.

MAIN ATTRACTIONS: Railway memorabilia and the district's pioneering history are preserved in the **Historical Museum** in Peel St. The museum is open Tuesday and Thursday, 2pm–4pm. The **Junee Roundhouse Museum** incorporates the largest

operational roundhouse in Australia. It features a 32m turntable, the original workshop, heritage transport displays, memorabilia and a large model train layout. Guided tours and light refreshments are available. **Memorial Park**, located beside the railway crossing, is an attractive spot for a picnic. **Endeavour Park**, on the Olympic Way south of the town centre, has an interesting hedge maze and a pond.

TOURIST INFO: Railway Refreshment Rooms, Railway Sq, Ph: (02) 6924 2522

■ Katoomba   POP 18 000

Map 80, E4

The major centre of the World Heritage-listed **Blue Mountains** west of Sydney, Katoomba has been a famous resort for lovers of the mountains since the end of the last century. It remains as popular today, with a variety of accommodation including charming guesthouses and beautifully restored hotels.

MAIN ATTRACTIONS: **The Three Sisters** are Katoomba's most famous natural attraction. This impressive rock formation is best seen from **Echo Point**, high above the **Jamison Valley**. An information centre is located at Echo Point. The **Scenic Railway**, located in Violet St, off Cliff Dr, is a heart-stopping ride for tourists. The **Scenic Skyway** and **Sceniscender** cable cars are also located in the **Scenic World** complex. For a step back in time, the **Paragon Cafe**, on Katoomba St, is the place to stop for morning or afternoon tea. Classified by the National Trust for its original Art Deco interiors, it is remembered by many generations for its delicious handmade chocolates. **The Edge** cinema, located on the Great Western Hwy, shows a spectacular movie of the Blue Mountains on a 6-storey-high screen.

NEARBY ATTRACTIONS: **Jenolan Caves**, 75km SW of Katoomba, offers a

spectacular system of limestone caves, icy rivers and limestone formations. The partially restored silver-mining ghost town of **Yerranderie** is worth a visit. It is located 200km south via **Oberon**, the drive itself is an adventure over the 73km dirt road.

TOURIST INFO: Echo Point, Katoomba; or Great Western Hwy, Glenbrook, Ph: 1300 653 408

■ Kempsey   POP 9200

Map 115, H6

The largest urban centre in the rural **Macleay Valley**, Kempsey is divided by the Pacific Hwy and the **Macleay River**. The town attracts business and tourists, and is growing as a retirement centre. Kempsey is also the home of Australia's famous **Akubra hats**, although the factory is not open to the public.

MAIN ATTRACTIONS: Kempsey's most interesting historic buildings are located mainly in **Kemp**, **Elbow** and **Sea sts**. Many of these 19th-century buildings are listed on the town's **heritage trail**. **South Kempsey Park** is the location of the **Kempsey Cultural Centre**. Here visitors will find the information centre and the **Macleay River Historical Museum**, which is open daily 10am–4pm. The museum displays feature an early settler's cottage and the local history of Aboriginal groups from the Macleay valley.

NEARBY ATTRACTIONS: One of Kempsey's main attractions is its proximity to the coastal resorts of **South West Rocks**, **Crescent Head**, **Hat Head**, **Stuarts Point** and **Grassy Head**, all offering unspoilt coastal scenery and clean beaches. **Wilay Bijarr Aboriginal Tours** offers cultural and historical tours of significant Aboriginal sites in the area, covering bush tucker and medicine. Ph: (02) 6562 5959

TOURIST INFO: Pacific Hwy, South Kempsey, Ph: (02) 6563 1555

THE BLUE MOUNTAINS

Named the Blue Mountains due to the blue haze that can be seen from Sydney—created by light interacting with the vapour emanating from the millions of eucalypt trees. This rugged region features dramatic cliffs, rock formations, waterfalls and caves. Once seen as a barrier to the infant colony's expansion westwards, the Blue Mountains is now a popular holiday or weekend destination due to its proximity to Sydney.

Located approximately 105km from Sydney, this spectacular wilderness area—now World Heritage-listed—can be enjoyed year round. Seasonal changes here are more marked than in Sydney, and temperatures can plummet very quickly, especially in winter, so it is wise to always be prepared for the cold. This climate makes the Blue Mountains an ideal location for **Yulefest**, a mid-winter 'Christmas' festival, held annually between June and August. Many quaint villages dot the landscape, offering excellent restaurants, cafes, pubs, gardens, galleries, antique stores and other shops to entertain less energetic visitors.

main attractions

◈ Blue Mountains NP
This very popular park offers sandstone cliffs, canyons, lookouts and a huge variety of walks.

◈ Echo Point Lookout
This lookout provides breathtaking views of Jamison Valley and The Three Sisters.

◈ Hydro Majestic
Built last century on the cliff edge, this hotel remains a popular retreat.

◈ Jenolan Caves
Limestone caverns lie underground, with icy rivers and impressive limestone formations.

◈ Leura
A picturesque town classified by the National Trust.

◈ Norman Lindsay Gallery and Museum
Formerly the home of the controversial artist, cartoonist and writer, it is now a gallery of Lindsay's works.

◈ Scenic World
Popular rides here are the Scenic Railway, Scenic Skyway and Scenicender.

◈ Zig Zag Railway
This railway was named in 1886, after a series of zig zags were constructed in the track enabling coal trains to descend into the valley.

Eastern water dragon, *Physignathus lesueurii*

World Heritage Area
The area was listed in 2000 as Australia's 14th World Heritage Area for its unique landforms, geological history, flora and fauna and its cultural significance to the Daruk and Gundungura Aboriginal people. Older than America's Grand Canyon, the area is home to living fossils like the Wollemi Pine. Bushwalking, rockclimbing, canyoning, abseiling, mountain biking and 4WDing are all possible.

i Tourist information

Echo Point Visitors Information Centre
Echo Point Rd, Echo Point,
Katoomba, NSW 2780

Glenbrook Visitor Information Centre
Great Western Hwy, Glenbrook, NSW 2773
Freecall: 1300 653 408

Blue Mountains NP
NSW Heritage Centre
Govetts Leap Rd, Blackheath, NSW 2785
Ph: (02) 4787 8877

Autumn garden in Mount Wilson, Blue Mountains

Scale 1:160 00

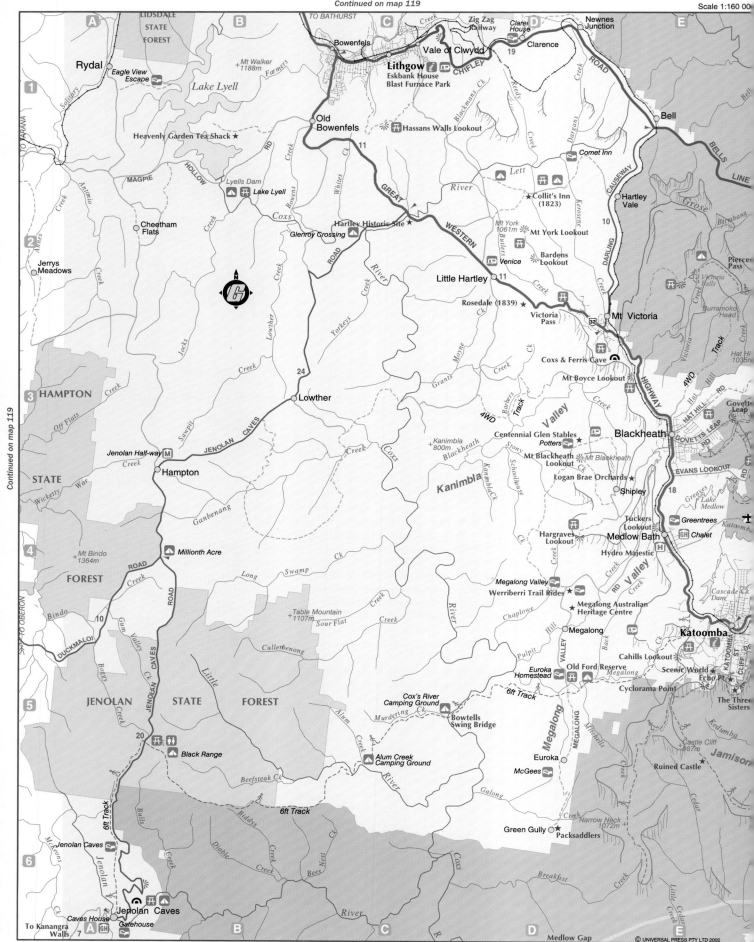

New South Wales

© UNIVERSAL PRESS PTY LTD 2002

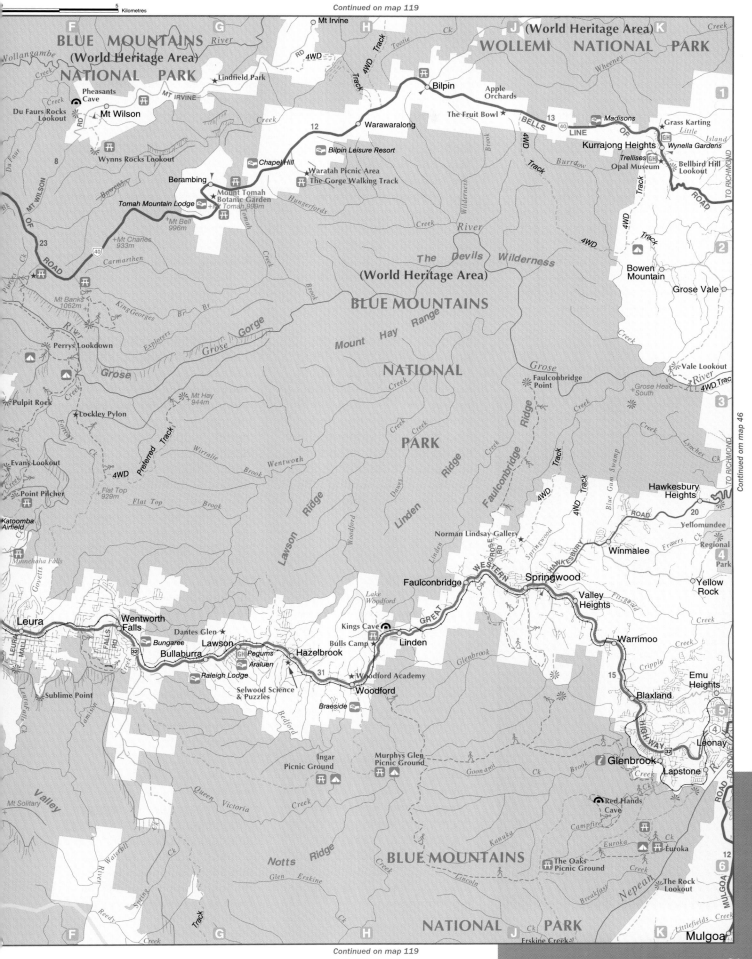

Continued on map 119

5 Kilometres

F   **G**   Mt Irvine   **H**   **J**   (World Heritage Area)   **K**

BLUE MOUNTAINS
(World Heritage Area)
NATIONAL PARK

WOLLEMI NATIONAL PARK

Lindfield Park

Pheasants Cave

Bilpin

Apple Orchards

1

Du Faurs Rocks Lookout

Mt Wilson

The Fruit Bowl ★

Madisons

Grass Karting

13

BELLS

Wynns Rocks Lookout

Warawaralong

12

Bilpin Leisure Resort

Burrdow

Kurrajong Heights

Wynella Gardens

Trellises

Bellbird Hill Lookout

Chapel Hill

Berambing

Waratah Picnic Area
The Gorge Walking Track

Opal Museum

LINE

40

Tomah Mountain Lodge

Mount Tomah Botanic Garden
+Mt Tomah 999m

+Mt Bell 996m

TO RICHMOND

ROAD

23

40

+Mt Charles 933m

Carmarthen

Hungerfords

The Devils Wilderness

Bowen Mountain

2

4WD

Grose Vale

Mt Banks 1062m

King Georges

Grose Gorge

River

(World Heritage Area)

BLUE MOUNTAINS

Mount Hay Range

4WD

Perrys Lookdown

Explorers

NATIONAL

Grose

Faulconbridge Point

Vale Lookout

3

Pulpit Rock

Mt Hay 944m

Grose Head South

Grose River

4WD Trac

TO RICHMOND

Lockley Pylon

PARK

Faulconbridge Ridge

Continued om map 46

Evans Lookout

Wirralie

Wentworth

4WD

Preferred Track

Flat Top 929m

Brook

Linden Ridge

Hawkesbury Heights

20

Point Pilcher

Flat Top

Brook

Lawson Ridge

Woodford

Norman Lindsay Gallery

ROAD

Yellomundee

Winmalee

Regional Park

Katoomba Airfield

Linden

WESTERN

HAWKESBURY

4

Minnehaha Falls

GROSE RD

Springwood

Yellow Rock

Faulconbridge

Govetts Ck

Lake Woodford

Valley Heights

Leura

Wentworth Falls

Dantes Glen ★

Kings Cave

GREAT

Warrimoo

Cripple Ck

LEURA MALL

Bungaree

Lawson

Bulls Camp

Linden

Glenbrook

Emu Heights

32

FALLS RD

Pegums

Hazelbrook

Araluen

Bullaburra

31

Woodford Academy

15

Blaxland

5

Raleigh Lodge

Selwood Science & Puzzles

Woodford

Braeside

HIGHWAY

32

Leonay

4

Sublime Point

Bedford

Glenbrook

Lapstone

Murphys Glen Picnic Ground

ROAD

Mt Solitary

Ingar Picnic Ground

Red Hands Cave

TO SYDNEY

Valley

Queen Victoria Creek

BLUE MOUNTAINS

The Oaks Picnic Ground

Euroka

Campfire

Euroka

6

Notts Ridge

Waterfall

Goon aroi

The Rock Lookout

Reedy Ck

Glen Erskine

Lincoln

Kanuka

Breakfast

Nepean

12

NATIONAL PARK

Erskine Creek

Littlefields Creek

Mulgoa

F   **G**   **H**   **J**   **K**

Continued on map 119

■ Kiama   POP 12 000
Map 107, C3

The centre of a rich dairying district, famous for its Illawarra shorthorn breed of cattle, Kiama is also a popular resort town. Located on the Princes Hwy, 119km south of Sydney, Kiama has a relaxed, country atmosphere as well as offering visitors excellent beaches, rockpools, fishing and a scenic rural hinterland.

MAIN ATTRACTIONS: The famous **Kiama Blowhole** is a fascinating yet unpredictable attraction. In calm weather it is fairly unimpressive, but when the seas are rough and running from the south-east, trapped water is forced to a height of 60m, creating a loud noise and spectacular sight. The Blowhole is floodlit until 9pm. **Kiama Family History (Genealogical) Centre** and **The Terrace** (art and craft shops) are historic buildings that are worthwhile visiting. A variety of fish can be caught around the town's rocky shoreline and there are plenty of fishing charters available.

NEARBY ATTRACTIONS: Brochures are available from the information centre about several scenic drives both along the coast and in the hinterland area. **Saddleback Mountain** can be reached by following the Jamberoo Rd from Kiama. The summit is 600m above sea level and views extend 240km along the coast and over farming land. The wonderful **Minnamurra Rainforest** and **Rainforest Centre** is close by in **Budderoo NP** which is also home to **Minnamurra Falls**.
TOURIST INFO: Blowhole Point, Ph: (02) 4232 3322

■ Kurri Kurri   POP 5510
Map 119, H4

Kurri Kurri is the centre of an agricultural and industrial region. Located midway between **Cessnock** and **Maitland**, Kurri Kurri was once a coal-mining town but the majority of residents are now employed at Capral Aluminium. The surrounding area is devoted to dairying and orchards. Kurri Kurri is a thriving little town despite the decline of coal mining.

MAIN ATTRACTIONS: **Kurri Regional Museum** is housed in the old timber Pokolbin Schoolhouse, located in the grounds of **Kurri Kurri High School**. The museum displays a collection of memorabilia covering daily life and work in the coalfields' region and is open Sunday, Wednesday and public holidays, 1pm–4pm, or by appointment.

Kiama Blowhole

NEARBY ATTRACTIONS: The **Buchanan Gallery**, east of Kurri Kurri in **Buchanan**, specialises in ceramics, paintings, outdoor pots and restored colonial furniture displayed in an old schoolhouse. Picnic facilities are available. Only a 20min drive from town are the wineries of the **Lovedale** region, including **Wandin Valley Estate**, **Sandalyn Estate** and **Allanmere Winery**.
TOURIST INFO: Hunter Wine Centre, Allandale Rd, Pokolbin, Ph: (02) 4990 4477

■ Kyogle   POP 2847
Map 115, H2

Located on **Summerland Way**, at the foot of **Fairymount**, is the township of Kyogle. Known as the 'Gateway to the Rainforest', Kyogle overlooks the **Richmond Valley** and the scenery of the tall **McPherson**, **Tweed** and **Richmond mountain ranges** to the north, east and west.

NEARBY ATTRACTIONS: The **Border Ranges World Heritage Area** lies 30km north and offers excellent views, waterfalls, deep gorges, clear creeks and steep escarpments. Highlights of the park's eastern section are the **Pinnacle Rock** formation and the view from **Blackbutt Lookout**. The **Rainforest Botanical Gardens** are located alongside **Fawcetts Creek**. Existing rainforest was enhanced and developed to create the gardens, which are well worth visiting. Parking is available near the tennis courts on Summerland Way.
TOURIST INFO: Roxy Gallery, 143 Summerland Way, Ph: (02) 6632 3518

■ Lake Macquarie   POP 170 495
Map 71, D2

The largest permanent saltwater lake in Australia, Lake Macquarie is an extensive coastal lagoon with 174km of foreshore. The lake is located in the northern section of the coastal strip separating **The Central Coast** and **Newcastle**.

Belmont Yacht Club, Lake Macquarie

A popular holiday resort, Lake Macquarie attracts thousands of visitors for the good fishing, sailing, swimming and year-round watersports.

MAIN ATTRACTIONS: Ocean beaches stretch for 20km from **Munmorah SRA** in the south to **Glenrock** in the north. All kinds of boats are available for hire—from outboard 'tinnies' to luxurious yachts and houseboats. With a boat, it is worthwhile visiting **Pulbah Island**, a wildlife sanctuary home to many native birds and animals.

NEARBY ATTRACTIONS: Munmorah SRA offers 12km of rugged coastline and on its western side, a frontage on to **Lake Munmorah**. Activities include surfing, sailing, fishing, picnicking and bushwalking. **Glenrock Lagoon** is a major feature of **Glenrock SRA**. The area is renowned for its attractive waterfalls, rockpools, beaches and striking headlands. To the west of Lake Macquarie lies **Watagan NP**. At the foot of the Watagans is the historic village of **Cooranbong**, which was settled in the late 19th century by members of the Seventh Day Adventist Church. **Sunnyside Museum**, open daily except Friday, 2pm–4pm, was originally the home of Ellen White, a pioneer of the church.

TOURIST INFO: 72 Pacific Hwy, Blacksmiths, Ph: (02) 4972 1172

■ Leeton   POP 11 031
Map 121, J1

The administrative centre of the **Murrumbidgee Irrigation Area**, Leeton is located 30km off the Newell Hwy. The first rice mill opened here in 1951 and Leeton is now the headquarters for Australia's rice industry, which exports rice to many Asian countries, including Japan.

MAIN ATTRACTIONS: The **Leeton SunRice Centre** at **Leeton Mill** is open to the public and gives presentations at 9.30am and 2.45pm on weekdays. The **Berri Juice Factory** offers guided tours at 10.45am on weekdays. **Toorak Wines** and **Lillypilly Estate**, 2 local wineries, are open for tastings and sales Mon–Sat. **Mountford Park**, near the town centre, is a relaxing spot for a picnic.

NEARBY ATTRACTIONS: Approximately 23km west is the historic village of **Whitton**. Worthwhile visiting is the **Court House and Historical Museum** which is open 1pm–4pm on weekends and 10am–1pm on Tuesdays, or by appointment. **Fivebough Swamp**, on the outskirts of town, is a popular spot for bird-watchers. The sanctuary is an important feeding and breeding ground for over 149 species of migratory waterbirds.

TOURIST INFO: 10 Yanco Ave, Ph: (02) 6953 6481

■ Lennox Head   POP 3200
Map 84, D3

Located 11km north of **Ballina**, Lennox Head is a small holiday town. Lying at the southern end of **Seven Mile Beach**, the town is renowned as a good surfing spot, but there are also calm areas for snorkelling and swimming.

NEARBY ATTRACTIONS: A good coastal road links Lennox Head to Ballina and also to **Byron Bay**, 20km north. **Forgotten Country Ecotours** offer a range of 1–5 day nature-based scenic adventures exploring the rainforests, rivers, gorges and wilderness areas of the **North Coast**. **Lake Ainsworth** is a unique freshwater lake only 50m from the ocean. This popular area is ideal for swimming, canoeing, sailing, windsurfing and fishing. South of the town is the **Pat Moreton Lookout**, which can be reached either via road or through the foreshore reserve. Between May and October migrating whales can frequently be seen offshore.

TOURIST INFO: Cnr Norton St and Las Balsas Plaza, Ballina, Ph: (02) 6686 3484

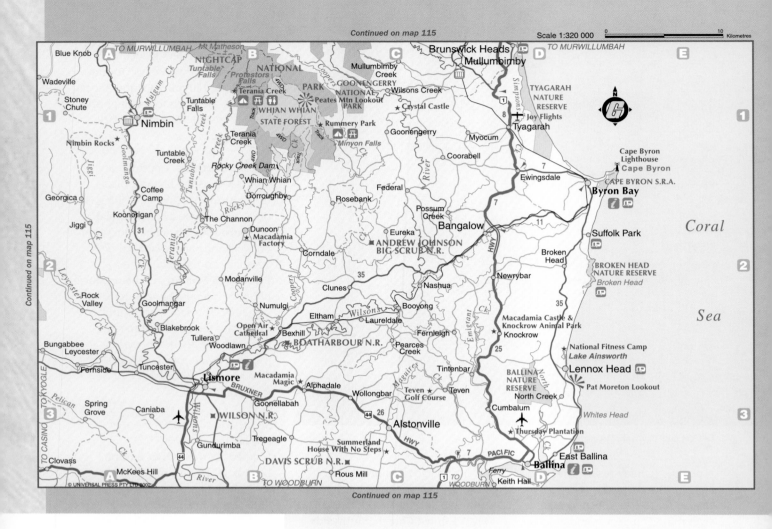

Continued on map 115

Scale 1:320 000

Continued on map 115

■ Lismore   POP 42 954

Map 84, B3

A bustling commercial centre and university city (Southern Cross), Lismore is located on the Bruxner Hwy and beside the **Wilsons River**, 760km north of Sydney. Lismore is in the heart of the **'Rainbow Region'** of northern New South Wales—referring not only to the district's many rainbows, but also to its reputation for attracting creative and alternative-lifestyle people.

MAIN ATTRACTIONS: The Lismore district is recognised as having some of the most unusual arts and crafts in the nation. The **Cultural and Heritage Gallery** at the Lismore Visitors Information Centre is one of the main attractions. The **Lismore Regional Art Gallery** is also located in Molesworth St and houses a permanent collection and regular local exhibitions. **Richmond River Historical Society Museum** is open from Monday to Friday, 10am–4pm; weekends and other times by appointment. Good picnic spots can be found in **Wade Park**, **Heritage Park** and **Lismore Lake**. Lismore's **Koala Hospital** cares for sick and injured koalas and a rehabilitation area is open daily. **Rotary Rainforest Reserve** is a 6ha area with a rainforest boardwalk, and an information centre.

NEARBY ATTRACTIONS: Koalas can also be seen in the wild at **Tucki Tucki Koala Reserve**, 15km south on the Woodburn Rd. **Macadamia Magic** farm and processing plant complex. is located 11km east at **Alphadale**.

TOURIST INFO: Cnr Ballina and Molesworth sts, Ph: (02) 6622 0122 or (02) 4385 4430

Totem Forest in Lismore's Heritage Park

New South Wales

Lithgow   POP 19 248

Map 80, C1

Located on the fringes of the **Blue Mountains**, Lithgow is a coal-mining town, with its coal-mining history dating back to 1841.

MAIN ATTRACTIONS: The most popular attractions in Lithgow are **Blast Furnace Park, Eskbank House** and the **Small Arms Museum**.

NEARBY ATTRACTIONS: The **Mount Piper Power Station** is open daily 10am–4pm and uses interactive exhibits to explain what electricity is and how it is made and distributed. Tour times are 10.30am and 1pm weekdays, and picnic and BBQ facilities are available. The **Zig Zag Railway** was built in 1869 to conquer the problem of transporting coal over the Blue Mountains. Considered one of the world's engineering marvels, the rail line crosses 3 huge sandstone viaducts and drops 150m into the **Lithgow Valley**. A section of the line has been restored and is now a major tourist attraction. The trains run daily at 11am, 1pm and 3pm. One of the most popular of the district's walks, the **Glow-Worm Tunnel Walk**, is accessed via 34km of dirt road through the **Wolgan Valley**. The walk follows the route of the railway that took shale from the mines at **Newnes** from 1906 until the 1930s. Lithgow is a good base for campers and bushwalkers wanting to explore the **Wollemi NP**, the second largest national park in New South Wales. Both **Lake Lyell** and **Lake Wallace** are excellent spots for picnics, sailing and fishing.

TOURIST INFO: 1 Cooerwull Rd, Old Bowenfels Station, Ph: (02) 6353 1859

Macksville   POP 3000

Map 62, C6

This **Nambucca River** town, only 10km upstream from Nambucca Heads, is a pleasant stop on your journey along the Pacific Hwy. Fishing and oyster farming are the main industries in Macksville. Crops grown in the surrounding district include bananas (the most southerly region where bananas are commercially grown) and other tropical fruit, macadamia nuts and vegetables. Grazing, dairying and timber are also important to the local economy.

MAIN ATTRACTIONS: The **Mary Boulton Pioneer Cottage** is a reminder of the settlement's early days. Stables on the property display tools, saddlery, harness and horse-drawn vehicles. The cottage is in River St and is open on Wednesdays and Saturdays, 2pm–4pm. Riverbank parks on either side of the Pacific Hwy bridge offer picnic tables. Boat launching ramps are also located on each side of the river. **Macksville Wharf**, a heritage project, was recently opened. The river provides ideal conditions for watersports and bottlenose dolphins are often seen swimming in these waters.

NEARBY ATTRACTIONS: The **Cosmopolitan Pub**, made famous in Slim Dusty's song, *A Pub with no Beer*, is located at **Taylor's Arm**, about 30km west of the town. In the same area **Bakers Creek Station** offers horse-riding, canoeing, BBQ and picnic areas. The old township of **Bowraville**, upstream on the Nambucca River, has the **Joseph and Eliza Newman Folk Museum** and the **Frank Partridge VC Military Museum**. **Yarahappini Mount Lookout**, 10km south, has excellent views and a rainforest. **Scotts Head**, 18km SE, is a scenic coastal town with great surfing conditions.

TOURIST INFO: Cnr Pacific Hwy and Riverside Dr, Nambucca Heads, Ph: (02) 6568 6954

Maclean   POP 3300

Map 115, H3

A fishing centre on the **Clarence River**, Maclean is also the southern gateway to Australia's sugarcane region, stretching north to Mossman.

Viaduct on the Zig Zag Railway, near Lithgow

Known as the **'Scottish Town in Australia'**, this little town celebrates the birthplace of many of its settlers with an annual **Highland Gathering** during Easter.

MAIN ATTRACTIONS: The **Bicentennial Museum**, in Wharf St, is open on Wednesday and Saturday, 1pm–4pm, and Friday, 10am–4pm. One building has displays reflecting the history and development of the district. The other, a stone cottage built in 1886, is furnished to reflect life at that time. Panoramic views of the town, coast, bushland and canefields can be seen from **Maclean Lookout**, 2km east at the top of Wharf St. Festivals include the **Aquatic Regatta**, held in August, and the **International Tartan Celebration**, held in July. The Lower Clarence Visitors Centre also incorporates a restaurant, and art and craft gallery.

NEARBY ATTRACTIONS: **Brooms Head**, edged by **Yuraygir NP**, is a small coastal village south-east of Maclean. The sandy beach with its grassy verges and shady pines is delightful. Much activity centres on the Clarence River with fishing, sailing and waterskiing being popular.

TOURIST INFO: Ferry Park, Pacific Hwy South, Ph: (02) 6645 4121

Walka Water Works, Maitland

■ Maitland   POP 49 941
Map 119, H4

Located on the **Hunter River**, 35km upstream from the port of Newcastle is the city of Maitland. Today, Maitland is the third largest provincial centre in New South Wales. This city began as 2 towns: **West Maitland** and **East Maitland**, and was not combined until 1944. East Maitland holds the most historic interest as it was a planned town, built above flood level, with spacious streets and fine public buildings. The area today still reflects the prosperity of the era in the mid-1800s when it served as the regional centre of the **Hunter Valley**.
MAIN ATTRACTIONS: Many of East Maitland's buildings were erected at a time when it was felt the new town could rival Sydney in size and power. Self-guided walks enable visitors to appreciate Maitland's architectural heritage. **Maitland Gaol** was built in 1844 and was modelled on London's Pentonville prison. Located in John St, East Maitland, it has a number of unique features including an elaborate stairway system. Antiques are popular in Maitland and there are many shops in Melbourne and High sts. Maitland has some of the best sport and recreation facilities in the region. Licensed clubs include Maitland Ex-Serviceman's, Citizens, Bowling and Sporting Club in Hunter St; East Maitland Bowling Club in Bank St; and Maitland Leagues Club in Bulwer St.
NEARBY ATTRACTIONS: The historic river port of **Morpeth**, 5km NE, has been classified by the National Trust. The village retains its 19th-century atmosphere, and is definitely worth visiting. **Walka Water Works Reserve**, located 1.5km north of Maitland, is the most intact waterworks complex remaining in New South Wales. BBQs, a children's playground and a walking trail make it a worthwhile recreational area for the entire family.
TOURIST INFO: Cnr High St and New England Hwy, Ph: (02) 4933 2611

■ Manilla   POP 2097
Map 114, D5

This small town is on the north-west slopes of the **Great Dividing Range**. A commercial centre, Manilla services the surrounding district of mixed farming, wheat, wool and cattle. The town is enhanced by a number of parks and is almost encircled by the **Namoi River**. The huge cartoon of a Murray cod outside the information centre announces Manilla is also a fishing destination.
MAIN ATTRACTIONS: Manilla is well-known among gliding, paragliding and hang-gliding enthusiasts. **Mount Baldwin** and **Red Jack Mountain** are the local take-off spots for hang-gliders. **Memorial Park** in the town centre is a pleasant place to wander and watch the birds in the aviary. **Royce Cottage** is a National Trust-classified building housing a local history museum. Located in Manilla St, the museum is open Monday, Wednesday and Friday afternoons, or by appointment.
NEARBY ATTRACTIONS: **Warrabah NP** is located north-east of the town. It is a small but attractive park on the Namoi River. Huge granite boulders, gorges and pools are the main features of this park. The park is popular for swimming, fishing, canoeing and bushwalking.
TOURIST INFO: 79 Arthur St, Ph: (02) 6785 1113

■ Merimbula   POP 4460
Map 122, D5

At the northern entrance of **Merimbula Lake**, 25km north of Eden, lies the fishing and tourist town of Merimbula. Popular for fishing, prawning and surfing, the town attracts many visitors. There are 3 surf beaches and sheltered lake beaches. Boats can be hired and reef- and game-fishing trips leave from Merimbula Lake. From late October to mid-December, there are whale-watching excursions.
MAIN ATTRACTIONS: An **aquarium** is housed in an historic wharf building on Lake St and is open daily from 10am–5pm. Arts and crafts are popular in the region and a number of outlets sell local works.
NEARBY ATTRACTIONS: **Magic Mountain Family Recreation Park** is located 5km north on **Sapphire Coast Drive** and is open daily 10am–4pm in summer and holidays. It features heated waterslides, mini golf, a toboggan run and a mini-grand prix. There are 2 national parks in the district—**Bournda** and **Ben Boyd**. Both are coastal parks and offer many walking tracks, swimming and fishing spots. At **Pambula Beach**, 10km south, there is a walking track, lookout and beach horseriding. Early morning and late afternoon if you are quiet and still, you may see kangaroos and wallabies on the foreshore.
TOURIST INFO: Beach St, Ph: (02) 6495 1129

New South Wales

SOUTHERN HIGHLANDS

Although the Illawarra and Southern Highlands are located on Sydney's south-west fringes and border each other (*see* pp.106–107), the Southern Highlands have their own distinct character. The cooler climate and picturesque villages lead to comparisons with rural England. In summer it is possible to experience the 4 seasons in a single daytrip by touring the many attractions in this diverse region. The towns and villages offer antique stores, arts and crafts, rustic cafes, B&Bs and museums. **Berrima**, founded in 1831, has several buildings listed on the National Estate. Other historic towns worthwhile visiting include **Bowral**, **Mittagong** and **Moss Vale**. There are also local national parks, caves at **Wombeyan** and the natural beauty of the **Kangaroo Valley**. The region's best known festival is **Bowral Tulip Time**, an annual

Tulips at Milton Park, Bowral Tulip Time

spring celebration with many thousands of tulips and other flowers in bloom. It is held late September until the October long weekend. There are mass plantings in **Corbett Gardens** and a number of private gardens are open to the public.

 Tourist information

**Southern Highlands Visitor
Information Centre**
62-70 Main St, Mittagong, NSW 2575
Ph: (02) 4871 2888
Freecall: 1300 657 559

■ Mittagong   POP 6000

Map 107, B2

Nestled in the valley of the **Nattai River**, Mittagong is the northern gateway to the **Southern Highlands**. It is an attractive town as many of the houses and public buildings have been built from the beautiful local sandstone.

MAIN ATTRACTIONS: Mittagong is well-known for its art and craft shops. Embroiderers will want to visit historic **Victoria House**, which has the largest display of embroidery and needlework kits in Australia. Located on the Hume Hwy, it is open daily, 9am–5pm. The **Sturt Craft Centre** in Range Rd holds workshops for pottery, weaving, glass, textiles, wood and jewellery. Its gallery displays quality local

crafts and is open daily, 10am–5pm. Mittagong is also a good base for walks in the Southern Highlands. One of the best walks in New South Wales begins here—the 7-day walk on the **Barallier Track** to **Katoomba**.

NEARBY ATTRACTIONS: **Wombeyan Caves** is located 65km SW of Mittagong. Renowned for their beauty and spectacular limestone formations, 5 caves are open to the public. Guided tours are run through 4 caves and **Figtree Cave** is open between 8.30am and 5pm daily for self-guided tours. Accommodation at the caves includes cottages, a caravan park, cabins and campsites.

TOURIST INFO: **62-70 Main St,** (Old Hume Hwy), Ph: (02) 4871 2888

■ Moree   POP 15 517

Map 114, C3

This wheat and wool town in the north-west of New South Wales has a landscape dominated by huge wheat silos. Sunflowers, pecan nuts and cotton are also grown in the area. Moree is a renowned spa area, with many visitors coming to ease aches their and pains in the famous artesian baths.

MAIN ATTRACTIONS: In 1895, the **Moree Spa Pool** was completed at **East Moree** and the town became a famous health resort. It was originally thought that the bore water tapped at Moree would be used for irrigation, but the heavy mineral content meant it was unsuitable. The spa complex offers 2 hot pools with temperatures of

Dolphin Beach at Moruya Heads

41°C, an Olympic-size pool, toddlers' pool and junior pool. Rheumatism and arthritis sufferers claim the water provides pain relief. The town has the largest Aboriginal population outside the major cities of New South Wales. The **Moree Plains Regional Gallery** houses a large number of artefacts and contemporary works with exhibitions changing every 6 weeks. **Moree Regional Library** has the largest collection of Aboriginal reference books and information within New South Wales. The library staff continually update and record Aboriginal family history and genealogy.

TOURIST INFO: Cnr Newell and Gwydir hwys, Ph: (02) 6757 3350

Moruya   POP 3000

Map 122, D4

On the Princes Hwy, 307km south of Sydney, this quiet, rural centre services the surrounding timber and cattle country and is the base for exploring many beautiful beaches and national parks.

MAIN ATTRACTIONS: There are many beautiful old buildings of much historical interest. **Moruya Museum** preserves regional history, including that of the gold period at **Mogo**. Located in Campbell St, the museum is open weekends and holidays, 10am–4.30pm. **Australia's Bush Orchestra** is a natural bush theme park located 2km west of the town. It emphasises the spiritual side of life and features the **Ironbark Walk**, colourful birdlife and native animals.

NEARBY ATTRACTIONS: **Deua NP**, inland from Moruya, is a rugged and interesting area. A belt of limestone running through the park has resulted in many caves. One of the park's major attractions is the **Big Hole**, a 96m chasm, which probably resulted from the collapse of a limestone cavern. Also interesting is the **granite quarry**, off North Head Dr on the north side of the river. Stone for the pillars and façade of the **Sydney GPO** building was taken from here in 1872 and the quarry was reopened in 1924 to supply the granite for the **Sydney Harbour Bridge** pylons and the **Cenotaph** in Martin Place, Sydney. When the Depression hit in the 1930s, the quarry was again closed.

TOURIST INFO: Rob Evans Real Estate, 73 Vulcan St, Ph: (02) 4474 4665

Moss Vale   POP 6000

Map 107, A2

A **Southern Highlands** market and tourist town, Moss Vale has become a popular retreat for retirees and home of the **Southern Highlands Country Fair**. The area is very scenic with sheep, cattle, horses, alpacas and goats feeding on the surrounding lush pastures.

MAIN ATTRACTIONS: **Throsby Park Homestead** was built by convicts in 1834, for the nephew of the explorer Charles Throsby. The fine Georgian sandstone and cedar home, now administered by the National Trust, is open for inspection by appointment. **Leighton Park**, in the centre of Moss Vale, is a perfect spot for a leisurely stroll. The landscaped gardens are lovely in autumn when the deciduous trees display their glorious colours.

NEARBY ATTRACTIONS: **Cecil Hoskins Nature Reserve** is located 3km NE of Moss Vale and here visitors will see a variety of birdlife.

TOURIST INFO: 62-70 Main St (Old Hume Hwy), Mittagong, Ph: (02) 4871 2888

Mudgee   POP 8413

Map 118, E3

Located 264km NW of Sydney, on the **Cudgegong River**, is the picturesque country town of Mudgee. The scenic landscape has attracted many artists to the region.

MAIN ATTRACTIONS: Mudgee is at the centre of one of the premium wine-growing areas of Australia. The wine industry dates back to the 1850s. The region is credited with introducing the chardonnay grape to Australia. Many of the surrounding wineries, including **Poets Corner** and **Huntington Estate**, are open

New South Wales

to the public offering tastings and cellar door sales. Other local produce includes fine wool, honey, livestock and gourmet foods. The profusion of flora in the region attracts bees and several honey-processing companies have taken advantage of this, with different kinds of honey produced at various times of the year by skilled beekeepers. **Mudgee Honey Haven**, cnr Gulgong and Hargraves rds; and **Mudgee Honey Company**, 28 Robertson St, both offer tastings and sales. There are many National Trust buildings in the town and all can be seen on a self-guided **historical town walk**. A brochure is available from the tourist office.

NEARBY ATTRACTIONS: **Gulgong**, the town on the old $10 note is only 28km north of Mudgee. Around 130 buildings in this town are classified by the National Trust. The streets are narrow and there are many reminders of its goldrush glory days. The **Pioneers Museum** is in the heart of town and includes a re-created bedroom, blacksmith shop, kitchen and bakehouse. The museum at 73 Herbert Rd is open 9am–5pm, 7 days a week. The **Henry Lawson Centre** is located at

147 Mayne St, Gulgong and is a memorial to Henry Lawson's life. **Windamere Dam**, 24km SE is a popular fishing and watersports venue with camping facilities.
TOURIST INFO: 84 Market St, Ph: (02) 6372 1020 or 1800 816 304

▦ Mullumbimby   POP 3200

Map 84, C1

The **North Coast** town of Mullumbimby is surrounded by sub-tropical countryside which supports dairying and cattle properties and produces a wide range of tropical fruits. The town has a well-deserved reputation as a centre for creativity and alternative lifestyles.

MAIN ATTRACTIONS: Mullumbimby's major annual event is the **Chincogan Fiesta**, held in September. The town's streets are closed for stalls and entertainment and the highlight is the **Chincogan Charge**, a foot race from the Post Office to the top of **Mount Chincogan** and back. **Brunswick Valley Historical Museum** preserves local history and memorabilia. Housed in the old timber Post Office (1907) in Stuart St, the museum is open weekdays, 11am–3pm.

NEARBY ATTRACTIONS: Only 8km east of Mullumbimby is **Brunswick Heads**, renowned for good surfing and excellent fishing. Further south, 15km away, is **Byron Bay** with its many attractions. The **Crystal Castle** is a popular attraction selling crystals from around the world, offering massage and meditation and also including a showroom, gallery and cafe. Housed in a 1920s-style homestead situated on the side of a hill at **Montecollum**, it is open daily 10am–4.30pm.
TOURIST INFO: Lyrebird Motel, Dalley St, Ph: (02) 6684 1725

▦ Murwillumbah   POP 8200

Map 115, J1

A picturesque town, Murwillumbah spreads across the western bank of the **Tweed River** and up into the hills of the **McPherson Ranges**. Formerly a red-cedar timber town, it is now a service town for the sugarcane and banana-growing district of the **Tweed Valley**.

MAIN ATTRACTIONS: The **Tweed River Regional Art Gallery** is home to the Doug Moran National Portraiture Competition, the richest portrait prize in the world. Past finalist and winning portraits are displayed. The gallery presents frequent exhibitions; open Wed–Sun, 10am–5pm.

NEARBY ATTRACTIONS: **Tropical Fruit World**, a plantation with a family entertainment and fauna park, is located about 15km north of Murwillumbah. The park is open daily from 10am to 5pm. **Pioneer Plantation**, at **Mooball**, is a working banana plantation with an animal nursery, native gardens and tearoom. During the harvest season from July to November the **Condong Sugar Mill** opens for the public to see sugarcane being processed. The mill opens between 9am and 3pm but closes in wet weather. Murwillumbah is the gateway to 5 World Heritage-listed national parks: **Mount Warning**, **Nightcap**, **Border Ranges**,

Fishing on the Tweed River, Murwillumbah, with Mount Warning in the distance

Wineries are a well-known feature of the Upper Hunter. Vines were originally planted in the area in the 1860's, but winemaking went into a long decline and farming took over the fertile valleys. Although dairy farming is still very important, the wine industry has made a come-back. Wineries such as **Rosemount** and **Arrowfield** offer wine tastings and cellar door sales.

The upper reach of the Hunter Valley, surrounding the pretty town of **Scone**, is widely regarded as Australia's premier thoroughbred and horse-breeding district. There are more than 30 stud farms in this part of the Hunter, some offering personalised tours. In May each year, Scone hosts **Scone Horse Week**, complete with rodeos— a must for equestrian types. Coal mining, vineyards and horse studs

have brought prosperity to the Upper Hunter—the site of some of Australia's oldest towns.

attractions

- Barrington Tops NP
- Denman
- Lake Glenbawn
- Muswellbrook
- Scone
- Wineries

Tourist information

Muswellbrook Visitors Centre
87 Hill St,
Muswellbrook, NSW 2333
Ph: (02) 6541 4050
www.muswellbrook.org.au

Bushwalker, Barrington Tops NP

Lamington and **Springbrook**. Information is available from the **NPWS World Heritage Rainforest Centre** incorporated with the visitors information centre. In Mount

Warning NP, a 4.4km walking track leads from **Breakfast Creek** to the summit for good all-round views.
TOURIST INFO: Cnr Pacific Hwy and Alma St, Ph: (02) 6672 1340

Muswellbrook   POP 15 562
Map 91, E1
Known primarily for its premium white wines, Muswellbrook is also a pastoral district with fodder crops, stud cattle, horses, sheep and dairy products. Open-cut coal mining is a major industry of this area.
MAIN ATTRACTIONS: **Muswellbrook Town Walk** includes significant historical buildings and other highlights. Brochures are available from the information centre. The **Regional Art Gallery** displays an extensive collection of contemporary art. The gallery is housed on the

first floor of the old Town Hall in Bridge St. Also in Bridge St and worth a visit is the **Upper Hunter Wine Centre** in the visitor centre.
NEARBY ATTRACTIONS: Major wineries, including **Rosemount Estate**, **Arrowfield Wines**, **Cruickshank Callatoota**, **Horseshoe Vineyard** and **London Lodge**, welcome visitors for tastings and sales. Many wineries in the area provide picnic and BBQ facilities and some have restaurants attached. The historic town of **Denman**, 36km SW of Muswellbrook, has changed little since the 1930s and a heritage order preserves the character of the main street. **Wollemi NP** is 30km SW and is the second largest national park and the biggest wilderness area in New South Wales. **Lake Liddell** lies 14km

Denman Hotel

New South Wales

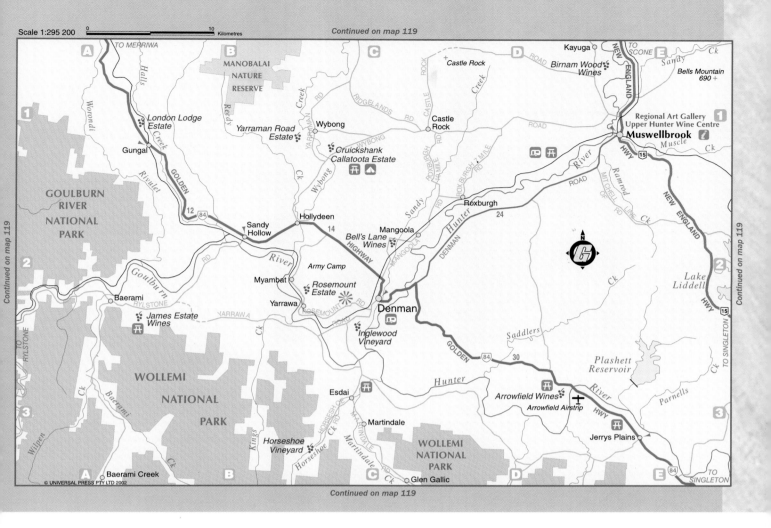

Continued on map 119

Scale 1:295 200

A

B

C

D

E

Continued on map 119

Continued on map 119

© UNIVERSAL PRESS PTY LTD 2002

south of the town and is a water storage and watersports area with facilities for boating, waterskiing, camping and picnics.
TOURIST INFO: 87 Hill St,
Ph: (02) 6541 4050

■ Nambucca Heads POP 6000
Map 62, C5
A holiday resort, fishing and oyster-farming town, Nambucca Heads lies at the mouth of the **Nambucca River**. One of the prettiest town-ships on the **North Coast**, Nambucca Heads offers a relaxed lifestyle, a subtropical climate and safe, clean beaches. Fishing, boating and swimming are popular pastimes.
MAIN ATTRACTIONS: Stunning views of the surf, river, hills and long stretches of bush and sand dunes

can be seen from 4 lookouts—**Rotary, Shelly, Pilot** and **Lions. Stuart Island Golf Course** is in the middle of the river and is the only island used exclusively as a golf course in Australia. A self-guided **historical walk** through the town is worthwhile exploring, including the river-foreshore walk past the sites of **Copenhagen Mill, Pioneer Well** and 19th-century shipyards. The **V Wall** is an outdoor gallery located in Wellington Dr. Here visitors are encouraged to paint a 'Postcard on Rock'. A 60m-long mosaic mural sculpture, depicting the journey of the Nambucca River, wraps around Nambucca Heads Police Station embankment in the centre of town.
NEARBY ATTRACTIONS: About 10km north of town is **Valla Beach**. Here

Nambucca River estuary, Nambucca Heads

the **Valla Smokehouse** makes delicious gourmet smoked products.
TOURIST INFO: Cnr Pacific Hwy and Riverside Dr, Ph: (02) 6568 6954

Sawn Rocks, Mount Kaputar NP, east of Narrabri

■ Narooma POP 3500
Map 122, D4

A small town overlooking **Wagonga Inlet**, Narooma is 70km south of Batemans Bay. Timber, fishing and tourism are the main industries in Narooma. The surfing, family beaches, waterways and surrounding state forests make the town an appealing holiday destination.

MAIN ATTRACTIONS: Of the 4 main surfing beaches, Narooma's **Main Beach** and **Dalmeny Beach** are patrolled in season. The **Glasshouse Rocks** can be seen south of Main Beach. Below **Bar Rock Lookout** is **Australia Rock**, so-called because a hole in the shape of Australia has been weathered into it.

NEARBY ATTRACTIONS: The historic gold-mining town of **Central Tilba** is 17km south of Narooma. Founded in 1894, the little mountain village has been classified by the National Trust. Late 19th-century buildings now house craft workshops and the **Old Cheese Factory** gives tastings of the famous Tilba Club cheese. **Montague Island**, 8km out to sea from Narooma, is popular for anglers in search of marlin. A flora and fauna reserve, the island is home to Australian fur seals and a variety of sea birds, including little penguins. Tours are run on the island by the National Parks and Wildlife Service and can be booked at the information centre. Diving schools also take people out to scuba dive with the seals off the island.

TOURIST INFO: Princes Hwy,
Ph: (02) 4476 2881

■ Narrabri POP 7900
Map 114, C4

This town lies in the fertile **Namoi River Valley**, at the junction of the **Narrabri Creek** and the Namoi River. Cotton is the major industry of Narrabri, although the rich, black soil of the valley supports a diversity of agricultural products. Cotton, sunflower and a variety of other crops are processed at the **Narrabri Oilseed Crushing Mill**, one of the largest of its type in the country.

MAIN ATTRACTIONS: During the cotton-picking season (April–July) tour guides explain the industry. Contact Narrabri Information Centre for details. The majority of the town's historic buildings are found in **Maitland St**, the main street, and **Dewhurst** and **Bowen sts**. The **Old**

Gaol is now the local history museum and is open Saturday 9am–4pm. **Town Walk** and **Town Drive** leaflets are available from the information centre.

NEARBY ATTRACTIONS: The **CSIRO Australia Telescope National Facility** at Culgoora, is located 23km west of Narrabri. The visitors centre is open daily 8am–4pm and has displays and offers hands-on experiences. **Mount Kaputar NP** is located 56km east of Narrabri. Ancient rock formations including **Sawn Rocks** and **Yullundunida Crater** are highlights. There are also scenic drives, bushwalks, campsites and cabins available.

TOURIST INFO: Tibbereena St (Newell Hwy), Ph: (02) 6799 6760

■ Narrandera POP 4785
Map 121, J2

Lying on the north bank of the **Murrumbidgee River**, Narrandera is surrounded by a district devoted to cereal crops, wool, fruit, lambs and cattle. It is the gateway to the **Murrumbidgee Irrigation Area** and is located 570km SW of Sydney.

MAIN ATTRACTIONS: **The Royal Doulton ceramic fountain**, located in Victoria Square, is a memorial for those people who served in WWI. **Narrandera Park** has picnic areas and features include aviaries, a miniature zoo and a fully restored DH82 Tiger Moth. The **Bundidgerry Walking Track**, which goes through the **Nature Reserve**, is the place to see koalas in the wild.

NEARBY ATTRACTIONS: **The John Lake Centre** at the **Inland Fisheries Research Station** is open to the public weekdays, 9am–4.30pm. Tours of the centre feature live exhibits, displays and audio-visual presentations. The centre is located 5km south of Narrandera. **Craigtop Deer Farm** is 8km NW and is open daily 9am–5pm. Tours are available and visitors can also hand-feed the pet deer.

Lake Talbot is a popular attraction for skiing, boating and fishing.
TOURIST INFO: Narrandera Park, Newell Hwy, Ph: (02) 6959 1766 or 1800 672 392

■ Narromine   POP 3520
Map 118, C3

A compact rural town on the southern bank of the **Macquarie River**, Narromine is located 40km west of Dubbo. The pastoral and wheat-growing country of the **Macquarie Valley** also produces cotton, citrus fruit, sorghum and vegetables (tomatoes and corn) as the area is so well irrigated.

MAIN ATTRACTIONS: The information centre has many details on tours, including visits to **Narromine Citrus-Packing Shed, Trangie Cotton Gin, Yates plant-breeding station**, historic **Narromine**

Boats on the Hunter River, Newcastle

Aerodrome, and **Auscott Cotton Gin and Cotton Fields**. There is a self-guided tour following the **Cobb & Co** route. The centre also sells a range of clothing made from locally grown cotton.

NEARBY ATTRACTIONS: Garden lovers will want to visit **Swane's Rose Nursery**, only 5km west of town. There are old-fashioned and heritage roses as well as modern and miniature forms. The nursery has also produced a special rose for Narromine called 'Heart of Gold'. Also worthwhile visiting is the **Narromine Iris Farm**, which displays over 700 varieties of the plant. There is a BBQ area and free coffee and tea. **Gin Gin Weir** is an attractive beach and picnic area on the banks of the Macquarie River, 30km NW of Narromine. Free bush-camping spots with toilets are available for public use.
TOURIST INFO: 37 Burraway St (Mitchell Hwy), Ph: (02) 6889 4596

■ Nelson Bay   POP 7000
Map 95, B3

Located on **Port Stephens**, 60km north of Newcastle on the **Mid-North Coast**, the resort town of Nelson Bay is the main centre on the **Tomaree Peninsula**. The region's commercial centre, Nelson Bay is a pretty town of gardens and galleries and home to the Port Stephens fishing fleet.

MAIN ATTRACTIONS: Nelson Bay has dolphin- and whale-watching cruises and fishing charters. Cruises also visit **Broughton Island, Myall River** and **Lakes**. Game fishing is especially good in the area and there are several major competitions held throughout the year. The Heritage Trust-listed **Inner Lighthouse** at **Little Beach** has heritage displays and a maritime museum. It also has alfresco dining with great views. **Toboggan Hill Park** on Salamander Way has a 700m slope and also offers mini-golf, Krazy cars, canoe rides and indoor rockclimbing.

NEARBY ATTRACTIONS: The nearby townships of **Shoal Bay, Fingal Bay, Anna Bay, Salamander Bay** and **Soldiers Point** provide a wide range of accommodation and activities year round. While most of the action is centred on Port Stephens, there are many other activities available, including 4WD tours, golf courses, beach and bush horseriding, camel riding, cycleways and tennis courts. The **Tomaree NP** is a good place to explore. The area is also noted for its colonies of koalas. The **Native Flora Grand Walk** at **Fly Point** has 15 vantage points to enjoy the wildflowers and views.
TOURIST INFO: Victoria Pde, Ph: 1800 808 900

■ Newcastle   POP 272 500
Map 119, H4

The second largest metropolitan area in New South Wales, Newcastle is an administrative, commercial, cultural and industrial centre for the **Hunter Region**. Located at the mouth of the **Hunter River**, Newcastle is one of the largest and busiest ports in the country, it is also a cosmopolitan tourist destination with a wide variety of restaurants, galleries, museums, beaches and parklands.

MAIN ATTRACTIONS: **The Town Walk**— brochure available from the information centre—features sites of heritage value to the city. This includes **Rose Cottage**, Newcastle's oldest building (1828); the **Convict Lumberyard** which is the site of the old convict barracks; and **Fort Scratchley**, which houses the **Newcastle Maritime Museum**. The **Newcastle Regional Museum**, housed in the former Castlemaine Brewery in Hunter St, includes permanent 'hands-on' science exhibits for children, **Supernova and Mininova**, as well as historical displays. **Shortland Wetland Centre** is well worth a visit. Newcastle has many excellent beaches that are great for surfing and family outings.

Described as **'Blue Water Paradise'**, Port Stephens is an expansive waterway two-and-a-half times the size of Sydney Harbour. It extends 24km inland from the sea and its sandy beaches, bays and sand dunes have proved a magnet to generations of holidaymakers. Capt James Cook, in May 1770, named the harbour in honour of Sir Phillip Stephens, Secretary of the Admiralty.

Pods of wild bottlenose dolphins are one of the region's most noted attractions. **Dolphin-spotting** and **whale-watching cruises** are popular. A number of lookouts on **Tomaree Headland** offer excellent vantage points for sighting the migrating whales during winter and spring. Fishing is popular within the waterway and offshore for a wide variety of species. Port Stephens hosts the world's largest game-fishing competition each year and several other fishing competitions. Not surprisingly, it is renowned for the quality of its fresh seafood. Port Stephens is one of the biggest oyster-growing areas in Australia.

main attractions

- Dolphin- and whale-watching cruises
- Inner Lighthouse, Tearooms and Museum
- Stockton sand dunes
- Toboggan Hill Park
- Tomaree National Park

i Tourist information

Port Stephens Visitors Information Centre
Victoria Pde,
Nelson Bay, NSW 2315
Ph: 1800 808 900
www.portstephens.org.au

Dolphin-spotting cruise, Port Stephens

NEARBY ATTRACTIONS: The wineries of the **Hunter Valley** are not far away. **Nelson Bay** is also nearby and visitors can come here to join daily dolphin-watching cruises and whale-watching cruises in season. On the drive to Nelson Bay visitors will pass the **RAAF's Williamtown base**. **Fighter World**, a display centre for military fighter aircraft is located here and is open daily, 10am–4pm. **Stockton Beach**, in the same area, has the largest sand dune system in the Southern Hemisphere.
TOURIST INFO: 363 Hunter St (Wheeler Place), Ph: (02) 4974 2999

▪ Nowra   POP 22 000
Map 97, B2
The commercial and tourist centre for the **Shoalhaven Region**, Nowra is located about 80km south of Wollongong on the southern bank of the **Shoalhaven River**. An 8-span steel bridge links the city with **Bomaderry** on the other side of the river. Bomaderry is the terminus of the rail link to Sydney. Nowra's main industries are milk processing, pulp and paper milling, fishing and flour milling.
MAIN ATTRACTIONS: **Nowra Animal Park**, located on the western bank of the Shoalhaven River, has birds, and native and farm animals—some of which can be patted and hand-fed. Camping and BBQ facilities are available and visitors can enjoy light lunches or Devonshire teas at the riverside coffee lounge. The park is open daily, 9am–5pm. Owned by the Historic Houses Trust, **Meroogal: Women's History Place**, built in 1885, contains the original contents collected by 4 generations of mostly women. It is open for guided tours. **Shoalhaven Historical Museum** is on the corner of Kinghorne and Plunkett sts.
NEARBY ATTRACTIONS: The **Australian Museum of Flight** at HMAS *Albatross* has an excellent collection of historic military aircraft, engines, uniforms and memorabilia. Located at the end of Albatross Rd, the museum is open daily, 10am–4pm.
TOURIST INFO: Cnr Princes Hwy and Pleasant Way,
Ph: (02) 4421 0778

▪ Nyngan   POP 2361
Map 118, B1
Nyngan is the regional centre for surrounding wheat farms, sheep and cattle studs. The town is close to the geographical centre of New

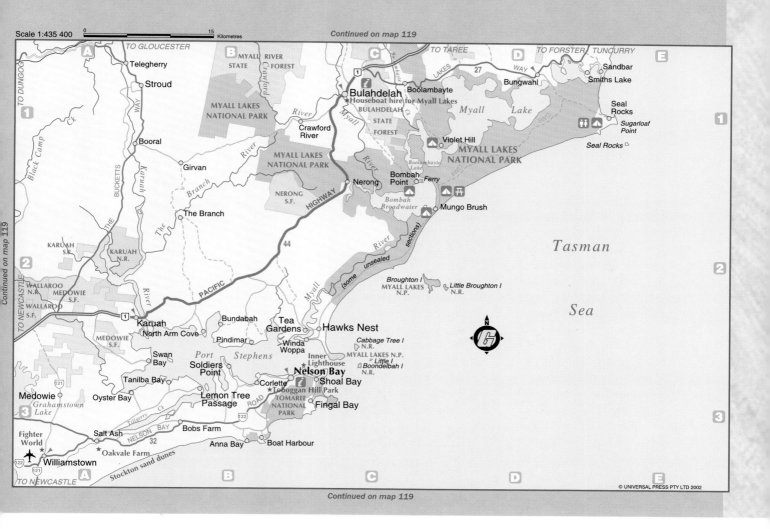

Continued on map 119

Scale 1:435 400

Continued on map 119

© UNIVERSAL PRESS PTY LTD 2002

South Wales, 603km NW of Sydney, beside the **Bogan River**.

MAIN ATTRACTIONS: Several public buildings, including the **Town Hall**, **Post Office** and **Court House** are testaments to the town's progressive phase in the 1880s and 1890s. They are all found on **Cobar St**, which runs parallel to the Mitchell Hwy. A tiled historic mural, located beside **Davidson Park**, records the history of the town and its pioneering families. Nyngan has an attractive 18-hole golf course and 2 licensed clubs: the RSL and Civic Club on Pangee St and the Bowling Club on Bogan and Terangion sts.

NEARBY ATTRACTIONS: Local landmarks include the grave of **Richard Cunningham**, a botanist with Sir Thomas Mitchell's exploration party. The grave is on a station near

Tottenham, 70km SE of Nyngan. The **Macquarie Marshes** is an extensive wetland area on the **Murray-Darling system**, 62km NE of Nyngan. A large part of this important bird and wildlife habitat is a wildlife sanctuary. Accommodation in the area includes a caravan park and campground, and bunk beds are available at **Willie's Retreat**.

TOURIST INFO: Nyngan Video Parlour, 105 Pangee St, Ph: (02) 6832 1155

■ Orange   POP 32 964

Map 118, D4

The sixth largest city in New South Wales, Orange is surrounded by fertile farming land that produces an abundance of fruit, wheat, wine grapes, sheep, cattle and pigs. Not known for its citrus, Orange does

produce well over half the State's apples. Cherry, pear and stone-fruit orchards also thrive in the red soil.

MAIN ATTRACTIONS: Wine tasting is a popular activity for those wanting to experience the cool-climate wines. A brochure on the wineries open to the public is available from the tourist office. The poet **Banjo Paterson** was born at Narrambla, near Orange in 1864. A memorial in **Banjo Paterson Park**, on the Ophir Rd, 5km east of Orange, marks his birthplace. Also worthwhile visiting are the **Orange Botanic Gardens**, located off Kearneys Dr, north of the city. They were first planted in 1981, and became established quickly. The **Regional Art Gallery**, in Byng St, houses a permanent art collection and also hosts touring exhibitions.

(CONTINUED P.98)

Located approximately 163km south of Sydney the Shoalhaven-Jervis Bay region offers the best of rural and coastal scenery. Dairying on the rich rolling hills, fishing and tourism are the main industries, creating a peaceful ambiance. The quaint rural villages, featuring teahouses, antique shops, galleries, cosy B&B cottages and old-fashioned pubs ooze with country charm.

From the massive coastal cliffs of the **Beecroft Peninsula** to around **Governor Head** in **Booderee NP**, the sheltered waters of Jervis Bay (10km wide and 15km long) provide a wonderful ocean 'playground'.

Hyams Beach is reputed to have the whitest sand in the world. Home to several pods of dolphins, the clear waters of Jervis Bay are also well-known for diving and watersports. Not surprisingly, fishing is one of the region's key industries and a pleasant pastime for amateur anglers. The headlands are renowned as being one of the few spots in the world where it is possible to catch game fish like marlin and sailfish from the shore. Dolphins, seals,

little penguins and seasonally migrating whales frequent the area, and there are many cruises on offer. **New South Wales Jervis Bay NP** and **Booderee NP** preserve the unique landforms, flora and fauna of this area as well as important Aboriginal sites.

A Safe Haven

Abraham's Bosom Beach, Jervis Bay, was the site where the shipwrecked passengers of the SS *Merimbula* found safety. It is named in the *Bible*, after the Bosom of Abraham described in the Old Testament, where children found shelter and safety.

 Tourist information

Shoalhaven Visitors Centre
Princes Hwy, Nowra, NSW 2541
Ph: (02) 4421 0778
www.shoalhaven@nsw.gov.au

Booderee NP Visitors Centre
Jervis Bay Rd, Jervis Bay, NSW 2540
Ph: (02) 4443 0977

Coolangatta Estate winery

main attractions

◈ **Berry**
This pretty hamlet boasts many charming buildings classified by the National Trust.

◈ **Bundanon**
Visit famous painter Arthur Boyd's scenic property, now a gallery; bookings required.

◈ **Coolangatta Historic Village**
This historic village was the first European South Coast settlement.

◈ **Jervis Bay**
This is a beautiful bay with a 50km shoreline of protected beaches.

◈ **Lady Denman Heritage Complex**
Once a ferry, *Lady Denman* is now housed within the maritime museum which is part of the complex.

◈ **Nowra Animal Park**
Native fauna is on show in a rainforest setting at Nowra Animal Park.

◈ **Nowra Historical Buildings**
St Andrews Church, the old Police Station and Meroogal House are all historical buildings in Nowra.

◈ **NSW Jervis Bay NP**
This national park boasts an array of pristine beaches.

◈ **Seven Mile Beach NP**
This national park has a long expanse of white, sandy beach flanked by sand dunes.

Slipway at Huskisson, Jervis Bay

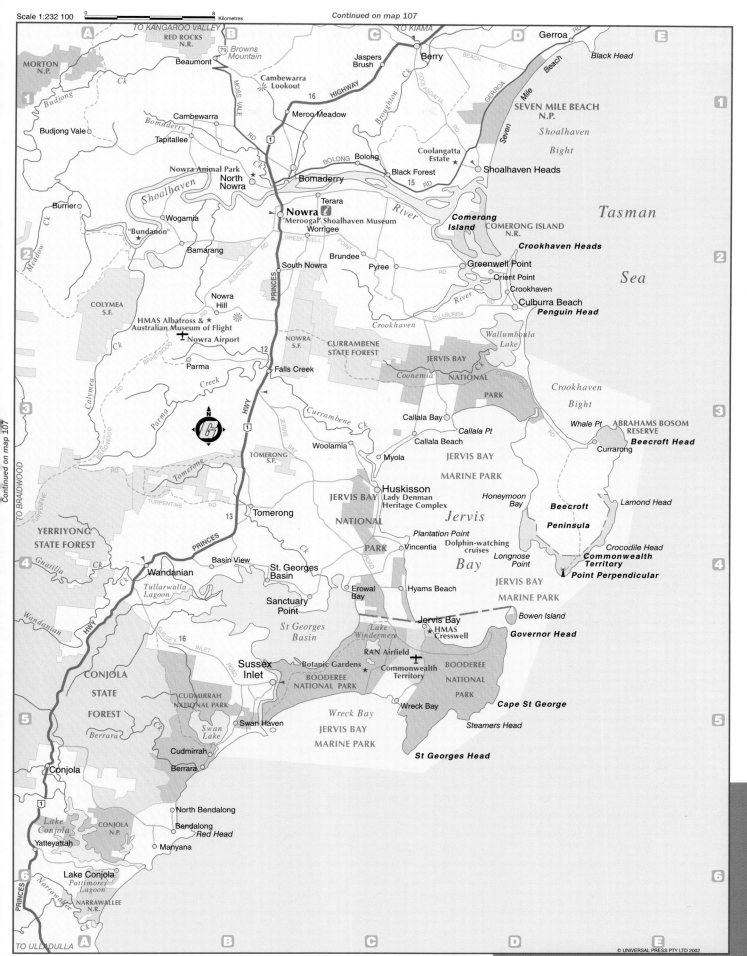

Scale 1:232 100

0   8

Kilometres

Continued on map 107

To Kangaroo Valley
TO KIAMA
TO BRAIDWOOD
TO ULLADULLA
Continued on map 107

MORTON N.P.
RED ROCKS N.R.
Budjong Vale
Burrier
"Bundanon"
COLYMEA S.F.
Beaumont
Browns Mountain
Cambewarra Lookout
Cambewarra
Tapitallee
Nowra Animal Park
North Nowra
Wogamia
Bamarang
Nowra Hill
HMAS Albatross & Australian Museum of Flight
Nowra Airport
Parma
Falls Creek
Meroo Meadow
Bolong
Bomaderry
Nowra
'Meroogal' Shoalhaven Museum
Worrigee
South Nowra
Brundee
Terara
Pyree
Jaspers Brush
Berry
Gerroa
Black Head
SEVEN MILE BEACH N.P.
Shoalhaven Bight
Coolangatta Estate
Black Forest
Shoalhaven Heads
Comerong Island
COMERONG ISLAND N.R.
Crookhaven Heads
Greenwell Point
Orient Point
Crookhaven
Culburra Beach
Penguin Head
Tasman Sea
Shoalhaven River
Crookhaven
CURRAMBENE STATE FOREST
NOWRA S.F.
JERVIS BAY NATIONAL PARK
Wallumboula Lake
Crookhaven Bight
Whale Pt
ABRAHAMS BOSOM RESERVE
Beecroft Head
Currarong
Lamond Head
Callala Bay
Callala Pt
Callala Beach
Woolamia
Myola
JERVIS BAY MARINE PARK
Huskisson
Lady Denman Heritage Complex
JERVIS BAY NATIONAL PARK
Beecroft Peninsula
Honeymoon Bay
Jervis Bay
Plantation Point
Dolphin-watching cruises
Vincentia
Longnose Point
Crocodile Head
Commonwealth Territory
Point Perpendicular
YERRIYONG STATE FOREST
Tomerong S.F.
Tomerong
Basin View
Wandanian
St. Georges Basin
Sanctuary Point
Erowal Bay
Hyams Beach
JERVIS BAY MARINE PARK
Jervis Bay
HMAS Cresswell
Bowen Island
Governor Head
CONJOLA STATE FOREST
Tullarwalla Lagoon
St Georges Basin
Lake Windermere
RAN Airfield
Botanic Gardens
Commonwealth Territory
BOODEREE NATIONAL PARK
Cape St George
Sussex Inlet
CUDMIRRAH NATIONAL PARK
Swan Haven
Swan Lake
Wreck Bay
JERVIS BAY MARINE PARK
Steamers Head
Cudmirrah
Berrara
St Georges Head
Conjola
North Bendalong
Bendalong
Red Head
Manyana
Yatteyattah
Lake Conjola
CONJOLA N.P.
Pattimores Lagoon
Lake Conjola
NARRAWALLEE N.R.
Narrawallee

© UNIVERSAL PRESS PTY LTD 2002

NEW SOUTH WALES   97

CSIRO Radio Telescope, north of Parkes

NEARBY ATTRACTIONS: **Borenore Caves Reserve** is located 17.5km west of Orange. A walking trail leads from **Arch Cave** and follows **Boree Creek** through to **Tunnel** and **Verandah Caves**. Take a good torch to explore the caves. The reserve also has picnic and BBQ facilities.
TOURIST INFO: Byng St, Ph: (02) 6361 5226

■ Parkes   POP 10 500
Map 118, C4
This **Central Western** town is surrounded by productive agricultural and grazing land. Parkes is an important bulkhead and wheat storage facility strategically placed on the state's north/south road and east/west rail links.
MAIN ATTRACTIONS: Parkes' major bicentennial project involved the restoration of the former Bushman's goldmine at **Bushman's Hill Reserve**, off the Newell Hwy. The main evidence of the mine's existence is an old chimney. Also

in the reserve is an Aboriginal walkway, and picnic and BBQ facilities. The **Henry Parkes Historical Museum** is open daily and features pioneering and gold-mining items. The most impressive exhibit is Sir Henry Parkes' library, which contains some 1000 books. Panoramic views of the town, **Goobang Valley** and the **Bumberry Mountains** can be seen from the **Shrine of Remembrance** on Memorial Hill.
NEARBY ATTRACTIONS: Popularised in the movie, *The Dish*, and located 20km north on the Newell Hwy is the **Parkes Radio Telescope**, one of the world's leading radio astronomy centres. The **Visitors Discovery Centre** has audio-visual and 3-dimensional displays, and BBQ facilities. The 64m-wide dish was built in 1961. **Bumberry Dam**, 24km east off the Orange Rd, is a popular boating and recreation area.
TOURIST INFO: Kelly Reserve, Newell Hwy, Ph: (02) 6862 4365

■ Port Macquarie   POP 32 760
Map 119, K1
Named after Governor Lachlan Macquarie, the town was established as a penal settlement in 1821. Present-day Port Macquarie is a fishing port and very popular tourist destination. Because of its pleasant year-round climate and lifestyle it is attracting increasing numbers of families and retirees to settle in the area.
MAIN ATTRACTIONS: Port Macquarie has an animal park, **Billabong Koala and Aussie Park**. Open daily 9am–5pm, the park is located off the Oxley Hwy. **Cassegrain Winery** is open daily for tastings and sales, and offers picnic, BBQ and children's play areas. Families will enjoy the **Fantasy Glades** theme park where children can see fairytale characters who live in places such as the Old Woman's Shoe and Snow White's Cottage. The park is open daily from

9am to 5pm. The award-winning **Hastings Historical Museum** on Clarence St, displays convict and pioneer relics in 15 different rooms. **St Thomas' Church** in Hay St was built by convicts in 1824 and is one of the oldest churches in Australia.
NEARBY ATTRACTIONS: South of Port Macquarie, beside the **Camden Haven River**, are the townships of **North Haven**, **Laurieton** and **Dunbogan**, together they make up the holiday area of **Camden Haven**. The clean waterways, lakes, forests, national parks and unspoilt coastline, make this a worthwhile place to stay.
TOURIST INFO: Cnr Clarence and Hay sts, Ph: (02) 6581 8000

■ Queanbeyan   POP 30 000
Map 135, D4
Situated at the junction of the **Molonglo** and **Queanbeyan rivers**, 12km SE of Canberra, Queanbeyan is the business centre of a wool-growing and mixed farming community.
MAIN ATTRACTIONS: The **Queanbeyan and District Historical Museum** and the **Queanbeyan Art Gallery** are interesting attractions. The sunken gardens of **Queanbeyan Park** and **Queen Elizabeth Park** beside the Queanbeyan River are ideal picnic spots. Good views can be had from the lookout in **Bicentennial Park**.
NEARBY ATTRACTIONS: Queanbeyan's location adjacent to the national capital, the snowfields, the scenic **South Coast** and historic towns make it an ideal base from which to explore. The major art and craft towns of **Bungendore** and **Braidwood**, both on Kings Hwy, have restored buildings, antique shops and lots of historic charm. **Bywong Town Gold Mining Village**, north of Queanbeyan, is a re-creation of the pioneering history of the 1850s. To the south-east at Captains Flat is **Captains Flat Museum**. For fishing, bushwalking, birdwatching

New South Wales

and picnicking visit **Googong Foreshores**, 10km south, and **Molonglo Gorge**, 1km north. (Canberra section pp.124–137)

Tourist Info: 1 Farrer Pl,
Ph: (02) 6298 0241 or 1800 026 192

■ Sawtell   POP 11 000
Map 62, D3

A resort town with surfing beaches, quiet swimming spots, excellent fishing, boating and camping sites, Sawtell is 537km north of Sydney. **Coffs Harbour** and all its attractions are only 8km further north.

Main Attractions: There are original buildings in Sawtell's main street reflecting the history of the area. The old **Sawtell Hotel** remains as does the picture theatre which shows both classic and modern movies. **Boambee Creek Reserve** has picnic and BBQ facilities. The reserve behind **Sawtell Beach** is also a popular picnic area.

Nearby Attractions: **Coffs Harbour Butterfly House and Maze** is home to hundreds of colourful Australian butterflies in a subtropical rainforest setting. There is also a maze, delightful gardens and a tearoom. Located on the Pacific Hwy at **Bonville**, the Butterfly House and Maze is open every day except Monday.

Tourist Info: Pacific Hwy, Coffs Harbour, Ph: (02) 6652 1522 and First Ave

■ Scone   POP 3500
Map 119, G2

This **Upper Hunter Valley** town is the commercial centre for an area of beautiful country famous for its prosperous horse stud farms. Kentucky in the USA is the only horse-breeding region in the world larger than Scone Shire. The importance of horses to Scone is represented by Gabriel Sterk's statue *Mare & Foal* that stands in **Elizabeth Park**, at the northern end of town. The surrounding area is also renowned for dairying and other primary products.

Main Attractions: For those visitors interested in working horses try the **Australian Stock Horse Museum** located in Guernsey St. The museum is also the national headquarters for the Australian Stock Horse Society. The **Historical Society Museum** is housed in the original town gaol; there are still 2 old cells at the back of the building. The museum documents the local history and opens by appointment.

Nearby Attractions: **Burning Mountain** is located on the New England Hwy, 20km north. Early settlers originally thought the mountain was a volcano after seeing smoke rising from it. The smoke is caused by a coal seam that has smouldered 30m underground for thousands of years.

Tourist Info: Cnr Kelly and Susan sts, Ph: (02) 6545 1526

■ Singleton   POP 12 500
Map 119, G3

This **Hunter River** town is 77km NW of Newcastle and historically has been the business centre for a rich dairying district. Beneath the farms are huge coal seams that have been mined since the beginning of the 19th century. More recently open-cut mining, supplying steaming and coking coals has transformed the region.

Main Attractions: **Rose Point Park**, beside the Hunter River, is the location of Singleton's **Bicentennial Sundial**. The sundial was a gift from a local mine and is reputed to be the largest of its kind in the world. There are many historical buildings in town. Some of the earliest are the **Post Office** and the **Court House** both built in 1841 and now occupied by the **Historical Museum**.

Nearby Attractions: The vineyards of the **Lower and Upper Hunter** are within easy reach of Singleton. (*see* pp. 58–59 and 90–91). Singleton is also ideally located as a stepping-off point for exploration of the largest wilderness area in New South Wales, **Wollemi NP**. The area also boasts some of the region's most beautiful scenery. **Lake St Clair** lies 26km NE of Singleton and is a wonderful recreation area, ideal for waterskiing, sailing and fishing. A picnic area, approximately 8km from the dam wall, has an electric BBQ, toilets and hot showers. Overnight camping is allowed.

Tourist Info: 57 George St, Ph: (02) 6571 5888 or 1800 449 888

Sawtell Beach

South West Rocks   POP 5000

Map 115, H5

The largest of **Macleay Valley's** seaside towns, South West Rocks lies on the shores of **Trial Bay**, near the mouth of the **Macleay River**. Stunning scenery and beaches combine to make this a most relaxing resort town.

MAIN ATTRACTIONS: **Everglades Aquarium** is a tropical fish centre and tourist attraction. It features fish feeding, display ponds and aquatic plants. The aquarium is located in Frank Cooper St, and is open daily, 9am–4.30pm. Fishing charter boats operate from **New Entrance**, and beach and estuary fishing are also popular. Scuba divers come to dive around **Fish Rock Cave**, some 2km SE of **Smoky Cape Lighthouse**. Apart from the beaches and watersports, the main attraction in town is the **Trial Bay Gaol**. The semi-ruined prison was built of local granite in 1886 by prisoners who had to build their own gaol while working on the breakwater. Abandoned in 1903, the gaol was used as an internment centre for 500 Germans during WWI. Surrounding the gaol is **Arakoon SRA**. Offering beaches, rainforest and coastal heathlands, there is much to explore, and advanced walkers can continue south along the coast as far as Smoky Cape Lighthouse in **Hat Head NP**.

TOURIST INFO: Historic Boatmans Cottage, Horseshoe Bay,
Ph: (02) 6566 7099

Sussex Inlet   POP 2700

Map 97, B5

A very popular holiday destination for families, Sussex Inlet is located on the channel that connects **St Georges Basin** with the Pacific Ocean. Sussex Inlet has not escaped the trend of residential canal development, which has almost made it an island but fortunately has not spoilt the charm of this peaceful town.

MAIN ATTRACTIONS: Sussex Inlet is famous among anglers for its very good fishing; a fishing carnival is held here annually during the July school holidays. South of the township, the beaches at **Berrara** and **Cudmirrah** provide some great surfing. The local golf course is a drawcard for visiting golfers who don't mind sharing the fairways with kangaroos and other wildlife.

NEARBY ATTRACTIONS: Before the turn-off to Sussex Inlet, the Princes Hwy passes through **Wandandian**, a village steeped in the history of the region's early timber industry. There are 2 craft shops and an art gallery located here, and the **Riverside Plant and Herb Nursery**.

TOURIST INFO: Cnr Princes Hwy and Pleasant Way, Nowra, Ph: (02) 4421 0778

Tamworth   POP 35 014

Map 114, E5

The commercial centre for the prosperous farming area of the **Peel Valley**, Tamworth is a progressive and growing city. There are fine restaurants, 4 licensed clubs, 2 major shopping centres and many specialty shops.

MAIN ATTRACTIONS: Renowned as the **'Country Music Capital of Australia'**, Tamworth has hosted the **Australasian Country Music Awards** for more than 20 years. Thousands of visitors arrive in Tamworth for the 10-day festival, which is held in January. There are more than 300 shows and much of the music is provided free-of-charge. **Bicentennial Park**, located alongside the **Peel River**, is a relaxing spot and a walk following the river's edge will reveal a war memorial, a distinctive fountain and busts of country music stars.

NEARBY ATTRACTIONS: **Nundle**, in the **Hills of Gold**, is an old gold-mining town with many original buildings to admire and craft shops to browse through. There is a re-created goldmine to inspect and many scenic outlooks in the district. **Lake Keepit** is located 57km west of Tamworth and is the place for powerboats, water-skiing and fishing. There are also children's facilities and a caravan park.

TOURIST INFO: Cnr Peel and Murray sts, Ph: (02) 6755 4300

Sailboats at Arakoon State Recreation Area, near South West Rocks

New South Wales

Diamond Head at Crowdy Bay NP, north of Taree

■ Taree   POP 17 250
Map 119, K2

This town is the commercial and administrative centre for the prosperous dairying, grazing, timber, fishing, oyster and tourist district of the **Manning Valley**. Located at the southern end of the **North Coast**, 326km north of Sydney, Taree is rewarding for both sightseers and shoppers and is just a short detour off the Pacific Hwy.

MAIN ATTRACTIONS: With 150km of navigable waterways, the **Manning River** is a popular venue for house-boating, cruising, rowing, sailing, waterskiing and fishing. In 1995, the river was the focus of worldwide media attention when a Brydes whale, 'Willy', stayed here for 100 days. **Queen Elizabeth Park**, edging the river, is an ideal spot for a picnic in the city centre. There is an interesting **art gallery** located on Macquarie St.

NEARBY ATTRACTIONS: Nearby beach resorts include **Old Bar Beach**, to the south, and **Crowdy Head** to the north. **Ellenborough Falls**, located 50km from Taree, is accessed on the Bulga Forest Dr. One of the highest-single drop waterfalls in the Southern Hemisphere, Ellenborough Falls plunges 200m into a rainforest gorge below. There are also walking trails with picnic areas clearly marked.

TOURIST INFO: Old Pacific Hwy, North Taree, Ph: (02) 6552 1900

■ Temora   POP 5 914
Map 121, K1

The rail centre for the rich wheat and sheep belt of the **Riverina**, Temora is located 460km SW of Sydney. The town is also recognised as a centre for harness racing and there are many trotting studs in the district. Races are held regularly.

MAIN ATTRACTIONS: Temora has a range of sporting clubs and venues. For the adventurous, a skydiving company operates from the airport. Visitors are welcome at the Temora Ex-Services Memorial Club, the Bowling Club and the Golf Club.

NEARBY ATTRACTIONS: **Lake Centenary**, 4km from Temora on the West Wyalong Rd, is a popular venue for picnics and watersports including boating, canoeing, sailing, swimming and fishing. **Ariah Park**, 34km west, is a village listed by the National Trust as a Conservation Area. Notable buildings include the **Lyons' Wool Store**, the **hotel**, and the **Westpac** and **National banks**. Therapeutic benefits are claimed for the **Mineral Pool** at nearby **Barmedman**.

TOURIST INFO: Shire Council, 105 Loftus St, Ph: (02) 6977 1099

■ Tenterfield   POP 3500
Map 115, G2

The northern gateway to the **New England** area, Tenterfield is the centre of a sheep- and cattle-grazing district. Autumn is a particularly beautiful time to visit as the banks of the **Tenterfield Creek** are covered with the gold and red leaves of the deciduous trees.

MAIN ATTRACTIONS: At weekends and holiday times, Tenterfield can be explored by **Cobb & Co coach**, which is drawn by 4 horses. Or the town can be investigated by taking the **Historic Walk**. The brochure for this tour is available at the information centre. Trains no longer run to Tenterfield Railway Station, and it is now the **Railway Museum**. Preserving railway memorabilia and history, the museum is open Thursday to Sunday and holidays, 10am–4pm. Handmade saddles are still made at the historic **Saddlers Shop** (1860s) in High St. The shop was made famous in Peter Allen's song, *Tenterfield Saddler*, commemorating his grandfather who was the saddler here for 50 years.

NEARBY ATTRACTIONS: **Thunderbolt's Hideout**, 13km east of town, is a small cave in high rocks where bushranger Captain Thunderbolt sheltered from the law.

TOURIST INFO: 157 Rouse St, Ph: (02) 6736 1082

Terrigal POP 10 760
Map 71, C4

Only a few kilometres from Gosford, Terrigal is an attractive **Central Coast** holiday resort.

MAIN ATTRACTIONS: The beach, with its esplanade, boutiques, cafes and international-standard resort, is the main attraction. **Terrigal Beach** and beaches both to the north and south attract surfers. Pedal boats, canoes and sailboards are available on the calm waters of **Terrigal Lagoon**. **The Skillion**, a headland, provides a good view over Terrigal. Deep-sea fishing, abseiling and rockclimbing are all available for those feeling adventurous. Contact **Central Coast Charters** for deep-sea fishing; and for canyoning, abseiling, bush-walking, orienteering and rock-climbing contact **Central Coast Bushworks**.

NEARBY ATTRACTIONS: The good surfing beaches around Terrigal include **Wamberal Beach**, 3km north; and **Avoca Beach**, 7.5km south. Half-way between Terrigal and Gosford is **Erina Fair**, the largest shopping centre on the Central Coast. Also at Erina is the **Fragrant Garden**, specialising in scented herbs and perfumed oils. **Matcham Valley** is a picturesque area just 8km from Terrigal Beach. Ken Duncan's **Australia Wide Gallery** is located here and well worth visiting. Ken Duncan is one of Australia's leading landscape photographers. The **Central Park Family Fun Centre** has a waterslide, fun cars and BBQ facilities. It is located 6km north at **Forresters Beach**.

TOURIST INFO: Rotary Park, Terrigal Dr, Ph: (02) 4385 4430

The Entrance POP 39 000
Map 71, C4

A commercial fishing centre and busy tourist resort, The Entrance is renowned for its fishing, surfing, swimming and picturesque scenery. Typical of many seaside resorts on the **Central Coast**, The Entrance is situated between the coast and the quiet waters of **Tuggerah Lake**.

MAIN ATTRACTIONS: Pelicans can be seen everywhere on Central Coast waterways and are now the tourist symbol of The Entrance. Hundreds of pelicans gather for the **Pelican Feeding** at 3.30pm daily, at **Memorial Park**, off Marine Pde. Another local attraction is the **Shell Museum** at **Dunleith Caravan Park**, where local memorabilia and old photographs complement the extensive shell collection. All forms of watersports are available at The Entrance. There are boat ramps on each side of **The Entrance Bridge** and picnic facilities can be found in the recreation areas facing the lake.

NEARBY ATTRACTIONS: **Wyrrabalong NP** covers much of the spit of land between The Entrance North and **Toukley**. The park is also known locally as **Red Gum Forest**.

TOURIST INFO: Marine Pde, Ph: (02) 4385 4430

Toukley POP 6800
Map 71, D3

With lakes to the west, the Tasman Sea to the east and national parks both north and south, this **Central Coast** town is an ideal location for boaties, fishermen and nature lovers. Toukley faces the narrow strip of land that separates **Tuggerah** and **Budgewoi lakes**. Both lakes offer excellent fishing, swimming, safe boating and wind-surfing. Foreshore prawning is a popular summer activity.

NEARBY ATTRACTIONS: **Munmorah SRA** is north of Toukley. The area edges **Lake Munmorah** and the Tasman Sea and encompasses many small beaches. It is worthwhile visiting in spring to see the wildflowers. There are 2 lookouts, both accessed by road. Close to town are many picnic areas: at **Canton Beach**, facing Tuggerah Lake; at **Osborne Park**, in Peel St; and in **Toukley Gardens**, facing Budgewoi Lake. **Edward Hargraves**, the first man to discover payable gold in Australia, built his all-cedar house in the 1860s. The house, in Elizabeth Dr, **Noraville**, still stands and can be seen from the road.

TOURIST INFO: Marine Pde, The Entrance, Ph: (02) 4385 4430

Pelican feeding at Memorial Park, The Entrance

New South Wales

Tumut POP 10 951

Map 122, A3

Located on the north-west slopes of the **Snowy Mountains**, Tumut is surrounded by forests and rich pastoral and agricultural land. The northern gateway to the Snowy Mountains, Tumut is the commercial centre for the district.

MAIN ATTRACTIONS: The town's history is reflected in its original buildings, including early homes; the Edmund Blacket-designed **All Saints Church** (1875); the stucco brick **Court House** (1878); and the historic **racecourse grandstand** framed by poplars and English oaks. Fishing is popular given the well-stocked rivers, dams and streams. Other activities available include white-water rafting, canoeing, horseriding, abseiling, hang-gliding and scenic flights. There are many walking trails, including the famous **Hume and Hovell Walking Track**, tempting walkers into **Kosciuszko NP**. Huge inland lakes created by the **Snowy Mountains Hydro-Electric Scheme** provide areas for watersports and many kinds of boating.

NEARBY ATTRACTIONS: Just over 20km west of Tumut is the historic gold town of **Adelong**. Here, the attractive **Adelong Falls** and old gold workings near the stream are to be found. Further afield is another historic gold-mining site at **Kiandra**, 95km south.

TOURIST INFO: Cnr Snowy Mountains Hwy and Gocup (Gundagai) Rd, Ph: (02) 6947 7025

Tweed Heads POP 39 630

Map 115, J1

Sitting on the New South Wales border next to **Coolangatta** in Queensland, Tweed Heads and Coolangatta have been labelled the **'Twin Towns'** and form a family holiday resort destination at the southern end of the **Gold Coast** tourist strip. Quieter than the Gold Coast, Tweed Heads is an ideal holiday base, with accommodation to suit all budgets and easy access to beaches and the towns and villages of the hinterland. For a change of pace, the Gold Coast with its nightlife and themed attractions is only a few kilometres north.

MAIN ATTRACTIONS: Morning and afternoon tea, and lunch cruises, flat-bottomed boat cruises and cruises with special activities are all available on the **Tweed River**. Deep-sea fishing charters are also offered.

NEARBY ATTRACTIONS: Not far to the north of town is the **Currumbin Sanctuary**, open daily, 8am–5pm. Here, at this famous wildlife park, visitors can hand-feed the native animals and brightly coloured lorikeets. Further south towards **Murwillumbah** there are major tourist attractions such as **Tropical Fruit World**, 15km south, off the Pacific Hwy. Open daily 10am–5pm, there is a huge plantation and visitors can see, touch, taste and smell a variety of fruits. **Crystal Creek Miniatures** is a miniature animal stud, located just outside Murwillumbah, toward Chillingham. Enjoy an informative and amusing tour of the stud and play with the miniature animals. The stud is open Wed–Mon. **Minjungbal Aboriginal Cultural Centre** is beside **Boyds Bay Bridge**. Inland there are many small mountain villages to explore and 3 World Heritage-listed national parks; **Mount Warning**, **Nightcap** and **Border Ranges**.

TOURIST INFO: 4 Wharf St, Ph: (02) 5536 4244

Ulladulla POP 7800

Map 107, B6

Known for its coastal waterways and excellent golf courses, Ulladulla and its twin town, **Mollymook**, form a pleasant holiday centre.

MAIN ATTRACTIONS: The annual Blessing of the Fleet in Ulladulla Harbour is one of a number of events held over the Easter

Fruits from Tropical Fruit World, south of Tweed Heads

weekend. **One Track For All** on the northern headland, is a fascinating trail with paintings and carvings illustrating Aboriginal and non-Aboriginal history of the area. White sandy beaches and clear water are the main attraction with surfers heading for Mollymook. Those looking for more sheltered swimming spots try the **Bogey Hole**, near the golf course, and **Narrawallee Inlet**.

NEARBY ATTRACTIONS: **Lake Conjola**, to the north, and **Burrill** and **Tabourie lakes** to the south, are good for swimming and fishing. Waterskiing is popular on Conjola and Burrill, while prawning takes place in the shallow waters of Tabourie.

Pigeon House Mountain is a distinctive landmark, located 26km inland, in the southern section of **Morton NP**. There are panoramic views from the summit, about a 4hr return trip from the car park. The **Coomie Nulunga Cultural Trail** is located at **Warden Head**. There is an iron lighthouse built on the headland and the walk features a totem man called Bunan and dream poles depicting local birds and animals.

TOURIST INFO: Civic Centre, Princes Hwy, Ph: (02) 4455 1269

■ Wagga Wagga   POP 57 000
Map 121, K2

The largest inland city in New South Wales, Wagga Wagga is known as the **'Garden City of the South'**. It is a university city and the commercial centre of the **Riverina** district which is devoted to wheat, lambs, dairying and mixed farming. The town's growth as a regional centre was assured by its position on the banks of the **Murrumbidgee River**, almost halfway between Sydney and Melbourne just off the Hume Hwy.

MAIN ATTRACTIONS: There are 3 **Historic Buildings' Walks**, varying in length from 40mins to 2hrs. Other attractions include **Charles Sturt University winery** and **cheese factory, RAAF Museum**, and the **Australian Army Base** and peace chapel at **Kapooka**. The **Wagga Wagga Regional Art Gallery** houses the superb **National Art Glass Collection**. Many public sculptures by notable local artists have been installed throughout the town centre. The **Botanic Gardens** includes a zoo, model trains, free-flight aviary and walking trails. The town hosts many events throughout the year covering fashion, jazz, horse racing, antiques, sports and gardens. Wagga Wagga has been home to many sporting champions, including Mark Taylor, Tony Roche, Steve Elkington, Wayne Carey and Paul Kelly.

TOURIST INFO: Tarcutta St, Ph: (02) 6926 9621

■ Walgett   POP 2100
Map 113, K4

Near the junction of the **Namoi** and **Barwon rivers**, Walgett is the centre of a vast pastoral area that stretches to the Queensland border.

MAIN ATTRACTIONS: Fishing has been a popular local sport since 1902, when 3 bridge workers camped on the river near Walgett caught a 115kg cod. Murray cod and golden perch are 2 of the many types of

Tourist train at Timbertown, Wauchope

fish to be caught in the local rivers. Picnic and BBQ facilities are located in the **Rotary Park** at the southern side of town. The river walk, linking the levee on the east bank of the river to the stock crossing, is a very pleasant 2km round trip.

NEARBY ATTRACTIONS: The opal-mining towns of **Lightning Ridge, Grawin, Glengarry** and the **Sheepyards** are within an hour's drive of the town. Lightning Ridge is the only place in the world where black opal is mined. Precious stones, including agate, jasper and topaz are also found in the surrounding area. Fossickers can venture out to the opal fields, but must remember these fields are undeveloped and there are no facilities. **Narran Lake**, a bird and wildlife sanctuary, is located 96km west of Walgett. There are no facilities, and visitors must get permission to enter.

TOURIST INFO: Council Office, 77 Fox St, Ph: (02) 6828 1399 or 1800 639 545

■ Wauchope   POP 4500
Map 119, K1

A timber town at the centre of the prosperous **Hastings River** dairying and cattle-raising region, Wauchope is 19km SW of **Port Macquarie**.

MAIN ATTRACTIONS: **Timbertown**, a working replica of a 19th-century village, is the main tourist attraction. Demonstrations of traditional skills,

such as shingle-splitting and wood-turning, and a steam locomotive, steam sawmill and bullock team bring the village to life. Timbertown is open daily, 9.30am–3.30pm. The **Hastings River** provides a venue for swimming, boating, fishing, canoeing, jet-skiing and waterskiing.

NEARBY ATTRACTIONS: Picnic spots and well-maintained recreation areas can be found in the state forests that surround Wauchope. Port Macquarie's hinterland is worthwhile visiting. The area is surrounded by valleys, mountains, waterfalls, rivers, eucalypt forests, rainforests and a number of excellent national parks. Wildlife includes wedge-tailed eagles, parrots, koalas, wallabies and platypus in the waterholes.

TOURIST INFO: Cnr Clarence and Hay sts, Port Macquarie, Ph: (02) 6581 8000

■ Wellington   POP 5325
Map 118, D3

Wellington is located at the junction of the **Macquarie** and **Bell rivers**. This **Central West** town services the surrounding agricultural and pastoral district.

MAIN ATTRACTIONS: **Cameron Park** occupies one side of the main street of Wellington. The Bell River flows through the park past picnic areas, a sunken garden and interesting landscaping. Brochures on the **historic town walk** are available

New South Wales

from the information centre and there is also a cycleway that runs through the local streets and along the highway to **Wellington Caves**.

NEARBY ATTRACTIONS: Wellington Caves, 9km south of the town, have been a popular tourist destination for many years. In 1826, the **Cathedral Cave** was painted by the travelling artist Augustus Earle, and in 1830, fossilised bones were discovered in the caves. Guided tours operate daily to the Cathedral and **Gaden caves**. There is also a phosphate mine located here. Holiday lodges and a caravan park form part of the caves complex. **Bakers Swamp Gallery** is a 100-year-old limestone house and is the home and studio of artist William O'Shea. The gallery is open daily 10am–5pm. **Lake Burrendong** is three-and-a-half times the surface area of Sydney Harbour. There are 2 small state parks on the western foreshore of the lake. Activities available include fishing and golf. Camping and caravanning is permitted. There are also cabins and a kiosk.

TOURIST INFO: Cameron Park, Nanima Cres, Ph: (02) 6845 1733

West Wyalong   POP 3600
Map 118, B5

A former gold-mining town, West Wyalong is now the business centre of a vast wheat-growing area. Located at the junction of the Mid Western and Newell hwys, 470km west of Sydney, the town is a convenient stopover for travellers. Today, eucalyptus oil is a lesser-known product of the town.

MAIN ATTRACTIONS: There is a pleasant 3.5km walking track known as the **Green Corridor**, which leads from the information centre to **Cooinda Bush Reserve**. Here, a simulated mine poppet head and a replica of the Neeld Family's bark hut are located near the picnic area. Gold was discovered on the Neeld property in the late 1800s. **West**

Wyalong Cemetery, 5km NE, holds many graves dating back to the late 1800s, including the Neeld family vault. The **Bland District Historical Museum** on the Newell Hwy displays a scale model of a working goldmine.

NEARBY ATTRACTIONS: The waters of **Barmedman Mineral Pool**, located 32km SE, are reputed to have healing properties. **Lake Cowal**, 48km NE, is a bird sanctuary and it is also possible to fish there.

TOURIST INFO: The Tourist Train, McCann Park, Mid Western Hwy, Ph: (02) 6972 3645

Wingham   POP 4600
Map 119, J2

A small rural town, Wingham services the rich dairying, timber and beef-cattle country of the **Manning Valley**. The town has been heritage-listed and is the oldest town along the **Manning River**, 13km upstream from Taree. A sawmill, an export abattoir, a horseshoe factory and a range of light engineering and service industries provide employment in the town.

MAIN ATTRACTIONS: The **Manning Valley Historical Museum** is located in an attractive village square, surrounded by historical buildings and is worthwhile visiting. A self-guided **historical walk** through

the town is also recommended and brochures are available from the museum. Located adjacent to the Manning River, **Wingham Brush** is a subtropical floodplain rainforest. There is a designated walkway where visitors can view giant Moreton Bay figs, which dominate the Brush, and see flying foxes, birds and native marsupials. A BBQ and picnic area is provided, and there is a boat-launching facility and a designated swimming area.

NEARBY ATTRACTIONS: For a scenic drive north through dairying and beef-cattle country, it is worthwhile visiting the high country of **Bulga Plateau** and the beautiful **Ellenborough Falls**. The falls are 40km NW of Wingham and are signposted from the village of **Elands**. They plunge 200m—one of the longest single-drop falls in the Southern Hemisphere.

TOURIST INFO: 21 Manning River Dr, Taree North, Ph: (02) 6552 1900 or 1800 801 522

Wollongong   POP 221 780
Map 107, C2

The third largest city in New South Wales, Wollongong is the administrative, commercial, cultural and industrial centre of the **Illawarra**. Steel and heavy industry were the

Wollongong Harbour

THE ILLAWARRA

The Illawarra—the name is an adaptation of an Aboriginal word meaning 'between the high place and the sea'—has **Wollongong** as its centre and is flanked by the Tasman Sea shores and the **Illawarra Escarpment**. The area is ideal for watersports and outdoor activities such as surfing at **North Beach**, hang gliding at **Stanwell Park**, fishing at **Lake Illawarra** and swimming at any one of the seventeen patrolled surf beaches. The spectacular shoreline is interrupted by rocky headlands, which provide panoramic views and sheltered beaches. There are also attractions away from the water, including **Minnamurra Falls** and the nearby **Minnamurra Rainforest Centre**, located in **Budderoo NP**, which has won many tourist awards and is definitely worthwhile visiting. The **Nan Tien Temple**, the largest Buddhist temple in the Southern Hemisphere, attracts visitors from around the world. The unspoilt bushland and rural scenery of **Kangaroo Valley** is breathtakingly beautiful. Some of the very best waterfalls in Australia are found in the national parks and reserves of the Illawarra, such as the 80m-high **Fitzroy Falls**.

Coastal view south from Stanwell Park to Wollongong

i **Tourist information**
Tourism Wollongong Visitors Centre
93 Crown St, Wollongong 2500
Ph: (02) 4227 5545 or 1800 240 737
www.tourismwollongong.com

Best Kept Secret
Wollongong Harbour is a major fishing port offering charters for game and offshore fishing as well as seasonal whale-watching.

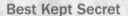
Lake Illawarra

initial growth areas for the city, although tourism and other industries have developed in recent times.
MAIN ATTRACTIONS: The **Historic Walk** explores the harbour area, which was a port for cargo and passenger vessels built in the 1860s. Today there are many seafood outlets, picnic areas and children's play facilities. **Illawarra Historical Society Museum** is housed in the city's first Post Office building at 11 Market St and is open Thursdays, 12pm–3pm; and weekends, 1pm–4pm. The museum contains authentically furnished rooms, and outside there is a blacksmith's shop and stockman's hut. From the museum visitors can also pick up the historic walk. The **Wollongong City Gallery**, on the corner of Kembla and Burelli sts, has a collection of Aboriginal, colonial and contemporary art by some of the best-known names in the Australian art world. The **Nan Tien Buddhist Temple** in the suburb of **Berkeley**, has beautifully landscaped gardens and views of the escarpment. Several sections, including a museum, meditation hall and other areas are open to the public 9am–5pm daily, except Monday.
NEARBY ATTRACTIONS: **Lake Illawarra**, a large saltwater lagoon 5km south of Wollongong, and home to many waterbirds, is popular for fishing, prawning, sailing, waterskiing, canoeing and windsurfing. There are parks with play facilities dotted along its shoreline, a cycle path and many walks along the shore. The **Botanic Gardens** are in **Keiraville**.
TOURIST INFO: 93 Crown St, Ph: (02) 4227 5545 or 1800 240 737

New South Wales

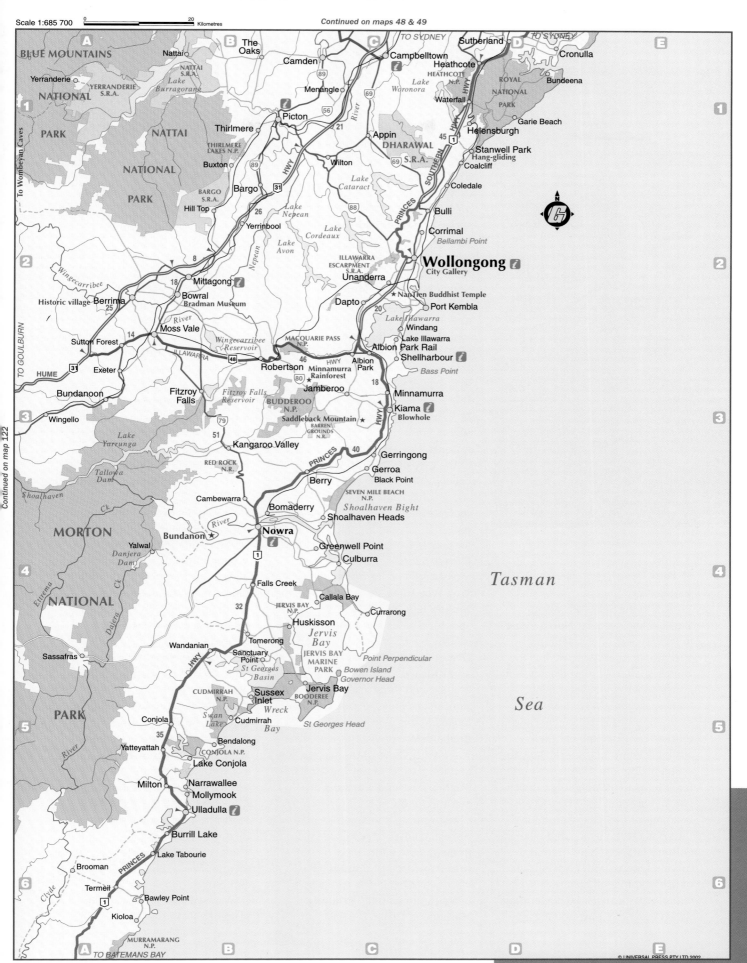

Scale 1:685 700

TO SYDNEY

BLUE MOUNTAINS

Yerranderie

NATIONAL

PARK

NATTAI

NATIONAL

PARK

Nattai

YERRANDERIE S.R.A.

NATTAI S.R.A.

Lake Burragorang

The Oaks

Camden

Menangle

Picton

Thirlmere

THIRLMERE LAKES N.P.

Buxton

Bargo

Hill Top

Yerrinbool

Mittagong

Historic village Berrima

Bowral

Bradman Museum

Moss Vale

Sutton Forest

Exeter

Bundanoon

Wingello

Campbelltown

Sutherland

Heathcote

HEATHCOTE N.P.

Cronulla

Bundeena

ROYAL NATIONAL PARK

Waterfall

Helensburgh

Garie Beach

Stanwell Park

Hang-gliding

Coalcliff

Coledale

Bulli

Corrimal

Bellambi Point

Appin

DHARAWAL S.R.A.

Wilton

Lake Cataract

Lake Nepean

Lake Cordeaux

Lake Avon

ILLAWARRA ESCARPMENT S.R.A.

Wollongong

City Gallery

Unanderra

Dapto

NanTien Buddhist Temple

Port Kembla

Windang

Lake Illawarra

Albion Park Rail

Shellharbour

Bass Point

Lake Illawarra

Macquarie Pass N.P.

Robertson

Minnamurra Rainforest

Jamberoo

Albion Park

Minnamurra

Kiama

Blowhole

Wingecarribee River

Wingecarribee Reservoir

ILLAWARRA HWY

HUME

Fitzroy Falls

Fitzroy Falls Reservoir

BUDDEROO N.P.

Saddleback Mountain

BARREN GROUNDS N.R.

TO GOULBURN

Lake Yarrunga

Kangaroo Valley

RED ROCK N.R.

PRINCES

Gerringong

Gerroa

Black Point

Berry

Cambewarra

SEVEN MILE BEACH N.P.

Shoalhaven Bight

Tallowa Dam

MORTON

NATIONAL

PARK

Shoalhaven

Bundanon

Yalwal

Danjera Dam

Bomaderry

Nowra

Shoalhaven Heads

Greenwell Point

Culburra

Shoalhaven River

Etrema

Sassafras

Wandanian

Falls Creek

Callala Bay

JERVIS BAY N.P.

Currarong

Huskisson

Jervis Bay

Tomerong

Sanctuary Point

JERVIS BAY MARINE PARK

Point Perpendicular

Bowen Island

Governor Head

Tasman

St Georges Basin

CUDMIRRAH N.P.

Sussex Inlet

BOODEREE N.P.

Jervis Bay

St Georges Head

Conjola

Swan Lake

Cudmirrah

Wreck Bay

Yatteyattah

Bendalong

CONJOLA N.P.

Lake Conjola

Sea

Milton

Narrawallee

Mollymook

Ulladulla

Burrill Lake

Brooman

Lake Tabourie

Termeil

Bawley Point

Clyde

Kioloa

MURRAMARANG N.P.

TO BATEMANS BAY

Continued on map 122

© UNIVERSAL PRESS PTY LTD 2002

Bushwalker at Girrakool, Brisbane Water NP

■ Woolgoolga   POP 4000
Map 62, E2

Known to the locals as 'Woopi', Woolgoolga is a quiet **North Coast** town with lots of character and spectacular coastal views. It is the centre of a fertile rural district that grows bananas and vegetables.

MAIN ATTRACTIONS: Wide bays and sandy beaches line the coast and tourists come for the excellent surfing, swimming, snorkelling and scuba diving. Conditions are perfect for fishing and **Woolgoolga Beach** has a boat ramp used by anglers heading for the fishing grounds on the reefs off the beach and near the **Solitary Islands**. Here there is a marine reserve with a vast array of fish and magnificent dive sites. Other activities include horseriding, whale-watching, bushwalking and golf. Woolgoolga is home to the largest Punjabi Sikh community in Australia. Members of the community are always keen to give visitors an understanding of their religion and culture through tours of the **Guru Nanak Temple**, which sits at the entrance to the town. Shady picnic spots are located in the reserve on the edge of **Woolgoolga Lake**, a safe swimming spot north of town where canoes and pedal boats are available for hire.

NEARBY ATTRACTIONS: **Mullaway**, **Arrawarra**, **Corindi** and **Red Rock** are quiet beaches located north of Woolgoolga. **Coffs Harbour** and its many attractions is 25km south.

TOURIST INFO: Boundary St, Ph: (02) 6654 8080

■ Woy Woy   POP 14 000
Map 71, B5

A **Central Coast** town that is part of the **City of Gosford**, Woy Woy covers a peninsula on the western shores of **Brisbane Water**. Over recent years the town has become part of the spreading residential area for people who commute back and forth to Sydney to work.

MAIN ATTRACTIONS: Surrounded by **Woy Woy Inlet**, Brisbane Water and **Broken Bay**, Woy Woy is an ideal spot for boaties and fishermen. Nearby beaches include **Ettalong**, **Ocean Beach**, **Umina**, **Pearl Beach** and **Killcare**. Pelican feeding is popular and there are many water-front picnic areas and picturesque lookouts. It is worthwhile visiting **Brisbane Water NP**. There are many walks with views of the waterways, and the park is renowned for its brightly coloured waratahs in autumn, and Christmas bells and Christmas bush in summer. Aboriginal rock carvings are also located in the park.

NEARBY ATTRACTIONS: **Bouddi NP** is worthwhile exploring and allows beachfront camping. **Ettalong Markets**, in Ocean View Rd, are the largest markets on the Central Coast. Every Saturday and Sunday there are over 150 stalls. **Old Sydney Town** and the **Australian Reptile Park** are located within a 30min drive of Woy Woy. (*see* Gosford, pp.69–70)

TOURIST INFO: 8-22 The Boulevard, Ph: (02) 4385 4430

■ Wyong   POP 4200
Map 71, C3

Formerly a centre for dairying, citrus-growing and timber-cutting, Wyong is now a commercial centre and commuter town on the northern **Central Coast**. The town is on the banks of the **Wyong River**, which flows into **Tuggerah Lake** a few kilometres east. Tuggerah Lake is linked to **Budgewoi** and **Munmorah lakes** and with this chain of lakes lying closely behind surf beaches, this area attracts many holiday-makers and permanent residents.

MAIN ATTRACTIONS: **Alison Homestead**, built in 1885, is a history museum with a family history resource and a good collection of local memorabilia. Located in Cape Rd, **West Wyong**, the museum is open weekends, 12pm–4pm. The **District Museum** incorporates displays about forest logging and the early services across the lakes. It is located in Cape Rd.

NEARBY ATTRACTIONS: The surrounding hinterland and state forests are popular for bushwalking and camping. For those interested in gardens, **Burbank Nursery** features 20ha of azaleas and is located 3km south. **The Forest of Tranquillity** is at nearby **Ourimbah**. During the **Firefly Festival** (mid-Nov–mid-Dec) the Forest remains open late on Friday and Saturday. Visitors should be there at dusk and bring a torch. The nearby **Watagan NP** and **Olney SF** offer bushwalks, picnic areas, camping and lookouts.

TOURIST INFO: Rotary Park, Terrigal Dr, Terrigal, Ph: (02) 4385 4430

New South Wales

Yamba POP 4000

Map 115, J3

This **North Coast** holiday resort and fishing town is located on the south side of the **Clarence River**, 693km north of Sydney.

MAIN ATTRACTIONS: The beaches of Yamba, considered to have the warmest waters in New South Wales, are a major drawcard for visitors. The main beach is patrolled all summer and there is a rockpool, offering safe swimming year-round. Fishing is one of the most popular activities with anglers choosing from rock, beach, estuary and deep-sea fishing. Boats can be hired and there are fishing charters. **Clarence River Ferries** operate a regular passenger service to **Iluka** where there are even more fishing spots. The local seafood shops and restaurants supply fish bought straight from the fishing boats based in the Clarence River. **Yamba Lighthouse** stands 41m above the sea and its automatic navigation light beams out as far as 17km. From here, the views are excellent and it is worthwhile visiting at dusk when the fishing fleet heads out to sea.

NEARBY ATTRACTIONS: There are 2 coastal national parks in close proximity to Yamba—**Yuraygir** and **Bundjalung**. Both parks offer bushwalks and access to pristine beaches. The famous **Blue Pool** is at the northern tip of Yuraygir NP.

South of Yamba, is the small village of **Angourie**, one of the best surfing spots in Australia.

TOURIST INFO: Ferry Park, Pacific Hwy, Maclean, Ph: (02) 6645 4121

Yass POP 4828

Map 122, B2

A quiet town on the **Yass River**, Yass is close to where the Barton Hwy to Canberra meets the Hume Hwy. An interesting and historic town, Yass is the service centre for the surrounding country which is famous for its merino sheep studs.

MAIN ATTRACTIONS: The area's history is represented by pioneer relics and historic photographs in the **Hamilton Hume Museum**. The museum is closed in winter and visitors should contact the tourist centre for opening times. The explorer Hamilton Hume and his wife bought **Cooma Cottage** in 1839. The weatherboard house, with its return verandah and fine cedar woodwork is now a National Trust property, open Thurs–Mon, 10am–4pm. The town drive includes a visit to the cemetery where Hamilton and Elizabeth Hume are buried.

NEARBY ATTRACTIONS: Some of Australia's best cool-climate wines are produced in the Yass region. Most of the wineries are found in the **Murrumbateman area** south of Yass and the majority welcome

visitors for tastings and sales. **Lake Burrinjuck** and **Burrinjuck Waters SP** are popular for watersports, picnics and cruises. **Careys Cave** in the **Wee Jasper Valley** is easily accessed and there are guided tours Mon–Fri, 12pm and 1.30pm; and on weekends and public holidays, 12pm, 1.30pm and 3pm.

TOURIST INFO: Coronation Park, Comur St (Old Hume Hwy), Ph: (02) 6226 2557

Young POP 11 046

Map 118, C6

The 'Cherry Capital of Australia', Young is the centre of a district that primarily produces cherries for the table, but also grows and processes plums and has a small number of wineries. It was once one of the richest and most populated goldfields in New South Wales.

MAIN ATTRACTIONS: Many of Young's cherry orchards invite visitors to pick their own cherries and other fruit in season—containers are supplied. Some orchards have BBQ areas and other facilities. **Burrangong Gallery** has many changing exhibitions; located next to the information centre, it is open Mon–Fri, 9am–5pm; and weekends, 9.30am–4pm. **Blackguard Gully**, at the end of Whiteman Ave, is a dedicated fossicking area where you can pan for gold. **J D's Jam Factory** processes fruit into jams and other products. There are factory and orchard tours, a gift shop and Devonshire teas. Located in Grenfell Rd, the factory is open daily, 8am–6pm.

NEARBY ATTRACTIONS: **Chinaman's Dam** is 3km from Young. A section of it is being dedicated as a 'Chinese Tribute Garden'. Wine produced in the **Hilltops Wine Region of Young**, **Harden** and **Boorowa**, is available in local outlets and some of the wineries have tastings and cellar door sales.

TOURIST INFO: Short St, Ph: (02) 6382 5433

Lake Burrinjuck, near Yass

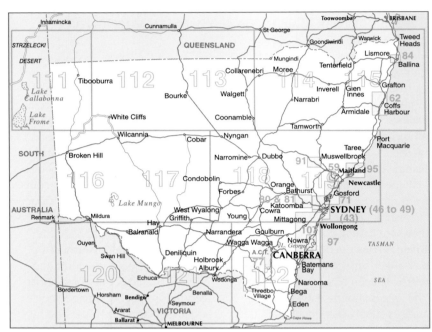

DISTANCE CHART

Approximate Distance	Albury	Bathurst	Bega	Bourke	Broken Hill	Canberra	Cooma	Dubbo	Goulburn	Grafton	Mildura VIC	Moree	Newcastle	Port Macquarie	Sydney	Tamworth	Tweed Heads	Wagga Wagga	West Wyalong	Wollongong
Albury		443	426	847	866	346	315	531	367	1162	569	904	693	935	562	866	1401	125	278	505
Bathurst	443		468	574	958	274	382	206	185	735	811	579	326	568	201	430	974	318	264	237
Bega	426	468		965	1292	222	111	604	283	1036	995	977	570	809	418	813	1275	393	501	336
Bourke	847	574	965		615	743	854	368	720	813	877	445	745	861	775	584	1052	722	572	811
Broken Hill	866	958	1292	615		1080	1181	752	1101	1328	299	1061	1129	1300	1159	1023	1567	863	846	1195
Canberra	346	274	222	743	1080		111	382	89	884	781	755	415	657	284	704	1123	244	271	227
Cooma	315	382	111	854	1181	111		493	197	992	882	866	523	765	392	815	1231	282	390	335
Dubbo	531	206	604	368	752	382	493		352	640	803	373	377	612	407	335	879	406	256	443
Goulburn	367	185	283	720	1101	89	197	352		795	802	725	326	568	195	569	1034	265	292	138
Grafton	1162	735	1036	813	1328	884	992	640	795		1513	368	479	249	618	305	239	1046	966	700
Mildura VIC	569	811	995	877	299	781	882	803	802	1513		1176	1137	1415	1012	1138	1682	564	547	940
Moree	904	579	977	445	1061	755	866	373	725	368	1176		490	498	610	272	568	779	629	692
Newcastle	693	326	570	745	1129	415	523	377	326	479	1137	490		252	152	275	718	591	590	234
Port Macquarie	935	568	809	861	1300	657	765	612	568	249	1415	498	252		391	277	488	833	868	473
Sydney	562	201	418	775	1159	284	392	407	195	618	1012	610	152	391		395	857	470	465	82
Tamworth	866	430	813	584	1023	704	815	335	569	305	1138	272	275	277	395		544	741	591	477
Tweed Heads	1401	974	1275	1052	1567	1123	1231	879	1034	239	1682	568	718	488	857	544		1299	1166	939
Wagga Wagga	125	318	393	722	863	244	282	406	265	1046	564	779	591	833	470	741	1299		153	403
West Wyalong	278	264	501	572	846	271	390	256	292	966	547	629	590	868	465	591	1166	153		430
Wollongong	505	237	336	811	1195	227	335	443	138	700	940	692	234	473	82	477	939	403	430	

All distances in this chart have been measured over highways and major roads, not necessarily by the shortest route.

New South Wales

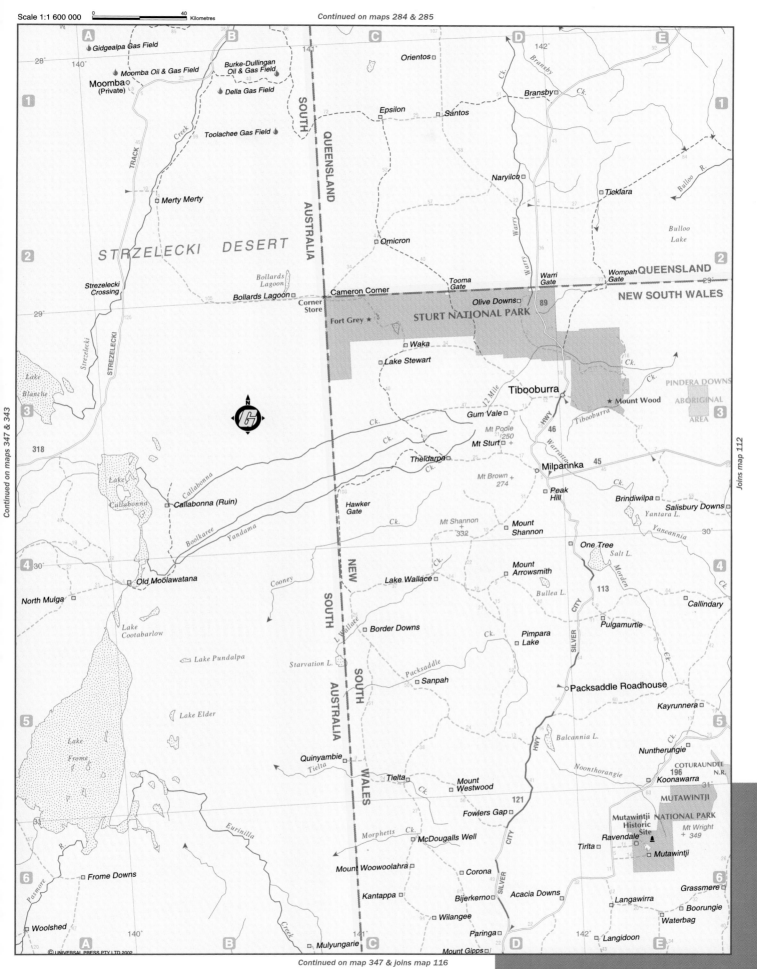

Scale 1:1 600 000

0 40 Kilometres

Continued on maps 284 & 285

A B C D E

1

28° 140°
Gidgealpa Gas Field
Moomba Oil & Gas Field
Moomba (Private)
Burke-Dullingan Oil & Gas Field
Della Gas Field
Orientos
Bransby Ck.

SOUTH AUSTRALIA
QUEENSLAND

Toolachee Gas Field
Epsilon
Santos
Creek
TRACK

Naryilco
Ticklara
Bulloo R.

Merty Merty

STRZELECKI DESERT

2

Omicron
Bulloo Lake

Bollards Lagoon
Tooma Gate
Warri Gate
Wompah Gate QUEENSLAND

Strzelecki Crossing
Bollards Lagoon
Cameron Corner
Olive Downs
29° NEW SOUTH WALES
Corner Store
Fort Grey ★
STURT NATIONAL PARK
89

3

Lake Blanche
Waka
Lake Stewart
Warratta Ck.
PINDERA DOWNS ABORIGINAL AREA

318
½ Mile
Tibooburra
Mount Wood ★

Gum Vale
Tibooburra
HWY
46
Warratta

Lake Callabonna
Mt Poole 250
Mt Sturt
Milparinka
45

Theldarpa
Mt Brown 274
Peak Hill
Brindiwilpa
Salisbury Downs

4

Callabonna (Ruin)
Yantara L.
30°
30° Hawker Gate
Mt Shannon 332
Mount Shannon
Yancannia

Boolkaree Yandama
One Tree
Salt L.
Old Moolawatana
Mount Arrowsmith
Morden
113

North Mulga
Cooney
Lake Wallace
Bullea L.
Callindary

Lake Cootabarlow
L. Wallace
Border Downs
Pulgamurtie

Lake Pundalpa
Pimpara Lake
SILVER

5

Starvation L.
Packsaddle
Sanpah
Packsaddle Roadhouse
Kayrunnera

Lake Elder
Balcannia L.
Nuntherungie
Quinyambie
Tielta
Noonthorangie
COTURAUNDEE N.R.

Lake Frome
Tielta
Mount Westwood
196
Koonawarra
31°

Quinyambie
Fowlers Gap
121
MUTAWINTJI
Mutawintji Historic Site
NATIONAL PARK

6

Eurinilla
Morphetts Ck.
McDougalls Well
CITY
Ravendale
Mt Wright 349
Grassmere

Frome Downs
Mount Woowoolahra
Corona
Tirlta
Mutawintji
Langawirra
Boorungie

Passmore R.
Kantappa
Bijerkerno
Acacia Downs
SILVER
Waterbag

Woolshed
140°
Mulyungarie
Wilangee
Paringa
142°
Langidoon

Mount Gipps
A B C D E

Continued on map 347 & joins map 116

Continued on maps 347 & 343

Joins map 112

© UNIVERSAL PRESS PTY LTD 2002

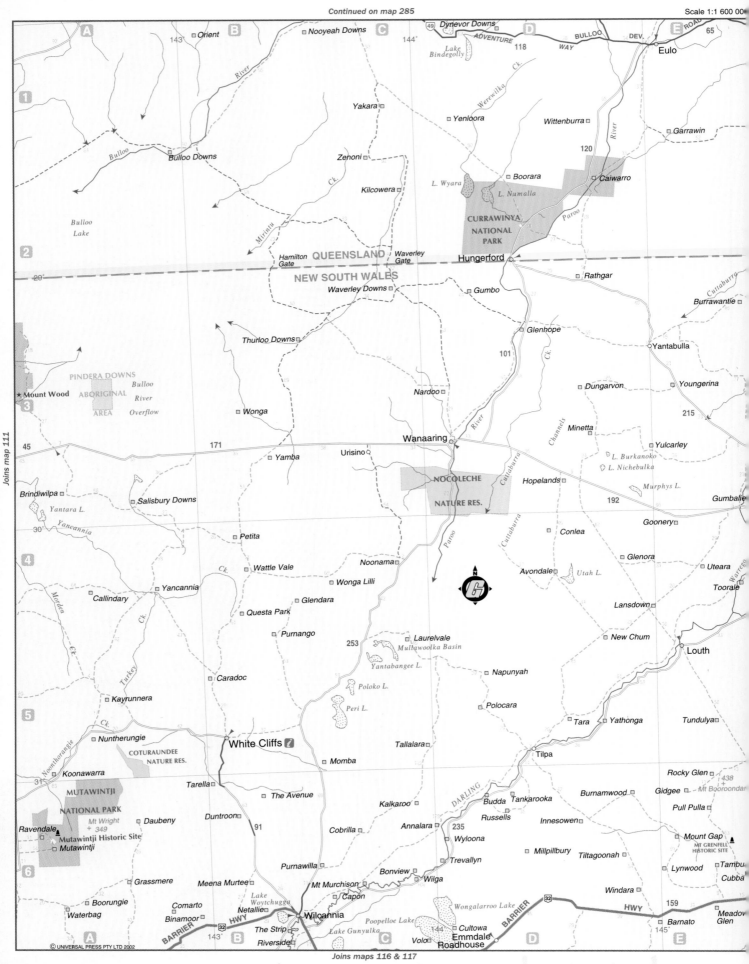

New South Wales

© UNIVERSAL PRESS PTY LTD 2002

40 Kilometres

Cunnamulla
F
33
146°
Weelamurra
G
147°
Murra Murra
H
Runnymede
J
148°
Mooramanna
K
1
R.
HWY
95
55
Noorama
Noondoo
Noondale
Hawston
Diranbandi

Burambil

Thurrulgoona
Noorama
184
Bundaleer
Coomburrah
Woolerina
Kyena
Ck
River
Balonne

71
89
MITCHELL

Tinnenburra

Ck

QUEENSLAND
NEW SOUTH WALES

Barringun
Widgee Downs
Gerara

CULGOA
FLOOD PLAIN
NATIONAL
PARK
CULGOA
72
NATIONAL PARK

Brenda Gate
39
Goodooga
66
Hebel
CASTLEREAGH
63
Angledool
Tuttawa
Briarie
Ballandool River
Bokhara River
29°
2

Nebine

Dongon Plains
Wallam
Mungallala
Creek

Enngonia
135
HWY

Ella Vale
River

Myuna
Weilmoringle
River
Bokhara
Narran

Imbergee
70
Opal mines
Lightning Ridge
73
CASTLEREAGH
Collarenebri
HWY
38
GWYDIR
73
Barwon
R.
3

Bullaroon
Collerina
122
Malabar
Grawin Opal Field
Glengarry Opal Field
NARRAN LAKE
NATURE RESERVE
Cumborah
Rosscommon
Narran Lake
Kia Ora

Fords Bridge
Lauradale
Culgoa River

96
Barwon
Brewarrina
The
Big

Joins map 114

North Bourke
KAMILAROI
Bogan
134
HWY
River
Walgett
KAMILAROI
Koothney
Cryon
30
94

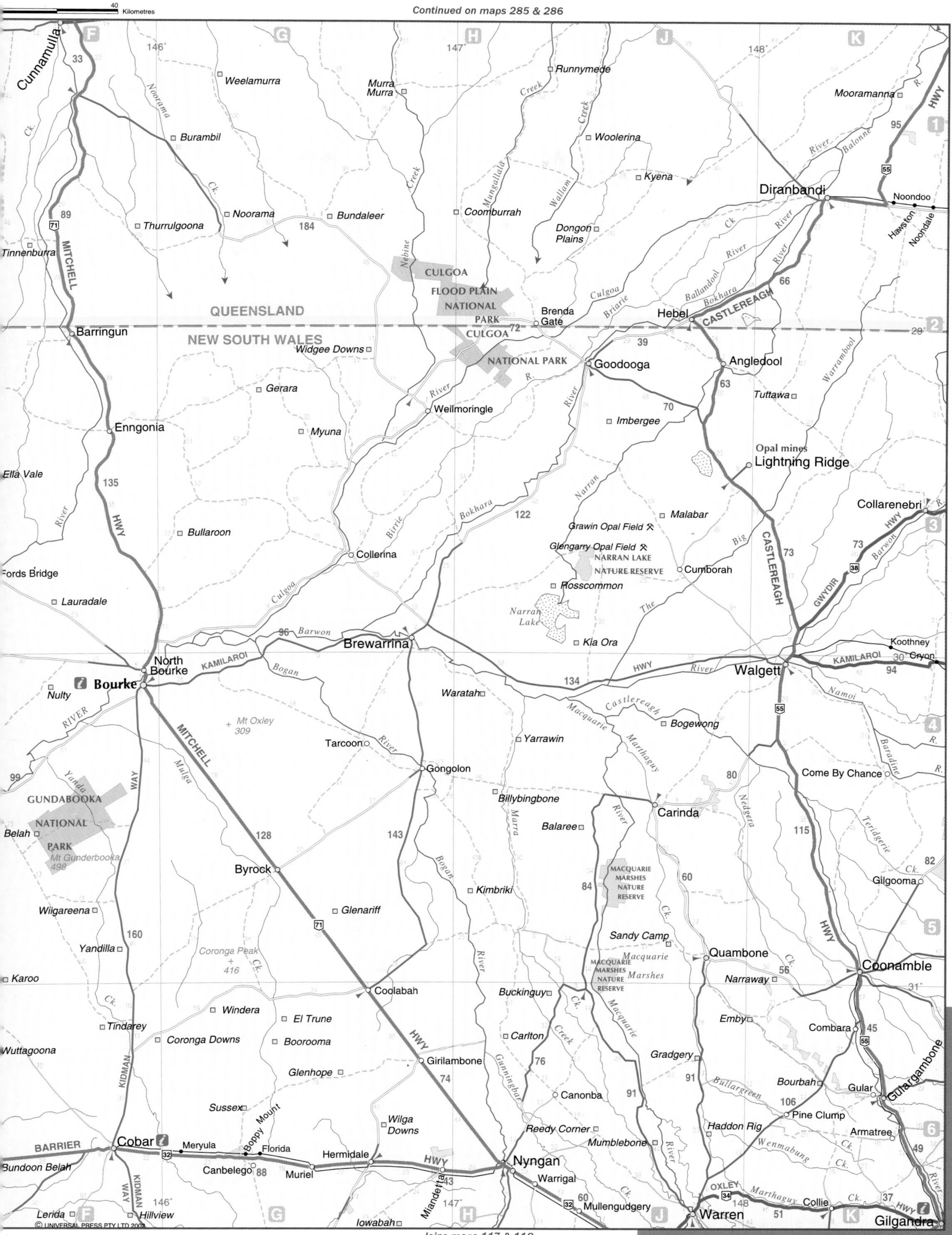

Bourke
Nulty
Waratah
Yarrawin
Macquarie
Castlereagh
Marthaguy
Bogewong
Come By Chance
Namoi
55
4
Baradine R.

RIVER
Mt Oxley
309
Tarcoon
River
Gongolon
Bogan
Billybingbone
Marra
Balaree
Carinda
80
115
82
Gilgooma

99
GUNDABOOKA
NATIONAL
PARK
Belah
Mt Gunderbooka
498
MITCHELL WAY
Mulga
128
143
Kimbriki
84
MACQUARIE MARSHES NATURE RESERVE
60
Ck
5

Wiigareena
Yandilla
160
Coronga Peak
+ 416
Byrock
71
Glenariff
River
Bogan
Sandy Camp
MACQUARIE MARSHES NATURE RESERVE
Marshes
Quambone
56
Narraway
Coonamble
31°

Karoo
Wuttagoona
Tindarey
Coronga Downs
Windera
El Trune
Boorooma
Coolabah
Buckinguy
76
Macquarie
Emby
91
Gradgery
Combara
45
55
6
Gulargambone

KIDMAN WAY
Glenhope
Girilambone
74
Carlton
Gunningbah Creek
91
Bourbah
106
Gular
Pine Clump
Armatree
49

Sussex
Boppy Mount
Wilga Downs
Canonba
Reedy Corner
Mumblebone
Haddon Rig
River
Bullargreen
Wenmabung
Ck

BARRIER
Cobar
Meryula
Florida
Muriel
Hermidale
HWY
Nyngan
Warrigal
OXLEY
34
148
Collie
37
HWY
Gilgandra

Bundoon Belah
32
Canbelego
88
Miandetta
43
32
Mullengudgery
60
Warren
51
K

Lerida
Hillview
F
146°
Iowabah
G
147°
H

KIDMAN WAY

© UNIVERSAL PRESS PTY LTD 2002

NEW SOUTH WALES   113

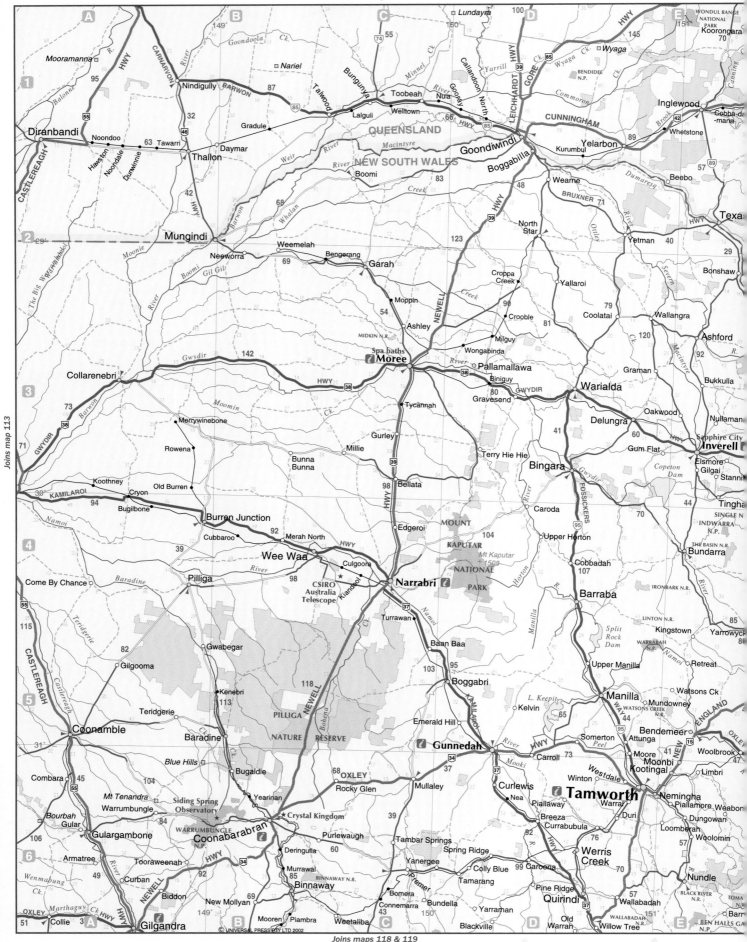

New South Wales

© UNIVERSAL PRESS PTY LTD 2002

40 Kilometres

154°

28°

Surfers Paradise

Tweed Heads ⓘ

1

Murwillumbah ⓘ

Pottsville Beach

Ocean Shores

Brunswick Heads

Nimbin

Bangalow

Byron Bay ⓘ

2

Lennox Head

Ballina ⓘ

CORAL

29°

QUEENSLAND

Warwick

Killarney

Legume

Urbenville

Stanthorpe

Amosfield

Wallangarra

Tenterfield

NEW SOUTH WALES

Torrington

Deepwater

Emmaville

Glen
Innes

Red Range

Guyra

Glencoe

Ben Lomond

Wandsworth

Llangothlin

Backwater

Aberfoyle

Armidale ⓘ

Uralla

Walcha

Woodenbong

Old Bonalbo

Bonalbo

Kyogle

Doubtful Ck

Mummulgum

Tabulam

Casino

Mallanganee

Coraki

Wyan

Rappville

Woodburn

Lismore

Alstonville

Broadwater

Evans Head

BROADWATER NATIONAL PARK

BUNDJALUNG

NATIONAL

PARK

Whiporie

Harwood

Iluka

Yamba

Maclean ⓘ

Gulmarrad

Brooms Head

Minnie Water

Wooli

Halfway Ck

Corindi

Red Rock

Corindi Beach

Arrawarra

Woolgoolga

Emerald Beach

Moonee Beach

Sapphire Beach

Coffs Harbour ⓘ

Sawtell

Raleigh

Urunga ⓘ

Valla Beach

Nambucca Heads

Scotts Head

Stuarts Point

South West Rocks ⓘ

Arakoon

Smoky Cape

Clybucca

Smithtown

Gladstone

Hat Head

Kempsey

Crescent Head

Kundabung

Copmanhurst

Lawrence

Cowper

Grafton

South Grafton

Ulmarra

Tucabia

Pillar Valley

YURAYGIR NATIONAL PARK

Coutts
Crossing

Glenreagh

Nymboida

Kungala

Coramba

Bellingen

Dorrigo

Ebor

Thora

Kalang

Missabotti

Bowraville

Macksville

Comara

Taylors Arm

Bellbrook

Eungai Creek

Millbank

Willawarrin

Frederickton

Sherwood

Rollands Plains

Birdwood

Pappinbarra

Bellangry

Pembrooke

Long Flat

Wauchope

Yarras

Ellenborough

Byabarra

Herons Ck

Lake
Cathie

Bonny Hills

Port Macquarie ⓘ

Telegraph Point

SEA

TASMAN

3

SEA

30°

4

5

31°

6

154°

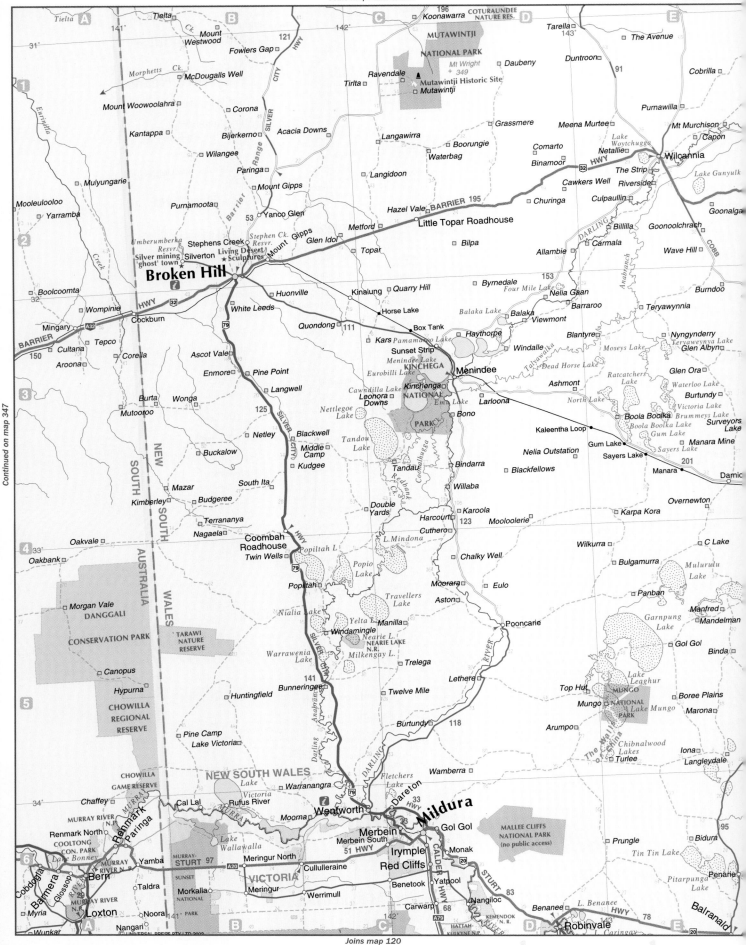

New South Wales

40 Kilometres

F · G · H · J · K

144° · 145° · 146° · 147°

Kalkaroo · Budda · Tankarooka · Burnamwood · Rocky Glen · Gidgee · Windera · El Trune · Coolabah
RIVER · 438 Mt Booroondarra · Coronga Downs · Booroma
Annalara · Russells · Pull Pulla · Wuttagoona · Glenhope · Girilambone
Bonview · Wyloona · Innesowen · Tiltagoonah · Mount Gap · ▲ MT GRENFELL HISTORIC SITE · Tindarey · Sussex · Mount Boppy · Wilga Downs
Wilga · Trevallyn · Millpillbury · Lynwood · Tambua · Cobar ℹ · Meryula · Boppy · Florida · Hermidale
BARRIER · Cubba · Meadow Glen · Canbelego · 88 · Muriel
Wongalarroo Lake · 32 · HWY · 159 · Bundoon Belah · Iowabah
Cultowa · Barnato · Lerida · Hillview · Mount Lewis · Gilgai · QUANDA N. R.
Volo · Poopelloe Lake · Emmdale Roadhouse · Noona · Kiaora · The Bluff · Osterley Downs · Creeper Gate · Babinda
Wongalara · Coomeratta · Kaleno · Pine Ridge · Bundycoola · Hartwood · Glengarry · Five Corners
Baden Park · Tiltagara · Bloomfield · Tara · Nymagee · Four Corners
Mount Kew · Box Valley · Belarabon · Bindi · Lachlan Downs · Overflow · Bobadah · Mogal Plain
Kewell East · Paddington · Taringo Downs · Manuka · Nangerybone · Walkers Hill
Yelta · Kiama · Keewong · Mirrabooka · Gilgunnia · Iris Vale · Avalon · Vermont Hill
Bambilla · Berangabah · Karwarn · Stanifords · Burthong · Tara · Kerein Hills
Tasman · Yalloch · YATHONG NATURE RESERVE · Romani · Bogolo · Tallebung · TOLLINGO N.R.
Mount Manara · Marfield · Kajuligah · Yathong · Woggoon N.R. · Wangangong
Gypsum Palace · KAJULIGAH N.R. · Moolah · Bundure · Yara
Walenda · Moondene · Morning Side · Tiarra · Coombie · Mount Hope · Matakana · ROUND HILL N.R. · Gunebang
Bonton · Orana · Waiko · NOMBINNIE NATURE RESERVE · NOMBINNIE N.R. · Euabalong West · Kiacatoo
Monivea · Ivandale · Ivanhoe · Conoble · Trida · Wee Elwah · Roto · Euabalong · LACHLAN VALLEY · Booberoi · Fairview
Beilpajah · Waverley · Lowlands · Gunniguldrie · Miami
Peneena · Moornanyah Lake · MORRISONS LAKE N.R. · WILLANDRA NATIONAL PARK · Lake Cargelligo · Wargambegal · Burgooney
Gunnaramby Swamp · Barneys Lake · Mossgiel · Boondara · Lake Brewster · Merri Merrigal · Tullibigeal
Clare · Alma Lake · Moolbong · Belingeramble · Weja
Culpataroo · COBB · Hillston · Dirrung · Monia Gap · Naradhan · Hannan · GUBBATA N.R. · Ungarie
Alma · LANGTREE N.R. · Langtree · Gubbata · Kikoira · Thulloo · Youngareen
Hatfield · Booligal · Goorawin · North Melbergen · Rankins Springs · Erigolia · Weethalle
Tarwong · Wongatoa · Merriwagga · Marong · Taleeban · Euratha · Narriah · Tallimba
One Tree · Gunbar · Goolgowi · PULLETOP N.R. · Buralyang · Buddigower
Oxley · Thelangerin · GOONAWARRA N.R. · HWY · Tabbita · COCOPARRA N.R. · Gunn
Wyoming · Carrathool · Warburn · COCOPARRA NATIONAL PARK · Barellan · Beckom
Nap Nap · Yerrinbool · Australian Shearers Hall of Fame · Beelbangera · Binya · Kamarah · Ardlethan
Maude · Hay ℹ · Tharbogang · Yenda · Koonandan · Gunn
Lake Tala · Ravensworth · STURT · Widgelli · Griffith ℹ · Yarmawl · Murrami
MURRUMBIDGEE · Hanwood · Yoogali · Whitton · Darlington Point · Leeton ℹ · Yanco
Willbriggie · Waddi · Roach · L. Coolah

© UNIVERSAL PRESS PTY LTD 2002

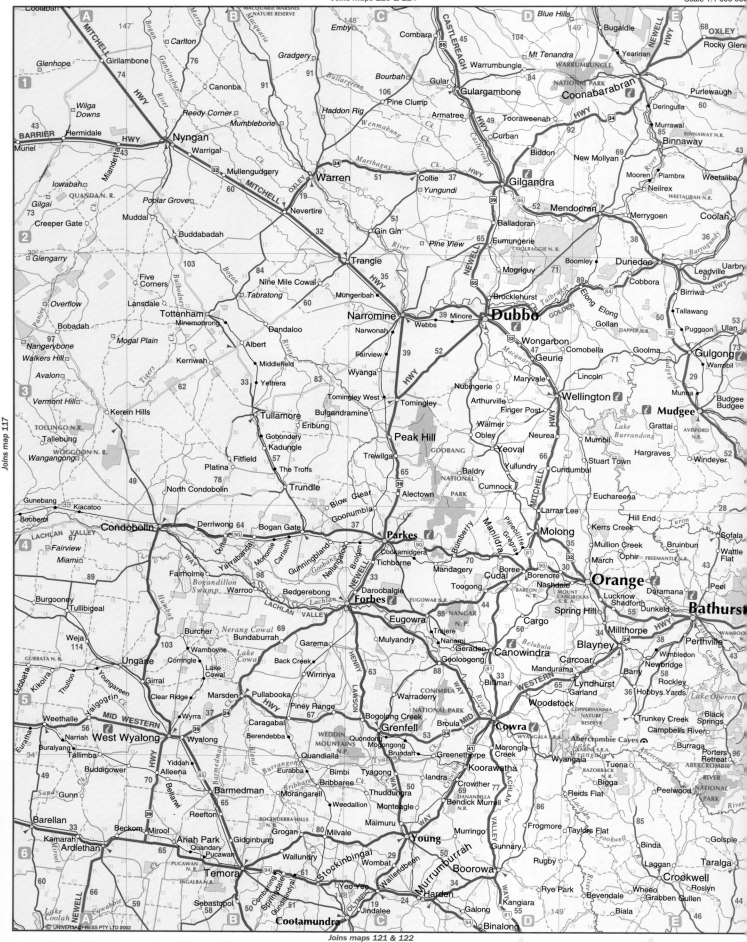

New South Wales

© UNIVERSAL PRESS PTY LTD 2002

40
Kilometres

F · 37 · HWY · 150° · Mullaley
Gunnedah
Curlewis
Nea
Carroll 73
Moore
Moonbi
Kootingal 151
Woolbrook
47 H 34
Walcha
OXLEY · CARRAI · FIFES KNOB N.R.
WILD RIVERS · WILLI WILLI
Willawarrin
THE CASTLES N.R.
Smithtown
Frederickton
64 K
HWY · 1
Winton
Westdale
Nemingha
Piallaway
Warral
Piallamore
Duri
Limbri
152
WERRIKIMBE
NATIONAL
Sherwood
Kempsey
Gladstone

39
Tambar Springs
Spring Ridge
Yanergee
Tremer
Bomera
onnemarra
Bundella
Breeza
Currabubula
Dungowan
Loomberah
Woolomin
Weabonga
Brackendale
Niangala
MUMMEL GULF · NGULIN N.R.
N.P.
Yarrowitch
Mount Seaview 176
MOUNT
SEAVIEW
N.R.
Birdwood
Rollands Plains
Pappinbarra
NATIONAL · PARK
KUMBATINE
N.P.
Crescent Head
Kundabung

Colly Blue
Tamarang
Pine Ridge
Old Warrah
Nundle
57
Wallabadah
BLACK RIVER
N.R.
NOWENDOC
Barry
147
Nowendoc
NATIONAL
Pembrooke
Bellangry
CREEK N.R.
Telegraph Poin
Port Macquarie
Wauchope
Byabarra
Herons Ck
Lorne
Kendall
Comboyne
Kew
Laurieton
North Haven
Bonny Hills
82
COOLAH TOPS
NATIONAL PARK
Yarraman
Blackville
Quirindi
Willow Tree
WALLABADAH
N.R.
BEN HALLS GAP
N.P.
TOMALLA
N.R.
WOKO
NATIONAL
PARK
BIRIWAL BULGA
N.P.
Elenborough
Falls
Ellenborough
Elands
KILLABAKH
N.P.
COORABAKH N.P.
Lansdowne
Coopernook
Moorland
Crowdy Head

Cassilis
Borambil
Turill
Murrurundi
Blandford
Kars Springs
Wingen
Parkville
Timor
Ellerston
Moonan Flat
BRETTI N.R.
Bretti
Mount George
Barrington
CARRAI
Wingham
Purfleet
Taree
Old Bar
WAY
TALAWAHL
N.R.
Manning Point
Harrington
32°
CROWDY BAY
N.P.
Watson Taylors Lake
Diamond Head

84 51
Merriwa
GOLDEN
Scone
62
Bunnan
Belltrees
Gundy
BARRINGTON
TOPS
NATIONAL PARK
Gloucester
Forbesdale
76
Krambach
72
Nabiac
THE GLEN
N.R.
Khappinghat N.R.
Hallidays Point
Failford
DARAWANK N.R.
Tuncurry
Forster
Coomba

GOULBURN RIVER
Wollar
MUNGHORN
GAP N.R.
Bylong
Aberdeen
Castle
Rock
MT ROYAL N.P.
Salisbury
Eccleston
Stratford
Craven
Wards River
Coolongolook
WALLAMBA N.R.
CHIN-DOO-EE
N.R.
BOOTI BOOTI N.P.
Cape Hawke
Elizabeth Beach

NATIONAL PARK
Gungal
Roxburgh
Sandy Hollow
Kerrabee
Baerami
Lake Glenbawn
50
26
Muswellbrook
24
Lake Liddell
Ravensworth
Lake
St Clair
Lake Lostock
KILLARNEY N.R.
Dungog
Bendolba
MONKERAI N.R.
Stroud Road
Wootton
56
WALLINGAT
N.R.
Bungwahl

Baerami
Creek
Holbrook
Denman
84
Jerrys Plains
Glen
Gailic
Camberwell
East Gresford
Wiragula
Booral
Stroud
Girvan
Bulahdelah
Seal Rocks

Lue 73
Rylstone
Olinda
Kandos
Clandulla
Bogee
Warkworth
Bulga
58
Singleton
21
Broke
22
Vacy
Paterson
Clarence
Town
WALLAROO
N.P.
Karuah
Port Stephens
MYALL LAKE NP
Tea Gardens
Hawks Nest
Broughton Island
MYALL LAKES NATIONAL PARK
Bombah Pt

Ilford
Running Stream
Glen Alice
WOLLEMI
NATIONAL
Howes Valley
Putty
165
Cessnock
Bellbird
45
Lochinvar
37
Maitland
31
Wallaroo
Erringhom
Lake
Karuah
Nelson Bay
Lemon Tree Passage

Capertee
68
Ben Bullen
N.P.
Cullen Bullen
86
Newnes
PARK
YENGO
NATIONAL
Millfield
Mulbring
Wollombi
Freemans
Waterhole
WATAGANS
N.P.
27
Kurri Kurri
Hexham
29
Williamtown
Raymond
Terrace
Port Hunter
Newcastle

Portland
Wallerawang
GARDENS OF STONE
N.P.
Glen Davis
PARR
S.R.A.
Cooranbong
26
Morisset
Toronto
Swansea
54
Belmont
33°
4

Lithgow
Tarana
Hampton
Oberon
Bell 91
MOUNTAINS
Mt Victoria
Blackheath
32
Bilpin
Kurrajong
Wollemi
Wentworth
Falls
Yarramalong
Kulnura
St Albans
Wyee
MUNMORAH S.R.A.
Munmorah Lake
Budgewoi
Toukley
WYRRABALONG N.P.

Katoomba
Edith
Jenolan Caves
Jenolan Caves
BLUE
Lawson
Springwood
Hazelbrook
Glenbrook
Wallacia
Richmond
Windsor
BEROWRA VALLEY
Berowra
Hornsby
Wyong
36
TUGGERAH
Tuggerah Lake
The Entrance
WAMBERAL LAGOON N.R.

KANANGRA BOYD
Kanangra
MOUNTAINS
Blaxland
Penrith
54
DHARUG
N.P.
Wisemans
Ferry
POPRAN
N.P.
Gosford
Woy Woy
BRISBANE
WATER
BOUDDI N.P.

NATIONAL
Lake
Burragorang
BENTS BASIN
S.R.A.
Liverpool
34
Parramatta
KU-RING-GAI CHASE
NATIONAL PARK
Mona Vale
GARIGAL N.P.
Broken Bay
Long Reef

BLUE
PARK
Walls
The Oaks
Oakdale
Camden
Campbelltown
20
SYDNEY
La Perouse
Kurnell
Botany
Bay
BOTANY BAY N.P.
Manly
SYDNEY HARBOUR
N.P.
Port Jackson
TASMAN
5

MOUNTAINS
Colong Caves
Wombeyan Caves
Picton
Thirlmere
YERRANDERIE
S.R.A.
NATTAI
S.R.A.
Appin
DHARAWAL
S.R.A.
Sutherland
HEATHCOTE
82
Voronora
ROYAL NATIONAL PARK
GARRAWARRA S.R.A.
Stanwell Park

NATIONAL
Buxton
Bargo
Yerrinbool
Berrima
Mittagong
Bowral
HUME
HWY
Dapto
20
Bulli
ILLAWARRA ESCARPMENT S.R.A.
Wollongong
Port Kembla
SEA

F · ARLO · RIVER · N.P. · Brayton
Moss Vale
Sutton Forest
Exeter
60
Robertson
Lake Illawarra
G · 151° · 152°
H
J
K · 153°
6

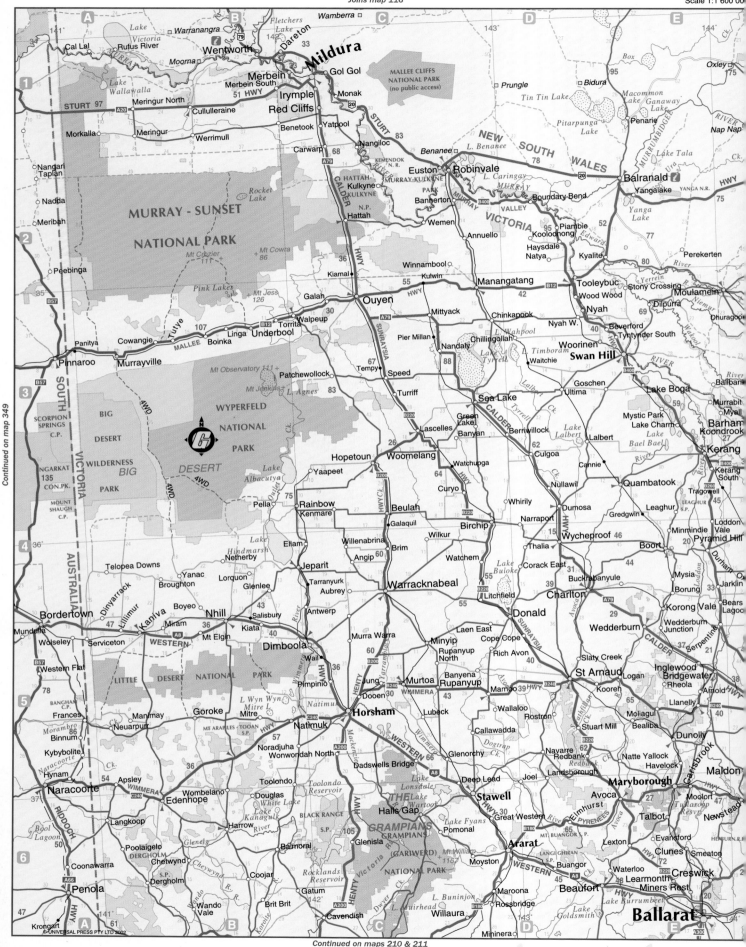

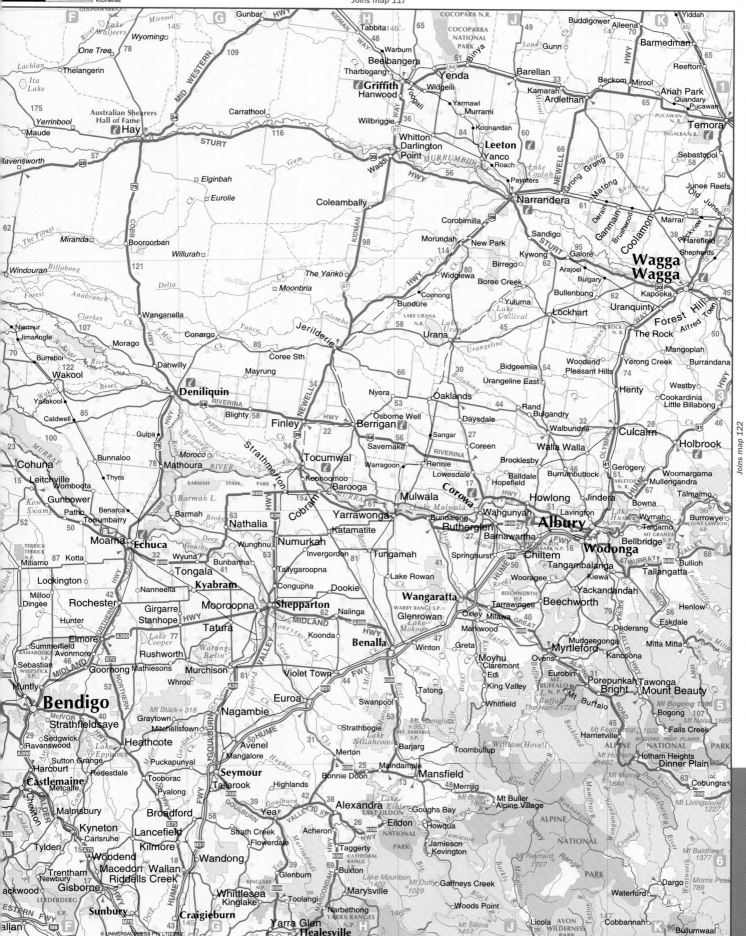

Joins map 122

A   B   C   D

The Oaks
Kanangra
Walls

Eurabba   Bimbi   Tyagong   Iandra   Crowther   Razorba   Tuena   Kanangra   Oakdale   Camden
Morangarell   Bribbaree   77   Bigga   Peelwood   Boyd   Picton   Thirlmere
Bribbaree   Thuddungra   50   Bendick Murrell   69   Reids Flat   Colong Caves   Appin
Weedallion   Monteagle   N.R.   86   Laggan   Wombeyan Caves   Buxton
Grogan   Milvale   Murringo   Frogmore   Taylors Flat   85   Golspie   Bargo
Wallundry   Young   Binda   Taralga   Mittagong   Bowral   Dapto
Stockinbingal   Wombat   Boorowa   Rugby   Crookwell   Berrima   Moss Vale   Lake Illawarra
Springdale   Yeo Yeo   Harden   Rye Park   Roslyn   Sutton Forest   Robertson
Combaning   Wallendbeen   Bevendale   Grabben Gullen   Brayton   Bundanoon   Kiama
Dirnaseer   Galong   Biala   Exeter   Wingello   Gerringong
Frampton   Cootamundra   Binalong   Bowning   Dalton   Kingsdale   Marulan   Kangaroo Valley   Berry   Gerroa
Brawlin   Bethungra   Muttama   Jugiong   Bookham   Gunning   Goulburn   Bungonia Caves   Shoalhaven Heads
Illabo   Coolac   Yass   Munboonen   Bungonia   Morton   Bomaderry
Junee   Eurongilly   Burrinjuck   Murrumbateman   Breadalbane   S.R.A.   Nowra   Yalwal
Nangus   Gundaroo   Collector   Inveralochy   National   Greenwell Pt Culburra
Gundagai   Wee Jasper   Sutton   Lake Bathurst   Wandandian   Currarong   Beach
Tumblong   Careys Caves   Hall   Butmaroo   Tarago   Sassafras   Jervis Bay
Gocup   Tumorrama   Canberra   Mt Fairy   Nerriga   Tomerong   Sussex Inlet
Mt Horeb   Brindabella   Queanbeyan   Lower Boro   Charleyong   Conjola N.P.   Lake Conjola
Tumut   Williamsdale   Bungendore   Milton   Ulladulla
Tarcutta   Adelong   Brindabella   Braidwood   Burrill Lake
Gilmore   Wondalga   Australian   Captains Flat   Majors Creek   Brooman   Lake Tabourie
Kyeamba   Batlow   Capital   Araluen North   Termeil
Humula   Talbingo   Territory   Michelago   Araluen   Bawley Point   Kioloa
Carabost   Laurel Hill   Tantangara   Nelligen   Durras   Murramarang National Park
Rosewood   Yarrangobilly Caves   Reservoir   Jerangle   Mogo   Batemans Bay
Mannus   Tumbarumba   Wyanbene Caves   Batehaven   Mossy Point
Munderoo   Kiandra   Shannons Flat   Deua   Broulee   Moruya Head
Jingellic   Cabramurra   Mt Selwyn   Bredbo   Moruya   Bergallia   Eurobodalla National Park
Walwa   Tooma   Adaminaby   Peakview   Bendethera Caves   Turlinjah   Coila Lake   Tuross Head
Welaregang   Eucumbene   Numeralla   Badja Swamps   Bodalla   Tuross Lake
Tintaldra   Towong   Buckenderra   Bunyan   Nerrigundah   Potato Point
Igewa   Khancoban   Cooma   Numeralla   Countegany   Eurobodalla   Dalmeny
Corryong   Kybeyan   Tilba Tilba   Narooma   Montague I.
Lucyvale   Perisher Valley   Berridale   Rock Flat   Dangelong N.R.   Cobargo   Central Tilba   Wallaga Lake
Nariel Creek   Guthega   Blue Cow Mtn   East Jindabyne   Cobargo   Bermagui   Bermagui South
Mt Kosciuszko   Smiggin Holes   Jindabyne   Dalgety   Quaama   Bermaguee N.R.
Thredbo   Bullocks Flat   Beloka   Maffra   Nimmitabel   Brogo   Brown Mountain   South East Forest   Tanja   Mimosa Rocks   Wapengo Lake
Ingebyra   Bemboka   Bega   Tathra
Benambra   Suggan Buggan   Ando   Candelo   Kameruka   Bournda National Park
Benambra   Bibbenluke   Cathcart   Wolumla   Wallagoot Lake
Hinnomunjie   Delegate River   Bombala   Wyndham   Merimbula   Pambula
Omeo   Wulgulmerang   Mila   Burragate   Pambula Lake
Tubbut   Craigie   South East Forest   Eden   Ben Boyd National Park
Swifts Creek   Gelantipy   Bendoc   Bonang   New South Wales   Wonboyn   Green Cape   Disaster Bay
Tongio West   Butchers Ridge   Victoria   Genoa   Ben Boyd National Park
Ensay   Murrindal   Erinundra   Combienbar   Gipsy Point   Cape Howe   Nadgee N.R.
Buchan   Malinns   Gabo I.
Club Terrace   Noorinbee   Mallacoota   Mallacoota Inlet
Cann River   Alfred N.P.

TASMAN

SEA

© UNIVERSAL PRESS PTY LTD 2002

The Australian Capital Territory has more to offer than just an insight into the political workings of the country, although it does this well. It's a place where Australia's history comes face-to-face with architectural modernity. You can discover the scientific workings of the universe, pay your respects to the soldiers who fought and died in the wars, venture back in time to the dinosaurs, create your own dollar coin or catch a close-up view of the fittest bodies on the continent. You can see artworks from all over the world, cycle around or sail on a large man-made lake, rise above it all in a hot-air balloon, visit Australia's only zooquarium, or stroll through the Australian National Botanic Gardens. The Australian Capital Territory has a diverse range of attractions and sights to suit everyones' taste.

Located on perhaps some of the best sheep and cattle grazing land in Australia, the national capital is bordered by farmland, bushland, national parks and the Boboyan, Tidbinbilla and Booth ranges. It is completely surrounded by New

Australian Capital Territory: The Federal Capital

◈ Population: 310 170
◈ Total area: 2358km^2
◈ % of Australia: 0.03%
◈ Length of border: 306km
◈ Floral emblem: Royal Bluebell
◈ Fauna emblem: Gang Gang Cockatoo

Photo above: Parliament House, Canberra

South Wales and was selected as the site of the national capital in 1909, eight years after Federation. Located inland, the creation of the Australian Capital Territory was a compromise to appease bitter interstate rivalry between New South Wales and Victoria.

The Australian Capital Territory encompasses only 0.03% of the entire continent, yet it is the political centre of the nation—rich with history and fine examples of modern architecture, art and culture. The capital city, Canberra, occupies around 15% of the Australian Capital Territory—a large percentage relative to the other capital cities of Australia. In addition to being Australia's only planned modern capital city, Canberra also has the distinction of being the only Australian capital city located inland.

Tourist information

Canberra Visitors Centre
330 Northbourne Ave,
Dickson, ACT 2602
Ph: (02) 6205 0044
www.canberratourism.com.au

Main ATTRACTIONS

◈ Australian War Memorial

The most visited building in Canberra and one of the most visited attractions in Australia, the War Memorial honours all Australians who fought and died for their country. It is the site for remembrance ceremonies and its museum contains historic information, artefacts and interactive displays. The volunteer guides are very passionate about the memorial.

◈ Lake Burley Griffin

Lake Burley Griffin is the geographic centre of the city, named after the American architect who won the international competition to design Canberra. Many of the city's attractions and most beautiful picnic spots are located on the 35km shoreline of the lake.

◈ National Gallery of Australia

This gallery houses a fine collection of Australian and international art, and displays major travelling exhibitions. There is a sculpture garden and a restaurant. Guided and audio tours are highly recommended.

◈ National Museum of Australia

The museum uses three main themes— Land, Nation and People, to focus on what it means to be an Australian. Cutting-edge technology, including a huge three-dimensional map of Australia, and displays of rare and unique objects, help tell the stories and cultural histories of Australians. Visitors can see the heart of racing legend Phar Lap, the sword of Governor Macquarie and much more.

◈ Parliament House

Completed in 1988 (in time for Australia's Bicentennial celebrations) Parliament House is now the focal point of the city. This impressive modern building forms part of Capital Hill, with extensive cityscape views from the entry forecourt.

THE FEDERAL CAPITAL

The Australian Capital Territory is home to **Canberra**, capital of Australia and seat of the Federal Government. It is situated 306km from Sydney and 655km from Melbourne. Before the original Parliament House was completed in 1927, Melbourne was the temporary home of government. **Old Parliament House** was used for 60 years until the new Parliament House was finished in 1988.

In 1913, construction began on the first public buildings and the rail link between Sydney and Canberra was completed in 1914. Canberra is renowned as one of the world's most planned cities—in 1911, an international competition for its design was won by American landscape architect **Walter Burley Griffin**. The **Molonglo River**, a tributary of the **Murrumbidgee River** that ran through the city, was damned in 1964 to create the centrepiece of the city—**Lake Burley Griffin** in honour of the first city planner. Canberra has continued to evolve around the 35km shoreline of the lake.

The name Canberra is thought to have originated from that of the homestead of the first European settler in the area, Joshua Moore. In 1824, his property of $25km^2$ was located by the Murrumbidgee River, and called 'Canberry'—the Aboriginal word for 'meeting place'.

The population of the Australian Capital Territory is very diverse. Although it is assumed that a large proportion of Canberra's workforce is politicians and bureaucrats, they in fact make up less than half the working population. With 99.4% of the population living in the Canberra urban area, the Australian Capital Territory is different from the other Australian states and territories in that it has a virtual city-state status.

There is huge ethnic diversity within the Australian Capital Territory, the diplomatic community itself adding to the character of the capital. Two out of five people are either immigrants or children of immigrants, which is higher than the average ratio for all of Australia. Canberra is a

Australian Institute of Sport

favoured site for international and national conferences and delegations, and the pursuit of excellence in all aspects of research (the **Australian National University**), science **(CSIRO)**, sport **(Australian Institute of Sport)** and culture, greatly influence the character of the city and surrounds.

The Australian Capital Territory is increasingly becoming home to younger people. With 2 world-class universities (Australian National University and the **University of Canberra**) as well as campuses of the **University of New South Wales (Australian Defence Force Academy)** and the **Australian Catholic University**, young students comprise a significant percentage of the population.

Sunrise over Lake Burley Griffin

Australian Capital Territory

NATIONAL PARKS

National Park Office

Environment ACT
Level 2, Macarthur House
12 Wattle St, Lyneham, ACT 2602
Ph: (02) 6207 9777   (02) 6207 2900
www.environment.act.gov.au

CANBERRA

facts

❖ Number of NPs: 1
❖ Area: 1059km^2
❖ % of territory: 48%

Kangaroos in Canberra Nature Park

A Namadgi NP (Map 137, B4)

Namadgi NP lies to the south of the city and borders the **Kosciuszko NP** and the **Bimberi Nature Reserve** of New South Wales. It is the most northern alpine environment in Australia and offers amazing views, Aboriginal rock art, rare sub-alpine species of flora and fauna, 160km of walking tracks, camping, BBQ and picnic facilities. There are 3 campgrounds, each with toilets, picnic tables and fireplaces, but no caravan facilities. Bush camping is allowed but fire permits are required; and a camping permit is needed for the **Cotter catchment**—part of Canberra's water supply.

Namadgi Visitor Centre, located on Naas Rd, offers a host of videos and exhibits, information on bushwalks, trails and paths for all adventure levels and ages. Guided tours are available if pre-booked.

Proclaimed a national park in 1984, Namadgi was expanded from 940km^2 to 1059km^2 in 1991. The most popular activities in Namadgi are bushwalking, picnicking and sightseeing.

B Molonglo Gorge Recreation Area

(Map 137, D2)

Smaller areas near Canberra City offer conveniently close walking trails and lunching spots. The Molonglo Gorge Recreation Area is to the east of the city and is known for its riverside picnic spots.

C Canberra Nature Park

(Map 135)

Canberra Nature Park is a series of hilltop nature reserves throughout Canberra. It includes **Black Mountain** (812m), **Mount Ainslie** (842m) and **Mount Majura** (890m). The lookout at Mount Ainslie is renowned for its extensive view of the city, day and night.

WINERIES

Vineyard at Lark Hill Winery, near Lake George

CANBERRA

key

A Murrumbateman/Yass
B Murrumbidgee River west of Hall
C Bungendore/Lake George

The wine industry around Canberra is both young and old. There were wineries in the area in the 1860s, but production ceased around the turn of the 19th century. The modern pioneers of Canberra district wines were scientists Dr John Kirk and Dr Edgar Riek, who planted vines at **Murrumbateman** and **Lake George** in 1971.

There are now 24 wineries within an hour's drive of the Australian capital. Nearly all of these are in New South Wales, just outside the Australian Capital Territory border.

The Canberra region has a variety of soils, mild temperatures and ample sunshine for ripening grapes. In table wines, riesling, pinot noir and chardonnay excel, as does premium sparkling wine. Other grape varieties, which are made into a range of wine styles, include cabernet sauvignon, merlot, shiraz and sauvignon blanc. Visit the **Kamberra Wine Tourism Complex** in the city for more information.

CANBERRA

Australian War Memorial and Anzac Parade

main attractions

◈ **National Capital Exhibition**

The extraordinary story of Canberra, from its indigenous heritage to modern-day political capital, is told with interactive displays, laser models and audiovisual presentations.

◈ **National Library of Australia**

The vast collection of beautiful, rare and unusual Australian books, manuscripts, newspapers, maps and paintings is held in more than 200km of shelving.

◈ **National Portrait Gallery**

Housed in Old Parliament House, the beautifully renovated gallery features portraits of people who have helped shape the nation. The permanent collection includes artists such as Arthur Boyd, David Moore, Howard Arkley and Nora Heysen.

◈ **Questacon — The National Science & Technology Centre**

Discover the science behind the fun in this interactive centre where lightning strikes several times a day and visitors can experience the force of an earthquake.

◈ **Royal Australian Mint**

See the minting process in action, trace the history of Australia's coinage and make your own special $1 coin at the Mint.

◈ **ScreenSound Australia**

Explore Australia's radio, film, television and sound recordings from the late 1800s to the present at McCoy Circuit, Acton. Displays include memorabilia from recent films like *Strictly Ballroom* and *Priscilla, Queen of the Desert* to original equipment from the early days.

Canberra is widely acclaimed as the best landscaped city in the world. Its geometrically circular street pattern, set around key urban planning elements, is complemented by millions of trees and shrubs, which give the city its ambience. Canberra is planned around Lake Burley Griffin and a 'parliamentary triangle' consisting of Parliament House, the High Court and other important public buildings. It extends more than 40km from the satellite towns of **Tuggeranong** in the south to **Gungahlin** in the north.

The best way to explore Canberra is by car, but make sure you have a good map. The city's attractions are quite spread out, but parking in Canberra is easy to find and inexpensive. If investigating by foot is appealing, then wander along King Edward Tce, or the Lake's shore and find the National Library, Questacon—The National Science and Technology Centre, Old Parliament House, High Court, Aboriginal Tent Embassy and the National Gallery of Australia—all within close proximity of each other. Visiting the city's other attractions will require you to travel through the wide, planned streets and the many roundabouts.

ⓘ Tourist information

Canberra Visitors Centre
330 Northbourne Ave, Dickson 2602
Ph: (02) 6205 0044
www.canberratourism.com.au

facts

◈ Population: 310 170
◈ Tallest building: MLC Tower (82m)
◈ Date founded: 1913—foundation stone laid and name 'Canberra' adopted
◈ Lake Burley Griffin: created in 1964 when the Molonglo River was dammed
◈ Average temperature: 21 C° (Jan), 6.5 C° (June)

Places of Interest

Anzac Parade Ⓐ E2
Australian National Botanic Gardens Ⓑ A1
Australian National University Ⓒ B2
Australian War Memorial Ⓓ E2
Blundell's Cottage Ⓔ E3
Canberra Theatre Centre Ⓕ D2
Captain Cook Memorial Water Jet Ⓖ C3
Casino Canberra Ⓗ D2
City Hill Lookout Ⓘ C2
Commonwealth Park Ⓙ D3
Gorman House Arts Centre Ⓚ D2
High Court of Australia Ⓛ D4
National Capital Exhibition Ⓜ D3
National Carillon Ⓝ E4
National Gallery of Australia Ⓞ D4
National Library of Australia Ⓟ C4
National Museum of Australia Ⓠ B3
Old Parliament House and
    National Portrait Gallery Ⓡ C4
Parliament House Ⓢ C5
Prime Minister's Lodge Ⓣ B5
Questacon — The National Science and
    Technology Centre Ⓤ D4
ScreenSound Australia Ⓥ C2

Questacon — The National Science and Technology Centre

Australian Capital Territory

Scale 1:25 000

0   750
Metres

A | B | C | D | E

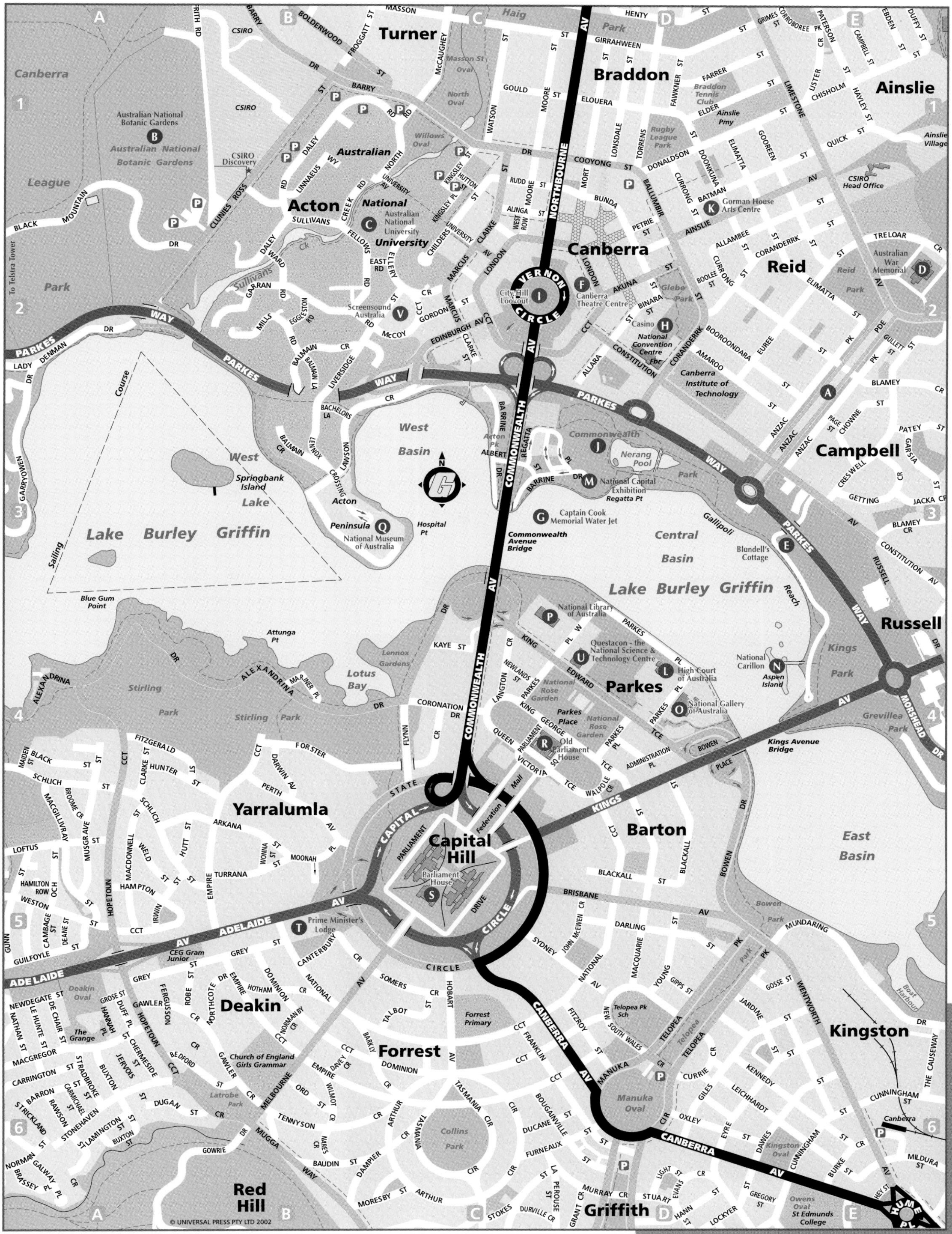

Turner

Braddon

Ainslie

Canberra

Australian National Botanic Gardens

Australian National Botanic Gardens

CSIRO

CSIRO Discovery ★

Australian

Acton

National

Australian National University

University

Screensound Australia V

CSIRO Head Office

Ainslie Village

Gorman House Arts Centre K

Canberra

City Hill Lookout I

Canberra Theatre Centre F

Casino H

National Convention Centre Fbr

Canberra Institute of Technology

Reid

Australian War Memorial D

Campbell

League

BLACK MOUNTAIN

To Telstra Tower

Park

Commonwealth Park

Commonwealth I

Nerang Pool

Regatta Pt M

National Capital Exhibition Regatta Pt

Captain Cook Memorial Water Jet G

Commonwealth Avenue Bridge

Russell

Blundell's Cottage E

Central Basin

Kings Park

West Basin

Acton Pk ALBERT

Springbank Island

Acton

Peninsula Q

National Museum of Australia

Hospital Pt

West Lake

Lake Burley Griffin

Blue Gum Point

National Carillon N

Aspen Island

Grevillea Park

Lake Burley Griffin

Attunga Pt

Lennox Gardens

Lotus Bay

Stirling Park

National Library of Australia P

Questacon - the National Science & Technology Centre U

High Court of Australia L

National Gallery of Australia O

National Rose Garden

Parkes

Parkes Place

National Rose Garden

Old Parliament House R

East Basin

Kings Avenue Bridge

Prime Minister's Lodge T

Yarralumla

CEG Gram Junior

Capital Hill

Parliament House S

Barton

Telopea Pk Sch

Kingston

Boat Harbour

Deakin

Deakin Oval

The Grange

Church of England Girls Grammar

Latrobe Park

Forrest

Forrest Primary

Manuka Oval P

Kingston Oval

Canberra P

Collins Park

Red Hill

© UNIVERSAL PRESS PTY LTD 2002

Griffith

Owens Oval St Edmunds College

Mildura ST

HUME

Historic Attractions

Australian National University

Occupying 145ha of Canberra City, the ANU was the first Australian research-based university; it was inaugurated in 1946. By 1960 ANU had begun to award undergraduate degrees. Three Nobel Prizes have been won by ANU researchers, and the **ANU Library** holds around 2 million books. Wander the landscaped campus dotted with native and exotic tree species, or perhaps drop into the **Drill Hall Gallery** and see some free exhibitions. Ph: (02) 6249 5111, or visit: www.anu.edu.au

Australian War Memorial

The Australian War Memorial—the most popular museum in the country—commemorates the sacrifices the men and women who served this country in war and in peacekeeping efforts made. The memorial is internationally recognised for its exhibitions. The Hall of Memory, the Tomb of the Unknown Australian Soldier, the Pool of Reflection and the Roll of Honour are the focal points of the memorial. **The ANZAC Hall**, completed in 2001, showcases a large technology collection. The redeveloped **World War II Gallery** and the Bradbury Aircraft Hall should not be missed. Ph: (02) 6243 4211 or visit: www.awm.gov.au

Blundell's Cottage

For more than 30 years this cottage has been a genuine museum of life before the city's existence. It was built in 1860 on the **Molonglo River**, and was originally part of the Campbell family's 'Duntroon' estate of 119km^2. Ph: (02) 6273 2667

Calthorpes' House

Built in 1927, Calthorpes' contains original furnishings, appliances and memorabilia, which reflect early life in Canberra. It is only open for tours at certain times. Ph: (02) 6295 1945

Hyatt Hotel Canberra

The Hyatt Hotel is Canberra's premier address, opened in 1924, it was originally named 'Hotel Canberra'. Today it is a sympathetically restored showcase of original Art Deco architecture. Surrounded by landscaped gardens, the Hyatt boasts comfort and luxury, modern casual cuisine and sophisticated restaurants, and also provides business and conference facilities. Ph: (02) 6270 1234 or visit: www.hyatt.com

Lanyon

This historic station homestead is surrounded by gardens and out-buildings, with guided and audio tours available. **The Sidney Nolan Gallery** is also located here and features the artist's works and changing exhibitions of modern Australian art. Enjoy a picnic in the garden or light meal in the cafe. Ph: (02) 6237 5136

National Archives of Australia

A visit to the National Archives is an exploration into the past; a place that holds the memories of the nation. Take a look at the evolving exhibitions, peruse original files, photographs, posters, maps and paintings in the reading room, or perhaps enjoy a film or audio recording. Located just behind **Old Parliament House**, the secrets of the nation are just waiting to be discovered. Ph: (02) 6212 3600 or visit: www.naa.gov.au

National Dinosaur Museum

Located in **Gold Creek Village** off the Barton Hwy, the National Dinosaur Museum displays full-sized dinosaur replicas, information panels, fossils of plants and fish dating to 500 million

Re-creation of the Battle of Lone Pine (1915), Australian War Memorial

Australian Capital Territory

National Museum of Australia on Acton Peninsula, Lake Burley Griffin

years ago, and a discovery area where children can build a dinosaur and investigate the process of their extinction. Ph: 1800 35 6000 or visit: www.nationaldinosaurmuseum. com.au

National Museum of Australia

Opened in March 2001 for the Centenary of Federation celebrations, the National Museum of Australia is an architecturally striking configuration of structures. Located on the **Acton Peninsula** it showcases the history of the nation, and has an outdoor amphitheatre, an Aboriginal Gallery, and evolving exhibition halls. Ph: (02) 6208 5000 or visit: www.nma.gov.au

Nature and Animal Attractions

Australian National Botanic Gardens

Located in **Acton** on the lower slopes of **Black Mountain**, the Australian National Botanic Gardens maintains and displays a diverse

collection of native Australian flora. With a visitor centre, bookshop, cafe and free guided walks, the gardens offer a wonderful outdoor experience. Take a picnic and wander through the Rainforest Gully, Rock Garden, Eucalypt Lawn and Mallee Shrublands. Ph: (02) 6250 9540 or visit: www.anbg.gov.au

Australian Reptile Park

Discover the history and evolution of our reptiles, or examine live specimens close up. The Australian Reptile Park, a fascinating place, is open 364 days a year and is an educational adventure for the whole family. It is located in **Gold Creek Village** off the Barton Hwy. Ph: (02) 6254 8533

Ginninderra Falls

The falls are located about a 20min drive from the city centre, situated in a bushland park on the **Murrumbidgee River** and **Ginninderra Gorge**. Picnic, BBQ, swim, hire a canoe, abseil or walk

along scenic trails that range from 10min to 2hrs. Ph: (02) 6278 4222 or visit: ginninderrafalls@cyberone.com.au

National Zoo and Aquarium

Australia's only zoo and aquarium combined, the National Zoo and Aquarium is situated on 8ha only 5min from the city centre at **Scrivener Dam**. The natural enclosures are vast and there are educational guided tours available. Ph: (02) 6287 1211 or visit: www.zooquarium.com.au

Cultural Attractions

Captain Cook Memorial Water Jet

Constructed by the Commonwealth Government in 1970, the Captain Cook Memorial Jet commemorates the bicentenary of James Cook's discovery of the east coast of Australia. Similar to the Jet d'eau in Geneva, Switzerland, the water jet is located in **Lake Burley Griffin** and can be seen from most points along the lake.

Embassies

There are around 80 diplomatic missions in Canberra, creating a cultural diversity and contributing architectural masterpieces to the cityscape. Some of the embassies and high commissions are open to visitors, but many are just open for business. Still, it is worth driving through **Yarralumla** to look at the different architectural styles of the buildings.

High Court of Australia

The highest point in the Australian judicial system, the High Court was permanently transferred from Sydney to Canberra in May 1980. Located on the shores of **Lake Burley Griffin**, it is adjacent to the National Gallery of Australia. Opened by Her Majesty Queen Elizabeth II, it is 40m tall at its highest point. The Public Hall is an unusual venue for functions and exhibitions, and a small theatre together with display cases offer an understanding of the court's history and the workings of the judicial system. Ph: (02) 6270 6811 or visit: www.hcourt.gov.au

National Carillon

A gift from the British Government for the 50th Anniversary of the National Capital, the carillon is situated on **Aspen Island**, Lake Burley Griffin. With 53 bronze bells, it is large by international standards. All styles of music are played by different carillonists throughout the year. Ph: (02) 6271 2888 or visit: www.nationalcapital.gov.au

National Gallery of Australia

The National Gallery of Australia is located on the shores of Lake Burley Griffin and contains one of the finest collections of art in the country. With travelling exhibitions, a children's gallery, sculpture garden, guided and audio tours, educational services, a cafe and restaurant, Gallery Shop and free parking both above and underground, the National Gallery is worth a whole day's outing. Ph: (02) 6240 6502 or visit: www.nga.gov.au

National Library of Australia

Situated on the shore of Lake Burley Griffin, the National Library offers free entry and a range of reading rooms, lounges, and changing exhibitions. There are facilities for people with a disability and the vision impaired. Ph: General; (02) 6262 1111, Events; (02) 6292 1699, or visit: www.nla.gov.au

National Portrait Gallery

Located in **Old Parliament House**, the National Portrait Gallery is one of only four in the world. Portraits of the famous, from Captain Cook, to sporting heroes, politicians, musicians, scientists, superstars and criminals adorn the walls of refurbished rooms in the building. Open every day except Christmas, a small entry fee applies. Ph: (02) 6270 8288 or visit: www.portrait.gov.au

Royal Australian Mint

The Mint is a fully functional money factory located in **Deakin**. With an extensive coin collection and an informative hands-on experience, the Mint is a fascinating destination for all ages. Ph: (02) 6202 6819 or visit: www.ramint.gov.au

Science and Technology Attractions

Australian Institute of Sport

The Australian Institute of Sport (AIS) is situated in **Bruce**. Visitors to the institute can take a tour with an elite Australian athlete; catch a glimpse of gymnasts and swimmers in training; test personal skills in the interactive sports exhibit,

18ft skiffs on Lake Burley Griffin

FLORIADE (AUSTRALIA'S CELEBRATION OF SPRING)

From mid-Sept to mid-Oct each year, a floral display that rivals all others in the country is held in **Commonwealth Park**. More than a million flowering bulbs and annuals bloom around the pools, streams, marsh gardens and sculptures of the park, which is located on the shores of Lake Burley Griffin. Private gardens are also opened and there are demonstrations and talks about flowers and gardening, as well as family entertainment. It is one of the major attractions of the city in spring and is accompanied by other events held throughout the capital. Visit: www.floriadeaustralia.com

Floriade Spring Festival, Commonwealth Park

Sportex; see the latest exhibitions in sporting technology, equipment and clothing; have a bite to eat at the Time Out Cafe; or visit the AIS shop for souvenirs and gifts. Ph: (02) 6214 1010 or visit: www.ausport.gov.au/aistours.html

Canberra Space Dome

Only a 5min drive from the city centre in **Dickson**, the Canberra Space Dome is one of Australia's best public observatories. The domed theatre offers unique shows to educate children and adults alike, while the 4 research-grade telescopes provide the opportunity to view the night sky. Ph: (02) 6248 5333 or visit: www.ctuc.asn.au/planetarium

CSIRO Discovery

This relatively new complex on the slopes of **Black Mountain** is 'an interactive showcase of Australian scientific innovation'. Exhibits explore CSIRO research in health, agriculture, manufacturing industries and the environment. Great for kids and anyone with an interest in science, the Discovery Centre is a place of Australian achievements in scientific research. Ph: (02) 6246 4646

Mt Stromlo Observatory

Open 9.30am–4.30pm, the observatory houses 3 working telescopes including a 188cm giant. A guided heritage tour around the observatory is provided. There is a gift shop, cafe and astronomy exhibits. Ph: (02) 6125 0232 or visit: www.mso.anu.edu.au/msovc

Questacon—The National Science and Technology Centre

Known as the 'hands on science and technology centre,' Questacon offers over 200 different exhibitions and programs. Officially opened in November 1988, it is the leading interactive science and technology centre in Australia, attracting approximately 300 000 visitors annually. Questacon certainly achieves its goal of 'making science fun and relevant for everyone'. Ph: (02) 6270 2800 or visit: www.questacon.edu.au

Telstra Tower

Soaring 195m above the peak of **Black Mountain**, Telstra Tower boasts an amazing 360^0 view of the Australian Capital Territory. The tower is open day and night, so visitors can venture onto the viewing platforms or the viewing gallery at their convenience. There is an exhibition gallery, theatrette, licensed revolving restaurant, cafe and gift shop. Admission charges apply. Ph: 1800 806 718

Political Attractions

Parliament House

The central point of the city, the flagpole of Parliament House is 81m high, and the flag itself is 12m by 6m. The landscaped gardens and lawns that surround the building are planted with native

AUSTRALIAN CAPITAL TERRITORY   **133**

species, while the more formal gardens feature exotics. Free tickets are available to Question Time in the **House of Representatives**; tickets are not required for Question Time in the **Senate**. Ph: (02) 6277 5399 or visit: www.aph.gov.au

Old Parliament House

Originally in use from 1927 until 1988, Old Parliament House is open for viewing and visitors can see the chambers where former Prime Ministers—Menzies, Evatt, Casey, Whitlam and Hawke among them—performed. Now housing the **National Portrait Gallery**, Old Parliament House is situated directly in front of Parliament House. The lawn in front of the building is the place of the **Aboriginal Tent Embassy**, and has been the site of many protests by conservationists, farmers and Vietnam War objectors.
Ph: (02) 6270 8222 or visit: www.oldparliamenthouse.gov.au

Cockington Green, Canberra

Hot-air balloon in flight near Black Mountain and Telstra Tower

Other Attractions

Canberra Tour Bus

A 24-hr valid ticket available from the bus, **Canberra Visitors Centre** or hotel, will secure easy hop on, hop off transport around the major city attractions. For more information on timetables and destinations, Ph: 0500 505 012 or visit: www.city-sight-seeing.com

Cockington Green

Located in **Gold Creek Village**, this award-winning land of miniature buildings (one-twelfth scale) and gardens is open 7 days a week. View the modellers' workshop, enjoy a steam train ride, have a coffee or light meal, picnic or BBQ, and even buy a souvenir to take home. With access and facilities for people with a disability, Cockington Green will provide opportunities to entertain the whole family. Ph: (02) 6230 2273 or visit: www.cockington-green.com.au

Ferry Cruises on the Lake

For a relaxed view of the city's attractions, why not take a ferry around Lake Burley Griffin. For more information contact the Canberra Visitors Centre.
(02) 6205 0044

Kamberra Wine Tourism Complex

This unique urban winery, just north of the city centre, is a focal point for the Canberra Region wine industry and local vineyards.
Ph: (02) 6262 2333

Trail Rides and Hot-Air Balloon Tours

For the more adventurous, take a horseride 10min from Parliament House, or a hot-air balloon flight above the city for a very different view of the sights. For more information contact the Canberra Visitors Centre.
Ph: (02) 6205 0044

Australian Capital Territory

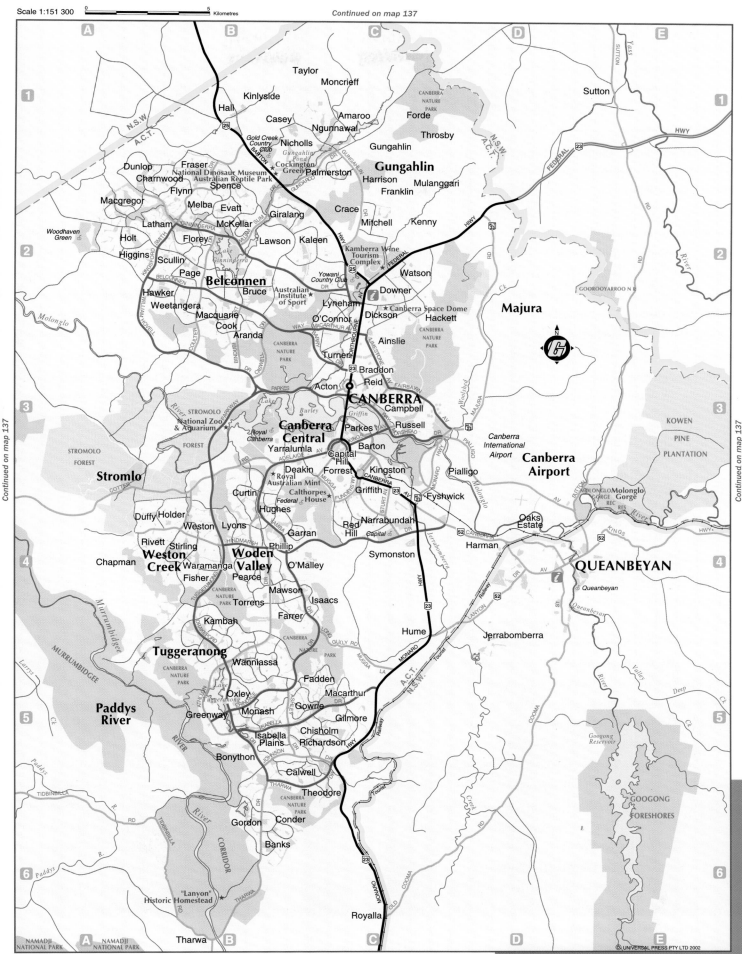

© UNIVERSAL PRESS PTY LTD 2002

REGIONAL ATTRACTIONS

Although the majority of the tourist attractions are in and around the city centre, there are a few regional attractions worth investigating in the surrounding area. These are mainly reserves, parklands and recreational spots, which some believe are the hidden wonders of the Australian Capital Territory.

Canberra Deep Space Communications Complex

Located in the countryside SW of Canberra, 5km from Tidbinbilla NR and off Tourist Route 5, is the only NASA deep space tracking station in the country. Within the grounds is the **Canberra Space Centre**, which showcases the history of space exploration and Australia's role in it. Tour the centre and see an Andy Thomas space suit, real space food, a piece of the moon obtained from *Apollo 11* astronauts and interactive exhibits and displays. Views from the centre take in the 4 large antennae used to communicate with spacecraft and for making radio investigations of space. One of them is 70m in diameter—the largest steerable antenna in the Southern Hemisphere. The centre has the Moonrock Cafe, picnic and BBQ facilities. Ph: (02) 6201 7880 or visit www.cdscc.nasa.gov

Corin Forest

Known as the Australian Capital Territory's '**mountain playground**', Corin Forest lies at an altitude of 1200m. The region averages 10 snowfalls a year, but with the resort's snowmaking facilities there is a reliable snow cover all winter. Corin Forest is a very accessible daytrip destination from the city (around 45min from Parliament House, and 18min from the Tuggeranong Valley). It boasts an 800m bobsled run, an alpine slide, cafe, and a dual 350m flying fox all year round, as well as tobogganing and snow play in winter. It is open weekends, public holidays and Australian Capital Territory school holidays. Ph: (02) 6247 2250 or visit: www.corin.com.au

Murrumbidgee River Corridor

The Murrumbidgee River Corridor runs from the mountains in the south through some of the most picturesque countryside that the Australian Capital Territory has to offer. Enjoy a picnic, walk along rocky gorges and planned trails, or have a splash in the cool waters of the river. The only place to camp along the Murrumbidgee is at **Cotter campground** where there are BBQ, toilet and hot shower facilities, but no power. Ph: (02) 6207 2425

Tidbinbilla Nature Reserve

Tidbinbilla NR is nestled in the slopes of the **Tidbinbilla Range** about 40min drive from Canberra city off Tourist Route 5. Experience Australian wildlife in specially designed enclosures. Walk amongst the koalas, kangaroos, wallabies, emus and waterbirds or maybe catch a glimpse of the elusive platypus. Regular ranger-guided tours are available but bookings are essential. Tidbinbilla is open every day, except Christmas Day, from 9am to 6pm (later in summer). There are walking trails, BBQs and picnic areas, a shop in the visitors centre and a cafe. Ph: (02) 6205 1233 or visit: www.environment.act.gov.au

Gilbraltar Rocks, Tidbinbilla Nature Reserve

Australian Capital Territory

Scale 1:400 000

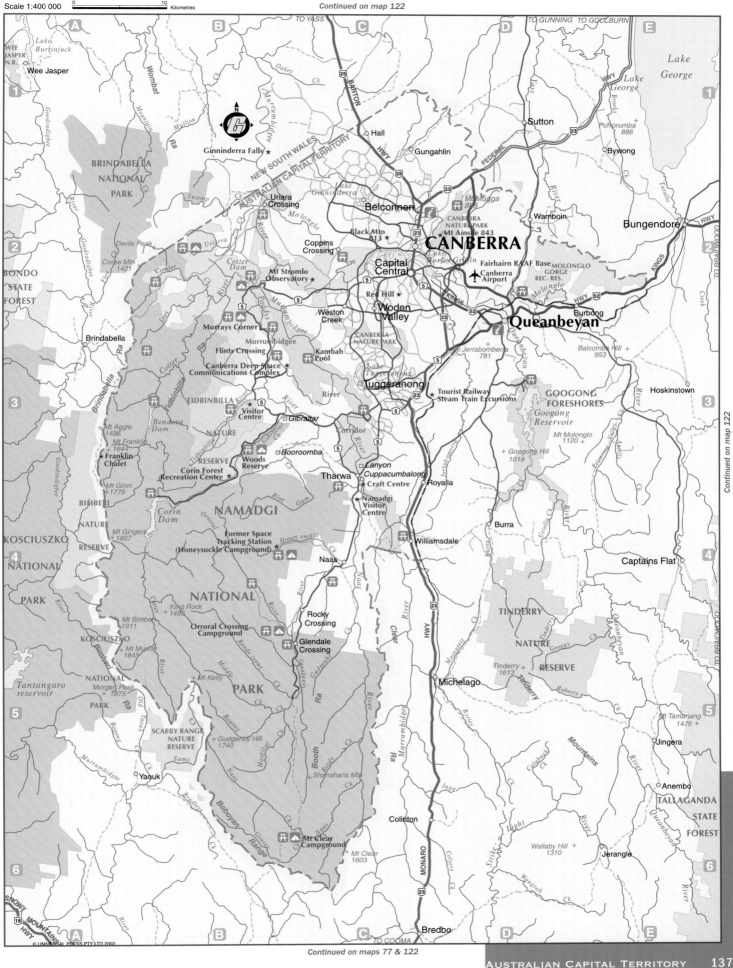

VICTORIA

Covering 227 416km² of the south-eastern corner of Australia, Victoria is a relatively compact state, the second smallest after Tasmania. The state's mostly temperate climate has four distinct seasons, each with its own attractions. As a result of its manageable size and efficient road system, travelling the state is easy and comfortable. Transport options are excellent: coaches, trains and planes carry visitors into and around the state, and for those who want to explore independently, touring by car is convenient. Most places can be reached within a day's drive of the capital city, Melbourne, and there is a huge array of natural, cultural and historic areas just waiting to be discovered.

Victoria packs a lot within its boundaries. The Murray River stretches along the border with New South Wales and is a delightful destination in itself. The southern coastline is spectacular and varied, taking in the Great Ocean Road to the west, Wilsons Promontory and the beautiful Gippsland Lakes area to the east. Victoria's magnificent

Victoria: The Garden State

◈ Population: 4 712 170
◈ Total area: 227 416km²
◈ % of Australia: 2.96%
◈ Length of coastline: 2512km
◈ Floral emblem: Pink Heath
◈ Fauna emblem: Leadbeaters Possum

 Tourist information

Melbourne Visitor Centre
Federation Square
Cnr Swanston and Flinders Sts
Melbourne, Vic 3000
Ph: (03) 9658 9658
www.visitvictoria.com

Victorian Tourism Information Service
Ph: 132 842

Main ATTRACTIONS

❖ The Dandenongs
Renowned for their green hills, lookouts and pretty townships, these ranges are only one hour from Melbourne.

❖ Echuca
On the banks of the Murray, Echuca is home to the largest collection of paddlesteamers in Australia.

❖ Gippsland Lakes
A boating and fishing paradise, this is the most extensive system of estuarine lagoons in Australia.

❖ The Goldfields
Ballarat, the goldfield capital since the 1850s, is dotted with ornate Victorian buildings and large parks.

❖ Grampians NP
Over 400 hundred million years old, this national park is a spectacular landscape of rock formations, lakes and waterfalls.

❖ Great Ocean Road
Beginning at Torquay and winding 285km west along the coast to Warrnambool, this is truly one of the world's most spectacular coastal routes.

❖ Phillip Island
Mostly known for its Penguin Parade, Phillip Island attracts 50 000 visitors annually.

❖ Spa Country
A region of historic towns, Spa Country is said to have mineral water springs with a quality equal to anywhere in the world.

❖ Victorian Alps
Home to some of Australia's premier ski resorts, the southernmost part of the Great Dividing Range is protected by national parks.

Alpine region has much to explore and the goldfields' districts reveal an exciting episode in the state's history. Tranquil lakes, an exciting selection of national parks, cool forests and fertile countryside await the visitor, with accessible cities, towns and villages offering their hospitality.

Victoria caters well for the discerning traveller. Fresh produce is a specialty all over the state, with specific gourmet focal points like the Milawa Gourmet Region near Wangaratta and the Gourmet Deli Trail in West Gippsland. Wine-lovers can select from 14 winery regions and over 350 wineries, ranging from the Grampians in the south-west to Rutherglen in the north-east. Victorian vineyards are renowned for producing excellent vintages for the Australian and international market.

Photo above: Twelve Apostles, Port Campbell NP, Great Ocean Road

THE GARDEN STATE

The 3rd British Colony to be established in Australia, Victoria was a collection of small, unauthorised settlements before 1834. In 1851, Victoria separated from New South Wales, so that it too did not end up becoming a penal settlement. When gold was discovered in **Ballarat** the same year, there was a rush of immigrants from all over the world, as well as from within the country, resulting in a explosion of Victoria's population within a year.

Cities such as **Melbourne** and **Bendigo** were originally built on wealth accumulated from the gold diggings. Interestingly, the land on which Melbourne is sited was 'bought' by John Batman in 1834 from its Aboriginal owners for 20 blankets, 30 knives, 12 red shirts, 4 flannel jackets and 50 handkerchiefs. It remained a small and slow-growing town until the discovery of gold, when it boomed and the population flourished.

Today, Victoria produces almost one-quarter of Australia's gross value of agricultural products. Together, the agriculture and food industry account for 31% of the state's export income. The main rural industries of the state are wheat, vegetables and wool. On a smaller scale, beef, dairy products, wine, dry vine fruits and timber are also important to its economy. Oil and gas fields in the **Bass Strait** produce more than 60% of the country's crude oil, and brown coal comes from the **Latrobe Valley** coalfields.

Like New South Wales, temperatures are moderate, though less predictable in some areas. The best times to tour this state are spring, late summer and autumn. The northern and western plains of Victoria are much hotter, drier and prone to drought.

Victoria can be broadly divided into 5 main regions. In the north-

Cattle in the Kiewa Valley

east highlands, the peaks of the **Great Dividing Range** attract skiers in winter and bushwalkers and climbers in the summer. The southeast is punctuated with lakes, caves, forests, waterways and coastal scenery, while the central west is a preserved goldfield heartland of goldrush and spa towns. Western districts are characterised by open pastoral lands and the striking **Grampians NP**. The 285km stretch of the **Great Ocean Rd** is a major attraction of this region, offering some of the most amazing coastal scenery in the world. The **Murray River region**, which forms the northern border of the state, boasts quaint old river ports, wineries and citrus groves.

Temperate rainforest, Lind NP

Victoria

TOURISM REGION HIGHLIGHTS

Victoria has a great deal to offer within its relatively small area. The southern coastline includes the world-famous Great Ocean Rd and the Gippsland Lakes region. The High Country offers superb mountain scenery and the goldfields recall a colourful past. A few hours' drive from Melbourne— the sophisticated 'cultural capital' of Australia—reveals rolling farmlands, picturesque winery regions, temperate forests and the mighty Murray River.

A Melbourne (pp.146–153)
Albert Park; Colonial Stadium; Crown Entertainment Complex; Federation Square; Fitzroy Gardens; Maritime Museum; Melbourne Aquarium; Melbourne Cricket Ground; Melbourne Museum; Melbourne trams; Melbourne Zoo; National Gallery; Queen Victoria Market; Royal Botanic Gardens; Southgate

B Goldfields (pp.158–159)
Ballarat; Bendigo; Castlemaine; Clunes; Maldon; Maryborough; Pyrenees Ranges; Sovereign Hill

C Goulburn Murray Waters
Alexandra; Euroa; Goulburn Valley; Lake Eildon; Nagambie Lakes; Nagambie Wineries; Shepparton; Strathbogie Ranges; Trawool Valley

D The Grampians (pp.194–195)
Ararat; Byaduk Caves; Grampians NP; Halls Gap; Hamilton; Little Desert NP; Mount Arapiles; Stawell

E Great Ocean Road (pp.199–201)
Apollo Bay; Cape Bridgewater; Lorne; Lower Glenelg NP; Melba Gully SP; Otway NP; Port Campbell NP; Port Fairy; Portland; The Shipwreck Coast; Torquay; Tower Hill; Warrnambool

F Lakes and Wilderness
Bairnsdale; Buchan Caves; Croajingolong NP; Gippsland Lakes; Lakes Entrance; Mallacoota; Mitchell River NP; Omeo; Orbost Rainforest Centre; Snowy River

G Legends Wine and High Country (pp.186–187)
Alpine NP; Beechworth; Benalla; Bright; Chiltern; Glenrowan; King Valley; Mansfield; Milawa Vineyards; Mount Beauty; Mount Buffalo NP; Mount Buller, Falls Creek, Mount Hotham and Dinner Plain Ski Resorts; Wangaratta; Yackandandah

H Macedon Ranges and Spa Country (pp.166–167)
Daylesford; Hanging Rock; Hepburn Springs; Macedon Ranges Wineries; Mount Macedon; Organ Pipes NP

I Melbourne's Bays and Peninsulas (pp.152–153)
Arthur's Seat; Bellarine Peninsula; Cape Schank; Frankston; Geelong; Hastings; Mornington Peninsula; Port Melbourne; Port Phillip; Portsea; Queenscliff; St Kilda; Sorrento; Werribee Park; Werribee Zoo

J Mildura and Murray Outback
Murray Sunset NP; Ouyen; Wyperfeld NP

K The Murray
Albury-Wodonga; Corryong; Lake Hume; Mildura; Murray River; Port of Echuca; Rutherglen Wineries; Swan Hill; Yarrawonga

L Phillip Island and Gippsland Discovery (pp.164–165 & 178–179)
Churchill Island; Coal Creek, Korumburra; Gippsland Heritage Park, Moe; Gourmet Deli Region; Latrobe Valley; Mount Baw Baw; Ninety Mile Beach; Penguin Parade; Phillip Island; PowerWorks, Morwell; Sale; Strzelecki Ranges; Tarra-Bulga NP; Walhalla; Wilsons Promontory; Wonthaggi State Coal Mine

M Yarra Valley, Dandenongs and the Ranges (pp.170–171)
Dandenong Ranges; Healesville Sanctuary; Lake Mountain; Marysville; Mystic Mountains; *Puffing Billy* Railway; William Ricketts Sanctuary; Yarra Valley Wineries

The Crags, near Port Fairy

NATIONAL PARKS

Victoria's national parks protect a great variety of landscapes—from beaches, rainforests and snowy mountains to semi-arid areas. They offer a range of scenery, natural features and cultural heritage, as well as a variety of recreational activities. A few of the most popular and diverse national parks are listed here.

A Alpine NP

(Map 209, G5)
Stretching to the New South Wales border, the Alpine NP is the largest park in Victoria at 6605km^2 and protects most of the state's High Country. The park offers spectacular gorges, waterfalls, wild rivers, green valleys and extensive winter snowfields. It is the perfect destination for downhill and cross-country skiers in winter. At other times of the year the park offers swimming, walking, 4WDing, cycling, horseriding, canoeing, and places of historical interest. Be prepared for sudden weather changes—snow can fall at any time, even in summer.

B Croajingolong NP

(Map 214, B5)
Located 450km east of Melbourne, Croajingolong NP is a pristine environment of eucalypt forests, rainforests, coastal heathlands, estuaries and sandy beaches. Created in 1979, the 875km^2 park

is home to over 1000 species of native plants as well as more than 300 bird species. Enjoy short or long walks, camping, swimming, diving, sailing and sea kayaking and the great 4WDing opportunities.

C Grampians NP **(Map 195, B3)**

In the central west of the state, the 1672km^2 Grampians NP has some of the state's most rugged and spectacular scenery. The Grampians are widely known for their spring-time display of wildflowers and their Aboriginal rock-art sites. Popular activities include walking, cycling, rockclimbing, nature studies and scenic driving. There are picnic and camping areas, toilet facilities and walking tracks. Visit the Grampians National Park and

Brambuk Cultural Centre at **Halls Gap** for park information.

D Little Desert NP

(Map 206, B4)
North-west of the Grampians, Little Desert NP is a great choice for 4WDing, camping and walking. Around 1320km^2, the park—a desert in name only—has many types of vegetation and abundant native fauna. Winter and spring are good times to visit the state's drier north-west parks as summer can be very hot. North of Little Desert NP, **Wyperfeld** and **Murray-Sunset** national parks protect extensive areas of mallee eucalypt vegetation, and **Hattah-Kulkyne** also has huge river red gum trees and lakes filled by the **Murray River**.

facts

❖ No. of parks/reserves: 108
❖ Total area: 30 900km2
❖ % of state: 13.6%

Rainbow lorikeets, *Trichoglossus haematodus*

Victoria

E Mornington Peninsula NP
(Map 152, D5)

Only 95km from Melbourne, Mornington Peninsula NP is a 40km sweep of ocean coastline and hinterland. With picnic areas, lookouts and other facilities, the park is a haven for swimmers, surfers, anglers and walkers. Walking tracks allow for both short easy strolls and more challenging hikes. The historic military fortifications at **Point Nepean**, which were out of bounds to the public for more than 100 years, are now one of the 27km^2 park's major attractions.

F Mount Buffalo NP
(Map 187, B2)

Mount Buffalo NP, established over 100 years ago, is 350km NE of Melbourne and covers 310km^2. It's a year-round family attraction, with snowsports in winter and wildflowers and walking in summer. It is notable as one of Victoria's top hang-gliding and rockclimbing spots, and offers wonderful views. Visitors can camp or stay in comfort at the historic Chalet or at Tatra Lodge. Facilities include picnic areas, BBQs, toilets and well-marked walking tracks.

G Port Campbell NP
(Map 200, D5)

Port Campbell NP, a narrow coastal strip along the **Great Ocean Rd**, has some of Australia's most recognised features, including the Twelve Apostles—towering rock islands rising out of the surf. There are also sheer cliffs, historic shipwreck sites and good walking opportunities.

H Wilsons Promontory NP
(Map 179, C3)

Wilsons Promontory NP, the southernmost tip of mainland Australia, is one of Victoria's most beautiful and popular parks. The park protects some 500km^2 of eucalypt forest, rainforest, heathland, sandy

Treeferns, Wilsons Promontory NP

beaches, granite peaks, headlands and their resident wildlife. It is 200km SE of Melbourne, about a 3hr drive, and is surrounded by marine parks that protect underwater ecosystems and historic shipwrecks. Swimming, surfing, snorkelling and scuba diving are popular attractions and walking opportunities range from short 1 or 2hr strolls to overnight hikes, which require permits. Camping, lodge and hut accommodation is available.

I Yarra Ranges NP
(Map 212, C2)

Established in 1995, Yarra Ranges NP, about 100km NE of Melbourne, is home to some of Australia's tallest trees. Much of the park's 760km^2 are set aside for water catchment and not open to the public. Elsewhere there are scenic drives, walking tracks and picnic areas. In winter, there are opportunities for cross-country skiing or snow play at **Mount Donna Buang** and **Lake Mountain**. Approach the park via Warburton, Healesville or Marysville.

National Park Head Office

Parks Victoria
Level 10, 535 Bourke St
Melbourne, VIC 3000
Ph: 13 19 63
www.parkweb.vic.gov.au

WINERIES

William Ryrie planted Victoria's first vines in the **Yarra Valley** in 1838. Largely through the efforts of Swiss immigrants, further vineyards were established in **Geelong**, the Yarra Valley and suburban Melbourne. Large suburban vineyards were located at South Yarra, **Toorak** and **Brighton** and by 1890 Victoria was the largest producer of wine in the country.

The Victorian wine industry was, however, devastated before the turn of the century, first by an economic downturn, then by an outbreak of *phylloxera*, a tiny vine eating aphid. Most vineyards had to be destroyed and their soils chemically sterilized.

The industry experienced a renaissance in the 1960s as table wines regained popularity. There are now over 350 wineries in Victoria, more than any other state. Over 200 of them welcome visitors to their cellar doors and about 100 of these are within an hour's drive from Melbourne.

Scotchmans Hill vineyard on the Bellarine Peninsula

A Alpine Valleys, King Valley and Glenrowan

This fertile region of north-east Victoria showcases century-old wineries such as Brown Brothers of Milawa and Baileys of Glenrowan. Several King Valley wineries had a much later start when Italian tobacco farmers switched to grape-growing in the 1970s. The area is renowned for complex red wines of great longevity. Recent innovations include Italian varietals such as sangiovese, nebbiolo and barbera.

B Ballarat (p.156, 158–159)

The wine history of this goldrush town began as recently as the 1970s. There are now about 10 wineries around the city offering mainly chardonnay and pinot noir. Yellowglen is one of Victoria's top-selling sparkling labels.

C Bendigo and Heathcote (p.158–160)

In 1893, this was the first Victorian region to be struck with the *phylloxera* problem. Nowadays it is prime red-wine country, producing superb shiraz and full-flavoured cabernet from small family-owned vineyards.

D Geelong (p.172)

Once the most significant wine region in Victoria, Geelong and the neighbouring **Bellarine Peninsula** still support a number of quality wineries. The region has a cool, maritime climate and an extended growing season producing cabernet sauvignon, shiraz and chardonnay.

E Gippsland

A number of small family wineries are spread across Gippsland from **Phillip Island** to **Lakes Entrance**. Some of the finest pinot noirs in Australia have come from these tiny vineyards, as well as classic varieties such as shiraz, cabernet sauvignon, chardonnay, riesling and sauvignon blanc.

F Goulburn Valley

The large region between **Seymour** and **Echuca** has a warm climate that is ideal for Rhone varietals. Marsanne, shiraz, viognier, grenache, roussanne, and mourvedre are all planted, as well as riesling, chardonnay, cabernet sauvignon, pinot noir and merlot. The beautiful old Chateau Tahbilk and Mitchelton are well-known historic wineries in this area.

Victoria

G Grampians (p.194-195)

Beneath the dramatic backdrop of the Grampian Mountains, wineries around **Ararat** produce fine shiraz, riesling, chardonnay, pinot noir and cabernet sauvignon. The Great Western district is synonymous with sparkling wine in Australia.

H Macedon Ranges

(p.166-167)

The rolling hills around **Kyneton**, **Lancefield** and **Woodend** have major plantings of chardonnay and pinot noir, much of which are used for methode champenoise wines. Shiraz does especially well in the cool climate and granite soils.

I Mornington Peninsula

(see p.152-153)

Blessed with rich soil, a cool climate, adequate rainfall during the growing season and high summer humidity, the Peninsula supports about 40 wineries producing fine table wines. Predominant varieties are chardonnay and pinot noir, used in table and sparkling wines, as well as cabernet sauvignon, merlot, shiraz, riesling, sauvignon blanc, semillon and pinot gris.

J Murray Valley and Swan Hill

The Murray River region between **Mildura** and Swan Hill basks in a sunny Mediterranean climate. Huge quantities of grapes are produced for the bulk wine and dried fruit markets, whilst smaller wineries offer high quality varietals.

K Pyrenees

Winemakers of the Pyrenees Ranges around **Avoca** and **Redbank** are famous for their minty reds, notably shiraz and cabernet sauvignon, as well as chardonnay and sauvignon blanc. The French Remy Martin group have specialised first in brandy and later in sparkling wines in the Pyrenees region.

L Rutherglen (p.191)

The Rutherglen wineries were established in the 1850s by German winemakers from the Barossa Valley. The region is best known for its unique muscats, tokays and rich red wines, but flavoursome whites and lighter reds are gaining popularity.

M Sunbury

This is the closest wine region to Melbourne, with a 150-year-old pedigree. The area is best known for shiraz, especially the Craiglee Shiraz. Other varieties include chardonnay, semillon, cabernet sauvignon, cabernet franc and pinot noir.

N Yarra Valley

The historical home of the Victorian wine industry has suffered the boom-and-bust cycle of other areas. After 80 successful years, most Yarra Valley vineyards had ceased operating by 1920. The cause was not the *phylloxera* scourge, from which the region was spared, but a growing fashion for fortified rather than table wines. After a resurgence in the 1960s there are now over 40 wineries in the area around **Yarra Glen**, **Lilydale** and **Healesville**, and the Yarra Valley attracts wine enthusiasts from around the world. Chardonnay and pinot noir are the most acclaimed grape varieties for both still and sparkling wines.

Domaine Chandon Winery in the Yarra Valley

MELBOURNE

State Orchestra of Victoria, Victorian Arts Centre

ℹ️ Tourist information

Melbourne Visitor Centre
Federation Square
Cnr Swanston and Flinders Sts
Melbourne, Vic 3000
Ph: (03) 9658 9658
www.visitvictoria.com

Victorian Tourism Information Service
Ph: 132 842

facts

- Population: 3 417 200
- Date founded: 1842
- Average temp: 20°C (Jan), 10.5°C (June)

main attractions

- **AFL (Australian Football League)**
  During the winter months, Aussie Rules Football is a Victorian obsession.

- **Lygon St**
  Renowned as one of the city's best 'eat streets', Lygon St is full of all things Italian, as well as a multicultural feast of Japanese, Lebanese, African, Greek, Chinese, Vietnamese and French flavours.

- **Old Melbourne Gaol**
  The old gaol now houses a museum with interesting exhibits.

- **Royal Botanic Gardens**
  Within walking distance of the CBD, the gardens are home to over 10 000 different plant species.

- **Shopping in Melbourne**
  Wander along Collins St, Bourke St and the streets running west off Swanston St, where most of the city's major stores, boutiques and designer label shops are found.

- **Southgate**
  On the banks of the Yarra River, there is an overwhelming selection of cafes, restaurants, bars and boutiques. Crown Casino is nearby.

- **Yarra River Cruises**
  The Yarra offers an array of cruises to enjoy year round.

The capital of the **'Garden State'**, Melbourne, is located on **Port Phillip**, with the picturesque **Yarra River** meandering through it. By any standard, it is a sophisticated and vibrant city.

The grand-scale city architecture, wide streets, symmetrical grid design and formally landscaped parks and gardens are all legacies of the goldrushes in nearby Ballarat and Bendigo. Melbourne's trams give the city an old-world charm. Quiet and pollution free, they are an efficient and attractive means of transport, quickly carrying passengers up and down the main thoroughfares. The free **City Circle Tram** transports visitors in a loop that takes in major CBD sights.

Melbourne's changeable climate is renowned, with the more marked seasonal changes giving the city its European feel. Large-scale immigration from Europe also adds to this atmosphere and, along with more recent immigration from South-East Asia, contributes to the diverse mix of cultures, foods and people, which make Melbourne the cosmopolitan city that it is today.

Places of Interest

Albert Park Ⓐ D6
Australian Grand Prix Ⓑ D6
Chinatown Ⓒ D2
Crown Casino Ⓓ B4
Federation Square Ⓔ D3
Gold Treasury Museum Ⓕ E2
Immigration Museum Ⓖ C3
Melbourne Aquarium Ⓗ C4
Melbourne Central Shopping Centre Ⓘ C2
Melbourne Cricket Ground Ⓙ E3
Melbourne Museum Ⓚ D1
Melbourne Park Ⓛ E4
Melbourne Observation Deck Ⓜ C3
Myer Music Bowl Ⓝ D4
National Gallery of Victoria Ⓞ D4
Old Melbourne Gaol Ⓟ C2
Parliament House Ⓠ D2
Polly Woodside Maritime Museum Ⓡ B4
Queen Victoria Market Ⓢ B2
Royal Botanic Gardens Ⓣ E5
Royal Exhibition Building Ⓤ D1
Shrine of Remembrance Ⓥ D5
Southgate Sheraton Towers Ⓦ C4
State Library of Victoria Ⓧ C2
Victorian Arts Centre Ⓨ D4

Princes Bridge over the Yarra River, Melbourne

Victoria

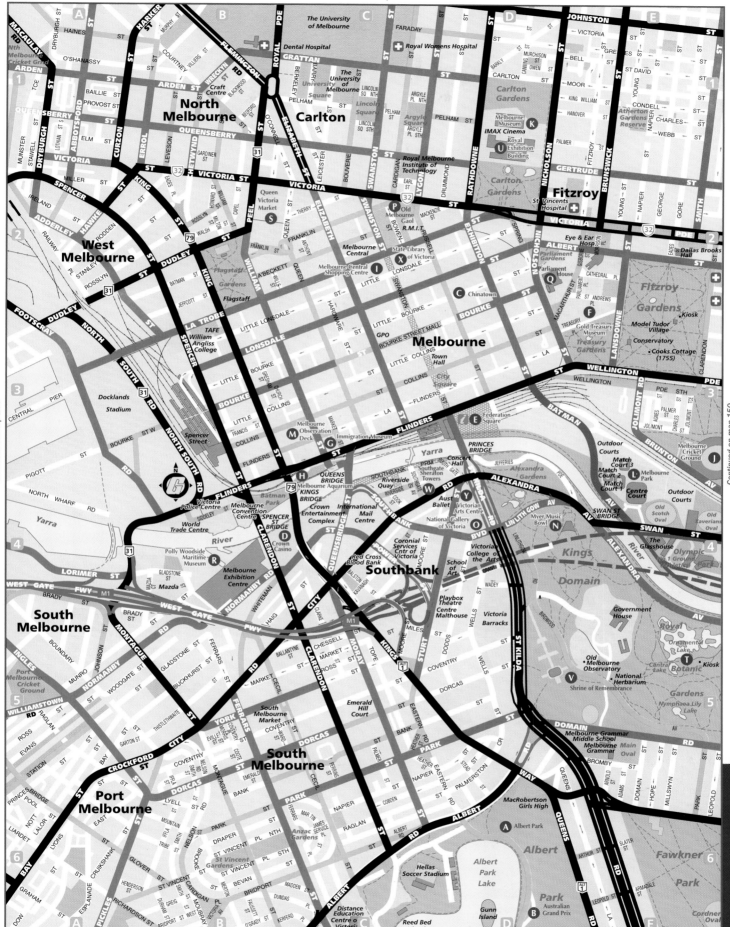

Continued on map 150

Continued on map 150

Continued on map 150

North Melbourne

Carlton

West Melbourne

Fitzroy

Melbourne

Southbank

South Melbourne

Port Melbourne

Albert Park

Fawkner Park

CBD & SUBURBS

With so much to see and do in the centre of this vibrant city, it is best explored in specific sections. For those wanting to shop there is the **Central Retail District** which is the heartbeat of Melbourne's shopping trade. **Bourke St Mall** is a popular site for big-name department stores. Not too far away, **Melbourne Central** is a 20-storey tower with cafes, restaurants and shops. Worth investigating are the **Royal Arcade** and **Centre Way** for their specialty shops and historic significance. The **Block Arcade** is very exclusive, while **Howey Place** and **Australia on Collins** are less so, but also popular shopping spots.

Chinatown is found in and around **Little Bourke St**, where Chinese business, commerce and culture have been thriving since the goldrushes of the 1850s. A popular destination for fans of authentic Chinese cuisine, Chinatown is also home to the **Chinese Museum**, an excellent showcase of Chinese culture, history and immigration.

The **Greek precinct**, at the top end of **Lonsdale St**, is a metropolis of Greek food, culture and specialty stores. With alfresco dining, visitors are tempted to sit and sample the delicacies, or just soak up some afternoon sun and traditional Greek music.

Swanston St is largely a pedestrian mall, overtaken by pavement cafes and shops. Meander along the mall and down the surrounding streets and view some of Melbourne's most historic buildings, such as **St Paul's Cathedral**, **Flinders Street Station**, **Young and Jackson's Hotel** and **Melbourne Town Hall.**

Definitely worth visiting is **Queen Victoria Market**, which contains over 1000 stalls in the indoor/outdoor area, ranging from fresh produce, deli goods, coffee stands to clothing, leather goods and manchester.

Further uptown are **Parliament House** and the **Gold Treasury Museum**. Some of the city's oldest churches are dotted along these streets, as well as many of its great old live theatres. North of the **Yarra River**, you'll find the innovative **Melbourne Aquarium** and the ultra-modern attractions of **Federation Square,** built over the railway lines.

South of the Yarra River, **Southgate** is the spot for arts and entertainment and the **Crown Entertainment Complex** includes a casino. Also in this precinct, the **Victorian Arts Centre**, with its famous spire, and the **Melbourne Concert Hall** are worth visiting. The refurbished **National Gallery of Victoria** is also situated here.

Part of the reason for Victoria's claim as the 'Garden State' is Melbourne's gracious parks, including **Flagstaff Gardens, Royal Botanic Gardens, Treasury Gardens** and **Parliament House Gardens**. Wander through these parks and discover manicured lawns and hedges, towering European trees and native Australian flora and landscapes. **Fitzroy Gardens** are home to historic **Capt Cook Cottage**.

To the North

The suburbs to the north of Melbourne are a multicultural delight, offering theatres, galleries and restaurants among the more bohemian bookshops, specialty stores and eateries. For more shopping, the streets of **Brunswick, Carlton, Collingwood, Fitzroy** and **Richmond** have an array of stores.

The **University of Melbourne** meant that **Carlton** was for a long time the place of student digs. Today, the dominant style is distinctly Italian, with restaurants, cafes, cinemas and shops lining the streets. Not too far from the university is **Melbourne Cemetery**, a unique attraction with fascinating theme tours and even an Elvis Presley memorial.

The domed **Royal Exhibition Building**, constructed in 1880 for the World Fair, is located in the picturesque **Carlton Gardens**. Today it is host to the many exhibitions, concerts, balls and expos of the city. Right next door, the very modern **Melbourne Museum** is innovative and interactive.

Leafy sea-dragon, *Phycodurus eques*, at Melbourne Aquarium

Victoria

THE MELBOURNE CUP

The most famous horse race in Australia, the Tooheys Melbourne Cup, is held at Flemington Racecourse and brings the entire country to a standstill for at least 3 minutes on the first Tuesday in November.

The Melbourne Cup has been a major sporting and social carnival since 1861. Past winners have included such legendary horses as Carbine and Phar Lap, but as a handicap race it has been won by colts and 7-year olds alike.

Almost everybody in Australia has a bet on the famous race. In Victoria the whole state takes an official holiday, as punters from around the country and overseas gather and raise their flutes of champagne to the horses, hats and fashions of the day.

Running of the Melbourne Cup at Flemington Racecourse

For lovers of nightlife, these northern suburbs are full of creative nights out. Everything from cinema, comedy, dance, theatre, jazz and rock, to world music can be found in these streets.

To the West

To the west is **Footscray** where it is worth taking the 6am breakfast tour of the **Wholesale Fruit and Vegetable Market** and the **National Flower Centre,** or perhaps a cruise on the **Maribyrnong River**.

To the East

Visit the **Melbourne Cricket Ground (MCG)**, home to Australian cricket and Aussie Rules Football, with its seating capacity of 100 000. Why not book a ticket to a cricket match or AFL game to see what the fuss is all about. Pop into the **Australian Gallery of Sport and**

Olympic Museum to find out about the stadium and history of the Olympic Games.

A must-see is the **Museum of Modern Art** at Heidelberg, where support was offered in the 1940s and 1950s to Australian artists such as Arthur Boyd, Albert Tucker, John Perceval and Sidney Nolan. The permanent exhibition is always a worthwhile experience, and there are also travelling exhibitions. The museum also has a cafe, sculpture park and beautiful gardens.

To the South

The art, culture and history of Melbourne are not limited to the CBD. In the south, galleries and shopping abound, with the added delight of beaches and parks.

St Kilda, one of the most well known spots in outer Melbourne, is not only a beachside address, but

also a cosmopolitan centre of food (don't miss the delicious cakes in Acland St), boutiques, art, entertainment and history. Some places of interest include **St Kilda Pier**; the fun attraction, **Luna Park**; the **Esplanade Hotel**; the **National** and **Astor theatres**; or perhaps even take a **Penguin Waters Cruise**.

Luna Park face, St Kilda

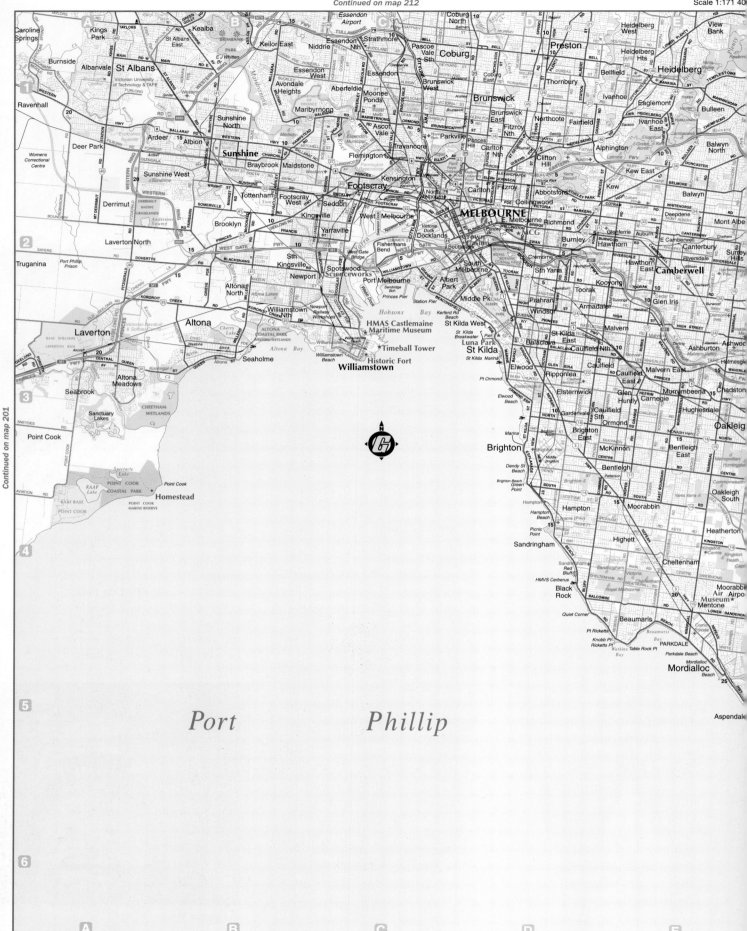

© UNIVERSAL PRESS PTY LTD 2002

Continued on map 212

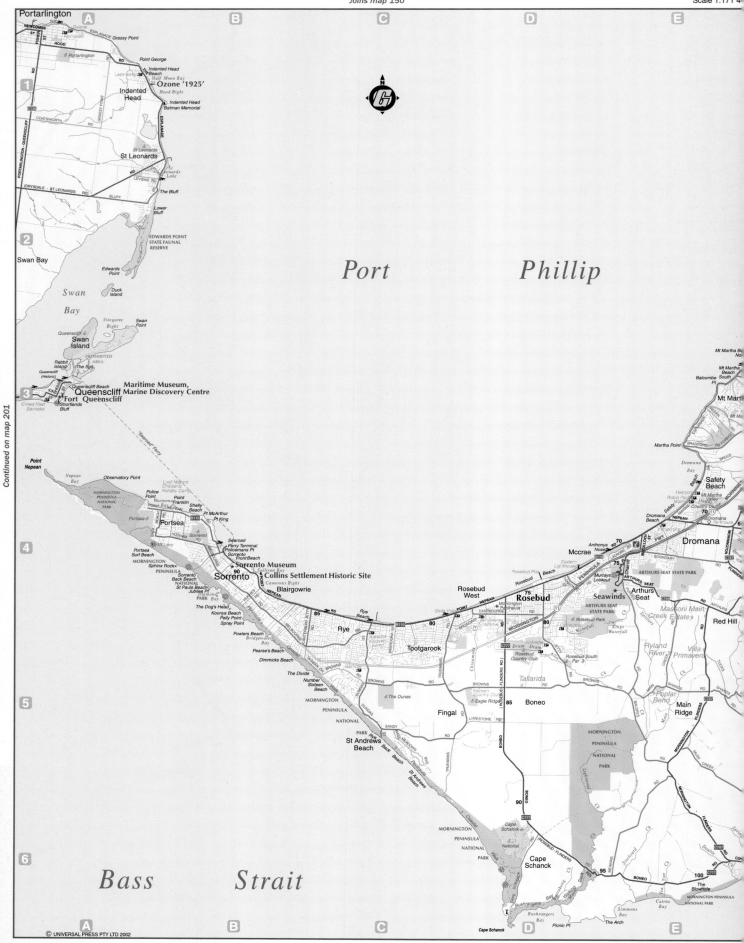

Portarlington

Grassy Point

Point George

Indented Head
Beach
Half Moon Bay
Ozone '1925'
Hood Bight
Indented Head
Batman Memorial

Indented
Head

St Leonards

St Leonards
Lake

The Bluff

Lower
Bluff

EDWARDS POINT
STATE FAUNAL
RESERVE

Swan Bay

Edwards
Point

Duck
Island

Swan
Bay

Stingaree
Bight

Swan
Point

Queenscliff &
Swan
Island

PROHIBITED
AREA

Rabbit
Island

The Spit

Queenscliff
(Historic)

Queenscliff Beach

Queenscliff **Maritime Museum,
Marine Discovery Centre**
Fort Queenscliff
Shortlands
Bluff

Crows Nest
Barracks

"SEAROAD" ferry

Port   Phillip

Mt Martha Be
No

Mt Martha
Beach
South
Balcombe
Pt

Mt Marti

Martha Point

Dromana
Bay

Safety
Beach

Point
Nepean

Nepean Bay

Observatory Point

Lord Marrys
Children's
Holiday Camp

Police
Point

Point
Franklin

Shelly
Beach
Pt McArthur

Pt King

MORNINGTON
PENINSULA
NATIONAL
PARK

Portsea

Mt Levy

Searoad
Ferry Terminal
Policemans Pt
Sorrento
Front Beach

Portsea
Surf Beach

MORNINGTON
PENINSULA
NATIONAL

Sphinx Rock

Sorrento
Back Beach

Sorrento Museum
Sullivan Bay
Collins Settlement Historic Site

Sorrento

90

St Pauls Beach
Jubilee Pt

Camerons Bight

Blairgowrie

Rosebud Pier

Hacketers

Robin Hood
Nepean Hwy
Country Club

Dromana
Beach

70 (11)

Dromana
Peninsula

70

Dromana

PARK
Bay

The Dog's Head
Koonya Beach
Pelly Point
Spray Point

85

RD

Rye
Beach

Rye

1110

80
RD

Bella Vista
POINT

Mornington
Peninsula

EASTBOURNE

Rosebud
West

Rosebud

75

Mccrae
Anthonys
Nose

Eastern
Lighthouse

80

Anthonys
Beach

70

75

Murrays
Lookout

Seawinds

Arthurs
Seat

ARTHURS SEAT STATE PARK

ARTHURS
SEAT
STATE
PARK

Rosebud Park

Kings
Waterfall

Masson Main
Creek Estate

Red Hill

Fowlers Beach
Bridgewater
Bay

Pearse's Beach

Dimmicks Beach

The Divide
Number
Sixteen
Beach

MORNINGTON

PENINSULA

NATIONAL

PARK

Tootgarook

BROWNS

BROWNS

TRUEMANS

Tallarida

Nepean Country Club

The Dunes

Eagle Ridge

Fingal

LIMESTONE

85

Boneo

Rosebud
Country Club

Drum Drum

Arthurs Seat
Golf Club

Rosebud South
Par 3

Ryland
River

Villa
Primavera

Poplar
Bend

Main
Ridge

St Andrews
Beach

SANDY

MORNINGTON

PENINSULA

NATIONAL

PARK

DUNDAS

BONEO

90

MORNINGTON

PENINSULA

NATIONAL

PARK

Cape
Schanck

National

Cape
Schanck

95

(ROSEBUD - FLINDERS) RD

MEAKINS

BONEO

100

The Blowhole

Cairns
Bay

MORNINGTON PENINSULA
NATIONAL PARK

Bushrangers

Bushrangers
Bay

Cape Schanck

Picnic Pt

The Arch

Bass   Strait

Gregory's Australia

Victoria

5 Kilometres

Frankston North
THE PINES
Cantenary Park
Cranbourne
East
Clyde
ROYAL BOTANIC GARDENS
Junction Village
Wylies Ck
Frankston
Long Island Country Club
Peninsula Country Club
Peninsula FLORA & FAUNA RESERVE
McClelland Art Gallery
Cranbourne South
BROWNS
Olivers Hill
Mornington Peninsula Fwy
Langwarrin
Five Ways
Devon Meadows
Mt Eliza
Point Davey Bay
Daveys Beach
Frankston Resvr
LANGWARRIN FLORA AND FAUNA RESERVE
MANKS
Ranelagh Beach
Canadian Bay
Mulberry Hill (National Trust)
Langwarrin South
Pearcedale
MANKS
Moondah Beach
North Sunnyside Beach
Frankston South
ROBINSONS
Cannons Creek
Blind Bight
Tooradin
National Antique Centre, World of Motorcycles Museum, Regional Gallery
Baxter
BAXTER
(LARNACH RD)
PEARCEDALE CONS. PK & MOONLIGHT SANCTUARY
BAXTER – TOORADIN (LARNACH RD)
Warneet
WARNEET NATURE RESERVE
Blind Bight
Mornington
Snapper Point
Red Bluff
Vintina
Disused Railway
Somerville
Watsons Inlet
Quail Island
QUAIL ISLAND WILDLIFE RESERVE
Chinaman Island
Warneet
GIPPSLAND HWY
Mooreduc
Bungower
Treetavan Equestrian Centre
Western Port
Stumpy Gully
Tyabb Scout Park Camp Fairnie
Tyabb
O'NEILLS
Mooreduc
Ermes
Devil Bend
Melbourne Water Dam
Western Port Airfield
DENHAM
Scrub Point
Devilbend Reservoir
Bittern Reservoir
River Point
RED BILL
FRENCH ISLAND NATIONAL PARK
Mt Martha
Mornington Peninsula Fwy
Tyabb Old Township
The Bays
Hastings
Reservoir
Loading Jetty
Long Island Point
Tuerong
Hastings Bight
Western Port Marina
Marina View
LINK
Mt Wellington
Osborns
Tanglewood Estate
Bittern
Sandstone Island
FRENCH ISLAND
Stockinbotham Dromana
Elan
Jacks Beach
Park Office
Bayview Chicory Kiln
BAYVIEW
Elgee Park
Willow Creek
BUCKLEY NATURE RESERVE
Kings Creek
MYERS
Woolleys Beach Crib Point
The Pinnacles
Craig Avon
Balnarring Racecourse
HMAS CERBERUS
Crib Point
MOSQUITO CREEK
Dromana Marina
Balnarring
Merricks North
Hanns Creek
Darling Park
Port Phillip Estate
Crib Point
Stony Point
TANKERTON
Red Hill Gallery
Coolart Valley
Merricks
Stanleys
Coolart Historic Homestead
Somers
Naval & Stony Point
Stony Point
Passenger Ferry
Tankerton
Red Hill South
Paringa Estate
Merricks Estate
Somers
HMAS CERBERUS
Tea Tree Point
Tortoise Head
Red Hill Estate
Merricks
Balnarring Beach
Somers Beach
South Beach
HMAS CERBERUS
Tucks Ridge
Ashcombe Maze
Point Leo
Merricks Beach
Merricks Beach
Sandy Point
Peck Point
Elizabeth Island
Shoreham
Point Leo (Bobbanaring Pt)
Point Leo Beach
Long Point
Shoreham Beach
Western Port
Cowes
Red Rocks Point
Mussel Rocks
Erehwon Point
Silverleaves
Observation Point
Finders
Kennon Cove
Rhylston Park Historic Homestead
VENTNOR
Conservation Hill
Rhyll Inlet
RHYLL INLET STATE WILDLIFE RESERVE
Lady Nelson Pt
West Head
McHaffie Point
Elizabeth Cove
Cowes
Rhyll
Fishermans Pt
West Head Gunnery Range
Wimbledon Heights
F OSWIN ROBERT KOALA RESERVE
Swan Bay
Reid Bight
Ventnor
Woolshed Bight
McHaffie Lagoon
Farm Beach
PHILLIP ISLAND
PHILLIP ISLAND NATURE PARK
Denne Bight
Long Point
Flynn Lagoon
Sunset Strip
Koala World
Pleasant Point
North Point
Churchill Island
Summerlands
Back Beach
Smiths Beach
Sunderland Bay
Chambers Point
Grants Monument
Historic Homestead
McLeod Point
Swan Lake
PHILLIP ISLAND NATURE PARK
Phillip Island
Cowrie Beach
Shelly Cat Bay
Swan Corner
Newhaven

© UNIVERSAL PRESS PTY LTD 2002

Continued on map 165
Continued on map 212

VICTORIA 153

VICTORIA A TO Z

Alexandra   POP 1978

Map 208, C5

Rich pastoral land and trout streams surround this **Goulburn River** town, located about 80km north of Melbourne. Gold discoveries in the 1850s and 1860s brought an influx of miners to the area. This prosperous period led to the construction of important civic buildings, including the Law Courts, Shire Hall, Post

Houseboat on Lake Eildon, near Alexandra

Office and the National Trust-classified **ANZ Bank building**. The town's economy relies on sawmilling—Gould's Timber mill exports to Japan; there are also 4 trout farms in the area.

MAIN ATTRACTIONS: Alexandra's main tourist attraction is the **Timber and Tramway Museum** housed in the old Railway Station, Station St. On the second Sunday of each month, and on public and school holidays, the restored narrow-gauge engines are steamed up for tourist trips. Bookings are essential. On the second Saturday of each month, Sept–June, a bush market is held in Perkins St.

NEARBY ATTRACTIONS: **McKenzie Flora Reserve**, located off Mount Pleasant Rd, has signposted walking tracks and visitors have the opportunity of spotting rare local wildflowers. Excavations and sites of past gold-mining activity dot the area. Alexandra is the gateway to **Eildon NP** (Frasers NP) on the shores of **Lake Eildon**. The park is a popular

family recreation area with holiday units, 2 caravan parks, camping areas, houseboats, boat-launching ramps and bushwalks. Trout fishing is popular in the Goulburn, **Acheron and Rubicon rivers**.

TOURIST INFO: 45a Grant St (opp Rotary Park), Ph: (03) 5772 1100 or 1800 652 298

Anglesea   POP 2250

Map 201, H4

A popular coastal resort and artists' colony, Anglesea lies on the **Great Ocean Rd**, 107km SW of Melbourne. Tourism is the main industry of this town with fishing, swimming, surfing and walking popular activities.

MAIN ATTRACTIONS: Views of the town, the coastline and the ocean are provided from the lookout behind **Front Beach**, Anglesea's main surfing spot. The **Heathland Cliff Walk** also offers scenic views; the walk begins at the carpark at the end of Purnell St. **Coogoorah Reserve**, located on the **Anglesea River**, offers waterways, islands, picnic areas, playground equipment

and walking tracks. The golf course attracts many visitors for a round of golf and unusual companions—tame kangaroos graze on its greens.
NEARBY ATTRACTIONS: **Angahook-Lorne SP** is close by and **Aireys Inlet**, 11km SW on the Great Ocean Rd, offers many activities including horseriding. Further south is the **Memorial Arch**, which commemorates the construction of the Great Ocean Rd, itself a memorial to the Australian soldiers killed in WWI.
TOURIST INFO: Surfworld Museum, Surf City, Beach Rd, Ph: (03) 5261 4219

Apollo Bay   POP 979
Map 201, F5
Apollo Bay is set on the coast with excellent surfing and swimming beaches and the **Otway Ranges** as a backdrop. Located 183km SW of Melbourne, it is a thriving tourist centre and the base for the local **Bass Strait** fishing fleet that supplies local and overseas markets.
MAIN ATTRACTIONS: The local historical museum is housed in the **Old Cable Station**, where the original telephone cable between Tasmania and the mainland came ashore. Situated on the Great Ocean Rd, it is open 2pm–5pm weekends, and school and public holidays. **Bass Strait Shell Museum**, in Noel St, displays a collection of shells and old photographs of shipwrecks, which litter the coast.
NEARBY ATTRACTIONS: Guided or self-guided scenic drives, walking or mountain biking tours are offered; details are available from the information centre. **Otway NP**, 13km SW, provides bushwalking trails throughout the park to the coast. **Cape Otway Lighthouse**, built in 1848, is also located in the park. Picnic spots are scattered throughout the **Barham Paradise Scenic Reserve**, part of the **Barham River Valley**, where many moisture-loving plants and trees thrive. **Melba Gully SP**, 56km west, has a glow-worm

habitat and there is a self-guided rainforest walk to explore.
TOURIST INFO: Ecotourism Centre, Great Ocean Rd, Ph: (03) 5237 6529

Ararat   POP 7000
Map 159, A2
Lying east of the **Grampian Ranges**, and 203km NW of Melbourne, Ararat is surrounded by rich farmland noted for producing top merino wool. It is also a grape-growing region, which produces excellent wines. The town is an ideal base for exploring the **Mount Cole Forest Range** and the **Grampians NP**. It is also the gateway to the **Pyrenees and Grampians Wine Trail**.
MAIN ATTRACTIONS: Details of the town's **Historic Walk** can be found at the tourist centre. Visitors can relax in the **Alexandra Gardens**, located in the centre of town. Nearby is the old bluestone **J Ward Gaol**, which housed the criminally insane from 1887 to 1991. In 1993, the gaol opened to the public and guided tours are available. **Langi Morgala Museum** was previously a Cobb & Co coach-changing station and woolstore. The museum has an Aboriginal history collection, and displays trace the stories of Chinese miners and Indian hawkers in the district, open weekends, 1pm–4pm. The **Gum San Chinese Heritage Centre** celebrates Ararat's gold-mining heritage.
NEARBY ATTRACTIONS: **Langi Ghiran SP**, 14km east of town, has rugged granite peaks and gentle sloping woodland. It offers scenic walks and a picnic and camping area. Many of the wineries surrounding the town are open for tastings and cellar door sales. **Seppelt Great Western Winery**, located 17km NW, was established in 1865 and specialises in dry red and sparkling wines. Its underground cellars are National Trust-classified.
TOURIST INFO: Railway Complex, Birdwood Ave, Ph: (03) 5352 2096

Ararat Town Hall

Bacchus Marsh   POP 11 279
Map 201, J1
This town is located between the **Werribee** and **Lerderderg rivers**, 49km west of Melbourne. Although close enough to Melbourne to be a commuter town, Bacchus Marsh is surrounded by orchards and market gardens sited on what once was marshland.
MAIN ATTRACTIONS: Many buildings, including the **Manor House** built by Capt William Henry Bacchus in 1846, are classified by the National Trust. Others include the sandstone **Court House**, built in 1858—and still used today; the **gaol**; and the **National Bank**. The avenue of English oaks, elms and plane trees called the **Avenue of Honour** was planted as a memorial to the citizens of Bacchus Marsh. An extension of Main St, it provides an impressive entrance to the town, and is claimed to be the best stand of elm trees in the world.
NEARBY ATTRACTIONS: **Lerderderg Gorge**, located 10km north, is a popular spot for swimming, picnics and bushwalking. **Brisbane Ranges NP**, with its many walking tracks and spring wildflowers, is 16km SW. Wineries in the area include **St Anne's Vineyard**, 6km west on the Western Fwy. This winery has a bluestone cellar built from the remains of the old Ballarat Gaol.
TOURIST INFO: 197 Main St, Ph: (03) 5366 7100

■ Bairnsdale POP 12 250
Map 177, C2

This **Gippsland** town lies on the **Mitchell River** flats at the tip of **Lake King**, 280km east of Melbourne. Bairnsdale and the surrounding district is promoted as the 'Victorian Riviera' with winter temperatures up to 6°C warmer than Melbourne. Situated at the junction of the Princes Hwy, the Great Alpine Rd and the road east to **Lakes Entrance**, Bairnsdale is a perfect base for exploring the surrounding region.

MAIN ATTRACTIONS: **St Mary's Catholic Church** is famous for its magnificent wall and ceiling murals painted by Italian artist, Francesco Floreani, in the 1930s. The local museum is located in the old **St Andrew's College** in Macarthur St. It is open on Wednesdays, Thursdays and Sundays, 1pm–4pm. **MacLeod Morass**, visible from the museum, is a deep freshwater marsh and reserve with more than 130 species of wildlife. Access to the reserve boardwalk is from Bosworth Rd. The **Bataluk Cultural Trail**, extending through **East Gippsland** from **Sale** to the **Cann River**, stops at an Aboriginal keeping place in Bairnsdale. **Krowathunkoolong**, located at 37 Dalmahoy St, has displays tracing Aboriginal culture from the Dreamtime to the present. **Bairnsdale Clocks**, in Nicholson St, has one of the largest collections of clocks in the country and is worth a visit.

NEARBY ATTRACTIONS: The information centre has details about self-guided scenic drives, walks and 4WD tours of the area. The picturesque town of **Metung**, 30km SE, is a fishing village on the shores of Lake King. **Mitchell River NP** is 45km west and offers excellent bushwalking tracks and the cavern known as the **Den of Nargun**, a significant site on the Bataluk Cultural Trail.

TOURIST INFO: 240 Main St,
Ph: (03) 5152 3444

■ Ballarat POP 66 480
Map 159, D3

Ballarat is the perfect spot for a short break or longer stay; it is an easy 112km drive from Melbourne. Victoria's largest inland city and regional centre has retained many of its classic Victorian buildings erected from the wealth of the goldrush. The town was also the site of Australia's only white uprising—in 1854, a group of miners led by Irishman Peter Lawlor refused to pay Government licence fees. The rebellion led to clashes with police and soldiers resulting in the deaths of 22 diggers and 3 soldiers. The event is now known as the **Eureka Stockade**.

MAIN ATTRACTIONS: The **Eureka Stockade centre**, located within the **Eureka Reserve** is a multi-million dollar interpretive centre. Many visitors come to **Sovereign Hill**, where the townsfolk have recreated Ballarat's first 10 years as an early gold town. This outdoor museum offers visitors the chance to purchase a licence, pan and wash for gold and shop in businesses just like those in the period 1851–1861. Or, there is the 27m-underground mining museum with the sound and light show, *Blood on the Southern Cross*, a re-creation of Eureka Stockade events. Adjoining Sovereign Hill is the **Gold Museum**, housing a unique collection and exhibits of the history of goldmining in the area. Australia's oldest (est 1884) and largest provincial gallery, the **Ballarat Fine Art Gallery**, in Lydiard St, has a truly impressive collection of Australian art, it also houses the original **Eureka Flag**. **Montrose Cottage**, in Eureka St, was the first mason-built cottage on the goldfields and is now an award-winning attraction. **Ballarat Wildlife and Reptile Park**, on the corner of York and Fussell sts, features native animals in a natural habitat; the park is allied to Melbourne Zoo.

'Gold prospector' at Sovereign Hill, Ballarat

NEARBY ATTRACTIONS: The well-known **Yellowglen Winery** is located at **Smythesdale**, 24km SW. Trout fishing is popular at **Lake Burrumbeet**, 22km NW. There are also many attractive picnic spots by the lake's shore. The **Flora and Bird Park**, 13km south at **Buninyong**, has a raised walkway and 60 colourful parrot aviaries.

TOURIST INFO: 39 Sturt St,
Ph: (03) 5320 5741 or 1800 648 450

■ Barwon Heads POP 2700
Map 201, K3

A popular fishing, boating and swimming holiday spot, Barwon Heads is located on the estuary of the **Barwon River**, about 100km from Melbourne. A bridge links Barwon Heads with neighbouring **Ocean Grove**, 2km away on the eastern side of the river. There is a limestone covered lava bluff protecting the town from the sea which at the same time is responsible for treacherous conditions that wrecked 12 ships on the 1800s. The town was also the 'home' of the ABC television series *Sea Change*.

MAIN ATTRACTIONS: A cairn commemorating the *Earl of Charlemont*, wrecked in this area in 1853, is located on the **Bluff Lookout**. The ship's anchor is mounted in a riverside park. **Thirteenth Beach**, located

Victoria

on the western edge of the township, is ideal for surfing. Calmer waters for swimming can be found at the mouth of the Barwon River. **Jirrahlinga Koala and Wildlife Sanctuary** is located in Taits Rd. Sick or wounded animals are nursed back to health at the hospital in the grounds. Visitors will find a variety of animals and birds as well as many koalas.

NEARBY ATTRACTIONS: Inland from Barwon Heads, the Barwon River fills **Lake Connewarre**. This large, shallow estuarine lagoon is home to cormorants, ibis, egrets, spoonbills, herons, bitterns, swamp hens and other wildlife. The area is popular for birdwatchers and bushwalkers.

TOURIST INFO: Caravan Park, Ewing Blyth Dr, Ph: (03) 5254 1115

■ Beechworth   POP 2953

Map 187, B1

Located in the foothills of the **Alpine region** and 270km NE of Melbourne, this well-preserved 1850s goldfields' town is famous for its fine honey-coloured granite buildings. Over 30 buildings are classified by the National Trust; the town is also notable for its colourful autumn foliage. Beechworth was once the centre of the Ovens gold-mining region and the National Trust has classified the whole town.

MAIN ATTRACTIONS: The **Beechworth Historic and Cultural Precinct** is a series of historically significant buildings from the goldrush era. There are interpretations on police life, the legal system and the history of the town's development. The recordings, heard in various buildings, are sometimes humorous sometimes sad but always instructive. They include messages from people such as Ellen Kelly and Elizabeth Scott and transport visitors to another time. **Burke Museum**, in Loch St, is named after ill-fated **Robert O'Hara Burke**, who at one time was officer-in-charge of

police in the town. There are relics of the goldrush on display at the museum and a 'strand of time', a re-creation of Beechworth's shops as they were over 100 years ago. The **Court House** (1858), was the scene of many trials involving bushrangers such as Ned Kelly and Harry Power. The **Carriage Museum**, in Last St, is located in **Murray Breweries**, which produces gourmet cordials, such as chilli punch and raspberry vinegar; open 7 days a week. Visitors can still fossick for gold and gems in the area, and maps for this and walking tours are available.

NEARBY ATTRACTIONS: **Beechworth Historic Park** surrounds the town and contains significant sites, including **Woolshed Falls**, **Beechworth Gorge** and the **Yedonbba** Aboriginal rock-art site. Nearby is the **Mount Pilot Lookout**, offering panoramic views of the **Murray Valley**. The **Gorge Scenic Drive** starts north of the town and passes through some gold-fossicking areas.

TOURIST INFO: 103 Ford St, Ph: (03) 5728 3233

■ Benalla   POP 9345

Map 208, D4

This town, 191km north of Melbourne, was **Sir Edward 'Weary' Dunlop's** hometown during his early years. The local Court House was the venue for a number of trials involving Ned Kelly.

MAIN ATTRACTIONS: Benalla has an Olympic-standard heated swimming pool in the **aquatic centre** located on Mair St. **Lake Benalla** is popular for swimming and sailing. The artificial lake was created by damming the **Broken River** in 1974. **Benalla Gardens**, located beside the lake, are worthwhile visiting for walks through the rose garden and along the lake's shores. The success of the rose garden, established in 1959, led to Benalla earning the title **'The Rose City on the Lake'**.

The **Benalla Art Gallery**, also located by the lake, houses the noted **Ledger Collection** of works by major Australian artists from colonial times to the 1960s. At the **Costume and Pioneer Museum**— incorporating the information centre—pioneer clothing and artefacts, including the cummerbund worn by Ned Kelly when he was captured at Glenrowan, are displayed.

NEARBY ATTRACTIONS: **Reef Hills Regional Park** offers 204km^2 of forest with a wide variety of native flora and fauna. It is located 4km south of the town. For moviegoers, the village of **Swanpool**, 23km south, shows classic films in a 1950s-style cinema.

TOURIST INFO: Costume and Pioneer Museum, 14 Mair St, Ph: (03) 5762 1749

■ Bendigo   POP 68 400

Map 159, E1

This elegant, old city is located in the geographic centre of Victoria. Its character and streetscapes were created during the gold boom years of the 1850s to 1870s, when the local goldfield was one of the world's richest. Less than a 2hr drive from Melbourne, Bendigo is a popular tourist destination surrounded by vineyards and wineries.

Historic Beechworth Post Office

THE GOLDFIELDS

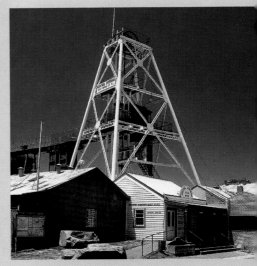

Situated in **Central Victoria**, just over 100km NW of Melbourne, the Goldfields region is filled with opportunities for those wanting to experience the heady days of the goldrush era.

In 1851, news of the discovery of gold spread like wildfire around the colonies of Victoria and New South Wales, and reached as far as China, England and the USA. A population explosion occurred—by October of that year, 8000 prospectors descended on the area; the number swelled to 30 000 a year later; and by 1856 a record number 100 000 people were at the goldfields. Tiny settlements became boom towns virtually overnight. Melbourne was almost deserted during 1851, after 20 000 of its 25 000 population left for the **Mount Alexander** diggings.

As prosperity spread to the trades, services and agricultural industries that supported the gold miners and developing mining companies, towns became thriving regional centres, bearing all the hallmarks of wealth.

The rich history of the Goldfields and Victorian architecture is evident everywhere and visitors can explore the area through activities such as prospecting, fossicking, camping and bushwalking.

The Goldrushes

The wealth from the gold diggings made Melbourne the largest city in Australia at that time. The status of the whole country was transformed. Australia changed from a colonial settlement with a dubious reputation to a respectable place for migration and investment.

Central Deborah Gold Mine, Bendigo

i Tourist information

Ballarat Visitor Information Centre
39 Sturt St, Ballarat Vic 3350
Ph: (03) 5320 5741
www.ballarat.com

Bendigo Visitor Information Centre
51–67, Pall Mall, Bendigo Vic 3550
Ph: (03) 5444 4445, 1800 813 153
www.bendigotourism.com

main attractions

◈ **Ararat**

Ararat was officially founded in 1857, when a group of 700 Chinese discovered alluvial gold in the area.

◈ **Ballarat**

This is the site of Sovereign Hill and the Eureka Stockade centre.

◈ **Ballarat Wildlife Park**

Meet emus, koalas, wallabies, wombats and other Australian animals at Ballarat Wildlife Park.

◈ **Bendigo**

Built on its goldrush prosperity, Bendigo is still a thriving and influential city.

◈ **Buda Historic Home and Gardens**

Visit this colonial home and see the best of 19th- and 20th-century landscaping.

◈ **Castlemaine**

Castlemaine is noted as much for its artistic endeavours as for its goldrush past. Castlemaine Art Gallery boasts a fine collection of Australian art.

◈ **Clunes**

This was Victoria's first gold town.

◈ **Golden Dragon Museum**

This Bendigo museum is a tribute to the Chinese gold miners.

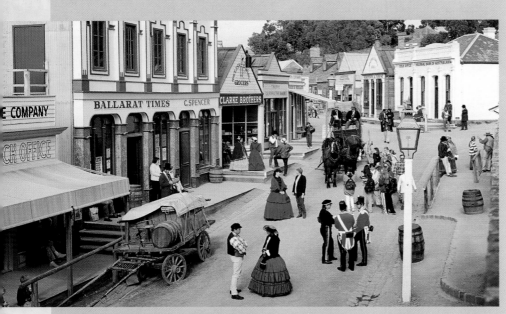

Sovereign Hill, Ballarat's re-creation of an early goldrush town

Victoria

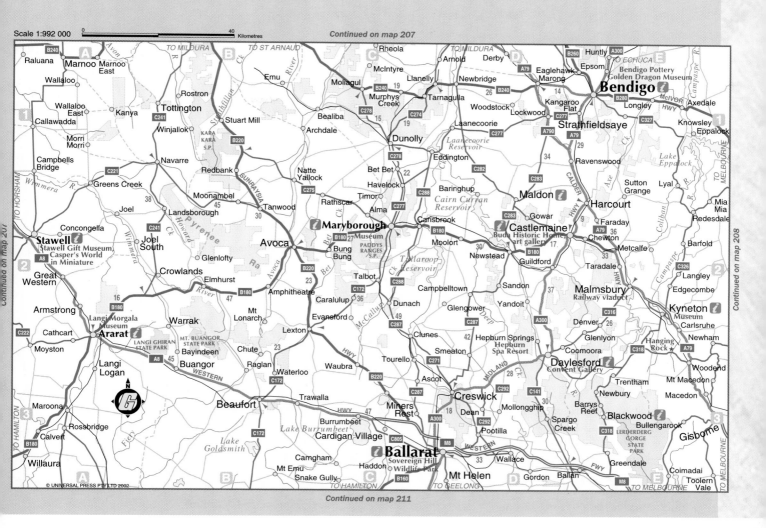

Continued on map 207

Scale 1:992 000

Continued on map 211

© UNIVERSAL PRESS PTY LTD 2002

MAIN ATTRACTIONS: Bendigo Pottery established in 1858, is Australia's oldest operating pottery and a major attraction. The centre also features a pottery museum. The **Heritage Walk** along the main street, Pall Mall, passes grand buildings, including the Post Office and Law Courts, **Alexandra Fountain** (1881), the **Beehive Store building** (1872) and **Shamrock Hotel** (1897). **Fortuna Villa**, a Baroque mansion renowned for its sculptured ceilings, stained glass, Italian-style garden and Roman bath was owned by George Lansell, the legendary 'quartz king'. An impressive collection of Australian and European art is displayed at the recently refurbished **Bendigo Art Gallery** in View St. The **Golden Dragon Museum**, located in the city centre, displays Chinese ceremonial regalia and 2 famous imperial dragons: Sun Loong and Loong.

NEARBY ATTRACTIONS: Wineries surrounding the town are open for tastings and cellar door sales. The information centre has maps for self-guided **Goldfields' tours**. Short camel rides or longer camel treks are available at **Sedgwick's Camel Farm**, located 20km SE at **Sedgwick**. The **Chinese Joss House**, about 3km north at **Emu Point**, was built by Chinese miners and has been refurbished and classified by the National Trust. **Whipstick SP**, 21km north, has a eucalyptus distillery and designated picnic and camping areas.

TOURIST INFO: Pall Mall, (old Post Office), Ph: (03) 5444 4445

Detail from the Alexandra Fountain (1881), Bendigo

■ Bright   POP 2130

Map 187, C2

Bright is a picturesque town situated on the **Ovens River**, 303km NE of Melbourne. The town is conveniently located to the **Victorian Alps** and the ski fields at **Mount Hotham**, **Mount Buffalo** and **Falls Creek**. Industries important to the local economy include tourism, timber and agriculture. Bright was established after the discovery of alluvial gold in the area.

MAIN ATTRACTIONS: Bright is worthwhile visiting in autumn and spring due to the variety of trees planted throughout the town, including Japanese maples, Lombardy poplars, oaks, elms, bunya pines and dogwoods. Each year the town celebrates the seasons with autumn and spring festivals. There is also an annual autumn art exhibition attracting artists and buyers from around Australia. The town and surrounding area is excellent for bushwalking, trout fishing and cycling. Worthwhile walks include the **Canyon Walk** along the **Ovens River** where visitors can see the remains of gold workings. **Centenary Park** has a children's

playground and a deep weir, popular for swimming in summer.

NEARBY ATTRACTIONS: The nearby **Alpine NP** is also ideal for bushwalkers, with many and varied tracks. **Mount Buffalo NP**, also nearby, has a variety of wildlife. **Boyntons of Bright Winery** is located at **Porepunkah**, 6km NW at the junction of the Ovens and **Bucklands rivers**. The information centre has details of lavender, deer, emu and berry farms in the district that are open to visitors

TOURIST INFO: 119 Gavan St, Ph: (03) 5755 2275

■ Buninyong   POP 1791

Map 211, H2

The small township of Buninyong is located 10km south of Ballarat. It was one of the first inland towns in Victoria and was also the site of the district's first gold find at **Hiscocks Gully** in 1851. After the goldrush, Buninyong once again became an agricultural centre.

MAIN ATTRACTIONS: Several buildings are of historic interest. The **Crown Hotel** claims to hold the oldest continuous licence, dating from 1842, although the first hotel on the site

burnt down in 1884. The Italianate Council Chambers and Court House were both built in 1882. Some walks in the town worthwhile taking include the **Town Walk**, picked up at the junction of Warrenheip and Learmouth sts. This route passes through the **Botanic Gardens**, planted in the 1860s, where there are picnic facilities. Another walk follows **Buninyong Creek**.

NEARBY ATTRACTIONS: A scenic drive in the area includes **Mount Buninyong**, an extinct volcano which offers panoramic views of the surrounding countryside; **Lal Lal Falls**, dropping 34m; and one of Australia's most important industrial archaeological sites, the ruins of the **Lal Lal Blast Furnace**, which once supplied smelted wrought iron to Ballarat. There are boardwalks enabling visitors to explore the area.

TOURIST INFO: Cnr Albert and Sturt sts, Ballarat, Ph: (03) 5320 5741 or 1800 648 450

■ Camperdown   POP 3240

Map 200, D3

Volcanic activity over 20 million years ago shaped the landscape of this **Western District** town. Surrounded by crater lakes and lying at the foot of extinct volcano, **Mount Leura**, Camperdown is in the centre of the world's third largest volcanic plain. The town is filled with elegant buildings and avenues of elms. In 1876, school children planted the avenue of elms running for 2km along **Manifold St**.

MAIN ATTRACTIONS: Camperdown has many statues, war memorials and monuments which commemorate the district's pioneers. The **town walk** takes in many of Camperdown's historic buildings, including the red-brick Court House (now the information centre), bluestone Post Office, Railway Station, commercial buildings and cottages. **Camperdown Buggy Museum** at 26 Ower St, houses 20 horse-drawn vehicles

Ovens River bridge at Bright in autumn

Victoria

collected from the district; it is open by appointment only. The **Historical Society Museum** at 241 Manifold St is open on Tuesdays, Fridays and Sundays, 2pm–4pm. The road to the top of Mount Leura leads to a lookout with panoramic views of the surrounding volcanic plain.

NEARBY ATTRACTIONS: There are 2 crater lakes lying side-by-side 3km west of Camperdown. Freshwater **Lake Bullen Merri** and **Lake Gnotuk**, are both popular spots for swimming and fishing. **Lake Corangamite** is Victoria's largest saltwater lake and is 13km east of the town. **Lake Purrumbete**, located 15km SE, is well stocked with Quinnat salmon, and also has excellent watersport facilities, picnic spots and a caravan park.

TOURIST INFO: The Court House, Manifold St, Ph: (03) 5593 3390

■ Casterton   POP 1870

Map 210, C2

Located halfway between Melbourne and Adelaide, and 42km east of the South Australian border, this picturesque town is noted for its heritage streetscape and surrounding countryside of agricultural and grazing land, forests and rivers. The **Glenelg River** runs beside **Island Park** and through the town.

MAIN ATTRACTIONS: Casterton's vibrant pioneering history can be seen in the many buildings dating back to the early days of European settlement. In the centre of town, a statue of a kelpie marks the district as the birthplace of this famous Australian working dog. The shopping centre offers an art gallery, bric-a-brac, craft shops and food outlets. A walk or drive to **Mickle Lookout**, off Robertson St, provides excellent views of the town and surrounding countryside. In 1941, a large **Scout emblem**, 91.5m high, was carved into the hillside overlooking Casterton. The symbol is surrounded by strip lighting and serves as a beacon for the town.

The Glenelg River flowing through Lower Glenelg NP

NEARBY ATTRACTIONS: The kelpie was originally bred 32km north of the town on **Warrock Homestead**. Today, the homestead comprises 33 National Trust-classified buildings dating from the 1840s, including a woolshed, belfry, blacksmith's shop, homestead and cottage. Open daily, the homestead provides an insight into pastoral life 150 years ago. Within a short drive of Casterton are wildflowers, native forests with kangaroos and emus, lakes and swamps for watersports, and picnic spots. **Bilston's Tree**, Australia's largest red gum—a mere sapling in 1200AD—stands on the road north of town. **Dergholm SP**, 50km to the north, has giant green boulders.

TOURIST INFO: Shiells Tce, Ph: (03) 5581 2070

■ Castlemaine   POP 7850

Map 159, C3

This is a prosperous industrial centre and a popular tourist destination, 120km NW of Melbourne. Castlemaine lies at the foot of **Mount Alexander** at the intersection of the Pyrenees and Midland hwys and is

surrounded by old goldfields. In the 1850s and 1860s, the area experienced a gold boom and the town grew rapidly. Many of the town's fine Victorian buildings were built during these boom years.

MAIN ATTRACTIONS: The **Castlemaine Market** is one of the most impressive buildings in the town. A produce market was held in the building until 1967 and it is now the town's information centre and a gold interpretive centre. Tours of **Old Castlemaine Gaol** are by appointment. Accommodation is available for visitors wishing to 'spend a night in gaol'. **Castlemaine Botanical Gardens** is one of Victoria's oldest provincial public gardens. **Barkers Creek**, located north of the town centre, is an attractive spot for a picnic. Works by many well-known Australian artists hang in the town's **Art Gallery and Historical Museum** in Lyttleton St.

NEARBY ATTRACTIONS: A guide to the gold digging sites in the area is available from the information centre. Close by are **Forest Creek Diggings** and **Herons Reef Gold**

Castlemaine Art Gallery

Diggings. At the **dingo farm** in **Chewton** visitors can learn all about this Australian wild dog. Natural mineral springs are quite common in the area and the most easily accessible is **Vaughan Spring**, accessed off the road to Guildford.
TOURIST INFO: Market Building, Mostyn St, Ph: (03) 5470 6200

■ Clunes   POP 943
Map 159, C3
The site of Victoria's first registered gold strike; Clunes is located 36km north of Ballarat. Extinct volcanoes surround the historic town, providing an interesting view.
MAIN ATTRACTIONS: The **Town Hall** and **Court House** give a sense of Clunes' influential past. Several buildings are classified by the National Trust. The **Bottle Museum**, located on Talbot Rd, boasts the largest collection of bottles in the Southern Hemisphere; it is also home to the information centre and tearooms. The **Creek Walk** takes visitors out to **Port Phillip Mine**, which crushed more than 1.3 million tons of quartz yielding 16 tons of gold.
NEARBY ATTRACTIONS: The historic town of **Talbot** is 18km NW and has many fine old Victorian buildings dating from the 1860s and 1870s.
TOURIST INFO: Bottle Museum, Talbot Rd, Ph: (03) 5345 3896

■ Cobram   POP 4567
Map 208, C2
This **Murray River** town is located 250km north of Melbourne on the Murray Valley Hwy. The town was established in 1887 to service the railway from Melbourne. After WWII, the area became part of a large Soldier-Settlement Scheme, which saw the growth of dairy farms and orchards—one of which was responsible for the development of the clingstone variety of peach.
MAIN ATTRACTIONS: With its wide sandy beaches, Cobram is popular for swimming, watersports, picnicking and fishing, and for houseboats and paddlewheeler cruises. The town's monthly market is held in Punt Rd on the first Saturday of each month.
NEARBY ATTRACTIONS: Wineries in the area include **Strathkellar Wines**, 8km east; **Fyffefield Wines**, 15km east; **Heritage Farm Wines**, 5km west; and **Monichino Winery** at **Katunga**. The wineries are open for tastings and cellar door sales.

Koonoomoo, 5km west, offers strawberry picking in season. Australia's largest cacti gardens, **Cactus Country**, is located at **Strathmerton**, 16km west. **Daveile Gallery**, located in **Barooga**, houses a fine collection of antiques including some 400 Victorian oil lamps.
TOURIST INFO: Cnr Station St and Punt Rd, Ph: (03) 5872 2132

■ Cohuna   POP 2510
Map 207, J2
Cohuna, 305km north of Melbourne, is located in the centre of a dairying district. The region is characterised by attractive landscapes created by the lagoons and waterways of the **Murray River**, including nearby **Gunbower Island**, which is encircled by the Murray River and **Gunbower Creek**.
MAIN ATTRACTIONS: **Cohuna Historical Museum** boasts some interesting exhibits. Each March, the **Bridge to Bridge Swim** is held, and in February the **Aquatic Festival** takes place in **Gunbower**.
NEARBY ATTRACTIONS: A bridge connects Cohuna to the **Gunbower Island SF**, which protects a river red gum and box habitat. Walking tracks and dirt roads penetrate the forest, which is home to emus, kangaroos, possums, gliders and a variety of birdlife. The *Wetlander* explores Gunbower Creek with regular, 2hr-long cruises from mid-August through to mid-May.
TOURIST INFO: Golden Rivers Tourism, Murray St, Barham, Ph: (03) 5453 3100 or 1800 621 882.

■ Colac   POP 10 270
Map 201, F4
Lying at the eastern edge of the world's third largest volcanic plain, Colac is located at the foothills of the **Otway Ranges**. The town is also the eastern gateway to the **Volcanic Discovery Trail** and is at the centre of some of Australia's richest farming areas.

MAIN ATTRACTIONS: Promoted as the **'Gateway to the Otways'**, Colac is also a good base for those exploring south to the **Great Ocean Rd**—it is an hour's drive to the **Twelve Apostles**—and north to **Ballarat**. Colac is located on the shores of **Lake Colac**: the largest freshwater lake in Victoria. The lake is popular for swimming, boating, waterskiing and fishing and there are many picnic spots dotted around its shores. A nature walk leads from the information centre to **Colac Botanic Gardens**, on the foreshore at the northern end of Queen St. Here, there are picnic and BBQ facilities, and a children's playground.

NEARBY ATTRACTIONS: **Lake Corangamite**, located 11km NW, is one of the district's many crater lakes. This very large lake has no outlet and is 3-times saltier than seawater. Boating is not allowed, as the lake is principally a wildlife habitat. **Red Rock Lookout**, 22km north, is located on twin volcanic peaks and offers a view of 30 volcanic lakes. At least 16 species of waterbirds have been recorded at **Floating Islands Reserve**, 18km west. There are 2 short walking trails giving access to the reserve and its unique islands. The scenic

Otway Ranges are 30km south and definitely worthwhile visiting. **Birregurra**, 20km east of Colac, has interesting old buildings.

TOURIST INFO: Cnr Queen and Murray sts, Ph: (03) 5231 3730

Coleraine   POP 1120
Map210, C2

This historic township in a lovely **Western District** valley, is located 323km west of Melbourne. Settled in 1839, this is mainly a pastoral district producing fine wool and beef cattle.

MAIN ATTRACTIONS: **Matthew Cookes Blacksmiths Shop**, built in 1888, and the **Historical Society** are both housed in the old Court House and open by appointment only. The **Chocolate Factory**, in Whyte St, is open for daily tastings. Local arts and craft are displayed in the historic **Railway Station**.

NEARBY ATTRACTIONS: A view of Coleraine and the surrounding countryside can be seen from the lookout in **Points Reserve Arboretum**, accessed off the Portland Rd. The reserve offers a picnic ground, shade house, walking tracks, children's playground, facilities and BBQs. The arboretum features the largest collection of

eucalyptus species in the country. **Konongwootong Reservoir**, about 9km north on Harrow Rd, is a good recreation and fishing spot, catches include rainbow trout. Between Coleraine and **Hamilton** are the **Nigretta Falls** and **Wannon Falls**, both on the **Wannon River**. These are popular recreation areas with facilities and walking trails. National Trust-classified historic homesteads in the area include **Glendinning Homestead and wildlife sanctuary**, located 49km to the north.

TOURIST INFO: Old Railway Station, Pilleau St, Ph: (03) 5575 2733

Corryong   POP 1420
Map 209, J3

Lying near the source of the **Murray River**, this town is the Victorian gateway to the **Snowy Mountains** and **Kosciuszko NP**.

MAIN ATTRACTIONS: The mountain location and excellent trout streams draw many visitors to the area. Other activities include scenic drives, canoeing, white-water rafting, cycling and 4WD tracks. Canoes and cycles can be hired at **Walwa**, 50km NW of Corryong. **Jack Riley**, the man generally accepted as the character in the *Man from Snowy River*, Banjo Paterson's epic poem, was buried at **Corryong Cemetery** in 1914. A granite headstone and snow gum logs mark his grave. There is also a **Man From Snowy River Museum**, which has both interior and exterior exhibits and an array of historical items from the area, including a ski collection dating from the 1870s.

NEARBY ATTRACTIONS: Information on horseriding trails and 4WDing tours is available from the information centre. Trout fishing is a popular pastime in **Nariel Creek**, 45km south of town. **Burrowa-Pine Mountain NP**, 27km west, offers many scenic bushwalks.

TOURIST INFO: 50 Hanson St, Ph: (02) 6076 2277

Mount Mittamatite, Corryong

PHILLIP ISLAND

Located in the calm waters of **Western Port** and a 1.5hr drive from Melbourne, Phillip Island is accessed by a bridge from the mainland at **San Remo**. It is Victoria's premier destination for international visitors and boasts superior surfing and unspoilt beaches, an array of wildlife, including colonies of koalas, seals and the famed **little penguins**— the island's major drawcard.

Phillip Island also has some outstanding geological formations, including **The Pinnacles**, ancient columns of pink granite; the **Forrest Caves**, large sea-eroded caverns; and **Pyramid Rock**, a column of basalt in the shape of a pyramid.

Cowes is the major town and administrative centre of the island and where the majority of the island's accommodation is to be found. The Australian leg of the 500cc world motorcycle championships is held at the Phillip Island Racing Circuit, not far from Cowes each October. The combined attractions of Phillip Island make it an ideal holiday location.

main attractions

❖ Cape Woolamai walk
❖ Koala Conservation Reserve
❖ Penguin Parade, Summerland Beach

i Tourist information

Phillip Island Information Centre
Phillip Island Tourist Rd
Newhaven Vic 3925
Ph: (03) 5956 7447
Freecall: 1300 366 422

Little penguins, *Eudyptula minor* on Summerland Beach

Safe swimming beach at Cowes

■ Cowes   POP 3500
Map 165, C1

Situated on the northern side of **Phillip Island**, Cowes is the main town on the island. The popular resort town is 15km from the bridge linking the island to the mainland. MAIN ATTRACTIONS: The Cowes fore-shore is a popular BBQ and picnic area and there are safe beaches for children to swim. The town's jetty is popular for fishing. Every Sunday there are markets in Settlement Rd. The town also offers shops, a cinema, cafes and restaurants. Ferries and bay cruises leave from Cowes. A walk to the end of the jetty provides views to **French Island** to the right and **Stony Point** to the left. NEARBY ATTRACTIONS: **Summerland Beach**, 11km SW on the southern shore, is best known for its nightly little penguin parade. The penguins are the world's smallest and they nest on the island. These delightful little creatures can be seen from a specially constructed viewing area. Bookings are essential in peak season. **Seal Rocks Sea Life Centre** has marine displays and colonies of fur seals on **Seal Rocks**, 13km SW, can be viewed live on the centre's giant screen. The centre is open daily, 10am–dusk. On the south-west corner of the island, in Berrys Beach Rd, **Phillip Island Winery** is open daily for tastings and cellar door sales. At the **Koala CR**, visitors walk around the reserve on elevated boardwalks for the best view of koalas in a natural habitat. TOURIST INFO: Phillip Island Tourist Rd, Newhaven, Ph: (03) 5956 7447 or 1300 366 422

Victoria

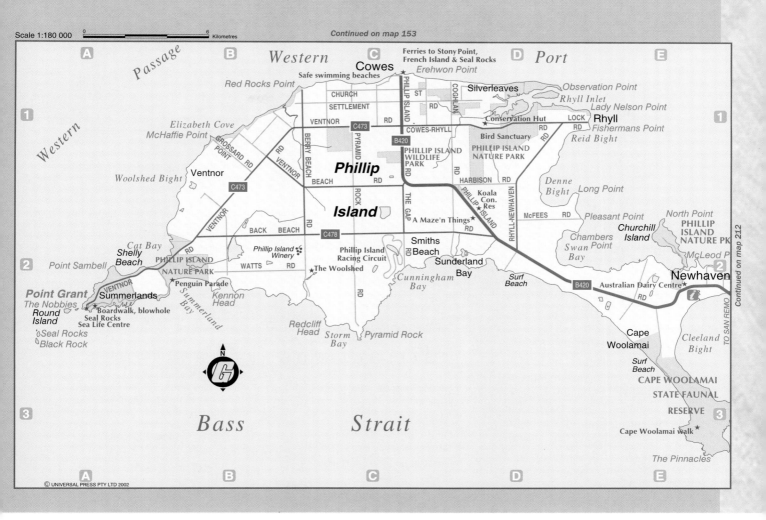

Continued on map 153

Western Passage

Western Port

Cowes
Ferries to Stony Point, French Island & Seal Rocks
Safe swimming beaches
Erehwon Point
Red Rocks Point
CHURCH
Silverleaves
Observation Point
SETTLEMENT
Rhyll Inlet
Lady Nelson Point
Elizabeth Cove
VENTNOR
C473
RD
Conservation Hut
LOCK
Rhyll
McHaffie Point
COWES-RHYLL
Bird Sanctuary
RD
RD
Fishermans Point
B420
Reid Bight
Woolshed Bight
Ventnor
BERRY BEACH
PYRAMID
PHILLIP ISLAND WILDLIFE PARK
PHILLIP ISLAND NATURE PARK
Denne Bight
Long Point
C473
VENTNOR
RD
BEACH
Phillip
ROCK
RD
HARBISON
RD
Koala Con. Res
McFEES
RD
Pleasant Point
North Point
Chambers Swan Bay
Churchill Island
PHILLIP ISLAND NATURE PK
Island
THE GAP
A Maze'n Things
RD
RHYLL-NEWHAVEN
McLeod P
BACK BEACH
C478
Smiths Beach
Cat Bay
Phillip Island Winery
WATTS
RD
Phillip Island Racing Circuit
Sunderland Bay
Newhaven
Shelly Beach
The Woolshed
Surf Beach
B420
Australian Dairy Centre
Point Sambell
PHILLIP ISLAND NATURE PARK
RD
Cunningham Bay
Point Grant
VENTNOR
Summerlands
Summerland Beach
Kennon Head
Cape Woolamai
Cleeland Bight
The Nobbies
Boardwalk, blowhole
Penguin Parade
Round Island
Seal Rocks Sea Life Centre
Surf Beach
Seal Rocks
Redcliff Head
Storm Bay
Pyramid Rock
CAPE WOOLAMAI STATE FAUNAL RESERVE
Black Rock

Bass Strait

Cape Woolamai walk

The Pinnacles

TO SAN REMO

Continued on map 212

Creswick   POP 3000

Map 159, D3

This historic gold-mining town is located 15km north of Ballarat, and contains some fine historic dwellings. Surrounded by pine plantations, Creswick is ideally positioned between the **Goldfields** and **Spa Country**.

MAIN ATTRACTIONS: Creswick was the birthplace of former Australian Prime Minister, **John Curtin** and also was home to the artistic **Lindsay family**. Norman, the most famous member, was born here in 1879. Works by the Lindsays and T G Moyle are exhibited in **Creswick Historical Museum**, in the Town Hall on Albert St. Walking tour notes, detailing the town's historic buildings, and a booklet on the **Buried Rivers of Gold Trail** are available.

NEARBY ATTRACTIONS: Visitors can try gold panning in **Slatey Creek**, 4km east of the town. For something different, see the lifesize models at the **World of Dinosaurs**, 1.5km east off the Midland Hwy. **Calembeen Park**, a recreational area on the Midland Hwy, offers a caravan park, picnic area, BBQs, playground and a natural lake, safe for swimming.

TOURIST INFO: 92 Vincent St, Daylesford, Ph: (03) 53481339

Daylesford   POP 3780

Map 167, A2

The **'Spa Centre of Australia'**, comprising the twin towns of Daylesford and **Hepburn Springs**. This is a popular destination for short breaks and is located 115km NW of Melbourne. A picturesque town, the surrounding area has

Boathouse, Lake Daylesford

MACEDON RANGES AND SPA COUNTRY

Boasting over 65 mineral springs concentrated within a relatively small area, this region is recognised as a premier boutique holiday destination due to the resurgence of belief in the healing properties of mineral water. Located a short distance from Melbourne, the Spa Country is an ideal locale for 'taking the waters'. This is a European tradition dating to the 1840s, when the large Swiss-Italian community realised the healing potential of the waters surrounding them. Mineral water has been bottled here since 1850 and the towns of **Daylesford** and **Hepburn Springs** have been spa resorts in the European-style since the 1880s. Alternative and natural therapies, including herbal baths and massages, are also offered.

The district also offers wineries and relics of the old goldfields. The surrounding rugged bushland is dotted with local reserves such as **Lerderderg SP** and the **Macedon Ranges**, which are ideal for bushwalking, horseriding, fishing and picnicking. The **Tipperary Walking Track** links Hepburn Springs and Daylesford, passing through old gold-mining areas. Surrounded by lakes and regional parks, this lovely area offers a relaxing holiday destination with a diversity of attractions.

main attractions

- Convent Gallery, Wombat Hill, Daylesford
- Hanging Rock
- Hepburn Springs Spa Resort
- Lake House Restaurant
- Lavandula Lavender Farm (outside Hepburn Springs)

 Tourist information

Daylesford Regional Visitor Information Centre
98 Vincent St, Daylesford, Vic 3460
Ph: (03) 5321 6123
www.visitdaylesford.com

Kyneton Visitor Information Centre
Jean Hayes Reserve
High St, Kyneton, Vic 3444
Ph: (03) 5422 6110

lakes, forests, relics from the gold-mining era and Australia's largest concentration of natural mineral springs. There are at least 65 mineral springs in the Daylesford and Hepburn Springs region.

MAIN ATTRACTIONS: A mineral bathhouse is located at **Hepburn Spa Resort**, in the **Hepburn Mineral Springs Reserve**. Both public and private baths, flotation tanks and a sauna are offered. There are a number of practitioners in the district providing massage and natural therapies. **Convent Gallery** houses fine art, pottery, antiques and a superb collection of jewellery. The town's history is displayed in the **Historical Society Museum** housed in the old School of Mines, which was once used for smelting and refining gold and is easily identified by the tall brick chimney. Maps of the **Tipperary Walking Track**—part of the **Great Dividing Trail**—from **Lake Daylesford** to Hepburn Mineral Springs Reserve, are available from the information centre. **Wombat Hill Botanic Gardens and Lookout** are popular. **Lavandula Lavender Farm** has a beautiful garden, farmyard animals, a restaurant and a variety of lavender-based products are offered for sale.

NEARBY ATTRACTIONS: There are other mineral springs in the surrounding area, including **Lyonville Spring**, 15km SE. The extinct volcano, **Mount Franklin**, is located 13km north, and 18km NW, is the attractive settlement of Swiss-Italian heritage, **Yandoit**.

TOURIST INFO: 98 Vincent St, Ph: (03) 5321 6123

▪ Donald   POP 1428

Map 207, F3

This town is situated on the **Richardson River**, 286km NW of Melbourne. Wheat has long been the principal product of this part of the **Wimmera**, and grain silos still dominate the skyline.

MAIN ATTRACTIONS: Donald's history is preserved at the old **Banyenong Police Camp**, now an historic precinct located on the Sunraysia Hwy, near the Richardson River. The old police building, constructed by Johann Meyer in 1874, now houses the information centre. Tours of local industries include the **Pea Company**, **Kooka's Country Cookies**, **Fair Mark Shirt Factory** and **The Belt Factory**. The **Agricultural Museum**, on the corner of Borung Hwy and Mill St,

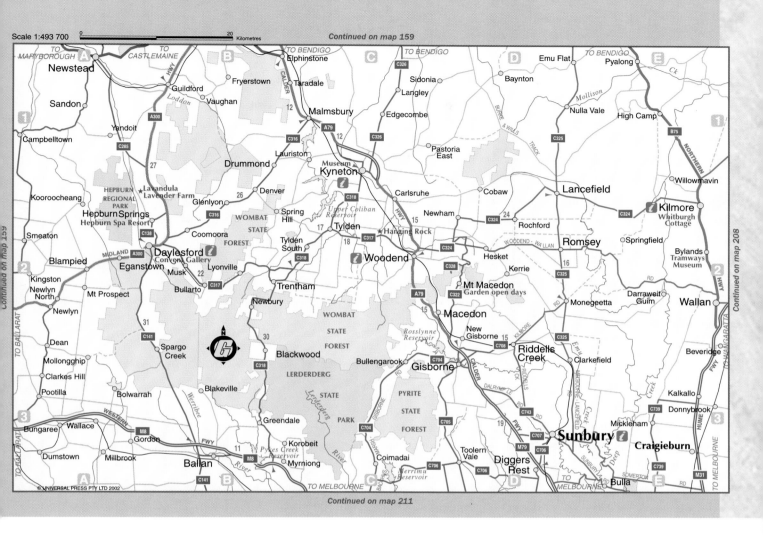

Continued on map 159

Continued on map 211

has displays which include hand chaffcutters, shearing tables, a grubbing machine and a stump-jump plough. **Lions Train Park**, across the road, is the site of the old J524 class steam locomotive; BBQ facilities are provided.

NEARBY ATTRACTIONS: **Apex Wayside Park**, adjacent to the highway, has picnic and BBQ facilities. Encircled by the Richardson River, there are walking tracks throughout the park. In Byrne St, also beside the river, is **Bullocks Head Lookout**, so-called because a large growth on a box tree resembles a bullock's head. The Richardson River flows into **Lake Buloke**, a wetlands' area that attracts an array of wildlife. The lake is 10km north of the town.

TOURIST INFO: Cnr Houston and McCulloch sts, Ph: (03) 5497 1300

■ **Drouin** POP 4790

Map 212, D3

This **West Gippsland** town is located in an agricultural and dairying district. Drouin is 94km east of Melbourne.

MAIN ATTRACTIONS: The region is renowned for the quality of its fresh produce. Many of the local producers of cheese, wine, fish, fruit, herbs and meat participate in the **Gourmet Deli Trail**, which also includes the towns of **Wonthaggi**, **Warragul** and **Foster**. Wineries, craft and antique shops complement the area. **Drouin NR** has 3km of walking tracks set in 14ha of natural bushland. In summer, the town is ablaze when the red-flowering gum trees (*Eucalyptus ficifolia*) are in full bloom. This beauty is celebrated with the **Ficifolia Festival** in February.

NEARBY ATTRACTIONS: **Glen Crombie Park,** 8km north of Drouin, is an attractive flora and fauna reserve offering bushwalking, camping and picnic spots on the **Tarago River**.

TOURIST INFO: Latrobe Information Centre, 'The Old Church', Southside Central, Princes Hwy, Traralgon, Ph: 1800 621 409

Gourmet Deli Trail produce

PS *Emmylou* paddlesteamer on the Murray River near Echuca

Drysdale   POP 1532
Map 211, K3

The small township of Drysdale, 18km east of Geelong, services the surrounding farming community on the **Bellarine Peninsula**.

MAIN ATTRACTIONS: Drysdale's many historic 19th-century buildings include the **Old Court House Museum**, the **Anglican Church** and the **War Veteran's Home**. The museum is open Sundays, Jan–April. The **Bellarine Peninsula Tourist Railway** offers rides on the steam train between Drysdale and **Queenscliff** on weekends and during summer holidays. There are locomotives and carriages dating back to the 1870s on display.

NEARBY ATTRACTIONS: Neighbouring **Clifton Springs** was a spa resort town in the 1880s, and featured a pier, baths and a kiosk for holiday-makers. Today, a modern sporting and public facilities complex stands on the site of the original spa hotel. There are several wineries in the area, including **Scotchmans Hill Winery**, 8km NE. The fishing and seaside resort of **Portarlington** is 8km NE. At the **Edwards Point**

Wildlife Reserve, 13km east, there is a memorial commemorating the landing by Matthew Flinders in 1802 and John Batman in 1835.

TOURIST INFO: A Maze'N Things, Cnr Bellarine Peninsula Hwy and Grubb Rd, Ph: (03) 5250 2669

Echuca   POP 10 870
Map 208, A2

Founded in 1863, Echuca is one of the state's oldest river towns. Echuca was originally a **Murray River** crossing point to and from its twin town, **Moama**, in New South Wales. An historic iron bridge still joins the 2 towns.

MAIN ATTRACTIONS: Echuca's interesting history, old paddlesteamers and picturesque setting have contributed to it becoming a thriving tourist destination. **Echuca Wharf**, built of red gum in 1865, was once 5 times its present size and is still a massive structure built on 3 levels to accommodate the rise and fall of the Murray River. There are also a number of paddlesteamers moored at the wharf, including the *Pevensey*, once used in a TV mini-series. The paddlesteamers are all available for cruises. A museum in the **Cargo Wharf Shed** houses dioramas portraying the life and activity of the port and runs a 10min audiovisual presentation on Echuca's history. The **Bridge Hotel**, built by the ex-convict founder of Echuca, Henry Hopwood, has some rooms furnished in period-style, the most interesting is the squatter's suite. **Echuca Historical Society Museum** is located in the old Police Station and gaol (1867). Fun attractions for families include the **Echuca Farmyard**, which has only small animals; the **Murray River Aquarium**; **Sharp's Magic Movie House and Penny Arcade**; **World in Wax**; **National Holden Museum**; and **Oz Maze**. Echucha hosts several festivals, including the **Heritage Steam Festival** in October, and the

Riverboat Jazz and Wine Festival in February.

NEARBY ATTRACTIONS: Just out of town, in the area registered as the **Perricoota Wine Region**, are several new wineries and a **Wine Trail** brochure is available. **Barmah SF**, with its ancient red gums is located 39km NE. Nearby, **Dharnya Aboriginal Interpretive Centre** has displays tracing the history and culture of the local Yorta Yorta people. **Barmah Lake** is ideal for fishing, canoeing, swimming or enjoying a wetlands' cruise.

TOURIST INFO: Echuca Historic Pump House, Cobb Hwy, Echuca, Ph: (03) 5480 7555 or 1800 804 446

Edenhope   POP 820
Map 206, B5

This small west **Wimmera** town is the administrative centre for sheep and cattle country that was first settled in 1845. Vast wetlands surround the town, which lies on the shores of **Lake Wallace**.

MAIN ATTRACTIONS: A cairn beside the lake commemorates the first Aboriginal cricket team to tour England (1868). The team was made up of players from the Edenhope and Harrow district and was coached on the shores of Lake Wallace, they also played in Melbourne and Sydney. Lake Wallace is 7m deep when full and is a habitat for many species of waterbirds. It is one of the best fly-fishing spots in the district with anglers targeting trout and redfin. There are 2 board-walks on the walking and cycling track around the lake for viewing the birdlife. Lake Wallace is also a popular recreational area with swimmers, anglers and boating enthusiasts. The endangered red-tailed black cockatoo can be seen around the golf course at certain times of the year.

NEARBY ATTRACTIONS: **Bailey's Rocks**, huge pink and green granite boulders, 30km south of Edenhope,

Victoria

is a significant local landmark and an impressive geological feature. It is a popular picnic area.
TOURIST INFO: Old Court House, 96 Elizabeth St, Ph: (03) 5585 1509

Eildon POP 725
Map 212, D1
In a region that once thrived on timber and goldmining, Eildon, 130km NE of Melbourne, was built in the 1950s to house employees of the **Lake Eildon Dam** project. Construction of the dam created **Lake Eildon**—officially opened 1956—the largest artificial lake in Victoria and the main storage for the vast **Goulburn Irrigation System**. The town is almost surrounded by **Lake Eildon NP** (Frasers NP).
MAIN ATTRACTIONS: Eildon has become a popular destination for inland waterskiers, wakeboarders, anglers, sailing enthusiasts, canoeists, sailboarders and jet skiers. Over 800 houseboats are moored on the lake, and at **Eildon Boat Harbour**, boats and equipment of all sorts, including houseboats, are available for hire. There are a variety of self-guided walks, drives and horse-riding trails available from the town.
NEARBY ATTRACTIONS: Part of Lake Eildon is contained within Lake Eildon NP. Watersports, fishing, walking and camping are popular

Puffing Billy steam train near Emerald

activities in the 300km² park, which is home to a variety of birds, kangaroos, wallabies and deer. Hand-feeding the deer is an attraction at **Eildon Deer Park**. The **Snobs Creek Discovery Centre and Freshwater Fish Hatchery**, 6km SW, breeds millions of fingerling trout to stock the state's waterways; it is open to the public. Nearby, the creek drops downhill in a series of cascades known as **Snobs Creek Falls**.
TOURIST INFO: Eildon Resource Centre, Main St, Ph: (03) 5774 2909

Emerald POP 4870
Map 171, D5
This picturesque township was the first white settlement in the **Dandenong Ranges**. Emerald, 49km east of Melbourne, attracts many visitors.
MAIN ATTRACTIONS: **Emerald Lake Park** offers a footbridge over the lake, waterslides, children's wading pool, picnic tables, BBQs, tearooms and walking trails; pedal boats can be hired here. A major attraction, the *Puffing Billy* steam train runs between **Belgrave** and **Gembrook**, Emerald and the park are two of the train's stopping points. In April the **Great Train Race** is held, where runners race *Puffing Billy* from Belgrave to Emerald Lake Park. Emerald is also home to the largest model railway in the Southern Hemisphere. **Emerald Lake Model Railway** has around 35 model trains, open Tues–Sun, 11.30am–5pm.
NEARBY ATTRACTIONS: The **Motorist Cafe and Museum** has many heritage cars on display and is located in Main St, Gembrook, 14km east of Emerald. **Sherbrooke Equestrian Park**, 3km west, organises horseriding treks. The **Puffing Billy Steam Museum** is at **Menzies Creek**, 4km NW of Emerald, and is open weekends, Wednesdays and public holidays.
TOURIST INFO: 1211 Burwood Hwy, Upper Ferntree Gully, Ph: (03) 9758 7522

Euroa POP 2940
Map 208, C4
Euroa, 140km from Melbourne, is a pleasant town set against a backdrop of the **Strathbogie Ranges**. Surrounded by one of the finest wool-producing regions in Victoria, albeit a shrinking industry. The amazing and tragically underrated Eliza Forlonge, with financial backing from Janet Templeton, personally selected core breeding stock of Saxon sheep from war-torn northern Europe in the 1820s and early 1830s. One flock was sold to John Macarthur, others went to Tasmania and Western Australia. Eliza eventually came to Australia and settled first in Goulburn, then walked her flock to Victoria and settled close to where the town now stands and built **Seven Creeks Station**. Her impact on the Australian economy was and is enormous.
MAIN ATTRACTIONS: A 19th-century inn houses the **Farmers' Arms Museum**, displaying historic items from the district, including patchwork quilts dating back to 1896. One room is dedicated to Eliza Forlonge and there are 2 machinery sheds where equipment from the past is on display. The museum, located at 25 Kirkland Ave West, is open Fri–Mon, 1pm–4pm. Starting from the museum is a 2.7km **heritage trail**, which explores Euroa township. **Seven Creeks Park** offers picnic and BBQ facilities. **Balloon Victoria** operates hot-air balloon flights in Euroa.
NEARBY ATTRACTIONS: A self-guided scenic drive leads visitors to **Gooram Falls**, 20km SE, and around the Strathbogie Ranges. Gliding and parachuting opportunities are available at **Locksley**, 20km SW. For a panoramic view of the **Victorian Alps** and surrounding country, visit **Mount Wombat lookout**, 25km SW, via a scenic drive.
TOURIST INFO: BP Service Station, 29 Tarcombe Rd, Ph: (03) 5795 3677

DANDENONG RANGES

Only a hour's drive from Melbourne, the beautiful Dandenong Ranges form a natural backdrop to Victoria's capital city, attracting hordes of city visitors annually to this green haven of hills and forests. Rising to an average elevation of 500–600m, the Dandenong Ranges peak at **Mount Dandenong**, 633m above sea level.

Colourful, inviting and cool, especially in summer, the Dandenongs are popular for daytrips, not only for their intrinsic beauty but also for the many beautiful gardens and great variety of European and native trees and shrubs. The Dandenongs are home to 6 of the **Great Gardens of Melbourne**. The rich volcanic soil and plentiful rain ensures that plants flourish here, and there are many nurseries and arboretums to visit. The smattering of restaurants, art galleries, antique shops and tearooms in the many townships of the Dandenongs provide excellent detours from exploring the region's stunning scenery.

Sculpture at William Ricketts Sanctuary, Mount Dandenong

Tourist information

Dandenong Ranges and Knox Visitor Information Centre
1211 Burwood Hwy
Upper Ferntree Gully, Vic 3156
Ph: (03) 9758 7522
www.yarrarangestourism.com

Puffing Billy

This vintage steam train has run almost continuously since its debut in 1900. With its open carriages and restaurant car, it is one of Victoria's top attractions. On total fire ban days, diesel locomotives replace it. The 25km journey between **Belgrave** and **Gembrook** and back again is beautiful and includes travelling over timber trestle bridges and through forests and tree ferns.

main attractions

◈ **Belgrave**
Home to the beloved vintage steam train *Puffing Billy*.

◈ **Dandenong Ranges NP**
See the world's tallest flowering plant in the Dandenongs—the mountain ash tree.

◈ **Mount Dandenong Observatory**
This lookout offers a breathtaking vantage point for panoramic views over Melbourne, Port Phillip and Western Port.

◈ **Olinda**
An ideal time to visit Olinda is in spring during the floral festival, when the town is a riot of colour.

◈ **Sassafras**
Picturesque Sassafras offers charming stores and galleries.

◈ **William Ricketts Sanctuary**
This sanctuary is a testimony to the work of Ricketts, who spent much time with the Aboriginal people of Central Australia. The setting of fern gardens and rock waterfalls provide a natural gallery for his kiln-fired sculptures of Aboriginal people.

Tesselaar's Tulip Festival, Silvan

Victoria

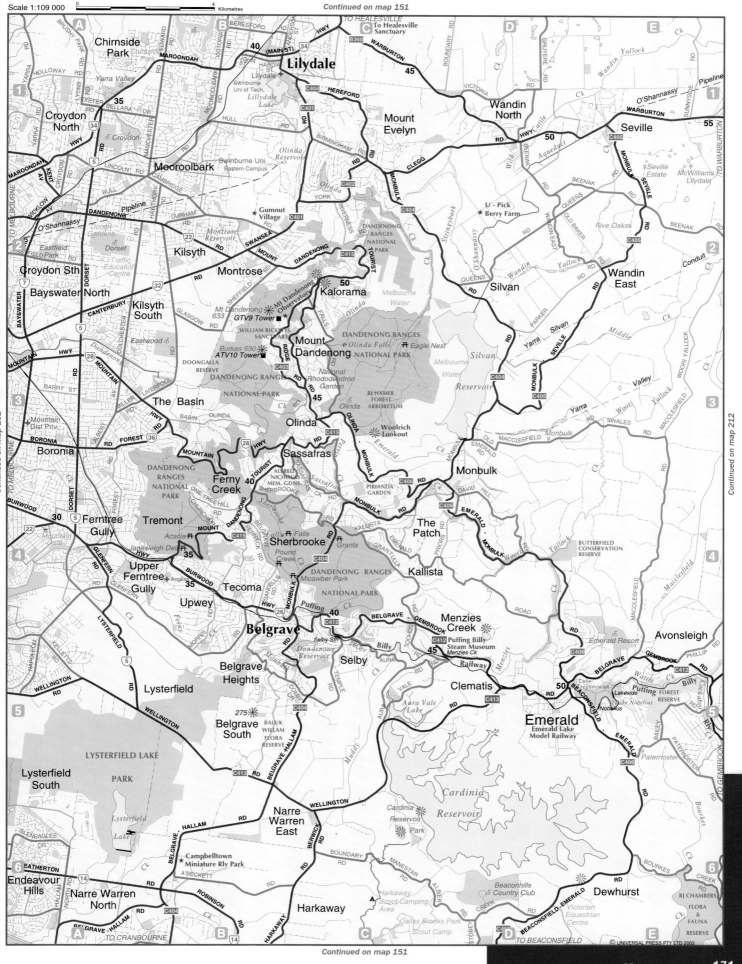

Scale 1:109 000

Continued on map 151

Continued on map 151

Continued on map 212

© UNIVERSAL PRESS PTY LTD 2002

Geelong   POP 146 166

Map 201, J3

The second largest provincial city in Victoria, Geelong is a deepwater port and industrial centre on the shores of **Corio Bay**. Much of Geelong's early wealth was created by wool exports and added to by thousands of gold-seekers passing through on their way to **Bendigo** and **Ballarat**; gold was exported through the port. Geelong is a well-planned city with many parks and open spaces.

MAIN ATTRACTIONS: The renowned botanist Ferdinand von Mueller laid out Geelong's fine **Botanic Gardens**, which overlook Corio Bay. A special feature is the historic first **Customs House**, prefabricated in Sydney and shipped to Geelong in 1838. **Eastern Beach** is in the same vicinity as the gardens. The 1930s beach facilities have been refurbished in recent years and the enclosed pool is a popular swimming area. **Geelong waterfront** is an attractive leisure precinct with restaurants and attractions. **The National Wool Museum** is one of more than 100 National Trust buildings in the city. There are displays in the bluestone

Geelong waterfront

museum telling the complete story of the Australian wool industry as well as recreated shearers' quarters. The museum is on the corner of Moorabool and Brougham sts. **Christ Church**, in Moorabool St, is the oldest Anglican Church in Victoria that is still in use. The **Geelong Art Gallery**, the largest regional gallery in Victoria, and the **Performing Arts Centre** are both located in Little Malop St.

NEARBY ATTRACTIONS: There are many wineries in the Geelong area, a number of them offer tastings of the local cabernet sauvignon, shiraz and chardonnay. Details are available from the information centre. **You Yangs Regional Park**, a range of granite hills 20km north, offers picnic grounds and walking tracks. The **Serendip Sanctuary**, close to the You Yangs, is 250ha of open grassy woodlands and wetlands. There are nature trails, bird hides and a visitors' centre with displays of brolgas, bustards and pademelons. **Brisbane Ranges NP**, located 34km north, offers the state's richest wildflower habitat. The old gold town of **Steiglitz**, 10km NW of **Anakie**, features the restored **Court House**; open Sundays.

TOURIST INFO: National Wool Museum, Cnr Moorabool and Brougham sts, Ph: 1800 620 888

Gisborne   POP 3578

Map 167, D3

Jacksons Creek flows through the town of Gisborne, which lies in the foothills of **Mount Macedon**. Gisborne is a pretty little town, about 52km from Melbourne.

MAIN ATTRACTIONS: There are many art and craft shops in the town. **Jacksons Creek** and **Gisborne Botanic Garden** offer recreation areas and picnic facilities. **Mount Gisborne Wines** in Watersun Rd specialises in chardonnay and pinot noir. The winery is open for tastings and sales on weekends. **Barringo**

Wildlife Reserve is an area of natural bushland which protects native wildlife. There are also deer, peacocks and a lake well stocked with trout.

NEARBY ATTRACTIONS: The township of **Mount Macedon** is north of Gisborne. Here, in the late 1800s, wealthy residents of Melbourne built estates to escape to during summer. Visitors continue to visit the old homes and grand European-style gardens, despite so many of them being devastated in the 1983 bush fires. Springtime flower shows and open garden days are a highlight of the area.

TOURIST INFO: Ampol Road Pantry, 4 Station Rd, Ph: (03) 5428 2541

Hamilton   POP 9879

Map 210, D2

A major centre for **south-west Victoria**, Hamilton is also known as the **'Wool Capital of the World'**. Around 294km west of Melbourne, it is located on the largest volcanic plain in the Southern Hemisphere. Hamilton is a good base from which to explore the area; both **Portland** and **Port Fairy**, to the south, are within easy reach.

MAIN ATTRACTIONS: **Lake Hamilton** is located on the eastern side of town and is a focus for local recreation. A walking track follows the lake and ends at a small swimming beach. **Ansett Transport Museum** is also beside the lake. The **Botanic Gardens**, in Thompson St, are ideal for picnics and relaxing. The **Pastoral Museum** is one of many historic buildings preserving the district's rural heritage. **Hamilton Art Gallery** has the impressive **Paul Sandby Collection**, which was donated by a local grazier. The **Big Woolbales Complex**, located in Coleraine Rd, displays woolshed memorabilia. **Hamilton Country Spun Woollen Mill and Factory**, in Peck St, offers sales and tours of the factory, Mon–Fri.

Victoria

NEARBY ATTRACTIONS: Hamilton is a 20min drive from the foothills of the **Grampians NP**. The town is an accommodation centre and service base for visitors to the national park. Features of **Mount Eccles NP**, 35km south, include 3 extinct volcanoes. Camping is permitted at Mount Eccles.
TOURIST INFO: Lonsdale St, Ph: (03) 5572 3746

Healesville   POP 8850
Map 212, C2
This attractive town is a popular destination for Melbourne residents as it is just over an hour's drive north-east, through the renowned vineyard country of the **Yarra Valley**. The wineries are not the only attraction. Healesville is also the gateway to the **Great Dividing Range** with its huge mountain ash forests and waterfalls.
MAIN ATTRACTIONS: One end of the **Yarra Valley Tourist Railway** is located in Healesville. On Sundays and public holidays, motorised trolleys travel every 30mins through an historic 100m brick-lined tunnel.
NEARBY ATTRACTIONS: The renowned **Healesville Sanctuary** is located 4km south of town at **Mount Riddell**. Over 200 species of native birds, mammals and reptiles are displayed in their natural habitat. There are over **30 wineries** throughout the Yarra Valley, all open for cellar door sales and tastings. Many of the larger wineries have restaurants attached. Wine tours of the Yarra Valley are also available. **Yarra Ranges NP** is east of the town and features mountain ash forest with an understorey of tree ferns. A rainforest gallery with an observation platform and walkway is provided on the slopes of **Mount Donna Buang**. Scenic drives include one through the forest over **Black Spur**, so-called because it was a route taken by displaced Aborigines. **Maroondah Reservoir**

and the **Badger and Donnelly weirs** offer many bushland walks as well as picnic and BBQ facilities.
TOURIST INFO: The Old Court House, Harker St, Ph: (03) 5962 2600

Heathcote   POP 2500
Map 208, A5
This town, 105km north of Melbourne, is located in picturesque countryside. Heathcote was a creation of the goldrush when the population reached 35 000. Today, its wide main streets with many historic buildings evoke feelings of the past.
MAIN ATTRACTIONS: **Pink Cliffs**, located in a reserve off Pink Cliffs Rd, are a local feature. The ever-changing pink shades of miniature gorges and pinnacles was created in the 1800s by mining activity. **McIvor Range Reserve** has basic picnic facilities and there are walking tracks to **Devils Cave** and **Viewing Rock**, which provide panoramic views of Heathcote and the surrounding countryside.
NEARBY ATTRACTIONS: Vineyards in the surrounding area supply grapes to winemakers throughout Victoria. Wineries in the immediate region include **Heathcote Winery** and **Wild Duck Creek Estate**. There are 2 yabby farms near Heathcote: **Central Victorian Yabby Farm** and **AV Yabbies**. Both farms are open for tours and offer visitors the chance to catch a yabby. **Dargile Flora and Fauna Reserve** is ideal for bushwalking and birdwatching. There is a picnic area, rotunda, BBQs and facilities. **Lake Eppalock** is popular for fishing and boating.
TOURIST INFO: Cnr High and Barrack sts, Ph: (03) 5433 3121

Heyfield   POP 1680
Map 213, F3
A prosperous timber-milling and tourist town, Heyfield is 195km SE of Melbourne. It is located in the centre of a dairying and beef cattle

Yarra Valley vineyard in the Healesville area

district based around the **Thomson River** and **Glenmaggie Weir**.
MAIN ATTRACTIONS: Heyfield offers many recreational activities, including golf, fishing, horse racing, yachting, power boating, bushwalking and trail bike riding. Local timber mills produce kiln-dried hardwood and several of them are open for inspection.
NEARBY ATTRACTIONS: Heyfield is ideally located as a departure point for tourist drives in the **Maffra** region. This region has many art and craft shops, markets, antique shops, general stores, galleries and pottery studios. The scenic drive to **Licola** offers many natural attractions. There are several tracks and river crossings for 4WDing. **Lake Glenmaggie**, 11km north, is popular for boating, swimming and fishing. Between June and September, excellent cross-country skiing conditions can usually be found north of Licola, in the region of **Mount Tamboritha** and **Mount Skene**.
TOURIST INFO: 1 Tyson Rd, Ph: (03) 5148 2356

Horsham POP 13 650

Map 206, D4

Situated 300km NW of Melbourne, Horsham is located in flat, open country and services a vast rural district producing wheat and livestock. Horsham is regarded as the capital of the **Wimmera** region and is a good base for travellers intent on exploring the **Grampians**, and **Little Desert NP** among others.

MAIN ATTRACTIONS: **Horsham Art Gallery** features the Mack Jost bequest and includes a Rembrandt, drawings by Hans Heysen and Lambert, several Charles Bush paintings and Charles Blackman's *Nocturnal Landscape*. The **Botanic Gardens** are laid out along the banks of the **Wimmera River**. A lemon-scented gum and a bunya pine stand sentinel at the entrance to the gardens, which were designed in the 1870s by William Guilfoyle, the curator of the Melbourne Royal Botanic Gardens.

NEARBY ATTRACTIONS: There are many daytrips visitors can make from Horsham. To the south there are **Black Ranges SP**, **Rocklands Reservoir** and the Grampians.

Climber on Mount Arapiles, west of Horsham

To the west, **Mount Arapiles** attracts climbers from around the world. Little Desert NP protects many endangered native plants and animals. Next to this national park, in the town of **Dimboola**, is the **Australian Pure Olive Oil Company**. The plantation of 20 000 trees, which is the largest in the Southern Hemisphere, was planted in 1945 and covers 121ha. Fishing for trout and redfin is popular in **Green Lake**, 13km SE and **Taylors Lake**, 18km SE.

TOURIST INFO: 20 O'Callaghan Pde, Ph: (03) 5382 1832

Inverloch POP 2678

Map 212, C4

This small seaside town is situated on **Anderson Inlet**, 150km SE of Melbourne. The many surfing beaches make Inverloch a popular destination for surfers and families.

MAIN ATTRACTIONS: Grouped together in the foreshore reserve are the **Environment Centre**, where **Inverloch Shell Museum** displays one of the best private collections of shells in Australia and **Rainbow Park**, a colourful children's play area and picnic spot. Inverloch is located in **South Gippsland** and its coastline has many attractions. Mangroves grow here at their southern limit, and, when the tide is out, it is possible to walk over the sands of the inlet and see the mangroves fully exposed. There are many rockpools to explore. Fishing, birdwatching, sailing and wind-surfing are also popular activities.

NEARBY ATTRACTIONS: For watching waterbirds both **Townsend Bluff** and **Mahers Landing** are good spots. The scenic drive from Inverloch to **Cape Paterson** offers stunning coastal views and edges the **Bunurong Marine Park**. The **Tarwin River**, 20km SE, provides good fishing opportunities.

TOURIST INFO: William St, Ph: (03) 5674 3510

Irymple POP 1150

Map 204, D2

In the heart of the **Sunraysia** district, 9km south of Mildura, Irymple is the centre of a citrus, dried fruit and winegrowing area.

MAIN ATTRACTIONS: Processing the region's crops into dried fruit is a major industry in Irymple. At **Australian Dried Fruit Sales** in Sunbeam Ave, guided tours show the processing and packaging of Sunbeam dried fruits. Fresh and dried-fruit recipe books and souvenirs can be purchased. There are many wineries in the region, but only one vineyard in Irymple. **Milburn Park Winery**, located in Campbell Ave, offers cellar door sales and tastings.

NEARBY ATTRACTIONS: Irymple offers easy access to many of the region's attractions, including the **Murray River** and **Mildura**.

TOURIST INFO: The Alfred Deakin Centre, 180 Deakin Ave, Mildura, Ph: (03) 5021 4424

Kerang POP 4375

Map 207, H1

Located 280km north of Melbourne and around 30km from the **Murray River**, Kerang is the centre of a large rural area. Lakes, waterways and swamps are around the town. The waterways are breeding grounds for many waterbirds, including the protected ibis—walking and flying pest controllers, especially valued for their appetite for locusts.

MAIN ATTRACTIONS: More ibis breed in the rookeries around Kerang than anywhere else in the world. An estimated 200 000 white ibis, straw-necked ibis and the rare glossy ibis nest each spring. There are major rookeries located at **Middle** and **Third lakes** to the west of Kerang. A hide at **Middle Lake** allows easier viewing. The best time to see birds soaring gracefully over the lakes and waterways is early morning or evening. Some of the lakes are

Victoria

suitable for watersports. **Lake Charm** is good for waterskiing, while **First Lake** offers a pleasant picnic area and the shallow water is ideal for swimming. **Lester Lookout Tower**, once the town's water storage, houses the **Gemstone Museum** and offers some regional information for visitors. The climb up the 83 steps to the top of the tower is worthwhile for the view.

NEARBY ATTRACTIONS: **Gunbower SF**, 25km north, is an important red gum habitat. **Murrabit**, 27km north, is a picturesque town on the Murray River. The **Murrabit markets** are held on the first Saturday of each month.

TOURIST INFO: Golden Rivers Country Visitor Information Centre, Murray St, Barham, Ph: (03) 5453 3100 or 1800 621 882

▪ Kilmore   POP 2950
Map 167, E2

Kilmore was founded in 1841 making it Victoria's oldest inland town. Located 60km north of Melbourne, Kilmore is known for its historic buildings. Many of the fine old stone buildings have been refurbished and some are now antique and specialty shops.

MAIN ATTRACTIONS: **Whitburgh Cottage**, built in 1857, is now a museum providing an insight into the lifestyle of a typical 19th-century family. The museum is open Sun, 2pm–4pm. Other historic buildings include the **Post Office** and old **Court House**, built in the early 1860s, and several main street shops and hotels dating back to the 1850s. Kilmore is renowned for its horseracing events and hosts the **Kilmore Racing Cup** and **Kilmore Pacing Cup**, Australia's richest provincial harness racing event.

NEARBY ATTRACTIONS: The **Tramways Museum** is located in **Bylands**, south of Kilmore. The museum has an extensive display of cable cars and early electric trams, and offers tram rides. It is open Sunday, 10am–5pm. On the **Mount Piper**

Rural scene in the Strzelecki Ranges, north of Korumburra

Walking Track—a 1hr return walk—visitors will see a variety of wildlife and wildflowers. **Strath Creek** and **Strath Creek Falls** are also worthwhile exploring. From here visitors are urged to take the scenic drive through the **Valley of a Thousand Hills**.

TOURIST INFO: 12 Sydney St, Ph: (03) 5781 1319

▪ Korumburra   POP 2949
Map 212, D4

Situated 118km SE of Melbourne, Korumburra is surrounded by dairying country and is a regional cattle-sales centre. The **Bass Valley**, north-east of Korumburra, is home to the rare and protected giant Gippsland earthworm, known as Karmai to the Aborigines. The worms can grow to an amazing 3m in length and 2.5cm in diameter.

MAIN ATTRACTIONS: **Coal Creek Heritage Village**, south of the town centre, is a re-creation of the coal-mining days of the 1890s. Features include the original Coal Creek Mine Tunnel, a bush tramway and authentic settlers' cottages. There is also a simulated mine explosion daily.

NEARBY ATTRACTIONS: The **South Gippsland Railway** operates train rides, which start at Korumburra

and travel 40km through the lower part of the **Strzelecki Ranges** to **Nyora**, stopping at **Loch**. This town, 14km NW of Korumburra, has many antique, art and craft shops.

TOURIST INFO: Cnr Silkstone Rd, south Gippsland Hwy, Ph: (03) 5655 2233 or 1800 630 704

▪ Kyabram   POP 6254
Map 208, B3

A friendly tree-lined country town in the dairying and fruit-growing region of the western **Goulburn Valley**, Kyabram is 192km north of Melbourne.

MAIN ATTRACTIONS: **Kyabram Fauna Park** is an award-winning 55ha reserve protecting wildlife, including free-roaming kangaroos and emus. Crocodiles are kept in a solar-heated reptile house. Wetlands support a variety of waterbirds, which can be observed from a raised hide. Also in the park are **Hazelmans Cottage**, a restored and refurnished settler's cottage, a restaurant, kiosk, and picnic and BBQ facilities. **Eddis Park Arboretum** is lovely for picnics under 200-year-old grey box gums, and for pleasant walks.

TOURIST INFO: Kyabram Fauna Park, 75 Lake Rd, Ph: (03) 5852 2883

GIPPSLAND LAKES

Lying parallel to **Bass Strait** and separated from the ocean by **Ninety Mile Beach**, the Gippsland Lakes are Australia's largest system of inland waterways. Stretching from **Yarram** in the west to **Lakes Entrance** in the east and the foothills of Victoria's **High Country** to the north, this region is a rich water playground. The area was once occupied by a clan of the Gunai/Kurnai Aboriginal people—evidence of their occupation can still be seen.

Five lakes cover around 400km²: **King**, **Coleman**, **Wellington**, **Reeve** and **Victoria**. These lakes parallel Ninety Mile Beach, providing a unique natural environment protected by **The Lakes NP** and **Gippsland Lakes Coastal Park**.

Promoted as the '**Victorian Riviera**', temperatures here can be up to 6°C warmer than in Melbourne. The region is dotted with holiday villages providing easy access to every imaginable form of water activity, including sailing, windsurfing and self-drive cruiser hire. Opportunities for fishing abound, making Gippsland Lakes a drawcard for lake, beach and offshore anglers seeking bream, flathead, whiting, skip jack, mullet, salmon and other species.

With the foothills of the High Country only a short drive away, visitors also have the chance to explore alpine mountains, forests and national parks and the many other attractions offered in this area.

Sailing on the Gippsland Lakes

 Tourist information

Central Gippsland Visitor Information Centre
8 Foster St, Sale, Vic 3850
Ph: (03) 5144 1108
Freecall: 1800 677 520

main attractions

- ◈ Bairnsdale
- ◈ Lakes NP
- ◈ Metung
- ◈ Ninety Mile Beach
- ◈ Paynesville

Railway viaduct at Malmsbury, NW of Kyneton

■ **Kyneton**   POP 4387
Map 167, C1

Kyneton, 86km north of Melbourne, is an attractive historic town featuring 19th-century bluestone architecture. Small-scale manufacturing and farming boomed in the 1850s and 1860s in the rush to feed the thousands of miners who flocked to the district.

MAIN ATTRACTIONS: Historic **Piper St** offers many specialty stores selling antiques, furniture, crafts and gourmet food. **Kyneton Museum**, a bluestone building that was once the Bank of New South Wales, recreates family life as it was in Victorian times. In the grounds are stables, a coach house and a drop-log cottage. The museum is open Fri–Sun and public holidays, 11am–4pm. Other buildings of note include **Willis Steam Mill**, the **Court House** and churches. **Kyneton Botanic Gardens**, in Clowes St, features a collection of rare and endangered trees, including a Chilean wine palm, blue atlas cedars and a golden English oak. The **Campaspe River** flows through the gardens and picnics on its banks are popular, as is the walking track from the gardens to the nearby racecourse.

NEARBY ATTRACTIONS: In recent years, the **Macedon wine region** has spread north-west to Kyneton and a number of wineries are within easy reach of the town. The township of **Malmsbury**, 10km NW, has a number of historic bluestone buildings, including a bluestone railway viaduct.

TOURIST INFO: Jean Haynes Playground, High St, Ph: (03) 5422 6110

Victoria

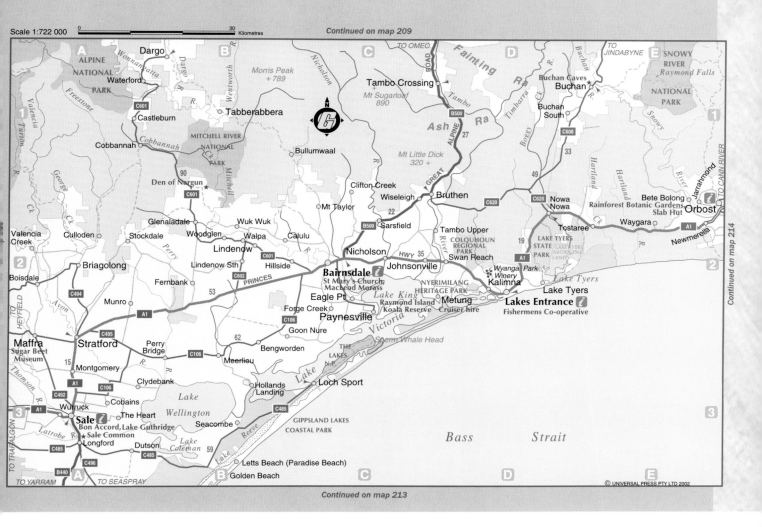

Continued on map 209

Scale 1:722 000

0   30 Kilometres

Continued on map 213

Continued on map 214

© UNIVERSAL PRESS PTY LTD 2002

■ Lakes Entrance   POP 5850

Map 177, D2

Situated on a permanent artificial opening to the **Gippsland Lakes** waterways, Lakes Entrance is a popular summer resort and active fishing port with 100 vessels, many of them engaged in deep-sea fishing. Lakes Entrance is located at the eastern end of the largest inland lakes system in Australia.

MAIN ATTRACTIONS: The greatest attractions of the area are the beaches and waterways. Famous **Ninety Mile Beach** (145km long) is a narrow stretch of sand, backed by extensive sand dunes, separating the Bass Strait and the lakes. A footbridge over **Cunningham Arm** connects the surf beach with the esplanade. Ferry services and cruise boats offer a variety of ways to explore the lakes. Boats of all kinds can be hired for sightseeing, sailing or fishing expeditions. There are also a number of excellent launching places around the lake. The **Fishermen's Cooperative** on **Bullock Island** offers freshly caught fish for sale.

NEARBY ATTRACTIONS: **Wyanga Park Vineyard and Winery** is 10km north and can also be reached by boat. **Nyerimilang Heritage Park** is 10km NW and the **East Gippsland Botanic Gardens**, also here, offer pleasant walks in relaxing surroundings and rose-pruning tips in July. **Lake Tyers Forest Park**, to the northeast, is an ideal spot for bushwalking, picnicking and camping.

TOURIST INFO: Cnr Marine Pde and The Esplanade, Princes Hwy, Ph: (03) 5155 1966 or 1800 637 060

Canoeing on the Tambo River, west of Lakes Entrance

WILSONS PROMONTORY

Once part of the ancient land bridge to Tasmania, Wilsons Promontory is the southernmost point of the Australian mainland. The area is protected by one of Victoria's oldest and most spectacular national parks, reserved in 1898. Its pristine beaches and coves framed by granite masses, rivers and creeks, and rugged mountain ranges, are pre-served by their remoteness. How-ever, the accommodation and camp-ing grounds at **Tidal River** are lively during summer and school holidays.

Visitors have always been intrigued by the majestic coastline and botanical abundance of Wilsons Promontory. **'The Prom'** contains the largest coastal wilderness area in Victoria. It features over 700 flowering native plant species growing in diverse habitats. There are tall eucalypts, moist fern gullies, groves of brown and yellow stringy-barks, copses of banksias and tea-trees, salt marshes and stands of white mangrove.

In spring, see the abundant wildflowers or visit in autumn when temperatures are cool and ideal for walking. Conditions can be cold and bleak but sometimes fresh and bracing in winter. In summer it is extremely crowded.

The 500km^2 national park has more than 150km of walking tracks. Permits are required for overnight hiking and a ballot system is used for the holiday cabins.

> **Tourist information**
>
> **Wilsons Promontory NP**
> **Park Office and Visitors Centre**
> Tidal River, Vic 3960
> Freecall: 1800 350 552
> www.parkweb.vic.gov.au

Norman Island viewed from Whisky Bay

■ Leongatha   POP 4144
Map 212, D4

Situated near the foothills of the **Strzelecki Ranges**, Leongatha is a service centre for the surrounding rural district. Dairying is a major industry here and the Murray Goulburn Cooperative Dairy is the largest in Australia.

MAIN ATTRACTIONS: The **Firelight Museum** displays a collection of antique lamps and firearms, some more than 400 years old. The **Historic Society Museum** contains some interesting displays worth-while investigating. **Leongatha Gallery** displays local arts and crafts and hosts changing exhibitions.

NEARBY ATTRACTIONS: The town is a good base for exploring **Wilsons Promontory** and the seaside and fishing villages along the coast. The **South Gippsland Railway** operates train rides from nearby **Korumburra** to **Loch** and **Nyora**. Departure times are available from the Korumburra information centre. The **Grand Ridge Brewing Company**, located at **Mirboo North**, 26km NE, offers tours of the beer-brewing process and sales. **Moss Vale Park** with its avenue of redwoods, is 16km NE, and offers good picnic and BBQ facilities. The **soundshell**, also located in the park, is the venue for a performance by the Victoria State Orchestra each February.
TOURIST INFO: Cnr Silkstone Rd, South Gippsland Hwy, Korumburra
Ph: (03) 5655 2233 or 1800 630 704

South Gippsland picnic, near Leongatha

Victoria

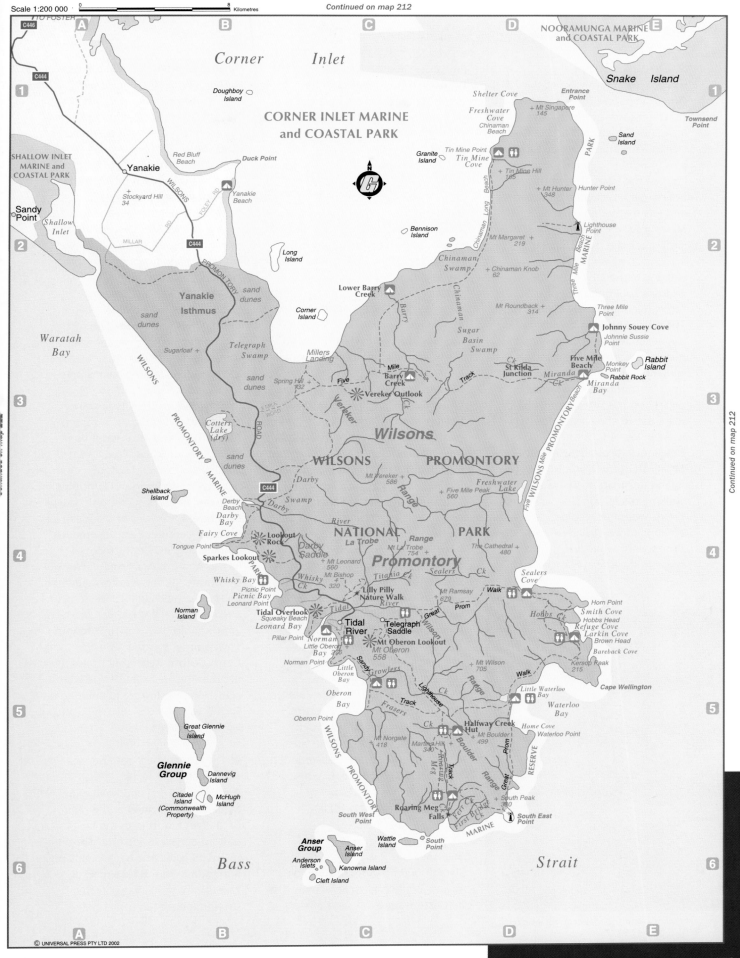

Scale 1:200 000   0 — 8 Kilometres

Corner   Inlet

CORNER INLET MARINE
and COASTAL PARK

Snake   Island

NOORAMUNGA MARINE
and COASTAL PARK

TO FOSTER

Doughboy
Island

Shelter Cove

Entrance
Point

+ Mt Singapore
145

Townsend
Point

Yanakie

Red Bluff
Beach

Duck Point

SHALLOW INLET
MARINE and
COASTAL PARK

Yanakie
Beach

+ Stockyard Hill
34

Sandy
Point

*Shallow
Inlet*

Freshwater
Cove

Chinaman
Beach

Tin Mine Point

Granite
Island

Tin Mine
Cove

Sand
Island

+ Tin Mine Hill
165

+ Mt Hunter
348

Hunter Point

Lighthouse
Point

Bennison
Island

Mt Margaret
219 +

Three
Mile
Point

*Waratah
Bay*

Long
Island

Yanakie
Isthmus

sand
dunes

Corner
Island

*Chinaman
Swamp*

+ Chinaman Knob
62

Lower Barry
Creek

Sugar
Basin
Swamp

Mt Roundback +
314

Three Mile
Point

Johnny Souey Cove

Johnnie Sussie
Point

St Kilda
Junction

Miranda
Ck

Five Mile
Beach

Monkey
Point

Rabbit
Island

sand
dunes

Telegraph
Swamp

Millers
Landing

Mile
Barry
Creek

Track

Rabbit Rock

*Miranda
Bay*

Sugarloaf +

sand
dunes

Spring Hill
132

Five

Vereker Outlook

Vereker

Wilsons

Cotters
Lake
(dry)

sand
dunes

WILSONS   PROMONTORY

Mt Vereker
586 +

Freshwater
Lake

+ Five Mile Peak
560

Shellback
Island

C444

Darby

Swamp

Darby

Mt La Trobe
754 +

La Trobe   *Range*

NATIONAL   PARK

The Cathedral +
480

Derby
Beach

*Darby
Bay*

Fairy Cove

River

Promontory

Sealers   Ck

Sealers
Cove

Lookout
Rock

Tongue Point

+ Mt Leonard
560

Sparkes Lookout

*Darby
Saddle*

Mt Bishop
320 +

Titania   Ck

Mt Ramsay
670 +

Prom

Walk

Horn Point

Smith Cove

Hobbs Ck

Hobbs Head
Refuge Cove

Whisky Bay

Picnic Point
Picnic Bay
Leonard Point

Whisky
Ck

Lilly Pilly
Nature Walk

River

Great

Larkin Cove

Brown Head

Bareback Cove

Norman
Island

Tidal Overlook

Squeaky Beach
Leonard Bay

Tidal
River

Telegraph
Saddle

+ Mt Wilson
705

Kersop Peak
215

Pillar Point

Norman
Bay

Little Oberon
775 +

Mt Oberon Lookout

Mt Oberon
558

Wilson   *Range*

Walk

Cape Wellington

Norman Point

*Little
Oberon
Bay*

Sandy   Growlers

Little Waterloo
Bay

*Waterloo
Bay*

*Oberon
Bay*

Frasers

Track

Lighthouse   Ck

Halfway Creek
Hut

Home Cove

Waterloo Point

Oberon Point

+ Mt Norgate
418

Martins Hill
340

+ Mt Boulder
499

Boulder

Range

Prom

RESERVE

Great Glennie
Island

*Glennie
Group*

Dannevig
Island

Citadel
Island
(Commonwealth
Property)

McHugh
Island

Roaring Meg
Ck

Roaring Meg
Falls

Fair Ck

First Bridge   Ck

WILSONS   PROMONTORY

South West
Point

Great

+ South Peak
490

South East
Point

MARINE

*Anser
Group*

Anderson
Islets

Anser
Island

Wattle
Island

South
Point

Kanowna Island

Cleft Island

Bass

Strait

© UNIVERSAL PRESS PTY LTD 2002

Continued on map 212

Lorne   POP 1230
Map 201, H4

One of Victoria's most attractive coastal resorts, Lorne, 137km SW of Melbourne, is located on the **Great Ocean Rd** with the **Otway Ranges** as a backdrop. Despite the popularity of the town as a tourist destination, it has retained its charm and has many fine old buildings.

MAIN ATTRACTIONS: Swimming and surfing are the most popular activities here, as well as bushwalking in the Otway Ranges. **Teddy's Lookout**, in George St, offers panoramic views of the bay. There is a **Shipwreck Walk** along the beach for people interested in history and exercise. Fresh fish, caught by the local fleet, can be bought from **Lorne Fisheries** on the pier. For those more interested in the creative arts, visit **Qdos Arts**, in Allenvale Rd.

NEARBY ATTRACTIONS: **Angahook-Lorne SP**, north of the town, is a popular inland destination. There are many walking tracks and the park offers rivers, waterfalls, rapids, cliffs and an abundance of native flora. Scenic drives worthwhile taking includes those to the Otway Ranges and

Erskine Falls in Angahook-Lorne NP, near Lorne

along the Great Ocean Rd. At **Gentle Annie Berry Gardens**, 26km NW, visitors are invited to pick-their-own berries in season (Nov–April).

TOURIST INFO: 144 Mountjoy Pde, Ph: (03) 52891152

Maffra   POP 4270
Map 177, A2

This town is located 228km east of Melbourne, and is surrounded by rich farming land. The 1890s saw the beginning of the sugar-beet industry in Maffra and the formation of the Maffra Sugar Beet Company. The company closed in 1946, and intensive dairying has since been the main industry on the irrigated land around Maffra.

MAIN ATTRACTIONS: The office building of the former sugar-beet factory has been moved to McMahon Dr, and is now the home of the **Maffra Sugar Beet Museum**, open Sun, 2pm–4pm. **Macalister Park** has excellent picnic facilities, BBQs and a playground. **Macalister Research Farm** is a commercially run dairy farm used for testing and demonstrating improved farming practices. The **Pino Deriu Mineral and Gemstone Collection** is housed in the old Maffra Court House, built in 1888.

NEARBY ATTRACTIONS: **Lake Glenmaggie**, 21km from Maffra, is popular for watersports and there are many scenic drives in the area. Horse trail-riding tours of the surrounding countryside and 4WD tours into the High Country are available. The **Blue Pool** on **Freestone Creek**, 10km from **Briagolong**, has a natural swimming hole surrounded by bushland; camping is permitted.

TOURIST INFO: The Court House, Johnson St, Ph: (03) 5141 1811

Maldon   POP 1255
Map 159, D2

Established in 1853, this uniquely preserved gold town lies 16km NW of **Castlemaine**, on the slopes of

Mount Tarrengower. Maldon is 136km NW of Melbourne, and is a popular destination for daytrips. The town has managed to retain its 19th-century streetscapes. Preservation is so complete that in 1996, the National Trust declared it the **'First Notable Town in Australia'**.

MAIN ATTRACTIONS: Maldon is a particularly popular destination during the **Maldon Easter Fair** and also in spring when the wildflowers put on a magnificent display. Today, Maldon's buildings and the renovated shops sell craft, pottery and antiques. Lookouts on Mount Tarrengower and **Anzac Hill** offer panoramic views of the town and surrounding districts. Brochures on a self-guided **walking tour** of the town are available from the information centre. **Clydesdale Treks and Tours** depart from the **Blacksmith and Wainwright's Shop** in High St. On Wednesdays, Sundays, public and school holidays, the **Victorian Goldfields Railway** operates steam train rides. In spring, the graves at the historic **Pioneer Cemetery** are covered with jonquils and wildflowers.

NEARBY ATTRACTIONS: **Carman's Tunnel Goldmine**, 2km SW, offers guided tours by candlelight on weekends and holidays. The reconstructed 1850s goldmining town, **Porcupine Township**, is located 3km NE. **Cairn Curran Reservoir**, 10km SW, provides picnic facilities and watersports and fishing are popular here.

TOURIST INFO: High St, Ph: (03) 5475 2569

Mallacoota   POP 1250
Map 214, D4

A tranquil fishing and holiday town, Mallacoota is located at the mouth of **Mallacoota Inlet** in the far eastern corner of Victoria. The surrounding estuaries, bays, headlands and promontories are especially scenic and many are protected by **Croajingolong NP**.

Skiing at Mount Buller

MAIN ATTRACTIONS: Swimming is popular along the foreshore reserve and there are safe swimming areas at all the beaches within Mallacoota. There are good surfing spots at **Bastion Point**, **Big Beach** and **Tip Beach**.

NEARBY ATTRACTIONS: Great bush and beach walks are within Croajingolong NP, which was declared a **World Biosphere Reserve** in 1977. This park has 100km of coastline, 320km of lake shoreline and many rivers and creeks to explore. There are many lake and river cruises available, and scenic drives and self-guided walks—brochures available from Parks Victoria. Birdwatching is particularly popular along the walking track to **Genoa Peak**, where there are over 300 species to spot, including the glossy-black cockatoo. **Gabo Island Lightstation Reserve** is 11km east. It can be enjoyed as a daytrip or visitors can arrange to stay in the Assistant Lightkeeper's residence.
TOURIST INFO: 57 Maurice Ave, Ph: (03) 5158 0788

■ Mansfield   POP 2779
Map 208, D5
The rural town of Mansfield lies in the foothills of the **Great Dividing Range**, 200km NE of Melbourne.

The area is renowned for its scenery. Summer visitors include bushwalkers, horseriders, anglers, watersports enthusiasts and those enjoying weekend getaways. Skiers descend on the area in winter. The region and some of its attractions have also been popular with film makers. The *Man from Snowy River*, as well as *Cool Change* and *The Far Country* were filmed here.
MAIN ATTRACTIONS: The town achieved notoriety when 3 policemen were ambushed nearby and shot dead by the notorious Kelly gang in 1878. Their graves are in **Mansfield Cemetery** and a monument in their memory stands at the centre of the town's roundabout. Local tour operators offer various ways to see the countryside and mountain scenery, including horseriding safaris into the Victorian Alps, camel treks, 4WD tours and hot-air balloon flights.
NEARBY ATTRACTIONS: Mansfield is the gateway to ski fields in **Merrijig**, **Mount Buller ski resort**, **Mount Stirling**, **Woods Point** and **Mount Samaria**. **Lake Eildon**, 15km south, is popular for fishing and all manner of watersports; houseboats are available for hire. The historic goldmining town of **Jamieson**, 37km south, is popular for gold fossicking and the **Jamieson River** is excellent for trout fishing. **Craig's Hut**, on **Clear Hills** near Mount Stirling, was used as Jim Craig's hut in *The Man from Snowy River* movies. A 1200m walk from the road gives access to the picnic area at the hut. However, there is no access in winter
TOURIST INFO: Historic Railway Station, Maroondah Hwy, Ph: (03) 5775 1464

■ Maryborough   POP 7600
Map 159, C2
A former goldmining town, Maryborough is situated on the northern slopes of the **Great Dividing Range**, 160km NW of

Melbourne. Today, Maryborough is the centre of a farming district and has several industries.
MAIN ATTRACTIONS: Legacies of gold boom times include many historic buildings, particularly the **McLandress Square** historic buildings, which includes the Court House, Town Hall and Post Office. Maryborough's jewel in the crown is its famous Railway Station. The information centre, an antique gallery and woodwork shop are located in the old station. Brochures on a self-guided **Historic Buildings Drive** are available from the information centre. The **Worsley Cottage Complex and Museum**, located in Palmerston St, is open on Tuesdays and Sundays. The **Central Goldfields Art Gallery**, located in Neill St in the old fire station, hosts travelling exhibitions.
NEARBY ATTRACTIONS: Brochures are also available on scenic drives of the surrounding area, which includes the **Golden Way Tourist Drive**. The once vital **Aboriginal wells**, carved out of granite rock, hold 107 litres of water and can be seen 4km south of the town.
TOURIST INFO: Railway Station Complex, off Station St, Ph: (03) 5460 4511

■ Melton   POP 30 304
Map 212, A2
Melton is 35mins from Melbourne's city centre, the Shire of Melton is an integral part of urban Melbourne. Despite its size, easy access to the airport, ports, and national road and rail networks, it has maintained its country atmosphere. There are a number of top harness racing operators here and Melton is recognised as one of the nation's foremost thoroughbred breeding areas.
MAIN ATTRACTIONS: **Warrensbrook Faire** is Melton's premier tourism precinct, featuring restaurants, wineries and equestrian facilities. **Melton Waves** leisure centre features Australia's first indoor wave

Mildura International Balloon Festival

pool, a rapid river, 25m pool, toddler pool, hydrotherapy pool and 2 outdoor pools. **Willows Historical Park and Homestead** is a museum of pioneer memorabilia and is accessed off McKenzie St. An ideal spot for picnics is **Hannah Watts Park**, beside **Toolern Creek**. Cycle paths and walking tracks follow the creek. A self-guided **heritage trail** passes the old town site, an Aboriginal canoe tree, Melton Hotel, The Willows and Darlingsford. The walk takes about 1.5hrs.

NEARBY ATTRACTIONS: Views across the town to the **You Yangs** and the **Macedon Ranges** are provided from **Mount Carberry Reserve** in Melton South.

TOURIST INFO: 323 High St, Ph: (03) 9747 7200

▪ Merbein POP 1860

Map 204, D2

This area of citrus orchards, vineyards and market gardens is located on the banks of the **Murray River**, 11km west of Mildura. Merbein was known as White Cliffs until 1909 when it was renamed.

MAIN ATTRACTIONS: **Mildara Wines** is situated on the edge of the towering cliffs rising from the Murray River. The winery's reputation was initially built on its sherries and brandies but has grown dramatically since

being taken over by Fosters. The winery is open 7 days a week for tastings and cellar door sales. Situated along the clifftop is the **Early Settlers Walk**, a short memorial walk in remembrance of the early settlers of the Merbein area. **McGowans Motor Bike Museum** has an impressive range of bikes and memorabilia that have been collected from Mildura and the surrounding districts. The museum is located at 46 Commercial St. **Chaffey** and **Kenny parks** both have electric BBQs and children's playgrounds. Kenny Park is adjacent to a swimming pool open all week throughout the summer months.

TOURIST INFO: 180 Deakin Ave, Mildura, Ph: (03) 5021 4424

▪ Mildura POP 25 486

Map 204, D2

The **Murray River** city of Mildura is surrounded by irrigated land that produces grapes, citrus, olives, avocados and asparagus. Its river setting, sunny winters and plentiful accommodation make this town a popular holiday destination.

MAIN ATTRACTIONS: Sandy beaches and swimming holes line the riverbanks. River cruises are available on the **PS Melbourne** Sun–Fri, 10.50am and 1.50pm. The **PV Rothbury** cruises at the same times on Saturdays.

Every Thursday this boat offers a day cruise to **Trentham Winery**. Bookings can be made through the information centre. In 1915, a series of 13 locks, weirs and water storages were built along the river. **Lock 11** is in Mildura and visitors can see it in operation as vessels move from one level of water to another. A walkway links the lock to **Lock Island**, created when the canal was constructed and now an ideal spot for picnics. **Old Mildura Homestead** has been relocated to a reserve on Cureton Ave, near the Murray River. There is a collection of pioneer-style buildings and a woolshed where displays illustrate the role of irrigation in the development of Mildura. **Rio Vista**, the original home of William Chaffey, the first mayor of Mildura, in Cureton Ave, is now a museum displaying colonial artefacts. The house is part of the **Mildura Arts Centre**, a complex with a theatre, museum and an art gallery with a good collection of paintings and sculptures; the centre is surrounded by parkland.

NEARBY ATTRACTIONS: The Sunraysia district can be explored on the 30km self-drive **Chaffey Heritage Trail** through the city and surrounding areas. There are many wineries in the area, including the huge **Lindemans Karadoc Winery**, 20km south. **Woodsies Gem Shop**, 6km east at **Nichols Point**, has rock cutting and grinding displays, 11am and 2.30pm daily. There is also a gift shop, garden maze and restaurant. **Murray-Sunset NP** and the smaller **Hattah-Kulkyne NP** lie south of Mildura. Birdlife is prolific in both parks but particularly so in Hattah-Kulkyne when the Murray River floods the **Hattah Lakes** system, creating a bird haven and transforming the landscape with carpets of wildflowers.

TOURIST INFO: 180–190 Deakin Ave, Ph: (03) 5021 4424

Victoria

Moe POP 16 772

Map 212, E3

The gateway to the **Latrobe Valley** and alpine region, Moe, 134km SE of Melbourne, is a major tourism centre in the region known as the **'Centre for Adventure'**.

MAIN ATTRACTIONS: Moe is home to **Gippsland Heritage Park**, a pioneer township with more than 35 buildings relocated from elsewhere in the Gippsland region. The park includes Bushy Park Homestead, the original home of Gippsland pioneer-explorer Angus McMillan; and an original Cobb & Co Coaching Inn from Pakenham East. Also part of the collection is a 2-storey iron-frame house, prefabricated (1850s) in England and shipped to Australia; the packing box was then used in the construction of the interior of the house. There is also an excellent collection of horse-drawn vehicles from the 1850s to the 1900s. All buildings are furnished in period-style. The **Edward Hunter Reserve** is an oasis in town featuring natural bushland with orchids. Brochures for self-guided walks around the town are available.

NEARBY ATTRACTIONS: Moe is a good base for tours to the wonderful

Sailboats on a Port Phillip beach, Mornington Peninsula

historic township of **Walhalla** with its narrow-gauge steam railway. Also nearby is the **Baw Baw Plateau** via **Mount Erica** or **Mount St Gwinear** and the **Thompson Dam**. There are easy or more difficult treks on offer in the Walhalla and **Mountain Rivers** district. Visitors can also travel through **Willow Grove** to the **Blue Rock Dam** for fishing and boating. A daytrip along Grand Ridge Rd takes visitors through the lush, picturesque timber and rural scenery of the **Strzelecki Ranges**.

TOURIST INFO: Gippsland Heritage Park, Lloyd St, Ph: (03) 5127 3082

Mornington POP 13 692

Map 153, F2

First settled in the 1840s, Mornington is now a growing residential area which retains its seaside village atmosphere. Its location makes it a good base for exploring the beautiful **Mornington Peninsula**.

MAIN ATTRACTIONS: The many historic buildings in town now house cafes and gift, book, antique and boating shops. **Mornington Peninsula Regional Gallery** houses a permanent collection of 1200 works and features many touring exhibitions. The collection includes works by Arthur Boyd, Brett Whiteley, Violet Teagul, Sidney Nolan and Russell Drysdale. The **National Antique Centre** and **World of Motorcycles Museum** are in Tyabb Rd. The old **Post Office** on the corner of High St and The Esplanade, houses a local historical display. Unspoilt beaches around the town include **Mothers Beach**, where the town's fishing fleet, yacht club and boatshed are located and **Fossil Beach**, which lies on the border with **Mount Martha**.

NEARBY ATTRACTIONS: There are many wineries on the Mornington Peninsula, including **Mount Eliza Estate**, **Morning Star Estate** and **Moorooduc Estate**. All are open for tastings and cellar door sales.

Festivals include the **Wine and Food Festival** in October and the **Winter Wine Weekend** in June, to name but a few. **Canadian Bay** beach, in nearby Mount Eliza, was made famous in the old film, *On the Beach*.

TOURIST INFO: Peninsula Visitor Centre, Point Nepean Rd, Dromana, Ph: (03) 5987 3078 or 1800 804 009

Morwell POP 14 560

Map 212, E3

A busy commercial centre in the heart of the famous coal-producing **Latrobe Valley**, Morwell is 150km SE of Melbourne.

MAIN ATTRACTIONS: Tours of **Hazelwood**, **Yallourn** and **Loy Yang open-cut mines and power stations** can be organised at the Powerworks Visitors Centre. Visitors can inspect the operations, see the dredgers working the coalfaces and the coal being conveyed to the power stations, and see the inside of a power station. Group bookings of 20 or more people can request an evening tour that includes dinner. The **Latrobe Regional Gallery** and the **Morwell Centenary Rose Garden** are both located in Commercial Rd. The rose garden is renowned for being the most significant in rural Victoria.

NEARBY ATTRACTIONS: 5km south of Morwell is **Hazelwood Pondage**. Heated by the power station, the warm waters provide a year-round venue for watersports. **Morwell NP**, 12km south, offers walking trails through a high ridge of stringybark forest and through moist areas studded with tree ferns and cool gullies with clear mountain streams—this is one of the few remaining areas of remnant vegetation in the **Strzelecki Ranges**. **Lake Narracan**, 15km NW, is popular for fishing and waterskiing.

TOURIST INFO: Powerworks Energy Technology Centre, Ridge Rd, Ph: (03) 5135 3415

The Cathedral in winter, Mount Buffalo NP, near Myrtleford

Mount Beauty   POP 2300
Map 209, G4

Situated at the foot of **Mount Bogong**, the highest peak in Victoria, Mount Beauty was built in the 1940s to house the workers on the Kiewa Hydro Electric Scheme. Located 338km NE of Melbourne, the town is one of Australia's best mountain-biking areas, it also attracts bushwalkers, especially in summer. In winter it is a popular base for skiers.

MAIN ATTRACTIONS: **Mount Beauty Museum** has a 'walk through time' exhibition, a variety of exhibits and historical information about the town. Beside the town is a large regulating pondage, created as part of the Hydro Electric Scheme. It is now a popular recreation area for fishing and watersports. Visitors can also borrow tape recorders and headsets from the information centre and listen to the history of the pondage, while they walk around it.

NEARBY ATTRACTIONS: In winter, Mount Beauty attracts skiers on their way to **Falls Creek**. Many ski hire businesses and affiliated enterprises service visitors and a coach service runs from the township to Falls Creek, allowing skiers to leave their cars below the slopes. The scenic road from the town to Falls Creek and the **Bogong High Plains** is worthwhile exploring. The drive takes in the **Clover Arboretum**, the village of **Bogong**, **Lake Guy** and Falls Creek. The Mount Beauty to **Bright** road passes **Sullivans Lookout**, offering panoramic views, before reaching **Tawonga Gap**, where there is a rocky picnic and BBQ area with views of the **Kiewa Valley** and Mount Bogong.

TOURIST INFO: Bogong High Plains Rd, Ph: (03) 5754 1962 or 1800 808 277

Myrtleford   POP 3270
Map 209, F4

Surrounded by the **Victorian Alps**, this town is located at the foot of **Mount Buffalo** and is the centre for a district that produces timber, hops, tobacco, grapes and many kinds of nuts. Myrtleford has some of the largest walnut groves in the Southern Hemisphere.

MAIN ATTRACTIONS: Interesting trees are a feature of the town. An ancient river red gum can be seen in Smith St. In the **Lions Club Park**, in Myrtle St, Hans Knorr's sculptured **Phoenix Tree**, symbolising the cycle of life, is displayed. In Albert St, a 100-year-old linden tree from Germany stands beside a historic home. Attractive parks abound in this town, including **Cundy Park**, on O'Donnell Ave, ideal for picnics and BBQs; **Rotary Park**, on the highway at the junction of a number of streams that flow into town, provides facilities and children's play equipment; and **Jubilee Park**, offering facilities, walkways and gardens. Historic items from the district are displayed in the **Old School Museum**, on the corner of Elgin and Albert sts, it is open Thurs–Sun, 2pm–4pm.

NEARBY ATTRACTIONS: Myrtleford is a gateway to the great granite plateau of **Mount Buffalo NP**, a favourite destination for skiers in winter and walkers in summer. **Lake Buffalo**, 22km south, is great for boating, waterskiing, fishing and swimming.

TOURIST INFO: 29-30 Clyde St, Ph: (03) 57521727

Nagambie   POP 1520
Map 208, B4

Situated on the shores of **Lake Nagambie** in the **Goulburn Valley**, Nagambie is surrounded by land devoted to sheep, cattle, cereal, grapes and horses. The town hosts several annual, water-based events, including rowing, canoeing, speed boating and waterskiing on Lake Nagambie.

MAIN ATTRACTIONS: Constructed in 1887 through the establishment of the **Goulburn Weir**, Lake Nagambie is a watery playground. **Nagambie Historical Museum**, housed in the old Court House and shire hall, features period-furniture, horse-drawn vehicles and a collection of old coins. The **Nut House**, located at the tourist information centre, displays and sells different varieties of nuts grown in Australia. There are antique and stained glass shops in town. Nagambie also offers skydiving, hot-air ballooning and gliding for the adventurous.

NEARBY ATTRACTIONS: There are many wineries within easy reach of the town. Classified by the National Trust, the **Chateau Tahbilk Estate**, located 6km SW, is the oldest winery in Victoria and overlooks the **Goulburn River**. Points of interest at this most charming winery includes the unique architecture of the old buildings, an avenue of mulberry trees, and old cellars. At **Mitchellstown**, 14km SW, the award-winning **Mitchelton Winery** has a good restaurant, underground cellars, museum and art gallery. The information centre offers a self-drive tour map of local wineries. The Goulburn River is popular with trout and redfin anglers, and canoeists who can hire boats here. **Goulburn River Cruises** offers daytrips on the *Major Mitchell* starting at Tahbilk Estate and finishing at Mitchelton Vineyard.

TOURIST INFO: 145 High St, Ph: (03) 5794 2647

Victoria

Nathalia   POP 1580

Map 208, B2

This small rural town located on the Murray Valley Hwy, 54km NW of Shepparton, is surrounded by agricultural land that was settled in 1843. Wheat, barley and dairying are the main agricultural activities of the district. Reflecting the local concern for the environment, the town has offices of the Dept of Natural Resources and Energy and the Rural Water Commission.

MAIN ATTRACTIONS: The town was set on each side of **Broken Creek** in 1879. Blake St, the main street, was modelled on Sturt St, Ballarat. This attractive street has a central plantation leading down to Broken Creek where several old buildings can be seen, including the **Court House Hotel** and a row of 19th-century shops with verandahs. The **historical museum** displays memorabilia, old photographs, maps and books. The museum is housed in what was once the Mechanics Institute, built in 1887.

NEARBY ATTRACTIONS: The region's waterways—the **Goulburn** and **Murray rivers** and Broken Creek—provide good fishing and camping opportunities. **Barmah SP**, the largest river red gum forest in the country, is easily accessible and provides camping areas.

TOURIST INFO: Nathalia Community Crafts (open weekends), Blake St, Ph: (03) 5866 3063

Nhill   POP 2215

Map 206, C3

Nhill, halfway between Melbourne and Adelaide, is a wheat and wool town in the **Wimmera** region. The town is surrounded by a number of national parks, wildlife areas and is within easy driving distance of **Lake Hindmarsh**, 45km north, and **Little Desert NP**.

MAIN ATTRACTIONS: The **Historical Museum** is located in McPherson St and is open by appointment. The

Draught Horse Memorial is located in the main street. Sculptured by Stanley Hammond, the memorial celebrates the Clydesdales that hauled the agricultural machinery and wagons in the past. The single-bin wheat silo, claimed to be the largest in the Southern Hemisphere, is located in Davis Av. There is a self-guided **historical walk** of the town and brochures are available from the information centre.

NEARBY ATTRACTIONS: A desert in name only, Little Desert NP, located 18km south, offers 600km of walking tracks to explore. To avoid temperature extremes, the best time to visit the park is late winter to early summer, this is also the time when the wildflowers bloom. There is a wildflower exhibition held here in October. A variety of accommodation is available, including motel, hotel, caravan and camping facilities. **Big Desert NP**, located 52km NW, is quite remote and access is via 4WD or on foot; tours are available. Some roads are impassible in wet weather.

TOURIST INFO: Goldsworthy Park, Victoria St, Ph: (03) 5391 3086

Numurkah   POP 3420

Map 208, C2

Numurkah is located 217km north of Melbourne, and a short distance from the attractions of the **Murray River**. The town serves irrigated farmlands supporting the dairy industry. A waterwheel, in the centre of a roundabout in Melville St, reminds passersby of the importance of irrigation to the region.

MAIN ATTRACTIONS: **Louis Hamon Rose Gardens** are located by **Broken Creek**, a tributary of the Murray. The **historical museum** is housed in the old National Bank building, on the corner of Melville and Knox sts, and is open Sunday, 2pm–4pm.

NEARBY ATTRACTIONS: **Monochino's Winery**, located 11km north, offers tastings of award-winning red and

white table wines, as well as dessert wines, port and muscat. **Strathmerton**, 26km north, is home to Australia's largest cactus farm. There are thousands of cacti growing in landscaped gardens. Visitors will also see pet alpacas and Mexican walking fish. There are tearooms and an art and craft shop. **Ulupna Island Flora and Fauna Reserve**, near Strathmerton, in addition to its other attractions the reserve has a large koala population; tours can be organised with **Red Gum Wildlife Tours**.

TOURIST INFO: 25 Quinn St, Numurkah, Ph: (03) 5862 3459

Ocean Grove   POP 9780

Map 201, K3

Situated at the mouth of the **Barwon River**, 96km SW of Melbourne, this resort town is a popular fishing and surfing destination. On the other side of the Barwon River is **Barwon Heads**, another popular holiday spot offering safe swimming along the shores of the river. A bridge over the Barwon River links both towns.

MAIN ATTRACTIONS: **Smiths Beach** is a fine surfing beach with a long stretch of sand, backed by a foreshore reserve with a number of walking tracks. Located in town are facilities for fishing, yachting, waterskiing and scuba diving. The

(CONTINUED P.187)

Point Lonsdale lighthouse, east of Ocean Grove

THE HIGH COUNTRY

The Victorian Alps are the southern-most part of the **Great Dividing Range**. These dramatic yet rounded mountains are far less challenging for skiers than the extremely jagged peaks of their Northern Hemisphere counterparts, the European Alps.

Located south-east of **Wangaratta**, the Victorian Alps cover a vast and rugged terrain that is mostly protected by national parks. The ski-resort towns dotting the mountains are within an hours radius of each other, so there are many opportunities for skiing. Resorts cater for different levels of skiers. **Mount Hotham, Falls Creek and Mount Buller** have ski runs for beginners, intermediate and advanced skiers, while **Mount Buffalo** caters for intermediate skiers. **Mount Baw Baw** is more suited to beginners. Around **Lake Mountain** there are some excellent cross-country runs.

The Victorian snow season usually starts in June and lasts until at least September, although some years it has extended as late as November. Bushwalking, horse-riding, paragliding, hang-gliding and trout fishing are some of the many recreational activities that attract visitors during the warmer months.

White-water rafting, Victorian High Country

Tourist information

Bright Visitor Information Centre
119 Gavan St (Great Alpine Rd)
Bright, Vic 3741
Ph: (03) 5755 2275

Wangaratta and Region Visitor Information Centre
Cnr Tone Rd and Handley St,
Wangaratta, Vic 3677
Ph: (03) 5721 5711

main attractions

◈ **Alpine NP**

This national park encompasses a large part of the Victorian Alps and is home to many of the region's ski resorts.

◈ **Beechworth**

Rich in history, this perfectly preserved goldfields' town is National Trust-classified.

◈ **Bright**

Bright is a picturesque town that began in the 1850s as a gold town. Today it is a centre for the local timber, agriculture and tourism industries.

◈ **Bogong**

The annual Bogong Moth Festival celebrates the town's namesake.

◈ **Falls Creek**

Falls Creek has what are considered to be Victoria's best ski runs. Spectacular views of Falls Creek can be seen from Roper's Lookout. The walk to Mount Nelse traverses colourful slopes covered with Alpine wildflowers.

◈ **Mount Buffalo NP**

This stunning national park covers the huge plateau surrounding Mount Buffalo.

Horse riders, Howqua River, near Mansfield

Victoria

Continued on map 209

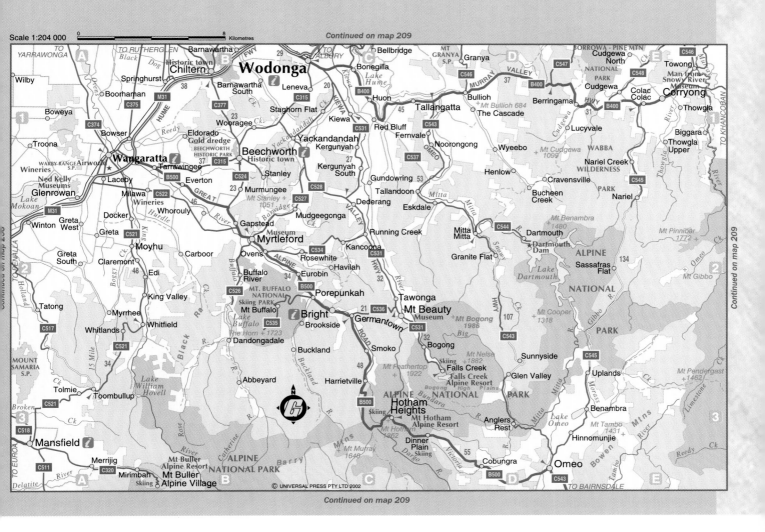

Scale 1:204 000

Continued on map 209

peninsula's last remaining stand of original bushland is located behind the town and is protected in the **Ocean Grove NR**. Native flora and fauna can be seen from 2 walking trails running through the reserve.

NEARBY ATTRACTIONS: **Jirrahlinga Koala and Wildlife Sanctuary** is in Taits Rd, Barwon Heads. **Wallington**, 8km north, is in the centre of the **Bellarine Peninsula**. **A Maze'N Things**, located here, features a giant wooden maze, mini golf, a puzzle centre, playground and BBQ areas. The **Country Connection Adventure Park**, also in Wallington, offers waterslides, pedal boats, aqua bikes, mountain bikes, golf, archery and go-karts.

TOURIST INFO: A Maze'N Things, 1570 Bellarine Hwy, Wallington, Ph: (03) 5250 2669

■ Omeo POP 298

Map 187, D3

Located 401km NE of Melbourne on the Great Alpine Rd, this lovely mountain township is the southern gateway to the magnificent scenery of the **Victorian Alps**. Omeo is a cattle township and tourist centre servicing the nearby **Alpine NP**.

MAIN ATTRACTIONS: **Omeo Historical Park**, is a precinct with a number of historic buildings, including the American Romanesque-style Court House (still in use) built in 1892 to dispense justice to what was reputed to be Australia's roughest goldfield. Positioned around the Court House are the log gaol, last used in the 1980s, stables, a blacksmith's shop, waterwheel and museum. **Oriental Claims**, in the old goldfields, offers interesting

walks around **Ah Fong's Loop**. For a magnificent collection of authentic cuckoo clocks, visit the German Cuckoo Shop.

NEARBY ATTRACTIONS: The district's streams are stocked with brown and rainbow trout, making angling a popular pastime. Omeo is an ideal base for bushwalkers attracted to the tracks in Alpine NP. White-water rafting is popular on the **Mitta Mitta River**. An excellent view of Omeo is provided from **Mount Mesley**. Access is via a walking track leading up from **Livingston Creek** that runs through the town. **McMillans Lookout**, on the road to **Benambra**, has 360° views of Omeo and the plains towards Benambra and the **Omeo Valley**.

TOURIST INFO: Omeo German Cuckoo Clock Shop, Great Alpine Rd, Ph (03) 5159 1552

Orbost POP 2185

Map 177, E2

A farming and administrative town on the **Snowy River**, Orbost is 374km east of Melbourne and 14km from Marlow Inlet, where the river reaches the sea. Orbost is surrounded by stunning coastal and mountain scenery.

MAIN ATTRACTIONS: The information centre is set in the **Rainforest Botanic Gardens**, in Lochiel St, and is run by Lakes and Wilderness Tourism. Combined with tourist information displays, there is an audiovisual exhibition, which interprets the ecosystems of the East Gippsland rainforests and rainforests in other parts of the world. The landscaped grounds feature rainforest species, creeks, waterfalls, pathways and boardwalks. **Orbost's Slab Hut** is a living museum. Originally built 40km away, it is now located in Forest Rd. The hut's humble furnishings illustrate the spartan lifestyle of pioneers. More local memorabilia can be seen in the **historical museum** located in the Orbost Business Centre, Nicholson St. The museum is open 9am–5pm weekdays. **Netherbyre Gallery**, in Browning St, displays woodwork, local paintings and a gemstone collection.

NEARBY ATTRACTIONS: There are 7 national parks within easy reach of Orbost. Walking tracks and forest drives explore scenic wilderness areas. **Raymond Creek Falls**, 42km north of town, has a 40min return walk to the falls and a further 1hr walk to the Snowy River. **Snowy River NP**, 25km NW, also offers a variety of walks. **Errinundra NP**, 54km NE, and has a rainforest boardwalk, and 4WD tours of the park are available.

TOURIST INFO: Cnr Lochiel and Browning sts, Ph: (03) 5154 2424

Ouyen POP 1360

Map 204, E5

This town, located 107km south of Mildura, began to grow in 1910, when the surrounding land was opened up for settlement and clearing for wheat, oats and sheep. Queues of trucks waiting to unload their grain at the silos are a common scene here at harvest time.

MAIN ATTRACTIONS: Ouyen's pioneers cleared many thousands of stumps in their efforts to create farming land from the mallee scrub, which covers the region. A memorial to their labour is the largest mallee stump in Australia, placed beside the Calder Hwy on the southern side of town. The **Local History Resource Centre** is located in the old Court House and comprises a significant collection of books, photographs, documents, maps, newspapers and cassettes.

NEARBY ATTRACTIONS: **Hattah-Kulkyne NP**, located 36km north, offers an extensive system of lakes and waterways that provide refuge for thousands of birds. Bushwalking and canoeing are popular activities here and the wildflower display is stunning in spring. **Murray-Sunset NP**, 60km west, contains unique **Pink Lakes**—under bright sunlight these salt lakes glitter white, while overcast conditions produce a dull pink hue. Vegetation in this park includes native pine and mallee scrub. Birdlife is abundant and bird-watchers can spot emus, red-rumped parrots, mulga parrots and pink cockatoos.

TOURIST INFO: 16 Oke St, Ph: (03) 5092 1000

Paynesville POP 2790

Map 177, C2

At the centre of the **Gippsland Lakes** system, surrounded by the waters of **Lake King** and **Lake Victoria**, Paynesville is the recreational-boating capital of the lakes.

MAIN ATTRACTIONS: Several operators offer a range of boats for hire or charters to explore the surrounding waterways, lagoons and islands. The **Church of St Peter-by-the-Lake** is located in Newlands Dr. Built in 1961, it has a seafaring theme, with a limestone brick spire designed to look like a lighthouse and a pulpit resembling the bow of a fishing boat. Lake Victoria can be seen through tall windows behind the altar.

NEARBY ATTRACTIONS: **Raymond Island**, on the other side of McMillan Strait, can be reached by car ferry from Paynesville. Popular with bushwalkers, the island is inhabited by native birds and animals, including koalas. Those with a boat can access **Rotamah Island**, south of the town, as well as the **Lakes NP** on **Sperm Whale Head**. The **Mitchell River Silt Jetties** are situated at Eagle Point. They stretch for nearly 10km towards the north-east shores of Lake King in the Gippsland Lakes. The silt jetties are second in size

Junction of the Snowy and Buchan rivers, NW of Orbost

Victoria

Petrified Forest, Cape Bridgewater, SW of Portland

only to those on the Mississippi River in the Gulf of Mexico. They were formed by the deposition of large quantities of silt brought down the Mitchell River in floods over the last million years.
TOURIST INFO: 240 Main St, Bairnsdale, Ph: (03) 5152 3444

■ Port Fairy   POP 2850
Map 200, A4
This former whaling port is located at the estuary of the **Moyne River**. Port Fairy is a holiday resort bordered by both river and ocean and is home to a large fishing fleet. It is well-known for rock lobster and abalone fishing. The town is more widely known for the famous **Port Fairy Folk Festival**.
MAIN ATTRACTIONS: One of Victoria's oldest towns, there are over 50 small stone cottages and bluestone buildings that are National Trust-classified. An **historic walk** leaflet is available from the information centre. There is a **history centre** in the old Court House, Gipps St. The old fort and signal station, **Battery Hill**, is located at the mouth of the Moyne River.
NEARBY ATTRACTIONS: Brochures are available on the **Mahogany Walk** to Warrnambool: a 6–7hr one-way walk with walkers able to return to

Port Fairy by bus. A causeway links **Griffiths Island** to the east of the town. Here, visitors can explore an area around the lighthouse where there are muttonbird rookeries. **Mount Eccles NP** is 56km NW. **Tower Hill State Game Reserve**, 14km east, is worthwhile exploring. There is an extinct volcano and crater lake with islands. A **Natural History Centre** is within the reserve where a nature walk begins.
TOURIST INFO: Bank St, Ph: (03) 5568 2682

■ Portland   POP 10 150
Map 210, C4
Located 366km south-west of Melbourne and close to the South Australian border, Portland is the only deepwater port between Melbourne and Adelaide. During the first half of the 19th century, Portland was a base for sealers and whalers. The town now has a fishing fleet concentrating on lobster and abalone. It is also a service centre for the pastoral hinterland. The town's major industry is now a huge aluminium smelter, which is also open for tours (check times).
MAIN ATTRACTIONS: As Victoria's first permanent settlement (1834), Portland has many interesting old buildings, some of them still used for their original purpose. Most of them are included on the self-guided **historical walk**. The local **museum** is located in the old Town Hall. Nearby is the still-used bluestone Customs House, built in 1849. The information centre is located at the **Portland Maritime Discovery Centre**. Displays include a 13m sperm whale skeleton and visitors can sit inside its rib cage. **Fawthrop Lagoon** is a unique wetland area within the city boundary. There are approximately 5km of walking tracks throughout the reserve. **Portland Botanic Gardens** (completed in 1857) feature stunning rose and dahlia gardens and a charming bluestone curator's cottage.

NEARBY ATTRACTIONS: **Cape Nelson SP**, 11km SW, features a National Trust-classified lighthouse. **Cape Bridgewater**, 21km SW, has many blowholes and freshwater springs; a walking track leads to the **Petrified Forest**, the remains of a forest that was covered by a sand dune thousands of years ago. Nearby, the cape's colony of fur seals can be seen from a viewing platform or by taking a boat trip. The 250km (around 10 days) **Great South West Walk** begins and ends in Portland. This walk can be undertaken in easy stages; it takes in a variety of landscapes and seascapes in a number of state, coastal and national parks through to **Discovery Bay** and **Cape Nelson**.
TOURIST INFO: Lee Breakwater Rd, Ph: (03) 5523 2671

■ Queenscliff   POP 4170
Map 152, A3
Surveyed in 1853, this seaside town has a noticeable 19th-century atmosphere generated by its old hotels, fishermen's cottages and public buildings. Queenscliff is located 107km south of Melbourne and 30km SE of Geelong on the **Bellarine Peninsula**.
MAIN ATTRACTIONS: The **Historical Centre**, in Hesse St, displays items relating to Queenscliff's marine, military and tourist heydays. The **Maritime Museum**, facing the bay, houses the last of the area's original lifeboats. The **Marine Discovery Centre**, the educational wing of the Marine and Fresh Water Research Institute, opens during school holidays and has living displays of marine life. **Fort Queenscliff** is Australia's largest and best preserved fortress; building began in the 1870s to protect investments from the threat—real or imagined—of foreign invasion. The most historic sections of the fort, the guardroom, cells, original lightkeeper's signal station, underground

Lake Hattah, Hattah-Kulkyne NP, west of Robinvale

magazines and a military museum are open for inspection. The Fort offers tours on weekends, public and school holidays at 1pm and 3pm with an extra tour at 11am in January. Fishing charters, seal and dolphin-watching tours, and 'swimming with the dolphins and seals' can all be organised through the information centre.

NEARBY ATTRACTIONS: The **Bellarine Peninsula Railway** originally linked Queenscliff and **Geelong**. Today the Geelong Steam Preservation Society displays its collection of vintage carriages and steam locomotives at the old station. The society also runs tourist trains along the 32km line to **Drysdale** on Sunday. Additional trips are run during school holidays. Queenscliff is linked to **Sorrento**, on the **Mornington Peninsula**, by vehicular and passenger ferries. The seaside holiday resort of **Point Lonsdale** is 6km SW.

TOURIST INFO: Hesse St, Ph: (03) 5258 4843

■ Red Cliffs   POP 2690
Map 204, D3

Located 559km NW of Melbourne and 8km south of Mildura, Red Cliffs was first considered for fruit growing in the 1880s. After WWI, the government assisted soldier settlers to clear large tracts of land for irrigated agriculture: the biggest venture of its kind ever undertaken in this country. A 45 tonne steam tractor, **Big Lizzie**, was built in Melbourne and was originally destined for Broken Hill. Instead, it cleared the mallee vegetation around Red Cliffs from 1917 to 1924.

MAIN ATTRACTIONS: Big Lizzie never made it to Broken Hill. The resting place of this huge piece of machinery is Barclay Square, opposite the Railway Station. **Cliff View Lookout** offers views of the 70m-high red cliffs from which the town gets its name.

NEARBY ATTRACTIONS: The Southern Hemisphere's largest winery, **Lindemans Karadoc**, is located 13km east of Red Cliffs. The winery is open for tastings and cellar door sales. There are also picnic and BBQ facilities. More wineries are located in the **Mildura region** to the north. On the tourist route drive, visitors will see the **Carringbush Glass Gallery**, **Homwood Estate** with its native wildflower farm, and artist **Alma Peterson's Gallery**.

TOURIST INFO: Kulkyne Creations, Calder Hwy, Ph: (03) 5024 2866

■ Robinvale   POP 1937
Map 205, F3

This small town is located 473km NW of Melbourne and 83km SE of Mildura. Robinvale is sited within a loop of the **Murray River** and is almost encircled by it. The town's economy is based on the production of wine grapes and dried fruits. The largest olive orchard in Australia is located here and produces 1500 tonnes of olives annually from its 20 000 trees.

MAIN ATTRACTIONS: Most of the grapes used in making McWilliams cream sherry are grown locally and processed at the huge **McWilliams Winery** in town. An original log cabin has become a tasting room, which is open weekdays. The information centre displays and sells locally made arts, crafts and produce. The recently restored old **Railway Station**, located close by, is now used as a sales outlet for ceramics. The **Machinery Museum** features steam engines and other farm machinery housed in a large split-log shed.

NEARBY ATTRACTIONS: **Robinvale Wines**, located 5km south, has a variety of alcoholic and non-alcoholic wines, juices and fortified wines to taste and buy. The winery is open daily. **Euston Weir**, 2km south of the town, has a specially constructed fish ladder allowing fish to jump their way up to higher water levels. The **Lock 15 gardens** nearby are a good spot for a picnic. **Kindalyn Almond Farm**, 22km SE, is worthwhile visiting in spring when the trees are in full bloom. On weekends, fresh almonds and almond products are for sale. Day-trips can be made from the town to **Hattah-Kulkyne NP**, where visitors can see the unique **Hattah Lakes** system with its prolific birdlife; the park has over 200 bird species.

TOURIST INFO: Bromley Rd, Ph: (03) 5026 1388

■ Rochester   POP 2742
Map 208, A3

Located 180km south of Melbourne and 29km NW of Echuca, Rochester is situated on the **Campaspe River**. The town is a service centre for surrounding dairy and small-crop farms. Rochester has the largest dairy factory in Australia.

MAIN ATTRACTIONS: There are many lakes and waterways in the region, making the town popular with fishing and watersports enthusiasts.

Victoria

Rochester was the birthplace of the renowned cyclist **Sir Hubert Opperman**, who achieved fame in the 1920s in the world of international cycling before becoming a politician. A statue opposite the Railway Station commemorates his achievements and a museum of memorabilia donated by Sir Hubert is located in the Railway Station and opens by request.

NEARBY ATTRACTIONS: **Random House**, located on Bridge Rd, is a stately 19th-century home beside the Campaspe River. It was originally built as a station homestead but now offers accommodation, lunches and Devonshire teas. Tours of the house and 4ha gardens, which extend down to the river, are available. The surrounding waterways yield redfin and carp. **Greens Lake** and **Lake Cooper**, located 14km SE, are popular with anglers and swimmers.

TOURIST INFO: Old Railway Station, Moore St, Ph: (03) 5484 2571

■ Rutherglen   POP 2180
Map 208, E2

Located 265km NE of Melbourne, Rutherglen is Victoria's leading wine producer. There are many vineyards in the area and all the way south to **Milawa** and the **King Valley**. The first vines were planted in 1859 and Hamilton's Clydeside Cellars was established after the discovery of gold in 1861. Seppelts bought the property from the Hamiltons in 1916 and established **Seppelts Clydeside Winery**.

MAIN ATTRACTIONS: Rutherglen's main street has retained its historic streetscape with all but 3 shopfronts dating back to the late 1880s and early 1900s. The **Victoria Hotel**, **Post Office** and old **Court House** are classified historic buildings. Brochures on **walking tours** of the town are available from the information centre. The local history museum is located in the town's first government school, known as

the **Common School** (1872), which is in the grounds of the local primary school. The museum opens Sundays, 10am–1pm, Oct–June. Australia's largest wine festival, **Winery Walkabout** is held on the Queens Birthday long weekend in June.

NEARBY ATTRACTIONS: Rutherglen is known for its full-bodied red wines, delicate whites, sherry, port and muscat. The region has 17 wineries, many within easy reach of the town. Maps are available from the information centre. Cycling tours of the wineries are popular and bicycles can be hired from the information centre. The **Rutherglen Wine Show** is held in late September.

TOURIST INFO: 13-27 Drummond St, Ph: 1800 622 871

■ St Arnaud   POP 2870
Map 207, G4

St Arnaud, 255km NW of Melbourne, is an old goldmining town between Donald and Avoca. The National Trust has classified many of the town's historic buildings. Modern facilities have been introduced, fortunately without detracting from the old-world character and charm of the town.

MAIN ATTRACTIONS: St Arnaud has many civic buildings, hotels and

stores with lavish iron lacework. The town's **Historic Precinct** includes the Court House, police lock-up, Crown Lands Office and the old Post Office. Napier St is a classified conservation area containing elegant red-brick buildings, evidence of wealth created in the goldmining period. The **historical museum** opens by appointment and is located in the house of the town's former water overseer and turncock. **Josephine Coppers Gallery** displays fine arts and is housed in the Old Post Office in Napier St. Sporting facilities in **Lord Nelson Park** are located on the site of the famous **Lord Nelson Mine**. **Wilsons Hill Lookout** provides good district views of forests and hills; under Wilsons Hill are deep shafts running north and south.

NEARBY ATTRACTIONS: **Kara Kara Vineyard** is located 10km south and is open for tastings and cellar door sales. **Berry's Bridge Vineyard**, 11km SE, is open weekends or by appointment. **Avoca River**, 28km south, offers good fishing. Maps for a self-guided **scenic drive** of the surrounding region are available from the information centre.

TOURIST INFO: 4 Napier St, Ph: (03) 5495 1268 or 1800 014 455

Daffodils in bloom, St Arnaud

St Leonards POP 1430

Map 152, A1

A coastal town on the **Bellarine Peninsula**, 110km south of Melbourne, St Leonards has long been a popular holiday destination for people from Melbourne. The town is twinned with **Indented Head**, another small holiday destination just 4km north.

MAIN ATTRACTIONS: St Leonards has many sheltered beaches ideal for swimming, boating and other watersports. **Harvey Park Foreshore** is a popular family recreation area overlooking **Port Phillip**. Just south of town, **Duck Island State Fauna Reserve** is a waterbird habitat and one of the few remaining homes for the rare orange-bellied parrot.

NEARBY ATTRACTIONS: **Batman Park**, located at Indented Head, offers a picnic and BBQ area and a boat ramp. A stone cairn marks the place where John Batman's expedition landed and camped in May 1835, before moving on to discover the site of Melbourne. Another memorial marks Matthew Flinders' landing in 1802.

TOURIST INFO: Queenscliff Visitor Information Centre, Hesse St, Queenscliff, Ph: (03) 5258 4843

Sale POP 13 980

Map 177, A3

Sale originally developed as a result of its strategic location on the route to major gold diggings. It is located 209km SE of Melbourne in the heart of **Gippsland**. The city is a gateway to an area of rich natural attractions, including the **High Country**, wetlands and **Ninety Mile Beach**.

MAIN ATTRACTIONS: Of historic interest is **Bon Accord homestead**, built in the 1860s, it is open Fri–Sun and Devonshire teas are available. Notable buildings include **St Pauls Cathedral and Rectory** (1885); **Bishops Court** (1903), the residence of the Bishop of Gippsland; and the

convent of **Notre Dame de Sion** (1892), designed by the convent's first Mother Superior. The **Botanic Gardens**, off Foster St, are located on the shores of **Lake Guthridge** which is connected by walkways to **Lake Guyatt**. This is a most pleasant walking and picnicking area. In the same street is the **Ramahyuck Aboriginal Corporation**, selling local arts and crafts. The **Bataluk Cultural Trail**, which begins at the Sale wetlands contains 12 sites of significance to the Gippsland Aboriginal people.

NEARBY ATTRACTIONS: **Sale Common Wetland and State Game Refuge**, is a protected wetland of mainly freshwater marsh. A 450m-long boardwalk provides views of permanent and migratory bird species' habitats. **Holey Plains SP**, 14km SW, has 530 species of native flora and fossils can be seen in a limestone quarry wall. Popular rivers for fishing include the **Avon**, **Thompson** and **La Trobe**.

TOURIST INFO: 8 Princes Hwy, Ph: (03) 5144 1108

Seymour POP 7056

Map 208, B5

A **Goulburn River** town, Seymour is located 89km north of Melbourne. The town services a prosperous rural community and a huge military base. The base is 10km west at **Puckapunyal**.

MAIN ATTRACTIONS: There is a 4km scenic **walking trail** along the Goulburn River. The **Royal Hotel**, in Emily St, has been immortalised in Russell Drysdale's painting, *Moody's Pub*. The old **Log Gaol**, originally built in 1858 and re-erected behind the old Court House in Emily St, is one of the town's prominent historic buildings. **Seymour Railway Heritage Centre**, Railway Pl, displays restored steam engines and carriages; occasionally steam train tours are organised. The centre is open Tuesdays and

Lake Guthridge, Sale

Thursdays. The information centre has brochures on the self-guided **historical walk**.

NEARBY ATTRACTIONS: Seymour is surrounded by fertile riverland supporting vineyards, including **Somerset Crossing Vineyards**, 2km south, **Hayward's Winery**, 12km SE and **Hankins Winery**, 10km north. All are open for tastings and cellar door sales. At Puckapunyal the **Royal Australian Armoured Corps Tank Museum** displays one of the largest collections of tanks in the world. At **Trawool**, 4WD tours into the National Trust-classified **Tallrook SF** are available.

TOURIST INFO: Old Court House, Emily St, Ph: (03) 5799 0233

Shepparton POP 51 902

Map 208, C3

Considered the capital of the **Goulburn Valley**, Shepparton is a thriving regional city, 180km north of Melbourne. Irrigated by the Goulburn Irrigation Scheme, Shepparton is known as the '**Food Business Hub of Australia**'.

MAIN ATTRACTIONS: **Shepparton Art Gallery**, in Welsford St, has an outstanding ceramics' reputation, housing 3000 works from the 19th

Victoria

century to the present day. In addition, it has works by notable artists, including Streeton, McCubbin and Perceval. The region's history is preserved in the **Shepparton Historical Society Museum** and is housed in Shepparton's first public hall, on the corner of High and Welsford sts. At **Victoria Park Lake**, the grassy banks invite visitors to picnic or enjoy a leisurely stroll along the foreshore. The **Shepparton Arts Festival**, held in March, is a major event spread over 2 weeks.

NEARBY ATTRACTIONS: The **Irrigation and Wartime Camps Museum** in **Tatura**, 13km SW, houses one of the best collections of memorabilia from the prisoner-of-war camps that were once located in the area. The annual **Taste of Tatura**, a food and wine festival, is held in March. **Ardmona KidsTown** is a 'must visit' for families, offering giant slides, a flying fox, miniature railway and much more; it is located between Shepparton and **Mooroopna**.

TOURIST INFO: 534 Wyndham St, Ph: (03) 5831 4400

■ **Sorrento**   POP 1862

Map 152, B4

This town, located on a strip of land between **Port Phillip** and **Bass Strait** on the **Mornington Peninsula**, has been a popular holiday destination since the 1890s. Then, people came to Sorrento via paddlesteamer and the steam tram. Sorrento has much to offer: surf and bayside beaches are easily accessible and there are upmarket shops and eateries along the main street.

MAIN ATTRACTIONS: Many of the shops are housed in historic limestone buildings. The peninsula's highest point, **Arthur's Seat**, can be seen from town. This area was the site of Victoria's first European settlement in 1803 (abandoned in 1804). The **Collins Settlement Historic Site** on

Sullivan Bay marks the site and there are also 4 early settlers' graves located here. There are several self-guided walks around Sorrento, passing many fine examples of Victorian architecture. The **Queenscliff–Sorrento Car and Passenger Ferry** departs from **Sorrento Pier**, on the front beach. Many other charter tours, including dolphin watching and seal watching also leave from here. **Sorrento Museum**, one of Victoria's top museums, displays memorabilia from pioneering days.

NEARBY ATTRACTIONS: Cruises to the **Pope's Eye Marine Reserve** are available. Here, there is a gannet rookery and snorkelling and diving opportunities. The seaside township of **Portsea** is 4km NW. Swimming and fishing from the pier are popular here. **Mornington Peninsula NP** protects much of the dramatic and diverse coastal environments. Tours of the former **Quarantine Station** on **Point Nepean**, established in 1852 to protect the colony from diseases brought in on ships. Tours are available on Sundays and public holidays. **Fort Nepean** has an extensive system of fortifications worthwhile touring.

TOURIST INFO: Point Nepean Rd, Dromana, Ph: (03) 5987 3078 or 1800 804 009

■ **Stawell**   POP 6580

Map 195, E2

A town with a rich history of gold-mining and pastoral activity, Stawell is 129km NW of Ballarat. It is an ideal base for exploring the **Grampians region**, including the western vineyards. Stawell is renowned for the annual **Stawell Gift**, the richest footrace in Australia.

MAIN ATTRACTIONS: From the Pioneers' Memorial on **Big Hill Lookout**, there are fine views over Stawell to the Grampians in one direction, and the wide flat **Wimmera** plain and the **Pyrenees** in the other. **Casper's World in Miniature Tourist Park**

displays scale models of world famous icons, including the Eiffel Tower. The park is located in London Rd. Other attractions include the **Stawell Gift Hall of Fame Museum** in Central Park; **Fraser Park**, which displays mining equipment; and **Stawell Ironbark Forest** showcases spring wildflowers and rare orchids.

NEARBY ATTRACTIONS: The **Sisters Rocks**, 3km SE, are huge granite boulders named after the Levi sisters whose mining family set up camp here. A rock shelter in the **Black Ranges**, 11km south, known as **Bunjil's Shelter**, is the most important Aboriginal art shelter in Victoria. A painting in the shelter depicts Bunjil, the All-Father and wise good spirit, and 2 dingoes. There is also a good view of the Grampians from here. The shelter is 11km south of Stawell. **Lake Bellfield**, 30km SW, is popular for canoeing, kayaking and fishing.

TOURIST INFO: 50-52 Western Hwy, Stawell west, Ph: (03) 5358 2314

Surfers at Sorrento

THE GRAMPIANS

This landscape of stark ridges and strangely shaped rocky outcrops rise spectacularly from western Victoria's plains and farmland. Known to Aboriginal people as Gariwerd, the area is renowned for its rock art and heritage. It has the largest proportion of rock-art sites in south-east Australia. Archaeologists have carbon-dated campfire charcoal in some rock shelters to approximately 22 000 years ago, although the earliest rock art suggests Aboriginal activity in the area may stretch back even further.

The landscape is punctuated by 4 main ranges—**Mount Difficult Range** to the north, and the parallel ridges of **Victoria Range**, **Serra Range** and **Mount William Range** in the south. Protected by one of Victoria's largest national parks, the Grampians cover 1671km^2 of stunning scenery, including wildflowers, panoramic mountain views and intricate ecosystems.

Almost one-third of Victoria's indigenous flora, 35 species of native mammals, 200 bird species and 27 reptile species reside in this unique habitat. Activities include rockclimbing and abseiling, bushwalking and camping out in the rugged bushland.

Aboriginal Art Sites

The Grampians NP is an important area for the history of Aboriginal rock art. Rock paintings are believed to serve many functions, such as recording days or visits, retelling stories, communicating laws and teaching spiritual principles.

 Tourist information

Grampians and Halls Gap Visitor Information Centre
Centenary Hall, Grampians Tourist Rd
Halls Gap, Vic 3381
Ph: (03) 5356 4616, 1800 065 599

Grampians National Park and Brambuk Cultural Centre
Grampians Tourist Rd
Halls Gap, Vic 3381
Grampians NP, Ph: (03) 5356 4381
Brambuk Cultural Centre, Ph: (03) 5356 4452
www.parkweb.vic.gov.au

Lake Bellfield, Grampians NP

main attractions

◈ **Aboriginal Art Tours**
Run by the Brambuk Cultural Centre, these tours incorporate excursions to the region's main art shelters.

◈ **Dunkeld**
This town is a convenient southern departure point for touring the Grampians.

◈ **Halls Gap Wildlife Park and Zoo**
See a diverse range of animals, including monkeys, red deer and kangaroos. This 8ha park also has BBQs and a playground.

◈ **MacKenzie Falls**
This spectacular waterfall is a worthwhile destination during a visit to the Grampians.

◈ **Mount William**
A steep walk will bring you to the highest point of the Grampians for breathtaking 360° views of the ranges and open plains.

◈ **The Balconies Lookout**
An easy walk leaves from Reed Lookout car park to spectacular rock formations and views across Grampians NP.

The Balconies Lookout, Grampians NP

Victoria

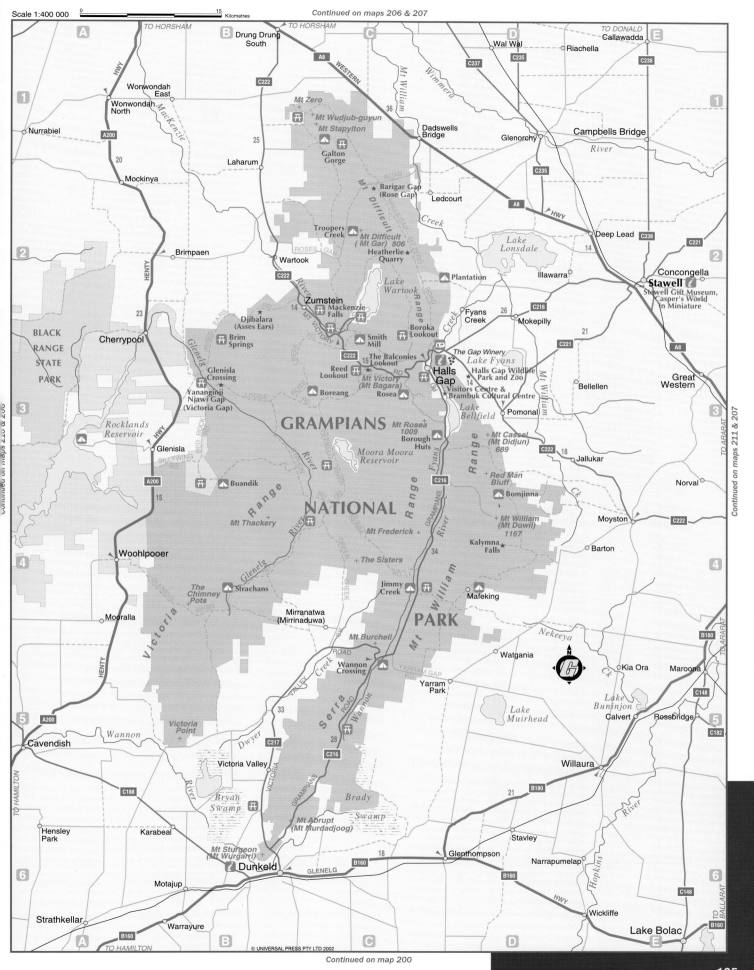

TO HORSHAM

TO HORSHAM

TO DONALD

A8

WESTERN

Drung Drung
South

Wal Wal   Callawadda
Riachella

C237   C235   C238

Wonwondah
East
Wonwondah
North

C222   Mt Zero
+ Mt Wudjub-guyun
Mt Stapylton

Nurrabiel   36

Glenorchy   Campbells Bridge

C235

Mockinya   25

Laharum

Galton
Gorge

Dadswells
Bridge

River

20

Brimpaen

Barigar Gap
(Rose Gap)

Ledcourt

A8   HWY

Deep Lead   C238   C221

Troopers
Creek

Mt Difficult
(Mt Gar) 806

Creek

Lake
Lonsdale

Wartook   ROSES GA   Heatherlie ★
Quarry

Illawarra

Concongella
Stawell
Stawell Gift Museum,
Casper's World
in Miniature

Cherrypool

C222

Zumstein   Mackenzie
Falls

Lake
Wartook

Plantation

Fyans
Creek

26

Mokepilly

BLACK
RANGE
STATE
PARK   23

Djibalara
(Asses Ears)
Brim
Springs

Smith
Mill

Boroka
Lookout

C216

C221   21

Great
Western

Glenisla
Crossing   C222

The Balconies
Lookout
Reed
Lookout   Mt Victory
(Mt Bagara)

Halls
Gap   The Gap Winery
Halls Gap Wildlife
Park and Zoo

A8

Yananginji
Njawi Gap
(Victoria Gap)   Boreang

Rosea   Visitors Centre &
Brambuk Cultural Centre

Lake Fyans

Bellellen

Rocklands
Reservoir

Glenisla   GRAMPIANS

Mt Rosea
1009
Borough
Huts   Lake
Bellfield   Pomonal

Mt Cassel
(Mt Didjun)
689   C222   18   Jallukar

Moora Moora
Reservoir   + Red Man
Bluff

Norval

A200   15   Buandik   NATIONAL

C216   Bomjinna

Range   Mt Thackery   + Mt William
(Mt Duwil)
1167   Moyston   C222

Woohlpooer   Mt Frederick +   Kalymna
Falls   Barton

+ The Sisters   34

The Chimney
Pots   Strachans   Jimmy
Creek   Mafeking

Mooralla   PARK

Mirranatwa
(Mirrinaduwa)   Nekeeya

Watgania   Kia Ora   Maroona

Mt Burchell   N
G   Lake
Buninjon   C148

Victoria
Point   Wannon
Crossing   Yarram
Park   Calvert   Rossbridge

A200   33   Dwyer   C217   C216   28

Cavendish

Victoria Valley   Lake
Muirhead   Willaura   B180   C182

Wannon

B180   21   River

Hensley
Park   Karabeal   Bryan
Swamp   Brady
Swamp   Stavley

C188

Mt Abrupt
(Mt Murdadjoog)   18   Narrapumelap   B160

Strathkellar   Motajup   Mt Sturgeon
(Mt Wurgarl)
Dunkeld   Glenthompson

GLENELG   B160   HWY   Wickliffe

Warrayure   C148

TO HAMILTON

Continued on map 200

Lake Bolac
TO BALLARAT

Continued on maps 211 & 207

TO ARARAT

Swan Hill POP 9950

Map 205, H5

Situated on the banks of the **Murray River** in the north of the state, Swan Hill is renowned for its pleasant climate, with more sunny days than Queensland's Gold Coast. This major holiday destination is 335km NW of Melbourne.

MAIN ATTRACTIONS: The river and surrounding waterways are popular for fishing, boating and watersports. Swan Hill's renowned **Pioneer Settlement** is a 7ha open-air living history museum. Set out as a Mallee township of the Riverland pioneers from the 1830s to the 1930s it has authentic buildings and the re-created streets include a replica 1860 coach house, a Post Office, an 1854 iron house, newspaper office and printery. It is also where traditional skills, such as printing, blacksmithing and woodturning are still practised. There are daily cruises offered on the paddleboat *Pyap*. The *Gem*, once one of the largest passenger boats on the river, rests at the entrance to the Pioneer Settlement. There are 6 golf courses in the region, including the excellent **Murray Downs Golf Course**. Many local walks offer stunning river scenery.

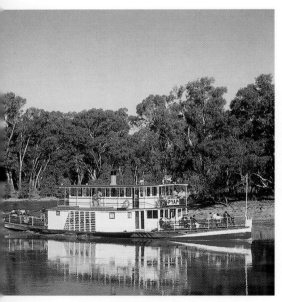

100 year-old PS *Pyap* on the Murray River, Swan Hill

NEARBY ATTRACTIONS: Historic **Tyntynder Homestead**, 17km NW, is Australia's oldest brick-veneer home (1846) and is surrounded by colonial gardens. Furnished as a typical squatters' residence, it features Aboriginal artefacts found on the property. The homestead is open for tours during public and school holidays or by appointment. There are 2 wineries close to Swan Hill: **Buller's Winery** at **Beverford** and **Best's Winery** near **Lake Boga**. Both are open for tastings and sales. Another 5 wineries are within a 140km radius of the town.
TOURIST INFO: 306 Campbell St. Ph: (03) 5032 3033 or 1800 625 373

Terang POP 2040

Map 200, D3

This **Western District** town, located 216km west of Melbourne, is a service centre for an irrigated farming district. Terang is noted for its horseracing facilities, early 20th-century architecture and wide tree-lined streets.

MAIN ATTRACTIONS: The National Trust has classified much of the town, particularly the broad, oak-lined High St with its Gothic-style sandstone Presbyterian Church. The **District Historical Museum** houses some interesting memorabilia. The **Lions Walking Track** is 4.8km long and passes alongside National Trust-classified dry **Lake Terang**.

NEARBY ATTRACTIONS: **Noorat**, 6km north of Terang, is the birthplace of Alan Marshall, author of the Australian classic novel, *I Can Jump Puddles*. The **Alan Marshall Walking Track** leads to the summit of an extinct volcano with excellent views extending to the **Grampians**. **Lake Keilambete**, 4km NW, is said to have therapeutic properties, as it is 2.5 times saltier than the sea. Also worth visiting is the **Ralph Illidge Wildlife Sanctuary**, 17km south.
TOURIST INFO: The Court House, High St, Ph: (03) 5592 1984

Torquay POP 6754

Map 201, J4

This fast-growing, busy resort, 96km SW of Melbourne, is renowned as the **'Surf Capital of Australia'**. **Jan Juc** and the world-famous **Bells Beach** are the main surf beaches.

MAIN ATTRACTIONS: **Lions Park**, situated on the Esplanade, has a children's playground, rotunda, picnic and BBQ areas. Natural parkland with walking tracks and a yabby pool can be found in **Taylors Park**, also on the Esplanade. Australia's only surfing museum, **Surfworld**, is located in the **Surf City Shopping Centre**. The museum is dedicated to surfing and incorporates a Hall of Fame, memorabilia, photographs, novel displays and working models.

NEARBY ATTRACTIONS: Torquay's location at the start of the **Great Ocean Rd** makes it an ideal base from which to explore the spectacular coastline and hinterland. This stretch of coastline is recognised as having the best waves outside of Hawaii. Bells Beach, just a few kilometres away, is the chosen venue for the international surf carnival, the **Rip Curl Pro Surfing Classic**, held each Easter. Jan Juc beach has a reputation for being a little wilder than Torquay. It is also the start of the 30km **Surf Coast Walk** to **Angahook-Lorne SP**. This walk takes in the beach, clifftop tracks and trails and travels through coastal bushland. Numerous access points allow walkers to leave or join the walk at any stage.
TOURIST INFO: Surfworld Museum, Surf City, Beach Rd, Ph: (03) 5261 4219

Traralgon POP 21 000

Map 212, E3

Once a supply depot for the goldfields to the north, Traralgon, 163km SE of Melbourne, is now a principal regional centre in the **Latrobe Valley**.

MAIN ATTRACTIONS: National Trust-classified buildings in the town include the **Post Office** and **Court House**, both dating from 1887, and **Ryan's Hotel** with its iron lacework balconies. **Victory Park**, on the banks of **Traralgon Creek**, offers a miniature railway for the young at heart.

NEARBY ATTRACTIONS: There are many **walking tours** and heritage drives around the district. The information centre has details. **The Festival of the Roses** is held in November at **Toongabbie**, a small town 19km NE of Traralgon. Tours of the **Loy Yang** power station—one of the area's major employers, are available.

TOURIST INFO: Latrobe Visitor Information Centre, 'The Old Church', Southside Central, Princes Hwy, Ph: 1800 621 409

Wangaratta   POP 16 780
Map 208, E3

This commercial and agricultural city is located 234km NE of Melbourne, at the junction of the **Ovens** and **King rivers**.

MAIN ATTRACTIONS: **Merriwa Park** is attractive with its sunken garden, mature river red gums, ferneries and ponds. The park is located on the King River. **Sydney Beach**, on the Ovens River, is a pleasant picnic and swimming area. The **Exhibition Gallery** features changing exhibitions. It is located in the old Presbyterian Church in Ovens St and is open 12pm–5pm. Infamous bushranger, Mad Dog Morgan's headless body was buried in Wangaratta's main cemetery, in Tone Rd.

NEARBY ATTRACTIONS: Wangaratta is an ideal base for exploring Victoria's **High Country**. **Airworld** displays aviation memorabilia, a collection of historic aircraft and Australia's largest collection of old civil aircraft. The museum is located at Wangaratta airport. **Eldorado**, 20km NE, is an interesting old gold town which has the largest gold

dredge in the Southern Hemisphere. Gold fossicking is popular in nearby **Reids Creek**. There are many scenic roads leading to quaint townships and natural attractions, such as **Powers Lookout** and **Paradise Falls** in the **King Valley**. **Milawa Gourmet Region** offers wineries, hand-made cheeses, trout, mustards, nuts and berry farms.

TOURIST INFO: Cnr Tone Rd and Handley St, Ph: (03) 5721 5711

Warracknabeal   POP 2675
Map 206, E3

Massive wheat silos mark Warracknabeal's status as the **'Cereal Capital of the Wimmera district'**. The town is 378km NW of Melbourne.

MAIN ATTRACTIONS: **The Historical Centre**, in Scott St, displays pioneer memorabilia, including furniture, pictures and documents. Highlights are a pharmaceutical collection from Woolcott's Pharmacy. Warracknabeal's historic streets and buildings can be seen on the **Black Arrow Tour**, a 5km walk or drive described in a leaflet available from the historical centre or the information centre. There are 23 points of interest, including the town's 6 National Trust-classified buildings: **Christ Church**, the **Commercial Hotel**, **railway water tower**, **Court House**, **log lock-up** and **Warracknabeal Hotel**.

NEARBY ATTRACTIONS: Exhibits in the **North Western Agricultural Machinery Museum**, just south of town, conveys the history of wheat farming in the district, with exhibits of farm machinery from the last 100yrs.

TOURIST INFO: 119 Scott Street, Ph: (03) 5398 1632

Warragul   POP 9740
Map 212, D3

Warragul, 104km SE of Melbourne, began as a construction camp for railway workers. It is now a dairying

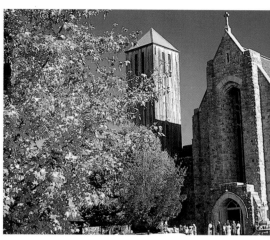
Cathedral Church of the Holy Trinity, Wangaratta

centre for the surrounding rich, green, rolling pastures of **West Gippsland**.

MAIN ATTRACTIONS: The region is renowned for the quality of its agricultural produce, supplying Melbourne with much of its milk. It boasts world-class cheese producers such as **Tarago River** and **Jindivick**. The **Gourmet Deli Trail** is a gastronomic tour of the countryside and visitors can stop to taste and purchase fresh bread, cheeses, smoked meats, wine and fruits. Brochures are available from the information centre. **Mount Worth SP** offers walking trails, picnic facilities and lookouts on the **McDonalds Track** provide views of the valley, the **Great Dividing Range** and **Western Port**. **Civic Park** offers a playground, picnic and BBQ facilities.

NEARBY ATTRACTIONS: There are many scenic drives around the area. The **Noojee Trestle Bridge** and **Tooronga Falls** are located on the road to **Mount Baw Baw**. **Darnum Musical Village**, 8km east, has a fine collection of antique player pianos, organs and other musical instruments. Visitors can play some of the instruments and see the workshop. **Yarragon**, 13km east, offers visitors boutique wineries, gourmet food, crafts and antiques.

TOURIST INFO: Latrobe Visitor Information Centre, Traralgon, Ph: 1800 621 409

■ Warrnambool POP 29 320

Map 200, B4

Warrnambool was an important port until the 1920s, when silting virtually ended commercial shipping. The city's early prosperity is reflected in the sandstone buildings of Liebig, Timor and Fairy sts. Today, Warrnambool is a coastal resort and Victoria's fifth largest city. It is at the western end of the **Great Ocean Rd**.

MAIN ATTRACTIONS: A superb attraction in Warrnambool is **Flagstaff Hill Maritime Museum**, an authentic replica of a typical 19th-century seaport. The village includes a group of lighthouse buildings, built in 1853 and still in use; an old fort and cannons, built in 1887, to fend off a perceived threat of invasion by Russia; and other commercial buildings associated with a busy port. The city's **Botanic Gardens** were laid out in 1872 and are worthwhile visiting. **Warrnambool Art Gallery** on the corner of Liebig and Timor sts displays a variety of works by 19th- and 20th-century European and Australian artists.

NEARBY ATTRACTIONS: **Lake Pertobe Adventure Playground** is a family venue, with pedal boats, islands, bicycles, walking tracks and an adventure playground for children.

Proudfoots boatshed on the Hopkins River, Warrnambool

Lady Bay, the main beach, offers a promenade edging the bay, recreation areas, safe swimming and surfing. **Whale watching** has become a popular winter pastime in Warrnambool. Between June and September each year, southern right whales return to breed in the sheltered waters off **Logans Beach**, 3km east and visitors can watch the whales from a viewing platform at the beach. **Tower Hill State Game Reserve** is located 14km west of Warrnambool. The reserve surrounds the peak and crater lake of an extinct volcano; wildlife which may be observed includes kangaroos, koalas and emus.

TOURIST INFO: 600 Raglan Pde, Ph: (03) 5564 7837

■ Wodonga POP 26 470

Map 209, F2

Wodonga lies on the south bank of the **Murray River**, close to the historic towns of **Yackandandah**, **Beechworth** and **Chiltern**, and the wineries of **Rutherglen**. Wodonga, on the Victorian side of the river, is twinned with **Albury**, on the New South Wales side.

MAIN ATTRACTIONS: A number of attractions can be found on the Lincoln Causeway, the only road link between Wodonga and Albury. The **Gateway Visitors Complex** features art, craft, woodturning, pottery and jewellery. Also popular are the **Fitness Trail** and the **Wiradjuri Walkabout Aboriginal Heritage Trail**. **Harvey's Native Fish Farm** with mini-golf, mini-train rides and animals is a perfect place for children. Visitors can also catch their own fish. On the third Sunday of each month, a miniature railway runs in **Diamond Park**, accessed off the Causeway. Another attraction is the **National Museum of Australian Pottery**, a museum dedicated to 19th-century Australian potters.

NEARBY ATTRACTIONS: There is much to do and see in areas close to

Wodonga, including winery tours, hot-air ballooning, fishing charters, horse trail-riding and canoeing; the information centre has details. Areas well worth touring include the Upper Murray; north-east Victoria, particularly the mountains; and the **Riverina** district.

TOURIST INFO: Gateway Village, Lincoln Causeway, Ph: (03) 6041 3875 or 1800 800 743

■ Wonthaggi POP 6270

Map 212, C4

Originally a black-coal mining town, today this **South West Gippsland** town is a prosperous industrial and commercial centre. In an area characterised by rugged coastline, beaches and fishing activity, Wonthaggi is a good tourist base within easy reach of **Phillip Island** and **Wilsons Promontory**.

MAIN ATTRACTIONS: The **State Coal Mine Historical Reserve** has reopened **Eastern Area Mine** and offers underground tours conducted by former coal miners. There is also a museum featuring mining activities. The historical reserve is open daily, 10am–3:30pm. The Wonthaggi Historical Society displays local memorabilia which is housed in the **Wonthaggi Railway Station**, it is open Saturdays 11am–1pm.

NEARBY ATTRACTIONS: **Cape Paterson**, 9km south, is located in the **Bunurong Marine Park**. The surf beach here is popular and there is a more sheltered beach for swimming. There are also excellent snorkelling and scuba-diving opportunities. From Cape Paterson to **Inverloch**, a scenic road winds 15km through the **Bunurong Cliffs Coastal Reserve**. A coastal track offers walkers an alternative route through the reserve. Brochures are available from the information centre on this and other walks in the area.

TOURIST INFO: Watt Street, Ph: (03) 5671 2444

Victoria

GREAT OCEAN ROAD

This legendary coastal route, starting at **Torquay** and extending 285km west to **Warrnambool**, is a journey along a stretch of spectacular coastline via seaside holiday towns, surf beaches, dramatic cliffs, expansive ocean, rainforest and woodlands.

Built between 1919 and 1932 as employment for returned servicemen and as a memorial to soldiers who died in WWI. The road was designed to be a tourist route of world repute in this wild, forested terrain. More than 100 and some believe as many as 700 ships have been sunk by reefs, foul weather and the treacherous waters of the **Southern Ocean**; the stretch to Peterborough is a stark reminder of the perils of this jagged coastline.

Historic seaside towns provide safe sandy beaches as well as many surfing beaches. Whale watching, horseriding, bushwalking and mountain bike riding, are just some of the activities of this remarkable region.

The Twelve Apostles

Within the **Port Campbell NP**, these majestic rock formations, seen from the Great Ocean Rd, were once part of the mainland's limestone cliffs, demonstrating the power of the coastline's waves. Rising 65m from the ocean and stretching along the coastline, the offshore sea-stacks are an impressive sight. Other attractions of the national park include **London Bridge**, **The Grotto** and **Loch Ard Gorge**.

 Tourist information

Geelong and Great Ocean Road Visitor Information Centre
Stead Park, Princes Hwy
Geelong, Vic 3214
Ph: (03) 5275 5797

Great Ocean Road Visitor Information Centre
Great Ocean Rd, Apollo Bay, Vic 3233
Ph: (03) 5237 6529
www.greatoceanrd.org.au

Great Ocean Road

main attractions

◈ **Anglesea**
Anglesea is renowned for its large population of grey kangaroos inhabiting Anglesea Golf Course.

◈ **Cape Otway Lightstation**
Built in 1848, this is Australia's oldest standing lighthouse.

◈ **Little penguins**
To observe a colony of little penguins, cross at low tide to Middle Island from Thunder Point Coastal Reserve, Warrnambool.

◈ **Lorne**
Surrounded by densely forested bushland with plunging waterfalls, Lorne is a prime holiday location.

◈ **Port Campbell NP**
This narrow strip of coastal park contains many spectacular rock formations, including the Twelve Apostles.

◈ **Torquay**
Torquay is the renowned centre of the surf culture on the Great Ocean Rd.

◈ **Whale watching**
From June to late Sept see southern right whales at Logan's Beach, Warrnambool.

Bay of Islands, off the Great Ocean Road, near Peterborough

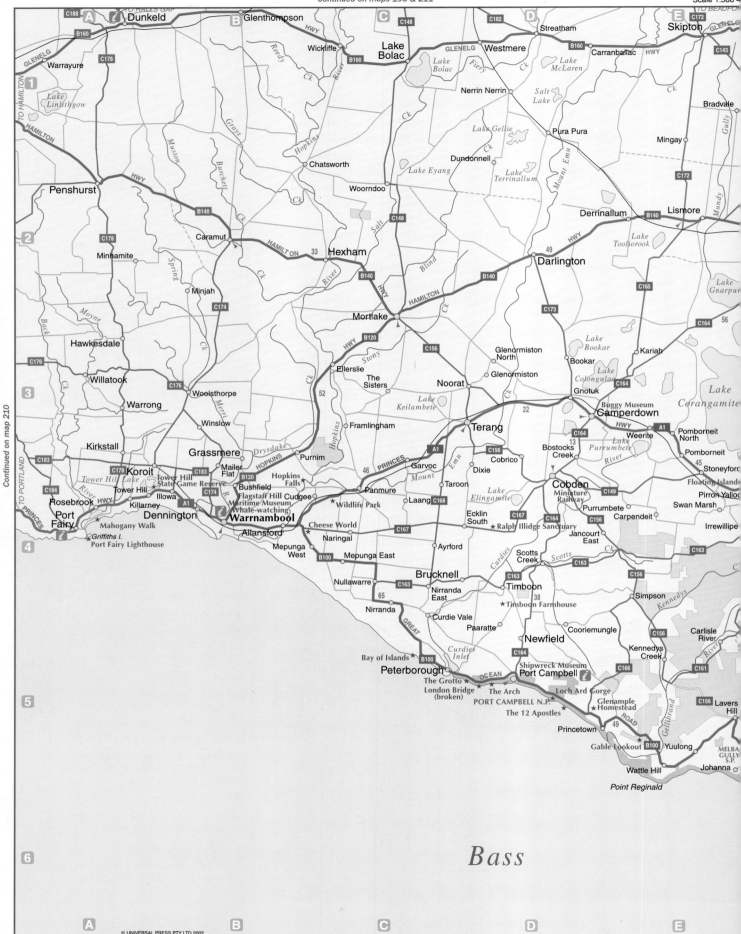

Gregory's Australia

Victoria

Bass

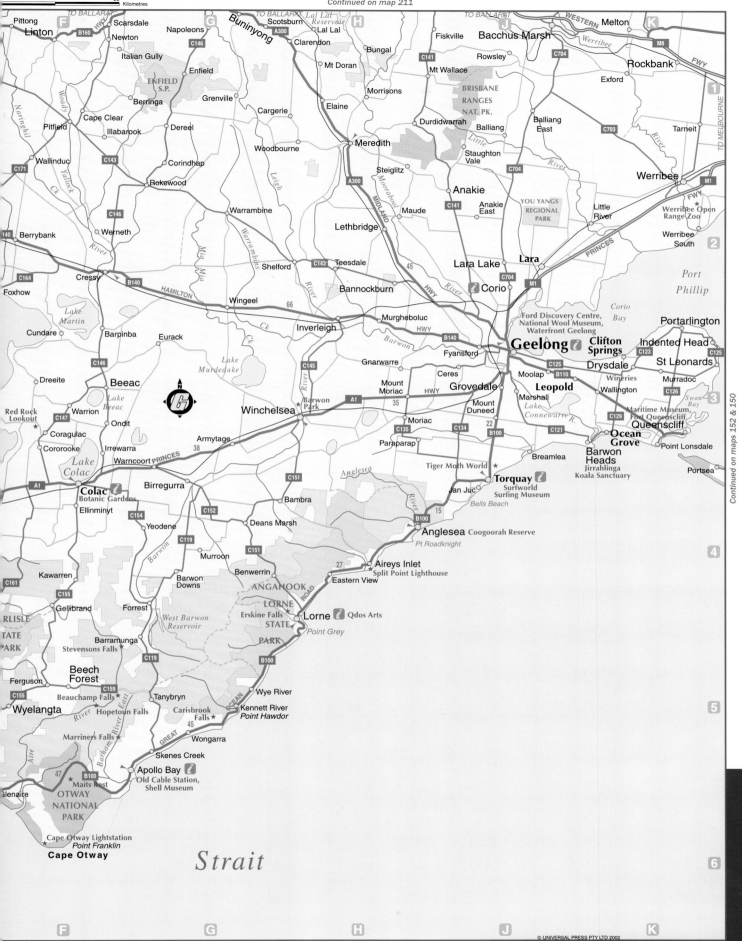

20
Kilometres

TO BALLARAT

Pittong
Linton
B160 HWY
Scarsdale
Newton
Napoleons
C146
Buninyong
Scotsburn
A300
Lal Lal
Reservoir
Lal Lal
TO BALLARAT
Clarendon
Fiskville
Bacchus Marsh
WESTERN
Melton
Werribee
M8
Italian Gully
Enfield
ENFIELD S.P.
Bungal
Rowsley
C141
Mt Wallace
C704
Exford
Rockbank
FWY
Berringa
Grenville
Mt Doran
Morrisons
BRISBANE RANGES NAT. PK.
Balliang
Balliang East
C703
Tarneit
Cape Clear
Illabarook
Dereel
Cargerie
Elaine
Durdidwarrah
Staughton Vale
C704
Pitfield
Cundare
TO MELBOURNE
Wallinduc
C143
Corindhap
Woodbourne
Steiglitz
Anakie
Anakie East
YOU YANGS REGIONAL PARK
Little River
Werribee
Werribee Open Range Zoo
M1 FWY
Rokewood
A300
Maude
C141
Werribee South
Warrambine
Lethbridge
Moorabool
Little
Woody
Naringhil
Narmeroo
C171
C146
Werneth
Shelford
Teesdale
C143
Lara Lake
Lara
M1
Berrybank
River
Warrambine
45
Corio
PRINCES
1
C164
Cressy
B140
HAMILTON
Wingeel
66
Murgheboluc
HWY
Ford Discovery Centre, National Wool Museum, Waterfront Geelong
Corio Bay
Portarlington
2
Foxhow
Lake Martin
Inverleigh
Barwon
B140
Geelong
Clifton Springs
Indented Head
C125
Cundare
Barpinba
Eurack
Ck
Gnarwarre
Fyansford
C125
Drysdale
St Leonards
Dreeite
C146
Lake Murdeduke
Ceres
Moolap
B110
Wineries
Murradoc
C126
Red Rock Lookout
Warrion
C147
Ondit
Lake Beeac
Beeac
Lake Colac
Mount Moriac
HWY
Grovedale
Marshall
Lake Connewarre R.
Wallington
C129
Swan Bay
Maritime Museum, Fort Queenscliff
Coragulac
Irrewarra
Armytage
38
Winchelsea
Barwon Park
A1
35
Mount Duneed
22
B100
C121
Queenscliff
Cororooke
Warncoort
PRINCES
Moriac
C135
Paraparap
C134
Breamlea
Barwon Heads
Ocean Grove
Point Lonsdale
Colac
Botanic Gardens
Birregurra
C151
Tiger Moth World
Jirrahlinga Koala Sanctuary
Portsea
Ellinminyt
Bambra
Anglesea
River
Torquay
Surfworld Surfing Museum
C154
Yeodene
C152
Deans Marsh
Jan Juc
B100
15
Bells Beach
C119
Murroon
C151
Anglesea
Coogoorah Reserve
Pt Roadknight
Kawarren
C161
Benwerrin
27
Aireys Inlet
Split Point Lighthouse
Eastern View
Gellibrand
C155
Barwon Downs
ANGAHOOK
LORNE
STATE
Forrest
West Barwon Reservoir
Erskine Falls
Lorne
Qdos Arts
Barramunga
Stevensons Falls
PARK
Point Grey
CARLISLE STATE PARK
Beech Forest
C119
B100
Ferguson
C159
Beauchamp Falls
Tanybryn
Wye River
C155
Wyelangta
Hopetoun Falls
Carisbrook Falls
Kennett River
Point Hawdor
Marriners Falls
45
Wongarra
Skenes Creek
GREAT
OCEAN
ROAD
47
B100
Apollo Bay
Old Cable Station, Shell Museum
Glenaire
Maits Rest
OTWAY NATIONAL PARK
Cape Otway Lightstation
Point Franklin
Cape Otway

Strait

3

4

5

6

© UNIVERSAL PRESS PTY LTD 2002

F   G   H   J   K

Continued on maps 152 & 150

Woodend POP 3127

Map 167, C2

This small township, 69km NW of Melbourne, is surrounded by the **Macedon Ranges**. Woodend became a resort town after the gold rush and has retained its old-world atmosphere.

MAIN ATTRACTIONS: Woodend is characterised by quaint shops in the main street, old hotels, a bluestone Anglican Church and a stone bridge built in 1862, which spans **Five Mile Creek**. The clock tower was built as a WWI memorial. The **Insectarium of Victoria** is located in town on the Calder Hwy. The Insectarium has expanded its exhibitions to become the largest insect and related invertebrate research centre in Australia.

NEARBY ATTRACTIONS: **Hanging Rock** is Woodend's most popular attraction. Located 6km NE of the town, this huge rock formation was made famous by Joan Lindsay's novel, *Picnic at Hanging Rock*, and then by the film of the same name. Visitors can discover the history, mystery and geology of the rock at the new **Hanging Rock Discovery Centre**. Nearby **Hanging Rock Winery**

produces a range of quality red, white and sparkling wines. It is open for tastings and cellar door sales. There are over 15 wineries in the region. **Mount Macedon** is located 10km east and there is a huge memorial cross at its summit. The area is renowned for beautiful gardens and many are open to the public in spring and autumn. There are numerous scenic drives and bushwalks around Mount Macedon.

TOURIST INFO: High Street, Ph:(03) 5427 2033

Yarram POP 1825

Map 213, F4

A **South Gippsland** town on the **Tarra River**, Yarram is 225km SE of Melbourne. Yarram offers easy access to the region's many coastal attractions as well as the rugged **Strzelecki Ranges**.

MAIN ATTRACTIONS: The **Regent Theatre**, built in 1930, has been restored and shows movies on weekends and during school holidays. It is located in Commercial Rd. The golf course, 3km east of the town centre, is very attractive with hundreds of ancient grass trees, it is also home to many kangaroos.

NEARBY ATTRACTIONS: **Tarra-Bulga NP**, north-west of Yarram, protects some of the best examples of cool temperate rainforest in the Strzelecki Ranges. There are many native birds and animals to be seen in the park. Just outside the town is **Port Albert**, an historic port with many fine old buildings. The **Maritime Museum** in the town is open weekends, 10:30am–4pm and also upon request. **White Woman Waterhole** is of immense natural beauty and is located in a bushland reserve in the **Won Wron SF**, 10km north of Yarram.

TOURIST INFO: Yarram Court House, cnr Commercial Rd and Rodger St, Ph: (03) 5182 6553

Yarrawonga POP 5630

Map 208, D2

Yarrawonga in Victoria and **Mulwala** in New South Wales are twin **Murray River** towns lying on the shore of **Lake Mulwala**. Both are popular holiday destinations.

MAIN ATTRACTIONS: **Lake Mulwala** is an ideal venue for watersports—on Anzac Day a large sailing regatta is held on the lake. The Yarrawonga foreshore is particularly attractive with abundant birdlife, willow trees, boat ramps, BBQs and picnic facilities. Trail rides through the forest and alongside the Murray River are available with **Red Gum Horse Tours**. The **Old Yarra Mine Shaft** displays a large collection of gems and fossils and is found at the information centre.

NEARBY ATTRACTIONS: At **Linley Park Animal Farm**, in Corowa Rd, visitors can feed the baby animals in the nursery. The *Paradise Queen* and *Lady Murray* both offer river cruises daily. Canoes and boats are also available for hire. The **Fyffefield Winery**, located 19km west on the Murray Valley Hwy, is open for tastings and sales.

TOURIST INFO: Cnr Irvine Pde and Belmore St, Ph: (03) 5744 1989

Tarra-Bulga NP, north-west of Yarram

Victoria

KEY MAP

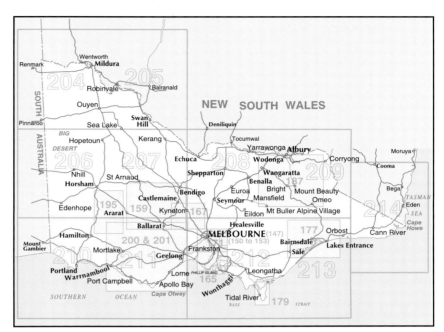

DISTANCE CHART

Approximate Distance	Albury NSW	Bairnsdale	Ballarat	Bega NSW	Bendigo	Bordertown SA	Cooma NSW	Geelong	Hamilton	Horsham	Melbourne	Mildura	Mount Gambier SA	Portland	Renmark SA	Shepparton	Swan Hill	Traralgon	Wangaratta	Warrnambool
Albury NSW		310	372	426	297	665	315	388	545	508	314	571	677	628	696	177	384	427	73	544
Bairnsdale	310		395	326	432	739	339	357	568	582	283	821	695	608	940	462	619	117	310	513
Ballarat	372	395		721	121	344	734	89	173	187	112	454	305	256	573	241	273	278	345	171
Bega NSW	426	326	721		709	1065	111	683	894	908	609	957	1026	934	1082	589	796	443	485	839
Bendigo	297	432	121	709		368	598	176	294	211	149	398	426	377	517	120	187	315	224	292
Bordertown SA	665	739	344	1065	368		966	433	259	157	456	411	183	281	279	488	396	622	592	365
Cooma NSW	315	339	734	111	598	966		696	907	921	622	1160	1039	947	1279	478	685	456	374	852
Geelong	388	357	89	683	176	433	696		238	276	74	543	338	251	662	253	362	240	315	156
Hamilton	545	568	173	894	294	259	907	238		129	285	439	132	83	558	414	368	451	526	112
Horsham	508	582	187	908	211	157	921	276	129		299	310	261	212	429	331	239	465	435	241
Melbourne	314	283	112	609	149	456	622	74	285	299		538	412	325	657	179	336	166	241	230
Mildura	571	821	454	957	398	411	1160	543	439	310	538		571	522	125	433	218	704	537	551
Mount Gambier SA	677	695	305	1026	426	183	1039	338	132	261	412	571		98	462	546	500	578	650	182
Portland	628	608	256	934	377	281	947	251	83	212	325	522	98		641	497	451	491	601	95
Renmark SA	696	940	573	1082	517	279	1279	662	558	429	657	125	462	641		558	343	657	662	676
Shepparton	177	462	241	589	120	488	478	253	414	331	179	433	546	497	558		215	345	104	412
Swan Hill	384	619	273	796	187	396	685	362	368	239	336	218	500	451	343	215		502	319	480
Traralgon	427	117	278	443	315	622	456	240	451	465	166	704	578	491	657	345	502		407	396
Wangaratta	73	310	345	485	224	592	374	315	526	435	241	537	650	601	662	104	319	407		471
Warrnambool	544	513	171	839	292	365	852	156	112	241	230	551	182	95	676	412	480	396	471	

All distances in this chart have been measured over highways and major roads, not necessarily by the shortest route.

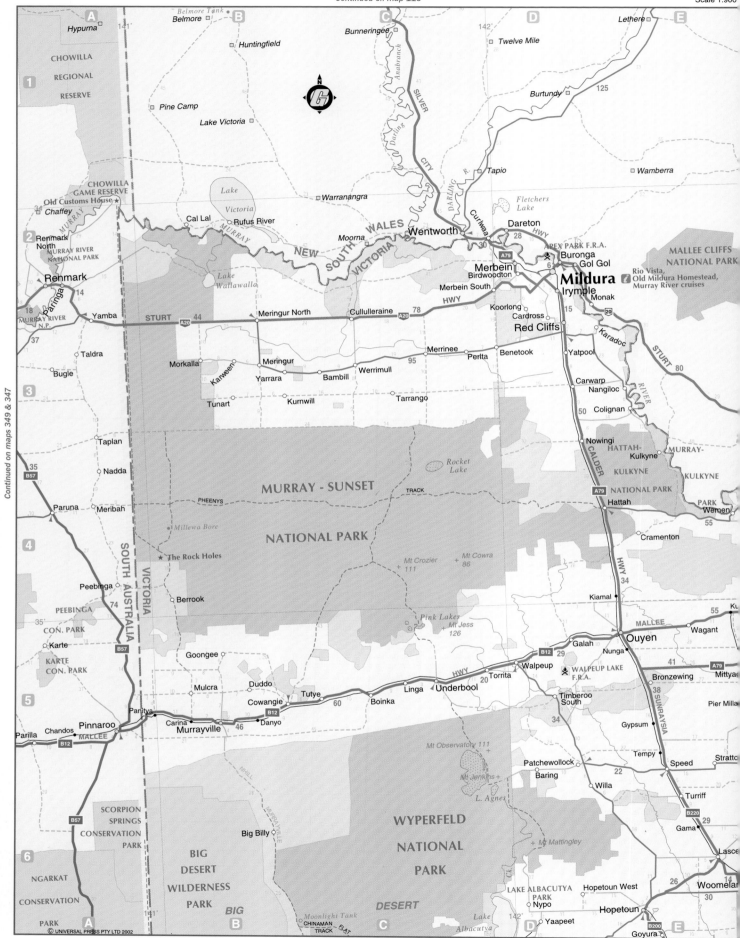

CHOWILLA
REGIONAL
RESERVE

Hypurna

141°

Belmore Tank
Belmore

Huntingfield

Pine Camp

Lake Victoria

Bunneringee

142°

Twelve Mile

Lethere

Burtundy   125

Wamberra

Fletchers Lake

CHOWILLA
GAME RESERVE
Old Customs House ★

Chaffey

Renmark
North
MURRAY RIVER
NATIONAL PARK

Renmark

Paringa

18
MURRAY RIVER
N.P.

14

Yamba

37

Taldra

Bugle

MURRAY

Lake Wallawalla

Cal Lal   *Rufus River*

STURT   A20   44

Morkalla

Karween

Meringur North

NEW   SOUTH   WALES

Moorna

VICTORIA

Warranangra

Cullulleraine   78   A20   HWY

Meringur

Yarrara   Bambill

Tunart   *Kurnwill*

Merrinee   95
Werrimull

Tarrango

Wentworth

Darling

SILVER   CITY

Tapio

Curlwaa   28   HWY
30   A79   Dareton
Merbein   6
Birdwoodton
Merbein South

Koorlong
Cardross

Red Cliffs

Perlta   Benetook

APEX PARK F.R.A.
Buronga
Gol Gol

Mildura
Irymple   Monak

15

Yatpool

*Rio Vista,
Old Mildura Homestead,
Murray River cruises*

MALLEE CLIFFS
NATIONAL PARK

Karadoc   STURT   80

Carwarp
Nangiloc

50   Colignan

Taplan

35   B57
Nadda

Paruna   Meribah

SOUTH   AUSTRALIA

VICTORIA

Rocket Lake

MURRAY - SUNSET

NATIONAL PARK

PHEENYS
Millewa Bore

★ The Rock Holes

TRACK

Mt Crozier
111   Mt Cowra
86

RIVER

Nowingi
Kulkyne

HATTAH-

KULKYNE

HWY   CALDER   A79   NATIONAL PARK

Hattah

MURRAY-
KULKYNE
PARK   55
Wemen

Cramenton

Peebinga

PEEBINGA
CON. PARK

35°   B57

Karte
CON. PARK

74

Berrook

Pink Lakes
Mt Jess
126

HWY   34

Kiamal

Mt Jess

MALLEE

55   Ku

Wagant

Goongee

Mulcra   Duddo
Cowangie   Tutye
Carina   B12
Murrayville   46   Danyo

Linga   Underbool
Boinka   20   Torrita

HWY   60

Galah   B12   29
Nunga

Walpeup
WALPEUP LAKE
F.R.A.

Ouyen

41   A79

Bronzewing   Mittyac

38   SUNRAYSIA

Pier Milla

Timberoo
South

34

Gypsum

Tempy

Speed

Stratto

Parilla   Chandos
Panitya
Pinnaroo

B57

MALLEE   B12

SCORPION
SPRINGS
CONSERVATION
PARK

NGARKAT
CONSERVATION

PARK

BIG
DESERT

WILDERNESS

PARK   *BIG*

111°

Big Billy

NHILL

MURRAYVILLE

Moonlight Tank
CHINAMAN
TRACK   FLAT

Mt Observatory 111

Mt Jenkins

L. Agnes

WYPERFELD

NATIONAL

PARK

DESERT

Patchewollock
Baring

Willa

Mt Mattingley

LAKE ALBACUTYA
PARK
Nypo

Hopetoun West

22

Turriff

B220   29

Gama

Lascel

Woomelar   14

142°   Yaapeet

Hopetoun

B200

Goyura

© UNIVERSAL PRESS PTY LTD 2002

30 Kilometres

F G H J K

1

2

3

4

5

6

Top Hut

143

Lake Leaghur

MUNGO

Mungo

NATIONAL

Boree Plains

PARK

Lake Mungo

Arumpo

The Walls of China

Chibnalwood Lakes

Turlee

Marona

Iona

Hatfield

Langleydale

Culpataroo

Alma

Tarwong

Merrowie Ck.

GOONAWARRA N.R.

COBB HWY

34

Prungle

Box

97

Bidura

Tin Tin Lake

Macommon Lake

Ganaway Lake

Penarie

Oxley

Lachlan

Thelangerin

One Tree

Ita Lake

Lake Waljeers

River

Pitarpunga Lake

MURRUMBIDGEE

RIVER

Nap Nap

Maude

Yerrinbool

L. Benanee

-manee

Lake Caringay

20

78

McWilliams Winery, Machinery Museum

HWY

Robinvale

20

B400

Bannerton

MURRAY

VALLEY

8

Boundary Bend

75

Lake Tala

Balranald

Yangalake

20

YANGA NATURE RESERVE

Yanga Lake

76

STURT

Ravensworth

HWY

20

57

Continued on maps 121 & 117

Ura Ck.

Ck.

Yungera

Koorkab

Piamble

Kenley

55

62

The Forest

Miranda

Booroorban

COBB

35

HWY

43

Annuello

Kooloonong

Haysdale

Winnambool

Bolton

Natya

Goodnight

Kyalite

80

Perekerten

Billabong

Windouran

Kulwyne

Prooinga

42

HWY

B12

Piangil

Tooleybuc

78

Yerrein

Edward

River

Moulamein

Anabranch

Manangatang

16

Cocamba

Miralie

40

Wood Wood

Koraleigh

Stony Crossing

Dhuragoon

Forest

Clarkes

106

Ck.

23

Chinkapook

Yarraby

64

Nyah

Nyah West

Vinifera

Dilpurra

69

Niemur

Niermur

70

Morago

L. Wahpool

Chillingollah

42

Nowie Nth

Pira

Beverford

Speewa

Tyntynder Central

Wakool

Jimaringle

Tyntynder Homestead

Tyntynder South

Burraboi

ndaly

Lake Tyrrell

L. Timboram

Woorinen

Swan Hill

Pioneer Settlement, Murray River cruises

River

46

Tyrrell Downs

Waitchie

Gowanford

31

Wakool

NEW

Ballbank

Wakool

rin

Long Plains

Lalbert

Ultima

Goschen

Lake Boga

Fish Pt

Banjeroop

VALLEY

Murrabit

Myall

Yallakool

-nda

Sea Lake

40

Lalbert Rd

Tresco

61

Murrabit

Capels Crossing

Caldwell

Tyrrell

36

Meatian

Kunat

Mystic Park

Culfearne

Barham

REEN AKE F.R.A.

Boigbeat

61

Lake Ck.Lalbert

Westby

Koondrook

SOUTH

Banyan

33

Berriwillock

Lalbert

Lake Charm

B400

Gemstone Museum

25

VICTORIA

WALES

Tantonan

56

A79

Bael Bael

Lake Bael Bael

Sandhill Lake

Kerang

Gannawarra

RIVER

Bunnaloo

Willangie

Culgoa

Cokum

Kalpienung

Tittybong

Cannie

57

Koroop

39

HWY

Watchupga

143°

Sutton

Warne

River

Dingwall

Kerang Sth

144°

37

HWY

Cohuna

Museum

CALDER

HWY

© UNIVERSAL PRESS PTY LTD 2002

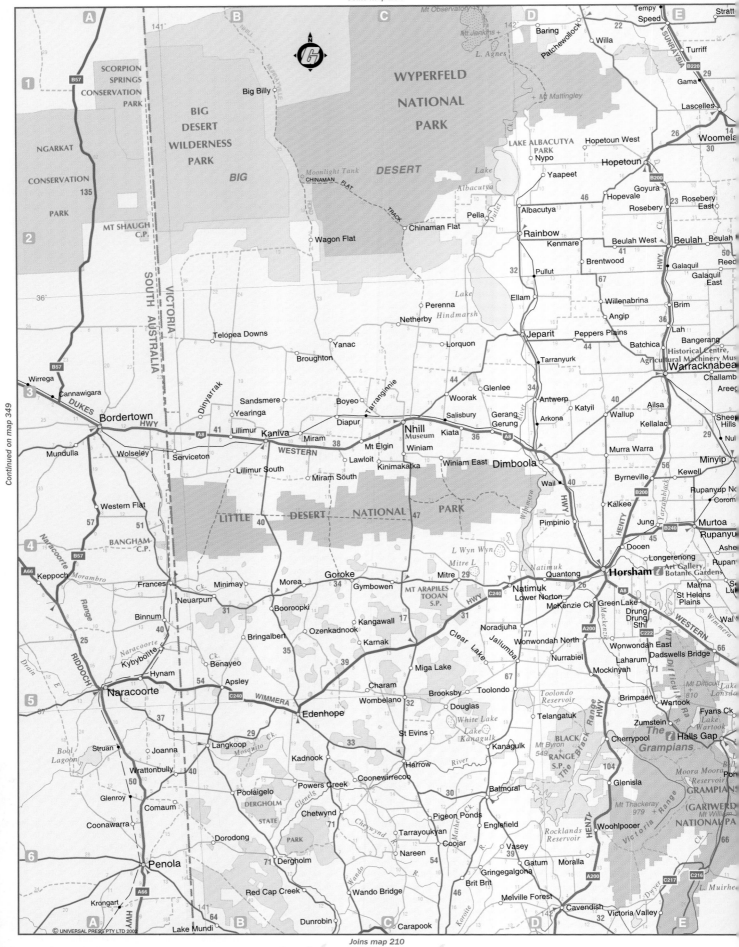

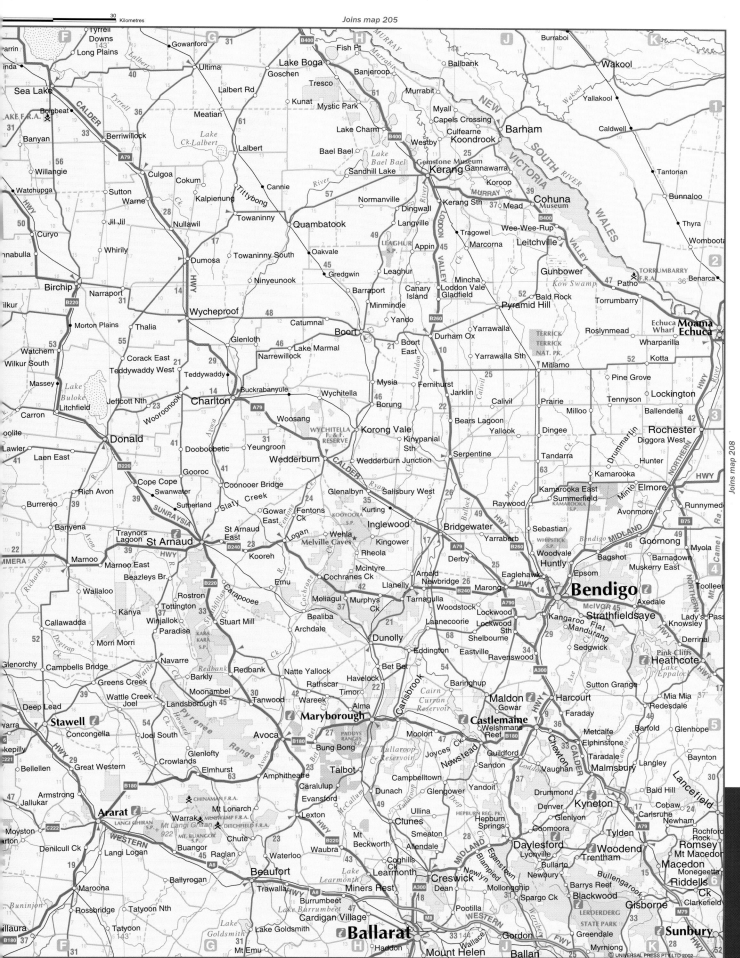

© UNIVERSAL PRESS PTY LTD 2002

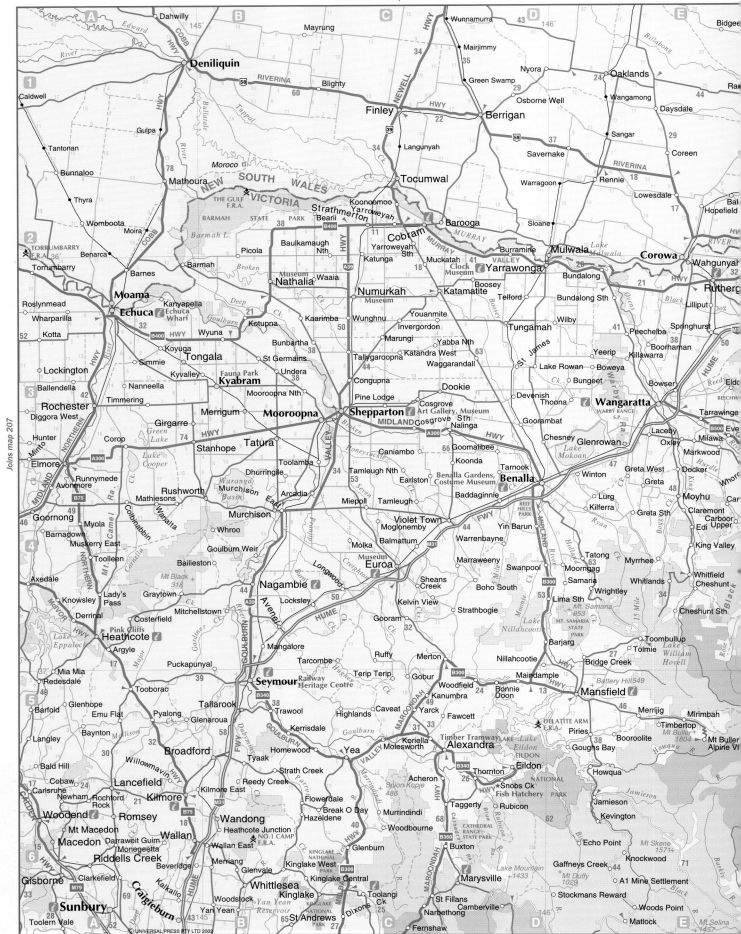

Victoria

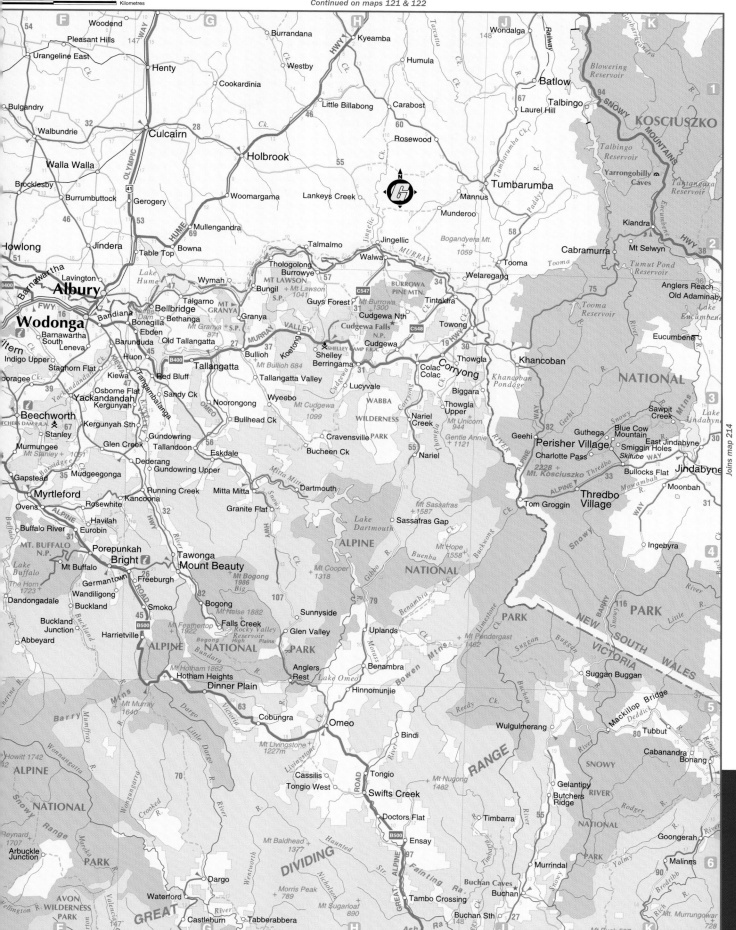

30 Kilometres

F

G

H

J

K

Woodend

Pleasant Hills

Urangeline East

Henty

Burrandana

Westby

Kyeamba

Humula

Batlow

Blowering Reservoir

KOSCIUSZKO

Bulgandry

Cookardinia

Little Billabong

Carabost

Laurel Hill

Talbingo

Walbundrie

Culcairn

Rosewood

Yarrongobilly Caves

Tantangara Reservoir

Walla Walla

Holbrook

Talbingo Reservoir

Brocklesby

Burrumbuttock

Gerogery

Woomargama

Lankeys Creek

Tumbarumba

Mannus

Kiandra

Howlong

Jindera

Table Top

Bowna

Mullengandra

Munderoo

Cabramurra

Mt Selwyn

Albury

Lake Hume

Talmalmo

Walwa

Jingellic

MURRAY

Tooma

Tumut Pond Reservoir

Anglers Reach

Old Adaminaby

Wodonga

Lavington

Bandiana

Bellbridge

Bethanga

Granya

MT LAWSON S.P.

Bungil

Mt Lawson 1041

Guys Forest

BURROWA PINE MTN.

Mt Burrowa 1300

Tintaldra

Welaregang

Tooma Reservoir

Lake Eucumbene

Eucumbene

Barnawartha South

Leneva

Ebden

Old Tallangatta

MURRAY

MT GRANYA S.P.

Mt Granya 871

Granya

Cudgewa Nth

Cudgewa Falls

Cudgewa

Towong

NATIONAL

Indigo Upper

Staghorn Flat

Huon

Barnuuda

Tallangatta

Bullioh

Mt Bullioh 684

Shelley

Berringama

Colac Colac

Corryong

Khancoban

Kewa

Kiewa

Red Bluff

Sandy Ck

Tallangatta Valley

Lucyvale

Thowgla

Khancoban Pondage

Beechworth

Osborne Flat

Kergunyah

Yackandandah

Noorongong

Wyeebo

Mt Cudgewa 1099

WABBA

Biggara

Thowgla Upper

Geehi

Guthega

Blue Cow Mountain

Sawpit Creek

Stanley

Kergunyah Sth

Bullhead Ck

WILDERNESS

Nariel Creek

Mt Unicorn 944

Perisher Village

Smiggin Holes

East Jindabyne

Murmungee

Mt Stanley 1057

Glen Creek

Tallandoon

Cravensville

PARK

Gentle Annie 1121

Charlotte Pass

Skitube

Gapstead

Mudgeegonga

Dederang

Gundowring Upper

Eskdale

Bucheen Ck

Nariel

Mt Kosciuszko 2228

Thredbo

Bullocks Flat

Jindabyne

Myrtleford

Rosewhite

Running Creek

Kancoona

Mitta Mitta

Dartmouth

RIVER

Tom Groggin

Thredbo Village

Moonbah

Ovens

Havilah

Eurobin

Granite Flat

ALPINE

Mt Sassafras 1587

Buffalo River

MT BUFFALO N.P.

Porepunkah

Tawonga

Sassafras Gap

Lake Dartmouth

Ingebyra

The Horn 1723

Bright

Mt Buffalo

Mount Beauty

NATIONAL

Mt Hope 1558

Dandongadale

Germantown

Freeburgh

Mt Bogong 1986 Big

Sunnyside

Mt Cooper 1318

Buckland Junction

Wandiligong

Buckland

Smoko

Bogong

Mt Nelse 1882

Falls Creek

Glen Valley

Uplands

NEW SOUTH WALES

Abbeyard

Harrietville

ALPINE

Mt Feathertop 1922

Rocky Valley Reservoir High Plains

Benambra

Mt Limestone

VICTORIA

PARK

Suggan Buggan

Mackillop Bridge

Mt Hotham 1862

Hotham Heights

Dinner Plain

NATIONAL

PARK

Anglers Rest

Lake Omeo

Mt Pendergast 1482

Wulgulmerang

Tubbut

Mt Murray 1640

Cobungra

Hinnomunjie

Bowen Mtns

Cabanandra

Bonang

Barry

Dargo

63

Omeo

Bindi

SNOWY

Mt Livingstone 1227m

Gelantipy

Howitt 1742

ALPINE

Cassilis

Tongio

Butchers Ridge

NATIONAL

Tongio West

Swifts Creek

RANGE

Goongerah

Arbuckle Junction

Doctors Flat

Timbarra

Malinns

NATIONAL

Reynard 1707

Waterford

Mt Baldhead 1377

Ensay

RIVER

PARK

Dargo

Morris Peak 789

Murrindal

Mt Murrungowar 728

AVON WILDERNESS PARK

Castleburn

Tabberabbera

Mt Sugarloaf 890

Tambo Crossing

Buchan Caves

Buchan

DIVIDING

Buchan Sth

Mt Buck 507

GREAT

Joins map 214

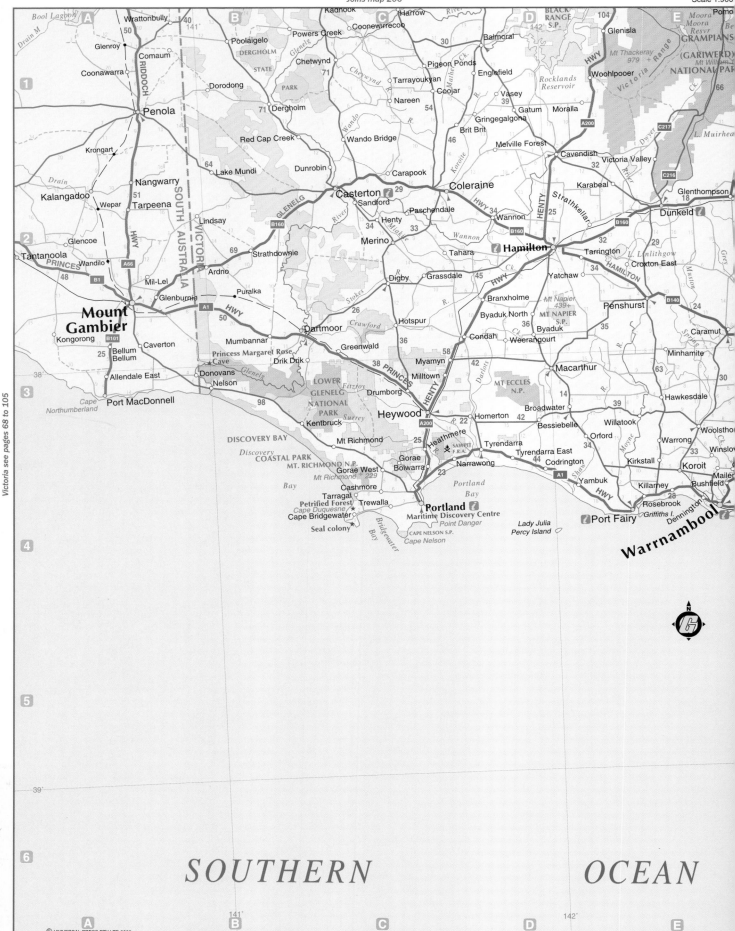

SOUTHERN OCEAN

Victoria

Victoria see pages 68 to 105

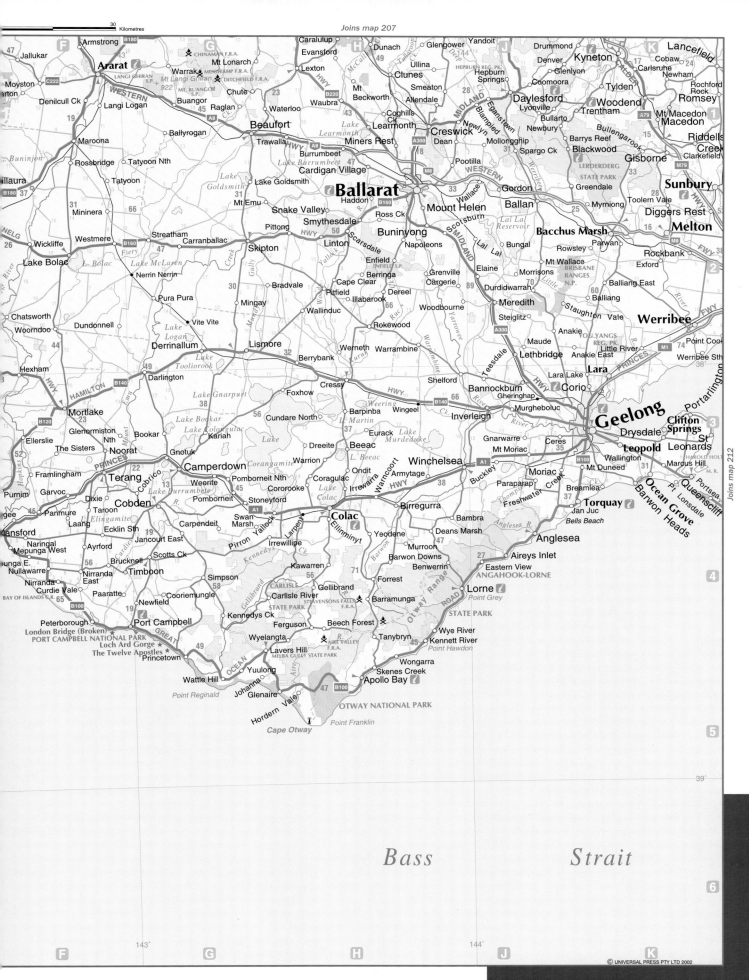

30 Kilometres

F

Jallukar
47
Armstrong

Moyston
arton
C222
Ararat
LANGI GHIRAN
S.P.
Warrak
CHINAMAN F.R.A.
Mt Lonarch
Mt Langi Ghiran
922
MT. BUANGOR
S.P.
MDEWAMP F.R.A.
DITCHFIELD F.R.A.

Denicull Ck
Langi Logan
Buangor
45
Raglan
Chute
A8
23
Waubra

Maroona
Rossbridge
Tatyoon Nth
19

Ballyrogan
Beaufort
Trawalla
Waterloo
B220
Lake
Learmonth

Buninjon
31
Tatyoon

Chatsworth
Mininera
66

Lake Burrumbeet
47

Cardigan Village

Ballarat
Haddon

Caralulup
Evansford
Lexton
Dunach
Glengower
Yandoit
Drummond
Denver
Kyneton
Lancefield

Clunes
Smeaton
Allandale
Hepburn
Springs
Lyonville
Glenlyon
Coomoora
Newham
Carlsruhe
Cobaw
Rochford
Rock
Romsey

Creswick
Dean
Mollongghip
Spargo Ck
Bullarto
Newbury
Barrys Reef
Blackwood
Gisborne
Clarkefield

Pootilla
Gordon
Greendale
Myrniong
Toolern Vale
Sunbury

Mount Helen
Ballan
Rowsley
Parwan
Rockbank
Melton
Exford
Balliang East

Bacchus Marsh
Bungal

FERNG
26
Wickliffe
Westmere
B160
Streatham
Carranballac
47

Lake Bolac
L. Bolac
Nerrin Nerrin
Lake McLaren
Skipton
Pittong

Pura Pura
Mingay
Bradvale

Vite Vite
Wallinduc

Lake
Logan
Dundonnell
Woorndoo
44

Hexham
Derrinallum
Lismore
Berrybank
32

Darlington
Lake
Tooliorook

Mortlake
Cressy
Foxhow
Wingeel

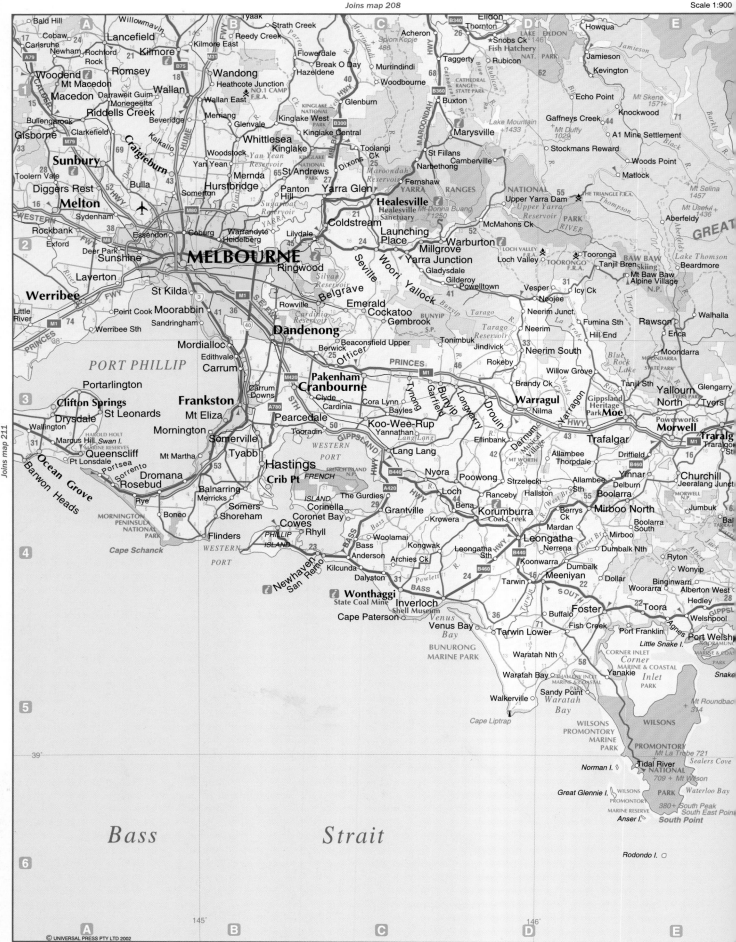

Bald Hill
Willowmavin
Tyaak
Strath Creek
Reedy Creek
Eildon
Thornton
Howqua

Cobaw
Lancefield
Kilmore East
Flowerdale
Acheron
Spion Kopje 488
Snobs Ck
Fish Hatchery

Carlsruhe
Newham
Rochford Rock
Kilmore
Hazeldene
Break O Day
Murrindindi
Taggerty
Rubicon
Jamieson

Woodend
Mt Macedon
Romsey
Wandong
Heathcote Junction
Glenburn
Woodbourne
Buxton
Kevington

Macedon
Darraweit Guim
Wallan
Wallan East
Merriang
Glenvale
Kinglake National Park
Toolangi Ck
St Fillans
Narbethong
Camberville
Echo Point

Riddells Creek
Beveridge
Woodstock
Kinglake West
Kinglake Central
Marysville
Lake Mountain 1433
Gaffneys Creek

Bullengarook
Clarkefield
Kalkallo
Yan Yean Reservoir
Kinglake
Dixons Ck
Maroondah Reservoir
Fernshaw
Stockmans Reward

Gisborne
Sunbury
Craigieburn
Yan Yean
Mernda
St Andrews
Yarra Glen
Healesville
Upper Yarra Dam
Woods Point
Matlock

Toolern Vale
Diggers Rest
Bulla
Hurstbridge
Panton Hill
Coldstream
Launching Place
Warburton
McMahons Ck
Upper Yarra PARK RIVER
Aberfeldy

Melton
Sydenham
Essendon
Coburg
Warrandyte Heidelberg
Lilydale
Millgrove
Loch Valley
Tanjil Bren

Rockbank
Exford
Deer Park
Sunshine
MELBOURNE
Ringwood
Seville
Woori Yallock
Yarra Junction
Gladysdale
Gilderoy
Powelltown
Vesper
Icy Ck
Mt Baw Baw Alpine Village

Laverton
St Kilda
Silvan Reservoir
Belgrave
Emerald
Neerim Junct.
Neerim
Fumina Sth
Rawson
Walhalla

Werribee
Point Cook
Moorabbin
Rowville
Cockatoo
Gembrook
Tarago Reservoir
Hill End
Neerim South
Erica

Little River
Sandringham
Dandenong
Beaconsfield Upper
Tonimbuk
Jindivick
Rokeby
Willow Grove
Moondarra

Werribee Sth
Mordialloc
Edithvale
Carrum
Berwick
Officer
Brandy Ck
Tanjil Sth

Portarlington
PORT PHILLIP
Carrum Downs
Pakenham
Cranbourne
Clyde
Cardinia
Cora Lynn
Bayles
Tynong
Bunyip
Garfield
Longwarry
Drouin
Warragul
Nilma
Yallourn North
Glengarry
Tyers

Clifton Springs
Drysdale
St Leonards
Frankston
Mt Eliza
Pearcedale
Tooradin
Koo-Wee-Rup
Yannathan
Lang Lang
Ellinbank
Darnum Musical Village
Moe
Morwell
Traralgon

Wallington
Marcus Hill
Queenscliff
Pt Lonsdale
Portsea
Sorrento
Mornington
Somerville
Tyabb
Hastings
Crib Pt
Nyora
Poowong
Strzelecki
Allambee Thorpdale
Driffield
Trafalgar
Yinnar
Churchill

Ocean Grove
Barwon Heads
Dromana
Rosebud
Rye
Balnarring
Merricks
Somers
Shoreham
Cowes
Rhyll
The Gurdies
Corinella
Grantville
Krowera
Loch
Bena
Ranceby
Hallston
Allambee Sth
Delburn
Boolarra
Mirboo North
Jumbuk

Boneo
Flinders
PHILLIP ISLAND
Bass
Anderson
Woolamai
Kongwak
Leongatha Sth
Korumburra
Coal Creek
Berrys Ck
Mardan
Mirboo
Boolarra South
Ryton

Cape Schanck
Newhaven
San Remo
Kilcunda
Dalyston
Archies Ck
Leongatha
Nerrena
Dumbalk Nth
Dumbalk
Dollar

Wonthaggi
State Coal Mine
Inverloch
Shell Museum
Koonwarra
Meeniyan
Tarwin
Foster
Fish Creek
Toora
Port Franklin
Welshpool

Cape Paterson
Venus Bay
Tarwin Lower
Buffalo
Port Welsh

BUNURONG MARINE PARK
Waratah Nth
Sandy Point
Yanakie

Waratah Bay
Walkerville
Cape Liptrap
Wilsons Promontory Marine Park

Bass Strait

Victoria

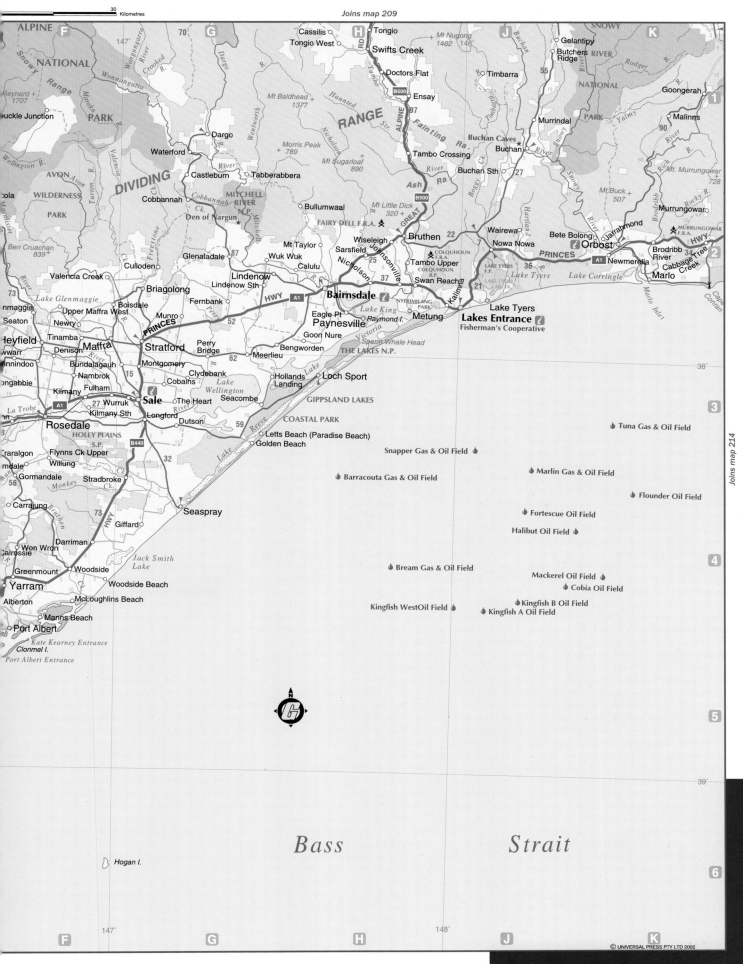

Joins map 214

Bass *Strait*

© UNIVERSAL PRESS PTY LTD 2002

Victoria

QUEENSLAN

The second largest state in Australia, Queensland is big, covering some 1 727 110km², and incredibly varied, stretching as it does from the tropics to the temperate zone. From north to south its greatest distance is 2092km and from east to west 1448km.

Shadowing the coastline for about 2000km, the stunning Great Barrier Reef is one of the natural wonders of the world and perhaps the state's greatest asset. Even so, the Reef is only one of the fabulous natural assets found throughout the state. Visitors to Queensland will also discover some of the world's most beautiful beaches, luxuriant tropical rainforests, paradisiacal islands, vast deserts, national parks and fascinating towns.

Evidence that Aboriginal people have lived in Queensland for many thousands of years can be seen in the traditional rock art found in such places as Carnarvon Gorge in the Central Highlands and Quinkan Galleries, located in the Laura River valley on Cape York. There are opportunities for visitors to inspect significant sites with Aboriginal guides, learn about indigenous

Queensland: The Sunshine State

- Population: 3 453 477
- Total area: 1 727 110km²
- % of Australia: 22.5%
- Length of coastline: 5207km
- Floral emblem: Cooktown Orchid
- Fauna emblem: Koala

Tourist information

Queensland Travel Centre
Tourism Queensland House
30 Makerston St,
Brisbane, Qld 4000
Ph: 138 833
www.tq.com.au

Main ATTRACTIONS

◈ Cairns

Cairns is a point of departure for the huge region known as Tropical North Queensland, including the northern section of the Great Barrier Reef and its islands, the Wet Tropics Rainforest, Atherton Tableland and Cape York Peninsula.

◈ Fraser Island

A World Heritage-listed national park, Fraser Island is the world's largest sand island and a fascinating holiday destination.

◈ Gold Coast

The fun-filled Gold Coast offers a range of world-class theme parks and great surf beaches, backed by high-rise developments and shopping centres.

◈ Great Barrier Reef

The most extensive coral reef system in the world is a blue-water panorama of colourful marine life, including around 1500 species of fish, 4000 species of molluscs, 350 species of echinoderms and 400 species of coral. It attracts divers and snorkellers as well as holiday-makers in every kind of boat.

◈ Sunshine Coast

This is a region of unhurried and unspoiled beaches within easy driving distance of Brisbane. There are also some very popular national parks and major family-oriented attractions.

◈ The Scenic Rim

Also within a few hours drive from the state capital, this is a lush region of mountainous national parks bordered by the Gold Coast and New South Wales.

◈ Whitsundays

A group of 74 idyllic islands in the balmy waters of the Coral Sea.

lifestyles at cultural centres such as the Dreamtime Centre near Rockhampton or be entertained by the world-renowned Tjapukai Dance Theatre near Cairns.

Touring Queensland by car is easy, although a 4WD is required to reach some of the more remote Outback regions. The Bruce Hwy links Brisbane with Cairns and gives access to all coastal areas in between. A sealed road continues to Mossman, but dirt roads take over further north into the pristine wilderness of Cape York. A network of roads covers the vast Outback areas, with convenient links to many points on the Bruce Hwy. The enormous distances can also be covered by rail or air. Brisbane, Cairns and Townsville have international airports and there are regional airports at many of the larger towns.

Photo above: Daydream Island, Whitsundays

THE SUNSHINE STATE

Seven times the size of Great Britain, twice the size of Texas and five times the size of Japan, Queensland occupies 22.5% of the mainland of Australia in the subtropical and tropical north-east of the continent. With beaches and islands among its key attractions, Queensland has 5207km of coastline, and from north to south its greatest distance is 2092km.

Known to Australians as the 'Sunshine State', the weather conditions vary greatly between the coastal plain and the inland environment. In the north, the tropical conditions mean that the Wet season Dec–March is extremely hot and humid. Inland, days are usually hot and dry throughout the year, while the nights can get cold and frosty in winter. The majority of the coast is bathed in sunshine and warmth most of the year. **Brisbane**, the capital, boasts an average summer temperature of 25°C as well as dry winters. The state's attractions and climate make it the perfect holiday destination.

With over 1000 species of vertebrates, 86% of which are native to the region, Queensland is a wildlife-watcher's paradise. There are around 572 bird species in the state, while the rainforest vegetation, banksias, eucalypts, and the Mitchell-grass plains and spinifex in the south-west also await keen explorers.

Pastoralism has always been important to Queensland's economy. Agriculture, originally in the form of sugarcane farms, now includes cotton, fruits, peanuts, grains and vegetables. Queensland dominates the sugarcane industry, growing almost the country's entire export crop. Around 37% of Australian beef is farmed in Queensland.

The state accounts for around 23% of Australia's mining industry with coal featuring prominently

Burning sugarcane in the Burdekin Valley, near Ayr

followed by copper, lead, bauxite and zinc. There are mineral deposits all over the state, but perhaps the largest and most well-known are located in the mining town of **Mount Isa**.

Tourism, the other dominant industry in Queensland, is very important to the state's economy, a brief visit to the Sunshine State attests to this fact. There are around 4.5 million international visitors annually. They are attracted to the sunny coast, offshore islands, the underwater marine wonderland of the **Great Barrier Reef**, the rainforests, the Outback, Aboriginal rock art and, in the gulf country, unrivalled river and estuary fishing. Three international airports—Brisbane, Cairns and Townsville—provide gateways to Queensland's manifold attractions.

Zillie Falls, Atherton Tableland

Queensland

TOURISM REGION HIGHLIGHTS

Queensland is a state of extraordinary diversity. It has 3 of Australia's most treasured natural wonders—the 2000km-long **Great Barrier Reef**, **Fraser Island** and the ancient **Daintree** rainforest. All of these are World Heritage-listed. There are literally hundreds of tropical beaches, islands and national parks to explore and a vast outback of rugged and austere beauty.

A Brisbane
Brisbane Forest Park; City Botanic Gardens; Ipswich; Lone Pine Koala Sanctuary; Moreton Bay; Moreton Island; Mount Coot-tha; Queen St Mall; Queensland Cultural Centre; Redcliffe; South Bank; Treasury Casino

B Bundaberg, Coral Isles and Country
Bundaberg Rum Distillery; Cania Gorge; Childers; Hinkler House; Lady Elliot Island; Lady Musgrave Island; Mon Repos Beach; Mystery Craters; Whale watching

C Capricorn
Dreamtime Cultural Centre; Gemfields; Great Barrier Reef; Great Keppel Island; Mount Morgan; Rockhampton; Yeppoon

D Fraser Coast South Burnett
Fraser Island; Hervey Bay; Kingaroy; Maryborough; Whale watching

Aboriginal hand-prints, Carnarvon NP

E Gladstone
Agnes Water; Calliope River Historical Village; Gladstone Marina; Great Barrier Reef; Heron Island; Kroombit Tops; Town of 1770

F Gold Coast
Currumbin Wildlife Sanctuary; Dreamworld; Jupiters Casino; Lamington NP; Movie World; Natural Arch; Sanctuary Cove; Sea World; Surfers Paradise

G Mackay
Brampton Island; Eungella NP; Finch Hatton Gorge; Great Barrier Reef; Hamilton Island; Lindeman Island; Sugar Mill tours

H Queensland's Outback
Barcaldine; Birdsville; Camooweal Caves; Hughenden Dinosaur Museum; Lark Quarry; Mount Isa Mine; Richmond Marine Fossil Museum; Simpson Desert; Stockman's Hall of Fame

I South East Queensland Country
Bunya Mountains; Crows Nest Falls; Darling Downs; Granite Belt Wineries; Ipswich; Scenic Rim; Toowoomba; Warwick

J Sunshine Coast
Australia Zoo; Blackall Range; Caloundra; Glass House Mountains; Gympie; Noosa Heads; Noosa NP; Rainbow Beach; The Big Pineapple; The Ginger Factory; Teewah Coloured Sands; UnderWater World

K Townsville
Bedarra Island; Charters Towers; Dunk Island; Great Barrier Reef; Hinchinbrook Island; Magnetic Island; Museum of Tropical Queensland; Orpheus Island; Reef HQ; Wallaman Falls

L Tropical North Queensland
Atherton Tableland; Cairns; Cape Tribulation; Cape York; Chillagoe Caves; Cooktown; Crater Lakes; Daintree NP; Gulf Savannah; Green Island; Great Barrier Reef; Johnstone River Crocodile Farm; Kuranda; Kuranda Scenic Railway; Lawn Hill Gorge; Mission Beach; Mossman Gorge; Port Douglas; Riversleigh Fossil Fields; Skyrail Rainforest Cableway; Tjapukai Aboriginal Cultural Centre; Undara Lava Tubes; Waterfall Circuit; White-water rafting, Wild World

M Western Downs
Carnarvon Gorge; Chinchilla Folk Museum; Goondiwindi; Miles; Roma

N Whitsundays
Airlie Beach; Conway NP; Daydream Island; Great Barrier Reef; Hamilton Island; Hayman Island; Lindeman Island; Proserpine; Whitehaven Beach; Whitsunday Passage

NATIONAL PARKS

Providing habitats for Queensland's diverse wildlife and plants and preserving some of the state's most unique scenery, the national parks of Queensland are distinctly beautiful samples of the state's natural landscapes and heritage. The national parks can be divided into 6 regions: the south-east, central coast, central highlands, western Queensland, north Queensland and far north Queensland (FNQ). Interestingly, most of the state's national parks are also the state's major tourist attractions. Camping is possible in most of the national parks, but a small fee does apply.

facts

◆ No. of parks/reserves: 494
◆ Area: 71 128km²
◆ % of state: 4.11%
◆ World Heritage Areas: Australian Fossil Mammal Site (Riversleigh), Central Eastern Rainforest Reserves, Great Barrier Reef, Fraser Island, and the Wet Tropics

A Brisbane Forest Park
(Map 230, A2)
On the western outskirts of the state's capital, Brisbane Forest Park covers 285km² and is made up of 4 small parks, forests and reserves. The place for birdwatchers, bushwalkers and campers, the park's convenient location and optional ranger-guided activities are the main attractions for a quick, quiet escape from the bustling city. Visit year-round to picnic, BBQ, walk, and explore the lakes, creeks, rainforests and eucalypt forests. To camp, prearrange a permit with the park ranger.

B Cooloola (Great Sandy NP)
(Map 255, C1)
Cooloola—part of Great Sandy NP—is located 200km north of Brisbane. Great to visit year-round, the national park offers the opportunity of watersports—canoeing, surf fishing, river fishing—as well as bushwalking, camping and 4WDing. Common fishing catches include bream, whiting and flathead. The 560km² park has a few unique features such as the coloured sands of Teewah Beach and Rainbow Beach, rainforests that grow in sand and 'perched' lakes found high in the sand dunes. Originally inhabited by the Kabi people, timber merchants arrived in the park in 1840, introducing diseases that almost wiped out the Aboriginal people.

C Daintree NP (Map 239, A1)
Daintree NP (565km²) is situated about 80km north of Cairns, and the **Cape Tribulation** section is a further 25km north (170km²). The best time to visit the lush rainforest and rugged mountain ranges of the park is from April to October (to avoid the Wet season). Known for its unique and rare bird, animal and plant life, the national park is in parts quite inaccessible to the amateur hiker or walker. Permits for camping are necessary. Visitors need to be careful of the saltwater crocodiles that are found in the creeks and rivers.

D Fraser Island (Great Sandy NP) (Map 259, D2)
Also part of Great Sandy NP, Fraser Island is administered as a separate park to Cooloola. Covering 1653km², the island is the largest sand island in the world and is listed as a World Heritage Area. Known for its variety of wildlife (over 230 bird species), Fraser Island is a popular destination with its amazing geographic heritage, coloured sands, perched dune lakes, desert-like sandblows, saltwater fishing, walking and hiking trails. Camping, cabin and resort accommodation is available. There are no formed roads on the island, so it is necessary to take a 4WD for any exploring. There are barges operating from 4 different points on the island and mainland, and it is possible to arrive via light plane.

White-lipped tree frog, *Litoria infrafrenata*

Queensland

Diving in the Great Barrier Reef Marine Park

There are prearranged tours and daytrips available for those interested in a guided service.

E Great Barrier Reef Marine Park (Map 279, K2)

The world's largest World Heritage Area and the largest structure made by living organisms, the Great Barrier Reef consists of 2900 reefs and around 600 islands. Located on the outer edge of Australia's north-eastern continental shelf (once part of the Queensland coast), the Reef extends for 2000km from Bundaberg/Maryborough in the

Big Red Sand Dune, Simpson Desert NP

south to beyond Cape York in the tropical north. Coral is formed from the hard chalky skeletons of tiny marine polyps, which are invertebrate animals related to jellyfish and sea anemones. Given the right conditions coral reefs are in a continual state of growth. The Reef attracts a multitude of brightly coloured fish and other sea creatures, as well as 215 species of birds, 6 species of turtles and the largest dugong population in the world. It offers some of the world's best diving and snorkelling sites. The entire area is managed by the Great Barrier Reef Marine Park Authority which was established in 1975. Many of the Barrier Reef's islands are listed as separate national parks.

F Lawn Hill NP (Map 280, B1)

Located 350km NW of Mount Isa, Lawn Hill NP borders the Northern Territory. Around 2820km², this national park is a haven for fresh-water crocodiles which are the 'friendlier' of the two varieties. It is best to visit the park in winter and early spring as access is quite difficult, especially during the Wet season. The gravel and dirt roads are easier to navigate with 4WDs. The rugged gorges, ancient creeks

and wildlife make this park a wonderland for nature lovers and explorers. Take a stroll, a hike, a canoe or inflatable boat and adventure through one of Queensland's northernmost national parks.

G Simpson Desert NP (Map 284, B1)

Bordered by South Australia and the Northern Territory, the Simpson Desert NP is the largest national park in Queensland at 10 120km² and is a suitable destination for 4WDs only. For those interested in remote desert camping, this national park should be top of the list. Red sand dunes carpeted with spinifex and broken intermittently by valleys spotted with wattles and scrub create a most wonderful Australian scene. Inhabited mainly by small reptiles, birds and dingoes, the national park is also home to beautiful salt lakes.

National Park Head Office
Queensland Parks and Wildlife Service
Environmental Protection Agency
PO Box 155,
Albert St
Brisbane, Qld 4002
Ph: (07) 3227 8185
www.epa.qld.gov.au

WINERIES

Queensland is generally regarded as a newcomer to the Australian wine industry, although wine grapes have been grown in the state since the 1860s. The oldest winery was established in the unlikely location of **Roma**, where **Samuel Bassett** planted vine cuttings from the Hunter Valley, New South Wales, in 1863. His **Romavilla** vineyard was a thriving business with several export markets and award-winning wines; it still exists today.

Vineyards were planted in other areas of south-east Queensland, however, it was not until the 1960s that the industry really burgeoned. **Ballandean Estate** was the first vineyard in the **Southern Downs**, which is now Queensland's most successful wine region. Experimentation with wine varieties, soils and microclimates has led to further successes in recent years. Continuing research is leading to new developments in coastal regions as far north as **Bundaberg** and **Gladstone**.

Queensland wines are distinctively light, crisp and fruity, and harmonise well with Queensland's light and fresh cuisine and the state's relaxed lifestyle.

Tasting room at Mount Tamborine Winery, Gold Coast hinterland

A Brisbane and Gold Coast (pp.234–235)

Several wineries have recently been established within a short drive of Brisbane, both in the **Brisbane Valley** and on the **Scenic Rim** region in the **Gold Coast hinterland**. Wines include semillon, chardonnay, shiraz, cabernet, merlot, chenin blanc, and sauvignon blanc.

B South Burnett

Fertile soils and elevation well above sea level have contributed to the eminence of this new winery region around **Kingaroy** and **Murgon**. High quality table wines are produced and include merlot, shiraz, traminer and full-bodied chardonnays.

C Southern Downs

The success of the region around **Stanthorpe** has been helped by a combination of high altitude, cool climate and decomposed granite soils. The 30 or so Southern Downs wineries have earned a reputation for full-bodied reds and very crisp premium whites.

D Sunshine Coast and D'Aguilar Ranges (pp.254–255)

This is another fast-growing wine region on the rich volcanic soils of the **Blackall** and **D'Aguilar ranges**. The excellent views are matched by a range of classic table wines, including chardonnay, sauvignon blanc, cabernet and shiraz.

E Toowoomba (pp.270–271)

A number of boutique wineries are scattered around Toowoomba, a region enjoying a renaissance. A wide selection of red and white table wines is produced as well as fortified wines. Rimfire Winery won an award for Australia's best chardonnay in 1997.

F Western Downs

Queensland's oldest wine region is in the Western Downs and has long been known for liqueur muscats, ports and sweet dessert wines. Merlot, chardonnay, cabernet sauvignon, shiraz, crouchen, chenin blanc, riesling, semillon and ruby cabernet are also produced.

Queensland

ISLANDS

Islands are magnets for tourists and Queensland has a wealth of beautiful tropical and subtropical islands, which cater for most tastes. While accommodation ranges from budget to luxury resorts, many islands are uninhabited and invite exploration.

Sandy Islands

South Stradbroke Island lies just off the Gold Coast, while North Stradbroke Island is a short ferry ride from Cleveland in Brisbane. The Moreton Bay islands, made up of Russell, Lamb, Macleay, Karragarra and other islands, are known for watersports, sailing, swimming and fishing. Moreton Island, north-east of Brisbane, is renowned for its huge sandhills, lakes, dolphins and 4WDing. Fraser Island, a World Heritage-listed national park with rainforests, perched lakes, great basalt headlands, salt pans and white-sand beaches is extremely popular. (*see* pp.258–259).

Great Barrier Reef Islands

Lady Elliot Island, north-east of Bundaberg, is an unspoiled coral cay known for its diving sites and birdlife. Heron Island is a true coral cay best known for diving, birdlife and turtles. Green Island has the only international 5-star resort found on a coral cay; it is a short boat trip from Cairns. Just north of Green Island, Michaelmas Cay is a protected sanctuary for 27 000 migratory birds and nesting place for 14 bird species. The tiny Low Isles are a popular destination with their magnificent coral gardens and coconut-palm-fringed beaches.

Continental Islands

Great Keppel Island lies offshore from Yeppoon. Only 8 of the 74 Whitsunday Islands, located between the Great Barrier Reef and Airlie Beach, are inhabited. Some of the most popular Whitsunday Islands include Lindeman, Hayman, Brampton, Daydream,

Red-tailed frigate bird, *Phaethon rubricauda*

South Molle, Long and Hamilton (*see* pp.262–263). Magnetic Island is Townsville's island playground—20min by Cat Ferry from the city. Hinchinbrook Island, off Cardwell, is a huge national park with a resort that caters for up to 50 guests at a time. Dunk Island has a large resort and is known for horseriding, watersports and rainforest walks. Nearby Bedarra and Orpheus islands are secluded and relaxing. Fitzroy Island caters for a range of budgets and is close to Cairns. Lizard Island north-east of Cooktown is bordered by sandy beaches and coral; it is also home to a marine research station. At the top of Cape York, the Torres Strait Islands showcase the distinctive culture of the Torres Strait Islanders. The main tourist centre is on Thursday Island.

Hayman Island Resort, Whitsundays

BRISBANE

City Botanic Gardens, Brisbane

main attractions

◈ **City Botanic Gardens**

Formal gardens, bicycle tracks and duck ponds are some of the gardens' attractions.

◈ **Fortitude Valley and Chinatown**

The cosmopolitan area to the north of the CBD boasts a wide range of cafes and restaurants as well as clubs and a shopping mall.

◈ **Mount Coot-tha Lookout**

Superb panoramic views over the city, bay and hinterland can be enjoyed here. Nearby, the Brisbane Botanic Gardens feature a scented garden and the Sir Thomas Brisbane Planetarium.

◈ **Queen St Mall**

With its blend of traditional and modern architecture, Queen St Mall brings to life the city's shopping centres.

◈ **Queensland Cultural Centre**

Located on Brisbane River's South Bank, the complex consists of the Queensland Museum, the Queensland Art Gallery, the State Library and the huge Performing Arts Complex.

◈ **South Bank**

This is a recreation area providing entertainment for all with gardens, waterways, a subtropical beach, riverside walkways, cafes, restaurants, BBQ facilities and an IMAX cinema.

The northernmost of Australia's state capitals, subtropical Brisbane is an attractive city lying 14km inland on the banks of the **Brisbane River**. It enjoys warm summers and clear mild winters. Although for many years Brisbane was a capital with the atmosphere of a large country town, the 1984 Commonwealth Games and the 1988 World Expo helped to change that image. Visitors now find a modern and sophisticated city that is full of life and vitality.

Settled in 1825 by a detachment of 45 convicts and their guards, Brisbane was originally a penal settlement situated at **Redcliffe**, north of the city's current location. The move to Brisbane's current site beside the river was mainly due to a lack of fresh water, the failure of introduced crops and unrest among the local Aboriginal people. The riverside position has since played a pivotal role in the life of the city. Paddlewheelers, yachts, floating restaurants, ferries, cruise boats and bridges can be seen from many vantage points on the river's picturesque banks.

ℹ Tourist information

Brisbane Visitor Information Centre
Queen St Mall,
Brisbane, Qld 4000
Ph: (07) 3229 5918
www.brisbanetourism.com.au

facts

◈ Population: 1 601 400
◈ Date founded: 1825
◈ Oldest building: The Old Windmill on Wickham Tce (1828)
◈ Average temp: 25°C (Jan), 16°C (June)

Places of Interest

Anzac Square Ⓐ D3
Brisbane City Hall and Tower Ⓑ C4
Brisbane Convention and Exhibition Centre Ⓒ B5
Brisbane Cricket Ground (Gabba) Ⓓ E6
City Botanic Gardens Ⓔ D4
Conrad International Treasury Casino Ⓕ C4
Customs House Ⓖ D3
Eagle St Pier and Riverside Markets Ⓗ D4
Festival Hall Ⓘ D4
Kangaroo Point Ⓙ E3
Old Commissariat Store Ⓚ C4
Old Government House Ⓛ D5
Old Windmill Observatory Ⓜ C3
Parliament House Ⓝ D4
Queen St Mall Ⓞ C4
Queensland Art Gallery and Museum Ⓟ B4
Queensland Maritime Museum Ⓠ C5
Queensland Performing Arts Complex Ⓡ C4
Queensland Sciencentre Ⓢ C4
Riverside Centre Ⓣ D3
South Bank Ⓤ C5
State Library of Queensland Ⓥ B4
Story Bridge Ⓦ E3
Victoria Barracks Ⓧ B3
Victoria Park Ⓨ C1

Brisbane CBD reflected in the Brisbane River

Queensland

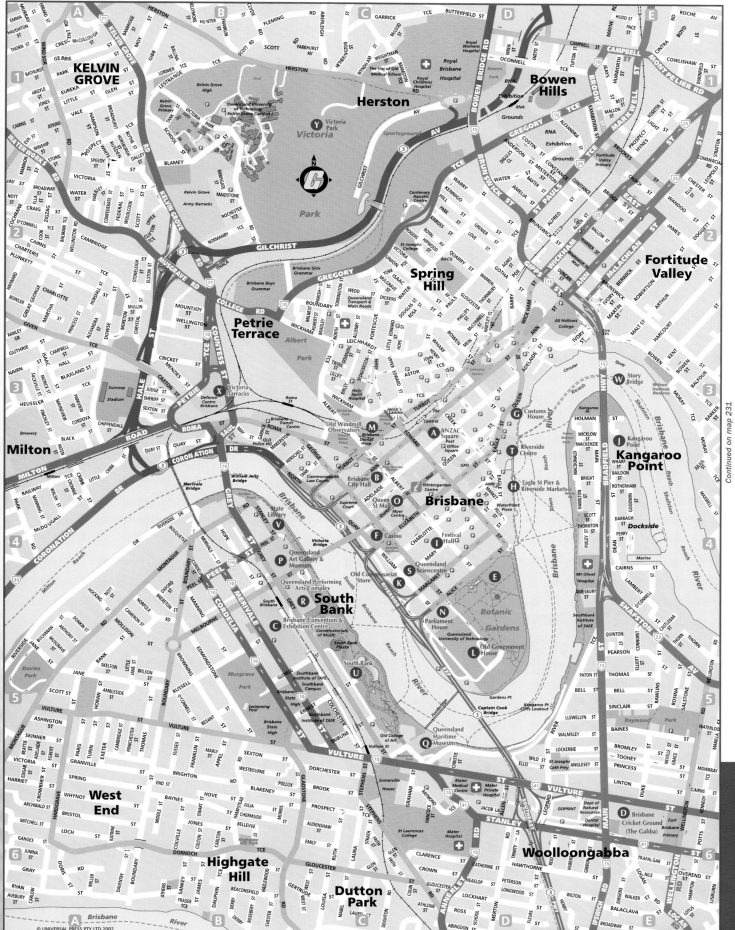

CBD & SUBURBS

CBD ATTRACTIONS

Although more of Brisbane's population live outside the city compared to other capital cities, it is still vibrant and economically and culturally alive. With a lot to see and do, and an atmosphere of lazy sunny days, a good way to tour Brisbane is on the specific buses. The **City Sights Tour** takes in modern and historical sites around the CBD, while stopping at 19 strategic locations. The ticket is valid all day and gives unlimited access to river ferries and Brisbane Transport's commuter bus fleet. The **City Nights Tour** includes floodlit landmarks, the illuminated cliff faces of **Kangaroo Point**, and breathtaking night views over the city from **Mount Coot-tha Lookout**. For more details and timetables, contact Transinfo, ph 13 1230.

For those who are more inclined to explore the city on foot, there is a **self-guided walk** through the CBD that begins at King George Square, along the way viewing **City Hall**, the **Shrine of Remembrance**, the 3-storey **Palace Backpackers** hostel and **Parliament House**.

Other attractions to take in are **Customs House**, which is now restored and is home to many cultural events, exhibitions and lectures. Not too far from here are **Eagle St Pier** and **Riverside Markets**—both popular for food and crafts and just strolling around. The paddlewheelers offer a variety of cruises on the **Brisbane River**; they depart from Eagle St Pier. The **Stamford Plaza Hotel** at the south end of the CBD has gardens and terraces worth wandering through, as well as bars and restaurants with views of the river and the **City Botanic Gardens**. Wandering to the south end of George St, **Parliament House**, constructed in 1868, is a beautiful French Renaissance-style building. Admission is free and includes a guided tour. **Queen St Mall**, located in the centre of the city, is brimming with retail shops, arcades and street performers. Not too far down the road is the **Queensland Sciencentre**, a hands-on centre with interactive displays for children and adults alike; it is open daily. To view a neo-Gothic style cathedral visit **St John's Anglican Cathedral**. Construction began in 1901 and continues to this day. **Conrad International Treasury Casino** in George St contains over 100 gaming tables and 1000 poker machines with a variety of entertainment and a buzzing nightlife.

SUBURBAN ATTRACTIONS

The suburbs surrounding the Brisbane CBD can be divided into the **Inner Suburbs**, **Southside**, **Bayside**, **Northside** and **Westside**.

Inner Suburbs

Originally a place of farming, shipping, commerce and industry, the inner suburbs are now alive with a diversity of people and nightlife to rival any other city in the country. **Fortitude Valley** is lined with indoor and outdoor eateries, shops and clubs. Also in the Valley is **Chinatown Mall**, a place of Chinese influence, with an array of clothes, shops, food and festivals. Visitors are attracted to this colourful area to sample authentic yum cha and Chinese culture.

For picnics and BBQs, visit **Kangaroo Point**, a magnificent outdoor reserve with abseiling and rockclimbing facilities, as well as great views from the clifftops. **New Farm**, once a prison farm, is now a

Chinese festival in Fortitude Valley

Queensland

leafy suburb brimming with grand houses and old cottages. Well-known for its parks, restaurants, bookshops and art galleries, New Farm is worth a visit. Take the **Hail and Ride** bus service for a tour of the 15 galleries in the area. The **Powerhouse Centre for Live Arts** is close by.

For lovers of Australia's colonial heritage, visit **Newstead House**, situated on the eastern side of Fortitude Valley and open Mon–Fri.

Southside

As one of the city's oldest suburbs, **South Brisbane** offers **South Bank**, 16ha of informal recreational gardens, as well as Brisbane's principal cultural precinct, with theatres, museums and an art gallery to explore.

Cricket lovers venture to **Woolloongabba**, the **Brisbane Cricket Ground** commonly known as the **Gabba**. You can sample the fresh fruit available at the **Brisbane Markets** in **Rocklea** or visit the famous rum distillery at **Beenleigh**. For a panoramic view of Brisbane city, try the **Mount Gravatt Lookout**, only 10km from the CBD.

Bayside

Situated on **Moreton Bay**, the bayside suburbs offer a relaxed ambience and water-based recreational activities. **Cleveland** has an historical precinct and is the departure point for ferries to **North Stradbroke Island**. **Manly** has a large marina and passenger ferry departures to **St Helena Island**. There is a mangrove boardwalk at **Wynnum** and a vehicular and passenger ferry links historic **Redcliffe** with the natural wonders of **Moreton Island**.

Pods of playful bottlenose dolphins are often seen riding the waves in Moreton Bay, and humpback whales sometimes venture into the bay during their winter

Beachfront at Tangalooma Wild Dolphin Resort, Moreton Island

migration (mid-June–Oct). **Fort Lytton**, at the mouth of the **Brisbane River**, played an important part in Queensland's defence for over 60 years. The 19th-century fort has a museum and guided tours are available on Sundays.

Northside

On the northside, the 'old money' suburbs of **Hamilton** and **Ascot** are 10km NE of the CBD. Ascot is home to famous **Eagle Farm Racecourse**. **Boondall Wetlands** is a magnificent reserve about 15km from the CBD. A nature-based recreation area, the wetlands can be explored from a bikeway, walking trails or by canoe. Brisbane's **Alma Park Zoo** and **Lake Samsonvale** are attractions in the far northern suburbs. The lake has several picnic spots and designated areas for shoreside fishing.

Westside

Visit the famous **Lone Pine Koala Sanctuary** close to the Brisbane River at **Fig Tree Pocket** and the many attractions around **Mount Coot-tha**. **Brisbane Forest Park** stretches through the western suburbs, offering bushwalking, picnicking, camping, scenic drives, horseriding and cycling; a permit is required. Lakes, mountains, eucalypt forest, lookouts, gullies, rainforest and waterfalls are all part of the park's natural environment. Park headquarters at **The Gap** has the **Walkabout Creek Wildlife Centre**, where platypus, turtles, lungfish, an aviary and nocturnal wildlife can be seen. Also worth visiting is the **Brisbane General Cemetery**, established in 1871. A pleasant place to wander around, it also offers an insight into the history of Brisbane.

Wamuran

Historical*
Village

Caboolture

Bellmere

Morayfield

Campbells Pocket

Mount Mee

Mt Mee
495

Bootawa

BYRON
CREEK
C.P.

Rocksberg

Upper
Caboolture

Ocean
View

Burpengary

Mount
Pleasant

Moorina

Narangba

King
Scrub

Laceys
Creek

Rush
Creek

Dayboro

Kurwongbah

Dakabin

Upper
Laceys
Creek

Kallangur

Lakeside
Motor Racing
Circuit

Alma Park Zoo
& Botanical Gardens

Samsonvale

Whiteside

Lake
Samsonvale

North Pine Historical Village

Petrie

BRISBANE

FOREST

PARK

Mt Kobble 364

Mt Samson
Emu Park

Mt Samson 689

Clear Mountain
State Forest

Cashmere

Lawnton

Joyner

Bray
Park

D'AGUILAR (MAIALA)

NATIONAL   PARK

Mt D'Aguilar 748

Mount
Samson

Clear Mtn 246

Strathpine

Clear
Mountain

CLEAR MOUNTAIN
STATE FOREST

Deer Farm*

Closeburn

Warner

Brendale

Mount
Glorious

Mt Glorious
819

Mt Lawson
473

Cedar
Creek

Bald
Hills

Greene's
Falls

Maiala
Recreation
Area

Eatons
Hill

Yugar

Draper

BRISBANE

Albany
Creek

FOREST

England Creek

Bunya

PARK

Westridge
Outlook

Mt O'Reilly
503

House   Mountain   Range

Samford Valley
Country Club

Bridgeman
Downs

Samford Valley

Samford
Village

Highvale

Mt Nebo
617

Manorina Bush Camp

Everton
Hills

McDowall

Cherms
West

Queensland

Continued on map 287

5 Kilometres

F   G   H   J   K

1
2
3
4
5
6

Ningi

Sandstone Point

Godwin Beach

BEACHMERE ENVIRONMENTAL PARK

Beachmere

Deception

Bay

Deception Bay

Bellara
Bribie Bridge
Sandstone Point
Welsby Bridge
Bongaree   *Bribie*
Island
Bribie Pines
FIRST

BRIBIE ISLAND N.P.
Woorim
AVENUE
Bribie Island

Skirmish Pt
Woody Bay

Buckleys Hole
South Pt
Red Beach
BUCKLEYS HOLE C.P.
Bald Pt

Vehicular Ferry

Moreton

North Reef
Castlereagh (or Reef) Pt
Scarborough Boat Harbour
Oyster Pt
Scarborough Pt
Scarborough Beach
Drury Pt
Scarborough
Queens Beach Nth
Osbourne Pt
Queens Beach
Queens Beach South
Redcliffe Jetty
Redcliffe Pt
Settlement Cove Lagoon

Bay

Redcliffe Aerodrome

Rothwell

NATHAN ROAD WETLANDS RESERVE

Rothwell Memorial
30

Kippa - Ring

HAYS INLET C.P. NO.2

Redcliffe   Museum
Margate
30
Clontarf
HAYS INLET C.P. NO.1

Griffin

Hays Inlet

Redcliffe

Scotts Pt
Woody Point
Bells Beach
Clontarf Beach
Clontarf Pt
Woody Point Beach
Picnic Pt
Woody Pt

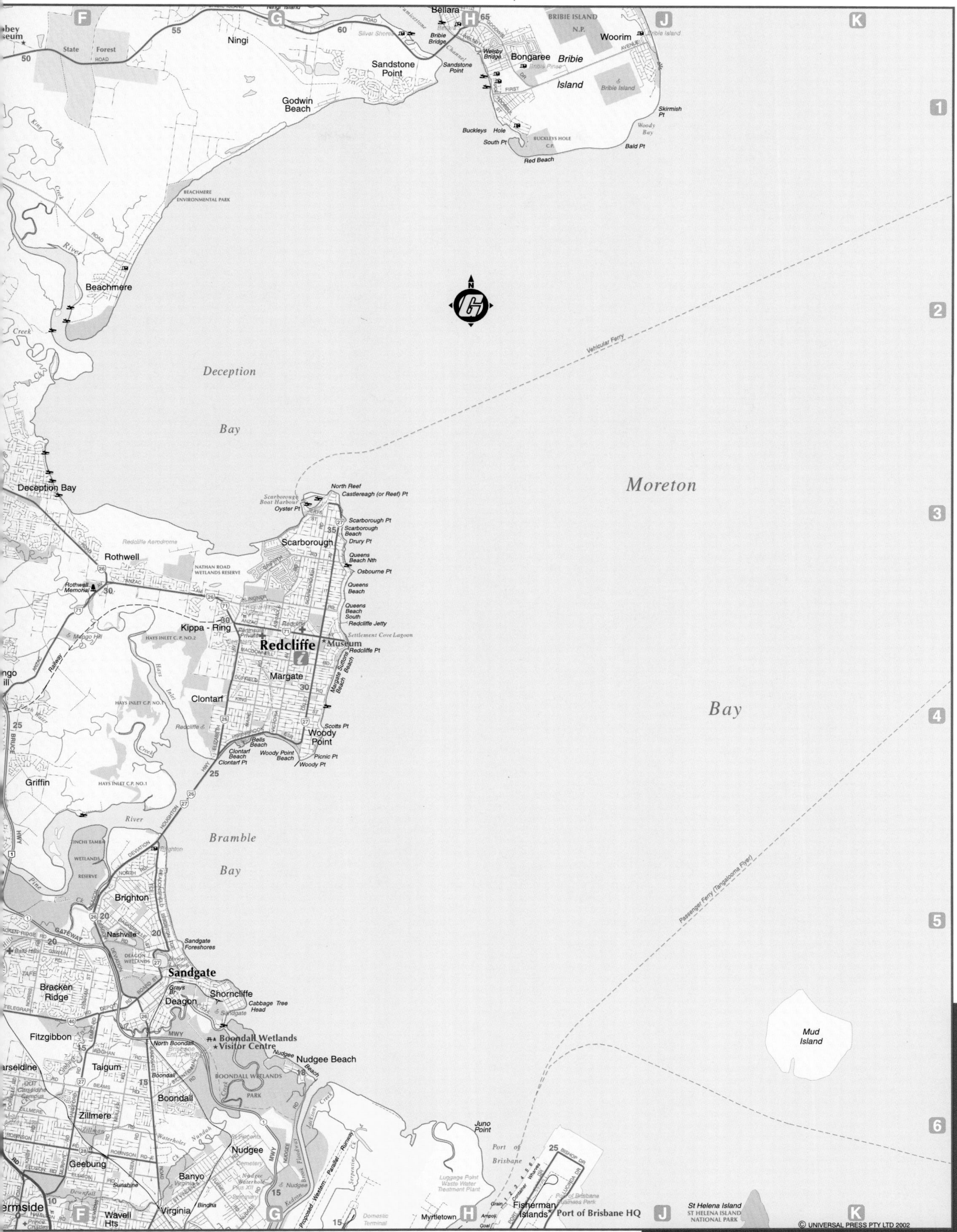

Mud Island

Bramble

Bay

River

PINE

Brighton
Nashville
Sandgate Foreshores

DEAGON WETLANDS

Sandgate
Deagon   Shorncliffe
Cabbage Tree Head

Bracken Ridge

Fitzgibbon

Boondall Wetlands Visitor Centre
Nudgee Beach
BOONDALL WETLANDS PARK

Taigum

Zillmere   Boondall

Nudgee

Banyo

Geebung

Virginia   Bindha

Juno Point

Port of Brisbane

Luggage Point Waste Water Treatment Plant

Myrtletown   Fisherman Islands   **Port of Brisbane HQ**

St Helena Island
ST HELENA ISLAND NATIONAL PARK

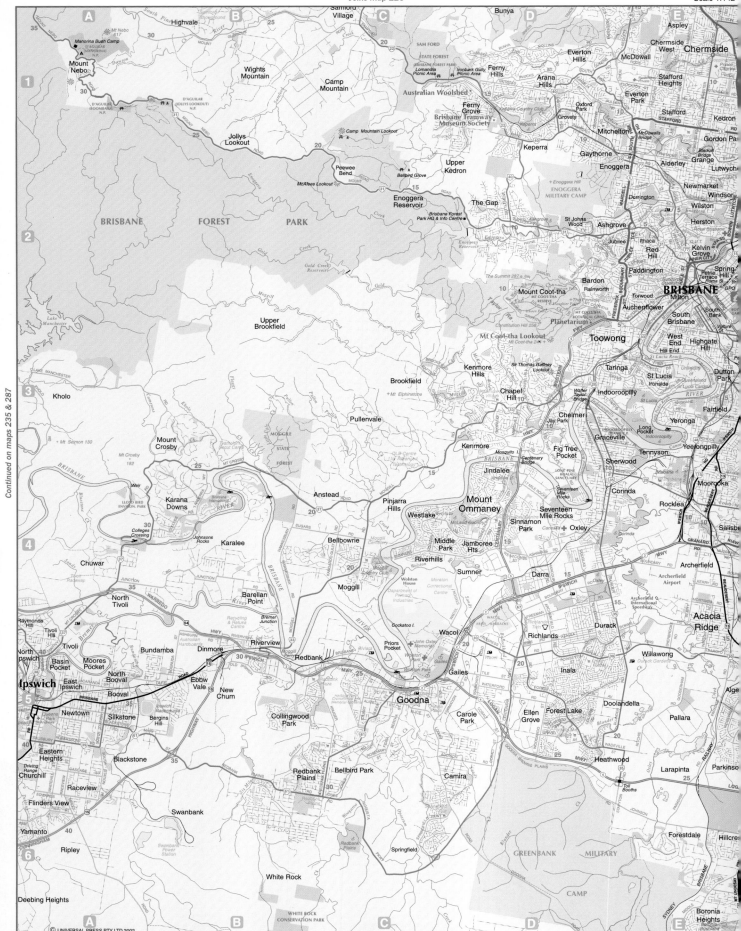

Continued on maps 235 & 287

Gregory's Australia

Queensland

Continued on map 235

© UNIVERSAL PRESS PTY LTD 2002

Continued on maps 235 & 247

QUEENSLAND A TO Z

■ Atherton POP 5860

Map 239, B5

Located at the heart of north Queensland's tropical **Atherton Tableland**, Atherton is an ideal base for exploring the region. The town is 91km SW of Cairns and is surrounded by rainforests, pasture lands and tropical crops.

Horseriding on the Atherton Tableland

MAIN ATTRACTIONS: The **Old Post Office Gallery** displays and sells a variety of local art and craft works; it is also the information centre. The **Chinese Joss House** is situated next to the Old Post Office Gallery and stands as a reminder of the once large Chinese population in Atherton. **Fascinating Facets and Crystal Caves** display minerals, high quality gemstones and valuable rocks. This popular tourist spot is a combination museum, gallery and jewellery store. The basement area displays crystals and has been constructed to resemble a cave.

NEARBY ATTRACTIONS: **Hallorans Hill CP** is a reminder of Atherton's volcanic past. The open eucalypt and rainforest walk (approx 1hr) winds up and around the slopes of an extinct volcano to a lookout at the summit. The reserve is a popular picnic spot. **Mount Hypipamee (The Crater) NP**, 26km south of Atherton, has a walking track leading to the stunning **Dinner Falls**.

TOURIST INFO: Old Post Office Gallery, Atherton–Herberton Rd, Ph: (07) 4091 4222

■ Ayr POP 8640

Map 282, D1

This sugar, mango and melon town, north-west of the **Burdekin River** delta, is the main commercial centre of Burdekin Shire. Known as the **'Silver Link'**, the Burdekin Bridge connects Ayr with nearby **Home Hill**. The **Burdekin River Irrigation Scheme** has enabled Ayr to become one of the largest horticultural areas in Australia. One result of this is that it has become a popular backpacker destination.

MAIN ATTRACTIONS: Ayr's most impressive building is the **Burdekin Theatre**, part of the **Burdekin Cultural Complex** in Queen St. The unusual award-winning design of the theatre and the 'Living Lagoon' sculpture in the theatre forecourt attracts many tourists. **Ayr Nature Display**, located on Wilmington St, exhibits an unusual collection of native fauna, butterflies, rocks and shells; a focal point at the centre is a colourful rock wall made from 9 400 pieces of Queensland rock.

NEARBY ATTRACTIONS: **Alva Beach**, 18km from Ayr, offers clean sand

The Boulders Wildland Park, Wooroonooran NP, west of Babinda

and calm waters, ideal for swimmers and anglers. Burdekin Shire attracts many native birds, including magpie geese, jabirus, pelicans, eagles, cockatoos and kingfishers. Spotting some of the 280 species identified in the area is a popular pastime. Fishing and crabbing in the Burdekin River and its estuaries are popular. **Hutchings Lagoon**, 5km NW, is a pleasant picnic spot and ideal for watersports.
TOURIST INFO: Plantation Park, Bruce Hwy and Kennedy St, Ph: (07) 4783 5988

■ **Babinda**   POP 1481
Map 239, D5
This small sugar town, located 60km south of Cairns, lies in the shadow of **Mount Bartle Frere** in **Wooroonooran NP**. Babinda has an average annual rainfall of 4238mm and holds a 30-yr record for the highest annual rainfall in Australia.
NEARBY ATTRACTIONS: Wooroonooran NP boasts the 2 highest mountain peaks in Queensland: Mount Bartle Frere (1622 m) and **Mount Bellenden Ker** (1598m). Fit and experienced walkers can climb Mount Bartle Frere via a walking

track, but Mount Bellenden Ker is not accessible. There are many scenic walks through the rainforest and the spectacular **Josephine Falls** is worthwhile visiting. **The Boulders Wildland Park** is 6km west of the town and offers a popular picnic and recreation spot. The park has many bushwalking tracks along **Babinda Creek**, at the base of Mount Bartle Frere. There are a series of waterfalls, mountain streams and swimming holes. Facilities in the park include change rooms, toilets and BBQs together with a basic camping area. **Deeral**, 14km north, is a departure point for cruises of the **Mulgrave** and **Russell rivers**, and the **Frankland Islands**. Visitors can cruise along the rainforest rivers and see saltwater crocodiles and other wildlife.
TOURIST INFO: Cnr Munro St and Bruce Hwy, Ph: (07) 4067 1008

■ **Barcaldine**   POP 1750
Map 281, J5
Located in the heart of a vast wool-growing and cattle-raising district, the town is 108km east of Longreach. Barcaldine is known as the '**Garden City of the West**'.
MAIN ATTRACTIONS: **Mad Mick's Funny Farm** offers tours of 9 restored and refurnished settlers' buildings and old shearing sheds. Hand-reared wildlife includes kangaroos and emus. There are wool-shearing demonstrations and Billy tea and damper lunches are available. The farm is located on the cnr of Pine and Bauhinia sts. **Barcaldine and District Folk Museum** houses a collection of memorabilia and is located on the cnr of Gidyea and Beech sts. **The Tree of Knowledge** is a ghost gum which stands in Oak St. In 1891, political history was made when 400 striking shearers gathered beneath this tree for a series of meetings, out of which the Australian Labour Party was formed. The **Australian Workers' Heritage**

Centre is located in Ash St. Centred around a billabong, there are heritage buildings with displays of art and history, an offering to the achievements of working men and women. Barcaldine has several National Trust buildings, including the **Masonic Lodge** and **Anglican Church**.
TOURIST INFO: Oak St, Ph: (07) 4651 1724

■ **Bargara**   POP 3600
Map 259, A1
This popular surf beach is the site of the world's first artificially created surfing point-break. Located 13km east of Bundaberg, Bargara is the largest and closest of Bundaberg's seaside townships.
MAIN ATTRACTIONS: A temperate climate and year-round sunshine provide ample opportunities to swim, surf, windsurf and sail at **Kelly's** and **Nielson Park beaches**. Bundaberg Surf Lifesaving Club patrols both beaches, but Kelly's is more attractive to families with small children due to its calm-water swimming area known as **Money's Creek**. Excellent diving and snorkelling is available just off **Bargara Beach**. Coral diving sites here are some of the closest to the Australian mainland.
NEARBY ATTRACTIONS: Panoramic views of the cane fields and ocean can be seen from **The Hummock**, an extinct volcano and the highest point in the district. A boardwalk travels through a patch of **Wongarra Scrub**—the last of the area's original vegetation—to the lookout. **Mon Repos Turtle Rookery**, Australia's best-known and most accessible sea turtle rookery, is a few kilometres north of town. Loggerhead, flatback, green and leatherback turtles come ashore after dark to lay their eggs. The nesting and hatching season occurs from November to March. Guided walks are conducted each night during this time.
TOURIST INFO: 271 Bourbong St, Bundaberg, Ph: (07) 4152 2333

Located south of Brisbane and on the border with New South Wales, the Scenic Rim's mountain rainforests form a barrier between the **Eastern Downs** and the coastal plains of the **Gold Coast**. A testament to nature's diversity, this lush expanse of sub-tropical rainforest hides national parks, the breathtaking **Lamington Plateau**, majestic waterfalls, remote river valleys and fertile farmlands, all with the backdrop of stunning mountain ranges. The national parks are part of the **Central Eastern Australian Rainforest Reserves World Heritage Area**. Cattle and dairy farms abound in the valleys and hills and there are quaint country towns with many galleries, shops and boutiques to explore.

A bushwalker's oasis, the Scenic Rim offers much to explore for daytrippers, campers and adventurers. The region combines well-trodden paths with more isolated tracks, so visitors have the choice of either joining or escaping the crowds. Three mountain groups dominate the landscape providing the source of the numerous rivers and streams that keep this verdant region well-watered.

Lamington blue-spiny crayfish, *Euastacus sulcatus*

Tree Top Walkway

The highlight of a visit to **O'Reilly's Rainforest Guesthouse**, in **Lamington NP**, is an exhilarating walk 16m above the rainforest canopy and along 9 suspension bridges spanning 160m. Anchoring one corner of the bridge is an ancient fig tree, where the adventurous can make the vertical climb to the crow's nest at the top of this forest giant. The reward is a magnificent view over the **Green Mountains**.

main attractions

◈ **Binna Burra**

Binna Burra is the north-east portion of Lamington NP. Binna Burra Lodge is a privately run resort in the middle of the rainforest.

◈ **Green Mountains**

This section of Lamington NP offers panoramic views of the park.

◈ **Lamington NP**

This national park protects Australia's largest remaining subtropical rainforest.

◈ **O'Reilly's Rainforest Guesthouse**

A feature of visiting this guesthouse, which has been open since the 1920s, is the Treetop Walk.

◈ **Springbrook NP**

This park showcases the Springbrook Plateau, Mount Cougal and Natural Bridge.

◈ **Tamborine Mountain**

The 3 villages of Tambourine Mountain feature galleries, cafes, gardens and sweeping views—some to the ocean.

 Tourist information

Beaudesert Historical Museum and Information Centre
Jubilee Park, Cnr Brisbane and McKee sts,
Beaudesert, Qld 4285
Ph: (07) 5541 3740

Natural Bridge, Springbrook NP

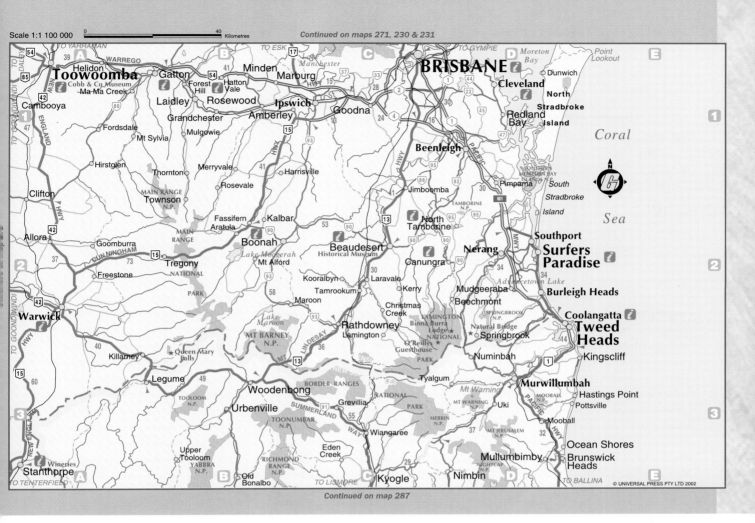

Continued on maps 271, 230 & 231

TO YARRAMAN
WARREGO
TO ESK
LAKE Manchester
BRISBANE
Moreton Bay
Point Lookout

Helidon
Toowoomba
Gatton
Minden
Marburg
Cleveland
Dunwich

Cambooya
Ma Ma Creek
Cobb & Co Museum
Forest Hill
Hatton Vale
North Stradbroke

Laidley
Rosewood
Ipswich
Redland Bay
Island

Grandchester
Amberley
Goodna
Beenleigh

Fordsdale
Mulgowie
Pimpama
South Stradbroke Island

Hirstglen
Thornton
Merryvale
Harrisville
TAMBORINE N.P.
Coral

Clifton
Rosevale
Jimboomba
North Tamborine
Nerang
Southport

Townson
MAIN RANGE N.P.
Fassifern
Aratula
Kalbar
Beaudesert Historical Museum
Surfers Paradise

Allora
Goomburra
MAIN RANGE
Boonah
Lake Moogerah
Mt Alford
Canungra
Sea

Freestone
Tregony
NATIONAL PARK
Laravale
Kooralbyn
Tamrookum
Kerry
Mudgeeraba
Beechmont
Burleigh Heads

Warwick
Maroon
Christmas Creek
LAMINGTON
Binna Burra Lodge
Natural Bridge
Springbrook
Coolangatta
Tweed Heads

Lake Maroon
MT BARNEY N.P.
Rathdowney
Lamington
O'Reillys Guesthouse
NATIONAL PARK
Numinbah
Kingscliff

Killarney
Queen Mary Falls
MT LINDESAY HWY
Tyalgum
Mt Warning
Murwillumbah
Hastings Point

Legume
Woodenbong
BORDER RANGES
MT WARNING N.P.
Uki
Mooball
Pottsville

TOOLOOM N.P.
Urbenville
SUMMERLAND WAY
Grevillea
NATIONAL PARK
MEBBIN N.P.
Mooball
Ocean Shores

TOONUMBAR N.P.
Wiangaree
Mullumbimby
Brunswick Heads

Upper Tooloom
YABBRA N.P.
RICHMOND RANGE N.P.
Eden Creek
NIGHTCAP N.P.

Stanthorpe
Wineries
Old Bonalbo
TO LISMORE
Kyogle
Nimbin
TO BALLINA

© UNIVERSAL PRESS PTY LTD 2002

Continued on map 287

Beaudesert POP 3982

Map 235, C2

Approximately an hour's drive from either **Brisbane** or the **Gold Coast**, Beaudesert is located in the middle of a vast region of rainforests, valleys and plains in the Gold Coast hinterland. A major market town, Beaudesert is also known for its dairying, agriculture and beef cattle.

MAIN ATTRACTIONS: The **Beaudesert Historical Museum** is located in Brisbane St and is open daily, 9am–4pm. Exhibits include the Pioneer Cottage, furnished in a style portraying early pioneering life, horse-drawn vehicles and farm implements. A prized exhibit is the buggy the Duchess of York rode in during her visit in 1927.

NEARBY ATTRACTIONS: Beaudesert is an ideal base for exploring national park areas, such as **Lamington**, **Mount Maroon** and **Mount Barney**. The Mount Barney area offers good walking tracks and the **Logan River** provides a great swimming spot. A caravan and camping area is provided at the bottom of Mount Barney, although campers must apply for a permit. **Tamborine Mountain** is a major tourist destination and comprises 3 small villages and several small national parks in centuries-old rainforest.

TOURIST INFO: Historical Museum and Info Centre, cnr Brisbane and McKee sts, Ph: (07) 5541 3740

Biloela POP 5340

Map 287, G1

This rural town, in the centre of the **Callide Valley**, is located 647km NW of Brisbane and is the largest town in the Banana Shire, which has no bananas.

Rainforest walk in Lamington NP, south of Beaudesert

MAIN ATTRACTIONS: A bus tour of local attractions leaves the information centre Mon–Fri, at 10am. The 1hr tour looks at **Greycliffe Homestead**, the meatworks and civic centre, and includes a running commentary. Greycliffe Homestead has been listed by the National Trust of Queensland and is filled with memorabilia of the early days. It is open by appointment only. The **SILO**—acronym for Simulated Interactive Learning Opportunities—is one of the most prominent features in Biloela and is located on Exhibition Ave. Displays focus on farming and mining technology and include electricity generation, alternative energy sources and ostrich farming.
NEARBY ATTRACTIONS: **Callide Dam**, 5km NE, is ideal for BBQ's, boating, swimming and fishing. **Callide 'B' Power Station** is 15km east of town. Free 1hr guided tours of the station operate from the main gate, Tues–Fri, at 1.30pm. **Mount Scoria** lies 14km south. Its name comes from scoriaceous basalt, a type of volcanic rock which resembles fingers from an outstretched hand.
TOURIST INFO: cnr Dawson Hwy and Callide St, Ph: (07) 4992 2405

■ Blackall   POP 1520

Map 281, J6

Located 106km south of Barcaldine and 969km NW of Brisbane, Blackall, on the **Barcoo River**, is at the centre of sheep-farming country. It is also the site of the state's first artesian bore—drilled in 1815.
MAIN ATTRACTIONS: A replica of the original **'Black Stump'** for this area is located in Thistle St. The tree stump was used as a key reference point when the area was surveyed in 1886. The **Jackie Howe Memorial**, on the cnr of Short and Shamrock sts, commemorates this shearer's record set in 1892, when he blade-sheared 321 sheep in 7hrs and 40mins. This astonishing record remained until 1950, but then it

was only broken by the use of mechanical shears.
NEARBY ATTRACTIONS: The **Blackall Wool Scour** is considered the most complete relic of the wool-scouring industry in Queensland. Located 5.5km north of town, the steam-driven scour was built in 1906. Guided tours are offered daily April–Nov, and by appointment at other times through the visitor information centre. **Idalia NP** is 100km SW of town and covers 1440km^2. The park is best known as the home of the rare and endangered yellow-footed rock wallaby.
TOURIST INFO: Short St, Ph: (07) 4657 4637

■ Blackwater   POP 8000

Map 282, E5

This leading coal-mining centre of Queensland is located 190km west of Rockhampton. Coal from open-cut mines is transported to **Gladstone** for export and steaming coal provides fuel to the **Gladstone Power Station**. The discolouration of the town's waterholes, from the tannins released by the plentiful ti-trees, has given Blackwater its name.
MAIN ATTRACTIONS: The town park has a lovely **Japanese garden** given by Blackwater's sister town in Japan.
NEARBY ATTRACTIONS: **Blackdown Tableland NP**, 34km SE of Blackwater, has deep gorges including spectacular **Carnarvon Gorge**, clear-water creeks and waterfalls. There are fireplaces, lookouts, a camping area and scenic walking tracks throughout the park.
TOURIST INFO: Clermont St, Emerald, Ph: (07) 4982 4142

■ Boonah   POP 2500

Map 235, B2

Surrounded by the hills of the **Great Dividing Range** known as the **Scenic Rim**, Boonah is located in the heart of the scenic Fassifern district, just over an hour's drive from Brisbane and one hour from the Gold Coast.

MAIN ATTRACTIONS: The town's **art gallery** is located in Highbury St and features leadlight displays, local artworks and sculptures. The information centre has details on a broad range of activities, including gliding and ultralight flight tours. Boonah is located in one of the most picturesque areas of Queensland and its rugged mountains, lakes and valleys attract many visitors. Bushwalking is popular given the many scenic walking tracks surrounding the town.
NEARBY ATTRACTIONS: **Main Range NP**, 35km west, is part of the Scenic Rim and offers many picturesque drives, bushwalking, trail riding, rockclimbing and various watersports. **Cunninghams Gap Lookout** offers panoramic views and **Lake Moogerah** has picnic areas and is a popular spot for sailing, fishing and waterskiing. South of the lake lies **Moogerah Peaks NP**, which is made up of several small parks, rocky cliffs and volcanic peaks, including **Mount French**.
TOURIST INFO: Bicentennial Park, Boonah–Fassifern Rd, Ph: (07) 5463 2233

Outback sunset near Blackall

Queensland

Bowen POP 9260

Map 282, E2

This holiday town on the coast halfway between Townsville and Mackay is also called the **'Climate Capital of the North'**. Bowen is the oldest town in north Queensland and was first settled in 1861. Year-round warm weather and 8 sandy beaches fringed by clear waters attract many visitors to Bowen.

MAIN ATTRACTIONS: The best-known beach is **Horseshoe Bay**, offering almost every kind of watersport. A highlight is scuba diving on the spectacular coral reef just offshore. There are many other secluded beaches close to town. Visitors can follow a number of signposted golden arrows on the **Golden Arrow Tour**, starting 200m on the town side of the salt works. This scenic driving tour takes in many points of interest in the town. The **Bowen Historical Museum** is one of the best country museums in Queensland. Located in Gordon St; it exhibits shells, minerals and Aboriginal artefacts. With 22 historic murals on the town walls and fishing, boating, snorkelling, diving and swimming, Bowen has much to offer visitors.

NEARBY ATTRACTIONS: The area surrounding Bowen is a birdwatcher's paradise with some 219 species to sight. Fossicking for gems is a popular activity, given the area's rich geology. Sapphires, amethysts, crystals, clear quartz, agate and jasper can be found in the area. **Binbee**, along the Collinsville Rd, is a good place to start fossicking.
TOURIST INFO: Bruce Hwy, Mount Gordon, Ph: (07) 4786 4494

Bundaberg POP 45 000

Map 259, A2

Surrounded by sugarcane fields, this city, which has many fine examples of Queensland architecture, is the southernmost approach to the **Great Barrier Reef**. Bundaberg,

Hinkler House, home of aviator Bert Hinkler, was transported from Southampton, England, to Bundaberg

368km north of Brisbane, is an important centre in the rich **Burnett River** plains. The Burnett River runs through the city and flows out into the ocean 11km beyond Bundaberg.
MAIN ATTRACTIONS: **Alexandra Park and Zoo** is on the riverbank in Quay St; admission to the zoo is free. The **Bundaberg Rum Distillery** is located next to Millaquin Sugar Mill. Tours of the plant show all aspects of the rum-making process. The distillery visitors centre, **Spring Mill House**, is a restored plantation house containing a museum, souvenir shop and tasting bar. **Schmeiders Cooperage and Craft Centre**, located near the distillery, offers an insight into local arts and crafts with glassblowing and wood-working demonstrations. The **Botanical Gardens**, in Mount Perry Rd, also contain **Hinkler House**, home of aviator Bert Hinkler and now a pioneer aviation museum; **Bundaberg Historical Museum**; and the **Fairymead House Sugar Museum**, which showcases the story of the sugar industry. Close to the gardens is **Tropical Wines**, which offer free tastings of fruit wines.
NEARBY ATTRACTIONS: There are many coastal and hinterland self-drive tours to explore. Whale-watching boat trips are available mid-August to mid-October. **Mon Repos CP** is 15km NE and contains the largest

and most accessible mainland sea turtle rookery in Australia. Turtles nest Nov–Jan and hatch Jan–March. **Lady Elliot** and **Lady Musgrave islands** are easily accessible from Bundaberg. The MV *Lady Musgrave* departs from Bundaberg Port Marina for Lady Musgrave Island. The island boasts the largest lagoon of the Great Barrier Reef. A permit is required for camping on the island. Lady Elliot Island is a 25min scenic flight from **Bundaberg Airport**. Island accommodation varies from tents to resort suites.
TOURIST INFO: 271 Bourbong St, Ph: (07) 4152 2333

Cairns POP 94 540

Map 239, C3

Lying at the centre of a tropical paradise on the shores of **Trinity Bay**, Cairns is full of natural attractions. It is a stepping-off point to so much, including the **Great Barrier Reef**, rainforests and scenic hinterland such as the **Cape York Peninsula**. Cairns is the premier holiday destination in northern Queensland. Its international airport is the sixth busiest in Australia, handling more than a million visitors each year.
MAIN ATTRACTIONS: **Trinity Wharf** offers shopping and eating venues, a tourist coach terminus and a place

(CONTINUED P.240)

Tropical North Queensland is bordered by the **Coral Sea islands** and the **Great Barrier Reef** to the east and the rainforest mountains that sweep down from the north-ernmost section of the **Great Dividing Range** to the west. Inland from the balmy, humid coast, the **Atherton Tableland** is elevated 600–900m above sea level. Known as the **'cool tropics'**, the weather is usually warm and sunny during the day, while nights are cool to cold.

The region offers waterfalls, lush **Wet Tropics World Heritage-listed rainforests**, idyllic palm-fringed tropical beaches and islands, the wonder of the Great Barrier Reef, extinct volcanoes and crater lakes—all waiting to be explored. Home to Queensland's most northerly city, eden-like Cairns, the region attracts millions of tourist dollars each year, taking pride of place as an inter-national holiday destination. The townships of tropical North Queensland feature an eclectic combination of colonial tropical architecture, modern resorts and a laid-back lifestyle. Visitors can choose from an array of outdoor activities from sunbathing to snorkelling.

Crater Lakes

Lake Barrine and **Lake Eacham** have formed in the craters of extinct volcanoes; volcanic activity ceased on the Tablelands around 20 000 years ago. Lake Eacham was an early settler's camp. Aborigines believed it to be haunted and steered clear of the vicinity calling it, 'No Man's Land of Devil Devils'. The lakes offer enchanting rainforest walks, accommodation, picnicking, swimming and cruises; they are also home to the unique rainbow fish. **Lake Euramo**, located nearby is a third crater lake filled with swamp.

main attractions

◈ **Daintree NP**

This wondrous park features ancient rainforest where activities include crocodile-spotting tours, forest walks and birdwatching. Cape Tribulation, where the rainforest meets the reef, is popular with visitors.

◈ **Great Barrier Reef**

One of the Seven Natural Wonders of the World, the reefs, coral cays and offshore islands are World Heritage-listed and accessed by cruise boats from Cairns and Port Douglas.

◈ **Kuranda**

This resort town's attractions include markets, the Australian Butterfly Sanctuary, Birdworld and a Scenic Railway.

◈ **Mossman Gorge**

This is a stunning river gorge filled with giant granite boulders and surrounded by rainforest. The Kuku Yalanji Aboriginal community conduct guided tours.

◈ **Port Douglas**

This quaint village is an upmarket tourist resort and the departure point for the Outer Reef and Low Isles.

◈ **Skyrail Rainforest Cableway**

The cable cars make their 7.5km journey from Smithfield near Cairns to Kuranda hovering above the treetops.

◈ **Tjapukai Aboriginal Cultural Park**

This park showcases the internationally acclaimed Tjapukai Aboriginal Dance Theatre. There is also a campsite, restaurant and history theatre.

◈ **Wooroonooran NP**

Within this mountain wilderness park are Josephine Falls, The Boulders, Walshs Peak (The Pyramid) and Queensland's highest peaks, Mount Bartle Frere and Mount Bellenden Ker.

 Tourist information

Tourism Tropical North Queensland
Visitor Information Centre,
51 The Esplanade, Cairns Qld 4870
Ph: (07) 4051 3588
www.tnq.org.au

Diver with a Maori wrasse, *Cheilinus undulatus*, Great Barrier Reef

Queensland

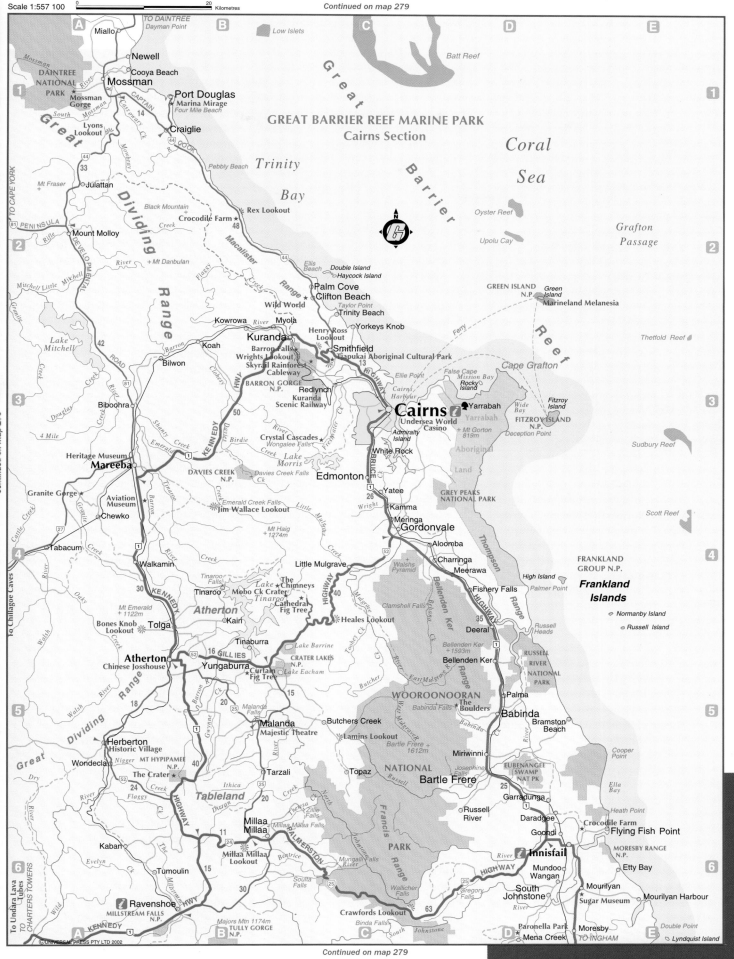

The century-old Flecker Botanic Gardens, Cairns

for international cruise liners to berth. **Pier Marketplace** is also on the waterfront. It is a retail and leisure complex with more than 90 outlets, including **Ben Cropp's Shipwreck Museum** and the **Undersea World Oceanarium**, home to over 1200 marine animals. All outlets are open 7 days a week. On weekends, local artists and craftspeople display their wares at the **Mud Market**, located in the main amphitheatre. Also popular with locals and visitors alike is **Rusty's Markets**. **Cairns Museum**, located on the cnr of Lake and Shields sts, has displays featuring the Aboriginal, timber, goldrush and sugarcane history of the area. **Flecker Botanic Gardens**, in Collins Ave, feature native plants and their traditional use by Aboriginal people. The gardens also have a very large collection of palm species. Cairns is famous for its tropical fruits, fresh seafood and relaxed ambience. It is

an international mecca for marlin and other big game fishermen.
NEARBY ATTRACTIONS: The lifestyle, history and culture of the indigenous people of the region is explored at the **Tjapukai Aboriginal Cultural Theme Park**. It showcases the world-renowned **Tjapukai Aboriginal Dance Theatre** and features a history theatre, campsite and restaurant. **Kuranda Scenic Railway** offers an amazing journey, weaving past canefields and jungle-covered mountains and valleys, then through the **Barron River Gorge** to the fern-covered station at **Kuranda**. **Skyrail Rainforest Cableway** complements the railway. Running from the suburb of **Smithfield**, the cable cars travel for 7.5km across the coastal range and over the rainforest canopy before arriving at Kuranda. The first stop, **Rainforest Station**, allows passengers to experience the forest floor, via boardwalks, while the second stop is located just a short walk from **Barron Gorge Falls**. Cairns is the departure point for many island and reef cruises visiting **Fitzroy** and **Green islands**, **Michaelmas Cay** and the **Outer Reef**.
TOURIST INFO: 51 The Esplanade, Ph: (07) 4051 3588

■ **Calliope**   POP 2414
Map 267, D6
Calliope, 20km SW of Gladstone, is a quiet rural town. Its principal industry centres on beef cattle, mainly Brahmans and Herefords. the town is the gateway to the **Boyne Valley**. National parks, creeks and trail riding are some of the attractions the region has to offer.
MAIN ATTRACTIONS: The **Calliope River** is popular for fishing and camping. **Calliope River Historical Village** displays houses and cottages, a pub, schoolhouse, blacksmith's shop, railway carriage and station. These historic buildings are from all over the shire and have been relocated to

this village. Markets are held in the village almost every month. The markets are famous for crafts and handmade goods.
NEARBY ATTRACTIONS: **Lake Awoonga**, south of **Benaraby**, supplies water to the region and also provides a recreation area and venue for watersports. There are nature walks with flora and fauna trails, picnic and BBQ facilities, a kiosk and caravan park. **Cedar Gallery Artists Village**, between Benaraby and Calliope, is worth a visit.
TOURIST INFO: Marina Ferry Terminal, Bryan Jordan Dr, Gladstone, Ph: (07) 4972 9922

■ **Caloundra**   POP 29 980
Map 255, D5
Caloundra is 95km north of Brisbane, it is one of the **Sunshine Coast's** most urbanised centres with a busy shopping district and a wealth of beautiful beaches.
MAIN ATTRACTIONS: The many beaches include: **Golden Beach** and **Bulcock Beach**, for boating, fishing and safe swimming; **Kings Beach** is a patrolled surfing beach with a fenced saltwater pool; **Shelley Beach** is a fishing beach with rockpools, but not safe for swimming; **Moffat Beach** is good for fishing and walking along; and **Dicky Beach** is a patrolled surfing beach with BBQ facilities and playground. **Queensland Air Museum** is at the airport and open daily. Scenic flights of the surrounding area are also available from the airport.
NEARBY ATTRACTIONS: There are many scenic drives to explore, including the coastal strip, **Blackall Range** and **Glass House Mountains NP**. **Currimundi Lake CP** lies 4km north and is a popular fishing and picnic spot. **Aussie World** and the famous **Ettamogah Pub** are 16km NW. The **Australia Zoo**, home of TV's *Crocodile Hunter*, is located 25km west of Caloundra.
TOURIST INFO: 7 Caloundra Rd, (07) 5491 0202

Queensland

Charleville POP 3420
Map 286, B3

The second largest town in Outback Queensland, Charleville is sited on the banks of the **Warrego River** in **mulga country**, 747km west of Brisbane. The town is the service centre for a prosperous sheep and cattle-raising district.

MAIN ATTRACTIONS: **Historical House**, in Alfred St, was once the old Queensland National Bank building, displays include local memorabilia, a working steam engine and a rail ambulance. Historic **Hotel Corones** is a National Trust-classified building furnished in period-style. The hotel operates a carvery Mon–Sat nights and a guided tour of the hotel takes place at 2pm most afternoons. The bilby, one of Australia's most endangered species, is bred at the **Charleville National Parks and Wildlife Office**. Yellow-footed rock wallabies are also bred here. There are bilby tours on Wednesday, Friday and Sunday nights. The Charleville **School of the Air** is located in the distance education building in Parry St and is open for guided tours at 9.15am and 11am on school days. Teachers explain how they teach via radio correspondence and visitors can listen to a lesson being broadcast. The **Outback Queensland Sky-watch** observatory, housed next to the airport's meteorology building, has nightly guided 'tours' of the sky, April–Oct, and 3 nights a week Nov–March, weather permitting, which is most of the time as the town has some of the clearest skies in the Southern Hemisphere. Book at the visitor information centre.

NEARBY ATTRACTIONS: **South-West Air Service** conducts regular tours of Outback Queensland and offers scenic flights over Charleville. There are many scenic drives around the area; brochures and maps are available from the information centre.

TOURIST INFO: Sturt St, Ph: (07) 4654 3057

Charters Towers POP 10 000
Map 282, C2

Located 132km SW of Townsville, Charters Towers is on the road and rail line to Mount Isa, in the pastoral district of the **Burdekin River Valley**. During the boom years of the goldrush era (1872–1916), Charters Towers was Queensland's second largest city.

MAIN ATTRACTIONS: Charters Towers has more National Trust buildings than any other place in Queensland, and many of these buildings have been restored to their former glory. Both **Gill** and **Mosman sts** are listed as heritage precincts. National Trust buildings worthwhile visiting include **Venus Gold Battery** on Milchester Rd, which offers guided tours daily, and **Zara Clark Folk and Military Museum** on the cnr of Mossman and Mary sts. **The Stock Exchange** in Mosman St is now home to the National Trust and the **Mining Museum**.

NEARBY ATTRACTIONS: The nearby historic gold-mining township of **Ravenswood** also has many National Trust buildings. **White Blow Environmental Park**, near Ravenswood, features a 300 million-year-old quartz-rock foundation. **Towers Hill**, 1.5km west, has old mine shafts and ammunition bunkers from WWII. The **Mount Leyshon goldmine** is 30km south and offers tours on Wednesdays.

TOURIST INFO: 74 Mosman St, Ph: (07) 4752 0314

Childers POP 2500
Map 287, H2

This small sugar town is located 53km south of Bundaberg. A National Trust town, Childers has many beautiful buildings and tree-lined streets. Although much of the town was destroyed by fire in 1902, the surviving buildings and re-building have resulted in a variety of architectural styles.

MAIN ATTRACTIONS: **Childers Art Gallery**, located above **Childers Pharmaceutical Museum**, is housed in what was once a dentist's surgery. It is considered one of the finest galleries in provincial Queensland and displays international, national and local art, and a collection of pottery and timber pieces. The Childers Pharmaceutical Museum, which retains its original cedar fittings, displays apothecary records and equipment. **Childers Multicultural Food, Wine and Arts Festival**, held on the last Sunday in July, is the largest of its kind in country Queensland. The **Historical Complex** in Taylor St, includes a century-old worker's cottage among its other old buildings housing the district's history.

NEARBY ATTRACTIONS: **Isis Central Sugar Mill**, 10km north near **Cordalba**, offers tours during the harvest season (July–Nov). **Burrum Coast NP** is situated 40km east of Childers.

TOURIST INFO: Pharmaceutical Museum, 90 Churchill St, Ph: (07) 4126 1994

The National Trust classified Hotel Corones, Charleville

Chinchilla POP 3500

Map 287, G4

Located in rugged country in the **Western Darling Downs**, 295km NW of Brisbane, Chinchilla is largely reliant on primary production from the excellent grazing and grain-growing pastures and on sawmilling.

MAIN ATTRACTIONS: **Chinchilla Folk Museum** is a complex of 10 buildings, including the original town gaol and school; an 1880s slab cottage with authentic furnishings and displays of photographs, memorabilia and fashion of the times.

NEARBY ATTRACTIONS: Chinchilla attracts many people to its gem and petrified-wood fossicking area—a stump of petrified wood is displayed outside the **Cultural Centre**. Fishing and canoeing on **Charley's Creek** and **Condamine River** are popular.

TOURIST INFO: Warrego Hwy (opposite Pioneer Cemetery) Ph: (07) 4668 9564

Clermont POP 2460

Map 282, D4

This rural town in the **Drummond Range** in Queensland's **Central Highlands** is 940km NW of Brisbane. Clermont is the commercial centre for the region's cattle and grain growing industries. The town was established in 1862, following the discovery of gold and copper at **Copperfield**, which was the first copper mine in Queensland. The town was relocated to higher ground in 1917 following the devastating floods of 1916.

MAIN ATTRACTIONS: A tour of the **Blair Athol Mine** can be organised through the information centre. **Hoods Lagoon**, located in Lime St, has a Walk Bridge; the **Mary MacKillop Grotto**—she visited a local convent; and a memorial to **Billy Sing**, the Anzac's crack sniper of WWI, who was born here.

NEARBY ATTRACTIONS: Fossicking for gold is a popular activity in the district. **Clermont and District Historical Museum** is 4km NW along the road to Charters Towers. The **Copperfield Store Museum**, 7km west, is housed in the original shop from the copper-mining era. **Copperfield Cemetery** is 10km SW and holds the 19th-century graves of copper miners. **Theresa Creek Dam**, 22km SW, is a popular spot for fishing and waterskiing, bushwalking and camping. There are picnic areas nearby.

TOURIST INFO: Capella St, Ph: (07) 4983 3001

Cloncurry POP 2540

Map 280, D2

Renowned as a colourful frontier-mining town, Cloncurry is 118km east of Mount Isa on the Overlander's Hwy. Cloncurry became the centre of a rich mineral field after copper deposits were discovered in 1867. By 1916 the area was the largest source of copper in Australia. Today, the Shire has a rural and mining-based economy; recent mining development has brought economic growth and diversity to the Shire.

MAIN ATTRACTIONS: **Cloncurry-Mary Kathleen Memorial Park and Museum**, in McIlwraith St, is home to one of the most comprehensive **Rock** and **Mineral Displays** in Australia. The park has preserved a unique chapter of north-west Queensland's mining history, with buildings and memorabilia from the former uranium-mining town of **Mary Kathleen**. Displays feature local history with the showpiece being Robert O'Hara Burke's (of Burke and Wills fame) water bottle. The outdoor museum has a traction engine, farm and mining machinery as well as the unusual 1941 Ford Rail Ambulance. There are BBQ and picnic areas in the park. **John Flynn Place**, in Daintree St, houses the **Royal Flying Doctor Service Museum** and **Fred McKay Art Gallery**. Displays of historic material in the centre include the first Traeger pedal wireless and automatic Morse keyboard used when the RFDS established its very first base in 1928.

NEARBY ATTRACTIONS: Tours to the newly developed **Ernest Henry Mine**, named after the founder of Cloncurry are available. The area is a fossicker's paradise, rich in minerals and gems, including garnets, amethysts and rare Maltese Crosses.

TOURIST INFO: Cloncurry-Mary Kathleen Memorial Park, McIlwraith St, Ph: (07) 4742 1361

Camel race at Boulia, south of Cloncurry

Collinsville   POP 2550

Map 282, D2

This coal-mining town lies 83km SW of Bowen. Modern open-cut mining by Thiess Contractors produces coal for export and Australian markets. The dry tropical climate offers a relaxed lifestyle.

MAIN ATTRACTIONS: Murals depicting historic figures and scenes of mining activities painted on building walls contribute to a street beautification scheme. The murals are part of a project linking Collinsville and Bowen, which has similar murals.

NEARBY ATTRACTIONS: From Collinsville it is a 45min drive to **Bowen's** beaches and 1.5hrs to the islands of the **Whitsunday coast**. Collinsville is a good base from which to explore the old gold- and coal-mining areas of **Ukalunda**, **Normanby**, and **Mount Coolan** where a hotel and a store still operate. Fossickers can spend hours in and around the area seeking fossilised wood, amethyst, jasper, agate and clear crystal. Fishing and camping are popular on the **Bowen River**.

TOURIST INFO: Cnr Stanley and Conway sts, Ph: (07) 4785 5366

Cooktown   POP 1580

Map 279, H2

The tropical port of Cooktown—gateway to the wilderness—lies on the banks of the **Endeavour River**. It was founded as a port in 1873 to service the Palmer River Goldfields. Cooktown is situated 240km NW of Cairns and is accessible via road, which is still unsealed in parts, and by boat or plane.

MAIN ATTRACTIONS: In 1770, Capt James Cook beached HMS *Endeavour* in what is now called Endeavour River and stayed for 7 weeks while the ship's hull was being repaired. A memorial marks the site of the mooring and each June, a re-enactment of the event takes place. **Grassy Hill** provides a good view of the **Great Barrier Reef**,

Campers at Kalpowar Crossing, Lakefield NP, west of Cooktown

Cooktown and the surrounding hinterland. Capt Cook climbed this hill to look for a clear passage through the Great Barrier Reef. **Cooktown Wharf**, dating from the 1880s, is a popular fishing venue. The **James Cook Historical Museum**, on the cnr of Helen and Walker sts, has displays of the area's maritime, natural and Aboriginal history; **Cooktown Botanic Gardens** are also in Walker St.

NEARBY ATTRACTIONS: Cooktown is a departure point for **Cape York Peninsula**; **Lizard Island**, 90km offshore via plane; **Lakefield NP**, 146km NE with good campsites accessible mainly by 4WD; **Cape Melville NP**, north of town and only accessible by 4WD; and the secluded beaches lying north-east of town. Fishing tours on the Great Barrier Reef also leave from town. The **Black Mountains**, 20km west, offer a scenic walking track. **Quinkan Reserve**, to the west, is renowned for its split-rock galleries containing the largest display of rock art in the world.

TOURIST INFO: Charlotte St, Ph: (07) 4069 5755

Cooroy   POP 1900

Map 255, C3

Located 25km inland from the Sunshine Coast resort town of Noosa Heads, Cooroy is primarily a timber and dairy town.

MAIN ATTRACTIONS: In Maple St in the heart of town is Cooroy's **Old Butter Factory**, which has been restored and is now a cultural and creative centre for artists and craftspeople to display and sell their work.

NEARBY ATTRACTIONS: Both Black Mountain Range and Sky Ring Creek roads provide scenic drives in the surrounding areas. Tours to and throughout Cooroy run from **Noosa** and can be booked through the information centre at Noosa Heads. **Lake MacDonald**, Noosa Shire's water storage area, lies close to the town. Fishing is popular as the lake is well stocked with Murray cod, eels, silver perch, golden perch and catfish. Picnic and BBQ areas are provided around the shore. Close to the lake is an amphitheatre that, from time to time, hosts a variety of entertainment performances.

TOURIST INFO: Hastings St, Noosa Heads, Ph: (07) 5447 4988

Ulysses butterfly, *Papilio ulysses*, in Daintree NP

■ Cunnamulla   POP 1430

Map 285, J5

First settled in the 1860s, Cunnamulla is situated on the **Warrego River**, 815km west of Brisbane. This town boasts the largest wool-loading station on the Queensland railway network. Surrounding land supports 2 million sheep, as well as beef cattle, Angora goats and yields opals.

MAIN ATTRACTIONS: The **Botanic Gardens** were only recently created. The first stage of the gardens, designed to showcase plants from the arid zone, was opened in 1998. The **Heritage Guide** is available from the information centre and takes visitors on a nostalgic tour of the town, walking in the footsteps of explorers and generations of locals. The **Bicentennial Museum** is located in John St. **Lost Generation Arts and Crafts** displays local Aboriginal art and is located in Stockyard St. **Centenary Park** in Jane St offers picnic and BBQ facilities.

NEARBY ATTRACTIONS: Wetlands in the area are home to abundant and varied birdlife. **Yowah**, 155km west of Cunnamulla, is an opal-mining town. There is a public fossicking area as well as a mine which is open Sun–Fri. A local tour operator in Cunnamulla also organises guided tours to Yowah, stopping at the mine and **Yowah Opal Fields**. The information centre has further details. **Eulo**, 65km west of the town on the **Paroo River**, is home to the **Palm Grove Date Winery**, unique in Australia because of its date-wine production and a variety of other date products which are offered for sale.

TOURIST INFO: Centenary Park, Jane St, Ph: (07) 4655 2481

■ Currumbin   POP 2984

Map 247, D5

Part of the **Gold Coast**, the town of Currumbin is located at the mouth of **Currumbin Creek**. It has a superb beach and bushland backdrop.

MAIN ATTRACTIONS: The National Trust's **Currumbin Wildlife Sanctuary** is the town's most popular attraction. The sanctuary covers 27ha of bushland and is home to the largest collection of Australian native animals in the world. Visitors are invited to handfeed lorikeets, be photographed with a koala, ride the mini-train and observe the animal nursery. Opposite the sanctuary is **Superbee Honey World**, where visitors are entertained by The Live Bee Show, and can sample various honey varieties. Honey-making products are also for sale.

NEARBY ATTRACTIONS: **David Fleay Wildlife Park** is 8km NW. Here visitors can see crocodile-feeding shows and also learn about Aboriginal culture. Set in beautiful surroundings, **Olson's Bird Gardens**, in the **Currumbin Valley** 9km SW, has many walk-through aviaries. **Springbrook NP**, 22km SW, offers delightful rainforest bushwalks.

TOURIST INFO: Shop 14b, Coolangatta Place, cnr Griffith and Warner sts, Coolangatta, Ph: (07) 5536 7765

■ Daintree   POP 240

Map 279, H3

Once a timber town, the village of Daintree is tucked into a bend of the **Daintree River** and is surrounded by the **McDowall Range**. The village is 119km NW of Cairns.

MAIN ATTRACTIONS: The area abounds with native animals, exquisite birds and tropical butterflies. Saltwater crocodiles are a feature of the creeks and tributaries of the Daintree River as well as the estuary. Glide through this paradise on a river cruise. **Daintree Timber Museum** displays local arts and crafts.

NEARBY ATTRACTIONS: **Daintree Rainforest Environmental Centre** has a boardwalk through the rainforest and a 23m-high viewing platform; the centre is 11km to the north. **Cape Tribulation** is 35km NE and features both rainforest and reef. It is renowned for its sheer beauty with pristine creeks, fan palms, colourful orchids and butterflies and ancient rainforest trees, some of which are the oldest flowering tree species in the world. Walking trails in the area include the **Dubuji Boardwalk**, a 1.2km walk, and **Murrdja Boardwalk** at **Noah Creek**.

TOURIST INFO: Port Douglas and Cooktown Tourist Information Centre, 23 Macrossan St, Port Douglas, Ph: (07) 4099 5599

■ Dalby   POP 10 348

Map 271, B3

This **Darling Downs** town is 212km NW of Brisbane. The area's rich volcanic soil ensures its prosperity. While cotton and grain are the main income-earners, the economy is broad-based and includes sheep, cattle and mining.

MAIN ATTRACTIONS: Contemporary Australian paintings are exhibited in the **Dalby Regional Gallery** and can be viewed Tues–Sun. Located in Black St the **Pioneer Park Museum** displays household memorabilia and agricultural machinery. Brochures are available from the

Queensland

information centre on self-guided walks and drives in the area.

NEARBY ATTRACTIONS: **Bunya Mountains NP** encompasses one of the most significant stands of bunya pine remaining in the world. The park features spectacular waterfalls and graded walking tracks, offering panoramic views of the Darling Downs. It is located 66km NE of Dalby. **Lake Broadwater CP** lies 29km SW of Dalby. The park protects native birds and plants and is an ideal spot for a picnic or BBQ, boating, waterskiing and overnight camping.

TOURIST INFO: Thomas Jack Park, Drayton St, Ph: (07) 4662 1066

■ Emerald   POP 9750

Map 282, D5

This busy **Central Highlands** town lies 270km west of Rockhampton. Emerald is the centre of a prosperous pastoral and mining region.

MAIN ATTRACTIONS: Built in 1900, **Emerald Railway Station**, with its beautiful facade, is one of the few remaining heritage buildings in the town. **Emerald Pioneer Cottage and Museum**, also classified by the National Trust, is a tribute to early settlement in the Highlands; open Mon–Fri, 2pm–4pm. Emerald's **Botanic Gardens** are located on the

Emerald Railway Station (1900)

banks of the **Nogoa River**. There are many different areas in the gardens, including **Palm Grove**, **Pine Plantation** and the **Rose Garden**, which is home to over 200 varieties of roses. The gardens also have **Marbles** and **Federation Pillars** and offer a BBQ area and playground. Near the information centre is a 23m-high (painting and easel) replica of one of Van Gogh's famous sunflower paintings. There is also a mosaic footpath depicting 100 years of Emerald's history.

NEARBY ATTRACTIONS: Around 45km west of Emerald are the gemfields of **Anakie**, **Sapphire** and **Rubyvale**, which have yielded some of the world's largest and most beautiful sapphires. These fields cover more than 100km^2 and visitors are offered the chance to fossick for gems and then have them cut by one of the many gem-cutters, jewellers or goldsmiths in the area. Visitors must obtain a license first. There are also many gem shops and galleries to browse through. At Rubyvale, there are tours of an underground sapphire mine and gem-cutting displays. **Lake Maraboon**, 19km south of Emerald, is a popular watersports and fishing area. Day tours of nearby cattle stations can be arranged through the information centre.

TOURIST INFO: Clermont St, Ph: (07) 4982 4142

■ Gatton   POP 6000

Map 271, E4

Located off the Warrego Hwy, 94km west of Brisbane and halfway to Toowoomba, Gatton is the business centre of the fertile **Lockyer Valley**. The valley is one of the most productive agricultural regions in Queensland. Industries include small crops, dairying, pork, beef, fruit and sawmilling.

MAIN ATTRACTIONS: **Lake Apex Fauna Sanctuary**, 1km from the town centre, is an attractive picnic area

with a wealth of bird species including pelicans and pygmy geese. It has a children's playground, BMX track and walking tracks. The town's visitor centre and a cafe are also in the park. **Gatton Historical Village** at the western end of the fauna sanctuary has a collection of historical buildings and more than 10 000 exhibits that trace the heritage of the Lockyer Valley. **Gatton Potato Carnival** is held in October. **Heavy Horse Field Days** are held at the showgrounds on the Labour Day long weekend in May.

NEARBY ATTRACTIONS: The town of **Laidley**, off the highway towards Ipswich, has many historic buildings, including **Das Neumann Haus**, which commemorates the contribution of German immigrants to the region. At the foot of the **Toowoomba Range** to the west of Gatton is the spa town of **Helidon**, also known for the high quality of its sandstone. **Helidon Natural Springs Resort**, on the Warrego Hwy outside Helidon, boasts a spa in every room. There are numerous scenic tourist drives throughout the Lockyer Valley. With 318 species on its official bird list, the valley attracts local and international birdwatchers.

TOURIST INFO: Visitor Centre and Cafe, Lake Apex, Ph: (07) 5462 3430

■ Gayndah   POP 1890

Map 287, H3

One of the oldest towns in Queensland, Gayndah was founded in 1848. Located 352km NW of Brisbane at a crossing on the **Burnett River**, it is known as the 'Orange Capital' of Queensland. It serves as a commercial centre for the surrounding district which produces cereal and grain crops, peanuts, fruit and beef cattle.

MAIN ATTRACTIONS: **Gayndah Historical Museum**, in Simon St, has a collection of relics and restored buildings, including a cottage built

(CONTINUED P.248)

THE GOLD COAST

Located an hour's drive south of Brisbane and stretching along 70km of coastline lies Australia's biggest, busiest and most vibrant tourist resort—the Gold Coast. The impressive coastal strip is dominated by high-rise accommodation, retail and tourist shops, international-standard resorts and restaurants, nightclubs and neon signs. The most famous stretch of Gold Coast beach is glittering **Surfers Paradise**.

The Gold Coast has a warm, balmy climate with over 300 sunny days per year. Together with the cooler subtropical rainforest ranges in the hinterland, with their wealth of scenic treasures, the Gold Coast is extremely popular with tourists and residents seeking a relaxed lifestyle in great surroundings.

Boasting more than 40 patrolled beaches in summer and several waterways, the Gold Coast offers a variety of watersports. Surfing, windsurfing, boogie boarding, swimming, sailing, scuba diving, jet skiing, fishing and canoeing contribute to its appeal. The quiet and peaceful hinterland offers opportunities for bushwalking, camping, freshwater-dam fishing and scenic drives.

A myriad of theme parks, including **Dreamworld**, **Sea World**, **Warner Bros Movie World**, and **Wet'n'Wild Water World** together with world-class shops, restaurants and outdoor activities attract well over 4 million visitors to the Gold Coast each year. This resort does not sleep; **Jupiters Casino**, nightclubs and bustling bars provide a hectic nightlife. For culture lovers, the **Gold Coast Arts Centre**, the largest regional centre in Australia, offers comedy nights, jazz, theatre, ballet and musicals.

Roadrunner rollercoaster at Warner Bros Movie World

 Tourist information

Gold Coast Tourism Information Centres
Cavill Walk (part of Cavill Ave),
Surfers Paradise, Qld 4217
Ph: (07) 5538 4419
Shop 14B, Coolangatta Place,
Coolangatta, Qld 4225
Ph: (07) 5536 7765

main attractions

◈ **Burleigh Head NP**

Several tracks wander through the rainforest, open forest and grassy tussocks of this park with magnificent 180° ocean views.

◈ **Coolangatta**

Greenmount Beach at Coolangatta is a delightfully calm beach, with shallow waters making it ideal for families.

◈ **Currumbin Wildlife Sanctuary**

Visitors to this wildlife sanctuary can feed colourful lorikeets, see koalas, visit the animal nursery and ride a mini-train.

◈ **Dreamworld**

This fantasy adventure park offers rides, a wildlife park, theme 'worlds' and a huge Imax cinema screen.

◈ **Sea World**

Sea World features a dolphin show, polar bears, fun rides and waterskiing displays.

◈ **Surfers Paradise**

With popular beaches and a waterfront promenade, this tourist hotspot is the heart of the Gold Coast.

◈ **Warner Bros Movie World**

Billed as 'Hollywood on the Gold Coast', this is a film and TV-based theme park.

Aerial view of Surfers Paradise

Queensland

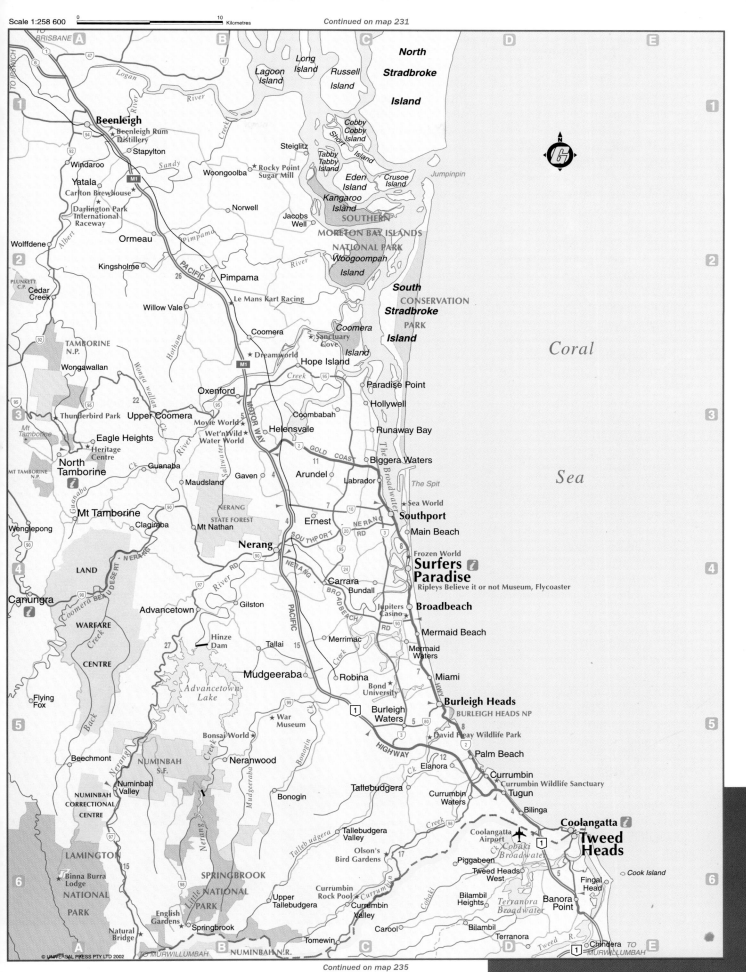

Scale 1:258 600

Continued on map 231

TO BRISBANE

A   B   C   D   E

Logan   River
Beenleigh
Beenleigh Rum Distillery
Stapylton
Windaroo
Yatala
Carlton Brewhouse
Darlington Park International Raceway
Wolffdene
Ormeau
Kingsholme
Cedar Creek
PLUNKETT C.P.
Willow Vale
Willow Vale
TAMBORINE N.P.
Wongawallan
Thunderbird Park
Eagle Heights
Heritage Centre
North Tamborine
MT TAMBORINE N.P.
Mt Tamborine
Wenglepong
Guanaba
Maudsland
Canungra
LAND WARFARE CENTRE
Advancetown
Flying Fox
Beechmont
Binna Burra Lodge
LAMINGTON NATIONAL PARK
Natural Bridge

Sandy   Creek
Woongoolba
Rocky Point Sugar Mill
Norwell
Jacobs Well
Steiglitz
Pimpama   River
Pimpama
Le Mans Kart Racing
Coomera
Sanctuary Cove
Dreamworld
Oxenford
Movie World
Wet'n'Wild Water World
Upper Coomera
Clagiraba
Mt Nathan
NERANG STATE FOREST
Nerang
Gilston
Hinze Dam
Tallai
Mudgeeraba
Neranwood
NUMINBAH S.F.
Numinbah Valley
NUMINBAH CORRECTIONAL CENTRE
War Museum
Bonsai World
Bonogin
English Gardens
Springbrook
SPRINGBROOK NATIONAL PARK
Upper Tallebudgera

Long Island
Lagoon Island
Russell Island
North Stradbroke Island
Cobby Cobby Island
Tabby Tabby Island
Eden Island
Crusoe Island
Kangaroo Island
SOUTHERN MORETON BAY ISLANDS NATIONAL PARK
Woogoompah Island
South Stradbroke Island
Coomera Island
Hope Island
Paradise Point
Hollywell
Coombabah
Runaway Bay
Helensvale
Biggera Waters
Arundel
Labrador
Gaven
Ernest
Sea World
Southport
Main Beach
Frozen World
Carrara
Bundall
Surfers Paradise
Ripleys Believe it or not Museum, Flycoaster
Jupiters Casino
Broadbeach
Merrimac
Mermaid Beach
Robina
Mermaid Waters
Bond University
Miami
Burleigh Waters
Burleigh Heads
BURLEIGH HEADS NP
David Fleay Wildlife Park
Palm Beach
Elanora
Currumbin
Tallebudgera
Currumbin Wildlife Sanctuary
Tugun
Currumbin Waters
Bilinga
Tallebudgera Valley
Olson's Bird Gardens
Coolangatta Airport
Coolangatta
Tweed Heads
Piggabeen
Currumbin Rock Pool
Currumbin Valley
Carool
Tomewin
Bilambil Heights
Bilambil
Terranora
Tweed Heads West
Banora Point
Fingal Head
Cook Island
Chinderah

Jumpinpin

Coral

Sea

CONSERVATION PARK

The Broadwater
The Spit

GOLD COAST
NERANG RD
SOUTHPORT
PACIFIC
MOTOR WAY
HIGHWAY

Cobaki Broadwater
Terranora Broadwater

TO IPSWICH
TO MURWILLUMBAH
NUMINBAH N.R.
TO MURWILLUMBAH

© UNIVERSAL PRESS PTY LTD 2002

Continued on map 235

of bricks made from clay, taken from the banks of the Burnett River in 1864. From April to November, a range of citrus fruits are packed at the cooperative packing shed for interstate and overseas markets. Tours to some private orchards and packing sheds are possible if booked in advance through the information centre. The town hosts a bi-annual **Orange Festival**.

NEARBY ATTRACTIONS: **Ban Ban Springs**, 26km south, offers a shady picnic area and birdwatching. The **Claude Weir Recreational Area**, 3km along Mundubbera Rd, is ideal for picnics, fishing and boating. **Archer's Lookout** on **Duke Mountain**, located behind the town, offers panoramic views of Gayndah, the Burnett River and surrounding district.

TOURIST INFO: Gayndah Museum, 8a Simon St, Ph: (07) 4161 2226

■ **Gladstone**   POP 28 150
Map 267, D5
Located 546km NW of Brisbane, Gladstone is one of the busiest ports in Australia, handling more than 30 million tonnes of cargo each year. The warm subtropical climate, beaches, rivers and reef islands ensure Gladstone is host to an increasing number of tourists each year.

MAIN ATTRACTIONS: With a coastline of beaches, headlands and estuaries, fishing is a popular activity and the fishing fleet regularly brings in catches of export-quality fish, bugs, prawns, sea scallops and mud crabs. It is worthwhile visiting one of the many fine restaurants in the city to taste the fresh seafood. The **Gladstone Regional Art Gallery and Museum** is located on the cnr of Goondoon and Bramston sts. Picnic and BBQ areas can be found in a number of city parks. **Reg Tana Park** includes **Railway Dam** which is inhabited by tame ducks, and closer to the city centre is **Central Park**, with a children's playground. **Gladstone Marina** is the departure

point for fishing and scuba-diving trips on the **Great Barrier Reef**, and also to ferry visitors to the islands such as **Heron Island**.

NEARBY ATTRACTIONS: At the foot of **Mount Biondello**, 8km from the city centre, are **Tondoon Botanic Gardens**, which specialise in plants of the **Port Curtis** region and far north Queensland. **Curtis Island**, in **Gladstone Harbour**, features a coastline of remote beaches and rugged headlands. There is a campground, picnic facilities, a shop and lodge accommodation. A regular barge service leaves from Gladstone taking an hour to reach the island. **Lake Awoonga**, 30km south, is popular for watersports and offers picnic and camping areas and walking trails. There are various national parks in the region and maps are available from the information centre.

TOURIST INFO: Ferry Terminal, Bryan Jordan Dr, Ph: (07) 4972 4000

■ **Goondiwindi**   POP 5000
Map 287, F6
Gateway to the **Western Downs**, this busy country town lies on the **MacIntyre River**. Goondiwindi is an administrative centre for the cotton, wheat, wool and beef industries.

MAIN ATTRACTIONS: The old **Customs House**, built around 1850, became the **Historical Museum** in 1974. It exhibits local memorabilia and is open Wed–Mon, 10am–4pm. Displays include a primitive wash-

ing machine and the first operating table from the district hospital. Beside the river in **Apex Park** is the statue, *Gunsynd, the Goondiwindi Grey*, the famous racehorse who won 29 of his 55 races. **MacIntyre Cotton Ginnery** claims to be the largest of its kind in the Southern Hemisphere. Tours can be booked in season (April–July).

NEARBY ATTRACTIONS: The **Botanical Gardens of the Western Woodland** are 1km west of the town. The 25ha gardens are being developed using plant communities native to the **Darling Basin**. The gardens offer BBQ facilities, toilets, a recreation area and an artificial lake. Self-drive tour brochures are available from the information centre. The **Paper Mill**, located at **Boggabilla**, is open for tours Mondays and Tuesdays.

TOURIST INFO: Cnr Bowen and McLean sts, Ph: (07) 4671 2653

■ **Gympie**   POP 11 462
Map 255, A2
The hub of the **Cooloola region**, Gympie is located 162km north of Brisbane. Gympie was established after gold was discovered in 1867. Today, it is the centre of the prosperous **Mary River Valley** agricultural district.

MAIN ATTRACTIONS: There are many attractive parks, gardens, art galleries and interesting craft shops to explore in the town. The self-guided **historical walk** takes in several examples of 19th-century

The *Valley Rattler* steam train, near Gympie

architecture. Exhibits at **Wood Works Forestry and Timber Museum** are run by the Queensland Department of Forestry and the Queensland Museum. There is a working replica of a steam-driven sawmill and a demonstration of early timber-cutting techniques. The museum is in Fraser Rd. The **Valley Rattler** is a steam train offering trips each Sunday and Wednesday from Gympie to **Imbil**.

NEARBY ATTRACTIONS: Much of the town's history is preserved at **Gympie Gold Mining and Historical Museum** at **Monkland**, 5km south. The museum comprises a number of buildings, each concentrating on a different aspect of the past. A display featuring gems and minerals from all over the world can be found at **Cooloola Rocks and Minerals**, 15km south. **Amamoor SF** is ideal for picnics and rainforest walks, and is located 30km south of town.

TOURIST INFO: Lake Alford, Bruce Hwy, Ph: (07) 5483 5554

■ Hervey Bay   POP 34 240
Map 259, C3

The setting and location combine to make this town a prime holiday destination. Situated between Maryborough and Bundaberg, the town, and bay of the same name, are protected by Fraser Island and lie at the southern tip of the **Great Barrier Reef**. Offering easy access to islands, wildlife and beaches, Hervey Bay is one of Australia's fastest growing regions.

MAIN ATTRACTIONS: There are 13 organisations operating **whale-watching tours**. From August to October, mainly mothers, calves and sub-adult humpback whales spend time in the waters of Hervey Bay on their return journey to the Antarctic. For 2 weeks in August Hervey Bay hosts a **Whale Festival** with many attractions, including a **Blessing of the Fleet**. Hervey Bay

is a popular destination for anglers and is the second largest fishing ground along the Queensland coastline. The 700m **Urangan Pier** is one of the town's landmarks and a favourite spot for fishing and strolling. **Vic Hislop's Shark Show** is located at **Urangan**. **Neptune's Reefworld**, also at Urangan, has seal shows. **Nature World Wildlife Park**, at **Pialba**, features koalas, snakes, birds, nocturnal animals and crocodiles. There are also picnic areas available, and the park is open daily, 9am–5pm.

NEARBY ATTRACTIONS: There are regular cruises to the World Heritage-listed **Fraser Island**, the world's largest sand island with its unique perched lakes, turpentine forests and miles of beaches. On the island are scenic 4WD and bushwalking tracks. **Lady Elliot Island**, the Great Barrier Reef's southernmost island, is only 45mins from Hervey Bay by air. **Hervey Bay Marine Park** is 40km north and the seaside resorts of **Toogoom** and **Burrum Heads** are 15km NW.

TOURIST INFO: 10 Bideford St, Torquay, Ph: (07) 4124 9609

■ Home Hill   POP 3281
Map 282, D1

Originally part of the Inkerman Downs cattle station, the land around this **Burdekin River Valley** town was turned over to sugarcane farms in 1911. Sugarcane is still the main product of this region, which is located 100km south of Townsville.

MAIN ATTRACTIONS: Home Hill is linked to its twin town, **Ayr**, by the district's best-known landmark, the **Burdekin Bridge**. Referred to as the 'Silver Link', it spans the **Burdekin River** and was the longest bridge in the country for many years. **Ashworth's Treasures of the Earth**, located in the main street, incorporates Treasures of the Earth gallery, the rock shop and Ashworth's Jewellers and Potters

Tranquil Lake Mackenzie, Fraser Island

Workshop. The centre has amazing and beautiful exhibits and is definitely worth visiting. Guided tours of the **Inkerman Sugar Mill** are run on weekdays during the crushing season, June–Nov.

NEARBY ATTRACTIONS: **Groper Creek**, south-east of town, is a popular fishing spot known for its huge gropers and mud crabs. Facilities include a boat ramp, picnic, camping and caravan areas. Local fishing tours are available. South of town is the WWII radar site with its forbidding concrete igloos. **Mount Inkerman** provides panoramic views of the district. The seaside community of **Wunjunga** is a renowned birdwatching site which is also great for fishing.

TOURIST INFO: Plantation Park, Bruce Hwy and Kennedy St, Ayr, Ph: (07) 4783 5988

■ Hughenden   POP 1590
Map 281, H2

This town lies on the banks of Queensland's longest river, the **Flinders**, 383km SW of Townsville. The town is located on the Flinders Hwy and significant fossil finds in the area have prompted the name 'Dinosaur Highway'.

MAIN ATTRACTIONS: There are pleasant parks in the area good for picnicking, a swimming pool and a range of accommodation. The **Dinosaur**

Orpheus Island, Great Barrier Reef, near Ingham

Display Centre, located at the rear of the information centre in Gray St, has a full size replica of *Muttaburrasaurus langdoni*, a prehistoric, bird-footed herbivorous dinosaur that once roamed the area.
NEARBY ATTRACTIONS: **Porcupine Gorge NP**, 63km north, with a diverse range of flora and fauna, offers camping, swimming and birdwatching in superb surrounds. Gemstone fossicking is a popular activity in **Chudleigh Park**, 138km north. The **Cobb and Co Yards**, at **Prairie**, 44km east, houses many historical relics.
TOURIST INFO: Grey St, Ph: (07) 4741 1021

■ **Ingham**   POP 5460
Map 279, J5
This sugar town is also the commercial centre of the **Herbert River Valley**, sometimes dubbed 'Australia's Sugar Bowl'. Ingham is positioned between a wilderness of parks, waterfalls and the waterways of the **Hinchinbrook Channel**, 110km north of Townsville.
MAIN ATTRACTIONS: **Victoria Sugar Mill**, in Forest Beach Rd, is the country's largest mill with the capacity to crush 4 million tonnes of cane. Guided tours are offered during the crushing season, around July–Dec. A **Country Music Festival** is held in the town in June and the **Australian-Italian Festival** in May. For a pleasant stroll or picnic, visit the **Botanic Gardens** in Palm Tce.
NEARBY ATTRACTIONS: **Forest Beach** offers a long stretch of beach

overlooking the **Palm Group** of islands, it is located 17km SE of town, and a marine-stinger net is installed at the beach each summer to protect swimmers. The resort islands of **Hinchinbrook** and **Orpheus** are located offshore. **Lumholtz NP**, 51km NW, offers walking tracks, swimming and picnic spots, campgrounds and the 305m-high **Wallaman Falls**. Camping is also allowed in **Broadwater SF**. Located 45km west in the Herbert River Valley is a 1.6km rainforest walk. **Paluma Range NP**, 25km south, features **Jourama Falls** and the quaint village of **Paluma**.
TOURIST INFO: Bruce Hwy, Ph: (07) 4776 5211

■ **Innisfail**   POP 9593
Map 239, D6
This lush tropical town is situated on the **North** and **South Johnston rivers** 88km SE of Cairns. Innisfail has been a sugar town since the 1880's and also grows tea and tropical fruits; aquaculture too is vital to the economy.
MAIN ATTRACTIONS: In addition to the **Botanical Gardens**, which offers bush tucker, there are numerous parks that are ideal for picnicking and for feasting on the delicious locally caught seafood. The Johnstone River is popular for fishing or for strolling along its picturesque bank. Brochures are available for a self-guided walk to see the influence of Italian migrant canecutters on the Art Deco architecture of the town.

NEARBY ATTRACTIONS: The **Johnstone River Crocodile Farm**, 3km NE, has over 3000 crocodiles, native fauna and endangered cassowaries that are part of a captive breeding program. The park has a number of facilities set in tropical surroundings. **Paronella Park** at **Mena Creek**, 18km south, is a rainforest heritage garden created by Jose Paronella in 1929. Guided tours of the castle, tropical gardens, 'Tunnel of Love' and waterfalls are offered. The **Australian Sugar Museum** at **Mourilyan**, 7km south, displays relics and memorabilia of the sugar industry, which is such an important part of the north. The museum also presents an audio-visual describing the history and processing of sugar. Innisfail is a base for exploring numerous islands, such as **Dunk** and **Bedarra** and national parks such as **Wooroonooran NP**, 25km NW. In this park stands **Mount Bartle Frere**, Queensland's highest peak. Also in the area are stunning **Josephine Falls**.
TOURIST INFO: 1 Edith St, Ph: (07) 4061 7422

■ **Ipswich**   POP 70 000
Map 230, A5
Ipswich is located 44km SW of Brisbane, set in the hills around the **Bremer River**. It is Queensland's oldest provincial city, which began as a convict settlement in 1827.
MAIN ATTRACTIONS: Maps for the areas' **heritage trails** can be obtained at the information centre. One of the trails is a guide to the **Ipswich City Centre** where there are numerous heritage buildings, while another leads to the city's many pubs and hotels. **Global Arts Link** is an interactive art gallery, open daily, 10am–5pm. Both the Bremer and **Brisbane rivers** provide excellent opportunities for canoeing and kayaking. The **Queens Park Nature Centre**, located on Goleby Ave,

Queensland

features a range of native wildlife, landscaped gardens and exhibits representing the local bushland and flora communities.

NEARBY ATTRACTIONS: **Swanbank Power Station**, 12km SE, conducts tours by appointment. The **Swanbank Vintage Steam Train** leaves from the Power Station for a 7km round trip. The train runs on the first Sunday of each month, April–Dec. **St Brigid's Church** is reputedly the largest wooden church in the South Pacific. It is located at **Rosewood**, 20km west, and guided tours are available by appointment.

TOURIST INFO: cnr Brisbane St and D'Arcy Doyle Place, Ph: (07) 3281 0555

Julia Creek   POP 557

Map 280, E2

This small service township is located 134km east of Cloncurry on the main route from Townsville to Mount Isa. Julia Creek is a stock-trucking and sales centre with impressive stockyards.

MAIN ATTRACTIONS: **MacIntyre Museum**, in Burke St, was named after Duncan MacIntyre, the first European settler in north-west Queensland. Displays include memorabilia of the township and McKinlay Shire. The area is home to

Grass-trees in Bunya Mountains NP, south-west of Kingaroy

the rare and endangered nocturnal marsupial, the Julia Creek dunnart. The **Dirt and Dust Triathlon** is Julia Creek's major sporting event and is held in April. The race attracts thousands of competitors and tourists.

NEARBY ATTRACTIONS: **Kynuna**, 115km to the south, is where **A B 'Banjo' Paterson** wrote the Australian ballad, *Waltzing Matilda*. A cairn now marks the spot where events in the ballad took place; a hut used by Paterson can be seen behind the **Kynuna Roadhouse**. Kynuna was once a staging post for Cobb & Co coaches and the original 1889 bush pub, **Blue Heeler Hotel**, still stands. West of Kynuna is **McKinlay**, best known for its pub, **Walkabout Creek Hotel**. This hotel and other buildings in the town featured in the movie, *Crocodile Dundee*.

TOURIST INFO: Shire Offices, Julia St, Ph: (07) 4746 7166

Kilcoy   POP 2500

Map 255, A5

This small town, 95km NW of Brisbane, is a good base for a variety of daytrips to cities and towns located within a 2hr drive, including **Brisbane**, **Toowoomba**, **Kingaroy** and **Caloundra**.

MAIN ATTRACTIONS: The hills surrounding this town are reputed to be the home of the legendary Yowie— the Australian version of North America's Bigfoot. Over 3000 sightings of the half-man-half-beast were recorded 1975–1979. A statue, based on the descriptions of those who claim to have seen the beast, stands in **Yowie Park** on Hope St. The **Craft Cottage**, located in Yowie Park, is home to a variety of crafts.

NEARBY ATTRACTIONS: **Peachester SF**, just north of Kilcoy, offers natural fresh-water swimming holes and bushwalking tracks. **Lake Somerset**, also close to the town, is well stocked with perch and bass, and is a popular fishing, waterskiing and sailing venue. Boat ramps, fish

cleaning facilities, camping and picnic areas line its western shore. Follow the **Kilcoy Shire Wine Trail** and sample the fruits of the vine along the way.

TOURIST INFO: The Craft Cottage, Yowie Park, Hope St, Ph: (07) 5497 1888

Kingaroy   POP 7500

Map 271, D1

Kingaroy is located 210km NW of Brisbane. It is the business and rural centre for the prosperous **South Burnett** district and is known as Australia's **'Peanut Capital'**, and indeed giant peanut silos dominate the landscape. Apart from peanuts, the town's economy is based on grain, fruit and manufacturing.

MAIN ATTRACTIONS: The **Heritage Museum** is housed in the old power station next to the information centre and displays early machinery used in association with the peanut industry. A **Peanut Festival** is held in September and a **Food and Wine Festival** is held each March. **Kingaroy Wines** is located in the Old Butter Factory at 57 William St, and is one of the largest wineries in the region. There are numerous other wineries offering tastings and cellar door sales.

NEARBY ATTRACTIONS: Views of the town and surrounding countryside are provided at the **Carroll Nature Area**, located off Fisher St. There are panoramic views from **Mount Wooroolin**, 3km west. **Bunya Mountains NP**, located 60km SW, and is worthwhile visiting. The park has picnic and camping facilities and numerous walking tracks to rainforests with spectacular flora, waterfalls and streams. The South Burnett region boasts a number of wineries, many open for tastings and sales. Nearby **Boondooma** and **Bjelke-Petersen dams** are popular fishing destinations and both host large annual fishing competitions.

TOURIST INFO: 128 Haly St, Ph: (07) 4162 3199

■ Kuranda   POP 1250
Map 239, B3

Located at the top of the **Macalister Range**, beside the **Barron River**, this appealing rainforest village is best known as a destination of the 34km-long **Kuranda Scenic Railway** and the 7.5km-long **Skyrail Rainforest Cableway** from **Cairns**. This superb skyrail is the longest gondola cableway in the world.

MAIN ATTRACTIONS: The cableway and scenic railway offer tourists 2 superb routes between Cairns and Kuranda, another is via the winding and scenic **Kuranda Range Road**. The tree-lined main street has galleries, craft shops and pubs. **Kuranda Markets** are famous for their arts, crafts and entertainment. The **Australian Butterfly Sanctuary** has a colourful collection of over 2000 butterflies in a large natural setting. **Birdworld**, in Rod Veivers Dr, houses a brilliant array of birds, many of them endangered. There are several rainforest walks in the area, including the **River Esplanade Walk** along the Barron River, the **Forest Walk** and the **Jungle Walk**.

NEARBY ATTRACTIONS: River cruises and guided rainforest walks depart from the Barron River. **Barron Falls** are located in **Barron Gorge NP**, 7km SE, and a platform provides views of the falls. **Rainforestation Nature Park** is 35km east of town. Tours of the rainforest are available. There is also a **Dreamtime Walk** and **The Koala and Wildlife Park**.

TOURIST INFO: Tourism Tropical North Qld, 51 The Esplanade, Cairns, Ph: (07) 4051 3588

■ Longreach   POP 3974
Map 281, H5

Situated on the banks of the **Thomson River** in the state's central-west, Longreach is the hub of a very prosperous wool and beef area. Considered the **'Gateway to the Outback'**, Longreach is 700km west of Rockhampton.

MAIN ATTRACTIONS: The **Australian Stockman's Hall of Fame and Outback Heritage Centre** is the most famous attraction in the town. The centre is dedicated to preserving Aboriginal and non-Aboriginal Outback history, to the arrival of the aeroplane and present-day technology. Traditional artefacts are displayed and there is a library, audiovisual presentations and a resource centre. The town was Qantas' first operational base 1922–34 and where the first of 6 DH-50 biplanes were built in 1926. **Qantas Founders Outback Museum** is at the airport, and **Qantas Park**, in Eagle St, has a replica of the original Qantas office, now the information centre. The **Powerhouse Museum**, in Swan St, houses the largest collection of rural power-generating equipment in Australia. Exhibits include a social history hall and the 1923 swimming baths.

NEARBY ATTRACTIONS: Cruises on the Thompson River are popular and can be booked through the information centre. Guided tours of sheep and cattle stations, such as **Oakley Station**, 17km north, are available. Historic **Toobrac Station** offers accommodation and camping; it is 107km SW.

TOURIST INFO: Qantas Park, Eagle St, Ph: (07) 4658 3555

■ Mackay   POP 45 450
Map 263, D6

Often referred to as the **'Sugar Capital of Australia'**, Mackay is located approximately halfway between Cairns and Brisbane. Its close proximity to the **Great Barrier Reef**, the islands of the **Whitsundays** and beautiful rainforests make Mackay a most desirable holiday destination.

MAIN ATTRACTIONS: A **Heritage Walk** brochure is available from the information centre, explores the city's architectural heritage and describes 21 buildings of interest. **Queens Park**, in the city centre, features a

Australian Stockman's Hall of Fame, Longreach

magnificent orchid house displaying more than 500 species of orchids, also ferns and other plants. **Mackay Marina**, one of the state's largest, is also home to one of the world's biggest bulk sugar terminals. Cruises and fishing trips to the islands and Great Barrier Reef depart from the marina. Both **Illawong** and **Harbour beaches** offer safe swimming along with picnic areas and playgrounds.

NEARBY ATTRACTIONS: During crushing season June–Dec, weekday tours of **Farleigh Sugar Mill** can be arranged. Demonstrations of planting, harvesting and cutting of sugarcane can be seen at **Polestone Cane Farm**, June–Dec. **Eungella NP**, located at the top of the **Clarke Range**, 79km west, offers stunning valley views, 20km of rainforest walks and the opportunity to see the elusive platypus. There are more than 30 beaches within a 45min drive from the city.

TOURIST INFO: The Mill, 320 Nebo Rd, Ph: (07) 4952 2677

Queensland

Malanda   POP 1500

Map 239, B5

Located at the heart of the **Atherton Tableland**, Malanda is almost encircled by the **Johnstone River**. The town, 20km SE of Atherton, is the centre of the only dairy industry in the tropics, and has the longest milk run in the world, supplying milk to Darwin and South-East Asia.

MAIN ATTRACTIONS: The historic **Majestic Theatre** is a much-loved feature of Malanda and the only original movie theatre on the Tableland with the original ticket office still standing. The historic **Malanda Hotel** is the largest all-timber structure in Queensland. The town's best-known attraction is **Malanda Falls CP** and **Scenic Reserve** where the Johnstone River 'falls' over a basalt lava flow into a natural swimming hole. The surrounding park offers 2 short rainforest walks that shelter many birds. The Malanda Falls Visitor Centre has much to offer, including the **'Volcano Experience'**, **Rainforest Room**, interactive touch-screen computer displays, and indigenous and non-indigenous historical displays. For a truly wonderful experience, visitors can book a guided **Rainforest Walk** with **Ernie Raymont**, a tribal elder with the Ngadjonji people.

NEARBY ATTRACTIONS: The Atherton Tableland provides many attractions, including **Bromfield Swamp**; the National Trust-classified village of **Yungaburra**; and the volcanic crater lakes, **Barrine** and **Eacham**, near Yungaburra. **Mount Hypipamee NP** (The Crater), to the SW on the Evelyn Tableland, has an extinct volcanic pipe crater with 58m sheer granite walls dropping down to a 82m-deep lake. **Eacham Historic Museum**, in **Millaa Millaa**, has displays depicting the life of early timber-cutters and the district's rural pioneers.

TOURIST INFO: Atherton-Malanda Rd, Ph: (07) 4096 6957

Mareeba   POP 7347

Map 239, A3

The largest town on the **Atherton Tableland**, Mareeba serves as the region's administrative centre and is the beginning of the Outback. It is a town of many cultures, reflected in its cafes and delicatessens; it is also a great place to shop. Crops grown include sugarcane, mangos, tea-trees and coffee; mining and horticulture are also important to the local economy.

MAIN ATTRACTIONS: Mareeba is famous for its annual **rodeo** in July that draws crowds from all over Australia. **Bicentennial Lakes** is a recreation area offering walking tracks, picnic areas, parklands and gardens. Brochures are available on the self-guided **historic town walk**. **Mareeba Heritage Museum** has displays tracing local history and features a rail ambulance. **Coffee Works** offer guided tours explaining how coffee is processed, from the bean to the cup. Tastings of several exotic coffees is included in the tour.

NEARBY ATTRACTIONS: **Beck's Aviation and Military Museum**, 5km south, is the largest privately owned collection of its type in Queensland. **Davies Creek NP**, 15km east, has a camping area with picnic tables and toilet facilities. A permit is required for overnight stays. **Emerald Creek**

Falls is a 20min drive from town. The return walk along a well-maintained path to the lookout over the falls is 1.9km. There is also a large grassy area beside a shallow creek which is ideal for picnics. The **WetLands** offer tours of the 120ha park, popular for birdwatching and observing native wildlife. Hot-air balloon flights over the Tablelands are available.

TOURIST INFO: Heritage Museum, Centenary Park, 345 Byrnes St, Ph: (07) 4092 5674

Maroochydore   POP 29 747

Map 255, C4

This popular beach resort, located 106km north of Brisbane, is also the administrative and business centre of the **Sunshine Coast**.

MAIN ATTRACTIONS: Surf beaches are a major attraction for visitors to this city. The surf beach on the ocean side is patrolled. **Maroochy River** is home to a variety of pleasure craft and waterbirds, including pelicans and swans. The river offers safe swimming year-round and it is possible to camp by the riverbank at **Cotton Tree** or by the beach at Maroochydore.

NEARBY ATTRACTIONS: There are cruises up the Maroochy River, which pass through sugarcane fields. **Bli Bli Castle** is a themed tourist

(CONTINUED P.256)

Hot-air balloon over Mareeba, Atherton Tableland

North of Brisbane, the 48km coastal stretch bound by **Caloundra** to the south and **Noosa Heads** to the north is called the Sunshine Coast. The name conjures vivid images of the region's many surf beaches stretching to the horizon; its picturesque lakes; unspoilt rainforests; and cliffs of rainbow coloured sand.

The Sunshine Coast offers a quieter, more relaxed alternative to the Gold Coast's excesses. With an average temperature that does not drop below 20°C year-round and a wide choice of accommodation, the Sunshine Coast invites visitors to experience its balmy, laid-back way of life. The once sleepy coastal villages and modest holiday destinations have become glamorous retreats for the glitterati; others retain the charm of quieter times. Attractions are varied and include theme parks such as **Australia Zoo**, **UnderWater World**, **The Big Pineapple** and **Aussie World**. For a different kind of holiday, there are many national parks and state forests to explore, including **Coochin Creek SF**, **Great Sandy NP**, **Mount Coolum NP** and **Noosa NP**.

Aboriginal legend of the coloured sands

According to the Kabi Kabi Aboriginal people, the coloured sands at **Rainbow Beach** were formed when the Rainbow Spirit was shattered by a boomerang in a fight over a woman. The pieces fell onto the sand cliffs, colouring them forever.

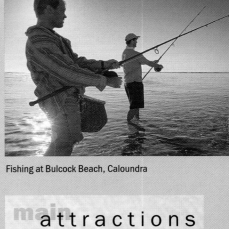

Fishing at Bulcock Beach, Caloundra

 Tourist information

Maroochy Tourism
Cnr Sixth Ave and Aerodrome Rd,
Maroochydore, Qld 4558
Ph: (07) 5479 1566 or 1800 882 032
www.maroochytourism.com

main attractions

◈ **Australia Zoo**
Located on the Glass House Mountains Tourist Route at Beerwah, this is the home of TV's Crocodile Hunter.

◈ **Dolphin viewing**
Tin Can Bay is a great place for viewing a pod of uncommon Indo-Pacific humpback dolphins (*Sina chinensis*).

◈ **Eumundi Markets**
These popular markets sell all manner of wares in a charming village setting.

◈ **Maroochydore**
The heart of the Sunshine Coast offers surfing beaches, excellent fishing, shopping and river cruises.

◈ **Mooloolaba**
This is a thriving beachside town. Two of its attractions are the 'Loo with a view' at the Esplanade and UnderWater World, which features a seal show.

◈ **Noosa Heads**
Noosa offers great beaches, world-class shopping and sophisticated restaurants, as well as Noosa NP.

◈ **Tewantin**
Tewantin is home to the House of Bottles, constructed from over 35 000 bottles, plus a giant beer bottle built from 17 000 stubbies.

◈ **The Big Pineapple**
This park is based on a working pineapple and macadamia plantation. The Big Pineapple itself is a tower with a lookout at the top.

Coastal pandanus, *Pandanus odoratissimus*, and Alexandria Bay, Noosa NP

Queensland

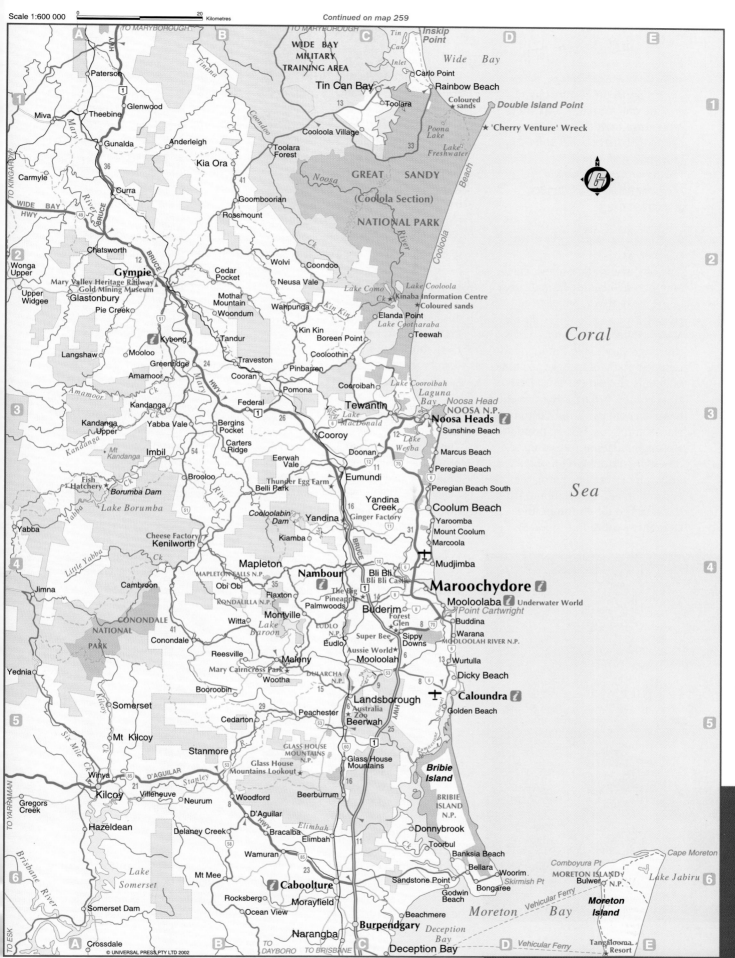

Scale 1:600 000

0   20
Kilometres

Continued on map 259

A   **B**   **C**   **D**   **E**

TO MARYBOROUGH   TO MARYBOROUGH   Tin Can   Inskip
Point

WIDE BAY
MILITARY
TRAINING AREA   *Wide*   *Bay*

Paterson   Carlo Point
Glenwood   Tin Can Bay   Rainbow Beach
Miva   Theebine   13   Toolara   Coloured   Double Island Point
    sands
Gunalda   Anderleigh   Cooloola Village   33   Poona   ★ 'Cherry Venture' Wreck
Carmyle   36   Kia Ora   Toolara   Lake   Lake
Curra   41   Forest   Freshwater
Goomboorian   **GREAT**   **SANDY**
WIDE BAY HWY   Rossmount   **(Cooloola Section)**

TO KINGAROY   **NATIONAL PARK**

Chatsworth   12   Wolvi   Coondoo   *Coral*
Wonga Upper   **Gympie**   Cedar Pocket   Neusa Vale   *Lake Como*   Kinaba Information Centre
Mary Valley Heritage Railway   Mothar   ★ Coloured sands
Upper Widgee   Gold Mining Museum   Mountain   Wahpunga   Elanda Point
Glastonbury   Woondum   *Lake Cootharaba*
Pie Creek   Kin Kin   Teewah

Kybong   Tandur   Boreen Point
Langshaw   Mooloo   24   Cooloothin
Greenridge   Traveston   *Sea*
Amamoor   Cooran   Pinbarren   *Lake Cooroibah*
Kandanga   Pomona   Cooroibah   *Laguna*
Federal   *Bay*   *Noosa Head*
Kandanga Upper   Yabba Vale   26   **Tewantin**   **NOOSA N.P.**
Bergins Pocket   *Lake MacDonald*   **Noosa Heads**
Carters   Cooroy   Sunshine Beach
Imbil   Ridge   Doonan   12   *Lake*
Mt 54   Eerwah   *Weyba*   Marcus Beach
Kandanga   Brooloo   Vale   11   Peregian Beach
Fish   Thunder Egg Farm ★   **Eumundi**   70   Peregian Beach South
Hatchery   Belli Park   *Borumba Dam*   Yandina   **Coolum Beach**
Yabba   *Lake Borumba*   16   Creek   Yaroomba
    Cooloolabin   Ginger Factory   Mount Coolum
    Dam   **Yandina**   11   31   Marcoola
Cheese Factory   Kiamba   Mudjimba
Kenilworth   10
    Little Yabba Ck   **Mapleton**   **Nambour**   Bli Bli   **Maroochydore**
Jimna   Cambroon   Obi Obi   35   Bli Bli Castle   **Mooloolaba**   Underwater World
Yednia   **MAPLETON FALLS N.P.**   Flaxton   The Big   Point Cartwright
    Palmwoods   Pineapple ★   8   Buddina
    KONDALILLA N.P.   14   **Buderim**   Warana
CONONDALE   Witta   Montville   Forest   70   **MOOLOOLAH RIVER N.P.**
    Lake   **EUDLO**   Glen
NATIONAL   41   Cononndale   *Baroon*   **N.P.**   Super Bee ★   Sippy   Wurtulla
PARK   Reesville   Eudlo   Downs
    Aussie World ★   13   Dicky Beach
    Maleny   **Mooloolah**   8
    Mary Cairncross Park ★   53   **Caloundra**
    Wootha   9   Golden Beach
    DULARCHA   8
Somerset   Booroobin   **N.P.**   15   **Landsborough**
Mt Kilcoy   Cedarton   Peachester   Australia   *Pumicestone Channel*
    29   ★ Zoo
    53   **Beerwah**   25
Stanmore   *Stanley R*   **GLASS HOUSE**   **Bribie**
    43   **MOUNTAINS**   60   **Island**
Winya   **D'AGUILAR**   **N.P.**   Glass House   **BRIBIE**
Kilcoy   Villeneuve   85   Glass House   Mountains   **ISLAND**
    21   Neurum   Mountains Lookout ★   16   **N.P.**
Gregors Creek   Woodford   Beerburrum
TO YARRAMAN   8   Donnybrook
Hazeldean   D'Aguilar   *Elimbah Ck*   Toorbul
    Delaney Creek   Bracalba   Elimbah   Banksia Beach
    58   11   *Comboyura Pt*   *Cape Moreton*
    Wamuran   85   Bellara
Brisbane River   Mt Mee   23   Sandstone Point   Woorim   **MORETON ISLAND**   *Lake Jabiru*
    Lake   **Caboolture**   Bongaree   *Skirmish Pt*   Bulwer   **N.P.**
    Somerset   Rocksberg   Godwin   *Moreton*
Somerset Dam   Morayfield   Beach   Vehicular Ferry   **Island**
    Ocean View   Beachmere   *Moreton*   *Bay*
TO ESK   **Narangba**   **Burpengary**   *Deception*   **Tangalooma**
Crossdale   TO DAYBORO   **Deception Bay**   *Bay*   Vehicular Ferry   **Resort**
TO BRISBANE

© UNIVERSAL PRESS PTY LTD 2002

1   **2**   **3**   **4**   **5**   **6**

Continued on maps 228 & 229

attraction, where visitors can explore a dungeon, torture chamber and the doll museum. **Top Shots Adventure Park** offers indoor rock-climbing, blaster boats and a 36-hole mini-golf course.
TOURIST INFO: cnr Sixth Ave and Aerodrome Rd, Ph: (07) 5479 1566 or 1800 882 032

Maryborough   POP 21 990

Map 259, B4

One of Queensland's oldest cities, Maryborough is nestled in a curve of the **Mary River**, 34km from Hervey Bay.
MAIN ATTRACTIONS: Known as a **'Heritage City'**, Maryborough has retained many of its historic public buildings and old Queenslander-style homes. **Wharf Street Precinct** has many old pubs, the Customs House and Court House. **Bond Store Heritage Museum** represents the development of Maryborough as an important river port during the pre-Federation era. The National Trust has restored the **Brennan and Geraghty's Store** in Lennox St.

City Hall, Maryborough

The **Heritage Walk** and **Drive Tour** brochure is available from the information centre. Each tour lasts 1.5hrs. **Elizabeth Park** is renowned for its display of more than 2000 roses. **Queens Park**, which is over 100 years old, has a fern house, waterfall, lily-pond and a lace-trimmed band rotunda. **Ululah Lagoon**, off Lions Dr, is a wildlife sanctuary and visitors are invited to handfeed the black swans, water hens, ducks and geese.
NEARBY ATTRACTIONS: Maryborough is a convenient base for exploring the attractions of the **Fraser Coast**, **Fraser Island**, **Hervey Bay** and **Lady Elliot Island**.
TOURIST INFO: BP South Tourist Complex, Bruce Hwy, Ph: (07) 4121 4111

Miles   POP 1250

Map 287, F4

This small rural town is 343km NW of Brisbane. Situated at the junction of the Leichhardt and Warrego hwys, Miles is an ideal stop for visitors travelling west to the **Stockman's Hall of Fame** or north to the **Great Barrier Reef** and tropical north Queensland.
MAIN ATTRACTIONS: The **Miles and District Historical Village** features 30 authentic buildings in a re-creation of a pioneer settlement. Original buildings include a church, hospital, general store, machinery shed, dairy and a slab hut. The village also has a war museum, and a memorabilia museum which features an extensive collection of shells, Aboriginal artefacts and lapidary. The museum is also the information centre.
NEARBY ATTRACTIONS: In early spring the wildflowers carpet the area and it is worthwhile doing the self-guided **wildflower drive**. Brochures on the drive are available. **Myall Park Botanical Gardens** are located at **Glenmorgan**, 134km SW.
TOURIST INFO: Miles Historical Village, Murilla St, Ph: (07) 4627 1492

Monto   POP 1436

Map 287, G2

Regarded as the southern gateway to central Queensland, Monto is 515km from Brisbane and 250km inland from Bundaberg. The town is at the centre of a rich agricultural, dairying and cattle district.
MAIN ATTRACTIONS: The **History and Cultural Centre**, in Flinders St, incorporates the **Ostwald Rock Collection**, and also a collection that traces local history.
NEARBY ATTRACTIONS: **Cania Gorge NP** is located 25km NW of Monto. It contains many interesting rock formations, including **The Leap**, **Dripping Rock**, **The Wool Bales**, **Castle Mountain** and **Mount Dowgo**. Walking tracks lead through the subtropical vegetation to **Cathedral** and **Dragon caves**. **Waruma Dam** is popular for fishing, swimming, waterskiing and sailing; it is 50km south of Monto.
TOURIST INFO: Three Moon Motel, 4 Flinders St, Ph: (07) 4166 1777

Moranbah   POP 6450

Map 282, D4

Situated on the **Denham Range**, Moranbah is 200km SW of Mackay. This town was purpose-built in the 1970s to service the employees of Goonyella and Peak Downs open-cut coal mines.
MAIN ATTRACTIONS: **Town Square** has a Mediterranean feel with many cafes and restaurants offering alfresco dining. There is a campdraft in July, which is a festival highlighting the traditional skills of stockmen, and a rodeo in October.
TOURIST INFO: Library, Town Square, Ph: (07) 4941 7221

Mossman   POP 2350

Map 239, A1

This small sugar town is situated in beautiful **Mossman River Valley**, overlooked by **Mount Demi** and a rainforest-clad mountain range. Mossman is 75km north of Cairns.

Queensland

Canoeing on Lawn Hill Creek, Lawn Hill NP, north-west of Mount Isa

MAIN ATTRACTIONS: **Mossman Sugar Mill Tours** operate daily during the crushing season, June–Nov, from **Mossman Central Mill**, the most northern mill in Australia. The town's Golf Course has a rainforest walk.

NEARBY ATTRACTIONS: The magnificent **Mossman Gorge**, 8km west, is the district's main attraction. It is part of **Daintree NP**, which in turn is part of the **Wet Tropics World Heritage Area**, and offers walking tracks, gorges, clear-water creeks and waterfalls. The Kuku Yalanji people conduct guided walks through the rainforest. Scenic roads through Mossman access 3 local beaches—**Cooya**, **Newell** and **Wonga**. To the north of Mossman is the quaint village of **Daintree**: the gateway to **Cape York**. Daintree NP, 64km north, has the largest area of tropical rainforest in Australia. For visitors wanting to see crocodiles

and other native fauna, it is worth-while visiting **Hartleys Creek Wildlife Reserve**, 35km south of Mossman. The resort town of **Port Douglas** is a short drive away and is a popular stepping-off point for cruises to the **Low Isles** and the **Outer Barrier Reef**.

TOURIST INFO: 23 Macrossan St, Port Douglas, Ph: (07) 4099 5599

■ Mount Isa   POP 22 251
Map 280, C2

Mount Isa is the largest and most important industrial provincial city west of the Great Dividing Range. It is located 887km west of Townsville. **Mount Isa Mines** is the largest single producer of copper, silver, lead and zinc in the world. The town is surrounded by cattle country and hosts one of the richest and largest rodeos in the world. The 3-day event is held in August.

MAIN ATTRACTIONS: The Mount Isa Mine offers underground mine tours. Visitors are taken on a 4WD adventure through some of the mine's 600km of tunnels and can experience the day-to-day oper-ations of a major underground mine. Tours operate twice daily, Mon–Fri, bookings required. Multi-award winning **Riversleigh Fossils Interpretive Centre** features displays of fossil discoveries from the Riversleigh area, some dating to over 30 million years. The infor-mation centre is also located here.

NEARBY ATTRACTIONS: Man-made **Lake Moondarra**, 15km north of Mount Isa, is an ideal recreational and picnic spot. The lake offers swim-ming, boating, canoeing, sailing and waterskiing and the surround-ing area is a wildlife sanctuary. **Lawn Hill NP**, 332km NW, offers around 20km of walking tracks, some leading to high peaks and others to swimming holes. Facilities include a camping area, tent accommodation and a shop with essential items. Tours of the World

Heritage-listed **Riversleigh Fossil Site** are available. The site is 267km NW of Mount Isa. **Lake Julius**, situ-ated along the **Leichhardt River**, 99km NE, offers the chance to see local wildlife, including freshwater crocodiles. Only a short distance from the lake are Aboriginal cave paintings, nature trails and an old goldmine. Camping at the lake is also possible.

TOURIST INFO: Riversleigh Fossils Centre, Centenary Park, Marian St, Ph: (07) 4749 1555

■ Mount Morgan   POP 2530
Map 267, B5

Located 38km SW of Rockhampton, the small and historic town of Mount Morgan has a history of gold and copper mining dating back over a century. **Mount Morgan Mine** is the largest open-cut gold mine in the Southern Hemisphere.

MAIN ATTRACTIONS: The Mount Morgan Mine was closed in 1981 but guided tours of the mine's old workings can still be booked. Tours run at 9.30am and 1.30pm, daily. **Mount Morgan Historical Museum**, located in Morgan St, has a large collection of historical pieces rep-resenting the town's early years. The National Trust has classified some historic buildings, including the **Court House**; and the **Railway Station**, which contains tearooms and a rail museum. A restored 1904 steam engine operates on week-ends and fettler's trolley-rides operate along a 4km-long track on weekdays. The diesel **Silver Bullet** also operates daily.

NEARBY ATTRACTIONS: The **Big Dam** is popular for boating and fishing, and is located about 3km north of Mount Morgan. The heritage town of **Wowan** is located 40km SW and is home to the **Scrub Turkey Museum**, which is housed in an old butter factory.

TOURIST INFO: Railway Station, Burnett Hwy, Ph: (07) 4938 2312

THE FRASER COAST

The magnificent natural playground of the Fraser Coast hosts diverse and unique landscapes, from intriguing coloured sands, rainforests, giant sand dunes and basalt headlands to tranquil lakes, beaches and national parks.

Boasting the world's largest sand island—120km long and an average of 15km wide—and magnificent waterways, the Fraser Coast offers a full range of watersports, including swimming, fishing and diving.

Apart from a few areas of private land, **Fraser Island** is a World Heritage-listed national park; the only place on earth where rainforest grows from sand. Most areas of interest are in the central part of the island, and 4WD tracks and walking tracks lead past major sites. **Lake Boomanjin** is a freshwater lake perched high up on the island's sand dunes—it is the largest perched lake in the world. Sandy beaches surround the lake and there are camping and picnic areas. Wildlife on the island is prolific, from dingoes to wild horses and wallabies to Jabirus.

The secluded seaside townships dotting the **Great Sandy Strait**, such as **Tuan**, **Boonooroo**, **Poona** and **Tinnanbar**, provide opportunities for more sedate and relaxed activities like fishing and boating.

A major attraction for visitors is the annual migration (Aug–Oct) of majestic humpback whales through the waters of **Hervey Bay** en route to feeding grounds in Antarctica.

Shipwreck Survivor

After the wreck of the *Stirling Castle* in 1836, Eliza Fraser was cast ashore on Fraser Island where she lived with the Dalungbara Aboriginal people. She was rescued by 'Wandi', the escaped convict, David Bracefell. The island is named in her honour.

 Tourist information

Maryborough/Fraser Island Visitor Information Centre
BP South Tourist Complex
Bruce Hwy, Maryborough, Qld 4650
Ph: (07) 4121 4111
www.frasercoast.org.au

Humpback whale, *Megaptera novaeangliae*, breaching in Hervey Bay Marine Park

main attractions

◈ **'The Cathedrals'**
These strikingly coloured sand cliffs at Cathedral Beach on Fraser Island change colour depending on the light and the time of day.

◈ **Eli Creek**
Crystalline Eli Creek is the largest creek on the east coast of Fraser Island, and is ideal for swimming.

◈ **Fraser Island**
This island is famous for its coloured sands, vast sand dunes, unique freshwater perched lakes and rainforests.

◈ **Great Sandy NP**
Bushwalking tracks offer opportunities to explore the 1650km² wilderness more closely, with 43 short walks ranging in levels of difficulty.

◈ **Hervey Bay**
Gateway to Fraser Island, Hervey Bay's sheltered waters are stinger-free, perfect for water-based activities.

◈ **Maryborough**
Picturesque Maryborough on the Mary River is known as 'Heritage City' because of its many historic buildings.

◈ **Whale watching**
A good time to see whales is August to October, when they rest and play en route back to their feeding ground in the Antarctic.

Wanggoolba Creek at Central Station, Fraser Island

Queensland

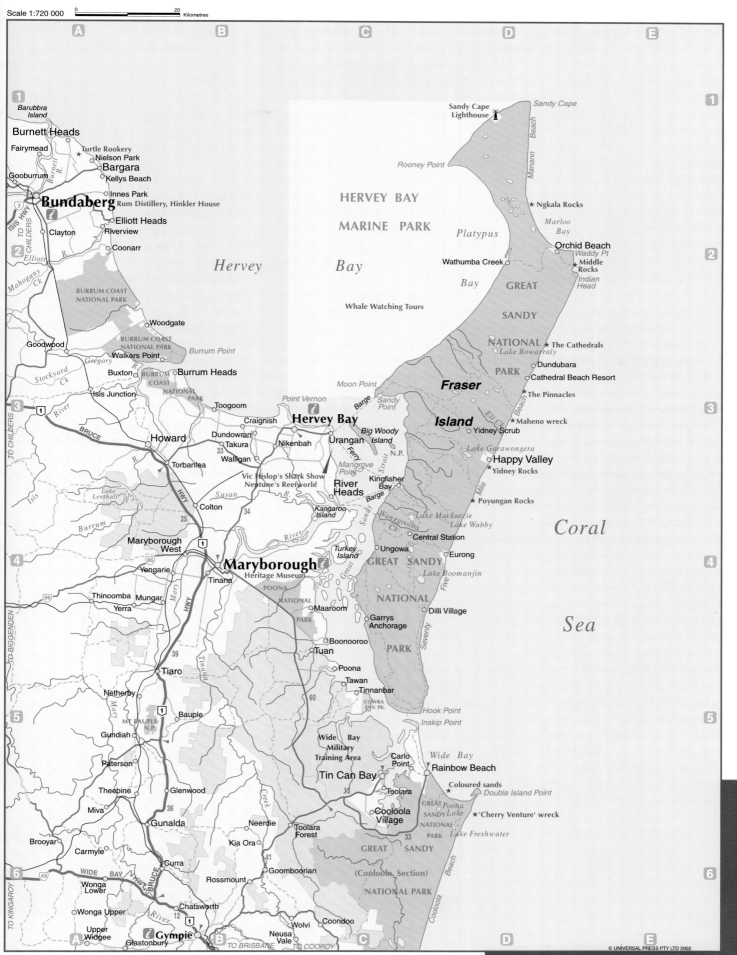

Continued on map 255

Moura POP 2500

Map 287, F2

This small town is located 69km from Biloela and lies in the heart of the **Dawson Valley**. Moura services the surrounding rural and coalmining communities. The town has a large and permanent storage depot for various grains, including wheat, sunflower, barley and maize. Cattle, cotton and peanuts are also important rural industries.

MAIN ATTRACTIONS: **Apex Park** at the **Dawson River**, a few kilometres from town, is a popular fishing, boating, swimming and picnic area. Unique to Moura is the local dairy where the family-owned business processes milk from cow to carton on the premises. A drive past the coal mine provides a good view of the huge dragline at work.

NEARBY ATTRACTIONS: **Banana Shire's Local History Museum** is located at **Theodore**, a small town 50km south of Moura. The museum is filled with historic memorabilia of Moura and the Dawson Valley. For keen hikers, **Mount Scoria**, **Carnarvon**, **Cania** and **Isla gorges** are within driving distance.

TOURIST INFO: 83 Dawson Hwy, Ph: (07) 4997 1411

Murgon POP 2230

Map 287, H3

This picturesque town is called the **'Beef Capital of the South Burnett'**. Murgon is nestled at the foot of **Boat Mountain**, about 96km west of Gympie. Murgon is famous for fossils—the area yielded the first evidence of marsupials in Australia, dating back 55 million years.

MAIN ATTRACTIONS: **Queensland's Dairy Industry Museum** displays trace the history of milk and cheese industries, with an emphasis on the production of butter as the basis of the industry. The museum is located on Gayndah Rd and is open weekends, 1pm–4pm or by appointment. Next door to the museum is the relocated **Trinity Homestead**, one of the district's original buildings.

NEARBY ATTRACTIONS: Murgon is the emerging wine area of the **Burnett Valley**. **Barambah Ridge** is being developed as a producer of premium wines and is set to become a leader in vineyard tourism. Located at **Redgate**, near Murgon, the winery offers tastings and sales of its award-winning wines, an entertainment area and picnic area. Cherbourg Aboriginal community is located south of Murgon and boasts the **Barambah Emu Farm**. This was the very first commercial emu farm in Queensland. It offers articles made from emu leather and Aboriginal artefacts. **Boat Mountain Environmental Park**, 14km north of Murgon, and **Jack Smith Scrub CP**, 15km NE, offer walking tracks and views. Both parks can be visited as part of a scenic drive in the area.

TOURIST INFO: 118 Lamb St, Ph: (07) 4168 1984

Nambour POP 12 834

Map 255, C4

Located just off the Bruce Hwy, 104km north of Brisbane in the heart of the **Sunshine Coast** sugar-growing area, is the agricultural service centre of Nambour. Macadamia nuts and lychees have recently joined the 3 main crops grown in the region—sugar, pineapples and bananas. It is thought the name for the town derives from 'namba' an Aboriginal word for the red flowers of the weeping bottlebrush (*Callistemon viminalis*), which is common in the region.

MAIN ATTRACTIONS: Sugar trains chug across the main street en route to Moreton Sugar Mill during the crushing season, about July–Dec. **Nambour Adventure Playground** on the corner of Matthew and Anne sts in **Quota Memorial Park** is a favourite with children.

NEARBY ATTRACTIONS: **The Big Pineapple**, the symbol of the Sunshine Coast, and **Macadamia Nut Factory** are 7km south. Visitors can see how pineapples and macadamias are grown and harvested on these working plantations. There is a train and nutmobile for kids, a fauna sanctuary and animal nursery. The Creatures of the Night exhibit has nocturnal rainforest animals that are rarely seen. **Superbee Honey Factory** with its Live Bee Show and the **Forest Glen Sanctuary**, which has deer and native animals, are located south on the **Tanawha-Forest Glen Tourist Drive**. The impressive **Glass House Mountains**, which are eroded volcanic pillars—Beerwah at 556m, is the highest—are also to the south. **Blackall Range Scenic Drive** to **Landsborough** is a worthwhile 70km trip.

TOURIST INFO: 5 Coronation Ave, Ph: (07) 5476 1933

View to the Glass House Mountains, south of Nambour

Queensland

Coloured sands of the Cooloola section of Great Sandy NP, north of Noosa Heads

Noosa Heads   POP 17 776
Map 255, C3

The well-known resort town of Noosa Heads is situated on the edge of **Noosa NP** and **Laguna Bay**. Not only does the town offer many beaches and safe swimming year-round, it is also the gateway to the stunning **Noosa River Everglades** and **Cooloola NP**.

MAIN ATTRACTIONS: Hastings St, the main street of Noosa Heads, offers many restaurants, cafes, galleries and boutiques. **Main Beach** offers safe swimming and is the most popular beach for families. Noosa NP is only a short walk from Hastings St. This 477ha park provides many walking tracks through rainforest, past small coves, rugged coastal rock formations and interesting coastal heathlands.

NEARBY ATTRACTIONS: The **Great Sandy NP** is 14km north, and although **Noosa River** separates it from Noosa Heads, it is accessible via ferry from **Tewantin**. The multi-coloured sand cliffs, known as the **Coloured Sands** are located in this park. Activities offered include bushwalking, camel riding, horse-riding and surfing. **Noosaville** is a family-style resort town, located 5km north. Parks surround the Noosa River, which is filled with pelicans, dinghies, catamarans and houseboats. **Eumundi**, 24km

SW, is best known for its Saturday morning markets.

TOURIST INFO: Hastings St Roundabout, Ph: (07) 5447 4988 or 1800 448 833

Normanton   POP 1398
Map 278, D4

Located on the **Norman River** and 72km inland from the Gulf of Carpentaria, Normanton is the capital of **Carpentaria Shire**. A major business and service centre, it serves a pastoral region covering 68 250km^2. Historic **Normanton Railway Station** is home to the *Gulflander* train which operates 2 days a week.

MAIN ATTRACTIONS: Brochures are available for the self-guided **scenic walks** and drives around the town. The **Gulfland Motel**, Landsborough St, has a giant barramundi out front. The **Shire Office Gardens**, in Haig St, displays a life-size replica of **Krys the Savannah King**, an 8.6m saltwater crocodile caught in the Norman River, which is also famous for its barramundi.

NEARBY ATTRACTIONS: Cruises on the Norman River offer the chance to see jabirus, brolgas, herons and saltwater crocodiles. **Shady Lagoon**, located 18km east, is popular for bush camping and birdwatching. Camping is also allowed at **Walkers Creek**, 32km NW, a popular spot for fishing. **Dorunda Station**, 197km

NE of Normanton, offers visitors the chance to stay on a working cattle station. The lakes and rivers on the station are good for barramundi and saratoga fishing. **Bang Bang Jump Up** rock formation is a solitary hill located 106km SW. A road goes to the top of the hill, which affords panoramic views of the district.

TOURIST INFO: Shire Offices, Haig St, Ph: (07) 4745 1166

Oakey   POP 4300
Map 271, C3

Situated around 30km from Toowoomba, Oakey is rich in historical and scenic attractions. National parks, the **Sunshine Coast** and **Gold Coast** are all within easy reach of the town. Oakey features the country's largest **Army Aviation Base**. Industries in the town include malting, engineering works and export abattoirs.

MAIN ATTRACTIONS: A life-size statue of the racehorse, **Bernborough**, stands near the town's library. This famous racehorse was bred near Oakey and raced during the 1940s. **Oakey Historical Museum** is located on the Warrego Hwy. The **Flypast Museum of Australian Army Flying** is located at the army base and displays a large collection of original and replica aircraft and aviation memorabilia.

NEARBY ATTRACTIONS: **Jondaryan Woolshed**, 22km NW of Oakey, is over 100 years old and is now an Australian heritage theme park. A complex of historic buildings house vintage machinery and memorabilia which commemorates pioneers of the wool industry. There are sheep-shearing demonstrations and visitors can buy goods at the wool store. National parks, including **Girraween**, **Stanthorpe** and **Cunningham's Gap** are ideal for daytrips as they are within easy reach of the town.

TOURIST INFO: Library, 64 Campbell St, Ph: (07) 4691 2306

WHITSUNDAY ISLANDS

Capt James Cook entered the waters of this group of idyllic islands on Whit Sunday, June 3, 1770. He spent much time charting these beautiful islands comprising 74 tropical islands, only 8 of which are inhabited. The Whitsunday Group lies off the stretch of coast between **Mackay** and **Bowen**. Paralleling the island group, further offshore in the **Coral Sea**, are the coral reefs and lagoons of the **Great Barrier Reef**—a wonderland of marine diversity. The islands have been compared with the beauty of the Caribbean Islands and are a favourite holiday destination for visitors from around the world.

With an estimated 8.25hrs of sunshine per day and an average yearly temperature of 25°C, the Whitsunday coast is an idyllic retreat. The region boasts unspoilt coral-fringed islands, beaches, turquoise waters, a tropical climate and alluring seaside resorts. Offer-ing consistently perfect conditions for swimming, snorkelling, scuba diving, fishing, sailing and cruising, the Whitsundays are a dream-holiday destination.

Charter and tour companies based on the mainland offer a wide variety of tour and recreation options. Explore the area by boat or seaplane, try parasailing and tandem skydiving. Take a cruise to the nearby Great Barrier Reef and see the migrating whales in season (around July–Sept). The Whitsundays offer a range of accommodation to suit most budgets, from camping on a deserted island to a suite in a luxurious five-star resort.

Snorkelling on the Hardy Reef

Airlie Beach

Within the exotic perimeters of the **Whitsunday Islands**, **Great Barrier Reef** and **Conway Range NP**, Airlie Beach is a prime holiday destination. There is a range of activities related to land, sea and air and all styles of accommodation. The village is the perfect base for exploring the region's many diversions. Airlie Beach boasts a year-round safe swimming lagoon surrounded by landscaped gardens.

 Tourist information

Whitsunday Information Centre
Bruce Hwy,
Proserpine Qld 4800
Freecall: 1800 801 252
www.whitsundayinformation.com.au

main attractions

◈ **Brampton Island**
The island resort is surrounded by national park and sandy beaches.

◈ **Daydream Island**
This is a popular resort island.

◈ **Great Barrier Reef**
This spectacular string of reefs and islands extends for more than 2000km along Australia's east coast. It offers superb diving and snorkelling opportunities.

◈ **Hamilton Island**
The island's resort is the key landmark offering a wide range of activities.

◈ **Hayman Island**
A luxurious resort island.

◈ **Hook Island**
A budget island retreat with an underwater observatory.

◈ **Lindeman Island**
This island is home to Australia's first Club Med resort.

◈ **Long Island**
Renowned as the Whitsunday's most natural and adventurous island, this is a secluded retreat not far from Shutehaven.

◈ **South Molle Island**
With unspoilt national park fringed by scenic beaches, this island is great for bushwalkers and family groups.

◈ **Whitehaven Beach**
A 7km-long white silica sand beach on Whitsunday Island.

Charter boat near Cid Island, Whitsunday Passage

Queensland

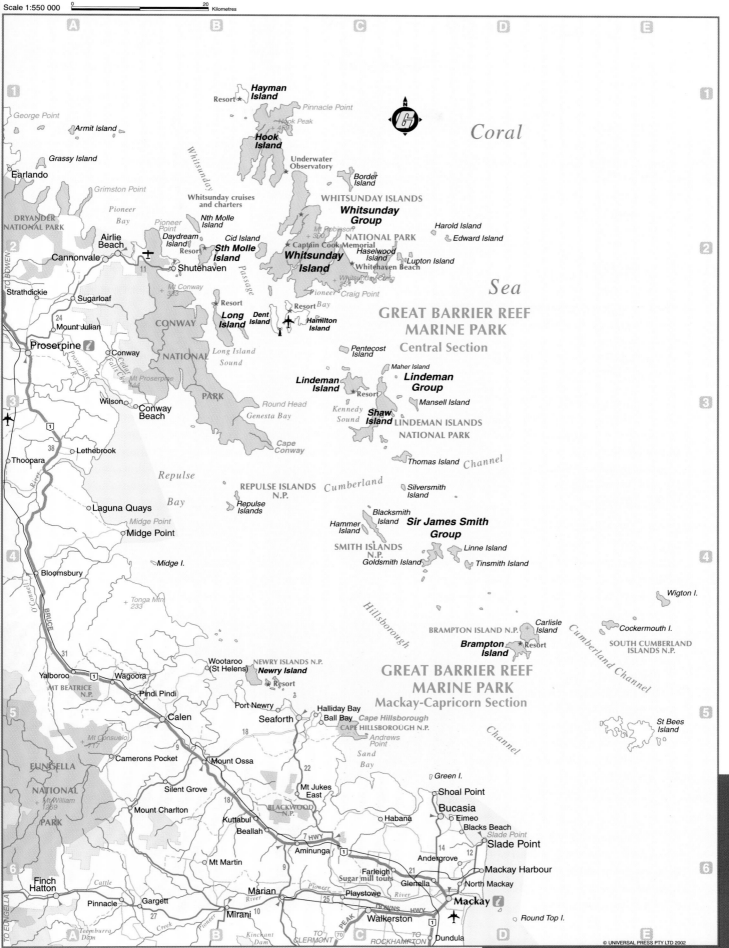

Coral

Sea

Whitsunday cruises
and charters

WHITSUNDAY ISLANDS

**Whitsunday
Group**

NATIONAL PARK

Captain Cook
Memorial

Whitehaven Beach

**Whitsunday
Island**

GREAT BARRIER REEF
MARINE PARK

Central Section

**Lindeman
Group**

**Lindeman
Island**

Mansell Island

**Shaw
Island**

LINDEMAN ISLANDS

NATIONAL PARK

Thomas Island Channel

Silversmith
Island

REPULSE ISLANDS
N.P.

Cumberland

Repulse
Islands

Blacksmith
Island

**Sir James Smith
Group**

Hammer
Island

SMITH ISLANDS
N.P.

Linne Island

Goldsmith Island

Tinsmith Island

Wigton I.

Hillsborough

BRAMPTON ISLAND N.P.

Carlisle
Island

Cockermouth I.

**Brampton
Island**

Resort

Cumberland Channel

SOUTH CUMBERLAND
ISLANDS N.P.

GREAT BARRIER REEF
MARINE PARK

Mackay-Capricorn Section

Channel

St Bees
Island

DRYANDER
NATIONAL PARK

George Point

Armit Island

Grassy Island

Earlando

Grimston Point

Pioneer
Bay

Airlie
Beach

Cannonvale

Shutehaven

Strathdickie

Sugarloaf

Mount Julian

Proserpine

Conway

Wilson

Conway
Beach

CONWAY

NATIONAL

PARK

**Hayman
Island**

Resort

Hook
Peak

**Hook
Island**

Pinnacle Point

Underwater
Observatory

Border
Island

Nth Molle
Island

Harold Island

Edward Island

**Sth Molle
Island**

Daydream
Island

Resort

Cid Island

Lupton Island

Haselwood
Island

Mt Robinson

Resort

**Long
Island**

Dent
Island

**Hamilton
Island**

Pioneer Bay

Craig Point

Pentecost
Island

Long Island
Sound

Maher Island

Resort

Kennedy
Sound

Round Head

Genesta Bay

Cape
Conway

Letherbrook

Thoopara

Laguna Quays

Midge Point

Midge I.

Repulse

Bay

Midge Point

Bloomsbury

Tonga Mtn
233

Yalboroo

MT BEATRICE
N.P.

Wagoora

Pindi Pindi

Calen

Wootaroo
(St Helens)

NEWRY ISLANDS N.P.

Newry Island

Resort

Port Newry

Halliday Bay

Ball Bay

Cape Hillsborough

CAPE
HILLSBOROUGH N.P.

Andrews
Point

Seaforth

Camerons Pocket

Mount Ossa

Silent Grove

Mount Charlton

Kuttabul

Beallah

Mt Jukes
East

BLACKWOOD
N.P.

Sand
Bay

Green I.

Shoal Point

Bucasia

Eimeo

Habana

Blacks Beach

Slade Point

Andergrove

Mackay Harbour

Aminunga

Mt Martin

FUNGELLA

NATIONAL

Mt William
1359

PARK

Finch
Hatton

Pinnacle Gargett

Marian

Mirani

Playstowe

Farleigh

Sugar mill tours

Glenella

North Mackay

Mackay

Round Top I.

Walkerston

Dundula

Continued on maps 282 & 283

■ Palm Cove   POP 2700
Map 239, C2

Located 27km north of Cairns, off the Bruce Hwy, this captivating resort town is situated on a tropical beach with views over the aqua waters to **Double Island** and **Scouts Hat Island**. There is a selection of accommodation and many art galleries, boutiques and shops in town.
NEARBY ATTRACTIONS: Dive tours to the **Great Barrier Reef** depart regularly from Palm Cove. Daytrip tours to the **Atherton Tableland** also leave from here. The town is a convenient base for exploring **Mossman** and **Port Douglas**. In **Smithfield**, 14km south, there is a bungy-jumping tower set in the rainforest. **Hartley's Creek Wildlife Reserve**, 15km north, has hundreds of crocodiles as well as other native fauna. There are crocodile and snake shows daily. For panoramic coastal views, visit **Rex Lookout**, 17km north.
TOURIST INFO: Tourism Tropical North Qld, 51 The Esplanade, Cairns, Ph: (07) 4051 3588

■ Port Douglas   POP 3850
Map 239, B1

Located 67km north of Cairns, Port Douglas is situated on the **Coral Sea** coastline with a backdrop of tropical mountains. With its close proximity to Australia's most popular tourist destinations, the **Daintree Rainforest** and **Cape Tribulation**, and the **Great Barrier Reef**, Port Douglas has become an internationally renowned tourist destination.
MAIN ATTRACTIONS: Port Douglas offers restaurants, art galleries, excellent shops, historic buildings, nightclubs, golf courses and beaches. The superb **Rainforest Habitat**, on Port Douglas Rd, is a wildlife sanctuary with a focus on biological conservation. **Flagstaff Hill**, Murphy St, offers panoramic views of **Four Mile Beach** and **Low Isles**. *Lady Douglas*, a paddlewheeler, offers cruises of **Dickson Inlet**.

NEARBY ATTRACTIONS: Many tours depart from Port Douglas, including 4WD safaris, horseriding and rainforest tours. Coach tours to **Mossman Gorge**, **Daintree NP**, Cape Tribulation and **Cooktown** are available. The Great Barrier Reef is the region's top tourist attraction. There are cruises to the **Outer Reef** and to the **Low Isles**.
TOURIST INFO: 23 Macrossan St, Ph: (07) 4099 5599

■ Proserpine   POP 4500
Map 263, A3

Lying close to the **Whitsunday coast**, Proserpine is the business centre for both **Airlie Beach** and **Shutehaven**. The town is located 264km SE of Townsville.
MAIN ATTRACTIONS: The **Historical Museum**, located on the Bruce Hwy next to the Whitsunday Information Centre, is housed in an old building, once part of a mill. The museum displays memorabilia highlighting the history of the district, including the sugar and mining industries and also has WWII displays.
NEARBY ATTRACTIONS: **Cedar Creek Falls** is a picturesque recreation area where, after rain, a creek drops over the falls into a large swimming hole lined with majestic Alexander palms. Nearby is **Peter Faust Dam**, 20km west of town. The dam was built to create **Lake Proserpine**, an area for watersports, including power boating, sailing, swimming, rowing, canoeing and waterskiing. The lake is also stocked with cod, barramundi, saratoga and sooty grunter. On weekends and holidays, boats can be hired and BBQ facilities are provided. **Conway NP**, 10km SE, offers views across the **Whitsunday Islands**.
TOURIST INFO: Bruce Hwy, Ph: (07) 4945 3711 or 1800 801 252

■ Rainbow Beach   POP 950
Map 255, C1

Situated near **Tin Can Bay**, 265km north of Brisbane, Rainbow Beach is a popular holiday town.
MAIN ATTRACTIONS: Activities, such as 4WDing on the beach, fishing or cruising down **Great Sandy Straits** on a houseboat are popular. A number of 4WD tours and safaris operate out of Rainbow Beach to the **Cooloola** area of **Great Sandy NP** and to the World-Heritage listed **Fraser Island**. The beautiful coloured sands in the cliff faces adjoining Rainbow Beach are one of Queensland's most popular tourist attractions.

Marina at Dickson Inlet, Port Douglas

Queensland

NEARBY ATTRACTIONS: The 400km² **Cooloola NP** has been listed in the Great Sandy NP region, which is World Heritage listed. A 30min walk through Cooloola NP leads to the **Carlo Sandblow**, 16ha of sand mass that, in windy conditions becomes a vast expanse of moving sand. Other signposted walking tracks lead through subtropical rainforests to coloured sand dunes and **Lake Poona** which is surrounded by a sandy beach. The freshwater lake is popular for swimming and camping is allowed in designated areas; permits can be obtained from the Rainbow Beach Dept of Environment Information Centre. The town is the southern gateway to Fraser Island. Vehicular ferries depart from **Inskip Point**, 13km north.

TOURIST INFO: 8 Rainbow Beach Rd, Ph: (07) 5486 3227

■ Richmond   POP 769
Map 281, G2
This small town lies 500km west of Townsville and 400km east of Mount Isa. It is situated beside Queensland's longest river, the **Flinders**. Richmond is the centre for a sheep and cattle district.
MAIN ATTRACTIONS: The main street is lined with bougainvilleas and has a fine display of federation-style buildings including hotels and churches. **Gidgee Wheel Arts and Crafts** is in Harris St. **Kronosaurus Korner** is part of the outstanding **Richmond Fossil Centre**. This museum exhibits world-class vertebrate fossils, all found in the area and which, 100 million years ago, was the site of an inland sea. There is also a cafe and public amenities in the centre.
NEARBY ATTRACTIONS: The countryside around Richmond is known for its **'moon rocks'**. These limestone rocks vary in size and can weigh tonnes. They carry the fossilised remains of fish, shells, and trees.

Kronosaurus Korner, Richmond Fossil Centre, Richmond

A display of moon rocks and a commemorative cairn can be seen at **Lions Park**, which is also a good place for picnicking. Moon rocks carrying fossilised remains are also displayed at the Richmond Fossil Centre. Fossils can be found at the designated fossicking site, 10km north. The **Cambridge Downs** ruins, about 30km north, are also worthwhile visiting.
TOURIST INFO: Kronosaurus Korner, 91 Goldring St, Ph: (07) 4741 3429

■ Rockhampton   POP 59 850
Map 267, B4
The city of Rockhampton is situated on the **Tropic of Capricorn**, 26km inland from the Pacific Ocean. The **Berserker Range** and the 607m-high **Mount Archer** surround the city. Rockhampton is the capital and cultural centre of **Central Queensland**, where the regional headquarters of most government departments and major commercial businesses are located.
MAIN ATTRACTIONS: Many of the town's original store buildings and churches are still standing. **Quay St**, which runs by the **Fitzroy River**, is Australia's longest National Trust-classified street with over 29

buildings. Brochures are available on the **Heritage Walk and Drive** tour around the city centre. With a near year-round tropical climate, Rockhampton is lush and green with many shady tree-lined streets and parks. Rockhampton's Heritage-listed **Botanic Gardens** were established in 1869 and are described as the best regional botanic gardens in Australia. The gardens cover an area of 39ha on the western slopes of the **Athelstane Range**. There is a fernery, orchid house, tropical fruit garden and a range of tropical plants. **Rockhampton Zoo** is located within the park and features chimpanzees, koalas, dingoes, kangaroos and wallabies and the rare bridled nail tail wallaby. A highlight is the koala feeding at 3pm. **Kershaw Native Gardens**, situated beside the Bruce Hwy were opened in 1988, as a Bicentenary Project. **The Spire**, in **Curtis Park**, on the southern outskirts of town marks the exact location of the Tropic of Capricorn. Enjoy a rodeo at the **Great Western Hotel**, the only hotel in Australia that hosts a rodeo. Anglers can fish for barramundi in the Fitzroy River that flows through the centre of Rockhampton.

(CONTINUED P.268)

THE CAPRICORN REGION

Straddling the **Tropic of Capricorn**, the Capricorn Region is an inviting combination of stunning beaches, rivers, subtropical reef islands and coastal rainforests. Inland, natural wonders include rugged volcanic outcrops, deep Outback gorges, estuarine mudflats, scenic headlands and wooded hills and vast cattle stations; the region is dotted with historic townships with elegant buildings that hint at the wealth of former times.

Rich in history, relics provide evidence that the region was once the site of a goldrush. The area flourished in the past and still does due to abundant natural resources—from gold, coal and copper mines to vast cattle and grain properties.

In the west of the region, fascinating sandstone gorges like **Blackdown Tableland** and the magnificent **Carnarvon Gorge** preserve unique ecosystems and are wonderful places to explore. Try your luck fossicking for rubies, sapphires and emeralds in the **Sapphire Gemfields**.

The region's interesting Aboriginal history is another drawcard for visitors: there are bora rings, museums and artefacts of the Darumbal people, whose territory once stretched from inland **Mount Morgan** to the **Keppel group of islands**. The Capricorn Region's diverse landscapes offer some of the world's best fishing, scuba diving, snorkelling, bushwalking, caving, camping and sightseeing experiences.

Rockhampton Court House

Dreamtime Cultural Centre

This large and diverse centre, 7km north of **Rockhampton**, is located on an important ancient site where Aboriginal people once gathered for tribal meetings. The museum aims to promote understanding of 40 000 years of Aboriginal history. Tours are available and include demonstrations of boomerang throwing and didgeridoo playing.

main attractions

◈ **Capricorn Caves**

A spectacular system of 16 limestone caves. A popular cavern is The Cathedral, which has extraordinary natural acoustics and old church pews to sit on.

◈ **Carnarvon Gorge NP**

A wonderful sandstone gorge with an impressive ancient Aboriginal art gallery.

◈ **Great Keppel Island**

This lively, sun-drenched island is accessible via ferry or cruises from Keppel Bay Marina and Rosslyn Bay Harbour near Yeppoon.

◈ **Rockhampton Heritage Village**

An active township museum where visitors can experience colourful history. There are working demonstrations on Sundays.

◈ **Koorana Crocodile Farm**

This farm is famed for breeding estuarine crocodiles. Don't miss the Big Croc Hatch Feb–April each year.

◈ **Mount Morgan**

Mount Morgan is an old gold-mining township with a local history and geology museum.

 Tourist information

Capricorn Tourism
Capricorn Information Centre
'The Spire', Gladstone Rd,
Rockhampton Qld 4700
Ph: (07) 4927 2055 or 1800 676 701

Moss Gardens in the Carnarvon Gorge section of Carnarvon NP

Queensland

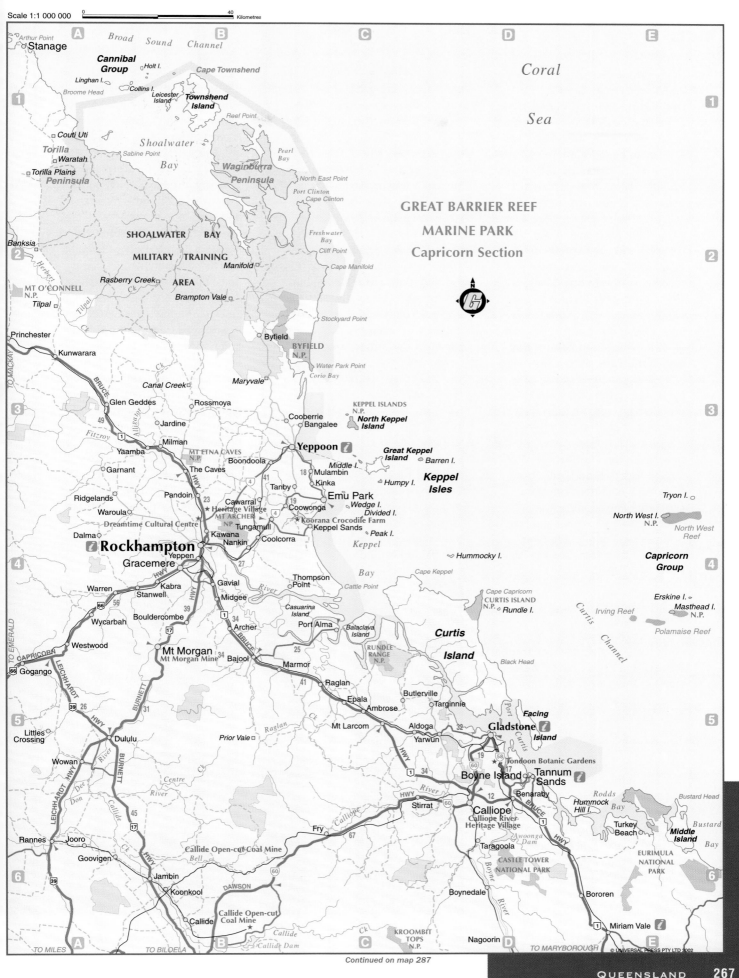

0   40
                Kilometres

A   B   C   D   E

Arthur Point
Stanage
**Cannibal
Group**   Holt I.
Linghan I.   Cape Townshend
Broome Head   Collins I.   Leicester
                            Island   **Townshend
                                      Island**

Broad   Sound   Channel

Coral

Sea

1   1

Couti Uti   Reef Point
Torilla   Shoalwater
Waratah   Sabine Point   Bay
Torilla Plains   **Waginburra
Peninsula**   **Peninsula**   Pearl
                                              Bay   North East Point
Banksia   Port Clinton
                                                Cape Clinton
MT O'CONNELL   **SHOALWATER   BAY**   Freshwater
N.P.   Bay
Tilpal   **MILITARY   TRAINING**   Cliff Point
Rasberry Creek   **AREA**   Manifold   Cape Manifold

2   Brampton Vale   2

GREAT BARRIER REEF

MARINE PARK

Capricorn Section

Princhester   Stockyard Point
Kunwarara   Water Park Point
            Canal Creek   Byfield   Corio Bay
Glen Geddes   Rossmoya   **BYFIELD
Jardine   N.P.**
Milman   Maryvale
Yaamba   The Caves   Boondoola   KEPPEL ISLANDS
Garnant   N.P.
Ridgelands   Pandoin   Tanby   18   **North Keppel
Waroula   Cawarral   Mulambin   Island**
              ★Heritage Village   Kinka   Middle I.   **Great Keppel   Barren I.
3   MT ARCHER   19   Coowonga   Island**   3
Dalma   NP   Tungamull   ★Koorana Crocodile Farm   Humpy I.   **Keppel**
            Kawana   Coolcorra   Keppel Sands   Wedge I.   **Isles**
Rockhampton   Nankin   Divided I.
Gracemere   Yeppen   Peak I.
                                   Emu Park
                                   Keppel
Warren   Kabra   Gavial   Bay   Cattle Point   Cape Keppel
Stanwell   Midgee   Thompson
Wycarbah   Bouldercombe   Point   Casuarina   Hummocky I.
                            Island   Cape Capricorn
Westwood   Archer   Port Alma   CURTIS ISLAND   Tryon I.
4   Balaclava   N.P.   Rundle I.   North West I.   4
Gogango   **Mt Morgan**   Bajool   Island   RUNDLE   **Curtis**   N.P.   North West
            Mt Morgan Mine   Marmor   RANGE   **Island**   Reef
                            Raglan   N.P.   **Capricorn
Littles   Epala   Black Head   Group**
Crossing   Dululu   Ambrose   Butlerville   Erskine I.
Wowan   Mt Larcom   Targinnie   Port   Irving Reef   Masthead I.
            Prior Vale   Aldoga   32   N.P.
                                      Yarwun   **Gladstone**   Curtis   Polamaise Reef
5   Rannes   Jooro   **Facing**   Channel   5
                                      19   Tondoon Botanic Gardens   **Island**
Goovigen   Benaraby   **Boyne Island**   **Tannum
            Callide Open-cut Coal Mine   Stirrat   12   Sands**   Rodds   Bustard Head
                                          Calliope   Hummock   Bay
                    Jambin   Fry   Calliope River   Hill I.
                    Koonkool   Heritage Village   Turkey   **Middle
6   Taragoola   Awoonga   Beach   Island**   6
            Callide Open-cut   Dam   Bustard
            Coal Mine   Boynedale   CASTLE TOWER   EURIMULA   Bay
            Callide   NATIONAL PARK   NATIONAL
                        Callide Dam   KROOMBIT   Boren   PARK
                                      TOPS   Bororen
                Callide   N.P.   Nagoorin   Miriam Vale
TO MILES   TO BILOELA   A   B   C   D   TO MARYBOROUGH   E   © UNIVERSAL PRESS PTY LTD 2002

Continued on map 287

NEARBY ATTRACTIONS: The Aboriginal and Torres Strait Islander **Dreamtime Cultural Centre** is 7km north of the city centre and located on an ancient traditional site, where Aboriginal people gathered for tribal meetings. **Rockhampton Heritage Village**, 11km north, is an active outdoor museum which includes slab huts, horse-drawn vehicles and a replica of an Egyptian water clock. On weekends there are working displays of steam and vintage machinery. **Capricorn Caves**, 23km north of town, are an award-winning system of 16 caves in a limestone mountain. The caves are open for inspection. **Mount Hay Gemstone Park**, 30min west of Rockhampton, offers fossicking for unique 118 million-year-old thundereggs and rainforest jasper; cutting and polishing is offered at the centre. Just 40km away are the beaches of the Capricorn Region. On the way to **Emu Park**, 30min from town is famous **Koorana Crocodile Farm**, offering an informative audiovisual and feeding of these fascinating 'dinosaurs'.
TOURIST INFO: The Spire, Gladstone Rd, Ph: (07) 4927 2055

■ **Roma**   POP 6500
Map 286, E3
Roma, 267km west of Dalby, is the commercial centre of the **Maranoa District** and capital of the **Western Downs**. Sheep and cattle form the basis of the area's economy.
MAIN ATTRACTIONS: **The Big Rig** is an authentic oil-drilling rig of the 1920s that stands at the eastern entrance to the town. Australia's oil and gas industry began in Roma in 1900, when the first natural gas strike was made at Hospital Hill. **Big Rig Research Centre**, next door, documents early oil exploration in the area. **Romavilla Winery**, Queensland's oldest winery, is located on the Northern Rd and visitors are welcome for cellar door

tastings and sales. An avenue of 94 bottle trees along Wyndham, Bungil and Station sts stands as a War Memorial. A tree was planted for every soldier from the area who died during WWI.
NEARBY ATTRACTIONS: **Meadowbank Station Museum**, located 15km west of town, is where visitors can experience life on a working property. The station's 2-storey hayloft houses a collection of artefacts, including 30 horse-drawn vehicles. **Carnarvon NP**, 244km NW, offers a variety of walks, camping, guided tours and accommodation. At **Carnarvon Gorge**, visitors can view significant Aboriginal cave paintings.
TOURIST INFO: Lower McDowall St, Ph: (07) 4622 4355

■ **St George**   POP 2580
Map 286, D5
Situated on the eastern bank of the **Balonne River**, 529km west of Brisbane, St George is in the heart of a cotton growing, grazing and farming district.
MAIN ATTRACTIONS: The town, known as the **'fishing capital of Queensland'**,

has many fishing spots, including the **Balonne River**, which contains Murray cod and yellowbelly. A huge mural in Scott St, painted by artist, Peter Caporn, depicts the history of transport in the area. Scenes include 'Racing the Storms' and 'Crossing the Balonne'. **Riversands Vineyard** is located in Whytes Rd and is open to the public.
NEARBY ATTRACTIONS: **Rosehill Aviaries** houses a large variety of birds as well as native animals. As well it holds the country's largest private collection of Australian parrots. It is located 64km west of St George. **Beardmore Dam** on the Balonne River, 21km north, provides excellent fishing, and picnicking in the surrounding parkland is popular. Koalas in their natural environment can be observed in the town of **Bollon**, 112km west. A large koala population can be seen in the trees along **Wallum Creek**. **Culgoa Floodplain NP** is 227km SW. The park offers 4WD access only and camping is permitted, however, there are no facilities.
TOURIST INFO: St George's Tce, Ph: (07) 4625 4996

School of Arts Hotel (1918) in Roma's CBD

Queensland

Sarina POP 3460

Map 283, F3

This attractive town is located in the foothills of the **Connors Range**, 36km south of Mackay.

MAIN ATTRACTIONS: The **Rose Gardens**, located in Broad St, form part of the **Sarina Tourist Art and Craft Centre** complex which is housed in the old Court House in Railway Sq. The centre offers arts and crafts and local and regional information. The **Field of Dreams** is a historical museum in Broad St. Waterways in the area yield barramundi, flathead, whiting, bream, grunter, salmon and cod. Prawns and crabs are plentiful in season.

NEARBY ATTRACTIONS: There are many unspoilt beaches within close proximity to Sarina, including **Sarina Beach**, 16km NE, fringed by high sand dunes; there is a lifesaving club, 2 boat ramps and sheltered bay that is ideal for fishing. Other beaches include **Armstrong, Grasstree, Salonika** and **Half Tide. Cape Palmerston NP** is located 78km SE, but offers 4WD access only. **Bartons Lookout**, 14km SW in the **Sarina Range**, offers panoramic views of the coastline and countryside.

TOURIST INFO: Railway Sq,
Ph: (07) 4956 2251

Stanthorpe POP 5000

Map 235, A3

This town is the commercial centre for the **Granite Belt**, 221km SW of Brisbane, close to the New South Wales border. Fruit growing is the main commercial enterprise and the town is well-known for its apples. Other produce includes stone and citrus fruits. Winemaking is an established and growing industry.

MAIN ATTRACTIONS: Browse the local art and craft markets or explore the historical sandstone buildings in town. **Stanthorpe Museum**, in High St, houses relics of Australian history. The **Art Gallery**, in Weroona Park, has an interesting collection

Granite boulders in Girraween NP, near Stanthorpe

and hosts travelling and community exhibitions. Accommodation in Stanthorpe suits most budgets.

NEARBY ATTRACTIONS: There are 4 national parks in the region. **Girraween NP**, 32km south, has huge granite outcrops and hills great for rockclimbing and which look stunning in springtime carpeted with wildflowers. **Sundown NP**, 79km SW, is a wilderness area with camping allowed along the **Severn River**. There is also a picnic area here. Australia's largest exposed granite rock is the centrepiece of **Bald Rock NP**. **Boonoo Bonoo NP**, 60km SE over the New South Wales border, features a 210m waterfall that plummets into a rainforest gorge. There are more than 30 **wineries** in the region, all offering tastings and cellar door sales.

TOURIST INFO: Visitor Information Centre, 26 Leslie Pde, Ph: (07) 4681 2057 or 1800 060 877

Tamborine Mountain

POP 4200

Map 247, A3

Tamborine Mountain is 30km inland from Queensland's **Gold Coast**. A volcanic plateau, it is 8km in length, 5km wide and is 560m above sea level. Tamborine Mountain consists of 3 villages. To the north lies **Eagle**

Heights and **North Tamborine** while the village of **Mount Tamborine** is south.

MAIN ATTRACTIONS: Each village offers a variety of craft and antique shops, galleries, restaurants and tearooms. Tamborine Mountain is also famous for its gardens, subtropical rainforests, waterfalls and magnificent scenic views.

NEARBY ATTRACTIONS: Nine national parks are easily accessible from Tamborine Mountain which protect a variety of native animals and birds, including lyrebirds, scrub turkeys, koalas and platypus. Flora within the parks includes fig trees, staghorns and orchids. All parks have picnic facilities. **Tamborine NP** can be accessed from many different points on the mountain and provides a range of facilities, lookouts and walking tracks.

TOURIST INFO: Doughty Park,
Nth Tamborine, Ph: (07) 5545 3200

Tin Can Bay POP 2000

Map 255, C1

This small fishing town, 229km north of Brisbane, near **Rainbow Beach**, is a quiet holiday spot.

MAIN ATTRACTIONS: The waters of Tin Can Bay are the town's main attraction and yachting, canoeing or hiring a houseboat are ideal ways of

(CONTINUED P.272)

THE DARLING DOWNS

Located 100km inland from Brisbane, the verdant plains of the **Darling Downs** are dotted with farmhouses, pastures, crops and grazing lands. The regions fertile black soil is a by-product of ancient volcanic activity, as are the mountain peaks of the **Great Dividing Range**, which form the eastern boundary of this region.

Sprawling from **Crows Nest** in the north to **Dalby** in the west, the Darling Downs offer visitors many diversions. Among the farmlands and cotton country there are also wineries, national parks, quaint villages, bustling townships, grand colonial architecture and remnants of the legends created by Arthur Hoey Davis alias **Steele Rudd**. Dad and Dave are the famous country characters created by Rudd. The Darling Downs are often associated with the grand old pastoralists of south-east Queensland. The region is ideal for combining outdoor activities—bushwalking, camping, cycling, horseriding and golf—with more refined and sedate pursuits such as shopping for antiques, farm stays, historical tours, enjoying Devonshire teas and exploring quaint rural villages.

Queensland's largest, and Australia's second largest, inland city, **Toowoomba** is the capital of the Darling Downs. Known as the 'Garden City of Queensland', Toowoomba has many historic buildings and excellent gardens, which are showcased in late September during the world-famous **Carnival of Flowers**.

St Patrick's Cathedral (1889), Toowoomba

Road Rules

The famous transport company **Cobb & Co** had rules for passengers displayed on notices in its carriages. These included 'no discussion of bushrangers, accidents, politics or religion, and no snoring or removal of shoes'.

 Tourist information

Toowoomba Visitor Information Centre
86 James St
Toowoomba
Qld 4350
Freecall: 1800 331 155

main attractions

◈ **Bunya Mountains NP**

This popular mountain retreat features rainforest walks and towering bunya pines.

◈ **Cobb & Co Museum, Toowoomba**

This museum houses Australia's finest collection of horse-drawn carriages, as well as historical displays of Toowoomba.

◈ **Crows Nest NP**

Not far inside the park's entrance lies the renowned Valley of Diamonds, named for the shimmering effect of sunlight streaming onto the rock-face of the gorge.

◈ **Empire Theatre, Toowoomba**

This heritage-listed theatre is the largest regional performance theatre in Australia.

◈ **Highfields to Crows Nest drive**

A picturesque drive from the Pioneer Village takes in an array of galleries, antique shops and museums.

◈ **Jondaryan Woolshed**

This sheep station features damper-making, sheepdog and blacksmithing demonstrations.

◈ **Rudd's Pub, Nobby**

Memorabilia line the walls of this pub, the birthplace of Arthur Hoey Davis, known as Steele Rudd—the creator of the fabled 'Dad 'n' Dave' tales.

◈ **Wineries**

Rimfire, Preston Peak and Governor's Choice are 3 of the many wineries in the region.

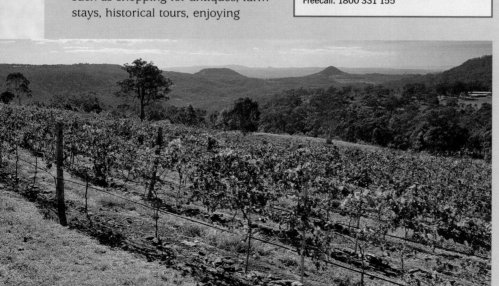
Preston Peak vineyard, Darling Downs

Queensland

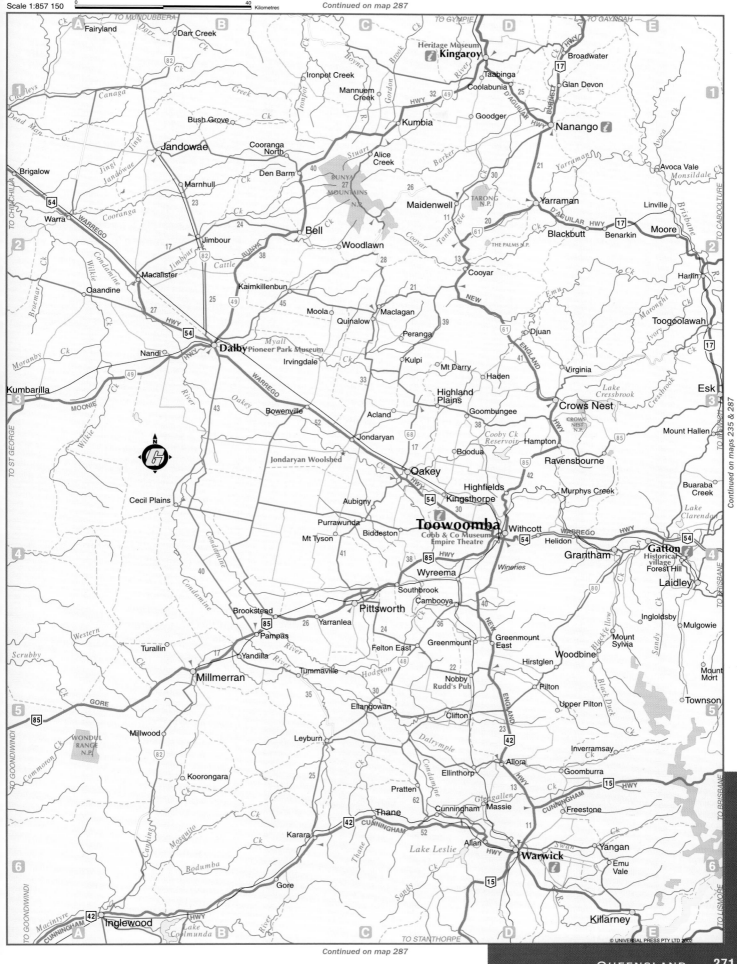

exploring the area. Fishing, crabbing and prawning are rewarding activities. A pod of uncommon Indo-Pacific humpback dolphins (*Sina chinensis*) come into the bay and can be seen from the **Norman Point** boat ramp.

NEARBY ATTRACTIONS: The coloured sands and beaches of the **Cooloola** section of **Great Sandy NP** are accessible via 4WD from Rainbow Beach. Ferries to **Fraser Island** leave from **Inskip Point**, 53km NE. There is also camping access along the point. **Carlo Point**, named by Capt Cook after his deckhand, Carlo, is 3km east, and offers fishing and swimming; yachts and houseboats are available for hire.

TOURIST INFO: 4 Gympie Rd,
Ph: (07) 5486 4333

■ Toowoomba   POP 87 644
Map 271, D4

Toowoomba, the capital of the **Darling Downs** region, is 128km west of Brisbane. Also known as the 'Garden City of Queensland', Toowoomba has 150 attractive parks and gardens. The best private gardens are open to the public during the city's famous **Carnival of Flowers**, a spring festival held in September. Accommodation is diverse and there are many interesting and historic B&Bs.

MAIN ATTRACTIONS: There are many art, craft and antique galleries to browse through. Garden shops and nurseries are also plentiful. **Cobb & Co Museum** offers visitors an introduction to the history of the Darling Downs. **Toowoomba Regional Art Gallery**, located in Ruthven St, exhibits paintings, fine art prints, and works by contemporary local artists. There are many **heritage walks** to take around the town and brochures are available from the information centre. The **Waterbird Habitat**, in MacKenzie St, provides 7.6ha of lakes and grassland for many bird species. This is a popular area for walks and picnics. Other parks worth visiting include **Queens Park Gardens**, located in Lindsay St and **Japanese Gardens** at the **University of Southern Queensland**. **Picnic Point Park** offers magnificent views of the **Lockyer Valley**.

NEARBY ATTRACTIONS: **Dad and Dave's Historic Rudds Pub** is located in **Nobby**, near Toowoomba. The theme behind the pub is based on Steele Rudd's famous collection of stories. Visitors can dine in the heritage lounge, view the collection of historical photographs or listen to the resident storyteller. There are many scenic drives around the region varying in length from 48km to 255km. Brochures are available from the information centre.

TOURIST INFO: 86 James St
or 476 Ruthven St, Ph: 1800 331 155

■ Townsville   POP 78 750
Map 279, K6

Townsville is located in the dry tropics, 1384km north of Brisbane around **Ross River**. Townsville is the region's centre for government and rural and mining industries; it is the business and commerce capital of the north.

MAIN ATTRACTIONS: The **Museum of Tropical Queensland**, in Flinders St East, is home to the largest display of tropical dinosaur fossils in Australia. The museum also features the *Pandora* **Shipwreck exhibition**. In the same street is **Reef HQ**, a living reef in a huge tank. It's the largest living coral reef on land. The **Imax Dome Theatre**, also in this building, offers an 18m-dome screen. Visitors can try their luck at **Jupiters Townsville Hotel and Casino**, located in Sir Leslie Thiess Dr. Boat cruises to the **Great Barrier Reef** and launches to **Magnetic, Orpheus, Dunk, Hinchinbrook** and **Bedarra islands** leave from Townsville's ferry terminal. The **Botanic Gardens** are located in Gregory St. The **Town Common and Environmental Park** is a birdwatchers' paradise. The **Palmetum**, located near James Cook University campus in Douglas, has a wide variety of palms from around the world. **The Strand** has a large rockpool and 2.5km landscaped promenade that is well suited to outdoor lifestyle. Children love the **Water Park**, near the **Tobruk Memorial Pool**, which is also on the Strand. Spectacular views of Townsville, Magnetic Island and the surrounding area are available from **Castle Hill**, the landmark granite outcrop in the centre of town; and also from **Mount Stuart**, around 10km to the SW.

Breakwater Marina and Castle Hill, Townsville

Queensland

Cunningham's Gap, Main Range NP, north-east of Warwick

NEARBY ATTRACTIONS: Many tours are possible from Townsville, including tours of the rainforest and Outback, white-water rafting, diving and sailing. The **Australian Institute of Marine Science** is located 30km east at **Cape Ferguson** and guided tours can be booked. **Billabong Sanctuary**, on the Bruce Hwy, has crocodile shows and visitors can also see the koalas being fed. **Magnetic Island**, in **Cleveland Bay**, can be seen from any point along the Townsville waterfront and is 20min from the city by fast cat ferry. The island has 23 bays and beaches, with well over half set aside as national park. There are many well-worn walking tracks and other activities offered, including fishing, snorkelling, golf and horseriding.
TOURIST INFO: Flinders Mall,
Ph: (07) 4721 3660

Tully   POP 2650

Map 279, J4
Tully is located at the base of **Mount Tyson**, on **Banyan Creek**, a tributary of the **Tully River**. The town is notable for having one of the

highest annual rainfalls in Australia. Tully's economic mainstays include sugar, bananas, tropical fruit, cattle, aquaculture and tourism.
MAIN ATTRACTIONS: Located in the heart of town, **Tully Sugar Mill** is open during the crushing season, June–mid-Nov. Daily tours are available and can be booked through the information centre. Tully is the base for one of the best white-water rafting adventures in Australia.
NEARBY ATTRACTIONS: An area of natural beauty, **Mission Beach** is located along the **Great Green Way**, 25km NE of Tully or a 2hr drive from Cairns and Townsville. Stretching along 14km of coastline, fringed by tropical rainforest and overlooking nearby **Dunk** and **Bedarra islands**, the Mission Beach area is worthwhile exploring. The rainforests of the **Wet Tropics World Heritage Area** are nearby and walking track maps are available from the Wet Tropics Visitor Centre. To explore the outer area of the **Great Barrier Reef**, boats leave daily from nearby **Clump Point Jetty**. White-water rafting, canoeing

and kayaking adventures are popular on the Tully River, as is swimming in the river's upper reaches. **Tully Heads**, 22km SE, is a good spot for fishing.
TOURIST INFO: Bruce Hwy,
Ph: (07) 4068 2288

Warwick   POP 11 000

Map 271, D6
Referred to as the **'Rose and Rodeo City'**, Warwick is situated near the **Great Dividing Range**, 162km SW of Brisbane, in the **Darling Downs** region of south-east Queensland. Established in 1849, the town is now the centre for the surrounding region famous for its horse and cattle studs and fine wool.
MAIN ATTRACTIONS: The floral emblem of Warwick is a red rose and there are many roses planted around the town, including a display in **Leslie Park**. **Warwick Regional Art Gallery** is located in Albion St. **Pringle Cottage**, built in the 19th century, is open to the public and displays old photographs, vehicles and machinery.
NEARBY ATTRACTIONS: Fossicking is a popular activity on the southern Downs and visitors can try gold-panning at **Thanes Creek**, 40km west. A fossicking license can be obtained from the Council. **Main Range NP** is located north-east of Warwick and is popular with hikers as there are rainforest slopes, open forest and high peaks. The main recreation area is at **Cunningham's Gap**, where there are picnic areas, a campground and graded walking tracks. **Leslie Dam**, 15km west, offers watersports, swimming, boating and fishing. There are also giant granite sculptures to see, and picnic and BBQ facilities are available. There are 4 signposted **tourist drives**, which leads visitors to the smaller country towns in the Warwick Shire.
TOURIST INFO: 49 Albion St,
Ph: (07) 4661 3401

Winton   POP 1285

Map 281, G4

Located in the 'red heart of Queensland', around 1400km NW of Brisbane, Winton is one of Australia's best-known Outback towns. It is also known as the home of bush poetry, hosting the annual **Bronze Swagman Award**—one of the country's most prestigious literary awards.

MAIN ATTRACTIONS: The **Ted Elliott Mineral and Gemstone and Mining Display** is one of Australia's best geological displays. It is located in the Corfield and Fitzmaurice building in Elderslie St. The display features thousands of specimens and works of art. The **Dinosaur Diorama** is made up of 12 life-size dinosaurs. Also located in the centre is **Combo Crafts**, where you can purchase original and handcrafted items. **The Waltzing Matilda Centre**, in Elderslie St, is dedicated to the song Banjo Paterson wrote on Dagworth Station near Winton in 1895. The centre has interactive and interpretive displays. **The Waltzing Matilda Bush Poetry Festival** is held annually. The historic **Royal Theatre**, located in Elderslie St, is an open-air picture theatre and museum, and one of the oldest of its kind still operating in Australia. Around town, there are sites commemorating **Qantas**, the country's flagship airline, which was formed in the town in 1920.

NEARBY ATTRACTIONS: **Lark Quarry CP** protects fossilised evidence of a dinosaur stampede some 93 million years ago. The park is on the eroded edge of the **Tully Range**, 110km SW. More than 5 000 dinosaur footprints, captured in rock, can be seen today. **Opalton**, 115km south, is an historic town where boulder opals are mined in nearby gemfields; there is also a public fossicking area. **Bladensburg NP** is 15km south and visitors can take a self-drive tour along the **Route of the River Gum**; there are campgrounds at the **Bough Shed Hole**.

TOURIST INFO: Waltzing Matilda Centre, Elderslie St, Ph: (07) 4657 1466

Wondai   POP 1250

Map 287, H3

This town, 250km NW of Brisbane, is almost the geographical centre of the **South Burnett** region. Wondai is surrounded by a rich agricultural region and produces grains, peanuts, cattle, dairying and mining.

MAIN ATTRACTIONS: **Dingo Creek Bicentennial Park**, located beside Bunya Hwy, is a pleasant place for a BBQ or picnic; there are also toilets and a playground. **Wondai Museum**, located behind the library in Mackenzie St, houses a collection of memorabilia from earlier times, including farm machinery, a fire engine, manual telephone exchange and early photographs.

NEARBY ATTRACTIONS: The town of **Proston**, 42km west, is home to **Boondooma Dam**. This dam provides the district's water supply and is a popular watersports area. The introduction of bass, golden perch and silver perch has made the dam attractive to anglers. Caravan, camping, picnic sites, BBQs and toilets are located in the area. Also located at Proston is **Sidcup Castle**. Built by Harold Douglas, it is a replica of his childhood home in England. There are 17 rooms in the castle filled with memorabilia.

TOURIST INFO: Council Chambers, cnr Scott and Mackenzie sts, Ph: (07) 4168 5155

Yandina   POP 987

Map 255, C4

Yandina is located 9km north of **Nambour** in the **Sunshine Coast** hinterland. The town is known as the **'Ginger Capital of the World'**.

MAIN ATTRACTIONS: Visitors are invited to see ginger being processed at the largest **Ginger Factory** in the world, located along Pioneer Rd. The historic **Queensland Cane Train** travels through the landscaped gardens. In January, the Ginger Factory hosts the **Ginger Flower Festival**. The **Nutworks Macadamia Factory and Tourist Complex**, opposite the Ginger Factory, gives demonstrations of the processing of macadamia nuts and offers tastings.

NEARBY ATTRACTIONS: The town of **Eumundi**, 10km north, is famous for its Saturday morning markets. The markets sell locally-grown fruit and vegetables, as well as arts and crafts. Fresh produce is also available on Wednesdays.

TOURIST INFO: Sunshine Coast Information, cnr Aerodrome Rd and Sixth Ave, Maroochydore, Ph: (07) 5479 1566

Rocky outcrop at sunset, near Winton

Queensland

Yeppoon   POP 12 000
Map 267, C3

Once a small centre for pineapple growers and sugarcane farmers, Yeppoon has developed into a popular resort town on the **Capricorn Coast**. The town is located 40km from Rockhampton and is within easy reach of **Great Keppel Island** and the **Great Barrier Reef**. Yeppoon itself is surrounded by attractive beaches and has a year-round warm climate and relaxed lifestyle.

NEARBY ATTRACTIONS: Cooberrie Park is a native flora and fauna sanctuary 15km north of town. Visitors can walk among the animals, handfeed the kangaroos and wallabies and hold a koala. **Byfield NP**, 32km north of Yeppoon, has mountains, rainforests, creeks and streams and is home to the unique Byfield ferns. Attractions in the park include **Ferns Hideaway Wilderness Restaurant**, **Waterpark Cabins**, **Nob Creek Pottery**, **Wompoo Gallery** and **Byfield Pottery**. Fascinating **Koorana Crocodile Farm** is located 38km SW. **Rydges Capricorn Resort**, 6km north, is surrounded by **The Wetlands**. There is a Wetlands Tour available and visitors may be able to spot over 150 species of birds. The **Keppel Group of islands** is one of the region's main features. Located 13km off-shore, daytrips to Great Keppel Island are offered. Cruise boats to the island and fishing charters leave from **Keppel Bay Marina** and **Rosslyn Bay Harbour**. The island has a resort, and activities on offer include snorkelling and scuba diving from the beaches. On the mainland at **Wreck Point**, south of **Cooee Bay**, a lookout offers panoramic views over the group of islands. At **Emu Park**, 19km south, is an interesting memorial to Capt Cook known as *The Singing Ship*, because when the wind blows the hidden organ pipes within the sculpture vibrate and seem to 'sing'.

TOURIST INFO: Ross Creek Roundabout, Yeppoon-Emu Park Rd, Ph: (07) 4939 4888

Yungaburra   POP 1137
Map 239, B5

The picturesque town of Yungaburra is 15km east of Atherton, high on the edge of the **Atherton Tableland**. The town is famous for its National Trust-classified **Historic Precinct** and award-winning restaurants.

MAIN ATTRACTIONS: The best way to explore the town is by following the route in the **Heritage Walk** leaflet prepared by the National Trust of Queensland and available from the information centre. A highlight of the Heritage Walk is the **Lake Eacham Hotel**, which has a display of historic photographs depicting the area's early sawmilling days. There are many art and craft galleries to browse through and the town also offers good restaurants. At **Peterson Creek**, on the Gillies Hwy, there is a platypus-viewing platform. Best times to visit are at sunrise and sunset.

NEARBY ATTRACTIONS: In **Crater Lakes NP** there are 2 volcanic crater lakes. **Lake Barrine**, 10km NE, is the largest of the crater lakes with clear blue waters 65m deep and fringed with lush rainforest. There is a 5.14km-circuit track beginning at the lake's edge. Daily flora and fauna cruises on the lake are available. **Lake Eacham**, 5km east, has a 2.8km track encircling the lake also surrounded by differing pockets of rainforests—the complexity of rainforest communities is primarily determined by soil fertility and rainfall. Swimming is popular and there are BBQ and picnic facilities. The famous and much photographed **Curtain Fig Tree** is located 2.5km SW of town in a small forestry reserve. **Lake Tinaroo**, 3km north, offers boating, fishing, waterskiing, sailing and swimming. On the eastern shores of Lake Tinaroo, there are **The Chimneys, Mobo Creek Crater** and **Cathedral Fig Tree**. **Malanda**, 20km south of Yungaburra, has its 19th-century **Majestic Theatre**. The **Malanda Falls CP** and **Scenic Reserve** offers a variety of sign-posted rainforest walks.

TOURIST INFO: Nick's Swiss-Italian Restaurant, Gillies Hwy, Ph: (07) 4095 3330

Cathedral Fig Tree near Yungaburra, Atherton Tableland

KEY MAP

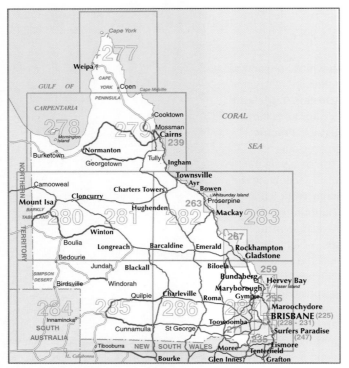

DISTANCE CHART

Approximate Distance	Bourke NSW	Bowen	Brisbane	Bundaberg	Cairns	Charleville	Charters Towers	Emerald	Gladstone	Longreach	Mackay	Maryborough	Moree NSW	Mt Isa	Rockhampton	Roma	Toowoomba	Townsville	Tweed Heads NSW	Warwick
Bourke NSW		1533	924	1102	1835	454	1353	966	1156	968	1346	1016	445	1610	1139	613	791	1488	1013	766
Bowen	1533		1181	812	542	1079	277	567	627	848	187	922	1292	1033	520	968	1160	195	1281	1244
Brisbane	924	1181		369	1701	754	1360	887	540	1186	980	259	479	1828	647	486	125	1376	100	158
Bundaberg	1102	812	369		1346	832	1025	560	185	973	617	110	714	1615	292	564	409	1007	469	493
Cairns	1835	542	1701	1346		1381	482	955	1169	1053	729	1442	1790	1117	1062	1356	1702	347	1801	1786
Charleville	454	1079	754	832	1381		899	512	811	514	892	762	629	1156	780	268	629	1034	832	713
Charters Towers	1353	277	1360	1025	482	899		473	848	571	464	1121	1308	756	741	874	1235	135	1438	1319
Emerald	966	567	887	560	955	512	473		375	413	380	648	835	1055	268	401	762	608	965	846
Gladstone	1156	627	540	185	1169	811	848	375		788	440	281	789	1430	107	543	544	822	640	628
Longreach	968	848	1186	973	1053	514	571	413	788		793	1061	1143	642	681	700	1061	706	1264	1145
Mackay	1346	187	980	617	729	892	464	380	440	793		713	1105	1220	333	781	973	382	1080	1057
Maryborough	1016	922	259	110	1442	762	1121	648	281	1061	713		628	1703	380	494	323	1117	359	407
Moree NSW	445	1292	479	714	1790	629	1308	835	789	1143	1105	628		1785	772	434	346	1443	568	321
Mt Isa	1610	1033	1828	1615	1117	1156	756	1055	1430	642	1220	1703	1785		1323	1342	1703	891	1906	1787
Rockhampton	1139	520	647	292	1062	780	741	268	107	681	333	380	772	1323		526	640	715	739	724
Roma	613	968	486	564	1356	268	874	401	543	700	781	494	434	1342	526		361	1009	564	445
Toowoomba	791	1160	125	409	1702	629	1235	762	544	1061	973	323	346	1703	640	361		1355	203	84
Townsville	1488	195	1376	1007	347	1034	135	608	822	706	382	1117	1443	891	715	1009	1355		1476	1454
Tweed Heads NSW	1013	1281	100	469	1801	832	1438	965	640	1264	1080	359	568	1906	739	564	203	1476		245
Warwick	766	1244	158	493	1786	713	1319	846	628	1145	1057	407	321	1787	724	445	84	1454	245	

All distances in this chart have been measured over highways and major roads, not necessarily by the shortest route.

Queensland

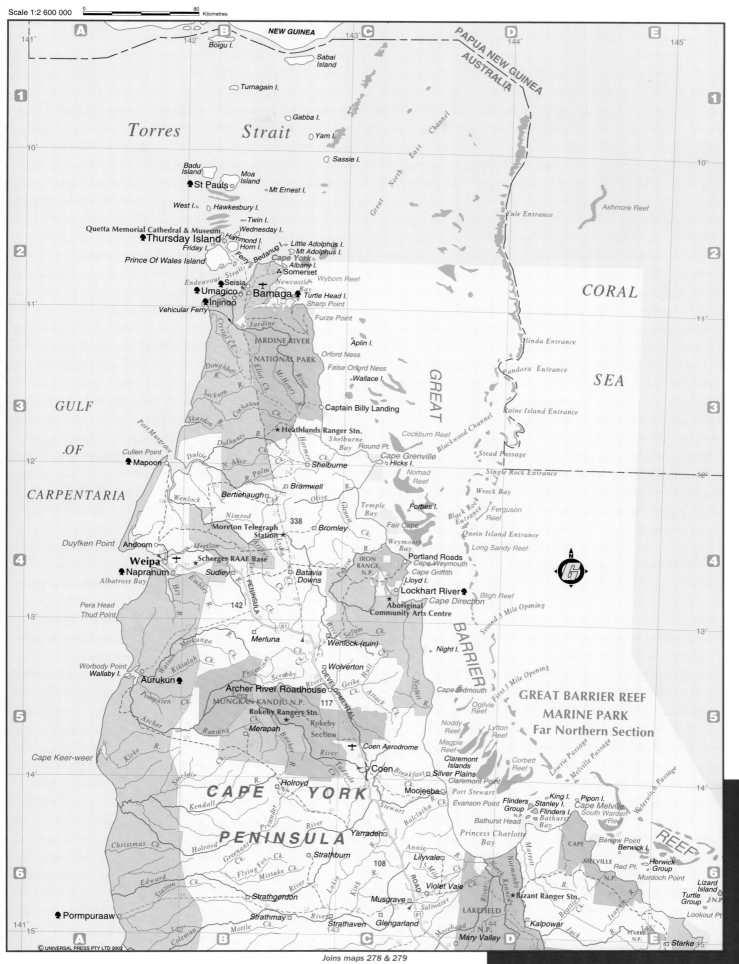

Scale 1:2 600 000

0   80
Kilometres

NEW GUINEA

Torres   Strait

Boigu I.

Sabai Island

Turnagain I.

Gabba I.

Yam I.

Sassie I.

Badu Island

Moa Island

St Pauls

Mt Ernest I.

West I.

Hawkesbury I.

Twin I.

Wednesday I.

Quetta Memorial Cathedral & Museum

Friday I.

Hammond I.

Horn I.

Thursday Island

Little Adolphus I.

Mt Adolphus I.

Prince Of Wales Island

Ferry Bedanug

Cape York

Albany I.

Somerset

Newcastle Bay

Wyborn Reef

Endeavour Strait

Seisia

Umagico

Bamaga

Turtle Head I.

Injinoo

Sharp Point

Vehicular Ferry

Furze Point

Jardine

Aplin I.

Orford Ness

JARDINE RIVER

False Orford Ness

NATIONAL PARK

Wallace I.

Captain Billy Landing

Heathlands Ranger Stn.

Shelburne Bay

Round Pt.

Cape Grenville

Hicks I.

Mapoon

Cullen Point

Shelburne

Nomad Reef

Wreck Bay

Bramwell

Forbes I.

Bertiehaugh

Temple Bay

Moreton Telegraph Station

338

Bromley

Fair Cape

Weymouth Bay

Duyfken Point

Andoom

Scherger RAAF Base

IRON RANGE N.P.

Portland Roads

Cape Weymouth

Weipa

Sudley

Batavia Downs

Cape Griffith

Lloyd I.

Napranum

Albatross Bay

Lockhart River

Cape Direction

Pera Head

142

Aboriginal Community Arts Centre

Thud Point

Merluna

Wenlock (ruin)

Night I.

Worbody Point

Wallaby I.

Aurukun

Wolverton

Archer River Roadhouse

MUNGKAN KANDJU N.P.

117

Cape Sidmouth

Rokeby Rangers Stn.

Rokeby Section

Ogilvie Reef

Noddy Reef

Lytton Reef

GREAT BARRIER REEF MARINE PARK Far Northern Section

Merapah

Coen Aerodrome

Magpie Reef

Claremont Islands

Corbett Reef

Cape Keer-weer

Coen

Breakfast

Silver Plains

Claremont Point

Holroyd

Moojeeba

Port Stewart

King I.

Pipon I.

Evanson Point

Stanley I.

Cape Melville

CAPE YORK

Flinders Group

Flinders I.

South Warden Reef

Strathburn

Bathurst Head

Bathurst Bay

CAPE MELVILLE

PENINSULA

Yarraden

108

Princess Charlotte Bay

Barrow Point

Berwick I.

Horwick Group

Lilyvale

Red Pt.

Murdoch Point

Strathgordon

Violet Vale

Lizard Island

Turtle Group

Pormpuraaw

Musgrave

LAKEFIELD N.P.

Bizant Ranger Stn.

Lookout Pt.

Strathmay

Strathaven

Glengarland

Mary Valley

Kalpowar

Starke N.P.

Starke

GULF OF CARPENTARIA

CORAL SEA

GREAT BARRIER REEF

PAPUA NEW GUINEA / AUSTRALIA

© UNIVERSAL PRESS PTY LTD 2002

Joins maps 278 & 279

QUEENSLAND   **277**

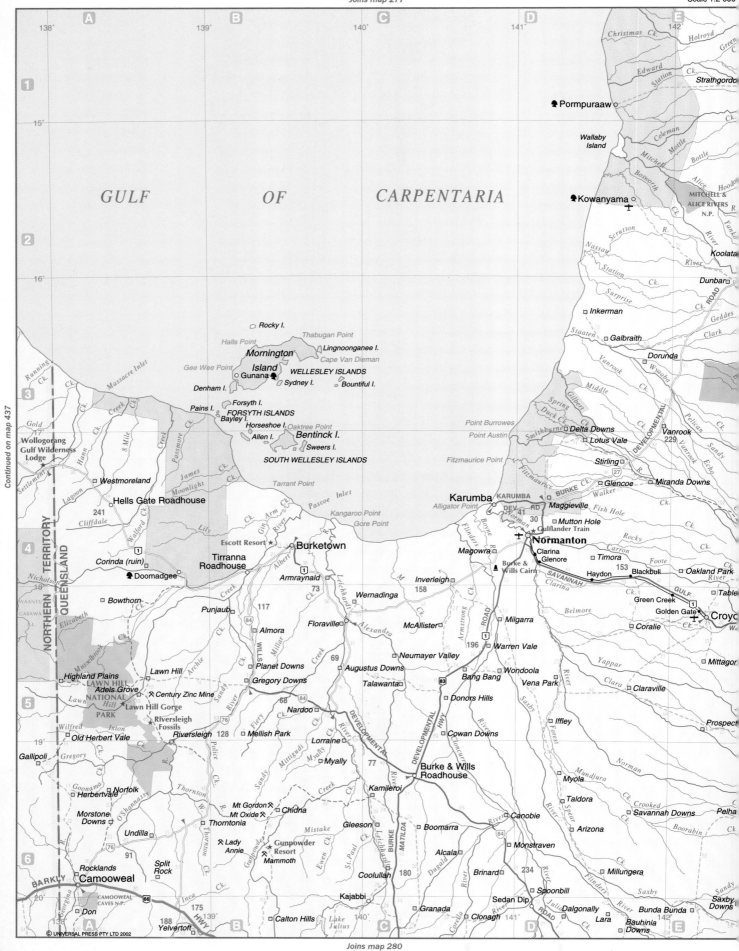

GULF OF CARPENTARIA

Gregory's Australia

Queensland

© UNIVERSAL PRESS PTY LTD 2002

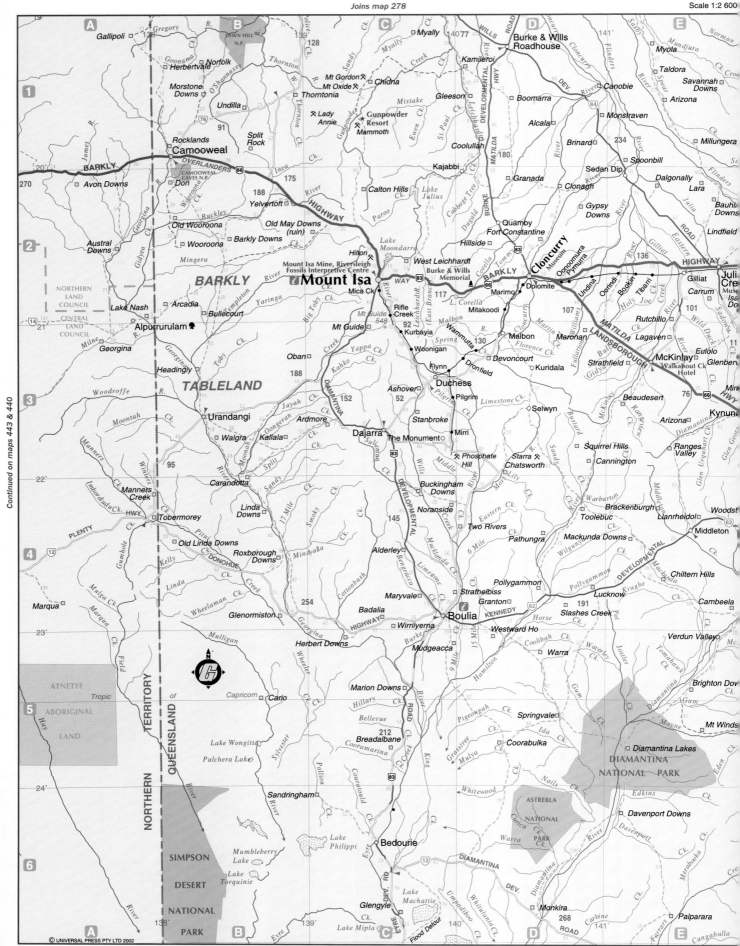

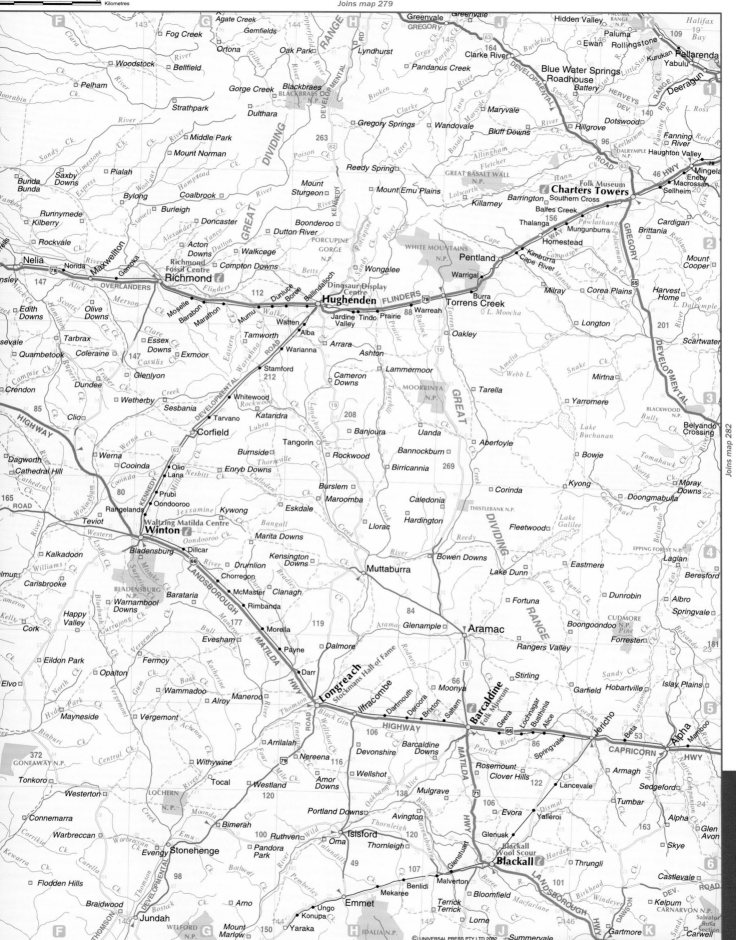

80 Kilometres

F | G | H | J | K

Greenvale Greenvale
Halifax
Hidden Valley PALUMA 19° Bay
GREGORY RANGE N.P.
Agate Creek
Gemfields
Ewan Paluma Rollingstone
Fog Creek
Ortona Oak Park
Lyndhurst
Clarke River
Blue Water Springs Roadhouse Kurukan Yabulu Pallarenda
109
Woodstock
Bellfield
Pandanus Creek
Battery Deeragun
1
Pelham
Gorge Creek
Blackbraes
BLACKBRAES N.P.
Maryvale HERVEYS RANGE DEV. 140
Strathpark
Dulthara
Gregory Springs
Wandovale Bluff Downs
Hillgrove 96
Dotswood
DALRYMPLE 46 HWY Haughton Valley
Fanning River
Macrossan Mingela Eneby
78
Middle Park
Mount Norman
263
Reedy Spring
GREAT BASALT WALL N.P.
Sellheim 20
Boorabin Saxby Downs Pialah
Mount Sturgeon
Mount Emu Plains
Folk Museum
Charters Towers
Southern Cross Cardigan 2
Bunda Bunda
Bylong Coalbrook
Doncaster
Boonderoo
Dutton River
Killarney Barrington
Balfes Creek
Thalanga 156 Mungunburra
Brittania
Mount Cooper
Runnymede Kilberry
Burleigh
WHITE MOUNTAINS N.P.
Pentland Homestead Kimburra Cape River
Milray
Corea Plains 55 Harvest Home
Rockvale Nelia Nonda
Richmond Fossil Centre
Compton Downs
Acton Downs
Walkcege
Wongalee
Warrigal
Burra Torrens Creek
Longton
Scartwater 201 3
147 Richmond
Flinders 112 FLINDERS 78 88 Warreah
Oakley
Edith Downs Olive Downs
Moselle Barabon Marathon Murmu Dunluce Boree Ballindalloch
Dinosaur Display Centre
Hughenden Jardine Valley Tindo Prairie
Bullock
L. Moocha
Essex Downs Coleraine Exmoor 147
Tamworth
Watten Alba Warianna
Arrara
Ashton
Lammermoor
Tarella
Mirtna Yarromere BLACKWOOD N.P.
Crendon Quambetook Glenlyon Wetherby Dundee Clio
Stamford 212
Cameron Downs
MOORRINYA N.P.
GREAT
Belyando Crossing
HIGHWAY 85 Sesbania Tarvano
Whitewood Rockwood Katandra
208 Banjoura
Uanda
Aberfoyle
Lake Buchanan Bowie
Tomahawk Moray Downs Doongmabulla 22
Corfield
Werna Cooinda
Lubra Tangorin
Rockwood Bannockburn
Birricannia 269
Corinda
Kyong DIVIDING
Dagworth Cathedral Hill
Olio Lana
Enryb Downs
Burnside Thorneville
Burslem
Caledonia
THISTLEBANK N.P. RANGE
Laglan 4
165 ROAD
Prubi Oondooroo Rangelands
Jessamine Kywong
Maroomba
Eskdale
Hardington
Fleetwood
Lake Galilee
Eastmere Dunrobin Albro EPPING FOREST N.P. Beresford
Teviot
Llorac Bowen Downs
Lake Dunn
Springvale
Winton Waltzing Matilda Centre
Bangall
Marita Downs
Muttaburra
80 Kalkadoon
Bladensburg Dillcar
Kensington Downs
Fortuna CUDMORE N.P. Boongoondoo Pine Springvale
BLADENSBURG N.P. Warnambool Downs Barataria
Drumlion Chorregon
McMaster Clanagh Rimbanda
84 Glenample
Aramac
Rangers Valley
Forresten 181 5
Carisbrooke Happy Valley
177
Morella
119
Cork
Evesham Payne
Dalmore
Stirling
Garfield Hobartville Islay Plains
Eildon Park Opalton Elvo
Fermoy Wammadoo Alroy Maneroo
Darr
Longreach Stockmans Hall of Fame
Ilfracombe Dartmouth Deroora Braxton Saltern
Moonya
Barcaldine Folk Museum
Lochnagar Busthinia Alice
Jericho
Beta 53 Alpha Mamboo
Mayneside Vergemont
Arrilalah
106
Barcaldine Downs
Geera 86 Springvale
CAPRICORN HWY
Alpha
372 GONEAWAY N.P.
Withywine Nereena 116
Devonshire
Wellshot
Rosemount Clover Hills 122 Lancevale
Armagh Sedgeford 24
Tonkoro Westerton
Tocal Westland 120
Amor Downs
Mulgrave 138 Avington
106 Evora
Tumbar
Alpha
Connemara Warbreccan
LOCHERN N.P.
Bimerah
Portland Downs
Thornleigh Yalleroi
Dismal Glen Avon
163 Skye
Flodden Hills
100 Ruthven Oma
Isisford 120
Thornleigh Glenusk
Blackall Wool Scour
Blackall Castlevale
Braidwood Evengy Stonehenge
Pandora Park
49
107 Glenstuart
Malvern Thrungli 101
98
Arno
Emmet Ungo Konupa
Mekaree Benlidi
Bloomfield Kelpum CARNARVON N.P.
Jundah WELFORD N.P.
Mount Marlow Yaraka 150
HIDALIAN.P. Lorne
Terrick Terrick
Macfarlane LANDSBOROUGH HWY
Summervale Gartmore Carwell
6

© UNIVERSAL PRESS PTY LTD 2002

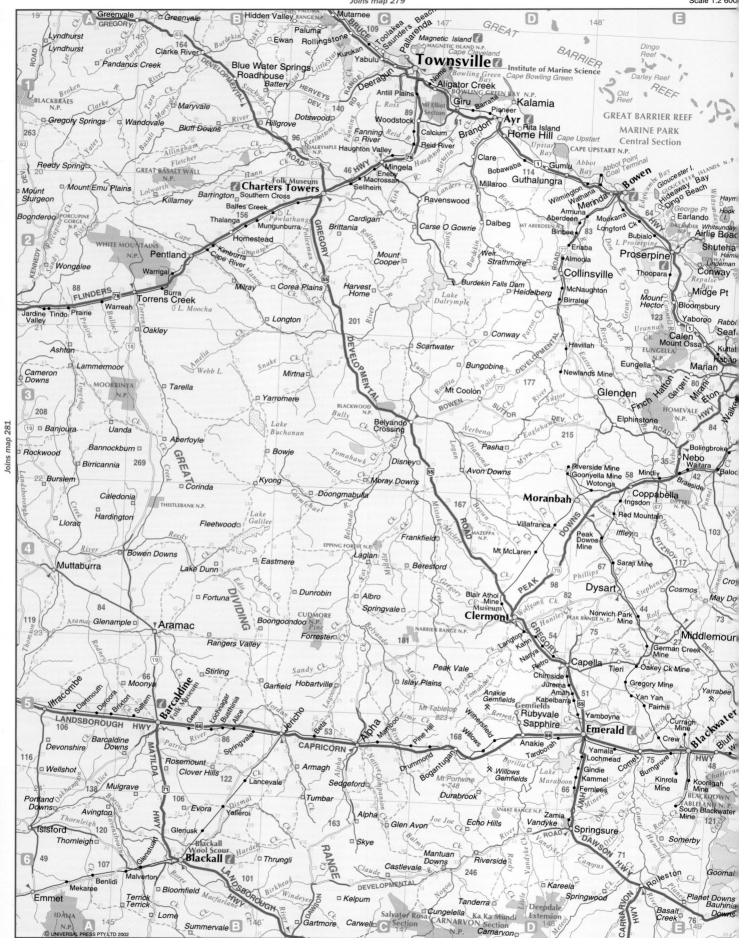

Queensland

© UNIVERSAL PRESS PTY LTD 2002

80
Kilometres

F   G   H   J   K

150°   151°   152°   153°

CORAL

Marion Reef

1

Hewitt Reef

Square Reef

WHITSUNDAY
WHITSUNDAY
ISLANDS N.P.
wood I.
GROUP

GREAT

Hunt Reef

Bax Reef

SEA

2

asell I.

Stevens Reef

Boulton Reef

anne I.
AMPTON IS. N.P.
rlisle I.   Wigton I.   Calder I.
Brampton
TH CUMBERLAND IS. N.P.
eswick I.   Scawfell I.
St Bees I.

Southhampton Reef

Chauvel Reefs

casia
Slade Point
Mackay

Derwent I.   *Penrith I.*

Pompey Reef

3

Hay Point
Sarina Beach
arina

Prudhoe I.

Double I.
Minster I.

BARRIER

21°

Yukan
Cape Palmerston
PALMERSTON N.P. GUARDFISH
oumala   Temple I.   Curlew I.
Koota   CLUSTER
Greenhill   Connor Islet
Orkabie   BEDWELL GROUP
West Hill I.   Poynter I.
WEST HILL N.P.
Carmila

Knight I.   Digby I.
Hotspur I.
Pine Peak I.
PERCY ISLES
Middle I.
North East I.
South I.

Swain

Reefs

Saumarez Reefs

154°

FLAT ISLES   Wild   DUKE ISLANDS
Elalie   Duck I.   Marble I.
airview   Quail I.   Hexham I.
194   Kalarka Long Arthur point
Broad Island Stanage
Sound   Linghan I.
Leicester I.

Berwick I.

Cheviot I.

Capricorn

G

4

22°

St Lawrence
Wumalgi
OLOOMBAH
CREEK C.P. Ogmore   Kooltandra
Marlborough
82

TORILLA
PENINSULA
Shoalwater
Bay
SHOALWATER BAY
MILITARY TRAINING
MT.O'CONNELL N.P. AREA

Townshend Island
Reef Point
Pearl Bay
WARGINBURRA
PEN.   Cape Clinton
Freshwater Bay
Cape Manifold

Channel

GREAT BARRIER REEF

MARINE PARK

Capricorn Section

REEF

Princhester
Kunwarara
Glen
Geddes
Glenroy
105
Gracemere

Byfield
BYFIELD N.P.
Corio Bay
Yaamba
The Caves
Yeppoon
Ridgelands

Cheviot I.

North Keppel I.
Great Keppel Island
KEPPEL ISLES

KEPPEL BAY ISLANDS N.P.

5

23°

GOODEDULLA
N.P.
Foleyvale
Stanwell
Westwood
Wycarbah
Kabra
Gracemere
Rockhampton
Gavial
Port Alma

Emu Park
Keppel Sands

North
West I.

Tryon I.

Wreck I.
Heron I.   CAPRICORN GROUP

North Keppel I.

onwara
Gogango
Bimbam
Bajool
107

55
69
Mt Morgan
26
17
Dululu
Marmor

Cape Capricorn
CURTIS ISLAND
N.P.
RUNDLE RANGE
Black Head

CAPRICORNIA CAYS N.P.   One Tree I.
Masthead I.

Tropic

of

Capricorn

nia   Wallaroo
Duaringa
55
CAPRICORN HWY
39
Wowan
Rannes
37
68
Kokotungo   Jooro
Baralba

Epala
Mount Larcom
Ambrose
Gladstone
Tannum Sands
Raglan
Yarwun

Fitzroy Reef

Llewellyn Reef

Hoskyn I.
BUNKER GROUP
Fairfax I.
CAPRICORNIA CAYS N.P.
Lady Musgrave I.

Woorabinda
75
Jimbin
Keentool
Calliope
100
Calliope

North Point
Facing Island

Bustard Head
Middle Island
Bustard Bay
61 N.P.
Round Hill Head

6

24°

2
Redcliffe
42
Callide
Callide Mine

Taragool
Boynedale

Bororen

Seventeen Seventy
Agnes Water
DEEPWATER N.P.

Moura
Banana
Biloela
Thangool
58

46
93 151 136
99
Nagoorin
Ubobo
Helen
Littlemore
Miriam Vale
Makowata
Lowmead

BROADWATER C.P.

DAWSON
93

F   G   H

Golembil
Many Peaks
L. CANIA
CANIA GORGE N.P.

152°   153°   154°

LITTABELLA N.P.

J   K

Joins map 287

© UNIVERSAL PRESS PTY LTD 2002

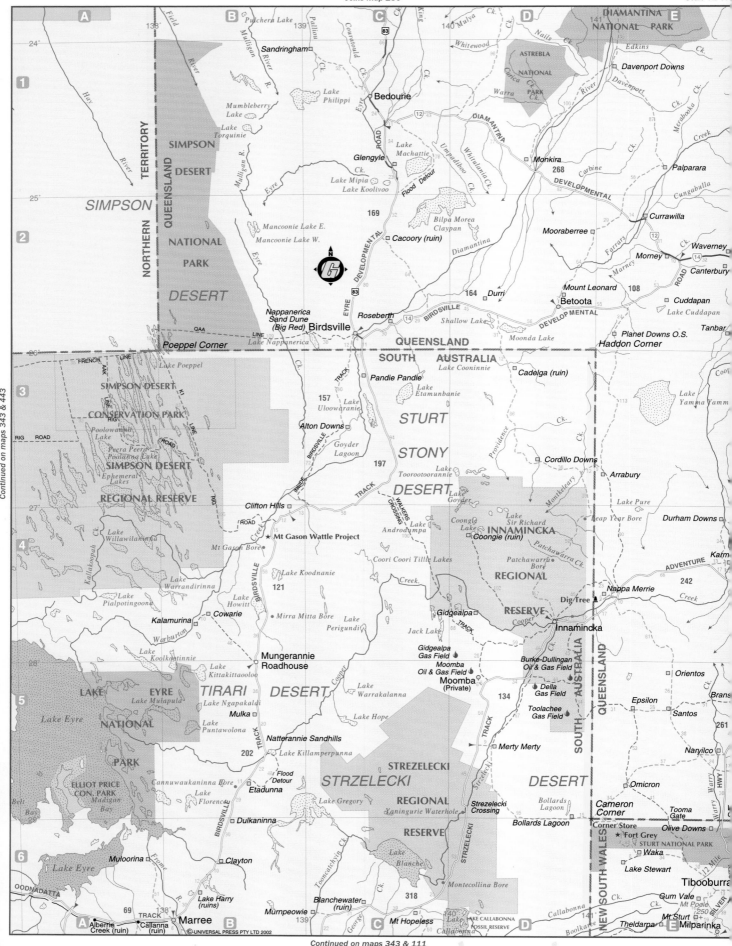

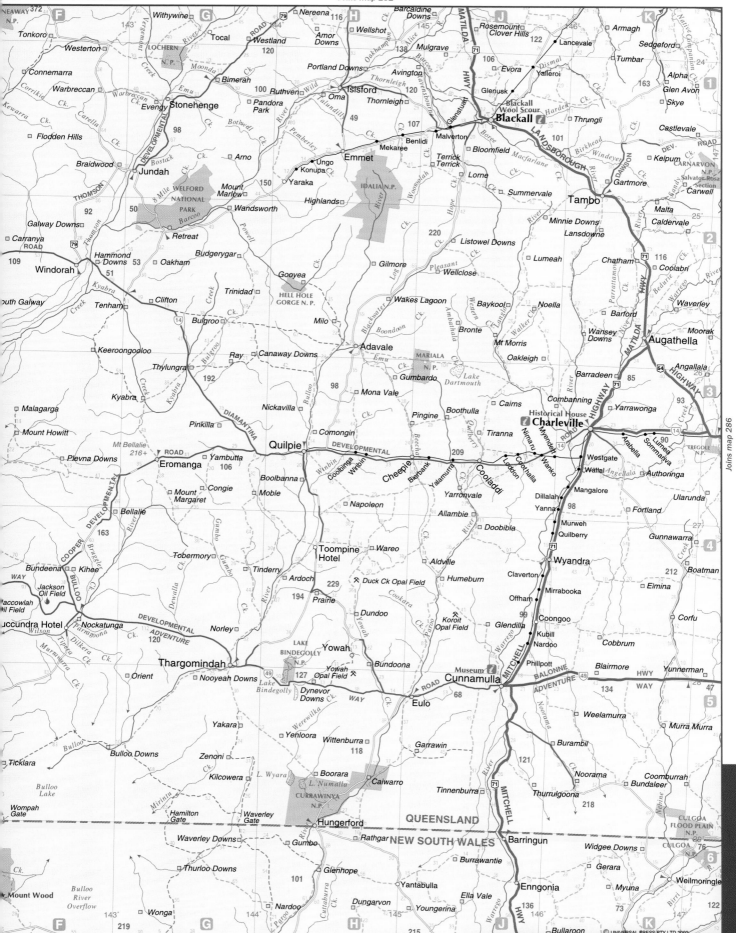

© UNIVERSAL PRESS PTY LTD 2002

Scale 1:2 600

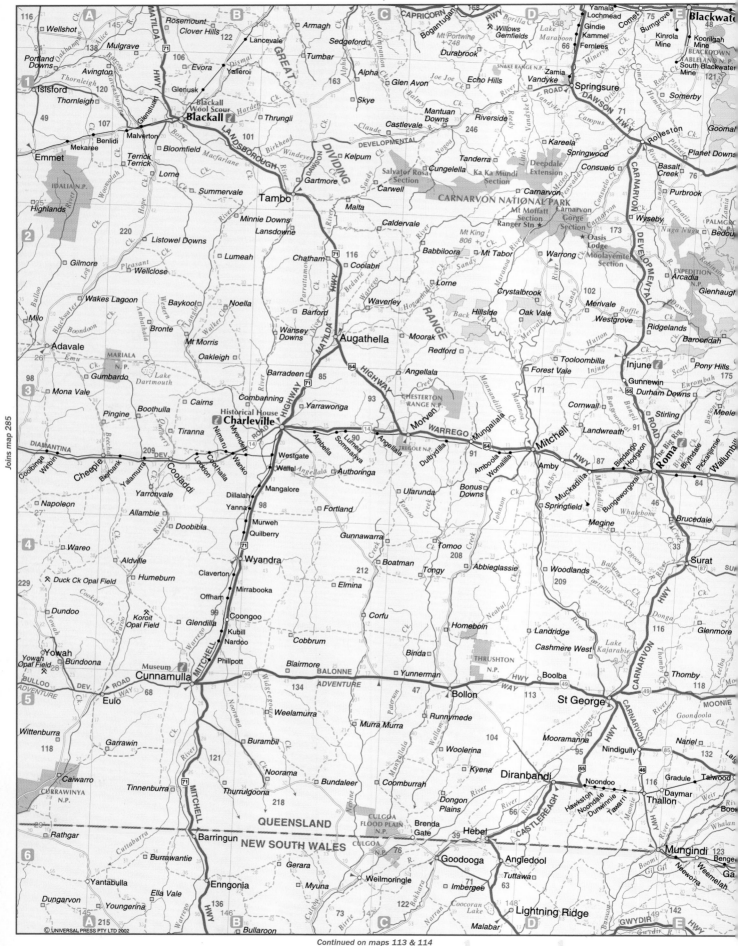

Continued on maps 113 & 114

286 *Gregory's Australia*

Queensland

© UNIVERSAL PRESS PTY LTD 2002

Continued on map 115

The fourth largest state (including the Northern Territory) and the driest in Australia, South Australia is a place of contrasts. In the unique position of bordering all the other mainland states, two-thirds of South Australia is dominated by a near-desert environment. Although conditions here are harsh and unrelenting, the varied landscapes of immense deserts, rugged mountains and dry lakes entice many visitors.

In contrast to the arid lands of the north and west are the gulf lands, which include the Eyre, Yorke and Fleurieu peninsulas, fringed by quiet beaches and fishing towns; the rolling hills of the Mount Lofty Ranges; and the dry south-east plains watered by the mighty Murray River, Australia's longest, as it flows to the sea. The extensive 3700km South Australian coastline offers scenic driving and walking routes along its many

indentations as well as offshore islands to explore, the largest being Kangaroo Island.

Touring South Australia by car is generally easy. From the state's

South Australia: The Festival State

- Population: 1 493 074
- Total area: 983 482km²
- % of Australia: 12.8%
- Length of coastline: 3700km
- Floral symbol: Sturt's Desert Pea
- Fauna symbol: Southern Hairy-Nosed Wombat

RALIA

ℹ Tourist information

South Australian Travel Centre
18 King William St,
Adelaide, SA 5000
Ph: 1300 655 276
www.southaustralia.com

Main ATTRACTIONS

◈ **Barossa Valley**

Only a short drive from Adelaide, this valley has long been reputed as one of Australia's premier wine-producing regions.

◈ **Coober Pedy**

This Outback town is famous for its lustrous opals and unusual underground accommodation.

◈ **Fleurieu Peninsula**

This striking peninsula features rolling hills and sandy beaches along Gulf St Vincent's picturesque coastline.

◈ **Flinders Ranges**

The distinctive landforms of the Flinders Ranges include colourful cliffs, granite peaks and deep gorges.

◈ **Kangaroo Island**

Accessible by ferry from Cape Jervis, this sparsely populated island offers secluded camping spots, bushwalking tracks, scenic coastal areas and magnificent wildlife.

◈ **Lake Eyre**

Usually a dry salt lake, Lake Eyre becomes a vast inland sea several times a century, teeming with waterbirds.

◈ **Limestone Coast**

In the south-east corner of the state, this coastal region offers many interesting parks and caves.

◈ **Nullarbor Plain**

This vast flat plain has numerous limestone caves and subterranean rivers. Spectacular cliffs up to 100m high border the waters of the Great Australian Bight.

◈ **Riverland**

The Murray River dominates this region. Cruise the river by houseboat or paddlesteamer, visit the wineries, orchards, quaint townships and historic ports.

sophisticated capital, Adelaide, there are links to the Barrier, Sturt, Ouyen, Dukes and Princes hwys to the eastern states; the Stuart Hwy, which crosses the continent to Darwin; and the Eyre Hwy, which traverses the virtually treeless Nullarbor Plain to Western Australia.

There are many reasons to visit South Australia, including the spectacular scenery, fishing, flora, fauna and the national, conservation and recreation parks that make up over

20% of the state. However, wine is usually top of the list. South Australia's wineries are legendary—the names Barossa Valley, McLaren Vale and Coonawarra are recognised by most Australians and overseas visitors. Four out of every ten glasses of Australian wine are produced from vineyards in the south-east corner of South Australia.

Photo above: Cliffs at Warren Gorge, Flinders Ranges

THE FESTIVAL STATE

South Australia represents one-eighth of the entire Australian continent and has a total area of 983 482km². While more than 50% of the state is pastoral land, the majority of the population live in the southern coastal zones below the 32nd parallel. Adelaide, the state's capital, has 73% of the state's population.

South Australia is the driest of the Australian states and territories and is mostly arid or semi-arid. However, the coastal zone, where the vast majority of the population live, has areas with a pleasant Mediterranean-like climate, ideal for outdoor pursuits and adventuring.

In contrast to the majority of Australian states, no convicts were ever sent to South Australia. The initial plan was for private settlement, however, South Australia was declared a province in 1836. After a faltering start, the discovery of copper in the 1840s and the success of the early wheat farms gave the new colony the economic boost

it needed in order to prosper. Today, agriculture, mining, fishing, tourism and manufacturing all contribute to the state's economy.

South Australia is regarded as the pre-eminent food and wine capital of Australia—the food industry is the state's largest export earner. The state also accounts for more than half of the Australian wine industry and is home to 44% of the country's vineyards.

Around 10% of Australian agricultural industry is based in South Australia. The main crop is wheat, followed by barley and oats. A wide range of fruit and vegetables are also grown in the state, including potatoes, onions, carrots, tomatoes, cauliflowers, peas, oranges, apples, apricots and peaches.

South Australia produces around 11% of Australia's sheep and over 4% of its cattle. The fishing industry has always been strong in South Australia and the growth of aquaculture farms, including oyster, rock

Historic Seppeltsfield winery, Barossa Valley

lobster, salmon, snapper and tuna, contribute to the development and expansion of overseas markets.

Crude oil and natural gas are now the major mining products, recently surpassing the coal and iron-ore output. Copper, uranium, silver and gold are also mined at **Roxby Downs**. Perhaps most commonly known are the mining towns of **Coober Pedy** and **Andamooka**, which account for 85% of the nation's opals.

The state is accessible by car, with around 95 000km of sealed and unsealed roads taking explorers to the furthest corners of South Australia. The **Trans Australian Railway** also runs through the state, originating in Kalgoorlie (Western Australia), and continuing to Broken Hill (New South Wales), Tarcoola (South Australia) and Alice Springs (Northern Territory).

Cape Willis, Whalers Way, Eyre Peninsula

South Australia

TOURISM REGION HIGHLIGHTS

A state of contrasts, South Australia varies dramatically from the arid lands and deserts of the north to the more fertile gulf lands of the south. These include the **Yorke** and **Fleurieu peninsulas** and the dry south-east plains through which the **Murray River** flows. South Australia's landscapes are stunning, particularly on the **Eyre Peninsula**, the **Flinders Ranges** and **Kangaroo Island**. South Australian wineries are legendary and names such as **Barossa**, **McLaren Vale** and **Coonawarra** are known and respected worldwide.

A Adelaide

Ayers House; Botanic Gardens; Central Market; Festival Centre; Glenelg Tram; Migration Museum; North Terrace; Port Adelaide; Rundle Mall; River Torrens

B Adelaide Hills

Adelaide Hills Wineries; Belair NP; Cleland Wildlife Park; Gumeracha Toy Factory; Hahndorf; Morialta CP; Mount Barker; Mount Lofty; National Motor Museum; Norton Summit; Onkaparinga Valley; Torrens Valley; Warrawong Sanctuary

Rocky River Mouth, Flinders Chase NP, Kangaroo Island

C Barossa

Barossa Valley Wineries; Eden Valley Wineries; Lyndoch; Menglers Hill Lookout; Museum of Mechanical Music; Nuriootpa; Tanunda

D Clare Valley

Auburn; Balaklava; Burra; Clare Valley Wineries; Gladstone; Jamestown; Kapunda; Laura; Mintaro; Mount Remarkable; Polish Hill Valley; Watervale

E Eyre Peninsula

Arno Bay; Ceduna; Coffin Bay NP; Cowell; Gawler Ranges; Lincoln Cove; Lincoln NP; Murphy's Haystacks; Nullarbor Cliffs; Nullarbor Plain; Point Lowly Lighthouse; Port Lincoln; Port Neill; Streaky Bay; Tumby Bay; Whalers Way; Whyalla

F Fleurieu Peninsula

Cockle Train; Deep Creek NP; Goolwa; Granite Island; Hallett Cove; Langhorne Creek; McLaren Vale Wineries; Old Noarlunga; Port Elliot; Strathalbyn; Victor Harbor; Willunga

G Flinders Ranges & Outback

Andamooka; Arkaroola Sanctuary; Birdsville Track; Coober Pedy Opal Mines; Coongie Lakes; Flinders Ranges NP; Gammon Ranges NP; Innamincka; Lake Eyre; Oodnadatta Track; Pichi Richi Railway; Port Augusta; Port Pirie; Quorn; Simpson Desert; Strzelecki Desert; Wilpena Pound; Yourambulla Caves

H Kangaroo Island

Admirals Arch; Cape Borda; Cape Gantheaume; Flinders Chase NP; Kingscote; Maritime Heritage Trail; Penneshaw; Ravine des Casoars; Remarkable Rocks; Seal Bay; Stokes Bay; Vivonne Bay

I Limestone Coast

Blue Lake, Mount Gambier; Bool Lagoon; Bordertown; Cape Jaffa Lighthouse; Canunda NP; Coonawarra Wineries; Crater Lakes; Kingston SE; Millicent; Naracoorte Caves; Padthaway; Penola; Pool of Siloam; Robe; Tantanoola Caves

J Murraylands

Coorong NP; Lake Albert; Lake Alexandrina; Mannum; Morgan; Murray Bridge; Murray River; Pinnaroo; Swan Reach; Yookamurra Sanctuary

K Riverland

Banrock Station; Barmera; Berri; Blanchetown; Loxton Historical Village; Renmark; The Big Orange; Waikerie

L Yorke Peninsula

Ardrossan; Edithburgh; Innes NP; Kadina Heritage Museum; Marion Bay; Moonta; Port Victoria; Port Vincent; Wallaroo Maritime Museum; Yorketown

NATIONAL PARKS

South Australia has a park system that ensures a great many natural areas are protected by a park or reserve and will, therefore, remain pristine and beautiful. From such places as the **Simpson Desert** and **Flinders Ranges**, to the flat plains of the **Nullarbor** that stretch to the rugged cliffs of the Great Australian Bight, the many national parks of South Australia are spectacular and awe-inspiring.

A Coffin Bay NP (Map 348, B1)

Coffin Bay NP is located 625km west of Adelaide on a peninsula bordered by the **Southern Ocean** and **Coffin Bay**. Known for its good fishing, swimming and surfing (check conditions first), the national park also offers walking trails that take in the coastal landscape—4WD access recommended. Camping facilities are found mainly near the Coffin Bay township where general stores and information are obtainable.

B Coorong NP (Map 323, B1)

Around 140km SE of Adelaide, Coorong NP is a line of shallow lagoons, protected from the rough Southern Ocean waters by a thin line of sand dunes known as the **Younghusband Peninsula**. At around 468km², the park stretches for 130km along the coast. The attractions of this park include good fishing (mulloway, whiting, flathead and shark), the wildlife (especially pelicans and other waterbirds), the unusual coastal walking trails and 4WD access. Camping and picnic spots are plentiful, but it is necessary to gain a camping permit from the ranger in Meningie.

C Flinders Ranges NP (Map 313, C1)

Covering 927km², Flinders Ranges NP is a campers' delight. Around 460km north of Adelaide, it was made famous by artist Hans Heysen's depiction of the ranges. Attractions of the park include the amazing sunrises and sunsets; **Wilpena Pound**, a huge natural amphitheatre 5km by 11km; the **Sacred Canyon**, a fantastic site of Aboriginal art; the wildflower display in early spring; and many stunning valleys and gorges. Some camping sites have toilet facilities; Wilpena Pound has a motel, ranger facilities and a general store.

D Lake Eyre NP (Map 342, D4)

Lake Eyre NP covers 12 250km² and is located 760km north of Adelaide. The park comprises Lake Eyre and the **Tirari Desert**, noted for its sand dunes and salt lakes. At 15m below sea level Lake Eyre is the lowest point in Australia, it is also the largest salt lake on the continent at over 340km². The area is considered one of the harshest environments in Australia; it is remarkably transformed when occasionally it fills with water. Then, it is home to fish and a multitude of waterbirds. Camping is permitted; permits are available at the National Parks and Wildlife office in Port Augusta or the William Creek store.

E Murray River NP (Map 333, C3)

Around 240km from Adelaide, 3 areas with similar habitats: **Katarapko**, **Lyrup Flats** and **Bulyong Island** form the Murray River NP. Three-quarters of the park is floodplain, containing permanent and semi-permanent wetlands. It is an important breeding area for many forms of life, including waterbirds. The park offers several recreational opportunities: birdwatching, fishing, camping and walking.

Common wallaroo, *Macropus robustus*, in the Flinders Ranges

facts

◈ No. of parks/reserves: 300

◈ Area: 200 000km²

◈ % of state: 20%

◈ World Heritage Area: Australian Fossil Mammal Site (Naracoorte)

South Australia

(Map 344, C3)

Nullarbor Cliffs fringe the Great Australian Bight Marine Park, Nullarbor NP

National Parks Head Office

National Parks and Wildlife South Australia
GPO Box 1047
Adelaide, SA 5001
Ph: (08) 8204 1910
Desert Parks Hotline: 1800 816 078
www.parks.sa.gov.au

F Nullarbor NP and Regional Reserve

(Map 344, C3)

The Nullarbor NP—meaning 'no tree'—and Regional Reserve is 950km west of Adelaide. The park is located on a coastal strip of the seemingly endless flat Nullarbor plain. The plain itself is a limestone plateau fringed by spectacular coastal cliffs shaped by the wild **Southern Ocean**. It is in these waters that it is possible to see mighty, but endangered, southern right whales. Southern rights come to the Bight in winter to breed and to calf. There are also sea-lion colonies along the **Great Australian Bight**. The park provides protected habitat for other wildlife including the southern hairy-nosed wombat. Besides wildlife-watching, the park and reserve protects the world's largest semi-arid karst (cave) landscape. It also offers Aboriginal art sites, and almost undisturbed camping, as this remote region sees few visitors.

G Witjira NP and Simpson Desert Regional Reserve

(Map 342, B1)

The furthest national park from Adelaide (1360km north), Witjira NP and Simpson Desert Regional Reserve adjoin on the South Australia/Northern Territory border. These 2 parks lure visitors with the distinctly beautiful desert landscape which includes dune systems, spinifex, dry playa lakes, gibber country and the Finke River flood-plains. Witjira NP also has the unusual Dalhousie mound-spring complex—the warm water is great for soaking in—it is claimed the spring resembles the finest oases in the world. There are also the ruins of historic **Dalhousie homestead** to investigate. Another wetland worth exploring is **Purnie Bore**, which attracts much wildlife. For access or camping rights to these parks, a **Desert Parks Pass** (or day/night permit) must be obtained.

Thorny devil, *Moloch horridus*

WINERIES

In 1837, just one year after the founding of South Australia, **J B Hach** and **George Stevenson** planted vine cuttings from Tasmania in **North Adelaide**. A few years later, German Lutheran immigrants arrived in the **Barossa Valley** and **Johann Gramp** planted his **Jacob's Creek Vineyard** there. By 1900, South Australia was the leading Australian wine producer. Labels such as **Hardy**, **Seppelt**, **Penfold**, **Orlando** and **Yalumba** had become internationally recognised, as indeed they are today. The state was fortunate to escape the vine aphid *phylloxera*, which devastated vineyards in Victoria, and to a lesser extent New South Wales in the late 19th century.

South Australia's wine regions encompass a wide variety of terrain, character and climate. They are today responsible for more than 50% of national wine production and 70% of international exports. They have also led Australia's success with international awards.

A Adelaide Hills

The state's oldest wine region produced its first vintage in 1841, and in 1845 a case of Echunga hock was sent to Queen Victoria in England. There are now at least 35 wine labels in the picturesque setting of the **Mount Lofty Ranges**. Varieties include chardonnay, pinot noir, riesling, semillon, sauvignon blanc, merlot, cabernet sauvignon, cabernet franc and shiraz.

B Adelaide Plains

This region between the Adelaide Hills and **Gulf St Vincent** has a Mediterranean climate with hot, dry summers and mild winters. The most common grape varieties are columbard and shiraz, as well as chardonnay, sauvignon blanc, riesling, cabernet and semillon. There are also plantings of Italian varietals—barbera, sangiovese and nebbiolo.

C Barossa Valley (pp.326–327)

Australia's most recognised wine region was established in 1842 by immigrants from Germany, Silesia and England. The main red varieties grown are cabernet sauvignon, shiraz and grenache; and riesling, semillon and chardonnay are the main white varieties. Famous labels include **Chateau Tanunda**, **Chateau Yaldara**, **Leo Buring**, **Orlando**, **Seppeltsfield**, **Yalumba** and **Wolf Blass**. **Penfold's Grange Hermitage** is rated one of the world's finest red wines.

D Clare Valley

More than 30 wineries are to be found in this historic region north of Adelaide. This is prime riesling country, with a consistency of style and quality possibly unmatched in Australia. Principal red wines are cabernet sauvignon and shiraz, with outstanding varietals.

E Coonawarra

With a predominantly maritime climate, Coonawarra is famous for its luscious red wines and the red soil (terra rossa) on which the vines flourish. Its superb cabernet sauvignons account for 50% of plantings, with 21% shiraz and lesser amounts of chardonnay, riesling, merlot and pinot noir.

F Eden Valley

The Barossa's neighbouring valley is at a higher altitude with a cooler climate, but an equal reputation for fine wines. Riesling, chardonnay, shiraz, merlot and cabernet grapes thrive in the long summer-ripening periods, assisted by innovative viticulture techniques. Premium wine labels include **Henschke's Hill of Grace**.

The Barrel Room at Orlando Wines, Rowland Flat, Barossa Valley

South Australia

Harvesting grapes in a McLaren Vale vineyard

shiraz and cabernet sauvignon with outstanding varietals. The local chardonnays are rich and fruity; other white varieties are also grown. **Padthaway Estate** has the only cellar door tastings and sales.

L Riverland (pp.332–333)

The prolific Murray River region between **Blanchetown** and **Paringa** is blessed with abundant sunshine and water supply, and rich, sandy loam soils. It produces about two-thirds of South Australia's wine grapes and almost one-third of the nation's total production. Its rich, velvety shiraz, cabernet sauvignon and merlot are very good. However, it is most famous for its outstanding flavoursome, fruity chardonnays.

M Wrattonbully

This rapidly growing region between **Padthaway** and **Coonawarra** shares their famous terra rossa soils. The majority of plantings are red grapes: cabernet sauvignon, shiraz, pinot noir, pinot meunier, merlot, cabernet franc and zinfandel. Whites include semillon, chardonnay, sauvignon blanc and riesling.

G Eyre Peninsula

This small region around **Port Lincoln** has a relatively cool maritime climate, with vines in places growing down to **Boston Bay**. Vineyards produce chardonnay, riesling, semillon, sauvignon blanc, cabernet sauvignon, merlot and shiraz.

H Langhorne Creek

Cooling breezes from the Southern Ocean and Lake Alexandrina help make Langhorne Creek a centre for fine cool-climate wines. It is known for superb cabernet sauvignon and full-flavoured shiraz with soft tannins. Verdelho, malbec, merlot and chardonnay grapes are also grown.

I McLaren Vale

There are more than 60 wineries in this **Fleurieu Peninsula** region, originally pioneered by pre-eminent winemakers such as **John Reynell** and **Thomas Hardy**. It is famous for ripe, generously flavoured wines,

especially shiraz, grenache, merlot, cabernet sauvignon, chardonnay, riesling and sauvignon blanc. There are also planting of varietals such as viognier, marsanne and sangiovese.

J Mount Benson

This small coastal region between **Kingston SE** and **Robe** was planted in 1989 by French winemakers from the Rhone Valley. Mount Benson wines are highly aromatic and predominantly red: cabernet franc, cabernet sauvignon, shiraz, grenache, merlot, petit verdot and pinot noir. There are also plantings of chardonnay and other white grape varieties.

K Padthaway

Padthaway shares the terra rossa soils of nearby Coonawarra, but has a warmer Mediterranean-like climate. Principal red wines are

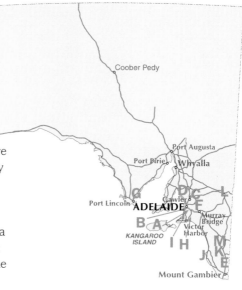

ADELAIDE

Plaza at Adelaide Festival Centre

main attractions

◈ **Adelaide Botanic Gardens**

These beautifully landscaped gardens contain the magnificently restored 19th-century Palm House and the Bicentennial Conservatory with its lush rainforest.

◈ **Adelaide Festival Centre**

This imposing building hosts a series of world-class productions during the biennial Adelaide Festival of the Arts as well as throughout the year.

◈ **Central Market**

The markets are a culinary adventure and reflect Adelaide's diverse ethnic population. Adelaide's Chinatown is in the market area.

◈ **Glenelg**

South Australia's first settlement was at Glenelg, which is now connected to the city by the Bay Tram. Glenelg Beach is the most popular of Adelaide's long, sandy beaches.

◈ **Gouger St**

One of Adelaide's premier 'eat streets', Gouger St features food from around the world.

◈ **Rundle Mall**

The retail hub of Adelaide is located here.

◈ **South Australian Museum**

This museum features a fascinating collection of Aboriginal artefacts and much more.

Named after Queen Adelaide, the wife of King William IV, Adelaide's boom times are evident in its glorious architecture. Adelaide's historic churches and gracious 19th-century buildings are interspersed with those built in the Italian-Renaissance style. **King William St** and the tree-lined **North Terrace** are excellent examples.

With a population of more than one million residents, this planned city is easy to navigate due to its grid design. The city is positioned on the banks of the picturesque **River Torrens**, among superb gardens, with the blue haze of the **Adelaide Hills** as a backdrop, giving it a relaxed atmosphere. Adelaide experiences 4 distinct seasons, adding to its charm.

Its long history of immigration has influenced the city's development and its ethnic diversity is reflected in the city's markets, restaurants and cafes. Adelaide is renowned for its fine restaurants, wines and colourful festivals.

 Tourist information

South Australian Travel Centre
18 King William St,
Adelaide, SA 5000
Freecall: 1300 655 276
www.southaustralia.com

facts

◈ Population: 1 083 074
◈ Date founded: 1836
◈ Tallest building: SANTOS House
◈ Average temp: 23°C (Jan), 12.5°C (June)

Places of Interest

Adelaide Botanic Gardens Ⓐ D3
Adelaide Festival Centre Ⓑ C3
Adelaide Town Hall Ⓒ D4
Adelaide Zoo Ⓓ D3
Art Gallery of South Australia Ⓔ D3
Ayers House Ⓕ D3
Central Market Ⓖ C4
Edmund Wright House Ⓗ C4
Elder Park Ⓘ C3
Government House Ⓙ D3
Light's Vision Ⓚ C3
Lion Arts Centre Ⓛ C3
Migration Museum Ⓜ D3
Mortlock Library of South Australia Ⓝ D3
National Wine Centre Ⓞ E3
Old Adelaide Gaol Ⓟ B3
Parliament House and
   Old Parliament House Ⓠ C3
Performing Arts Collection Ⓡ C3
Skycity Adelaide Ⓢ C3
South Australian Museum Ⓣ D3
Tandanya Ⓤ D4

River Torrens, Adelaide

South Australia

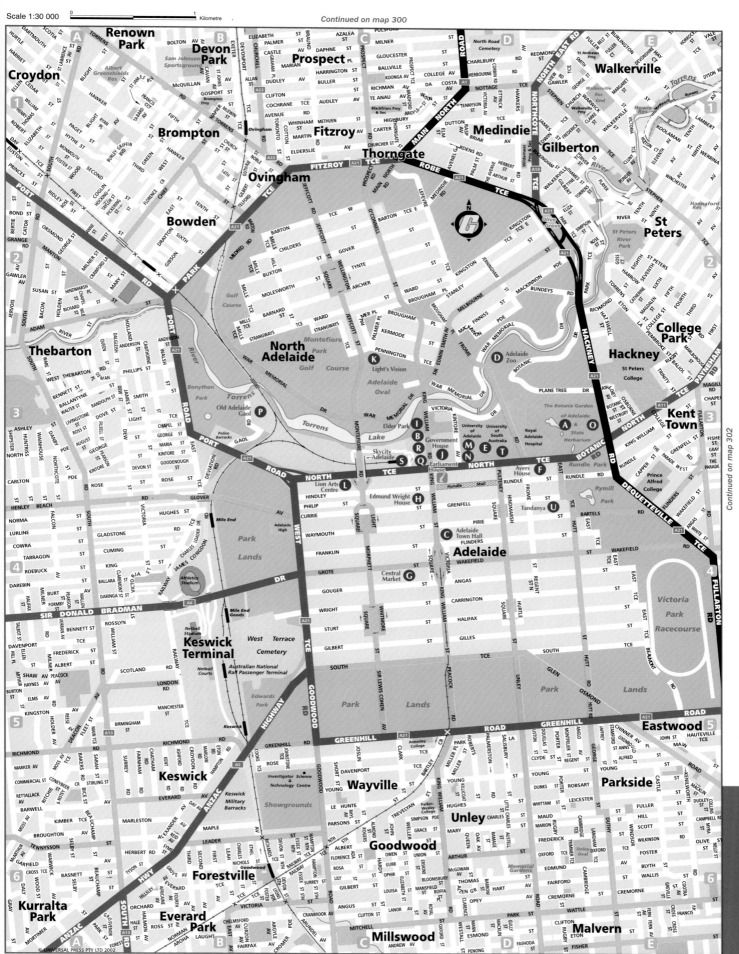

CBD & SUBURBS

CBD ATTRACTIONS

To explore the CBD of Adelaide, it is best to leave the car behind and walk or take the **City Free bus**. The centre of town is well planned and it is easy to wander along the wide, attractive streets lined with cafes, restored Edwardian and Victorian buildings and shops. Small and compact, this in an elegant, cultured, cosmopolitan but unhurried city.

Begin at **North Terrace**, the city's most attractive boulevard, and wander along the street and find the casino at **Skycity Adelaide**, **Government House**, **Parliament House** (with its award-winning museum of state history), the **State Library of South Australia** and the **Mortlock Library**. The **Art Gallery of South Australia** houses a collection divided into 4 parts: prints and drawings, Australian decorative arts, European and Asian decorative arts and paintings and sculptures. The **University of Adelaide** is between North Tce and the Torrens River and the neo-Gothic buildings are worth inspecting. The **Migration Museum** is close by, and the **Tate Museum** is on the ground floor of the **Mawson Laboratory**, home to a collection of rocks, minerals and fossils. For a peek into Adelaide's past, drop into **Ayers House** (opposite the **Royal Adelaide Hospital**), and view the mansion of former South Australia Premier, Sir Henry Ayers.

Further along North Tce, are the **Botanic Gardens**, renowned for the magnificent Moreton Bay figs that create a pathway to the main lake. The gardens themselves back onto the **Adelaide Zoo**. One of the country's most historic zoological gardens, Adelaide Zoo is an immaculately landscaped area with large grassy enclosures and many walk-through aviaries. Next to the Botanic Gardens, the **National Wine Centre** represents every wine region in Australia and the stunning **International Rose Garden** is close by. These parks and gardens reflect Colonel William Light's (the first surveyor-general) original urban design, which was to surround Adelaide with a pleasant expanse of greenery.

Behind Parliament House off King William St is the **South Australian Theatre Museum**. This performing arts' collection is a living history, holding over 40 000 pieces, from old posters to puppets and videos. Also located here, overlooking the Torrens River, are the **Adelaide Festival Centre**, the focus of the city's cultural life, and **Elder Park**, with its historic rotunda.

A shopper's paradise, **Rundle Mall** is located adjacent to North Tce, between King William and Pulteney sts, and is lined with department stores, boutiques, cafes and cinemas. For fresh produce, explore the **Central Market** in Grote St or the **East End Market** in Rundle St.

Located above North Tce to the west is the **Old Adelaide Gaol**— definitely worth a visit. Other attractions of the city include **Edmund Wright House**, where the History Trust of South Australia promotes the state's history; the **Lion Arts Centre**, containing 9 different arts organisations; and **Tandanya**, the National Aboriginal Cultural Institute.

Elder Park's historic rotunda at sunset

South Australia

SUBURBAN ATTRACTIONS

Two kilometres north of the CBD, **North Adelaide** is lined with grand Victorian and Edwardian homes made of bluestone and sandstone. There is an abundance of hotels, motels and B&Bs in this suburb, with exotic restaurants, cafes and welcoming pubs all within walking distance.

Around 20–30min from the CBD, Adelaide's beaches are popular seaside escapes. Well-known areas include **Henley Beach**, **West Beach** and **Brighton**.

The site of the first mainland settlement in South Australia in 1836, **Glenelg** is a seaside suburb with a 5-star hotel, beachfront apartments, shops and restaurants on the shoreline. **Jetty Road** is a hive of activity as the main precinct for shopping and alfresco dining. **Rodney Fox's Shark Museum** is located in the Town Hall. For the adventurous, attractions include helicopter rides and parasailing, with other outdoor activities like beach volleyball available.

South of Adelaide (2km), the suburb of **Wayville** is home to the **Investigator Science and Technology Centre** and the Royal Adelaide Show at Wayville Showground. A small suburb to the south-east of Adelaide, **Hyde Park** is a known shopping destination with designer and international labels available, great bars and eateries. Further to the south are **Carrick Hill**, a Tudor mansion set in manicured English gardens; and **Belair NP**, only 20min from the city. **Hallett Cove**, on the coast, is one of Australia's most significant geological sites.

Port Adelaide is perhaps one of the more visited suburbs and boasts a maritime history both on and off the water. There are many imposing buildings as well—like the old **Court House**—definitely worth wandering around. The port is a

World's largest rocking horse at the Gumeracha Toy Factory

relic from a bygone era and the **South Australian Maritime Museum** is spread over 7 sites. The **Railway Museum**, not far away, is also worth a look. After the history lesson, retreat to the seaside and take a boat trip to watch the Port River dolphins. Another suburb, **West Lakes**, plays an important part in the sporting life of Adelaide by housing both **Football Park Stadium** and the **South Australian Rowing Association**.

Burnside in the foothills of the **Mount Lofty Ranges** is 6km east of Adelaide. Originally a settlement of 4 houses in 1840, the suburb flourished in 1849 when land lots were auctioned. Today, the suburb offers a glimpse into Adelaide's past; pamphlets are available from the local library on the historic sites of **Rose Park**, **Knightsbridge** and **Waterfall Gully**. Further to the east, the former South Australian

Governor's summerhouse, **Marble Hill**, has been restored after fires destroyed it in 1955, and is now open to the public. Apart from their beauty, especially in autumn, the **Adelaide Hills** have many attractions including the craft galleries of **Hahndorf**, **Lobethal** and **Strathalbyn**; **Cleland CP** and **Cleland Wildlife Park**; **Mount Lofty Botanic Garden** and **Mount Lofty Summit** provide stunning 360° views over Adelaide city, coast and hills. **Warrawong Sanctuary** is an award-winning ecotourism complex dedicated to preserving endangered native animals. The world's largest rocking horse is at the Gumeracha Toy Factory.

Another interesting spot, 14km NW from the city centre, is **Fort Glanville**. The buildings are all that remain of the city's commitment to Britain, and consist of a line of forts along the coast of **Gulf St Vincent**.

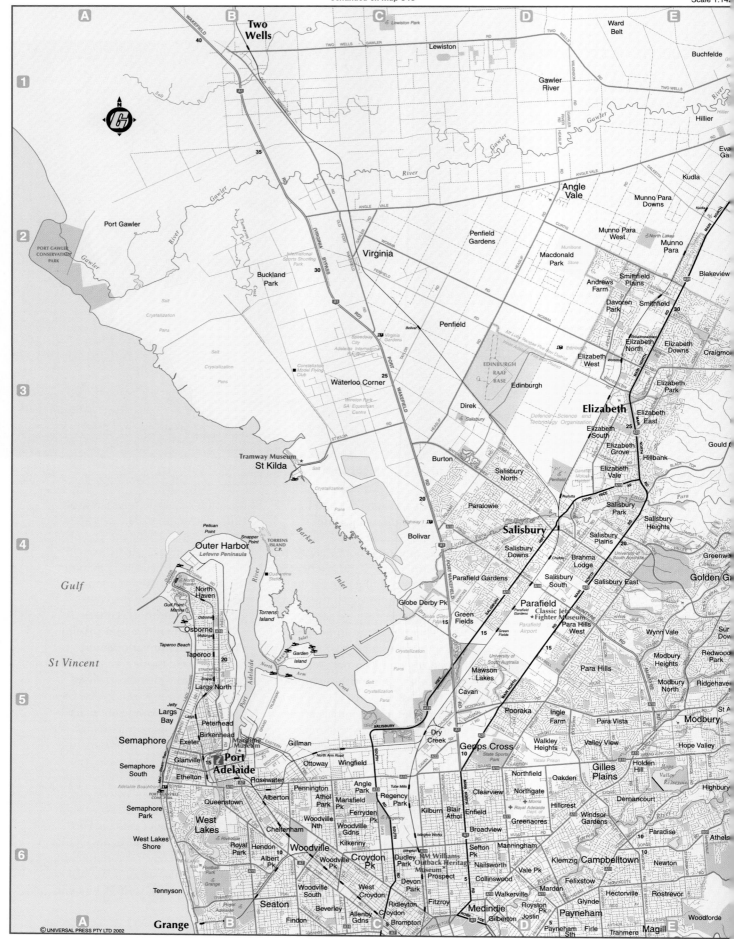

Scale 1:14

South Australia

Continued on map 327

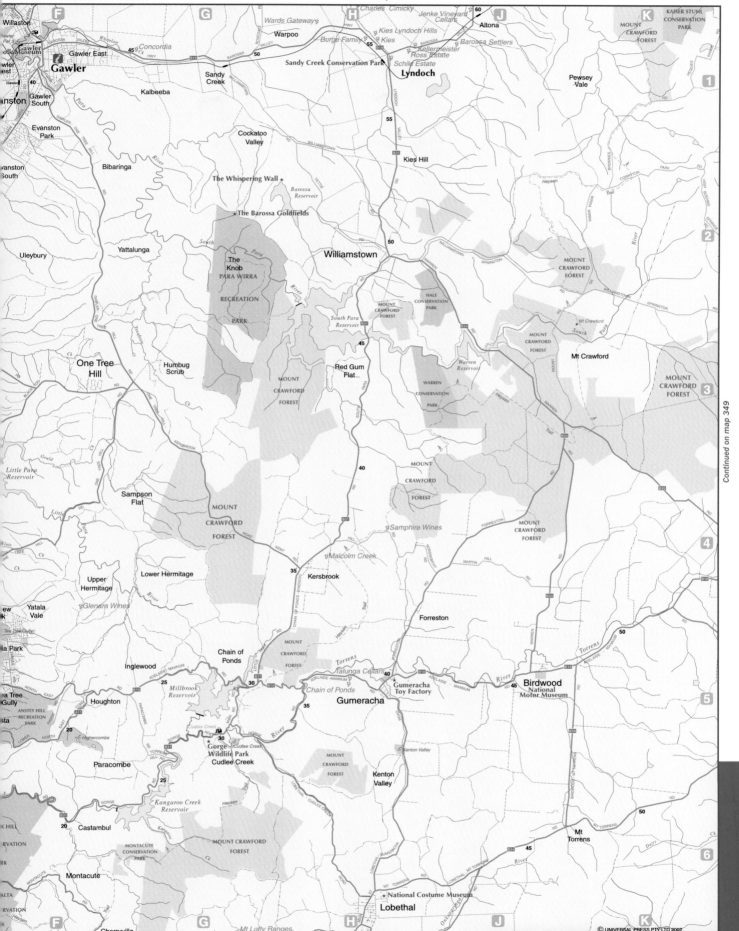

Continued on map 349

Joins map 303

© UNIVERSAL PRESS PTY LTD 2002

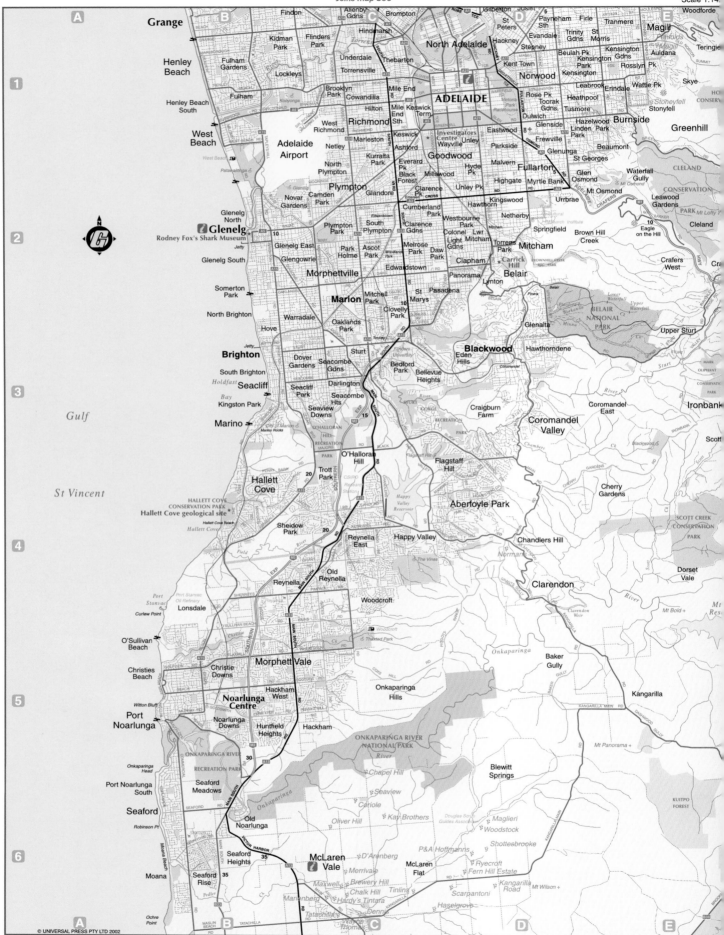

Gregory's Australia

South Australia

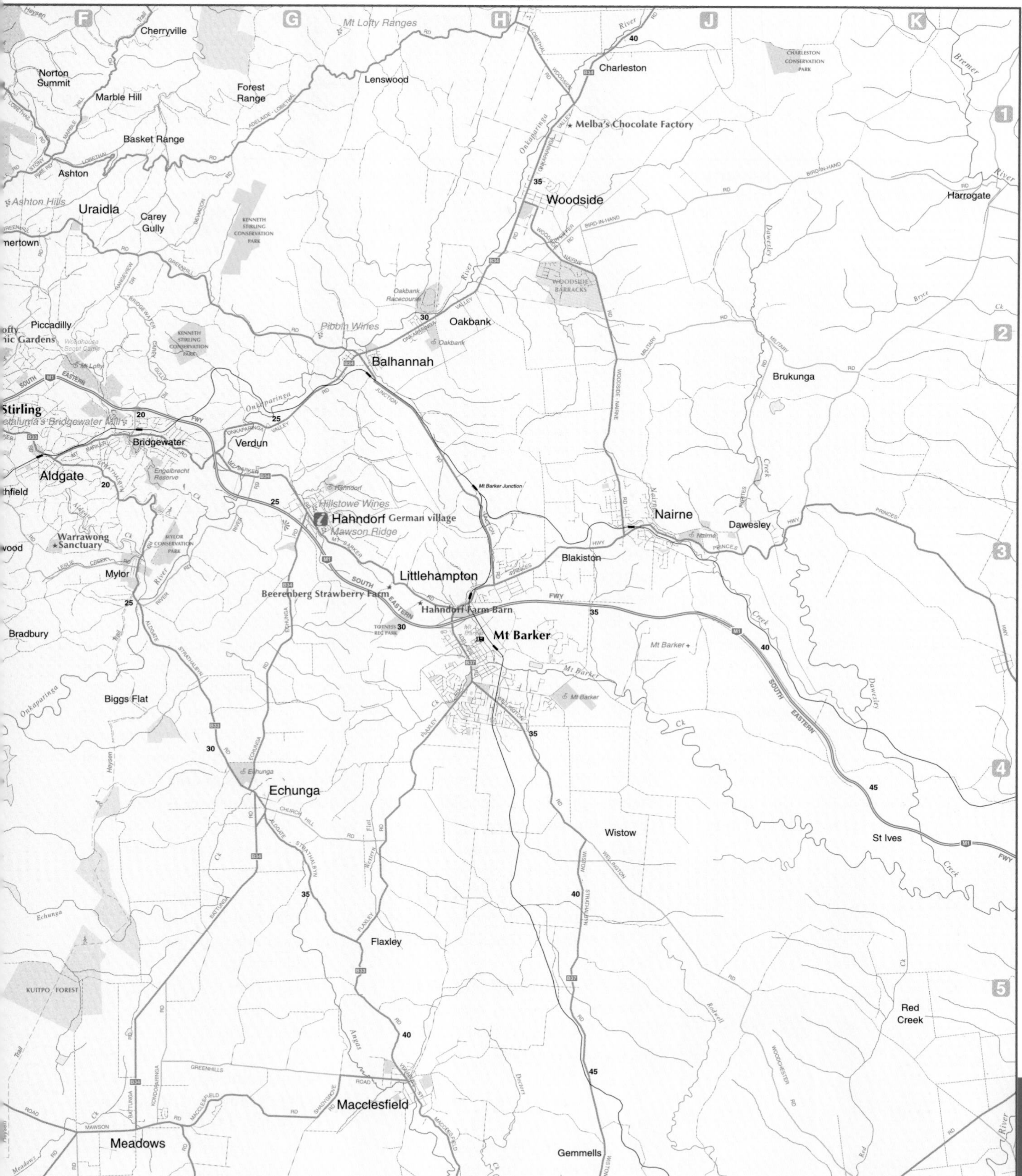

5 Kilometres

F   G   H   J   K

Cherryville

Norton Summit

Marble Hill

Forest Range

Mt Lofty Ranges

Lenswood

Charleston

CHARLESTON CONSERVATION PARK

Basket Range

★ Melba's Chocolate Factory

Ashton

Uraidla

Carey Gully

KENNETH STIRLING CONSERVATION PARK

Woodside

Harrogate

Ashton Hills

WOODSIDE BARRACKS

merton

Piccadilly

nic Gardens

KENNETH STIRLING CONSERVATION PARK

Oakbank Racecourse

Pibbin Wines

Oakbank

Brukunga

Balhannah

Stirling

etalunga's Bridgewater Mills

Bridgewater

Verdun

Mt Barker Junction

Nairne

Dawesley

Aldgate

thfield

Engelbrecht Reserve

Hahndorf   German village

Hillstowe Wines

Mawson Ridge

Blakiston

MYLOR CONSERVATION PARK

Warrawong ★ Sanctuary

Mylor

Littlehampton

Mt Barker +

wood

Beerenberg Strawberry Farm

Hahndorf Farm Barn

Mt Barker

Bradbury

TOTNESS REC PARK

Biggs Flat

Mt Barker

St Ives

Echunga

Wistow

KUITPO FOREST

Flaxley

Red Creek

Macclesfield

Meadows

Gemmells

Woodchester

Prospect Hill

Bletchley

Continued on map 349

■ Angaston   POP 1950

Map 327, D3

A picturesque rural town in the rolling countryside of the Barossa Valley, Angaston is a showcase of colonial architecture. In 1841 the town was named after George Fife Angas an early settler and large landholder.

MAIN ATTRACTIONS: The tree-lined main street, **Murray St**, is lined with art and craft shops and tearooms. Visit the **Angas Park Fruit Co** and try some of the local produce. Around

Diver in the Gulf St Vincent, near Ardrossan

the corner is **Artfully Yours Studio and Gallery** for local arts and crafts. A shady park with picnic and BBQ facilities adjacent to **Angaston Creek** complements the village atmosphere of this little town.

NEARBY ATTRACTIONS: Around 8km south on the Eden Valley Rd the historic National Trust property, **Collingrove** (built for George Angas' son, John), is open for inspection, 11am–4pm. For a spectacular view of the **Barossa Valley** travel 8km south-west of the town to **Menglers Hill** where there is a lookout and sculpture garden. Wineries close by are **Yalumba** (2km south), **Saltram** (1km west) and **Henschke Cellars** (10km SE).

TOURIST INFO: Barossa Wine and Visitor Centre, 66–68 Murray St, Tanunda, Ph: (08) 8563 0600 or 1800 812 662 www.barossa-region.org

■ Ardrossan   POP 1156

Map 348, E1

Ardrossan, on the east coast of the **Yorke Peninsula** and 140km from Adelaide, was proclaimed in 1873. The town sits above 25m cliffs that, although red, are in many ways reminiscent of the famous white cliffs of Dover. Ardrossan is a thriving seaport, shipping dolomite and grain all over the world. Named by Governor Fergusson after the seaport in Ayrshire, Scotland, the name is derived from the Gaelic words 'ard' meaning 'height' and 'ros', a 'prominent rock' or 'headland'.

MAIN ATTRACTIONS: The cliff-top reserve has a lookout, BBQs and a walking track. **Ardrossan and District Historical Museum** is housed in the old powerhouse factory in Fifth St. A room is devoted to *Zanoni*, a wheat clipper that sank off the coast in the 19th century. There is also information on the Australian invention, the stump jump plough, as well as a good collection of farm and agricultural equipment, the town's maritime history and general historical items.

NEARBY ATTRACTIONS: The salt and dolomite mines are definitely worth visiting. Fishing in **Gulf St Vincent** is rewarding all year round for a variety of species. Diving around the wreck of *Zanoni*, 20km off the coast, (for which a permit is necessary) is an exciting experience.

TOURIST INFO: BP Road House, Main Coast Rd, Ph: (08) 8837 3048

Coastal scenery at Beachport

Balaklava POP 1500
Map 349, F1

This town is 91km north of Adelaide on the banks of the **Wakefield River**. Balaklava services a rich pastoral area in the fertile region where the **Adelaide Plains** become the **Mid North**. Farming around Balaklava is diverse, producing wheat, wool, barley, oats, pigs, sheep, poultry and cattle. Local industries include 2 hay processing plants and another for processing legumes and grain for local and overseas markets.

MAIN ATTRACTIONS: Interesting places to visit include the **Court House Gallery** for quality arts and crafts, and the **Local History Museum**, housed in the **Centenary Hall** and open on the second and fourth Sunday of each month. Starting in Elizabeth St, the **Lions Walking Trail** follows the Wakefield River for approximately 2.5km and is popular with residents and visitors alike.

NEARBY ATTRACTIONS: Experience the natural beauty of the **Rocks Reserve** with its abundant flora and fauna. There is a swimming hole on the Wakefield River, where water has sculpted unusual shapes into the rocks. **Port Wakefield**, 26km west, is an historic beachside town.

TOURIST INFO: Wakefield Regional Council, 10 Edith Tce, Ph: (08) 8862 1811

Barmera POP 1963
Map 333, C2

Around 215km NE of Adelaide, Barmera sits on the shore of **Lake Bonney** and is an ideal destination for windsurfing, waterskiing, canoeing, fishing, enjoying a round of golf or sitting and watching the pelicans on the manicured foreshore. Original settlers were attracted by the expanse of fresh water, and by 1846 there were several cattle runs in the area. After WWI, Barmera was opened up for soldier-settlement and a second wave of settlers arrived in 1922.

MAIN ATTRACTIONS: Barmera's picturesque setting and beautiful beaches draw many visitors, and canoes, pedal boats and jet skis can be hired. For an all-over tan, visit the nudist beach at **Point Pelican**. The **Barmera Theatre Gallery** is an outlet for locally executed paintings, crafts and pottery. A boutique winery, **Bonnyview Wines** located on the Sturt Hwy, is open daily for tours and tastings. Close by is **Highway Fern Haven**, a specialist nursery offering ferns and many other plants, and a coffee shop in a lush tropical setting. For fans of country music, pop into **Rockys Hall of Fame**, which showcases country music memorabilia.

NEARBY ATTRACTIONS: **North Lake** is the site of the ruins of **Nappers Accommodation House** (1850), one of the earliest buildings in the area. The town of **Cobdogla** is a small settlement 6km west of Barmera. Of interest here is the **Irrigation and Steam Museum**, home of the famous Humphrey Pump and other engines. **Bookmark Biosphere Reserve** located at Loch Luna, is a wetlands' area of creeks and swamps popular with nature lovers and birdwatchers.

TOURIST INFO: Barwell Ave, Ph: (08) 8588 2289

Beachport POP 455
Map 323, C4

In the 1830s this small coastal town was a whaling station that also serviced rural land opened up by the Henty brothers. Agriculture is still one of the district's sustaining industries but lobster fishing has taken over from whaling. Forestry, vineyards and tourism are now also important to the township.

MAIN ATTRACTIONS: The long screw-pile jetty that juts out into **Rivoli Bay** is a prominent feature of the town and popular with recreational anglers. The 2 museums in town—the **National Trust Museum** (Railway Tce) and the **Artefacts Museum** (McCourt St), explore the town's whaling and Aboriginal heritage. **Centenary Park**, in the centre of town, is a good lunch spot with picnicking and BBQ facilities.

NEARBY ATTRACTIONS: To the northwest of town, the **Beachport CP** protects coastal vegetation and sand dunes between **Lake George** and

The landmark Big Orange, near Berri

the coast. The park has some interesting walking trails. **Bowman Scenic Dr**, commencing at the end of Foster St, reveals magnificent coastal views of rugged, weathered, limestone cliffs contrasting with secluded white sandy beaches and a profusion of native vegetation. The **Pool of Siloam**, located just behind the town, is a small lake claimed to have healing qualities because of its high salt content.
TOURIST INFO: Millicent Rd, Ph: (08) 8735 8029

■ Berri   POP 5950
Map 333, C2
Founded in 1911, the town of Berri owes its existence to irrigation. It is built on the site of what was originally a refuelling stop for traffic on the **Murray River** in the 1880s. The town is now known as the 'Heart of the Riverland' and has become an important regional centre. The name 'Berri' comes from the Aboriginal word 'ber-beri' meaning 'wide bend in the river'.

MAIN ATTRACTIONS: Berri has the largest shopping complex in the **Riverland**, and excellent facilities for a range of sports including golf, tennis, bowling, fishing, canoeing and waterskiing. Visit **Earth Works** and the **Berri Art Gallery** for local arts and crafts. For a great view of the town try the **Water Tower Lookout** on Fiedler St. To cruise the Murray, houseboats are for hire from the large local fleet. Close to the marina there is a memorial sculpture garden to **Jimmy James**, one of Australia's most famous and respected Aboriginal trackers.
NEARBY ATTRACTIONS: On the highway at **Glossop**, **Berri Estates Winery** has cellar door sales. The **Murray River NP** is 10km SW of town and offers fishing, birdwatching, walking trails and camping. Between Berri and **Renmark** lies the **Big Orange** tourist attraction—a sales outlet with souvenirs, refreshments and a children's playground.
TOURIST INFO: 24 Vaughan Tce, Ph: (08) 8582 5299

■ Bordertown   POP 2324
Map 323, E1
Bordertown is about 20km from the state border at the junction of the road linking Adelaide and Melbourne and the north–south route from the **Riverland** to **Mount Gambier**. Established in 1852 adjacent to the **Tatiara Creek**, the town was originally the site of a base camp. The camp was created by Police Inspector Alexander Tolmer, who was in charge of the gold escorts from the Victorian goldfields to Adelaide. At one time the border between South Australia and Victoria was not very far from the town—hence its name.
MAIN ATTRACTIONS: There are parks and gardens, which are good for picnics or BBQs. **Tolmer Park** has an interpretative walk that explains the history of the area. For a swim in an Olympic-sized pool, **Memorial**

Park is the place. A **Wildlife Park** on North Tce exhibits rare white kangaroos, as well as friendly wallabies, emus and waterbirds. **Hawke House Museum**, the birthplace of former Australian Prime Minister **Robert J Hawke**, is on the corner of Farquhar and Binnie sts and is open weekdays, 9am–5pm.
NEARBY ATTRACTIONS: **Clayton Farm**, 3km from the town centre, is an historic site and agricultural museum. The heritage-listed **Old Mundulla Hotel**, 10km west at **Mundulla**, offers memorabilia, arts, crafts and refreshments. Just north off the hwy, **Recreation Lake** is another good spot for BBQs, canoeing and fishing. **Poocher Swamp**, 8.5km to the west, is noted for its magnificent red gums and prolific birdlife.
TOURIST INFO: Tolmer Park, 81 North Tce, Ph: (08) 8752 0700

■ Burra   POP 1065
Map 347, F6
Burra is located 154km north of **Adelaide**. A treasure, it is listed on the National Estate and is a declared State Heritage Area. The first mining-company town, known as Kooringa, was established by 1851. With a population of more than 5000 people, many of whom lived in small satellite villages based around a different British regional identity. In time, the settlements merged to become Burra. Today tourism and pastoral industries form the town's economic base.
MAIN ATTRACTIONS: As there is so much to see in this small town it is worthwhile using the guide *Discovering Historic Burra*. Walks around the town and through the cemetery are a good introduction to Burra's heritage. The town's museums are well worth visiting, including the **Burra Mine Open Air Museum**, once a copper mine, it features a powder magazine dating to 1847. Also worth a look are historic sites

South Australia

such as the underground cellars of the old **Unicorn Brewery**; **Redruth Gaol**, which was used in the 1979 film, *Breaker Morant*; the **old copper mines**; and **miners' dugouts**—by 1851 almost 2000 miners lived in caverns dug into the banks of the Burra Creek until forced out by floods.

NEARBY ATTRACTIONS: Go horseriding with **Burra Trail Rides**, tour the **Mongolata Gold Mine** by appointment, or take a trip up **Burra Gorge**, a scenic picnic and camping area 27km east of the town.

TOURIST INFO: 2 Market Sq, Ph: (08) 8892 2154

Bute POP 300

Map 346, E6

Proclaimed in 1884, this quiet little town at the northern end of the **Yorke Peninsula** caters for the needs of the surrounding agricultural and pastoral districts. Local industries include the manufacture of farm machinery and a working tannery.

MAIN ATTRACTIONS: The public is welcome at the **Bute Tannery**, which is located off Port Broughton Rd. A range of skins, hides and a variety of personal goods including ugg boots, belts, bags and sheepskin jackets are available. A picnic area with a fauna park housing native and other animals is located at Railway Tce. **Gunner Bill's Gallery** on Railway Tce has displays of arts and crafts and an historical gallery. An old well just off Kulpara Rd, used for watering stock in times past, is now of historic interest.

NEARBY ATTRACTIONS: Bute was finally put on the map by the famous **Yorke Peninsula Machinery Field Days**, which were first held near the township in 1895, making them the oldest event of their kind in Australia. Now a multimillion dollar biennial event, the field days are held in **Paskeville** to the south-west.

TOURIST INFO: Bay St, Port Broughton, Ph: (08) 8635 2261

Ceduna POP 2637

Map 345, H4

Spread along the shores of beautiful **Murat Bay**, Ceduna is the eastern gateway to the **Nullarbor Plain**. Established in 1896, it is a fishing and oyster farming town, as well as the commercial centre for the pastoral and cereal-growing area of the **Far West**. The town is a popular stopover prior to, or after crossing the vast Nullarbor Plain.

MAIN ATTRACTIONS: The **Old School House Museum** in Park Tce exhibits pioneer memorabilia and items from **Maralinga**, site of British atomic testing. **Ceduna Arts and Cultural Centre**, on Poynton St, features local art and craftwork. **The Sea Dragon Art Gallery** and the **Memorial Hall** also showcase works by local artists. The white sandy beaches of Ceduna are perfect for swimming and watersports.

NEARBY ATTRACTIONS: In winter, whale-watching excursions to the **Great Australian Bight** can be arranged through the visitor information centre. **Whale Air** also offers visitors a stunning birdseye view of whales and the coastal cliffs. At **Denial Bay** (13km west) are the **McKenzie Ruins**—site of the

original settlement. Tours of **Clear Water Oyster Farm** are available. East of Ceduna, **Wittelbee CP** is an attractive combination of fine sandy beaches broken by low rocky headlands. **Laura Bay CP** is south-east of the town and offers a great walking track that explores the rocky headland, sandy cove and rockpools at low tide. **Paul's Fish Factory** at **Thevenard Boat Haven** has fresh seafood for sale.

TOURIST INFO: 58 Poynton St, Ph: (08) 8625 2780 or 1800 639 413

Clare POP 3365

Map 347, F6

Clare lies at the northern end of the **Clare Valley**, renowned as one of South Australia's premium wine-producing regions. Close enough to **Adelaide** to be accessible to day-trippers, the picturesque valley offers a full range of accommodation. Settled in 1842, the town is named after County Clare in Ireland.

MAIN ATTRACTIONS: The many National Trust-classified buildings can be seen on the **historic town walk**, including **Wolta Wolta Homestead** (1846) and the **Old Police Station Museum** in Neagles Rock Rd, which holds memorabilia and early records

Sandy Cove, Laura Bay CP, south-east of Ceduna

of the district. There are a number of shady parks perfect for picnics and BBQ's and walking trails at **Inchiquin Lake**, Clare's main water-storage area. Not too far from the town centre, **Billy Goat Hill** provides good views of the region. NEARBY ATTRACTIONS: Many appealing galleries and restaurants can be found throughout the Clare Valley. As well there are tours of the working **Bungaree Sheep Station**, which was established in 1841. Most popular of course are the wineries found in the region. The first vines planted were at **Sevenhill**, 7km south of Clare, by a Jesuit priest from Austria. Now there are more than 30 wineries in the valley, including **Tim Adams, Knappstein, Eldredge, Wilson Vineyard, Stringy Brae, Waninga, Mitchell, Crabtree of Watervale, Olssen** and **Taylors**. The **Clare Valley Riesling Trail**, a pathway suitable for cyclists and walkers, runs 27km from Clare to **Auburn** and is an ideal way to experience the picturesque countryside. A few kilometres from historic **Mintaro** is **Martindale Hall**, one of South Australia's finest mansions. It offers accommodation and meals. TOURIST INFO: Town Hall, 229 Main North Rd, Ph: (08) 8842 2131

■ Cleve   POP 750
Map 346, C6

The large rural district surrounding this **Eyre Peninsula** town produces mainly wheat and sheep. Cleve is a neat and interesting town surrounded by rolling hills. First settled in 1883 as **Wangaraleednie Station** by Scotsman James McKenzie and his brothers, the farming community grew and eventually the town of Cleve was proclaimed. MAIN ATTRACTIONS: Recreation areas fringe 3 sides of the town and include an 18-hole golf course, sports ovals, swimming pool, tennis and basketball courts and a bowling green. TOURIST INFO: Cleve Newsagency and Garden Centre, Fourth St, Ph: (08) 8628 2183

■ Coffin Bay   POP 430
Map 348, B1

This delightful holiday retreat and fishing village is located 51km north-west of **Port Lincoln**. Coffin Bay was named (1802) by Matthew Flinders to honour Sir Isaac Coffin. Ironically though, many shipwrecks and drownings have occurred on the exposed coastline. In the 1840s, oysters and scale fish were harvested and shipped to markets in Adelaide. Oyster farming is now important to the community.

MAIN ATTRACTIONS: The 12km **Oyster Walk** along the foreshore to **Long Beach** gives an excellent view of the entire bay. It provides an opportunity for both visitors and locals to relax and enjoy the picturesque coastline with seats, pergolas and BBQ facilities along the way. Watersports, relaxing on the beach or in charter boats are the main attractions in the town. NEARBY ATTRACTIONS: **Coffin Bay NP** is a diverse landscape ranging from ancient granite hills and outcrops, high windswept sandstone and limestone cliffs, mobile sand dune systems and long white beaches with pounding surf to the sheltered waters of **Yangie** and Coffin Bay. Bushwalking, camping, boating, swimming in sheltered waters and guided 4WD tours are all popular activities in the area. TOURIST INFO: Beachcomber Mobil Service Station, Esplanade, Ph: (08) 8685 4057

■ Coober Pedy   POP 3500
Map 342, A5

Coober Pedy, known as the last frontier and '**Australia's opal mining capital**', is a modern mining town. Well-known for its unusual 'dugouts'—underground accommodation which enables the inhabitants to escape scorching summer heat. The Aboriginal name, 'Kupa piti', means 'uninitiated man', or 'white man hole'. MAIN ATTRACTIONS: With 2 hotels, the aboveground **Opal Inn** and underground **Desert Cave**, as well as other accommodation, the town caters well for visitors. Experience the underground mining museums, mine tours and opal cutting demonstrations on a range of tours of the town. Attractions include the **Old Timers Mine** off Crowders Gully Rd; **Umoona Museum** on Hutchison St, which concentrates on local Aboriginal heritage; **Coober Pedy Underground Pottery; Underground Books & Gallery;** and the **Big**

Avoid Bay, Coffin Bay NP

South Australia

Underground church at Coober Pedy

Winch Lookout, accessed off Italian Club Rd, is spectacular after dark or during one of the region's frequent lightning storms.

NEARBY ATTRACTIONS: **Breakaways Reserve**, 23km north on the Sturt Hwy, protects an area featuring unique flora and fauna, best viewed at sunrise or sunset. Visitors are requested to stay on the marked tracks, as the ecosystem is very fragile. Locals and visitors can go 'noodling', that is searching through mullocks (mounds of dirt and rock) for overlooked pieces of opal. Permission must first be obtained from the owner. Extreme care must be taken in the opal fields to avoid falling into abandoned shafts.

TOURIST INFO: Council Offices, Hutchinson St, Ph: (08) 8672 5298 or 1800 637 076

■ Cowell   POP 767
Map 346, D6

Located on **Franklin Harbour**, Cowell was first settled in 1853; the town was known as Flinders Lakes until 1880. Nearby **Minbrie Ranges** have large deposits of jade. Local industry includes jade and granite mining and processing, agriculture, and aquaculture based on oyster, snapper and kingfish farming in Franklin Harbour.

MAIN ATTRACTIONS: Watersports are popular, including swimming, waterskiing, sailing and fishing for snapper and King George whiting. The old Post Office is home to the **Franklin Harbour Historical Museum**. Restored by the National Trust the museum displays old photographs, documents, books, memorabilia and geological specimens. There is an open-air **Agricultural Museum** on the Lincoln Hwy, and a restored Ruston Proctor steam tractor in the parklands opposite the St John's Ambulance building. With more than 40% of South Australia's oysters grown in Cowell, dining alfresco on fresh seafood is popular.

NEARBY ATTRACTIONS: **Franklin Harbour CP** is south of the town and home to great fishing, swimming and picnic spots. Both north and south of Cowell there are beaches worth visiting—**Lucky Bay** (16km north) and **The Knob** (13km south). Seals are often seen at **Point Price**, south of Cowell.

TOURIST INFO: District Council of Franklin Harbour, Main St, Ph: (08) 8629 2019

■ Crystal Brook   POP 1800
Map 346, E5

Proclaimed in 1874, the township of Crystal Brook is located where the southern **Flinders Ranges** begin. Today, the rolling plains surrounding this quiet and picturesque country town produce barley and wheat as well as sheep and cattle.

MAIN ATTRACTIONS: The National Trust **Old Bakehouse Museum** on Brandis St displays pioneering artefacts, photographs and memorabilia. It also has an underground baker's oven, a relic of the building's original purpose. Local crafts are available at **Crystal Crafts** in Bowman St. Both of the town's hotels were built in the 1800s, and there are many attractive old stone homes to wander past. Picnic and BBQ areas are found in **Adelaide Square**—in the town centre—and in **Jubilee Park**.

NEARBY ATTRACTIONS: Only 5km east of town are the remains of historic **Bowman Homestead**, which has been incorporated into **Bowman Park**, an attractive recreation area with extensive facilities including a wildlife park, marked bushwalking tracks and a section of the superb **Heysen Trail**. At **Redhill**, 25km away, the riverside walk, museum, craft shop and antique shop are the main attractions.

TOURIST INFO: Port Pirie Regional Tourism and Arts Centre, 3 Mary Elie St, Ph: (08) 8633 0439 or 1800 000 424

■ Cummins   POP 750
Map 348, B1

Serving an important agricultural district on the **Lower Eyre Peninsula**, Cummins is a small town established in 1902. In 1907 the railway from **Port Lincoln** arrived, providing a direct link to the region's main economy. The only operating flour mill on the peninsula is located here. The town was named after William Patrick Cummins, a member of the South Australian House of Assembly.

MAIN ATTRACTIONS: The unusual double railway line through the centre of town is the venue for the annual **Kalamazoo Classic** event in April. Kalamazoos are trolleys manually operated with a pumping action that race up and down the dual tracks. Craft, souvenirs and gifts are available at **Palm Court Crafts** in Bruce Tce. Close by, the **Railway Triangle** has picnic and BBQ facilities as well as a playground.

NEARBY ATTRACTIONS: Cummins is a good base for touring the Lower Eyre Peninsula. There are magnificent surfing and fishing beaches only 30min to the east and west of town. The **Kapinnie Lakes**, **Mount Greenly** and the drystone walls around **Lake Hamilton** are popular attractions in the region. The town of **Koppio** is south-east of Cummins and the home of **Koppio Smithy Museum**.

TOURIST INFO: Palm Court Crafts, 64 Bruce Tce, Ph: (08) 8676 2522

■ Edithburgh   POP 475
Map 348, E2

Located at the heel of the **Yorke Peninsula**, Edithburgh is an attractive tourist and fishing township overlooking **Gulf St Vincent** and **Troubridge Island**. The town enjoys a good reputation for the high standard and range of food available in local restaurants. Settled in the 1870s, the first 2 hotels—**Troubridge** and **Edithburgh**—are still standing in their original form. The town was once the centre of a thriving salt extraction industry based around **Lake Fowler**, one of the many salt lakes in the region.

MAIN ATTRACTIONS: **Edithburgh Museum** concentrates on the official maritime history of the town as well as the history of salt scraping and the settlement's pioneers. The 17ha **Native Flora Park** on Ansty Tce, located near the town centre, is a haven for people, plants and birdlife. Of interest are the town jetty built in 1873 and the natural tidal pool.

Coastal dunes near West Cape, Innes NP, west of Edithburgh

NEARBY ATTRACTIONS: **Innes NP** is an easy drive to the south-west tip of the peninsula and is famous for its magnificent coastal scenery and wildflowers in spring. Guided tours of Tourbridge Island are available and visitors can marvel at the array of resident seabirds, including little penguins. For keen anglers, **Tourbridge Point** offers catches of tommy ruff, mullet and whiting, as well as stunning views of the notorious shipwreck-littered coastline where the *Clan Ranald* and *Iron King* went down.

TOURIST INFO: Post Office, Edith St, Ph: (08) 8852 6295

■ Eudunda   POP 915
Map 349, F1

The township of Eudunda is just off the main road, in the rich farming area of the **Lower Mid North**. The town grew from a watering stop for stock brought overland from Queensland and New South Wales en route to Adelaide. It was the town's fresh-water springs that attracted the drovers.

MAIN ATTRACTIONS: The **Eudunda Town Walk** passes by many heritage homes and public buildings, including historic **Laucke Flour Mill**, which still operates producing chaff. Maps of the walk are available from the **Eudunda Family Heritage Gallery**, 19 Bruce St, open Fri–Sun. A life-size sculpture of **Colin Thiele**, poet and writer of children's books, who was born in the town in 1920, is in **Centenary Gardens** opposite the **Memorial Town Gardens**. The town offers a number of sporting facilities.

NEARBY ATTRACTIONS: At **Point Pass**, a small town 10min north, the **Old Emmanuel College**, **manse** and **church**, are a reminder of the religious strength of the settlement years. The more energetic explorers may want to climb the 100 steps to the top of the town lookout and view the wheat and grazing lands and mallee scrubs extending east towards the **River Murray**. **Burra Creek Gorge** picnic and camping grounds, 25min north of Eudunda via Point Pass and heading towards **Burra**, is a nature lover's paradise with small waterfalls and wildlife.

TOURIST INFO: Eudunda Heritage Gallery, 19 Bruce St, Ph: (08) 8581 1218

South Australia

■ Freeling   POP 1080

Map 349, F1

This town is positioned to take advantage of 2 worlds. Its location at the northern edge of the **Barossa Valley**, close to **Gawler** and only 60km from Adelaide, means that residents are able to commute to the larger Barossa towns or the capital for employment and facilities, while remaining in peaceful and serene surroundings. The town has an agricultural machinery manufacturer, stockfeed mill and other small industries.

MAIN ATTRACTIONS: The old stone buildings of the town date back to the 1860s, and are definitely worth a look. Of main interest to visitors is the **railway precinct**, which offers guided tours of the railway and town. To obtain tour information and bookings, contact the Council Office. There is a 'town breakfast' held on Australia Day, and Christmastime brings a carnival and Carols by Candlelight.

TOURIST INFO: Council Offices, 12 Hanson St, Ph: (08) 8525 2028

■ Gawler   POP 17 540

Map 301, F1

Around 44km NE of Adelaide, the town of Gawler began as a supply centre for the copper-mining towns of **Kapunda** and **Burra**. In the 1870s and 1880s, when entrepreneurs built flour mills to process grain grown by pioneer agriculturalists, the town boomed. The rural depression at the beginning of the 20th century was a prelude to Gawler's decline and in the 1930s with the Great Depression, the town's manufacturing industries closed. However, due to its strategic position, Gawler survived and today is largely a commercial service centre for the surrounding farmlands.

MAIN ATTRACTIONS: The sporting facilities—2 golf courses, bowling and croquet lawns, a heated pool, tennis courts, trotting grounds, and a racecourse—attract visitors to the town. The town walking routes are popular activities, the **Church Hill Estate Area Walk** being a very interesting walk through the original town centre. The busy Thursday morning market held in **Gawler South Hall** attracts many shoppers and browsers. The **National Trust and Gawler Heritage Museum** has interesting exhibits. **Para Para Historic Mansion** can be viewed from Penrith Ave.

NEARBY ATTRACTIONS: The wineries of the **Barossa Valley** are only a 15min drive east of the town centre. **Roseworthy Campus, University of Adelaide**, was established in 1883 as Australia's first agricultural teaching college and research centre. Today the college is famous for its wine industry research. **Dryland Farming Museum**, located on the campus, is open Wednesday and the third Sunday of every month, although tours can be arranged at other times by appointment.

TOURIST INFO: 2 Lyndoch Rd, Ph: (08) 8522 6814

■ Gladstone   POP 860

Map 347, F5

Originally there were 2 separate towns—Gladstone (east) and **Booyoolee** (west)—which officially merged in 1940. In earlier times, the town was an important railway junction that serviced the surrounding rural area, but more recently it has grown as the hub of a prosperous farming and pastoral community. The silos here are South Australia's largest inland grain storage facilities, capable of holding 500 000 tonnes of grain from the region.

MAIN ATTRACTIONS: The lovely old sandstone homes and historic gaol are favourite points of interest in town. **Gladstone Gaol** was built in the 1880s and is well worth visiting—the 'complete' history of the town is held within its walls; it is open daily 9am–5pm.

NEARBY ATTRACTIONS: **Beetaloo Valley** offers scenic drives to picnic grounds at **Beetaloo Dam**, the **Heysen Trail** and **Bundaleer Forest Reserve**, which has excellent walks and picnic areas.

TOURIST INFO: Post Office, Ph: (08) 8662 2103

■ Goolwa   POP 3950

Map 337, E2

Located on the **Murray River**, the town of Goolwa is a popular holiday spot within easy reach of **Adelaide**. This charming old river port is steeped in steam and riverboat history. In its heyday between the 1850s and the 1880s, the town was a prosperous port where riverboats from New South Wales and Victoria unloaded at Goolwa wharf. From here, wool and grain were shipped to Victor Harbor, Port Adelaide and beyond. However, this early prosperity did not last after the Morgan to Port Adelaide railway opened in 1878 and the river trade on the lower reaches dwindled.

MAIN ATTRACTIONS: Goolwa is a haven for watersports like fishing, windsurfing, yachting, jet skiing and power boating. There are many well-preserved stone and brick buildings and history-lovers will enjoy the **heritage walks**; details at the information centre. **Signal Point Murray Interpretive Centre** showcases all facets of the river's history, open 9am–5pm daily.

Corio Hotel, Goolwa

FLINDERS RANGES

Renowned for its rugged mountain scenery, deep gorges and tranquil valleys, this is a land of legends, telling tales of adventure, hardship, success and failure. Located north of Adelaide, the ancient landscape of the Flinders Ranges has constantly been reshaped over the ages—granite, dating to 600 million years, has been found. The superb **Brachina Gorge** offers up secrets of its geological history. Seashell remains have been found in the midst of rocky inland deserts and there are remnants of fossilised palm trees. The walls of the gorge at **Mount Billy Creek** have fossils embedded in them, meaning this area was once an ancient seabed.

For more than 40 000 years Aboriginal people lived in this area; ceremonial grounds, cave paintings and carvings testify to their cultural and spiritual links with the land.

There are a great many natural attractions to explore in this region, including vast salt lakes, historic mining areas, rock formations, gorges and picturesque waterholes and a range of flora and fauna—some of it rare.

main attractions

❖ Arkaroola Wilderness Sanctuary
❖ Flinders Ranges NP
❖ Gammon Ranges NP
❖ Wilpena Pound

i Tourist information

Wadlata Outback Centre/Flinders Ranges and Outback Interpretive Centre
41 Flinders Tce,
Port Augusta, SA 5700
Ph: (08) 8641 0793
wadlata@portaugusta.sa.gov.au

Cazneaux Tree, near Wilpena, Flinders Ranges NP

NEARBY ATTRACTIONS: **The Bird Sanctuary** east of Goolwa is home to swans, pelicans and other water-birds. A visit to **Hindmarsh Island** gives visitors a feel for the Aboriginal and colonial heritage of the area—it is a very important site for local Aboriginal people, especially the women. A bridge links the island to the mainland. The wide expanse of **Coorong NP** stretches to **Kingston**. This unique wetland area's name is from the Aboriginal word 'karangh', meaning 'narrow neck'. The park comprises a chain of saltwater lagoons separated from the sea by the narrow **Younghusband Peninsula**. Day cruises around the wetland are available on the *Wetland Explorer* and the *Spirit of the Coorong*.
TOURIST INFO: Signal Point, The Wharf, Ph: (08) 8555 1144

■ Hawker   POP 450
Map 313, B3

This is an ideal base from which to explore the stunning scenery of the **Flinders Ranges** and surrounding area. The town of Hawker was proclaimed in 1880, and was once a thriving railway town, this role changed in the mid-1950s when the railway line was moved further west. Hawker then became more tourist-orientated, offering accommodation and services for people visiting the Flinders Ranges.
MAIN ATTRACTIONS: **Hawker Motors Museum** has information on all of the town's attractions as well as a small display of fossils, minerals and pioneer memorabilia. The historic buildings of the town are identified in the **Historic Walk** pamphlet, and include the **Post Office**, **Hawker**

Hotel and the old **Railway Station**. There are also 4WD tours of the area.
NEARBY ATTRACTIONS: **Jarvis Hill**, 6km SW, has a walking track and lookout. There are fine views from the **Yourambulla Caves**, 11km south, which also contain Aboriginal rock art. The ruins of **Hookina** and the old **Kanyaka Homestead** are good examples of the region's abandoned settlements. Close by are the spectacular landscapes of **Quorn**, **Pichi Richi Pass**, **Wilpena**, **Brachina** and **Bunyeroo gorges**, the **Leigh Creek Coalfields** and **Aroona Dam**. A popular tourist route, the **Moralana Scenic Drive**, links the roads to **Wilpena Pound** and **Leigh Creek**. There are scenic flights from **Rawnsley Park** and Wilpena.
TOURIST INFO: Hawker Motors, Cnr Cradock and Wilpena rds, Ph: (08) 8648 4283

South Australia

Continued on map 347

Scale 1:750 000

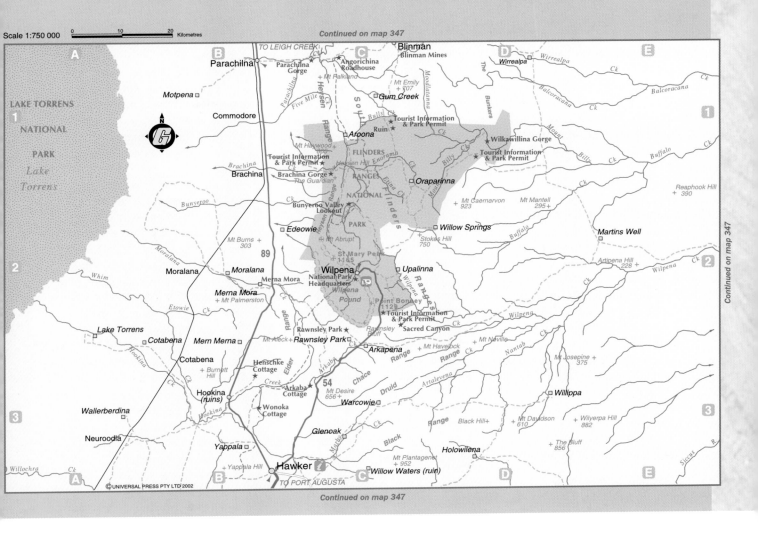

Continued on map 347

Continued on map 347

■ Jamestown POP 1589

Map 347, F5

Around 205km from Adelaide, Jamestown is a picturesque town that serves a prosperous area in the state's **Mid North**. Farmers here produce sheep, cattle, wheat, barley and legumes. Timber from pine and eucalypt plantations at nearby **Bundaleer Forest** is also important to the local economy. Sir James Fergusson, Governor of South Australia 1869–1873, named the town after himself.

MAIN ATTRACTIONS: The **National Trust Museum** preserves the past in the old Railway Station complex. Displays include mementos of the district's pioneering days as well as vintage railway equipment. There are self-guided **town** and **cemetery walks** worth taking. **Belalie Creek**,

a beautiful, permanent watercourse, flows through Jamestown and creates a pleasant setting for picnics and BBQs.

NEARBY ATTRACTIONS: **Bundaleer Forest Reserve**, first established in 1875, is 9km south of the town. Here, forest walks, picnics and BBQs are popular activities, and there is a playground for children. Bushwalkers using the **Heysen Trail** may come upon the restored **Curnow's Hut**, which is available as accommodation. **The Old Bundaleer Homestead**, a classic rural mansion, is also located in the reserve. Beyond the forest, **New Campbell Hill** provides panoramic views towards **Mount Remarkable**.

TOURIST INFO: Country Retreat Caravan Park, 103 Ayr St, Ph: (08) 8664 0077

■ Kadina POP 3772

Map 346, E6

The largest of the 3 towns on the **Yorke Peninsula** which make up the **Copper Triangle**, Kadina was proclaimed in 1862, after the discovery of copper ore nearby. The mines in the area were productive for about 60 years; they closed in the 1920s, and Kadina became the peninsula's regional service centre, with wheat, barley and sheep forming the basis of its prosperity.

MAIN ATTRACTIONS: Old stone buildings—hotels, churches, houses and mine sites have all been preserved and can be viewed via the **Kadina Heritage Trail**. The trail takes in 38 historic sites and begins at the **Railway Station**, heads west to the **Wallaroo Mine Historic Site** and then returns to the town centre via

the **National Dryland Farming Centre**. The centre includes **Matta House**, an original mine manager's house built in 1863, and thematic and photographic displays. The **Banking and Currency Museum** is an award-winning display of banking history located in a splendid old bank building in Graves St.
NEARBY ATTRACTIONS: The biennial **Kernewek Lowender (Cornish Festival)** is held in May of odd numbered years. This is a joint festival of the 3 towns of the Copper Triangle celebrating their Cornish heritage. Kadina, **Wallaroo** and **Moonta** together attract thousands of visitors for a 3-day long festival of fairs, dancing, games and processions. **Yorke Peninsula Field Days** are also held biennially in September in odd years. The Copper Coast is renowned for its excellent fishing, crabbing and safe beaches.
TOURIST INFO: National Dryland Farming Centre, Moonta Rd, Ph: 1800 654 991

■ Kapunda   POP 2418
Map 349, F1

After green copper ore was discovered (1842) the town of Kapunda was established (1845). It is located 80km north of Adelaide on the edge of the **Barossa Valley**. The Great Kapunda Mine opened in 1844 and in a period of 40 years produced about 14 000 tonnes of copper ore.
MAIN ATTRACTIONS: The 8m bronze figure, *Map of Kernow*, (son of Conwall), is a tribute to Cornish miners who arrived in large numbers in the 19th century. There is an excellent **Museum and Mine Interpretation Centre** in Hill St that brings the mining heritage to life. It is possible to walk around the mine site. Kapunda's heritage-listed buildings are a striking feature, especially the magnificent cast-iron lacework adorning them. Many trails, such as the **Mawson Cycling Trail** and **Heysen Walking Trail** may be

joined at Kapunda, as well as a **Heritage Trail** (visitors can walk or drive the trail). The **Sir Sidney Kidman Trail** takes in the cattle king's former home, Eringa, the burial site of his children, and places where he conducted the largest horse sales in the Southern Hemisphere. **Kapunda Gallery** showcases travelling exhibitions and artworks of the region.
NEARBY ATTRACTIONS: A scenic drive links Kapunda with the small town of **Eudunda**, 28km NE, and continues on to **Morgan** and the **Riverland** region. **Pines Reserve**, 6km NW, is a good picnic and wildlife-watching spot. **Scholz Park Museum** at Riverton (30km NW) and historic **Anlaby Station** (16km NE) are worth visiting. Anlaby Station has restored buildings, beautiful gardens and a collection of 40 horse-drawn vehicles.
TOURIST INFO: 7 Hill St, Ph: (08) 8566 2902

■ Keith   POP 1124
Map 349, H4

Known as the **'Gateway to the south-east'**, the modern rural town of Keith was once part of the arid **Ninety Mile Desert**. In the 1950s the CSIRO carried out experiments that showed the land could be made to be fertile. Modern farming methods then opened up the land to agriculture and now some of the state's leading cattle studs are established in the district.
MAIN ATTRACTIONS: One of the most impressive of the early buildings in Heritage St is the former **Congregational Church** (1910). Built of local stone, it has some original leadlight windows and some new ones portraying pioneering history. The park in Heritage St has a rotunda and playground and is popular with visitors. On the southeast edge of town lies **Lions Club Park**, with picnic areas and a children's playground. There is an 18-hole golf course 5km east on Emu Flat Rd, where the large licensed clubhouse commands views of the township.
NEARBY ATTRACTIONS: **Ngarkat CP** is the largest unspoiled wilderness in the south-east. Native flora and fauna abound in this park, which is ideal

The Cornish festival Kernewek Lowender is celebrated every 2 years in Kadina and other towns of the Copper Triangle

South Australia

National Trust and Folk Museum, Kingscote, Kangaroo Island

for bushwalking and has designated camping areas. **Mount Monster CP** is a much smaller park 14km south of town. Here, birds and animals share their home with picnickers. **Kelvin Prowrie Reserve**, 8km to the north, is another good picnic area.
TOURIST INFO: Penny Farthing Coffee and Crafts, 15 Heritage St, Ph: (08) 8755 1061

Kimba   POP 742

Map 346, C5
The township of Kimba promotes itself as the place 'halfway across Australia', although this is not entirely accurate. The town was proclaimed in 1914, after mallee was cleared to make way for the planting of wheat. Before then, huge sheep and cattle properties, established by settlers in the 1870s, occupied the land.
MAIN ATTRACTIONS: The **Halfway Across Australia Gem Shop** is identified by a 8m-high pink and grey galah, an attraction that provides tourist information as well as natural and cut rocks, gemstones, gifts and souvenirs. The main street of town, **High St**, is lined with good shops and cafes, including the **Pine 'n' Pug Gallery**. Sporting facilities include a golf course, swimming pool, bowling green, tennis court, croquet lawn, sports ovals and horse and harness race tracks. Experience a Pioneer House, school and blacksmith's shop at **Kimba Historical Museum**.
NEARBY ATTRACTIONS: The **Gawler Ranges** are not far to the north of town and can be visited in a day; take in the natural beauty and prolific birdlife of this area. However, the area must be treated as private property, so visitors should keep to the main roads and seek permission to camp or travel across the land. On the highway, 19km east of Kimba, **Lake Gillies CP** is a protected habitat for a variety of birdlife including mallee fowl; activities in the park are restricted to picnicking and bushwalking.
TOURIST INFO: Kimba Halfway Across Australia Gem Shop, Eyre Hwy, Ph: (08) 8627 2766

Kingscote   POP 1595

Map 317, D2
The largest town on **Kangaroo Island** (110km south-west of Adelaide), Kingscote was actually the first European settlement in the state (1836). The island can be accessed from **Cape Jervis** to **Penneshaw** via the *Kangaroo Island SeaLink* vehicular ferry, or fly from Adelaide to Kingscote.
MAIN ATTRACTIONS: For a historic look at the town, wander by **Hope Cottage**; the **National Trust and Folk Museum**; **St Alban's Church** with stained-glass windows and pioneer memorials; and the **town cemetery**, the oldest in the State. There is a variety of hotels, restaurants and cafes in town and for transport; cars, bicycles and scooters can be hired. The carved-out **Rock Pool** is a good swimming spot; for fishing try the jetty which is great for squid, tommy ruff, trevally, garfish, whiting and snook. Tours to see the little penguins depart from **Ozone Seafront Hotel**. **The Kangaroo Island Marine Centre** at **Kingscote Wharf** has displays of seahorses, sea anemones and wrasse and daily pelican feeding at 5pm, as well as penguin tours.
NEARBY ATTRACTIONS: The national park and conservation areas abound with opportunities to swim, surf, dive and fish. As well, there is the option of joining a guided coach or surf tour, 4WD adventure, wilderness excursion, fishing trip or diving charter. On the west of the island is the pristine **Flinders Chase NP** a sanctuary for some of the country's rarest wildlife. There are guided tours for **Seal Bay**, **Kelly Hill Caves**, **Cape Borda** and **Cape Willoughby**. About 20km south on Wilson Rd is a **eucalyptus oil distillery** and slightly further on is **Clifford's Honey Farm**. For spectacular views it is worth the 50km journey to **Prospect Hill Lookout**. **A Maze 'N' Fun**, 10min drive from Kingscote, has Australia's largest hedge maze, a 'Rainbow Special' railway ride, crazy golf, BBQs, picnic facilities and a kiosk.
TOURIST INFO: Howard Dr, Penneshaw, Ph: (08) 8553 1185

Kingston SE   POP 1575

Map 323, B2
This once small village, located on the shores of **Lacepede Bay**, is now a regional centre for an area producing sheep, lambs, cattle and crops, with some producers diversifying into viticulture, horticulture and aquaculture. Crayfishing is also an important part of Kingston SE's economy. The town is known as Kingston SE (South East) to avoid confusion with Kingston-on-Murray.

KANGAROO ISLAND

The third largest island off the Australian coastline, Kangaroo Island is 155km long and 55km at its widest point—many visitors are surprised by its large size and its scenic beauty. Its reputation as a haven for native wildlife and flora is well deserved, with 30% of its total area covered by national parks.

Even in the peak summer season the island's size protects it from feeling crowded, although its small townships swell considerably. It offers a relaxed lifestyle and endless opportunities for water-based activities such as fishing, swimming, sailing, surfing, scuba diving and boating. Wildlife is very visable with the opportunity to see little penguins, Australian sea-lions, New Zealand fur seals, platypus, 240 bird species, an abundance of koalas, and the kangaroos that the island is named after.

main attractions

- ◈ Cape Borda Lighthouse
- ◈ Cape Willoughby Lighthouse
- ◈ Emu Bay
- ◈ Flinders Chase NP
- ◈ Kangaroo Island Marine Centre
- ◈ Kingscote
- ◈ Little penguin tours
- ◈ Prospect Hill Lookout
- ◈ Remarkable Rocks
- ◈ Seal Bay Conservation Park
- ◈ Stokes Bay

 Tourist information

Gateway Information Centre
Howard Dr,
Penneshaw, SA 5222
Ph: (08) 8553 1185
www.tourkangarooisland.com.au

Australian sea-lion, at Seal Bay CP, Kangaroo Island

MAIN ATTRACTIONS: Fishing is a major attraction with good catches of a variety of species possible from the surf, jetty or from a boat. The **National Trust Pioneer Museum** is worth seeing, as well as **Lions Park**, **Apex Park** and the **Aboriginal burial ground** in Dowdy St. Historic **Cape Jaffa Lighthouse** was moved to the foreshore in 1975 from Margaret Brock Reef. The lighthouse is usually open for inspection on weekends and school holidays.

NEARBY ATTRACTIONS: **Butchers Gap** and **Jip Jip conservation parks** are both within easy reach of the town. The unique rock formation—**The Granites**—is located on a beach about 18km north. **Coorong NP** isn't too far either and is renowned for the prolific birdlife on the **Younghusband Peninsula**. There

are scenic drives scattered throughout the region, and **Mount Scott CP**, 20km to the east, has good walking trails.

TOURIST INFO: Council Office, 29 Holland St, Ph (08) 8767 2033

■ Laura   POP 520

Map 347, F5

Located near the southern slopes of the **Flinders Ranges**, the small township of Laura is situated beside the **Rocky River**. Author and poet **C J Dennis** spent his boyhood here when his father owned the long-gone Beetaloo Hotel. Laura is a service town for the surrounding rural area, but cottage crafts and tourism also play an important role in the local economy.

MAIN ATTRACTIONS: A **walking tour** takes you to places of special

interest in the town, including the charming little **Court House** and the **old brewery**, which is now B&B accommodation. Some of the early buildings have become galleries and antique shops, and Laura boasts a silversmith, shoemaker and potter. Perhaps taste South Australia's famous **Golden North Ice Cream**, which is made in the town. For picnicking and BBQs, there are facilities beside the Rocky River and lawns alongside the **Civic Centre**. In April the town hosts a large folk fair.

NEARBY ATTRACTIONS: **Beetaloo Reservoir** is around 15km west of town and is a picturesque recreation spot with picnic and BBQ areas. It is also a good spot for birdwatching and lazy strolls. **Laura Lookout** in the ranges about 5km west of town

South Australia

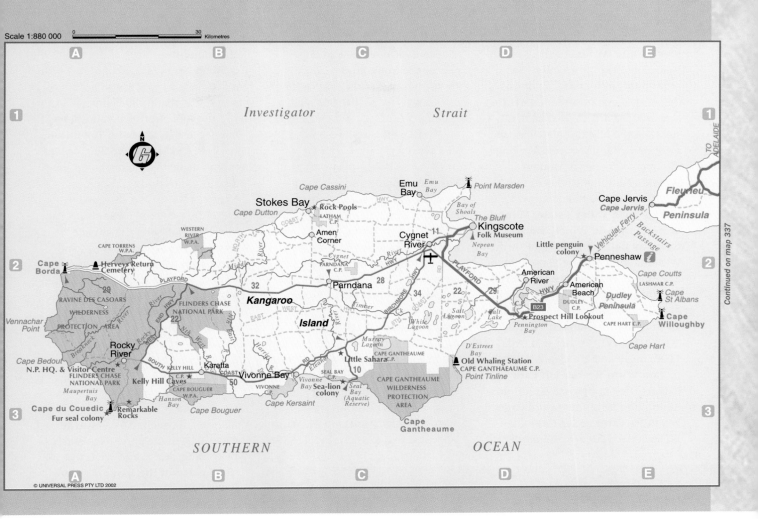

Scale 1:880 000   0 ___ 30 Kilometres

Investigator   *Strait*

Cape Cassini

Emu Bay   *Emu Bay*   ⚓ Point Marsden
Stokes Bay   Rock Pools   *Bay of Shoals*   *The Bluff*
Cape Dutton   LATHAM C.P.   ⚓ Kingscote
WESTERN   Amen Corner   Cygnet River   ✠ Folk Museum
RIVER W.P.A.   *Nepean Bay*
CAPE TORRENS   *Cygnet PARNDANA C.P.*   Little penguin colony
Cape Borda   ★ Herveys Return Cemetery   ★ Penneshaw ℹ
RAVINE DES CASOARS   PLAYFORD   32   Parndana   28   American River   American Beach
WILDERNESS   DUDLEY C.P.   *Dudley Peninsula*
Vennachar Point   PROTECTION AREA   22   *Kangaroo*   34   22   29   B23   ★ Prospect Hill Lookout   CAPE HART C.P.
FLINDERS CHASE NATIONAL PARK   *Island*   *Salt Lagoon*   *Salt Lake*   *Pennington Bay*
Cape Bedout   Rocky River   SOUTH KELLY HILL   Karatta   *White Lagoon*
N.P. HQ. & Visitor Centre   KELLY HILL C.P.   Vivonne Bay   *Murray Lagoon*   Little Sahara   CAPE GANTHEAUME C.P.
FLINDERS CHASE NATIONAL PARK   50   VIVONNE C.P.   Vivonne Bay   SEAL BAY   10   CAPE GANTHEAUME WILDERNESS PROTECTION AREA   Old Whaling Station
Maupertuis Bay   CAPE BOUGUER W.P.A.   Sea-lion colony   *Seal Bay (Aquatic Reserve)*   *Point Tinline*
Cape du Couedic   Remarkable Rocks   *Hanson Bay*   *Cape Bouguer*   *Cape Kersaint*   Cape Gantheaume
Fur seal colony

SOUTHERN   *OCEAN*

© UNIVERSAL PRESS PTY LTD 2002

---

also has picnic facilities and a lovely view of the town and scenic **Beetaloo Valley** countryside.
TOURIST INFO: Ticke's Old Style Lolly Shop, 51 Herbert St, Ph: (08) 8663 2419

■ **Loxton**   POP 3580
Map 333, C3
Loxton is a lovely little **'garden town'** in the **Riverland** region. It is one of the area's most prosperous centres. Located on the south bank of the **Murray River** and surrounded by vineyards, fruit orchards and olive groves, the town was proclaimed in 1907 and has grown significantly since. The post-WWII Soldier Settlement Scheme contributed to the town's growth.
MAIN ATTRACTIONS: The river provides opportunities for many recreational activities including camping,

fishing, swimming, cruising, waterskiing and canoeing. **Loxton Historical Village** is an award-winning attraction of 30 fully furnished buildings on the river-front. Art galleries and craft shops are in abundance, and the town's **Heritage Walk** is definitely worth the effort.
NEARBY ATTRACTIONS: The Murray River scenery that surrounds the town is perfect for picnics. **Banrock Station Wine and Wetland Centre** on Holmes Rd, **Kingston-on-Murray** has magnificent views over restored wetlands, wine tasting, a bistro, walking trails, a boardwalk and birdwatching hides. A number of other wineries can be found in the Riverland region.
TOURIST INFO: Bookpurung Tce, Ph: (08) 8584 7919

■ **Lyndoch**   POP 1240
Map 327, A5
Located on the south-west edge of the **Barossa Valley**, Lyndoch is the first of the Barossa towns to be reached by most visitors; it is only 1hr from **Adelaide**. Lyndoch is named after Lord Lynedoch, a friend of Colonel Light who carried out the first survey of the valley. Settlers arrived in 1839, and vineyards as well as farms were established in the early years, but the first winery, in a converted flour mill, was not operational until 1896.
MAIN ATTRACTIONS: **Lyndoch Recreation Park** has picnic facilities, toilets and a children's playground. The **Stone Mill Wheel** (1855) and other locally quarried ironstone buildings from the mid-1800s can be viewed on the self-guided **historical walk**.

Kies Family Wines, on the Barossa Valley Hwy 1km from town, has cellar door sales and functions as the local tourist information centre. NEARBY ATTRACTIONS: Wineries of all sizes dot the hills around Lyndoch, most being family owned. Among the many wineries is **Yaldara Wines**, one of the largest in the Barossa. Other well-known wineries include **Twin Valley Estate**, **Miranda Wines**, **Orlando Wines**, **Wards Gateway Cellar** and **Burge Family Winemakers**. Around 8km south of town is the **Barossa Reservoir** with its **Whispering Wall**, which has an amazing acoustic effect—words whispered at one end of the wall are carried to the other end over 100m away and are clearly audible. In **Para Wirra Recreation Park** explore the old **Barossa Goldfields**. About 7km SE of the town, **Lyndoch Lavender Farm** grows more than 50 lavender varieties and produces

excellent olive oil in beautiful peaceful surroundings.
TOURIST INFO: Kies Family Wines Pty Ltd, Barossa Valley Hwy, Ph (08) 8524 4110

■ Maitland POP 1050
Map 348, E1
Lying in the golden heart of the **Yorke Peninsula** and serving a prosperous rural community, Maitland is rich in limestone soils, which support lambs, barley, wheat and oats. Governor Fergusson named the town after one of his ancestors, Lady Jean Maitland, the wife of Lord Kilkerran of Scotland.
MAIN ATTRACTIONS: Maitland offers a **Town Heritage Walk** that includes significant sites with plaques outside the buildings explaining their history. In particular, **St John's Anglican Church** (1876), in Caroline St, is notable for its beautiful stained-glass windows. **Maitland Museum** is located in a former school (1877)

and features displays of the town's German heritage, agricultural machinery, as well as the history of schools on the Yorke Peninsula. A key, available from the council, allows access to **Maitland Town Hall**, where a spectacular wool-on-canvas mural, depicting the history of the district, takes pride of place.
NEARBY ATTRACTIONS: A central location for touring the Yorke Peninsula, the town isn't far from the seaside towns of **Port Victoria** (west) and **Ardrossan** (east), as well as the Copper Triangle towns of **Kadina**, **Moonta** and **Wallaroo**. The coastal town of **Balgowan**, 15km west, is a good fishing spot.
TOURIST INFO: Council Offices, 8 Elizabeth St, Ph: (08) 8832 2701

■ Mannum POP 2070
Map 349, G2
Mannum developed as a **Murray River** port in the early days of the river trade, and is known as the **'Birthplace of the River Murray Paddlesteamers'**. It was here, in 1853, that William Randell launched the **PS Mary Ann** and in doing so opened up a new era in trade for the colony that eventually involved dozens of paddlesteamers plying Australia's longest river system, the **Murray-Darling**.
MAIN ATTRACTIONS: Popular activities include houseboating, fishing, waterskiing, canoeing and jet skiing. There are week-long and weekend cruises on the **PS Murray Princess**. Randell St in the town centre is home to attractions like the **Cottage Window** craft shop, and the **Butter Factory** and **Mannum Institute**, both selling old wares and bric-a-brac. A lookout at the end of **Crawford Crescent** has scenic river views in both directions. All that is left of the historic paddle-steamer *Mary Ann* is her boiler, and that is located in the new **Mannum Dock Museum** at 6 Randell St. Another original paddlesteamer

PS *Murray Princess* paddlesteamer on the Murray River near Mannum

South Australia

Australian pelican, *Pelecanus conspicillatus*, Coorong NP

more than a century old is the wood-fired **PS Marion**, moored off the site of William Randell's original dock at **Arnold Park** near the ferry. She is now restored and open for display and river cruises.

NEARBY ATTRACTIONS: **Mannum Waterfalls**, only 10km from town along Murray Bridge Rd, is a pretty place of cascading water over black granite rocks. The 12km strip of swampy land between Purnong Rd and the river is a designated bird sanctuary with a scenic drive—a birdwatcher's paradise. The marina 8km NE of the town is the largest river marina in the state. About 20km north is the excellent scenic drive from **Wongulla** to **Cambrai**.

TOURIST INFO: 6 Randell St, Ph: (08) 8569 1303

■ Meningie   POP 1000

Map 349, G3

Meningie is located on the eastern shore of **Lake Albert**, about 160km from Adelaide. It is a small rural and holiday town, the service centre for an irrigated fodder-cropping area that also produces wheat, barley, sheep, cattle and dairying. It is also a thriving fishing town and has an abundance and variety of birdlife.

MAIN ATTRACTIONS: Perfect for water-sports like canoeing, waterskiing, windsurfing, sailing, swimming and fishing, Meningie is in the heart of the **Coorong NP**. Not far from the town, on Narrung Rd, is a great pelican-viewing spot. **Lions Park**, in town, is perfect for a lunchtime picnic or BBQ. The **Cheese Factory** is now a museum and restaurant.

NEARBY ATTRACTIONS: Coorong NP is a major district attraction that can be explored on the nature trail at **Salt Creek**. This trail displays the diversity of the national park's environment and passes **Chinaman's Well**, a vital stop on the route taken by Chinese prospectors travelling from South Australia to the Victorian goldfields.

TOURIST INFO: Melaleuca Centre, 76 Princes Hwy, Ph: (08) 8575 1259

■ Millicent   POP 4890

Map 323, D5

Built on land reclaimed from swamp, Millicent is a busy rural centre in the south-east corner of the state. The drainage scheme begun in 1863 transformed the marsh into arable land that today supports pasture and seed crops. Pine forests maintain a pulp mill, paper mill and sawmill.

MAIN ATTRACTIONS: The **Resource Centre** in town is a modern complex that features a civic centre; performance area; library; and art gallery that presents first-class travelling exhibitions. The **Living History Museum** is also a popular attraction, with a reputation for being one of the best regional museums in South Australia. Occupying the site and buildings of the old primary school, it features Victoriana, Aboriginal, maritime and natural history displays and the largest collection of horse-drawn vehicles in South Australia. The **Millicent Wildlife Park**, on Adelaide Rd, is home to many native animals and birds in a lovely garden setting.

NEARBY ATTRACTIONS: **Tantanoola Caves CP**, 21km SE, its famous for its caves, which are carved out of the limestone cliff face. The park is also renowned for the legend of the 'Tantanoola Tiger'—a visit to the park reveals all. An historic **woolshed** (1863) is located in the township of **Glencoe**; a key must be obtained from the general store to see the woolshed. **Millicent Swimming Lake**, off Rendelsham Rd, is open for swimming Oct–April. Further along the road is the picnic area of **Lake McIntyre**, home to boardwalks and birdwatching hides.

TOURIST INFO: 1 Mount Gambier Rd, Ph: (08) 8733 3205

■ Minlaton   POP 750

Map 348, E2

The town of Minlaton was originally known as Gum Flat because of the naturally occurring red gums in this area of the **Yorke Peninsula**. Today it is the commercial centre for a thriving agricultural region. The surrounding district is known as the 'Barley Capital of the World'.

MAIN ATTRACTIONS: The **National Trust Museum**, **Harry Butler Memorial**, a **fauna park** and **Harvest Corner Information and Crafts** are all located on Main St in town. Minlaton events of note are the **Minlaton Agricultural Show** (first Wednesday of October) and the **Minlaton Australiana Night** held on the Friday before Australia Day.

NEARBY ATTRACTIONS: Several art and craft galleries are located in or near Minlaton. **Port Vincent**, 25km east, and **Port Rickaby**, **The Bluff** and **Barkers Rocks** are good for swimming, fishing and watersports.

TOURIST INFO: Harvest Corner Information and Craft, 59 Main St, Ph: (08) 8853 2600

■ Moonta POP 3120

Map 348, E1

Part of the historic **Copper Triangle** towns (with **Kadina** and **Wallaroo**), Moonta is located at the northern end of the **Yorke Peninsula**, 163km NW of Adelaide. A popular seaside town, with excellent fishing and golden beaches, the town centre is surrounded by parklands and open space and in the middle is **Queen Square**.

MAIN ATTRACTIONS: The town is dotted with historic stone buildings including the **Town Hall** and **All Saints Church**. There are galleries and gift shops to browse in and maps are available for self-guided scenic drives and walks around the town and mines.

NEARBY ATTRACTIONS: Both the **State Heritage Area of Moonta Mines** and the old primary school, which is now **Moonta Mines National Trust Museum**, showcase mining artefacts and memorabilia as well as the history of the Cornish miners. The **Moonta Mines Railway Tour** goes right through the mine area and is a good way to take in the area's mining heritage. The **Wheel Hughes Mine**, about 3km north of town, has tours at 1pm daily; bookings are through the tourist information centre.

TOURIST INFO: Moonta Station, Kadina Rd, Ph: (08) 8825 1891

■ Morgan POP 520

Map 349, G1

In its heyday Morgan was briefly one of the busiest river ports on the **Murray-Darling** river system, where paddlesteamers met the railway line to Adelaide. Now that the railway line is closed and river traffic is reduced to houseboats and water-skiers, Morgan is a much quieter place. The township is a service centre for the local wine, sheep and fruit growing industries as well as catering for the holiday-home community by the Murray.

MAIN ATTRACTIONS: A self-guided **walking trail** covers the town's historic sites, mainly clustered around the **Railway Station** and the remains of the **old jarrah wharf**. Maps are available as well as audio commentary on the area. The **Port of Morgan Museum** is housed in the old Railway Station and displays a paddlesteamer, old engines and a range of memorabilia. Picnic and BBQ facilities are located on the riverfront lawn next to the museum. Remember to stroll along **Railway Tce** where a charming row of 1880s shops, Carmine's Antiques and 2 pubs are located.

NEARBY ATTRACTIONS: **Morgan CP** is located on the other side of the river where rough riverbank camping and fishing are the main attractions. Only 1km from the town on the Blanchetown Rd, there is a fossil quarry where fossickers will often find fossil shells and very occasionally a shark's tooth. **White Dam CP** is 9km NW of town, and the **Nor-West Bend Private Museum** is 8km east and has a very large collection of horse-drawn vehicles and buggies.

TOURIST INFO: Shell Roadhouse, 14 Fourth St, Ph: (08) 8540 2205

■ Mount Compass POP 507

Map 337, D1

Overlooking the **Nangkita** and **Tooperang valleys**, the small farming community of Mount Compass is located less than an hour's drive from Adelaide. The town is known for its warm country hospitality, clean air and rolling hills. The district is renowned for its range of agricultural, aquacultural and horticultural products.

MAIN ATTRACTIONS: The many art and craft galleries are worth investigating. Australia's only cow race, **The Compass Cup**, is held in February, and the **Mount Compass Agricultural Field Day**, in March.

NEARBY ATTRACTIONS: Situated in the heart of South Australia's **Fleurieu Peninsula** region and nestled between the world-renowned **McLaren Vale wineries** and the beautiful beaches of the southern peninsula, Mount Compass is a perfect centre from which to explore the wineries or beaches in the area.

TOURIST INFO: The Wharf, Goolwa, Ph: (08) 8555 3488

Murray River ferry at Morgan

South Australia

Mount Gambier   POP 22 580
Map 323, E5

Located 460km SE of Adelaide and 450km west of Melbourne, Mount Gambier is located on the slopes of an extinct, 3-cratered volcano. **Centenary Tower**, on the highest point 190m above sea level, overlooks the picturesque craters, which were last active 5000 years ago. The unofficial capital of **The Limestone Coast**, Mount Gambier is at the heart of a rich agricultural district known for its pine plantations, dairy farming, wool, vineyards and meat production.

MAIN ATTRACTIONS: **Blue Lake** is believed to be the only lake in the world that changes each year from grey-blue in winter to a brilliant turquoise blue in summer—a road and walking track encircle the lake. A popular tour is the 45min **Aquifer Tour**, which takes visitors via a lift and tunnel close to the surface of the lake. Nearby, within the **Valley Lake** crater is a wildlife park and boardwalk. A sinkhole in the city centre, **Cave Garden**, is renowned for its rose garden, which features heritage roses. **Engelbrecht Cave**, off the Jubilee Hwy, offers tours showing where experienced divers enter the underground water to dive under the city. **Umpherston Sink hole** has lovely terraced gardens which become a hive of activity at night when possums come out to feed in the floodlight.

NEARBY ATTRACTIONS: **Port MacDonnell**, 30km south of Mount Gambier, is **'Australia's Southern Rock Lobster Capital'** and a favourite destination for surfers and anglers alike. The quiet township of **Nelson** is 37km SE of Mount Gambier in Victoria. It offers a range of cruises and recreational activities. Both the **Princess Margaret Rose Cave** and **Tantanoola Caves** are within a 30min drive.

TOURIST INFO: The Lady Nelson Visitor and Discovery Centre, Jubilee Hwy East, Ph (08) 8724 9750 or 1800 087 187

Murray Bridge   POP 13 500
Map 349, G2

This town was known as Mobilong then Edwards Crossing and finally Murray Bridge when the railway bridge connected both sides of the river in 1924. This rural city is the centre of a major agricultural region. Whilst the first road bridge was being built—completed in 1879—a community grew to support the builders. This community grew rapidly and became an important river port when the railway line linked the paddlesteamer trade with Adelaide in 1885.

MAIN ATTRACTIONS: A perfect holiday spot, Murray Bridge has facilities for most sports, particularly watersports. River cruising and houseboating are popular as well as the Go Kart Park and the Bunyip in **Sturt Reserve**. **Captain's Cottage Museum**, in Thomas St, has a collection of farm equipment, pioneering artefacts and historical records. Murray Bridge also boasts the smallest cathedral in Australia—**St John the Baptist Anglican Cathedral** on Mannum Rd. The **Art Gallery** housed in the **Town Hall** on Sixth St is worth investigating.

NEARBY ATTRACTIONS: **Monarto Zoological Park** on the Old Princes Hwy is an open-range zoo where a safari bus tours around giraffes, antelopes, deer, bison, cheetahs and other free-roaming animals. Visitors can also stroll along well-defined nature trails. The **Willow Point Winery** is 10km south of town and the historic railway town of **Tailem Bend** is 25km SE. For beautiful surrounds of citrus and stone fruit orchards visit **Mypolonga**, 14km north. Riverside reserves abound in the surrounding area—**Thiele**, **Swanport** and **White Sands** are all good spots for picnics and relaxation. **Puzzle Park**, located on Jervois Rd near the Murray Bridge/ Wellington exit off the south-east Fwy, has more than 30 fun rides.

Alexandra Cave, Naracoorte Caves

Dundee's Wildlife Park, located nearby has fresh and saltwater crocodiles, bird aviaries, a nocturnal house and a children's zoo.

TOURIST INFO: 3 South Tce, Ph: (08) 8532 6660

Naracoorte   POP 6500
Map 323, E3

Around 330km from Adelaide, Naracoorte is at the geographical heart of the **Limestone Coast** region. Settled in the 1840s, the area is famous for its World Heritage-listed and fossil-filled limestone caves. Primary industries include sheep, beef cattle, grains and vineyards. The name 'Naracoorte' is derived from the Aboriginal word meaning 'running water'.

MAIN ATTRACTIONS: **The Museum and Snake Pit**, in Jenkins Tce, houses a collection of snakes and artefacts. For woollen products and history, explore the **Sheep's Back Wool**

LIMESTONE COAST

The Limestone Coast, in the south-east corner of South Australia, is rich in natural attractions, with an arc of beaches and lobster-fishing ports stretching along the coastline to the Victorian border. The region, which centres on **Mount Gambier**, is named after its incomparable concentration of limestone craters, caves and cliffs, and offers visitors a range of activities and attractions in a spectacular natural setting.

Volcanic activity sculpted the landscape, with the **Crater Lakes** among its most stunning natural attractions. Inland, the World Heritage-listed **Naracoorte Caves** is a major fossil cave system—re-creations of prehistoric mammals, that once inhabited the caves, are displayed at **Wonambi Fossil Centre**. Limestone also gives the famous **Coonawarra** its terra rossa soil.

main attractions

- Blue Lake
- Camp Coorong
- Coonawarra wine region
- Coorong NP
- Engelbrecht Cave
- Kingston SE
- Mount Gambier
- Naracoorte Caves
- Robe
- Umpherston Sinkhole

Tourist information

Lady Nelson Visitor and Discovery Centre
Jubilee Hwy East,
Mount Gambier, SA 5290
Ph: (08) 8724 9750 or 1800 087 187
www.mountgambiertourism.com.au

Lady Nelson Visitor and Discovery Centre, Mount Gambier

Museum and the **Mini Jumbuck Factory**. For walks, swimming and picnicking visit **Jubilee Park**, off Park Tce.

NEARBY ATTRACTIONS: **Naracoorte Caves NP** is 12km SE of Naracoorte. The national park was listed in 1994 as a World Heritage site for its extensive fossil deposits. The **Wonambi Fossil Centre** has life-like moving models of extinct animals, and the Bat Cave Teleview Centre allows visitors to view the inside of a Bat Cave via infrared cameras. The nearby **Heathfield Ridge Winery** offers guided tours while the wine regions of **Coonawarra**, **Padthaway** and **Wrattonbully** are all close to Naracoorte.

TOURIST INFO: The Sheep's Back Wool Museum, MacDonnell St, Ph: (08) 8762 1518

■ Normanville   POP 590
Map 337, B2

Established in 1849, the seaside town of Normanville is located near the mouth of the **Bungala River** on the **Fleurieu Peninsula**. In the early years, this scenic stretch of coastline witnessed several shipwrecks; the *Mary Smith* in 1856, the cutter *Teaser* in 1859, and *The Rose* in 1875. Today, the town makes up part of the holiday triangle that includes **Yankalilla**, 3km west, and **Carrickalinga**, 2km north. The area is very popular with beach lovers and anglers and the 2 large caravan parks are often booked out in summer months.

MAIN ATTRACTIONS: The extensive beaches are ideal for swimming, surfing, boating, fishing and horse-riding. Walking tracks penetrate the sand dunes behind the beaches, which are heritage listed. The historic **Court House** (1855) has been converted into a restaurant (open Wed–Sun). The town also boasts the **Fleurieu Fishing Festival** and **Surf Lifesaving Triathlon** in summer.

NEARBY ATTRACTIONS: South of Normanville is the huge **Marina St Vincent**, the **Paradise Wirrina Cove Resort** and the **Links Lady Bay Golf** development. **Rapid Bay** is known for its imposing cliffs, caves and beaches and for the long wharf, where anglers love to drop a line. It is also a renowned diving spot. The RAN's scuttling of **HMAS *Hobart*** in **Yankalilla Bay** provides an excellent wreck dive.

TOURIST INFO: 106 Main Rd, Yankalilla, Ph: (08) 8558 2999

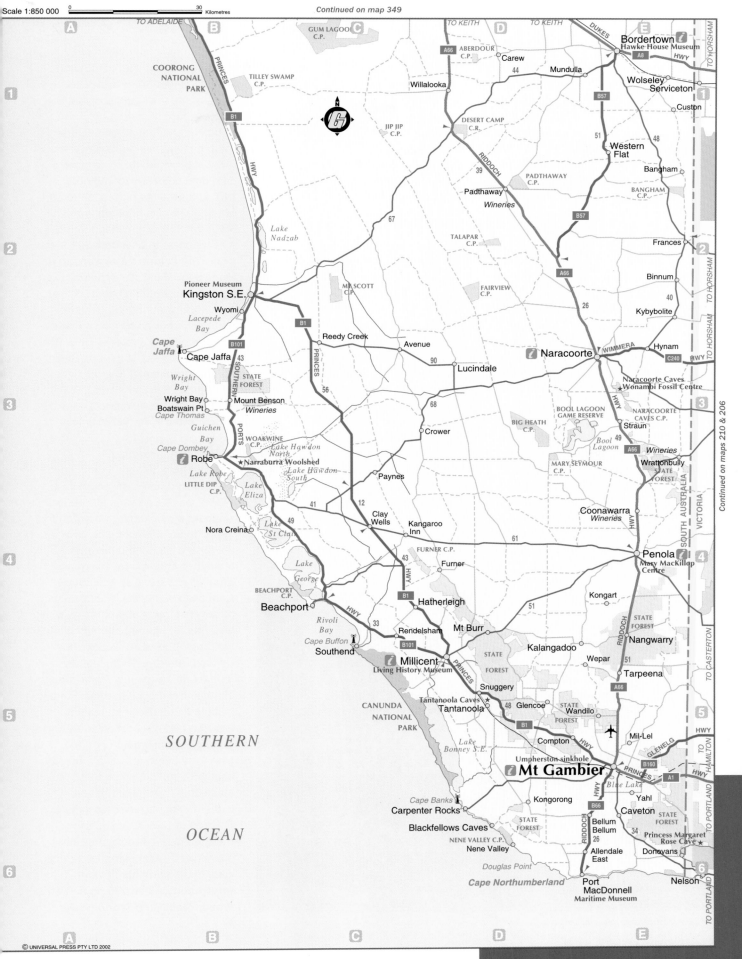

TO ADELAIDE

TO KEITH   TO KEITH

COORONG
NATIONAL
PARK

GUM LAGOO
C.P.

ABERDOUR
C.P.

Carew

Mundulla

Bordertown
Hawke House Museum

TO HORSHAM

TILLEY SWAMP
C.P.

Willalooka

44

Wolseley
Serviceton

Custon

DESERT CAMP
C.R.

JIP JIP
C.P.

51

48

Western
Flat

Bangham

PADTHAWAY
C.P.

Padthaway
Wineries

BANGHAM
C.P.

67

39

Frances

TALAPAR
C.P.

26

Binnum

Pioneer Museum
Kingston S.E.

FAIRVIEW
C.P.

40

Kybybolite

Wyomi

Lacepede
Bay

MI SCOTT
C.P.

Reedy Creek

Avenue

Naracoorte

WIMMERA

Hynam

TO HORSHAM

Cape Jaffa

43

Cape
Jaffa

STATE
FOREST

90

Lucindale

Naracoorte Caves
Wonambi Fossil Centre

Wright
Bay

56

68

NARACOORTE
CAVES C.P.

Wright Bay
Boatswain Pt
Cape Thomas

Mount Benson
Wineries

Crower

BIG HEATH
C.P.

BOOL LAGOON
GAME RESERVE

Straun

49

Wineries

Guichen
Bay
Cape Dombey

WOAKWINE
C.P.

Lake Hawdon
North

Wrattonbully

Robe

Narraburra Woolshed

Lake Hawdon
South

Paynes

MARY SEYMOUR
C.P.

STATE
FOREST

Lake Robe

LITTLE DIP
C.P.

Lake
Eliza

12

Clay
Wells

Kangaroo
Inn

Coonawarra
Wineries

Nora Creina

Lake
St Clair

41

49

43

FURNER C.P.

Furner

61

Penola
Mary MacKillop
Centre

Lake
George

BEACHPORT
C.P.

Kongart

STATE
FOREST

Beachport

33

B1

Hatherleigh

51

Nangwarry

Rivoli
Bay
Cape Buffon

Rendelsham

Mt Burr

Kalangadoo

Wepar

51

Tarpeena

Southend

Millicent
Living History Museum

PRINCES

STATE
FOREST

Snuggery

SOUTHERN

CANUNDA
NATIONAL
PARK

Tantanoola Caves
Tantanoola

48

Glencoe

Wandilo

STATE
FOREST

Mil-Lel

Lake
Bonney S.E.

Compton

HWY

Mt Gambier

Umpherston sinkhole

GLENELG

TO HAMILTON

OCEAN

Cape Banks

Carpenter Rocks

Blue Lake

Yahl

Caveton

Kongorong

Blackfellows Caves

STATE
FOREST

Bellum
Bellum

34

Princess Margaret
Rose Cave

NENE VALLEY C.P.
Nene Valley

Allendale
East

Donovans

Douglas Point

Cape Northumberland

Port
MacDonnell
Maritime Museum

Nelson

TO PORTLAND

Nuriootpa   POP 3670
Map 327, D2

Located on the **North Para River** at the northern end of the **Barossa Valley**, Nuriootpa is a commercial and service centre with a number of government agencies and offices. Production facilities and huge tanks sited alongside the railway line attest to the fact that winemaking is big business in the district. A viticultural research station is located on the outskirts of town.

MAIN ATTRACTIONS: The early influence of German settlers is still reflected in the food outlets of the town, with locally produced food and wine featured on the menus. **Coulthard Reserve**, a short distance from the Para River, is perfect for picnicking. For some local history, drop into **Luhrs Pioneer German Cottage** on Light Pass Rd.

NEARBY ATTRACTIONS: Numerous wineries are located in the surrounding area. Among them are **Southcorp**, the valley's largest winery complex and **Wolf Blass**, another famous winery, established in 1970. Other well-known wineries in the surrounding area include **Elderton Wines, Hamilton's Ewell**

Vineyards, Yunbar Estate, Penfolds Wines, Heritage Wines, Greenock Creek Cellars, the Willows Vineyard and Barossa Cottage Wines. Most wineries are open for tastings and cellar door sales.

TOURIST INFO: Barossa Wine and Visitor Centre, 66–68 Murray St, Tanunda, Ph: (08) 8563 0600

Orroroo   POP 557
Map 347, F5

Orroroo is a pretty little town lying on the edge of the Southern **Flinders Ranges**. It is a service centre for the surrounding agricultural region. Proclaimed a town in 1876, the name comes from the Aboriginal word 'oorama'. There is controversy over whether the name means 'meeting place of the magpie' or 'early start'.

MAIN ATTRACTIONS: Many beautifully restored 1870s buildings and shopfronts are to be found in Orroroo's wide tree-lined streets including **Cellar Antiques** (Main St), **Yesteryear Costume Gallery** (Adelaide Rd) and **Solly's Hut**, an early settler's cottage built of pug and pine containing furniture and relics from the 1870s (inspection

by appointment). **Tank Hill Lookout**, off Pekina Rd, provides scenic views of the town and surrounding countryside.

NEARBY ATTRACTIONS: Around 12km south of town lies the 'almost' ghost town of **Black Rock**. A signpost here directs drivers to **Magnetic Hill**, an intriguing natural phenomenon where cars apparently roll uphill when they are stopped on what appears to be a downhill slope. The **Pekina Reservoir** can be found by walking along the trail from Lions Picnic and BBQ area. Walkers pass ancient Aboriginal carvings, natural springs and a poem that was carved into a rock in 1896. The walk continues past the remains of **Pekina Homestead**, the district's first permanent settlement.

TOURIST INFO: Orroroo Carrieton Council Offices, Second St, Ph: (08) 8658 1434

Penola   POP 1250
Map 323, E4

The oldest town in the south-east, Penola was founded as a travellers' stopover by Alexander Cameron in 1850. Today it is a service town for the local pastoral and forestry industries and also for the growing number of vineyards at nearby **Coonawarra**. Penola is a destination for lovers of Australian history, with well-preserved and restored colonial buildings. The word 'Penola' is derived from the Aboriginal word 'penaoorla', meaning 'big swamp'. The history of wine in the area goes back to Penola pastoralist John Riddoch and his Coonawarra Fruit Colony establishment of 1890.

MAIN ATTRACTIONS: Australia's already beatified and likely first saint, **Mary MacKillop**, started her teaching career in Penola, educating the children of settlers regardless of their financial or social position. Memorabilia relating to her can be seen in the **Mary MacKillop Interpretative Centre** and in the **Woods MacKillop Schoolhouse**,

Elderton Wines, near Nuriootpa

both on the corner of Petticoat La and Portland St. The **Penola Heritage Walk** begins at the information centre and is a sign-posted trail that passes 33 heritage sites. NEARBY ATTRACTIONS: Worth a visit is **Yallum Park**, John Riddoch's house built between 1878 and 1880, which is privately owned. Inspection times are available from the visitor information centre. **Penola CP**, 10km west, has a woodland and wetland walk. The Coonawarra district lies a few kilometres north of Penola and visitors can taste and buy premium red and white table wines at more than 20 cellar door outlets.
TOURIST INFO: 27 Arthur St,
Ph: (08) 8737 2855

■ Peterborough   POP 1930
Map 347, F5
An historic railway town located on the main south-east approach to the **Flinders Ranges**, Peterborough is a popular stop for travellers en route to the ranges and especially for those interested in steam trains. There are 4 unique hand-made model steam trains located at each of the 4 entrances to the town. Surrounded by grain-growing and pastoral country, Peterborough is the main service town on the Port Pirie to Broken Hill railway line.
MAIN ATTRACTIONS: An easy way to see the main attractions is on the guided **bus tour**, which leaves from Peterborough Caravan Park. **The Gold Battery** has been crushing ore for small mines in the region for over 100 years and is still operational. **Iven Ley's Museum**, in Queen St, is a small museum featuring bottle and mineral collections, memorabilia and a superb display of dolls. **Ranns Museum** in Moscow St specialises in working and non-working stationary engines and other artefacts dating to the 1800s. Both museums are generally open daily. **The Steamtown Museum** holds memorabilia in the old rail-

St Joseph's Convent School, Peterborough

way workshops and is a must for steam train enthusiasts. In Callary St, **St Cecilia** is a 20-room restored mansion with a 2-storey coach house. The house is now a private hotel that specialises in Murder Mystery weekends.
NEARBY ATTRACTIONS: The historic railway township of **Terowie** is 24km SE, and is home to many heritage buildings. Peterborough is not far from the town of **Black Rock** and the strange **Magnetic Hill**.
TOURIST INFO: Railway Carriage, Main St,
Ph: (08) 8651 2708

■ Pinnaroo   POP 620
Map 349, J2
Pinnaroo is the first South Australian town to be encountered by travellers from New South Wales and Victoria using the Mallee Hwy. This little oasis in the middle of the **Mallee** owes its 'greenness' to the availability of good underground water that supports an olive plantation, mixed farming and potato growing. Other primary production in the region includes wheat, barley, poultry, sheep, pigs, lambs and beef cattle.

MAIN ATTRACTIONS: The town offers excellent sporting facilities, a number of pleasant picnic spots and a small fauna park on the corner of South Tce and Mann St. **Mallee Tourist and Heritage Centre** brings together 4 museum collections; the **Historical Museum**; the **Heritage Centre** with printing machinery and equipment and a farm machinery collection; the **Gum Family Collection** of stationary engines; and the unusual **DA Wurfel Cereal Collection**, comprising over 1300 varieties of grain from around the world.
NEARBY ATTRACTIONS: Pinnaroo makes a good base for those interested in flora and fauna. There are a number of conservation parks in the area which were set aside to preserve unique local environments. Walks of varying distances can be taken in **Ngarkat CP**, a wilderness that adjoins **Scorpion Springs** and **Mount Shaugh parks** to the south of Pinnaroo, while to the north are **Billiatt** and the smaller **Karte** and **Peebinga conservation parks**.
TOURIST INFO: Mallee Tourist and Heritage Centre, Railway Tce, Ph: (08) 8577 8644

THE BAROSSA VALLEY

Although relatively small in area, the Barossa Valley is Australia's best-known wine region. Each year thousands of visitors tour the region, tasting the wines and making cellar-door purchases.

The Barossa's Mediterranean-type climate and differing soils make it an ideal place for growing diverse varieties of grapes, producing consistently high quality wines. German immigrants initially settled the region and in 1847, the valley's first vines were planted at the **Orlando vineyards**.

While the Barossa Valley boasts more than 50 wineries, ranging from household names such as **Penfolds** to boutique wineries like **Charles Melton** and **Grant Burge Wines**, the region also offers lots of other attractions, including its history and scenery. This lovely, closely settled valley is dotted with small Lutheran churches, yet another legacy of the German settlers who escaped religious persecution. As well, there are quaint townships featuring antique stores, bakeries and old-fashioned pubs.

The Barossa Valley's proximity to Adelaide makes it an ideal daytrip destination, and with a range of great accommodation options and attractions available, it is worthwhile staying a few days.

main attractions

◈ **Angaston**

This small rural town in the Barossa Valley is home to some of the Barossa's oldest wineries.

◈ **Bethany Wines**

Located in an old quarry, Bethany produces wine and port.

◈ **Chateau Yaldara Estate**

Specialising in sweet and sparkling European-style wines, this winery is housed in a 19th century flour mill.

◈ **Lyndoch**

One of South Australia's oldest towns, Lyndoch was settled in 1839. Although wine has always been produced here, wheat was the primary crop until 1896.

◈ **Penfolds Wines**

Established in 1844, Penfolds is the Barossa's largest winery, showcasing some of Australia's best-known wines.

◈ **Seppeltsfield**

Founded in 1851, this winery is the Barossa's most spectacular.

◈ **Wolf Blass Wines**

This winery produces prize-winning wines of consistent quality.

ℹ Tourist information

Barossa Wine and Visitor Centre
66-68 Murray St, Tanunda SA 5352
Ph: (08) 8563 0600 or 1300 852 982
www.barossa-region.org

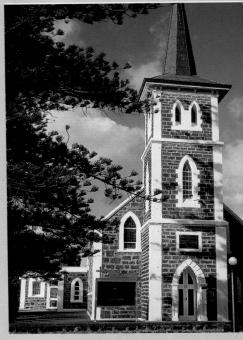

Lutheran church, Barossa Valley

Barossa Festivals

German influence is very much alive in some of the Barossa festivals. The biennial **Barossa Vintage Festival**, held from Easter Monday during odd-numbered years attracts more than 100 000 people. Other festivals in the region include **Barossa Under the Stars** (Feb), **Melodienacht** (May) and **Barossa International Music Festival** (Oct).

Vineyards in Tanunda area, Barossa Valley

South Australia

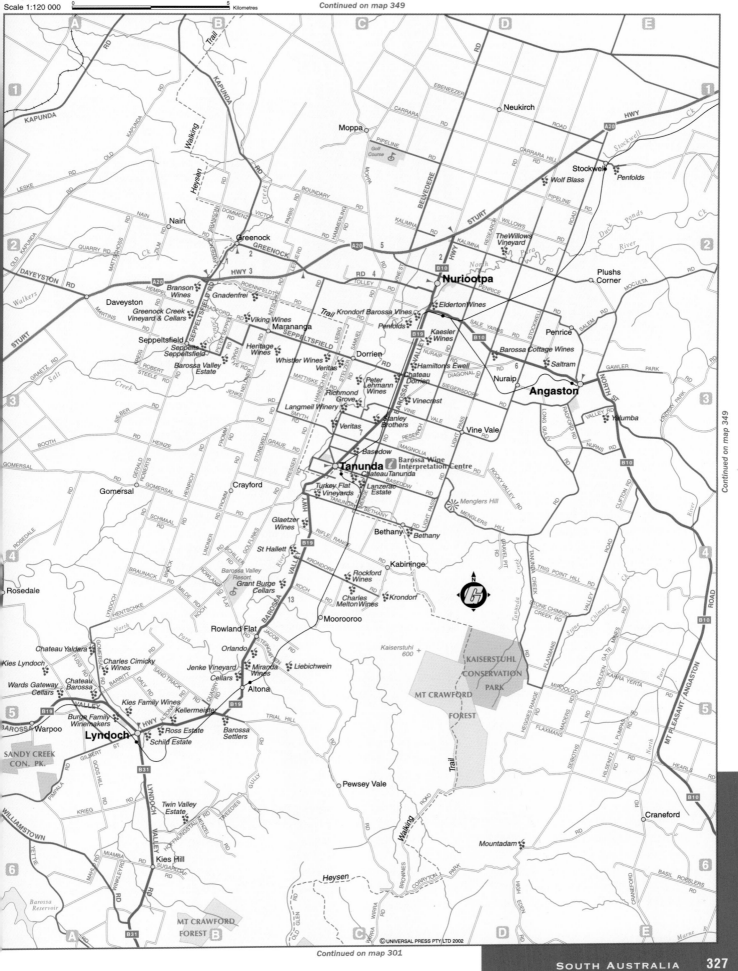

Continued on map 349

Continued on map 349

Continued on map 301

Uniting Church, Port Augusta

■ Port Augusta POP 15 000

Map 346, E4

The most northerly point on the **Spencer Gulf**, Port Augusta is often referred to as the **'Crossroads of Australia'**. Major highways of the north, south, east and west meet here, and the city is an important link for the **Indian Pacific** and **Ghan railway lines**. With the **Flinders Ranges** to the east, Port Augusta attracts many tourists en route to this scenic outback wonderland.

MAIN ATTRACTIONS: Beaches are popular attractions; **Redbanks Beach** off Gardiner Ave is especially lovely. A 2hr **heritage walk** and a scenic drive highlight the city's many historic buildings. Take the time to visit the **Wadlata Outback Centre**, an interpretative centre where audio-visuals and interactive displays trace the history of the region from its geological development, through to Aboriginal culture, European exploration, the development of transport and technological achievements. The **Royal Flying Doctor Service** (RFDS) and the **School of Air** both have bases in Port Augusta and visitors are welcome. The **Curdnatta Art and Pottery Gallery** on Commercial Rd is an outlet for weaving, pottery, painting and other local crafts. The **Homestead Park Pioneer Museum** is housed in the old Yudnapinna Station pine-log homestead. The city's scenic lookouts—**McLellan**, Whiting Pde; **Water Tower**, Mitchell Tce; and **Flinders/Redbank** in McSporan Cres provide great views to the Flinders Ranges at the top of Spencer Gulf. Nearby, on the Stuart Hwy, is the **Australian Arid Lands Botanic Gardens** which exhibit Australia's most beautiful arid-land plants, birds and animal life.

NEARBY ATTRACTIONS: The townships of **Stirling North**, **Quorn** and **Hawker** are all in the vicinity of Port Augusta.

TOURIST INFO: Wadlata Outback Centre, 41 Flinders Tce, Ph: (08) 8641 0793

■ Port Broughton POP 655

Map 346, E6

Around 170km from Adelaide this peaceful seaside village has much to offer its visitors. The town, built on the **Mundoora Arm Inlet**, is protected from the **Spencer Gulf**, and is the home base for a prawn-fishing fleet. The town was named after William Grant Broughton, who was consecrated Anglican bishop of Australia in 1836.

MAIN ATTRACTIONS: A popular recreation area is the grassed foreshore reserve, where picnic and BBQ facilities are located adjacent to a children's playground. Swimming is possible near the jetty and sporting facilities include tennis courts, a bowling green and golf course. A **Heritage Walking Trail** takes in the places of historic interest in the town and there are also **fishlab tours**, by appointment, where visitors can see a variety of aquatic organisms, both plant and animal.

NEARBY ATTRACTIONS: **Clements Gap NP** isn't too far away, and visitors can see a range of native animals such as kangaroos, echidnas, lizards, over 66 bird species, snakes, insects and rare flowers. **The Copper Triangle** towns of **Moonta**, **Kadina** and **Wallaroo** are close by, while to the east, the wineries of the **Clare Valley** are within easy reach.

TOURIST INFO: Bay St, Ph: (08) 8635 2261

■ Port Elliot POP 1490

Map 337, D2

This town is an ideal holiday destination within easy reach of Adelaide. Port Elliot was surveyed in 1852, and was briefly the major ocean port for goods moving up and down the **Murray River**. There are extensive beaches in the area that offer surfing and swimming opportunities.

MAIN ATTRACTIONS: Water-based leisure activities are well catered for and there is a range of accommodation overlooking **Horseshoe Bay**. The township boasts one of the smallest council chambers ever constructed and the National Trust has created a local **Heritage Walk** that passes quaint buildings and historic sites. **Freeman's Knob**, a small promontory at the southern end of the bay, is an excellent vantage point for coastal views. In winter it is a good spot for whale sightings.

South Australia

NEARBY ATTRACTIONS: The town of **Middleton** lies 4km east of Port Elliot and is the state's most popular surf beach. A number of surfing competitions are held here every year and facilities for competitors and spectators alike are excellent. Middleton also has the **Heritage Bakery** and **old flour mill**, as well as **Middleton Winery** a further 5km away. **Crows Nest Lookout** has excellent views of the bays and the coast of **Encounter Bay**.

TOURIST INFO: Signal Point Interpretive Centre, Goolwa Wharf, Ph: (08) 8555 1144

■ Port Lincoln   POP 13 500
Map 348, B1

Port Lincoln is located on extensive **Boston Bay** and was originally considered as a site for the capital of South Australia. The Bay provides an idyllic setting at the southern tip of the **Eyre Peninsula**. The city is 650km west of Adelaide. It is now the base for a large fishing industry including Australia's biggest commercial tuna-fishing fleet. As well, Port Lincoln is an export centre for wheat, wool, lambs, lobsters, prawns and abalone.

MAIN ATTRACTIONS: Boston Bay is the perfect place for water and other sports, as well as scenic walking trails—in particular the **Parnkalla Walking Trail**, which edges the bay all the way from **Billy Lights Point** to **North Shields**. Two city lookouts, **Puckridge Park** and **The Old Mill**, offer excellent but different views. For superb timber furniture, Port Lincoln's world-renowned **Constantia Designer Craftsmen** on Proper Bay Rd offer a guided tour, which reveals the creative processes involved from the raw timber state to finished pieces. There are several museums in Port Lincoln; the **Axel Stenross Maritime Museum** centres on the workshop and home of Axel Stenross, a Finnish boat builder who established his business here in the 1920s. Three small museums

are located in Flinders Park; **Mill Cottage Museum** features artefacts from the early days of settlement; the **Settler's Cottage Museum** houses local memorabilia; nearby is the **Rose-Wal Memorial Shell Museum**. The **MB Kotz Collection of Stationary Engines** and the **Step'n Back Relic Collection** are 2 private museums of farming and folk memorabilia. In the old Railway Station at Railway Pl, is the **Railway Museum**. Tours of the **Seahorse Farm**, which supplies the aquarium market, can be booked through the visitor information centre.

NEARBY ATTRACTIONS: Around 15min west lies **Glenforest Animal Park**, which is home to native and farm animals including kangaroos, camels, wombats, donkeys, deer, dingoes, goats and many more. **Lincoln NP** is south of the city and consists of secluded beaches, rugged cliffs, sand dunes, native fauna and sheltered camping spots. North, off the Lincoln Hwy, **Tod Reservoir** is a good spot for a picnic and a visit to the **Tod Reservoir Museum** with its marvellous heritage display telling the history of water supply on the Eyre Peninsula. The 14km tourist drive known as

Whaler's Way provides spectacular views of the cliffs, blowholes, crevasses, caves and beaches of the area, and between May and November there is an amazing wildflower display. A permit and key, available from Port Lincoln Visitor Centre, are necessary to enter the area. For wine lovers there are 4 wineries in the region, including **Boston Bay Wines** and **Delacolline Estate Winery**.

TOURIST INFO: 3 Adelaide Pl, Ph: (08) 8683 3544 or 1800 629 911

■ Port MacDonnell   POP 680
Map 323, E6

About 28km south of Mount Gambier, Port MacDonnell is known as **'Australia's Southern Rock Lobster Capital'** and is a favourite destination for surfers and anglers. The Port was also home to poet **Adam Lindsay Gordon** who wrote *Dingley Dell*, a poetic depiction of life in the early 1860s. It is said the Port MacDonnell area was the inspiration behind much of his poetry. In the early days, Port MacDonnell was a thriving trade port and today a breakwater (built in 1975) shelters Australia's largest southern rock-lobster fishing fleet.

Lincoln Cove Marina, Port Lincoln

MAIN ATTRACTIONS: The **Maritime Museum** displays artefacts salvaged from ships wrecked on reefs in the vicinity as well as a photographic display tracing the town's heritage. Port MacDonnell also offers many activities—bushwalking, golf, boating, fishing, sailing, diving, snorkelling, surfing, waterskiing, lawn bowls and tennis.

NEARBY ATTRACTIONS: **Dingley Dell CP** is located just outside of town and protects the rare Dingley Dell blue-gum and local vegetation. Nature walks and picnic facilities are available. Also within the park is the restored and refurnished cottage of poet, Adam Lindsay Gordon. Visitors can step back in time to the 1860s and take a glimpse of Gordon's life. Located 15km north of the town, **Mount Schank** is actually the crater of Australia's youngest volcano, classified as dormant, yet it erupted as recently as 2000 years ago. A walking trail takes visitors to the top, where there are wonderful panoramic views of the surrounding countryside.

TOURIST INFO: 5 Charles St, Ph: (08) 8738 2100

■ Port Pirie   POP 14 580
Map 346, E5

South Australia's first provincial city began in 1845 as a caretaker's cottage and 3 crude woolsheds on the banks of what was then known as Tarparrie Creek, on the eastern side of **Spencer Gulf**. Over the years, Port Pirie has grown to become one of the state's largest industrial and commercial centres—its skyline is dominated by the world's largest lead smelter. The city forms the southern point of the Spencer Gulf triangle completed by **Whyalla** and **Port Augusta**. It has rail connections to the **Indian Pacific** and **The Ghan**.

MAIN ATTRACTIONS: The city is a good base for walkers and drivers to explore the scenic southern **Flinders Ranges**. There is a 2hr **Heritage Walk** through the CBD, with many buildings of note, including **Sampson's Cottage** (1890s), and the **National Trust Museum** at the northern end of Ellen St. **Memorial Park** in Gertrude St is home to the **Northern Festival Centre**, a complex of theatre, ballroom and conference rooms. The park itself is also a popular recreation area.

NEARBY ATTRACTIONS: **Mount Remarkable NP** is a pleasant scenic drive, with a detour to **Telowie Gorge** revealing deep ravines and giant red-river gums. **Alligator Gorge** at the northern end of the park, offers a series of steps into the gorge bounded by sheer red quartzite cliffs. About 24km south of the city is the small beachside resort of **Port Germein** which has attractive swimming areas and a long wooden jetty, ideal for fishing and strolling along. **Solomontown Beach** is another great area for families, with picnic and BBQ spots and a playground.

TOURIST INFO: 3 Mary Elie St, Ph: (08) 8633 8700 or 1800 000 424

■ Port Victoria   POP 320
Map 348, D1

Known as the '**Last of the Windjammer Ports**', this tourist and fishing township on the west coast of the **Yorke Peninsula** is one of the original grain ports. Settled in the 1870s, the port was named by the first European explorers in the area after their ship, *Victoria*.

MAIN ATTRACTIONS: Swimming and jetty fishing are popular, with good catches of whiting and snapper to be had. The **National Trust Maritime Museum** is housed in the old grain shed near the partially restored jetty, and displays feature artefacts and photographs relating to the early shipping and grain industries. The **Port Victoria Geology Trail** is a 4km path that heads south from the jetty to explore the quiet foreshore where 2000 million years ago volcanoes spewed ash and red-hot lava into the atmosphere and earthquakes shook the ground. Picnic tables, BBQs and toilets are located on the foreshore and an interpretation shelter details the locations and histories of 9 shipwrecks in the vicinity of **Wardang Island**. There is also a **Maritime Heritage Trail** to follow.

Alligator Gorge, Mount Remarkable NP

South Australia

The restored paddlesteamer PS *Industry* at Renmark

NEARBY ATTRACTIONS: **Goose Island**, a small island off the northern end of Wardang Island, is home to a colony of Australian sea-lions. Divers can dive with the animals. Overnight camping is permitted—obtain a permit from the Innes National Parks and Wildlife Service. TOURIST INFO: Port Victoria Kiosk and Post Office, Main St, Ph: (08) 8834 2098

Quorn POP 1500
Map 346, E4

Located in a valley in the southern **Flinders Ranges**, the old railway town of Quorn is an important gateway to the ranges and a fascinating destination in its own right. Originally, in the 1850s, the district thrived on wheat production. This gave way to sheep and cattle when the good rains of the early years failed. Quorn was established as a railway town in 1878, today it is in a position to cater to a diverse tourist trade, which ensures its existence and prosperity.

MAIN ATTRACTIONS: Many pre-1900 buildings remain in the town and can be viewed on the town's 45min **Historic Buildings Walk**. The **Quorn Mill** (1878) now operates as a motel and restaurant. Several other local outlets sell arts and crafts. A collection of farm machinery is located in **Lions Park** on the Port Augusta Rd. From April to November the **Pichi Richi Railway** offers a link to the past with a steam-train trip on a section of narrow-gauge line from Quorn Station to **Woolshed Flat**, **Stirling North** and **Port Augusta**.

NEARBY ATTRACTIONS: Quorn is an ideal base for exploring the historic ruins of **Kanyaka**, **Willochra**, **Gordon**, **Wilson** and **Simmonston**—all reminders of the harsh conditions encountered by early pioneers. Spectacular mountain scenery can be seen in **Yarrah Vale** and **Warren gorges** and from **Buckaringa Scenic Lookout**. Both **Dutchmans Stern CP**, 8km west, and **Mount Brown CP**, 16km away are worth a visit. TOURIST INFO: 3 Seventh St, Ph: (08) 8648 6419

Renmark POP 4650
Map 333, D1

Australia's oldest irrigation town, Renmark was settled in 1887. It was pioneered by the Canadian Chaffey brothers, who reached an agreement with the government for a grant of land on which to test their irrigation scheme. The scheme proved successful, and the town and district still flourish using water pumped from the **Murray River** to irrigate the vineyards, orchards and other crops that line the river.

MAIN ATTRACTIONS: **Olivewood**, the pine-log home of pioneer, George Chaffey, is run by the National Trust and holds a collection of relics and photographs of Renmark's early days. There are a number of galleries that display locally produced paintings, pottery and crafts. An **Interpretive Centre** located within the Renmark/Paringa Visitors Centre links the past with the present by tracing the river's history from ancient times. Moored close to the centre is the fully restored 1911 paddlesteamer **PS *Industry***. This wonderful old paddlesteamer cruises on the first Sunday of each month. Cruises on the modern **Big River Rambler** depart from the town wharf daily.

NEARBY ATTRACTIONS: About 3km east of Renmark is the town of **Paringa**, its attractions include historic **Customs House** (1884), now a general store, a **suspension bridge** that is one of only 4 still spanning the river and **Lock 5**, built in the 1920s to regulate the waterflow of the river. There are 2 major wineries southwest of town: **Renmano Winery** and **Angove's Winery**. The 9000km^2 **Bookmark Biosphere Reserve** is to the north and south of the town. **Bredl's Wonder World of Wildlife** is 7km south on the Sturt Hwy. TOURIST INFO: Murray Ave, Ph: (08) 8586 6704

Robe POP 880
Map 323, B3

Previously, one of the most important ports in the state, Robe was settled in 1846 and is now a holiday destination and the home port of a commercial crayfishing fleet. The town is located on **Guichen Bay**, 336km south of Adelaide, and was named after Governor Fredrick Robe, who sailed along the coast and chose this site as a suitable location for a port.

RIVERLAND

This region features about 300km of the **Murray River**, one of the world's great waterways, meandering through a changing landscape. Not only does the river dominate the region's landscape, it also influences its economy—providing the life-blood to irrigate its many orchards and vineyards.

Riverland produces close to half of South Australia's wine grapes and is becoming increasingly known as a wine area in its own right. Riverland is the heart of the fruit bowl of South Australia, where more than 90% of the state's citrus, stone fruit and nuts are grown; local produce can be sampled from stalls along the roadside.

There is no better way to explore the might of the Murray River than by travelling on it—houseboats fully equipped with home comforts are an ideal holiday option. The river is ideal for anglers, where catches of the day include Murray cod, redfin and callop. Riverland is dotted with tiny towns rich in the history of pioneering days. This is a fragile region that offers much to explore.

main attractions

- ◈ Banrock Station
- ◈ Fresh and Dried Fruit Outlets
- ◈ Loxton Historical Village
- ◈ River Cruises
- ◈ Ruston's Rose Garden
- ◈ The Big Orange

 Tourist information

Renmark/Paringa Visitors Centre
84 Murray Ave, Renmark SA 5341
Ph: (08) 8586 6704

Murray River cliffs near Paringa, Riverland

MAIN ATTRACTIONS: The **Historic Walk** takes in the charm and character of the town as it passes the old cottages and historic buildings of the old port area. In particular, the **Star of Sea Catholic Church** (1868), and a number of the early homes now offer accommodation or house galleries and specialty shops. Built in 1863, **Robe Customs House** in Royal Circus is a National Trust museum displaying nautical items and local memorabilia. The **Historical Interpretive Centre** is worth a visit and is part of the library and tourist information complex in Mundy Tce. Fresh, locally caught crayfish and fish are popular with residents and visitors to the port.
NEARBY ATTRACTIONS: This is a wonderful area for fishing, surfing and swimming holidays, Robe has a very safe beach only 2km north of town. **Long Beach**, on Guichen Bay, stretches for 11km and at the northern end it is possible to drive onto the white sand beach. It is not safe to swim in the ocean beaches as many of them have dangerous rips. For an interesting walk take the Obelisk Rd to **Cape Dombey**, where a clifftop track leads to the ruins of an old gaol and the **Obelisk**, once a beacon for early mariners. Robe borders **Little Dip CP**. Around 14km SE of Robe, **Narraburra Woolshed** has displays of shearing and wool sorting. Group bookings are required. For wine lovers, the **Limestone Coast region** offers **Mount Benson** and **Cape Jaffa wineries**.
TOURIST INFO: Public Library, Mundy Tce, Ph: (08) 8768 2465

■ **Roxby Downs**   POP 4000
Map 346, D2
Nestled in rich red sand dunes clad in native pine, Roxby Downs is a delightful town. A young modern mining town, it was purpose-built to house and service employees and their families of the **Olympic Dam Mining** project. The mine produces gold, copper, uranium oxide concentrate and silver.
MAIN ATTRACTIONS: From March to November, surface mine tours depart from the town centre. Bookings are essential. The town boasts a range of excellent accommodation. Retail and leisure facilities include a 3-star motel with restaurant, a tavern, modern shopping centre, bowls and golf course. Visitors are welcome at the community's leisure centre which

South Australia

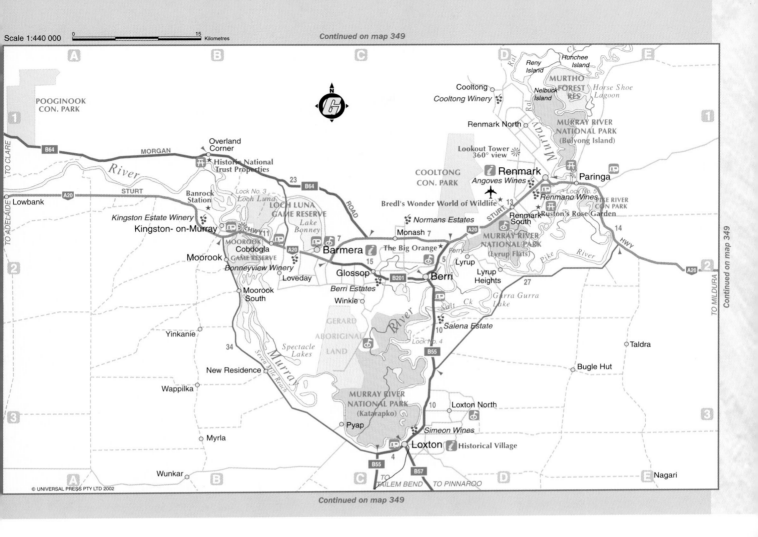

Continued on map 349

Scale 1:440 000

A

POOGINOOK
CON. PARK

TO CLARE
TO ADELAIDE

B64

MORGAN

Overland
Corner

River

STURT

A20

Lowbank

Banrock
Station

Kingston Estate Winery

Kingston- on-Murray

Historic National
Trust Properties

Lock No. 3
Loch Luna

23

B64

LOCH LUNA
GAME RESERVE

Lake
Bonney

HWY

11

MOOROOK

Cobdogla

A20

Moorook

GAME RESERVE

Bonneyview Winery

Loveday

7

Barmera

i

15

The Big Orange

Glossop

B201

Berri

Moorook
South

Yinkanie

34

Spectacle
Lakes

Seven Mile Reach

Murray

Berri Estates

Winkie

GERARD
ABORIGINAL
LAND

River

New Residence

Wappilka

Myrla

Pyap

MURRAY RIVER
NATIONAL PARK
(Katarapko)

Lock No. 4

10

Loxton

Simeon Wines

Historical Village

Wunkar

B

C

B55

TO
TAILEM BEND

B57

TO PINNAROO

© UNIVERSAL PRESS PTY LTD 2002

D

Reny
Island

Hunchee
Island

MURTHO
FOREST
RES

Horse Shoe
Lagoon

Cooltong

Cooltong Winery

Nelbuck
Island

MURRAY RIVER
NATIONAL PARK
(Bulyong Island)

E

Renmark North

COOLTONG
CON. PARK

Lookout Tower
360° view

Renmark

Angoves Wines

Paringa

Lock No. 5

Renmano Wines

Renmark
South

Ruston's Rose Garden

Bredl's Wonder World of Wildlife

13

STURT

Normans Estates

Monash

7

A20

MURRAY RIVER
NATIONAL PARK
(Lyrup Flats)

Pike River

14

HWY

A20

TO MILDURA

Lyrup

Ferry

5

Lyrup
Heights

27

Salt Ck

Gurra Gurra
Lake

Salena Estate

10

B55

Taldra

Bugle Hut

Loxton North

10

Nagari

Continued on map 349
Continued on map 349

has a swimming pool, squash court and tennis court.

NEARBY ATTRACTIONS: The **Olympic Dam and Mining Complex** is 16km north of Roxby Downs. The opal fields of **Andamooka** are 30km east of town and offer an easy side trip. East of Andamooka (13km) is the northern tip of **Lake Torrens**, a vast, normally dry salt lake that stretches south, almost all the way to **Port Augusta**.

TOURIST INFO: Roxby Downs Council, Richardson Place, Ph: (08) 8671 0010

■ Stansbury   POP 532

Map 348, E2

Located on the **Yorke Peninsula**, halfway between Port Vincent and Edithburgh, Stansbury looks across **Oyster Bay** to the waters of **Gulf St Vincent**. Stansbury is a pleasant

holiday destination nurturing a growing tourist industry. Grain-growing and pastoral activities and the state's largest limestone quarry at **Klein Point**, also support the local economy.

MAIN ATTRACTIONS: The **School House Museum** is located in historic Stansbury school (1878) on North Tce, and offers a look into 19th-century education. Jetty fishing is a popular activity and in May, the **Sheep Dog Trials** draw quite a crowd.

NEARBY ATTRACTIONS: About 15km NW, **Lake Sundown** is, as the name implies, absolutely stunning at sunset. **Klein's Point Quarry** is located 5km south and has daily tours of the limestone quarry.

TOURIST INFO: Dalrymple Store, St Vincent St, Ph: (08) 8852 4400

The unusual tent-shaped Oasis Motel at Roxby Downs

Murphy's Haystacks, 40km SE of Streaky Bay

■ Strathalbyn POP 3120
Map 349, F2

The north-east gateway to the **Fleurieu Peninsula**, Strathalbyn lies on the banks of the **Angas River** and is acknowledged as one of South Australia's most attractive rural towns. When they settled in the district in 1839, the Scottish Rankine brothers commenced building **St Andrew's Uniting Church**, overlooking the river.
MAIN ATTRACTIONS: The wide streets, numerous historic buildings and the stately old homes contribute to Strathalbyn's status as a **Heritage Town**. A browsers' and shoppers' paradise, the main areas in town are **Albyn Tce/Dawson St** and **High St**, which are lined with shops selling antiques, arts and crafts and all manner of collectables. The old Police Station and Court House are now home to the **National Trust Museum**, which displays photographs, clothing and appliances that depict the life of the pioneers. The pleasant walk through the **Soldier's Memorial Gardens** and along the river bank is highly recommended.
NEARBY ATTRACTIONS: The old riverboat port of **Milang** lies on the shores of **Lake Alexandrina**, the largest freshwater lake in Australia. Conditions on the lake are ideal for sailing, windsurfing and boating. A network of roads leads from this inland town to all parts of the Fleurieu Peninsula. Just 15km east are the wineries of the **Langhorne Creek District**. About 35km NW are the old diggings at **Jupiter Creek Goldfields**.
TOURIST INFO: Old Railway Station, 20 South Tce, Ph: (08) 8536 3212.

■ Streaky Bay POP 1250
Map 345, J5

Streaky Bay is a picturesque town servicing thriving rural and fishing communities and also the granite-mining industry. Around 727km NW of Adelaide, the town attracts a growing number of visitors to the local bays, beaches and coves. The town was originally named Flinders, after Capt Matthew Flinders. In 1940, it changed to that of the bay, which Flinders named in 1802 because of its streaky colours—it is now known the colours are created from oils given off by seaweed.
MAIN ATTRACTIONS: The oldest building, **Hospital Cottage** (1864), is made of mud brick and **St Canute's Catholic Church** is a lovely old sandstone building. **The Old School Museum** in Montgomerie Tce displays the area's pioneering memorabilia as well as botanical and geological exhibits. The **Powerhouse Restored Engine Centre**, Alfred Tce, has displays of working engines. A replica of the world's largest great white shark caught on rod-and-reel is on display at **Stewart's Shell Roadhouse Tourist Centre**.
NEARBY ATTRACTIONS: Located opposite **Pelubie Beach**, **Felchillo Oasis** is 20km NE of Streaky Bay and offers a self-guided tour of an orchard and propagation nursery. Two groups of huge, wind-eroded, pink granite rocks, known as **Murphy's Haystacks**, are a distinctive landmark 40km SE of Streaky Bay. For those wishing to explore the coastline, **Point Labatt CP** is about 55km south of town and offers a sea-lion viewing area as well as panoramic views of the rugged coastline.
TOURIST INFO: Stewart's Shell Roadhouse Tourist Centre, Ph: (08) 8626 1126

■ Tailem Bend POP 2000
Map 349, G2

Perched on a cliff overlooking the **Murray River**, Tailem Bend was proclaimed in 1887 and became a major railway town with lines servicing the **Murray-Mallee** area. With the reduction of railway passenger and freight services, Tailem Bend gained a new lease of life providing facilities for the steady stream of road traffic to and from the south-east and eastern states.
MAIN ATTRACTIONS: There is a shopping centre in Railway Tce, opposite the station, and alongside the station, a large park features a stationary engine and adventure playground for children. A picnic spot with river views is located near the ferry landing and there are 2 antique shops for browsers.
NEARBY ATTRACTIONS: Many hours can be spent wandering the streets of **Old Tailem Town Historical Village**, 5km NW of town. This village, on a former sheep run, has been 'created' by importing old buildings and restoring them, and

South Australia

erecting new 'old' buildings. The 12 streets in the village contain a school, church, railway station, general store and police station, also a barber, watchmaker and saddler. The Murray River is an excellent location for boating, sailing, rowing, swimming and fishing and 3km downstream, **Freds Landing** has a concrete boat ramp. The **Riverside Walking Trail** leads past a cliff face where it is possible to see fossils and evidence of early Aboriginal habitation.
Tourist Info: Railway Tce,
Ph: (08) 8572 4277

■ Tanunda   POP 3600
Map 327, C3
This busy, properous town developed from the village of Langmeil, the valley's second German settlement in 1843. The town is in the heart of the **Barossa wine region**, an important stopover for visitors to the area. Tanunda offers history, art and a vine-to-wine display.
Main Attractions: The town's German heritage has been preserved in its fine churches, specialty bakeries and small-goods shops. The art and craft shops feature locally-produced painted woodware, pottery and glassware. In St Hallet Rd, the **Keg Factory** produces handcrafted kegs and barrels. **Historic Goat Square** is located at the centre of the original town and the old streets are fascinating and best explored on foot. **Barossa Historical Museum**, in Murray St, is housed in the former Post Office (1865). **Tanunda Recreation Reserve**, located in Elizabeth St, is home to a swimming pool, bowling and RSL clubs.
Nearby Attractions: **Kaiser Stuhl CP** lies in the ranges beyond **Bethany**. Bushwalkers here pass through original vegetation that supports a variety of native birds and animals. Wineries and vineyards encircle the town. Some of the better known are: **Chateau Tanunda, Peter**

Lehmann Wines, Richmond Grove and **Basedow Wines**. Most have cellar door tastings and sales.
Tourist Info: Barossa Wine and Visitor Centre, 66–68 Murray St,
Ph: (08) 8563 0600

■ Tumby Bay   POP 1350
Map 348, C1
Around 50km from Port Lincoln, Tumby Bay is situated on the east coast of the **Eyre Peninsula**. It is a quiet rural centre servicing a wheat and sheep-farming area and a local fishing industry. Popular with holidaymakers, the sheltered bay is lined with a white sandy beach and provides a scenic view for a variety of water-based activities, including excellent fishing.
Main Attractions: There are several art and craft outlets in town that welcome browsers, in particular **Rotunda Art Gallery** and **Tumby Cottage Crafts**. A recreation area edges the foreshore of Tumby Bay and there are picnic and BBQ facilities at the southern lookout reserve. **The Interpretive Mangrove Boardwalk**, near the causeway at the southern end of the bay, crosses the mangroves and has signs explaining their ecological importance. There are 2 museums in the town centre, the **C L Alexander National Trust Museum** and the **Excell**

Blacksmith and Engineering Workshop Museum, both are well worth investigating.
Nearby Attractions: **Tumby Bay Charters** offer fishing cruises and trips to **Sir Joseph Banks Group Islands** lying some way offshore. The islands are recognised for their excellent fishing grounds and wealth of birdlife. There is also the opportunity to observe sea-lions basking in the sun or an aquatic ballet of dolphins. The town of **Koppio** is 30km SW where visitors can discover the **Koppio Smithy Museum**. It features an authentic blacksmith's shop, cottages, schoolhouse and heritage hall with stationary engines and horse-drawn vehicles. Located nearby is the **Tod Reservoir Museum** and picnic ground.
Tourist Info: Council Office, Mortlock Tce,
Ph: (08) 8688 2101

■ Victor Harbor   POP 10 184
Map 337, D2
Only an hour's drive from Adelaide, Victor Harbor is one of the state's major tourist destinations. On the **Fleurieu Peninsula**, it nestles in a sandy curve of **Encounter Bay**. Because of its accessibility, the population swells on weekends and can increase up to 80 000 during the peak holiday season.

Disused jetty at Tumby Bay

FLEURIEU PENINSULA

Its close proximity to Adelaide and outstanding combination of seaside resorts surrounded by idyllic rural townships, set among rolling hills and vineyards, make the Fleurieu Peninsula an ideal holiday destination. The region starts near the southern coast of **Adelaide** and continues to **Cape Jervis**, a small town situated at the tip of the Peninsula, which offers excellent views across **Backstairs Passage** to **Kangaroo Island**.

Both sides of the Peninsula's coast offer a full range of waterfront attractions. It boasts great surfing and swimming beaches; islands, which are home to little penguins; and waters frequently visited by southern right whales.

In contrast, the lush green interior hosts 20 or more conservation parks, 1500km of nature trails, historic villages and the world-class wineries of **McLaren Vale**. The region's noted natural beauty has made it a haven for artists and craftspeople, whose works are showcased in galleries and at weekend craft markets. The attractions of the Fleurieu Peninsula can be enjoyed in any season.

main attractions

❖ Cape Jervis
❖ Granite Island, Victor Harbor
❖ Deep Creek Conservation Park
❖ McLaren Vale wineries

 Tourist information

McLaren Vale and Fleurieu Visitor Centre
Main Rd, McLaren Vale SA 5171
Ph: (08) 8323 9944
www.visitorcentre.com.au

Granite Island, Victor Harbor

MAIN ATTRACTIONS: The area enjoys a mild Mediterranean-type climate and extensive coastline, so recreational activities can be enjoyed most of the year. On Sunday, Monday, public holidays, and school holidays, the historic **Cockle Train** runs between **Goolwa** and Victor Harbor. Rolling past beaches and sandhills on Australia's oldest public railway is a nostalgia trip for history lovers. There are many historic buildings in Victor Harbor—take a look at **Congregational Church** (1869), the **Adare House** (1852), **St Augustines Church** (1869) and **Old Customs House** (1867). The **South Australian Whale Centre** on Railway Tce has displays to increase awareness about dolphin and whale conservation. Three favourite attractions with kids are within a 5min drive of Victor Harbor;

they are **Greenhills Adventure Park**, offering canoeing and waterslides; **Urimbirra Wildlife Park**, which has birds, mammals and reptiles; and **Wild Rose Miniature Village** featuring scale models of buildings set in lovely gardens.

NEARBY ATTRACTIONS: Conservation parks and nature reserves abound around Victor Harbor. The **Heysen Trail**, South Australia's premier walk, passes through **Deep Creek CP**. The neighbouring towns of **Port Elliot**, **Middleton** and **Goolwa** are within easy reach of Victor Harbor as are the wineries of **McLaren Vale**, the beaches of **Gulf St Vincent**, **Cape Jervis** and the pretty town of **Strathalbyn**. Access to **Granite Island** is via a causeway built in 1875. Every afternoon at dusk, the **Penguin Interpretive**

Centre runs guided tours to view the hundreds of little penguins that have made the island their home. Take a look at the **Aquarium** off Granite Island, which has an underwater viewing area.
TOURIST INFO: Causeway Kiosk near Horse Tram, Ph: (08) 8552 5738

■ Waikerie   POP 3500
Map 349, G1

Waikerie is known as the '**Citrus Centre of Australia**', with more than 5000ha of irrigated vineyards, citrus and stone-fruit orchards on the banks of the **Murray River**. About 170km NE of Adelaide, the town has been turned from mallee scrubland into productive farming land. It is thought the name 'Waikerie' is a corruption of the Aboriginal word 'weikari' which

South Australia

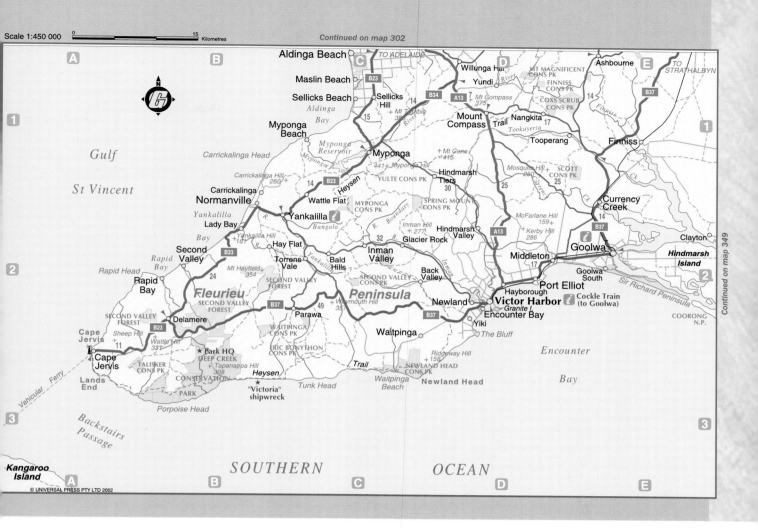

Continued on map 302

Scale 1:450 000

Continued on map 349

refers to the giant swift moths found in the area.

MAIN ATTRACTIONS: The **Waikerie Golf Club** is among the top 10 South Australian golf clubs. Starting near the ferry, a scenic 2km **Clifftop Walkway** runs along sandstone cliffs edging the river. On the way, take in the spectacular views from **Waikerie Lookout Tower**. The walkway runs from the lookout to **Lions Riverfront Reserve**, which provides lawns by the water's edge, shady trees, picnic and BBQ facilities and a playground. Gliding is also a popular activity as the conditions in the area around Waikerie are ideal.

NEARBY ATTRACTIONS: There are 3 protected wetland areas near the town—**Stockyard Plains**, **Hart Lagoon** and **Maize Island CP**—all

with an abundance of birdlife, fauna and flora. **Broken Cliffs** offer a fossicking spot around 7km north on the river. Crystallised gypsum fossils can be found in great numbers here. A short drive away is the popular **Lock 2**, used to control water levels in the Murray. It has BBQ and picnic facilities in a lovely setting.

TOURIST INFO: Orange Tree Giftmania, Sturt Hwy, Ph: (08) 8541 2332

■ Wallaroo   POP 2670

Map 346, E6

The principal port of the **Yorke Peninsula**; the main commodities Wallaroo handles are fertiliser imports and seed and grain exports. The town is also a popular tourist resort, attracting visitors to its safe beaches and excellent fishing. Wallaroo is around 155km NW of

Adelaide. It was the discovery of copper in the late 1880s that led to the settlement; it is one of the 3 towns in the **Copper Triangle**. Declining copper prices saw the demise of the mines in the early 1920s.

MAIN ATTRACTIONS: There are many National Trust-listed buildings and 44 of these sites are featured on the town's 90min **Heritage Walk** that starts at the museum and ends at the **Smelting Works Offices**. **Hughes Chimney Stack** (1861) contains more than 300 000 bricks and is the only one of the smelter's many chimneys to survive. The **National Trust Wallaroo Heritage and Nautical Museum** is located on Jetty Rd and is worth a look to gain an understanding of the town's maritime history. **Jubilee Square** on John Tce is a perfect picnic spot with electric BBQ facilities and a children's playground.

NEARBY ATTRACTIONS: The other Copper Triangle towns of **Moonta** and **Kadina** are both within easy reach. Dotted about the Triangle are Cornish-style cottages, built by hard-rock miners from Cornwall who flocked to this area in the 19th century. About 10km south is **Bird Island**, its shallow waters renowned for an abundance of tasty blue-swimmer crabs.

TOURIST INFO: Moonta Station, Kadina Rd, Moonta, Ph: (08) 8825 1891

■ Whyalla   POP 24 490
Map 346, E5

South Australia's largest regional city, Whyalla is located near the top of **Spencer Gulf**. It prospered on iron ore discovered at nearby **Iron Knob** in the late 1880s. A rapid period of expansion followed when BHP set up their fully integrated steelworks in the town. Today, Whyalla is one of the nation's best-known industrial cities. Originally known as Hummock Hill, after the hill named by Matthew Flinders in 1802, the town was proclaimed Whyalla, from an Aboriginal word of unknown meaning, in 1914.

MAIN ATTRACTIONS: Visit **Whyalla Maritime Museum** with its impressive displays, including **HMAS *Whyalla***, the largest ship in Australia permanently 'docked' on dry land. The museum also houses collections, displays and artefacts relating to BHP shipbuilding and WWII. The **Onesteel Steelworks** (previously BHP) is an interesting but unconventional tourist attraction; tours run Mondays and Wednesdays. The formal landscaping of **Ada Ryan Gardens** and extensive open areas with recreational facilities line Whyalla's **foreshore beach** area. On the other side of the jetty, **Whyalla Marina** has a 4-lane launching ramp and offers every facility to boat owners. A drive up **Hummock Hill**

and walk to the lookout was developed by BHP to commemorate the company's centenary—the lookout offers magnificent 360° views over the town and Onesteel. **Mount Laura Homestead Museum** houses pioneering memorabilia, folk history and a telecommunications museum. **Whyalla Wildlife and Reptile Park** covers 100ha of bushland near the airport and is home to a range of native animals, monkeys and local venomous snakes.

NEARBY ATTRACTIONS: **Whyalla CP** protects original Myall and bluebush woodland of the northern **Eyre Peninsula**. Walk up **Wild Dog Hill** for a great view of the park and surrounding areas. Other tracks lead to **Point Douglas** and to the lighthouse and beach at **Point Lowly**. The temperate waters around Whyalla create a diverse marine ecosystem for divers to explore. Each year from early May to mid-August, the shallow waters around the coast witness the annual migration of the giant Australian cuttlefish, known as the 'chameleons of the sea'.

TOURIST INFO: Lincoln Hwy, Ph: (08) 8645 7900

■ Woomera   POP 1480
Map 346, D2

Located 502km NW of Adelaide, the interdependent **Long Range Weapons Establishment** and Woomera village were established in 1947. They were the result of a joint project between Britain and Australia to set up a remote rocket range. Although much reduced in size, the range itself is a prohibited area, even for the traditional Aboriginal owners.

MAIN ATTRACTIONS: A particular point of interest in the town is the **Missile Park** where rockets, aircraft and weapons associated with the testing range are displayed. The town's facilities include a hotel, caravan park and camping areas. There is a

modern shopping centre, cinema, fitness centre, sports facilities and the **Heritage Centre**, which features the **Woomera Heritage Museum**, snack bar and bowling alley. At **Old Guard Gate** there are opal sales and **Breen Park** is a perfect picnic area.

TOURIST INFO: Heritage Centre, Banool Ave, Ph: (08) 8673 7042

■ Yorketown   POP 720
Map 348, E2

Settled in 1872, Yorketown is the main town of the southern **Yorke Peninsula**. It is the administrative, business and service centre for the area. It was one of the earliest pastoral settlements on the peninsula and although not a seaside town, it has easy access to 3 major bodies of water.

NEARBY ATTRACTIONS: **Gulf St Vincent** and the townships of **Edithburgh** and **Stansbury** are just a few kilometres east. **Innes NP** is 77km SW and offers walking tracks and rugged coastal scenery with tranquil hinterland. About 50km west is **Daly Head**, and **Corny Point** is on the north-west tip of the Peninsula, 55km NW of town. **Hardwicke Bay** and **Spencer Gulf** are a little further away to the west, while to the south is **Investigator Strait**.

TOURIST INFO: Moonta Station, Kadina Rd, Moonta, Ph: (08) 8825 1892

Point Lowly Lighthouse at Port Bonython, near Whyalla

South Australia

KEY MAP

Capital city CBD map
Adelaide p.297

Adelaide suburban maps
pp. 300–303

Region maps
Flinders Ranges p.313
Kangaroo Island p.317
Limestone Coast p.323
The Barossa Valley p.327
Riverland p.333
Fleurieu Peninsula p.337

State maps
pp. 340–349

Merty Merty sand dunes, Strzelecki Desert

DISTANCE CHART

Approximate Distance	Adelaide	Bordertown	Broken Hill NSW	Ceduna	Coober Pedy	Eucla WA	Innamincka	Kulgera NT	Leigh Creek	Mount Gambier	Murray Bridge	Peterborough	Pinnaroo	Port Augusta	Port Lincoln	Port Pirie	Renmark	Streaky Bay	Whyalla	Woomera
Adelaide		267	514	769	837	1256	1033	1251	548	435	74	261	236	305	642	223	247	695	378	484
Bordertown	267		781	1036	1104	1523	1300	1518	815	183	193	528	132	572	909	490	279	962	645	751
Broken Hill NSW	514	781		878	946	1365	1064	1360	579	870	588	281	674	414	751	387	424	804	487	593
Ceduna	769	1036	878		996	487	1213	1410	728	1204	843	597	972	464	404	546	861	107	449	643
Coober Pedy	837	1104	946	996		1483	896	414	487	1272	911	665	1040	532	869	614	923	922	605	369
Eucla WA	1256	1523	1365	487	1483		1700	1897	1215	1691	1330	1084	1459	951	891	1033	1392	594	936	1130
Innamincka	1033	1300	1064	1213	896	1700		1310	485	1468	1107	783	1204	749	1086	817	1087	1139	822	789
Kulgera NT	1251	1518	1360	1410	414	1897	1310		901	1686	1325	1079	1454	946	1283	1028	1337	1336	1019	783
Leigh Creek	548	815	579	728	487	1215	485	901		983	622	298	719	264	601	332	602	654	437	380
Mount Gambier	435	183	870	1204	1272	1691	1468	1686	983		361	696	315	740	1077	658	462	1130	813	919
Murray Bridge	74	193	588	843	911	1330	1107	1325	622	361		335	162	379	716	297	207	769	452	558
Peterborough	261	528	281	597	665	1084	783	1079	298	696	335		421	133	470	106	300	523	206	312
Pinnaroo	236	132	674	972	1040	1459	1204	1454	719	315	162	421		508	845	437	147	898	581	687
Port Augusta	305	572	414	464	532	951	749	946	264	740	379	133	508		337	82	391	390	73	179
Port Lincoln	642	909	751	404	869	891	1086	1283	601	1077	716	470	845	337		419	724	294	264	420
Port Pirie	223	490	387	546	614	1033	817	1028	332	658	297	106	437	82	419		316	472	155	261
Renmark	247	279	424	861	923	1392	1087	1337	602	462	207	300	147	391	724	316		777	460	566
Streaky Bay	695	962	804	107	922	594	1139	1336	654	1130	769	523	898	390	294	472	777		375	569
Whyalla	378	645	487	449	605	936	822	1019	437	813	452	206	581	73	264	155	460	375		252
Woomera	484	751	593	643	369	1130	789	783	380	919	558	312	687	179	420	261	566	569	252	

All distances in this chart have been measured over highways and major roads, not necessarily by the shortest route.

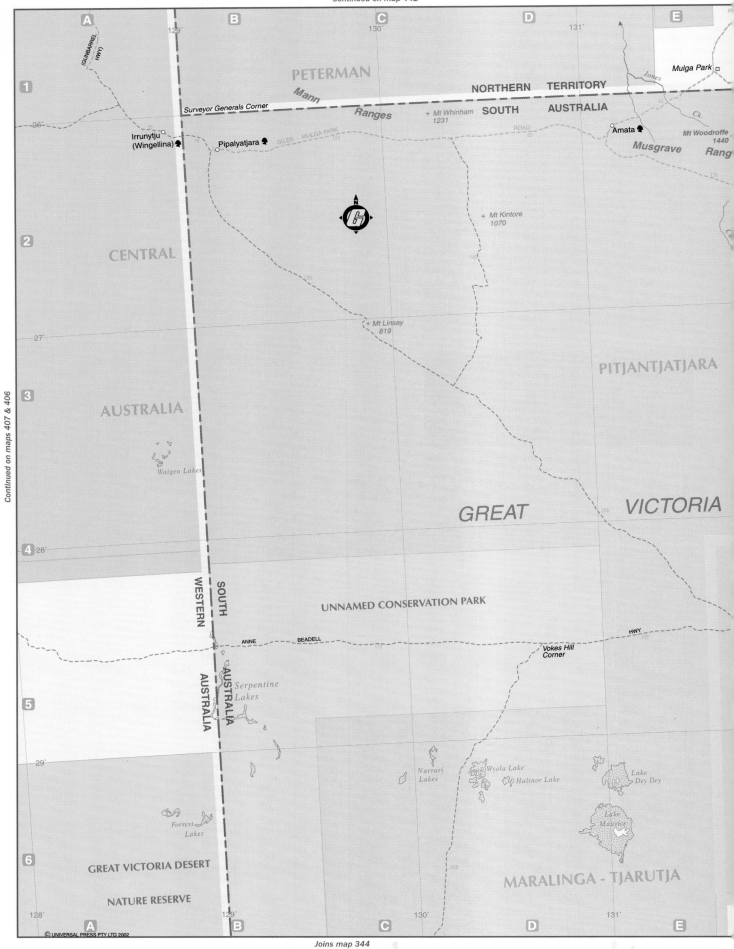

Scale 1:1 90

A   B   C   D   E

Continued on maps 407 & 406

PETERMAN

Mann   Ranges

Surveyor Generals Corner

+ Mt Whinham
1231

NORTHERN   TERRITORY

SOUTH   AUSTRALIA

ROAD

Mulga Park

Jones

Ck.

Amata

Mt Woodroffe
1440

Musgrave   Rang

Irrunytju
(Wingellina)

Pipalyatjara

GILES - MULGA PARK

CENTRAL

AUSTRALIA

Waigen Lakes

+ Mt Kintore
1070

+ Mt Linsay
819

PITJANTJATJARA

GREAT   VICTORIA

UNNAMED CONSERVATION PARK

SOUTH

WESTERN

AUSTRALIA

ANNE   BEADELL

HWY

Vokes Hill
Corner

Serpentine
Lakes

Nurrari
Lakes

Wyola Lake

Halinor Lake

Lake
Dey Dey

Forrest
Lakes

Lake
Maurice

GREAT VICTORIA DESERT

NATURE RESERVE

MARALINGA - TJARUTJA

South Australia

50
Kilometres

New Crown

F | 132°
G | 133°
H | 134°
J

Umbeara

Kulgera Roadhouse
Kulgera Siding
Johnstone Geodetic
Mount Cavenagh

NORTHERN

145

Mt Beddome

Beddome Range

Charlotte Waters (ruin)

McDills Bore

Finke

Mount Dare

Victory Downs

SOUTH

TERRITORY

AUSTRALIA

Goyder

Mt Daning
541

Carralutha

Mt Anderson
358

Abminga
(ruin)

WITJIRA

1

Hamilton

Marryat

Marryat

Mt Howe
515

Tieyon

Stevenson

Lindsay

Eringa
(ruin)

Bloods Ck
Bore

Federal
(ruin)

NATIONAL

PARK

Pukatja
(Ernabella)

Inyarinya
(Kenmore Park)

182
Agnes Creek

Earferingiana

Taroonyinna

Alberga

Bagot

Range

Mt Walter
361

Creek

OLD

Dalhousie (ruin)

Pedirka (ruin)

GHAN

2

Fregon

STUART

Ck.

Chandler

Granite Downs

PEDIRKA DESERT

Mt Rebecca
288

Mount Sarah

Hamilton

ROUTE

Everard   Ranges

Mimili

Indulkana (Iwantja)

Chambers
Bluff 592

Yoolperlunna

Lambina

Nicholson Hill
404

CENTRAL

Ammannodinna

Coongra

OODNADATTA

Todmorden

Fogarty's
Claypan

River

27°

Mintabie
Opal Fields

Marla

HWY

Welbourne Hill

Olaninna

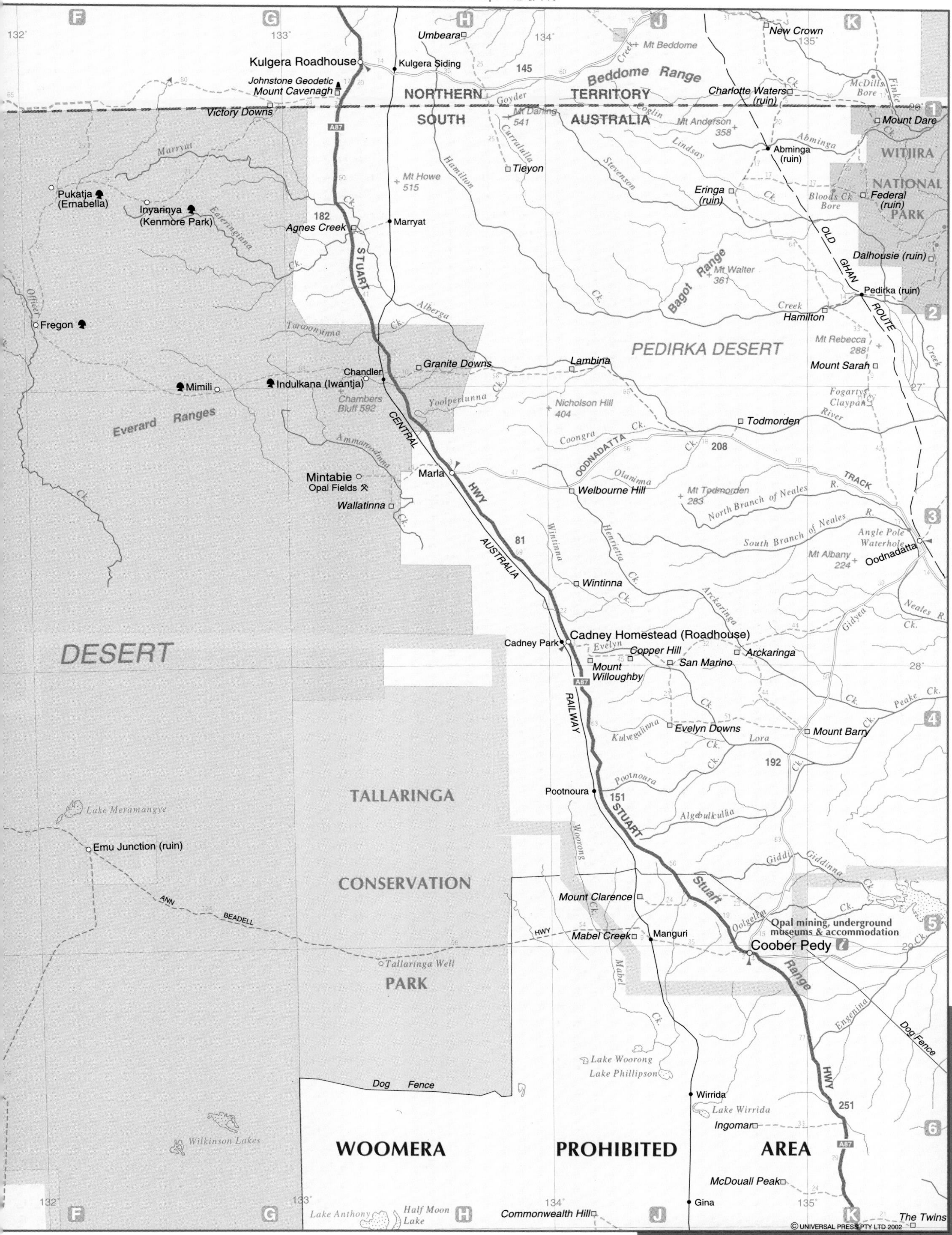

208

North Branch of Neales

TRACK

Angle Pole
Waterhole

3

Wallatinna

AUSTRALIA

81

Wintinna

Mt Todmorden
283

Mt Albany
224

South Branch of Neales

R.

Oodnadatta

Neales R.

DESERT

Wintinna

Henrietta Ck.

Arckaringa

Gidyea

Joins map 342

Cadney Park

Cadney Homestead (Roadhouse)

Evelyn

Copper Hill

San Marino

Arckaringa

28°

RAILWAY

A87

Mount
Willoughby

Ck.

Peake   Ck.

4

Evelyn Downs

Mount Barry

Lake Meramangye

TALLARINGA

Kulvegalinna

Lora

192

Ck.

Emu Junction (ruin)

Pootnoura

151

Pootnoura

STUART

Algebulkulla

Giddi

Giddinna

ANN

CONSERVATION

Woorong

Mabel

Range

BEADELL

HWY

Mount Clarence

Mabel Creek

Manguri

Stuart

Oolgelima

Opal mining, underground
museums & accommodation

Ck.

5

Tallaringa Well

PARK

Coober Pedy

Range

Wilkinson Lakes

Dog   Fence

Lake Woorong
Lake Phillipson

Wirrida

Lake Wirrida

Engenina

HWY

Dog Fence

Ingomar

251

A87

6

WOOMERA

Lake Anthony

Half Moon
Lake

PROHIBITED

Commonwealth Hill

McDouall Peak

Gina

AREA

The Twins

© UNIVERSAL PRESS PTY LTD 2002

F
G | 133°
H | 134°
J
K | 135°

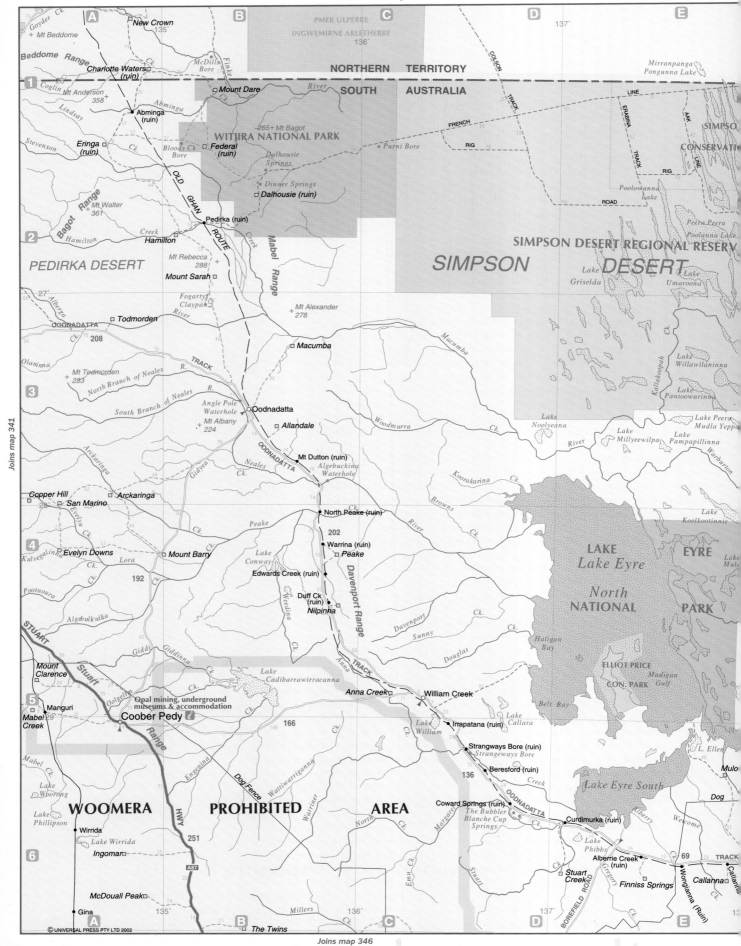

South Australia

50
Kilometres

SIMPSON DESERT
NATIONAL PARK

Simpson Desert

Keppel
Corner

Flood
Detour
LINE

Nappanerica
Sand Dune
(Big Red)

Roseberth

Durri

Mount Leonard
Betoota

ROAD

DEVELOPMENTAL

Cuddapan

Lake
Cuddapan

Birdsville

Shallow Lake

Moonda Lake

Planet Downs O.S.

QUEENSLAND

SOUTH AUSTRALIA

L. Nappanerica

Pandie Pandie

Lake Cooninnie

Haddon Corner

Lake Short

Cadelga (Ruin)

Karrathunka
Waterhole

Lake
Etamunbanie

STURT

165

Alton Downs

157

Lake
Uloowaranie

Goyder
Lagoon

197

STONY

Koonchera
Waterhole

Koonchera
Sandhill

DESERT

L Goyder
L Lady Blanche
L Sir Richard

Cordillo Downs

Lake Surprise
Sandhill

Arrabury

Clifton Hills

Warburton
Crossing

Coongie
Lake

L Marroocutchanie

Candmdecka

Leap Year
Bore

Lake
Pure

Mt Gason Wattle Project

Coongie (ruin)

INNAMINCKA

ADVENTURE

WY

242

Mt Gason
Bore

121

Lake Koodnanie

REGIONAL

Patchawarra

142

Patchawarra
Bore

RESERVE

Nappa
Merrie

Walkers
Crossing

Lake
Howitt

Mirra Mitta Bore

Dig Tree

Gullyamurra
Waterhole

Lake Perigundi

Gidgealpa

Burkes Mem.

Mungerannie Gap

Wills Mem.

Innamincka

Mungerannie
Roadhouse

Gidgealpa Gas Field

TRACK

Lake Kittakittaooloo

TIRARI

DESERT

Moomba Oil & Gas Field

Moomba (Private)

130

Burke-Dullingari
Oil & Gas Field

Orientos

Lake Warrakalanna

Lake Ngapakaldi

Mulka

Della Gas Field

116

Epsilon

Lake Puntewolona

Lake Hope

Toolachee Gas Field

Santos

Natterannie
Sandhills

Gas

Lake
Killamperpunna

Pipeline

Cooper

Flood
Detour

STREZELECKI

Merty Merty

DESERT

Omicron

Lake
Palankarinna

Etadunna

Cannuwaukaninna
Bore

202

Lake
Florence

Lake Kopperekoppinna

STRZELECKI

Bollards
Lagoon

REGIONAL

Lake Gregory

Yaningurie
Waterhole

Strzelecki
Crossing

Bollards Lagoon

Cameron Corner

Tooma
Gate

Dulkaninna

Corner Store

Lindon

Fort Grey

Olive Downs

SOUTH AUSTRALIA

NEW SOUTH WALES

STURT NATIONAL PARK

Clayton

RESERVE

Lake
Blanche

Waka

Clayton

Lake Harry

Lake Stewart

Lake Harry (ruin)

Gum Vale

Lake Arthur

Blanchewater (ruin)

317

Montecollina Bore

Tilcha

Hewart Downs

Mt Poole 250

Murnpeowie

STRZELECKI

Mundowdna

Mt Hopeless

LAKE CALLABONNA
FOSSIL RESERVE

Callabonna (Ruin)

Mt Sturt

Theldarpa

Dog Fence

140

Milparinka

Moolawatana

Hawker
Gate

Mt Brown 274

© UNIVERSAL PRESS PTY LTD 2002

Continued on maps 111 & 284

South Australia

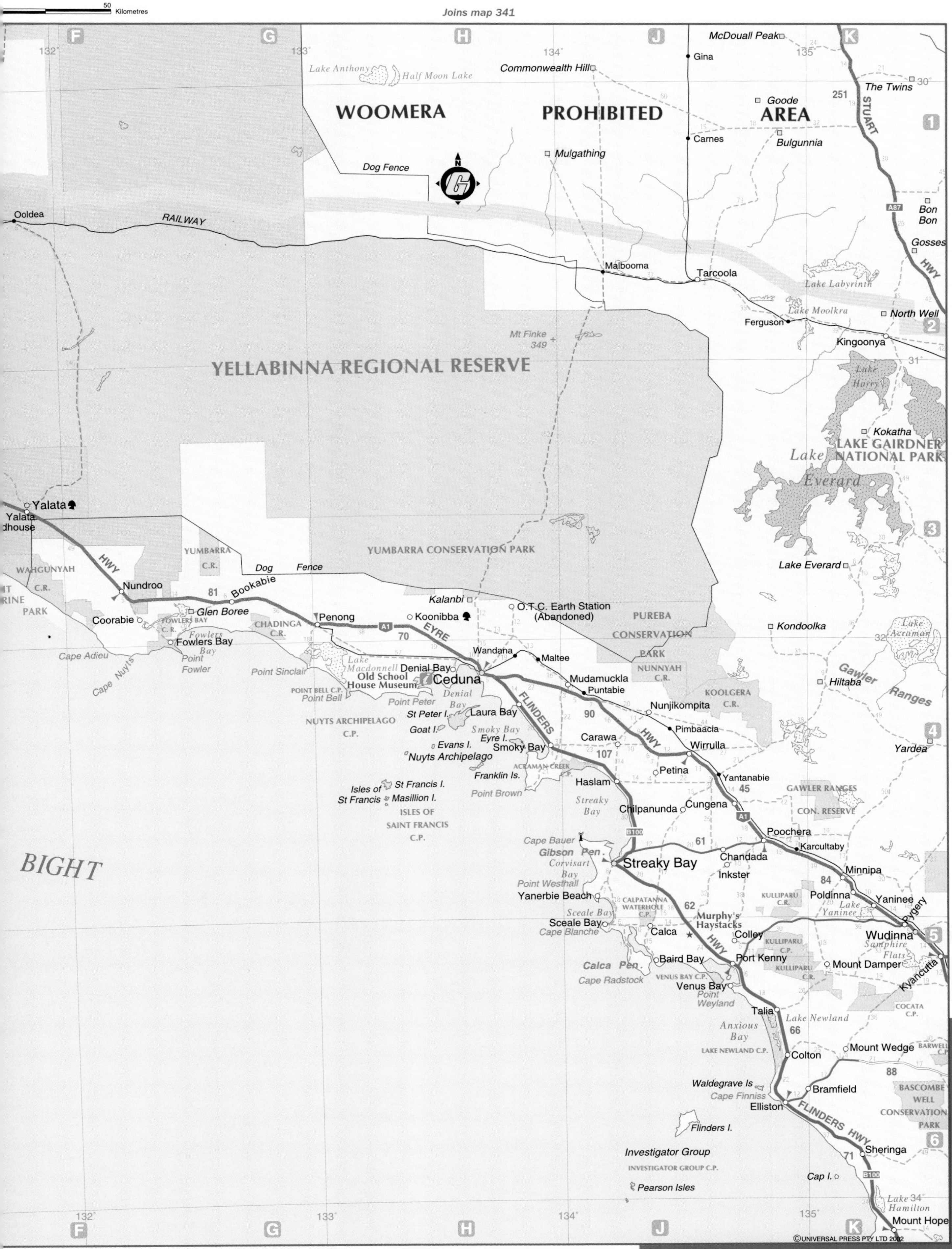

50
Kilometres

F 132° G 133° H 134° J K

Lake Anthony Half Moon Lake

WOOMERA   **PROHIBITED**   **AREA**

McDouall Peak
Gina
Commonwealth Hill
The Twins
30°
1
Goode
251
Bulgunnia
Carnes
A87
Bon Bon
Mulgathing
Gosses

Ooldea
RAILWAY
Dog Fence
Malbooma
Tarcoola
Lake Labyrinth
North Well
2
Ferguson
Lake Moolkra
Kingoonya

Mt Finke
349
YELLABINNA REGIONAL RESERVE
31°
Lake Harry
Lake Gairdner
Kokatha
LAKE GAIRDNER
NATIONAL PARK
Lake Everard

Yalata
Yalata
Roadhouse
HWY
Lake Everard
3
Lake Acraman

WAHGUNYAH
C.R.
YUMBARRA
C.R.
Dog Fence
YUMBARRA CONSERVATION PARK
32°
MT
RINE
PARK
Nundroo
Bookabie
Kalanbi
O.T.C. Earth Station
(Abandoned)
PUREBA
Kondoolka
Gawler Ranges
81
Glen Boree
Koonibba
CONSERVATION
Hiltaba
Coorabie
CHADINGA
C.R.
Penong
A1
70
Koonibba
PARK
NUNNYAH
Fowlers Bay
Fowlers
Bay
EYRE
Wandana
Maltee
C.R.
KOOLGERA
Kondoolka
Cape Adieu
Point
Fowler
Lake
Macdonnell
Old School
House Museum
Denial Bay
Ceduna
Mudamuckla
Puntabie
C.R.
4
Cape Nuyts
Point Sinclair
POINT BELL C.P.
Point Bell
Denial
Bay
FLINDERS
Nunjikompita
Yardea
Point Peter
St Peter I.
Laura Bay
Pimbaacia
NUYTS ARCHIPELAGO
C.P.
Goat I.
Smoky Bay
90
Wirrulla
Cape
Evans I.
Smoky Bay
Carawa
HWY
Petina
GAWLER RANGES
Nuyts Archipelago
107
Yantanabie
CON. RESERVE
Franklin Is.
Haslam
45
Point Brown
ACRAMAN CREEK
Cungena
Poochera
Isles of
St Francis
St Francis I.
Masillion I.
Streaky
Bay
Chilpanunda
A1
Karcultaby
Minnipa
ISLES OF
SAINT FRANCIS
C.P.
Cape Bauer
B100
Chandada
84
BIGHT
Gibson Pen.
61
Streaky Bay
Inkster
KULLIPARU
C.R.
Poldinna
Yaninee
Corvisart
Bay
Point Westhall
Yanerbie Beach
Lake
Yaninee
Pygery
CALPATANNA
WATERHOLE
C.P.
Murphy's
Haystacks
Colley
KULLIPARU
C.P.
Wudinna
Scale Bay
Cape Blanche
Calca
62
Samphire
Flats
Mount Damper
Calca Pen.
Baird Bay
HWY
Port Kenny
KULLIPARU
C.R.
Kyancutta
5
Cape Radstock
VENUS BAY C.P.
Venus Bay
Point
Weyland
Talia
COCATA
C.P.
Mount Wedge
BARWELL
C.P.
66
Lake Newland
Anxious
Bay
LAKE NEWLAND C.P.
Colton
BASCOMBE
WELL
Waldegrave Is
Cape Finniss
Bramfield
88
Elliston
FLINDERS HWY
CONSERVATION
PARK
Flinders I.
71
Sheringa
Investigator Group
6
INVESTIGATOR GROUP C.P.
Cap I.
B100
Lake
Hamilton
34°
Pearson Isles
Mount Hope

F 132° G 133° H 134° J 135° K

© UNIVERSAL PRESS PTY LTD 2002

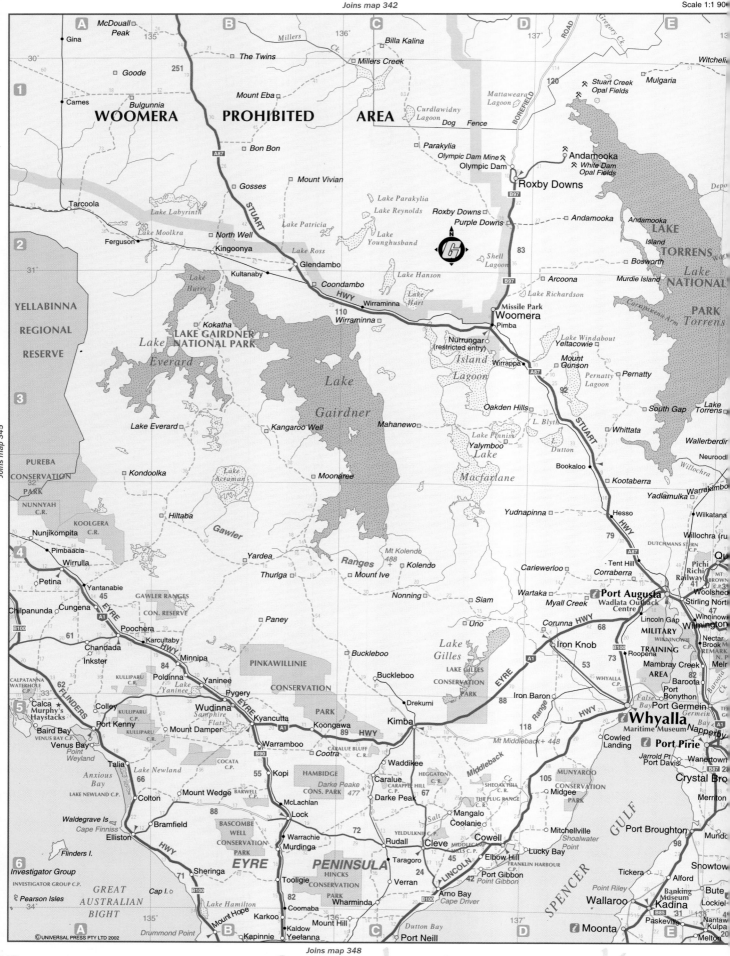

WOOMERA   PROHIBITED   AREA

YELLABINNA
REGIONAL
RESERVE

PUREBA
CONSERVATION
PARK

NUNNYAH
C.R.

KOOLGERA
C.R.

LAKE GAIRDNER
NATIONAL PARK

Lake
Everard

Lake
Gairdner

Gawler
Ranges

GAWLER RANGES
CON. RESERVE

PINKAWILLINIE
CONSERVATION
PARK

EYRE   HWY

KULLIPARU
C.R.

EYRE
PENINSULA

HAMBIDGE
CONS. PARK

Darke Peake
CONS. PARK

BASCOMBE
WELL
CONSERVATION
PARK

HINCKS
CONSERVATION
PARK

LAKE GILLES
CONSERVATION
PARK

LAKE
TORRENS
NATIONAL
PARK

Lake
Torrens

Lake
Macfarlane

MILITARY
TRAINING
AREA

MUNYAROO
CONSERVATION
PARK

GREAT
AUSTRALIAN
BIGHT

SPENCER   GULF

© UNIVERSAL PRESS PTY LTD 2002

Gregory's Australia

South Australia

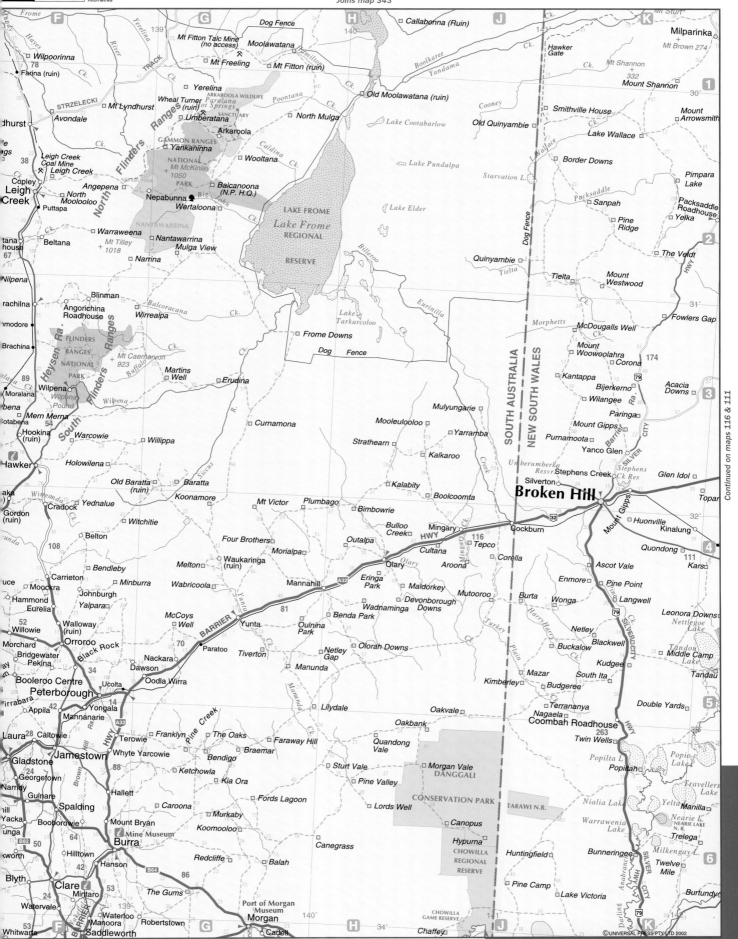

50 Kilometres

© UNIVERSAL PRESS PTY LTD 2002

Milparinka
Mt Brown 274
Hawker Gate
Mt Shannon
332
Mount Shannon
Mount Arrowsmith
30°
Callabonna (Ruin)
Smithville House
Old Quinyambie
Border Downs
Lake Wallace
Pimpara Lake
Packsaddle Roadhouse
Yelka
Sanpah
Pine Ridge
The Veldt
Quinyambie
31°
Tielta
Fowlers Gap
Mount Westwood
Morphetts
McDougalls Well
Mount Woowoolahra
Corona
174
Kantappa
Bijerkerno
Wilangee
Acacia Downs
Paringa
Mount Gipps
Purnamoota
Yanco Glen
Stephens Creek
Glen Idol
Silverton
Broken Hill
32
Cockburn
Topar
Huonville
Kinalung
Quondong
Kars
111
Ascot Vale
Enmore
Pine Point
Burta
Wonga
Langwell
Leonora Downs
Nettlegoe Lake
Netley
Blackwell
Buckalow
Kudgee
Tandou
Middle Camp
Mazar
South Ita
Tandou Lake
Kimberley
Budgeree
Double Yards
Terrananya
Nagaela
Coombah Roadhouse
263
Twin Wells
Oakbank
Oakvale
Popilta L.
Popio Lake
Popiltah
Travellers Lake
Morgan Vale
DANGGALI
Nialia Lake
Yelta
Manilla
Nearie L.
NEARIE LAKE N.R.
Warrawenia Lake
Trelega
CONSERVATION PARK
Lords Well
Canopus
Hypurna
TARAWI N.R.
Milkengay L.
Bunneringee
Huntingfield
CHOWILLA REGIONAL RESERVE
Pine Camp
Lake Victoria
Twelve Mile
Burtundy
34°
Chaffey
CHOWILLA GAME RESERVE

Continued on maps 116 & 111

SOUTH AUSTRALIA / NEW SOUTH WALES

Dog Fence
Mt Fitton Talc Mine (no access)
Moolawatana
Mt Freeling
Mt Fitton (ruin)
Callabonna (Ruin)
Bootkaree Ck
Yandama
Cooney
Wilpoorinna
Farina (ruin)
78
STRZELECKI
Mt Lyndhurst
Avondale
Yerelina
Wheal Turner (ruin)
Umberatana
ARKAROOLA WILDLIFE SANCTUARY
Paralana Springs
Poontana
North Mulga
Old Moolawatana (ruin)
Lake Cootabarlow
Leigh Creek Coal Mine
38
Leigh Creek
Copley
Angepena
North Moolooloo
Puttapa
GAMMON RANGES
Yankaninna
Arkaroola
NATIONAL
Mt McKinlay 1050
PARK
Wooltana
Caldina Ck
Lake Pundalpa
Starvation L.
67
Beltana
Balcanoona (N.P. H.Q.)
Nepabunna
Big John
Wertaloona
Warraweena
NANTAWARRINA
Mt Tilley 1018
Nantawarrina
Mulga View
Narrina
LAKE FROME REGIONAL RESERVE
Lake Frome
Lake Elder
Billeroo
Blinman
Angorichina Roadhouse
Wirrealpa
Balcoracana Ck
Eurinilla Ck
rachilna
Frome Downs
Lake Tarkarcooloo
89
FLINDERS RANGES NATIONAL PARK
Mt Caernarvon 923
Buffalo
Martins Well
Erudina
Dog Fence
Heysen Ra.
Wilpena
Moralana
Wilpena Pound
Wilpena
Mern Merna
54
Curnamona
Mulyungarie
Hookina (ruin)
Warcowie
Holowilena
Willippa
Mooleulooloo
Yarramba
Strathearn
Hawker
Old Baratta (ruin)
Baratta
Koonamore
Kalkaroo
Gordon (ruin)
Yednalue
Cradock
Witchitie
Mt Victor
Plumbago
Bimbowrie
Kalabity
Boolcoomta
108
Belton
Bulloo Creek
Mingary
Four Brothers
Outalpa
Cultana
116
Tepco
Belton
Morialpa
Aroona
Corella
Melton
Waukaringa (ruin)
Olary
Olary
Minburra
Wabricoola
Mannahill
Eringa Park
Maldorkey
Mutooroo
Johnburgh
Yalpara
Benda Park
Wadnaminga
Devonborough Downs
81
Carrieton
Moockra
McCoys Well
Yunta
Oulnina Park
Netley Gap
Olorah Downs
Hammond
Eurelia
Willowie
Walloway (ruin)
Paratoo
Tiverton
Manunda
Orroroo
Black Rock
Nackara
Dawson
52
BARRIER
70
Morchard
Bridgewater
Pekina
Ucolta
Oodla Wirra
34
Booleroo Centre
Peterborough
Yongala
Lilydale
Oakvale
Appila
Mannanarie
14
42
Caltowie
A32
Laura
28
Jamestown
Terowie
Franklyn
The Oaks
Faraway Hill
Quandong Vale
Gladstone
Whyte Yarcowie
Bendigo
Braemar
Georgetown
88
Ketchowla
Kia Ora
Sturt Vale
Pine Valley
Narridy
Hallett
Fords Lagoon
Gulnare
Caroona
Spalding
24
Booborowie
Murkaby
Koomooloo
Canegrass
Mount Bryan
Mine Museum
64
Hilltown
Burra
Redcliffe
Balah
Hanson
86
Blyth
B64
Clare
Mintaro
The Gums
Port of Morgan Museum
Watervale
Waterloo
Manoora
Robertstown
Morgan
53
Whitwarta
Saddleworth
BARRIER
139
Cadell

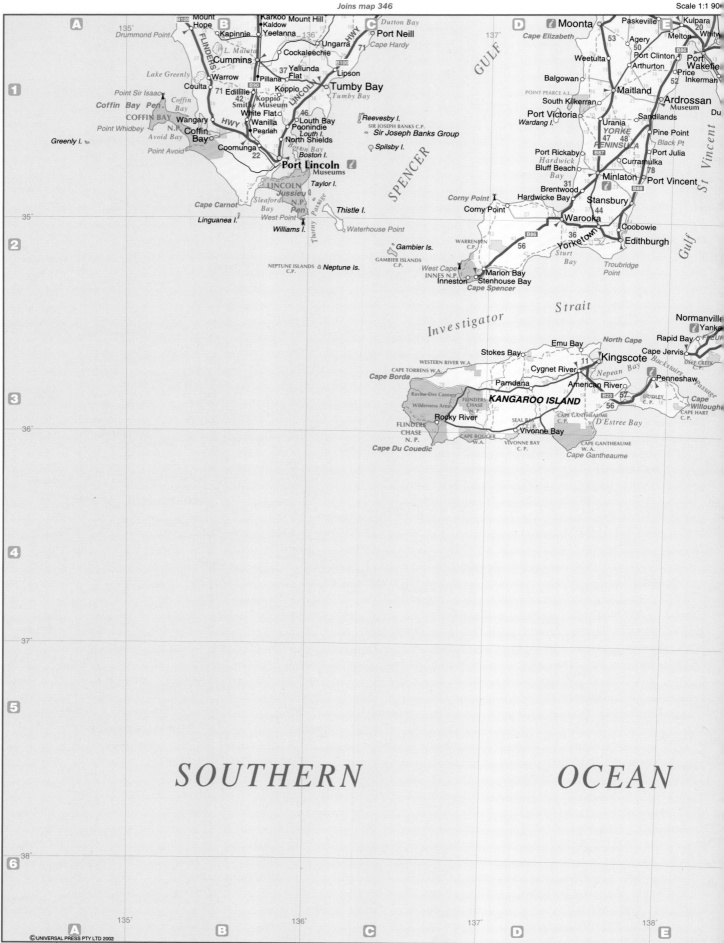

Scale 1:1 90

A
135°
Drummond Point

B
Mount Hope
Kapinnie
Karkoo
Kaldow
Yeelanna
Mount Hill

C
Dutton Bay
Port Neill
Cape Hardy

D
137°
Cape Elizabeth

Moonta
Paskeville
Agery
53
50

E
Kulpara
20
Melton
Whitw

Port Wakefie

FLINDERS
Cummins
Ungarra
Cockaleechie
71

HWY
LINCOLN

Weetulta
Port Clinton
Arthurton
Price
Inkerman
52

GULF

Balgowan
Maitland

Warrow
Coulta
71
Edillilie
42
Koppio
White Flat
Wanilla
Pearlah
B90
Pillana
Koppio
37
Yallunda
Flat
Lipson
Tumby Bay
Tumby Bay
46
Louth Bay
Poonindie
Louth I.

Reevesby I.
SIR JOSEPH BANKS C.P.
Sir Joseph Banks Group
Spilsby I.

POINT PEARCE A.L.
South Kilkerran
Port Victoria
Wardang I.
YORKE
PENINSULA
47 48
Urania
Sandilands
Ardrossan
Museum
Du

Pine Point

Coffin Bay Pen.
Point Sir Isaac
COFFIN BAY
Coffin
Bay
Lake Greenly
Smith
Museum
North Shields
Boston
Bay
Boston I.

Port Rickaby
Port Julia
Bluff Beach
Curramulka
78
Minlaton
Port Vincent

Point Whidbey
Greenly I.
Wangary
N.P.
Coffin
Bay
Coomunga
22

HWY

Avoid Bay
Point Avoid

Port Lincoln
Museums

Hardwick
Bay

Brentwood
31
Hardwicke Bay
Stansbury
B88

35°

Cape Carnot
Taylor I.
LINCOLN
Jussieu
N.P.
Pen
Sleaford
Bay
West Point

Thistle I.

SPENCER

Corny Point
Corny Point
Warooka
27
44
Yorketown
Coobowie
Edithburgh

Linguanea I.
Williams I.

WARRENBEN
C.P.
56
B86
Sturt
Bay
Troubridge
Point

Waterhouse Point

Gulf

Gambier Is.
GAMBIER ISLANDS
C.P.

NEPTUNE ISLANDS
C.P.
Neptune Is.

West Cape
INNES N.P.
Inneston
Marion Bay
Stenhouse Bay
Cape Spencer

St Vincent

Strait

Investigator

Normanville
Yanka

North Cape
Rapid Bay
FLEUR

WESTERN RIVER W.A.
Stokes Bay
Emu Bay
Cygnet River
11
Kingscote
Nepean
Bay
Cape Jervis
DEEP CREEK
Penneshaw

CAPE TORRENS W.A.
Cape Borda
Parndana
American River
B23
57
Cape
Willough
CAPE HART

FLINDERS
CHASE
Ravine-Des Casuary
Wilderness Area
FLINDERS
CHASE
N.P.
KANGAROO ISLAND
56
DUDLEY
C.P.
D'Estree Bay
CAPE GANTHEAUME
C.P.

Rocky River
SEAL BAY
C.P.
CAPE BOUGER
W.A.

Vivonne Bay
VIVONNE BAY
C.P.
CAPE GANTHEAUME
W.A.
Cape Gantheaume

Cape Du Couedic

36°

37°

4

5

38°

6

SOUTHERN   OCEAN

A   B   C   D   E
135°   136°   137°   138°

©UNIVERSAL PRESS PTY LTD 2002

South Australia

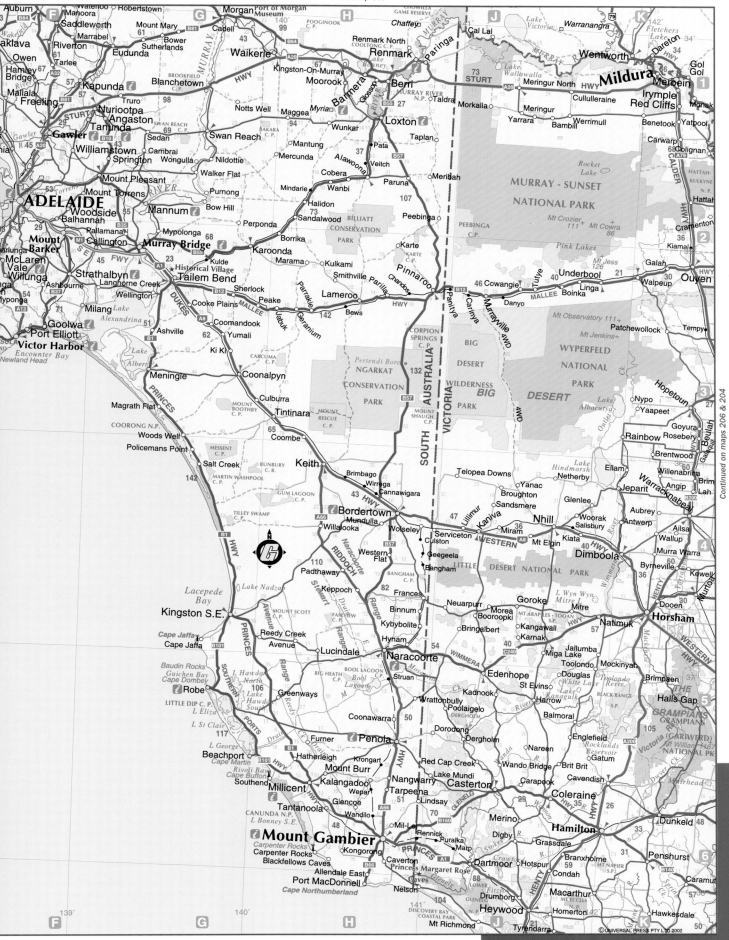

50
Kilometres

Auburn
Manoora
Saddleworth
Hobertstown
Morgan
Port of Morgan Museum

Waleva
Owen
Riverton
Marrabel
Eudunda
Mount Mary
Bower
Sutherlands
Cadell
Waikerie

Hamley Bridge
Kapunda
Tarlee
Truro
Blanchetown
Kingston-On-Murray
Moorook
Renmark North
Renmark
Paringa
Cal Lal

Mallala
Freeling
Nuriootpa
Angaston
Sedan
Swan Reach
Notts Well
Barmera
Berri
Murray River
Loxton
Taldra
Morkalla

Gawler
Tanunda
Cambrai
Wongulla
Nildottie
Maggea
Myria
Glossop
Wunkar
Mantung
Mercunda
Alawoona
Pata
Veitch
Meribah

Williamstown
Springton
Walker Flat
Purnong
Mindarie
Wanbi
Cobera
Paruna

ADELAIDE
Woodside
Mount Torrens
Mount Pleasant
Mypolonga
Bow Hill
Halidon
Sandalwood
Perponda
Peebinga

Mount Barker
Balhannah
Mannum
Borrika
Karoonda
Karte
Peebinga

McLaren Vale
Strathalbyn
Langhorne Creek
Wellington
Murray Bridge
Kulde
Marama
Kulkami
Smithville
Parilla
Chandos
Pinnaroo

Myponga
Ashbourne
Tailem Bend
Sherlock
Cooke Plains
Peake
Jabuk
Parrakie
Lameroo
Bews

Goolwa
Milang
Lake Alexandrina
Ashville
Coomandook
Yumali
Geranium
Ki Ki

Victor Harbor
Encounter Bay
Newland Head
Meningie
Coonalpyn
Culburra
Tintinara
Coombe

Magrath Flat
Woods Well
Policemans Point
Salt Creek
Keith
Brimbago
Wirrega
Cannawigara

Kingston S.E.
Bordertown
Mundulla
Willalooka
Wolseley
Serviceton
Culston

Cape Jaffa
Reedy Creek
Avenue
Padthaway
Keppoch
Frances
Geegeela
Bangham

Robe
Greenways
Lucindale
Naracoorte
Struan

Beachport
Furner
Penola
Coonawarra

Millicent
Tantanoola
Mount Burr
Kalangadoo
Nangwarry
Tarpeena
Casterton

MURRAY - SUNSET NATIONAL PARK

WYPERFELD NATIONAL PARK

BIG DESERT

Mildura
Merbein
Irymple
Red Cliffs

Wentworth

Ouyen
Underbool
Walpeup

Rainbow
Brentwood
Nhill
Dimboola
Horsham

Mount Gambier
Carpenter Rocks
Blackfellows Caves
Port MacDonnell

© UNIVERSAL PRESS PTY LTD 2002

Western Australia is the giant of Australian states, occupying about one-third of the continent. Its vast coastline takes in the remote Kimberley in the north, the iron 'shoulder' of the Pilbara, and runs past the Ningaloo coral reef, Shark Bay, the Houtman Abrolhos Islands and Perth's sandy plain. After turning east at the rocky capes of the south-west, it takes in granite shores facing the wild Southern Ocean and the limestone cliffs of the Great Australian Bight.

Perth, Western Australia's capital, is a modern city situated on the Swan River within easy reach of ocean beaches and the forested Darling Ranges. The city is a tourist attraction in its own right and, with its port of Fremantle, is the gateway to the state. In the south of the state, visitors seek out the famous wildflower displays, the majestic karri forests, the Stirling and Porongurup ranges, the inland goldfields and the coastal national parks. Further north, many are drawn to the Pinnacle Desert,

Western Australia: The Wildflower State

◈ Population: 1 861 020
◈ Total area: 2 529 875km²
◈ % of Australia: 33%
◈ Length of border: 1862km
◈ Length of coastline: 20 781km
◈ Floral emblem: Kangaroo Paw
◈ Fauna emblem: Numbat

STRALIA

Geraldton's wildflowers, Batavia Coast and the natural wonders of the Shark Bay World-Heritage area, the Ningaloo Reef, the Pilbara's iron ranges, and to Broome and the Kimberley.

Touring this vast state with its multitude of outstanding attractions requires planning and time. The south-west area around Perth is relatively easy to get around by car, with a network of good roads and accessible features. The rest of

Western Australia has fewer road options. Flying to different parts of the state can cut out some long drives, but despite the daunting distances touring by car is a rewarding experience. A 4WD vehicle is essential for touring in the Kimberleys or the desert tracks of the state's centre, such as the Canning Stock Route and the Gunbarrel Hwy.

Photo above: The Pinnacle Desert, Nambung NP

i **Tourist information**

Western Australia Visitor Centre
Forrest Place, cnr Wellington St
Perth, WA 6000
Freecall: 1300 361 351
www.westernaustralia.net

Main ATTRACTIONS

◈ **Broome**
Located at the southern end of the Kimberleys, Broome was once the pearling capital of the world.

◈ **Caves District**
This area is characterised by caves, wineries, fine restaurants and secluded hideaways.

◈ **Fremantle**
Perth's historic port city has developed an alternative, arty atmosphere in recent years.

◈ **Kalgoorlie-Boulder**
A once-notorious frontier town, Kalgoorlie has many reminders of its rip-roaring goldfields' past.

◈ **Mandurah-Pinjarra**
This region is renowned for its idyllic beaches, waterways and the karri forests of the Darling Range.

◈ **Nambung NP**
The myriad spires of the Pinnacle Desert are a favourite with photographers, especially at sunrise and sunset.

◈ **Nullarbor Plain**
The world's longest stretch of dead-straight railway line runs for 478km across this virtually treeless plain between Nurina in Western Australia and Watson in South Australia.

◈ **Purnululu NP**
'Discovered' relatively recently, the orange-striped beehive domes of the Bungle Bungles are an outstanding attraction.

◈ **Rottnest Island**
This island near Perth is a popular holiday resort with secluded beaches and beautiful coves.

THE WILDFLOWER STATE

The largest state, Western Australia comprises one-third of the continent's landmass and travelling may involve huge distances. The state consists of mainly dry plateaus ranging from 300m to 600m above sea level and bordered by a coastal plain. Despite its vast area Western Australia has a relatively small population—less than one-tenth of the nation's total. Around 80% of West Australians live in Perth and the south-west corner of the state. The other 20% are scattered in coastal towns and small outback communities.

The state was not formally annexed until Lt Governor James Stirling established the Swan River settlement and proclaimed the colony of Western Australia in June 1829. The settlement expanded to become Perth but isolation from other settlements held back development. The discovery of gold at **Coolgardie** in the 1890s caused the first economic boom. Hugely rich in minerals and with more than 270 operating mines, Western Australia

now exports iron ore, alumina, nickel, mineral sands, gold and diamonds. Extensive gas reserves have developed markets in Taiwan, Korea and Japan. Western Australia is also one of the major sources of petroleum in Australia.

Cereal crops grown in the **Mid West** are the largest primary industry. This huge area of the state provides the space and soils for large-scale agricultural production. Exports range from wool, beef, lambs and leather, to wine, ice-cream, barley, malt and noodles. The fisheries of Western Australia are also major world suppliers of lobsters, prawns and pearls. The forestry industry produces both hard and softwood timbers as well as woodchips.

Today, like many other Australian states, the fastest growing industry is tourism. As popular with Australians as with overseas visitors, Western Australia offers a wide range of experiences and adventures throughout the year. Those who venture to the north of

Hamersley Iron Open-Cut Mine, Tom Price

Perth will find the landscape offers great diversity, including paddocks of cereal crops and the unique wind-carved limestone formations known as the **Pinnacles**.

Further north still, is the ancient gorge country of the **Pilbara**, which can be seen at its best in **Karijini NP**. At the top of the state, in the **Kimberley region**, the **King Leopold Range**, **Purnululu NP**, **Geikie** and **Windjana gorges** create uniquely spectacular landscapes.

Within the **Goldfields region**, the city of **Kalgoorlie-Boulder**, in its heyday the 'richest square mile of earth in the world', retains its frontier atmosphere. South of Perth, visitors are attracted to the **Caves District**, the imposing karri forests and an exciting array of coastal national parks.

The whole state is famed for its dazzling display of spring wildflowers, which has led to it being called the 'Wildflower State'.

Walpole Inlet, Walpole

Western Australia

TOURISM REGION HIGHLIGHTS

Western Australia occupies over 2.5million km² of the Australian continent. Travellers in this vast, rugged state come for its natural marvels, like the beehive domes of the Bungle Bungles, the extraordinary spires of the Pinnacle Desert and the stark, red gorges of the Kimberleys. They come to ride camels at Cable Beach, swim with dolphins at Monkey Mia or dive with whale sharks at Ningaloo Reef. When you add historic goldfields, spring wildflowers, wineries, caves and stunning national parks there's a lot to see in Western Australia for those who have the time.

A Perth and Fremantle
Burswood Casino; Cottesloe Beach; Fremantle Arts Centre; Kings Park; London Court; Mundaring Weir; Old Observatory; Old Perth Port; Perth Zoo; Rottnest Island; Swan River; Swan Valley Wineries; The Old Mill; Western Australian Museum; Western Australian Maritime Museum; Yanchep NP

B Esperance
Bay of Isles, Esperance; Cape Arid NP; Cape Le Grand NP; Hopetoun; Peak Charles NP; Pink Lake; Ravensthorpe

C Gascoyne (Outback Coast)
Cape Range NP; Carnarvon; Dirk Hartog Island; Exmouth; Francois Peron NP; Hamelin Pool; Kennedy Ranges; Monkey Mia dolphins; Mount Augustus; Ningaloo Reef; Shark Bay

D Goldfields
Coolgardie; Golden Mile; Hannan's North Mine; Kalgoorlie; Kookynie; Norseman; Nullarbor Plain, WA Museum Kalgoorlie-Boulder

E Great Southern
Albany; Denmark; Elephant Cove; Katanning; King George Sound; Mount Barker; Nornalup; Porongorup NP; Stirling Range NP; Torndirrup NP; Valley of the Giants; Whale watching; Whale World

F Heartlands
Avon Valley NP; Badgingarra NP; Cervantes; Coomberdale Wildflower Farm; Dura-Koppin Wildlife Sanctuary; Kellerberrin; Lake Dumbleyung; Mount Lesueur NP; New Norcia; Pinnacle Desert, Nambung NP; Wagin Historical Village; Wave Rock; Wickepin; York

G Kimberley
Argyle Diamond Mine; Broome; Bungle Bungles, Purnululu NP; Cable Beach; Derby; Fitzroy River; Gantheaume Point dinosaur footprints; Geikie Gorge; Halls Creek; Kununurra; Lake Argyle; Ord River; Piccaninny Creek; Willie Creek Pearl Farm; Windjana Gorge; Wolfe Creek Meteorite Crater; Wyndham

H Mid West
Batavia Coast; Canning Stock Route; Dongan-Denison; Geraldton; Greenough Hamlet; Gunbarrel Highway; Houtman Abrolhos Islands; Kalbarri; Meekatharra; Wiluna

I Peel
Bibbulmun Track; Darling Range; Dwellingup; Hotham Valley Railway; Jarrahdale; Mandurah; Peel Inlet; Pinjarra; Waroona Dam; Yalgorup NP

J Pilbara
Burrup Peninsula; Dampier; Dampier Archipelago; Hamersley

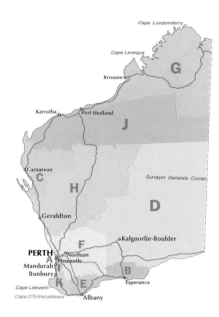

Range; Karijini NP; Karratha; Marble Bar; Millstream-Chichester NP; Mount Bruce; Tom Price

K South West
Augusta; Bunbury; Busselton; Cape Leeuwin Lighthouse; D'Entrecasteaux NP; Donnybrook; Geographe Bay; Jewel Cave; Lake Cave; Leeuwin-Naturaliste NP; Manjimup; Margaret River Wineries; Ngilgi Cave; Pemberton Tramway; Whale watching; Willyabrup Valley

Geikie Gorge, in the Kimberleys

NATIONAL PARKS

As the largest state in Australia, it is not surprising that Western Australia has an enormous diversity of environments and landscapes. From the coastal coral marine reserves to the inland semi-arid desert and the lush south-west, it could take several visits to Western Australia to be able to see and appreciate the dramatic differences in the state's national parks.

A Cape Arid NP (Map 407, B5)

Located 120km east of Esperance, Cape Arid NP is 2794km^2 of beach, sea, headland and heathland. Attractions range from walking and climbing trails to idyllic swimming and fishing spots. A wildlife watcher's paradise, the park is home to many species of birds and wallabies in the heathlands. A great place to spot whales and sea lion colonies, the coastline has many lookout points over the ocean.

B Cape Range NP and Ningaloo Marine Park (Map 400, B2)

Cape Range NP and Ningaloo Marine Park are located 400km north of Carnarvon. The marine park is known for its amazing coral reef and recreational diving, with the opportunity to sight, or even swim with, the whale shark (*Rhincodon typus*), the world's largest fish. On land, Cape Range NP covers 506km^2, and has great walking trails which cater for all levels and preferences. Camping is a popular pastime here and a number of secluded beaches and other good sites are available once a camping permit is obtained.

C Drysdale River NP (Map 399, J1)

In the northern Kimberley region, Drysdale River NP covers 4483km^2. It is a remote park with rugged ranges, cliffs and escarpments. Only accessible by 4WD, the national park offers walking trails and canoeing possibilities for the experienced adventurer. Known for the Carson Escarpment and the Carson and Drysdale Rivers, the national park is also home to many bird species, mammals, reptiles and freshwater fish. It is a good area for camping, however, permission is required from the local Aboriginal community.

D Gibson Desert NR (Map 401, K3)

The Gibson Desert NR is located in central Western Australia, around 1540km NE of Perth. Covering 18 429km^2 (only a small section of the southern Gibson Desert), the nature reserve is home to the Young, Alfred and Marie Ranges and numerous salt lakes. A few small and endangered marsupials dwell in this arid environment, which can only be accessed by 4WD. There are no specific camping areas, but with local ranger advice it is possible to find an ideal spot for a desert camping experience.

E Leeuwin-Naturaliste NP (Map 404, A4)

Leeuwin-Naturaliste NP is a well-known park that caters for many interests with its huge variety of attractions. Around 265km south of Perth, the park offers not only a

facts

❖ No. of parks/reserves: 909
❖ Area: 166 146km^2
❖ % of state: 6.57%
❖ World Heritage Area: Shark Bay

Greater bilby, *Macrotis lagotis*

Western Australia

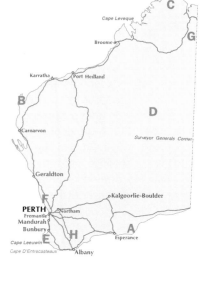

Striped 'beehive' domes of the Bungle Bungles, Purnululu NP

glimpse of a rugged and dramatic coastline, but some amazing rock formations and underground limestone caves. Over 100 caves have been found in the park, some with animal remains dating back 37 000 years. Also known for its swimming, diving, walking and fishing, the national park boasts excellent 4WDing opportunities and camping areas.

F Nambung NP (Map 402, A3)

Situated around 230km north of Perth, Nambung NP is famous for the Pinnacles—limestone rock formations—that lie in the heart of the park and number over 150 000. A combination of water, quartz, limestone and sand has interacted to create these unique and varying rock columns that appear to be growing out of golden desert sands. A photographer's paradise, the park is also home to a variety of native flora and fauna and offers fishing, bushwalking and swimming opportunities.

G Purnululu (Bungle Bungle) NP (Map 399, K3)

One of the most famous national parks in Western Australia, it is located in the north of the state, around 3000km from Perth. Limited to 4WD drive access, the 2397km^2 park is most spectacular from the air. Both helicopter and light plane flights are available. From above, the full effect of the Bungle Bungle Range is obvious: huge orange striped rock domes protruding from the landscape. Other attractions of the Purnululu NP are the gorge walks, particularly the Cathedral Gorge, Echidna Chasm and Froghole walking trails.

H Stirling Range NP (Map 404, E4)

Stirling Range NP is located in the south-west corner of the state, 450km from Perth. The mountain range itself rises out of vast wild-flower plains, the deep blue peaks dominating the horizon from every angle. There is a popular 42km drive through the centre of the 1159km^2 park, with lookout stops along the way. Bushwalks are another attraction. There are designated camping sites and areas available to caravans as well.

National Park Head Office

Western Australia Conservation and Land Management (CALM)

17 Dick Perry Ave, Western Precinct
Kensington, WA 6151
Ph: (08) 9334 0333
www.naturebase.net

Ornate burrowing frog, *Limnodynastes tasmaniensis*

WILDFLOWERS

Every year between July and November the Western Australian landscape undergoes a startling transformation. A multicoloured patchwork of wildflowers spreads out across the state. Western Australia has often been referred to as the 'Wildflower State', little wonder since about 12 000 wildflower species thrive here.

The wildflower season commences in the northern **Pilbara** region in July, begins slightly later further south and concludes in the southern part of the state in November. Whilst rain and sunshine influence seasonal variations, generally speaking there is a profusion of wildflowers throughout the state between July and November.

Northern regions

These are home to many species of coastal and inland wildflowers, but are best known for everlastings. These lollipop-shaped flowers form carpets of brilliant colour that may well stretch to the horizon. The 1860km² **Kalbarri NP** also teems with kangaroo paws, banksias, flowering eucalypts and grevilleas.

Further north, the **Gascoyne** and **Cape Range** regions are covered with wattles, hakeas, dampiera, purple peas and Shark Bay daisies. The Pilbara blossoms with yellow native hibiscus, bluebells, sticky cassia, mulla mulla and native fuchsias, to name a few. To the east, fields of everlastings, acacias, hakeas and Sturt's desert pea enliven the plains of the **Kalgoorlie-Goldfields region**.

Southern regions

Many rare and dainty flowers cover the southern areas, including orchids, milkmaids, honeypots, green kangaroo paws and mountain bells. There are over 50 orchid species and over 80 species of carnivorous plants such as the Albany pitcher plant, mistletoes like the Western Australian Christmas tree, heady, scented plants like brown boronia, and the unique grass tree *Kingia australis*.

Desert wildflowers in Mount Augustus NP

Visitors to Perth can simply go to Kings Park for a dazzling display. The **Kings Park Wildflower Festival** is an extremely popular event in early October. Many other regions also hold special wildflower events.

Package tours to wildflower country

Relaxing wildflower experiences can be booked from Perth or interstate during the peak season. Packages involve coach, rail or air transport with wildflower tour options that may include other natural attractions such as the famous dolphins of **Monkey Mia**, the **Pinnacles** and **Wave Rock**.

Self drive wildflower country

Hiring a car is a great way to tour the wildflower regions at one's own pace. Full details and maps are available from Western Australia tourist centres, motoring organisations and many of the state's service stations.

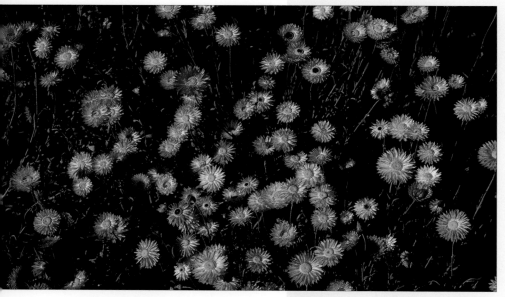

Wildflowers in Kings Park, Perth

356 *Gregory's Australia*

Western Australia

WINERIES

Viticulture in Western Australia followed very quickly after the first settlers arrived in 1829. The oldest winery, **Olive Farm**, near the present Perth Airport, was established in 1830 and is still going strong. **George Fletcher Moore** also planted vines in the Swan Valley, with cuttings from the Cape of Good Hope in South Africa. The Swan Valley has remained commercially viable, and, since the 1960s, has been joined by 5 other regions that have been successfully developed in the southwest corner of the state.

Western Australian wines are generally of exceptional quality. Although the state produces less than 2% of Australian wine, it accounts for about 20% of the nation's premium bottled wine.

A Coastal Plains

There are a number of wineries on the fertile coastal soils, both on the northern outskirts of Perth and southward between **Rockingham** and **Capel**. Wines include shiraz, cabernets, grenache, chardonnay, chenin blanc, sauvignon blanc, riesling, merlot and pinot noir.

B Great Southern
(pp.368–369)
This picturesque area around **Mount Barker**, **Albany** and **Denmark** is one of Australia's largest wine regions. More than 30 wineries flourish here, producing all the major grape varieties. Rieslings with an intense limey flavour have been a great success, also premium quality shiraz, pinot noir and chardonnay.

C Margaret River
(pp.370–371)
The 50 or so Margaret River vignerons have gained an impressive reputation for world-class premium wines, in an area extending from **Dunsborough** and **Busselton** to **Augusta**. Outstanding reds include cabernet sauvignon, cabernet franc and merlot. Semillon, sauvignon blanc, chardonnay and verdelho are the most successful whites.

D Pemberton/Manjimup

This is an exciting new region deep in karri, jarrah and red-gum country with a fast-growing reputation for premium wines. Varieties grown include pinot noir, shiraz, merlot, chardonnay, cabernet sauvignon, cabernet franc, verdelho, malbec and sauvignon blanc.

E Perth Hills (p.363)

A number of boutique wineries are to be found in the **Darling Range**, to the east of Perth. Classic wines such as cabernet sauvignon, shiraz, merlot and chardonnay are available for tasting, as well as sparkling wines.

F Swan Valley (p.363)

Winemaking has been continuous here since 1830 and has involved such famous labels as Houghton, Sandalford and Evans & Tate. In 1937, vigneron **Jack Mann** produced the first vintage of Houghton's White Burgundy, the earliest widely-accepted table wine in Australia. Nearly all classic wine varieties are now represented. **Swan River cruises** from Perth offer a very pleasant way to visit the historic wineries.

Cellar door entrance, historic Houghton Winery

PERTH

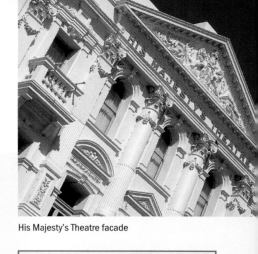

His Majesty's Theatre facade

main attractions

❖ **Fremantle**

Perth's port city is the western gateway to Australia, with beautiful beaches, historic buildings, old-world charm and a fascinating heritage that dates back to 1829.

❖ **Government House**

Completed in 1864 and home to the State Governor, Government House is set in romantic English-style gardens and includes an elegant ballroom.

❖ **Kings Park**

Affording excellent views from Mount Eliza over Perth and the Swan River, the 400ha parkland, includes natural bushland and showcases Western Australia's famed wildflowers in spring.

❖ **London Court**

This Tudor-style shopping arcade between Hay St Mall and St George's Tce is Perth's most photographed tourist attraction.

❖ **Perth Mint**

Visit the past in the Mint's Old Melting House, see molten gold being poured, watch coins being minted and view natural gold in one of Western Australia's oldest buildings.

❖ **Rottnest Island**

A popular holiday island off the coast, Rottnest offers crystal water, white beaches, fishing, golf, surfing, walks and wildlife, including the quokka, *Setonix brachyurus*.

Founded in 1829 on the banks of the **Swan River**, Perth's fortunes received a substantial boost in the 1890s when gold was discovered at **Coolgardie** and **Kalgoorlie** to the east. Today, Perth is a scenic and sophisticated city, renowned for its abundant sunshine, relaxed lifestyle and easy-going manner. The city's modern skyline blends with magnificent colonial architecture, housing excellent retail outlets particularly around **Hay** and **Murray sts** and the malls running between them. **King St**, a historic and lovingly restored commercial precinct, is known for its fashion houses, cafes, art galleries and specialist book stores.

Within minutes of the CBD is the world's oldest operating mint as well as a number of art galleries and museums, historic buildings and parklands. Perth's prime position, flanking the broad reaches of the Swan River, provides an excellent setting for enjoying alfresco dining in one of the many outdoor restaurants and cafes. Perth residents have a choice of more than 80km of white sandy beaches within easy reach.

 Tourist information

Western Australia Visitor Centre
Forrest Place, cnr Wellington St,
Perth, WA 6000
Ph: 1300 361 351
www.westernaustralia.net

facts

❖ Population: 1 381 070
❖ Date founded: 1 June, 1829
❖ Tallest building: Central Park (261.7m)
❖ Oldest building: The Old Court House (1836)
❖ Average temp: 24°C (Jan), 14.5°C (June)

Places of Interest

Art Gallery of Western Australia Ⓐ C3
Barracks Archway Ⓑ B3
Fire Safety Education Centre and Museum Ⓒ C3
Francis Burt Law Education Centre and Museum Ⓓ C4
His Majesty's Theatre Ⓔ B3
Kings Park Ⓕ A4
London Court Ⓖ C3
Parliament House Ⓗ B3
Perth Cultural Centre Ⓘ E4
Perth Institute of Contemporary Arts Ⓙ C3
Perth Mint Ⓚ D4
Perth Town Hall Ⓛ C3
Perth Zoo Ⓜ B6
Queens Gardens Ⓝ E4
Scitech Discovery Centre Ⓞ B2
Stirling Gardens Ⓟ C4
Supreme Court Gardens Ⓠ C4
The Old Mill Ⓡ B5
The Swan Bells Ⓢ C4
WACA Oval Ⓣ E4
Western Australia Museum Ⓤ C3

Perth at night, seen from the Swan River

Western Australia

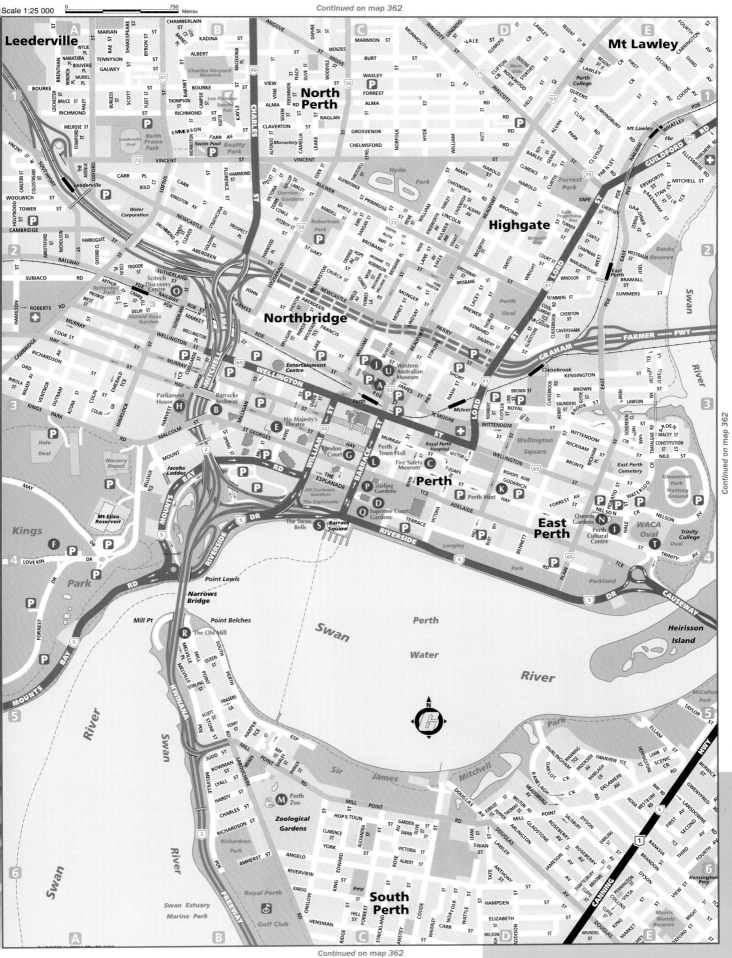

Scale 1:25 000

Leederville

Mt Lawley

North Perth

Highgate

Northbridge

Perth

East Perth

Kings Park

Swan River

Perth Water

Swan River

Mill Pt

The Old Mill

Point Belches

Narrows Bridge

Point Lewis

Heirisson Island

Swan River

Sir James Mitchell Park

Perth Zoo

Zoological Gardens

Royal Perth Golf Club

Swan Estuary Marine Park

South Perth

CBD & SUBURBS

CBD ATTRACTIONS

Exploring Perth's CBD is an easy task. The city is compact and well planned, even though its location on a broad stretch of the Swan River gives it a spacious feeling. In addition, Perth has one of the best public transport systems in the country.

Perhaps the best place to start is the western edge of the CBD, in **Kings Park** and the **Botanic Gardens**. From here, along Kings Park Rd and onto Malcolm St, the attractions of the CBD are waiting to be explored. Take a look at **Parliament House** with an education officer and discover the history of the Westminster system. Continuing along Malcolm St to St Georges Tce brings you to the **Barracks Archway**, originally built in 1863 and the only relic of the old Guards Barracks. Divert to **Hay St** via **Cloisters Square** to find **His Majesty's Theatre**, home to the city's premier theatre and musical productions. Drop into the pedestrian mall on Hay St for a break and then explore **London Court**, a spectacular Tudor-style arcade catering for tourists and window shoppers alike. Turn right into Barrack St, then left into St George's Tce, passing **Perth Town Hall**, **Stirling Gardens** and several stately churches. Continuing onto Adelaide Tce, turn left into Hill St and visit the **Perth Mint**. Since the goldrush, Australia's gold has been refined here into legal tender, gold bars and jewellery, however, the Mint itself has only been open to the public in recent years.

Other interesting attractions of the CBD area include the **Fire Safety Education Centre and Museum** in the original Perth City Fire Station; **Francis Burt Law Education Centre and Museum** near the **Supreme Court Gardens**; and the **Scitech Discovery Centre** on Railway Pde.

On the banks of the Swan River, **Barrack Square** was originally built as a military parade facility. Today it is an attractively manicured garden square surrounding the unique **Bell Tower**, with a surrounding jetty of cafes, shops and a busy ferry terminal. **The Swan Bells** in the Tower include 12 original bells from St Martin-in-the-Fields Church in London, celebrated in the old nursery rhyme *Oranges and Lemons*. Jump on a ferry across the Swan River to the **South Perth Esplanade** where the renowned **Perth Zoo** is located a few minutes away. It has one of Australia's best collections of native and exotic animals, which are in enclosures resembling their natural habitats. Wandering back along the Swan the length of the **Sir James Mitchell Park**, take a look at **Heirisson Island**, access is via the bicycle path from the City of Perth Causeway Carpark. The island contains a memorial to Yagan, an Aboriginal leader killed in 1833.

Returning to **East Perth** after visiting Heirisson Island, wander by **Trinity College** and the **WACA Oval**, home to Western Australia's leading cricket and football matches. Finally, a little further up Hay St, the **Perth Cultural Centre**, located in **Queens Gardens**, is definitely worth a visit.

SUBURBAN ATTRACTIONS

Closest to the CBD, the suburb of **Northbridge** is a popular restaurant and entertainment precinct. A complex of imposing buildings between William St and Beaufort St includes the **Western Australian Museum, Alexander Library, Perth Institute of Contemporary Arts** and the **Art Gallery of Western Australia**. The **Galleria Art and Craft Markets** specialise in local arts and crafts and are open weekends.

Miners' statue outside the Perth Mint

Western Australia

KINGS PARK

Perth's largest and best-loved park overlooks the Swan River and is only 5mins from the CBD. The park is not only an attractive garden of native Australian wildflowers and parkland, but also a haven for children and the young at heart. The park offers playgrounds, scenic walking and driving tours, the presentation of special events, local and Aboriginal live performances and the **State War Memorial**. And then there are the amazing views of the city itself from **Mount Eliza Lookout**—Kings Park and the **Botanic Gardens** are truly the heart and soul of the City of Perth.

Underneath the lookout, the **Artist in Residence Gallery** provides a venue for local Aboriginal artists to work and sell their unique art. The spectacular **Kings Park Wildflower Festival** in October is extremely popular.

Perth CBD viewed from Kings Park

Perth residents boast that their beaches are the 'best surf beaches in Australia'. Some of the more popular are **Cottesloe**, **Port**, **Scarborough** and the nudist beach, **Swanbourne**.

A cruise on the Swan River to discover the **Swan Valley** is a worthwhile side trip. This was the site of the state's first permanent vineyards and there are are now over 40 wineries offering tours and tastings of top quality wines. A number of the wineries offer excellent alfresco or restaurant dining. Some wineries, like **Houghton** and **Sandalford** are over 100 years old.

Only 20mins from Perth, **Sorrento Quay** at **Hillarys Boat Harbour** is a marina-style complex packed with shopping and leisure options, as well as providing a fast ferry service to **Rottnest Island**. The **Aquarium of Western Australia** (**AQWA**) will introduce you to the beauty and wonder of Western Australia's marine environments. There are many other reasons to explore the suburban areas of Perth: the **Armadale Reptile Centre**, **Burswood International Resort Casino**, **Kalamunda History Village Museum**, the **Museum of Childhood** at Edith Cowan University and **Perth Observatory**, 25km east of the city.

Popular natural getaways for Perth residents and visitors include **Whiteman Park**, **the Hills Forest** and **John Forrest NP**. Whiteman Park is an ideal place to spend the day with the family. It is centred around **Mussel Pool**, a picnic area and playground, and attractions include an animal enclosure, pony rides, trams, steam trains, sheep shearing, a live snake display, sporting fields, a Craft Village and cafe. Whiteman Park has a constant programme of special events such as bush dances and picnic days for the public. The Hills Forest encompasses national parks and state forests, historic townships, **Mundaring Weir**, and a **Discovery Centre** with an exciting programme of outdoor experiences for visitors such as bushwalking, Aboriginal storytelling, camping and rock-climbing. Within the Hills Forest, John Forrest NP is particularly popular, with fine views of Perth, scenic bushwalking, a tavern, picnic areas and BBQ facilities.

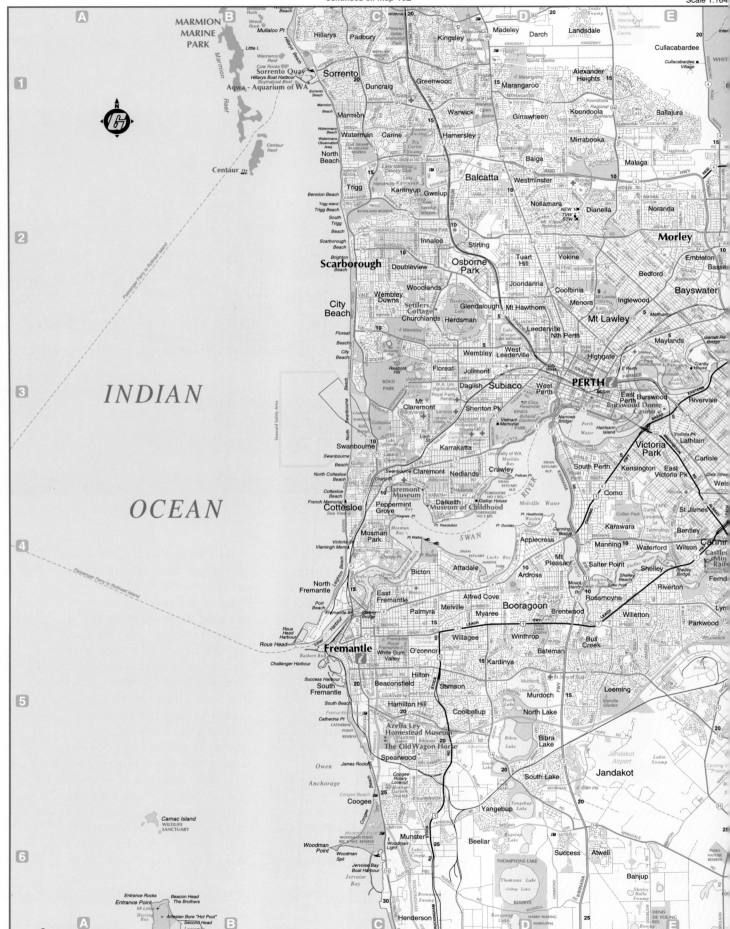

MARMION
MARINE
PARK

Hillarys
Padbury
Kingsley
Madeley
Darch
Landsdale
Cullacabardee

Mullaloo Pt

Sorrento
Duncraig
Greenwood
Marangaroo
Girrawheen
Koondoola
Ballajura

Aqwa - Aquarium of WA

Marmion
Waterman
Carine
Hamersley
Warwick
Alexander
Heights
Mirrabooka
Malaga

North
Beach

Balga

Trigg
Karrinyup
Gwelup
Balcatta
Westminster
Nollamara
Dianella
Noranda

Morley

INDIAN

Scarborough
Doubleview
Osborne
Park
Stirling
Tuart
Hill
Yokine
Coolbinia
Menora
Inglewood
Bedford
Embleton
Basse

Bayswater

Woodlands
Joondanna
Mt Lawley
Maylands

City
Beach
Wembley
Downs
Glendalough
Mt Hawthorn
Leederville
Nth Perth
Highgate

Herdsman

Churchlands
Herdsman

West
Leederville
Wembley

OCEAN

Floreat
Jolimont
Daglish
Subiaco
West
Perth
PERTH
East
Perth
Burswood
Rivervale

Mt
Claremont
Shenton Pk
Burswood Dome
Casino

Swanbourne
Karrakatta
Victoria
Park
Lathlain
Carlisle

Claremont
Nedlands
Crawley
South Perth
Kensington
East
Victoria Pk
Wels

Cottesloe
Peppermint
Grove
Dalkeith
Como
Karawara
Bentley
St James

Mosman
Park
Applecross
Manning
Waterford
Wilson
Cannir

North
Fremantle
Bicton
Attadale
Mt
Pleasant
Ardross
Salter Point
Shelley
Riverton
Fernd

East
Fremantle
Palmyra
Melville
Myaree
Alfred Cove
Booragoon
Brentwood
Willetton
Parkwood
Lyn

Fremantle
White Gum
Valley
O'connor
Willagee
Winthrop
Bateman
Bull
Creek

South
Fremantle
Beaconsfield
Hilton
Samson
Kardinya
Leeming

Hamilton Hill
Coolbellup
North Lake
Murdoch

Azelia Ley
Homestead Museum
The Old Wagon Horse
Spearwood
Bibra
Lake
South Lake
Jandakot
Jandakot
Airport

Coogee
Yangebup
Yangebup
Lake
Success
Atwell

Woodman
Point
Munster
Beeliar
Banjup

Henderson
THOMPSONS LAKE
RESERVE

Western Australia

Motor
Museum
Tractor
Museum

Henley
Brook

Millendon

Swan Valley
Wineries

Windy Creek

Mt Oakover

Red Hill

ADELAIDE

Gidgegannup

RECREATION
RESERVE

Adventure
Centre
Lake Leschenaultia
Camp School

DEPT of
AGRICULTURE

LESCHENAULTIA
CONSERVATION
PARK

Chidlow

West
Swan

Tanjanich

Edwardes
Bridge

Sittella

Vindara

Ambrook

Oakover

Herne
Hill

Swan Valley
Highway

JOHN FORREST

Parkerville

Hilston
Youth
Camp

Stoneville

Mt Helena

Caversham

Pinelli

Houghton

Middle
Swan

Jane
Brook

Garbin

Stratton

NATIONAL PARK

Youth Camp

Clutterbuck

YMCA Camp Pickering

Carosa

Lilac
Hill

Banara

Viveash

RiverBank
ESTATE

Midland

SWAN
REGIONAL
HEALTH

National Park
Falls

Rocky
Pool

Glen
Brook
Dam

Hovea
Falls

Sunninghill
Equestrian
Centre

Sawyers
Valley

Midvale

Swan View
Rly Stn

Swan View

Greenmount

Hovea

Barkers
Bridge

Guildford

West
Midland

Bellevue

GREAT EASTERN

Mahogany
Creek

GREAT EASTERN

Mundaring

South Guildford

Hazelmere

Koongamia

GREENMOUNT
N.P.

Boya

Helena
Valley

Darlington

Glen Forrest

Pimelia
Mycumbene
Picnic Area

Guildford
Cemetery

West Aviat

Darlington
Estate

Heritage
Rose Garden

Grevillea
Mycumbene
Picnic Area

Perth International Airport

High Wycombe

GOOSEBERRY HILL
NATIONAL PARK

Pipehead
Dam

PARKLANDS

Helena

STATE FOREST

Maida
Vale

Gooseberry Hill

KALAMUNDA
NATIONAL
PARK

Paulls Valley

O'Connor
Museum

Gallery
CY O'Connor

CALM District Office

Helena River
Reservoir

Forrestfield

Calamunnda
Camel Farm

The Dell Picnic Area

Mundaring
Weir

Kalamunda History Village

Kalamunda

Piesse Brook

Hacketts Gully

Gungin Gully
Picnic Area

Mt Gungin

Reservoir

Sawyers
Valley

Kewdale
Freight
Terminal

LESMURDIE FALLS
NATIONAL
PARK

Piesse Brook

Walliston

Brookside

Lawnbrook

STATE   FOREST

Murdos

East
Cannington

Hartfield
Country Club

Lesmurdie

LESMURDIE FALLS
NATIONAL PARK

Halnault

Perth Observatory

Wattle Grove

Crystal Brook

Bickley

Carmel

Cosham

Carilla

Beckenham

Woodloes Homestead

Kenwick

Orange
Grove

New Victoria Dam

Victoria
Reservoir

Pickering Brook

Pickering Brook

Bartons Mill
Prison

Kenwick

Jadran

STATE FOREST

Maddington

Canning
Mills

STATE FOREST

Thornlie

Gosnells

GOSNELLS
REGIONAL
OPEN SPACE

Martin

Carinyah

Huntingdale

Seaforth

COHUNU
WILDLIFE PARK

Southern River

CHEVIN

BROOKTON

Karragullen

STATE FOREST

Kelmscott

Staaton
Cascades

Westfield

Roleystone

ARALUEN
BOTANIC
PARK

Araluen
Country Club

Lesley

Mount Nasura

Armadale Kelmscott
Lakeside Country Resort

Elizabeth Village

Canning
Dam

Canning
Reservoir

STATE FOREST

Armadale
History House

Botanic
Garden &
Arboretum

Churchman Brook
Reservoir

Brookdale

Armadale Settlers
Common

Willow Springs

©UNIVERSAL PRESS PTY LTD 2002

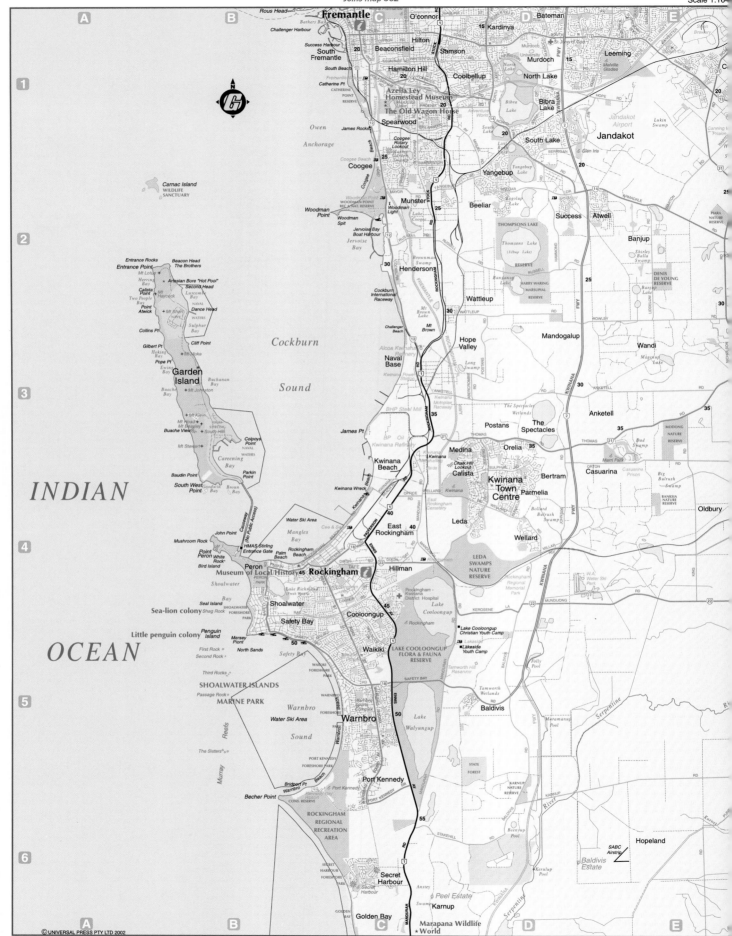

Continued on map 402

Western Australia

Thornlie
Gosnells
Huntingdale
Southern River
Westfield
Kelmscott
Forrestdale
Mount Nasura
Elizabethan Village
Armadale History House
Brookdale
Armadale Reptile Centre
Wungong
Darling Downs
Byford
Karrakup
Cardup
Whitby
Mundijong
Whitby Falls Coach House
Mardella
Karrup
Serpentine
Cowerin
Curralong
Jarrahdale
Gooralong

Martin
Canning Mills
Roleystone
Karragullen
Carinyah
STATE FOREST
Lesley
Illawarra
Ashendon
Bedfordale
Willow Springs
Bungendore Park
Wungong Dam
Wungong Reservoir
Canning Reservoir
Canning Dam
Rangers House

Korrbinjal
Century Log
Alcoa Jarrahdale Mine
Mundiman Swamp
Gleneagle
STATE FOREST
Serpentine National Park
Pipehead Dam
Serpentine Reservoir
Serpentine Dam
STATE FOREST

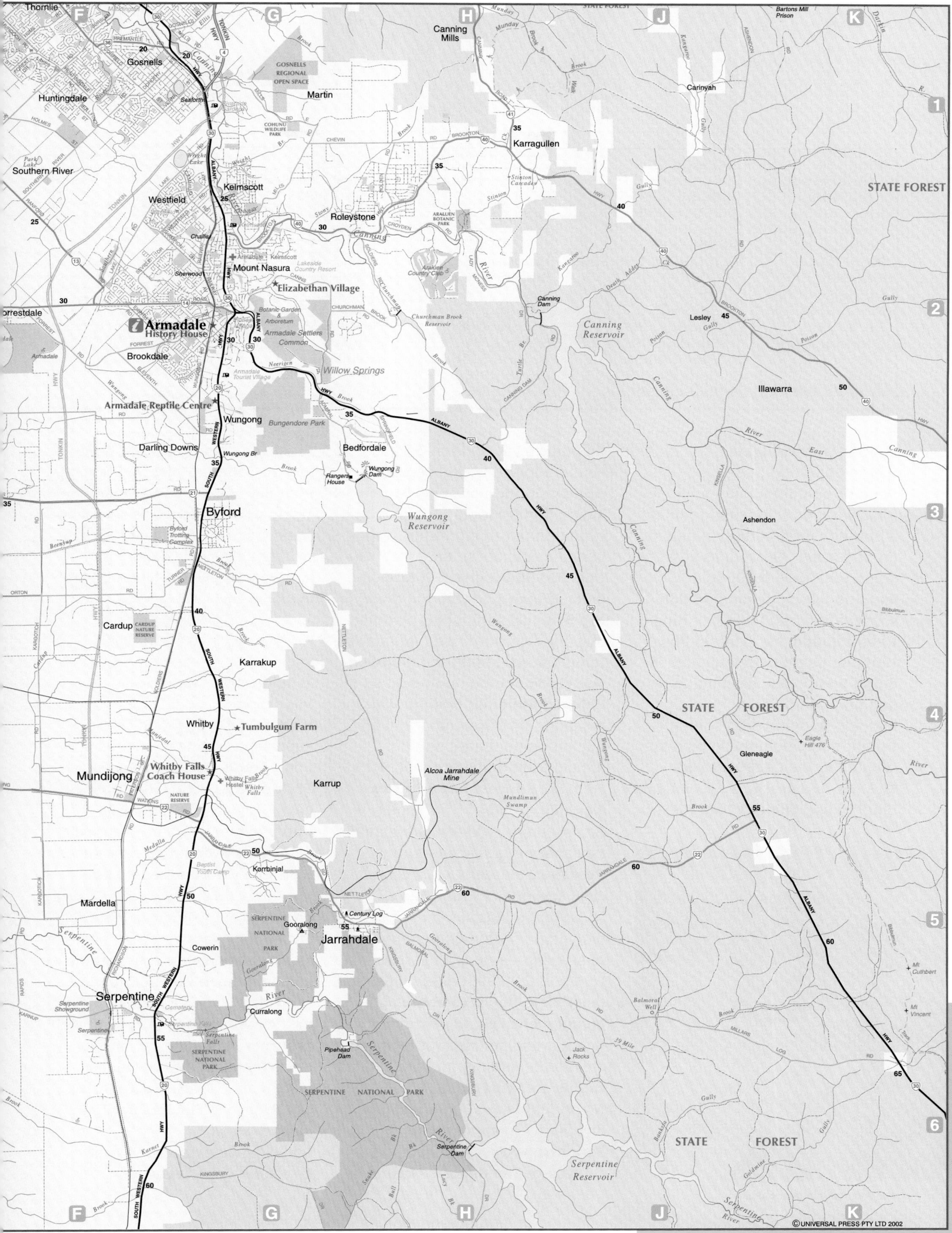

Continued on map 402
Continued on map 402

© UNIVERSAL PRESS PTY LTD 2002

■ Albany   POP 29 000

Map 369, C3

Western Australia's oldest town, Albany was established in 1826 as a British military outpost. It now attracts many visitors to its beautiful scenery, heritage buildings and excellent fishing. Located 409km south of Perth at the edge of **King George Sound** and **Princess Royal Harbour**, its port today services the **South West Coast**, handling grain and silica sand.

MAIN ATTRACTIONS: Stirling Tce is a historic street featuring Victorian shopfronts, the **Old Post Office Museum** and nearby, an operational Court House. **The Old Gaol** (1851)

Two Peoples Bay, east of Albany

was constructed by convicts and houses a folk museum. Reputedly the town's oldest building, **Patrick Taylor Cottage** (circa 1832) has been restored and furnished with period memorabilia. National Trust-classified **Strawberry Hill Farm**, on Middleton Rd, is the site of an experimental farm (1836). Architectural highlights in York St include **St Johns Church** (1848) and the **Town Hall** (1886), now a theatre. A **Colonial Buildings Historic Walk** brochure, available from the information centre, guides visitors around these important sites. Off Forts Rd, **Princess Royal Fortress** was built to defend King George Sound and has daily tours, a nature trail and spectacular views. **Residency Museum** was a convict store converted in 1873 into a house for magistrates. Its displays— of the era of European exploration of Australia—include a full-scale replica of the 1826 settlement ship, the *Amity*. **Mount Clarence** and **Mount Melville** have panoramic lookouts and **Middleton Beach** has areas for picnicking, swimming, surfing and windsurfing.

NEARBY ATTRACTIONS: Renowned for its spectacular coastal views **Torndirrup NP**, 17km south, encompasses **The Gap** and **Natural**

Bridge, the **Blowholes**, the **Gorge** and the **Salmon Holes**. At **Frenchman Bay**, 25km SE, is **Whale World** which operated as a whaling station until 1978. Now it houses a museum exhibiting hundreds of artefacts. Whale-watching trips are available July–Oct.

TOURIST INFO: Old Railway Station, Proudlove Pde, Ph: (08) 9841 1088

■ Augusta   POP 1123

Map 371, C6

Western Australia's third oldest European settlement, Augusta is in the **South West** region about 320km SW of Perth. This fishing town is situated on the slopes of **Hardy Inlet** overlooking the mouth of the **Blackwood River**, and surrounded by pristine countryside.

MAIN ATTRACTIONS: Local history is well preserved at the **Augusta Historical Museum** in Blackwood Ave; of architectural interest nearby is the modern **Lumen Christi Church**. A cairn off Albany Tce marks where the first settlers landed in 1830 and in **Turner Park** there are huge fig trees planted by a town founder more than 170 years ago. Whales can be seen in **Flinders Bay** from June to August.

NEARBY ATTRACTIONS: Built of local limestone, **Cape Leeuwin**

Lighthouse (1896), 9km south, is a 39m-high sentinel and also operates as a meteorological station on the most south-westerly point of mainland Australia. Nearby is a calcifying waterwheel built in 1895 to supply the lighthouse keeper's cottages. Other points of interest include: **Hillview Lookout**, 8km west; **Cosy Corner picnic spot**; former mill town **Old Karridale**; a picnic area east of Karridale at **Alexandra Bridge** which is renowned for its spring wildflowers; and **Boranup Maze**, 18km north in a karri forest. **Jewel Cave**, 9km NW, is notable for exquisite limestone formations.
Tourist Info: 70 Blackwood Ave, Ph: (08) 9758 1695

■ Australlind   POP 5854
Map 375, C4

Australlind is a small coastal resort situated on the **Leschenault Inlet**, 11km NE of Bunbury. Bordered by the inlet and the **Collie** and **Brunswick rivers**, it is a popular destination for watersports enthusiasts who enjoy fishing, prawning, crabbing, boating, sailing and windsurfing. A curious note of history, the town's name originates from the 1840s proposed port venture with India (Australia-India).
Main Attractions: The compact jarrah-built **Church of St Nicholas** (1840), located on Paris Rd, measures 3.8m by 6.7m, claiming the distinction of being the state's smallest church. Opposite is **Henton Cottage** built in 1841. It was originally the Prince of Wales Hotel and now houses a real estate agency. **The Featured Wood Gallery**, on Piggot Dr, has works fashioned from old and new timbers.
Nearby Attractions: A scenic drive north to **Binningup** follows the shore of the Leschenault Inlet where access to picnic and crabbing spots is provided.
Tourist Info: Old Railway Station, Carmody Pl, Bunbury, Ph: (08) 9721 7922

■ Beverley   POP 798
Map 402, D5

Beverley is an historic township, 130km east of Perth on the **Avon River**, it was founded in 1831 and named after a township in Yorkshire, England. The town is in the heart of a wheat and sheep-farming district.
Main Attractions: Western Australia's aviation achievements feature at the **Aeronautical Museum**, in Vincent St, and includes a locally built bi-plane, *Silver Centenary*, constructed 1929–1930. On Brooking St is the grave of **Bill Noongale**, a local Aboriginal who accompanied Sir John Forest on his 1870 trek from Perth to Adelaide. Beverley has the largest range of architectural styles in any Western Australian rural town, from Federation to Art Deco to post-modern. Architectural sites of interest include the **Court House** (1897), **Town Hall** and **Beverley Hotel** (Art Deco).
Nearby Attractions: Historical farm machinery, a museum, homestead and Clydesdale horses can be seen at **Avondale Discovery Farm**, 6km SW. Other attractions include wildflowers in season, **Barrie's private collection** and the **Dead Finish Museum**, built as an inn in 1872, it is now a historical museum.
Tourist Info: 139 Vincent St, Ph: (08) 9646 1555

■ Boyup Brook   POP 750
Map 404, C3

Boyup Brook sits at the junction of the **Blackwood River** and **Boyup Creek**, in the heart of the **South West's** mixed farming and timber country. This pleasant little town is around 270km south of Perth.
Main Attractions: The **Pioneer Museum**, in Jayes Rd, provides an appreciation for local history, including a display of vintage clover seed-harvesting machinery. A **Heritage Trail Walk** of the township is signposted while the **Bicentennial**

Ornamental stalagmites in Jewel Cave, near Augusta

Trail follows the course of the Blackwood River and undulating hills. The information centre holds the **Carnaby Collection** of beetles—many of them rare specimens—and butterflies, and is an outlet promoting local art and handicrafts. **Sandy Chambers Art Studio**, in Gibbs St, has a unique hologram statue, artworks and aviaries. **Perup Forest Ecology Centre**, Cranbrook Rd, has an abundance of rare wildlife.
Nearby Attractions: **Harvey Dickson's Country Music Centre** is 5km NE at Easington Farm on Arthur River Rd. Its attractions include horse-drawn vehicles, boats and Elvis Presley memorabilia. A highlight of driving in the area is the spring wildflower display. The **Haddleton Flora Reserve**, 50km NE, is renowned for its pink and brown boronias. Two well-established wineries are **Blackwood Crest** and **Scots Brook Winery**.
Tourist Info: Cnr Bridge and Abel sts, Ph: (08) 9765 1444

Blessed with natural beauty, the Great Southern region is ideal for holidaymakers. Its diverse landscape incorporates sweeping rural vistas, rugged coastlines, gentle coves and bays, rivers and dramatic mountain ranges. Unspoilt national parks of majestic karri and tingle forest are dotted with ancient rock formations, while the tranquil bays provide the perfect environment for calving southern right and humpback whales to give birth to their young. Some of Western Australia's most beautiful wildflowers grace the 1000 million-year-old granite ranges, that offer excellent hiking and bushwalking opportunities.

This region was settled before Perth—its de facto capital, **Albany** was Western Australia's first European settlement. Now, the region is being increasingly feted for its produce—it is fast becoming one of Australia's largest wine-growing regions, with over 30 wineries to visit.

main attractions

- ◈ Albany Whale World
- ◈ Middleton Beach
- ◈ Mount Barker wine-producing region
- ◈ Porongurup and Stirling Range NPs
- ◈ Valley of the Giants and Tree Top Walk

ℹ Tourist information

Albany Visitor Centre
Old Railway Station, Proudlove Pde,
Albany, WA 6330
Ph: (08) 9841 1088
Freecall: 1800 644 088
www.albanytourist.com.au

Lighthouse, Albany

■ Bridgetown   POP 2420

Map 404, C4

Picturesque Bridgetown, 94km SE of Bunbury, is situated in the **Blackwood River Valley** area on the banks of the Blackwood River. A temperate climate and high rainfall support karri forests, farmland, plantations and wildflowers, which attract many people, including photographers and artists.

MAIN ATTRACTIONS: **Bridgedale** was built by one of the town's first European settlers. Restored by the National Trust, it is a good example of an 1850s homestead. **Blackwood River Park** near Blackwood Bridge, is an ideal picnic spot. **Memorial Park** on Hampton St is another pleasant recreation area and panoramic views are provided from **Suttons Lookout**, off Phillips St.

Bridgetown Pottery and Restaurant in Hampton St, is a working studio, and the information centre houses a local history display and the fascinating **Brierley Jigsaw Gallery**, with its amazing collection of jigsaw puzzles. A pamphlet details a self-guided walking tour of historic buildings, including **St Paul's Church** (1911), notable for its Gordon Holdsworth collection, including an award-winning lectern.

NEARBY ATTRACTIONS: Local agricultural, mining and timber histories can be discovered driving along the 52km **Geegelup Heritage Trail**. Approximately 20km south is the 19th-century **Donnelly Well**, sunk to water horses on the mail run. Beautiful **Bridgetown Jarrah Park**, 25km west, is an educational and recreational park, demonstrating

the unique ecosystem of jarrah forests; there are walking trails and a BBQ area.

TOURIST INFO: 154 Hampton St, Ph: (08) 9761 1740

■ Broome   POP 11 876

Map 398, E4

The western gateway to the northern **Kimberley Region**, Broome is a sunny paradise of white sandy beaches and pristine turquoise waters that now attracts tourists from around the world. Its well-known pearling industry has contributed richly to the town: Broome supplied 75% of the world's mother-of-pearl in the early 1900s till war and plastic buttons undermined demand. The industry has since revived with the development of cultured-pearl farming.

Western Australia

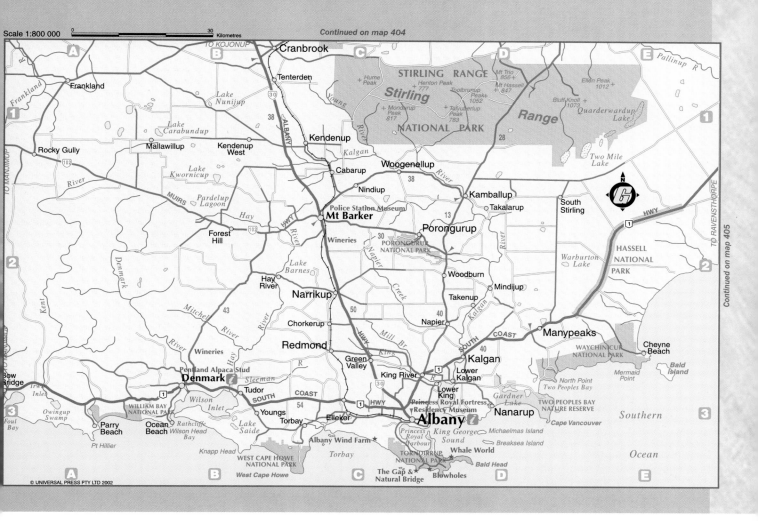

Continued on map 404

Scale 1:800 000 0   30 Kilometres

© UNIVERSAL PRESS PTY LTD 2002

MAIN ATTRACTIONS: Remnants and records documenting the town's colourful history can be uncovered: at **Chinatown**, also renowned for its contemporary pearl showrooms, jewellers and restaurants; and at the **Broome Historical Society Museum**, Saville St, one of the best regional museums in the country. **Bedford Park** features an old train coach; at **Captain Gregory's House** (now a gallery), home of the most successful pearler; and at the elegant **Court House** (1888), which was originally the Cable Station. **Sun Pictures** (1916) is one of the world's oldest open-air theatres and offers a memorable excursion to the movies. Headstones at the **Japanese Cemetery** stand as testament to the many contributions made by Asian pearlers. Worthwhile walks in the

area include a **Mangrove Walk** and **Remnant Rainforest Walk**, located off Gubinge Rd, with entry points signposted. Equally diverse are the excellent tours, including sunset beach camel rides, cruises, and hovercraft rides to remote beaches. Visit **Roebuck Bay** at full moon to witness mudflats reflecting luminous light, a phenomenon known as 'Staircase to the Moon'. Anglers should inquire about good local fishing spots.

NEARBY ATTRACTIONS: Only 6km NW is **Cable Beach**, a 22km stretch of sand and clear turquoise waters ideal for swimming. It was named in 1889 when an underwater telegraph cable linked the town with Java, Indonesia. Nearby is the **Malcolm Douglas Crocodile Park**, home to more than 1000 reptiles.

(CONTINUED ON P.372)

Japanese Cemetery headstones, Broome

CAVES DISTRICT

The Caves District boasts one of the world's most extensive limestone cave systems. It is also known as the **'Cape to Cape'** area because it lies in the region from **Cape Naturaliste** in the north to **Cape Leeuwin** in the south.

The district offers much to adventurous visitors, with a combination of caves and rolling pastures in the hinterland, bordered by a spectacular coastline of reefs and bays. The infamous Roaring Forties winds that create challenging surf conditions, make the coastline a beacon for surfers and windsurfers from other parts of Australia and beyond. The tranquil waters of **Geographe Bay** attract anglers, waterskiers, snorkellers, windsurfers and beach lovers, while the network of caves draws abseilers, cavers and bushwalkers from

around the globe. Jewel Cave, Lake Cave and Mammoth Cave are 3 of the most popular caves. Wine enthusiasts will appreciate the district's close proximity to the vineyards and wineries of one of Australia's up-and-coming wine-producing regions, and gourmet dining opportunities are also easy to find.

Sugarloaf Rock, Leeuwin-Naturaliste NP

The Magical Cave System

Weathering over the eons has resulted in the formation of caves in the long, limestone range between Cape Naturaliste and Cape Leeuwin. Of the 120–200 known caves, 7 of the most spectacular are open to the public.

main attractions

◈ **Augusta**

This is a beautiful fishing town.

◈ **Busselton**

With 30km of white sandy beaches, this premier seaside resort town has twice been voted 'Western Australia's Top Tourism Town'.

◈ **Dunsborough**

Home of the *Swan* dive wreck and artificial reef, its sheltered waters, peaceful coves and scenic bushland make it an ideal family holiday retreat.

◈ **Jewel Cave**

Regarded as the region's best cave, it features fragile calcite formations such as helictites.

◈ **Lake Cave**

An ancient karri tree guards the cave and inside a unique 'table' is suspended over a subterranean lake.

◈ **Mammoth Cave**

This historic cave features a self-guided tour; there is disabled access.

◈ **Margaret River Vineyards**

The success of the vineyards here, only established in the early 1970s, has been extraordinary.

 Tourist information

Margaret River Tourist Bureau
Bussell Hwy,
Margaret River, WA 6285
Ph: (08) 9757 2911

Lake Cave, south-west of Margaret River

Western Australia

Scale 1:400 000

0   15

Kilometres

Continued on map 404

A   B   C   D   E

Cape Naturaliste

Lighthouse & Museum
Rocky Point

Sugarloaf Rock

Eagle Bay
Point Picquet
Meelup

★ HMAS Swan dive site

Geographe

TO BUNBURY

Peppermint Grove
Beach

Penola

Capel

Whaling Station Site
Point Darling

LEEUWIN - NATURALISTE
NATIONAL PARK

Dunsborough

Quindalup

250

Ngilgi
Cave

Yallingup

250

Gunyulgup

Quindalup
Fauna Park

CAVES

15

250

RD

Busselton Jetty,
Underwater Observatory,
Old Butter Factory Museum

Bay

Wonnerup

TUART
FOREST
N.P.

HWY

Wonnerup
Estuary

Ludlow

14

Ludlow River

Busselton

10

Smiths Point

16

Happs

Marybrook

Vasse
Estuary

BUSSELL

Vasse

9

8

Abba

Canal Rocks

Deep
Woods

Rivendell

Yallingup
Shearing Shed

Marybrook

Wildwood

Cape Clairault

Amberley

Clairault

18

Carbunup
River
North

Jindong

Island Brook

Jindong

VASSE

11

6

Ambergate

Sabrina

HWY

Yoongarillup

Abbeys

LEEUWIN -
NATURALISTE
NATIONAL
PARK

STATE

FOREST

Driftwood

Injidup Point

Yelverton

Mary

Becketts
Flat

Boallia

Walsall

RD

River

Range

Moss Brothers

Lenton Brae

Chapmans
Creek

Metricup

Woody Nook
The Grove

Acton
Park

North

Moss Wood

Walburra
Fermoy

Evans & Tate

Pierro

Sandalford
Willespie

20

Harmans

Hay Shed Hill

Ashbrook

Whicher

River

Margaret

State

Woodlands

Ribbon Vale

Gralyn

18

Bettenay

Arlewood

Treeton

Palandri

SUES

Cullen

Vasse Felix

Juniper

Stellar
Ridge

7

Howard Park

Cape Grace

River

52

FOREST

North Point

Cowaramup Point

Gracetown

LEEUWIN -
NATURALISTE
NATIONAL
PARK

250

ROAD

BUSSELL

Cowaramup

Ellensbrook
Homestead

Adinfern

Edwards

Wirring

10

Osmington

Indian

13

STATE
FOREST

Margaret

Old Settlement Museum

Cape
Mentelle

Margaret
River

Rosa
Brook

FOREST

Jalbarragup

Cape Mentelle

Xanadu

5

8

Eagle's Heritage

Minot

Voyager

9

East
Witchcliffe

Marron
Farm

Berry
Farm

Rosa Glen

STATE

Prevelly

Ocean

Redgate

Leeuwin

Shell
Museum

Swallows
Welcome

Rockfield

Serventy

FOREST

Witchcliffe

7

10

S.F.

Upper Chapman

Blackwood

Rosa

River

"Georgette" Wreck ★

Cape Freycinet

Mammoth
Cave

Lake Cave

Forrest
Grove

250

Green Valley

McLeod

BUSSELL

STATE
FOREST

Br

River

SUES

STATE

Warner
Glen

HWY

LEEUWIN -

NATURALISTE

20

Alexandra
Bridge

BROCKMAN

10

FOREST

NATIONAL

North Point

27

Creek

Hamelin
Bay

Alexandra
Bridge

30

PARK

Botanup
Maze

10

Hamelin
Bay

Karridale

Glenarty

HWY

Ck

SCOTT

10

Kudardup

Milyeannup

Foul Bay

Knobby Head

5

12

ROAD

Jewel
Cave

16

250

Hardy
Inlet

NATIONAL

Scott

River

GINGILUP SWAMPS
NATURE
RESERVE

Cosy Corner

Cape Hamelin

Hillview Lookout

PARK

Historical Museum,
Lumen Christi Church

Hamelin
Bay

Augusta

Duke Head

Finders   Bay

Gingilup
Swamps

Lake
Quitjup

White Point

LEEUWIN - NATURALISTE

NATIONAL PARK

250

Cape Leeuwin

Point Matthew

Cape Leeuwin Lighthouse

D'ENTRECASTEAUX
N.P.

Southern   Ocean

Black Point

TO NANNUP

TO PEMBERTON

Broome Bird Observatory, 18km east on Roebuck Bay, is one of Australia's premier sites for observing wading waterbirds; habitats are diverse which ensures a variety of birds; tours are available. Visible at low tide at **Gantheaume Point**, 5km SW, are dinosaur footprints dating back 120 million years. To the north of Gantheaume Point is a rockpool called Anastasia's Pool. This rockpool was built by the former lighthouse keeper for his arthritic wife. **Willie Creek Pearl Farm**, 35km north (18km unsealed road), provides rare insight into a working pearl farm.
Tourist Info: Cnr Great Northern Hwy and Bagot St, Ph: (08) 9192 2222

■ **Bunbury**   POP 29 000
Map 375, B5
Western Australia's second largest town, Bunbury is 185km south of Perth on the **Leschenault Inlet** at the junction of the **Preston** and **Collie rivers**. With a temperate climate, accessibility to attractions, and its natural harbour, Bunbury is both a thriving port town—exporting timber, mineral sands, alumina and other regional cargo—and a popular holiday destination.
Main Attractions: **Koombana Bay**, protected by a breakwater, has ideal conditions for waterskiing, boating and fishing; a historic jetty runs parallel. A highlight of the **Dolphin Discovery Centre**, in Koombana Dr, is supervised swimming with regularly visiting dolphin pods, which can also be seen from harbour cruises. Opposite is a **Mangrove Boardwalk** through the southernmost mangroves in Western Australia and habitat for more than 60 bird species. Signs on the **Shipwreck Trail** provide details of the area's early explorers. **King Cottage** (1880) is a museum furnished with items from 1870 to 1920. Opposite is **Forest Park** with a miniature railway running every

third Sunday. **Big Swamp Wildlife Park**, in Prince Philip Dr, includes a penguin pool and walk-in aviary. **Centenary Gardens**, in Princep St, with its wishing-well, is a favoured spot for picnics. The distinctive chequered **Lighthouse** on Ocean Dr, **Boulters Heights**, and **Marlston Hill** are popular lookout points.
Nearby Attractions: **St Marks Church** (1842), 5km SE at Picton, is Western Australia's second oldest church, while north-east at **Australind** in Paris Rd is **St Nicholas**, the state's smallest church. **Boyanup Transport Museum**, 20 minutes NE, exhibits a vintage steam train among other early forms of transport. Gem enthusiasts can visit the **Gem Museum**, north on Old Coast Rd, or the **Rock and Gem Museum** on Bussell Hwy.
Tourist Info: Old Railway Station, Carmody Pl, Ph: (08) 9721 7922

■ **Busselton**   POP 15 500
Map 371, D1
This fishing town built on the shores of **Geographe Bay** and the **Vasse River** is 228km south of Perth. Busselton's 30km of sandy beaches are one of its principal attractions.
Main Attractions: Measuring 2km in length **Busselton Jetty** is the Southern Hemisphere's longest wooden structure. It is a favourite site for walks, snorkelling, scuba diving and fishing and offers miniature train rides that travel its length. Also part of the jetty complex are **Busselton Jetty Interpretive Centre**, and **Busselton Underwater Observatory** which features unique corals and marine life. Historic buildings include the **Old Butter Factory Museum**, in Peel St, which recounts the early days of the town's history. **St Mary's Anglican** Church, Peel Tce, was built in 1844 of stone—making it the oldest stone church in the state. The **Old Court House**, in Queen St, houses an arts complex.

Nearby Attractions: **Ludlow Tuart Forest**, 7km east, is a popular picnic and walking retreat and is the world's only natural tuart forest. Nearby on Layman Rd is **Wonnerup House** (1859), a National Trust-restored and furnished colonial period home. A scenic drive along Geographe Bay to **Cape Naturaliste** journeys through **Dunsborough**, **Eagle Bay** and **Meelup** and provides an opportunity to visit **Ngilgi Cave** and **Cape Naturaliste Lighthouse**.
Tourist Info: 38 Peel Tce, Ph: (08) 9752 1288

■ **Carnarvon**   POP 6587
Map 400, B3
Just south of the **Tropic of Capricorn** and 904km north of Perth, sunny, palm-lined Carnarvon utilises the **Gascoyne River** and its subsurface waters to irrigate its flourishing plantations of tropical fruits and a wide range of vegetables.
Main Attractions: Signposts of Carnarvon's past are detailed in a **Heritage Walk** pamphlet. The **Maritime Heritage Precinct** includes **One Mile Jetty** (1904), a tramway and Kimberley steam loco-

Gantheaume Point, near Broome, where dinosaur footprints can be seen at low tide

Western Australia

motive, and a **lighthouse keeper's cottage** which houses the local history museum. **Town Beach** is popular for swimming and picnics.
NEARBY ATTRACTIONS: On **Babbage Island**, connected by a causeway, are both **Pelican Point**, a beach popular for fishing, swimming and windsurfing, and the **Nor-west Seafoods Prawning Factory** (the information centre can arrange tours). Anglers fish from the **Prawning Jetty** opposite the factory. Between 1964 and 1974, NASA operated a satellite tracking station here, and the remnant 29m-dish, 8km east, provides an excellent vantage for viewing the township. **Westoby Plantation**, 5km east, and **Munro's Banana Plantation**, 10km east, offer samples and plantation tours. On the Gascoyne River and set amidst ghost gums is **Chinaman's Pool**, suitable for picnics and swimming. Around 76km north are the dramatic **Blowholes** that sometimes reach 20m in height. A kilometre south is a protected beach with a variety of marine life to observe.
TOURIST INFO: 11 Robinson St, Ph: (08) 9941 1146

■ Collie   POP 7346
Map 375, E5
This town is nestled in jarrah timber country, 57km east of Bunbury. Collie produces 3.25 million tonnes of coal annually from nearby open-cut mines.
MAIN ATTRACTIONS: Several attractions reflect the town's central position in the State's only coal-producing region. The excellent **Coalfields Museum** displays pioneering and mining memorabilia together with a large doll collection. The **Steam Locomotive Museum** and the informative **Collie Tourist Coal Mine**—a replica of an underground mine, are worthwhile visiting. There are several parks for picnics and leisurely strolls including **Soldiers Park**, in Steere St, with an **Arboretum** opposite,

Camel farm, Coolgardie

and in Throssell St, are **Baarnimar Reconciliation Park**, with fine examples of Aboriginal art, and **Finlay Gardens**. A **Historic Walk** brochure highlights notable sites and an **Art and Craft Gallery** is situated behind the information centre.
NEARBY ATTRACTIONS: Showcasing jarrah forests and seasonal wildflowers is the **Collie Scenic River Drive**, which starts 5km west of town. **Wellington Dam**, 28km SW, is perfect for picnics, fishing and bushwalking, while north is **Harris Dam**, the town's scenic reservoir. **Muja Power Station**, 24km SE, offers guided tours; book through the information centre. **Muja Mine**, 21km SE, can be viewed from the Coalfields Hwy.
TOURIST INFO: Throssell St, Ph: (08) 9734 2051

■ Coolgardie   POP 1457
Map 403, J4
A goldrush town born out of an alluvial strike at **Fly Flat** in 1892, Coolgardie in its heyday supported 23 hotels and 7 newspapers. Though the population dwindled as the gold ran out, today the town, 560km east of Perth, preserves an important history.
MAIN ATTRACTIONS: On Bayley St, a **Pharmacy Museum** displays tools-of-the-trade in a recreated turn-of-the-century pharmacy. Adjacent is

the **Goldfields Exhibition Museum** (1898) staging the state's most comprehensive goldfields exhibition, and the **old Coolgardie Gaol**. **The Gaol Tree**, complete with replica leg-irons, pre-dates the gaol and is located on Hunt St. The old **Railway Station Museum** recounts local and transport history, including the Varischetti mine rescue. Relics of the gold-mining era are also housed here. Also of interest are the **Lindsay Pit Lookout**; **Ben Prior's Open Air Museum** of machinery, mining equipment and assortment of relics; **Warden Finnerty's House** (1895) restored by the National Trust and open to the public; **Lions Bicentennial Lookout**; **Coolgardie Cemetery**; and the **Old Pioneer Cemetery**, in Forrest St, has graves from 1892 to 1894.
NEARBY ATTRACTIONS: **Coolgardie Camel Farm**, 3km west, offers camel rides. **Kurrawang Emu Farm**, 20km east, offers tours and emu products. Picnic areas south of the town are at **Gnarlbine Rocks** (30km); **Victoria Rocks** (48km), known for its excellent views; and **Burra Rock** (55km). **Rowles Lagoon**, a 2km wide freshwater lake and reserve ideal for picnics and camping, is 60km to the north.
TOURIST INFO: 62 Bayley St, Ph: (08) 9026 6090

The waters of the capital of the region known as the South West and Western Australia's second largest population centre, **Bunbury**, mark the point where the warm **Indian Ocean** waters collide with those of the cooler **Southern Ocean**. This area is renowned for its abundant wildlife, as well as its bountiful rivers.

The city was named more than 150 years ago after Lt Henry William St Pierre Bunbury, who was sent to explore the lands south of Fremantle in 1836. It now provides visitors with an excellent base for their own regional explorations, although the city itself offers many attractions—a stretch of beaches, caves and inlets, beach-and sea-fishing opportunities, lagoons, superior yachting facilities, picturesque picnic spots and dolphin cruises.

The surrounding hinterland features superb karri forests, spectacular coastline, pretty orchards, verdant grassland and farmstay opportunities. The surrounding towns are worthwhile exploring. **Donnybrook** is known for its apple orchards, wineries, arts and crafts, while at **Harvey** visitors will find some of Western Australia's prime beef and best oranges.

Manjimup

This region is best known for its towering karri and jarrah forests and is also home to the **'Four Aces'**—4 giant karri trees over 400 years old. The other karri trees here are hundreds of years old and grow over 75m tall.

 Tourist information

Bunbury Visitor Information Centre
Old Railway Station,
Carmody Pl,
Bunbury WA 6230
Ph: (08) 9721 7922
www.justsouth.com.au

Harvesting apples at Donnybrook

main attractions

◈ **Australind**

This historic town is popular for boating, sailing, fishing, prawning, crabbing and windsurfing.

◈ **Bunbury**

Bunbury offers a cosmopolitan seaside atmosphere of beaches, cafes and shopping and many nature-based attractions, such as the Mangrove Boardwalk.

◈ **Dolphin Discovery Centre**

Experience the sight and sounds of these amazing sea mammals through an audiovisual show.

◈ **Koombana Bay dolphins**

The bay is famed for its dolphins, which frolic in its protected waters.

◈ **Mangrove Boardwalk**

Mangroves have been growing here for about 25 000 years.

◈ **Old Goldfields Orchard and Cider Factory**

Here the workings of Donnybrook's historic goldrush era are recreated, with gold panning just one of the activities available. There is a boutique cider factory where adults can taste different brews.

Eucalyptus diversicolor in a karri forest near Manjimup

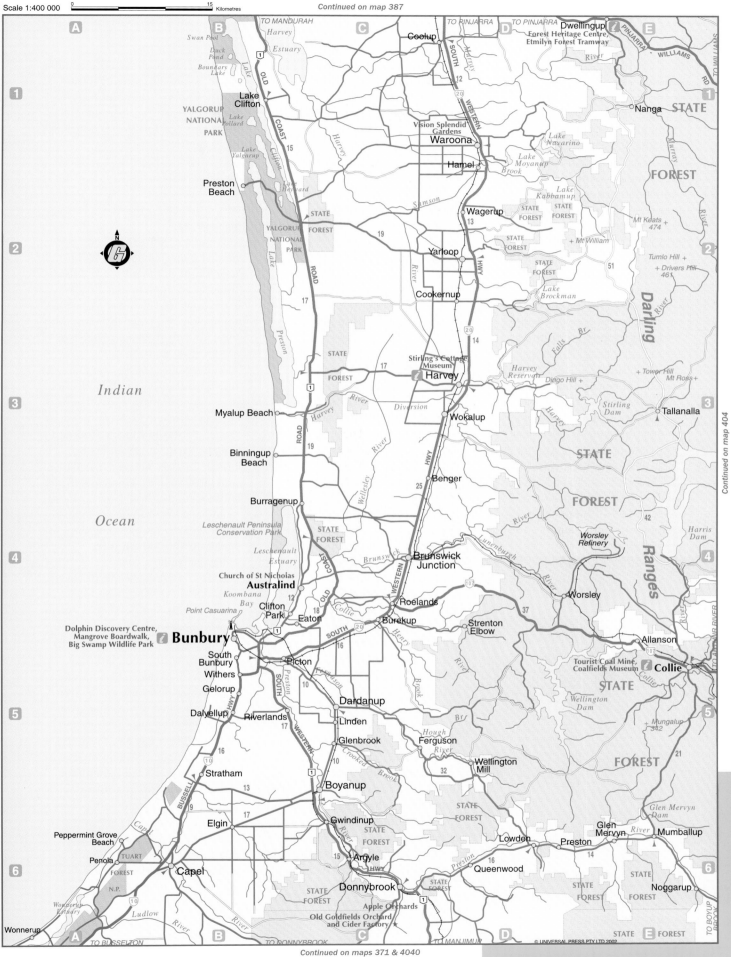

Scale 1:400 000

Continued on map 387

TO MANDURAH

Swan Pool
Duck Pond
Boundary Lake

Harvey
Estuary

TO PINJARRA
TO PINJARRA

Dwellingup
Forest Heritage Centre,
Etmilyn Forest Tramway

Coolup

Lake Clifton

YALGORUP
NATIONAL
PARK

Lake Pollard

Lake Yalgorup

Nanga

STATE

Preston Beach

Lake Hayward

Harvey

Vision Splendid
Gardens

Waroona

Hamel

Lake
Navarino

Lake
Moyanup
Brook

FOREST

STATE
FOREST

Lake
Kabbamup

Mt Keats
474 +

STATE
FOREST

Samson

Wagerup

STATE
FOREST

+ Mt William

YALGORUP
NATIONAL
PARK

Yarloop

STATE
FOREST

Tumlo Hill +

+ Drivers Hill
461

51

Indian

STATE

FOREST

Cookernup

Lake
Brockman

Darling

River

Stirling's Cottage
Museum

Harvey

Falls Br

+ Tower Hill
Mt Ross+

Dingo Hill +

Stirling
Dam

Myalup Beach

Harvey

River

Diversion

Wokalup

Harvey
Reservoir

Tallanalla

Binningup
Beach

Harvey

River

STATE

Wellesley

River

Benger

FOREST

River

42

Harris
Dam

Burragenup

Leschenault Peninsula
Conservation Park

Ocean

STATE
FOREST

Brunswick

Brunswick
Junction

Lunenburgh

Worsley
Refinery

Leschenault
Estuary

River

Ranges

Church of St Nicholas

Australind

Koombana
Bay

Point Casuarina

Clifton
Park

Eaton

Collie

Roelands

Burekup

Strenton
Elbow

Worsley

37

Allanson

Dolphin Discovery Centre,
Mangrove Boardwalk,
Big Swamp Wildlife Park

Bunbury

South
Bunbury

Withers

Picton

Henry

Tourist Coal Mine,
Coalfields Museum

Collie

Gelorup

Dardanup

Brook

River

Wellington
Dam

State

Dalyellup

Riverlands

Linden

Hough

Ferguson

Br

Mungalup
342

FOREST

Glenbrook

Ferguson River

Wellington
Mill

21

Stratham

Boyanup

Crooked

Brook

32

Glen Mervyn
Dam

Elgin

Gwindinup

STATE

FOREST

Glen
Mervyn

River

Mumballup

Peppermint Grove
Beach

Preston

Capel

River

Argyle

Lowden

Preston

Queenwood

14

STATE

FOREST

Penola

TUART

FOREST

N.P.

Capel

STATE

FOREST

Donnybrook

STATE
FOREST

Noggarup

Wonnerup
Estuary

Ludlow

River

Capel

River

Apple Orchards
Old Goldfields Orchard
and Cider Factory ★

STATE
FOREST

STATE E FOREST

Wonnerup

TO BUSSELTON

TO DONNYBROOK

TO MANJIMUP

© UNIVERSAL PRESS PTY LTD 2002

TO BOYUP
BROOK

Continued on maps 371 & 4040

Dampier   POP 2000

Map 398, B6

A port town built in the 1960s, Dampier overlooks **Hampton Harbour** in **King Bay**, 20km from Karratha. Water recreation activities and accessibility to the islands of the **Dampier Archipelago** are premier attractions. Exports from Dampier's busy harbour include iron ore, natural gas and salt.

MAIN ATTRACTIONS: Loading 400 million tonnes of ore annually **Hamersley Iron Port Facilities** conducts tours by arrangement with the Karratha Tourist Centre. Recreation is popular in the area, including boating, windsurfing, fishing and diving. Popular swimming spots include **Dampier Back Beach** and nearby **Hearsons Cove**.

NEARBY ATTRACTIONS: North-east is the **Burrup Peninsula** renowned for its 10 000 Aboriginal rock-art sites, best viewed on a tour. Also on the Peninsula is the **Northwest Shelf Gas Project** onshore operations, which pipes natural gas from offshore fields 130km north of Dampier. Its information centre

is open weekdays. **Dampier Archipelago NP** comprises 42 islands within a radius of 45km of Dampier and is considered one of the country's best fishing spots. Archipelago tours and fishing charters depart from Dampier boat ramps.

TOURIST INFO: Lot 4548, Karratha Rd, Karratha, Ph: (08) 9144 4600

Denham   POP 1264

Map 400, B4

Denham, 831km north of Perth, is the commercial centre for the extraordinary **Shark Bay World Heritage Region**. Historically a pearling town, but now is best known for its eco-tourism and its thriving fishing industry.

MAIN ATTRACTIONS: **Pioneer Park**, off Hughes St, is a pleasant picnic spot with gas BBQ and an unusual whale-bone arch. Locally organised excursions include tours of **Shark Bay Fisheries**; a glass-bottom boat cruise to a pearl farm; and chartered flights and boat trips to **Dirk Hartog Island**, where the famed Dutch navigator landed in 1616, and where turtles hatch during April. Both the deep-sea and game fishing here are superb.

NEARBY ATTRACTIONS: **Monkey Mia**, 25km NE, is where close-encounters with wild bottlenose dolphins occur. Rangers and an information centre shed light on this friendly exchange, which has occurred since the 1960s. To the north, **Francois Peron NP** covers 400km²; **Peron Homestead**, in the park, has a 'hot tub' filled by warm artesian waters; it is accessible by 2WD. Other parts of the park can be reached by 4WD only, including **Cape Peron** where dugongs (sea cows) and other marine life can be observed. **Shell Beach**, 50km south, is one of only 2 mainland beaches in the world comprised entirely of seashells. **Stromatolites**, found nowhere else in the world and of

enormous scientific interest, can be found 100km SE, thriving in the warm waters of **Hamelin Pool**—tours are available. Nearby are the **Telegraph Station** (1884) and shell block quarry.

TOURIST INFO: 83 Knight Tce, Ph: (08) 9948 1253

Denmark   POP 4250

Map 369, B3

Denmark, 414km SE of Perth, is an idyllically situated retreat on the **Denmark River** beside **Wilson Inlet**. In addition to its scenic attractions the town has earned a reputation as a creative centre, with local artisans producing excellent works of art and craft.

MAIN ATTRACTIONS: Aboriginal and other art galleries can be found in and around Denmark. Riverside markets are held Dec–Jan and at Easter. **Pentland Alpaca Stud and Tourist Farm**, on Scotsdale Rd, breeds alpacas, and also has native and farm animals. Popular activities include windsurfing, fishing, water-skiing and horseriding, and there are several walks including the **Moakare** and **Wilson Inlet Heritage trails**.

NEARBY ATTRACTIONS: Scenic drives in the area are rewarding and lookouts are at **Mount Shadforth** and **Wilson Head**. Local wineries include **Catherine Hill** and **Howard Parks**, both 2km north; and **Matilda's Meadow**, 5km north. **Bartholomew's Meadery**, 20km west, makes bee produce, including mead, an alcoholic drink made from honey and water. **William Bay NP**, 17km SW, protects unique coastal scenery including **Greens Pool**, **Elephant Rocks**, **Tower Hill**, **Madfish Bay** and **Waterfall Beach**; both Greens Pool and Madfish Bay are safe swimming spots. **Parry's Inlet**, 25km west, has good swimming and seasonal salmon fishing.

TOURIST INFO: 60 Strickland St, Ph: (08) 9848 2055

A friendly bottlenose dolphin at Monkey Mia, near Denham

Western Australia

Tunnel Creek in the Kimberley region, east of Derby

Derby   POP 2643

Map 399, F3

Located on the **King Sound**, Derby is known for its boab trees which give the town its distinctive character. Derby is around 2643km NE of Perth, and is a service centre for the rich pastoral and mining hinterland and a gateway to exploring the **Kimberley**.

MAIN ATTRACTIONS: Anglers are often found at the **Fitzroy River** and on **Derby Wharf**. The wharf is also a good place to comprehend the magnitude of the tidal range here— 1.3m at low tide and 11.8m at high tide. Other points of interest in the town include the local history museum at **Wharfinger House**, **Kimberley School of the Air**, the **Botanic Gardens**, and the **Joonjoo Botanical Trail**. An administrative centre for several Aboriginal communities, Derby has a number of outlets selling traditional and contemporary indigenous art.

NEARBY ATTRACTIONS: **The Boab Prison Tree**, 7km south, is a massive hollowed boab, believed to have been used as a temporary cell for prisoners en route to Derby. **Myall's**

Bore, nearby, is an astonishing 120m-long cattle trough. The self-drive **Pigeon Heritage Trail** highlights sites of interest between Derby and **Windjana Gorge** and **Tunnel Creek NP**. Derby is also a base for cruises, tours and scenic flights to **Cockatoo Island**, **Buccaneer Archipelago** and **King Leopold Ranges**.

TOURIST INFO: 2 Clarendon St, Ph: (08) 9191 1426

Dongara/Port Denison

POP 1964

Map 402, A2

Settled in the early 1850s, Dongara is one of the state's oldest settlements. It, and Port Denison nearby are located on the **Batavia Coast**, 359km north of Perth. Local industries are agriculture and fishing, though natural gas, 6km east, also contributes to the region's economy.

MAIN ATTRACTIONS: **Dongara's Heritage Trail** takes in 14 attractions including the old **Police Station** (1870), the **Royal Steam Flour Mill** (1894), and **Russ Cottage** (1870), a farm worker's cottage furnished in period-style. Port Denison is famed for its rock lobsters, excellent fishing, beautiful bays and safe beaches such as **South Beach**.

NEARBY ATTRACTIONS: Excellent views of the harbour can be seen from **Fisherman's Lookout** near **Point Leander**.

TOURIST INFO: 5 Waldeck St, Ph: (08) 9927 1404

Donnybrook   POP 1764

Map 375, C6

Originally a timber town, and for a short period a gold town. Today, Donnybrook, 210km south of Perth, is a mixed farming area known for its horticulture and orchards especially its apples.

NEARBY ATTRACTIONS: **The Old Goldfields Orchard and Cider Factory**, 5km south, offers tours of its orchard and cider factory

and has picnic areas, a restaurant, a goldmine and gold-panning facilities. Two potteries in the area are **Cedar Shed**, 10km SE, and **Old Stables Pottery**, 25km SE. **Balingup**, 30km SE, is a hub for arts and crafts, including **The Old Cheese Factory** craft centre, **Village Pedlars** home crafts and **Tinderbox** herb products. Nearby are the **Golden Valley Tree Park**, and **Birdwood Park Fruit Winery** on Nannup Rd.

TOURIST INFO: The Harvest Office, South Western Hwy, Ph: (08) 9731 2400

Dunsborough   POP 4000

Map 371, B1

Dunsborough is located on **Geographe Bay**, 26km west of Busselton, The town's attractions include beaches, coastal scenery and seasonal wildflowers. It is also a gateway to **Cape Naturaliste** and **Leeuwin-Naturaliste NP**.

MAIN ATTRACTIONS: Adventurous recreational options include scuba diving, canoeing, horseriding and caving. Local craft outlets are **Dunsborough Gallery** showcasing woodcraft; **Goanna Gallery**; **Happ's Pottery and Vineyard**, which sells pottery; and **Bush Cottage Crafts** featuring a variety of wares.

NEARBY ATTRACTIONS: In the north-west, beautiful bay-fronting towns with good swimming and boating beaches are **Meelup** (5km), **Eagle Bay** (8km) and **Bunker Bay** (12km). Wreck dive tours of **HMAS** *Swan*, south of Eagle Bay at **Point Picquet**, are available. **Cape Naturaliste Lighthouse and Museum**, 13km NW, offers tours, walking trails and whale-watching platforms set amidst spectacular coastal scenery. Diverse animal encounters can be enjoyed at **Country Life Farm** nearby, at **Quindalup Fauna Park**, 4km east, and south-east at **Yallingup Shearing Shed**.

TOURIST INFO: Seymour Blvd, Ph: (08) 9755 3299

Esperance   POP 9268

Map 405, K3

The South Coast's pristine beaches, good fishing, and access to the **Archipelago of the Recherche** have contributed much to Esperance's popularity as a holiday destination. Situated 720km SE of Perth, the town is a commercial and service centre for nearby farming districts.

MAIN ATTRACTIONS: **Esperance Municipal Museum**, James St, has a collection of farm equipment, a marine exhibit, and remnants of *Skylab*, the US space station that fell to earth in the area in July 1979. For a distinctive souvenir, **Mermaid Marine Leather** processes and sells fashion accessories made from fish skins. **Tanker Jetty** is recommended for angling and seal watching. A 10km shorefront walking and cycling track follows the **Bay of Isles**. Fishing and diving tours and scenic cruises are also on offer.

NEARBY ATTRACTIONS: The spectacular 36km **Great Ocean Drive** takes a round-trip passing attractions such as: **Pink Lake**, a salt lake coloured pink by algae; **Observatory Point and Lookout**; **Twilight Beach**; a power-generating **Wind Farm**; **Rotary Lookout**; and the Archipelago of the Recherche (Bay of Isles), 105 islands that provide sheltered habitats for seals,

Yardie Creek, Cape Range NP

penguins and birdlife. Cruises are available to **Woody Island** where camping is allowed Sept–April. **Telegraph Farm**, 21km NW, is a commercial protea farm that has buffalo, camels and other animals. Boardwalks facilitate birdwatching at **Monjinup Lake Botanical Park**, 20km west. White-sand swimming beaches and hilly scrublands are features of **Cape Le Grand NP**, 56km east. Beaches of note include **Hellfire Bay**, **Thistle Cove** and **Lucky Bay**; there are also scenic walks and sensational wildflower displays in spring. **Cape Arid NP**, 120km east, is a rugged setting for bushwalking, camping, fishing and 4WDing.

TOURIST INFO: Museum Park, Dempster St, Ph: (08) 9071 2330

Exmouth   POP 3124

Map 400, B1

Exmouth was established on the **North West Cape** in 1967, primarily as a US Naval Communications Station that has since ceased operating. Ecotours are well rewarded as the town's proximity to **Ningaloo Reef**, protected within **Ningaloo Marine Park** and **Cape Range NP** guarantees sightings of some extraordinary marine life.

MAIN ATTRACTIONS: Excellent tours include glass-bottom, coral-viewing boat cruises, fishing charters, safaris, diving and sea kayaking. Inquire about turtle nesting (Nov–Jan), humpback whale watching (August–Nov) and swimming with the whale sharks (April–June).

NEARBY ATTRACTIONS: Tours are offered of **Vlaming Head Lighthouse**, 17km north, and the views are spectacular. The wreck of the ill-fated **SS Mildura**, sunk in 1907, is 100m offshore. Ningaloo Marine Park, to the west, is the largest fringing coral reef in Australia with more than 220 coral species. Highlights of the park include swimming with giant whale sharks, greenback

turtle nesting, and coral spawning that occurs after the March full moon. Within Cape Range NP is magnificent **Shothole Canyon**, 16km south, and **Charles Knife Canyon**, 23km south. **Milyering Visitor Centre**, 52km SW, is an environmentally friendly building with displays on the area's natural history and culture. Also not to be missed are **Bundegi Beach**, **Turquoise Bay** and **Yardie Creek**.

TOURIST INFO: Murat Rd, Ph: (08) 9949 1176

Fitzroy Crossing   POP 1200

Map 399, H4

Fitzroy Crossing, located beside the **Fitzroy River**, is a growing outback centre providing services and supplies to Aboriginal communities and the Kimberley's cattle and mining industries. A base for visiting **Kimberley** attractions, local conditions should be checked first as roads are subject to seasonal flooding.

MAIN ATTRACTIONS: The oldest hotel in the Kimberley, the legendary **Crossing Inn** (1897), was a stopping point for travellers poised to make the sometimes perilous river crossing. Nearby is the **Pioneer Cemetery**. The original site for Fitzroy Crossing was 5km NE of its present location—the move occurred with construction of the bridge and re-routing of the highway. Remnants of the old town site are worth visiting.

NEARBY ATTRACTIONS: Part of a 350-million-year-old Devonian coral reef, the limestone cliffs of **Geikie Gorge NP** contain layers of fossilised fish and are dotted with caves. This 14km gorge, 18km north of the town, is best seen from a boat cruise or Aboriginal Heritage cruise, both can be booked at the information centre. Crocodiles, and stingrays and sawfish adapted to fresh water, can be seen in the river.

TOURIST INFO: Cnr Great Northern Hwy and Forrest Rd, Ph: (08) 9191 5355

Western Australia

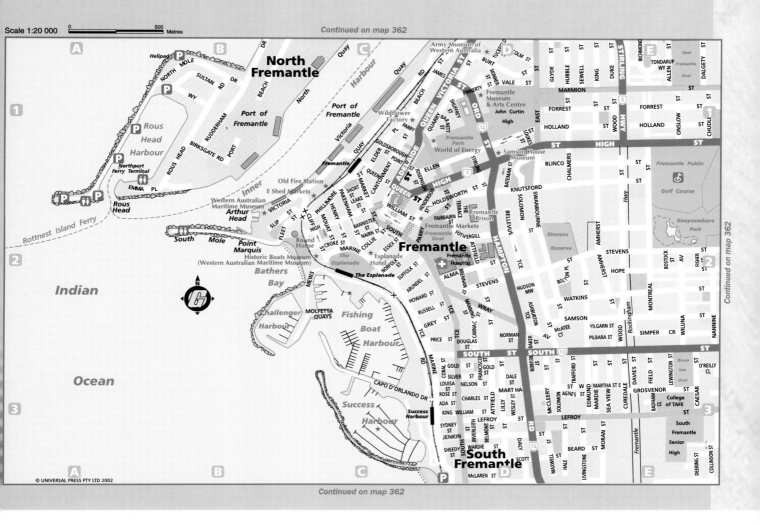

Scale 1:20 000

Continued on map 362

North Fremantle

Port of Fremantle

Rous Head Harbour

Rous Head

Indian

Ocean

Fremantle

South Fremantle

Continued on map 362

Continued on map 362

© UNIVERSAL PRESS PTY LTD 2002

Fremantle   POP 24 950

Map 379, C2

The historic city of Fremantle lies 19km SW of Perth at the mouth of the **Swan River**. Now merged with suburban Perth, 'Freo', as the locals call it, is a major fishing and shipping port with a vibrant multicultural society. It has lovingly preserved its 19th-century heritage and created a relaxed ambience. In 1986–87, the city hosted the first America's Cup yacht races held outside the USA. This major event triggered the rejuvenation of many of the historic 19th-century buildings—there are more than 3000 buildings of historical significance and the National Trust has classified 150 of these.

MAIN ATTRACTIONS: National Trust-classified **Fremantle Markets**, 84

South Tce, was established in 1897 and offers an array of goods, from fish to antiques. The **E Shed Markets**, at Victoria Quay, contain more than 100 specialty shops. **Tram West** offers tours of historical buildings, the harbour and other attractions in Fremantle. Tickets are available on board. The **Western Australian Maritime Museum**, in Cliff St, has an internationally important collection of shipwreck relics dating from early 17th-century Dutch ships, including the *Batavia*. A large new section of the museum, tracing the state's maritime history, is at Victoria Quay. The submarine, *Ovens*, located nearby off Slip St, is open to the public. **Fremantle History Museum and Arts Centre**, located in the Fremantle Arts Centre in Finnerty St, is in a convict-built

former lunatic asylum. The **Town Hall**, completed in 1887 and remodelled in the 1950s, is an important heritage building. **The Round House Precinct**, at Arthurs Head overlooking **Cockburn Sound**, preserves Western Australia's most historic site. The Round House, originally a gaol, was built in 1831 and is Western Australia's oldest public building. It is built from local limestone. At 1pm daily, the **Signal Station** fires the Jardine's Time Gun; an honorary gunner is selected to fire the gun. The Gun Deck provides wonderful views to Rottnest and Garden Islands and the Fremantle harbour areas. Other buildings with interesting architecture are the **Esplanade Hotel**, on the corner of Marine Tce and Essex St, the **Old Fremantle Fire Station** at

18 Phillimore St and the **Fremantle Chamber of Commerce**, located next door. Tours are available of **Fremantle Prison**, 1 The Terrace, this was the last convict prison to be built in Australia and is a fascinating experience. For the cafe society, don't miss Fremantle's popular South Tce, known as the 'capuccino strip'.

NEARBY ATTRACTIONS: Ferries to **Rottnest Island**, a favourite playground, leave from Victoria Quay. Fremantle is close to beaches to the south and all of Perth's attractions.

TOURIST INFO: Town Hall, cnr William and Adelaide sts, Ph: (08) 9431 7878

■ Geraldton   POP 25 850
Map 402, A1

Rock lobsters, wildflowers, year-round sunshine and white sandy beaches are trademarks of the attractive mid-western port city of Geraldton, 424km north of Perth on **Champion Bay**.

MAIN ATTRACTIONS: The **Geraldton Museum**, located on Marine Tce, has an outstanding maritime display, with relics from the 17th-and 18th-century Dutch shipwrecks, *Batavia*, *Zuytdorp* and *Zeewijk*, together with natural and cultural heritage exhibits. The eclectic **St Francis Xavier Cathedral**, completed 1938, is one of John Hawes'

St Francis Xavier Cathedral, Geraldton

architectural masterpieces. A pamphlet describing the **Monsignor Hawes Heritage Trail** is available and includes **The Hermitage**, the monsignor's former residence. Other notable buildings in town are the prefabricated **Point Moore Lighthouse** (1878); **Lighthouse Keeper's Cottage** (1870); and the **Bill Sewell Complex** (1887), formerly the Victoria District Hospital, then prison, and presently incorporating the **Old Gaol Craft Centre**. **Geraldton Art Gallery** has well-regarded permanent and touring exhibitions. **Marra Indigenous Art Gallery**, located at the old Railway Station on Chapman Rd, displays Aboriginal artworks. There are several lookouts providing good views, including **Mount Scott**, which is the site of the **HMAS *Sydney* Memorial**. Fishermen unload huge rock lobster hauls on **Fisherman's Wharf** and the lobster processing plant conducts tours of its operations Dec–June. Activities in the area include windsurfing, diving, walking, fishing, kite flying and cycling.

NEARBY ATTRACTIONS: Seasonal wild-flowers are a highlight of the hinterland—a spectacular sight not to be missed. Air, diving and bird-watching tours visit the impressive 122-island chain of the **Houtman Abrolhos Islands**, 64km offshore. **Mungala Eco Farm Tours** provide insight into farming life. **Chapman Valley Wines**, 35km NE, offer tastings daily.

TOURIST INFO: Cnr Bayley St and Chapman Rd, Ph: (08) 9921 3999

■ Greenough (shire)   POP 7652
Map 402, A1

The **Shire of Greenough** surrounding the city of **Geraldton** is one of Australia's most prosperous sheep and wheat districts. Emblematic in the area are the leaning trees, *Eucalyptus camaldulensis*, shaped by the strong salt winds from the sea.

MAIN ATTRACTIONS: Restored by the National Trust, **Greenough Historical Hamlet** is a collection of 11 buildings from the 1880s; tours are conducted through these buildings. North of the hamlet is the **Pioneer Cemetery**, and the **Pioneer Museum** is housed in a 120-year-old farmhouse and has an excellent folk collection. **Cliff Grange**, opposite an 1858 flour mill, is a National Trust restored property. The mouth of the **Greenough River** is a good swimming and fishing spot.

NEARBY ATTRACTIONS: Pamphlets are available on the **Greenough to Walkaway Heritage Trail** and the **Greenough River Nature Walk Trail Guide**. **Ellendale Pool**, located 21km from Walkaway, is a popular permanent waterhole framed by cliffs. It has picnic and BBQ areas and camping is permitted. **Walkaway Station Museum**, housed in the old Railway Station, has a large collection of local family records, regional transport items, weapons and military relics.

TOURIST INFO: Historic Greenough Hamlet, Brand Hwy, Ph: (08) 9926 1660

■ Halls Creek   POP 1280
Map 399, J4

Halls Creek is the site of Western Australia's first payable gold discovery in 1885. The township, 2855km NE of Perth, is located at the centre of the **Kimberley**, adjacent to the **Great Sandy Desert**. Today it services local Aboriginal communities, pastoralists, and tourists seeking access to nearby national parks.

MAIN ATTRACTIONS: **Russian Jack Memorial**, on Thomas St, is a tribute to a gold digger who pushed his sick friend 300km in a wheelbarrow to seek medical help in Wyndham. Also in town is an art outlet on the Duncan Hwy selling quality local Aboriginal art.

NEARBY ATTRACTIONS: **China Wall**, 6km east, is a natural white quartz rock

Wave Rock, Hyden

formation. A further 9km east is **Caroline Pool**, an ideal picnic and swimming spot. Past the ruins of the original Halls Creek town site (16km east), are 2 swimming and picnic spots: **Palm Springs**, 41km east, and **Sawpit Gorge**, 43km east, both are on the **Black Elvire River**. Halls Creek serves as a base for excursions to **Purnululu NP (Bungle Bungles)**, with its spectacular ancient rock formations (155km NE) and to **Wolfe Creek Crater**, 148km south. The 50 000 year-old meteorite crater is the world's second largest, measuring 800m wide and 49m deep.
TOURIST INFO: Great Northern Hwy, Ph: (08) 9168 6262 (Open April–Sept)

■ **Harvey**   POP 2670
Map 375, D3
Bordered by the **Darling Range** and the Indian Ocean, Harvey, 139km south of Perth, is blessed with some of the state's most fertile farmland which supports dairy and beef cattle.
MAIN ATTRACTIONS: The Old Railway Station building houses **Harvey's Historical Society Museum** and on the South West Hwy is the **Harvey Internment Camp Memorial**, built by prisoners-of-war during the

1940s. Collect the key to the shrine from the information centre. Within the information centre, the **Moo Shoppe** is home to all things Friesian, promoting the region's dairying industry. Nearby is **Stirling's Cottage**, a replica of James Stirling's hunting lodge— Capt Stirling selected the town site for settlement in 1829. The cottage also has commentary on **May Gibbs**, author of the children's classic, *Snugglepot and Cuddlepie*, who lived in Harvey briefly during her childhood.
NEARBY ATTRACTIONS: The region's picturesque irrigation dams are also recreation and picnic stops, including **Harvey Dam**, 3km east, **Stirling Dam**, 17km east, and **Five Mile Bridge**, 12km east on the **Harvey River**. **Logue Brook Dam**, 15km east, offers opportunities for swimming, waterskiing and good trout fishing.
TOURIST INFO: South Western Hwy, Ph: (08) 9729 1122

■ **Hyden**   POP 157
Map 405, F2
A small wheat belt township, 344km east of Perth, Hyden's most distinctive and most photographed nearby attraction is the geologically stunning **Wave Rock**.
NEARBY ATTRACTIONS: Situated 4km east of the township is a 15m-high granite outcrop curling into a surf-like wave formation. Dated at 2700 million years old, the effects of weathering have fashioned Wave Rock's unique shape and natural chemical reactions with rainwater runoff have striped the granite red and grey. Other rock formations in the vicinity are the **Breakers**, **Hippo's Yawn**, **The Falls** and **The Humps**. At the information centre is **Lace Place**, reputedly showcasing the largest lace collection in the Southern Hemisphere. The **Salt lakes**, 1km east of the centre, are popular for picnics and swimming.

Mulka's Cave, 18km to the north, contains Aboriginal rock paintings.
TOURIST INFO: Wave Rock Visitors Centre, 4km east on Wave Rock Rd, Ph: (08) 9880 5182

■ **Jurien**   POP 650
Map 402, A3
Lobster fishing, safe beaches, boating, and access to the spectacular **Pinnacles** and regional national parks are some of the main attractions of this fishing town situated beside the sheltered waters of Jurien Bay, 266km north of Perth.
MAIN ATTRACTIONS: Jurien is a haven for water-based activities such as boating, swimming and fishing. Seasonal tours are offered through the **lobster-processing factory** on Roberts Rd.
NEARBY ATTRACTIONS: **Lions Lookout**, 4km from town, has sweeping views of the bay. Bountiful wildflowers bloom at **Cockleshell Gully**, 31km north, a reserve popular with bushwalkers and photographers. **Lesueur NP**, 23km NE, has more than 900 species of flora and is one of the most important flora reserves in the state. It also has a lookout with amazing views. **Stockyard Gully NP**, 50km north, is 4WD accessible only, and has a 300m ancient underground tunnel walk, requiring torches. Tours are available. The coastal **Nambung NP**, 40km south, contains the remarkable limestone pillars, **The Pinnacles**. Dated at 30 000 years old, the beautifully weathered calcified spires vary from 1 to 4m in height and cover approximately 400ha of variably coloured sands in an area known as the **Pinnacle Desert**. Driving conditions should be confirmed and organised tours operate daily. West of the Brand Hwy, **Badgingarra NP** has a worthwhile 2km walk through heathlands.
TOURIST INFO: 110 Bashford St, Ph: (08) 9652 1444

The ornate York Hotel, Kalgoorlie

■ Kalbarri POP 1854

Map 400, B5

On the southern bank of the **Murchison River** estuary, almost surrounded by national park, the coastal town of Kalbarri, 591km north of Perth, is a popular holiday destination in a region famous for its fishing, wildly beautiful scenery and Mediterranean climate.

MAIN ATTRACTIONS: Leisure activities range from adventurous abseiling, horse and camel riding, and canoe safaris, to scenic flights, dolphin-watching cruises, and boat rides on the Murchison River. Whale-watching trips run July–Nov. **Black Rock Café and Museum** on Grey St has a small collection featuring dolls, shells and gemstones. Pelicans are handfed daily on the river foreshore.

NEARBY ATTRACTIONS: A highly recommended surfing beach is **Jakes Corner**, 3.5km south. Close by is **Red Bluff** for swimming and climbing. **Rainbow Jungle** is an Australian parrot breeding centre and rainforest bird park. In 1629, 2 mutinous seamen from the *Batavia* were banished to the shore, making it the first European settlement in the country and a unwitting prelude

to later events—a cairn at **Wittecarra Creek** marks the site. The 1860km² **Kalbarri NP** contains intricately-carved sandstone river gorges, rugged coastal cliffs and more than 850 recorded species of wildflower. Highlights are **The Loop Gorge** and **Z Bend Gorge**, 30km NE, and views from **Hawks Head** and **Ross Graham Lookouts**, 39km east. The park has both short and strenuous walking trails.

TOURIST INFO: Grey St, Ph: (08) 9937 1104

■ Kalgoorlie-Boulder POP 31 000

Map 403, K4

Irish prospector **Paddy Hannan's** lucky strike in 1893 started the last great goldrush in Australia's history, leading to the establishment of the twin towns of Kalgoorlie and Boulder, 597km east of Perth. **Kalgoorlie-Boulder's Golden Mile**, believed to be the world's richest square mile of gold-bearing ore, still yields gold.

MAIN ATTRACTIONS: **Hannans North Tourist Mine** is a fascinating historic mining site that operates surface and underground tours revealing miners' methods and machinery. It forms part of the

Australian Prospectors and Miners Hall of Fame that houses 5 interactive galleries. Views of a massive modern operation can be seen from **Super Pit Lookout** off Eastern Bypass Rd. A 1hr ride on the 'Rattler' on the **Golden Mile Loopline Railway**, with commentary, travels along a line that in the 1890s was reputed to be the busiest and best. Comprehensive coverage can be found at the **Western Australia Museum Kalgoorlie-Boulder** with its underground gold vault and lift-ride to views from the mine headframe. A replica statue of miner Paddy Hannan, situated outside the town hall, provides a novel photo opportunity (the original is inside). On Burt St the **Goldfields War Museum** features armoured vehicles and war memorabilia. **Heritage Walks** inform visitors about mining-town architecture. Geological specimens of all kinds can be found in the **School of Mines Mineral Museum** on Cassidy St. Nearby, the **Goldfields Art Centre** holds regular exhibitions. The **Mount Charlotte Reservoir** remains as a tribute to engineer C Y O'Connor's ingenious feat and world first—in 1903 he constructed a 563km pipeline to carry water from Perth to the goldfields. The lookout here offers excellent sunset views. **Hammond Park** on Lyall St is a wildlife reserve with a mini-Bavarian castle. **Kalgoorlie Arboretum** has over 100 eucalypt species and **Karlkurla Bushland Park** has walking paths and a lookout. The history of Kalgoorlie's notorious red light district—**Hay St**—is recounted at the **Bordello Brothel Museum**.

NEARBY ATTRACTIONS: Fortunes rest on the outcome of a penny toss at the **Bush 2-up School** (7km north on the Leonora Rd), the town's only legal gambling den. Organised **Goldfields Tours** take in Kalgoorlie, Coolgardie, nature reserves and

ghost towns. Scenic flights, prospecting, Aboriginal culture and bush tucker tours as well as seasonal wildflower trips are available. Tours of the working gold mine, **Kanowna Belle Gold Mine**, are also available. **Kurrawang Emu Farm**, 18km west, offers guided tours.
TOURIST INFO: 250 Hannan St, Kalgoorlie, Ph: (08) 9021 1966

■ Kambalda   POP 3598
Map 403, K4
Kambalda is a mining town on the shores of the giant saltpan, **Lake Lefroy**, 58km south of Kalgoorlie. Originally born out of an 1887 gold find, the town dwindled in 1907 when the strike seemed exhausted but was resurrected by WMC (Western Mining Corporation) when nickel was discovered in 1966, and gold deposits have more recently been uncovered.
MAIN ATTRACTIONS: Though known as Lake Lefroy, this 510km^2 saltpan rarely contains water, despite deceptive mirages. Views of the lake are provided from **Red Hill Lookout**, off Gordon Adams Rd. WMC mining structures are visible from **John Hill viewpoint**, off Serpentine Rd. Places to picnic are at **Kambalda Memorial Garden** and at the **Lions Park** and playground, both on Barnes Dr.
TOURIST INFO: Cnr Emu Rocks and Marianthus rds, Kambalda West, Ph: (08) 9027 0192

■ Karratha   POP 10 469
Map 398, B6
Established in the late 1960s to service the needs of iron ore, salt and natural gas industry projects, Karratha derives its name from an Aboriginal word meaning 'good country'. An ideal base for exploring the **Pilbara**, Karratha is an administrative centre and boasts 'city style' shopping and services.
NEARBY ATTRACTIONS: The picturesque clear-water **Miaree Pool**, 30km

south, is surrounded by shady trees—a perfect place to picnic and swim. North-west of Karratha, the **Burrup Peninsula** has over 10 000 Aboriginal art sites best viewed on a self-drive or organised tour. Used extensively by early European settlers as a pastoral station, an oasis at the centre of **Millstream-Chichester NP**, 124km south, has unique **Pilbara Palms** and permanent freshwater pools. The state's second largest park, **Karijini NP** has spectacular gorges, waterfalls, rockpools, graded walking trails and ancient rock formations. Just 20km from Karratha, **Dampier** offers access to the 42 islands of the **Dampier Archipelago**.
TOURIST INFO: Lot 4548 Karratha Rd, Ph: (08) 9144 4600

■ Katanning   POP 4127
Map 404, E3
A thriving agricultural town 295km SE of Perth, Katanning has the second largest saleyards in Australia (Wagga Wagga in New South Wales has the largest), and is renowned for producing fine merino sheep.
MAIN ATTRACTIONS: A **Heritage Trail** pamphlet highlights some of the town's notable buildings including the Piesse family home **Kobeelya** (1902); the **Winery Ruins**, on Warren Rd, with its historic vats and equipment; and the National Trust-restored roller flour mill (1891), which now incorporates the **Mill Museum** displaying roller flour-milling machinery. A **Historical Museum** of local memorabilia is housed in the first government school and an **Art Gallery** and **Library** are situated next to the Shire Offices. Another notable landmark is the **Islamic Mosque**. **All Ages Playground** has huge slides and operates a miniature steam train every second and fourth Sunday (from 1pm, weather permitting). Katanning also boasts one of Western Australia's largest

recreation and leisure centres. **Metro Meat Works** offers tours by appointment, and the **Police Pools Memorial** is a fine place to picnic.
NEARBY ATTRACTIONS: Local lakes provide venues for watersports, including waterskiing and boating. The **Kattaning-Piesse Heritage Trail** is a 20km self-guided driving tour. **Stirling Range NP**, 80km south, is notable for a 65km-long chain of peaks, excellent bushwalking trails and prolific wildflowers in season.
TOURIST INFO: Cnr Austral Tce and Clive St, Ph: (08) 9821 2634

■ Kellerberrin   POP 855
Map 402, E5
Wheat and sheep farming are the mainstays of this small country township. Kellerberrin is located along the Great Eastern Hwy 203km from Perth.
MAIN ATTRACTIONS: The town's **International Art Space Kellerberrin Australia (IASKA)** features international and national contemporary artists on 3-month residencies—the nation's only gallery of its kind. A **Folk Museum** of local memorabilia is situated in the old Agricultural Hall and a 2hr **Heritage Trail** takes in notable sites, including **Kellerberrin Hill Lookout**.

Sheep grazing near the Stirling Range, south of Katanning

Lake Argyle, part of the Ord River Scheme near Kununurra

Farming implements and machinery displayed around **Pioneer Park** provide an interesting backdrop for picnics. **Centenary Park** in the centre of town has shaded playground equipment, BBQs, in-line skate and BMX tracks, a heritage walkway and maze.
NEARBY ATTRACTIONS: Constructed from local field stone in 1871, **Milligan Homestead**, located 10km north on Trayning Rd, is an example of building methods of the period (private property). A massive granite outcrop, **Kokerbin Rock**, 30km south, is reputed to be Australia's third largest monolith and has a vehicle access road to the top of the rock. Great views are also assured from **Mount Stirling** and **Mount Caroline**, 22km south. Kellerberrin's countryside is covered in wildflowers during spring, but 2 particular places to enjoy the flora are **Durakoppin Wildlife Sanctuary**, 27km north, and **Charles Gardner NP**, 35km SW.
TOURIST INFO: 110 Massingham St, Ph: (08) 9045 4006

Kojonup   POP 1075
Map 404, D3
Kojonup, 256km SE of Perth, was originally established in 1837 as a military post of Pensioner Guards with responsibility for protecting travellers. Today, it is the centre of a farming and agricultural district.
MAIN ATTRACTIONS: **The Kojonup Spring and Picnic Area** is the site of a natural spring to which the original surveyor Alfred Hillman was directed to by local Aborigines. Other historic landmarks are **Elverds Cottage** (1851) and the **Barracks** (1845). The **Kodja Place Interpretative Centre** features an **Australian Rose Maze** as its centre-piece. Additional local attractions include a working farm and harness display.
NEARBY ATTRACTIONS: Wildflowers are prolific in the region, including more than 60 orchid species. Established sites for enjoying the flora and fauna include the **Australian Bush Heritage Block** on Mission Rd, **Cherry Tree Pool**, **Myrtle Benn Flora and Fauna Sanctuary** on Tunney Rd, and **Farrar Reserve**, 7km west on Blackwood Rd. **Proandra Flower Farm**, 20km north, has fresh and dried proteas and offers tours of its operations.
TOURIST INFO: Albany Hwy, Ph: (08) 9831 1686

Kununurra   POP 4962
Map 399, K2
Two key local ventures contributing to the character of Kununurra, 3214km north of Perth, are the **Argyle Diamond Mine** and the **Ord River Scheme**, a massive irrigation project harnessing the rivers of the **Kimberley**. With good accessibility to the striped formations of the Bungle Bungles in **Purnululu NP**, the township also serves as a base for exploring the region's many other attractions.
MAIN ATTRACTIONS: Visitors can learn about diamonds from local retailers selling a range of Argyle Diamonds, including white, champagne, cognac and rare, and expensive, pink varieties. Authentic Kimberley art can be purchased at **Waringarri Aboriginal Arts Centre** or **Red Rock Art**. Kununurra's highest point, **Kellys Knob Lookout**, offers impressive views of the **Ord Valley** and **Lake Kununurra**, an artificial lake convenient for swimming, sailing, rowing, waterskiing and birdwatching. **Mirima (Hidden Valley) NP** contains ancient sandstone formations known as the 'Mini Bungles'; Aboriginal rock paintings, engravings and artefacts; and a natural amphitheatre once used for corroborees. Local tours include canoe trips and cruises on the **Ord River**, barramundi-fishing trips, ecotours, and flights over **Purnululu NP**.
NEARBY ATTRACTIONS: Argyle Diamond Mine, 250km south, is the world's largest diamond mine. Access is by organised tours only. A scenic 12km drive travels north to **Ivanhoe Crossing**—a local fishing hole—and returns via the natural sandstone **City of Ruins** on Weaber Plains Rd. Another rock formation **Sleeping Buddha (Elephant Rock)** is 10km south of town. Situated 70km from town on the Wyndham Rd is a deep swimming hole known as **The Grotto**. Massive **Lake Argyle**, 72km south, is the nation's second largest storage reservoir, at 1000km^2 it holds 9 times the volume of water in Sydney Harbour and was formed by the damming of the Ord River. **Argyle Homestead**, on the shore, contains a pioneer museum and is the departure point for lake cruises. The turn-off to **Gibb River Rd**, a popular 4WD outback exploration route, is 60kms from Kununurra. The Victoria Hwy to the east leads to Katherine and the attractions of the Northern Territory.
TOURIST INFO: Coolibah Dr, Ph: (08) 9168 1177

Western Australia

Laverton POP 676

Map 407, A2

Located at the western end of the **Great Victoria Desert** and the Great Central Hwy, 957km NE of Perth, Laverton's present gold-mining operations began with a lucky find back in 1896. Nickel was discovered in the late 1960s and is presently mined south-west of the town at **Anaconda Murrin Murrin Nickel Operations**. The town has a typical desert climate with minimal rainfall.

MAIN ATTRACTIONS: A 20m climb up **Billy Goat Hill** to the scenic lookout provides panoramic views of the surrounding district. Situated in the town's centre, the **Old Gaol and Police Station** (1900) serves as the tourist information centre and Telecentre.

NEARBY ATTRACTIONS: Wildflowers are a highlight of the area, particularly in spring, though the Sturt desert pea flourishes year round. **Windarra Heritage Trail**, 28km NW, has an informative walking tour of local nickel mining history and offers excellent views from **Mount Windarra Lookout**. Laverton is also the starting point for travelling the **Outback Highway** through the Great Victoria Desert to Uluru and Alice Springs. No desert driving should be undertaken without thorough and informed preparation. Escorted Great Victoria Desert 4WD tours are available.

TOURIST INFO: Shop 4, Laver Pl, Ph: (08) 9031 1750

Leonora POP 1170

Map 403, K1

Railhead for the gold, copper and nickel mines in **Laverton** and **Leinster**; Leonora is an administrative centre 237km north of Kalgoorlie servicing the surrounding district's mining operations and sheep properties. The town has retained a 19th-century appearance and is close to some interesting historical sites.

MAIN ATTRACTIONS: Views of the town are available from **Mount Leonora**, named after the niece of explorer John Forrest during his search for the Leichhardt expedition.

NEARBY ATTRACTIONS: Adjoining Leonora is the ghost town of **Gwalia**, former home of the Sons of Gwalia Goldmine, the state's second largest gold-mining operation after Kalgoorlie. Closed in 1963, the mine was managed in the late 1890s by Herbert Hoover, who later became President of the United States of America. **The Mine Office** (1898) houses an interesting local museum. There is also a 1km **Historic Gwalia Heritage Trail**—a pamphlet details sites of interest.

TOURIST INFO: 16 Tower St, Ph: (08) 9037 6044

Mandurah POP 37 250

Map 387, C1

The **Indian Ocean** and beautiful beaches have long lured holiday-makers to Mandurah, 74km south of Perth, where the **Murray**, **Harvey** and **Serpentine rivers** flow into the **Peel Inlet** and the **Harvey Estuary**. Once an important trading site for indigenous groups, 'Mandurah' is derived from an Aboriginal word '*mandjar*' meaning 'meeting place'.

MAIN ATTRACTIONS: Water-based attractions and activities include estuary cruises (dolphins are regularly sighted), boating, swimming, waterskiing, jetskiing and fishing. A **Historic Heritage Trail** highlights significant buildings including the restored **Hall's Cottage** (1832) and **Christ Church** (1870), with its graveyard featuring pioneers' headstones. An old School (1898) houses the **Community Museum**. More active endeavours can be enjoyed on the western foreshore at **King Carnival Amusement Park**.

NEARBY ATTRACTIONS: Popular with families, **Linga Longa Park** and **Marapana Wildlife World** are at **Karnup**, 12km north. Nearby, on Pinjarra Rd, are the **Murray Mandurah Weekend Markets**. An impressive collection of native parrots can be seen at **Bellawood Parrot Park**, located at **Ravenswood Sanctuary**, 16km east on the banks of the Murray River, incorporating Redcliffe Barn, an animal enclosure, suspended bridge, plus plentiful lakes and picnic spots. **Cooper's Mill**, south-east at **Yunderup**, was the first flour mill in the region and one of only 2 wind-driven mills in Western Australia. Access is only by boat; guided tours are available. For travellers on the winery trail, **Cape Bouvard Wineries** can be found 22km south. **Yalgorup NP**, 15km south, has bushwalking tracks through tuart trees.

TOURIST INFO: Mandurah Tce, Ph: (08) 9550 3993

State Hotel, previous HQ for the Sons of Gwalia Goldmine in the ghost town of Gwalia, near Leonora

PEEL REGION

Just an hour's drive south of Perth, the Peel Region encompasses 5500km² of diverse landscapes, ranging from rolling farm pastures and striking jarrah forests in the east to the calm waters of **Peel Inlet** and **Harvey Estuary** in the west and the white sandy beaches that fringe the **Indian Ocean**. With a combination of popular attractions and its close proximity to Perth, this is one of Western Australia's premier tourist destinations.

The protected inlet waters provide an aquatic playground that offers excellent opportunities for sailing, cruising, canoeing, swimming, fishing and crabbing. The area is famous for blue-swimmer crabs that can be easily caught by scoop or drop net. Locals rejoice when the 'crab run' begins, as boat owners armed with drop nets arrive to lure away the bountiful crabs.

Golf is also a popular pastime: the region boasts 3 world-renowned golf courses—designed by Ian Baker-Finch, Graham Marsh and Robert Trent Jones Jnr, respectively—and the Peel Region has often been labelled the Golf Coast. Other attractions include wineries; white-water rafting on the **Murray River**; and **Yalgorup NP**, containing several lakes—havens for birdlife.

Fishing at Mandurah Beach

main attractions

- ◈ Dwellingup
- ◈ Forest and river trails
- ◈ Harvey Estuary
- ◈ Hotham Valley Tourist Railway
- ◈ Jarrah forest wildflowers
- ◈ Peel Inlet
- ◈ Peel wineries
- ◈ Pinjarra Heritage Trail

 Tourist information

Mandurah Visitor Centre
75 Mandurah Tce,
Mandurah WA 6210
Ph: (08) 9550 3993
www.peeltour.net.au

■ Manjimup   POP 4480
Map 404, C4
Wooden arches welcome visitors to Manjimup, 129km SE of Bunbury, and gateway to the tall-timber country of the jarrah and karri forests of the **South West region** of Western Australia. Founded in 1910 to exploit the forest resources, this is both a timber town and thriving agricultural centre.
MAIN ATTRACTIONS: The town's principal attraction, **Manjimup Timber Park** complex is a theme park museum with highlights such as **Bunnings Age of Steam** display, an historical reconstructed hamlet, the state's only **Timber Museum** and a working blacksmith. The town's natural assets can also be enjoyed by bushwalking, fishing, or on a forest or ecology tour.

NEARBY ATTRACTIONS: A well-felled karri tree was used to construct **One Tree Bridge** (1904), found in a picturesque spot 22km west. Close by are the **Four Aces**, a stand of towering karri trees averaging 73m, believed to be about 400 years old. **King Jarrah**, 4km east, is an equally well-aged specimen. Enthusiasts can climb **Diamond Tree Fire Lookout**, 9km south, a 52m-high karri tree utilised for fire spotting from 1941 to 1974; there is a nature trail close by. **Fontys Pool**, 10km south, is a popular swimming hole. Adjacent is **Fontaninis Nut Farm** growing chestnuts, walnuts and hazelnuts (March–May). Just 7km SW, **Deanmill** is a working jarrah saw mill offering free tours 3 times a week. **Diamond Woodchip Mill**, 12km south, also has guided tours

of its complex. A scenic heritage trail takes a 19km loop drive through **Dingup**, taking in its historic church (1896) and pioneer cemetery. **Perep Forest Ecology Centre**, 50km east, offers nocturnal spotlight forest tours.
TOURIST INFO: Cnr Rose and Edward sts, Ph: (08) 9771 1831

■ Margaret River   POP 6000
Map 371, B3
The centre of Western Australia's renowned wine-growing region, Margaret River is renowned for its wines, surfing beaches, stunning coastal scenery and awesome cave systems. Built on the banks of the **Margaret River**, it also provides an ideal base for exploring the South West peninsula from **Cape Naturaliste** to **Cape Leeuwin**.

Western Australia

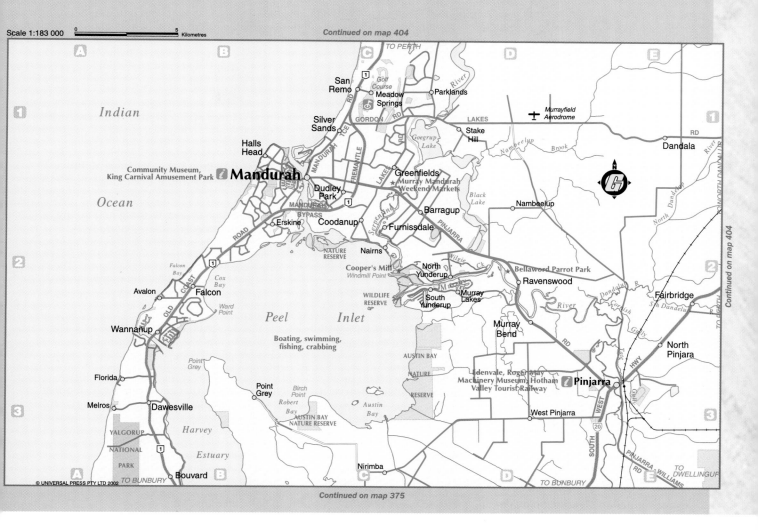

Continued on map 404
TO PERTH

Scale 1:183 000

Indian

Ocean

Mandurah

Community Museum,
King Carnival Amusement Park

Halls
Head

San
Remo

Golf
Course

Meadow
Springs

GORDON

Silver
Sands

Dudley
Park

Erskine

MANDURAH
BYPASS

Coodanup

Cooper's Mill
Windmill Point

Falcon
Bay

Cox
Bay

Avalon

Falcon

Ward
Point

Wannanup

Florida

Melros

Dawesville

YALGORUP

NATIONAL

PARK

Bouvard

Point
Grey

Point
Grey

Birch
Point

Robert
Bay

Austin Bay
NATURE RESERVE

Austin
Bay

Harvey

Estuary

Peel   Inlet

Boating, swimming,
fishing, crabbing

NATURE
RESERVE

Nairns

WILDLIFE
RESERVE

AUSTIN BAY

NATURE

RESERVE

Nirimba

Parklands

Stake
Hill

Goegrup
Lake

Greenfields
Murray Mandurah
Weekend Markets

Barragup

Furnissdale

North
Yunderup

South
Yunderup

Black
Lake

Wilgie   Ck.

Bellswood Parrot Park

Murray
Lakes

Ravenswood

Murray
Bend

Edenvale, Rogermay
Machinery Museum, Hotham
Valley Tourist Railway

West Pinjarra

PINJARRA

Murrayfield
Aerodrome

LAKES

Nambeelup   Brook

Nambeelup

River

Dandala

North
Dandalup

RD

Fairbridge

North
Pinjara

Pinjarra

SOUTH

WEST

PINJARRA-WILLIAMS
RD

TO
DWELLINGUP

TO BUNBURY

© UNIVERSAL PRESS PTY LTD 2002   TO BUNBURY

Continued on map 404
Continued on map 375

MAIN ATTRACTIONS: Rotary Park and Historical Settlement is a pleasant riverside park for picnics and the starting point for **Heritage Walks**. An **Old Settlement Historical Museum** is on Bussell Hwy. Galleries featuring local wares include **Margaret River Gallery**, **Kookaburra Crafts**, **Melting Pot Glass Studio** and **Margaret River Pottery**. A free surfing guide brochure outlines the best beaches and general conditions. Additional active options include surfing lessons, canoeing, forest secrets tours, caving trips, abseiling, and winery tours.

NEARBY ATTRACTIONS: Brochures trace the trail to the region's wineries, which are concentrated in **Cowaramup**, 10km NE, and **Willyabrup**, 20km north. Other

regional produce includes cheese outlets along the Bussell Hwy and at the **Cheese Factory**, 4km north. National Trust-administered **Ellensbrook Homestead** (1853), pioneer home of the Bussell family, is 15km NW. Birds of prey can be seen at **Eagles Heritage**, 5km south. Nearby is the **Bellview Shell Museum**. **Marron Farm**, 9km SE, has trout fishing and delicacies made from marron while, 15km SE, the **Berry Farm and Winery** has fresh seasonal berries and produce. **Ten Mile Brooks Dam**, south-east, is popular for bushwalking. Four of the region's more than 150 known caves are open to the public by guided tour: **Mammoth Cave**, 21km SW, has fossilised remains; **Lake Cave** features an underground stream and interactive caving

Ellensbrook Homestead, near Margaret River

centre 'CaveWorks'; **Jewel Cave** has a 5m straw stalactite; and **Ngilgi Cave** at Yallingup has shawl limestone formations. Adventure caving tours are taken through **Moondyne Cave**.

TOURIST INFO: Cnr Tunbridge Rd and Bussell Hwy, Ph: (08) 9757 2911

■ Meekatharra   POP 1295
Map 400, E4

Servicing a widespread mining, sheep and cattle station community, Meekatharra, 768km NE of Perth, started as a gold town in the 1890s and later became the railhead for transporting overland cattle from the Northern Territory and East Kimberley until the railway ceased operation in 1978.

MAIN ATTRACTIONS: One gold-era architectural remnant is the **Court House** (1912) on Darlot St. One of the **Flying Doctor Service** bases is open for inspection, as is the local **School of the Air** (only during school term).

NEARBY ATTRACTIONS: An interesting rock formation, **Peace Gorge (The Granites)** is found 5km west. **Bilyuin Pool**, 88km NW, becomes a swimming hole when filled in late winter and spring and wildflowers bloom prolifically in season. **Mount Gould's** restored historic **police station** is 156km west.

TOURIST INFO: Shire Offices, Main St, Ph: (08) 9981 1101

■ Merredin   POP 3500
Map 403, F5

Merredin, 259km east of Perth, is the commercial centre for this region which grows 40% of Western Australia's wheat. It is a major station along the Kalgoorlie to Perth railway route.

MAIN ATTRACTIONS: As the second line of defence in the event of a WWII westerly invasion, Merredin's **Military Museum** recounts an interesting era. It is also the starting point for the self-guided **Merredin**

Peak Heritage Trail, which takes in such notable sites as **Cummins Theatre** (1926) and the **Old Town Hall** (1913). Highlights among the rail memorabilia featured at the **Old Railway Station Museum** include a G117 steam engine built around 1897. The wheat storage depot in Gamenya Ave is proudly the Southern Hemisphere's largest horizontal wheat silo with a storage capacity of 220 000 tonnes. Recent additions to the depot facility have earned it fame as Australia's largest inland port.

NEARBY ATTRACTIONS: Noted goldfields engineer C Y O'Connor designed the **No. 4 Pumping Station**, 3km west. **Hunts Dam**, 5km north, is popular for bushwalking and picnics while spring wildflowers abound at **Totadgin Dam Reserve**, 16km SW. Interesting rock formations in the area include **Kangaroo Rock**, **Burracoppin Rock** and **Sandford Rocks**. Further afield, 40km NW is **Mangowine Homestead**, a restored National Trust property.

TOURIST INFO: Barrack St, Ph: (08) 9041 1666

■ Moora   POP 1644
Map 402, C3

Situated on the **Moora River**, 172km north of Perth, Moora is the commercial centre for surrounding farming districts and the most sizeable town between Perth and Geraldton.

MAIN ATTRACTIONS: Local talent and handiwork can be seen in Padbury St at the **Moora Tin Shed Pottery**, at **Yuat Artifacts**, which displays and sells locally made Aboriginal arts and crafts, and at the **Moora Fine Arts Gallery** situated in Gardiner St. **Apex Park** located beside the river is a grassy park set among salmon gums and **Federation Park** features a memorial to the Australian draught horse.

NEARBY ATTRACTIONS: Brochures outline an 80km **Heritage Trail**, which

includes **Berkshire Valley Homestead** (1847) a restored flour mill complex with a folk museum located 19km east. **Watheroo NP**, 50km north, protects rare and common flora and some unusual geological features found at **Jingemia Cave**. **Western Wildflower Farm** at **Coomberdale**, 16km north, provides insight into export flower farming and drying. **New Norcia**, 55km SE, is an extraordinary monastic village, established as a mission in 1846 by Spanish Benedictine monks and operated today by the same order. The National Trust has classified 27 of the Spanish-style buildings, 2 of which house a museum and art gallery. A self-guided walk and daily tours are available. A stay at the **Monastic Guesthouse**, which offers a bed, meals and prayers, adds much to the experience.

TOURIST INFO: 34 Padbury St, Ph: (08) 9651 1401

■ Mount Barker   POP 1670
Map 369, C2

Since vines were planted in the late 1960s Mount Barker, 50km NW of Albany, has enjoyed a growing

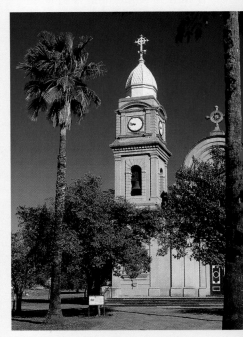

The Spanish-style Abbey Church at New Norcia, south-east of Moora

Western Australia

reputation as a wine-producing region. Central to **Porongurup** and **Stirling Range national parks**, the town is also known for its agriculture and commercial wildflower production.

MAIN ATTRACTIONS: A **Police Station Museum** is housed in the convict-built station and gaol (1868). The **Old Station House Craft Shop** is a gallery featuring quality arts and crafts and the **Shire Art Gallery** on Lowood Rd exhibits works by local artists. Information on hiking trails, the **Great Southern Wineries** and tours of a banksia farm are available from the tourist bureau.

NEARBY ATTRACTIONS: **Mount Barker Lookout**, 5km SW, has sweeping views of the ranges. **Werburghs Way Tourist Drive** takes in **St Werburghs Chapel** (1872), 12km SW. Historic **Kendenup**, 16km NE, is the site where gold was first found in Western Australia. **Porongurup NP**, 24km east, has bushwalking trails ranging in duration from 10min to 3hrs through dramatic ranges, karri tree stands, and seas of seasonal wildflowers. The highest peak in Stirling Range NP, 80km NE, is **Bluff Knoll** (1073m). Qualified operators run rockclimbing and abseiling trips to the national park.
TOURIST INFO: Unit 6, Lot 622 Albany Hwy, Ph: (08) 9851 1163

■ Mount Magnet   POP 750
Map 400, E5
Situated in pastoral country along the route to Port Hedland, 562km north of Perth, Mount Magnet began as a gold town. Today more modern operations are undertaken at **Hill 50 Mine**.
MAIN ATTRACTIONS: A **Heritage Walk** provides some historical background, supplemented by the **Pastoral Museum** in Hepburn St that covers the local heritage, including gold mining and pioneering endeavours.

NEARBY ATTRACTIONS: A map outlines the route for a 37km **Tourist Drive** providing directions to dramatic views of the open-cut mines from **Warramboo Hill**, to gold ghost towns, such as **Lennonville**, 11km north, and to **The Granites**, an Aboriginal art site and picnic stop, 7km north. Wildflowers are a highlight in the spring. Further afield near **Sandstone**, 166km east, is a natural basalt archway, **London Bridge**, and a cave that was converted into a now historic brewery. At **Yalgoo**, 127km west, is the **Dominican Chapel of St Hyacinth**, designed by the famous Monsignor John Hawes.
TOURIST INFO: Hepburn St, Ph: (08) 9963 4172

■ Narrogin   POP 4650
Map 404, D2
In the heart of Western Australia's wheat belt, 192km SE of Perth, Narrogin is a major railway junction and a thriving service centre for the surrounding farmlands.
MAIN ATTRACTIONS: **The Court House Museum** (1894) focuses on the industry and daily life of early settlers, while the **Restoration Group Museum** houses locally restored cars and machines. Other notable buildings are listed in the 14km **Township Heritage Trail** leaflet. Quality local art and visiting exhibitions are displayed at the **Town Hall Art Gallery** on Federal St. Narrogin's various parks for picnics or rest stops include **Apex** and **Memorial parks**, but worth a look are **Gnarojin Park** with its commemorative tiles and Aboriginal art, and **Foxes Lair**, a 45ha bushland reserve off Williams Rd. For a panoramic view of Narrogin and district go to **Lions Lookout** in Kipling St.
NEARBY ATTRACTIONS: A **District Heritage Trail** traces a 117km drive highlighting historic farms. Bushwalking and birdwatching are popular at **Dryandra Forest Reserve**,

Weano Gorge in the iron-rich Hamersley Ranges, Karijini NP, west of Newman

26km north, also habitat for Western Australia's rare fauna emblem, the numbat. Unusual rock formations featuring wildflowers in spring are **Yilliminning Rock** and **Birdwhistle Rock**, 11km east. **Albert Facey Homestead**, 39km east, is a significant site in the life of Albert Facey, author of the well-known autobiography, *A Fortunate Life*. An 86km self-drive **Albert Facey Heritage Trail** pamphlet is also available.
TOURIST INFO: 23 Egerton St, Ph: (08) 9881 2064

■ Newman   POP 4980
Map 401, F2
Newman, 450km south of Port Hedland, is a **Pilbara** iron-ore mining town originally built by Mount Newman Mining Company in the 1960s as a base for its employees.
MAIN ATTRACTIONS: Located at the information centre is the **BHP Iron Ore Silver Jubilee Museum and Gallery**, recounting local mining history through memorabilia and displays. The centre is also the departure point for tours through **Mount Whaleback Mine**, the world's largest open-cut iron-ore

mine, and the starting place for a 30min walk to **Radio Hill Lookout** with views of the town and **Opthalmia Ranges**.

NEARBY ATTRACTIONS: When water levels are adequate, **Opthalmia Dam**, 19km south, provides an oasis for swimming, sail boating and picnics. A 4WD only **Waterhole Circuit Trail** highlights local waterholes and Aboriginal art sites. Rugged **Karijini NP (Hamersley Range)**, 2hrs NW, features walks to spectacular gorges and contains Western Australia's highest peak, **Mount Meharry**. Organised ecotours of the Pilbara region can be booked in Newman.

TOURIST INFO: Cnr Newman Dr and Fortescue Ave, Ph: (08) 9175 2888

■ Norseman   POP 1546
Map 403, K6

Gateway for travellers crossing the **Nullarbor** via the Eyre Hwy, Norseman, 190km south of Kalgoorlie, has been a gold-mining town since 1894.

Horse in a field of wildflowers near Northam

MAIN ATTRACTIONS: The goldrush was started by a horse—so the mythology goes. And 'Norseman', the horse reputed to have turned up gold while pawing with its hoof at the dirt, is commemorated with a statue in Roberts St. A **Historical Collection** of local mining and other memorabilia is on Battery Rd and the 33km **Norseman's Heritage Trail** follows a route once travelled by the Cobb & Co Coachline. A toy museum, **Dollykissangel**, is on Roberts St. Gem fossicking permits are available from the tourist information centre.

NEARBY ATTRACTIONS: Vantage points for viewing the town, salt lakes and massive mine tailings dumps include **Beacon Hill Lookout**, 2km east, and **Mount Jimberlana**, 5km east. A pleasant picnic area, the **Dundas Rocks**, 22km south, have been dated at more than 2 million years old. **Buldania Rocks**, 28km east, is also a picturesque picnic spot renowned for its seasonal wildflowers. **Peak Charles NP**, 90km south (including an unsealed 40km access road) has challenging walks and excellent views from the peak summit.

TOURIST INFO: 68 Roberts St, Ph: (08) 9039 1071

■ Northam   POP 7000
Map 402, D5

Gazetted as a town in 1836, picturesque Northam in the **Avon Valley** sits at the junction of the **Avon** and **Mortlock rivers**, servicing a rich agricultural region.

MAIN ATTRACTIONS: Heritage buildings covered in a **Town Walk** pamphlet reflect the town's early settlement, such as the **Town Hall** (1897), **Old Police Station** (1866), **Flour Mill** (1871), National Trust-classified **Sir James Mitchell House** (1905) and the restored **Shamrock Hotel** (1886). **The Avon Valley Arts Society Gallery** is also included on the route and early settlers' graves can be

found near the golf course. **Morby Cottage** (1836) functioned as the first church and school and is now a museum. **The Old Train Station Museum** is on Fitzgerald St. The very pretty Avon River, ideal for picnics, has one of Australia's longest suspension bridges and is home to Northam's famous white swans—descendants of a flock brought here from England by an early settler.

NEARBY ATTRACTIONS: Dramatic valley views can be seen hot-air ballooning, available April–Nov. **Avonlea Alpaca Tourist Farm** is 12km NW.

TOURIST INFO: 2 Grey St, Heaton Ave, Ph: (08) 9622 2100

■ Northampton   POP 832
Map 400, C6

Heritage-listed Northampton is 51km north of Geraldton in the **Nokanena Brook Valley**. The town's heyday came in the mid-1800s after the discovery of local copper and lead deposits; many historic buildings date from this era.

MAIN ATTRACTIONS: A former mine manager's residence, the construction of **Chiverton House**, now a museum of pioneer memorabilia, was completed by convicts in 1875. Other buildings of note are the **Old Convent, Church of Our Lady in Ara Coeli**, designed by Monsignor John Hawes, and **Gwalla St miners' cottages**. Early headstones can be perused at the **Old Cemetery and Pioneer Memorial** opposite the Gwalla Church ruins.

NEARBY ATTRACTIONS: A relic from the Lead Mining Company, **Warribanno Chimney** is a National Trust smelter relic, 65km NW. District labour shortages during 1853–56 were resolved by the establishment of a convict hiring station at **Lynton**, the remnants of which can be seen 47km NW near **Port Gregory**. Fishing and surfing are popular at **Horrocks Beach**, 20km west.

TOURIST INFO: Hampton Rd, Ph: (08) 9934 1488

Beedelup Falls in Beedelup NP, near Pemberton

■ Northcliffe   POP 225
Map 404, C5

Nestled near awe-inspiring karri forests in the south-west corner of Western Australia, Northcliffe lies 31km south of Pemberton and offers visitors sightseeing, as well as myriad leisure and recreational activities—bushwalking, climbing and fishing, photography, canoeing and swimming.

MAIN ATTRACTIONS: Located on Wheatley Coast Rd, **Northcliffe Pioneer Museum** recounts the town's history through photographs and memorabilia, while nearby **Forest Park** is home to the **Hollowbutt Karri Tree**, **Twin Karris**, the **Perfect Tree** and numerous walking trails. Mountain bike hire and horseriding operators offer active opportunities to enjoy the scenic terrain.

NEARBY ATTRACTIONS: **Mount Chudalup**, 15km south, is a massive granite outcrop with a walking trail to a lookout. Set in karri forest, 16km east of Boorara Rd is **Lane Poole Falls**, spectacular in winter and spring. **Windy Harbour**, 27km south, has a sheltered beach suitable for surfing, swimming, fishing, and snorkelling and

providing access to the cliffs of **D'Entrecasteaux NP**. **Salmon Beach** has spectacular views as well as salmon fishing from April to June. A 6km-long 2WD coastal drive travels the scenic route to **Point D'Entrecasteaux**, which features walking trails and lookouts. An excellent 48km **Great Forest Trees Drive** follows a gravel road taking in giant karri stands at **Snake Gully** and **Big Tree Grove**. Camping and bushwalking can be enjoyed at **Shannon NP**, 27km east.

TOURIST INFO: Wheatley Coast Rd, Ph: (08) 9776 7203

■ Onslow   POP 625
Map 400, C1

Originally settled in 1883 at the mouth of the **Ashburton River**, the town of Onslow moved to its present location in 1925 as a result of repeated cyclone damage and the subsequent silting of the river. Pearling, gold mining, agriculture and British nuclear testing (on Montebello Islands in the 1950s) dot its history, but today it primarily serves as a base-town for offshore gas and oil exploration.

MAIN ATTRACTIONS: The **Goods Shed Museum** in Second Ave is a repository for relics from the early days, while the **Karinjini Aboriginal Corporation** on Third Ave is an outlet for Aboriginal artefacts and artworks. A **Town Heritage Trail** brochure is available.

NEARBY ATTRACTIONS: The ruins of **Old Onslow**, 48km SW, and its history are described in a pamphlet. Fishing is excellent, particularly in winter, with **Beadon Creek Groyne** and the mouth of the Ashburton River recommended. About 20km offshore are the 10 **Mackerel Islands**, a resort attracting anglers to the plentifully stocked waters. Termite mounds can be seen 10km south on Onslow Access Rd.

TOURIST INFO: Second Ave (April–Oct), Ph: (08) 9184 6644

■ Pemberton   POP 1125
Map 404, C4

Pemberton is a forest timber town in southern Western Australia. It sits in a valley encircled by karri, jarrah and marri forests. Handcrafted timber products are a regional specialty.

MAIN ATTRACTIONS: The Karri Visitors Centre incorporates a **Pioneer Museum and Forest Discovery Centre**. The many craft outlets create and sell hardwood wares and the **Pemberton Sawmill** offers guided tours. **Pemberton Tramway** operates a 1907 replica tram daily from Pemberton Station through scenic tall-timber country. Two trails, called **Rainbow** and **Tramway**, follow the former log transport route and include stops at the **Big Brook Arboretum** and at **Big Brook Dam**, which is a favourite fishing, swimming, canoeing and sailboarding spot.

NEARBY ATTRACTIONS: Forest Discovery Tours, hiking, horseriding, fishing and 4WD trails provide interesting options for exploring. **Gloucester NP**, 1km south, encompasses the picturesque **Cascades**, bushwalking trails and fishing sites, and **Gloucester Tree**, which is the world's highest fire lookout stretching 61m with 153 rungs to climb (access off Brockman St). **Brockman Saw Pits**, 13km south, consists of 4 original sawpits (1865) reconstructed to display original timber sawing methods. Once a wheat field, **Founders Forest** of tall karri trees is an excellent example of regeneration 13km from town. **Warren NP**, 9km SW, has an 89m karri tree, walking trails and picnic facilities surrounded by virgin karri forest, while 18km west is **Beedelup NP**, with pretty **Beedelup Falls** and a 400-year-old 'walk-through' karri tree. Pamphlets provide details on local wineries.

TOURIST INFO: Brockman St, Ph: (08) 9776 1133

Coppins Gap, south-east of Port Hedland

■ Perenjori POP 250

Map 402, C2

Bordering the Murchison goldfields and Midwestern wheat farms and sheep-stations, Perenjori lies on the Wubin–Mullewa Hwy or **'Wildflower Way'**, 352km NE of Perth.

MAIN ATTRACTIONS: **Perenjori Museum** displaying pioneering memorabilia is located behind the tourist centre in Fowler St. On Carnamah Rd is the **Catholic Church of St Joseph**, another architectural creation of Monsignor John Hawes.

NEARBY ATTRACTIONS: Spectacular spring **Wildflower Trails** are a must July–Oct. Situated 47km east is **Camel Soak**, a waterhole utilised originally by Aboriginal peoples and later by travelling camel trains. The 180km **Perenjori–Rothsay Heritage Trail** traces the area's gold-mining history visiting old mining areas and gold ghost towns. Gold and gemstone fossickers are often well rewarded for their efforts. Waterbirds can be seen at **Mongers Lake**, a salt lake 50km NE.

TOURIST INFO: Fowler St (July–Oct),
Ph: (08) 9973 1105

■ Pinjarra POP 1942

Map 387, E3

One of the oldest towns in Western Australia, picturesque Pinjarra is located on the **Murray River**, 84km south of Perth in a region supported by farming, bauxite mining and timber milling.

MAIN ATTRACTIONS: The **Pinjarrah Heritage Trail** takes in such sites as **St Johns Anglican Church** (1861), the **Original School House** (1862), a **Heritage Rose Garden** featuring 360 heritage roses, including the oldest known variety in cultivation, and the McLarty family home **Edenvale** (1888). Within the **Edenvale Complex** is the **Roger May Machinery Museum**, the **Murray Arts and Crafts Centre**, quilt displays and sales, and tearooms. The Murray River has picnic facilities and is used in summer for swimming and canoeing. A suspension bridge crosses the river at **Pioneer Memorial Park**.

NEARBY ATTRACTIONS: From May to October the **Hotham Valley Tourist Railway** runs steam train trips between Pinjarra and **Dwellingup**. Australia's largest alumina operation, **Alcoa Refinery**, 4km NE, conducts bus tours on Wednesdays. The **Alcoa Scarp Lookout**, 14km east, offers an overview of the massive plant. **Coopers Mill** on **Culeenup Island** was the first flour mill in the region and is accessible by boat only. Tours of the mill are available. **Tumbulgum Farm**, 38km north at **Mundijong** has native and farm animals, farm shows and product sales. **North Dandalup Dam**, 16km NE, **South Dandalup Dam** at **Dwellingup**, and **Waroona Dam**, 33km south, are pleasant picnic and recreational areas. The many attractions of **Mandurah**, the **Peel Inlet** and **Harvey Estuary**, also **Yalgorup NP**, are a short drive west.

TOURIST INFO: Cnr George and Henry sts,
Ph: (08) 9531 1438

■ Port Hedland POP 13 420

Map 398, C5

Renowned for handling Australia's largest amount of iron ore for export and for its mammoth salt exports, Port Hedland sits in a mangrove-lined inlet discovered in 1863 by Capt Peter Hedland.

MAIN ATTRACTIONS: Tours of the bustling port area and the **Nelson Point** iron ore site depart from the tourist centre. A 26m-high **Observation Tower** behind the centre provides an excellent vantage of the port, town and shipping traffic. Relics of old manganese mines and BHP railway locomotives are some of the memorabilia on display at **Don Rhodes Mining Museum** on Wilson St. In Sutherland St is the **Pioneer and Pearlers Cemetery** where Japanese and Chinese nationals are buried. Aboriginal petroglyphs carved into a limestone ridge can be viewed with permission from Aboriginal Affairs and visitors are welcome at the **Royal Flying Doctor Service** and **School of the Air**. Whale-watching and flatback turtle nesting ecotours operate seasonally.

NEARBY ATTRACTIONS: Visible from **Cooke Point** March–Oct, the rising full moon creates an illusory reflection descriptively known as **'Stairway to the Moon'**. **Pretty Pool**, a nearby tidal pool, is a safe swimming and fishing spot, though beware of stonefish. Stockpiled conical dunes of salt produced by solar evaporation can be seen 8km SE at **Cargill Salt**.

TOURIST INFO: 13 Wedge St,
Ph: (08) 9173 1711

■ Rockingham POP 52 100

Map 364, C4

From Rockingham's founding in 1872 until the opening of the Fremantle harbour in 1897 this town operated as one of Western Australia's timber ports. Today it is a seaside resort city, conveniently

Western Australia

located 47km south of Perth, capitalising on its pristine beaches and protected waterways.

MAIN ATTRACTIONS: Beach-based recreation is a major attraction, including swimming, boat harbour tours, 'watch and swim with the dolphins' cruises, and diving excursions to offshore wrecks and reefs. On Kent St is the **Museum of Local History** and exhibitions can be viewed at the **Art Gallery** on Civic Blvd. Western Australia's grain industry history is recounted at **The Granary** on Rockingham Rd, which is open by appointment. A coastal scenic lookout worth visiting is at **Cape Peron** on Peron Rd.

NEARBY ATTRACTIONS: Islands in nearby waters offer a variety of excellent excursions: **Penguin Island** has a colony of little penguins and a **Penguin Experience Island Discovery Centre** (access prohibited June–August during breeding season); **Seal Island** has a colony of sea-lions; **Garden Island** is the site of the HMAS *Stirling* naval base

Grass trees, *Xanthorrhoea preisii*, at Shoalwater Bay, Rockingham

and features pleasant beaches accessible by private boat; and **Shoalwater Bay Island Marine Park** offers park cruises. **Lake Richmond**, 4km SW, has interesting walks and domed thrombolites (unlayered stromatolites). **Marapana Wildlife World**, 15km south, and **Tumblegum Farm**, 29km east, are popular with families. A waterski park is 5km east at **Baldivis** and **Peel Estate Winery** offers cellar door sales. Seasonal wildflowers make the scenic drive to **Serpentine Dam** and **Serpentine Falls**, 48km SE, particularly worthwhile in spring.

TOURIST INFO: 43 Kent St, Ph: (08) 9592 3464

■ Roebourne   POP 940
Map 398, B6

Established in 1864 and named after Western Australia's first Surveyor-General, John Septimus Roe, Roebourne is the oldest town in the **Pilbara**.

MAIN ATTRACTIONS: Historic buildings reflect an earlier era when Roebourne served as an important administrative centre, and include the **Holy Trinity Church** (1894), **Union Bank** (1889), **Victoria Hotel** (1866) and 4 stone buildings constructed in 1887—the **Post Office, Hospital, Court House** and the **Old Gaol** which now houses the **Roebourne Museum**. A lookout is located along Fisher Dr at **Mount Welcome**.

NEARBY ATTRACTIONS: **Emma Withnell Heritage Trail** is a 52km self-guided walk/drive tour through the historic coastal towns of **Cossack, Point Samson** and **Wickham. Cossack**, 14km north, was originally known as Tien Tsin Harbour and retains many interesting restored buildings from its brief era as a port. It was once connected to Roebourne by horse-drawn tram. **Point Samson**, 19km north, has good onshore and offshore fishing, boat hire, swimming and snorkelling. Local anglers

also recommend visitors try **Cleaverville**, 25km north. **Millstream–Chichester NP**, 150km south, is a 2000km² park with fascinating features—**Pyramid Hill**, a volcanic remnant; freshwater **Python Pool** and **Chinderwarriner Pool**; and **Mount Herbert lookout** (366m). Directions to bushwalking trails and self-drive tours can be obtained from the **Millstream Homestead** off Hamersley Iron Rd, which functions as the park's information centre.

TOURIST INFO: Old Gaol, Queen St, Ph: (08) 9182 1060

■ Southern Cross   POP 1200
Map 403, G4

A service centre for the surrounding pastoral and gold mining districts, Southern Cross was founded after a gold-find in 1888, though the rush was short-lived. Situated 368km east of Perth, its streets—like the town itself—are named after stars and constellations.

MAIN ATTRACTIONS: Notable historical buildings are the **Post Office** (1891), **Railway Tavern** (1890s), **Palace Hotel** (1912) and the **Court House** (1893), which houses the local **Historical Museum**. Off the Great Eastern Hwy is the **Old Cemetery** where town pioneers are buried.

NEARBY ATTRACTIONS: Prolific wildflowers on the sand plains make springtime scenic drives more than memorable. **Koolyanobbing**, 53km north, became a 'modern ghost town' after its iron-ore mine closed in 1983; however, the town revived in 1994 when iron-ore and salt mining recommenced. Rock formations with nearby picnic spots are **Hunts Soak**, 7km north, constructed by convicts in 1865; **Frog Rock**, 15km south, shaped in a wave-like outcrop; **Karalee Rock** and **Dam**, 37km east; and **Baladjie Rock**, 45km NW.

TOURIST INFO: Shire Offices, Antares St, Ph: (08) 9049 1001

ROTTNEST ISLAND

This limestone island is home to **quokkas**, small indigenous marsupials mistakenly identified as rats in 1696 by a Dutch explorer, who subsequently named the island 'Rats Nest'. Thousands of holiday-makers are drawn to Rottnest Island each year. Bicycles, available for hire, are the main mode of transport on the island—so there is little motorised traffic.

'Rotto', 19km west of Fremantle, is only 11km long and less than half that wide. Its beaches are a major drawcard, as they boast crystal-clear water and some of the world's southernmost coral reefs. Over 360 species of fish and 20 species of coral are found within Rottnest waters and the sheltered bays provide idyllic conditions for snorkelling, surfing, scuba diving, swimming or just soaking up the sun. Colonial streetscapes and architecture are also a feature of this historic island. Due to its close proximity to Perth and Fremantle, by ferry or aeroplane, Rottnest is an ideal daytrip destination, but has much to offer visitors who choose to stay.

main attractions

- ❖ Rottnest's colonial architecture
- ❖ Rottnest Museum
- ❖ Island coach tour (2hr)
- ❖ Oliver Hill gun battery and train

Tourist information

Rottnest Island Visitor and Information Centre
Thomson Bay, Rottnest Island WA 6161
Ph: (08) 9372 9752
www.rottnest.wa.gov.au

Snorkelling at Cape Vlamingh, Rottnest Island

◼ Tom Price   POP 3200
Map 400, E2

The discovery in 1962 of iron ore deposits at **Mount Tom Price** soon led to the Hamersley Iron Company establishing the town of Tom Price to support and service its mining operation. Situated on the edge of the **Hamersley Range** at an altitude of 747m, it is the highest town in Western Australia.

MAIN ATTRACTIONS: Tours of the huge **Hamersley Iron open-cut mine** depart from the information centre.

NEARBY ATTRACTIONS: **Mount Nameless**, 6km west, has an elevation of 1128m, affording panoramic views of the town and mine. Its summit is accessible via 4WD or from the walking track at the base of the hill. Bushwalking and scenic drives are popular pursuits in the rugged **Karijini (Hamersley Range) NP**, 50km east. Renowned for its spectacular and colourful gorges and prolific wildlife, highlights include **Dales Gorge**, a giant termite mound, **Circular Pool** and **Fortescue Falls**, **Oxers Lookout**, swimming pools at **Hamersley Gorge**, and an Aboriginal interpretive centre in the south-east. Tour operators also run day trips, camping safaris and helicopter flights.

TOURIST INFO: Central Rd,
Ph: (08) 9188 1112

Note: *Travellers should not venture to the town of **Wittenoom** to the north-east of the park, which has been declared no longer habitable due to the significant health risk from asbestos fibres, a legacy of the town's asbestos mine that closed in the 1960s.*

◼ Wagin   POP 1300
Map 404, D3

A 9m-high statue of a merino ram is an appropriate icon for the rural service town of Wagin, 177km east of Bunbury. Originally established in 1889 as an important point on the Great Southern Railway, the town is today surrounded by thriving sheep, cattle, grain and emu farms.

MAIN ATTRACTIONS: **Wagin Historical Village** on Kitchener St recreates the daily life as it would have been 100 years ago in the settlement town. A one-room school, black-smith, settlers' cottages and wool museum are among the interesting and informative attractions in the village. Heritage trails trace these and other historic town buildings including the **Little Gem Theatre**.

Western Australia

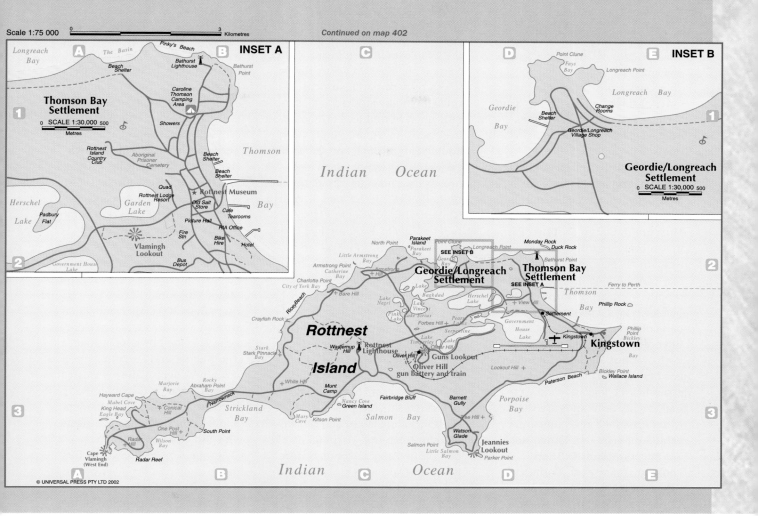

Continued on map 402

Scale 1:75 000

INSET A

Thomson Bay Settlement
SCALE 1:30,000

INSET B

Geordie/Longreach Settlement
SCALE 1:30,000

Indian Ocean

Rottnest Island

Indian Ocean

© UNIVERSAL PRESS PTY LTD 2002

NEARBY ATTRACTIONS: Emu chick incubation and hatching are among highlights sometimes seen at the **Corralyn Emu Farm**, 4km north. Rocky outcrops in the area, often with lookouts, picnic facilities and walks include **Puntapin Rock** which functions as a water catchment, 6km SE, and **Mount Latham**, 6km west. **Lake Norring**, 13km SE, is a popular recreation area. For speed enthusiasts, Donald Campbell set a world water-speed record in 1964 at **Lake Dumbleyung**, 18km east.

TOURIST INFO: Wagin Historical Village, Kitchener St, Ph: (08) 9861 1232

■ **Waroona**   POP 2500
Map 375, D1
Conveniently close to the **Preston** and **Clifton lakes**, **Yalgorup NP**, and other picturesque forested

areas, the rural town of Waroona, 112km south of Perth, provides an excellent base for exploring. Settlers arrived in the district in the 1830s and a township (at the time known as Drakesbrook) was established about 40 years later. Timber milling and the arrival of the railway boosted the growth of the area.

MAIN ATTRACTIONS: **The Vision Splendid Gardens** on Parnell St is an exceptional private garden featuring more than 400 rose bushes and creative landscape architecture. Plantation pine toys, dolls houses and household wares can be found at **The Puzzleman** on McLarty St.

NEARBY ATTRACTIONS: **Lane Pool Reserve** is a forest recreation area with camping, picnic and swimming areas, including **Scarp Pool**, **Baden Powell Water Spout**, and

Island Pool. Nearby, to the north, in the town of **Dwellingup** is the **Forest Heritage Centre** promoting timber and the trees through exhibits, a treetops walk and wood products. The **Etmilyn Forest Tramway**, a steam train venturing into the jarrah forest, also departs from town. **Preston Beach**, 34km west, offers good ocean swimming and fishing. Off Preston Beach Rd is Yalgorup NP with well-developed bushwalking trails through the tuart trees. **Drakesbrook Weir**, 5km SE, has good fishing, swimming and non-power boating. Situated in 2.5ha of bushland in Thomson Cres at Armstrong Hills, is **Cherubijn Gallery and Studio** featuring the works of local artists.

TOURIST INFO: Cnr South Western Hwy and Millar St, Ph: (08) 9733 1506

Wongan Hills POP 813
Map 402, D4

This township is situated in the north-east wheat belt, 184km from Perth. The name, Wongan Hills, originates from an Aboriginal word for 'whispering hills'.

MAIN ATTRACTIONS: Improvised furniture and implements are among the memorabilia from the early days displayed at the **Pioneer Museum** in Camm St. **Town Park**, in Fenton Pl, has BBQ facilities and a children's play area.

NEARBY ATTRACTIONS: During the spring months Wongan Hills and district blossoms into a spectacular sea of wildflowers, best seen at **Reynoldson's Flora Reserve**, 15km north. **Mount Matilda**, 10km west, is a flora and fauna reserve with an ecowalk trail. In stark contrast to the region's flat farmlands are various rock formations also popular for wildflower sightings: **Dingo Rock**, 26km east, **Mount O'Brien Lookout**, 10km west, **Gathercole Reserve** on Moonijin Rd, and **Christmas Rock**, an old water catchment area closer to town, accessed off Wandoo Cres. **Lake Ninnan**, 10km west, provides a venue for waterskiing, sailing and swimming.

TOURIST INFO: Fenton Pl,
Ph: (08) 9671 1247

Wyndham POP 920
Map 399, K2

Western Australia's northernmost town, Wyndham supported a sizeable meatworks industry till its closure in 1985. Today the port town services pastoral, mining and Aboriginal communities and exports diverse cargoes including grain, raw Kununurra sugar, and live cattle shipments to south-east Asia.

MAIN ATTRACTIONS: A landing port for prospectors during the 1880s goldrushes, Wyndham's port heritage is traced in a pamphlet noting other historic town highlights including the **Old Post Office** (now privately owned) and the **Old Court House**, which serves as an **historical museum**. Saltwater crocodiles can be sighted from the wharf (observed from a distance), or at the **Zoological Gardens and Crocodile Park** on Barytes Rd, which also breeds the endangered Indonesian Komodo Dragon. Located in **Warriu 'Dream Time' Park** are large monuments of an Aboriginal family.

NEARBY ATTRACTIONS: **Five Rivers Lookout**, 5km north on **Bastion Range**, is renowned for its spectacular views, which are highly recommended at sunrise or sunset. Aboriginal rock paintings are 18km SW and an unusual temporary prison cell from the 1890s, a **Boab Prison Tree** believed to be 2000–4000 years old, is 22km SW. A wetland sanctuary for migratory birds including jabiru and brolga, **Marglu Billabong**, 15km SE, is part of the **Parry Lagoons Nature Reserve**. A 100m-deep natural swimming hole, **The Grotto** is located 36km east and is a popular picnic area, as is the water catchment reservoir **Moochalabra Dam**, 20km from town. Fresh and saltwater fishing are popular in the **King River** area, though 4WD access is recommended. Tours offered in the region include mustering, horseriding treks, scenic boat cruises, and for an unforgettable Outback station stay, **El Questro Station**, located 100km south.

TOURIST INFO: 6 Great Northern Hwy,
Ph: (08) 9161 1281

York POP 1985
Map 402, D5

This is the oldest inland town in Western Australia, settled in 1831, just two years after the Swan River Colony. York prospered as a result of the 1889 gold discoveries at **Southern Cross** and has since become the main commercial centre for the **Avon Valley**.

MAIN ATTRACTIONS: Awarded the National Trust classification of **Historic Town**, York has many significant buildings: the **Old Gaol**, **Court House** and **Police Station** (1850), **Sandalwood Yards** and **Tipperary School** (1874), **Town Hall** (1911), **Castle Hotel** (1853), and **Holy Trinity Church** (1854), with its rare pipe organ and Robert Juniper-designed glass and paintings. **Residency Museum** (1843) on Brook St houses a collection of records and memorabilia from early colonial life. York's highly regarded **Motor Museum** in Avon Tce exhibits more than 200 classic and vintage cars, motorcycles and horse-drawn vehicles. Open by appointment is **The Needle and I**, featuring period costumes. **Avon Valley Historical Rose Garden** on Osnaburg Rd has fragrant and spectacular blooms and is open weekends in season. **The Old Mill Gallery** in Avon Tce sells and displays fine jarrah furniture and artworks. At **Avon Park** there are picnic facilities and a river-crossing **Suspension Bridge** originally built in 1906.

NEARBY ATTRACTIONS: Spectacular views can be seen from **Mount Brown Lookout**, 3km SE, which is also popular for picnics.

TOURIST INFO: 81 Avon Tce,
Ph: (08) 9641 1301

York's Romanesque Town Hall

Western Australia

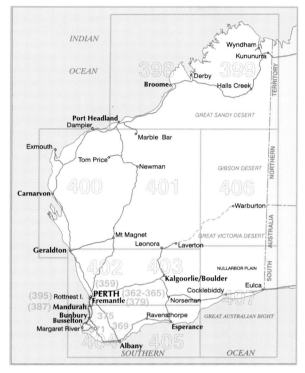

Capital city
CBD map
Perth p.359

Perth suburban
maps
pp.362–365

Fremantle map
p.379

Region maps
Great Southern
  Region p.369
Caves District p.371
South West Region
  p.375
Peel Region p.387
Rottnest Island
  p.395

State maps
pp.398–407

Boab tree in the Kimberleys

DISTANCE CHART

Approximate Distance	Albany	Broome	Bunbury	Busselton	Carnarvon	Derby	Esperance	Eucla	Geraldton	Halls Creek	Kalgoorlie/Boulder	Kununurra	Mandurah	Meekatharra	Merredin	Narrogin	Norseman	Northam	Perth	Port Hedland
Albany		2582	361	372	1292	2736	474	1386	819	3196	799	3554	468	1116	463	269	676	439	406	1988
Broome	2582		2538	2592	1461	222	912	3082	1934	682	2185	1040	2441	1466	2304	2313	2372	2143	2372	614
Bunbury	361	2538		54	1069	2554	687	1599	596	3004	764	3362	1027	924	422	170	889	261	182	1796
Busselton	372	2592	54		1123	2608	698	1610	650	3058	818	3416	161	978	482	224	900	315	236	1850
Carnarvon	1292	1461	1069	1123		1615	1600	2300	473	2075	1161	2433	972	620	1125	1078	1590	964	903	867
Derby	2736	222	2554	2608	1615		2728	3236	2088	544	2267	902	2447	1620	2458	2467	2526	2297	2378	768
Esperance	474	912	687	698	1600	2728		912	1319	3188	389	3486	710	1108	562	535	202	828	714	1980
Eucla	1386	3082	1599	1610	2300	3236	912		1827	3696	897	4054	1502	1616	1175	1433	710	1336	1433	2488
Geraldton	819	1934	596	650	473	2088	1319	1827		2548	988	2906	499	540	652	605	1117	491	430	1340
Halls Creek	3196	682	3004	3058	2075	544	3188	3696	2548		2799	358	2907	2080	2918	2927	2986	2757	2838	1228
Kalgoorlie/Boulder	799	2185	764	818	1161	2267	389	897	988	2799		3157	663	719	336	594	187	497	594	1591
Kununurra	3554	1040	3362	3416	2433	902	3486	4054	2906	358	3157		3265	2438	3276	3285	3344	3115	3196	1586
Mandurah	468	2441	1027	161	972	2447	710	1502	499	2907	663	3265		827	327	175	792	166	75	1698
Meekatharra	1116	1466	924	978	620	1620	1108	1616	540	2080	719	2438	827		838	847	906	677	758	872
Merredin	463	2304	422	482	1125	2458	562	1175	652	2918	336	3276	327	838		258	465	161	258	1710
Narrogin	269	2313	170	224	1078	2467	535	1433	605	2927	594	3285	175	847	258		723	170	192	1719
Norseman	676	2372	889	900	1590	2526	202	710	1117	2986	187	3344	792	906	465	723		626	723	1778
Northam	439	2143	261	315	964	2297	828	1336	491	2757	497	3115	166	677	161	170	626		97	1549
Perth	406	2372	182	236	903	2378	714	1433	430	2838	594	3196	75	758	258	192	723	97		1630
Port Hedland	1988	614	1796	1850	867	768	1980	2488	1340	1228	1591	1586	1698	872	1710	1719	1778	1549	1630	

* All distances in this chart have been measured over highways and major roads, not necessarily by the shortest route.

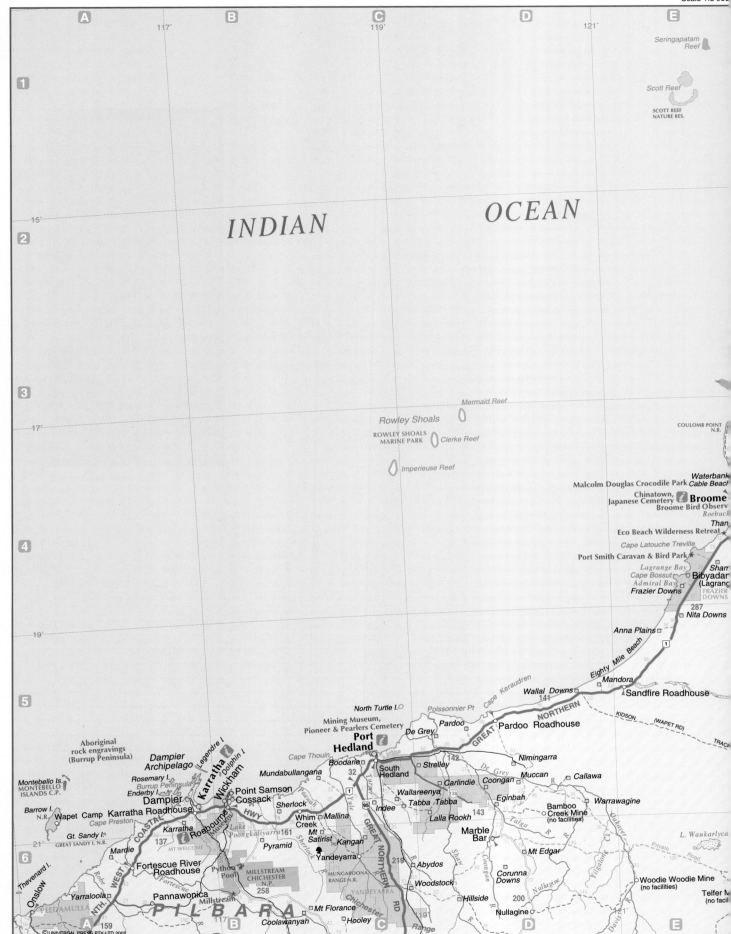

Scale 1:3 900

INDIAN OCEAN

Seringapatam Reef

Scott Reef

SCOTT REEF NATURE RES.

Mermaid Reef

Rowley Shoals

ROWLEY SHOALS MARINE PARK   Clerke Reef

Imperieuse Reef

COULOMB POINT N.R.

Waterbank
Malcolm Douglas Crocodile Park Cable Beach
Chinatown, i **Broome**
Japanese Cemetery Broome Bird Observ
Broome Bird Observ
Roebuck
Than
Eco Beach Wilderness Retreat
Cape Latouche Treville
Port Smith Caravan & Bird Park
Lagrange Bay
Cape Bossut Sham
Bibyadar
Admiral Bay (Lagrang
Frazier Downs FRAZIER
DOWNS
287
Nita Downs
Anna Plains

Eighty Mile Beach
Mandora
Wallal Downs
NORTHERN KIDSON (WAPET RD)
Sandfire Roadhouse
TRACK

North Turtle I.
Poissonnier Pt
Mining Museum, Pardoo
Pioneer & Pearlers Cemetery De Grey Pardoo Roadhouse
Port i Nimingarra
Aboriginal **Hedland** 142
rock engravings Cape Thouin Boodarie De Grey Coongan Muccan Callawa
(Burrup Peninsula) 32 South Strelley
Dampier Legendre I. i Hedland Carlindie
Archipelago Dolphin I. Wallareenya 138 Eginbah
Rosemary I. **Karratha** Mundabullangana Tabba Tabba Bamboo Warrawagine
Montebello Is. Burrup Peninsula **Wickham** 95 Creek Mine
MONTEBELLO Enderby I. Indee 143 (no facilities)
ISLANDS C.P. **Dampier** Point Samson Lalla Rookh
Cossack Marble
Barrow I. Wapet Camp Karratha Roadhouse Sherlock Bar Mt Edgar
N.R. Cape Preston Whim Mallina
Gt. Sandy Is. Karratha Creek Kangan Corunna Woodie Woodie Mine
GREAT SANDY I. N.R. Roebourne 161 Mt Downs (no facilities)
137 Museum Poongkaliyarra Satirist 219 Abydos 200 Telfer M
Thevenard I. MT WELCOME Pyramid Yandeyarra Hillside (no facil
Mardie Woodstock
Onslow Fortescue River Python MILLSTREAM MUNGAROONA Nullagine
YEEDAMULLA Roadhouse Pool CHICHESTER RANGE N.R. YANDEYARRA
Pannawonica N.P. Mt Florance
159 Yarraloola 117 258 Coolawanyah Hooley
PILBARA

Joins maps 400 & 401

© UNIVERSAL PRESS PTY LTD 2002

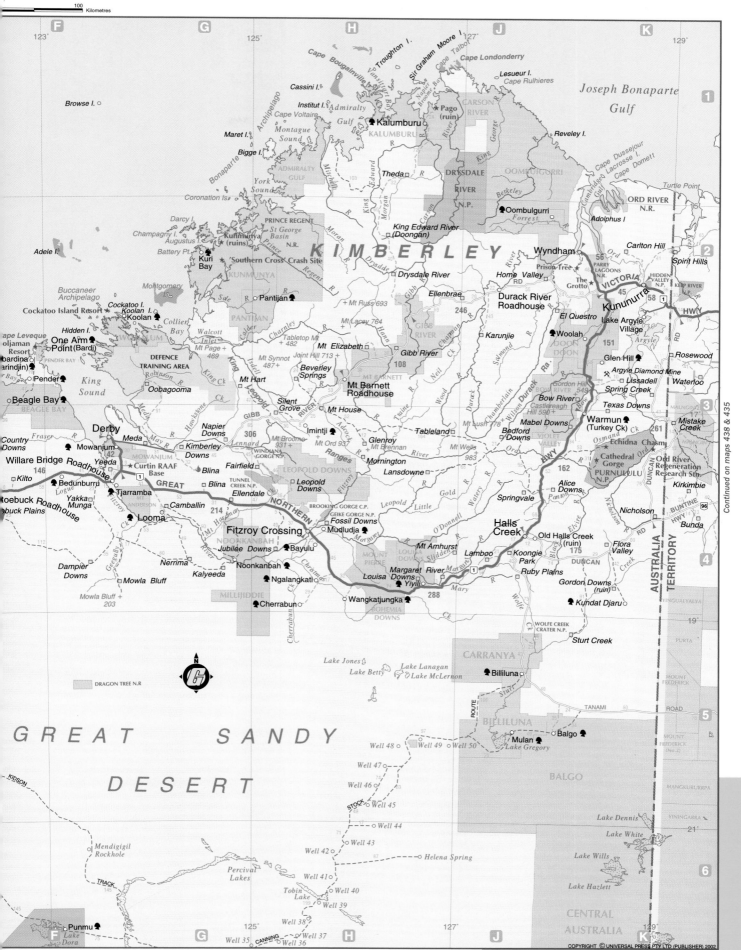

100
Kilometres

Browse I.

Cape Bougainville I.
Cassini I.
Troughton I.
Cape Talbot
Sir Graham Moore I.
Cape Londonderry
Lesueur I.
Cape Rulhieres

Joseph Bonaparte Gulf

Institut I.
Admiralty
Pago (ruin)
CARSON RIVER
Reveley I.

Cape Voltaire
Gulf
Kalumburu
KALUMBURU
Cape Dussejour
Cape Lacrosse I.
Cape Domett

Maret I.
Montague Sound
Theda
DRYSDALE RIVER N.P.
OOMBULGURRI

Bigge I.
Bonaparte
Adolphus I.
ORD RIVER N.R.

Adele I.
Coronation Is.
Oombulgurri
Turtle Point

Darcy I.
PRINCE REGENT N.R.
Spirit Hills

Champagny I.
St George Basin
King Edward River (Doongan)
Carlton Hill

Augustus I.
Kunmunya (ruins)
Wyndham
Prison Tree
VICTORIA
KEEP RIVER N.P.

Battery Pt.
Southern Cross Crash Site
KIMBERLEY
56
HIDDEN VALLEY N.P.

Kuri Bay
Home Valley
The Grotto
45
Kununurra
58

Buccaneer Archipelago
Montgomery
Drysdale River
Durack River Roadhouse
El Questro
HWY

Cockatoo Island Resort
Cockatoo I.
Koolan I.
Pantijan
246
Karunjie
Lake Argyle Village
151

Koolan
Collier Bay
Mt Russ 693
GIBB RIVER
Woolah
DOON DOON

Hidden I.
Walcott Inlet
Mt Lacey 764
Glen Hill
Rosewood

One Arm Point (Bardi)
DEFENCE TRAINING AREA
Mt Page 469
Mt Elizabeth
Gibb River
108
Argyle Diamond Mine
Lissadell
Waterloo

Pender
Oobagooma
Mt Synnot 487+
Joint Hill 713+
Spring Creek

Beagle Bay
Mt Hart
Beverley Springs
MT BARNETT
Gordon Hill 549
Bow River
Texas Downs

King Sound
Silent Grove
Mt House
Mabel Downs
Warmun (Turkey Ck)
Mistake Creek

Country Downs
Napier Downs
Mt Barnett Roadhouse
Mt Broome 931+
Imintji
Tableland
Bedford Downs
261
Echidna Chasm

Willare Bridge Roadhouse
Meda
Kimberley Downs
306
Mt Ord 937
Glenroy
Mt Brennan
Mt Wells 983
162
Cathedral Gorge
PURNULULU N.P.
Ord River Regeneration Research Stn.

Derby
Mowanjum
Yeeda
Blina
Fairfield
Mornington
Lansdowne
Alice Downs
Kirkimbie

Kilto
Bedunburru
Curtin RAAF Base
Blina
LEOPOLD DOWNS
Springvale
Nicholson
Bunda

Yakka Munga
Tjarramba
GREAT
TUNNEL CREEK N.P.
Leopold Downs
BROOKING GORGE C.P.
Halls Creek
Old Halls Creek (ruin)
Flora Valley

Roebuck Roadhouse
Camballin
214
Ellendale
GEIKE GORGE N.P.
Lamboo
175

ebuck Plains
Looma
NOONKANBAH
Fossil Downs
Mudludja
Margaret River
Koongie Park
Gordon Downs (ruin)

Dampier Downs
Jubilee Downs
Bayulu
Louisa Downs
Yiyili
Ruby Plains

Mowla Bluff
Nerrima
Noonkanbah
Kalyeeda
Ngalangkati
288

Mowla Bluff 203
MILLIJIDDIE
Cherrabun
Wangkatjungka
Kundat Djaru

DRAGON TREE N.R
WOLFE CREEK CRATER N.P.

CARRANYA
Billiluna

GREAT SANDY
Lake Jones
Lake Lanagan
Lake McLernon
BILLILUNA
Sturt Creek

DESERT
Well 48
Well 49
Well 50
Mulan
Balgo
MOUNT FREDERICK (No.2)

Well 47
Lake Gregory
BALGO

Well 46
MANGKURURRPA

KIDSON
Well 45
Lake Dennis

Well 44
Lake White

Mendigigil Rockhole
Well 43

Percival Lakes
Well 42
Helena Spring
Lake Wills

TRACK
Well 41
Lake Hazlett

Tobin Lake
Well 40

Punmu
Well 39
CENTRAL

Lake Dora
Well 38
AUSTRALIA

Well 35
CANNING
Well 37
Well 36

Continued on maps 438 & 435

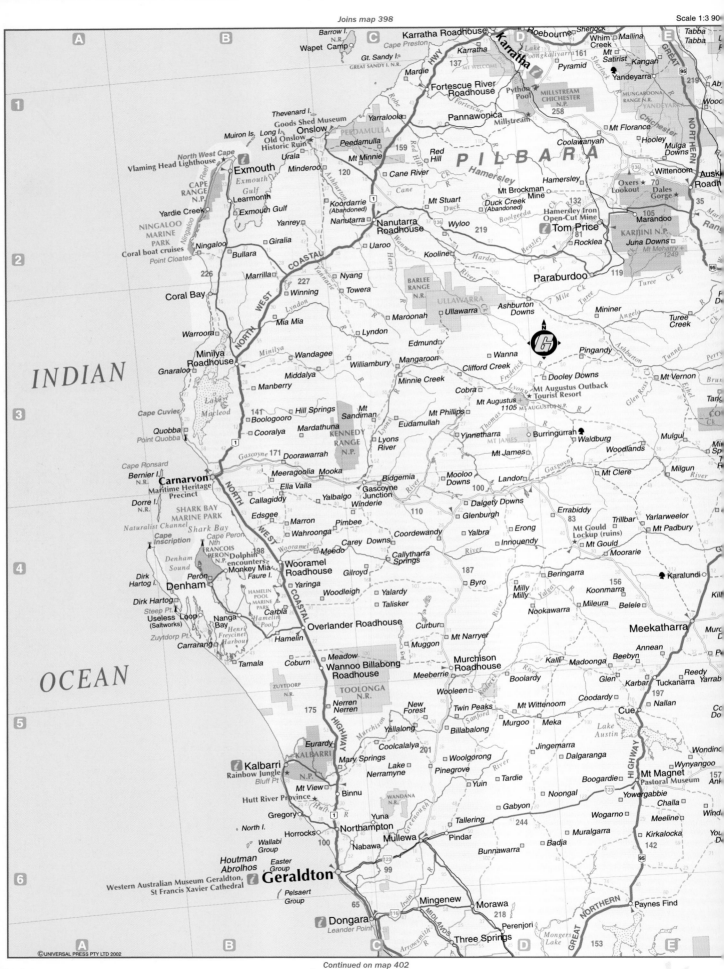

Western Australia

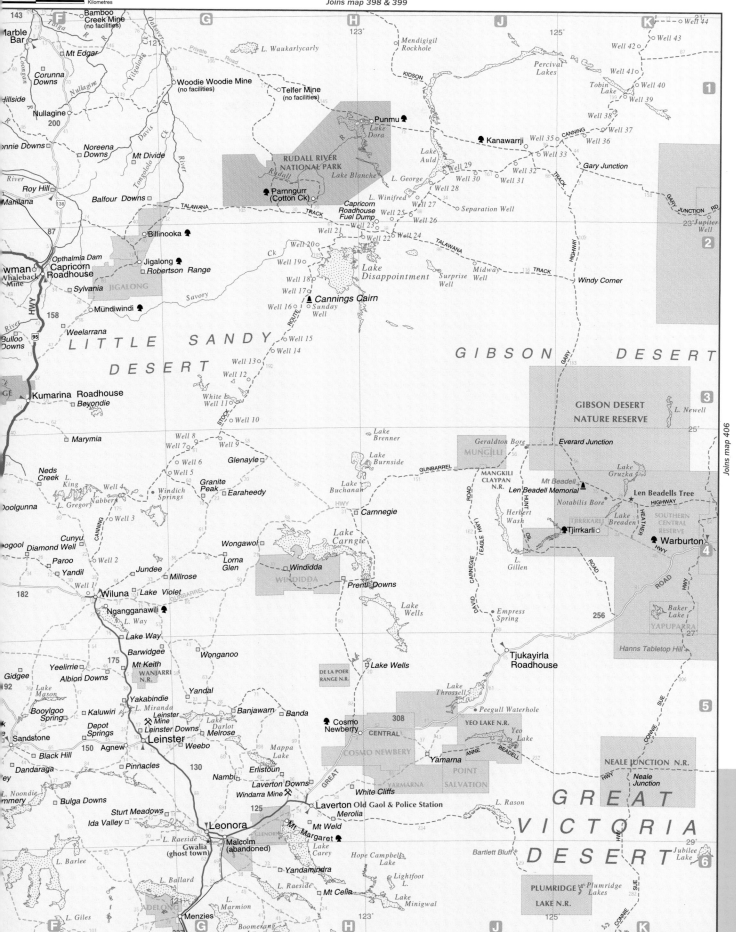

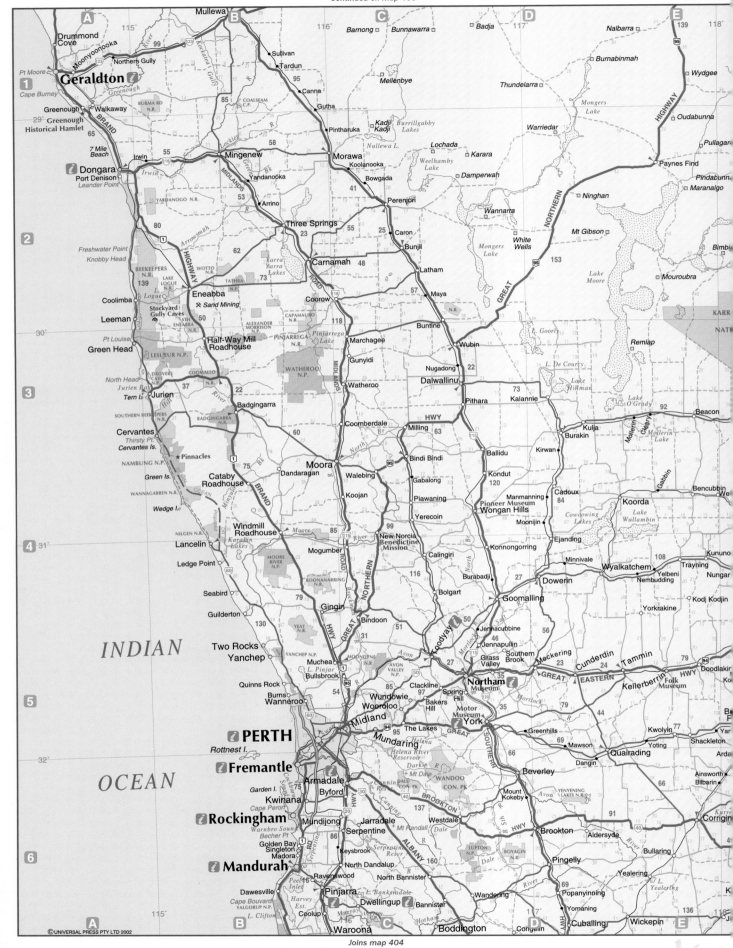

Western Australia

INDIAN

OCEAN

© UNIVERSAL PRESS PTY LTD 2002

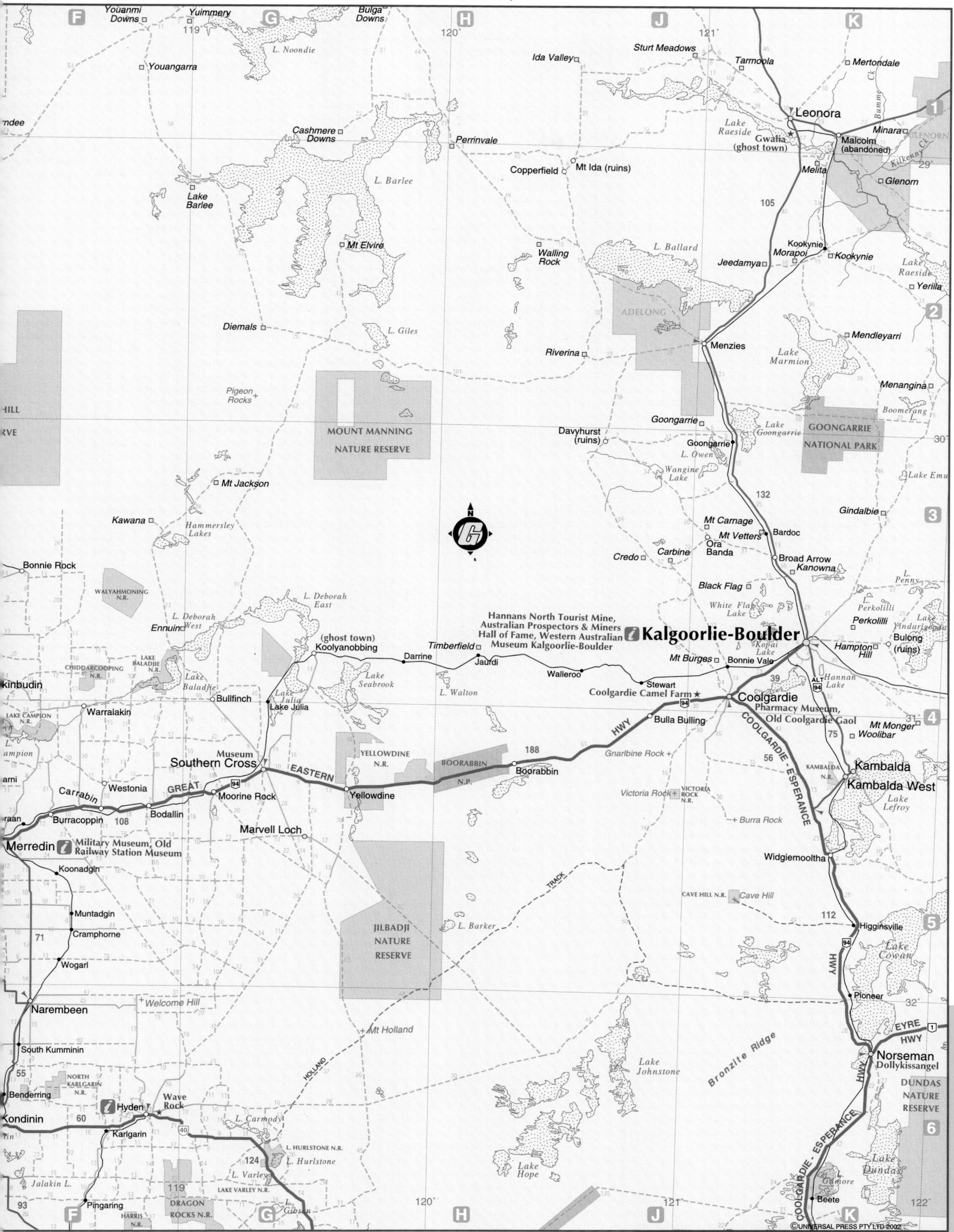

100 Kilometres

Youanmi Downs
Yuimmery
Bulga Downs
Ida Valley
Sturt Meadows
Tarmoola
Mertondale

Youangarra
L. Noondie
119
Leonora
Minara
GLENORN

Cashmere Downs
Perrinvale
Gwalia (ghost town)
Malcolm (abandoned)
Glenorn
29°

L. Barlee
Copperfield
Mt Ida (ruins)
Melita

Lake Barlee
Morapoi
Kookynie
Yerilla
105
Lake Raeside

Mt Elvire
L. Ballard
Kookynie
Jeedamya
Menangina

Diemals
L. Giles
ADELONG
Lake Marmion
Mendleyarri
Boomerang

Walling Rock
Riverina
Menzies

Pigeon Rocks
Goongarrie
Lake Goongarrie
GOONGARRIE NATIONAL PARK
30°

MOUNT MANNING NATURE RESERVE
Davyhurst (ruins)
Goongarrie
L. Owen
Lake Emu

Mt Jackson
Wangine Lake
Gindalbie
132

Kawana
Hammersley Lakes
Mt Carnage
Mt Vetters
Bardoc
L. Penny

Bonnie Rock
Credo
Carbine
Ora Banda
Broad Arrow
Kanowna
Perkolilli
3

WALYAHMONING N.R.
L. Deborah East
Black Flag
White Flag Lake
Bulong (ruins)

Ennuin
L. Deborah West
(ghost town) Koolyanobbing
Hannans North Tourist Mine, Australian Prospectors & Miners Hall of Fame, Western Australian Museum Kalgoorlie-Boulder
Kalgoorlie-Boulder
Hampton Hill

LAKE BALADJIE N.R.
Darrine
Timberfield
Jaurdi
Mt Burges
Bonnie Vale
Kopai Lake
Hannan Lake

CHIDDARCOOPING N.R.
Lake Baladjie
Bullfinch
Lake Julia
Lake Seabrook
Walleroo
Stewart
Coolgardie Camel Farm
Coolgardie
Pharmacy Museum, Old Coolgardie Gaol
Mt Monger
Woolibar
39
ALT 94

LAKE CAMPION N.R.
Warralakin
L. Walton
Bulla Bulling
Gnarlbine Rock
56
KAMBALDA N.R.
Kambalda
Kambalda West

Southern Cross
Museum
EASTERN
YELLOWDINE N.R.
BOORABBIN N.P.
Boorabbin
188
Victoria Rock
VICTORIA ROCK
Burra Rock
Lake Lefroy
31°
75

Westonia
GREAT
Moorine Rock
Yellowdine
Lake Julia

Carrabin
Bodallin
Marvell Loch
Widgiemooltha

Burracoppin
108

Merredin
Military Museum, Old Railway Station Museum
Koonadgin
TRACK
CAVE HILL N.R.
Cave Hill
112
Higginsville
94
Lake Cowan
5

Muntadgin
Cramphorne
JILBADJI NATURE RESERVE
L. Barker
Pioneer
32°
71
Wogarl

Narembeen
Welcome Hill
Mt Holland
EYRE HWY

South Kumminin
Lake Johnstone
Bronzite Ridge
Norseman
Dollykissangel
DUNDAS NATURE RESERVE
55

NORTH KARLGARIN N.R.
HOLLAND
Benderring
Hyden
Wave Rock
L. Carmody
Lake Hope
COOLGARDIE - ESPERANCE
Lake Dundas

Kondinin
60
Karlgarin
40
L. Hurlstone N.R.
L. Hurlstone
124
L. Varley
LAKE VARLEY N.R.
93
Pingaring
119
DRAGON ROCKS N.R.
HARRIS N.R.
L. Gibson
120°
121°
122°
6

© UNIVERSAL PRESS PTY LTD 2002

Continued on map 407

WESTERN AUSTRALIA 403

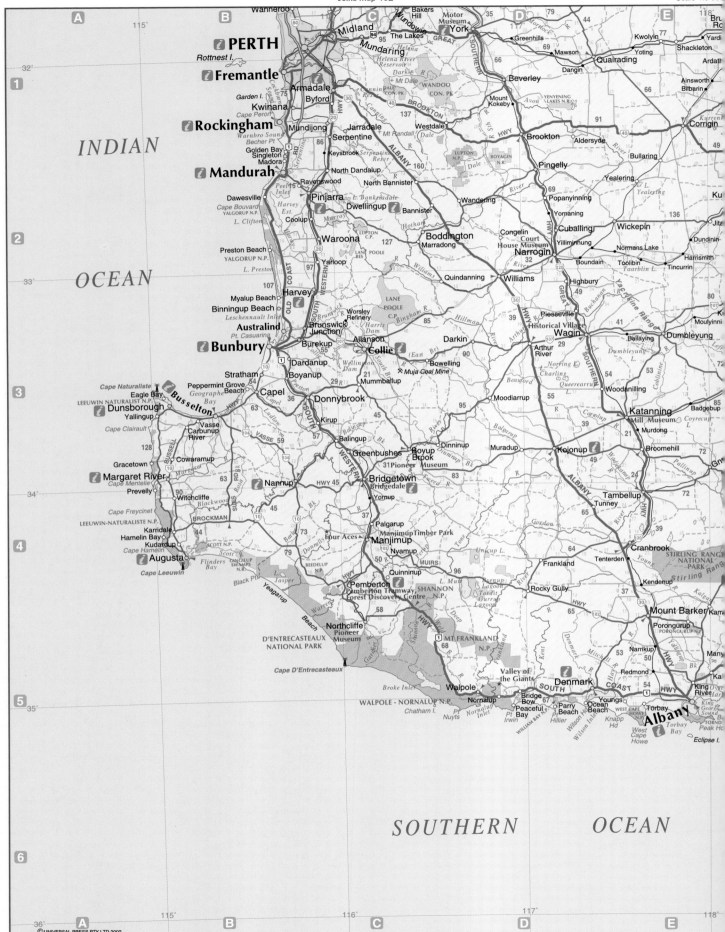

Scale 1:3 900

INDIAN

OCEAN

PERTH
Rottnest I.
Fremantle
Garden I.
Kwinana
Cape Peron
Rockingham

Mandurah

Bunbury

Busselton
Cape Naturaliste
Eagle Bay
LEEUWIN NATURALIST N.P.
Dunsborough
Yallingup
Cape Clairault

Margaret River
Cape Mentelle
Prevelly
Cape Freycinet
LEEUWIN-NATURALISTE N.P.
Karridale
Hamelin Bay
Kudardup
Cape Hamelin
Augusta
Cape Leeuwin

D'ENTRECASTEAUX
NATIONAL PARK

Cape D'Entrecasteaux

WALPOLE - NORNALUP N.P.

SOUTHERN   OCEAN

Wanneroo
Midland
Mundaring
Armadale
Byford
Mundijong
Jarrahdale
Serpentine
Keysbrook
Golden Bay
Singleton
Madora
North Dandalup
Ravenswood
North Bannister
Pinjarra
Dwellingup
Bannister
Waroona
Yarloop
Harvey
Myalup Beach
Binningup Beach
Australind
Brunswick
Junction
Burekup
Dardanup
Boyanup
Stratham
Peppermint Grove Beach
Capel
Donnybrook
Kirup
Vasse
Carbunup River
Cowaramup
Balingup
Greenbushes
Boyup Brook
Pioneer Museum
Nannup
Bridgetown
Bridgedale
Yornup
Palgarup
Manjimup
Nyamup
Quinninup
Pemberton
Pemberton Tramway
Forest Discovery Centre
Northcliffe
Pioneer Museum
Walpole
Nornalup
Bridge Bow
Peaceful Bay

York
The Lakes
Greenhills
Mawson
Beverley
Mount Kokeby
Westdale
Brookton
Aldersyde
Pingelly
Wandering
Yornaning
Boddington
Marradong
Congelin Court House Museum
Yilliminning
Narrogin
Quindanning
Williams
Highbury
Collie
Bowelling
Muja Coal Mine
Darkin
Arthur River
Wagin
Woodanilling
Moodiarrup
Katanning
Dinninup
Muradup
Kojonup
Broomehill
Tambellup
Tunney
Frankland
Rocky Gully
Cranbrook
Tenterden
Kendenup
Mount Barker
Porongurup
Narrikup
Redmond
Denmark
Youngs
Ocean Beach
Torbay
Albany
King River

Greenhills
Dangin
Quairading
Kwolyin
Yoting
Shackleton
Ardath
Corrigin
Bullaring
Yealering
Popanyinning
Cuballing
Wickepin
Normans Lake
Dundinin
Boundain
Toolibin
Harrismith
Tincurrin
Piesseville
Ballaying
Dumbleyung
Moulyinni

STIRLING RANGE
NATIONAL PARK

SOUTH COAST

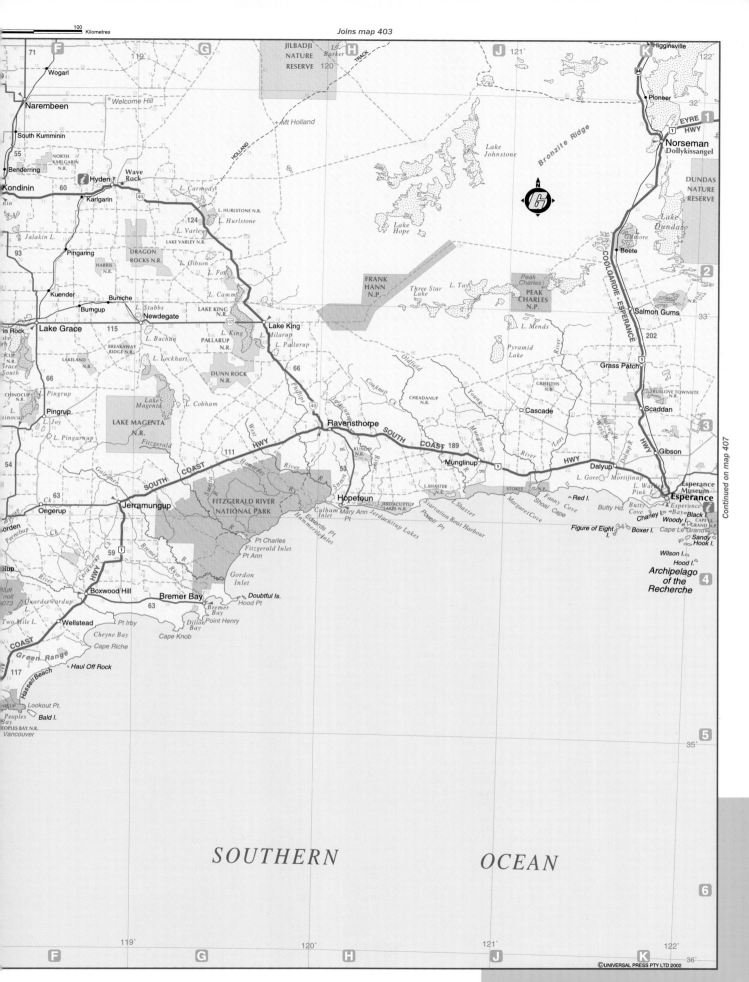

100 Kilometres

F 71

Wogarl

Narembeen

South Kumminin

55

Benderring

NORTH
KARLGARIN
N.R.

Hyden

Wave
Rock

Kondinin 60

Karlgarin

(40)

L. Carmody

L. HURLSTONE N.R.

124

L. Hurlstone

L. Varley

Lake Varley N.R.

G 119

+ Welcome Hill

+ Mt Holland

HOLLAND

DRAGON
ROCKS N.R.

L. Gibson

L. Fox

L. Camm

JILBADJI
NATURE
RESERVE 120

TRACK

Lake
Barker

H

Lake
Johnstone

Bronzite Ridge

Lake
Hope

J 121°

K

Higginsville

94

Pioneer

32°

Norseman
Dollykissangel

EYRE
HWY

1

DUNDAS
NATURE
RESERVE

Lake
Dundas

2

Jalakin L.

93

Pingaring

HARRIS
N.R.

FRANK
HANN
N.P.

Three Star
Lake

L. Tay

Peak
Charles

PEAK
CHARLES
N.P.

Gilmore

Beete

N.R.

Salmon Gums

33°

Kuender

Burngup

Buniche

L. Stubbs

Newdegate

LAKE KING
N.R.

(107)

Lake King

Milarup

L. Mends

Pyramid
Lake

202

Grass Patch

1

in Rock

Lake Grace 115

L. Buchan

L. King

PALLARUP
N.R.

L. Pallarup

Oldfield

River

Young

Griffiths R.

GRIFFITHS
N.R.

TRUSLOVE TOWNSITE

Scaddan

3

CHINOCUP
N.R.

Grace Lake
South

66

L. Joy

Pingrup

LAKELAND

BREAKAWAY
RIDGE N.R.

L. Lockhart

66

DUNN ROCK
N.R.

Coujinup Ck

CHEADANUP
N.R.

Maaling

Lort

R.

Cascade

HWY

Dalyup R.

Gibson

hinocup

Pingrup

L. Pingarnup

Lake
Magenta

L. Cobham

Phillips

(40)

West

River

Fitzgerald

KUNDIP
N.R.

River

R.

SOUTH COAST 189

Munglinup

1

Dalyup

L. Warden
Pink

Esperance
Museum

Esperance

54

LAKE MAGENTA
N.R.

Gairdner

111

SOUTH

COAST

HWY

Hamersley

Steere

R.

Ravensthorpe

53

R.

Hopetoun

L. SHASTER
N.R.

Shaster

L. Gore

Mortijinup

Butty Hd.

Charley Is.

Black I.

CAPE LE
GRAND N.P.

63

Ongerup

Jerramungup

FITZGERALD RIVER
NATIONAL PARK

R.

Culham
Inlet

Mary Ann
Edwards
Inlet

Jerdacuttup Lakes

JERDACUTTUP
LAKES N.R.

Powell
Pt.

Starvation Boat Harbour

STOKES
N.P.

Margaret Cove

Fanny Cove

Shoal Cape

Red I.

Butty
Cove

Bay

Figure of Eight
I.

Boxer I.

34°

Cape Le Grand

Sandy
Hook I.

orden

Peenebup

59

1

Bremer
River

Pt Charles
Fitzgerald Inlet
Pt Ann

Gordon
Inlet

Hammersley Inlet

Wilson I.

Hood I.

Archipelago
of the
Recherche

4

lup

Quaarderwardup
L.

073

Two Mile L.

Boxwood Hill

Cranbrook

HWY

River

63

Bremer Bay

Doubtful Is.
Hood Pt

Bremer
Bay

Dillon
Bay

Point Henry

Wellstead

Pt Irby

Cheyne Bay

Cape Riche

Cape Knob

COAST

Green Range

117

Hassell Beach

Haul Off Rock

NKLUP

Peoples
Bay

PEOPLES BAY N.R.

Vancouver

Lookout Pt.

Bald I.

5

35°

6

SOUTHERN   OCEAN

F 119°

G 120°

H

J 121°

K 122°

36°

Continued on map 407

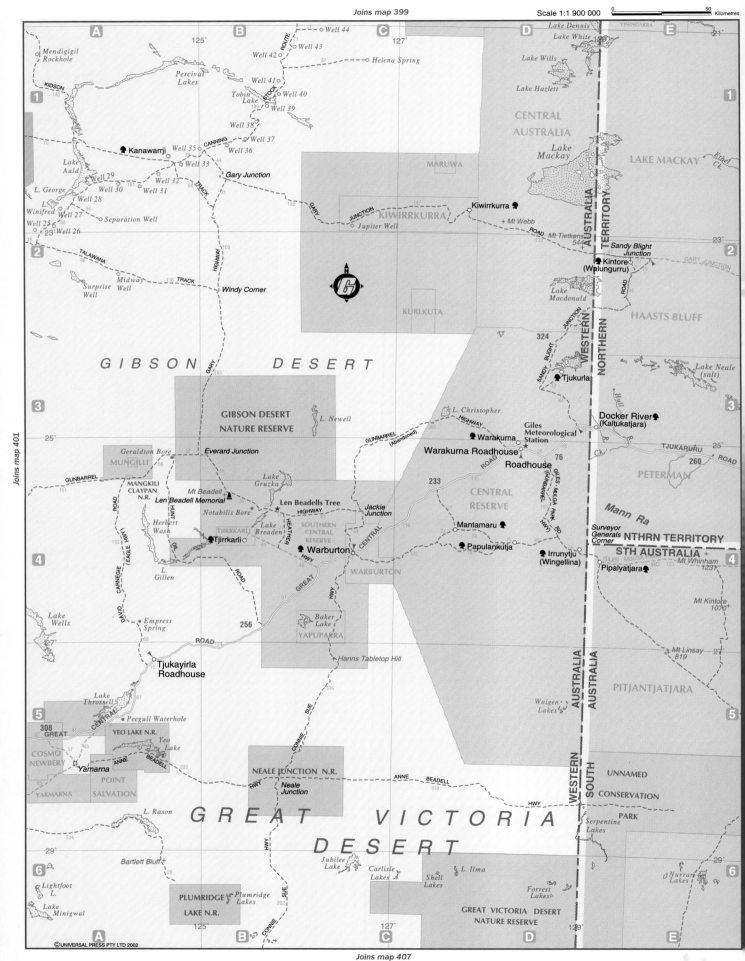

Western Australia

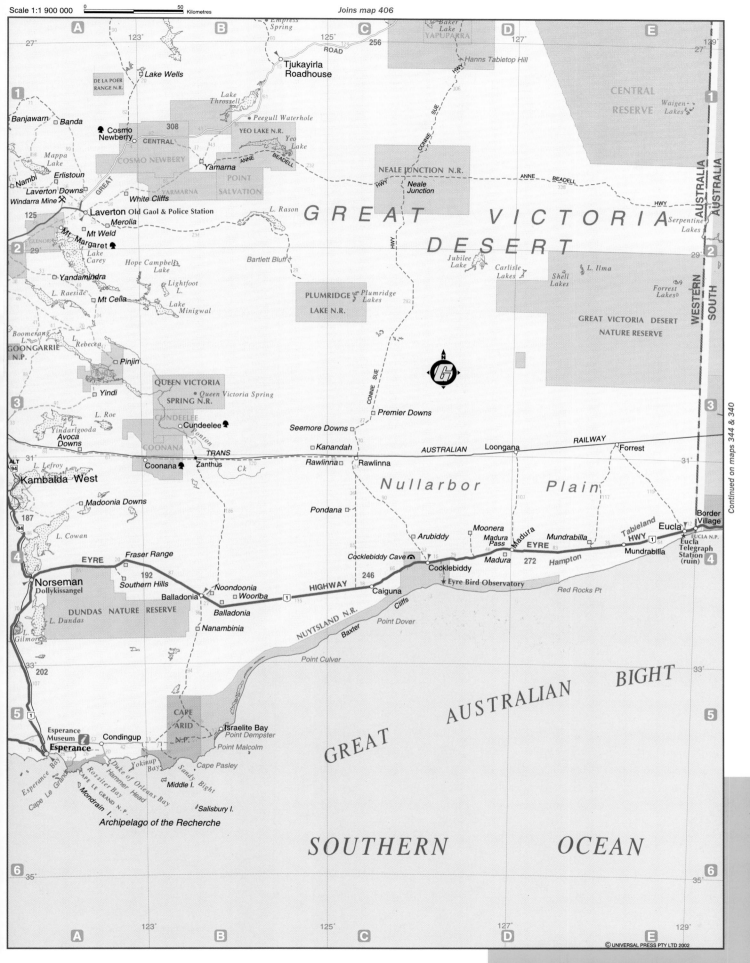

NORTHERN

The Northern Territory is Australia's most barren region and it covers approximately one-sixth of the continent. The Territory's rich Aboriginal past dates back some 60 000 years. Ceremonies, stories, rock art and intimate knowledge of the land and its seasons attest to the Aboriginal people's special link with the Territory. About 50 % of the Territory's terrain is classified Aboriginal land, and visitors are required to obtain a special permit to enter many of these areas.

The vibrant ochre and red sands of the Centre characterise the stunning MacDonnell Ranges and Simpson Desert; in contrast are the verdant greens of the rainforests and savanna woodlands of the northern lands that merge into the monsoonal Timor and Arafura seas.

The remoteness and diversity of the Northern Territory make it an ideal location for exploring beyond the beaten track. It is excellent for 4WD touring, and camel treks can be organised from Alice Springs— one option is a 2-week journey to Rainbow Valley. Bushwalkers will

Northern Territory: Outback Australia

◈ Population: 170 000
◈ Total area: 1 349 129km^2
◈ % of Australia : 17.5%
◈ Length of coastline: 10 953km
◈ Length of border: 3179km
◈ Floral emblem: Sturt's Desert Rose
◈ Fauna emblem: Red Kangaroo

TERRITORY

i **Tourist information**

Tourism Top End
Cnr Mitchell and Knuckey sts,
Darwin, NT 0800
Ph: (08) 8936 2499

**Central Australia Tourism Visitors
Information Centre**
Gregory Terrace, Alice Springs, NT 0870
Ph: (08) 8952 5800

Main ATTRACTIONS

◈ **Alice Springs**

Surrounded by the signature Northern Territory red desert, Alice Springs is the Territory's second largest centre. It is the base for exploration of the Red Centre.

◈ **Devil's Marbles**

These red and grey granite rocks perch precariously on and around each other—a very dramatic sight to explore about 400km north of Alice Springs.

◈ **Kakadu NP**

One of Australia's most famous regions. It is a World Heritage-listed national park for both its natural and cultural significance.

◈ **Kings Canyon**

Sandstone cliffs up to 100m high frame this spectacular canyon in the Watarrka NP. Relict vegetation still exists in the canyon.

◈ **Nitmiluk NP**

This national park is home to the magnificent 12km-long Katherine Gorge. Over time, the Katherine River carved out 13 gorges, which are separated by rapids.

◈ **Uluru-Kata Tjuta NP**

Uluru (Ayers Rock)—the Australian outback's most famous international landmark—is a sacred site for the local Anangu Aboriginal people.

◈ **Litchfield NP**

The national park encompasses the Tabletop Range and has spectacular waterfalls and generally crocodile-free swimming spots.

◈ **Simpson Desert**

Partly accessible by 4WD, the world's largest sand dune system has a beauty matched by its remoteness. Chambers Pillar, a 50m sandstone butte, is a major attraction.

find much to discover. Many areas in the Territory offer a variety of walking tracks of varying degrees of difficulty. Scenic flights are a more leisurely sightseeing option, while the Centre's dry heat creates ideal conditions for hot-air ballooning.

Near the geographical centre of the continent, are the iconic Uluru and Kata Tjuta. These Aboriginal sacred sites are also World Heritage-listed and are synonymous with the red heart of Australia. Nearby,

Mount Connor, a giant tabletop mountain, is also impressive in scale.

The spectacular sights, ancient landscapes and vast, formidable terrain of the Northern Territory— often subject to droughts, bushfires, flash flooding and cyclones— epitomise the description 'Outback Australia'. Adventure and discovery are constant companions in this frontier land.

Photo above: Cliffs reflected in a seasonal pool in Rainbow Valley Conservation Area

OUTBACK AUSTRALIA

Aboriginal people have occupied the Northern Territory for at least 60 000 years. Macassan seafarers regularly visited the shoreline seeking bêche-de-mer or trepang (sea cucumbers), a delicacy in Asia. They probably introduced the dingo to Australia. In 1623, a Dutch ship, the *Arnhem* also sailed offshore.

The Northern Territory was originally part of the colony of New South Wales. European settlers began to arrive in larger numbers in the Territory after the building of the Overland Telegraph in 1872. The communications line spanned the country, north to south, from Port Augusta (in South Australia) to **Palmerston** (as **Darwin** was then known). The Territory was governed by South Australia from 1862 to 1911, after which, administration was transferred to the Commonwealth Government. Self-government was granted in 1978. However, at a referendum in 1998 Territorians rejected the chance for statehood. Extensively bombed by the Japanese in WW11, Darwin has survived the ravages of tropical cyclones, especially Cyclone Tracy in 1974, to become a flourishing modern city.

Although the population is small in comparison with other Australian states, it is currently growing at a higher rate than any other state or territory. The 170 000 inhabitants represent a great ethnic diversity, including a large proportion of Aboriginal people (around 40%).

This vast Territory is often divided into 3 main geographical regions: the **Top End**, the dry **central plateaus and basins**, and the **Red Centre**. When planning a holiday to the Territory it is advisable to consider the season—climate in the Northern Territory is extreme. There are 2 main seasons in the Top End, the **Wet** season (Nov–April) with monsoonal rain and the **Dry** (May–Oct). The Dry is perhaps the best time to visit the Top End—less rain and less chance of a tropical cyclone! By contrast the Red Centre has 4 distinct seasons, with cold winters and hot, dry summers.

In the early years of European settlement, the main industry in the Territory was pastoralism, but this has now been overtaken by mining and tourism. Mineral and hydrocarbon production have impacted greatly on the state's

Western bearded dragon, *Pogona minor*

economic development in more recent years with uranium, bauxite, gold, manganese, zinc, lead, silver, copper, diamonds, opals, tin and turquoise mining adding to the state's export market. Oil and natural gas provide a massive contribution to the country's energy resources and are extracted onshore and offshore.

Tourism is also a major industry in the Northern Territory. The draw-cards are the spectacular landscapes, the unique native flora and fauna, as well as the abundant **Aboriginal rock-art** sites. Sport fishing attracts visitors from all over the world particularly those seeking the acrobatic barramundi, Australia's best fighting freshwater fish, and other tropical species. Major tourism developments have been established at **Yulara**, **Darwin**, **Alice Springs** and **Kakadu**. Other industries of importance to the Northern Territory economy are aquaculture, pearl farming and crocodile farming.

Anbangbang Gallery painting, Nourlangie Rock, Kakadu NP

Northern Territory

TOURISM REGION HIGHLIGHTS

The Northern Territory is seen as one of the world's last wild frontiers, and it is, perhaps, the expectation of adventure that draws visitors every year from around the globe. Yet touring this vast area is surprisingly easy—all-weather sealed roads reach most of the better-known tourist attractions.

A Darwin (pp.416–419)
Aquascene; Australian Pearling Exhibition; Charles Darwin NP; Crocodylus Park; Darwin Botanic Gardens; Darwin Wharf Precinct; Deck Chair Cinema; East Point Reserve; Fannie Bay Gaol; Howard Springs; Indo-Pacific Marine; Majestic Orchid Farm; Mindil Beach Sunset Markets; Museum and Art Gallery of the Northern Territory; Territory Wildlife Park

B Alice Springs
(pp.420–421 and 424)
Alice Springs Cultural Precinct; Alice Springs Desert Park; Alice Springs School of the Air; Alice Springs Telegraph Station; Anzac

Chambers Pillar at sunset

Hill; Chateau Hornsby Winery; Frontier Camel Farm; Olive Pink Botanic Garden; Royal Flying Doctor Service; School of the Air; The Date Gardens

C Central Australia
(pp.422–423)
Arltunga Historical Reserve; Chambers Pillar; Corroboree Rock; Ellery Creek Big Hole; Ewaninga Rock Carvings; Finke Gorge; Glen Helen Gorge; Henbury Meteorite Craters; Hermannsburg; Larapinta Trail; MacDonnell Ranges; N'Dhala Gorge; Ormiston Gorge; Palm Valley; Rainbow Valley; Redbank Gorge; Ross River Homestead; Serpentine Gorge; Simpson Desert; Simpsons Gap; Standley Chasm; Tanami Desert; Tnorala (Gosse Bluff); Trephina Gorge; Watarrka NP (Kings Canyon)

D Kakadu NP
(pp.412 and 426–427)
Aboriginal rock art; Bowali Visitor Centre; Gunlom Falls (Waterfall Creek); Jabiru; Jim Jim Falls; Maguk (Barramundi Gorge); Mamukala; Nourlangie Rock; Twin Falls; Ubirr; Warradjan Aboriginal Cultural Centre; Yellow Water

E Katherine (pp.427–428)
Borroloola; Cape Crawford; Cutta Cutta Caves; Daly River; Daly Waters; Elsey Homestead; Flora River Nature Park; Gregory NP; Katherine Hot Springs; Katherine Low Level Nature Reserve; Katherine Museum; Keep River NP; Leliyn (Edith Falls); Lost City; Manyallaluk; Mataranka Thermal Pool; Never Never Museum; Nitmiluk NP (Katherine Gorge); O'Keefe House; Pine Creek; Roper Bar; Springvale Homestead; Timber Creek

F Tennant Creek (pp.429–430)
Attack Creek; Barkly Tablelands; Barrow Creek; Battery Hill Mining Centre; Central Mount Stewart; Devil's Marbles; Mary Ann Recreational Dam; The Pebbles; Tuxworth Fullwood House

G The Top End
Adelaide River War Cemetery; Arnhem Land; Batchelor; Butterfly Gorge; Cobourg Peninsula; Corroboree Billabong; Douglas Hot Springs; Fogg Dam; Gove Peninsula; Lake Bennett; Litchfield NP; Magnetic Termite Mounds; Mary River NP; Nhulunbuy; Tiwi Islands (Melville and Bathurst); Umbrawarra Gorge; Window on the Wetlands

H Uluṟu – Kata Tjuṯa NP
(pp.413 and 422–423)
Kata Tjuṯa (The Olgas); Uluṟu (Ayers Rock); Uluṟu–Kata Tjuṯa Cultural Centre; Yulara

NATIONAL PARKS

The national parks of the Northern Territory are home to some of the most spectacular environments, scenery and natural formations in the country, ranging from the tropical lushness of **Kakadu** and **Katherine Gorge**, to the sands of the Centre, with Uluru rising 350m out of a sea of red sand and tufts of spinifex grass.

Primarily an area of national park attractions, the Northern Territory is a photographer's dream, with the light constantly changing the colours and shadows of these uniquely beautiful landscapes. Whilst 4 of the most popular national parks are detailed here, there are many more worth investigating. Out of the 17 national parks in the Northern Territory, only Uluru–Kata Tjuta NP and Kakadu NP have entrance fees.

facts

- No. of parks/reserves: 93
- Area: 48 129km^2
- % of state: 3.6%
- World Heritage Areas: Kakadu NP, Uluru–Kata Tjuta NP

A Kakadu NP (pp.426–427)

Kakadu NP is located 150km SE of Darwin and is Australia's largest national park covering 19 757km^2. It is owned by the Gagudju Aboriginal people and is home to around 10 000 species of insects, 1600 plant species, 275 bird species, 75 reptile species and 25 species of frogs. The diverse landscape is affected dramatically by the changing Wet and Dry seasons. As the tropical rain-fed floodplains fill, millions of birds arrive to feed and mate. The Aboriginal heritage of the park is hugely significant. Artefacts such as grindstones, shelters and stone tools, some dating back 50 000 years can be found along with ochre, used in ceremonial painting. Some of the main attractions in the national park are **Gunlom Falls**, a waterfall and plunge pool which has become a popular picnic spot; **Jabiru**, the famous town set against the spectacular backdrop of the **Arnhem Land Escarpment**; **Nourlangie Rock**, an ancient Aboriginal shelter with impressive art sites; and **Yellow Water**, a spectacular and diverse wetland ecosystem.

B Litchfield NP (pp.424–425)

The most visited park near Darwin, Litchfield NP covers 1651km^2 of monsoonal rainforest, weather-beaten sandstone, huge termite mounds, historic ruins and spring-fed streams. Around 250 000 people annually discover, or rediscover, this exciting national park. Attractions include the magnificent waterfalls, walking tracks, and magnetic termite mounds, which are not magnetic, but built by termites in a way that controls the natural temperature inside the mounds. Also, historic **Blyth Homestead** and the **Lost City**, a stunning sight which appears as a city of free-standing weathered sandstone formations jutting out of the otherwise flat landscape. The spring-fringed sandstone plateau of the **Tabletop Range** feeds the park's waterfalls; the waterholes are excellent for swimming and generally crocodile-free but observe warning signs. A number of camping spots requiring permits can be found throughout the park, with hotel accommodation at nearby **Adelaide River**. Rivers and waterholes also provide ample opportunities for anglers.

Great egret, *Ardea alba*, in Kakadu NP

Northern Territory

Uluṟu (Ayers Rock), Uluṟu-Kata Tjuṯa NP

C Nitmiluk NP (pp.428–429)

Nitmiluk NP is known mainly for the amazing **Katherine Gorge** and is located only 32km east of Katherine. Covering 2920km^2, the national park offers 120km of walking tracks varying in length from short strolls to overnight walks. As well, there is canoeing, cruises, plane and helicopter flights, swimming and wildlife spotting. The **Jatbula Trail** running through the park is internationally regarded as one of Australia's best walks. The national park is divided into 2 sectors: Katherine Gorge and **Edith Falls**. The **Katherine River** winds through the **Arnhem Land plateau** and has formed 13 water-filled gorges, some with cliffs 100m in height on either side. The main camping area in Katherine Gorge— **Nitmiluk Tours**—has all major facilities, including powered sites and a kiosk. The **Edith Falls** area also has a camping site with most facilities and a kiosk, but no power.

D Uluṟu–Kata Tjuṯa NP
(pp.422–423)

Uluṟu-Kata Tjuṯa NP, covering 1325km^2, is perhaps the most talked about national park in the country. The home of Uluṟu (Ayers Rock), as well as the magnificent Kata Tjuṯa (The Olgas), this national park has a distinctly spiritual heritage with Aṉangu Aboriginal history dating to at least 22 000 years. The rock itself, some say, is an incomparable beauty, dwarfing the surrounding desert landscape with its immensity. Around 9.4km in circumference and rising 350m above the plain, Uluṟu is a giant monolith amidst the flat, arid desert plains. Kata Tjuṯa is a group of 36 enormous weathered domes, described by explorer Ernest Giles as 'monstrous pink haystacks', the highest rises 546m into the sky. Giles named them after Queen Olga of Wurttemberg. The domes cover an area of 35km^2 and may once have been a super dome larger than Uluṟu. Their Aboriginal name, 'Kata Tjuṯa' means 'many heads'.

Each feature of the 2 landforms has great cultural and spiritual significance to the traditional Aṉangu owners. A basic knowledge of the Aboriginal mythology surrounding these sacred places and their true spiritual meaning will greatly enhance any visit to the area. Information on the area is widely available in tourist offices and visitor centres throughout the Territory. Whilst certain ceremonial sites in the national park have been declared out-of-bounds for tourists, there are special guided tours hosted by local Aborigines that are worth experiencing. (*see* pp.414–415)

National Park Head Office

Parks and Wildlife Commission
Goyder Centre,
25 Chung Wah Tce
Palmerston, NT 0830
Ph: (08) 8999 5511
www.nt.gov.au/paw

ABORIGINAL TOURISM

The oldest living culture in the world, Australia's Aboriginal people boast a heritage that is ancient and spiritual. Archaeological dating reveals evidence of human occupation for at least 60 000 years.

The relationship between Aboriginal culture and the land is deeply spiritual. Aboriginal society comprises many regional groups whose dialects, stories, ceremonies and practices differ greatly.

Today, visitors can experience Aboriginal culture and gain insight into Australia's ancient past by viewing Aboriginal rock art, listening to Dreamtime stories and mythology, watching ceremonial dancing and singing, hearing the unique sounds of the didgeridoo and experiencing sacred sites and even tasting a witchetty grub.

In the Northern Territory there are 4 particularly powerful places for visitors to experience firsthand the world's oldest culture.

Alice Springs
(pp.420–421 and 424)
The Aboriginal Art and Cultural Centre at 86 Todd St has an

Aboriginal art, Daly River region

Arrernte gallery, an Aboriginal music museum with the world's only **Didgeridoo University** as well as spear-throwing demonstrations and bush tucker. **The Alice Springs Cultural Precinct**, located at the corner of Larapinta Dr and Memorial Ave has several attractions with an Aboriginal theme. **The Araluen Centre** has a 500-seat theatre and major art galleries, including one featuring works of Albert Namatjira and his contemporaries. **The**

Museum of Central Australia, also in the precinct, has excellent natural history exhibits and the **Strehlow Collection**, which displays non-culturally sensitive material from Professor Ted Strehlow and the Arrernte Aboriginal people of Central Australia.

Kakadu NP (pp.426–427)
The **Bininj** people have established the **Warradjan Aboriginal Cultural Centre** at **Yellow Water** in Kakadu NP. Here, histories, stories and mythology are all depicted along with a showcase of Aboriginal arts and crafts of the Top End region. The **Bowali Visitor Centre**, in the main visitor centre in Kakadu NP, gives a deeper insight into the indigenous and non-indigenous history of Kakadu, including an audio-visual presentation of the park's highlights. For more information contact:

Northern Land Council
9 Rowling St, Casuarina,
Northern Territory 0811
Ph: (08) 8920 5100
www.nlc.org.au

Witchetty grubs, Aboriginal cultural tour, Wallace Rockhole Community

Northern Territory

Tiwi Islands

The Tiwi Islands are also a very significant region for Northern Territory Aboriginal people. The islands of **Bathurst** and **Melville** are only a short 80km flight from Darwin and are home to the Tiwi community. The total land area of the islands is 7450km^2 with an estimated population of 1800. Predominantly self-sufficient, the group resisted control by the Dutch and British in the past. Relative isolation has enabled the Tiwi people to preserve their culture. Since 1977, the Tiwi Islands have been regarded as Aboriginal land under the administration of the Tiwi Land Council.

Aboriginal crafts, Tiwi Islands

Pukumani carved burial poles, Bathurst Island

The islands' income is provided by both the sprawling pine plantations and tourist attractions such as stunning white sand tropical beaches bordering dense rainforests, which conceal pristine waterfalls and streams.

The Tiwi people have preserved many aspects of their distinctive culture and art, including plaited bangles, painted shells, pottery, carvings, batik and silk-screened clothing, and the unique Pukumani burial poles—originally placed around graves. Today, the poles are still commissioned, but placed on the ground where the funeral dances take place. At the end of the Wet season, the Tiwis hold the 'Kurlama', or yam ceremony, a ritual to invoke a good hunting season. The older men of the community sing songs to the ancestors and the women harvest and cook yams. Organised 1–2 day tours are the only way to see the islands.

For more information contact:
Tiwi Land Council
U5/3 Bishop St,
Stuart Park,
Northern Territory 0820
Ph: (08) 8981 4898

Uluṟu–Kata Tjuṯa

(pp.422–423)

The Aṉangu people have established the **Uluṟu-Kata Tjuṯa Cultural Centre** near **Yulara** to help visitors appreciate the history of the Aboriginal culture. Offering guided tours of 'the Rock' and its sacred areas, interpretive art, videos and oral histories, the centre is a great stop for an introduction to, and the appreciation of, the Aboriginal culture of Central Australia.

For more information contact:
Central Land Council
33 Stuart Hwy, Alice Springs,
Northern Territory 0871
Ph: (08) 8951 6320
www.clc.org.au

DARWIN

Smith St Mall, Darwin

attractions

◈ Aquascene
Witness the daily spectacular sight of hundreds of fish such as mullet, milkfish, and catfish competing for hand-fed white bread at high tide.

◈ Australian Pearling Exhibition
Provides an insight into the workings (and romance) of the local pearling industry.

◈ Darwin Botanic Gardens
Explore the 42ha gardens and discover mangroves, orchids, rainforest, open woodlands and other tropical habitats.

◈ East Point Reserve
Visit around dusk and see Fannie Bay's amazing sunset, and wallabies coming out to roam the 200ha reserve. The reserve features natural mangroves and forest, parklands and safe saltwater swimming.

◈ Indo Pacific Marine
Visitors can view living coral reef eco-systems; the night program offers a torchlight tour and a seafood buffet dinner.

◈ Mindil Beach Sunset Markets
The markets feature myriad stalls, including the very popular food stalls reflecting the city's eclectic multicultural mix.

◈ Wharf Precinct
Once the domain of anglers and skateboarders; now the old wharves are a tourist attraction, with restaurants, museums and tours.

Darwin, the Territory's capital, is perched on a picturesque harbour and lies closer to Jakarta and Singapore than to Sydney and Melbourne. First settled by Europeans in 1869, when South Australian Surveyor-General Goyder arrived to establish a city in the Top End. Palmerston, as it was then known, became the terminus for the **Overland Telegraph** link to England, which began in 1872. Darwin now serves primarily as an administration centre for government and the mining and agricultural industries.

Its isolation and steamy tropical climate gives Darwin a relaxed, easygoing atmosphere and lifestyle for its residents. On Christmas Day 1974, however, this peace was dramatically shattered, when **Cyclone Tracy** struck, making Darwin the site of Australia's worst natural disaster. During WWII, Darwin was attacked and heavily bombed by the Japanese. Today, few historic buildings remain making it one of Australia's most modern cities.

Almost half the Northern Territory population live within 50km of Australia's only tropical capital city. The population, which consists of more than 50 different cultures, has an average age younger than the rest of Australia.

Tourist information

Tourism Top End
Beagle House, cnr Mitchell and Knuckey sts, Darwin, NT 0800
Ph: (08) 8936 2499
www.ntholidays.com.au

facts

- ◈ Population: 90 011
- ◈ Date founded: 1911
- ◈ Tallest building: NT House (13 stories)
- ◈ Oldest building: Government House (1878–79)
- ◈ Average temp: 28.5°C (Jan), 25.5°C (June)

Places of Interest

Aquascene Ⓐ C5
Australian Pearling Exhibition Ⓑ E5
Chinese Temple Ⓒ D5
Darwin Botanic Gardens Ⓓ D3
Darwin Entertainment Centre Ⓔ D5
Darwin Wharf Precinct Ⓕ E6
Fannie Bay Gaol Museum Ⓖ C1
Government House Ⓗ D5
Indo Pacific Marine Ⓘ E5
MGM Grand Darwin (Casino) Ⓙ C3
Mindil Beach Lookout Ⓚ B3
Mindil Beach Market Ⓛ C3
Museum and Art Gallery of the NT Ⓜ C2
Old Court House Ⓝ D5
Parliament House Ⓞ D5
Smith St Mall Ⓟ D5
Vesteys Beach Ⓠ C2

Timor Sea, Nightcliff, Darwin

Northern Territory

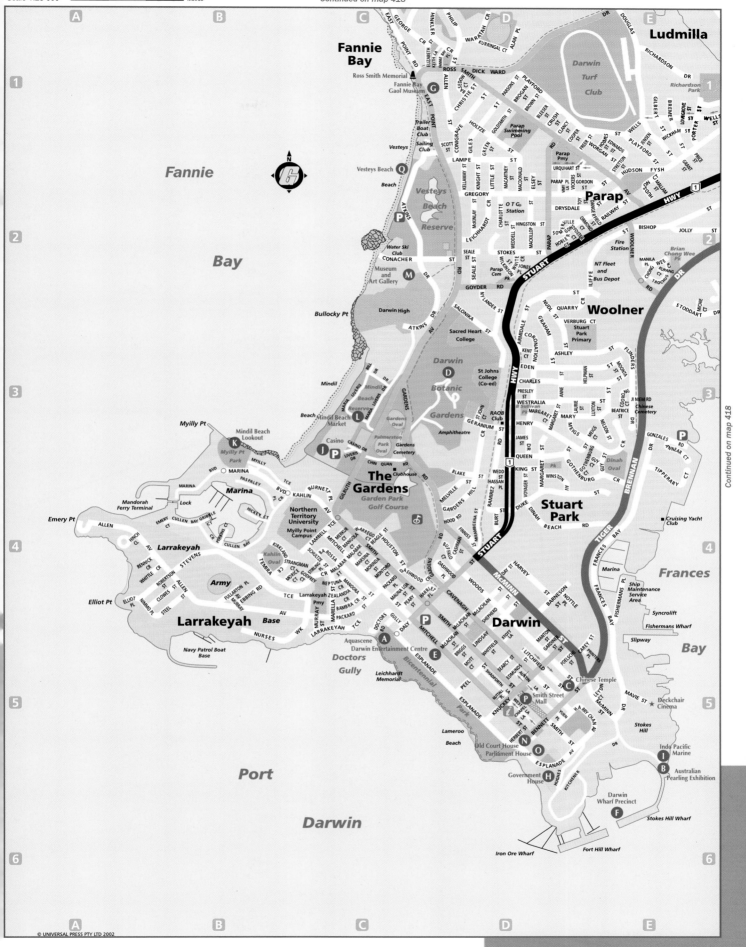

Fannie Bay

Ludmilla

Ross Smith Memorial
Fannie Bay Gaol Museum

Darwin Turf Club

Richardson Park

Trailer Boat Club
Sailing Club

Parap Swimming Pool

Fannie

Vesteys

Vesteys Beach

Parap Pmy

Parap

Beach

Vesteys Beach Reserve

Bay

Water Ski Club
CONACHER

Fire Station

NT Fleet and Bus Depot

Brian Chong Wee Pk

Woolner

Museum and Art Gallery

Bullocky Pt

Darwin High

Verburg Ct
Stuart Park Primary

Sacred Heart College

Stoddart

Mindil

Darwin Botanic Gardens

St Johns College (Co-ed)

Chinese Cemetery

Beach

Mindil Beach Reserve

RAOB Club

Myilly Pt

Mindil Beach Lookout

Mindil Beach Market

Gardens Oval

Amphitheatre

Dinah Oval

Myilly Pt Park

Casino

Palmerston Park Oval

Gardens Cemetery

Stuart Park

Clubhouse

Cruising Yacht Club

Emery Pt

MARINA

Marina

Northern Territory University
Myilly Point Campus

The Gardens
Garden Park Golf Course

Frances

Larrakeyah

Mandorah Ferry Terminal
Lock

Marina

Ship Maintenance Service Area

Syncrolift

Fishermans Wharf

Army

Elliot Pt

Larrakeyah Base

Darwin

Bay

Aquascene
Darwin Entertainment Centre

NURSES

Doctors Gully

Leichhardt Memorial

Bicentennial Park

Chinese Temple

Mavie St

Deckchair Cinema

Smith Street Mall

Stokes Hill

Lameroo Beach

Old Court House
Parliament House

Indo Pacific Marine

Australian Pearling Exhibition

Port

Government House

Darwin Wharf Precinct

Darwin

Stokes Hill Wharf

Iron Ore Wharf

Fort Hill Wharf

Continued on map 418

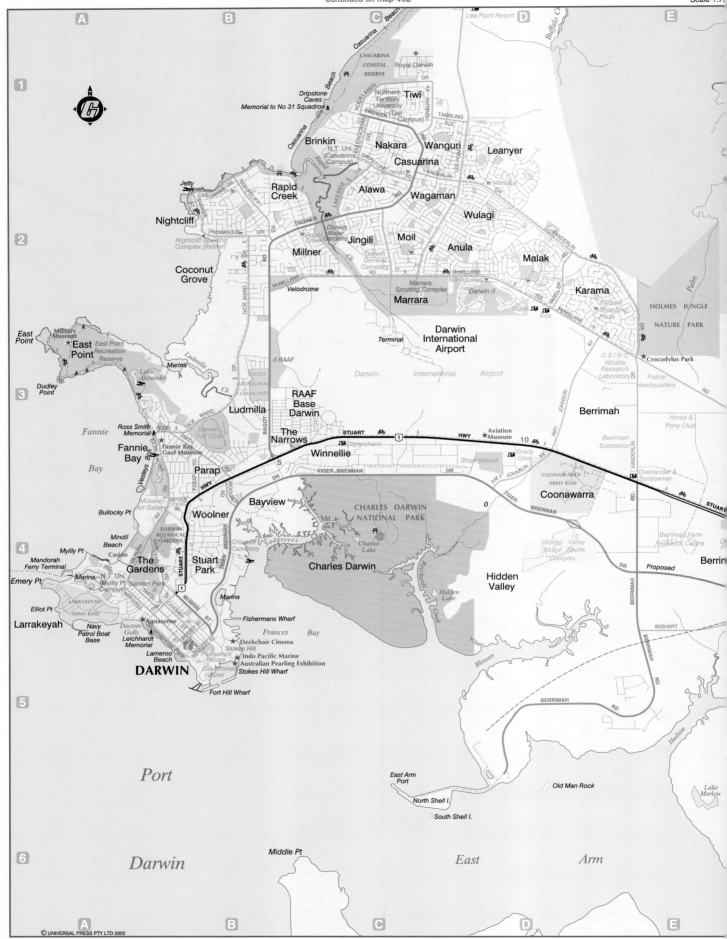

East
Point

East
Point

Dudley
Point

Fannie

Bay

Emery Pt

Elliot Pt

Larrakeyah

Myilly Pt

Mandorah
Ferry Terminal

Navy
Patrol Boat
Base

DARWIN

Port

Darwin

Middle Pt

East

Arm

Nightcliff

Coconut
Grove

Rapid
Creek

Brinkin

Millner

Jingili

Ludmilla

Fannie
Bay

Parap

Woolner

Bayview

The
Gardens

Stuart
Park

Nakara

Casuarina

Alawa

Moil

Wagaman

RAAF
Base
Darwin

The
Narrows

Winnellie

Charles Darwin

Tiwi

Wanguri

Leanyer

Wulagi

Anula

Malak

Karama

Marrara

Darwin
International
Airport

Berrimah

Coonawarra

Hidden
Valley

Charles Darwin
NATIONAL
PARK

Holmes Jungle
Nature Park

Crocodylus Park

Police
Headquarters

Berri

East Arm
Port

Old Man Rock

Lake
Marlow

F G H J K

1

Hope

Inlet

*Howards
Peninsula*

MILITARY AREA

(FORMER RAAF BOMBING AND GUNNERY RANGE)

NO PUBLIC ACCESS

*Noogoo
Swamp*

2

Mickett

ckett
reek

ckett Creek
ting Complex

*Thorak
Cemetery*

Thorak
Reserve

Milner   Swamp

Kings

3

ROBERTSON BARRACKS

(MILITARY AREA)

Kings

Howard

River

Continued on map 432

Knuckey
Lagoon

Pinelands

HWY

Holtze

Ck

*Howard
Springs*

*Howard Springs
Nature Park*

4

Northern
Territory
University

ROYSTONEA

20

Durack

Palmerston

Yarrawonga

TCE

Palmerston
Town Centre

STUART

GUNN POINT

RD

HALY Park

*Dutchie
Lagoon*

5

Marlow
Lagoon

Driver

Palmerston

Gunn

Mitchell

Marlow
Lagoon
Recreation
Area

Gray

Bakewell

Creek

HOWARD SPRINGS

25

LAMBRICK

*Wadham
Lagoon*

Howard
Springs

6

Woodroffe

Moulden   Rosebery

Sewage
Treatment
Works

Bellamack

Virginia   HWY

Archer
Sporting
Complex

F G H J K

©UNIVERSAL PRESS PTY LTD 2002

NORTHERN TERRITORY   419

■ Adelaide River   POP 279

Map 425, D2

The location for 30 000 Australian and US soldiers during WWII, this small town lies 112km SE of Darwin on the Stuart Hwy.

MAIN ATTRACTION: The **Adelaide River War Cemetery**, with the graves of 434 servicemen, is just to the north.

NEARBY ATTRACTIONS: Historic **Mount Bundy Station**, 3km NE, offers a rural Territory experience, with fishing, walking and accommodation. **Robin Falls**, 15km south, flows for most of the year. **Daly River Roadhouse** and region, 114km SW, is a good locale for fishing and Aboriginal arts and crafts. **Litchfield NP** is close by, although the main entrance is via the Litchfield Park Rd, 27km north.

TOURIST INFO: Tourism Top End, Darwin, Ph: (08) 8936 2499

■ Alice Springs   POP 22 488

Map 421 and 442, E2

European settlement in Alice Springs dates back to 1871 with the building of the Overland Telegraph line linking Australia with Europe. **'The Alice'**, as it is affectionately known, is almost at the geographical centre of Australia, and around 1500km from Darwin and Adelaide.

MAIN ATTRACTIONS: The heart of Alice Springs is **Todd Mall**, with many attractions in the vicinity. There are galleries selling Aboriginal art, crafts, textiles and pottery, with the opportunity to see the artists at work, and an **Aboriginal Art and Culture Centre**. The **Adelaide House Museum** has an exhibit explaining the origins and workings of **The Royal Flying Doctor Service** and daily tours are available at the Stuart Terrace base. The **National Pioneer Women's Hall of Fame** is in the old Court House. Close by, the **Sounds of Starlight Theatre** has a show April–Nov depicting a musical journey through Central Australia. Also nearby are **Minerals House**, with geological displays; **Old Stuart Gaol**; and **Anzac Hill**, with views over the town. The **Todd River** doesn't flow much. In fact, it's usually dry and the venue for the **Henley-on-Todd Regatta**, an unusual 'sailing' event where competitors carry their 'boats' for the whole course of the race.

In the northern suburbs are the **School of the Air**, Australia's first radio school for children in remote areas, and the **Alice Springs Telegraph Station Historical Reserve**. The painstakingly restored stone buildings of the reserve have displays of photographs and documents portraying life in the early days of settlement. West of the mall are the **Araluen Arts Centre**, the **Museum of Central Australia** and, further along Larapinta Dr, the **Alice Springs Desert Park**. The latter features animals and plants in a natural desert habitat and explains their traditional use by Aboriginal people. There are also 8 walk-through aviaries and the world's largest nocturnal house. To the south-east, across the Todd River, are **Lasseter's Casino** and the 16ha **Olive Pink Botanic Gardens**, which is the most developed arid-zone botanic garden in Australia. For visitors wanting to make a circuit of the many local attractions the green and yellow **Alice Wanderer Bus** service provides a pleasant and easy way to see the sights. Hot-air balloon flights from Alice Springs are very popular, as are tours by bus, 4WD, Harley Davidson motorcycle, helicopter, light aircraft and, for the more adventurous, camel treks.

NEARBY ATTRACTIONS: Alice Springs is the ideal base from which to travel around the entire **Red Centre** region. At **Gemtree**, 135km NE, visitors can prospect for zircons and join guided fossicking tours. To the east (7km), the **Frontier Camel Farm** offers camel rides. The Ross Hwy also leads to **The Date Gardens**,

(CONTINUED P.424)

Alice Springs Telegraph Station

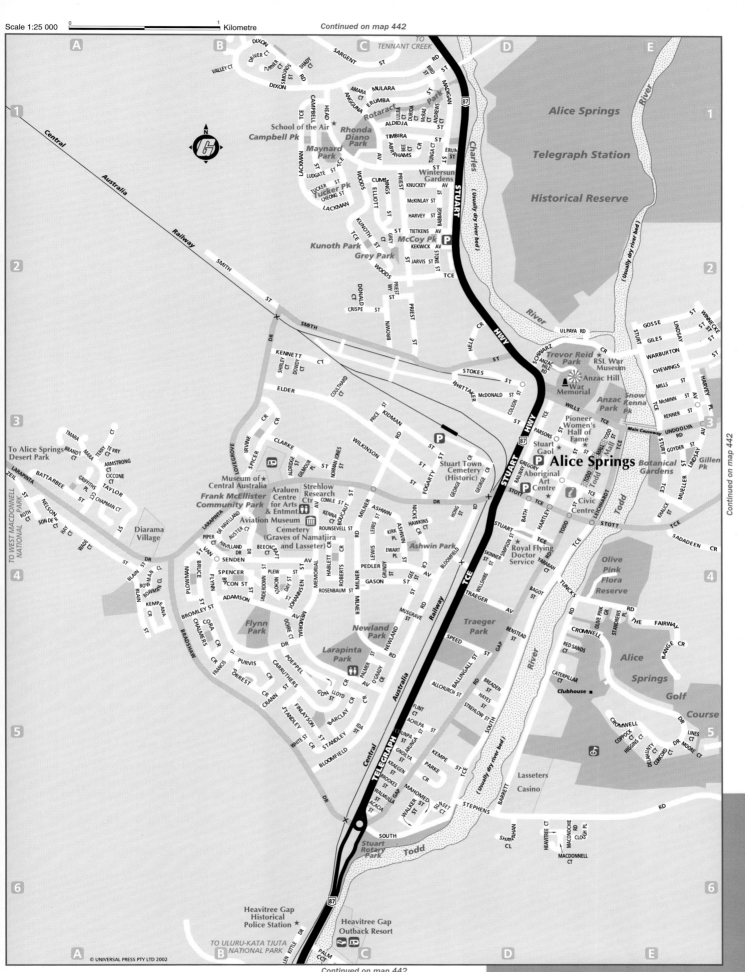

Continued on map 442

TO TENNANT CREEK

Central

Australia

Railway

Alice Springs
Telegraph Station
Historical Reserve

School of the Air ★
Campbell Pk

Rhonda Diano Park

Maynard Park

Tucker Pk

Wintersun Gardens

Kunoth Park

McCoy Pk

Grey Park

To Alice Springs Desert Park

TO WEST MACDONNELL NATIONAL PARK

Diarama Village

Museum of Central Australia ★
Frank McEllister Community Park

Araluen Centre for Arts & Entmnt.
Strehlow Research Ctr

Aviation Museum
Cemetery (Graves of Namatjira and Lasseter)

Trevor Reid Park

RSL War Museum
Anzac Hill
★ War Memorial

Anzac Park

Snow Kenna

Pioneer Women's Hall of Fame

Stuart Gaol ★

Alice Springs
Aboriginal Art Centre

Civic Centre

Botanical Gardens

Stuart Town Cemetery (Historic)

Royal Flying Doctor Service

Olive Pink Flora Reserve

Ashwin Park

Flynn Park

Newland Park

Larapinta Park

Traeger Park

Clubhouse ■

Alice Springs Golf Course

Lasseters Casino

Heavitree Gap Historical Police Station ★

TO ULURU-KATA TJUTA NATIONAL PARK

Heavitree Gap Outback Resort

Stuart Rotary Park

Todd

© UNIVERSAL PRESS PTY LTD 2002

CENTRAL AUSTRALIA (THE RED CENTRE)

The terrain west of Alice Springs to **Uluru-Kata Tjuta NP** is the heart of the Red Centre, spanning the western section of the **MacDonnell Ranges**. This vast and stunning but rugged landscape encompasses an ancient and unique terrain dotted with gorges, waterholes, unusual geological formations, tranquil creeks and strange landforms, carved out over hundreds of millions of years.

The arid and seemingly inhospitable landscape is home to an array of flora and fauna—springtime sees the blossoming of colourful wildflowers, and rock wallabies are often seen around the steep ridges and rocky outcrops of **Simpsons Gap**.

Uluru-Kata Tjuta NP covers 1325km² and contains 2 of the world's greatest natural wonders, Uluru (Ayers Rock) and Kata Tjuta (The Olgas). This national park is one of the most visited sites in Australia. The park also offers much more, including spectacular views,

Desert wildflowers west of Alice Springs

guided walks, and an insight into Anangu Aboriginal heritage. With 500 plant species, 150 bird species, 24 endemic mammals, and the 72 species of reptiles, (making it the richest reptile fauna on Earth), it received international recognition in 1977, when it was declared an **International Biosphere Reserve** by UNESCO. In 1987, Uluru-Kata Tjuta NP was listed as a **World Heritage Area**. Extensions to the park were listed in 1994.

main attractions

◈ **Finke Gorge NP**

This national park's main attraction is Palm Valley. Prehistoric cycads and red cabbage palms have survived the barren terrain for more than 10 000yrs, relics of a wetter time.

◈ **Kata Tjuta**

These extraordinary rock formations and 36 domes rise from the ground and, like Uluru, their colours change with the light throughout the day. None of the domes are safe to climb. The 7km Valley of the Winds walk is spectacular.

◈ **Standley Chasm**

Sunlight bathes the 80m high walls of this narrow chasm around noon. The chasm was formed by erosion of the softer rock from the red, quartzite walls.

◈ **Uluru**

At 350m high, Uluru is the world's largest monolith. The Mala and Kuniya guided walks provide an excellent grounding in the cultural significance of Uluru as a sacred site of the Anangu people.

◈ **Yulara (Ayers Rock Resort)**

This tourist resort and village is within close proximity to the district's major attractions.

Tourist information

Uluru–Kata Tjuta Cultural Centre
Uluru–Kata Tjuta NP
Yulara, NT 0872
Ph: (08) 8956 2299

Garden of Eden in Watarrka NP (Kings Canyon)

Northern Territor

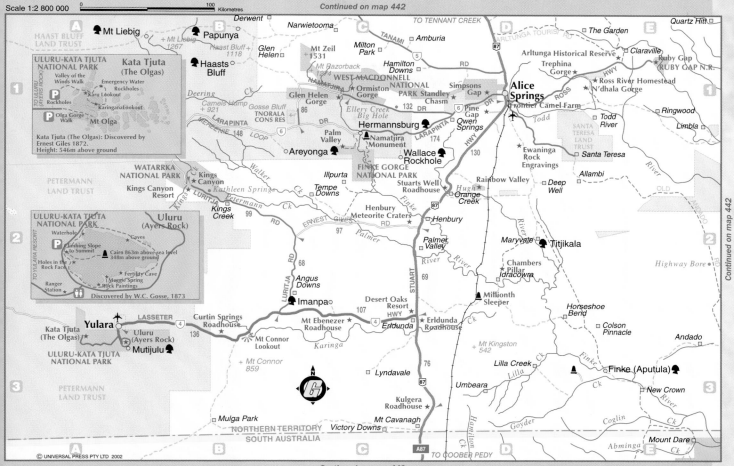

Continued on map 442

Scale 1:2 800 000

ULURU-KATA TJUTA NATIONAL PARK
Kata Tjuta (The Olgas)

Valley of the Winds Walk
Emergency Water
Rockholes
Karu Lookout
Rockholes
Olga Gorge Walk
Karingana Lookout
Mt Olga

Kata Tjuta (The Olgas): Discovered by Ernest Giles 1872.
Height: 546m above ground

ULURU-KATA TJUTA NATIONAL PARK
Uluru (Ayers Rock)

Waterhole
Caves
Climbing Slope to Summit
Holes in the Rock Face
Fertility Cave
Moggie Spring
Rock Paintings
Ranger Station
Cairn 863m above sea level
348m above ground

Discovered by W.C. Gosse, 1873

HAAST BLUFF LAND TRUST

Mt Liebig
+ Mt Liebig 1267
Papunya
Haasts Bluff
Haast Bluff + 1118

PETERMANN LAND TRUST

WATARRKA NATIONAL PARK
Kings Canyon
Kings Canyon Resort
Kings Creek
Kathleen Springs

Yulara
LASSETER
Kata Tjuta (The Olgas)
Uluru (Ayers Rock)
Mutijulu
ULURU-KATA TJUTA NATIONAL PARK

PETERMANN LAND TRUST

Mulga Park

Derwent
Narwietooma
Glen Helen
Mt Zeil +1531
Milton Park
Amburia
Mt Razorback
Hamilton Downs
WEST MACDONNELL NATIONAL PARK
Ormiston Gorge
Simpsons Gap
Standley Chasm
Gosse Bluff TNORALA CONS RES
Glen Helen Gorge
Ellery Creek Big Hole
Pine Gap
Owen Springs
Palm Valley
Hermannsburg
Namatjira Monument
Areyonga
Wallace Rockhole
Illpurta
FINKE GORGE NATIONAL PARK
Tempe Downs
Stuarts Well Roadhouse
Henbury Meteorite Craters
Henbury
Orange Creek
Palmer Valley
Angus Downs
Imanpa
Desert Oaks Resort
Erldunda
Erldunda Roadhouse
Millionth Sleeper
Mt Ebenezer Roadhouse
Curtin Springs Roadhouse
Mt Connor Lookout
+ Mt Connor 859
Karinga
Lyndavale
Kulgera Roadhouse
Mt Cavanagh
Victory Downs
NORTHERN TERRITORY
SOUTH AUSTRALIA

TO TENNANT CREEK
The Garden
Quartz Hill
ARLTUNGA TOURIST RD
Arltunga Historical Reserve
Claraville
Trephina Gorge
Ruby Gap
RUBY GAP N.R.
Alice Springs
Ross River Homestead
N'dhala Gorge
Frontier Camel Farm
Todd River
Ringwood
Limbla
Ewaninga Rock Engravings
Santa Teresa
SANTA TERESA LAND TRUST
Rainbow Valley
Deep Well
Allambi
Maryvale
Titjikala
Chambers Pillar
Idracowra
Horseshoe Bend
Highway Bore
Colson Pinnacle
Andado
+ Mt Kingston 542
Lilla Creek
Finke (Aputula)
New Crown
Umbeara
Coglin Ck
Goyder River
Abminga
Mount Dare

TO COOBER PEDY

© UNIVERSAL PRESS PTY LTD 2002

Continued on map 442

Continued on map 442

Kata Tjuta (The Olgas) at sunset, Uluru-Kata Tjuta NP

LITCHFIELD NP

Home to the Wagait Aboriginal people; the area was mined for tin and copper before being used as a pastoral lease. The 1651km² area was proclaimed a National Park in 1986. Located 129km from Darwin and 268km from Katherine, this popular park has many natural and historic attractions. Access to some of the more remote attractions such as the unusual sandstone pillars of the **Lost City** is by 4WD only and most tracks are closed during the Wet season.

Thousands of 3m-high **magnetic termite mounds** exist in the park. Several waterfalls punctuate the escarpments and provide a refreshing opportunity to swim in the pools below. The most popular attraction in Litchfield is **Wangi Falls**, which also has a 3km-long walking track through monsoonal forest to the top of the falls. Other falls include **Tjaynera Falls (Sandy Creek)**, **Tolmer Falls**, **Buley Rockhole** and **Florence Falls**. Camping facilities are available at Wangi Falls, **Walker Creek**, Tjaynera Falls, Florence Falls, Buley Rockhole and **Surprise Creek**.

main attractions

- Blyth Homestead
- Lost City
- Magnetic termite mounds
- Waterfalls

ℹ Tourist information

Tourism Top End
cnr Mitchell and Knuckey sts
Darwin, NT 0800
Ph: (08) 8936 2499

Magnetic termite mounds

Australia's first commercial date farm; **Chateau Hornsby Winery** (11km); **Emily Gap** (13km); and **Jessie Gap** (18km). Further into the **East MacDonnell Ranges**, the highway also leads to **Corroboree Rock**; **Trephina** and **N'dhala Gorges**; **Ross River Homestead**; and **Arltunga Historical Reserve**. To the west are **Rev John Flynn's grave** (5km), **Simpsons Gap** (17km), **Standley Chasm** (50km), **Ellery Creek Big Hole** (93km), **Serpentine Gorge** (104km), **Ochre Pits** (119km), **Ormiston** and **Glen Helen gorges** (about 132km) and **Redbank Gorge** (170km, 4WD only). Most of these are in the **West MacDonnell NP**, as is the acclaimed walking track, the **Larapinta Trail**. Larapinta Dr also leads to **Hermannsburg** (125km) and **Palm Valley** in **Finke Gorge NP** (140km, 4WD only).

To the south are the **Transport Hall of Fame** and the **Ghan Preservation Society's Rail Museum** at **MacDonnell Siding** (10km). The Ghan railway was replaced in 1980, but visitors can still travel the **Old Ghan** to **Ewaninga**. Side roads from the Stuart Hwy to the south lead to **Ewaninga Rock Carvings Conservation Reserve** (35km), an Aboriginal cultural site; the magnificent **Rainbow Valley** (99km); **Henbury Meteorite Craters** (147km); and **Chambers Pillar** (149km), a 50m-high sandstone pillar, which served as a landmark for early explorers.
TOURIST INFO: 60 Gregory Tce,
Ph: (08) 8952 5800

■ Batchelor   POP 645

Map 425, C1

Once the service centre for Australia's first uranium mine, Rum Jungle (now closed), Batchelor is the gateway to **Litchfield NP**.
MAIN ATTRACTIONS: **Coomalie Cultural Centre** at Batchelor College has an extensive display of Aboriginal artworks. There is a mini replica of Bohemia's **Karlstein Castle** on the Rum Jungle Rd.
NEARBY ATTRACTIONS: **Lake Bennett Wilderness Resort**, 25km NE, offers fishing, swimming, windsurfing, boating, bushwalking and accommodation. Swimming is also popular at **Rum Jungle Lake**, 10km west. Litchfield NP, a magnificent wilderness area, is 20km to the west. Most of Litchfield's main attractions, such as the magnetic

Northern Territory

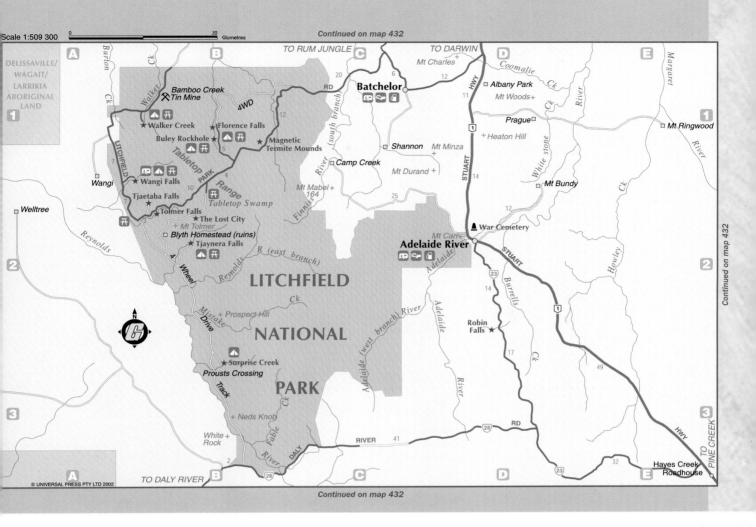

Continued on map 432

termite mounds, Florence, Tolmer and Wangi falls and Buley Rockhole can be accessed via the sealed Litchfield Park Rd. A 4WD is required to reach the unusual and enticing sandstone rock formations of The Lost City, Tjaynera Falls and the ruins of the old **Blyth Homestead**; during the Wet season the tracks can become impassable and may be closed. The park has rainforest walks and camping grounds.
TOURIST INFO: Tarkarri Rd,
Ph: (08) 8976 0444

■ Borroloola   POP 551

Map 437, H2

Borroloola is an Aboriginal community on the **Carpentaria Hwy** which is popular with 4WD and fishing enthusiasts. Tourists do not need a permit to visit the town.

MAIN ATTRACTIONS: Scenic flights can be made over the town and the **Sir Edward Pellew Island Group**. Fishing for barramundi, trevally and other tropical species and succulent mud crabs is very popular. River and island tours are available. The old **Police Station**, built in 1886, has a small museum.
NEARBY ATTRACTIONS: **Cape Crawford**, 110km SW, is a base from which to visit extraordinary ancient sandstone rocks in remote areas to the east. The **Bukalara Rock Formations** can be reached by 4WD, it is highly recommended to travel with a guide. The strange rock formations of **The Lost City** can only be reached by helicopter and a guide is essential.
TOURIST INFO: Borroloola Community Government Council,
Ph: (08) 8975 8799

■ Hermannsburg   POP 462

Map 442, C2

Home to an Aboriginal community, Hermannsburg lies 125km west of Alice Springs on the site of a Lutheran Mission—the first Aboriginal mission in the Northern Territory. It was once the home of painter **Albert Namatjira** for many years and while visitors are welcome they are restricted to the historic precinct, shop and petrol station.
MAIN ATTRACTIONS: The historic precinct includes **Strehlow's House** (1897); the **Old Manse** (1888), now a gallery showcasing Aboriginal watercolours of the Hermannsburg School; mission station buildings; and a museum in the **Old Colonists House** (1885).
NEARBY ATTRACTIONS: There is a monument to the famous Aboriginal

KAKADU NP

This World Heritage-listed national park is internationally famous for the breathtaking natural beauty of its wetlands, escarpments and spectacular waterfalls as well as its more than 50 000-year-old Aboriginal cultural heritage. Aboriginal people own and co-manage the huge park, which covers almost 20 000km^2 and encompasses a huge variety of Top End habitats. The park has an equally diverse number of plants and animals, including 1600 plant species, 25 frog species, 75 reptile species and 275 species of bird.

There are more than 5000 Aboriginal cultural sites in the park. The ancient rock-art galleries of Kakadu are the oldest in the world and record extinct species like the *thylacine* (Tasmanian Tiger) as well as depicting sacred creation beings like Namarrgon the Lightning Man and Ngalyod the Rainbow Serpent.

Several styles are represented including x-ray paintings showing the internal structure of animals fish and birds.

main attractions

- Gunlom Falls
- Jim Jim Falls
- Nourlangie Rock
- Ubirr Rock
- Warradjan Aboriginal Cultural Centre
- Yellow Water

ℹ Tourist information

Tourism Top End
cnr Mitchell and Knuckey sts
Darwin, NT 0800
Ph: (08) 8936 2499

Nourlangie Creek, Kakadu NP

---

painter Albert Namatjira, 2km east on Larapinta Dr. Aboriginal cultural tours are available at the **Wallace Rockhole** community, 46km SE. **Finke Gorge NP** is 20km south. The park features many rare plants unique to the area including red fan palms (*Livistona mariae*) in **Palm Valley** and extraordinary rock formations—4WD country. **Tnorala (Gosse Bluff)** meteorite crater is 35km west, with a **Mereenie Loop Pass** required for access (available at Hermannsburg petrol station).
TOURIST INFO: Kata-Anga
Tearooms, Ph: (08) 8956 7402

▪ Howard Springs   POP 3207
Map 419, K6
This Darwin satellite township lies 34km to the east. The springs were Darwin's main water supply before the construction of **Manton Dam**.

MAIN ATTRACTION: A beautiful spring-fed swimming pool, fringed by rainforest, is the central feature of **Howard Springs Nature Park**. A wildlife and recreation area since WWII, it has picnic sites and a kiosk.
NEARBY ATTRACTIONS: There are several orchid farms and exotic nurseries nearby. **Darwin Crocodile Farm**, 18km south on the Stuart Hwy, is Australia's largest, with a population of 7000 saltwater and freshwater crocodiles and even some American alligators. Cox Peninsula Rd, further south, leads to several interesting places, such as the **Berry Springs Nature Park** (57km from Darwin), which offers safe swimming in a monsoon forest pool. The adjacent **Territory Wildlife Park** is home to Top End native wildlife in a 400ha bushland setting. To the south of **Lakes Resort** are **Southport Siding**

Exotic Fruit Farm, **Majestic Orchids Farm**, **Tumbling Waters Tourist Park** and Manton Dam.
TOURIST INFO: Tourism Top End, Darwin, Ph: (08) 8936 2499

▪ Jabiru   POP 1696
Map 427, D2
Jabiru is on the Arnhem Hwy 80km from Darwin. The town was established after uranium mining began. It is situated on 13km^2 of leased land in **Kakadu NP**. When mining ceases in the area it will be restored.
MAIN ATTRACTIONS: **Gagudju Crocodile Hotel** is built in the shape of a crocodile, a totem of the local Gagudju people. Fishing and safari tours are available.
NEARBY ATTRACTIONS: Arnhem Hwy, the main tourist route from Darwin passes the superb waterlily-covered **Fogg Dam**, **Window on the**

Northern Territory

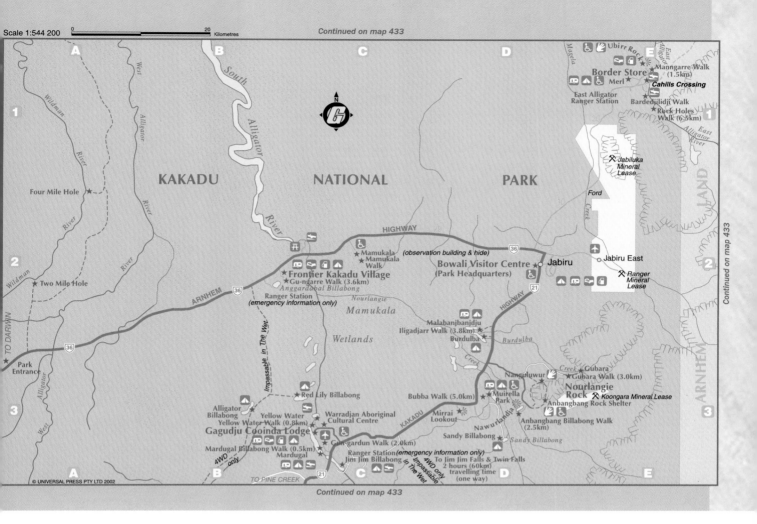

Continued on map 433

Scale 1:544 200
0   20 Kilometres

KAKADU   NATIONAL   PARK

Four Mile Hole ★

Two Mile Hole ★

Park Entrance

TO DARWIN

ARNHEM

Mamukala ★ Mamukala Walk

(observation building & hide)

Bowali Visitor Centre (Park Headquarters)

Jabiru

Jabiru East

○ Ranger Mineral Lease

Jabiluka Mineral Lease

Ford

Ubirr Rock

Border Store

Manngarre Walk (1.5km)

Merl ★ Cahills Crossing

East Alligator Ranger Station

Bardedjilidji Walk

Rock Holes Walk (6.5km)

ARNHEM LAND

Frontier Kakadu Village
★ Gu-ngarre Walk (3.6km)
Anggardabal Billabong
Ranger Station
(emergency information only)

Mamukala

Wetlands

HIGHWAY

Malabanjbanjdju
Iligadjarr Walk (3.8km) ★
Burdulba

Burdulba

Creek

Gubara
★ Gubara Walk (3.0km)

Nanguluwur
★ Nourlangie Rock
✕ Koongara Mineral Lease

Anbangbang Rock Shelter

Anbangbang Billabong Walk (2.5km)

Bubba Walk (5.0km) ★

Muirella Park

Mirrai ★ Lookout

Sandy Billabong

Nawurlandja

Impassable in The Wet

Red Lily Billabong

Alligator Billabong
Yellow Water ★
Yellow Water Walk (0.8km)
Gagudju Cooinda Lodge

Warradjan Aboriginal Cultural Centre

Gun-gardun Walk (2.0km)

Mardugal Billabong Walk (0.5km)
Mardugal
Jim Jim Billabong

Ranger Station (emergency information only)
To Jim Jim Falls & Twin Falls
2 hours (60km)
travelling time (one way)

4WD only

4WD only
Impassable in The Wet

TO PINE CREEK

© UNIVERSAL PRESS PTY LTD 2002

Continued on map 433

Continued on map 433

Wetlands display centre, **Djukbinj** and **Mary River NPs**. The many attractions of world-famous Kakadu NP are close to Jabiru, including Aboriginal rock-art sites at **Nourlangie Rock** and **Ubirr** and numerous billabongs with prolific wildlife. **Bowali Visitors Centre** can be reached by road or short walk. It is only 1.5km from Jabiru. **Yellow Water**, 55km SE, is a spectacular large billabong, where tourist cruises guarantee sightings of waterbirds and other wildlife, including crocodiles. **Warradjan Aboriginal Cultural Centre** is nearby. **Jim Jim** and **Twin Falls** can be reached by a track only accessible to 4WDs, though it may be impassable after heavy monsoonal rain when the falls are at their best.

The Kakadu landscape can be viewed on scenic flights departing from Jabiru airport. There are daily tours to **Ranger Uranium Mine**, 6km east; and the **Injalak Art and Craft Centre** at **Oenpelli**, in nearby Arnhem Land, is worth a visit (a permit is necessary). During the Wet season (approx Nov–April), roads to Ubirr, Jim Jim and Twin Falls, Ranger Mine and Arnhem Land are usually impassable, but alternative transportation may be available to some attractions. Landscapes and wildlife are particularly spectacular during the Wet.

TOURIST INFO: 6 Tasman Plaza, Ph: (08) 8979 2548 or Tourism Top End, Darwin, Ph: (08) 8936 2499

■ **Katherine**   POP 11 300
Map 429, C3
Lying 310km from Darwin, Katherine is a centre for beef-cattle properties, produce farms and the Tindal RAAF

Base. Katherine is also the gateway to **Nitmiluk NP**.

MAIN ATTRACTIONS: Katherine boasts 2 museums; **Katherine Museum** off Gorge Rd and the **Railway Station Museum** (hours of opening from visitors centre). The **School of the Air** in Giles St is usually open on school days, with tours available. Historic **O'Keefe House** is in Riverbank Dr. For swimming, fishing or bushwalking in shady riverbank parkland, head for **Katherine Low Level Nature Park**. The pools are fed by natural hot springs located nearby.

NEARBY ATTRACTIONS: Renowned **Katherine Gorge** in Nitmiluk NP, 29km SE, can be viewed by canoe, flat-bottomed tour boat, scenic flight or helicopter. **Edith Falls**, 62km to the north, is also in Nitmiluk NP and worth a visit.

NITMILUK NP

'Nitmiluk' is the traditional Jawoyn owners' word for 'Cicada Dreaming', an important Aboriginal Creation story. Located 29km from Katherine on sealed road, the 2920km² park, on the southernmost end of the **Arnhem Land Plateau**, contains a series of 13 beautiful gorges carved out over time by the **Katherine River** and separated by rapids. Rock art adorns the gorge walls and the park is home to prolific wildlife, including freshwater crocodiles and 168 species of birds. Walking, swimming, fishing (lures only), canoeing and cruising along the river are popular activities.

The park is a bushwalkers paradise with 120km of walking trails, ranging from 400m to the 65km one-way **Jatbula Trail**, from **Katherine Gorge** to **Leliyn-Edith Falls** (accessed via the Stuart Hwy). Guided walking tours and extended camping bushwalks are available. For information on these and other park details, see the excellent national park information sheets. If bushwalking sounds too strenuous, why not take a helicopter tour for a birdseye view of the gorge and surrounding country.

main attractions

- Edith Falls
- Jatbula Trail
- Katherine Gorge
- Katherine River

Tourist information

Nitmiluk Visitors Centre
Gorge Rd,
Nitmiluk NP, NT 0851
Ph: (08) 8972 1886

Tour boat in Nitmiluk NP (Katherine Gorge)

So too is **Springvale Homestead**, 8km west, the oldest remaining homestead in the Territory, built by Alfred Giles in 1878. **Cutta Cutta Caves**, 500-million-year-old limestone caves 27km south, are the home of the rare orange horseshoe bat, with cave tours available year-round. **Flora River Nature Park**, 86km SW, features unique tufa dams, pools and cascades. Aboriginal cultural tours are available at **Manyallaluk, Eva Valley**.
TOURIST INFO: Cnr Katherine Tce (Stuart Hwy) and Lindsay St, Ph: (08) 8972 2650

■ Mataranka POP 667
Map 433, G6
Mataranka is a small town 106km SE of Katherine on the Stuart Hwy.
MAIN ATTRACTIONS: The **Museum of the Never Never** has historical displays of railway history and outback life. Statuary representing characters from the Australian classic outback pioneering novel *We of the Never Never* (by Jeannie Gunn) can be seen in **Stan Martin Park**. Visitors can see barramundi being fed every morning at **Territory Manor** and the works of local artists are on show at **Stockyard Gallery**.
NEARBY ATTRACTIONS: **Elsey NP**, 5km east, offers bushwalking and camping, as well as boating, canoeing and barramundi fishing on the **Roper River**. A swim in the clear waters of **Mataranka Thermal Pool**, surrounded by lush forest, is a must. From here, a walking trail leads to the **Mataranka Falls** and the tufa limestone formations. **Mataranka Homestead Tourist Resort** has a replica of historic **Elsey Station Homestead** (where Jeannie Gunn lived). Further north, the **Bitter Springs** section of Elsey NP has another thermal pool, waterways and BBQ facilities. **Elsey Cemetery**, 20km south, contains the graves of local pioneers, including Jeannie Gunn.
TOURIST INFO: Stockyard Gallery, Stuart Hwy, Ph: (08) 8975 4530

■ Palmerston POP 22 700
Map 419, G5
Palmerston, named after the British prime minister of the time, was the original name for **Darwin**. Now it is a satellite town, just 22km along the Stuart Hwy. Palmerston is the fastest-growing community in the Territory.
MAIN ATTRACTIONS: **Marlow Lagoon Regional Park** attracts birdlife and provides an attractive recreation area for picnicking and year-round swimming. Palmerston's multi-

Northern Territory

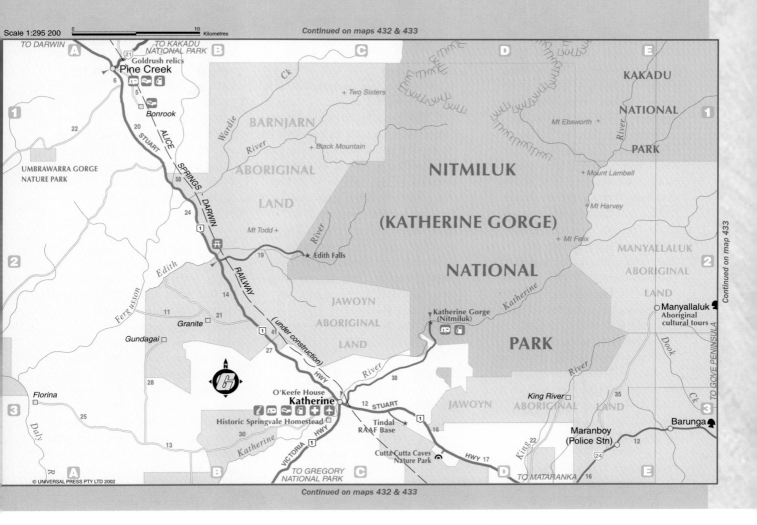

Continued on maps 432 & 433

Scale 1:295 200

Continued on maps 432 & 433

© UNIVERSAL PRESS PTY LTD 2002

cultural society is reflected in the colourful **Frances Mall markets** held every Friday evening in the Dry season.
TOURIST INFO: Tourism Top End, Darwin, Ph: 8936 2499

Pine Creek POP 624

Map 429, A1

Pine Creek, 90km NW of Katherine at the junction of the Kakadu and Stuart hwys, was a goldrush town in the 1870s. Still a gold-mining town, it has one of the largest open-cut gold mines in the Territory.
MAIN ATTRACTIONS: The town contains historic buildings and reminders of the goldrush days—**Miners Park**, the **Museum in Railway Tce**, **Mine Lookout**, **Gun Alley Gold Mining** and **Old Timers Rock Hut**. Try your luck at some of the sites—fossicking for gold is permitted under licence.

Bird Park displays tropical birds in a lush setting. The **Railway Station Museum** contains the veteran steam train used in the film adaptation of *We of the Never Never*.
NEARBY ATTRACTIONS: Pine Creek is the southern gateway to **Kakadu NP** via the Kakadu Hwy. The closest attractions in the park are the **Rock Hole**, 65km NE (4WD only), and **Gunlom Falls** (Waterfall Creek, 113km NE) with beautiful falls and a permanent waterhole. **Copperfield Dam**, 6km SW, is ideal for picnics on the foreshore. **Umbrawarra Gorge Nature Park**, 22km SW, offers swimming, rockclimbing and walks. **Butterfly Gorge NR**, 113km NW (4WD only), is noted for the large number of common crow butterflies found in the area.
TOURIST INFO: Diggers Rest Motel, 32 Main Tce, Ph: (08) 8976 1442

Tennant Creek POP 3856

Map 439, H2

Tennant Creek is one of Australia's most isolated towns, 506km north of Alice Springs on the Stuart Hwy. A charming modern town, it is the country's third largest gold producer.
MAIN ATTRACTIONS: The old **Australian Inland Mission**, built of prefabricated corrugated iron in 1934, and **Tuxworth Fullwood House**, a WWII army hospital and now a museum, are 2 places of interest on the town's **heritage walk**. Aboriginal arts and crafts are sold at **Anyinginyi Congress Art Gallery** in Paterson St. **Jurnkurakurr Mural** is a community project illustrating both men's and women's 'Dreaming'.
NEARBY ATTRACTIONS: **Mary Ann Dam**, 5km NE, offers shady picnic areas, swimming and boating—a pleasant surprise in an arid landscape. The

old **Telegraph Station** still stands, 12km to the north. **The Pebbles**, in a desert 16km NW, glow red at sunset. **Attack Creek Historical Reserve**, 73km north, marks a confrontation between explorer John McDouall Stuart and local Aboriginal people. A tourist drive 1.5km east along Peko Rd takes visitors to **Battery Hill Regional Centre** and **Gold Stamp Battery**, which features an underground mine and a mining museum. Guided tours are conducted daily. **Bill Allen Lookout** provides district views. Travel a further 106km south on the Stuart Hwy, to a collection of unusual and magnificent granite boulders called the **Devil's Marbles**—of spiritual importance to Aborigines, they are one of the Territory's top tourist attractions.
TOURIST INFO: Battery Hill Regional Centre, Peko Rd, Ph: (08) 8962 3388

■ **Timber Creek** POP 556
Map 435, C2
Timber Creek is 285km SW of Katherine on the Victoria Hwy midway to **Kunnunurra** in Western Australia.
MAIN ATTRACTIONS: The **1908 Timber Creek Police Station** is now a museum, open May–Oct. Fishing enthusiasts may want to organise

a barramundi fishing tour on the **Victoria River**.
NEARBY ATTRACTIONS: **Gregory NP**, one of the Territory's largest, is 15km west. The park features **Limestone Gorge**, wild scenery, boab trees, Aboriginal and European heritage sites and a network of 4WD tracks. **Keep River NP**, 175km west, has red sandstone cliffs, boab trees and exceptional Aboriginal rock art. Information on both parks can be obtained from the Conservation Commission in Timber Creek. Also worth a visit is scenic **Jasper Gorge**, 48km SW, which has an enticing permanent waterhole.
TOURIST INFO: Timber Creek Hotel, Victoria Hwy, Ph: (08) 8975 0722

■ **Yulara (Ayers Rock Resort)** POP 1100
Map 423, A3
Yulara was established to cater for the information and touring needs of the thousands of visitors who come to see Uluru (Ayers Rock), Australia's most enduring and internationally recognised landmark, within **Uluru–Kata Tjuta NP**.
MAIN ATTRACTION: **The Ayers Rock Visitors Centre** has displays and information on the history, geology, flora and fauna of the region, and organises tours such as the **Uluru Experience Night Sky Show**.

NEARBY ATTRACTIONS: On the approach road to Uluru, **Uluru–Kata Tjuta Cultural Centre** provides information on the attractions in the national park. Local Aboriginal history, culture and beliefs are explained through videos, interactive displays, arts, crafts and performance. Uluru–Kata Tjuta NP is jointly managed by the **Anangu** people (traditional owners of the land) and Environment Australia–Parks Australia North. Uluru (Ayers Rock) is 20km SE of Yulara. Uluru can be explored on one's own or via an organised tour, by Harley Davidson, by helicopter or plane, but probably the most rewarding is with an Aboriginal guide who can explain the deep cultural significance the site has for the local people. The 9.4km **Uluru Circuit Walk** is popular, as are sunrise and sunset viewings when the monolith undergoes dramatic changes of colour. **Kata Tjuta (The Olgas)** lies 50km west of Uluru— these 36 weathered domes are spectacular at any time of day. Walking tracks lead through **Olga Gorge** and the **Valley of the Winds**. Travel 110km from Yulara on the Lasseter Hwy, and you reach a lookout with distant views of **Mount Connor**, another large mountain. The Luritja Rd, 136km east, links with the unsealed **Mereenie Loop** as an alternative route to Alice Springs. A permit is required to travel the Loop as large sections pass through Aboriginal land reserves (it is available from the tourist information centre in Alice Springs, Glen Helen Resort, Kings Canyon Resort and Hemannsburg). The route accesses another major Red Centre attraction, **Watarrka NP (Kings Canyon)**. The 6km circuit **Rim Walk** features a boardwalk through prehistoric cycads in the **Garden of Eden**, canyon views and unusual rock formations such as those at the **Lost City**.
TOURIST INFO: Ayers Rock Resort, Ph: (08) 8957 7377

The Devil's Marbles, south of Tennant Creek

Northern Territory

KEY MAP

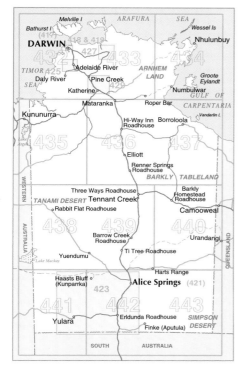

Yellow Water Billabong, Kakadu NP

DISTANCE CHART

Approximate Distance	Adelaide River	Alice Springs	Ayers Rock/Yulara	Borroloola	Camooweal QLD	Darwin	Erldunda	Hi-Way Inn	Jabiru	Katherine	Kulgera	Kununurra WA	Mataranka	Nicholson WA	Pine River SA	Tennant Creek	Ti-Tree	Top Springs	Tobermorey	Wauchope
Adelaide River		1385	1827	585	1293	107	1584	477	288	202	1660	714	308	902	111	871	1180	492	1799	985
Alice Springs	1385		442	1214	988	1492	199	908	1468	1183	275	1695	1077	1464	1274	514	205	1054	570	400
Ayers Rock/Yulara	1827	442		1656	1430	1934	243	1350	1910	1625	319	2137	1519	1906	1716	956	647	1496	1012	842
Borroloola	585	1214	1656		746	967	1413	383	943	658	1489	1151	552	1011	749	700	1009	601	1628	814
Camooweal QLD	1293	988	1430	746		1400	1187	816	1376	1091	1263	1603	985	1372	1182	474	783	962	1402	588
Darwin	107	1492	1934	967	1400		1691	584	243	309	1767	821	415	1009	218	978	1287	599	1906	1092
Erldunda	1584	199	243	1413	1187	1691		1107	1667	1382	76	1894	1276	1663	1473	713	404	1253	769	599
Hi-Way Inn	477	908	1350	383	816	584	1107		560	275	1183	768	169	628	366	394	703	218	1322	508
Jabiru	288	1468	1910	943	1376	243	1667	560		285	1743	797	391	985	194	954	1263	575	1882	1068
Katherine	202	1183	1625	658	1091	309	1382	275	285		1458	512	106	700	91	669	978	290	1597	783
Kulgera	1660	275	319	1489	1263	1767	76	1183	1743	1458		1970	1352	1739	1549	789	480	1329	845	675
Kununurra WA	714	1695	2137	1151	1603	821	1894	768	797	512	1970		618	327	603	1181	1490	550	2109	1295
Mataranka	308	1077	1519	552	985	415	1276	169	391	106	1352	618		797	197	563	872	396	1491	677
Nicholson WA	902	1464	1906	1011	1372	1009	1663	628	985	700	1739	327	797		791	950	1259	410	1878	1064
Pine River SA	111	1274	1716	749	1182	218	1473	366	194	91	1549	603	197	791		760	1069	381	1688	874
Tennant Creek	871	514	956	700	474	978	713	394	954	669	789	1181	563	950	760		309	540	928	114
Ti-Tree	1180	205	647	1009	783	1287	404	703	1263	978	480	1490	872	1259	1069	309		849	619	195
Top Springs	492	1054	1496	601	962	599	1253	218	575	290	1329	550	396	410	381	540	849		1468	654
Tobermorey	1799	570	1012	1628	1402	1906	769	1322	1882	1597	845	2109	1491	1878	1688	928	619	1468		814
Wauchope	985	400	842	814	588	1092	599	508	1068	783	675	1295	677	1064	874	114	195	654	814	

All distances in this chart have been measured over highways and major roads, not necessarily by the shortest route.

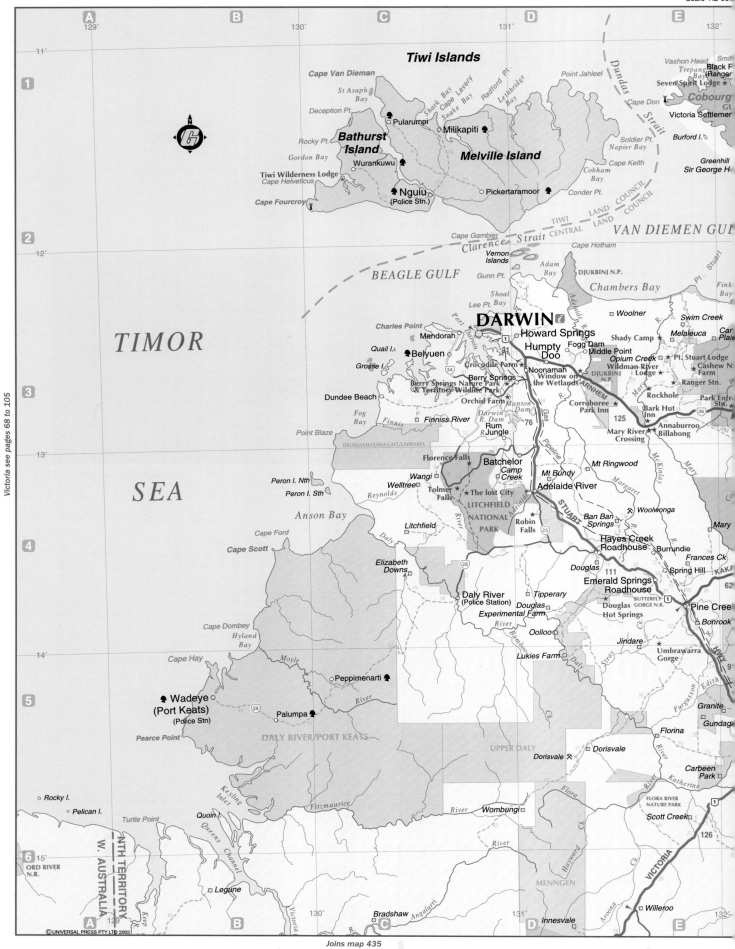

Tiwi Islands

Cape Van Dieman

St Asaph Bay

Deception Pt.

Rocky Pt.

Bathurst Island

Gordon Bay

Wurankuwu

Tiwi Wilderness Lodge
Cape Helveticus

Cape Fourcroy

Shark Bay
Cape Lavery
Snake Bay
Radford Pt.
Leithbridge Bay

Point Jahleel

Pularumpi

Milikapiti

Melville Island

Pickertaramoor

Nguiu
(Police Stn.)

Cape Gambier

Cape Hotham

Clarence

Strait

CENTRAL
LAND
COUNCIL

TIWI
LAND
COUNCIL

Vashon Head
Trepang Bay
Ranger

Seven Spirit Lodge

Cape Don

Victoria Settlement

Soldier Pt.
Napier Bay

Cape Keith

Cobham Bay

Conder Pt.

Smit

Black P

Cobourg
GU

Burford I.

Greenhill
Sir George H

VAN DIEMEN GU

TIMOR

SEA

BEAGLE GULF

Vernon Islands

Gunn Pt.

Shoal Bay

Lee Pt.

Adam Bay

DJUKBINJ N.P.

Chambers Bay

Pt. Stuart

Fink Bay

Charles Point

Quail I.

Grosse I.

Mahdorah

DARWIN

Howard Springs

Belyuen

Berry Springs
Berry Springs Nature Park
& Territory Wildlife Park

Dundee Beach

Fog Bay

Point Blaze

Finniss River

Crocodile Farm

Orchid Farm

Humpty Doo

Noonamah

Fogg Dam
Middle Point
Window on
the Wetlands

Woolner

Shady Camp

Opium Creek
Wildman River
Lodge

DJUKBINJ
N.P.

Swim Creek

Melaleuca

Pt. Stuart Lodge

Mary

Cashew N
Farm

Ranger Stn.

Car
Plai

DELISSAVILLE/WAGAIT/LARRAKIA

Peron I. Nth

Peron I. Sth

Reynolds

Daly

River

Finnis

Darwin R. Dam

Manton Dam

Rum Jungle

ARNHEM

Gas

Pipeline

Corroboree
Park Inn

Mary River
Crossing

Rockhole

Bark Hut
Inn

125

Annaburroo
Billabong

Park Entr.
Stn.

Florence Falls

Wangi

Welltree

Tolmer Falls

The lost City

LITCHFIELD

NATIONAL
PARK

Batchelor

Camp Creek

Robin Falls

Mt Bundy

Adelaide River

STUART

Adelaide

Mt Ringwood

Margaret

Ban Ban
Springs

McKinlay

Mary

Woolwonga

Mary

SEA

Anson Bay

Cape Ford

Cape Scott

Elizabeth Downs

Litchfield

Daly River
(Police Station)

Douglas
Experimental Farm

Tipperary

River

Oolloo

Douglas

Hayes Creek
Roadhouse

Burrundie

Frances Ck

Emerald Springs
Roadhouse

Douglas
Hot Springs

BUTTERFLY
GORGE N.R.

111

Spring Hill

Jindare

Pine Cree

Bonrook

KAKA

62

Cape Dombey
Hyland Bay

Cape Hay

Moyle

Peppimenarti

Wadeye
(Port Keats)
(Police Stn)

Palumpa

Pearce Point

DALY RIVER/PORT KEATS

River

UPPER DALY

Lukies Farm

Daly

Stray

Umbrawarra
Gorge

Florina

Dorisvale

Dorisvale

Carbeen
Park

Fergusson

Granite

Gundag

9

FLORA RIVER
NATURE PARK

Edith

Rocky I.

Pelican I.

Turtle Point

Quoin I.

Keyling Inlet

Queens Channel

Fitzmaurice

River

River

Wombungi

Flora

Hayward

Scott Creek

River

Katherine

126

Victoria

HWY

132

ORD RIVER
N.R.

129

NTH TERRITORY

W. AUSTRALIA

Legune

Keep

Bradshaw

Angalarri

130

Innesvale

131

Arcona

MENNGEN

VICTORIA

Willeroo

E

Victoria see pages 68 to 105

Northern Territor

F · G · H · J · K

ARAFURA SEA

Croker Point · 133°

134°

135°

11°

1

Danger Pt.
Croker Island
Lawson I.
McCluer I.
Minjilang
Darch I.
Grant I.
Templer I.

OBOURG
RINE PARK
Morse I.
Endyalgout I.

Peninsula
TIONAL PARK

Valencia I.
Mountnorris Bay

Murgenella
(Ranger Stn.)

Brogden Pt.

Aurari Bay

Turner Pt.
Arla Bay

Nth Goulburn I.
Goulburn Islands
Sth Goulburn I.

Warruwi

Cape Cockburn
De Courcy Head

Junction Bay
Braithwaite Pt.
Cuthbert Pt.
Goomandeer Pt.
Hawkesbury Pt.

Cape Stewart

North Crocodile Reef

N.W. Crocodile I.

Crocodile Islands
Mooroongga I.

Elcho Island
Galiwinku

12°

2

Field I.
Point Farewell

Cooper Creek

East Alligator

Entrance I.
Skirmish Pt.

Boucaut Bay

Maningrida
(Police Stn.)

Milingimbi

Rabuma I.
Milingimbi I.

Castlereagh Bay

Howard I.

Banyan I.

Ramingining

Woden R.

West Alligator Hd.

King River

Goomadeer River

Nungbalgarri

River

Blyth River

Glyde

Goyder R.

Mitchell Range

Maidjula R.

Ubirr Rock
Border Store
(Manbiyarri)

Oenpelli
(Police Stn.)

Nabarlek

Tin Camp Ck.

KAKADU

Jabiluka M.L.
Ranger M.L.

Jabiru
Bowali Visitor Centre
(Park H.Q.)

Cadell

Imimbar

Liverpool River

Blyth

River

13°

3

87
Frontier Kakadu Village
Nourlangie HWY
ooinda Lodge
Nourlangie Rock
Koongarra Mineral Lease

132
NATIONAL

Jim Jim Billabong

River

Mann

Guyuyu

Annie River

CENTRAL

ARNHEM LAND

Parsons Ra.

Bath Ra.

Koolatong

Walker River

21

Maguk
(Barramundi Gorge)

Jim Jim Creek

ARNHEM LAND

Rose River

Harris

4

PARK
Gunlom Falls
Jarrangbarnmi
(Koolpin Gorge)
Gimbat

Gimbet Ck.

River

Wilton River

Bulman

Wukayiwanya

Park Entrance Stn.
y River
adhouse

MANYALLALUK

Mainoru River

Flying Fox Creek

ROAD
Lindsay Ck.

70

Phelp River

14°

5

NITMILUK
h Falls
KATHERINE GORGE)
N.P.

Katherine

Katherine Gorge
(Nitmiluk)

Manyallaluk

Mountain Valley

Mainoru

Malboi

ARNHEM

Turkey Lagoon

156

River

Katherine River

King River

West Branch

Dook Ck.

247

24

Maiwok

CENTRAL

River

King River
Tindal RAAF Base
52
Barunga
Maranboy
(Police Stn.)
Beswick

BESWICK

Chambery R.

Creek

Creek

Roper River

Urapunga (Police Stn.)
Roper Bar
Ngukurr

Port Roper
Limmen Bight

6

Cutta Cutta Caves

STUART

61

Roper

Waterhouse Ck.

Goondooloo
Roper
Moroak

176

ELSEY N.P.

HWY
20

Mataranka Resort
Thermal Pool
Mataranka

Elsey

ROPER

River
Hodgson River

YUTPUNDJI-DJINDIWIRRITJ

Roper Valley

River

Port Roper

Maria I.

MARRA

15°

ALICE SPRINGS - DARWIN RAILWAY
Under Construction

1

HWY

133°

Elsey Ck.
Elsey Cemetery
MANGARRAY

Strangeways River

134°

Miniyeri
ALAWA

Towns River

Limmen Bight R.

Cox River

135°

Dry River
y River

Joins map 434

© UNIVERSAL PRESS PTY LTD 2002

NORTHERN TERRITORY   433

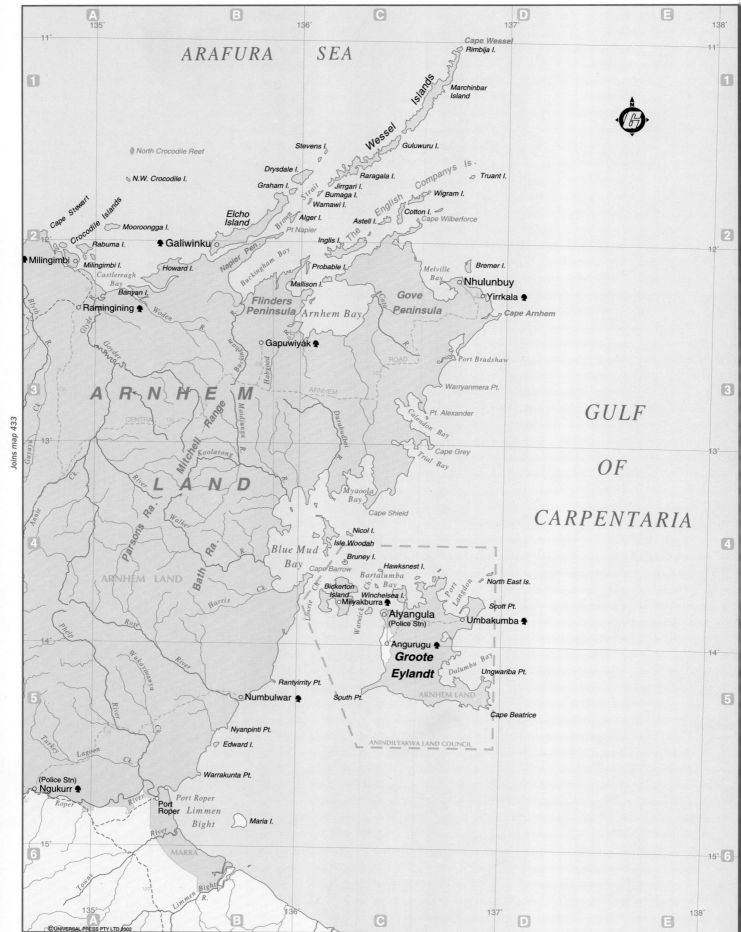

Scale 1:2 000 000

ARAFURA SEA

Wessel Islands

Cape Wessel
Rimbija I.

Marchinbar Island

North Crocodile Reef

Stevens I.
Guluwuru I.

N.W. Crocodile I.
Drysdale I.
Raragala I.
Truant I.

Graham I.
Jirrgari I.
Bumaga I.
Wigram I.
Wamawi I.

Cape Stewart
Crocodile Islands
Mooroongga I.
Elcho Island
Alger I.
Astell I.
Cotton I.
Cape Wilberforce

Rabuma I.
Pt Napier
Inglis I.

Milingimbi
Milingimbi I.
Howard I.
Probable I.
Melville Bay
Bremer I.
Nhulunbuy

Castlereagh Bay
Mallison I.
Yirrkala

Banyan I.
Flinders Peninsula
Arnhem Bay
Gove Peninsula
Cape Arnhem

Ramingining
Port Bradshaw

Gapuwiyak
ROAD

A R N H E M
Warryanmera Pt.

CENTRAL
Pt. Alexander

Mitchell Range
Calendon Bay

L A N D
Koolatong
Cape Grey
Trial Bay

Parsons Ra.
Walker
Myaoola Bay

ARNHEM LAND
Cape Shield

Harris
Nicol I.
Isle Woodah
North East Is.

Blue Mud Bay
Bruney I.
Hawksnest I.
Bartalumba Bay

Cape Barrow
Bickerton Island
Winchelsea I.
Scott Pt.

Milyakburra
Umbakumba

Alyangula
(Police Stn)

Rantyirrity Pt.
Angurugu
Groote Eylandt
Dalumbu Bay
Ungwariba Pt.

Numbulwar
South Pt.
ARNHEM LAND

Nyanpinti Pt.
Cape Beatrice

Edward I.
ANINDILYAKWA LAND COUNCIL

Warrakunta Pt.

(Police Stn)
Ngukurr

Port Roper
Port Roper
Limmen Bight
Maria I.

MARRA

GULF OF CARPENTARIA

434 Gregory's Australia

Joins map 437

Northern Territory

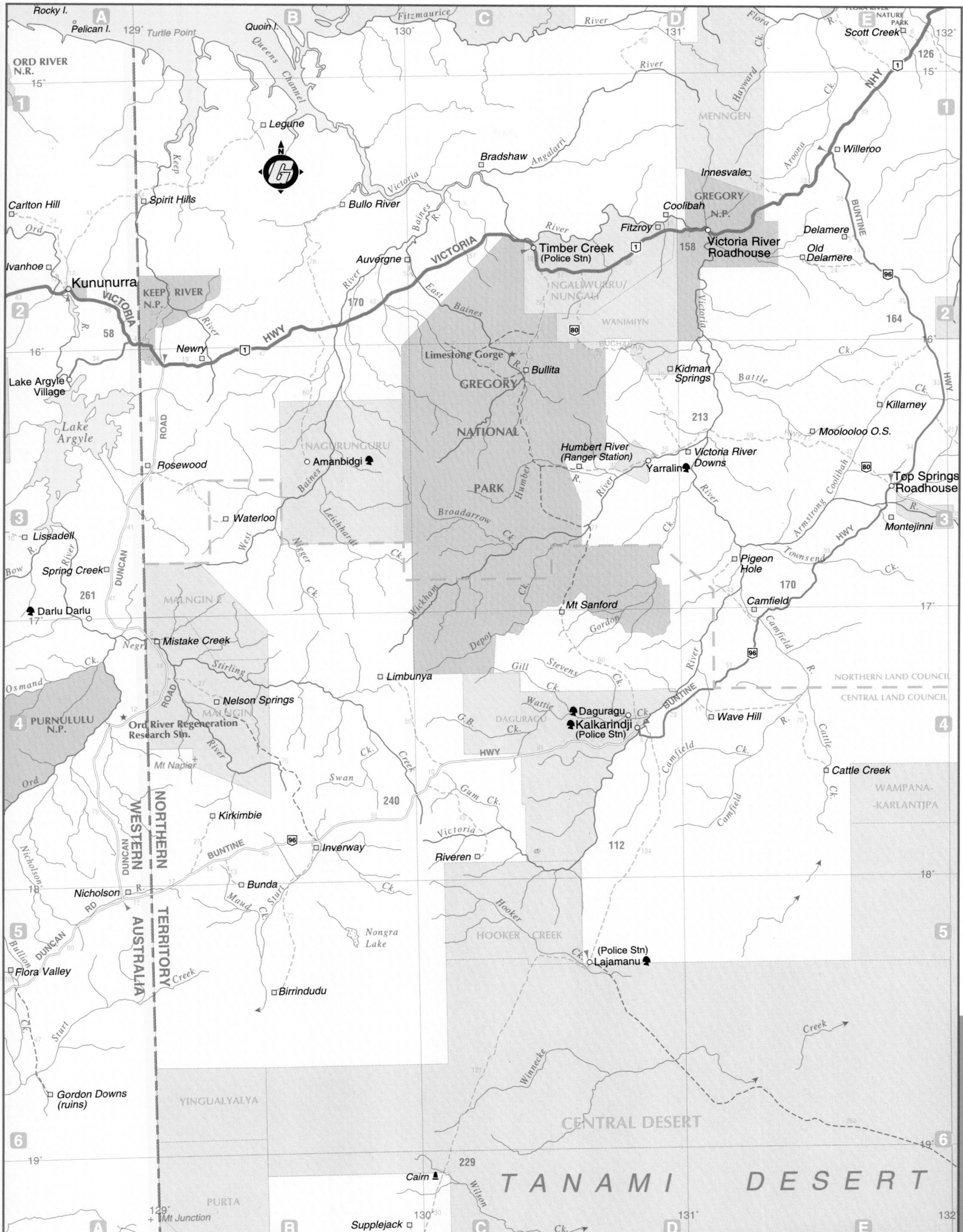

0   50   Kilometres

A   B   C   D   E

Rocky I.
Pelican I.   129°   Turtle Point   Quoin I.   130°   Fitzmaurice   River   131°   Flora   R.   132°
FLORA RIVER NATURE PARK
Scott Creek
ORD RIVER N.R.   River   NHY   126
15°   1

1

MENNGEN
Legune
Bradshaw   Angalarri
Willeroo
Spirit Hills   Bullo River   Victoria   Baines   R.   Innesvale   Aroona
Carlton Hill   GREGORY N.P.
Coolibah   Delamere
Ivanhoe   Auvergne   VICTORIA   River   Fitzroy   158   Victoria River   Old Delamere
Timber Creek   1   Roadhouse   96
Kununurra   HWY   (Police Stn)   164
2   VICTORIA   170   East   Baines   NGALIWURRU/   Victoria   2
58   40   NUNGALI
Newry   1   47   80   WANIMIYN   BUNTINE
16°   R.   DUCHANAN   16°
Lake Argyle   Limestone Gorge   R.   Kidman   Battle   Ck.
Village   Bullita   Springs   213   Killarney   HWY
ROAD   GREGORY   Molooloo O.S.
Rosewood   NATIONAL   Humbert River   Victoria River   80
Amanbidgi   (Ranger Station)   Downs   Top Springs
3   NAGURUNGURU   Baines   PARK   Humber   Yarralin   Roadhouse   3
Waterloo   Letichhardt   R.   River   Townsend   Montejinni
West   Broadarrow   R.   Ck.   HWY   R.
MALNGIN   Ck.   Pigeon   170
Lissadell   Niggger   Wickham   Hole   Camfield
Spring Creek   261   Ck.   Mt Sanford   96   Camfield   17°
17°   Darlu Darlu   Gordon   NORTHERN LAND COUNCIL
Mistake Creek   Negri   Depot   Gill   Stevens   Ck.   CENTRAL LAND COUNCIL
PURNULULU   Stirling   Ck.   River   Wave Hill
4   N.P.   Ord River Regeneration   Nelson Springs   Wattie   Daguragu   BUNTINE   4
Research Stn.   MALNGIN   Limbunya   DAGURAGU   Kalkarindji   Cattle Creek
Mt Napier   G.B.   Ck.   (Police Stn)   WAMPANA-
Ord   River   HWY   112   -KARLANTJPA
Kirkimbie   Swan   Camfield   Ck.   R.
Osmand   240   Gum Ck.   Camfield
NORTHERN   BUNTINE   Victoria   18°
18°   Nicholson   96   Inverway   Riveren   R.
WESTERN   DUNCAN   Bunda   Ck.   Hooker   Cattle   Ck.
Nicholson   R.   Maud   Ck.   Sturt
5   Flora Valley   AUSTRALIA   TERRITORY   Nongra   HOOKER   CREEK   (Police Stn)   5
Bullion   Lake   Ck.   Lajamanu   Winnecke
DUNCAN   Birrindudu   Creek
RD   Creek
Sturt
19°   Gordon Downs   CENTRAL DESERT
6   (ruins)   YINGUALYALYA   229   6
PURTA   Cairn   TANAMI   DESERT
129°   Mt Junction   Supplejack   130°   Wilson   131°   Ck.   132°

A   B   C   D   E

Joins map 436

Scale 1:2 000

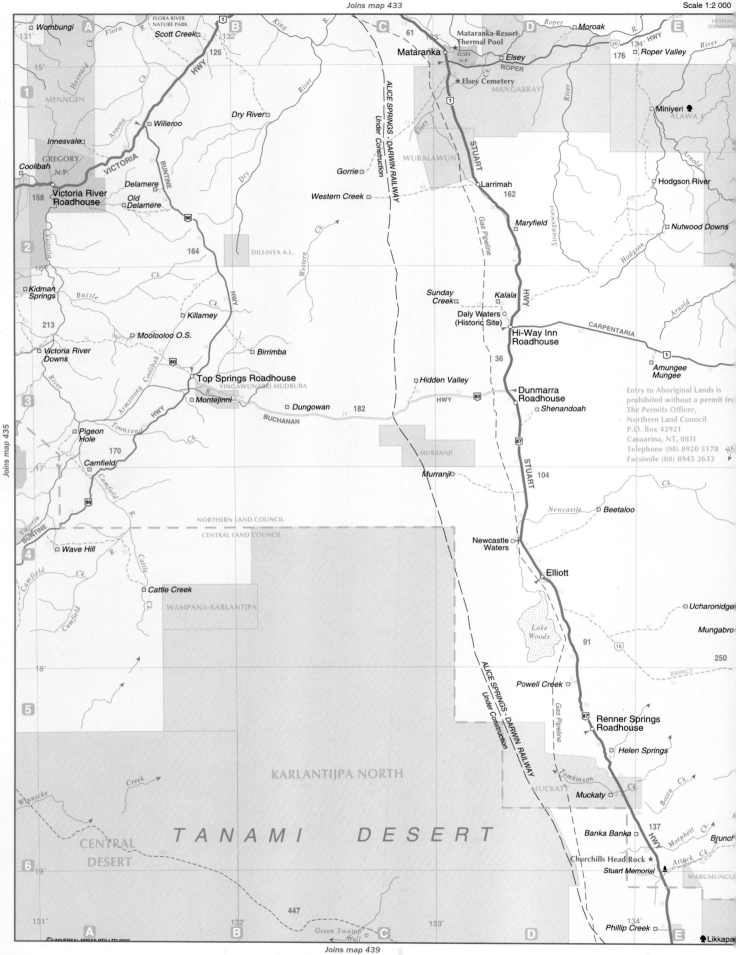

MENNGEN

Wombungi

Scott Creek

Willeroo

Dry River

Innesvale

GREGORY N.P.

Coolibah

Delamere

Old Delamere

Victoria River Roadhouse

158

VICTORIA

BUNTINE

96

164

Kidman Springs

213

Killarney

Moolooloo O.S.

Victoria River Downs

Birrimba

80

Top Springs Roadhouse

YINGAWUNARRI MUDBURA

Montejinni

Dungowan

182

BUCHANAN

Pigeon Hole

170

Camfield

96

BUNTINE

Wave Hill

Cattle Creek

WAMPANA-KARLANTJPA

NORTHERN LAND COUNCIL

CENTRAL LAND COUNCIL

KARLANTIJPA NORTH

CENTRAL DESERT

Winnecke

Creek

T A N A M I   D E S E R T

Mataranka

61

Mataranka Resort Thermal Pool

Roper

Moroak

ELSEY N.P.

Elsey

Elsey Cemetery

ROPER

MANGARRAY

WUBALAWUN

STUART

Larrimah

162

Maryfield

Gorrie

Western Creek

ALICE SPRINGS - DARWIN RAILWAY

Under Construction

DILLINYA A.L.

Sunday Creek

Kalala

Daly Waters (Historic Site)

Hi-Way Inn Roadhouse

36

Hidden Valley

HWY

80

Dunmarra Roadhouse

Shenandoah

87

STUART

104

MURRANJI

Murranji

Newcastle

Beetaloo

Newcastle Waters

Elliott

Lake Woods

91

16

250

BARKLY

Powell Creek

Gas Pipeline

Tomkinson

ALICE SPRINGS - DARWIN RAILWAY

Under Construction

MUCKATY

87

Renner Springs Roadhouse

Helen Springs

Muckaty

Banka Banka

137

HWY

Morphett

Churchills Head Rock

Stuart Memorial

WARUMUNGU

Phillip Creek

Likkapa

Roper

20

134 HWY

176

Roper Valley

Miniyeri

ALAWA

Hodgson River

Nutwood Downs

Strangways

CARPENTARIA

Amungee Mungee

1

Ucharonidge

Mungabro

Brunch

Attack Ck.

Entry to Aboriginal Lands is prohibited without a permit fro The Permits Officer, Northern Land Council P.O. Box 42921 Casuarina, NT, 0811 Telephone (08) 8920 5178 Facsimile (08) 8945 2633

Northern Territory

© UNIVERSAL PRESS PTY LTD 2000

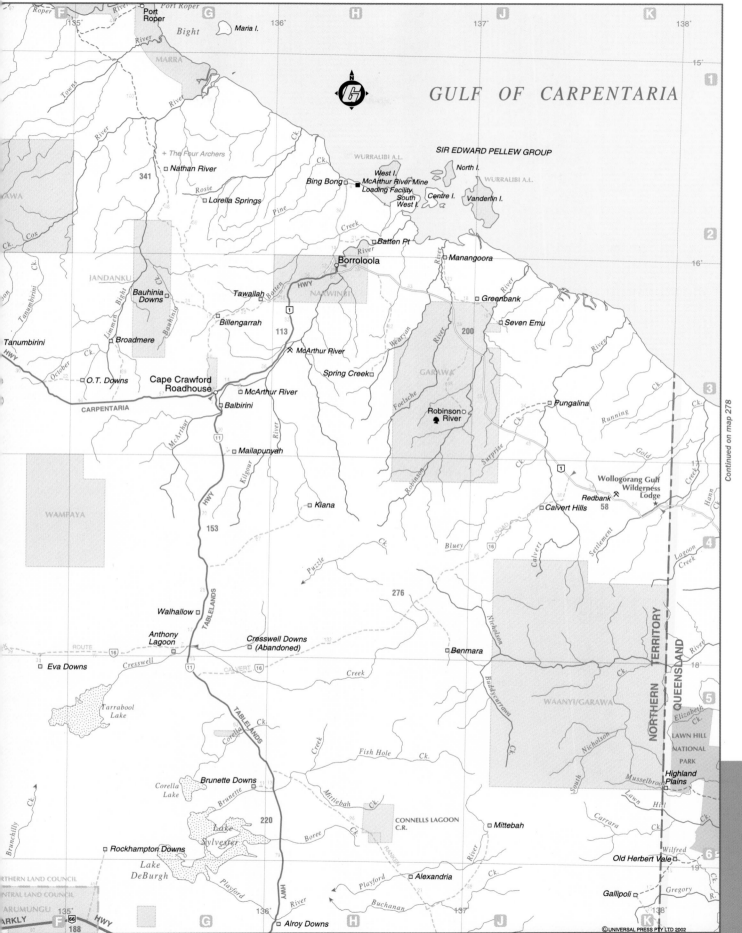

50
Kilometres

GULF OF CARPENTARIA

SIR EDWARD PELLEW GROUP

Port Roper
Port Roper
Bight
Maria I.
MARRA

Towns River
Roper
River

+ The Four Archers

Nathan River
341
Lorella Springs
Rosie

WURRALIBI A.L.
West I.
Bing Bong   McArthur River Mine
Loading Facility
South
West I.
North I.
Centre I.
WURRALIBI A.L.
Vanderlin I.

Pine   Creek
Batten Pt

Borroloola
Manangoora
River
HWY
NARWINBI
Greenbank
200
Seven Emu

JANDANKU
Bauhinia
Downs
Tawallah
Billengarrah
1
113
Broadmere
McArthur River
Spring Creek
GARAWA
River
Foelsche

Tanumbirini
HWY
October   Ck.
O.T. Downs
Cape Crawford
Roadhouse
Balbirini
11
CARPENTARIA
McArthur
Robinson   Ck.
Robinson
River
Pungalina
Running
Gold   Ck.

WAMPAYA
Mailapunyah
Kilgour
River
Surprise   Ck.
1
Wollogorang Gulf
Wilderness
Lodge
Redbank
Calvert Hills
58
HWY
153
Kiana
Puzzle
Bluey   Creek
16
276
Calvert

Walhallow
TABLELANDS
Anthony
Lagoon
Cresswell Downs
(Abandoned)
Benmara
Nicholson
Setzlement
Hann

ROUTE   16
Eva Downs
Cresswell   Ck.
11
CALVERT   16
Creek
Tarrabool
Lake
TABLELANDS
Fish Hole   Ck.
Buddycurrawa
WAANYI/GARAWA
Nicholson
Elizabeth   Ck.
LAWN HILL
NATIONAL
PARK

Corella
Lake
Brunette Downs
Brunette   Ck.
11
Mittebah   Ck.
CONNELLS LAGOON
C.R.
Mittebah
South   Nicholson
Carrara
Musselbrook
Highland
Plains
Lawn   Hill   Ck.

Lake
Sylvester
220
Rockhampton Downs
Boree   Creek
RANGE
Playford
Alexandria
Old Herbert Vale
Wilfred   Ck.

Lake
DeBurgh
NORTHERN LAND COUNCIL
CENTRAL LAND COUNCIL
ARUMUNGU
Playford
River
Buchanan
Gallipoli
Gregory   R.
BARKLY
66
188
HWY
HWY
Alroy Downs

NORTHERN TERRITORY
QUEENSLAND

Continued on map 278

© UNIVERSAL PRESS PTY LTD 2002

Scale 1:2 000

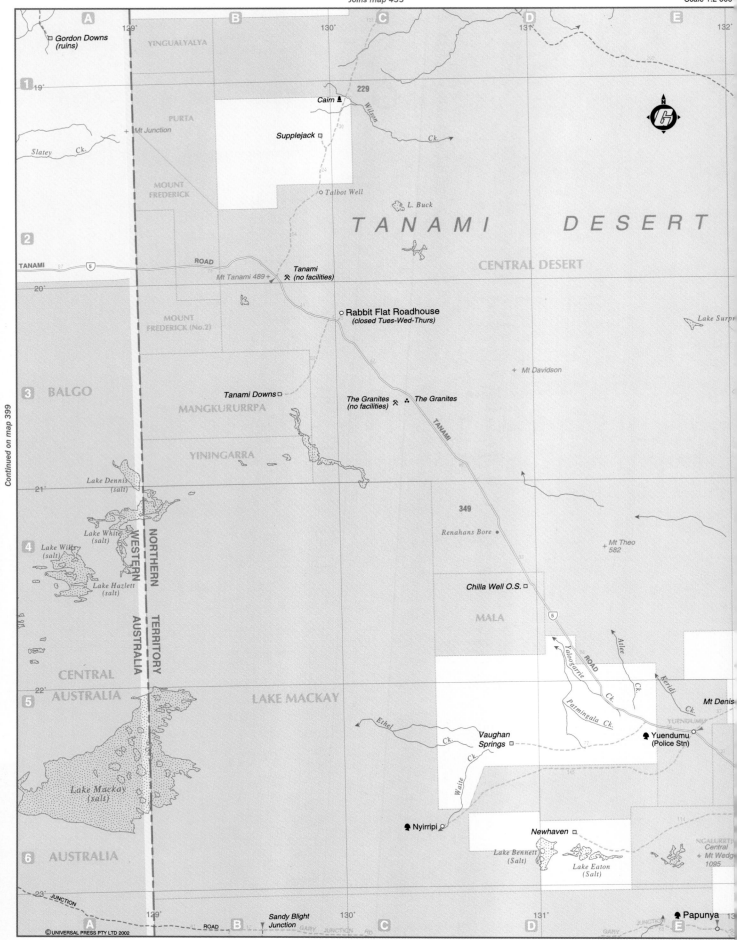

Gordon Downs
(ruins)

A

129°

YINGUALYALYA

B

130°

C

D

131°

E

132°

1 19°

PURTA

+ Mt Junction

Cairn ▲

229

Wilson

Slatey Ck.

Supplejack □

Ck.

MOUNT
FREDERICK

○ Talbot Well

L. Buck

T A N A M I   D E S E R T

2

TANAMI

ROAD

Mt Tanami 489 +

Tanami
(no facilities)

CENTRAL DESERT

20°

MOUNT
FREDERICK (No.2)

○ Rabbit Flat Roadhouse
(closed Tues-Wed-Thurs)

+ Mt Davidson

3 BALGO

MANGKURURRPA

Tanami Downs □

The Granites
(no facilities)

The Granites

TANAMI

YININGARRA

Lake Dennis
(salt)

21°

349

Renahans Bore •

+ Mt Theo
582

Lake Surpr

4 Lake Wills
(salt)

Lake White
(salt)

Lake Hazlett
(salt)

NORTHERN

Chilla Well O.S. □

WESTERN

MALA

5

TERRITORY

AUSTRALIA

CENTRAL

22° AUSTRALIA

LAKE MACKAY

Yaloogarrie

ROAD

Atlee

Ck.

Kerridi

Ck.

Mt Denis

YUENDUMU

Patmingala Ck.

Ethel

Ck.

Vaughan
Springs □

Ck.

♣ Yuendumu
(Police Stn)

Lake Mackay
(salt)

Waite

Ck.

6 AUSTRALIA

♣ Nyirripi ○

Newhaven □

Lake Bennett
(Salt)

Lake Eaton
(Salt)

NGALURRT
Central
+ Mt Wedge
1095

23° JUNCTION

ROAD

Sandy Blight
Junction

GARY   JUNCTION   RD

♣ Papunya

A

129°

B

130°

C

131°

D

E

Northern Territor

Continued on map 399

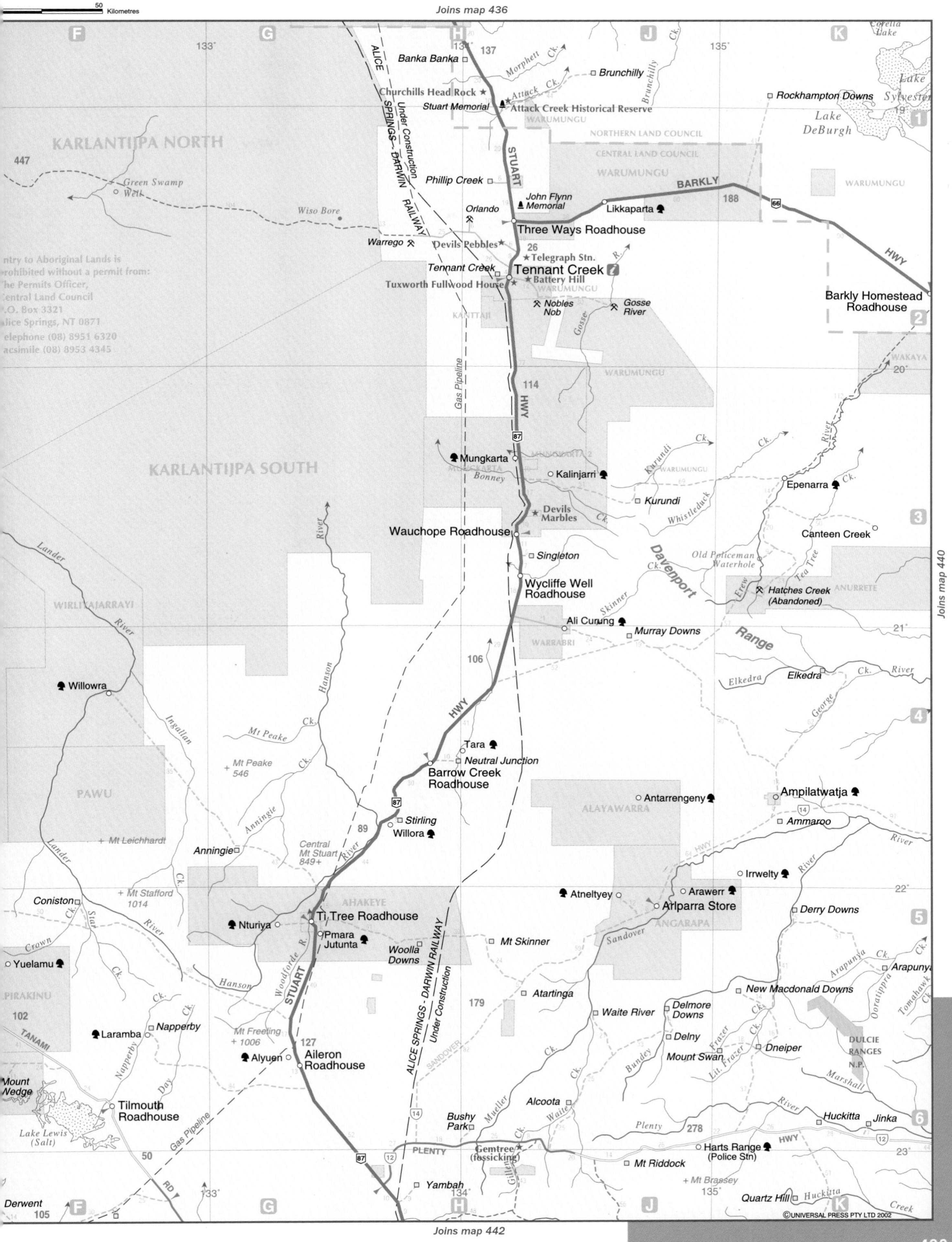

50 Kilometres

F G H J K

133° 133° 137 135°

Banka Banka

Brunchilly

Churchills Head Rock ★
Stuart Memorial ★ ★ Attack Creek Historical Reserve

Rockhampton Downs

Lake Sylvester

Corella Lake

Lake DeBurgh

WARUMUNGU

NORTHERN LAND COUNCIL

KARLANTIJPA NORTH

447

Green Swamp Well

Wiso Bore

Phillip Creek

Orlando

John Flynn Memorial ▲

Three Ways Roadhouse

CENTRAL LAND COUNCIL

WARUMUNGU

BARKLY

Likkaparta ♣

188

66

Warrego ⚒

Devils Pebbles ⚒

26

★ Telegraph Stn.

Tennant Creek
Tennant Creek ★ Battery Hill

Tuxworth Fullwood House ★

HWY

WARUMUNGU

WARUMUNGU

20°

WAKAYA

Barkly Homestead Roadhouse

Nobles Nob

Gosse River ⚒

Gosse

KANTTAJI

114

Entry to Aboriginal Lands is prohibited without a permit from:
The Permits Officer,
Central Land Council
P.O. Box 3321
Alice Springs, NT 0871
Telephone (08) 8951 6320
Facsimile (08) 8953 4345

KARLANTIJPA SOUTH

Gas Pipeline

87

Mungkarta ♣

Kalinjarri

Kurundi ⚒

Kurundi

Ck.

Ck.

WARUMUNGU

Epenarra ♣

River

Canteen Creek

3

Bonney

★ Devils Marbles

Wauchope Roadhouse

Singleton

Old Policeman Waterhole

Erew

Ck.

Whistleduck

Davenport

ANURRETE

Wycliffe Well Roadhouse

Hatches Creek (Abandoned) ⚒

Skinner

River

Lander

WIRLIYAJARRAYI

River

Ali Curung ♣

Murray Downs

WARRABRI

Range

21°

Elkedra

Elkedra Ck. River

Willowra ♣

Ingallan

River

106

HWY

Mt Peake Ck.

+ Mt Peake 546

Tara ♣

Neutral Junction

Barrow Creek Roadhouse

Anningie Ck.

PAWU

+ Mt Leichhardt

Antarrengeny ⚒

ALAYAWARRA

Ampilatwatja ♣

14

Ammaroo

River

22°

Lander

Ck.

87

89

Stirling

Willora ♣

Anningie ▫

Central Mt Stuart 849+

River

AHAKEYE

HWY

Irrwelty ♣

+ Mt Stafford 1014

Coniston

Atneltyey ♣

Arawerr ♣

Arlparra Store

ANGARAPA

Derry Downs

PIRAKINU

102

Yuelamu ♣

Nturiya ♣

Ti Tree Roadhouse

Pmara Jutunta ♣

Woolla Downs

Mt Skinner

Sandover

Crown Ck.

River

New Macdonald Downs

Arapunya ▫

Arapunja

Oratippa

Tomahawk

TANAMI

Laramba ♣

Napperby ▫

Napperby

Day Ck.

STUART

Woodforde R.

Alyuen ♣

Aileron Roadhouse

Hanson

ALICE SPRINGS – DARWIN RAILWAY

Under Construction

Atartinga ▫

179

Waite River

Delmore Downs

Delny

Mount Swan

Dneiper

Fraser Ck.

Lit. Frazer Ck.

Frazer

River

DULCIE RANGES N.P.

5

Mt Freeling + 1006

127

Gas Pipeline

Sandover

Mueller Ck.

Alcoota

Waite Ck.

Bundey

Marshall River

Mount Wedge

Lake Lewis (Salt)

50

87

12

RD

133°

PLENTY

14

Bushy Park

Gemtree (fossicking)

Gillen Ck.

Mt Riddock ▫

Plenty

278

Harts Range (Police Stn) ♣

HWY

12

Huckitta

Jinka

6

Yambah ♣

134°

Mt Brassey +

135°

Quartz Hill

Huckitta

Creek

23°

Derwent

105

© UNIVERSAL PRESS PTY LTD 2002

Joins map 440

Scale 1:2 000 000

0   50 Kilometres

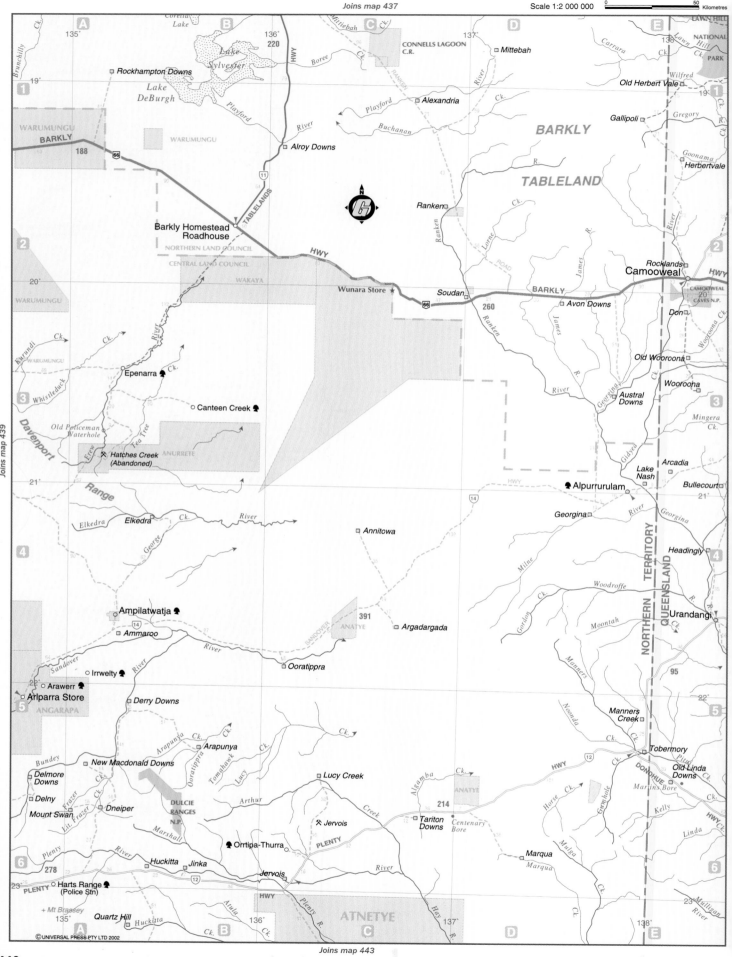

Ck.   135°

Brunchilly Ck.

Corella Lake

Lake Sylvester

136° 220

Joins map 437

Boree

Playford

CONNELLS LAGOON C.R.

Mittebah

Carrara

Ck.

LAWN HILL NATIONAL PARK

137°

138°

Old Herbert Vale

Wilfred

Rockhampton Downs

Lake DeBurgh

Playford

River

Alexandria

Ck.

Buchanan

Gallipoli

Gregory

Goonama Ck.

Herbertvale

WARUMUNGU

BARKLY

188

66

WARUMUNGU

Playford

River

Alroy Downs

Ranken

Ranken

BARKLY

TABLELAND

R.

Ck.

Lorne

11

TABLELANDS

Barkly Homestead Roadhouse

NORTHERN LAND COUNCIL

CENTRAL LAND COUNCIL

WAKAYA

HWY

ROAD

James

Wunara Store

Soudan

Rocklands

Camooweal

HWY

BARKLY

260

Ranken

Avon Downs

James

CAMOOWEAL CAVES N.P.

Don

WARUMUNGU

20°

66

Karundi Ck.

Ck.

Whistleduck

WARUMUNGU

River

Epenarra

Ck.

Tea Tree

Old Policeman Waterhole

Erew

Hatches Creek (Abandoned)

ANURRETE

Canteen Creek

River

James

Old Wooroona

Georgina

Austral Downs

Wooroona

Mingera Ck.

Arcadia

Lake Nash

Bullecourt

Joins map 439

Davenport

Range

Elkedra

Elkedra

George

Ck.

River

Annitowa

HWY

Gidyea

Alpurrurulam

14

Georgina

Headingly

21°

Milne

Woodroffe

Ampilatwatja

14

Ammaroo

Sandover

ANATYE

391

Argadargada

River

Gordon

Ck.

Moontah

Manners

Urandangi

R.

Irrwelty

River

Ooratippra

NORTHERN TERRITORY

QUEENSLAND

95

22°

Arawerr

Arlparra Store

ANGARAPA

Derry Downs

Arapunya Ck.

Ck.

Arapunya

Ooratippra

Tomahawk

Lucy

Ck.

Ck.

Alsamba

Ck.

Noonda

Manners Creek

Tobermory

HWY

12

Old Linda Downs

Bundey

New Macdonald Downs

Delmore Downs

Delny

Fraser Ck.

Lit. Fraser

Dneiper

DULCIE RANGES N.P.

Arthur

Lucy Creek

Jervois

Creek

ANATYE

214

Tariton Downs

Centenary Bore

DONOHUE

Martins Bore

Greenhole

Horse Ck.

Kelly

Mulga

Pitu

Ck.

HWY

Linda Ck.

Mount Swan

Marshall

Orrtipa-Thurra

PLENTY

River

Marqua

Marqua

Plenty

Huckitta

Jinka

Jervois

HWY

12

PLENTY

River

Hoy

R.

Harts Range (Police Stn)

278

23°

135°

+ Mt Brassey

Quartz Hill

Huckitta

Ck.

ATNETYE

136°

HWY

Plenty R.

137°

138°

Mulligan River

© UNIVERSAL PRESS PTY LTD 2002

A   B   C   D   E

Gregory's Australia

Joins map 443

Northern Territory

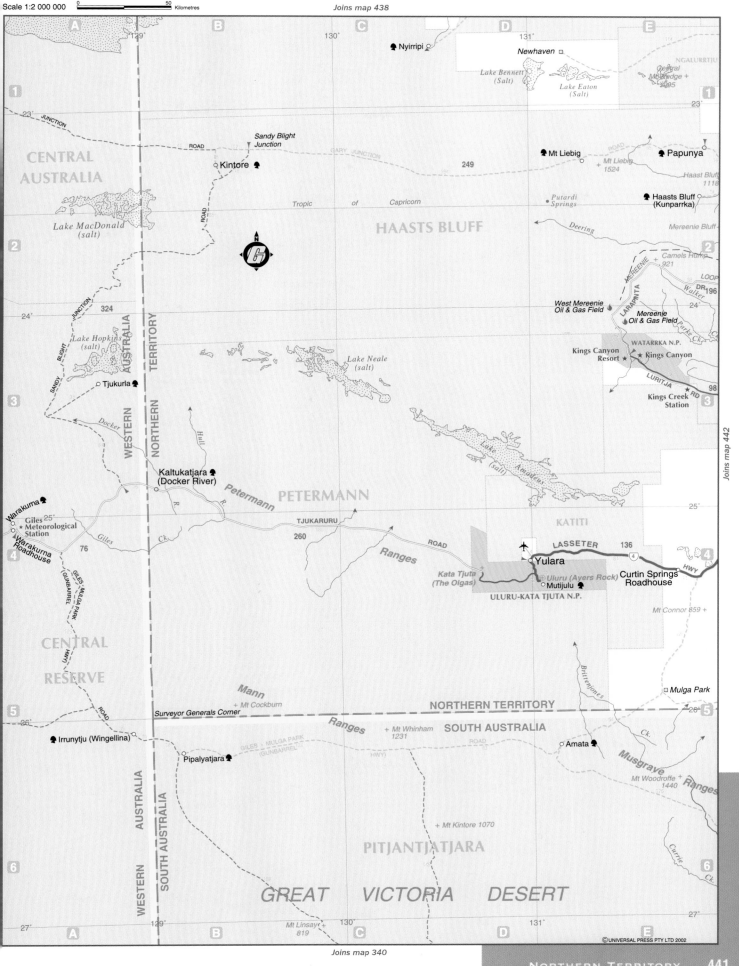

Scale 1:2 000 000

Joins map 438

A · B · 130° C · 131° D · E

1

Nyirripi

Newhaven

Lake Bennett (Salt)

Lake Eaton (Salt)

NGALURRTJU

Central Mt Wedge + 995

23°

CENTRAL AUSTRALIA

JUNCTION ROAD

Sandy Blight Junction

Kintore

GARY JUNCTION 249

Mt Liebig

Mt Liebig + 1524

Papunya

Haast Bluff 1118

2

Tropic of Capricorn

HAASTS BLUFF

Putardi Springs

Haasts Bluff (Kunparrka)

Mereenie Bluff

Lake MacDonald (salt)

Deering

Camels Hump + 921

LOOP DR 196

Walker

24°

JUNCTION 324

Lake Hopkins (salt)

West Mereenie Oil & Gas Field

Mereenie Oil & Gas Field

LARAPINTA

Parke Ck

WATARRKA N.P.

Kings Canyon Resort

Kings Canyon

LURITJA RD 98

3

WESTERN AUSTRALIA

NORTHERN TERRITORY

SANDY BLIGHT

Tjukurla

Docker

Hull

Lake Neale (salt)

Lake Amadeus (salt)

Kings Creek Station

Kaltukatjara (Docker River)

Petermann R.

R.

PETERMANN

KATITI

4

Warakurna

Giles 25° Meteorological Station

Warakurna Roadhouse

GILES 'MULGA PARK (GUNBARREL) HWY

Giles Ck.

76

TJUKARURU 260

ROAD

Petermann Ranges

LASSETER 136

Yulara

Kata Tjuta (The Olgas)

Uluru (Ayers Rock)

Mutijulu

ULURU-KATA TJUTA N.P.

HWY

Curtin Springs Roadhouse

Mt Connor 859 +

CENTRAL RESERVE

Mann Ranges

+ Mt Cockburn

Surveyor Generals Corner

NORTHERN TERRITORY

Brittenjones Ck

Mulga Park

5

26°

Irrunytju (Wingellina)

Ranges

+ Mt Whinham 1231

SOUTH AUSTRALIA

ROAD

Amata

Musgrave

Ck.

Pipalyatjara

GILES · MULGA PARK (GUNBARREL) HWY

Mt Woodroffe + 1440

Ranges

Currie

WESTERN AUSTRALIA

SOUTH AUSTRALIA

+ Mt Kintore 1070

6

PITJANTJATJARA

GREAT VICTORIA DESERT

Ck

27°

A 129° B Mt Linsay + 819 C 130° D 131° E

Joins map 340

Joins map 442

NORTHERN TERRITORY 441

Alice Springs

NORTHERN TERRITORY

SOUTH AUSTRALIA

GREAT VICTORIA
DESERT

PITJANTJATJARA

Musgrave

Ranges

ULURU-KATA TJUTA N.P.

WATARRKA N.P.

MacDonnell Ranges

James Ranges

FINKE GORGE N.P.

442

Gregory's Australia

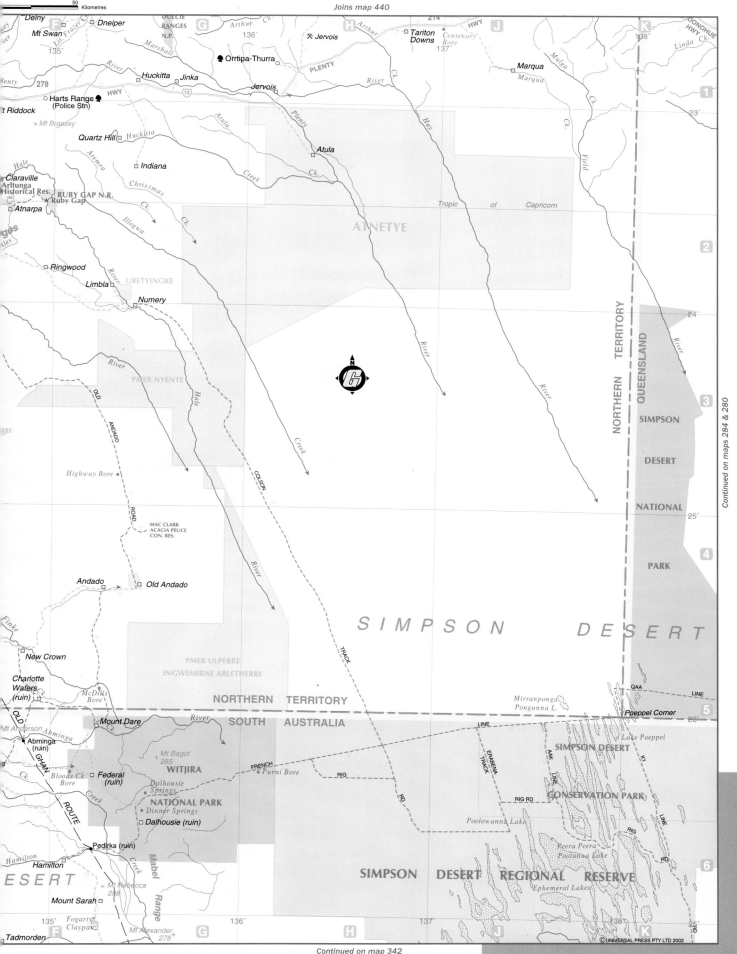

50 Kilometres

Delny
Mt Swan □ □ Dneiper
DULCIE
RANGES
N.P.
Arthur Ck.
136°
214
HWY
138°
DONOHUE
Linda Ck.

F
Jervois
G
Arthur
H
Tariton Downs
J
Centenary Bore
137°
K

135°
♣ Orrtipa-Thurra
PLENTY
Marqua □
Marqua Ck.

Huckitta □ Jinka
River
Jervois
Field Ck.
23°
1

278
HWY
12

t Riddock
Harts Range ♣
(Police Stn)
+ Mt Brassey

Quartz Hill □
Huckitta
Atula □
Tropic of Capricorn
2

Claraville
Arltunga
Historical Res.
RUBY GAP N.R.
Indiana □
Christmas
ATNETYE

Atnarpa □
Ruby Gap
Illogwa
URETYINGKE
24°

Ringwood
Limbla □
Numery □
River
N
G
River
3

PMER NYENTE
Hale
River
SIMPSON

OLD
Creek
River
DESERT

ANDADO
Highway Bore □
COLSON
25°
4

ROAD
MAC CLARK
ACACIA PEUCE
CON. RES.
NATIONAL

Andado □
Old Andado □
River
TRACK
PARK

New Crown
PMER ULPERRE
INGWEMIRNE ARLETHERRE
S I M P S O N   D E S E R T

Charlotte
Waters
(ruin)
McDills Bore
NORTHERN TERRITORY
Mirranponga
Pongunna L.
QAA
LINE
Poeppel Corner
26°
5

OLD
Mt Anderson Abminga
Mount Dare □
River
SOUTH AUSTRALIA
LINE
Lake Poeppel
SIMPSON DESERT

Abminga
(ruin)
Mt Bagot
265
WITJIRA
FRENCH
Purni Bore
RIG
ERABENA TRACK
AAK LINE
CONSERVATION PARK

GHAN
Bloods Ck
Bore
Federal
(ruin)
Dalhousie
Springs
NATIONAL PARK
Dinner Springs
RD
RIG RD
Poolowanna Lake
RIG
LINE

ROUTE
Dalhousie (ruin)
Pedirka (ruin)
Peera Peera
Poolanna Lake
RD
6

Hamilton
Hamilton
Mabel Range
+ Mt Rebecca
SIMPSON   DESERT   REGIONAL   RESERVE
Ephemeral Lakes

ESERT
Mount Sarah □
135°
Fogarty
Claypan
136°
Mt Alexander
278
137°
138°

F
G
H
J
K

Tadmorden

Continued on map 342
Continued on maps 284 & 280

© UNIVERSAL PRESS PTY LTD 2002

NORTHERN TERRITORY   443

TASMANIA

Tasmania is the smallest of the Australian states. It is an island 240km from the mainland and surrounded by the turbulent Bass Strait, Southern Ocean and Tasman Sea. Its compactness makes it an ideal touring destination, as only relatively short distances separate its many attractions. Tasmania is a land of diversity with beaches encircling its coastline, while national parks and reserves protect its spectacular landmass, which features more than 2000km of world-class walking tracks.

This is the most mountainous Australian state, as well it has the highest percentage of national parks, comprising about one-third of the island. Tasmania boasts stunning and often remote World Heritage Areas. There are fertile plains and open bushland, mountains and valleys, rare flora and fauna, rustic ports and historic villages all crammed into a comparatively small area.

Of all the Australian states, Tasmania has the smallest population and the lowest immigration rate. As

Tasmania: The Holiday Isle

- Population: 470 1000
- Total area: 68 401km²
- % of Australia: 1%
- Length of coastline: 4882 km
- Floral emblem: Blue Gum
- Fauna emblem: Tasmanian Devil

ℹ️ Tourist information

Tasmanian Travel and Information Centre
20 Davey St, Hobart, Tas 7000
Ph: (03) 6230 8233
Freecall: 1800 806 846
www.tourism.tas.gov.au

Main ATTRACTIONS

◈ Bruny Island

A small isthmus connects North and South Bruny Islands. Adventure Bay, South Bruny Lighthouse and little penguins at The Neck Reserve are highlights.

◈ Cradle Mountain– Lake St Clair NP

This World Heritage-listed national park is one of Tasmania's best-known and most popular attractions — deep, trout-filled lakes and bushwalks attract visitors from around the world.

◈ East Coast

The East Coast is where Tasmanians go for their holidays. A mild climate, surfing beaches, excellent fishing and spectacular scenic attractions make this region an ideal holiday destination.

◈ Flinders Island and King Island

Flanking Bass Strait's eastern and western sides, these islands are secluded and an idyllic holiday destination. Both islands are rich in colonial history.

◈ Launceston

Tasmania's second city, Launceston, is sometimes known as the Garden City and offers museums, galleries, parks and gardens among its many attractions.

◈ Port Arthur

This infamous convict settlement is well preserved and maintained. Located past Eaglehawk on the Tasman Peninsula, it is a fascinating step back in time. The coastline itself is a physical reminder of the rugged and dramatic history of the port.

◈ Strahan

A former timber and copper mining town on Macquarie Harbour, Strahan is the West Coast at its prettiest and offers access to the scenic Franklin-Gordon Wild Rivers NP.

a result, its society is not as multi-cultural as other states. The small Aboriginal population is actively involved in maintaining its cultural identity through language and land management projects.

Unlike most of Australia, Tasmania enjoys 4 distinct seasons, which are a perfect complement to the other attractions of the state. Magnificent scenery is provided on both the Cradle Mountain-Lake St Clair NP walks and the cruise on the Gordon River in the south-west. Historic villages that have hardly changed since the 1800s together with convict-built bridges and old gaols are reminders of colonial days. The wide variety of attractions make the smallest state the perfect holiday destination deserving of the epithet 'The Holiday Isle'.

Photo above: Cradle Mountain reflected in Dove Lake in winter, Cradle Mountain-Lake St Clair NP

THE HOLIDAY ISLE

Abel Tasman, the Dutch explorer, called this island **Van Diemen's Land** when he sighted it in 1642; and the island's European colonisation began in 1803. The first settlement was at **Risdon**, now a suburb of **Hobart**. In 1830, the penal settlement of **Port Arthur** was built to house troublesome convicts. The living conditions were brutal, and the convicts suffered great hardship. Great hardship was visited too, on the original Aboriginal population, most of whom died out in the wake of European settlement.

Tasmania became a colony in its own right by breaking away from New South Wales in 1825, but continued to receive convicts until 1853. Free settlers were attracted by the island's rich farming land and because of its resemblance to Britain. Many of them established successful enterprises that continue to contribute to Tasmania's diverse rural economy. Today, agricultural establishments cover around 30% of the state's total area. Beef cattle are farmed throughout the state, while sheep are found mainly in the Midlands and south-east region and dairy cattle and pigs are run mainly in the north and north-west areas.

Apples and potatoes remain the most significant crops for the Tasmanian food industry, and in more recent years the state has become well-known for producing gourmet fare; dairy, meat and fish products. Tasmanian dairy foods, particularly those from **King Island**, enjoy a very high reputation. The **Tamar Valley** produces about 70% of the island's cool-climate wines. Many towns have fishing fleets which ensures fresh seafood is nearly always available.

Tasmania has a good store of natural resources, particularly timber. Hardwood forests are established throughout the island, and plantations of softwood are

Sheep grazing near Copping on the East Coast

also being planted. The wood is used for building and construction as well as paper, wood pulp, hardboard and plywood. There are also rich mineral deposits of iron ore, scheelite, coal, zinc, tin, copper, silver and gold.

The state's economy is also boosted by a healthy tourist industry, worth millions of dollars per year and growing. This isn't surprising—visitor access to the island is easy. Options include fly-drive packages; the *Spirit of Tasmania* car-and-passenger ferry between **Melbourne** and **Devonport**; and the *Devil Cat* car-and-passenger ferry between Melbourne and **George Town**. Visitors can do a relatively comprehensive tour of the island in 2 weeks on well-surfaced roads (sometimes narrow and winding). Accommodation is plentiful with a special feature being the many quaint guesthouses offering B&B.

Lichen-covered rocks, Rocky Cape NP

Tasmania

TOURISM REGION HIGHLIGHTS

Australia's **'Natural State'**, the island of Tasmania crams a great many attractions into a small space. There are World Heritage-listed wilderness areas with spectacular scenery, historic towns, wineries, farms and dairies in a lush green landscape. The state's convict and colonial past is reflected at **Hobart**, the ruins of **Port Arthur** and **Sarah Island**. World-renowned national parks, such as **Cradle Mountain-Lake St Clair** attract bushwalkers, outdoor adventurers and anglers from all over the world.

A Hobart

Antarctic Adventure; Battery Point; Boronong Park Wildlife Centre; Cascade Brewery; Nelson Signal Station; Mount Wellington; Old Hobart Gaol; Old Hobart Town Model Village; Richmond; Royal Tasmanian Botanical Gardens; Salamanca Place and Markets; Tasmanian Museum and Art Gallery

B Central North and Cradle Mountain

Cradle Mountain; Deloraine; Devonport; Don River Railway; Latrobe's Axeman's Hall of Fame; Liffey Falls; Marakoopa Caves; Meander Valley; Mole Creek;

Narawntapu (Asbestos Range) NP; Overland Track; Port Sorell; Sheffield murals

C Derwent Valley and Central Highlands

Australian Golf Museum; Bothwell; Bushy Park; Hamilton; Lake St Clair; Mount Field NP; New Norfolk; Ouse; Salmon Ponds; Strathgordon; Russell Falls

D East Coast

Bicheno; Douglas-Apsley NP; Evercreech Forest Reserve; Freycinet NP; Maria Island; Orford; Swansea Bark Mill; The Hazards; Wineglass Bay

E Flinders Island

Strzelecki NP; Trousers Point; Wybalenna Historic Site

F Huon Valley and Bruny Island

Apple and Heritage Museum; Cockle Creek; Forest and Heritage Centre; Geeveston; Hartz Mountains NP; Hastings Caves; Huonville; Kettering; Talune Wildlife Park

G King Island

Cape Wickham Lighthouse; Currie; Grassy; King Island Dairies; Lavinia Nature Reserve; Stokes Point

H Launceston and Tamar Valley

Cataract Gorge; Country Club Casino; Grubb Shaft Gold and Heritage Museum; National Automobile Museum; Penny Royal World; Planetarium; Queen Victoria Museum; Seahorse World; Tamar Valley Wineries

I Midlands

Campbell Town; Clarendon Homestead; Evandale; Longford;

Russell Falls, Mount Field NP

Oatlands; Ross Bridge; Tasmanian Wool Centre

J North East

Bay of Fires; Ben Lomond; Bridestowe Lavender Farm; Bridport; Derby Tin Mine Centre; Eddystone Point Lighthouse; Mount William NP; St Columba Falls; St Helens

K North West

Arthur River; Burnie; Cape Grim; Dip Falls; Rocky Cape NP; Stanley; The Nut; Waratah

L South East

Bush Mill; Copping Colonial and Convict Exhibition; Port Arthur; Remarkable Cave; Sorell; Tasman Arch; Tasmanian Devil Park; Tessellated Pavement

M West Coast

Abt Railway; Gordon River; Montezuma Falls; Mount Lyell Mine; Queenstown; Queenstown Chairlift; Sarah Island; Strahan; Teepookana Plateau; Zeehan

NATIONAL PARKS

From the wild waters of the **West Coast** and the quiet tranquillity of the **East Coast**, to the unchartered wilderness, Tasmania's landscape may be confined, but it is still as diverse as that of mainland Australia. The state's national parks provide a glimpse of this environmental diversity, as well as an opportunity to relax, explore and appreciate the charm of the Tasmanian wilderness. Many unique animal (*see* pp.450) and plant species, like the Tasmanian devil and the ancient Huon pines, are preserved in Tasmania's parks.

facts

- No. of parks/reserves: 395
- Area: 20 500km^2
- % of state: 30%
- World Heritage Areas: Macquarie Island, Tasmanian Wilderness

A Ben Lomond NP

(Map 481, G3)

A 1300m high plateau, Ben Lomond NP is Tasmania's main winter ski resort. Within the national park itself, there are 8 ski tows, with cross-country skiing and other skiing amenities on offer. When the snow clears, the park is a popular destination for bushwalkers as well as picnicking day-trippers. The 165km^2 national park is not abundant with native wildlife (like other areas in the state), yet its unspoiled beauty is invigorating.

B Cradle Mountain-Lake St Clair NP

(Map 473, B3)

One of the most famous national parks in Tasmania, Cradle Mountain-Lake St Clair NP is a precious part of Australia's natural history and wilderness. World Heritage-listed, the national park offers spectacular scenery of rugged mountains, tree-filled gorges, glacial lakes, rainforests and moorlands. Sprawling across 1612km^2 in **Central North** Tasmania, Cradle Mountain-Lake St Clair NP is home to many of the state's unique animals, including the Tasmanian devil and quoll. With possibilities for fishing, walking, rockclimbing, canoeing, windsurfing, cycling and 4WD tours, the park is an exciting source of holiday escapism. With an accessible resort, backpacking and camping facilities, the park is well worth exploring.

C Franklin-Gordon Wild Rivers NP

(Map 483, D3)

Located only 180km from Hobart, the 4463km^2 Franklin-Gordon Wild Rivers NP is home to Tasmania's longest river, the **Franklin**, as well as the **Collingwood**, **Gordon**, **Jane**, **Governor** and **Denison rivers**.

Myrtle beeches and Huon pine dominate the rainforests while elsewhere there are eucalypt forests, heaths, boglands and buttongrass plains. Access to the northern end of the park is via the Lyell Hwy. A 4WD track from **Queenstown**, requiring a permit, ends near the Franklin River. The best way to explore the surrounds is by foot; enjoying one of the many walks that leave the Lyell Hwy. Alternatively, cruises and float-planes depart from **Strahan** for the lower Gordon River.

D Freycinet NP **(Map 481, J6)**

Freycinet NP is a protected area of coastal heathland and white sand beaches washed by vibrant blue waters. Located on the **East Coast** of Tasmania, 180km SE of Launceston, the 168km^2 national park boasts granite mountain

Wilderness Seeker cruise on the Gordon River, Franklin-Gordon Wild Rivers NP

Sleepy Bay, Freycinet NP

peaks, including **Amos**, **Dove** and **Mason**, which can be seen from any point within the park. The park offers great coastal walking paths as well as summit climbs and bushwalking. Watersports are popular in the summer months, with fishing and cruising the main attractions. Worth exploring is **Bluestone Bay**, a beach with bluish rocks, some up to 1m in length, that many believe resemble dinosaur eggs. Campsites, youth hostels and B&Bs are all available for the weary explorer.

E Mount Field NP

(Map 484, D2)

Located 80km NW of Hobart, this 159km² NP is Tasmania's oldest and home to the much photographed 40m-high **Russell Falls** and stands of magnificent **swamp gums** (*Eucalyptus regnans),* the world's tallest hardwood. King Billy and pencil pines, unique to Tasmania, are also found here as well as abundant wildlife.

F Mount William NP

(Map 481, J1)

In the north-east corner of the state, Mount William NP covers 184km² of heathland, beach and dry forest. Not as well known as other Tasmania parks, Mount William is home to some of the state's most pristine and beautiful beaches and a great variety of native flora and fauna. Swimming, surfing, diving and fishing are popular recreations, as are the coastal walks and the views from **Mount William**. Camping sites and picnic facilities are found throughout the park.

G Southwest NP

(Map 484, B4)

Bordered on one side by the **Southern Ocean**, Southwest NP is a region of unspoiled coastline, rivers, rainforest and mountains. Offering an array of activities for the visitor, the 6180km² national park is well-known for its wilderness drive, 82km of sealed road, which takes in the northern part of the park and much of the flora. The park can also be accessed via cruises and flights to **Bathurst Harbour**. There are a number of walking tracks and, importantly, the trout fishing here is said to be the best in the country. Sailing and canoeing are popular activities in summer. There are several campsites and numerous picnicking spots.

H Walls of Jerusalem NP

(Map 480, B5)

Wild and unspoiled, Walls of Jerusalem NP, 90km south of Devonport, is dominated by a high plateau of dolerite peaks, conifer forests and alpine vegetation. Also part of the World Heritage Area and covering 518km², the park has no vehicle access, so it remains a destination for energetic and fit hikers, skiers and rockclimbers. Worth exploring are: **Solomon's Jewels** (a row of small lakes), **Herod's Gate** (2 giant rocks which seem to create an entrance to **Lake Salome**) and the surrounding **West Wall** (300m), and **Mount Jerusalem** (1458m). There are no camping facilities in the park, however bush camping is allowed.

National Park Head Office

Tasmania Parks and Wildlife Service
GPO Box 44
Hobart, Tas 7001
Ph: 1300 368 550
www.parks.tas.gov.au

UNIQUE WILDLIFE

Tasmania's isolation from the main-land has created a refuge, a preservation area, in which many animal species, some of which are now extinct on the mainland, have been able to thrive. As home to some of the country's most unusual wildlife, Tasmania is proud of its natural heritage and wilderness status.

Perhaps the best known of Tasmania's unique animals is the **Tasmanian devil** (*Sarcophilus harrisii*). Affectionately termed the **'Tassie devil'**, this little creature, generally the size of a small dog, is famous for its screeches, reputed bad temper and fierce looking mouth. With powerful jaws and teeth to devour its prey (bones, fur and all), the devil is the world's largest surviving carnivorous marsupial. It is thought to have become extinct on the mainland 600 years ago, but today is commonly seen in **Asbestos Range NP**, **Mount William NP** and **Cradle Mountain-Lake St Clair NP**.

Although it is believed extinct, the **Tasmanian tiger** (*Thylacinus cynocephalus*) is a symbol of the state, now immortalised on the label of one of the state's leading beers, Cascade. The tiger, was once widespread on the Australian continent, but after the arrival of the dingo 3500–4000 years ago, it gradually became extinct on the mainland. Feared by Tasmanian settlers, who blamed the creature for killing sheep, it was hunted to extinction. The last known Tasmanian tiger died in Beaumaris Zoo, Hobart on 7 Sept 1936. However, unsubstantiated sightings of the animal continue, particularly in the north of the state.

The **eastern quoll** (*Dasyurus viverrinus*), sometimes called the **native cat**, is considered rare on the mainland but found in abundance in Tasmania. Quolls feed on insects, small mammals and birds and are commonly found in **Mount Field NP**. The **red-bellied pademelon** or rufous wallaby (*Thylogale billardierii*) is a stocky creature with a short tail and legs. It makes its home in the thick vegetation of forests and rainforests during the day and is mainly nocturnal and solitary. Feeding mostly on herbs, green shoots and grasses, the pademelon is extinct on the mainland but found over most of the state of Tasmania.

The eastern half of the state is home to the **Tasmanian bettong** (*Bettongia gaimardi*) of the kangaroo

Tasmanian wedge-tailed eagle (juvenile), *Aquila audax fleayi*

family. This small animal weighs on average 2kg, is covered in grey-brown fur on its back and white fur below, and has a grasping tail that it uses to carry nesting materials. Bettongs live in dry, open eucalypt forests and grassy woodlands, and feed on seeds, fungi, roots and small insects.

Extinct on the mainland, the **Tasmanian native hen** (*Gallinula mortierii*) is quite common on the island. The rare **ground parrot** (*Pezoporus wallicus*) is one of only three ground-dwelling parrots in the world. The **Tasmanian wedge-tailed eagle** (*Aquila audax fleayi*) has been isolated for 10 000 years from its smaller mainland counterparts and is viewed as a separate sub-species. However, with only 100 breeding pairs in Tasmania, the eagle is now considered endangered.

Tasmanian devil cubs, *Sarcophilus harrisii*

Tasmania

WINERIES

Tasmania was the second colony to develop a wine industry. In 1823 **Bartholomew Broughton** established his vineyard at **New Town**, north of **Hobart** and soon began producing quality wines—one of his wines won an award at the Paris Exhibition of 1848. Several Silesian immigrants also planted vineyards, but by 1890, the Tasmanian winemaking industry had virtually wound up, the general assumption being that the island was too cold and too wet for profitable grape growing.

In the late 1950s, however, this was repudiated by the success of **Claudio Alcorso's Moorilla vineyard** in the **Derwent Valley**. Today over 100 vineyards flourish in suitable microclimates throughout Tasmania, producing outstanding cool-climate wines. Visitors can enjoy hours of pleasure traversing the **Tasmanian Wine Routes** that have been drawn up from Hobart and **Launceston**.

A East Coast

The scenic coastline between **St Helens** and **Orford** is home to a number of wineries, linked by the **East Coast Gourmet Trail**. The family-owned vineyards produce prize-winning chardonnays and velvety, rich pinot noirs and cabernets.

B Hobart and Coal River

This historic gourmet food and wine region around the **River Derwent** and **Coal River** can be explored on the **Southern Tasmanian Wine Route**. Elegant local wines include pinot noir, riesling, chardonnay, sauvignon blanc, cabernet sauvignon, merlot, schonburger and gewurztraminer.

C Huon/Channel

The orchard region that gave Tasmania its 'Apple Isle' epithet also offers some attractive waterside wineries. Pinot noir, chardonnay, riesling, sauvignon blanc, semillon, pinot gris, cabernet sauvignon, sylvaner and methode champenoise sparkling wines can be sampled on the **Southern Tasmanian Wine Route**.

D North West

One of Tasmania's richest agricultural regions, the North West (which includes King Island) is famous for its magnificent cheeses. The area around **Sheffield**, en route to **Cradle Mountain** also produces fine wines to accompany them. Varieties include chardonnay, pinot noir, riesling, gewurztraminer and gamay.

E Pipers Brook

The rich, red soil region north-east from Launceston now accounts for 70% of Tasmania's wine production and the original Pipers Brook Vineyard is the state's largest. Poplar windbreaks protect the vines from westerly winds and provide a dazzling display of colour in autumn.

Wines include chardonnay, sauvignon blanc, pinot noir, riesling, pinot grigio, white frontignac, cabernets and semillon.

F Tamar Valley

Set between the **Tamar Estuary** and alpine peaks, this wine region is often considered the prettiest in Australia and, with Pipers Brook, forms the **Northern Tasmanian Wine Route**. Cabernets, chardonnay, pinot noir, pinot grigio and methode champenoise wines are the standout varieties.

Picnickers at Pipers Brook Vineyard

HOBART

Victoria Dock reflections

◈ **Battery Point**

Hobart's oldest district was once home to sailors, fishermen, prostitutes and shipwrights. It is now a fashionable inner-city neighbourhood.

◈ **Cadbury Chocolate Factory**

Hobart is home to this well-known chocolate manufacturer—a tour of the factory at Claremont is a must for chocoholics.

◈ **Cascade Brewery**

Australia's oldest brewery produces some of the finest beer in the country. Tours of both the brewery and museum are available daily.

◈ **Constitution Dock**

The final destination for the annual Sydney to Hobart Yacht Race is part of Hobart's picturesque waterfront area.

◈ **Royal Tasmanian Botanical Gardens**

Established in 1818, these gardens house an extensive collection of native and exotic plants. Features include a cactus house, herb garden and Japanese garden.

◈ **Runnymede**

Set in tranquil gardens, this National Trust homestead was built in 1837. Open to the public, many items in the home are original and the rooms have been lovingly restored.

Founded in 1804 and declared a city in 1842, Hobart is rich in reminders of its colonial past. It is Australia's second-oldest city (after Sydney) and more than 90 of the city's buildings are National Trust-classified.

Hobart is nestled on the western shore of the **River Derwent** and at the foot of **Mount Wellington**, which is often snowcapped in the winter months. There are panoramic vistas of the city available from the mountain's superb lookouts.

Like most Australian capitals, Hobart's lifestyle is defined by water; it is a riverside city with a bustling harbour, surrounded by picturesque harbourside warehouses. The harbour remains integral to the city's economy. Only metres from the business district are the docks where overseas ships moor, supplies are loaded for Australia's Antarctic bases and fishing vessels return with their catch. The waterfront area is the focal point for visitors to Hobart, as it is the site for many of the city's tourist attractions.

i Tourist information

Tasmanian Travel and Information Centre
Cnr Davey and Elizabeth sts
Hobart, Tas 7000
Ph:(03) 6230 8233
Freecall: 1800 806 846

facts

◈ Population: 218 000
◈ Date founded: 1804
◈ Tallest building: AMP Building
◈ Oldest building: Commissariat (1808–1810)
◈ Average temperature: 17°C (Jan), 9°(June)

Places of Interest

Allport Library and
    Museum of Fine Arts Ⓐ C4
Anglesea Barracks Ⓑ C4
Antarctic Adventure Ⓒ C4
Battery Point Ⓓ D4
Cascade Brewery Ⓔ A5
Elizabeth Mall Ⓕ C4
Government House Ⓖ C2
Maritime Museum of Tasmania Ⓗ D4
Narryna Folk Museum Ⓘ C4
Parliament House Ⓙ C4
Princes Park Ⓚ D4
Rosny Hill Lookout Ⓛ E2
Royal Tasmanian Botanical Gardens Ⓜ C2
Runnymede Ⓝ B1
St David's Park Ⓞ C4
Salamanca Place and Markets Ⓟ C4
State Library of Tasmania Ⓠ C4
Sullivans Cove Ⓡ C4
Tasmanian Museum and Art Gallery Ⓢ C4
Wrest Point Hotel and Casino Ⓣ D6

Battery Point, Hobart

Tasmania

Continued on map 456

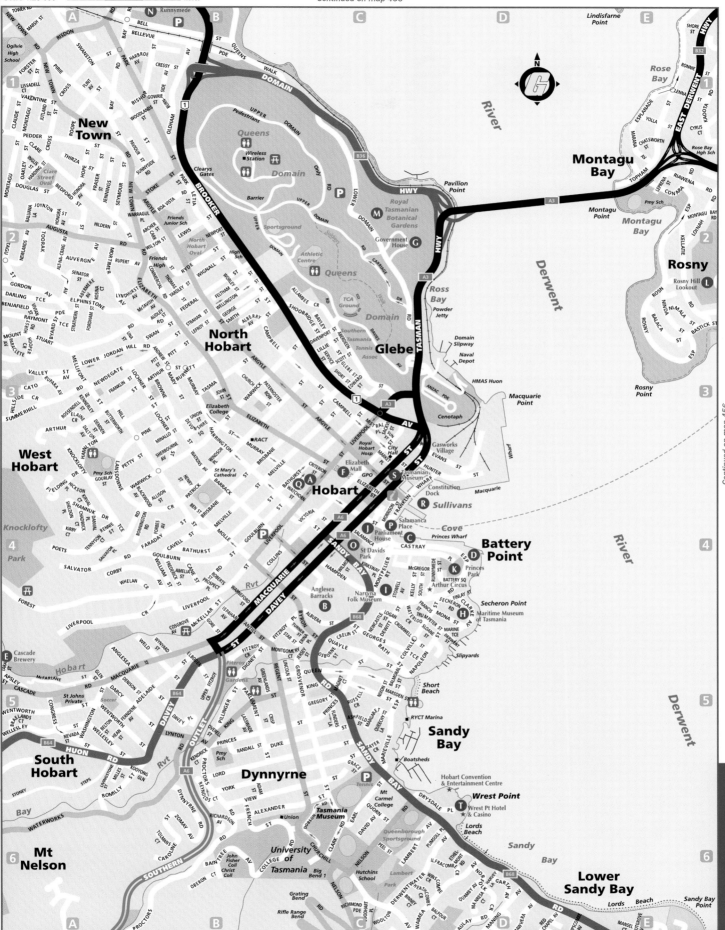

Continued on map 456

© UNIVERSAL PRESS PTY LTD 2002

CBD & SUBURBS

CBD ATTRACTIONS

Most of Hobart's attractions are concentrated in a relatively small area within easy walking distance of **Sullivans Cove** and **Constitution Dock**. Close to the northern end of the Cove, **Gasworks Shopping Village** has shops and restaurants in restored 19th-century buildings. Tours can be made of Australia's only commercial whisky distillery here. A stroll along Campbell St takes you to the **Theatre Royal**, built in the 1830s, and the **Penitentiary Chapel** at the **Criminal Courts**, where guided tours (including ghost tours) are conducted. Opposite Constitution Dock is the **Tasmanian Museum and Art Gallery**. The Museum explores Tasmanian identity with a variety of displays covering history, science and the natural environment. The art collection focuses on colonial art, contemporary Australian painting and changing exhibitions. Hobart's Italianate **Town Hall** is close by. Further down Davey St, a walk along Murray St will take you past **St David's Cathedral** to the **Allport Library and Museum of Fine Arts**, part of the **State Library of Tasmania** complex.

At the southern end of Sullivans Cove, ferries and cruises depart from **Brooke St Pier** on **Franklin Wharf**. **Salamanca Place** is an excellent example of how Hobart's historic buildings have been preserved to play a vital part in city life. Sandstone merchant warehouses from the 1830s are now used as restaurants, shops and galleries. On Saturdays, traffic is blocked off to make way for the **Salamanca Market**; a colourful collection of 300 stalls selling all manner of things. Also at Salamanca Pl, **Antarctic Adventure** explores the fragile ecosystem of the southern continent with a penguin theatre, fossils, weather station, theatrette and planetarium. Connected to Salamanca Pl by **Kellys Steps**, **Battery Point** is another historic section of Hobart with heritage buildings such as the ring of houses at **Arthur Circus**.

Three further attractions in the Battery Point area are **'Narryna' Folk Museum**, in a beautiful Georgian building built 1833–36 by sea captain Andrew Haig; the **Maritime Museum of Tasmania** which displays historic vessels, shipwreck relics, whaling implements, paintings, photographs and models; and **Anglesea Barracks**, the oldest military establishment in Australia still in use.

SUBURBAN ATTRACTIONS

Hobart's boundary extends to the foot of **Mount Wellington** in the west—certainly the city's most prominent landmark. From the top of the mountain the view of the city and surrounding countryside is breathtaking, and on very clear days it is possible to see parts of the south-west corner of the state. Walk, drive or cycle the paths of the mountain to get a dramatic view of the landscape. Walkers should be prepared for sudden weather changes and the peak is often covered in snow in winter.

After an exploration of the mountain views, a stop into **Cascade Brewery** at the mountain foot is highly recommended. The brewery is known for premium quality beer and, established in 1832, is the oldest in Australia. Tours are available of the brewery and attached museum, as well as the adjoining **Woodstock Gardens**.

North of the city, the **Royal Tasmanian Botanical Gardens** have many interesting features, including the conifer collection, fernery, Japanese Garden, historic Arthur Wall, Conservatory, Subantarctic House and a Chinese section. The restored National Trust homestead,

Pleasure craft at Sandy Bay

Tasmania

SYDNEY TO HOBART YACHT RACE

The world-famous Sydney to Hobart Yacht Race has occurred annually since 1949 and is now considered a premier event on the international yachting circuit. The gun fires at **Rushcutters Bay**, **Sydney** at 1pm each Boxing Day. Thousands of Sydneysiders fight for a glimpse of the boats as they sail out of **Sydney Harbour**. The boats' arrival into Hobart, generally just before New Year's Day, is a charged occasion, with thousands of locals and visitors turning out to see the yachts sail up the **River Derwent estuary**. With the tension of the race over, traditional champagne celebrations are unleashed as the fleet rests at Constitution Dock. The **Taste of Tasmania Food and Wine Festival** is also held on the dock to coincide with the conclusion of the race.

Maxi yacht *Brindabella* nearing the finish line of the 1997 Sydney to Hobart Yacht Race

Runnymede, can be found at **New Town** and the **Cadbury Chocolate Factory** at **Claremont** can be reached by road or cruise from Hobart. Tours offer visitors the chance to see the factory's chocolate-making process and to taste samples along the way. Chocolate can be bought afterwards for those who have completed the tour. Bookings are essential and enclosed footwear must be worn. Not far away, **Alpenrail** provides a unique alpine experience with a model railway running through a realistic Swiss model village. At **Brighton**, 25min drive north of Hobart, **Bonorong Wildlife Park** has Tasmanian devils, koalas, common wombats, eastern quolls and native birds as well as kangaroos which are free to roam the park.

On the other side of the Derwent River, accessed by the **Bowen Bridge**, is **Risdon Cove Historic Site**, where Hobart's first European settlement began. Also on the eastern side are **Cambridge Aerodrome**, **Rosny Hill Lookout** and **Hobart Airport**. Visitors are welcome to the **Royal Hobart Golf Course** as well as the **Tasmanian**, **Airport** and **Llanherne** courses. There are a number of pretty beaches on both sides of the Derwent and **Clifton Beach** is a popular summer-surfing destination.

Located south of the CBD in **Sandy Bay**, the convention and entertainment centre at **Wrest Point** is the site of Australia's first gambling casino. **Wrest Point Hotel Casino** not only provides gaming such as roulette, blackjack, poker,

keno and electronic gambling, but also offers hotel and motel accommodation, restaurants and bars, nightclubs and shops. Sandy Bay is also home to Tasmania's university and the prestigious **Royal Yacht Club**, where hundreds of yachts are moored.

In the Lower Sandy Bay area, there are lookouts near **Long Beach** and at the **Mount Nelson Signal Station Reserve** with Derwent estuary views. Further south are **Truganini Reserve**, dedicated to the last full-blood Tasmanian Aborigine, **Tudor Court Model Village**, and the convict-built **Shot Tower**, which provides a superb view of the Derwent estuary and includes a small museum. The **Australian Antarctic Division** is at **Kingston**.

Scale 1:7

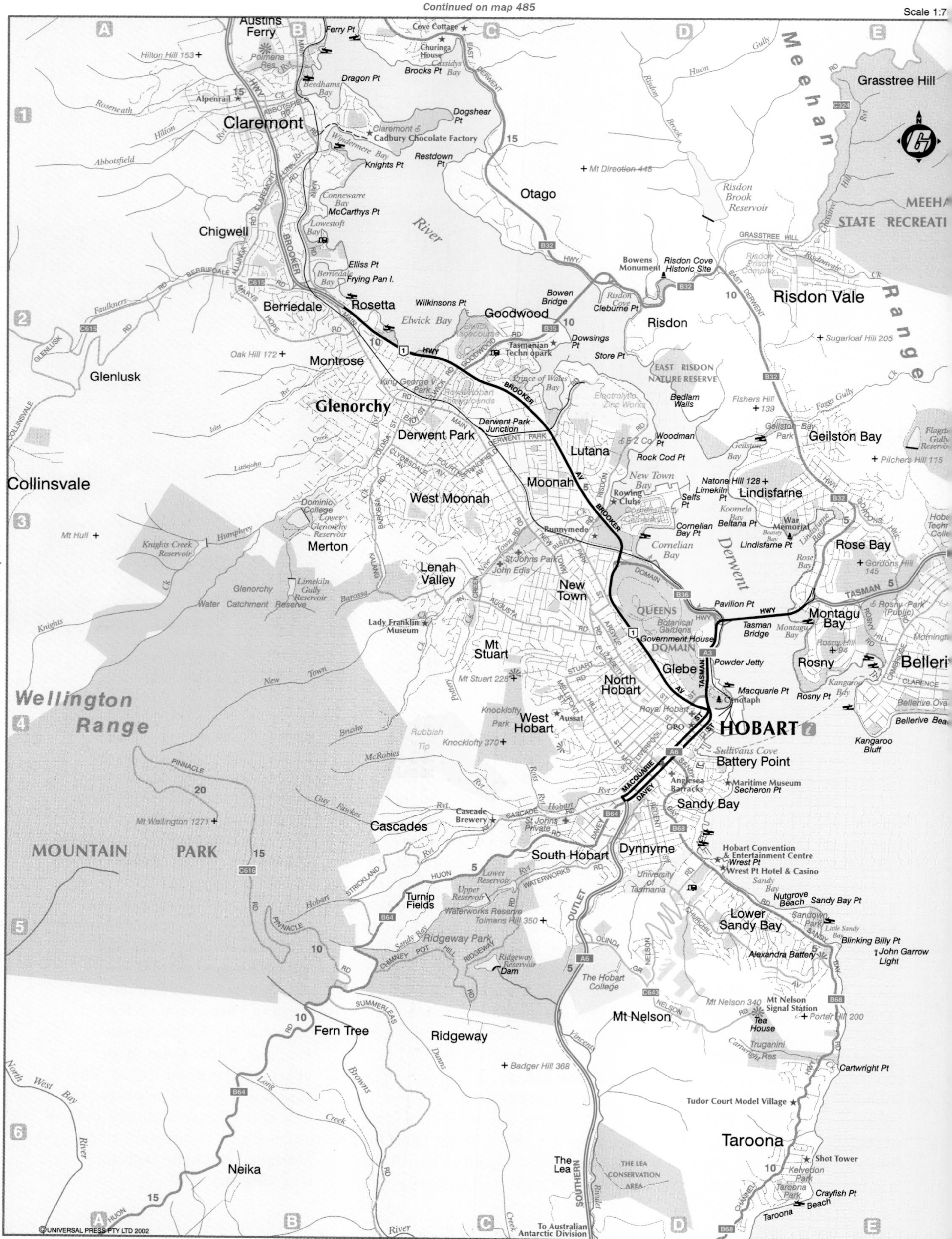

Austins Ferry
Hilton Hill 153
Polmena Res
Alpenrail
Ferry Pt
Cove Cottage
Churinga House
Cassidys Bay
Dragon Pt
Brocks Pt
Dogshear Pt
Grasstree Hill
Claremont
Rosebeath
Abbotsfield
Hilton
Abbotsfield
Claremont
Cadbury Chocolate Factory
Windermere Bay
Knights Pt
Restdown Pt
Otago
Mt Direction 448
Risdon Brook Reservoir
MEEHAN STATE RECREATI
Chigwell
Connewarre Bay
McCarthys Pt
Lowestoft Bay
Bowens Monument
Risdon Cove Historic Site
Risdon Prison Complex
GRASSTREE HILL
Risdon Vale
Berriedale
Elliss Pt
Frying Pan I.
Rosetta
Wilkinsons Pt
Elwick Bay
Goodwood
Bowen Bridge
Cleburne Pt
Risdon
Dowsings Pt
Store Pt
Sugarloaf Hill 205
Meehan Range
Glenlusk
Oak Hill 172
Montrose
Elwick Racecourse
Tasmanian Technopark
Prince of Wales Bay
Electrolytic Zinc Works
EAST RISDON NATURE RESERVE
Bedlam Walls
Fishers Hill 139
Geilston Bay Park
Geilston Bay
Flagste Gully Reservoir
Glenlusk
King George V Park
Royal Hobart Showgrounds
Glenorchy
Derwent Park Junction
Derwent Park
Lutana
Woodman Pt
Rock Cod Pt
EZ Co
New Town Bay
Cornelian Bay
Natone Hill 128
Limekiln Pt
Selfs Pt
Koomela Bay
Beltana Pt
Lindisfarne
Pilchers Hill 115
Rose Bay
Hobe Tech Colle
Collinsvale
Moonah
West Moonah
Runnymede
Cornelian Bay Pt
War Memorial
Lindisfarne Pt
Gordons Hill 145
Rose Bay
Dominic College
Lower Glenorchy Reservoir
Merton
Lenah Valley
St Johns Park
John Edis
New Town
Cornelian Bay
Derwent
Rosny Park (Public)
Mt Hull
Knights Creek Reservoir
Lady Franklin Museum
Mt Stuart
Mt Stuart 228
Botanical Gardens
Government House
QUEENS DOMAIN
Pavilion Pt
Tasman Bridge
Montagu Bay
Rosny Hill 94
Morningto
Glenorchy Water Catchment Reserve
Limekiln Gully
Barossa
North Hobart
Glebe
Powder Jetty
Rosny
Rosny Pt
Belleri
CLARENCE
Wellington Range
Knocklofty Park
Knocklofty 370
West Hobart
Aussat
Royal Hobart
Macquarie Pt
Cenotaph
HOBART
Kangaroo Bay
Bellerive Ova
Bellerive Bea
PINNACLE
20
Mt Wellington 1271
Brushy
McRobies
Rubbish Tip
Cascade Brewery
St Johns Private
South Hobart
Battery Point
Anglesea Barracks
Maritime Museum
Secheron Pt
Sandy Bay
Kangaroo Bluff
Cascades
Dynnyrne
Hobart Convention & Entertainment Centre
Wrest Pt
Wrest Pt Hotel & Casino
Nutgrove Beach
Sandy Bay Pt
MOUNTAIN PARK
15
Lower Reservoir
WATERWORKS
University of Tasmania
Sandown Park
Little Sandy Bay
Lower Sandy Bay
Blinking Billy Pt
John Garrow Light
Turnip Fields
Upper Reservoir
Waterworks Reserve
Tolmans Hill 350
Ridgeway Park
Ridgeway Reservoir
Dam
The Hobart College
Mt Nelson
Mt Nelson 340
Mt Nelson Signal Station
Tea House
Porter Hill 200
Fern Tree
Summerleas
Ridgeway
Badger Hill 368
Truganini Res
Cartwright Pt
Tudor Court Model Village
Neika
Taroona
The Lea
THE LEA CONSERVATION AREA
Shot Tower
Kelvedon Park
Taroona Park
Crayfish Pt
Taroona Beach
North West Bay River

Tasmania

© UNIVERSAL PRESS PTY LTD 2002

To Australian Antarctic Division

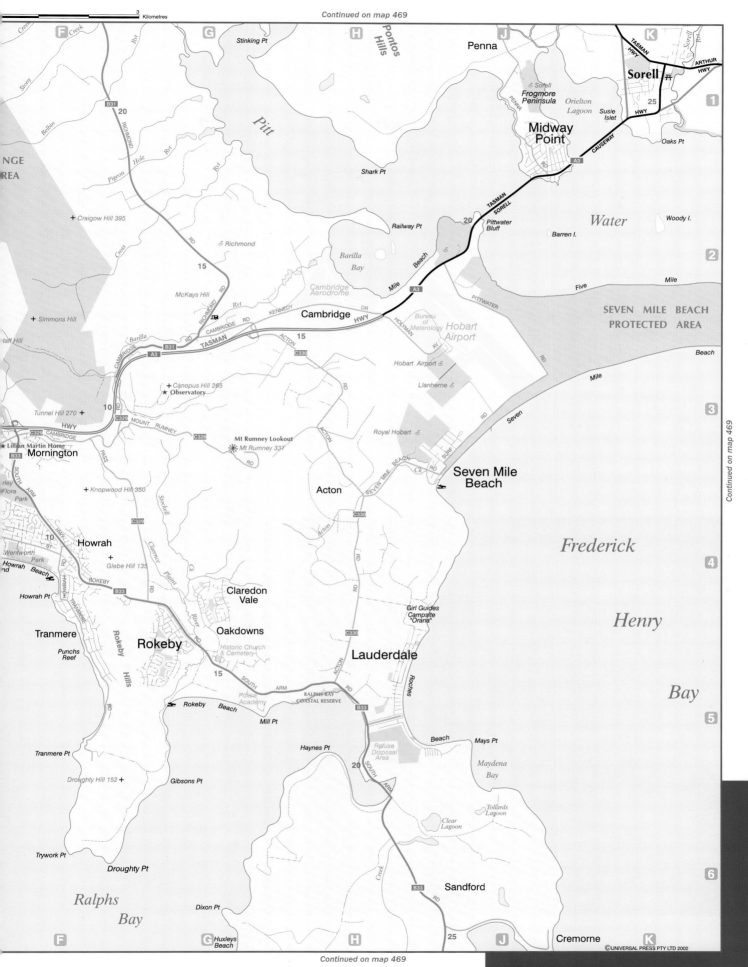

F Creek

Stinking Pt

G

Pontos
Hills

H

J

Penna

TASMAN
HWY

K

ARTHUR
HWY

Sorell

Stony

Belbin

B31

20

RICHMOND

Pigeon

Hole

Pitt

Rvr

RD

Craigow Hill 395

Richmond

15

McKays Hill

Cambridge
Aerodrome

Simmons Hill

Barilla
Bay

RICHMOND

Cross

RD

Barilla

RD

CAMBRIDGE

B31

Richmond
Rvr

KENNEDY

Canopus Hill 285
Observatory

10

CAMBRIDGE

C325

Tunnel Hill 270

RD

MOUNT

CAMBRIDGE

RD

RUMNEY

B33

Lillian Martin Home

Mornington

Knopwood Hill 350

C329

10

ST

SOUTH

ARM

Howrah

Glebe Hill 135

Wentworth

Park

Howrah

Beach

ROKEBY

TRAMWAY

Howrah Pt

B33

Tranmere

Rokeby
Hills

Rokeby

Clarence

Plains

Stockell

Ck

Claredon
Vale

Oakdowns

Historic Church
& Cemetery

Punchs
Reef

River

RD

15

SOUTH

Rokeby

Beach

Police
Academy

Mill Pt

RALPHS BAY
COASTAL RESERVE

B33

Tranmere Pt

Droughty Hill 152

Gibsons Pt

20

SOUTH

ARM

Trywork Pt

Droughty Pt

Ralphs
Bay

Dixon Pt

Huxleys
Beach

F

G

25

H

J

Cremorne

Shark Pt

Railway Pt

Mile

Beach

A3

TASMAN

20

SORELL

A3

Cambridge

HWY

HOLYMAN

Bureau
of
Meteorology

Hobart
Airport

Hobart Airport

Llanherne

Royal Hobart

ACTON

RD

Mt Rumney Lookout
Mt Rumney 337

C328

Acton

Acton

C330

SEVEN MILE BEACH

SURF

CK

RD

Seven Mile
Beach

RD

Acton

RD

C330

RD

ACTON

RD

Lauderdale

Girl Guides
Campsite
"Orana"

Roches

B33

Sandford

Frogmore
Peninsula

Sorell

PENNA

Midway
Point

RD

A3

Orielton
Lagoon

Susie
Islet

Oaks Pt

Pittwater
Bluff

PITTWATER

Water

Barren I.

Woody I.

Five

Mile

SEVEN   MILE   BEACH
PROTECTED   AREA

Beach

Mile

Seven

Frederick

Henry

Bay

Beach

Mays Pt

Maydena
Bay

Tollards
Lagoon

Clear
Lagoon

Haynes Pt

Refuse
Disposal
Area

Creek

B33

25

1
2
3
4
5
6

Continued on map 469

© UNIVERSAL PRESS PTY LTD 2002

3 Kilometres

TASMANIA A TO Z

■ Beaconsfield POP 1020

Map 480, D2

An historic mining town 43km NW of Launceston, Beaconsfield has a number of relics and ruins that are reminders of the town's gold-mining past. Gold was discovered at what was then called Cabbage Tree Hill in 1869. The mine closed in 1914, but gold fever has recently reignited with the reopening of the **Beaconsfield Gold Mine**.

MAIN ATTRACTIONS: **Grubb Shaft Gold and Heritage Museum** in West St features working models, gold-mining relics and displays. Opposite are the original **Flowery Gully schoolhouse** and a restored miner's cottage. The original Tasmania Bank (1880s) in Weld St is now **Van Diemen's Gallery**, selling locally made arts and crafts.

NEARBY ATTRACTIONS: **York Town monument** is 9km north at the site of the first European settlement in northern Tasmania. At **Sidmouth**, 13km east, are **Auld Kirk**, a church (1843) built by free and convict labour. The 100m-high **Batman Bridge** was the world's first cable-stayed truss bridge. The nearby **Kayena** and **Rowella** wine-producing areas offer cellar door sales.

TOURIST INFO: Tamar Visitor Centre, Main Rd, Exeter, Ph: 1800 637 989

■ Beauty Point POP 2000

Map 480, D2

Beauty Point lies 48km NW of **Launceston** on the **Tamar River**, and was originally established as a port for the Beaconsfield gold mine. The port facilities now service the **Australian Maritime College**.

MAIN ATTRACTIONS: This is a popular centre for fishing and yachting. A seahorse farm, the world's first, breeds common and endangered seahorses. These fascinating sea creatures can be viewed at **Seahorse World**, with its many other attractions which include a restaurant and wine centre.

NEARBY ATTRACTIONS: The holiday destinations of **Kelso** and **Greens Beach** are to the north-west on **Port Dalrymple**. **Narawntapu (Asbestos Range) NP**, 25km NW, has exhilarating coastal walks and views.

TOURIST INFO: Tamar Visitors Centre, Main Rd, Exeter, Ph: 1800 637 989

Grubb Shaft Gold and Heritage Museum, Beaconsfield

Bicheno POP 750

Map 481, J5

Bicheno is a popular resort and busy commercial fishing port 195km NE of Hobart. It was a sealing and whaling town in the early 19th century, and later a centre servicing a nearby coal mine. Today, the main industries are shellfish culture, crayfishing and tourism.

MAIN ATTRACTIONS: Some of the marine life found in the clear waters around Bicheno can be seen at the **Bicheno Sea Life Centre**. **Bicheno Penguin and Adventure Tours** has nightly tours of a nearby penguin rookery. Also a glass-bottom boat tours the sheltered waters of Bicheno's **Marine Park** and **Gulch**, providing close-up views of underwater life, including a spectacular kelp forest. The grave of **Waubedebar** can be seen near **Waubs Beach**. Waubedebar was an Aboriginal woman enslaved by sealers, some of whom she subsequently saved from drowning. Bicheno's attractive setting can be appreciated from **Whalers Lookout** off Foster St or the scenic foreshore walkway that runs from the **Blowhole** in the south all the way to **Redbill Point**.

NEARBY ATTRACTIONS: The **East Coast Nature World**, 8km north, exhibits Tasmanian fauna. **Freycinet** and **Springvale vineyards** are 18km SW on the Tasman Hwy. Ocean views can be enjoyed from the lookout at **Douglas-Apsley NP**, 14km NW.

TOURIST INFO: Charles St and Esplanade West, Triabunna, Ph: (03) 6257 4090

Bridport POP 1250

Map 481, F1

Bridport on Anderson Bay, 85km NE from Launceston, developed as a port for the timber, agricultural and mining industries; it still retains its seaport atmosphere.

MAIN ATTRACTIONS: Bridport is a popular holiday destination and most visitors come for the pristine sandy beaches and excellent river and

Fishing boats in The Gulch, Bicheno

ocean fishing. **Bridport Wildflower Reserve** is at its best in spring when plants are in full bloom.

NEARBY ATTRACTIONS: The **Bowood Homestead** (1838), 8km west, and its magnificent gardens are open by appointment and at selected times during the year. **Pipers Brook Vineyard** the most recognised Tasmanian wine label, is 18km SW. Bridport is an ideal base for exploring the rugged north-east coastline. **Flinders Island**, the largest of the **Furneaux Group** in Bass Strait, is accessible either by car ferry or light plane. This holiday island for the adventurous has beautiful beaches, unique wildlife, fishing, diving, bushwalks and **Strzelecki NP**, dominated by **Mount Strzelecki** (756m).

TOURIST INFO: 2000 Plus Info Shop, Main St, Ph: (03) 6356 0280

Bruny Island POP 600

Map 485, F5

Separated from the mainland by the **D'Entrecasteaux Channel**, Bruny Island is virtually 2 islands, **North** and **South Bruny**, joined by a strip of sandhills. In the 17th and 18th centuries, the island was logged by

notable explorers and navigators including Abel Tasman, Tobias Furneaux and James Cook. The island was an important 19th-century whaling station, but is now reliant on agriculture and tourism. Access to Bruny is via vehicular ferry from **Kettering** to **Batnes Bay**.

MAIN ATTRACTIONS: Activities on the island include boating, fishing, scuba diving, kayaking, bushwalking and camel riding. Wildlife and scenery can be enjoyed from walking tracks through 5 state reserves and **South Bruny NP**. Notable landmarks include the ruins of a convict-built church at **Variety Bay** (viewed on the **Cape Queen Elizabeth Walk**), old brick kilns and **South Bruny Lighthouse** (1836)— the second oldest in Australia. Little penguins and muttonbirds can be seen on the sandy isthmus. There is also a memorial to **Truganini**, the last full-blood Tasmanian Aborigine, who died in 1876. **Bligh Museum** at scenic **Adventure Bay** highlights the island's history, with a collection of early volumes on the voyages of Cook, Bligh and Flinders.

TOURIST INFO: Ferry Rd, Kettering, Ph: (03) 6267 4494

FLINDERS & KING ISLANDS

Perched above the east and west of Tasmania's north coast, Flinders and King islands were once centres of the long-banned sealing industry, but now support celebrated agricultural industries of their own.

Flinders Island is the largest in the **Furneaux Group**. Since its colonial settlement, the island has witnessed many changes: in the 1950s a Soldier/Farmer Settlement Scheme was initiated, leading to 336km^2 of land being cleared and sown. The island is now an ideal place for tourists to escape the stresses of city life, offering many attractions, most of them natural and some man-made or a combination of both such as wreck-diving.

King Island lies on the western edge of **Bass Strait** and covers 1260km2. The mining of gold and tin were once the island's primary industries; this has shifted to dairy products of international repute, livestock farming, crayfishing, abalone harvesting and even kelp processing. With more than 145km of picturesque coastline and abundant natural attractions, King Island is an idyllic holiday destination.

History of King Island

The first European thought to have discovered this island was **Capt James Black**. He named it after Phillip King, the Governor of New South Wales in 1801. There were once thriving fur seal and sea-lion colonies but these have suffered from extensive sealing and hunting in the past.

Cape Barren goose, *Cereopsis novaehollandiae*, in Strzelecki NP, Flinders Island

i **Tourist information**

Tasmanian Travel and Information Centre
20 Davey St,
Hobart, Tas 7000
Ph: (03) 6230 8233
Freecall: 1800 806 846

main attractions

Flinders Island   POP 850

❖ **Emita Museum**

This museum displays the history of various groups of pioneer settlers.

❖ **Logan Lagoon Wildlife Sanctuary**

This sanctuary has been included on the list of Wetlands of International Importance.

❖ **Strzelecki NP**

This 422km^2 park offers many recreational opportunities including bushwalking.

❖ **Wybalenna**

An historic, culturally significant and tragic site for Tasmanian Aborigines who were settled there in the 1830s.

King Island   POP 1500

❖ **Cape Wickham Lighthouse**

Australia's tallest lighthouse was built in 1861 to guide travellers safely into the often stormy waters of Bass Strait.

❖ **King Island Dairies**

The world famous dairy was established in 1902 because dairy products were easier to transport than livestock.

❖ **Grassy**

Well-known for its little penguin rookery.

Southern rock lobsters, *Jasus novaehollandiae*, from King Island

Tasmania

Burnie POP 19 700

Map 480, A1

Tasmania's fourth largest city is on the **North Coast** 148km NW of Launceston. Its deepwater port has long served the silver mines of the west coast, but its recent prosperity is partially due to its location for **Australian Paper**, one of the state's largest enterprises.

MAIN ATTRACTIONS: The **Civic Centre** is the hub of tourist activity with an information centre, art gallery and **Burnie Pioneer Village**, a museum with a re-creation of Burnie as it was a century ago. The information centre books free guided tours of the huge **Amcor paper mill**. **Lactos Cheese Factory** welcomes visitors to its cheese-tasting centre in Old Surrey Rd. Views over the city are available from lookouts on **Mount St** and **Round Hill**. There is a **loop walk** around Burnie that includes a waterfront boardwalk, the **Romaine Track**, and **Fernglade Recreation Reserve** on the **Emu River**, a good place to see platypus.

NEARBY ATTRACTIONS: **Emu Valley Rhododendron Gardens**, 6km south off Cascade Rd, will delight garden lovers, as will the English-style **Annsleigh Gardens**, 9km south on Mount Rd (closed in winter). **Guide Falls** are the best known of several waterfalls near **Ridgley**, 17km south. **Guide Falls Alpaca Farm** is close by. **Upper Natone Forest Reserve**, 20km to the south, is a favourite picnic spot.

TOURIST INFO: Civic Centre precinct, Little Alexander St, Ph: (03) 6434 6111

Campbell Town POP 840

Map 481, G5

Campbell Town is 66km SE of Launceston on the Midland Hwy. It was established as an early garrison town on the route between Hobart and Launceston, but its inhabitants were nevertheless harassed by 3 notorious bushrangers, Matthew Brady, Martin Cash and John Quigley. In 1820 Saxon merinos were introduced to the area, and the town is still a centre renowned for its fine wool and stud sheep, as well as beef cattle and timber.

MAIN ATTRACTIONS: There are many National Trust-classified buildings and sites that can be seen on a self-guided **heritage walk**, including **Campbell Town Inn** (1840) and convict-built **Red Bridge** (1837). In High St, there is a memorial to **Harold Gatty**, the first round-the-world flight navigator, and the **Heritage Highway Museum** showcases colonial history.

NEARBY ATTRACTION: **Lake Leake**, 30km east, is popular for trout fishing.

TOURIST INFO: Heritage Highway Museum, 103 High St, Ph: (03) 6381 1353

Cygnet POP 851

Map 485, F4

Cygnet is a small rural town at the head of **Port Cygnet**, 52km SW of Hobart. Apple orchards and mixed farming are the main industries, with flower farms and wineries established in recent years.

MAIN ATTRACTIONS: Art and craft shops are worth visiting, and the **Cygnet Guest House** in Mary St has woodcraft and an art gallery.

NEARBY ATTRACTIONS: Excellent beaches can be found at **Verona Sands**, **Randalls Bay** and **Eggs and Bacon Bay**. Other activities include boating, fishing, gem-fossicking and visiting orchards and wineries. Apple, pear and wattle blossoms colour the local landscape from September to October. The spectacular free-falling **Pelverata Falls** are 20km north on Sandfly Rd. **The Deepings Woodturners**, at **Nicholls Rivulet** 10km east, make beautiful high-quality dolls, bowls and other items from Tasmanian timbers, especially sassafras. **Talune Wildlife Park and Koala Gardens**, 6km SE at **Gardners Bay**, is a mostly free-range wildlife park with native wildlife, including platypus, wombats and of course Tasmanian devils.

TOURIST INFO: Talune Wildlife Park, Gardners Bay, Ph: (03) 6295 1775

Deloraine POP 2250

Map 480, D3

Deloraine is a rich agricultural centre nestling in a valley encircled by **Quamby Bluff** and the **Western Tiers** and renowned for its stunning scenery. Artists and craftspeople are attracted to the district.

MAIN ATTRACTIONS: **Deloraine Folk Museum** is housed in an old coaching inn (circa 1860). There are many other buildings of historic interest, including the attractive 1853 colonial building that is now **Bowerbank Mill Gallery**. The impressive *Yarns Artwork in Silk*, created by more than 300 people and depicting the area's history, hangs in the **Community Complex** in Alveston Dr.

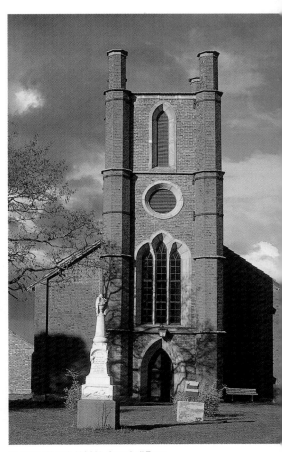

St Lukes Church (1839), Campbell Town

NEARBY ATTRACTIONS: At **Elizabeth Town**, 10km NW, English-style cheeses can be sampled at **Ashgrove Farm** and raspberry products at **Christmas Hills Raspberry Farm**. A **honey factory**, **Trowunna Wildlife Park** and **Mole Creek Caves** (including the glow-worm filled **Marakoopa Cave** and **King Solomon's Cave**) are among the attractions around **Mole Creek**, 20km west. There are many pretty waterfalls in the district, including **Lobster Falls** (15km west), **Westmoreland Falls** (10km SW), **Montana Falls** (9km SW), **Meander Falls** in **Meander Forest Reserve** (22km SW) and **Liffey Falls** (29km south). A scenic drive south through **Golden Valley** to the **Central Highlands** leads to **Great Lake**, where the trout fishing is excellent.
TOURIST INFO: Deloraine Folk Museum, 98 Emu Bay Rd, Ph: (03) 6362 3471

■ **Devonport**   POP 22 756
Map 480, C2
The third largest city in Tasmania is a busy port for agricultural and industrial exports. As it has an airport and terminal for the *Spirit of Tasmania* from **Melbourne**, Devonport is the point of entry for many of the state's visitors.
MAIN ATTRACTIONS: **Bluff Lighthouse** (1889) stands on the dramatic **Mersey Bluff** beaming its light 27km out to sea. **Tiagarra Aboriginal Culture and Museum Centre** was established to preserve a superb collection of Aboriginal rock carvings. There are also a number of displays and over 2000 artefacts. Paintings by Tasmanian artists are exhibited at the **Gallery and Arts Centre** in Stewart St. **The Maritime and Folk Museum** off Victoria Pde illustrates shipping history with model ships, photographs and souvenirs. The house museum **Home Hill** (1916), administered by the National Trust, was the home of former Premier of Tasmania (1923–1928) and later Prime Minister, Joseph Lyons and Dame Enid Lyons. **Don River Railway and Museum** runs vintage and steam train trips 7 days a week and has a large collection of railway memorabilia. A 7km walking and cycling track links the city with Mersey Bluff and the Don River Railway and Museum.

NEARBY ATTRACTIONS: **Braddon's Lookout**, 9km west near **Forth**, has panoramic coastal views. The **Tasmanian Arboretum**, 10km south at **Eugenana**, has tree plantings representing different geographic areas of the world. It also offers picnic facilities around a picturesque lake inhabited by swans and shy platypus.
TOURIST INFO: 92 Formby Rd, Ph: (03) 6424 8176

■ **Eaglehawk Neck**   POP 220
Map 469, D4
This small town sits on the very narrow isthmus that separates **Tasman** and **Forestier peninsulas**. In convict times it was blockaded by police, soldiers and a line of chained savage dogs to prevent escape from the **Port Arthur** penal settlement. It is now known as a fishing spot, with a tuna-fishing fleet operating from **Pirates Bay**.
MAIN ATTRACTIONS: A museum in the restored **Officers Quarters**, off Arthur Hwy, tells the story of Port Arthur escapee, bushranger Martin Cash. A bronze sculpture marks the site of the infamous dogline.
NEARBY ATTRACTIONS: Sailing is popular in Pirates Bay. Many of the attractions of the 2 peninsulas are close by. The **Tessellated Pavement**, 1km north, looks man-made, yet it results from the earth's movement and wave erosion. **Pirates Bay Lookout** is just a little further north. Some of the most striking formations of **Tasman NP** are about 4km to the south: **Tasman Blowhole**, **Tasman Arch** and **Devil's Kitchen**. The **Tasmanian Devil Park and Wildlife Rescue Centre** is 12km SW on the road to Port Arthur. To the south, there is a coastal walking track in Tasman NP from **Waterfall Bay** to **Fortescue Bay**. **Port Arthur Historic Site** is 21km SW.
TOURIST INFO: Officers Mess, Arthur Hwy, Ph: (03) 6250 3635

Rainforest creek near Liffey Falls

Tasmania

Contestants in Evandale's Penny Farthing Bicycle Race

■ Evandale   POP 1095
Map 481, F4

Evandale is one of Australia's most beautifully preserved historic villages, with buildings dating to 1809. It lies in a delightful rural setting, just 20km from Launceston, that has attracted notable artists such as John Glover and Tom Roberts.

MAIN ATTRACTIONS: There are numerous historic buildings in the village, and these can be admired on a self-guided **heritage walk. Evandale Tourism and History Centre** has displays of local significance, and most of the old shops now house quality art, craft and antique galleries, cafes and restaurants. Evandale's famous **Penny Farthing Bicycle Race** in February attracts many visitors from interstate and overseas.

NEARBY ATTRACTIONS: **Tasmanian Glassblowers** is one of several craft shops in the area. Recognised as one of the country's great Georgian houses, **Clarendon** (1838), with its extensive formal gardens, is 8km south near **Nile**.

TOURIST INFO: 18 High St,
Ph: (03) 6391 8128

■ Exeter   POP 870
Map 480, E2

Exeter, a large fruit-growing and wine-producing area, lies 24km NW of Launceston.

MAIN ATTRACTIONS: Historic **Exeter Bakery** has a wood-fired oven and **Kerrisons Orchard** offers sales of locally grown fruit.

NEARBY ATTRACTIONS: To the south, **Rosevears** has extensive vineyards with tastings and cellar door sales. At **Waterbird Haven**, birds can be observed in their wetland's habitat. **Notley Fern Gorge**, 11km SW off the Frankford Hwy, offers scenic walks in a pristine rainforest reserve. **Brady's Lookout**, 5km SE, once used by bushranger Matthew Brady, has panoramic views of the **Tamar Valley** and its farmlands.

TOURIST INFO: Tamar Visitor Centre,
Main Rd, Ph: 1800 637 989

■ Geeveston   POP 1500
Map 484, E4

Geeveston developed as a business centre for the timber industry based on the eucalypts and rainforests of its rugged hinterland. It is also a gateway to Tasmania's **Southwest World Heritage Area**.

MAIN ATTRACTIONS: **The Forest and Heritage Centre** presents a vibrant window on the local timber industry, with visual and interactive displays. **Hartz Gallery** exhibits antique machinery and the works of local craftspeople. **Geeveston Highlands Salmon and Trout Fishery** allows fly-fishing sport for Atlantic salmon, rainbow and brown trout on a catch-and-release basis.

NEARBY ATTRACTIONS: There are picnic and BBQ facilities at **Arve River** (10km) and **Tahune Forest Reserve** (27km), accessible from Arve Rd to the west. **Tahune Forest AirWalk**, 570m long and up to 45m above the ground, provides unique views of the forest canopy. Other highlights of this area include **Keoghs Creek Walk**, **Big Tree**

Lookout, **West Creek Lookout**, **Zig Zag Walk** and **Huon Pine Walk**. **Hartz Mountain NP**, 23km SW, offers birdwatching, walking trails to waterfalls and glacial tarns, wildflowers and the splendid **Waratah Lookout**. **Huon River Cruises** operate daily from **Point Huon**, 4km NE, visiting Atlantic salmon fish farms on the way.

TOURIST INFO: Forest and Heritage Centre,
Church St, Ph: (03) 6297 1836

■ George Town   POP 4570
Map 480, D2

Situated at the mouth of the **Tamar River** and bordering Bass Strait, George Town is the oldest town (1811) in the north of the island. It is an important commercial centre today, mainly due to the large industrial plants at **Bell Bay**. It is also the Tasmanian port for the fast vehicular *Devil Cat* ferry connection with Victoria (Dec–April).

MAIN ATTRACTIONS: A monument on the **Esplanade** honours Lt Colonel William Paterson whose ship was driven ashore in 1804. **The Grove**, a mansion built in 1830, was a port officer's residence; it is open daily.

NEARBY ATTRACTIONS: Tours are available of the **Comalco Aluminium Smelter** and **TEMCO Ferro Alloy Plant** at **Bell Bay**, 6km south. The rural hamlet of **Hillwood**, 24km SE, is known for its fruit, gourmet products and cottage industries. A lookout from **Mount George**, 1km east, gives views over the town. Further east are the vineyards of the **Pipers Brook region**. There are beautiful beaches at **Low Head**, a village 5km north. The **Pilot Station and Maritime Museum**, has operated continuously since 1805; existing buildings date from 1835. Visits can be made to the nearby lighthouse, and also to a little penguin colony. There are cruises to an Australian fur seal colony at the Tamar River mouth.

TOURIST INFO: Main Rd, Ph: (03) 6382 1700

Huonville POP 1775
Map 484, E4

Huonville is the commercial centre for the **Huon Valley** fruit-growers, with apples available year-round; and cherries, blueberries, strawberries and raspberries in season. Dairy farming and Atlantic salmon fish farming are also important.

MAIN ATTRACTIONS: The **Huon River** provides a venue for watersports and trout fishing. Visitors can ride the Huon River in jet boats over rapids to **Glen Huon**, 12km west.

NEARBY ATTRACTIONS: Fruit can be bought in season from roadside stalls and at pick-your-own-fruit farms. Apples carved into character heads are novelties at **Glen Huon's Appleheads Village. The Huon Apple and Heritage Museum** at **Grove**, 6km NE, displays an astonishing 500 varieties of apples. **Snowy Ranges Trout Fishery**, 25km NW, allows anglers to catch their own trout from a series of ponds.

TOURIST INFO: Huon River Jet Boats, Esplanade, Ph: (03) 6264 1838

Latrobe POP 2890
Map 480, C2

This historic township dates from 1851 and its 19th-century street-scapes give it plenty of character. Located a 15min drive from **Bass Strait Searoad Terminal** and **Devonport Airport**, it is an ideal base for discovering the attractions of northern Tasmania.

MAIN ATTRACTIONS: Old buildings, many National Trust-classified, have been rejuvenated as restaurants, boutiques and antique galleries. Local history is conserved at the **Court House Museum** with prints and artefacts on display. **Bells Parade Park** is a delightful riverside picnic spot on the **Mersey River**. The shingle-roofed pioneer house, **Sherwood Hall**, can be inspected here. The **Australian Axemans Hall of Fame**, celebrating Tasmanian woodchopping achievements, is nearby. **Teddy Sheean Memorial Walk** is accessed from Gilbert St and guided platypus-viewing tours are available at dawn and dusk. One of Australia's most important cycling carnivals is held at Latrobe every Christmas.

NEARBY ATTRACTIONS: **Henry Somerset Orchid Reserve** is 7km south. The rural hinterland is an ever-changing tapestry of colour, with paddocks of vegetables, grains, cereals, tulips, sweet peas, pyrethrum and poppies.

TOURIST INFO: 70 Gilbert St, Ph: (03) 6426 2693

Launceston POP 70 560
Map 480, E3

Tasmania's second largest city is located in scenic countryside at the headwaters of the **Tamar River**. This garden city is the perfect base for exploring northern Tasmania.

MAIN ATTRACTIONS: The famous **Cataract Gorge** on the **South Esk River**, with its adjacent reserves, is close to the city. Attractions here include a chairlift and suspension bridge, historic **King's Bridge** (1867), floral and peacock gardens, walking trails and views. **Penny Royal World** is an impressive tourist development near Cataract Gorge. Attractions include tramway rides, an early 19th-century gunpowder mill, cannon foundry, arsenal, underground armoury and windmill in a landscaped setting. The *Lady Stelfox* paddlesteamer cruises on the Tamar River. Opposite is a gallery in historic **Ritchie's Mill**. The *Tamar Odyssey*, which leaves from nearby **Home Point**, also offers river cruises. Launceston city centre has very attractive street-scapes including **Yorktown Square**, which is a quaint shopping centre designed to echo the past, and **Princes Square** with its magnificent baroque fountain. The **Old Umbrella Shop** in George St is a genuine period shop preserved by the National Trust. Colonial history and art can be explored at **Queen Victoria Museum and Art Gallery** in Wellington St, and a range of classic cars can be admired at the **National Automobile Museum** in Cimitiere St. **City Park** has shady lawns, a conservatory, duck pond and monkey island. Just over the Tamar St Bridge is the **Inveresk Railyard** redevelopment, a focal point for arts and events, including the **Esk Market** on Sundays.

NEARBY ATTRACTIONS: **Trevallyn Dam**, 6km west, is a picnic spot with an exhilarating but safe cable hang-gliding facility close by. Fly-fishing lessons are available at **Launceston Lakes Trout Fishery**, 17km west. Launceston's **Country Club Casino** is 7km SW. Tours can be made of the **Waverley Woollen Mills**, 5km east. Three National Trust historic houses are within easy driving distance: **Entally House**, 18km SW at **Hadspen**; **Franklin House**, 6km south; and **Clarendon**, 28km SE near Nile. The **Northern Tasmanian Wine Route** winds its way to the **Tamar Valley** and **Pipers Brook**

Gunpowder Mill, Penny Royal World, Launceston

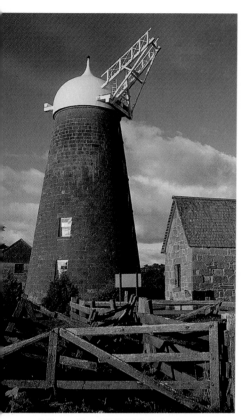

Callington Flour Mill (1837), Oatlands

vineyard regions. **Grindelwald Swiss Village**, also to the north, is about a 15min drive away. During winter, skiers head for the alpine village in **Ben Lomond NP**, 60km SE, but the park is worth visiting at any time of the year.
TOURIST INFO: Cnr St John and Paterson sts, Ph: (03) 6336 3122

▓ Longford   POP 3058
Map 480, E4
One of Tasmania's oldest towns, Longford was established in 1813 by settlers from Norfolk Island. Now it is the centre for a fertile agricultural district.
MAIN ATTRACTIONS: There are many historic buildings, some convict-built. **Christ Church** (1839) has beautiful stained-glass windows and is surrounded by pioneer graves. **Heritage Corner** complex on Marlborough St includes **Tom Roberts Gallery** and tearooms. **The Village Green** is a popular picnic and BBQ spot.

NEARBY ATTRACTIONS: **Brickendon**, an 1824 homestead 2km south, is now a working farm village. **Woolmers Estate** (circa 1816) 5km SE, has a rose garden, colonial cottages, tearooms and guided tours.
TOURIST INFO: Cnr St John and Paterson sts, Launceston, Ph: (03) 6336 3122

▓ Mole Creek   POP 245
Map 480, C3
Mole Creek is located 74km south of Devonport, nestled at the foot of the **Great Western Tiers**. It is the heart of the surrounding farming and forestry district.
MAIN ATTRACTION: **Stephen's Honey Factory** in Pioneer Dr specialises in honey from a leatherwood tree unique to this area.
NEARBY ATTRACTIONS: **Mole Creek Karst NP** has several spectacular limestone caves, of which the best known are **Marakoopa Cave**, 8km west which has a wonderful glowworm display, and **King Solomons Cave**, 16km west. Guided tours of these caves as well as to wild undeveloped caves are available. **Devils Gullet**, 40km SE, is an impressive natural lookout over the **Fisher River Valley**. **Trowunna Wildlife Park** is 4km east and **Alum Cliffs Gorge** 3km NE. There are 4WD tours to the **Mersey Valley** and fly-fishing tours to local streams. Experienced bushwalkers head for **Walls of Jerusalem NP**, 45km SW.
TOURIST INFO: Mole Creek Guest House, Pioneer Dr, Ph: (03) 6363 1399

▓ New Norfolk   POP 5249
Map 484, E3
This historic town, 33km NW of Hobart on the **Derwent River**, was pioneered around 1808 by Norfolk Island free settlers. The district produces most of the hops used by Australian breweries, although the main industry in the region is paper manufacture.
MAIN ATTRACTIONS: New Norfolk has many fine examples of colonial

architecture, including **Bush Inn** (1815), **Old Colony Inn** (1835), now a museum, and **St Matthew's Church** (1823), reputedly the state's oldest church. These can be seen on a **heritage walk** that also includes **Denmark Hill** (1830) and **Rosedown Gardens** (1840), which feature over a 1000 roses. **The Oast House** is the only hops' museum in Australia. Jet boats leave daily for the **Derwent River rapids** and **Derwent Valley Railway** has several excursions every month. There are scenic lookouts at **Peppermint Hill** and **Pulpit Rock**, and BBQ facilities in **Esplanade** and **Tynwald parks**. Browsers will enjoy the **Drill Hall Markets** in Stephen St, Tues–Sat.
NEARBY ATTRACTIONS: Group tours of the newsprint mills at **Boyer**, 5km east, can be arranged in advance. **Salmon Ponds**, 11km NW, at **Plenty**, is where rainbow and brown trout were first bred in Australia. The complex includes a restaurant and **Museum of Trout Fishing**. **Mount Field NP**, 40km NW, features spectacular mountain scenery and the much-photographed **Russell Falls**, surrounded by giant swamp gums.
TOURIST INFO: Circle St, Ph: (03) 6261 0700

▓ Oatlands   POP 551
Map 485, G1
The historic lakeside township of Oatlands, 84km north of Hobart, was proclaimed by Governor Macquarie in 1827.
MAIN ATTRACTIONS: The Georgian sandstone buildings are a big attraction and there are 87 of them in **High St** alone! The convict-built **Court House** (1829), **St Peters Church** (1888), **St Pauls Church** (1850) and **Callington Flour Mill** (1837) are notable. Extra local colour is provided on evening 'ghost' tours by lantern light. **Dulverton Wildlife Sanctuary** is a lakeside picnic and camping reserve. There are antique and craft shops in town and guided tours of the **Aquaculture Centre**.

The Guard Tower, Port Arthur Historic Site

NEARBY ATTRACTIONS: **Jericho**, 13km south, has convict-built mud walls and the remains of a convict probation station. The cemetery has a memorial to **John Hutton Bisdee**, the first Australian to be awarded the Victoria Cross. Trout fishing is available at **Lake Sorell**, 29km NW, and the adjacent **Lake Crescent**.
TOURIST INFO: The Stables, 85 High St, Ph: (03) 6254 1212

■ Orford   POP 461
Map 469, D1
In 1825 the **East Coast** town of Orford was a shore station servicing whalers, the local garrison and the penal settlement on **Maria Island**. It is now a holiday and fishing resort.
MAIN ATTRACTIONS: Boating, fishing and swimming are popular activities. Scuba divers are attracted to the clear waters of **Prosser Bay** and sandy swimming beaches are within easy walking distance. A scenic walking track from **Shelly**

Beach to **Spring Beach** passes old sandstone quarries.
NEARBY ATTRACTIONS: A ferry from **Louisville Point** takes visitors to Maria Island. The island is now a national park and wildlife sanctuary, with convict ruins, historic buildings and interesting walks. A scenic route south to **Sorell** and **Hobart** takes in the **Thumbs picnic area and lookout** over **Mercury Passage** and Maria Island, and the blue gum forest at **Sandspit River Reserve**.
TOURIST INFO: Charles St and Esplanade West, Triabunna, Ph: (03) 6257 4090

■ Penguin   POP 3187
Map 480, B2
Penguin developed in the late 19th century as an iron-ore mine and timber town, shipping timber throughout Australia and New Zealand. It was named after the little penguin rookeries that are common along the coast.
MAIN ATTRACTIONS: BBQs and duck ponds are located in **Hiscutt Park**, which also features a Dutch windmill. The much-photographed **Big Penguin** and 2 National Trust classified churches are in **Main St**. A miniature railway runs along the foreshore on the second and fourth Sunday each month. Little penguin viewing tours are conducted nightly by appointment Sept–March.
NEARBY ATTRACTIONS: There are magnificent views from the summit of **Mount Montgomery**, 5km south. **Ferndean Glow Worm Cave**, 6km south, has a BBQ area and walks to the hop fields of **Gunns Plains**. **Pioneer Park**, 10km SW at **Riana**, offers gardens and walks, and **Pindari Deer Farm** is a further 5km. The **Old Bass Hwy** between Penguin and **Ulverstone** has scenic views of the rugged coastline including the **Three Sisters** which are offshore islands with seabird sanctuaries.
TOURIST INFO: 78 Main St, Ph: (03) 6437 1421

■ Port Arthur   POP 215
Map 469, C5
Sited on the beautiful but remote **Tasman Peninsula**, historic Port Arthur was one of Australia's most infamous penal settlements from 1830 to 1877. (*see* pp.468-469)
MAIN ATTRACTIONS: **Port Arthur Historic Site** has more than 30 sandstone buildings, ruins and sites open for inspection. These include the church, penitentiary, model prison, asylum, guard tower and period-furnished houses. The visitors centre has an interpretation gallery and restaurant and takes bookings for the popular evening ghost tours. Daily cruises are available on the harbour and to the **Isle of the Dead**, the island's cemetery.
NEARBY ATTRACTIONS: Just 1km from the historic site is **The Bush Mill Steam Railway and Settlement**, where visitors can experience life in a pioneer timber camp and enjoy a steam-train ride. There is a nature walk to nearby **Stewarts Bay**. **Coal Mines Historic Site** is 30km NW. **Palmers Lookout**, 3km south, has views over the harbour and coastline. **Remarkable Cave** is 6km south in the rugged **Tasman NP**.
TOURIST INFO: Historic Site, Arthur Hwy, Ph: (03) 6251 2310

■ Port Sorell   POP 1910
Map 480, C2
Port Sorell, together with **Hawley** and **Shearwater** form a holiday resort 18km east of Devonport. It was one of the first towns established on the **North Coast**.
MAIN ATTRACTIONS: Fishing, sailing, boating and waterskiing are popular on the beautiful estuary. There are walking tracks and picnic facilities in the reserve beside **Freers Beach** and views over the town from **Watch House Hill**, off Meredith St.
NEARBY ATTRACTIONS: **Hawley Beach** has safe swimming, good fishing and historic **Hawley House** (1878). **Narawntapu (Asbestos Range) NP**

Tasmania

is just across the estuary. This is a favourite destination for daytrippers and campers, offering nature walks, isolated sandy beaches, summer wildflowers and views to the mountains of the **Western Tiers**.

TOURIST INFO: 70 Gilbert St, Latrobe, Ph: (03) 6426 2693

■ Queenstown POP 2773
Map 483, C2

Queenstown emerged as a boom-town of the 1890s when gold and minerals were discovered at **Mount Lyell**. The strange but arresting 'moonscape' that surrounds the town was caused by acid-rain during the mining era. Arguably the pink, purple and grey rocky hills do have a certain beauty.

MAIN ATTRACTIONS: Queenstown's wide streets, old buildings and mountain setting give it a Wild West look, which can be appreciated from **Spion Kop Lookout**, off Bowes St.

Mining mural, Rosebery

More than 1000 old photographs, documents and memorabilia make a visit to the **Galley Museum** worthwhile. A chairlift from Penghana Rd to old silica and limestone quarries gives magnificent views, especially at sunset. The restored historic **Abt Railway** which uses a rack and cog system designed for steep hills, runs to **Lynchford**, **Rinadeena** and on to **Strahan**.

NEARBY ATTRACTIONS: There are good views from the Lyell Hwy as it climbs out of town. The Mount Lyell field to the east produced more than 670 000 tonnes of copper, 510 tonnes of silver and 20 tonnes of gold between 1893 and 1994. Surface and underground copper-mine tours that commence in Queenstown. The original **Iron Blow goldmine** (1883) is 6km east at **Gormanston**, and the ghost town of **Linda** a further 3km. Scenic **Mount Jukes Rd** to the south passes the old mining settlement of Lynchford, **Crotty Dam** and the southern end of **Lake Burbury**. Near **Lake Margaret**, 12km north, is an historic 1914 hydroelectric power station that is still operating. There is excellent trout fishing at Lake Burbury and Lake Margaret.

TOURIST INFO: Lyell Tours, 1 Driffield St, Ph: (03) 6471 2388

■ Richmond POP 854
Map 469, A2

This lovely old town is located 26km from Hobart. Richmond is one of Tasmania's earliest settlements.

MAIN ATTRACTIONS: Richmond has dozens of historic buildings, some of which have been converted into restaurants, shops and galleries. Highlights of the local **heritage tour** include convict-built **Richmond Bridge** (1823), the oldest of its kind in Australia; the original **Post Office** building; **St Luke's Anglican Church** (1836); and **St John's Catholic Church** (1837), with cemetery headstones dating back

to 1823. Guided tours are available for **Old Richmond Gaol** (1825), in Bathurst St, one of the best-preserved convict establishments in the country. **Saddlers Court** (circa 1848) and **Peppercorn Gallery** (circa 1850) feature local arts and crafts. The Georgian mansion **Prospect House** (1830s), off Hobart Rd, is said to be haunted. Tourist attractions include **Richmond Maze and Tearooms**, and award-winning **Old Hobart Town Model Village** which shows Hobart as it was in the 1820s. Picnic facilities on the riverbank are near the famous Richmond Bridge.

NEARBY ATTRACTIONS: There is a scenic drive north through **Campania** (8km) and **Colebrook** (19km) with over 30 vineyards in the area.

TOURIST INFO: Saddlers Court Gallery, 48 Bridge St, Ph: (03) 6260 2132

■ Rosebery POP 1493
Map 483, C1

Rosebery is a **West Coast** mining town 29km NE of **Zeehan**. Gold was discovered here in 1893, and later zinc, lead and copper were found. Rosebery township evolved following the involvement of the Mount Lyell Company in 1927.

MAIN ATTRACTIONS: Parts of the aerial ropeway system that carried ore 7km from the Hercules Mine at Williamsford to Rosebery can be seen near the Murchison Hwy. **Lake Pieman** and **Lake Rosebery** are noted fishing spots.

NEARBY ATTRACTIONS: Surface tours of the **Pasminco Mine** can be arranged. Tracks for 4WD vehicles and walking tracks diverge from the Williamsford site for the impressive **Montezuma Falls** at 110m, the highest waterfall in Tasmania. There is a picturesque lake at **Tullah**, 12km NE, and the historical **Wee Georgie Wood Railway** is nearby (check operating times).

TOURIST INFO: West Coast Pioneers Museum, Zeehan, Ph: (03) 6471 6225

TASMAN PENINSULA

The Tasman Peninsula's landscape is rugged—like much of its history. The coastline features geological curiosities, fascinating seascapes and spectacular seaside walks, while the inland and the offshore islands are protected habitats for a rich variety of flora and fauna.

The coastline offers many opportunities for adventure—abseiling, rockclimbing, scuba diving and sea kayaking. There is a vast array of walking trails, horseriding and mountain-biking tracks.

Aboriginal people occupied the Peninsula for thousands of years and the region is also scattered with some of Tasmania's oldest colonial and penal sites, including **Port Arthur** and **Eaglehawk Neck**. It is believed that the only prisoners who escaped did so by sea.

Eaglehawk Neck

The 100m-wide isthmus was once guarded by vicious dogs in an attempt to turn the Tasman Peninsula into a natural prison. Today, Eaglehawk Neck Historic Site is a must to visit. Nearby, there are many natural wonders including the extraordinary Tessellated Pavement wave platform, Tasman Blowhole, Tasman Arch and Devil's Kitchen.

 Tourist information

Port Arthur Visitor Centre
Port Arthur Historic Site,
Port Arthur, Tas 7182
Ph: (03) 6251 2371
www.portarthur-region.com.au

Tessellated Pavement, near Eaglehawk Neck

Cape Pillar and Tasman Island, Tasman NP

main attractions

◈ **Bush Mill Steam Railway and Settlement**

A reconstructed timber-mill settlement near Oakwood, with a 4km miniature railway.

◈ **Isle of the Dead**

Cruises are available across the bay from Port Arthur to the historic cemetery.

◈ **Port Arthur Historic Site**

This is the site of Australia's longest established penal colony, operating between 1830 and 1877. The area is now filled with sandstone ruins as well as restored buildings and gardens. Evening lantern-lit ghost tours are available.

◈ **Tasman NP**

This park boasts some of Australia's best coastal walks. Australian fur seal colonies breed along the rugged coastline.

◈ **Tasmanian Devil Park**

This centre near Taranna offers an opportunity to get close to Australian native animals and enjoy the 'Kings of the Wind' free-flight birds of prey show.

Tasmania

Continued on map 485

10 Kilometres

A **B** **C** **D** **E**

C342

Poulters Hill
670
STATE
FOREST

Mt Hobbs
823

BUCKLAND MILITARY
TRAINING AREA

STATE
FOREST

STATE
FOREST

TO SWANSEA

Triabunna

Cape
Bougainville

Moreys Hill
153

Lords Bluff

1

Craigbourne
Dam

Levendale

Rowlands Hill
458

C318

Ryton Hills
577

Double Creek
Louisville

Point Home
Lookout

Cape Boullanger

Ile du Nord

Fossil
Bay

1

STATE
FOREST

C312

Brown Mtn
792

Buckland

Orford

Shelly Beach
Spring Beach

Quarry Point

Prosser Bay

Penal Settlement
Darlington

MARIA

ISLAND

Mt Maria
710

NATIONAL

PARK

Campania

Runnymede

A3

Three Thumbs
549
Three Thumbs
Picnic Area

Johnsons
Point

*Maria
Island*

Mistaken
Cape

2

C321

Enfield

C350

Richmond
Historic town

Orielton

Pawleena

Nugent

647
Prossers
Sugarloaf

Eatlham Hill
309

STATE

FOREST

SANDSPIT
FOREST RESERVE

Rheban

Carrickfergus
Bay

Lachlan
Island

Sandspit
Point

Point
Lesueur

Returns
Point

Little Raggedy
Head

Riedle
Bay

2

C322

Penna

Sorell

Wattle Hill

Mt Elizabeth
235

C331

Mt Jacob
522

Point
des Galets

Point
Mauge

Shoal
Bay

Big Hill

Point
Cape
Bernier

Cape Maurouard

3

Dulcot

B31

Midway
Point

A3

Lewisham

C334

Forcett

ARTHUR

A9

Mother Browns
Bonnet 405

HWY

C349

Copping
Convict
Exhibition

Kellevie

Bream
Creek

239 Allanbys
Hill

Steeles Hill
247

Marion

Bay

The Long Spit

Cape Paul Lamanon

Bottom
Hill

Barren
Head

Cape Peron

Tasman

3

Cambridge

Hobart
Airport

SEVEN MILE BEACH
PROTECTION AREA

Sandy
Point

Dodges
Ferry

Connellys
Marsh

Blackman
Bay

North
Bay

Cape
Frederick Hendrick

Lagoon Bay

4

B33 C329

Howrah

Rokeby

Seven Mile
Beach

Park
Beach

Carlton

Carlton Bluff

Connellys
Bay

Fulham
Point

Dunalley

ARTHUR

Mt Forestier
319

Tasman
Hill

Kelly Island

Humper Bluff

High Yellow Bluff

ABEL TASMAN
FOREST RESERVE

Cape Surville

Deep Green Bluff

Sea

4

Lauderdale

Mays Point

Frederick

Henry

Primrose
Sands

Primrose
Point

Fulham
Island

Dunbabin
Point

Dunalley
Bay

Smooth
Island

King George
Island

Chronicle
Point

Forestier

Peninsula

FOREST

Hawks Hill

Macgregor Peak
591

5

Sandford

Cremorne

Pipe Clay Point

Clifton Beach

Sloping
Island

Green
Head

LIME BAY

Lime
Bay

Whitehouse
Point

Monk Bay

Ironstone
Point

NATURE

RESERVE

Mt Stewart
130

Coal Mines
Historic Site

FLINDERS BAY
COASTAL RESERVE

Flinders Bay

Norfolk

Bay

EAGLEHAWK BAY
COASTAL RESERVE

Eaglehawk Bay

Murdunna

A9

Lookout

TESSELLATED PAVEMENT STATE RESERVE

Tessellated Pavement

Pirates
Bay

Eaglehawk Neck

Officers Quarters Museum

Tasman Arch & Blowhole

5

Opossum
Bay

South
Arm

Cape
Direction

Iron
Pot

Ralphs

Bay

Mortimer
Bay

Gellibrand
Pt

Droughty
Pt

Pipe
Clay
Lagoon

Cape Deslacs

North West
Head

Mt Wilmot

Gwandalan

Saltwater
River

Deer
Point

Prices
Bay

Dart Island

Penzance

Tarana

Tasman
Arch
State
Reserve

Doo Town

TASMAN ARCH
STATE RESERVE

Waterfall Bay

Tatnells Hill
438

O'Hara Bluff

TASMAN N.P.

6

BETSEY ISLAND
NATURE RESERVE

Betsey Island

Little Betsey Island

Mt Communication
344

Outer North
Head

ROARING BEACH
COASTAL RESERVE

Roaring Beach Bay

Premaydena

B37

Koonya

C341

C343

Halfway
Bluff

Cascades
Bay

Tasmanian Devil Park

My Koonya
488

Nubeena

STATE

FOREST

Tasman

Oakwood

Bush Mill
Steam
Railway

STATE

FOREST

Signal Hill

HWY

A9

Peninsula

Thumbs Point

Dolomieu Point

The Lanterns

Cape Hauy

Simmonds
Hill

Fortescue

6

Storm

White Beach

Wedge
Bay

Wedge
Island

B37

Radnor

Highcroft

Stormlea

STATE

FOREST

TASMAN

N.P.

Curio
Bay

Salters Point

Two Islands Bay

Mt Arthur

Palmers Hill
Lookout

Remarkable
Cave

C347

Port Arthur
Historic Site

**Port
Arthur**

Pt Puer Historic Site

Isle of the Dead

Port

Arthur

Blowhole

BROWN MTN/
REMARKABLE CAVE
STATE RESERVE

West Arthur
Head

Mt Fortescue

Tasman

Munro

Bight

Haines
Bight

Black
Head

C344

Cape Pillar

Tasman Passage

*Tasman
Island*

Bruny

Island

Variety Pt

BRUNY I. NECK
GAME RESERVE

Moorina
Bay

Cape
Queen Elizabeth

Trumpeter
Bay

Bay

Mt Raoul
462

Raoul
Bay

Cape Raoul

Maingon
Bay

Historic Ross Bridge

Ross POP 289

Map 481, G5

Ross is an historic, picturesque township on the Midland Hwy in the heart of Tasmania's premier wool-growing area.

MAIN ATTRACTIONS: **Ross Bridge** (1836) is one of Australia's most elegant bridges; it was built by convict labour. The **Female Factory Site**, off Bond St, operated as a probation station for female convicts between 1847 and 1854. The **Tasmanian Wool Centre**, a 1988 bicentennial project, includes a heritage museum and sells a wide range of woollen products. Historic sandstone buildings include **churches**, **Man O'Ross Hotel**, **Ross Bakery Inn**, **Scotch Thistle Inn** and the **Old General Store**.

NEARBY ATTRACTIONS: Some of Tasmania's finest trout fishing locations are within 1 hour's drive: the **Macquarie River**, **Lake Sorell** and **Lake Crescent** to the west; **Lake Leake** to the east; and **Tooms Lake** to the south-east.

TOURIST INFO: Tasmanian Wool Centre, Church St, Ph: (03) 6381 5466

St Helens POP 1776

Map 481, J2

St Helens is a popular beach and fishing resort on the inlet of **Georges Bay**; it was a whaling base in the early 19th century. Commercial fishing, timber and tourism play an important part in the economy.

MAIN ATTRACTIONS: Watersports such as swimming, waterskiing and sailing are enjoyed at safe bay beaches. Charter boats make deep-sea fishing excursions, and smaller boats can be hired for bay fishing. Fresh fish is available from a fish-processing plant and is a specialty at local restaurants. **St Helens History Room** is a comprehensive museum and information centre.

NEARBY ATTRACTIONS: There are scenic coastal walks at **Humbug Point Reserve**, **St Helens Point SRA** and **Bay of Fires Coastal Reserve** to the north. **Binalong Bay**, 11km NE, has excellent rock fishing. Inland, the **Goblin Forest Walk** (with wheelchair access) and other walking trails explore old tin-mining sites on the **Blue Tier** via **Lottah**. **Healey's Cheese Factory** is at **Pyengana**, 28km west, and **St Columba Falls** is close by. The holiday town of **Scamander**, 17km south, offers fishing, swimming and forest drives, and the nearby **Trout Creek Reserve** has picnic facilities.

TOURIST INFO: St Helens History Room, 61 Cecilia St, Ph: (03) 6376 1744

St Marys POP 575

Map 481, J4

St Marys is a small town on the Esk Hwy, 12km from the **East Coast**, surrounded by glorious mountains and forests.

MAIN ATTRACTIONS: **Rivulet Park** has picnic and BBQ facilities, where sightings of platypus are possible and Tasmanian native hens likely. Historic **St Marys Railway Station** became the terminus for the East Coast railway in 1866.

NEARBY ATTRACTIONS: The road north to **Scamander** via **St Marys Pass** and the road south to **Bicheno** via **Elephants Pass** provide spectacular mountain and coastal scenery. There are great views of the **Fingal Valley** from the top of **South Sister**, 3km NW. The coal-mining and coastal township of **Falmouth**, 14km NE, has a number of buildings of historic interest, fine beaches and fishing.

TOURIST INFO: Coach House Restaurant, 34 Main St, Ph: (03) 6372 2529

Scottsdale POP 1972

Map 481, G2

The largest town in north-east Tasmania is the centre for a prosperous agricultural area and a thriving pine forest industry. Other industries include food processing, and the cultivation of oil poppies and hops.

MAIN ATTRACTIONS: **Settlers Museum** in King St operated as a theatre from 1924 to 1972. **Scottsdale Forest EcoCentre** has interactive displays showcasing the regional forest industry. Tours of the dried-fruit laboratory, **MRL**, in George St are available on request. Scottsdale is also a base for **Pepper Bush Peaks** wildlife and wilderness tours, and **Sapphire Safari** gem-fossicking tours to nearby areas.

NEARBY ATTRACTIONS: A visit to **Bridestowe Lavender Farm**, 13km west, is a unique experience as it is the only one of its kind in Australia. The flowering season is mid-Dec–late Jan. **Sideling Lookout**, 16km west, provides views of the countryside. **Golconda**, 20km west, is the venue for the **Tasmanian Circus Festival** in February. **Derby Tin Mine Centre**, 30km east, provides horse-drawn coach rides to the 1885 granite tunnel. **Shanty Town**, next door, features a miner's cottage, general store, butcher's shop, mine office and the original Derby gaol. About 1 hour's drive

Tasmania

south-east of town, **White Gum Reserve** has giant white gum trees up to 89m high and 3000 years old. The **South Esk River**, for brown trout fishing, is close to town, as are **Cuckoo** and **Mathinna waterfalls**.
TOURIST INFO: Scottsdale Forest EcoCentre, 86–88 King St, Ph: (03) 6352 6465

■ Sheffield   POP 1059
Map 480, C3
Sheffield is a mixed farming community 30km south of Devonport, and lies in the foothills of **Mount Roland**, (1234m), in an area of lovely natural scenery.
MAIN ATTRACTIONS: The town's most famous feature is the series of more than 30 murals—mainly illustrating the town's early history—painted on almost every available wall. **Mural Town World** in Main St is home to the 'Walls of Fame', an exhibition featuring famous Tasmanians. Pioneering memorabilia is housed in the **Kentish Museum**. Redwater Creek Steam and Heritage Society operates steam train trips from **Apex Park** on the first weekend of the month and daily in the summer school holidays.
NEARBY ATTRACTIONS: The region's beauty is enhanced by thousands of flowering daffodils in spring. The many lakes and dams of the **Mersey-Forth Hydro-Electric Development** are to the west. These include the international rowing venue **Lake Barrington** and the semi-circular **Devil's Gate Dam**. Close to Lake Barrington is the world's largest maze complex, **Tasmazia**, with a lavender farm and model village. **Lake Barrington Estate Vineyard** is also in the area. **Stoodley Forest Reserve** is 7km NE. Sheffield is also the gateway to the bushwalks and stunning scenery of the internationally renowned **Cradle Mountain-Lake St Clair NP**, 61km SW. (pp. 472-473)
TOURIST INFO: 5 Pioneer Cr, Ph: (03) 6491 1036

■ Smithton   POP 3350
Map 479, C2
Smithton is situated at the mouth of the **Duck River** in north-west Tasmania. The region is known for its blackwood swamp forests, which have yielded the fossilised bones of extinct giant marsupials. Dairy farming, vegetable-growing, forestry and fishing are the main industries.
MAIN ATTRACTIONS: The **Apex lookout tower** on **Tier Hill** takes in a panoramic view over **Duck Bay**, **Robbins Island** and **Three Hummock Island** in Bass Strait. **The Smithton-Circular Head Heritage Centre**, in the old Billings Store building, is run by volunteers.
NEARBY ATTRACTIONS: Fishing and boating are popular at Duck River and Duck Bay, 2km north. **Lacrum Dairy Farm**, 6km west at **Mella**, offers milking demonstrations and cheese tasting, Nov–May. Neighbouring **Wombat Tarn** has BBQs, bushwalks and a lookout. Tours can be arranged to visit the huge **Gunns Timber Mill**, and the historic Van Diemen's Land Company property, **Woolnorth**. The **Sumac Lookout**, 4km south, gives views over eucalypt forests. The great forests of north-west Tasmania can also be seen on a 60km circular drive into **South Arthur Forest**. River cruises are available at **Arthur River**, 70km south-west.
TOURIST INFO: Council Offices, 33 Goldie St, Ph: (03) 6452 4800

■ Sorell   POP 3248
Map 457, K1
Founded in 1821, Sorell played an important part in Tasmania's early European history, by supplying most of the colony's grain. The settlement was brazenly captured in 1824 by bushranger Matthew Brady, who imprisoned the garrison and most of the citizens. Sorell is an important tourist link between **Hobart**, the **Tasman Peninsula** and the **East Coast**.

MAIN ATTRACTIONS: Interesting buildings from colonial times include **St George's Church** (1826), **Scotts Church** (1842) and **Blue Bell Inn** (circa 1863). **Pioneer Park** is popular for BBQs and picnics. **Orielton Lagoon** is a significant bird sanctuary with many species.
NEARBY ATTRACTIONS: **Sorell Fruit Farm** is 2km east off the Arthur Hwy and there are several wineries in the region. **Dodges Ferry** and **Carlton**, 18km south, are popular beach areas. **Weilangta Forest Drive** to **Orford** via **Copping** winds through forests and coastal mountains. **Bream Creek**, 25km east, has vineyards and stunning rural and coastal scenery. The village of **Dunalley**, 35km SE, is known for antiques, arts and crafts.
TOURIST INFO: Know How Travel, 25 Main Rd, Ph: (03) 6265 3377

■ Stanley   POP 543
Map 479, C2
The charming north-west coastal township of Stanley is located on a peninsula and is overlooked by a 150m-high basalt rock formation known as **The Nut**. The original port for the Van Diemen's Land Company from 1826, it is known for fresh fish, crayfish and oysters.

(CONTINUED P.474)

The Nut at Stanley

CRADLE MOUNTAIN-LAKE ST CLAIR NP

Located approximately 85km south of Devonport, Cradle Mountain, and the national park, are drawcards for Australian and international visitors alike. This national park is renowned for its excellent bushwalking tracks, including the wonderful 80km **Overland Track** and shorter circuits taking just a few hours to cover.

The park's founding father, Austrian immigrant **Gustav Weindorfer**, was overwhelmed by the other-worldliness of this area, proclaiming that it 'must be a national park for the people of all time'. It is now part of the acclaimed **Tasmanian Wilderness World Heritage Area**, protecting a diversity of environments just waiting to be explored by the adventurous. Its 1612km^2 boasts stunning scenery, wild landscapes, buttongrass plains, primordial rainforests and alpine heathlands. The rugged terrain is interspersed with glacial lakes, while icy rivers and streams cascade from the

mountains. Natural attractions include the **Enchanted Walk**, **Forgotten Lake**, **Ballroom Forest**, and **Shadow Lake**.

Facilities include picnic shelters fitted with electric BBQs, toilets in a few locations, campgrounds, lodges and track huts, Cradle Mountain Lodge Store and Cradle Mountain Wilderness Cafe.

Lake St Clair

This lake was formed by a glacier and is Australia's deepest natural freshwater lake, 17km long and 200m deep. It is the source of the **Derwent River** on which Hobart is situated.

Tourist information

Cradle Mountain Visitors Centre
Park entrance, Cradle Mountain Rd,
Cradle Mountain–Lake St Clair NP
Ph: (03) 6492 1110
www.dpiwe.tas.gov.au

Lake St Clair in winter

main attractions

◈ **Ballroom Forest**

Nestled on the slopes of Cradle Mountain, this temperate-climate rainforest is a highlight of the Dove Lake Loop Track Walk.

◈ **Dove Lake**

The shores of this picturesque lake are ideal for observing Cradle Mountain.

◈ **Overland Track**

The Overland Track is reputed to be one of Australia's premier wilderness walking tracks. The 5-day expedition covers 80km. Highlights include a side-trip to Tasmania's highest peak, Mount Ossa.

◈ **Waldheim Chalet**

The name of this chalet means 'forest home', Waldheim is located at the northern end of the Overland Track. Waldheim Cabins offer an authentic experience in the wilderness of this pristine area.

Bushwalkers at Pelion Gap on the Overland Track

Tasmania

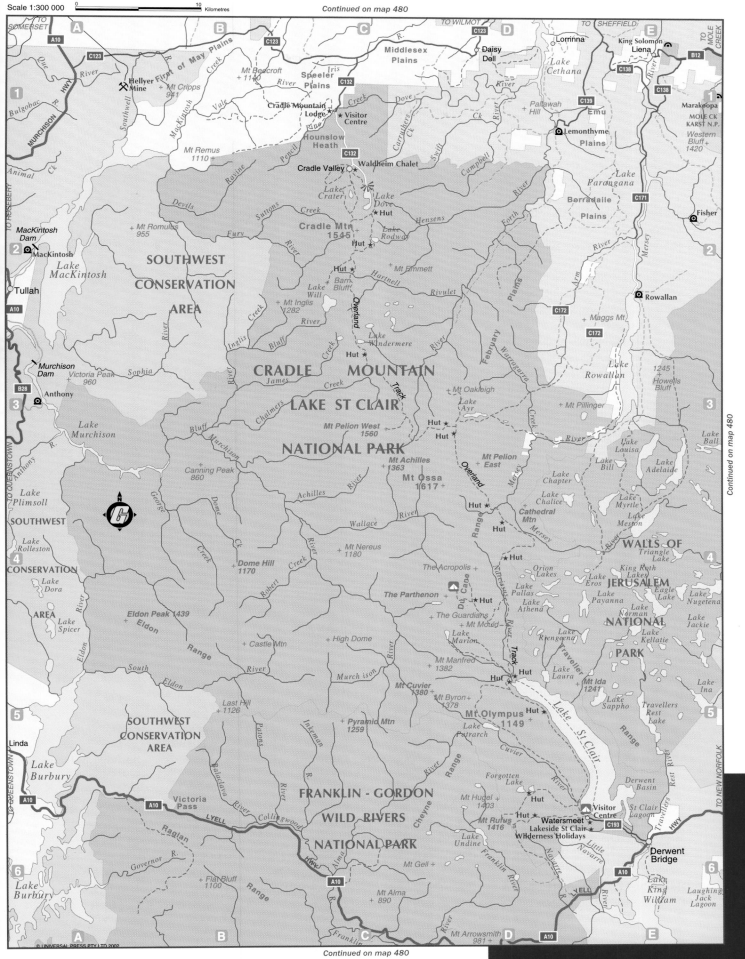

0   10
Kilometres

Continued on map 480

TO SOMERSET

A10

C123

MURCHISON HWY

Que River

Bulgobac R.

Animal Ck

TO ROSEBERY

MacKintosh Dam

Lake MacKintosh

MacKintosh

Tullah

A10

Murchison Dam

B28

Anthony

Victoria Peak 960

TO QUEENSTOWN

Lake Murchison

Lake Plimsoll

SOUTHWEST

CONSERVATION

AREA

Lake Dora

Lake Spicer

Lake Rolleston

Linda

Lake Burbury

A10

Lake Burbury

Hellyer Mine

+ Mt Cripps 941

First of May Plains

MacKintosh River

Vale

Southwell Creek

Mt Remus 1110 +

SOUTHWEST

CONSERVATION

AREA

Devils Ravine

Pencil Creek

Suttons Creek

Fury River

Mt Romulus 955

Inglis River

Sophia River

George River

Bluff

Murchison River

Chelmers Creek

Canning Peak 860

Dome Ck

Dome Hill 1170

Castle Mtn +

Eldon Peak 1439 +
+ Eldon

Eldon Range

South Eldon River

Robert Creek

Last Hill + 1126

SOUTHWEST

CONSERVATION

AREA

Patons River

Baladava River

Collingwood River

Victoria Pass

LYELL

Raglan Range

Governor R.

Flat Bluff + 1100

Range

Mt Beecroft + 1140

Speeler Plains

C132

Cradle Mountain Lodge

Visitor Centre

Iris R.

Hounslow Heath

C132

Cradle Valley

Waldheim Chalet

Lake Crater

Lake Dove

★ Hut

Cradle Mtn 1545

Hut ★

Lake Rodway

Hut ★ Barn Bluff

+ Mt Emmett

Lake Will

+ Mt Inglis 1282

Overland Track

Hartnell Rivulet

Lake Windermere

Hut ★

CRADLE MOUNTAIN

Creek

James Creek

LAKE ST CLAIR

NATIONAL PARK

Mt Pelion West 1560

Achilles River

Mt Achilles + 1363

Mt Ossa 1617 +

Wallace River

Murchison River

Mt Nereus + 1180

The Acropolis +

The Parthenon +

Du Cane

★ Hut

+ The Guardians
+ Mt Mould

Lake Marion

High Dome +

Mt Manfred + 1382

Mt Cuvier 1380 +

Mt Byron + 1378

Pyramid Mtn + 1259

Inkerman R.

Cheyne Range

FRANKLIN - GORDON

WILD RIVERS

NATIONAL PARK

Alma River

A10

Mt Gell +

Mt Alma + 890

S Franklin

Middlesex Plains

TO WILMOT

C123

Daisy Dell

Dove R.

Carruthers Ck

Swift R.

Campbell R.

Hut ★

Forth River

Mt Oakleigh +

Lake Ayr

Overland

Mersey

Pelion Plains

Waragurra Creek

February

C172

Maggs Mt +

C172

Lorrinna

Lake Cethana

C138

Pallawah Hill

C139

Emu

Lemonthyme

Borradaile Plains

Lake Parangana

C171

Mersey River

Mersey Arm

Rowallan

Lake Rowallan

1245

Howells Bluff

King Solomon

Liena

B12

C138

Marakoopa

MOLE CK KARST N.P.

Western Bluff + 1420

Fisher

TO SHEFFIELD

TO MOLE CREEK

Du Cane Range

Mt Pelion East +

★ Hut

Cathedral Mtn +

★ Hut

★ Hut

Orion Lakes

Lake Pallas

Lake Athena

Lake Riengeena +

Narcissus River

Lake Chapter

Lake Chalice

Traveller Range

Lake Laura

Lake Norman

Lake Payanna

King Roth Lakes

Lake Eros +

Triangle Lake

WALLS OF

JERUSALEM

NATIONAL

PARK

Lake Louisa

Lake Bill

Lake Myrtle

Lake Meston

Lake Adelaide

Lake Ball

Lake Nugetena

Lake Jackie

Eagle Lake

Lake Kellatie

Lake Ina

Lake Sappho

Travellers Rest Lake

Travellers Rest Range

Track

Hut ★

★ Hut

Mt Ida + 1241

Mt Olympus 1149 +

Lake Petrarch

Forgotten Lake

Mt Hugel + 1403

Hut ★

Mt Rufus + 1416

Lake Undine

Lake St Clair

Cuvier River

Navarre River

Franklin River

Derwent Basin

St Clair Lagoon

Visitor Centre

Watersmeet

Lakeside St Clair Wilderness Holidays

C193

Derwent Bridge

A10

Little Navarre R.

Rest River

TO NEW NORFOLK

Lake King William

Laughing Jack Lagoon

Mt Arrowsmith + 981

A10

Continued on map 480

Continued on map 480

© UNIVERSAL PRESS PTY LTD 2002

MAIN ATTRACTIONS: There are many historic buildings, particularly near the waterfront. Old bluestone buildings include the **Van Diemen's Land Company store**, now an art gallery. In Church St are the **Union Hotel** (1849), and **Commercial Hotel** (1842), now a private residence. The **Plough Inn** (1850s) has been restored as an antiques' gallery with an adjacent craft shop. The nearby **Discovery Centre Folk Museum** is a repository for local history. The summit of The Nut can be reached by chairlift or walking track and provides spectacular views over the coastline and **Bass Strait islands**. **Lyons Cottage** in Alexander Tce, the birthplace of **Prime Minister Sir Joseph Lyons**, is open to the public. The burial-ground, off Browns Rd, has early colonial graves, and there are little penguin and muttonbird rookeries in the area.

NEARBY ATTRACTIONS: The gracious colonial property **Highfield** and its original outbuildings are 2km north on Scenic Dr. **Dip Falls**, 40km SE via **Mawbanna**, is a pretty double-drop waterfall surrounded by rain-forest. Nearby are a picnic area, walking trails and a giant stringy-bark known as the **Big Tree**.

TOURIST INFO: Nut Reserve, Ph: (03) 6458 1286

■ **Strahan** POP 723

Map 483, B2

This historic fishing and timber port on **Macquarie Harbour** is the only town sited on Tasmania's forbidding **West Coast**. Its colourful history is linked with the **Sarah Island** penal colony and the Mount Lyell mining boom. As a tourist centre, it is the gateway to the **Gordon River** and the **South West Wilderness Area**.

MAIN ATTRACTIONS: Strahan's 19th-century streetscapes feature such buildings as the grand old **Customs House** and the **Union Steamship Building**. The visitor centre on the

Macquarie Harbour, Strahan

Esplanade has an excellent historical display on south-west Tasmania, including the fight to save the **Franklin River**. A nightly play features the convict escape story, *The Ship that Never Was*. The adjacent **Morrisons Mill**, a Huon pine sawmill, features woodturning, arts and crafts. Historic **Ormiston House** is also on the Esplanade. Harbour views can be had from **Water Tower Hill**, and **Peoples Park** features a walk to **Hogarth Falls**.

NEARBY ATTRACTIONS: **Ocean Beach**, 6km to the west, has areas for horseriding and beach fishing as well as muttonbird rookeries, which are active Oct–March. **Teepookana Plateau**, 16km SE, with its 10m-high viewing platform, can be reached by helicopter. **Henty Dunes**, 12km north, are vast sandhills popular with sailboarders and quad bikers. There is also a lagoon and picnic area. Boat trips can be taken on Macquarie Harbour to visit the convict ruins on Sarah Island, the setting for Marcus Clarke's novel, *For the Term of His Natural Life*. A huge range of sightseeing options

are available for the magnificent **Franklin-Gordon Wild Rivers NP**, including cruises, helicopter and seaplane flights, yacht charters, horseriding, jet boat rides and fishing excursions. Other local activities include kayaking and canoeing on the **Gordon** and **Henty rivers**.

TOURIST INFO: Wharf Complex, The Esplanade, Ph: (03) 6471 7622

■ **Swansea** POP 512

Map 481, J6

Formerly one of many whaling stations on Tasmania's **East Coast**, Swansea is a popular fishing and tourist resort overlooking beautiful **Great Oyster Bay**. It is a handy base for exploring **Freycinet** and **Maria Island NPs**.

MAIN ATTRACTIONS: A **heritage walk** reveals several old buildings that are still used for their original purpose, including the **Council Chambers** (1860), **Morris' General Store** (1838) and the **Swan Inn** (1841). There are 3 attractions at the information centre on the Tasman Hwy: **Swansea Bark Mill** (1885) processed black wattle bark for

Tasmania

leather tannins until 1935, it is now a centre for Tasmanian crafts; **Yesteryear Museum** charts local history; and the **Wine and Wool Centre** is an outlet for Tasmanian wines. The museum at the **Community Centre** (circa 1860) includes the immense slate billiard table made for the 1880 World Exhibition. The walking track around **Waterloo Point** takes in Aboriginal middens, views to **Freycinet Peninsula** and muttonbird viewing at dusk.

NEARBY ATTRACTIONS: There is a small colony of little penguins at **Coswell Beach**, 1km south. **Kate's Berry Farm**, 2km south has fresh berries in season and fruit wines. There are a number of vineyards in the region for wine tasting and cellar door sales. **Duncombes Lookout**, 3km south, offers splendid views. **Spikey Beach**, 7km south, has picnic grounds, rock fishing and the convict-built **Spikey Bridge** (1843). **Mayfield Beach**, 14km south, has safe swimming and a walking track to **Three Arch Bridge**. **Dolphin Sands** and the **Swan River** picnic area, 4km north, are popular recreation spots. **Meetus Falls** and **Lost Falls** are 50km NW.

TOURIST INFO: Swansea Bark Mill, 96 Tasman Hwy, Ph: (03) 6257 8382

◼ Triabunna   POP 771
Map 469, D1

Triabunna is located on **Spring Bay**, 86km NE of Hobart. Once it was a whaling base and garrison town for the nearby **Maria Island** penal settlement. Today, the town's mainstays are the woodchipping, scallop and abalone industries.

MAIN ATTRACTIONS: A **town walk** from the visitor centre takes in 17 heritage buildings, the oldest being the **Police Watch-house** and **Magistrates Office** (both 1840s). The visitor centre has interpretative displays and interesting tapestries. A **Seafarers' Memorial** on the Esplanade commemorates sailors

lost in Tasmanian waters. **Pioneer Park** has displays of historic farm machinery from the region.

NEARBY ATTRACTIONS: Informal tours of **North Products woodchip mill** at **Freestone Point** can be arranged on arrival. Boats can be chartered for fishing expeditions. Ferries leave daily from **Eastcoaster Resort**, 7km south, for Maria Island, where the main highlights are penal settlement ruins at **Darlington**, painted cliffs, fossil deposits and walking trails in **Maria Island NP**.

TOURIST INFO: Charles St and Esplanade West, Ph: (03) 6257 4090

◼ Ulverstone   POP 9819
Map 480, B2

The beachside town of Ulverstone, 19km west of Devonport, is a popular tourist destination, especially in summer. It is the centre for a dairy farming and agricultural district.

MAIN ATTRACTIONS: Ulverstone's beaches, memorial parks, antique and craft shops are big drawcards. Dominating the town is the **Shrine of Remembrance clock tower** in Reibey St. There are 4 memorial parks: **Tobruk Park** in Hobbs Pde; **Anzac Park** by the River Leven;

Legion Park in West Ulverstone; and **HMAS *Shropshire* Naval Memorial Park** in Dial St. **Fairway Park** has an adventure playground and a giant waterslide in summer. The **History Museum** in Main St displays local memorabilia in the form of shop windows (open Tue, Thurs and weekends). The **NW Woodcraft Guild Workshop and Gallery** is open Tue, Thurs and Sat. A lookout off Upper Maud St in **West Ulverstone** gives views across the river to the **Bass Strait beaches**.

NEARBY ATTRACTIONS: There is a miniature railway 2km east, and little penguins can be seen at dusk at **Leith**, 12km east. **Goat Island Sanctuary**, 5km west, can be reached by a walkway at low tide. **Gunns Plains Caves**, 24km SW, feature limestone formations, an underground river and glow-worms; guided tours are available. **Gunns Plains Hop Farm** is nearby. Scenic waterfalls in the area include **Preston** (19km south) and **Castra falls** (30km south). **Leven Canyon**, 41km south, is a magnificent gorge with interesting walking tracks.

TOURIST INFO: Car Park La, (behind Post Office), Ph: (03) 6425 2839

The Hazards on Freycinet Peninsula, east of Swansea

Westbury   POP 1307

Map 480, D3

This small quaint town 35km SW of Launceston on the Bass Hwy, has a European history dating to 1828. Westbury's original Georgian and early Victorian buildings clustered around a village green is very much in the style of an English village. MAIN ATTRACTIONS: Facing the Village Green, the **White House** (1841) is now a colonial museum, with a magnificent antique-Georgian doll's house and several original outbuildings (closed July–August). Lovers of handcrafts and collect-ables will find plenty to interest them in Westbury's fascinating side streets. Three historic build-ings offer B&B accommodation. The beautiful English garden, **Culzean**, in William St is open Sept–June. **Westbury Maze** on Bass Hwy is a traditional hedge maze, with more than 3000 privet bushes; there is also a tearoom. **Pearn's Steam World** has a large collection of working steam-traction engines, which steam up at Easter and during November. **Tractor Shed** in Veterans Row is a museum of old farm ma-chinery. **Animal Haven** is a zoo where children can pet the animals. NEARBY ATTRACTIONS: **St Marys Anglican Church** at **Hagley**, 5km east, has a superb east-facing window. Trout fishing enthusiasts head for **Brushy Lagoon**, 15km NW, or **Four Springs Creek**, 15km NE. TOURIST INFO: Clarke's Antiques, 52 William St, Ph: (03) 6393 1140

Wynyard   POP 4983

Map 479, E3

The pretty north-west coast town of Wynyard is the centre of a pros-perous farming district. It is also a popular tourist centre, with an airport on the edge of town. MAIN ATTRACTIONS: **Gutteridge Gardens** are attractive parklands beside the **Inglis River**. There is a Tasmanian tiger (*thylacine*)

interpretive sculpture at the infor-mation centre. Scenic walks include a riverside ramble to amazing **Fossil Bluff**, where the sea cliffs contain thousands of fossils. In the mid-1800s a 20 million-year-old fossil marsupial was discovered at the Bluff—the oldest ever found. NEARBY ATTRACTIONS: Scenic flights over the coastline and north-west wilderness areas are available at the airport. The drive or walk to **Table Cape**, a 170m volcanic plug, passes a colourful patchwork of vegetables, poppies and tulips, with **Cape Tulip Farm** open for inspection in Oct-ober. Table Cape, 5km north, has an historic lighthouse and stunning views over a vast stretch of the coastline. **Boat Harbour**, 15km NW, is considered one of Australia's most beautiful beaches, with white sand, crystal-clear blue water, coral formations, rocky outcrops for fishing and tidal pools. Seals usually visit the bay in late summer. Further west, **Rocky Cape NP** has many excellent walks, Aboriginal relics, a marine park and lighthouse. TOURIST INFO: Hogg and Goldie Sts, Ph: (03) 6442 4143

Zeehan   POP 1098

Map 483, B1

This once booming mining town, named after one of Abel Tasman's ships, is 36km NW of Queenstown. After silver-lead deposits were discovered in 1882, Zeehan's population rose to around 10 000 in 1901. By 1909 it was almost deserted, but has recently revived with the reopening of the **Renison Bell Tin Mine**. MAIN ATTRACTIONS: Main St has many buildings from the boom years (1890–1908). **The Gaiety Grand** building contains the Grand Hotel and the Gaiety Theatre, which is much as it was in its heyday, when it seated 1000 and showcased such stars as Enrico Caruso and Nellie Melba. The Old School of Mines

building (1894) now houses the **West Coast Pioneers Memorial Museum**, with perhaps the best mineral collection in the Southern Hemisphere, including the finest specimens of rare crocoite, which is Tasmania's mineral emblem. Excellent old steam engines and carriages used on the **West Coast** are displayed outside. From the museum a 7km round-trip drive heads out through a low mining tunnel to the old **Spray Silver Mine**. **Frank Long Memorial Park** marks the first silver-lead deposit. A **pioneer cemetery** lies off Zeehan–Strahan Rd. NEARBY ATTRACTIONS: There are old mine workings at **Dundas**, 13km east. Tasmania's highest waterfall **Montezuma Falls** (110m) is 17km NE, accessible by walking track or 4WD. An unsealed scenic drive leads to the fishing village of **Granville Harbour**, 35km NW, once the port for Zeehan. **Corinna**, formerly a gold-mining town 48km NW, is now a base for gold panning, bushwalking and trout-fishing with a car ferry crossing the **Pieman River**. Fishing and boating are popular on **Lake Pieman** to the north. Trout fishermen head for the Henty River, 25km south. TOURIST INFO: West Coast Pioneers Museum, Main St, Ph: (03) 6471 6225

Granville Harbour, 35km from Zeehan

KEY MAP

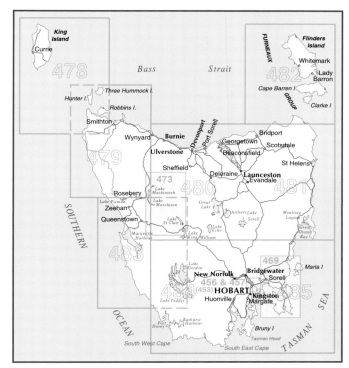

Capital city CBD map
Hobart p.453

Hobart suburban map
pp.456–457

Region maps
Tasman Peninsula
   p.469

Region maps (continued)
Cradle Mountain-
   Lake St Clair NP
   p. 473

State maps
pp. 478–485

Frozen ferns, Cradle Mountain

DISTANCE CHART

Approximate Distance	Burnie	Campbell Town	Deloraine	Devonport	Geeveston	George Town	Hobart	Launceston	New Norfolk	Oatlands	Port Arthur	Queenstown	Rosebery	St Helens	St Marys	Scottsdale	Smithton	Sorell	Swansea	Triabunna
Burnie		198	100	50	381	152	328	137	290	246	386	148	109	293	259	197	88	316	264	314
Campbell Town	198		98	148	184	120	131	70	127	48	188	253	308	120	85	130	286	118	66	116
Deloraine	100	98		50	281	87	228	51	190	146	286	204	209	207	159	111	188	216	164	214
Devonport	50	148	50		331	102	278	87	240	196	336	198	159	243	209	147	138	266	214	264
Geeveston	381	184	281	331		304	53	254	91	136	148	312	367	304	269	314	469	78	189	139
George Town	152	120	87	102	304		251	50	259	168	308	300	261	170	205	74	240	238	186	236
Hobart	328	131	228	278	53	251		201	38	83	95	259	314	251	216	261	416	25	136	86
Launceston	137	70	51	87	254	50	201		197	118	258	251	246	156	131	60	225	188	136	186
New Norfolk	290	127	190	240	91	259	38	197		79	133	221	276	247	212	257	378	63	174	124
Oatlands	246	48	146	196	136	168	83	118	79		140	261	316	168	133	178	334	70	114	131
Port Arthur	386	188	286	336	148	308	95	258	133	140		354	409	299	268	318	474	70	181	131
Queenstown	148	253	204	198	312	300	259	251	221	261	354		55	407	338	311	236	284	395	345
Rosebery	109	308	209	159	367	261	314	246	276	316	409	55		401	368	306	197	339	450	400
St Helens	293	120	207	243	304	170	251	156	247	168	299	407	401		35	96	381	229	118	168
St Marys	259	85	159	209	269	205	216	131	212	133	268	338	368	35		131	347	198	87	137
Scottsdale	197	130	111	147	314	74	261	60	257	178	318	311	306	96	131		285	248	214	264
Smithton	88	286	188	138	469	240	416	225	378	334	474	236	197	381	347	285		404	352	402
Sorell	316	118	216	266	78	238	25	188	63	70	70	284	339	229	198	248	404		111	61
Swansea	264	66	164	214	189	186	136	136	174	114	181	395	450	118	87	214	352	111		50
Triabunna	314	116	214	264	139	236	86	186	124	131	131	345	400	168	137	264	402	61	50	

All distances in this chart have been measured over highways and major roads, not necessarily by the shortest route.

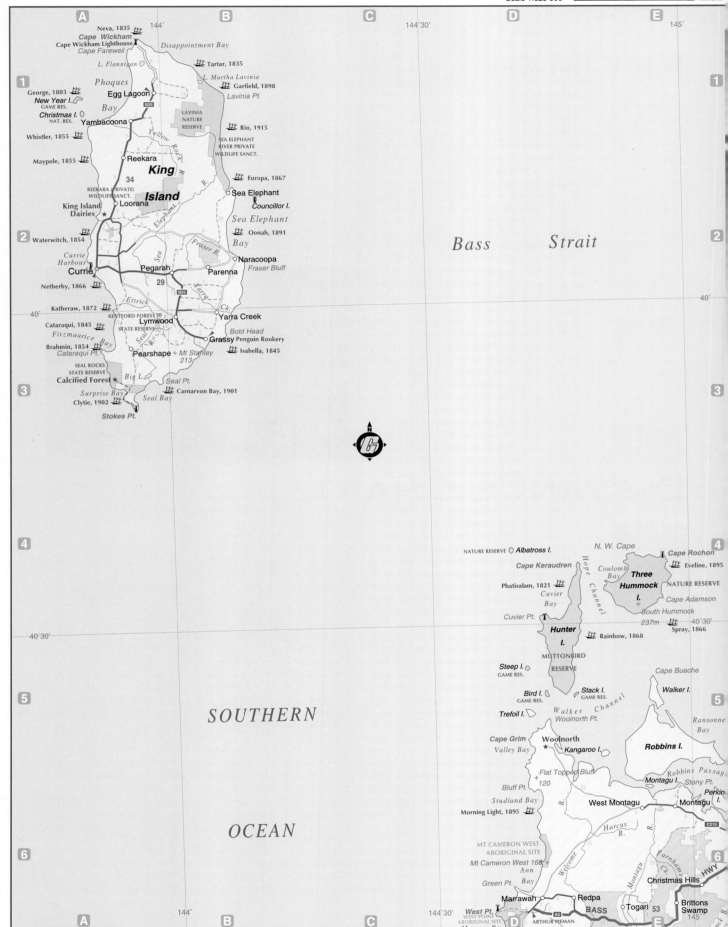

0   20 Kilometres

A   **B**   **C**   144°30'   **D**   **E**   145°

Neva, 1835 144°
Cape Wickham
Cape Wickham Lighthouse
Cape Farewell
Disappointment Bay

1
Tartar, 1835
L. Martha Lavinia
Phoques   *L. Flannigan*
George, 1803
New Year I.   Egg Lagoon
Christmas I.   *Bay*
NAT. RES.
Yambacoona
Whistler, 1855
Garfield, 1898
Lavinia Pt.
LAVINIA
NATURE
RESERVE
Rio, 1915
SEA ELEPHANT
RIVER PRIVATE
WILDLIFE SANCT.

Maypole, 1855
Reekara
King
34
REEKARA (PRIVATE)
WILDLIFE SANCT.
Island
King Island   Loorana
Dairies ★
Europa, 1867
Sea Elephant
Councillor I.
Sea Elephant

2
Waterwitch, 1854   *Fraser R.*   Oonah, 1891   *Bay*
Currie   *Sea*
Harbour   Pegarah   Naracoopa
Currie   Parenna   *Fraser Bluff*
Netherby, 1866   29
Ettrick   B25   *Yarra*
Katheraw, 1872   KENTFORD FOREST   Yarra Creek   *Ck.*
Cataraqui, 1845   STATE RESERVE   Lymwood   *Bold Head*
Fitzmaurice   Grassy   Penguin Rookery
Brahmin, 1854   *Bay*
Cataraqui Pt.   Pearshape   + *Mt Stanley*   Isabella, 1845
SEAL ROCKS   213
STATE RESERVE   *Big L.*

3
Calcified Forest ★   *Seal Pt.*
Surprise Bay   Carnarvon Bay, 1901
Clytie, 1902   *Seal Bay*
Stokes Pt.

Bass   *Strait*

4
NATURE RESERVE   *Albatross I.*   *N. W. Cape*   Cape Rochon
Cape Keraudren   *Hope*   *Coulomb*   Eveline, 1895
Channel   *Bay*   **Three**
Phatisalam, 1821   **Hummock**
Cuvier   **I.**   NATURE RESERVE
Bay   Cape Adamson
Cuvier Pt.   *South Hummock*   40°30'
237m   Spray, 1866
40°30'   **Hunter**   Rainbow, 1868
I.
MUTTONBIRD
Steep I.   RESERVE   Cape Buache

5
GAME RES.
SOUTHERN   *Bird I.*   Stack I.   Walker I.
GAME RES.
GAME RES.   *Walker*   *Channel*   *Ransonne*
Trefoil I.   Woolnorth Pt.   *Bay*
Cape Grim   Woolnorth
Valley Bay   Kangaroo I.   **Robbins I.**
★
Flat Topped Bluff   *Robbins Passage*
OCEAN   + 120   Montagu I.   Stony Pt.
Bluff Pt.   *Perkin*
Studland Bay   West Montagu   Montagu   *I.*
Morning Light, 1895   C215

6
MT CAMERON WEST   *Harcus R.*
ABORIGINAL SITE
Mt Cameron West 168 +   Christmas Hills
Ann   *HWY*
Green Pt.   *Bay*   *Montagu R.*
Marrawah   Redpa   Togari   Brittons
West Pt.   **BASS**   53   Swamp
WEST POINT   A2   145
ABORIGINAL SITE
Mawson Bay   ARTHUR PIEMAN   *Duck R.*
CONSERVATION AREA

A   144°   **B**   **C**   144°30'   **D**   **E**

© UNIVERSAL PRESS PTY LTD 2002

Scale 1:625 000

0   20   Kilometres

144°30'

Bass   *Strait*

Albatross I.
NATURE RESERVE
Cape Keraudren
N. W. Cape
Coulomb Bay
Cape Rochon
Eveline, 1895
145'

Phatisalam, 1821
Cuvier Bay
Cuvier Pt.

Three Hummock I.
NATURE RESERVE
Cape Adamson
South Hummock
237m
Spray, 1866

Hunter I.
MUTTONBIRD RESERVE

Rainbow, 1868

40°30'

Steep I.
GAME RES.

Bird I.
GAME RES.
Stack I.
GAME RES.

Trefoil I.

Walker Channel
Woolnorth Pt.

Cape Buache

Walker I.

Ransonnet Bay
Guyton Pt.

Cape Grim
Valley Bay
Woolnorth
Kangaroo I.

Robbins I.

Cape Elie

Elizabeth, 1864
North Pt.
The Nut Chairlift
Half Moon Bay
Highfield
Stanley
Circular Head (The Nut) 143

Flat Topped Bluff
120

Montagu I.
Robbins Stony Pt.
Passage

Perkins I.

Bluff Pt.
Studland Bay
Morning Light, 1895

West Montagu
Montagu

Perkins I.

Perkins Bay
Anthony Beach

Sawyer Bay

MT CAMERON WEST
ABORIGINAL SITE
Mt Cameron West 168
Ann

Green Pt.
Bay

Marrawah
Redpa

Togari

West Pt.
WEST POINT
ABORIGINAL SITE

Mawson Bay

Bluff Hill Pt.

ARTHUR PIEMAN
CONSERVATION AREA

Mella
Smithton
Forest
Smokers Bank
South Forest
Wiltshire
Black River
Port Latta
Hellyer
Prairie, 1856
Rocky Cape

Christmas Hills
Irishtown
Mengha
Crayfish Creek
Rocky Cape
Sisters Beach
Boat Harbour

Brittons Swamp
Alcomie
Mawbanna
Montumana
Sisters Creek
Flowerdale
Myalla
Moorleah

Table Cape
Emma Prescott, 1867
Wynyard

Edith Creek
Lileah
Milabena
Lapoinya
Seabrook

Nabageena
Giant Eucalypts
Dip Falls
Mt Dipwood 519
Calder
Lower Mt Hicks
Somerset

Roger River
Meunna
Kellatier
Oldina
Elliott

Roger River West
Trowutta
Preolenna
Yolla

Arthur River
River Cruise
Rebecca, 1853

Milkshake Hills
Lake Chisholm

Takone
Henrietta
West Ridgley
Ridgley

Alert, 1854

Julius River

Kanunnah Bridge

Little Rapid
Takone West
Oonah
Highclere
Tewkesbury

Couta Rocks

SUNDOWN POINT
ABORIGINAL SITE
Nelson Bay

Hampshire

Richardson Pt.
Temma
Eva, 1880

Balfour
Mt Frankland 448

Hellyer Gorge
HELLYER GORGE
STATE PARK
Parrawe

St. Valentines Pk 1106

Wild Wave, 1894
Yolla, 1898
Sandy Cape

Mt Bertha 703

SAVAGE RIVER N.P.

Baretop Ridge

Guildford
Talbots Lagoon

Mt Norfolk 760

ARTHUR PIEMAN CONSERVATION AREA

Mt Sunday 699

Mt Cleveland 858
Waratah
Waratah Reservoir

Luina
Mt Pearse 1002

Mayday Mt 1140
Hellyer

Savage River

Mt Meredith 810

Mt Ramsay 856

Mt Remus 1110

Rupert Pt.
Ethel Cuthbert, 1878
Pieman Heads
Hardwicke Bay
Conical Rocks Pt.
Dolphin, 1867

Mt Donaldson 837
Corinna

Mt Livingstone 781

Mackintosh Dam
Mackintosh
Mt Romulus 955
Lake Mackintosh

Reece Reece Dam

Bastyan Dam
Bastyan
Tullah
Tullah
Murchison Dam

GRANITE TOR
Wee Georgie Wood Railway
CONSERVATION AREA

SOUTHERN OCEAN

Rosebery
Renison Bell

Joins map 480

© UNIVERSAL PRESS PTY LTD 2002

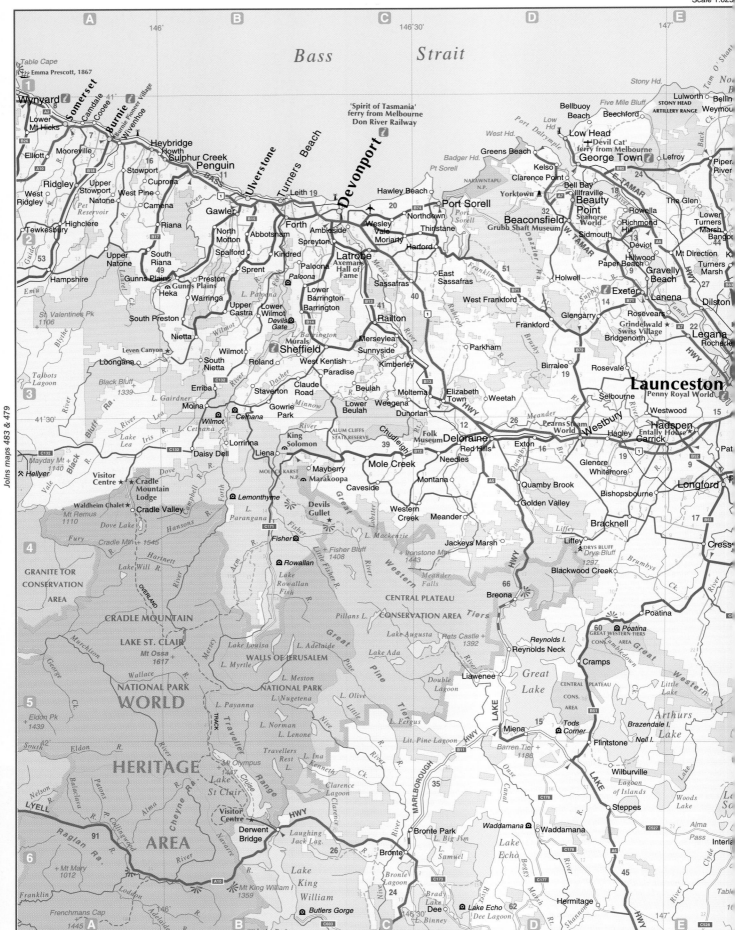

Scale 1:625

Bass Strait

Tasmania

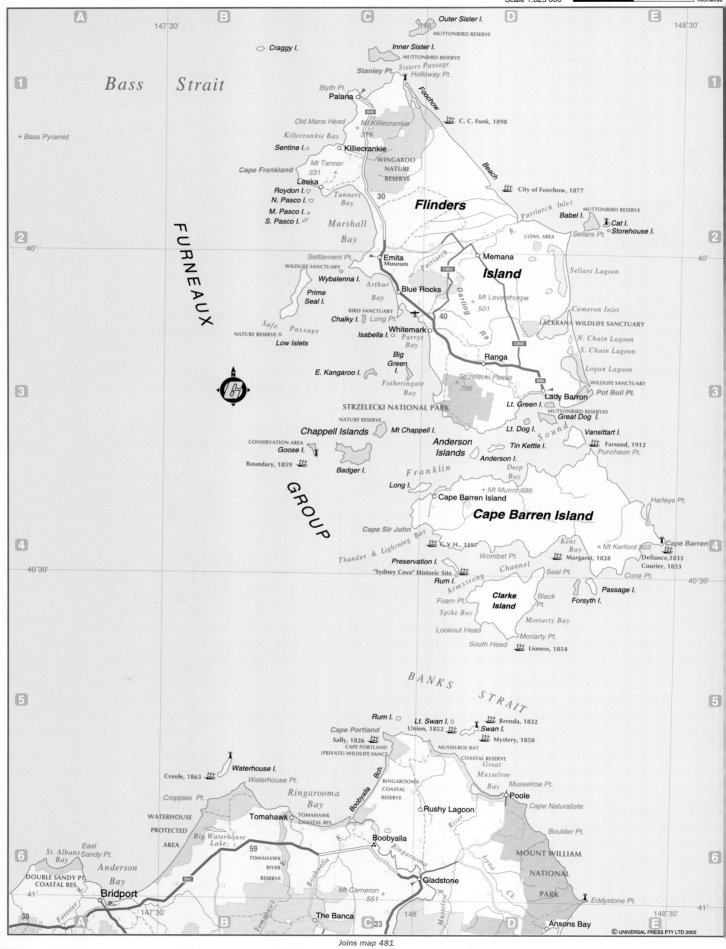

Bass Strait

A   B   C   D   E

Craggy I.

Outer Sister I.
MUTTONBIRD RESERVE
Inner Sister I.
MUTTONBIRD RESERVE
Sisters Passage
Stanley Pt.   Holloway Pt.
Blyth Pt.
Palana
C.C. Funk, 1898
Old Mans Head
Mt Killiecrankie
376
Killecrankie Bay
Sentine I.   Killiecrankie   Beach
Cape Frankland   Mt Tanner   WINGAROO   City of Foochow, 1877
Leeka   331   NATURE
Roydon I.   RESERVE
N. Pasco I.   Tanners   Flinders   Patriarch Inlet   MUTTONBIRD RESERVE
M. Pasco I.   Bay   Babel I.   Cat I.
S. Pasco I.   R.   Sellars Pt.   Storehouse I.
Marshall   CONS. AREA
Bay
Settlement Pt.   Emita   Memana   Sellars Lagoon
WILDLIFE SANCTUARY   Museum   Island
Wybalenna I.   Arthur   C803
Prime   Bay   Blue Rocks   Mt Leventhorpe   LACKRANA WILDLIFE SANCTUARY
Seal I.   501   Cameron Inlet
BIRD SANCTUARY   N. Chain Lagoon
Chalky I.   Long Pt.   40   S. Chain Lagoon
Safe   Whitemark   C803
NATURE RESERVE   Isabella I.   Parrys   Logan Lagoon
Low Islets   Passage   Bay   Ranga   WILDLIFE SANCTUARY
Big   Pot Boil Pt.
Green   Lady Barron
I.   Strzelecki Peaks   B85
E. Kangaroo I.   756   Lt. Green I.
Fotheringate   Vansittart I.
Bay   STRZELECKI NATIONAL PARK   Great Dog I.   Farsund, 1912
MUTTONBIRD RESERVES   Puncheon Pt.
NATURE RESERVE   Lt. Dog I.   Sound
Chappell Islands   Mt Chappell I.   Anderson   Tin Kettle I.
CONSERVATION AREA   Islands   Deep
Goose I.   Anderson I.   Bay
Boundary, 1859   Franklin   Mt Munro 686   Harleys Pt.
Badger I.   Long I.
Cape Barren Island   Cape Barren Island
Cape Sir John   Kent   Mt Kerford 303   Cape Barren
Bay   Margaret, 1828   Defiance, 1833
Thunder & Lightning Bay   G.V.H., 1897   Wombat Pt.   Courier, 1833
Preservation I.   Channel   Seal Pt.   Cone Pt.
"Sydney Cove" Historic Site   Armstrong   Black   Passage I.
Rum I.   Foam Pt.   Clarke   Pt.   Forsyth I.
Spike Bay   Island   Moriarty Bay
Lookout Head   Moriarty Pt.
South Head   Lioness, 1854

BANKS   STRAIT

Rum I.   Lt. Swan I.   Brenda, 1832
Cape Portland   Union, 1852   Swan I.
Sally, 1826   Mystery, 1850
CAPE PORTLAND   MUSSELROE BAY
(PRIVATE) WILDLIFE SANCT.   COASTAL RESERVE
Creole, 1863   Waterhouse I.   RINGAROOMA   Great
Waterhouse Pt.   COASTAL   Musselroe   Musselroe Pt.
Croppies Pt.   Ringarooma   RESERVE   Bay   Poole
WATERHOUSE   Bay   Rushy Lagoon   Cape Naturaliste
PROTECTED   Tomahawk   River
AREA   TOMAHAWK   Boulder Pt.
Big Waterhouse   COASTAL RES.   Boobyalla
East   Lake   59   MOUNT WILLIAM
St. Albans   TOMAHAWK   Ck.   NATIONAL
Bay   RIVER   Mt Cameron   PARK
Anderson   B82   RESERVE   551   Gladstone
DOUBLE SANDY PT.   Bay   Eddystone Pt.
COASTAL RES.
Bridport   The Banca   Ansons Bay

FURNEAUX   GROUP

Tasmania

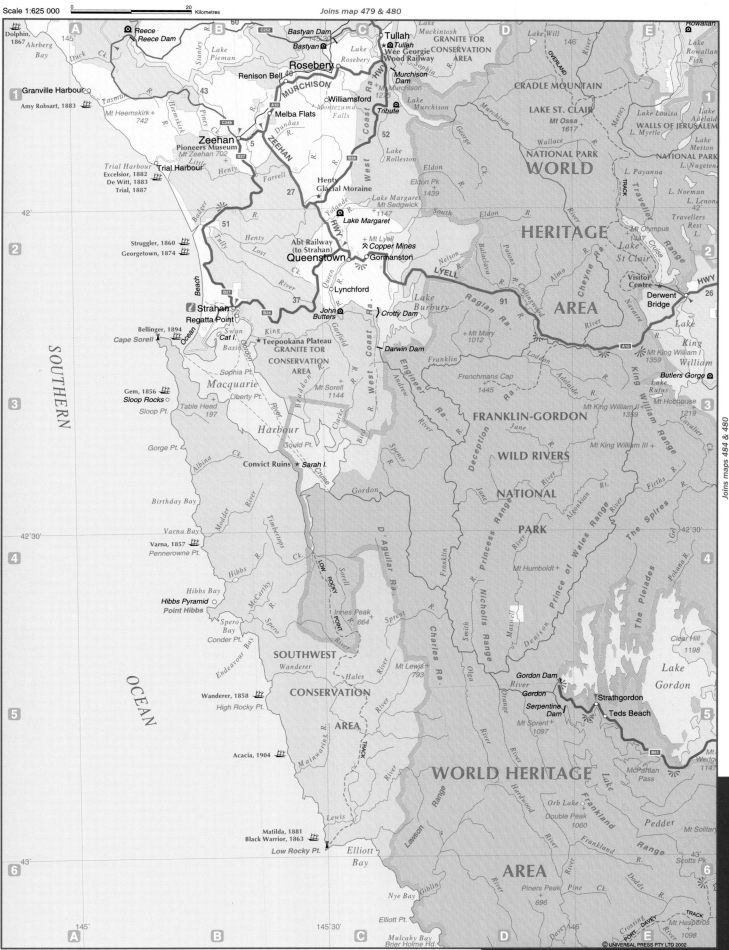

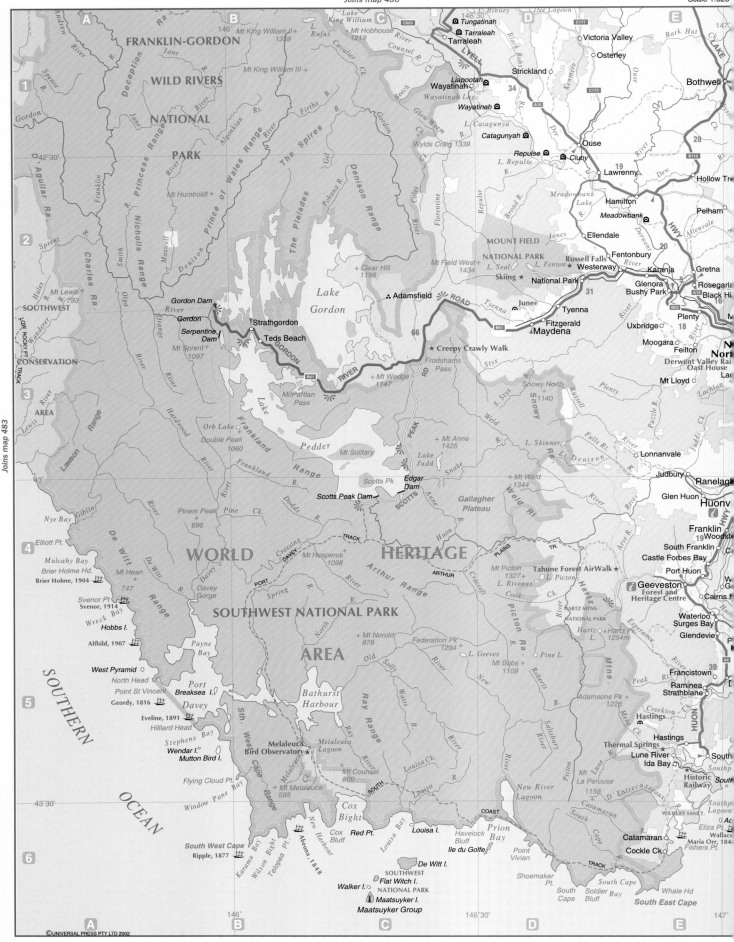

Tasmania

Joins map 483

20 Kilometres

F   **G** 47°30'   **H**   148°   **J** 148°30'   **K**

York Plains
Nala
L. Dulverton
Lemont
Lisdillon
Buxton Pt.
Schouten
Passage
1

Oatlands
Historic town
Andover
Little Swanport
Harriet, 1849
Little Swanport
Seaford Pt.
Cape Faure
Schouten I.
FREYCINET NATIONAL PARK
Chain Locker Bay
Cape Sonnerat

Parattah
Jericho
Mt Seymour
+739
Crichton
Pt. Bailly
Cape Sonnerat
Taillefer Rocks

Apsley
20
Stonor
Mt Seymour
Stonehenge
Sarah Ann Bay
Ile des Phoques

17
MIDLAND
Baden
Whitefoord
BUCKLAND MILITARY
BOLTONS BEACH
COASTAL RESERVE
Grindstone Pt.

Black Tier
+775
Melton
Mowbray
Rhyndaston
Tunnack
Woodsdale
TRAINING AREA
42°30'
2

Kempton
Colebrook
Levendale
Triabunna
Cape Bougainville
Okehampton

Dysart
Elderslie
Quoin Mtn.
899
Craigbourne
Dam
Brown Mtn.
+791
Buckland
63
Three Thumbs
550
Orford
Louisville
Apollo, 1827
Ile du Nord
Cape Boullanger
Darlington Penal Settlement

Bagdad
Lowdina
Runnymede
Spring
Beach
Maria
Island

Broadmarsh
Mangalore
Rekuna
Campania
Rheban
Mistaken Cape

Pontville
Upper
Dromedary
Brighton
Orielton
Pawleena
Nugent
MARIA ISLAND NATIONAL PARK

Bridgewater
Richmond
Historic town
Wattle Hill
Kellevie
Shoal
Bay
Riedle Bay
Cape Maurouard

Granton
Old Beach
Sorell
Forcett
31
Bream Creek
Cape
Bernier
Marion
Bay
Cape Peron

Boyer
Malbina
Risdon
Vale
Midway
Point
Lewisham
ARTHUR
Copping
Zephyr, 1852
Cape Paul Lamanon
North
Bay
Cape Frederick Hendrick
42°30'
3

Molesworth
Cambridge
Dodges Ferry
Carlton
Dunalley
Tasman Monument
Cape Surville

HOBART
Rokeby
Seven
Mile Beach
Primrose
Sands
Dunalley
Bay
Green Hd.
FORESTIER
PENINSULA
TASMAN N.P.
MacGregor Peak
591m

Fern Tree
Lauderdale
Sloping I.
Smooth I.
Murdunna
Tessellated Pavement
43°

Neika
Cremorne
Henry
Bay
LIME BAY
NATURE RES.
Norfolk
Bay
30
Eaglehawk Neck
Penzance
Tasman Arch & Devils Kitchen

Leslie Vale
Sandford
Clifton Beach
Saltwater
River
Taranna
O'Hara Bluff
TASMAN N.P.

Kingston
Opossum
Bay
Premaydena
Koonya
TASMAN
Oakwood

Blackmans
Bay
Howden
South Arm
Cape
Direction
Betsey I.
Tasmanian
Devil Park
PEN.
26
Port Arthur
Fortescue Bay
Cape Hauy
4

Margate
Electrona
Snug
Tinderbox
Dennes Pt
NATURE RES.
Outer North
Hd.
Nubeena
Highcroft
White
Beach
Munro Bight
TASMAN N.P.

Pelverata
Killora
Storm
Wedge Bay
Amelia, 1833
Wedge I.
Stormlea
Remarkable Cave
Cape Pillar

Oyster Cove
Barnes Bay
One Tree Pt.
Yellow Bluff
TASMAN
N.P.
Raoul
Bay
Maingon Bay
Cape Raoul
Tasman I.

Kettering
Roberts Point
Australian, 1834
Trumpeter Bay
Contest, 1831

Nicholas
Rivulet
Woodbridge
Great
Bay
BRUNY I. NECK
GAME RESERVE
Cape Queen Elizabeth
Moorina Bay

Flowerpot
Middleton
Garden I.
Ck
Gordon
SEA

Verona
Sands
Adventure
Bay
D'Entrecasteaux

Alonnah
Adventure
Bay
Captain Cooks Landing Place
Cookville
Bligh Museum
TASMAN
5

Lunawanna
Bruny
Island
Partridge I.
Bay of Islands
Mangana Bluff
Cloudy Bay
Lagoon

SOUTH
BRUNY
N.P.
Cloudy
Bay
South Bruny
Lighthouse
Mt Bruny 504
Boreal Hd

Cape
Bruny
SOUTH
BRUNY
N.P.
Tasman Head
The Friars
James Lucas, 1829
43°30'
6

INDEX

This alphabetical index covers the cities, suburbs, towns, localities and homesteads shown in this publication, as well as national parks, selected topographical features and selected places of interest.

The indexed entries are followed by the state, the page number in the case of text references, and the page number and grid reference in the case of maps. All page references are in numerical order, e.g. Adelaide Zoo, SA 297 D3, 298

Entries under one word are grouped together. Where entries consist of two words or more, the alphabetical sequence is governed by the first, then the second word, e.g. Little Swanport, Little Topar Roadhouse, Little Wobby, Littlehampton, Littlemore, Littles Crossing

References in bold type indicate locations to be found on the state maps at the end of the chapters, e.g. Adamsfield, TAS **484 C2**

Entries in italic type indicate homesteads, e.g. *Acacia Downs*, NSW 111 D6

Entries beginning with *Mc* are treated as though they are spelt *Mac*, similarly *Mt* is indexed as *Mount* and *St* is indexed as *Saint*.

The following state abbreviations are used in this index: ACT—Australian Capital Territory; NSW—New South Wales; NT—Northern Territory; QLD—Queensland; SA—South Australia; TAS—Tasmania; VIC—Victoria; WA—Western Australia

Note: this index does not purport to include every city, suburb, town, locality or homestead in Australia.

Bargara, QLD 233, 259 A1, **287 J2**
Bargo, NSW 107 B2, **119 G6**
Barham, NSW **120 E3**
Baring, VIC **204 D5**
Baringhup, VIC 159 D2, **207 J5**
Barjarg, VIC **208 D5**
Bark Hut Inn, NT **432 E3**
Bark Mill & Museum, TAS **481 H6**
Barkly, VIC **207 G5**
Barkly Downs, QLD **280 B2**
Barkly Homestead Roadhouse, NT **440 B2**
Barmah, VIC **208 B2**
Barmedman, NSW **118 B6**
Barmera, SA 305, 333 C2, **349 H1**
Barnadown, VIC **207 K4**
Barnato, NSW **117 G2**
Barnawartha, VIC 187 B1, **209 F2**
Barnawartha South, VIC 187 B1, **209 F3**
Barnes Bay, TAS **485 G4**
Barnong, WA **402 C1**
Barooga, NSW **121 H4**
Barool NP, NSW **115 G3**
Baroondah, QLD **286 E3**
Baroota, SA **346 E5**
Barossa Valley, SA 289, 326, 327
Barpinba, VIC 201 F3, **211 H3**
Barraba, NSW **114 D4**
Barracks Archway, Perth, WA 359 B3, 360
Barracouta Gas & Oil Field, VIC **213 H3**
Barradeen, QLD **286 B3**
Barragup, WA **387 C2**
Barramunga, VIC 201 G5, **211 H4**
Barraport, VIC **207 H2**
Barraroo, NSW **116 D2**
Barratta, QLD **282 D1**
Barrington, NSW **119 J2**
Barrington, QLD **282 B2**
Barrington, TAS **480 B2**
Barrington Tops NP, NSW **119 H2**
Barringun, NSW **113 F2**
Barrow Creek Roadhouse, NT **439 H4**
Barry, NSW 118 E5, **119 H2**
Barrys Reef, VIC 159 E3, **211 J1**
Bartle Frere, QLD **239 D5**
Barton, ACT 129 D5, 135 C3
Barton, VIC 195 E4, **211 F1**
Barunduda, VIC **209 F3**
Barunga, NT 429 E3, **433 F5**
Barwidgee, WA **401 G5**
Barwon Downs, VIC 201 G4, **211 H4**
Barwon Heads, VIC 156–7, 201 K3, **211 K3**
Baryugil, NSW **115 H3**
Basalt Creek, QLD **286 E2**
Basin Pocket, QLD **230 A5**
Basin View, NSW **97 B4**
Baskerville, WA **363 G1**
Basket Range, SA **303 F1**
Basket Swamp NP, NSW **115 G2**
Bass, VIC **212 C4**
Bass Hill, NSW **48 E2**
Bass Strait 140, 460, 478
Bassendean, WA **362 E2**
Batavia Downs, QLD **277 B4**
Batchelor, NT 424–5, 425 C1, **432 D3**
Batchica, VIC **206 E3**
Bateau Bay, NSW **71 C4**
Batehaven, NSW **122 D3**
Bateman, WA **362 D5**
Batemans Bay, NSW 52, **122 D3**
Bathurst, NSW 52, **118 E4**
Bathurst Island, NT 415
Batlow, NSW 77 A1, **122 A3**
Batten Pt, NT **437 H2**
Battery, QLD **279 J6**
Battery Hill, NT **439 J2**
Battery Point, TAS 452, 453 D4, 454, 456 D4
Bauhinia Downs, NT **437 G2**
Bauhinia Downs, QLD **280 E2**
Baulkamaugh North, VIC **208 C2**
Baulkham Hills, NSW **46 E5**
Bauple, QLD **259 B5**
Baw Baw NP, VIC **212 E2**
Bawley Point, NSW 107 A6, **122 E3**
Baxter, VIC **153 G2**

Bayindeen, VIC **159 B3**
Baykool, QLD **285 J2**
Bayles, VIC **212 C3**
Baynton, VIC 167 D1, **208 A5**
Bayswater, VIC **151 H2**
Bayswater, WA **362 E2**
Bayswater North, VIC 151 H2, **171 A2**
Bayulu, WA **399 H4**
Bayview, NSW **47 K3**
Bayview, NT **418 B4**
Beachmere, QLD 229 F2, **255 C6**
Beachport, SA 305–6, 323 C4, **349 G5**
Beacon, WA **402 E3**
Beacon Hill, NSW **47 J4**
Beaconsfield, NSW **49 H2**
Beaconsfield, TAS 458, **480 D2**
Beaconsfield, VIC **151 J5**
Beaconsfield, WA **362 C5**
Beaconsfield Upper, VIC 151 J5, **212 C3**
Beagle Bay, WA **399 F3**
Bealiba, VIC 159 C1, **207 H4**
Beallah, QLD **263 B6**
Beardmore, VIC **212 E2**
Bearii, VIC **208 C2**
Bears Lagoon, VIC **207 J3**
Beaudesert, QLD 235, 235 C2, **287 J5**
Beaudesert, QLD **280 E3**
Beaufort, VIC 159 B3, **211 G1**
Beaumaris, TAS **481 J3**
Beaumaris, VIC **150 E4**
Beaumont, NSW **97 B1**
Beaumont, SA **302 E1**
Beauty Point, NSW **47 J5**
Beauty Point, TAS 458, **480 D2**
Beazleys Bridge, VIC **207 G4**
Beckenham, WA **363 F4**
Beckom, NSW **118 A6**
Bedford, WA **362 E2**
Bedford Downs, WA **399 J3**
Bedford Park, SA **302 C3**
Bedfordale, WA **365 G3**
Bedgerebong, NSW **118 B4**
Bedourie, QLD **280 C6**
Bedourie, QLD **286 E2**
Bedunburru, WA **399 F3**
Beeac, VIC 201 F3, **211 H3**
Beebyn, WA **400 E5**
Beech Forest, VIC 201 F5, **211 H4**
Beechboro, WA **363 F2**
Beechford, TAS **480 E1**
Beechmont, QLD 235 D2, **247 A5**
Beechworth, VIC 157, 186, 187 B1, **209 F3**
Beecroft, NSW **47 F4**
Beedelup NP, WA **404 C4**
Beelbangera, NSW **117 J6**
Beenleigh, QLD 227, 235 D1, 247 A1, **287 J5**
Beeliar, WA **362 D6**
Beerburrum, QLD **255 C5**
Beerwah, QLD 255 C5, **287 J4**
Beetaloo, NT **436 D4**
Beete, WA **405 K2**
Bega, NSW 53, **122 D5**
Beilpajah, NSW **117 F4**
Beilpajah, NSW **117 F4**
Belah, NSW **113 F5**
Belair, SA **302 D2**
Belair NP, SA 299, 302 D3
Belarabon, NSW **117 G2**
Belconnen, ACT 135 B2, **137 C2**
Belele, WA **400 E4**
Belfield, NSW **49 G2**
Belford, NSW **59 B1**
Belgrave, VIC 151 J3, 170, 171 B4, 171 B5, **212 C2**
Belgrave South, VIC 151 J4, 171 B5
Belingeramble, NSW **117 H4**
Bell, NSW 80 E1, **119 F5**
Bell, QLD 271 C2, **287 G4**
Bell Bay, TAS **480 D2**
Bella Vista, NSW **46 E4**
Bellalie, QLD **285 F4**
Bellangry, NSW **119 K1**
Bellara, QLD 229 H1, **255 D6**
Bellarwi, NSW **118 B6**

Bellata, NSW **114 C4**
Bellbird, NSW 59 C6, **119 H4**
Bellbird Park, QLD 230 C5
Bellbowrie, QLD 230 C4
Bellbridge, VIC 187 C1, **209 G2**
Bellbrook, NSW **115 G5**
Bellbuoy Beach, TAS **480 D1**
Bellellen, VIC 195 D3, **207 F5**
Bellenden Ker, QLD **239 D5**
Bellerive, TAS **456 E4**
Bellevue, WA **363 G2**
Bellevue, QLD **279 G3**
Bellevue Heights, SA 302 C3
Bellevue Hill, NSW **49 J2**
Bellfield, QLD **279 F6**
Bellfield, VIC **150 E1**
Belli Park, QLD 255 B4
Bellingen, NSW 62 B4, **115 H5**
Bellinger River NP, NSW **115 G5**
Belltrees, NSW **119 H2**
Bellum Bellum, SA 323 E6
Belmont, NSW 71 E1, **119 H4**
Belmont, QLD **231 G3**
Belmont, WA **363 F3**
Belmore, NSW **49 G2**
Beloka, NSW 77 D6, **122 B5**
Belrose, NSW **47 J4**
Beltana, SA **347 F2**
Beltana Roadhouse, SA **347 F2**
Belton, SA **347 F4**
Belyando Crossing, QLD **282 C3**
Belyuen, NT **432 C3**
Bemboka, NSW **122 C5**
Bemm River, VIC **214 A5**
Ben Boyd NP, NSW 38, 122 D5, **122 D6**
Ben Buckler, NSW **49 K2**
Ben Bullen, NSW **119 F4**
Ben Halls Gap NP, NSW **119 H2**
Ben Lomond, NSW **115 F4**
Ben Lomond NP, TAS 448, **481 G3**
Ben Lomond Ski Village, TAS **481 G3**
Bena, VIC **212 C4**
Benalla, VIC 157, **208 D4**
Benambra, VIC 187 E3, **209 H5**
Benanee, NSW **120 C1**
Benaraby, QLD 267 D6, **287 G1**
Benarca, NSW **121 F4**
Benarkin, QLD 271 E2, 271 E4
Benayeo, VIC **206 A3**
Bencubbin, WA **402 E4**
Benda Park, SA **347 H4**
Bendalong, NSW 97 B6, 107 B5
Bendemeer, NSW **114 E5**
Benderring, WA **405 F1**
Bendethera Caves, NSW **122 C4**
Bendick Murrell, NSW **118 C6**
Bendidee NP, QLD **287 G5**
Bendigo, SA **347 G5**
Bendigo, VIC 140, 157, 158, 159, 159 E1, **207 J4**
Bendleby, SA **347 F4**
Bendoc, VIC **214 A3**
Bendolba, NSW **119 H3**
Benetook, VIC **204 D3**
Benger, WA **375 C3**
Bengerang, NSW **114 C2**
Bengworden, VIC 177 B3, **213 G3**
Benlidi, QLD **285 H1**
Benmara, NT **437 J5**
Bentleigh, VIC **150 E3**
Bentleigh East, VIC **150 E3**
Bentley, NSW **115 H2**
Bentley, WA **362 E4**
Benwerrin, VIC 201 G4, **211 J4**
Berajondo, QLD **287 H 2**
Berala, NSW **49 F2**
Berambing, NSW **81 G2**
Berangabah, NSW **117 G3**
Berendebba, NSW **118 B5**
Beresford, QLD **282 C4**
Beresford (Ruin), SA **342 D5**
Bergallia, NSW **122 D4**
Bergins Hill, QLD 230 A5
Bergins Pocket, QLD 255 B3
Beringarra, WA **400 D4**

Berkeley Vale, NSW **71 C4**
Berkshire Park, NSW **46 B3**
Bermagui, NSW **122 D4**
Bermagui South, NSW **122 D5**
Berowra, NSW 47 G2, 71 A6, **119 G5**
Berowra Heights, NSW **47 G2**
Berowra Waters, NSW 44, 47 G2
Berrara, NSW **97 B5**
Berri, SA 306, 333 C2, **349 H1**
Berridale, NSW 77 D5, **122 B4**
Berriedale, TAS **456 B2**
Berrigan, NSW **121 H3**
Berrilee, NSW **47 G2**
Berrima, NSW 53, 107 A2, **122 E1**
Berrimah, NT **418 E3**
Berrinba, QLD **231 F6**
Berringa, VIC 201 F1, **211 H2**
Berringama, VIC **187 D1**
Berriwillock, VIC **207 F1**
Berrook, VIC **204 B4**
Berry, NSW 53–4, 96, 97 C1, 107 C3, **122 E2**
Berry Springs, NT **432 D3**
Berry Springs Nature Park & Territory Wildlife Park, NT **432 D3**
Berrybank, VIC 201 F2, **211 H3**
Berrys Creek, VIC **212 D4**
Bertiehaugh, QLD **277 B4**
Bertram, WA **364 D4**
Berwick, VIC 151 J5, **212 C3**
Bessiebelle, VIC **210 D3**
Beswick, NT **433 G5**
Bet Bet, VIC 159 C1, **207 H5**
Beta, QLD **282 C5**
Bete Bolong, VIC 177 E2, **213 K2**
Bethanga, VIC **209 G3**
Bethania, QLD **231 H6**
Bethany, SA **327 C4**
Bethungra, NSW **122 A2**
Betoota, QLD **284 D2**
Beulah, TAS **480 C3**
Beulah, VIC **206 E2**
Beulah East, VIC **206 E2**
Beulah Park, SA **302 D1**
Beulah West, VIC **206 E2**
Bevendale, NSW **118 D6**
Beverage, VIC **167 E3**
Beverford, VIC **205 G5**
Beveridge, VIC **212 B1**
Beverley, SA **300 C6**
Beverley, WA 367, **402 D5**
Beverley Springs, WA **399 H3**
Beverly Hills, NSW **49 G3**
Beverly Park, NSW **49 G3**
Bews, SA **349 H2**
Bexhill, NSW **84 B2**
Bexley North, NSW **49 G3**
Bexley, NSW **49 G3**
Beyondie, WA **401 F3**
Biala, NSW **122 C2**
Biamanga NP, NSW **122 D5**
Bibaringa, SA **301 F2**
Bibbenluke, NSW **122 C5**
Biboohra, QLD 239 A3, **279 J3**
Bibra Lake, WA 362 D5, 364 D1
Bibyadanga (Lagrange), WA **398 E4**
Bickensfield, WA **364 C1**
Bickley, WA **363 H4**
Bicheno, TAS 459, **481 J5**
Bicton, WA **362 C4**
Biddeston, QLD **271 C4**
Biddon, NSW **118 D1**
Bidgeemia, NSW **121 J3**
Bidgemia, WA **400 C3**
Bidura, NSW **120 D1**
Bidwill, NSW **46 C4**
Bierbank, QLD **285 J3**
Big Billy, VIC **206 B1**
Big Pineapple, QLD 254
Bigga, NSW **118 D6**
Biggara, NSW **77 A5**
Biggara, VIC 187 E1, **209 J3**
Biggenden, QLD **287 H3**
Biggera Waters, QLD **247 C3**
Biggs Flat, SA **303 F4**

Bowen, QLD 237, 262, **282 E2**
Bowen Downs, QLD **281 J4**
Bowen Hills, QLD 225 D1, 230 E2
Bowen Mountain, NSW 81 K2
Bowenfels, NSW 80 C1
Bowenville, QLD 271 C3, **287 G4**
Bower, SA **349 G1**
Boweya, VIC 187 A1, **208 D3**
Bowgada, WA **402 C2**
Bowie, QLD **282 B3**
Bowling Green Bay NP, QLD **282 D1**
Bowna, NSW **121 K4**
Bowning, NSW **122 B2**
Bowral, NSW 55, 107 B2, **122 E1**
Bowraville, NSW 62 B6, **115 H5**
Bowser, VIC 187 A1, **208 E3**
Bowthorn, QLD **278 A4**
Box Hill, NSW **46 D3**
Box Hill, VIC **151 F2**
Box Hill North, VIC 151 F2
Box Hill South, VIC 151 F2
Box Tank, NSW **116 C3**
Box Valley, NSW **117 F2**
Boxgrove, QLD **287 F2**
Boxwood Hill, WA **405 F4**
Boya, WA **363 G2**
Boyanup, WA 375 C5, **404 B3**
Boyeo, VIC **206 C3**
Boyer, TAS **485 F3**
Boyne Island, QLD **267 D5**
Boynedale, QLD 267 D6, **287 G1**
Boyup Brook, WA 367, **404 C3**
Bracalba, QLD **255 B6**
Brachina, SA 313 B1, **347 F3**
Brachina Gorge, SA 312
Bracken Ridge, QLD **229 F5**
Brackenburgh, QLD **280 E4**
Brackendale, NSW **119 H1**
Bracknell, TAS **480 E4**
Bradbury, NSW **48 C5**
Bradbury, SA **303 F3**
Braddon, ACT 129 D1, 135 C3
Bradman Museum, Bowral, NSW 55, 107 B2
Bradshaw, NT 432 C6, **435 C1**
Bradvale, VIC 200 E1, **211 G2**
Braemar, SA **347 G5**
Braemar Bay, NSW **77 D4**
Braeside, QLD **282 E4**
Braeside, VIC **151 F5**
Brahma Lodge, SA **300 D4**
Braidwood, NSW **122 D3**
Braidwood, QLD **285 F2**
Bramfield, SA **346 A6**
Brampton Island, QLD 262, 263 D5
Brampton Island NP, QLD **283 F2**
Brampton Vale, QLD **267 B2**
Bramston Beach, QLD 239 D5, **279 J4**
Bramwell, QLD **277 B4**
Brandon, QLD **282 D1**
Brandy Creek, VIC **212 D3**
Bransby, QLD **284 E5**
Branxholm, TAS **481 H2**
Branxholme, VIC **210 D2**
Branxton, NSW 59 D1, **119 H3**
Brawlin, NSW **122 A2**
Braybrook, VIC **150 B1**
Brayton, NSW **122 D2**
Breadalbane, NSW **122 C2**
Breadalbane, QLD **280 C5**
Break O Day, VIC **212 C1**
Breakfast Creek, QLD **231 F2**
Breakfast Point, NSW 47 G6, 49 G1
Bream Creek, TAS 469 C3, **485 H3**
Breamlea, VIC 201 J3, **211 K3**
Bredbo, NSW 122 J3, **137 C6**
Breeza, NSW **114 D6**
Bremer Bay, WA **405 G4**
Brenda Gate, QLD **286 C6**
Brendale, QLD **228 E5**
Brentwood, SA **348 D2**
Brentwood, VIC **206 D2**
Brentwood, WA **362 D4**
Breona, TAS **480 D4**
Bretti, NSW **119 J2**

Brewarrina, NSW **113 H4**
Briagolong, VIC 177 A2, **213 G2**
Bribbaree, NSW **118 C6**
Bribie Island, QLD 229 J1, **255 D5**
Bribie Island NP, QLD **287 J4**
Bridestowe Lavender Farm, TAS 470, **481 F2**
Bridge Creek, VIC **208 D5**
Bridgeman Downs, QLD 228 E6
Bridgenorth, TAS **480 E3**
Bridgetown, WA 368, **404 C4**
Bridgewater, SA 303 F3, **347 F5**
Bridgewater, TAS **485 F2**
Bridgewater, VIC **207 J4**
Bridport, TAS 459, **481 F1**
Brierfield, NSW 62 B4
Brigalow, QLD 271 A2, **287 G4**
Bright, VIC 160, 186, 187 C2, **209 F4**
Brighton, QLD **229 F5**
Brighton, SA 299, 302 B3
Brighton, TAS 455, **485 F2**
Brighton, VIC **150 D3**
Brighton Downs, QLD **280 E5**
Brighton East, VIC 150 D3
Brighton Le-Sands, NSW 49 H3
Brim, VIC **206 E2**
Brimbago, VIC **349 H4**
Brimpaen, VIC 195 B2, **206 E5**
Brinard, QLD **278 D6**
Brindabella, NSW 122 B3, **137 A3**
Brindabella NP, NSW **122 B2**
Brindiwilpa, NSW **111 E4**
Bringalbert, VIC **206 B5**
Bringelly, NSW **48 A3**
Brinkin, NT **418 C1**
Brinkworth, SA **347 F6**
Brisbane, QLD 218, 224–31, 225 D4, 230 E2, 231 F2, 235 C1, **235 J5**
Brisbane Airport, QLD **231 G1**
Brisbane Cricket Ground, QLD 225 E6, 227
Brisbane Forest Park, QLD 220, 227, 230 A2
Brisbane Ranges NP, VIC **211 K2**
Brisbane River, QLD 225, 226, 227
Brisbane Water NP, NSW **119 H4**
Brit Brit, VIC **210 D1**
Brittania, QLD **282 C2**
Brittons Swamp, TAS **479 B3**
Brixton, QLD **281 H5**
Broad Arrow, WA **403 K3**
Broadbeach, QLD **247 C4**
Broadford, VIC **208 B5**
Broadmarsh, TAS **485 F2**
Broadmere, NT **437 F3**
Broadview, SA **300 D6**
Broadwater, NSW **115 J2**
Broadwater, QLD **271 D1**
Broadwater, VIC **210 D3**
Broadwater NP, NSW **115 J2**
Broadway, NSW **43 B6**
Brocklehurst, NSW **118 D2**
Brocklesby, NSW **121 J3**
Brodribb River, VIC **213 K2**
Brogo, NSW **122 D5**
Broke, NSW **119 G3**
Broken Head, NSW 84 D2
Broken Hill, NSW 55, **116 B2**
Brolgan, NSW **118 C4**
Bromley, QLD **277 C4**
Brompton, SA 297 B1, 302 C1
Bronte, NSW **49 J2**
Bronte, QLD **285 J3**
Bronte, TAS **480 C6**
Bronte Park, TAS **480 C6**
Bronzewing, VIC **204 E5**
Brookdale, WA 363 F6, 365 F2
Brookfield, QLD **230 C3**
Brooklana, NSW 62 B3
Brooklyn, NSW 47 J1, 71 B5
Brooklyn, VIC **150 B2**
Brooklyn Park, SA 302 C1
Brooksby, VIC **206 D5**
Brookside, VIC 187 C2
Brookstead, QLD 271 B4, **287 G5**
Brookton, WA **404 D1**

Brookvale, NSW **47 J5**
Brooloo, QLD **255 B3**
Brooman, NSW 107 A6, **122 D3**
Broome, WA 351, 368–9, 372, **398 E4**
Broome Bird Observatory, WA **398 E4**
Broomehill, WA **404 E3**
Brooms Head, NSW **115 J3**
Brooweena, QLD **287 H3**
Brooyar, QLD 259 A6
Broughton, VIC **206 B3**
Broula, NSW **118 D5**
Broulee, NSW **122 D4**
Brovinia, QLD **287 G3**
Brown Hill Creek, SA 302 D2
Browns Plains, QLD **231 F6**
Bruce, ACT 132, 135 B2
Bruce, SA **347 F4**
Bruce Rock, WA **402 E5**
Brucedale, QLD **286 E4**
Brucknell, VIC 200 D4, **211 F4**
Bruinbun, NSW **118 E4**
Brukunga, SA 303 J2
Brunchilly, NT **436 E6**
Brundah, NSW **118 C5**
Brundee, NSW **97 C2**
Brunette Downs, NT **437 G6**
Brunswick, VIC **150 D1**
Brunswick East, VIC 150 D1
Brunswick Heads, NSW 56, 84 D1, 115 J2, 235 D3
Brunswick Junction, WA 375 C4, **404 C3**
Brunswick West, VIC 150 C1
Bruny Island, TAS 445, 459
Brushwood, NSW **121 K2**
Bruthen, VIC 177 C2, **213 H2**
Bryah, WA **400 E4**
Buangor, VIC 159 B3, **211 G1**
Bubialo, QLD **282 E2**
Bucasia, QLD 263 D6
Buchan, VIC 177 E1, **213 J1**
Buchan Caves, VIC **213 J1**
Buchan South, VIC 177 D1, **213 J1**
Bucheen Creek, VIC 187 D1, **209 H3**
Buchfelde Belt, SA 300 E1
Buckalow, NSW **116 B3**
Buckenderra, NSW 77 D4, **122 B4**
Bucketty, NSW **71 A2**
Buckingham Downs, QLD **280 C4**
Buckinguy, NSW **113 H5**
Buckland, TAS 469 C1, **485 H2**
Buckland, VIC 187 B3, **209 F4**
Buckland Flat, VIC **209 F4**
Buckland Junction, VIC **209 F5**
Buckland Park, SA 300 B2
Buckleboo, SA **346 C5**
Buckleboo, SA **346 C5**
Buckley, VIC **211 J3**
Buckrabanyule, VIC **207 H3**
Budawang NP, NSW **122 D3**
Budda, NSW **112 D6**
Buddabadah, NSW **118 B2**
Budderoo NP, NSW 106, **122 E2**
Buddigower, NSW **118 A5**
Buddina, QLD **255 D4**
Buderim, QLD **255 C4**
Budgeree, NSW **116 B4**
Budgerygar, QLD **285 G2**
Budgewoi, NSW 71 D3, **119 H4**
Budjong Vale, NSW **97 A1**
Buffalo, VIC **212 D4**
Buffalo River, VIC 187 B2, **209 F4**
Bugaldie, NSW **114 B5**
Bugilbone, NSW **114 A4**
Bugle Hut, SA **333 D3**
Bukkulla, NSW **114 E3**
Bulga, NSW **119 G3**
Bulga Downs, WA **401 F6**
Bulgamurra, NSW **116 E4**
Bulgandramine, NSW **118 C3**
Bulgandry, NSW **121 J3**
Bulgary, NSW **121 K2**
Bulgroo, QLD **285 G3**
Bulgunnia, SA **345 K1**
Bulimba, QLD **231 F2**

Bulimba, QLD **279 G3**
Bulingary, NSW 62 A6
Bull Creek, WA **362 D5**
Bulla, VIC **212 A2**
Bulla Bulling, WA **403 J4**
Bullaburra, NSW 81 G5
Bullara, WA **400 B2**
Bullaring, WA **404 E2**
Bullaroon, NSW **113 F3**
Bullarto, VIC 167 B2, **211 J1**
Bullecourt, QLD **280 B2**
Bulleen, VIC **150 E1**
Bullenbalong, NSW **77 D5**
Bullenbung, NSW **121 K2**
Bullengarook, VIC 159 E3, 167 C3, **211 K1**
Bulleringa NP, QLD **279 G4**
Bullfinch, WA **403 G4**
Bullhead Creek, VIC **209 G3**
Bulli, NSW 107 C2, **119 G6**
Bullioh, VIC 187 D1, **209 G3**
Bullita, NT **435 C2**
Bullo River, NT **435 B1**
Bullocks Flat, NSW **122 B4**
Bulloo Creek, SA **347 H4**
Bulloo Downs, QLD **285 F5**
Bulloo Downs, WA **401 F3**
Bullsbrook, WA **402 C5**
Bullumwaal, VIC 177 B1, **213 H2**
Bulman, NT **433 H4**
Bulong (Ruin), WA **403 K4**
Bulwer, QLD **255 E6**
Bulwer Island, QLD **231 G1**
Bumberry, NSW **118 C4**
Bunarba, VIC **208 B3**
Bunbury, WA 372, 374, 375 B5, **404 B3**
Bunda, NT **435 B5**
Bunda Bunda, QLD **278 E6**
Bundabah, NSW **95 B2**
Bundaberg, QLD 237, 259 A2, **287 H2**
Bundaberg Rum Distillery, QLD 237, 259 A2
Bundaburrah, NSW **118 B5**
Bundalagauh, VIC **213 F3**
Bundaleer, QLD **286 C6**
Bundall, QLD **247 C4**
Bundalong, VIC **208 D2**
Bundalong South, VIC **208 E2**
Bundamba, QLD **230 A5**
Bundanoon, NSW 107 A3, **122 E2**
Bundarra, NSW **114 E4**
Bundeena, NSW 49 H5, 107 D1
Bundeena, QLD **285 F4**
Bundella, NSW **119 F1**
Bundjalung NP, NSW **115 J3**
Bundoon Belah, NSW **117 H1**
Bundoona, QLD **285 H5**
Bundure, NSW **117 J3**
Bundure, NSW **121 H2**
Bundycoola, NSW **117 H2**
Bung Bong, VIC 159 C2, **207 H5**
Bungabbee, NSW 84 A3
Bungal, VIC 201 H1, **211 J2**
Bungaree, VIC 167 A3
Bungawalbin NP, NSW **115 H2**
Bungeet, VIC **208 D3**
Bungendore, NSW 122 C3, **137 E2**
Bungeworgorai, QLD **286 E4**
Bungil, VIC **209 G2**
Bungle Bungles see Purnululu (Bungle Bungle) NP, WA
Bungobine, QLD **282 D3**
Bungonia, NSW **122 D2**
Bungonia Caves, NSW **122 D2**
Bungunya, QLD **287 F5**
Bungwahl, NSW 95 D1, **119 J3**
Buniche, WA **405 F2**
Buninyong, VIC 160, 201 G1, **211 H2**
Bunjil, WA **402 C2**
Bunna Bunna, NSW **114 B3**
Bunnaloo, NSW **121 F3**
Bunnan, NSW **119 G2**
Bunnawarra, WA **402 C1**
Bunneringee, NSW **116 C5**
Buntine, WA **402 C3**
Bunya, QLD 228 D6, 230 D1

Carlisle, WA 362 E3
Carlisle River, VIC 200 E5, **211 G4**
Carlo, QLD **280 B5**
Carlo Point, QLD 255 C1, 259 C5
Carlsruhe, VIC 159 E2, 167 C2, **212 A1**
Carlton, NSW 49 G3
Carlton, NSW **113 H6**
Carlton, TAS 469 B3, **485 G3**
Carlton, VIC 147 C1, 148, 150 D2
Carlton Hill, WA **399 K2**
Carlton North, VIC 150 D1
Carmala, NSW **116 D2**
Carmel, WA 363 H4
Carmila, QLD 283 F4
Carmor Plains, NT **432 E3**
Carmyle, QLD 255 A1, 259 A6
Carnamah, WA 402 C2
Carnarvon, QLD **286 D2**
Carnarvon, WA 372-3, **400 B3**
Carnarvon NP, QLD 266, **286 D2**
Carnegie, VIC 150 E3
Carnes, SA 345 J1
Carnes Hill, NSW 48 C3
Carngham, VIC 159 C3
Carnnegie, WA **401 H4**
Caroda, NSW **114 D4**
Carole Park, QLD 230 D5
Caroline Springs, VIC 150 A1
Caron, WA 402 C2
Carool, NSW 247 C6
Caroona, NSW **119 G1**
Caroona, SA **347 G6**
Carpendeit, VIC 200 E4, **211 G4**
Carpentaria Downs, QLD **279 G5**
Carpenter Rocks, SA 323 D6, **349 H6**
Carrabin, WA **403 F4**
Carrai NP, NSW **115 G5**
Carrajung, VIC **213 F4**
Carramar, NSW 48 E2
Carranballac, VIC 200 D1, **211 G2**
Carranya, QLD **285 F2**
Carrara, QLD 247 C4
Carrarang, WA **400 B4**
Carrathool, NSW **121 G1**
Carrick, TAS **480 E3**
Carrickalinga, SA 337 B1
Carrieton, SA **347 F4**
Carroll, NSW **114 D5**
Carron, VIC **207 F3**
Carrum, QLD **280 E2**
Carrum, VIC 151 F6, **212 B3**
Carrum Downs, VIC 151 F6, **212 B3**
Carse O Gowrie, QLD **282 C2**
Carseldine, QLD 229 F6
Carss Park, NSW 49 G3
Carters Ridge, QLD 255 B3
Cartwright, NSW 48 D2
Carwarp, VIC **204 D3**
Carwell, QLD **286 C2**
Cascade, NSW 62 B3
Cascade, WA **405 J3**
Cascade Brewery, Hobart, TAS 452, 453 A5, 454
Cascade NP, NSW **115 H4**
Cascades, TAS 456 C4
Casey, ACT 135 B1
Cashew Nut Farm, NT **432 E3**
Cashmere, QLD 228 D5
Cashmere Downs, WA **403 G1**
Cashmere West, QLD **286 D5**
Cashmore, VIC **210 C4**
Casino, NSW 60, **115 H2**
Cassilis, NSW **119 F2**
Cassilis, VIC **209 H5**
Castambul, SA 301 F6
Casterton, VIC 161, **210 C2**
Castle Cove, NSW 47 H5
Castle Forbes Bay, TAS **484 E4**
Castle Hill, NSW 46 E4
Castle Rock, NSW 91 C1, **119 G3**
Castleburn, VIC 177 A1, **213 G2**
Castlecrag, NSW 47 J5
Castlemaine, VIC 158, 159 D2, 161-2, **207 J5**
Castlevale, QLD **286 C1**

Casuarina, NT 418 C2
Casuarina, WA 364 D4
Casula, NSW 48 D3
Cataby Roadhouse, WA 402 B4
Catamaran, TAS **484 E6**
Cataract Gorge, Launceston, TAS 464, **480 E3**
Cathcart, NSW 122 C5
Cathcart, VIC 159 A3
Cathedral Gorge, WA **399 K3**
Cathedral Beach Resort, QLD 259 D3
Cathedral Hill, QLD **281 F3**
Cathedral Rock NP, NSW **115 G5**
Catherine Field, NSW 48 B4
Catherine Hill Bay, NSW 71 D2
Cattai, NSW 46 D1
Cattle Creek, NT **436 A4**
Catumnal, VIC **207 H2**
Caulfield, VIC 150 D3
Caulfield East, VIC 150 E3
Caulfield North, VIC 150 D3
Caulfield South, VIC 150 E3
Cavan, SA 300 D5
Caveat, VIC **208 C5**
Cavendish, VIC 195 A5, **210 D1**
Caversham, WA 363 F2
Caverton, SA **349 H6**
Caves Beach, NSW 71 E2
Caveside, TAS **480 C4**
Caveton, SA 323 E6
Cawarral, QLD 267 B4
Cawdor, NSW 48 A5
Cawkers Well, NSW **116 D2**
Cecil Hills, NSW 48 C2
Cecil Park, NSW 48 C2
Cecil Plains, QLD 271 B4, **287 G5**
Cedar Bay NP, QLD **279 J2**
Cedar Brush Creek, NSW 71 B2
Cedar Creek, QLD 228 B5, 247 A2
Cedar Pocket, QLD 255 B2
Cedar Point, NSW **115 H2**
Cedarton, QLD 255 B5
Ceduna, SA 307, **345 H4**
Centennial Park, NSW 49 J2
Central (Station), NSW 43 B6, 49 J2
Central Market, Adelaide, SA 296, 297 C4
Central Mountain, NSW 71 B3
Central Station, QLD 259 C4
Central Tilba, NSW 122 D4
Ceradotus, QLD **287 G2**
Ceres, VIC 201 J3, **211 J3**
Cervantes, WA **402 A3**
Cessnock, NSW 59 D6, 60, **119 H4**
Chadstone, VIC 150 E3
Chaelundi NP, NSW **115 G4**
Chaffey, SA **347 J6**
Chain of Lagoons, TAS **481 J4**
Chain Of Ponds, SA 301 G5
Chalky Well, NSW **116 C4**
Challa, WA **400 E6**
Challambra, VIC **206 E3**
Chambers Pillar, NT 423 D2, **442 E4**
Chandada, SA **345 J5**
Chandler, QLD 231 H3
Chandler, SA **341 H2**
Chandlers Creek, VIC **214 B3**
Chandlers Hill, SA 302 D4
Chandos, SA **349 H2**
Chapel Hill, QLD 230 D3
Chapman, ACT 135 A4
Charam, VIC **206 C5**
Charles Darwin NP, NT 418 C4
Charleston, SA 303 J1
Charleville, QLD 241, **286 B3**
Charleyong, NSW **122 D3**
Charlotte Pass, NSW 76, 77 B6, **122 B4**
Charlotte Waters (Ruin), NT **443 F5**
Charlton, VIC **207 G3**
Charmhaven, NSW 71 D3
Charnwood, ACT 135 B2
Charringa, QLD 239 C4
Charters Towers, QLD 241, **282 C2**
Chatham, QLD **286 C2**
Chatham Village, NSW 48 D3
Chatswood, NSW 47 H5

Chatswood West, NSW 47 H5
Chatsworth, NSW 46 B5
Chatsworth, QLD 255 A2, 259 B6
Chatsworth, QLD **280 D3**
Chatsworth, VIC 200 B2, **211 F2**
Cheepie, QLD **285 H3**
Cheetham Flats, NSW 80 A2
Chelmer, QLD 230 D3
Chelsea, VIC 151 F5
Chelsea Heights, VIC 151 F5
Cheltenham, NSW 47 G5
Cheltenham, SA 300 B6
Cheltenham, VIC 150 E4
Cherbourg, QLD **287 H3**
Chermside, QLD 229 F6, 230 E1
Chermside West, QLD 228 E6, 230 E1
Cherrabun, WA **399 H4**
Cherry Gardens, SA 302 E4
Cherrybrook, NSW 47 F4
Cherrypool, VIC 195 A3, **206 D5**
Cherryville, SA 303 F1
Cheshunt, VIC **208 E4**
Cheshunt South, VIC **208 E4**
Chesney, VIC **208 D3**
Chester Hill, NSW 48 E2
Chesterton Range NP, QLD **286 C3**
Chetwynd, VIC **210 C1**
Chewko, QLD 239 A4
Chewton, VIC 159 D2, **207 J5**
Cheyne Beach, WA 369 E3
Chidlow, WA 363 K1
Chidna, QLD **278 B6**
Chifley, NSW 49 J3
Chigwell, TAS 456 B2
Childers, QLD 241, **287 H2**
Chilla Well O.S., NT **438 D4**
Chillagoe, QLD **279 H3**
Chillagoe Caves, QLD **279 G3**
Chillagoe-Mungana Caves NP, QLD **279 G3**
Chillingollah, VIC **205 F5**
Chilpanunda, SA **345 J4**
Chiltern, VIC 187 B1, **209 F3**
Chiltern Hills, QLD **280 E4**
Chinaman Flat, VIC **206 C2**
Chinatown, Brisbane, QLD 224, 225 E2, 226
Chinatown, Melbourne, VIC 147 D2, 148
Chinatown, Sydney, NSW 42, 43 B5, 44
Chinchilla, QLD 242, **287 G4**
Chindera, QLD 247 E6
Chinkapook, VIC **205 F5**
Chippendale, NSW 43 A6, 49 H2
Chipping Norton, NSW 48 E2
Chirnside, QLD **282 D5**
Chirnside Park, VIC 151 H1, 171 A1
Chisholm, ACT 135 C5
Chiswick, NSW 47 G6, 49 G1
Chorkerup, WA 369 C2
Chorregon, QLD 281 G4
Chowey, QLD **287 H3**
Christies Beach, SA 302 A5
Christies Downs, SA 302 B5
Christmas Creek, QLD 235 C2
Christmas Hills, TAS **479 B3**
Chudleigh, TAS **480 C3**
Chullora, NSW 49 F2
Church Point, NSW 47 K3, 71 B6
Churchill, QLD 230 A5
Churchill, VIC **212 E3**
Churchills Head Rock, NT **436 E6**
Churchlands, WA 362 C2
Churinga, NSW **116 D2**
Chute, VIC 159 B3, **211 G1**
Chuwar, QLD 230 A4
Circular Quay, NSW 43 C2, 44, 47 H6, 49 H1
City Beach, WA 362 C2
City Botanic Gardens, Brisbane, QLD 224, 225 D4, 226
Clackline, WA **402 C5**
Clairview, QLD **283 F4**
Clanagh, QLD **281 G4**
Clandulla, NSW **119 F4**
Clapham, SA 302 D2
Claraville, NT 423 E1, **443 F2**

Claraville, QLD **278 E5**
Clare, NSW **117 F4**
Clare, QLD **282 D1**
Clare, SA 307-8, **347 F6**
Claredon Vale, TAS 457 G4
Claremont, TAS 455, 456 B1
Claremont, VIC 187 A2, **208 E4**
Claremont, WA 362 C4
Claremont Meadows, NSW 46 B5
Clarence, NSW 80 D1
Clarence Gardens, SA 302 C2
Clarence Park, SA 302 C2
Clarence Point, TAS **480 D2**
Clarencetown, NSW **119 H3**
Clarendon, SA 302 D4
Clarendon, TAS **481 F4**
Clarendon, VIC 201 H1
Clareville, NSW 47 K3
Clarina, QLD **278 D4**
Clarinda, VIC 151 F4
Clariraba, QLD 247 A4
Clarke River, QLD **279 H6**
Clarkefield, VIC 167 D3, **212 A1**
Clarkes Hill, VIC 167 A3
Claude Road, TAS **480 B3**
Claverton, QLD **285 J4**
Clay Wells, SA 323 C4
Clayfield, QLD 231 F1
Claymore, NSW 48 C4
Clayton, QLD 259 A2
Clayton, SA 337 E2
Clayton, SA **343 F6**
Clayton, VIC 151 F3
Clayton South, VIC 151 F4
Clear Lake, VIC **206 D5**
Clear Mountain, QLD 228 C5
Clear Ridge, NSW **118 B5**
Clearview, SA 300 D6
Cleary, WA **402 E3**
Cleland, SA 302 E2
Cleland Wildlife Park, SA 299, 302 E2
Clematis, VIC 151 K3, 171 D5
Clermont, QLD 242, **282 D4**
Cleve, SA 308, **346 C6**
Cleveland, QLD 227, 231 K4, 235 D1
Cleveland, TAS **481 F4**
Clifford Creek, WA **400 D3**
Clifton, QLD 235 A2, 271 D5, **287 H5**
Clifton, QLD **285 G2**
Clifton Beach, QLD 239 C2, **279 J3**
Clifton Beach, TAS 455, 469 A4, **485 G4**
Clifton Creek, VIC 177 C2
Clifton Gardens, NSW 47 J6, 49 J1
Clifton Hill, VIC 150 D1
Clifton Hills, SA **343 G2**
Clifton Park, WA 375 C4
Clifton Springs, VIC 201 K3, **211 K3**
Clio, QLD **281 F3**
Clonagh, QLD **280 D2**
Cloncurry, QLD 242, **280 D2**
Clontarf, NSW 47 J5
Clontarf, QLD 229 G4
Closeburn, QLD 228 C5
Clouds Creek, NSW **115 G4**
Clouds Creek State Forest, NSW 62 A1
Clovass, NSW 84 A3
Clovelly, NSW 49 J2
Clovelly Park, SA 302 C2
Clover Hills, QLD **282 B5**
Cloverdale, WA 363 F3
Cloyna, QLD **287 H3**
Club Terrace, VIC **214 A4**
Clunes, NSW 84 C2
Clunes, VIC 158, 159 C2, 162, **211 H1**
Clybucca, NSW **115 H5**
Clyde, VIC 153 K1, **212 C3**
Clyde North, VIC 151 J6
Clydebank, VIC 177 A3, **213 G3**
Clytie, 1902, TAS **478 A3**
Coalbrook, QLD **281 G2**
Coalcliff, NSW 107 D1
Coal Creek Heritage Village, Korumburra, VIC 175, **212 D4**
Coaldale, NSW **115 H3**
Coasters Retreat, NSW 47 K2

Cowes, VIC 153 H5, 164, 165 C1, **212 B4**
Cowled Landing, SA **346 E5**
Cowper, NSW **115 H3**
Cowra, NSW 64–5, **118 D5**
Cowra Japanese Garden, NSW 64, **118 D5**
Cowwarr, VIC **213 F3**
Crabtree, TAS **485 F3**
Crace, ACT **135 C2**
Cracow, QLD **287 F2**
Cradle Mountain Lake St Clair NP, TAS 445, 448, 472, 473 C3, **480 A4**, **483 D1**
Cradle Mountain Lodge, TAS **480 A4**
Cradle Valley, TAS 473 C1, **480 A4**
Cradoc, TAS **484 E4**
Cradock, SA **347 F4**
Crafers, SA **302 E2**
Crafers West, SA **302 E2**
Craigburn Farm, SA **302 D3**
Craigie, NSW **122 C6**
Craigieburn, VIC 167 E3, **212 B2**
Craiglie, QLD 239 B1, **279 J3**
Craigmore, SA **300 E3**
Craignish, QLD **259 B3**
Cramenton, VIC **204 E4**
Cramphorne, WA **403 F5**
Cramps, TAS **480 D5**
Cranbourne, VIC 151 H6, 153 J1, **212 B3**
Cranbourne East, VIC **151 H6**
Cranbourne North, VIC **151 H6**
Cranbourne South, VIC **153 H6**
Cranbourne West, VIC **151 G6**
Cranbrook, TAS **481 J5**
Cranbrook, WA 369 B1, **404 E4**
Cranebrook, NSW **46 A4**
Craneford, SA **327 E6**
Craven, NSW **119 J3**
Cravensville, VIC 187 D1, **209 H3**
Crawford River, NSW **95 B1**
Crawley, WA **362 D4**
Crayfish Creek, TAS **479 D3**
Crayford, SA **327 B4**
Credo, WA **403 J3**
Creeper Gate, NSW **118 A2**
Creepy Crawly Walk, TAS **484 D3**
Cremorne, NSW 47 J6, 49 J1
Cremorne, TAS 457 K6, 469 A4, **485 G3**
Cremorne, VIC **150 D2**
Cremorne Junction, NSW 47 J6, 49 J1
Cremorne Point, NSW 47 J6, 49 J1
Crendon, QLD **281 F3**
Crescent Head, NSW 65, **115 H6**
Cresswell Downs, NT **437 G5**
Cressy, TAS **480 E4**
Cressy, VIC 201 F2, **211 H3**
Creswick, VIC 159 D3, 165, **211 H1**
Crew, QLD **282 E5**
Crib Point, VIC 153 H4, **212 B4**
Croajingolong NP, VIC 142, **214 C4, 214 C5**
Cromer, NSW **47 J4**
Cromer Heights, NSW **47 J4**
Cronulla, NSW 49 H5, **107 D1**
Crooble, NSW **114 D3**
Crookhaven, NSW **97 D2**
Crookwell, NSW 65, **122 C1**
Croppa Creek, NSW **114 D2**
Crossmaglen, NSW **62 C3**
Crowdy Bay NP, NSW **119 K2**
Crowdy Head, NSW **119 K2**
Crower, SA **323 C3**
Crowlands, VIC 159 B2, **207 G5**
Crown Entertainment Complex, Melbourne, VIC 147 B4, 148
Crows Nest, NSW 47 H6, 49 H1
Crows Nest, QLD 270, 271 D3, **287 H4**
Crows Nest NP, QLD 270, **287 H4**
Crowther, NSW **118 D6**
Croxton East, VIC **210 E2**
Croydon, NSW **49 G2**
Croydon, QLD **278 E4**
Croydon, SA 297 A1, **300 C6**
Croydon, VIC 151 H1, 171 A2
Croydon Hills, VIC 151 H1, 171 A1
Croydon North, VIC 151 H1, 171 A1
Croydon Park, NSW **49 G2**
Croydon Park, SA **300 C6**

Croydon South, VIC 151 H2, 171 A2
Cryon, NSW **114 A4**
Crystal Brook, SA 309, **346 E5**
Crystal Kingdom, NSW **114 B6**
Crystalbrook, QLD **286 D2**
CSIRO Australia Telescope, NSW **114 C4**
CSIRO Discovery, ACT 133
Cuballing, WA **404 D2**
Cubba, NSW **117 H1**
Cubbaroo, NSW **114 B4**
Cudal, NSW **118 D4**
Cuddapan, QLD **284 E2**
Cudgee, VIC 200 C4, **211 F4**
Cudgewa, VIC 187 E1, **209 H3**
Cudgewa Falls, VIC **209 H3**
Cudgewa North, VIC 187 E1, **209 H2**
Cudlee Creek, SA **301 G5**
Cudmirrah, NSW 97 B5, **107 B5**
Cudmore NP, QLD **282 C4**
Cue, WA **400 E5**
Culburra, NSW **107 C4**
Culburra, SA **349 G3**
Culburra Beach, NSW 97 D2, **122 E2**
Culcairn, NSW **121 K3**
Culfearne, VIC **207 J1**
Culgoa, VIC **207 G1**
Culgoa Flood Plain NP, QLD **286 C6**
Culgoa River, NSW **113 H2**
Culgoora, NSW **114 C4**
Cullacabardee, WA **362 E1**
Cullen Bullen, NSW **119 F4**
Culloden, VIC 177 A2, **213 G2**
Cullulleraine, VIC **204 C3**
Culpataroo, NSW **117 F5**
Culpaullin, NSW **116 E2**
Culston, SA **349 H4**
Cultana, SA **347 J4**
Cultowa, NSW **112 C6**
Cumbalum, NSW **84 D3**
Cumberland Park, SA **302 C2**
Cumborah, NSW **113 J3**
Cummins, SA 309–10, **348 B1**
Cumnock, NSW **118 D4**
Cundare, VIC 201 F3, **211 H3**
Cundeelee, WA **407 B3**
Cunderdin, WA **402 D5**
Cundumbul, NSW **118 D3**
Cungelella, QLD **286 C2**
Cungena, SA **345 J4**
Cunnamulla, QLD 244, **285 J5**
Cunnawarra NP, NSW **115 G5**
Cunningham, QLD 271 C6, **287 H5**
Cunyu, WA **401 F4**
Cuppacumbalong, ACT **137 C4**
Cuprona, SA **480 A2**
Curban, NSW **118 D1**
Curbur, WA **400 C4**
Curdie Vale, VIC 200 C4, **211 F4**
Curdimurka (Ruin), SA **342 D6**
Curl Curl, NSW **47 K5**
Curlewis, NSW **114 D6**
Curnamona, SA **347 G3**
Curra, QLD 255 A2, **259 B6**
Currabubula, NSW **119 G1**
Curragh Mine, QLD **282 E5**
Curralong, WA **365 G5**
Curramulka, SA **348 E1**
Currans Hill, NSW **48 B4**
Curraong, NSW **107 C4**
Currarong, NSW 97 E3, **122 E2**
Currawilla, QLD **284 E2**
Currawinya NP, QLD **285 H6**
Currawong Beach, NSW **47 K2**
Currency Creek, SA **337 E2**
Currie, TAS **478 A2**
Currumbin, QLD 244, 247 D5
Currumbin Valley, QLD 247 C6
Currumbin Waters, QLD 247 D5
Currumbin Wildlife Sanctuary, QLD 246, 247 D5

Curyo, VIC **207 F2**
Customs House, Brisbane, QLD 225 D3, 226
Custon, SA **323 E1**
Cuthero, NSW **116 C4**
Cutta Cutta Caves, NT **433 F5**
Cygnet, TAS 461, **485 F4**
Cygnet River, SA 317 C2, **348 D3**

D

Daceyville, NSW **49 J2**
Dadswells Bridge, VIC 195 C1, **206 E5**
Daglish, WA **362 D3**
D'Aguilar, QLD **255 B6**
Daguragu, NT **435 D4**
Dagworth, QLD **279 G4**
Dahwilly, NSW **121 G3**
Daintree, QLD 244, **279 H3**
Daintree NP, QLD 220, 238, 239 A1, **279 H3, 279 J2**
Daisy Dell, TAS 473 D1, **480 B3**
Daisy Hill, QLD **231 H5**
Dajarra, QLD **280 C3**
Dakabin, QLD **228 E4**
Dalbeg, QLD **282 D2**
Dalby, QLD 244–5, 270, 271 B3, **287 G4**
Dales Gorge, WA **400 E2**
Dalgaranga, WA **400 D5**
Dalgety, NSW 77 D6, **122 B5**
Dalgety Downs, WA **400 D4**
Dalgonally, QLD **278 D6**
Dalhousie (Ruin), SA **342 B2**
Dalkeith, WA **362 C4**
Dalma, QLD **267 A4**
Dalmeny, NSW **122 D4**
Dalmore, QLD **281 H5**
Dalmorton, NSW **115 G4**
Dalrymple NP, QLD **282 C1**
Dalton, NSW **122 C2**
Dalveen, QLD **287 H6**
Dalwallinu, WA **402 D3**
Daly River (Police Stn), NT **432 C4**
Daly Waters, NT **436 D2**
Dalyellup, WA **375 B5**
Dalyston, VIC **212 C4**
Dalyup, WA **405 K3**
Damperwah, WA **402 D2**
Dampier, WA 376, **398 B6**
Dampier Downs, WA **399 F4**
Dandala, WA **387 E1**
Dandaloo, NSW **118 B3**
Dandaraga, WA **401 F5**
Dandaragan, WA **402 B4**
Dandenong, VIC 151 G5, **212 B3**
Dandenong North, VIC **151 G4**
Dandenong Ranges, VIC 170
Dandenong Ranges NP, VIC 139, 170
Dandenong South, VIC **151 G5**
Dandongadale, VIC 187 B2, **209 F4**
Dangar Island, NSW **47 J1**
Dangin, WA **402 D5**
Danyo, VIC **204 B5**
Dapto, NSW 107 C2, **119 G6**
Daradgee, QLD **239 D6**
Darch, WA **362 D1**
Dardanup, WA 375 C5, **404 B4**
Dareton, NSW **116 C6**
Dargo, VIC 177 B1, **213 G1**
Darke Peak, SA **346 C6**
Darkin, WA **404 D3**
Darling Downs, QLD 270
Darling Downs, WA **365 F3**
Darling Harbour, NSW 42, 43 B5, 44, 47 H6, 49 H1
Darling Point, NSW 47 J6, 49 J1
Darlinghurst, NSW **49 J2**
Darlington, NSW **49 H2**
Darlington, SA **302 C3**
Darlington, TAS **469 E1**
Darlington, VIC 200 D2, **211 G3**
Darlington, WA **363 H2**
Darlington Penal Settlement, TAS **485 J2**
Darlington Point, NSW **121 H1**
Darnick, NSW **116 E4**

Darnum, VIC **212 D3**
Daroobalgie, NSW **118 C4**
Darr, QLD **281 H5**
Darr Creek, QLD **271 B1**
Darra, QLD **230 D4**
Darraweit Guim, VIC 167 E2, **212 A1**
Darriman, VIC **213 F4**
Darrine, WA **403 H4**
Dartmoor, VIC **210 B3**
Dartmouth, QLD **282 A5**
Dartmouth, VIC 187 D2, **209 H4**
Darwin, NT 410, 416–9, 417 D4, 418 B5, **432 D3**
Darwin Botanic Gardens, NT 416, 417 D3
Darwin Crocodile Farm, NT **432 D3**
Darwin International Airport, NT 418 C3
Darwin wharf precinct, NT 416, 417 E6
Daubeny, NSW **116 D1**
Davenport Downs, QLD **280 E6**
Daveyston, SA **327 A2**
Davidson, NSW **47 H4**
Davidson Whaling Station Historic Site, NSW **122 D6**
Davoren Park, SA **300 E2**
Davyhurst (Ruins), WA **403 J3**
Daw Park, SA **302 C2**
Dawes Point, NSW **43 B1**
Dawesley, SA **303 J 3**
Dawesville, WA 387 A3, **404 B2**
Dawson, SA **347 G5**
Dawson Park, QLD **287 F2**
Dayboro, QLD 228 B3, **287 J4**
Daydream Island, QLD 262
Daylesford, VIC 159 D3, 165–6, 167 A2, **211 J1**
Daymar, QLD **286 E6**
Daysdale, NSW **121 J3**
De Grey, WA **398 C5**
Deagon, QLD **229 G5**
Deakin, ACT 129 B5, 132, 135 B3
Dean, VIC 159 D3, 167 A3, **211 J1**
Dean Park, NSW **46 C4**
Deans Marsh, VIC 201 G4, **211 J4**
Deception Bay, QLD **229 F3**
Deddington, TAS **481 F4**
Dederang, VIC 187 C2, **209 F3**
Dee, TAS **480 C6**
Dee Why, NSW **47 K4**
Dee Why Beach, NSW **47 K4**
Deebing Heights, QLD **230 A6**
Deep Lead, VIC 195 E2, **207 F5**
Deep Well, NT 423 D2, **442 E3**
Deepdene, VIC **150 E2**
Deepwater, NSW **115 F3**
Deepwater NP, QLD **283 H6**
Deer Park, VIC 150 A1, **212 A2**
Deeragun, QLD **279 K6**
Deeral, QLD 239 D4, **279 J4**
Delamere, NT **436 A2**
Delamere, SA **337 B2**
Delaney Creek, QLD **255 B6**
Delburn, VIC **212 E4**
Delegate, NSW **122 B5**
Delegate River, VIC **214 A3**
Delmore Downs, NT **439 J5**
Delny, NT **439 J6**
Deloraine, TAS 461–2, **480 D3**
Deloraine Folk Museum, TAS **480 D3**
Delta Downs, QLD **278 D3**
Delungra, NSW **114 E3**
Den Barm, QLD **271 C2**
Denham, WA 376, **400 B4**
Denham Court, NSW **48 C3**
Denial Bay, SA **345 H4**
Denilcull Creek, VIC **211 F1**
Deniliquin, NSW 65–6, **121 G3**
Denison, VIC **213 F3**
Denistone, NSW **47 G5**
Denistone East, NSW **47 G5**
Denman, NSW 91 C2, **119 G3**
Denmark, WA 369 B3, 376, **404 D5**
Dennes Pt, TAS **485 F4**
Dennington, VIC 200 B4, **210 E4**
D'Entrecasteaux NP, WA **404 B5**
Denver, VIC 159 E2, **207 J6**

Edith Creek, TAS 479 C3
Edith Downs, QLD 281 F2
Edith Falls, NT 433 F5
Edithburgh, SA 310, 348 E2
Edithvale, VIC 150 E5, 212 B3
Edmondson Park, NSW 48 C3
Edmonton, QLD 239 C3, 279 J3
Edmund, WA 400 C3
Edmund Kennedy NP, QLD 279 J4
Edmund Wright House, Adelaide, SA 297 C4, 298
Edsgee, WA 400 B4
Edungalba, QLD 283 F5
Edwards Creek (Ruin), SA 342 C4
Edwardstown, SA 302 C2
Eerwah Vale, QLD 255 C3
Eganstown, VIC 167 A2, 211 J1
Egg Lagoon, TAS 478 A1
Eginbah, WA 398 D6
Ehlma, QLD 287 G4
Eidsvold, QLD 287 G2
Eight Mile Plains, QLD 231 F4
Eildon, VIC 169, 208 D5
Eildon Park, QLD 281 F5
Eimeo, QLD 263 D6
Einasleigh, QLD 279 G5
Ejanding, WA 402 D4
Ekibin, QLD 231 F3
El Arish, QLD 279 J4
El Questro, WA 399 J2
El Trune, NSW 113 G5
Elaine, VIC 201 H1, 211 J2
Elalie, QLD 283 F4
Elanda Point, QLD 255 C2
Elands, NSW 119 J2
Elanora, QLD 247 D5
Elanora Heights, NSW 47 J4
Elbow Hill, SA 346 D6
Elder Park, Adelaide, SA 297 C3, 298
Elderslie, NSW 48 A5
Elderslie, TAS 485 F2
Eldorado, VIC 187 B1, 208 E3
Electrona, TAS 485 F4
Elgin, WA 375 B6
Elgin Vale, QLD 287 H4
Elginbah, NSW 121 G2
Elimbah, QLD 255 C6
Elizabeth, SA 300 E3
Elizabeth Bay, NSW 47 J6, 49 J1
Elizabeth Beach, NSW 119 K3
Elizabeth Downs, NT 432 C4
Elizabeth Downs, SA 300 E3
Elizabeth East, SA 300 E3
Elizabeth Grove, SA 300 E3
Elizabeth North, SA 300 E3
Elizabeth Park, SA 300 E3
Elizabeth South, SA 300 E3
Elizabeth Town, TAS 480 C3
Elizabeth Vale, SA 300 E3
Elizabeth West, SA 300 D3
Elkedra, NT 440 A4
Ella Bay NP, QLD 279 J4
Ella Vale, NSW 113 F3
Ella Valla, WA 400 B4
Ellam, VIC 206 D2
Ellangowan, QLD 271 C5
Elleker, WA 369 C3
Ellen Grove, QLD 230 D5
Ellenborough, NSW 119 K1
Ellenbrae, WA 399 J2
Ellendale, TAS 484 D2
Ellendale, WA 399 G4
Ellerslie, VIC 200 C3, 211 F3
Ellerston, NSW 119 H2
Ellery Ck Gorge, NT 442 D2
Ellinbank, VIC 212 D3
Ellinminyt, VIC 201 F4, 211 H4
Elliott, NT 436 D4
Elliott, QLD 287 H2
Elliott, TAS 480 A1
Elliott Heads, QLD 259 A2, 287 J2
Elliston, SA 345 K6
Elmhurst, VIC 159 B2, 207 G5
Elmina, QLD 286 C4

Elmore, VIC 208 A3
Elong Elong, NSW 118 D2
Elphinstone, QLD 282 E3
Elphinstone, VIC 167 B1, 207 J5
Elsey, NT 433 G6
Elsey Cemetery, NT 433 G6
Elsey NP, NT 433 G6
Elsmore, NSW 114 E3
Elsternwick, VIC 150 D3
Eltham, NSW 84 C2
Elvina Bay, NSW 47 J3
Elvo, QLD 281 F5
Elwood, VIC 150 D3
Embleton, WA 362
Emby, NSW 113 J5
Emerald, QLD 282 D5
Emerald, VIC 119 J4, 151 K4, 169, 171 D5, 212 C2, 245
Emerald Beach, NSW 62 D2, 115 H4
Emerald Hill, NSW 114 C5
Emerald Springs Roadhouse, NT 432 E4
Emerton, NSW 46 B4
Emita, TAS 482 C2
Emita Museum, TAS 482 C2
Emmaville, NSW 115 F3
Emmdale Roadhouse, NSW 117 F2
Emmet, QLD 285 H1
Empire Bay, NSW 71 C5
Emu, VIC 159 B1, 207 G4
Emu Bay, SA 317 C2, 348 D3
Emu Flat, VIC 167 D1, 208 A5
Emu Heights, NSW 81 K5
Emu Junction (Ruin), SA 341 F5
Emu Park, QLD 267 C4, 283 G5
Emu Vale, QLD 271 E6
Enarra, QLD 287 F5
Encounter Bay, SA 337 D2
Endeavour Hills, VIC 151 H4, 171 A6
Endeavour River NP, QLD 279 J2
Eneabba, WA 402 B2
Eneby, QLD 282 C2
Enfield, SA 300 D6
Enfield, TAS 469 A2
Enfield, VIC 201 G1, 211 H2
Enfield South, NSW 49 G2
Engadine, NSW 48 E5
Engineer Barracks, NSW 48 D3
England Creek, QLD 228 A6
Englefield, VIC 210 D1
Enmore, NSW 49 H2
Enmore, NSW 116 D4
Enngonia, NSW 113 F3
Ennuin, WA 403 G4
Enoggera, QLD 230 E2
Enoggera Reservoir, QLD 230 C2
Enryb Downs, QLD 281 G3
Ensay, VIC 213 H1
Entally House, TAS 480 E3
Epala, QLD 267 C5, 283 G6
Epenarra, NT 439 K3
Eppalock, VIC 159 E1
Epping, NSW 47 F5
Epping Forest, TAS 481 F4
Epping Forest NP, QLD 282 C4
Epsilon, QLD 284 E5
Epsom, VIC 159 E1, 207 J4
Erarind, NSW 71 D1
Eriaba, QLD 282 D2
Eribung, NSW 118 B3
Erica, VIC 212 E3
Erigolia, NSW 117 J5
Erina, NSW 71 C4
Erindale, SA 302 E1
Eringa (Ruin), SA 341 J1
Eringa Park, SA 347 H4
Erinundra, VIC 214 A4
Erldunda, NT 423 C2, 442 D4
Erldunda Roadhouse, NT 423 D3, 442 D4
Erlistoun, WA 401 H5
Ermington, NSW 47 F6, 49 F1
Ernest, QLD 247 C4
Eromanga, QLD 285 G3
Erong, WA 400 D4
Erowal Bay, NSW 97 C4
Errabiddy, WA 400 D4

Erriba, TAS 480 B3
Erringibba NP, QLD 287 F4
Errinundra NP, VIC 214 B3
Erskine, WA 387 B2
Erskine Park, NSW 46 B5
Erskinville, NSW 49 H2
Erudina, SA 347 G3
Eschol Park, NSW 48 B4
Escott Resort, QLD 278 B4
Esdai, NSW 91 C3
Esk, QLD 287 H4
Eskdale, QLD 281 H4
Eskdale, VIC 187 C2, 209 G3
Esmeralda, QLD 279 F5
Esperance, WA 378, 405 K3
Essendon, VIC 150 C1, 212 B2
Essendon North, VIC 150 C1
Essendon West, VIC 150 C1
Essex Downs, QLD 281 G3
Etadunna, SA 343 F5
Ethelton, SA 300 B5
Eton, QLD 282 E3
Ettalong Beach, NSW 71 B5
Etty Bay, QLD 239 E6
Euabalong, NSW 117 K4
Euabalong West, NSW 117 J4
Euchareena, NSW 118 D4
Eucla, WA 407 E4
Eucla NP, WA 407 E4
Eucla Telegraph Station (Ruin), WA 407 E4
Eucumbene, NSW 122 B4
Eucumbene Dam, NSW 77 C4
Eudamullah, WA 400 C3
Eudlo, QLD 255 C4
Eudunda, SA 310, 349 F1
Eugowra, NSW 118 C4
Eulo, NSW 116 D4
Eulo, QLD 285 H5
Eulolo, QLD 280 E3
Eumemmerring, VIC 151 G5
Eumundi, QLD 255 C5, 287 J4
Eumungerie, NSW 118 D2
Eungai Creek, NSW 115 H5
Eungella, QLD 281 H4
Eungella NP, QLD 282 E3
Eurabba, NSW 118 C5
Eurack, VIC 201 G3, 211 H3
Eurardy, WA 400 C5
Euratha, NSW 117 K5
Eureka, NSW 84 C2
Eurelia, SA 347 F4
Eurimbula NP, QLD 287 H1
Euroa, VIC 169, 208 C4
Eurobin, VIC 187 C2, 209 F4
Eurobodalla, NSW 122 D4
Eurobodalla NP, NSW 122 D4
Euroka, NSW 80 D5
Eurolie, NSW 113 G2
Eurong, QLD 259 D4, 287 J3
Eurongilly, NSW 122 A2
Euston, NSW 120 C2
Eva Downs, NT 437 F5
Evandale, SA 302 D1
Evandale, TAS 463, 481 F4
Evans Head, NSW 115 J2
Evansford, VIC 159 C2, 207 H6
Evanston, SA 301 F1
Evanston Gardens, SA 300 E1
Evanston Park, SA 301 F1
Evanston South, SA 301 F2
Evatt, ACT 135 B2
Eveleigh, NSW 49 H2
Evelyn Downs, SA 341 J4
Evengy, QLD 281 G6
Everard Park, SA 297 B6, 302 C2
Everton, VIC 187 B1, 208 E3
Everton Hills, QLD 228 E6, 230 D1
Everton Park, QLD 230 E1
Evesham, QLD 281 G5
Evora, QLD 282 B6
Ewan, QLD 279 J5
Ewaninga, NT 423 D1, 442 E2
Ewingsdale, NSW 84 D1
Exeter, NSW 107 A3, 122 E2
Exeter, SA 300 B5

Exeter, TAS 463, 480 E2
Exford, VIC 201 K1, 212 A2
Exmoor, QLD 281 G3
Exmouth, WA 378, 400 B1
Exmouth Gulf, WA 400 B2
Expedition NP, QLD 286 E2
Exton, TAS 480 D3
Eyre Bird Observatory, WA 407 D4

F

Fadden, ACT 135 C5
Failford, NSW 119 J2
Fairbairn RAAF Base, ACT 137 D2
Fairbridge, WA 387 E2
Fairfield, NSW 46 E6, 48 E2
Fairfield, QLD 230 E3
Fairfield, VIC 150 D1
Fairfield, WA 399 G3
Fairfield East, NSW 46 E6, 48 E2
Fairfield Heights, NSW 46 D6, 48 D1
Fairfield West, NSW 46 D6, 48 D1
Fairhill, QLD 282 E5
Fairholme, NSW 118 B4
Fairleigh, QLD 263 C6
Fairlight, NSW 47 J5
Fairlight, QLD 279 G2
Fairview, NSW 118 A4
Fairview, NSW 118 C3
Fairview, QLD 279 G2
Fairview Park, SA 301 F4
Fairyland, QLD 271 A1
Fairymead, QLD 259 A1
Falcon, WA 387 B2
Falls Creek, NSW 97 B3, 107 B4, 122 E2, 186
Falls Creek, VIC 187 D3, 209 G4
Falmouth, TAS 481 J3
Fannie Bay, NT 417 C1, 418 A3
Fanning River, QLD 282 C1
Faraday, VIC 159 E2, 207 J5
Faraway Hill, SA 347 G5
Farina (Ruin), SA 347 F1
Farrer, ACT 135 B4
Fassifern, NSW 71 D1
Fassifern, QLD 235 B2
Faulconbridge, NSW 81 J4
Fawcett, VIC 208 C5
Federal, NSW 84 C1
Federal, QLD 255 B3
Federal (Ruin), SA 342 B1
Federation Square, Melbourne, VIC 147 D3, 148
Feilton, TAS 484 E3
Felixstow, SA 300 D6
Felton East, QLD 271 C5
Female Factory Site, TAS 481 G5
Fentonbury, TAS 484 E2
Fentons Creek, VIC 207 H4
Ferguson, SA 345 K2
Ferguson, VIC 201 F5, 211 H4
Ferguson, WA 375 C5
Fermoy, QLD 281 G5
Fern Tree, TAS 456 B5, 485 F3
Fernbank, VIC 177 B2, 213 G2
Ferndale, WA 362 E4
Fernihurst, VIC 207 H3
Fernlees, QLD 282 D6
Fernleigh, NSW 84 C2
Fernmount, NSW 62 C4
Fernshaw, VIC 212 C2
Fernside, NSW 84 A3
Ferntree Gully, VIC 151 H3, 171 A4
Fernvale, QLD 287 J5
Fernvale, VIC 187 C1
Ferny Creek, VIC 151 J3, 171 B4
Ferny Grove, QLD 230 D1
Ferny Hills, QLD 230 D1
Ferryden Park, SA 300 C6
Fig Tree Pocket, QLD 227, 230 D3
Finch Hatton, QLD 263 A6, 282 E3
Findon, SA 300 B6
Fingal, TAS 481 H4
Fingal, VIC 152 C5
Fingal Bay, NSW 95 C3

Gisborne, VIC 159 E3, 167 D3, 172, **212 A1**
Glacier Rock, SA 337 C2
Gladesville, NSW 47 G6, 49 G1
Gladfield, VIC **207 J2**
Gladstone, NSW **115 H6**
Gladstone, QLD 248, 267 D5, **287 G1**
Gladstone, SA 311, **347 F5**
Gladstone, TAS **481 H1**
Gladysdale, VIC **212 C2**
Glan Devon, QLD 271 D1
Glandore, SA 302 C2
Glanville, SA 300 B5
Glass House Mountains, QLD 255 C5
Glastonbury, QLD 255 A2
Glebe, NSW 49 H2
Glebe, TAS 453 C3
Gleeson, QLD **278 C6**
Glen, WA **400 E5**
Glen Albyn, NSW **116 E3**
Glen Alice, NSW 119 F4
Glen Alpin, QLD **287 H6**
Glen Alpine, NSW 48 B5
Glen Avon, QLD **282 C6**
Glen Boree, SA **345 G3**
Glen Creek, VIC **209 F3**
Glen Davis, NSW 119 F4
Glen Forrest, WA 363 H2
Glen Gailic, NSW 119 G3
Glen Geddes, QLD 267 A3, **283 F5**
Glen Helen, NT 423 B1, **442 B2**
Glen Helen Gorge, NT 423 C1, **442 C2**
Glen Hill, WA **399 K3**
Glen Huntly, VIC 150 E3
Glen Huon, TAS **484 E4**
Glen Idol, NSW **116 C2**
Glen Innes, NSW 68–9, **115 F3**
Glen Iris, VIC 150 E2
Glen Mervyn, WA 375 E6
Glen Ora, NSW **116 E3**
Glen Osmond, SA 302 D2
Glen Ruth, QLD **279 H4**
Glen Valley, VIC 187 D3, **209 H5**
Glen Waverley, VIC 151 F3
Glenaire, VIC 201 F6, **211 G5**
Glenaladale, VIC 177 B2, **213 G2**
Glenalbyn, VIC **207 H4**
Glenalough, VIC 362 D3
Glenalta, SA 302 D3
Glenample, QLD **282 A4**
Glenariff, NSW **113 G5**
Glenaroua, VIC 208 B5
Glenayle, WA **401 G3**
Glenbervie, QLD **280 E3**
Glenbrook, NSW 81 K5, **119 G5**
Glenbrook, WA 375 C5
Glenburgh, WA **400 D4**
Glenburn, VIC **212 C1**
Glencoe, NSW **115 F4**
Glencoe, QLD **278 D4**
Glencoe, SA 323 D5, **349 H6**
Glendale Crossing, ACT 77 E2, **137 C5**
Glendambo, SA **346 B2**
Glendara, NSW **112 B4**
Glenden, QLD **282 D3**
Glendenning, NSW 46 C5
Glendevie, TAS **484 E5**
Glendilla, QLD **285 J5**
Gleneagle, WA 365 K4
Glenelg, SA 296, 299, 302 B2
Glenelg East, SA 302 B2
Glenelg North, SA 302 B2
Glenelg South, SA 302 B2
Glenella, QLD 263 D6
Glenferrie, VIC 150 E2
Glenfield, NSW 48 D3
Glengarland, QLD **279 F1**
Glengarry, NSW **117 K2**
Glengarry, TAS **480 D3**
Glengarry, VIC **212 E3**
Glengower, VIC 159 D2, **207 H5**
Glengowrie, SA 302 B2
Glengyle, QLD **280 C6**
Glenhaughton, QLD **286 E2**
Glenhaven, NSW 46 E4

Glenhope, NSW **112 D3**
Glenhope, VIC **207 K5**
Gleniffer, NSW 62 B4
Glenisla, VIC 195 A3, **210 E1**
Glenlee, VIC **206 D3**
Glenlofty, VIC 159 B2, **207 G5**
Glenloth, VIC **207 G3**
Glenlusk, TAS 456 A2
Glenlyon, QLD **281 F3**
Glenlyon, VIC 159 D2, 167 B2, **207 J6**
Glenmaggie, VIC **213 F2**
Glenmore, QLD **286 E5**
Glenmorgan, QLD **287 F4**
Glenoak, SA 313 C3
Glenora, NSW **112 E4**
Glenora, QLD **279 F5**
Glenora, TAS **484 E2**
Glenorchy, TAS 456 B2
Glenorchy, VIC 195 D1, **207 F5**
Glenore, QLD **278 D4**
Glenore, TAS **480 E3**
Glenorie, NSW 46 E2
Glenormiston, QLD **280 B4**
Glenormiston, VIC 200 D3
Glenormiston North, VIC 200 D3, **211 F3**
Glenorn, WA **403 K1**
Glenreagh, NSW 62 C1, **115 H4**
Glenrowan, VIC 187 A2, **208 E3**
Glenroy, QLD **283 F5**
Glenroy, WA **399 H3**
Glenside, SA 302 D1
Glenstuart, QLD **282 A6**
Glenthompson, VIC 195 D6, 200 A3, 200 B1, **210 E2**
Glenunga, SA 302 D1
Glenusk, QLD **282 B6**
Glenvale, VIC **212 B1**
Glenwood, NSW 46 D4
Glenwood, QLD 255 A1, 259 B5
Globe Derby Park, SA 300 C4
Glossodia, NSW 46 B1
Glossop, SA 333 C2, **349 H1**
Gloucester, NSW 69, **119 J2**
Gloucester Islands NP, QLD **282 E2**
Glynde, SA 300 D6
Gnaraloo, WA **400 B3**
Gnarware, VIC 201 H3, **211 J3**
Gnotuk, VIC 200 D3, **211 G3**
Gnowangerup, WA **404 E3**
Gobondery, NSW 118 B3
Gobur, VIC **208 C5**
Gocup, NSW **122 A2**
Godwin Beach, QLD 229 G1, 255 D6
Gogango, QLD 267 A5, **283 F5**
Gol Gol, NSW **116 C6**
Gol Gol, NSW **116 E5**
Golconda, TAS **481 F2**
Gold Coast, QLD 217, 234, 246
Gold Creek Village, ACT 131, 134
Gold Treasury Museum, Melbourne, VIC 147 F2, 148
Golden Bay, WA 364 C6, **404 B1**
Golden Beach, QLD 255 D5
Golden Beach, VIC 177 B3, **213 G3**
Golden Gate, QLD **278 C4**
Golden Grove, SA 300 E4
Golden Valley, TAS **480 D4**
Golembil, QLD **287 G2**
Gollan, NSW **118 D3**
Golspie, NSW 118 E6
Gomersal, SA 327 A4
Goneaway NP, QLD **281 F5**
Gongolon, NSW 113 H4
Goobang NP, NSW **118 C3**
Gooburrum, QLD 259 A2
Goode, SA **345 K1**
Goodedulla NP, QLD **283 F5**
Goodger, QLD 271 D1
Goodna, QLD 230 C5, 235 C1
Goodnight Scrub NP, QLD **287 H2**
Goodooga, NSW 113 J2
Goodwood, QLD 259 A3
Goodwood, SA 297 C6, 302 D1
Goodwood, TAS 456 C2
Goolgowi, NSW **117 H5**

Goolma, NSW 118 E3
Goolmangar, NSW 84 A2
Gooloogong, NSW 118 C5
Goolwa, SA 311–2, 337 E2, **349 F3**
Goolwa South, SA 337 E2
Goomalibee, VIC **208 D3**
Goomalling, WA **402 D4**
Goomally, QLD **286 E 1**
Goombi, QLD **287 F4**
Goomboorian, QLD 255 B2, 259 B6
Goombungee, QLD 271 D3, **287 H4**
Goomburra, QLD 235 A2, 271 D5
Goomeri, QLD **287 H3**
Goon Nure, VIC 177 B2, **213 H3**
Goonalga, NSW **116 E2**
Goondi, QLD 239 D6
Goondiwindi, QLD 248, **287 F6**
Goondooloo, NT **433 G6**
Goondoon, QLD **287 H2**
Goonellabah, NSW 84 B3
Goonengerry, NSW 84 C1
Goonengerry NP, NSW **115 J2**
Goonery, NSW **112 E4**
Goongarrie, WA **403 J3**
Goongarrie, WA **403 J3**
Goongarrie NP, WA **403 K3**
Goongee, VIC **204 B5**
Goongerah, VIC **214 A3**
Goonoolchrach, NSW **116 E2**
Goonumbla, NSW 118 C4
Goonyella Mine, QLD **282 D4**
Gooralong, WA 365 G5
Gooram, VIC **208 C4**
Goorambat, VIC **208 D3**
Goorawin, NSW **117 H5**
Gooray, QLD **287 F5**
Goornong, VIC **207 K4**
Gooroc, VIC **207 G3**
Gooseberry Hill, WA 363 G3
Goovigen, QLD 267 A6
Gooyea, QLD **285 H2**
Gorae, VIC **210 C3**
Gorae West, VIC **210 C4**
Goranba, QLD **287 G4**
Gordon, ACT 135 B6
Gordon, NSW 47 H5
Gordon, TAS **485 F5**
Gordon, VIC 159 D3, 167 A3, **211 J1**
Gordon (Ruin), SA **347 F4**
Gordon Downs, WA **399 K4**
Gordon Park, QLD 230 E1
Gordonvale, QLD 239 C4, **279 J3**
Gore, QLD 271 B6, **287 G5**
Gore Hill, NSW 47 H6, 49 H1
Gorge Creek, QLD **279 G6**
Gormandale, VIC **213 F3**
Gormanston, TAS **483 C2**
Gorokan, NSW 71 D3
Goroke, VIC **206 C4**
Gorrie, NT **436 C2**
Gosses, SA **346 B2**
Goschen, VIC **207 G1**
Gosford, NSW 69, 71 B4, **119 H5**
Gosnells, WA 363 F5
Gosses, SA **346 B2**
Goughs Bay, VIC **208 D5**
Goulburn, NSW 69–70, **122 D2**
Goulburn River NP, NSW **119 F3**
Goulburn Weir, VIC **208 B4**
Gould Creek, SA 300 E3
Goulds Country, TAS **481 J2**
Government House, Adelaide, SA 297 D3, 298
Government House, Perth, WA 358
Gowanford, VIC **205 G5**
Gowar, VIC 159 D2, **207 J5**
Gowar East, VIC **207 G4**
Gowrie, ACT 135 C5
Gowrie, QLD **287 H5**
Gowrie Park, TAS **480 B3**
Goyura, VIC **206 E2**
Grabben Gullen, NSW **122 C1**
Gracemere, QLD 267 B4, **283 G5**
Gracetown, WA 371 B3, **404 A3**
Graceville, QLD 230 E3
Gradgery, NSW **118 C1**

Gradule, QLD **286 E6**
Grafton, NSW 70, 72, **115 H3**
Graman, NSW **114 E3**
Grampians (Gariwerd) NP, VIC 142, 194, 195, 195 B3, **206 E6**
Granada, QLD **278 C6**
Grandchester, QLD 235 B1, **287 H5**
Grange, QLD 230 E2
Grange, SA 300 B6
Granite, NT 429 B2, **432 E5**
Granite Downs, SA **341 H2**
Granite Flat, VIC 187 D2, **209 G4**
Granite Island, SA 336, 337 D2
Granite Peak, WA **401 G4**
Grantham, QLD 271 E4, **287 H5**
Grantleigh, QLD **283 F5**
Granton, QLD **280 D4**
Granton, TAS **485 F3**
Grantville, VIC **212 C4**
Granville, NSW 46 E6, 48 E1
Granville Harbour, TAS **483 A1**
Granya, VIC 187 D1, **209 G2**
Grass Patch, WA **405 K3**
Grass Valley, WA **402 D5**
Grassdale, VIC **210 C2**
Grassmere, NSW **116 D1**
Grassmere, VIC 200 B3, **210 E3**
Grasstree Hill, TAS 456 E1
Grassy, TAS **478 B3**
Grassy penguin rookery, TAS **478 B3**
Grattai, NSW 118 E3
Gravelly Beach, TAS **480 E2**
Gravesend, NSW **114 D3**
Gray, NT 419 G6
Gray, TAS **481 J4**
Grays Point, NSW 49 G5
Graysholme, QLD **287 G6**
Graytown, VIC **208 B4**
Great Barrier Reef, QLD 217, 218, 223, 238, 262, 277
Great Barrier Reef Marine Park, QLD 221, **279 K2**
Great Basalt Wall NP, QLD **281 J2**
Great Dividing Range 36, 76, 140, 186, 238, 270
Great Keppel Island, QLD 266, 267 C3
Great Mackerel Beach, NSW 47 K2
Great Ocean Road, VIC 199
Great Sandy NP, QLD 220, 255 C1, 258, **287 J3**, **287 K2**
Great Western, VIC 159 A2, 195 E3, **207 F5**
Gredgwin, VIC **207 H2**
Green Creek, QLD **278 E4**
Green Fields, SA 300 D4
Green Gully, NSW 80 D6
Green Head, WA **402 A3**
Green Lake, VIC **206 E4**
Green Mountains, QLD 234
Green Valley, NSW 48 C2
Green Valley, WA 369 C3
Greenacre, NSW 49 F2
Greenacres, SA 300 D6
Greenbank, NT **437 J2**
Greenbushes, WA **404 C3**
Greendale, VIC 159 E3, 167 B3, **211 J1**
Greenethorpe, NSW 118 C5
Greenfield Park, NSW 48 D2
Greenfields, WA 387 C1
Greenhill, QLD **283 F3**
Greenhill, SA 302 E1
Greenhills, WA **402 D5**
Greenmount, QLD 271 D5, **287 H5**
Greenmount, VIC **213 F4**
Greenmount, WA 363 G2
Greenmount East, QLD 271 D5
Greenock, SA 327 B2
Greenough, WA 380, **402 A1**
Greenough Hamlet Historic Site, WA **402 A1**
Greenridge, QLD 255 B3
Greens Beach, TAS **480 D1**
Greens Creek, VIC 159 A1, **207 F5**
Greenslopes, QLD 231 F3
Greenvale, QLD **279 H5**
Greenvale, QLD **279 H5**

High Camp, VIC 167 E1
High Court of Australia, ACT 129 D4, 132
Highbury, QLD 279 F3
Highbury, SA 300 E6
Highbury, WA 404 D2
Highclere, TAS 479 E4
Highcroft, TAS 469 C5, 485 H4
Highett, VIC 150 E4
Highfield, TAS 479 C2
Highfields, QLD 271 D4
Highgate, SA 302 D2
Highgate, WA 359 D2, 362 E3
Highgate Hill, QLD 225 B6, 230 E3
Highland Plains, QLD 271 D3
Highland Plains, QLD 278 A5
Highlands, QLD 285 H2
Highlands, VIC 208 C5
Highvale, QLD 228 B6, 230 B1
Highwycombe, WA 363 F3
Hill End, NSW 118 E4
Hill End, QLD 230 E3
Hill End, VIC 212 D3
Hill Springs, WA 400 B3
Hill Top, NSW 107 B2
Hillarys, WA 362 C1
Hillbank, SA 300 E3
Hillcrest, QLD 230 E6
Hillcrest, SA 300 D6
Hillgrove, NSW 115 F5
Hillgrove, QLD 279 J6
Hillier, SA 300 E1
Hillman, WA 364 C4
Hillsdale, NSW 49 J3
Hillside, NSW 46 E2
Hillside, QLD 280 D2, 286 D3
Hillside, VIC 177 B2
Hillside, WA 398 D6
Hillston, NSW 117 H5
Hilltown, SA 347 F6
Hillview, NSW 117 J2
Hillwood, TAS 480 E2
Hiltaba, SA 346 B4
Hilton, SA 302 C1
Hinchinbrook, NSW 48 C2
Hinchinbrook Island NP, QLD 279 K5
Hindmarsh, SA 302 C1
Hindmarsh Tiers, SA 337 D1
Hindmarsh Valley, SA 337 D2
Hines Hill, WA 402 E5
Hinnomunjie, VIC 187 D3, 209 H5
Hirstglen, QLD 235 A1, 271 D5
Hivesville, QLD 287 H3
Hi-Way Inn Roadhouse, NT 436 D3
HMAS Cerberus, VIC 153 H5
Hobart, TAS 446, 452-7, 453 C4, 454-5, 456 D4, 485 F3
Hobartville, QLD 282 C5
Hobbys Yards, NSW 118 E5
Hodgson, QLD 286 E4
Hodgson River, NT 436 E2
Holbrook, NSW 119 F3
Holbrook, NSW 121 K3
Holden Hill, SA 300 E5
Holder, ACT 135 B4
Holgate, NSW 71 C4
Holland Park, QLD 231 F3
Holland Park West, QLD 231 F3
Hollands Landing, VIC 177 B3, 213 G3
Hollow Tree, TAS 484 E2
Hollydeen, NSW 91 B2
Hollywell, QLD 247 C3
Holmesglen, VIC 150 E3
Holowilena, SA 313 D3, 347 F3
Holroyd, NSW 46 E6, 48 E1
Holroyd, QLD 277 B5
Holsworthy, NSW 48 D4
Holsworthy Barracks, NSW 48 E3
Holt, ACT 135 A2
Holtze, NT 419 H4
Holwell, TAS 480 D2
Home Hill, QLD 249, 282 D1
Home Valley, WA 399 J2
Homeboin, QLD 286 C5
Homebush, NSW 47 G6, 49 G1
Homebush West, NSW 47 F6, 49 F1

Homerton, VIC 210 D3
Homestead, QLD 282 B2
Homevale NP, QLD 282 E3
Homewood, VIC 208 C5
Hook Island, QLD 262, 263 B1
Hookhams Corner, NSW 47 G3
Hookina (Ruin), SA 313 B3, 347 F3
Hooley, WA 400 E1
Hope Island, QLD 247 C3
Hope Valley, SA 300 E5
Hope Valley, WA 364 C3
Hopefield, NSW 121 J4
Hopeland, WA 364 E6
Hopelands, NSW 112 D3
Hopetoun, VIC 206 E2
Hopetoun, WA 405 H4
Hopetoun West, VIC 206 D1
Hopevale, QLD 279 H2
Hopevale, VIC 206 D2
Hordern Vale, VIC 211 H5
Horningsea Park, NSW 48 C3
Hornsby, NSW 47 G4, 71 A6, 119 G5
Hornsby Heights, NSW 47 G3
Horrocks, WA 400 C6
Horse Lake, NSW 116 C2
Horseshoe Bend, NT 423 D2, 442 E4
Horsham, VIC 174, 206 D4
Horsley Park, NSW 46 C6, 48 C1
Hoskinstown, NSW 137 E3
Hotham Heights, VIC 187 C3, 209 G5
Hotham Valley Tourist Railway, WA 387 D3, 392
Hotspur, VIC 210 C3
Houghton, SA 301 F5
Hove, SA 302 B3
Hovea, WA 363 H2
Howard, QLD 259 A3, 287 J2
Howard Springs, NT 419 K6, 426, 432 D3
Howden, TAS 485 F4
Howes Valley, NSW 119 G4
Howlong, NSW 121 J4
Howqua, VIC 208 D5
Howrah, TAS 457 F4
Howth, TAS 480 A1
Hoxton Park, NSW 48 C3
Huckitta, NT 440 A6
Hughenden, QLD 249-50, 281 H2
Hughes, ACT 135 B4
Hughesdale, VIC 150 E3
Humbert River (Ranger Stn), NT 435 D3
Humbug Scrub, SA 301 G3
Hume, ACT 135 C4
Humeburn, QLD 286 A4
Humphrey, QLD 287 H3
Humpty Doo, NT 432 D3
Humula, NSW 122 A3
Hungerford, NSW 112 D2
Hungerford, QLD 285 H6
Hunter, VIC 207 K3
Hunter Valley, NSW 35, 58, 90
Hunters Hill, NSW 47 H6, 49 H1
Huntfield Heights, SA 302 B5
Huntingdale, VIC 151 F3
Huntingdale, WA 363 F5
Huntingfield, NSW 116 B5
Huntingwood, NSW 46 D5
Huntleys Point, NSW 47 G6, 49 G1
Huntly, VIC 159 E1, 207 J4
Huon, VIC 187 C1, 209 G3
Huonville, NSW 116 B2
Huonville, TAS 464, 484 E4
Hurlstone Park, NSW 49 G2
Hurricane, QLD 279 H3
Hurstbridge, VIC 212 B2
Hurstville, NSW 49 G3
Hurstville Grove, NSW 49 G3
Huskisson, NSW 74, 97 C4, 107 B4, 122 E2
Hutt River Province, WA 400 B5
Hyams Beach, NSW 97 C4
Hyde Park, SA 302 D2
Hyde Park, Sydney, NSW 43 C4, 44
Hyden, WA 381, 405 F1
Hyland Park, NSW 62 C5

Hynam, SA 323 E3, 349 H5
Hypurna, SA 347 J6

I

Iandra, NSW 118 C6
Icy Creek, VIC 212 D2
Ida Bay, TAS 484 E5
Ida Valley, WA 403 J1
Idalia NP, QLD 285 H2
Idracowra, NT 423 D2, 442 D4
Iffley, QLD 278 D5, 282 E4
Ilford, NSW 119 F4
Ilfracombe, QLD 282 A5
Illabarook, VIC 201 F1, 211 H2
Illabo, NSW 122 A2
Illawarra, VIC 195 D2, 207 F5
Illawarra, WA 365 K2
Illawong, NSW 49 F4
Illfraville, TAS 480 D2
Illowa, VIC 200 B4
Illpurta, NT 423 C2
Iluka, NSW 74-5, 115 J3
Imanpa, NT 432 C2, 442 C4
Imbergee, NSW 113 J2
Imbil, QLD 255 B3, 287 J4
Imintji, WA 399 H3
Impadna Siding, NT 442 D4
Inala, QLD 230 D5
Indee, WA 398 C6
Indented Head, VIC 152 A1, 201 K3
Indiana, NT 443 G1
Indigo Upper, VIC 209 F3
Indo Pacific Marine, Darwin, NT 416, 417 E5
Indulkana (Iwantja), SA 341 G2
Indwarra NP, NSW 114 E4
Ingebyra, NSW 122 B5
Ingham, QLD 250, 279 J5
Ingle Farm, SA 300 E4
Ingleburn, NSW 48 C4
Ingleburn Military Camp, NSW 48 C3
Ingleside, NSW 47 J3
Inglewood, NSW 271 A6, 287 G6
Inglewood, SA 301 F5
Inglewood, VIC 207 H4
Inglewood, WA 362 E2
Ingoldsby, QLD 271 E4
Ingomar, SA 341 K6
Ingsdon, QLD 282 E4
Injinoo, QLD 277 B2
Injune, QLD 286 E3
Inkerman, QLD 278 D2
Inkerman, SA 348 E1
Inkster, SA 345 J5
Inman Valley, SA 337 C2
Innaloo, WA 362 C2
Innamincka, SA 343 J4
Innes NP, SA 348 C2
Innes Park, QLD 259 A2
Innesowen, NSW 117 G1
Inneston, SA 348 D2
Innesvale, NT 435 D1
Innisfail, QLD 239 D6, 250, 279 J4
Innouendy, WA 400 D4
Institute of Marine Science, QLD 282 D1
Inveralochy, NSW 122 D2
Inverell, NSW 75, 114 E3
Inverell Pioneer Village, NSW 75, 114 E3
Invergordon, VIC 208 C3
Inverleigh, QLD 278 C4
Inverleigh, VIC 201 H2, 211 J3
Inverloch, VIC 174, 212 C4
Inverramsay, QLD 271 E5
Inverway, NT 435 B5
Inyarinya (Kenmore Park), SA 341 F1
Iona, NSW 116 E5
Iowabah, NSW 118 A2
Ipswich, QLD 230 A5, 235 C1, 250-1, 287 J5
Iris Vale, NSW 117 J3
Irishtown, TAS 479 C3
Iron Baron, SA 346 D5
Iron Knob, SA 346 D5
Iron Range NP, QLD 277 C4

Ironbank, SA 302 E3
Ironhurst, QLD 279 F4
Ironpot Creek, QLD 271 C1
Ironside, QLD 230 E3
Irrapatana (Ruin), SA 342 C5
Irrewarra, VIC 201 F3, 211 H3
Irrewillipe, VIC 200 E4, 211 G4
Irrunytju (Wingelinna), WA 406 D4
Irrwelty, NT 439 J5
Irvinebank, QLD 279 H4
Irvingdale, QLD 271 C3
Irwin, WA 402 A2
Irymple, VIC 174, 204 D2
Isaacs, ACT 135 C4
Isabel Downs, QLD 280 E2
Isabella, 1845, TAS 478 B3
Isabella Plains, ACT 135 B5
Isis Junction, QLD 259 A3
Isisford, QLD 281 H6
Isla Gorge NP, QLD 287 F2
Island Bend, NSW 77 C5
Islay Plains, QLD 282 C5
Israelite Bay, WA 407 B5
Italian Gully, VIC 201 F1
Ithaca, QLD 230 E2
Ivandale, NSW 117 F3
Ivanhoe, NSW 117 F4
Ivanhoe, VIC 150 E1
Ivanhoe East, VIC 150 E1
Iwupataka, NT 442 D2

J

Jabiru, NT 426-7, 427 D2, 433 F3
Jabiru East, NT 427 E2
Jabuk, SA 349 H2
Jackadgery, NSW 115 G3
Jackeys Marsh, TAS 480 D4
Jacobs Well, QLD 247 C2
Jallukar, VIC 195 D3, 207 F6
Jallumba, VIC 206 D5
Jamberoo, NSW 107 C3, 122 E2
Jambin, QLD 267 B6
Jamboree Heights, QLD 230 D4
Jamestown, SA 313, 347 F5
Jamieson, VIC 212 D1
Jan Juc, VIC 201 J4, 211 J4
Jancourt East, VIC 200 D4, 211 G4
Jandakot, WA 362 E6
Jandowae, QLD 271 B1, 287 G4
Jane Brook, WA 363 G1
Jannali, NSW 49 F4
Jardine, QLD 267 B3
Jardine River NP, QLD 277 B3
Jardine Valley, QLD 281 H2
Jarklin, VIC 207 J3
Jarradale, WA 365 G5, 404 C1
Jarrahmond, VIC 177 E2, 213 K2
Jarrangbarnmi (Koolpin Gorge), NT 433 F4
Jaspers Brush, NSW 97 C1
Jaurdi, WA 403 H4
Jay Park, QLD 230 D3
Jeedamya, WA 403 K2
Jeeralang Junction, VIC 212 E4
Jeffcott North, VIC 207 G3
Jennacubbine, WA 402 D5
Jennapullin, WA 402 D5
Jenolan Caves, NSW 79, 80 A6, 119 F5
Jeogla, NSW 115 G5
Jeparit, VIC 206 D3
Jerangle, NSW 122 C4, 137 E6
Jericho, QLD 282 B5
Jericho, TAS 485 F1
Jerilderie, NSW 121 H3
Jerrabomberra, NSW 135 D4
Jerramungup, WA 405 F4
Jerry Meadows, NSW 80 A2
Jerrys Plains, NSW 91 E3, 119 G3
Jervis Bay, NSW 96, 97 C4, 107 C5, 122 E2
Jervis Bay Marine Park, NSW 97
Jervis Bay NP, NSW 96, 97
Jervois, NT 443 H1
Jetsonville, TAS 481 G2
Jewel Cave, WA 370, 371 B5
Jigalong, WA 401 G2

Kilcoy, QLD 251, 255 A5, **287 J4**
Kilcunda, VIC **212 C4**
Kilferra, VIC **208 D4**
Kilkenny Park, SA **300 C6**
Kilkivan, QLD **287 H3**
Killara, NSW 47 H5
Killara, WA **400 E4**
Killarney, NT **436 B2**
Killarney, QLD 235 A3, 271 E6, **287 H5**
Killarney, QLD **279 G2**, **282 A2**
Killarney, VIC 200 A4, **210 E4**
Killarney Heights, NSW 47 J5
Killarney Vale, NSW 71 C4
Killawarra, VIC **208 E3**
Killer Whale Museum, Eden, NSW
  67, **122 D6**
Killiecrankie, TAS **482 C1**
Killora, TAS **485 F4**
Kilmany, VIC **213 F3**
Kilmany South, VIC **213 F3**
Kilmore, VIC 167 E2, 175, **212 B1**
Kilmore East, VIC **212 B1**
Kilsyth, VIC 151 H2, 171 B2
Kilsyth South, VIC 151 H2, 171 A2
Kilto, WA **399 F3**
Kimba, QLD **279 G2**
Kimba, SA 315, 346 C5
Kimberley, NSW **116 B4**
Kimberley, TAS **480 C3**
Kimberley Downs, WA **399 G3**
Kimbriki, NSW **113 H5**
Kimburra, QLD **282 B2**
Kin Kin, QLD 255 C2
Kinalung, NSW **116 C2**
Kinchega NP, NSW **116 C3**
Kinchenga, NSW **116 C3**
Kincumber, NSW 71 C4
Kindred, TAS **480 B2**
King Edward River (Doongan), WA **399 H2**
King Island, TAS 445, 446, 460, **478 B2**
King Island Dairies, TAS **478 A2**
King Junction, QLD **279 G2**
King River, NT **429 D3**
King River, NT **433 F5**
King River, WA 369 C3, **404 E5**
King Scrub, QLD **228 B3**
King Solomon's Cave, TAS **480 B3**
King Valley, VIC 187 A2, **208 E4**
Kingaroy, QLD 251, 271 D1, **287 H4**
Kingfisher Bay, QLD 259 C4
Kinglake, VIC **212 C1**
Kinglake Central, VIC **212 B1**
Kinglake NP, VIC **212 C1**
Kinglake West, VIC **212 B1**
Kingoonya, SA **346 B2**
Kingower, VIC **207 H4**
Kings Canyon, NT 409, 423 B1, **442 B3**
Kings Canyon Resort, NT 423 B1, **442 A3**
Kings Creek Station, NT **442 B3**
Kings Cross, NSW 45
Kings Langley, NSW 46 D4
Kings Park, NSW 46 D4
Kings Park, Perth, WA 358, 359 A4,
  360, 361
Kings Park, VIC 150 A1
Kings Plains NP, NSW **115 F3**
Kingscliff, NSW **115 J1**, 235 D3
Kingscote, SA 315, 317 D2, **348 E3**
Kingsdale, NSW **122 D2**
Kingsford, NSW 49 J2
Kingsgrove, NSW 49 G3
Kingsholme, QLD 247 A2
Kingsley, WA 362 D1
Kingsthorpe, QLD 271 D4
Kingston, ACT 129 E6, 135 C3
Kingston, QLD 231 G6
Kingston, TAS 455, **485 F3**
Kingston, VIC 167 A2
Kingston Park, SA 302 B3
Kingston SE, SA 315–6, 323 B2, **349 G4**
Kingston-on-Murray, SA 333 B2, **349 H1**
Kingstown, NSW **114 E5**
Kingstown, WA 395 E3
Kingsville, VIC 150 C2
Kingswood, NSW 46 A5

Kingswood, SA 302 D2
Kinimakatka, VIC **206 C3**
Kinka, QLD 267 C3
Kinlyside, ACT 135 B1
Kinnabulla, VIC **207 F2**
Kinrola Mine, QLD **282 E5**
Kintore, NT **441 B1**
Kinypanial South, VIC **207 H3**
Kioloa, NSW 107 A6, **122 E3**
Kirkalocka, WA **400 E6**
Kirkham, NSW 48 A4
Kirkimbie, NT **435 B4**
Kirkstall, VIC 200 A3, **210 E3**
Kirrawee, NSW 49 F4
Kirribilli, NSW 47 J6, 49 J1
Kirup, WA **404 C3**
Kirwan, WA **402 D3**
Kiwirrkurra, WA **406 D2**
Klemzig, SA **300 D6**
Knockrow, NSW 84 D2
Knockwood, VIC **212 E1**
Knowsley, VIC 159 E1, **207 K4**
Knoxfield, VIC 151 G3
Koah, QLD 239 B3, **279 J3**
Kodj Kodjin, WA **402 E4**
Koetong, VIC **209 H3**
Kogan, QLD **287 G4**
Kogarah, NSW 49 G3
Kogarah Bay, NSW 49 G3
Kojonup, WA 384, **404 D3**
Kokatha, SA **346 B3**
Kokotungo, QLD **287 F1**
Kolan South, QLD **287 H2**
Kolendo, SA **346 C4**
Kondinin, WA **405 F2**
Kondoolka, SA **345 K3**
Kondut, WA **402 D4**
Kongart, SA 323 E4
Kongorong, SA 323 D6, **349 H6**
Kongwak, VIC **212 C4**
Konnongorring, WA **402 D4**
Konupa, QLD **285 H2**
Kooemba, QLD **287 F1**
Koojan, WA **402 C4**
Kookynie, WA **403 K2**
Kookynie, WA **403 K2**
Koolan, WA **399 F2**
Koolanooka, WA **402 C2**
Koolburra, QLD **279 G2**
Koolewong, NSW 71 B4
Kooline, WA **400 D2**
Kooljaman Resort, WA **399 F3**
Kooloonong, VIC **205 G4**
Kooltandra, QLD **283 F4**
Koolunga, SA **347 F6**
Koolyanobbing, WA **403 G4**
Koombooloomba, QLD **279 J4**
Koomooloo, SA **347 G6**
Koonadgin, WA **403 F5**
Koonalda, SA **344 C3**
Koonamore, SA **347 G4**
Koonandan, NSW 121 J1
Koonawarra, NSW **112 A5**
Koonda, VIC **208 C3**
Koondola, WA 362 E1
Koondrook, VIC **207 J1**
Koongamia, WA 363 G2
Koongawa, SA **346 C5**
Koongie Park, WA **399 J4**
Koonibba, SA **345 H3**
Koonkool, QLD 267 B6, **287 G1**
Koonmarra, WA **400 E4**
Koonoomoo, VIC **208 C2**
Koonorigan, NSW 84 A2
Koonwarra, VIC **212 D4**
Koonya, TAS 469 C5, **485 H4**
Kooralbyn, QLD 235 C2
Koorawatha, NSW **118 D5**
Koorda, WA **402 E4**
Koordarrie, WA **400 C2**
Kooreh, QLD **207 G4**
Koorilgah Mine, QLD **282 E5**
Koorkab, VIC **205 G4**
Koorlong, VIC **204 D2**
Koorongara, QLD 271 B5

Koorongara, QLD **287 G5**
Kooroocheang, VIC 167 A2
Koota, QLD **283 F3**
Kootaberra, SA **346 E4**
Koothney, NSW **114 A4**
Kootingal, NSW **114 E5**
Koo-Wee-Rup, VIC **212 C3**
Kooyong, VIC 150 E2
Kopi, SA **346 B5**
Koppio, SA **348 B1**
Koreelah NP, NSW **115 G1**
Koriella, VIC **208 C5**
Korobeit, VIC 167 B3
Koroit, VIC 200 A3, **210 E4**
Korong Vale, VIC **207 H3**
Koroop, VIC **207 J1**
Kororo, NSW 62 D3
Korrbinjal, WA **365 G5**
Korumburra, VIC 175, **212 D4**
Kosciuszko NP, NSW 38, 76, 77, **122 B4**
Kotta, VIC **207 K3**
Kotupna, VIC **208 B3**
Koumala, QLD **283 F3**
Kowanyama, QLD **278 E2**
Kowguran, QLD **287 F4**
Kowrowa, QLD 239 B3
Koyuga, VIC **208 A3**
Krambach, NSW **119 J2**
Krongart, SA **349 H5**
Kroombit Tops NP, QLD **287 G1**
Krowera, VIC **212 C4**
Kubill, QLD **286 B5**
Kudardup, WA 371 C5, **404 B4**
Kudgee, NSW **116 B3**
Kudla, SA **300 E2**
Kuender, WA **405 F2**
Kukerin, WA **404 E2**
Kulde, SA **349 G2**
Kulgera Roadhouse, NT **442 D5**
Kulgera Siding, NT **442 D5**
Kulin, WA **404 E2**
Kulja, WA **402 D3**
Kulkami, SA **349 H2**
Kulkyne, VIC **204 E3**
Kulnura, NSW 71 B3, **119 H4**
Kulpara, SA **348 E1**
Kulpi, QLD 271 C3, **287 H4**
Kultanaby, SA **346 B2**
Kulwin, VIC **204 E4**
Kulwyne, VIC **205 F4**
Kumarina Roadhouse, WA **401 F3**
Kumbarilla, QLD 271 A3, **287 G4**
Kumbatine NP, NSW **115 G6**
Kumbia, QLD 271 C1, **287 H4**
Kunat, VIC **207 H1**
Kundabung, NSW **115 H6**
Kundat Djaru, WA **399 K4**
Kungala, NSW **115 H4**
Kunmunya (Ruin), WA **399 G2**
Kununoppin, WA **402 E4**
Kununurra, WA 384, **399 K2**
Kunwarara, QLD 267 A3, **283 F5**
Kupunn, QLD **287 G4**
Kuraby, QLD 231 G5
Kuranda, QLD 238, 239 B3, 252, **279 J3**
Kuranda Scenic Railway, QLD 239 C3, 252
Kurbayia, QLD **280 C3**
Kuri Bay, WA **399 G2**
Kuridala, QLD **280 D3**
Ku-ring-gai Chase NP, NSW **119 H5**
Kurmond, NSW 46 A1
Kurnell, NSW 49 H4, **119 H5**
Kurnwill, VIC **204 B3**
Kurrajong, NSW **119 G5**
Kurrajong Heights, NSW 81 K1
Kurralta Park, SA 297 A6, 302 C1
Kurri Kurri, NSW 82, **119 H4**
Kurting, VIC **207 H4**
Kurukan, QLD **279 K5**
Kurumbul, QLD **287 F6**
Kurundi, NT **439 J3**
Kurwongbah, QLD **228 D4**
Kuttabul, QLD 263 B6, **282 E3**
Kwinana, WA 364 D4, **402 B6**
Kwolyin, WA **402 E5**

Kyabra, QLD **285 G3**
Kyabram, VIC 175, **208 B3**
Kyalite, NSW **120 D2**
Kyancutta, SA **346 B5**
Kybeyan, NSW **122 C4**
Kybong, QLD 255 B3
Kybybolite, SA 323 E2, **349 H5**
Kyeamba, NSW **122 A3**
Kyeemagh, NSW 49 H3
Kyena, QLD **286 D5**
Kyle Bay, NSW 49 G3
Kyneton, VIC 159 E2, 167 C1, 176, **207 K5**
Kynuna, QLD **280 E3**
Kyogle, NSW 82, 115 H2, 235 C3
Kyong, QLD **282 B4**
Kyvalley, VIC **208 B3**
Kywong, NSW **121 J2**
Kywong, QLD **281 G4**

L

La Perouse, NSW 49 J3, **119 H5**
Laanecoorie, VIC 159 D1, **207 H4**
Laang, VIC 200 C4, **211 F4**
Labrador, QLD 247 C3
Laceby, VIC 187 A1, **208 E3**
Laceys Creek, QLD **228 A3**
Lachlan Downs, NSW **117 H2**
Lady Barron, TAS **482 D3**
Lady Bay, SA 337 B2
Lady Elliot Island, QLD 223, 237
Lady Musgrave Island, QLD 237, **287 J1**
Lady's Pass, VIC **208 A4**
Laen East, VIC **207 F3**
Lagaven, QLD **280 E3**
Laggan, NSW **122 C1**
Laglan, QLD **282 C4**
Laguna, NSW 71 A1
Laguna Quays, QLD 263 A4
Lah, VIC **206 E3**
Laharum, VIC 195 B1, **206 E5**
Laidley, QLD 235 B1, 271 E4, **287 H5**
Lajamanu (Police Stn), NT **435 D5**
Lake Argyle Village, WA **399 K2**
Lake Barlee, WA **403 G1**
Lake Barrine, QLD 238
Lake Bathurst, NSW **122 D2**
Lake Bindegolly NP, QLD **285 H5**
Lake Boga, VIC **207 H1**
Lake Bolac, VIC 195 E6, 200 C1, **211 F2**
Lake Burley Griffin, ACT 125, 126,
  129 A3, 131
Lake Cargelligo, NSW **117 J4**
Lake Cathie, NSW **119 K2**
Lake Cave, WA 370, 371 B4
Lake Charm, VIC **207 H1**
Lake Clifton, WA 375 B1
Lake Conjola, NSW 97 A6, 107 B5, **122 E3**
Lake Cowal, NSW **118 B5**
Lake Dunn, QLD **282 B4**
Lake Eacham, QLD 238
Lake Eildon NP, VIC **208 D6**
Lake Euramo, QLD 238
Lake Everard, SA **346 B3**
Lake Eyre, SA 289
Lake Eyre NP, SA 292, **342 D4**
Lake Gairdner NP, SA **346 B3**
Lake Goldsmith, VIC **211 G1**
Lake Grace, WA **405 F2**
Lake Harry (Ruin), SA **343 F6**
Lake Illawarra, NSW 106, 107 C3, **119 G6**
Lake Julia, WA **403 G4**
Lake King, WA **405 G2**
Lake Leake, TAS **481 H5**
Lake Macquarie, NSW 70, 82–3
Lake Marmal, VIC **207 H3**
Lake Mundi, VIC **210 B2**
Lake Munmorah, NSW 71 D2
Lake Nash, NT **440 E4**
Lake Nerramyne, WA **400 C5**
Lake Rowan, VIC **208 D3**
Lake St Clair, TAS see Cradle Mountain -
  Lake St Clair NP
Lake Stewart, NSW **111 C3**
Lake Tabourie, NSW 107 A6, **122 E3**

Louisville, TAS 469 D1, **485 H2**
Louth, NSW **112 E5**
Louth Bay, SA 348 B1
Loveday, SA 333 B2
Lovett Bay, NSW 47 J2
Low Head, TAS **480 D1**
Lowanna, NSW 62 B2
Lowbank, SA 333 A2
Lowden, WA 375 D6
Lowdina, TAS **485 G2**
Lower Barrington, TAS **480 B2**
Lower Beulah, TAS **480 C3**
Lower Boro, NSW **122 D2**
Lower Glenelg NP, VIC **210 C3**
Lower Hermitage, SA **301 G4**
Lower Hunter NP, NSW **119 H4**
Lower Hunter Valley, NSW 59
Lower Kalgan, WA 369 D3
Lower King, WA 369 D3
Lower Mangrove, NSW 71 A4
Lower Mitcham, SA 302 D2
Lower Mount Hicks, TAS **479 E3**
Lower Norton, VIC **206 D4**
Lower Plenty, VIC 151 F1
Lower Sandy Bay, TAS 453 E6, 456 D5
Lower Turners Marsh, TAS **480 E2**
Lower Wilmot, TAS **480 B2**
Lowesdale, NSW 121 J4
Lowlands, NSW **117 H4**
Lowmead, QLD **287 H2**
Lowood, QLD **287 H5**
Lowther, NSW 80 B3
Loxton, SA 317, 333 C3, **349 H1**
Loxton Historical Village, SA 317, 333 C3
Loxton North, SA 333 D3
Lubeck, VIC **206 E4**
Lucas Heights, NSW 48 E4
Lucinda, QLD **279 J5**
Lucindale, SA 323 D3, **349 H5**
Lucknow, NSW **118 D4**
Lucknow, QLD **280 D4**
Lucky Bay, SA 346 D6
Lucky Downs, QLD **287 F3**
Lucy Creek, NT **440 C5**
Lucyvale, VIC 187 D1, **209 H3**
Luddenham, NSW 48 A2
Ludlow, WA 371 E1
Ludmilla, NT 417 E1, 418 B3
Lue, NSW **119 F3**
Lugarno, NSW 49 F3
Luina, TAS **479 D5**
Lukies Farm, NT **432 D5**
Lumeah, QLD **286 B2**
Lumholtz NP, QLD **279 J5**
Lunawanna, TAS **485 F5**
Lundayra, QLD **287 F5**
Lune River, TAS **484 E5**
Lupton NP, WA **404 D1**
Lurg, VIC **208 D4**
Lurnea, NSW 48 D3
Lurnea, QLD **286 C3**
Lutana, TAS 456 D3
Lutwyche, QLD 230 E2
Lyal, VIC 159 E1
Lygon St, Melbourne, VIC 146, 147 C2
Lymwood, TAS **478 B3**
Lynchford, TAS **483 C2**
Lyndavale, NT 423 C3, **442 C4**
Lyndbrook, QLD **279 G4**
Lyndhurst, NSW 118 D5
Lyndhurst, QLD **279 G5**
Lyndhurst, SA **347 F1**
Lyndhurst, VIC 151 G5
Lyndoch, SA 301 H1, 317–8, 326, 327 A5
Lyndon, WA **400 C2**
Lyneham, ACT 135 C2
Lynton, SA 302 D2
Lynwood, WA 362 E4
Lynwood, NSW **117 G1**
Lyons, ACT 135 B4
Lyons River, WA **400 C3**
Lyonville, VIC 167 B2, **211 J1**
Lyrup, SA 333 D2
Lyrup Heights, SA 333 D2

Lysterfield, VIC 151 H4, 171 B5
Lysterfield South, VIC 151 H4, 171 A5
Lytton, QLD 231 G2

M

Ma Ma Creek, QLD 235 A1
Maaroom, QLD 259 C4
Mabel Creek, SA **341 J5**
Mabel Downs, WA **399 J3**
Macalister, QLD 271 A2, **287 G4**
McAllister, QLD **278 C4**
Macarthur, ACT 135 C5
Macarthur, VIC **210 D3**
McArthur River, NT **437 G3**
Macclesfield, SA 303 G6
McCoys Well, SA **347 G4**
McCrae, VIC 152 D4
Macdonald Park, SA 300 D2
MacDonnell Ranges, NT 422
McDouall Peak, SA **341 K6**
McDougalls Well, NSW 116 B1
McDowall, QLD 228 E6, 230 E1
Macedon, VIC 159 E3, 167 C2, **211 K1**
Macedon Ranges, VIC 166
McGraths Hill, NSW 46 C2
Macgregor, ACT 135 A2
Macgregor, QLD 231 F4
McIntyre, VIC 159 C1, **207 H4**
Mackay, QLD 252, 262, 263 D6
Mackay Harbour, QLD 263 D6
McKees Hill, NSW 84 A3
McKellar, ACT 135 B2
Mackenzie, QLD 231 G4
McKenzie Creek, VIC **206 D4**
Mackillop Bridge, VIC **209 K5**
McKinlay, QLD **280 E3**
McKinnon, VIC 150 E3
Macknade, QLD **279 J5**
Macksville, NSW 62 C6, 85, **115 H5**
Mackunda Downs, QLD **280 E4**
McLachlan, SA **346 B6**
Maclagan, QLD 271 C2
McLaren Flat, SA 302 C6
McLaren Vale, SA 302 C6, **349 F2**
Maclean, NSW 85, **115 H3**
McLoughlins Beach, VIC **213 F4**
McMahons Creek, VIC **212 D2**
McMahons Point, NSW 49 H1
McMaster, QLD **281 G4**
MacMasters Beach, NSW 71 C5
McNaughton, QLD **282 D2**
Macquarie, ACT 135 B2
Macquarie Fields, NSW 48 D3
Macquarie Links, NSW 48 D3
Macquarie Park, NSW 47 G5
Macquarie Pass NP, NSW **119 G6**
Macquarie St, Sydney, NSW 42, 43 C3, 44
Macquarie University, NSW 47 G5
Macrossan, QLD **282 C2**
Macumba, SA **342 B3**
Maddington, WA 363 F5
Madeley, WA 362 D1
Madoonga, WA **400 E5**
Madoonia Downs, WA **407 A4**
Madora, WA **404 B2**
Madura, WA **407 D4**
Madura, WA **407 D4**
Mafeking, VIC 195 D4
Maffra, NSW 77 E6, **122 B5**
Maffra, VIC 177 A2, 180, **213 F3**
Maggea, SA **349 H1**
Maggieville, QLD **278 D4**
Magill, SA 302 E1
Magnetic Island NP, QLD **279 K5**
Magowra, QLD **278 D4**
Magrath Flat, SA **349 G3**
Maguk (Barramundi Gorge), NT **433 F4**
Mahanewo, SA **346 C3**
Mahogany Creek, WA 363 H2
Maianbar, NSW 49 G5
Maida Vale, WA 363 G3
Maidenwell, QLD 271 D2, **287 H4**
Maidstone, VIC 150 B1
Mailapunyah, NT **437 G3**

Mailer Flat, VIC 200 B3, **210 E3**
Maimuru, NSW **118 C6**
Main Beach, QLD 247 C4
Main Range NP, QLD **287 H5**
Main Ridge, VIC 152 E5
Maindample, VIC **208 D5**
Mainoru, NT **433 H5**
Maitland, NSW 58, 86, 119 H3
Maitland, SA 318, **348 E1**
Maitland Downs, QLD **279 H3**
Majestic Orchid Farm, NT 426, **432 D3**
Majors Creek, NSW **122 D3**
Majura, ACT 135 D2
Makowata, QLD **287 H2**
Malabar, NSW 49 J3
Malabar, NSW **113 J3**
Malacura, QLD **279 F5**
Malaga, WA 362 E2
Malagarga, QLD **285 F3**
Malak, NT 418 D2
Malanda, QLD 239 B5, 253, **279 J4**
Malbina, TAS **485 F3**
Malbon, QLD **280 D3**
Malbooma, SA **345 J2**
Malcolm (Abandoned), WA **403 K1**
Maldon, VIC 159 D2, 180, **207 J5**
Maldorkey, SA **347 H4**
Maleny, QLD 255 B5, **287 J4**
Malinns, VIC **213 K1**
Mallacoota, VIC 180–1, **214 C4**
Mallala, SA **349 F1**
Mallanganee, NSW **115 H2**
Mallanganee NP, NSW **115 H2**
Mallawillup, WA 369 B1
Mallee Cliffs NP, NSW **116 D6**
Mallina, WA **398 C6**
Malmsbury, VIC 159 E2, 167 C1, **207 K5**
Malta, QLD **286 C2**
Maltee, SA **345 H4**
Malvern, SA 297 E6, 302 D2
Malvern, VIC 150 E3
Malvern East, VIC 150 E3
Malverton, QLD **282 A6**
Mamboo, QLD **282 C5**
Mambray Creek, SA 346 E5
Manangatang, VIC **205 F4**
Manangoora, NT **437 J2**
Manara, NSW 116 E3
Manara Mine, NSW 116 E3
Manberry, WA **400 B3**
Mandagery, NSW **118 C4**
Mandalond, NSW 71 C2
Mandelman, NSW 116 E4
Mandogalup, WA 364 D3
Mandora, WA **398 D5**
Mandorah, NT **432 D3**
Mandurah, WA 385, 387 C1, **404 B2**
Mandurama, NSW 118 D5
Mandurang, VIC **207 J4**
Maneroo, QLD **281 G5**
Manfred, NSW 116 E4
Mangalo, SA 346 C6
Mangalore, QLD **286 B4**
Mangalore, TAS **485 F2**
Mangalore, VIC **208 B5**
Mangana, TAS **481 H4**
Mangaroon, WA **400 C3**
Mango Hill, QLD 229 F4
Mangoola, NSW 91 C2
Mangoplah, NSW **121 K3**
Mangrove Mountain, NSW 71 A3
Manguri, SA **341 J5**
Manifold, QLD 267 B2
Manildra, NSW **118 D4**
Manilla, NSW 86, **114 D5**
Manilla, NSW **116 C4**
Maningrida (Police Stn.), NT **433 H2**
Manjimup, WA 374, 386, **404 C4**
Manly, NSW 44, 47 K5, **119 H5**
Manly, QLD 227, 231 H2
Manly Vale, NSW 47 J5
Manly West, QLD 231 H2
Manmanning, WA **402 D4**
Mannahill, SA **347 H4**
Mannanarie, SA **347 F5**

Mannering Park, NSW 71 D2
Manners Creek, NT **440 E5**
Manning, WA 362 D4
Manning Point, NSW **119 K2**
Manningham, SA 300 D6
Mannuem Creek, QLD **271 C1**
Mannum, SA 318–9, **349 G2**
Mannus, NSW **122 A3**
Manoora, SA **347 F6**
Mansfield, QLD 231 G4
Mansfield, VIC 181, 187 A3, **208 D5**
Mansfield Park, SA 300 C6
Mantamaru, WA **406 C4**
Mantuan Downs, QLD **282 C6**
Mantung, SA **349 H1**
Manuka, NSW **117 J3**
Manunda, SA **347 H5**
Many Peaks, QLD **287 G2**
Manyallaluk, NT 429 E2, **433 F5**
Manyana, NSW 97 A6
Manypeaks, WA 369 D2
Mapleton, QLD 255 B4
Mapoon, QLD **277 B3**
Maragle, NSW 77 A3
Marakoopa, TAS **480 C4**
Maralinga, SA 344 E1
Marama, SA **349 H2**
Maranalgo, WA **402 E2**
Marananga, SA 327 B3
Maranboy, NT 429 E3
Maranboy (Police Stn), NT **433 F5**
Marandoo, WA **400 E2**
Marangaroo, WA 362 D1
Marathon, QLD **281 G2**
Maraylya, NSW 46 D2
Marayong, NSW 46 D4
Marble Bar, WA **398 D6**
Marble Hill, SA 303 F1
March, NSW **118 D4**
Marchagee, WA **402 C3**
Marcoola, QLD 255 C4
Marcorna, VIC **207 J2**
Marcus Beach, QLD 255 D3
Marcus Hill, VIC **211 K3**
Mardan, VIC **212 D4**
Mardathuna, WA **400 B3**
Mardella, WA 365 F5
Marden, SA 300 D6
Mardie, WA **398 A6**
Mareeba, QLD 239 A3, 253, **279 J3**
Marfield, NSW **117 F3**
Margaret, 1828, TAS **482 E4**
Margaret River, WA 370, 371 B3, 386–8, **404 B4**
Margaret River, WA **399 J4**
Margate, QLD 229 G4
Margate, TAS **485 F4**
Maria Island NP, TAS **485 K2**
Maria NP, NSW **115 H6**
Mariala NP, QLD **285 J3**
Marian, QLD 263 B6, **282 E3**
Maribyrnong, VIC 150 C1
Marillana, WA **401 F2**
Marimo, QLD **280 D2**
Marino, SA 302 B3
Marion, SA 302 C2
Marion Bay, SA **348 D2**
Marion Downs, QLD **280 C5**
Marita Downs, QLD **281 G4**
Maritime Discovery Centre, Portland, VIC 189, **210 C4**
Maritime Museum of Tasmania, Hobart, TAS 453 D4, 454
Markwood, VIC **208 E3**
Marla, SA **341 H3**
Marlborough, QLD **283 F5**
Marleston, SA 302 C1
Marlo, VIC **213 K2**
Marlow Lagoon, NT 419 F5
Marma, VIC **206 E4**
Marmion, WA 362 C1
Marmor, QLD 267 B5, **283 G5**
Marnoo, VIC 159 A1, **207 F4**

Minlaton, SA 319, **348 E2**
Minmindie, VIC **207 H2**
Minnamoolka, QLD **279 H4**
Minnamurra, NSW 106, 107 C3
Minnie Creek, WA **400 C3**
Minnie Downs, QLD **286 B2**
Minnie Water, NSW **115 H4**
Minnies O.S., QLD **279 F4**
Minnipa, SA **346 B5**
Minnivale, WA **402 D4**
Minore, NSW **118 C3**
Mintabie, SA **341 G3**
Mintaro, SA **347 F6**
Minto, NSW 48 C4
Minto, VIC **207 K3**
Minto Heights, NSW 48 C4
Minyip, VIC **206 E3**
Miralie, VIC **205 G5**
Miram, VIC **206 B3**
Miram South, VIC **206 B4**
Miranda, NSW 49 G4
Miranda, NSW **121 F2**
Miranda Downs, QLD **278 E4**
Mirani, QLD 263 B6, **282 E3**
Mirboo, VIC **212 E4**
Mirboo North, VIC **212 D4**
Miriam Vale, QLD 267 E6, **287 H1**
Mirimbah, VIC 187 A3, **208 E5**
Miriwinni, QLD **239 D5**
Mirool, NSW **118 A6**
Mirrabooka, NSW **117 J3**
Mirrabooka, QLD **286 B4**
Mirrabooka, WA 362 D1
Mirranatwa (Mirrinaduwa), VIC 195 C4
Mirri, QLD **280 C3**
Mirtna, QLD **282 B3**
Missabotti, NSW 62 B5, **115 H5**
Mission Beach, QLD **279 J4**
Mistake Creek, NT **435 A4**
Mitakoodi, QLD **280 D2**
Mitcham, SA **302 D2**
Mitcham, VIC 151 G2
Mitchell, ACT **135 C2**
Mitchell, NT **419 H5**
Mitchell, QLD **286 D3**
Mitchell & Alice Rivers NP, QLD **278 E2**
Mitchell Park, SA 302 C2
Mitchell River NP, VIC **213 G2**
Mitchellstown, VIC **208 B4**
Mitchellville, SA **346 D6**
Mitchelton, QLD 230 E1
Mitiamo, VIC **207 J3**
Mitre, VIC **206 C4**
Mitta Mitta, VIC 187 D2, **209 G4**
Mittagong, NSW 87, 107 B2, **119 F6**
Mittagong, QLD **278 E5**
Mittebah, NT **437 J6**
Mittyack, VIC **204 E5**
Miva, QLD 255 A1, 259 A6
Moble, QLD **285 G4**
Moama, NSW **121 F4**
Moana, SA **302 B6**
Mobbs Hill, NSW 47 F5
Mockinya, VIC 195 A2
Mockinyah, VIC **206 D5**
Modanville, NSW 84 B2
Modbury, SA **300 E5**
Modbury Heights, SA **300 E5**
Modbury North, SA **300 E5**
Moe, VIC 183, **212 E3**
Mogal Plain, NSW **118 A3**
Moggill, QLD **230 C4**
Moglonemby, VIC **208 C4**
Mogo, NSW **122 D3**
Mogongong, NSW **118 C5**
Mogriguy, NSW **118 D2**
Mogumber, WA **402 C4**
Moil, NT **418 C2**
Moina, TAS **480 B3**
Mokepilly, VIC 195 D2, **207 F5**
Mole Creek, TAS 465, **480 C3**
Mole Creek Karst NP, TAS **480 B4**
Molesworth, TAS **485 F3**
Molesworth, VIC **208 C5**
Moliagul, VIC 159 C1, **207 H4**

Molka, VIC **208 C4**
Mollerin, WA **402 E3**
Mollongghip, VIC 159 D3, 167 A3, **211 J1**
Mollymook, NSW 107 B5
Molong, NSW **118 D4**
Molonglo Gorge Recreation Area, ACT 127, 135 E4
Molonglo River, ACT 126
Moltema, TAS **480 C3**
Momba, NSW **112 C5**
Mona Vale, NSW 47 K3, 71 B6, **119 H5**
Mona Vale, QLD **285 H3**
Monak, NSW **116 C6**
Monash, ACT **135 B5**
Monash, SA **333 C2**
Monbulk, VIC 151 K3, 171 D3
Moncrieff, ACT **135 C1**
Monegeetta, VIC 167 D2, **212 A1**
Monia Gap, NSW **117 J5**
Monivea, NSW **117 F3**
Monkey Mia, WA **400 B4**
Monkira, QLD **284 D2**
Monomie, NSW **118 B4**
Monstraven, QLD **278 D6**
Mont Albert, VIC 150 E2
Mont Albert North, VIC 151 F2
Montacute, VIC 301 F6
Montagu, TAS **479 B2**
Montagu Bay, TAS 453 E1, 456 E3
Montague Island, NSW 92, **122 D4**
Montana, TAS **480 C4**
Monteagle, NSW **118 C6**
Montejinni, NT **436 B3**
Monterey, NSW 49 H3
Montgomery, VIC 177 A3, **213 G3**
Monto, QLD 256, **287 G2**
Montrose, TAS **456 B2**
Montrose, VIC 151 J2, 171 B2
Montumana, TAS **479 D3**
Montville, QLD **255 C4**
Mooball, QLD 235 D3
Mooball NP, NSW **115 J1**
Moockra, SA **347 F4**
Moodiarrup, WA **404 D3**
Moogara, TAS **484 E3**
Moojeeba, QLD **277 D5**
Mooka, WA **400 C3**
Mookarra, QLD **282 E2**
Moola, QLD 271 C2
Moolah, NSW **117 G3**
Moolap, VIC 201 J3
Moolawatana, SA **347 H1**
Moolbong, NSW **117 G4**
Mooleulooloo, SA **347 J3**
Mooloo, QLD 255 A3
Mooloo Downs, WA **400 C3**
Mooloolaba, QLD 254, 255 D4
Mooloolah, QLD 255 C5
Mooloolerie, NSW **116 D4**
Moolooloo O.S., NT **436 A3**
Moolort, VIC 159 D2, **207 J5**
Moomba (Private), SA **343 H4**
Moonah, TAS 456 C3
Moonambel, VIC 159 B2, **207 G5**
Moonan Flat, NSW **119 H2**
Moonaree, SA **346 C4**
Moonbah, NSW 77 C6
Moonbi, NSW **114 E5**
Moonbria, NSW **121 G2**
Moondarra, VIC **212 E3**
Moondene, NSW **117 F3**
Moonee Beach, NSW 62 D2, **115 H4**
Moonee Ponds, VIC 150 C1
Moonera, WA **407 D4**
Mooney, NSW 71 A5
Mooney Mooney, NSW 47 H1
Moonie, QLD **287 F5**
Moonijin, WA **402 D4**
Moonta, SA 320, **346 E6**
Moonya, QLD **282 A5**
Moonyoonooka, WA **402 A1**
Moora, WA 388, **402 C3**
Moorabbin, VIC 150 E4, **212 B2**
Moorabbin Airport, VIC 150 E4
Mooraberree, QLD **284 D2**

Moorak, QLD **286 C3**
Mooralla, VIC 195 A4
Mooramanna, QLD **286 D5**
Moorara, NSW **116 D4**
Moorarie, WA **400 E4**
Moore, NSW **114 E5**
Moore, QLD 271 E2, **287 H4**
Moore Park, NSW 49 J2
Moore Park, QLD **287 H2**
Moore River NP, WA **402 B4**
Moorebank, NSW 48 D3
Moorebank Village, NSW 48 D3
Mooren, NSW **118 E2**
Moores Pocket, QLD 230 A5
Mooreville, TAS **480 A1**
Moorina, QLD 228 C2
Moorine Rock, WA **403 G4**
Moorland, NSW **119 K2**
Moorleah, TAS **479 E3**
Moorna, NSW **116 C6**
Moorngag, VIC **208 D4**
Moorooduc, VIC 153 G2
Moorook, SA 333 B2, **349 H1**
Moorook South, SA 333 B2
Moorooka, QLD **230 E4**
Mooroolbark, VIC 151 H1, 171 B1
Mooroopna, VIC **208 C3**
Mooroopna North, VIC **208 B3**
Moorooroo, SA 327 C4
Moorrinya NP, QLD **281 H3**
Mootwingee, NSW **116 C1**
Moppa, SA 327 C1
Moppin, NSW **114 C2**
Morago, NSW **121 F3**
Moralana, SA **313 B2**
Moralana, SA 313 B2, **347 F3**
Moralla, VIC **210 D1**
Moranbah, QLD 256, **282 D4**
Morangarell, NSW **118 B6**
Morapoi, WA **403 K2**
Morawa, WA **402 C1**
Moray Downs, QLD **282 C4**
Morayfield, QLD 228 E1, 255 C6
Morchard, SA **347 F5**
Mordialloc, VIC 150 E5, **212 B3**
Morea, VIC **206 B4**
Moree, NSW 87–8, **114 C3**
Morella, QLD **281 G4**
Moresby, QLD **239 D6**
Moreton Bay, QLD 227
Moreton Island, QLD 255 E6
Moreton Island NP, QLD **287 K4**
Moreton Telegraph Station, QLD **277 B4**
Morgan, SA 320, **349 G1**
Morgan Vale, SA **347 H5**
Moriac, VIC 201 H3, **211 J3**
Morialpa, SA **347 H4**
Moriarty, TAS **480 C2**
Morisset, NSW 71 C2, **119 H4**
Morkalla, VIC **204 B3**
Morley, WA 362 E2
Morney, QLD **284 E2**
Morning Bay, NSW 47 J2
Morning Side, NSW **117 G3**
Morningside, QLD 231 F2
Mornington, TAS 457 F3
Mornington, VIC 153 F2, 183, **212 B3**
Mornington, WA **399 H3**
Mornington Peninsula NP, VIC 143, **212 A4**
Moroak, NT **433 H6**
Moroco, NSW **121 G3**
Morongla Creek, NSW **118 D5**
Morpeth, NSW 58
Morphett Vale, SA 302 B5
Morphettville, SA 302 C2
Morri Morri, VIC 159 A1, **207 F4**
Morrisons, VIC 201 H1, **211 J2**
Morstone Downs, QLD **280 B1**
Mortdale, NSW 49 F3
Mortlake, NSW 47 G6, 49 G1
Mortlake, VIC 200 C3, **211 F3**
Mortlock Library of SA, Adelaide, SA 297 D3, 298
Morton NP, NSW **122 D2**
Morton Plains, VIC **207 F2**

Morundah, NSW **121 J2**
Moruya, NSW 88, **122 D4**
Moruya Head, NSW **122 D4**
Morven, QLD **286 C3**
Morwell, VIC 183, **212 E3**
Morwell NP, VIC **212 E4**
Moselle, QLD **281 G2**
Mosman, NSW 47 J6, 49 J1
Mosman Park, WA 362 C4
Moss Vale, NSW 88, 107 B2, **122 E1**
Mossgiel, NSW **117 G4**
Mossman, QLD 239 A1, 256–7, **279 J3**
Mossman Gorge, QLD 238
Mossy Point, NSW **122 D4**
Motajup, VIC 195 B6
Mothar Mountain, QLD **255 B2**
Motpena, SA **313 B1**
Moulamein, NSW **120 E2**
Moulden, NT 419 G6
Moulyinning, WA **404 E3**
Mount Aberdeen NP, QLD **282 D2**
Mount Ainslie, ACT **137 D2**
Mount Alexander, VIC 158
Mount Alford, QLD **235 B2**
Mount Amhurst, WA **399 J4**
Mount Annan, NSW 45, 48 B5
Mount Arrowsmith, NSW **111 D4**
Mount Augustus NP, WA **400 D3**
Mount Augustus Outback Tourist Resort, WA **400 D3**
Mount Barker, SA 303 H3, **349 F2**
Mount Barker, WA 369 C2, 388–9, **404 E4**
Mount Barnett Roadhouse, WA **399 H3**
Mount Barney NP, QLD **287 H5**
Mount Barry, SA **342 A4**
Mount Baw Baw Alpine Village, VIC **212 E2**
Mount Beauty, VIC 184, 187 C2, **209 G4**
Mount Beckworth, VIC **211 H1**
Mount Benson, SA 323 B3
Mount Brockman Mine, WA **400 D2**
Mount Bryan, SA **347 F6**
Mount Buffalo, VIC 143, 186, 187 B2, **209 F4**
Mount Buffalo NP, VIC 143, 184, **209 F4**
Mount Buller Alpine Village, VIC **208 E5**
Mount Bundy, NT **425 D1**
Mount Bundy, NT **432 D4**
Mount Burges, WA **403 J2**
Mount Burr, SA 323 D4, **349 H5**
Mount Carbine, QLD **279 H3**
Mount Carnage, WA **403 J3**
Mount Cavenagh, NT **442 D5**
Mount Celia, WA **407 A2**
Mount Charlton, QLD 263 A6
Mount Claremont, WA 362 C3
Mount Clarence, SA **341 J5**
Mount Clere, WA **400 E3**
Mount Clunie NP, NSW **115 G1**
Mount Colah, NSW 47 G3
Mount Compass, SA 320, 337 D1
Mount Connor Lookout, NT **423 B3**
Mount Coolon, QLD **282 B3**
Mount Coolum, QLD 255 C4
Mount Cooper, QLD **282 C2**
Mount Coot-tha, QLD 224, 226, 230 D2
Mount Cotton, QLD 231 J5
Mount Crawford, SA 301 K3
Mount Crosby, QLD 230 B3
Mount Damper, SA **346 B5**
Mount Dandenong, VIC 151 J2, 170, 171 C3
Mount Dare, SA **342 B1**, 423 E3
Mount Darry, QLD 271 D3
Mount Direction, TAS **480 E2**
Mount Divide, WA **401 G2**
Mount Doran, VIC 201 H1
Mount Doris, NSW **117 G2**
Mount Druitt, NSW 46 C5
Mount Duneed, VIC 201 J3, **211 K3**
Mount Eba, SA **346 B1**
Mount Ebenezer Roadhouse, NT 423 C2, **442 C4**
Mount Eccles NP, VIC **210 D3**
Mount Edgar, WA **398 D6**
Mount Elgin, VIC **206 C3**

Mutchilba, QLD **279 H3**
Mutijulu, NT 423 A3, **441 D4**
Mutooroo, SA **347 J4**
Muttaburra, QLD **282 A4**
Muttama, NSW **122 A2**
Mutton Hole, QLD **278 D4**
Myall, VIC **207 J1**
Myall Creek, SA **346 D4**
Myall Lakes NP, NSW 39, 56, **119 K3**
Myalla, TAS **479 D3**
Myally, QLD **278 C5**
Myalup, WA **404 B2**
Myalup Beach, WA **375 B3**
Myambat, NSW **91 B2**
Myamyn, VIC **210 C3**
Myaree, WA **362 D4**
Myendett, QLD **286 B3**
Mylor, SA **303 F3**
Mylsetom, NSW **62 C4**
Myocum, NSW **84 D1**
Myola, NSW **97 C3**
Myola, QLD **239 B3**
Myola, QLD **278 D5**
Myola, VIC **208 A4**
Mypolonga, SA **349 G2**
Myponga, SA 337 C1, **349 F2**
Myponga Beach, SA **337 C1**
Myria, SA 333 B3, **349 H1**
Myrniong, VIC 167 B3, **211 K2**
Myrrhee, VIC 187 A2, **208 E4**
Myrtle Bank, SA **302 D2**
Myrtle Springs, SA **347 F1**
Myrtleford, VIC 184, 187 B2, **209 F4**
Myrtletown, QLD 229 H6, 231 G1
Mysia, VIC **207 H3**
Mystery, 1850, TAS **482 D5**
Myuna, NSW **113 G3**

N

Naas, ACT **137 C4**
Nabageena, TAS **479 C3**
Nabawa, WA **400 C6**
Nabiac, NSW **119 J2**
Nabowla, TAS **481 F2**
Nackara, SA **347 G5**
Nagaela, NSW **116 B4**
Nagambie, VIC 184, **208 B4**
Nagari, SA **333 E3**
Nagoorin, QLD **287 G1**
Nailsworth, SA **300 D6**
Nairne, SA **303 J 3**
Nairns, WA **387 C2**
Nakara, NT **418 C1**
Nala, TAS **485 G1**
Nalbarra, WA **402 E1**
Nalinga, VIC **208 C3**
Nallan, WA **400 E5**
Namadgi NP, ACT 127, **137 B4**
Namadgi Visitor Centre, ACT **137 C4**
Namatjira Monument, NT **423 C1**
Nambeelup, WA **387 D2**
Nambi, WA **407 A2**
Nambour, QLD 255 C4, 260, **287 J4**
Nambrok, VIC **213 F3**
Nambucca Heads, NSW 62 C5, 91, **115 H5**
Nambung NP, WA 351; 355, **402 A3**
Nana Glen, NSW **62 C2**
Nanambinia, WA **407 B4**
Nanami, NSW **118 C5**
Nanango, QLD 271 D1, **287 H4**
Nandaly, VIC **205 F5**
Nandi, QLD 271 B3, **287 G4**
Nanga Bay, WA **400 B4**
Nangar NP, NSW **118 D4**
Nangerybone, NSW **117 K3**
Nangiloc, VIC **204 E3**
Nangkita, SA **337 D1**
Nangus, NSW **122 A2**
Nangwarry, SA 323 E5, **349 H5**
Nankin, QLD **267 B4**
Nanneella, VIC **208 A3**
Nannup, WA **404 B4**
Nantawarrina, SA **347 G2**

Nanutarra, WA **400 C2**
Nanutarra Roadhouse, WA **400 C2**
Nanya, QLD **282 B5**
Nap Nap, NSW **117 F6**
Napier, WA **369 D2**
Napier Downs, WA **399 G3**
Napoleon, QLD **285 H4**
Napoleons, VIC 201 G1, **211 H2**
Nappa Merrie, QLD **284 E4**
Napperby, NT **439 F6**
Napperby, SA **346 E5**
Napranum, QLD **277 B4**
Napunyah, NSW **112 D5**
Naracoopa, TAS **478 B2**
Naracoorte, SA 321–2, 323 E3, **349 H5**
Naracoorte Caves, SA 322, 323 E3
Naracoorte Caves NP, SA 322, 323 E3
Naradhan, NSW **117 J5**
Narangba, QLD 228 E3, 255 C6
Narara, NSW **71 B4**
Narawntapu NP, TAS **480 D2**
Nardoo, NSW **112 C3**
Nardoo, QLD **278 C5**
Nardoo, QLD **286 B5**
Nareen, VIC **210 C1**
Narellan, NSW **48 A4**
Narellan Vale, NSW **48 B5**
Narembeen, WA **403 F5**
Naremburn, NSW 47 H6, 49 H1
Nargoorin, QLD **267 D6**
Nariel, QLD **286 E5**
Nariel, VIC 187 E2, **209 H3**
Nariel Creek, VIC 187 E1, **209 H3**
Naringal, VIC 200 C4, **211 F4**
Narndee, WA **403 F1**
Narooma, NSW 92, **122 D4**
Narrabeen, NSW 47 K4, 71 B6
Narrabeen Peninsula, NSW **47 K4**
Narrabri, NSW 92, **114 C4**
Narrabundah, ACT **135 C4**
Narrandera, NSW 92–3, **121 J2**
Narraport, VIC **207 F2**
Narrapumelap, VIC **195 D6**
Narrawallee, NSW **107 B5**
Narraway, NSW **113 K5**
Narraweena, NSW **47 J4**
Narrawong, VIC **210 C3**
Narre Warren, VIC **151 H5**
Narre Warren East, VIC 151 J4, 171 B6
Narre Warren North, VIC 151 H4, 171 A6
Narre Warren South, VIC **151 H6**
Narrewillock, VIC **207 G3**
Narriah, NSW **118 A5**
Narridy, SA **347 F6**
Narrien Range NP, QLD **282 C5**
Narrikup, WA 369 C2, **404 E5**
Narrina, SA **347 F2**
Narrogin, WA 389, **404 D2**
Narromine, NSW 93, **118 C3**
Narwee, NSW **49 F3**
Narwietooma, NT 423 C1, **442 C1**
Narwonah, NSW **118 C3**
Naryilco, QLD **284 E5**
Nashdale, NSW **118 D4**
Nashua, NSW **84 C2**
Nashville, QLD **229 F5**
Nathalia, VIC 185, **208 B2**
Nathan, QLD **231 F4**
Nathan Heights, QLD **230 E4**
Nathan River, NT **437 G2**
Natimuk, VIC **206 D4**
National Archives of Australia, ACT **130**
National Capital Exhibition, ACT
   128, 129 D3
National Carillon, ACT 129 E4, 132
National Dinosaur Museum, ACT 130–1,
   135 B2
National Gallery of Australia, ACT
   125, 129 D4, 132
National Gallery of Victoria, Melbourne,
   VIC 147 D4, 148
National Library of Australia, ACT
   128, 129 C4, 132

National Museum of Australia, ACT
   125, 129 B3, 131
National Portrait Gallery, ACT 128,
   129 C4, 132, 134
National Wine Centre, Adelaide, SA
   297 E3, 298
National Zoo & Aquarium, ACT 131, 135 B3
Natone, TAS **480 A2**
Nattai NP, NSW **119 F6**
Natte Yallock, VIC 159 B1, **207 G5**
Nattie, NSW **107 B1**
Natya, VIC **205 G4**
Naval Base WA **364 C3**
Navarre, VIC 159 B1, **207 G5**
N'Dhala Gorge, NT 423 E1, **442 E2**
Nea, NSW **114 D6**
Nebo, QLD **282 D3**
Nectar Brook, SA **346 E5**
Nedlands, WA **362 D4**
Neds Creek, WA **401 F4**
Needles, TAS **480 C3**
Neerdie, QLD **259 B6**
Neerim, VIC **212 D3**
Neerim Junction, VIC **212 D2**
Neerim South, VIC **212 D3**
Neeworra, NSW **114 B2**
Neika, TAS 456 B6, **485 F3**
Neilrex, NSW **118 E2**
Nelia, QLD **281 F2**
Nelia Gaan, NSW **116 D2**
Nelia Outstation, NSW **116 D3**
Nelligen, NSW **122 D4**
Nelson, NSW **46 D3**
Nelson, SA **323 E6**
Nelson, VIC **210 B3**
Nelson Bay, NSW 93, 95 B3, **119 J3**
Nelson Springs, NT **435 B4**
Nelungaloo, NSW **118 C4**
Nembudding, WA **402 E4**
Nemingha, NSW **114 E6**
Nene Valley, SA **323 D6**
Nepabunna, SA **347 G2**
Nerang, QLD 235 D2, 247 B4, **287 J5**
Neranwood, QLD **247 B5**
Nereena, QLD **281 H5**
Nerong, NSW **95 C1**
Nerren Nerren, WA **400 C5**
Nerrena, VIC **212 D4**
Nerriga, NSW **122 D2**
Nerrigundah, NSW **122 D4**
Nerrima, WA **399 G4**
Nerrin Nerrin, VIC 200 D1, **211 F2**
Netallie, NSW **116 E1**
Netherby, QLD **259 A5**
Netherby, SA **302 D2**
Netherby, VIC **206 C3**
Netley, NSW **116 B3**
Netley, SA **302 C1**
Netley Gap, SA **347 H5**
Neuarpurr, VIC **206 B4**
Neukirch, SA **327 D1**
Neumayer Valley, QLD **278 C5**
Neurea, NSW **118 D3**
Neuroodla, SA **313 A3**
Neurum, QLD **255 B6**
Neusa Vale, QLD 255 B2, 259 C6
Neutral Bay, NSW 47 J6, 49 J1
Neutral Junction, NT **439 H4**
Nevertire, NSW **118 B2**
New Chum, NSW **112 D5**
New Chum, QLD **230 B5**
New Crown, NT 423 E3, **443 F5**
New England NP, NSW **115 G5**
New Farm, QLD 226–7, 231 F2
New Forest, WA **400 C5**
New Gisborne, VIC **167 D2**
New Laura Ranger Stn., QLD **279 H1**
New Macdonald Downs, NT **439 J5**
New Mollyan, NSW **118 E1**
New Norcia, WA **402 C4**
New Norfolk, TAS 465, **484 E3**
New Park, NSW **121 J2**
New Residence, SA **333 B3**
New South Wales 34–123
New Town, TAS 453 A1, 455, 456 C3

Newbridge, NSW **118 E5**
Newbridge, VIC 159 D1, **207 H4**
Newbury, VIC 159 E3, 167 B2, **211 J1**
Newcastle, NSW 93–4, **119 H4**
Newcastle Waters, NT **436 D4**
Newdegate, WA **405 G2**
Newee Creek, NSW **62 C6**
Newell, QLD 239 A1, **279 J3**
Newfield, VIC 200 D5, **211 G4**
Newham, VIC 159 E2, 167 D2, **212 A1**
Newhaven, NT **438 D6**
Newhaven, VIC 153 K6, 165 E2, **212 C4**
Newington, NSW 47 F6, 49 F1
Newland, SA **337 D2**
Newlands Mine, QLD **282 D3**
Newlyn, VIC 167 A2, **211 J1**
Newlyn North, VIC **167 A2**
Newman, WA 389–90, **401 F2**
Newmarket, QLD **230 E2**
Newmerella, VIC 177 E2, **213 K2**
Newnes, NSW **119 F4**
Newnes Junction, NSW **80 D1**
Newport, NSW **47 K3**
Newport, VIC **150 D2**
Newport Beach, NSW **47 K3**
Newry, NT **435 B2**
Newry, VIC **213 F2**
Newrybar, NSW **84 D2**
Newstead, QLD **231 F2**
Newstead, VIC 159 D2, 167 A1, **207 J5**
Newton, SA **300 E6**
Newton, VIC **201 F1**
Newton Boyd, NSW **115 G3**
Newtown, NSW **49 H2**
Newtown, QLD **230 A5**
Ngalangkati, WA **399 H4**
Ngangganawili, WA **401 F4**
Nguiu (Police Station), NT **432 C2**
Ngukurr (Police Stn.), NT **433 J6**
Ngunnawal, ACT **135 C1**
Nhill, VIC 185, **206 C3**
Nhulunbuy, NT **434 D2**
Niagara Park, NSW **71 C4**
Niangala, NSW **119 H1**
Nicholas Rivulet, TAS **485 F4**
Nicholls, ACT **135 B1**
Nicholson, VIC 177 C2, **213 H2**
Nicholson, WA **399 K4**
Nickavilla, QLD **285 H3**
Niddrie, VIC **150 C1**
Nielson Park, QLD **259 A1**
Niermur, NSW **121 F3**
Nietta, TAS **480 B3**
Nightcap NP, NSW **115 J2**
Nightcliff, NT **418 B2**
Nikenbah, QLD **259 B3**
Nildottie, SA **349 G2**
Nile, TAS **481 F4**
Nillahcootie, VIC **208 D5**
Nilma, VIC **212 D3**
Nilpena, SA **347 F2**
Nilpinna, SA **342 C4**
Nimaru, QLD **286 B3**
Nimbin, NSW 84 A1, **115 J2**
Nimingarra, WA **398 D5**
Nimmitabel, NSW **122 C5**
Ninda, VIC **207 F1**
Nindigully, QLD **286 E5**
Nindiup, WA **369 C1**
Nine Mile Cowal, NSW **118 C2**
Ningaloo, WA **400 B2**
Ningaloo Marine Park, WA 354, **400 B2**
Ninghan, WA **402 D2**
Ningi, QLD **229 G1**
Ninyeunook, VIC **207 G2**
Nipan, QLD **287 F2**
Nirimba, WA **387 C3**
Nirranda, VIC 200 C4, **211 F4**
Nirranda East, VIC 200 C4, **211 F4**
Nita Downs, WA **398 E4**
Nitmiluk (Katherine Gorge) NP, NT
   409, 413, 428, 429, **433 F5**
Noarlunga, SA **349 F2**
Noarlunga Centre, SA **302 B5**
Noarlunga Downs, SA **302 B5**

Orelia, WA 364 D3
Orford, TAS 466, 469 D1, **485 H2**
Orford, VIC **210 D3**
Orielton, TAS 469 A2, **485 G2**
Orient, QLD **285 F5**
Orient Point, NSW 97 D2
Orientos, QLD **284 E5**
Oriners, QLD **279 F2**
Orkabie, QLD **283 F4**
Ormeau, QLD 247 B2
Ormiston, QLD 231 J3
Ormiston Gorge, NT 423 C1, **442 C2**
Ormley, TAS **481 H4**
Ormond, VIC 150 E3
Ororoo, SA 324, **347 F5**
Orrtipa-Thurra, NT **440 B6**
Ortona, QLD **279 F5**
Osborne, SA 300 B5
Osborne Flat, VIC **209 F3**
Osborne Park, NSW 47 H6, 49 H1
Osborne Park, WA 362 D2
Osborne Well, NSW 121 H3
Osmington, WA 371 C3
Osterley, TAS **484 D1**
Osterley Downs, NSW 117 J2
O'Sullivan Beach, SA 302 A5
Otago, TAS 456 C1
Ottoway, SA 300 C5
Otway NP, VIC **211 H5**
Oudabunna, WA **402 E1**
Oulnina Park, SA **347 H4**
Ourimbah, NSW 71 C4
Ouse, TAS **484 D1**
Outalpa, SA **347 H4**
Outer Harbor, SA 300 B4
Ouyen, VIC 188, **204 E5**
Ovens, VIC 187 B2, **209 F4**
Overflow, NSW **118 A2**
Overland Corner, SA 333 B1
Overlander Roadhouse, WA **400 C4**
Overnewton, NSW **116 E4**
Ovingham, SA 297 B1
Owen, SA **349 F1**
Owen Springs, NT 423 D1, **442 D2**
Oxenford, QLD 247 B3, **287 J5**
Oxers Lookout, WA **400 E2**
Oxford Falls, NSW 47 J4
Oxford Park, QLD 230 D1
Oxley, NSW **117 F6**
Oxley, QLD 230 D4
Oxley, VIC **208 E3**
Oxley Park, NSW 46 B5
Oxley Wild Rivers NP, NSW **115 F5**
Oyster Bay, NSW 49 G4, 95 A3
Oyster Cove, TAS **485 F4**
Ozenkadnook, VIC **206 B5**

P

Paaratte, VIC 200 D5, **211 F4**
Packsaddle Roadhouse, NSW **111 D5**
Padbury, WA 362 C1
Paddington, NSW 43 E6, 49 J2
Paddington, NSW **117 G2**
Paddington, QLD 230 E2
Paddys River, ACT 135 A5
Padstow, NSW 49 F3
Padstow Heights, NSW 49 F3
Padthaway, SA 323 D2, **349 H4**
Page, ACT 135 B2
Pagewood, NSW 49 J3
Pago (Ruin), WA **399 J1**
Pakenham, VIC 151 K6, **212 C3**
Palana, TAS **482 C1**
Palgarup, WA **404 C4**
Pallamallawa, NSW **114 D3**
Pallamana, SA **349 F2**
Pallara, QLD 230 E5
Pallarenda, QLD **279 K6**
Palm Beach, NSW 44, 47 K2, 71 B5
Palm Beach, QLD 247 D5
Palm Cove, QLD 239 C2, 264
Palm Island, QLD **279 K5**
Palm Valley, NT 423 C1, **442 C2**
Palma, QLD 239 D5

Palmer River Roadhouse, QLD **279 H2**
Palmer Valley, NT 423 C2, **442 D3**
Palmerston, ACT 135 C1
Palmerston, NT 419 G5, 428–9
Palmerville, QLD **279 G2**
Palmswood, QLD 255 C4
Palmyra, WA 362 C4
Paloona, TAS **480 B2**
Palparara, QLD **284 E2**
Paluma, QLD **279 J5**
Paluma Range NP, QLD **279 J5**
Palumpa, NT **432 B5**
Pambula, NSW **122 D5**
Pampas, QLD 271 B5
Panania, NSW 48 E3
Panban, NSW **116 E4**
Pandanus Creek, QLD **279 H6**
Pandie Pandie, SA **343 G1**
Pandoin, QLD 267 B4
Pandora Park, QLD **281 G6**
Paney, SA **346 B4**
Panitya, VIC **204 A5**
Panmure, VIC 200 C4, **211 F4**
Pannawonica, WA **400 C1**
Panorama, SA 302 D2
Pantijan, WA **399 G2**
Panton Hill, VIC **212 B2**
Paper Beach, TAS **480 E2**
Pappinbarra, NSW **115 G6**
Papulankutja, WA **406 D4**
Papunya, NT 423 B1, **442 B1**
Para Hills, SA 300 D5
Para Hills West, SA 300 D5
Para Vista, SA 300 D5
Paraburdoo, WA **400 D2**
Parachilna, SA 313 B1, **347 F2**
Paracombe, SA 301 F5
Paradise, SA 300 E6
Paradise, TAS **480 C3**
Paradise, VIC **207 G4**
Paradise Beach (Letts Beach), VIC 177 B3, **213 G3**
Paradise Point, QLD 247 C3
Parafield, SA 300 D4
Parafield Gardens, SA 300 D4
Parakylia, SA **346 C1**
Paralowie, SA 300 D4
Parap, NT 417 E2, 418 B3
Paraparap, VIC 201 H3, **211 J3**
Paratoo, SA **347 G5**
Parattah, TAS **485 G1**
Parawa, SA 337 C2
Pardoo, WA **398 D5**
Pardoo Roadhouse, WA **398 D5**
Parenna, TAS **478 B2**
Parilla, SA **349 H2**
Paringa, NSW **116 B2**
Paringa, SA 333 E1, **349 J1**
Park Beach, TAS 469 B3
Park Holme, SA 302 C2
Park Orchards, VIC 151 G1
Parkdale, VIC 150 E5
Parkerville, WA 363 H2
Parkes, ACT 129 D4, 135 C3
Parkes, NSW 98, **118 C4**
Parkes Radio Telescope, NSW 98, **118 C4**
Parkham, TAS **480 D3**
Parkinson, QLD 230 E5
Parklands, WA 387 C1
Parklea, NSW 46 D4
Parkside, SA 297 E5, 302 D1
Parkside, TAS **481 J3**
Parkville, NSW **119 G2**
Parkville, VIC 150 C1
Parkwood, WA 362 E4
Parliament House, ACT 125, 126, 129 C4, 129 C5, 132, 133–4, 417 E6
Parliament House, Adelaide, SA 297 C3, 298
Parliament House, Brisbane, QLD 225 D4, 226
Parliament House, Darwin, NT 417 D5
Parliament House, Hobart, TAS 453 C4
Parliament House, Melbourne, VIC 147 D2, 148

Parliament House, Perth, WA 359 B3, 360
Parliament House, Sydney NSW 43 D3
Parma, NSW 97 B3
Parmelia, WA 364 D4
Parndana, SA 317 C2, **348 D3**
Parnella, TAS **481 J3**
Parnngurr (Cotton Ck), WA **401 H2**
Paroo, WA **401 F4**
Parrakie, SA **349 H2**
Parramatta, NSW 45, 47 F6, 49 F1, **119 G5**
Parrawe, TAS **479 E4**
Parry Beach, WA 369 A3, **404 D5**
Paruna, SA **349 H2**
Parwan, VIC **211 K2**
Pasadena, SA 302 C2
Paschendale, VIC **210 C2**
Pascoe Vale South, VIC 150 C1
Pasha, QLD **282 D3**
Paskeville, SA **346 E6**
Pastoria East, VIC 167 C1
Pata, SA **349 H1**
Patchewollock, VIC **204 D5**
Pateena, TAS **480 E3**
Paterson, NSW **119 H3**
Paterson, QLD 255 A1, 259 A5
Patersonia, TAS **481 F3**
Patho, VIC **207 K2**
Pathungra, QLD **280 D4**
Patonga, NSW 47 J1, 71 B5
Patterson Lakes, VIC 151 F6
Paulls Valley, WA 363 H3
Pawleena, TAS 469 B2, **485 G2**
Payne, QLD **281 G5**
Payneham, SA 300 D6
Payneham South, SA 302 D1
Paynes, SA 323 C3
Paynes Find, WA **402 E2**
Paynesville, VIC 177 C2, 188–9, **213 H2**
Paynters, NSW 121 J2
Peaceful Bay, WA **404 D5**
Peachester, QLD 255 C5
Peak Charles NP, WA **405 J2**
Peak Downs Mine, QLD **282 D4**
Peak Hill, NSW **111 D4**
Peak Hill, NSW **118 C3**
Peak Range NP, QLD **282 D4**
Peak Vale, QLD **282 D5**
Peake, SA **342 C4**
Peake, SA **349 G2**
Peakhurst, NSW 49 F3
Peakhurst Heights, NSW 49 F3
Peakview, NSW **122 C4**
Pearce, ACT 135 B4
Pearcedale, VIC 153 H2, **212 B3**
Pearces Corner, NSW 47 G4
Pearces Creek, NSW 84 C3
Pearl Beach, NSW 47 K1, 71 B5
Pearlah, SA **348 B1**
Pearns Steam World, TAS **480 D3**
Pearshape, TAS **478 A3**
Peats Ridge, NSW 71 B3
Pedirka (Ruin), SA **342 B2**
Peebinga, SA **349 J2**
Peechelba, VIC **208 E3**
Peedamulla, WA **400 C1**
Peelwood, NSW **118 E6**
Peewee Bend, QLD 230 C2
Pegarah, TAS **478 B2**
Pekina, SA **347 F5**
Pelham, QLD **281 F1**
Pelham, TAS **484 E2**
Pelican, NSW 71 E1
Pella, VIC **206 D2**
Pelverata, TAS **485 F4**
Pemberton, WA 391, **404 C4**
Pembrooke, NSW **115 H6**
Penarie, NSW **120 E1**
Pender, WA **399 F3**
Pendle Hill, NSW 46 E5
Penfield, SA 300 C3
Penfield Gardens, SA 300 D2
Penguin, TAS 466, **480 B2**
Penna, TAS 457 J1, 469 A3
Pennant Hills, NSW 47 F4

Penneshaw, SA 317 E2, **348 E3**
Pennington, SA 300 C6
Penny Royal World, Launceston, TAS 464, **480 E3**
Penola, SA 323 E4, 324–5, **349 H5**
Penola, WA 371 E1, 375 A6
Penong, SA **345 G3**
Penrice, SA 327 D3
Penrith, NSW 46 A5, **119 G5**
Penshurst, NSW 49 G3
Penshurst, VIC 200 A2, **210 E2**
Pentland, QLD **282 B2**
Penzance, TAS 469 D5, **485 H4**
Peppermint Grove Beach, WA 371 E1, 375 A6, **404 B3**
Peppers Plains, VIC **206 D3**
Peppimenarti, NT **432 C5**
Peranga, QLD 271 C3
Peregian Beach, QLD 255 C3
Peregian Beach South, QLD 255 C3
Perekerten, NSW **120 E2**
Perenjori, WA 392, **402 C2**
Perenna, VIC **206 C2**
Perisher Valley, NSW 76, 77 B5, **122 B4**
Perkolilli, WA **403 K4**
Perlta, VIC **204 D3**
Pernatty, SA **346 E3**
Peron, WA 364 B4
Peron, WA **400 B4**
Perponda, SA **349 G2**
Perrinvale, WA **403 H1**
Perry Bridge, VIC 177 B3, **213 G3**
Perth, WA 358–65, 359 D4, **402 C5**
Perth Cultural Centre, WA 359 E4, 360
Perth Institute of Contemporary Arts, Perth, WA 359 C3, 360
Perth International Airport, WA 363 F3
Perth Mint, WA 358, 359 D4, 360
Perth Zoo, WA 359 B6, 360
Perthville, NSW **118 E5**
Peterborough, SA **347 F5**
Peterborough, VIC 200 C5, **211 F4**, 325
Peterhead, SA 300 B5
Petersham, NSW 49 H2
Petford, QLD **279 H4**
Petina, SA **345 J4**
Petita, NSW **112 B4**
Petrie, QLD 228 E4
Petrie Terrace, QLD 225 B3, 230 E2
Pewsey Vale, SA 301 K1, 327 C5
Phatisalam, 1821, TAS **478 D4**
Phillip, ACT 135 B4
Phillip Bay, NSW 49 J3
Phillip Creek, NT **439 H1**
Phillip Island, VIC 164, 165 C1
Phillpott, QLD **286 B5**
Pialah, QLD **279 F6**
Piallamore, NSW **119 G1**
Piallaway, NSW **119 G1**
Pialligo, ACT 135 D3
Piamble, VIC **205 G4**
Piambra, NSW **118 E2**
Piangil, VIC **205 G4**
Piawaning, WA **402 C4**
Piccadilly, SA 303 F2
Pickanjinnie, QLD **286 E4**
Pickering Brook, WA 363 H4
Pickertaramoor, NT **432 D2**
Picnic Point, NSW 48 E3
Picola, VIC **208 B2**
Picton, NSW 107 B1, **119 G6**
Picton, WA 375 B5
Pie Creek, QLD 255 A2
Pier Millan, VIC **204 E5**
Piesse Brook, WA 363 H3
Piesseville, WA **404 D2**
Pigeon Hole, NT **435 D3**
Pigeon Ponds, VIC **210 C1**
Piggabeen, NSW 247 D6
Pikedale, QLD **287 G6**
Pilbara, WA 352, 356
Pilgrim, QLD **280 C3**
Pillana, SA **348 B1**
Pillar Valley, NSW **115 H4**
Pilliga, NSW **114 B4**

Rainworth, QLD 230 D2
Raleigh, NSW 62 C4, **115 H5**
Raluana, VIC 159 A1
Raminea, TAS **484 E5**
Ramingining, NT **433 J2**
Ramornie NP, NSW **115 H3**
Ramsgate, NSW 49 G3
Ranceby, VIC **212 D4**
Rand, NSW **121 J3**
Randwick, NSW 49 J2
Ranelagh, TAS **484 E4**
Ranga, TAS **482 D3**
Rangelands, QLD **281 G4**
Rangers Valley, QLD **282 B5**
Ranken, NT **440 D2**
Rankins Springs, NSW **117 J5**
Rannes, QLD 267 A6, **287 F1**
Ransome, QLD 231 H3
Rapid Bay, SA 337 B2, **348 E3**
Rapid Creek, NT 418 B2
Rappville, NSW **115 H2**
Rasberry Creek, QLD 267 B2
Rathdowney, QLD 235 C2, **287 J5**
Rathgar, NSW **112 D2**
Rathscar, VIC 159 C2, **207 H5**
Ravendale, NSW **116 C1**
Ravenhall, VIC 150 A1
Ravensbourne, QLD 271 E3
Ravensdale, NSW 71 B2
Ravenshoe, QLD 239 B6, **279 J4**
Ravensthorpe, WA **405 H3**
Ravenswood, QLD **282 C2**
Ravenswood, VIC 159 D1, **207 J5**
Ravenswood, WA 387 D2, **404 B2**
Ravensworth, NSW **119 G3**
Ravensworth, NSW **121 F2**
Rawlinna, WA **407 C3**
Rawlinna, WA **407 C3**
Rawnsley Park, SA 313 C3
Rawson, VIC **212 E3**
Ray, QLD **285 G3**
Raymond Terrace, NSW **119 H3**
Raymonds Hill, QLD 230 A4
Raywood, VIC **207 J4**
Red Bluff, VIC 187 C1, **209 G3**
Red Cap Creek, VIC **210 B1**
Red Cliffs, VIC 190, **204 D3**
Red Creek, SA 303 K5
Red Gum Flat, SA 301 H3
Red Hill, ACT 129 B6, 135 C4, **137 C2**
Red Hill, QLD 230 E2
Red Hill, VIC 152 E4
Red Hill, WA 363 G1
Red Hill, WA **400 C1**
Red Hill South, VIC 153 F5
Red Hills, TAS **480 C3**
Red Mountain, QLD **282 E4**
Red Range, NSW **115 F3**
Red Rock, NSW 62 E1, **115 H4**
Redbank, QLD 230 B5
Redbank, QLD **287 G3**
Redbank, VIC 159 B1, **207 G5**
Redbank Gorge, NT **442 C2**
Redbank Plains, QLD 230 B5
Redcliffe, QLD 224, 227, 229 G4, **287 J4**
Redcliffe, WA 363 F3
Redcliffe, QLD **287 F1**
Redcliffe, SA **347 G6**
Redesdale, VIC 159 E2, **207 K5**
Redfern, NSW 49 H2
Redford, QLD **286 D3**
Redhill, SA **347 F6**
Redland Bay, QLD 231 K5, 235 D1
Redlynch, QLD 239 C3
Redmond, WA 369 C3, **404 E5**
Redpa, TAS **479 B3**
Redwood Park, SA 300 E5
Reedy, WA **400 E5**
Reedy Corner, NSW **118 B1**
Reedy Creek, SA 323 C3, **349 G5**
Reedy Creek, VIC **208 B6**
Reedy Dam, VIC **206 E2**
Reedy Spring, QLD **279 H6**
Reefton, NSW **118 B6**
Reekara, TAS **478 A1**

Reesville, QLD 255 B5
Regatta Point, TAS **483 B2**
Regency Park, SA 300 C6
Regents Park, NSW 49 F2
Regents Park, QLD 231 F6
Reid, ACT 129 E2, 135 C3
Reid River, QLD **282 C1**
Reids Flat, NSW **118 D6**
Rekuna, TAS **485 G2**
Relbia, TAS **481 F3**
Remarkable Cave, TAS **485 H4**
Remlap, WA **402 E3**
Rendelsham, SA 323 C5
Renison Bell, TAS **483 B1**
Renmark, SA 331, 333 D1, **349 H1**
Renmark North, SA 333 D1, **349 H1**
Renmark South, SA 333 D2
Renner Springs Roadhouse, NT **436 D5**
Rennie, NSW **121 H3**
Renown Park, SA 297 A1
Repton, NSW 62 C4
Reservoir, WA 363 J4
Retreat, NSW **114 E5**
Retreat, QLD **285 G2**
Retro, QLD **282 D5**
Revesby, NSW 49 F3
Revesby Heights, NSW 49 F3
Reynella, SA 302 B4
Reynella East, SA 302 C4
Reynolds Neck, TAS **480 D5**
Rheban, TAS 469 D2, **485 H2**
Rheola, VIC 159 C1, **207 H4**
Rhodes, NSW 47 G6, 49 G1
Rhyll, VIC 153 J6, 165 E1, **212 B4**
Rhyndaston, TAS **485 G1**
Riachella, VIC 195 D1
Riana, TAS **480 A2**
Rich Avon, VIC **207 F4**
Richlands, QLD 230 D5
Richmond, NSW 46 A2, **119 G5**
Richmond, QLD 265, **281 G2**
Richmond, SA 302 C1
Richmond, TAS 467, 469 A2, **485 G2**
Richmond, VIC 150 D2
Richmond Hill, TAS **480 E2**
Richmond Range NP, NSW **115 H2**
Riddells Creek, VIC 167 D3, **212 A1**
Ridgehaven, SA 300 E4
Ridgelands, QLD 267 A4, **283 G5**
Ridgelands, QLD **286 E3**
Ridgeway, TAS 456 C6
Ridgley, TAS **480 A2**
Ridleyton, SA 300 C6
Rifle Creek, QLD **280 C2**
Rimbanda, QLD **281 G4**
Ringarooma, TAS **481 G2**
Ringwood, NT 423 E1, **443 F2**
Ringwood, VIC 151 G2, **212 B2**
Ringwood East, VIC 151 G2
Ringwood North, VIC 151 G2
Ripley, QLD 230 A6
Ripponlea, VIC 150 D3
Risdon, TAS 446, 455, 456 D2
Risdon Vale, TAS 456 E2, **485 F3**
Rita Island, QLD **282 D1**
River Heads, QLD 259 C4, **287 J3**
River Torrens, SA 296, 297
Riverdale, WA 362 E3
Riveren, NT **435 C5**
Riverhills, QLD 230 C4
Riverina, WA **403 J2**
Riverland (Murray River region), SA
   289, 332, 333
Riverlands, WA 375 B5
Riversdale, VIC 150 E2
Riverside, NSW **116 E2**
Riverside, QLD **282 D6**
Riverside Markets, Brisbane, QLD
   225 D4, 226
Riverside Mine, QLD **282 D3**
Riversleigh, QLD **278 B5**
Riversleigh Fossils, QLD **278 B5**
Riverstone, NSW 46 C3
Riverton, SA **349 F1**
Riverton, WA 362 E4

Riverview, NSW 47 H6, 49 H1
Riverview, QLD 230 B5, 259 A2
Riverwood, NSW 49 F3
Rivett, ACT 135 A4
Roach, NSW **121 J2**
Robe, SA 323 B3, 331–2, **349 G5**
Roberts Point, TAS **485 F4**
Robertson, NSW 107 B3, **122 E2**
Robertson, QLD 231 F4
Robertson Range, WA **401 G2**
Robertstown, SA **347 G6**
Robin Falls, NT **432 D4**
Robina, QLD 247 C5
Robinhood, QLD **279 G5**
Robinson River, NT **437 J3**
Robinvale, VIC 190, **205 F3**
Rochedale, QLD 231 G4
Rochedale South, QLD 231 G5
Rocherlea, TAS **480 E3**
Rochester, VIC 190–1, **207 K3**
Rochford, VIC 167 D2
Rochford Rock, VIC **212 A1**
Rock Flat, NSW **122 C4**
Rock Valley, NSW 84 A2
Rockbank, VIC 201 K1, **212 A2**
Rockdale, NSW 49 H3
Rockhampton, QLD 265, 266, 267 B4,
   268, **283 G5**
Rockhampton Downs, NT **439 K1**
Rockhole, NT **432 E3**
Rockingham, WA 364 C4, 392–3, **404 B1**
Rocklands, QLD **280 B1**
Rocklea, QLD 227, 230 E4
Rocklea, WA **400 D2**
Rockley, NSW **118 E5**
Rocksberg, QLD 228 C1, 255 B6
Rockvale, QLD **281 F2**
Rockview, NSW **121 K2**
Rockwood, QLD **281 H3**
Rocky Cape, TAS **479 D3**
Rocky Cape NP, TAS **479 D3**
Rocky Crossing, ACT 77 E1, **137 C4**
Rocky Glen, NSW **112 E5**
Rocky Glen, NSW **114 C6**
Rocky Gully, WA 369 A1, **404 D4**
Rocky Hills Convict Station, TAS **481 J6**
Rocky Plains, NSW 77 D4
Rocky River, NSW **115 F5**
Rocky River, SA 317 A3, **348 D3**
Rodd Point, NSW 47 G6, 49 G1
Roebourne, WA 393, **398 B6**
Roebuck Plains, WA **399 F4**
Roebuck Roadhouse, WA **399 F4**
Roelands, WA 375 C4
Roger River, TAS **479 C3**
Roger River West, TAS **479 C3**
Rokeby, TAS 457 G5, 469 A3, 469 A4,
   485 G3
Rokeby, VIC **212 D3**
Rokeby Rangers Stn, QLD **277 B5**
Rokewood, VIC 201 G2, **211 H2**
Roland, TAS **480 B3**
Roleystone, WA 365 G2
Rollands Plains, NSW **119 K1**
Rolleston, QLD **286 E1**
Rollingstone, QLD **279 J5**
Roma, QLD 268, **286 E4**
Romani, NSW **117 J3**
Romsey, VIC 167 D2, **212 A1**
Rookwood, NSW 49 F2
Rookwood, QLD **279 G3**
Roopena, SA **346 E5**
Rooty Hill, NSW 46 C5
Roper Bar, NT **433 J6**
Roper Valley, NT **433 H6**
Rosa Brook, WA 371 C3
Rosa Glen, WA 371 C4
Rosanna, VIC 150 E1
Rose Bay, NSW 47 J6, 49 J1
Rose Bay, TAS 456 E3
Rose Bay North, NSW 47 K6, 49 K1
Rose Park, SA 302 D1
Rosebank, NSW 84 C2
Roseberth, QLD **284 C3**
Rosebery, NSW 49 H2

Rosebery, NT **419 G6**
Rosebery, TAS 467, **483 C1**
Rosebery, VIC **206 E2**
Rosebery East, VIC **206 E2**
Rosebrook, VIC 200 A4, **210 E4**
Rosebud, VIC 152 D4, **212 A4**
Rosebud West, VIC 152 D4
Rosedale, NSW 77 E3
Rosedale, QLD **287 H2**
Rosedale, SA 327 A4
Rosedale, VIC **213 F3**
Rosegarland, TAS **484 E2**
Rosehill, NSW 47 F6, 49 F1
Roselands, NSW 49 G3
Rosemount, QLD **281 J5**
Rosetta, TAS 456 B2
Rosevale, NSW 235 B1
Rosevale, QLD **281 F3**
Rosevale, TAS **480 E3**
Rosevears, TAS **480 E2**
Roseville, NSW 47 H5
Roseville Chase, NSW 47 H5
Rosewater, SA 300 B6
Rosewhite, VIC 187 C2, **209 F4**
Rosewood, NSW **122 A3**
Rosewood, NT **435 A3**
Rosewood, QLD 235 B1, **287 H5**
Roslyn, NSW **122 C1**
Roslynmead, VIC **207 K2**
Rosny, TAS 453 E2, 456 E4
Ross, TAS 470, **481 G5**
Ross Bridge (1836), TAS 470, **481 G6**
Ross Creek, VIC **211 H2**
Ross River Homestead, NT 423 E1, **442 E2**
Rossarden, TAS **481 G4**
Rossbridge, VIC 159 A3, 195 E5, **211 F1**
Rosscommon, NSW **113 H3**
Rosslyn, QLD **287 G2**
Rosslyn Park, SA 302 E1
Rossmore, NSW 48 B5
Rossmount, QLD 255 B2, 259 B6
Rossmoya, QLD 267 B3
Rossmoyne, WA 362 D4
Rossville, QLD **279 H2**
Rostrevor, SA 300 E6
Rostron, VIC 159 B1, **207 G4**
Rothbury, NSW 59 C3
Rothwell, QLD 229 F3
Roto, NSW **117 H4**
Rottnest Island, WA 351, 358, 361, 394,
   395 C3
Round Corner, NSW 46 E 4
Rous Mill, NSW 84 C3
Rouse Hill, NSW 46 D3
Rowella, TAS **480 E2**
Rowena, NSW **114 B3**
Rowland Flat, SA 327 B5
Rowsley, VIC 201 J1, **211 K2**
Rowville, VIC 151 H3, **212 B2**
Roxborough Downs, QLD **280 B4**
Roxburgh, NSW 91 D2, **119 G3**
Roxby Downs, SA 290, 332–3, **346 D2**
Roxby Downs, SA **346 D2**
Roy Hill, WA **401 F2**
Royal Australian Mint, ACT 128, 132,
   135 B3
Royal Botanic Gardens, Melbourne, VIC
   146, 147 E5, 148
Royal Botanic Gardens, Sydney, NSW
   42, 43 D3
Royal Exhibition Building, Melbourne, VIC
   147 D1, 148
Royal George, TAS **481 H5**
Royal NP, NSW **119 H6**
Royal Park, SA 300 B6
Royal Tasmanian Botanical Gardens,
   Hobart, TAS 452, 453 C2, 454
Royalla, ACT 135 C6, **137 C4**
Royles, QLD **283 F5**
Royston Park, SA 300 D6
Rozelle, NSW 47 H6, 49 H1
Rubicon, VIC **212 D1**
Ruby Gap, NT 423 E1, **443 F2**
Ruby Plains, WA **399 J4**

Sinnamon Park, QLD 230 D4
Sippy Downs, QLD 255 C4
Sisters Beach, TAS 479 D3
Sisters Creek, TAS 479 D3
Skenes Creek, VIC 201 G5, 211 H5
Skipton, VIC 200 E1, 211 G2
Skycity Adelaide, SA 297 C3, 298
Skye, QLD 282 C6
Skye, SA 302 E1
Skye, VIC 151 G6
Skyrail Rainforest Cableway, QLD 238, 239 B3, 252
Slacks Creek, QLD 231 G5
Slade Point, QLD 263 D6, 283 F3
Slashes Creek, QLD 280 D4
Slaty Creek, VIC 207 G4
Smeaton, VIC 159 D3, 167 A2, 211 J1
Smeaton Grange, NSW 48 B4
Smiggin Holes, NSW 76, 77 C5, 122 B4
Smithfield, NSW 46 D6, 48 D1
Smithfield, QLD 239 C3, 279 J3
Smithfield, SA 300 E2
Smithfield Plains, SA 300 E2
Smiths Beach, VIC 153 J6, 165 C2
Smiths Lake, NSW 95 D1
Smithton, TAS 471, 479 C2
Smithtown, NSW 115 H6
Smithville, SA 349 H2
Smokers Bank, TAS 479 C3
Smoko, VIC 187 C3, 209 G4
Smoky Bay, SA 345 H4
Smythesdale, VIC 211 H2
Snake Gully, VIC 159 C3
Snake Range NP, QLD 282 D6
Snake Valley, VIC 211 H2
Snobs Creek Fish Hatchery, VIC 208 D6
Snowtown, SA 346 E6
Snowy Mountains, NSW 35, 76, 77
Snowy River NP, VIC 209 K5, 214 A3
Snug, TAS 485 F4
Snuggery, SA 323 D5
Sofala, NSW 118 E4
Somerby, QLD 282 E6
Somers, VIC 153 G5, 212 B4
Somersby, NSW 71 B4
Somerset, QLD 255 A5, 277 B2
Somerset, TAS 480 A1
Somerset Dam, QLD 255 A6
Somerton, NSW 114 D5
Somerton, VIC 212 B2
Somerton Park, SA 302 B2
Somerville, VIC 153 G2, 212 B3
Sommariva, QLD 285 K3, 286 C3
Sorell, TAS 457 K1, 469 B3, 471, 485 G3
Sorlie, NSW 47 J4
Sorrento, VIC 152 B4, 193, 212 A4
Sorrento, WA 361, 362 C1
Soudan, NT 440 D2
South Arm, TAS 485 G4
South Australia 288–349
South Australian Museum, Adelaide, SA 296, 297 D3
South Bank, QLD 224, 225 C4, 225 C5, 227, 230 E2
South Blackwater Mine, QLD 282 E6
South Brighton, SA 302 B3
South Brisbane, QLD 227, 230 E3
South Bruny Lighthouse, TAS 485 F6
South Bruny NP, TAS 485 F5, 485 F6
South Bunbury, WA 375 B5
South Coogee, NSW 49 J2
South Cumberland Island NP, QLD 283 F3
South East Forest NP, NSW 122 C5, 122 C6
South Forest, TAS 479 C3
South Franklin, TAS 484 E4
South Fremantle, WA 362 C5, 379 D3
South Galway, QLD 285 F2
South Gap, SA 346 E3
South Glen, QLD 287 F4
South Grafton, NSW 115 H3
South Granville, NSW 46 E6, 48 E1
South Guildford, WA 363 F2
South Hedland, WA 398 C5
South Hobart, TAS 453 A5, 456 C5

South Hurstville, NSW 49 G3
South Ita, NSW 116 B4
South Johnstone, QLD 239 D6, 279 J4
South Kilkerran, SA 348 E1
South Kingsville, VIC 150 B2
South Kumminin, WA 403 F6
South Lake, WA 362 D6
South Melbourne, VIC 147 A4, 147 B5, 150 D2
South Mission Beach, QLD 279 J4
South Molle Island, QLD 262, 263 B2
South Nietta, TAS 480 B3
South Nowra, NSW 97 B2
South Penrith, NSW 46 A5
South Perth, WA 359 C6, 362 E3
South Plympton, SA 302 C2
South Preston, TAS 480 B3
South Riana, TAS 480 A2
South Springfield, TAS 481 G2
South Stirling, WA 369 D2
South Stradbroke Island, QLD 247 C2
South Turramurra, NSW 47 G4
South Wentworthville, NSW 46 E6, 48 E1
South West Rocks, NSW 100, 115 H5
South Windsor, NSW 46 B3
South Yanderup, WA 387 C2
South Yarra, VIC 150 D2
Southbank, VIC 147 C4, 150 D2
Southbrook, QLD 271 C4
Southend, SA 323 C5, 349 G6
Southern Brook, WA 402 D5
Southern Cross, QLD 282 B2
Southern Cross, WA 393, 403 G4
Southern Cross (Crash Site), WA 399 G2
Southern Highlands, NSW 35, 87, 107
Southern Hills, WA 407 A4
Southern River, WA 363 F5
Southgate, Melbourne, VIC 146, 147 C4, 148
Southport, QLD 235 D2, 247 C4
Southport, TAS 484 E5
Southwest NP, TAS 449, 473 A2, 473 A5, 484 B4, 484 C6
Southwood NP, QLD 287 F5
Sovereign Hill, Ballarat, VIC 156, 158, 159 C3
Spalding, SA 347 F6
Spalford, TAS 480 B2
Spargo Creek, VIC 159 D3, 167 B3, 211 J1
Spearwood, WA 362 C5
Speed, VIC 204 E5
Speewa, VIC 205 G5
Spence, ACT 135 B2
Spencer, NSW 71 A4
Spiky Bridge, TAS 481 H6
Spirit Hills, NT 435 A1
Spit Junction, NSW 47 J6, 49 J1
Split Rock, QLD 280 B1
Spoonbill, QLD 278 D6
Spotswood, VIC 150 C2
Sprent, TAS 480 B2
Spreyton, TAS 480 C2
Spring Beach, TAS 469 D1, 485 H2
Spring Creek, NT 437 H3
Spring Creek, QLD 279 H5
Spring Creek, WA 399 K3
Spring Farm, NSW 48 A5
Spring Grove, NSW 84 A3
Spring Hill, NSW 118 D4
Spring Hill, NT 432 E4
Spring Hill, QLD 225 C2, 230 E2
Spring Hill, WA 402 D5
Spring Ridge, NSW 119 F1
Springbrook, QLD 235 D2, 247 B6
Springbrook NP, QLD 234, 287 J5
Springdale, NSW 118 B6
Springfield, QLD 230 C6
Springfield, QLD 279 G4, 286 D4
Springfield, SA 302 D2
Springfield, TAS 481 G2
Springfield, VIC 167 E2
Springhurst, VIC 187 B1, 208 E3
Springsure, QLD 282 D6
Springton, SA 349 F2
Springvale, NT 429 C3

Springvale, QLD 282 B5
Springvale, VIC 151 F4
Springvale, QLD 279 H2
Springvale, QLD 280 D5
Springvale, QLD 282 C4
Springvale, WA 399 J4
Springvale South, VIC 151 F4
Springwood, NSW 81 J4, 119 G5
Springwood, QLD 231 G5
Springwood, QLD 286 D1
Squirrel Hills, QLD 280 D3
Stafford, QLD 230 E1
Stafford Heights, QLD 230 E1
Staghorn Flat, VIC 187 C1, 209 F3
Stake Hill, WA 387 D1
Stamford, QLD 281 G3
Stanage, QLD 267 A1, 283 F4
Stanbroke, QLD 280 C3
Standley Chasm, NT 422, 423 D1, 442 D2
Stanhope, VIC 208 B3
Stanhope Gardens, NSW 46 D4
Stanifords, NSW 117 J3
Stanley, TAS 471, 474, 479 C2
Stanley, VIC 187 B1, 209 F3
Stanley Park, NSW 46 B1
Stanmore, NSW 49 H2
Stanmore, QLD 255 B5
Stannifer, NSW 114 E4
Stansbury, SA 333, 348 E2
Stanthorpe, QLD 235 A3, 269, 287 H6
Stanwell, QLD 267 A4, 283 F5
Stanwell Park, NSW 106, 107 D1, 119 G6
Stapylton, QLD 247 A1
Starke, QLD 279 H1
Starke NP, QLD 279 H1
Staughton Vale, VIC 201 J1, 211 J2
Staverton, TAS 480 B3
Stavley, VIC 195 D6
Stawell, VIC 159 A2, 193, 195 E2, 207 F5
Steiglitz, VIC 201 H2, 211 J2
Stenhouse Bay, SA 348 D2
Stephens Creek, NSW 116 B2
Stepney, SA 302 D1
Steppes, TAS 480 E6
Stewart, WA 403 J4
Stieglitz, TAS 481 J2
Stirling, ACT 135 B4
Stirling, SA 303 F2
Stirling, WA 362 D2
Stirling, NT 439 H5
Stirling, QLD 278 E3, 282 B5, 286 E3
Stirling Gardens, Perth, WA 359 C4, 360
Stirling North, SA 346 E4
Stirling Range NP, WA 355, 404 E4
Stirrat, QLD 267 C5
Stockdale, VIC 177 A2
Stockinbingal, NSW 122 A1
Stockmans Reward, VIC 212 D1
Stockwell, SA 327 E1
Stockyard Gully Caves, WA 402 B2
Stokes Bay, SA 317 C2, 348 D3
Stokes NP, WA 405 J3
Stonehenge, QLD 285 G1
Stonehenge, TAS 485 G1
Stones Corner, QLD 231 F3
Stoneville, NSW 84 A1
Stoney Chute, NSW 84 A1
Stoneyford, VIC 200 E4, 211 G4
Stonor, TAS 485 G1
Stony Crossing, NSW 120 E2
Stony Point, VIC 153 H4
Stonyfell, SA 302 E1
Stormlea, TAS 469 C6, 485 H4
Storys Creek, TAS 481 G4
Stowport, TAS 480 A2
Stradbroke, VIC 213 F3
Strahan, TAS 445, 474, 483 B2
Strangways Bore (Ruin), SA 342 D5
Stratford, NSW 119 J2
Stratford, VIC 177 A2, 213 G3
Strath Creek, VIC 212 B1
Strathalbyn, SA 334, 349 F2
Stratham, WA 375 B5, 404 B3
Strathaven, QLD 279 F1
Strathblane, TAS 484 E5

Strathbogie, VIC 208 C4
Strathburn, QLD 279 F1
Strathdickie, QLD 263 A2
Strathdownie, VIC 210 B2
Strathearn, SA 347 H3
Strathelbiss, QLD 280 C4
Strathfield, NSW 45, 47 G6, 49 G2
Strathfield, QLD 280 E3
Strathfield South, NSW 49 F2
Strathfieldsaye, VIC 159 E1, 207 K4
Strathgordon, QLD 277 B6
Strathgordon, TAS 484 B3
Strathkellar, VIC 195 A6, 210 D2
Strathleven, QLD 279 F2
Strathmay, QLD 277 B6
Strathmerton, VIC 208 C2
Strathmore, QLD 279 F4, 282 D2
Strathmore, VIC 150 C1
Strathpark, QLD 279 F6
Strathpine, QLD 228 E5, 287 J5
Stratton, VIC 204 E5
Stratton, WA 363 G2
Straun, SA 323 E3
Streaky Bay, SA 334, 345 J5
Streatham, VIC 200 D1, 211 G2
Strelley, WA 398 C5
Strenton Elbow, WA 375 D4
Stretton, QLD 231 F5
Strickland, TAS 484 D1
Stromlo, ACT 135 A3
Stroud, NSW 95 A1, 119 J3
Stroud Road, NSW 119 J3
Struan, SA 349 H5
Strzelecki, VIC 212 D4
Strzelecki NP, TAS 460, 482 C3
Stuart Creek, SA 342 D6
Stuart Mill, VIC 159 B1, 207 G4
Stuart Park, NT 417 C4, 418 B4
Stuart Town, NSW 118 D3
Stuarts Point, NSW 115 H5
Stuarts Well Roadhouse, NT 423 C2, 442 D3
Sturt, SA 302 C3
Sturt Creek, WA 399 K4
Sturt Meadows, WA 403 J1
Sturt NP, NSW 39, 111 D2
Sturt Vale, SA 347 H5
Subiaco, WA 362 D3
Success, WA 362 D6, 364 D2
Sudley, QLD 277 B4
Suffolk Park, NSW 84 D2
Sugarloaf, QLD 263 A2
Suggan Buggan, VIC 209 K5
Sujeewong, QLD 287 G3
Sullivan, WA 402 B1
Sullivans Cove, TAS 453 C4, 454
Sulphur Creek, TAS 480 B1
Summer Hill, NSW 49 G2
Summerfield, VIC 207 J4
Summerlands, VIC 165 A2
Summertown, SA 303 F2
Summervale, QLD 285 J2
Sumner, QLD 230 D4
Sunbury, VIC 167 D3, 212 A1
Sunday Creek, NT 436 C2
Sunderland Bay, VIC 153 J6, 165 D2
Sundown NP, QLD 287 G6
Sunnybank, QLD 231 F4
Sunnybank Hills, QLD 231 F5
Sunnyside, TAS 480 C3
Sunnyside, VIC 187 D3, 209 H4
Sunset Strip, NSW 116 C3
Sunset Strip, VIC 153 J6
Sunshine, VIC 150 B1, 212 A2
Sunshine Beach, QLD 255 D3
Sunshine Coast, QLD 217, 254
Sunshine North, VIC 150 B1
Sunshine West, VIC 150 B2
Supplejack, NT 438 C1
Supreme Court Gardens, Perth, WA 359 C4, 360
Surat, QLD 286 E4
Surf Beach, VIC 153 J6, 165 D2
Surfers Paradise, QLD 235 D2, 246, 247 C4, 287 J5

The Spectacles, WA 364 D3
The Spit, NSW 47 J5
The Strip, NSW 116 E2
The Swan Bells, Perth, WA 359 C4, 360
The Troffs, NSW 118 B4
The Twins, SA 346 B1
The Yanko, NSW 121 H2
Thebarton, SA 297 A3, 302 C1
Theda, WA 399 H2
Theebine, QLD 255 A1, 259 A5, 287 J3
Thelangerin, NSW 117 G6
Theldarpa, NSW 111 D3
Theodore, ACT 135 C5
Theodore, QLD 287 F2
Theresa Creek, NSW 115 H2
Thermal Springs, TAS 484 E5
Thinoomba, QLD 259 A4, 287 H3
Thirlmere, NSW 107 B1, 119 G6
Thirlmere Lakes NP, NSW 119 G6
Thirlstane, TAS 480 C2
Thistlebank NP, QLD 281 J4
Thologolong, VIC 209 G2
Thomby, QLD 286 E5
Thompson Point, QLD 267 B4
Thompsons Corner, NSW 47 F4
Thomson Bay Settlement, WA 395 D2
Thoona, VIC 208 D3
Thoopara, QLD 263 A3, 282 E2
Thora, NSW 62 B4, 115 H5
Thornbury, VIC 150 D1
Thorneside, QLD 231 H3
Thorngate, SA 297 C1
Thornlands, QLD 231 K4
Thornleigh, NSW 47 F4
Thornleigh, QLD 282 A6
Thornlie, WA 363 F5
Thornton, QLD 235 B1
Thornton, VIC 208 D6
Thorntonia, QLD 278 B6
Thorpdale, VIC 212 D3
Thowgla, VIC 187 E1, 209 J3
Thowgla Upper, VIC 187 E1, 209 J3
Thredbo, NSW 76, 77 B6, 122 B5
Three Sisters, NSW 79, 80 E5
Three Springs, WA 402 B2
Three Ways Roadhouse, NT 439 H2
Throsby, ACT 135 C1
Thrungli, QLD 282 B6
Thrushton NP, QLD 286 D5
Thuddungra, NSW 118 C6
Thulloo, NSW 118 A5
Thundelarra, WA 402 D1
Thurlga, SA 346 B4
Thurloo Downs, NSW 112 B3
Thurrulgoona, QLD 286 B6
Thursday Island, QLD 277 B2
Thylungra, QLD 285 G3
Thyra, NSW 121 F4
Ti Tree Roadhouse, NT 439 G5
Tiaro, QLD 259 B5, 287 J3
Tiarra, NSW 117 G3
Tibarri, QLD 280 E2
Tibooburra, NSW 111 D3
Tichborne, NSW 118 C4
Tickera, SA 346 E6
Ticklara, QLD 285 F5
Tidal River, VIC 179 C4, 212 E5
Tidbinbilla Nature Reserve, ACT 136, 137 B3
Tielta, NSW 111 C5
Tieri, QLD 282 E5
Tieyon, SA 341 H1
Tilba Tilba, NSW 122 D4
Tilcha, SA 343 J6
Tilmouth Roadhouse, NT 439 F6
Tilpa, NSW 112 D5
Tilpal, QLD 267 A2
Tiltagara, NSW 117 G2
Tiltagoonah, NSW 117 G1
Timbarra, VIC 213 J1
Timber Creek, NT 430, 435 C2
Timberfield, WA 403 H4
Timberoo South, VIC 204 D5
Timbertop, VIC 208 E5
Timboon, VIC 200 D4, 211 F4

Timmering, VIC 208 A3
Timmsvale, NSW 62 B2
Timor, NSW 119 G2
Timor, VIC 159 C2, 207 H5
Timora, QLD 278 D4
Tin Can Bay, QLD 255 C1, 259 C5, 269, 272, 287 J3
Tinaburra, QLD 239 B5
Tinamba, VIC 213 F3
Tinana, QLD 259 B4
Tinaroo, QLD 239 B4
Tincurrin, WA 404 E2
Tindal RAAF Base, NT 433 F5
Tindarey, NSW 113 F6
Tinderbox, TAS 485 F4
Tinderry, QLD 285 G4
Tindo, QLD 282 A2
Tingalpa, QLD 231 G3
Tingha, NSW 114 E4
Tingoora, QLD 287 H4
Tinnanbar, QLD 259 C5
Tinnenburra, QLD 285 J6
Tintaldra, VIC 209 J2
Tintenbar, NSW 84 D3
Tintinara, SA 349 G3
Tipperary, NT 432 D4
Tiranna, QLD 285 J3, 286 B3
Tirlta, NSW 116 C1
Tirranna Roadhouse, QLD 278 B4
Titjikala (Maryvale), NT 423 D2, 442 E3
Tittybong, VIC 207 G2
Tiverton, SA 347 G5
Tivoli, QLD 230 A5
Tivoli Hill, QLD 230 A5
Tiwi, NT 418 C1
Tiwi Islands, NT 415
Tiwi Wilderness Lodge, NT 432 B2
Tjakupai Aboriginal Cultural Park, QLD 238, 239 C3, 240
Tjarramba, WA 399 F4
Tjirrkarli, WA 406 B4
Tjukayirla Roadhouse, WA 406 A5
Tjukurla, WA 406 D3
Tobermory, NT 440 E5
Tobermory, QLD 285 G4
Tocal, QLD 281 G5
Tocumwal, NSW 121 H3
Todd River, NT 423 E1, 442 E2
Todmorden, SA 341 J3
Togari, TAS 479 B3
Tolga, QLD 239 B4, 279 J4
Tolmer Falls, NT 432 C4
Tolmie, VIC 187 A3, 208 E5
Tom Price, WA 394, 400 E2
Tomahawk, TAS 481 H1
Tomaree NP, NSW 94, 119 J4
Tomerong, NSW 97 B4, 107 B4, 122 E2
Tomewin, QLD 247 C6
Tomingley, NSW 118 C3
Tomingley West, NSW 118 C3
Tomoo, QLD 286 C4
Tongala, VIC 208 B3
Tonganah, TAS 481 G2
Tongio, VIC 209 H5
Tongio West, VIC 209 H6
Tongy, QLD 286 C4
Tonkoro, QLD 281 F5
Toobanna, QLD 279 J5
Toobeah, QLD 287 F5
Tooborac, VIC 208 A5
Toodyay, WA 402 C5
Toogong, NSW 118 D4
Toogoolawah, QLD 271 E3, 287 H4
Toogoom, QLD 259 B3
Toolakea, QLD 279 K6
Toolamba, VIC 208 C3
Toolangi, VIC 212 C1
Toolara, QLD 255 C1, 259 C5
Toolara Forest, QLD 255 B1, 259 B6
Toolebuc, QLD 280 D4
Toolern Vale, VIC 159 E3, 167 D3, 212 A2
Tooleybuc, NSW 120 D2
Toolibin, WA 404 E2
Tooligie, SA 346 B6

Toolleen, VIC 208 A4
Toolondo, VIC 206 D5
Tooloom, NSW 115 G2
Tooloom NP, NSW 115 G1
Tooloombilla, QLD 286 D3
Tooma, NSW 77 A3, 122 A4
Toombul, QLD 231 F1
Toombullup, VIC 187 A3, 208 E5
Toompine Hotel, QLD 285 H4
Toongabbie, NSW 46 E5
Toonumbar NP, NSW 115 H1
Tooperang, SA 337 D1
Toora, VIC 212 E4
Tooradin, VIC 153 K2, 212 C3
Toorak, VIC 150 D2
Toorak Gardens, SA 302 D1
Toorale, NSW 112 E4
Tooraweenah, NSW 118 D1
Toorbul, QLD 255 C6
Toormina, NSW 62 D3
Tooronga, VIC 212 D2
Tootgarook, VIC 152 C5
Toowong, QLD 230 E3
Toowong Upper, NSW 77 A4
Toowoomba, QLD 235 A1, 270, 271 D4, 272, 287 H5
Toowoon Bay, NSW 71 D4
Top Hut, NSW 116 D5
Top Springs Roadhouse, NT 436 B3
Topar, NSW 116 C2
Topaz, QLD 239 C5
Torbanlea, QLD 287 J3
Torbay, WA 369 C3, 404 E5
Torilla Plains, QLD 267 A1
Torndirrup NP, WA 404 E5
Toronto, NSW 71 D1, 119 H4
Torquay, VIC 196, 199, 201 J4, 211 K4
Torrens, ACT 135 B4
Torrens Creek, QLD 282 A2
Torrens Park, SA 302 D2
Torrens River, SA *see* River Torrens, SA
Torrens Vale, SA 337 C2
Torrensville, SA 302 C1
Torrington, NSW 115 F3
Torrita, NSW 204 D5
Torrumbarry, VIC 207 K2
Torwood, QLD 230 E2
Torwood, QLD 279 G4
Tostaree, VIC 177 E2
Tottenham, NSW 118 B2
Tottenham, VIC 150 B2
Tottington, NSW 159 B1, 207 G4
Toukley, NSW 71 D3, 102, 119 H4
Tourello, VIC 159 C3
Towaninny, NSW 207 G2
Towaninny South, VIC 207 G2
Towarri NP, NSW 119 G2
Tower Hill, VIC 200 A4, 210 E4
Towera, WA 400 C2
Town Hall, Sydney, NSW 43 C4
Townson, QLD 235 B2, 271 E5, 287 H5
Townsville, QLD 272–3, 282 C1
Towong, VIC 187 E1, 209 J3
Trafalgar, VIC 212 D3
Tragowel, VIC 207 J2
Trajere, NSW 118 C5
Trangie, NSW 118 C2
Tranmere, SA 302 E1
Tranmere, TAS 457 F4
Traralgon, VIC 196–7, 212 E3
Traralgon South, VIC 212 E3
Travancore, VIC 150 C1
Traveston, QLD 255 B3
Trawalla, VIC 159 B3, 211 H1
Trawool, VIC 208 B5
Traynors Lagoon, VIC 207 F4
Treasury Casino, Brisbane, QLD 225 C4, 226
Trebonne, QLD 279 J5
Tregeagle, NSW 84 B3
Tregear, NSW 46 B4
Tregole NP, QLD 286 C3
Tregony, QLD 235 B2
Trelega, NSW 116 C5

Tremont, VIC 151 H3, 171 B4
Trentham, VIC 159 E3, 167 B2, 211 J1
Trephina Gorge, NT 423 D1, 442 E2
Tresco, VIC 207 H1
Trevallyn, NSW 117 F1
Trewalla, VIC 210 C4
Trewilga, NSW 118 C3
Triabunna, TAS 469 D1, 475, 485 H2
Trial Harbour, TAS 483 B1
Trida, NSW 117 G4
Trigg, WA 362 C2
Trillbar, WA 400 E4
Trinidad, QLD 285 G2
Trinity Beach, QLD 239 C2
Trinity Gardens, SA 302 D1
Troona, VIC 187 A1
Trott Park, SA 302 C3
Trowutta, TAS 479 C3
Truganina, VIC 150 A2
Trundle, NSW 118 B4
Trunkey Creek, NSW 118 E5
Truro, SA 349 F1
Tryphinia, QLD 283 F5
Tuan, QLD 259 C5, 287 J3
Tuart Hill, WA 362 D2
Tubbut, VIC 209 K5
Tucabia, NSW 115 H3
Tuckanarra, WA 400 E5
Tudor, WA 369 B3
Tuena, NSW 118 E5
Tuerong, VIC 153 G4
Tuggerah, NSW 71 C3
Tuggeranong, ACT 128, 135 B5, 137 C3
Tugun, QLD 247 D5
Tulendeena, TAS 481 G2
Tullagrie, QLD 287 F4
Tullah, TAS 473 A2, 479 E6
Tullamore, NSW 118 B3
Tullera, NSW 84 B2
Tullibigeal, NSW 118 A4
Tully, QLD 273, 279 J4
Tully Heads, QLD 279 J4
Tulmur, QLD 281 F4
Tumbar, QLD 282 B6
Tumbarumba, NSW 77 A2, 122 A3
Tumblong, NSW 122 A2
Tumby Bay, SA 335, 348 C1
Tummaville, QLD 271 C5
Tumorrama, NSW 122 B2
Tumoulin, QLD 239 B6
Tumut, NSW 103, 122 A3
Tunart, VIC 204 B3
Tunbridge, TAS 481 F6
Tuncester, NSW 84 A3
Tuncurry, NSW 119 K3
Tundulya, NSW 112 E5
Tungamah, VIC 208 D3
Tungamull, QLD 267 B4
Tunnack, TAS 485 G1
Tunnel, TAS 481 F2
Tunnel Creek NP, WA 399 G4
Tunney, WA 404 D4
Tuntable Creek, NSW 84 B1
Tuntable Falls, NSW 84 B1
Turallin, QLD 271 B5
Turee Creek, WA 400 E2
Turill, NSW 119 F2
Turkey Beach, QLD 267 E6
Turlee, NSW 116 E5
Turlinjah, QLD 122 D4
Turner, ACT 129 C1, 135 C3
Turners Beach, TAS 480 B2
Turners Marsh, TAS 480 E2
Turnip Fields, TAS 456 C5
Tuross Head, NSW 122 D4
Turramurra, NSW 47 G4
Turrawan, NSW 114 C4
Turrella, NSW 49 G2
Turriff, VIC 206 E1
Tusmore, SA 302 D1
Tuttawa, NSW 113 K2
Tutye, VIC 204 C5
Tuxworth Fullwood House, NT 439 H2
Tweed Heads, NSW 103, 115 J1, 235 D2, 247 D6

Wangan, QLD 239 D6
Wanganella, NSW **121 F3**
Wangangong, NSW **118 A3**
Wangarabell, VIC **214 C4**
Wangaratta, VIC 186, 187 A1, 197, **208 E3**
Wangary, SA **348 B1**
Wangi, NT 424, 425 A1
Wangi, NT **432 C4**
Wangi Wangi, NSW 71 D1
Wangkatjungka, WA **399 H4**
Wanguri, NT **418 C1**
Wanilla, SA **348 B1**
Wanko, QLD **286 B3**
Wanna, WA **400 D3**
Wannanup, WA 387 B2
Wannarra, WA **402 D2**
Wanneroo, WA **402 B5**
Wanniassa, ACT **135 B5**
Wannon, VIC **210 D2**
Wannoo Billabong Roadhouse, WA **400 C5**
Wansey Downs, QLD **286 B3**
Wantirna, VIC **151 G2**
Wantirna South, VIC **151 G3**
Wapet Camp, WA **398 A6**
Wappilka, SA **333 B3**
Warakurna, WA **406 D3**
Warakurna Roadhouse, WA **406 D3**
Waramanga, ACT **135 B4**
Warana, QLD **255 D4**
Waratah, NSW **113 H4**
Waratah, QLD **267 A1**
Waratah, TAS **479 D5**
Waratah Bay, VIC **212 D5**
Waratah North, VIC **212 D5**
Warawaralong, NSW **81 H1**
Warbreccan, QLD **281 F6**
Warburn, NSW **117 J6**
Warburton, VIC **212 C2**
Warburton, WA **406 C4**
Warcowie, SA 313 C3, **347 F3**
Ward Belt, SA **300 E1**
Wards River, NSW **119 J3**
Wareek, VIC **207 H5**
Wareo, QLD **285 H4**
Wargambegal, NSW **117 K4**
Warialda, NSW **114 D3**
Warianna, QLD **281 H3**
Warkworth, NSW **119 G3**
Warnambool Downs, QLD **281 F4**
Warnbro, WA **364 C5**
Warncoort, VIC 201 G3, **211 H3**
Warne, VIC **207 G2**
Warneet, VIC **153 J2**
Warner, QLD **228 E5**
Warner Bros Movie World, Gold Coast, QLD 246, 247 B3
Warner Glen, WA **371 C5**
Warnervale, NSW 71 C3
Warooka, SA **348 D2**
Waroona, WA 375 D1, 395, **404 C2**
Waroula, QLD **267 A4**
Warpoo, SA 301 H1, 327 A5
Warra, QLD 271 A2, **287 G4**
Warra, QLD **280 D5**
Warra NP, NSW **115 F4**
Warrabah NP, NSW **114 E5**
Warrachie, SA **346 B6**
Warracknabeal, VIC 197, **206 E3**
Warradale, SA 302 B3
Warraderry, NSW **118 C5**
Warragoon, NSW **121 H3**
Warragul, VIC 197, **212 D3**
Warrak, VIC 159 B2, **211 G1**
Warrakimbo, SA **346 E4**
Warral, NSW **114 E6**
Warralakin, WA **403 F4**
Warrambine, VIC 201 G2, **211 H3**
Warramboo, SA **346 B5**
Warranangra, NSW **116 B6**
Warrandyte, VIC 151 G1, **212 B2**
Warrandyte South, VIC **151 G1**
Warrane, TAS **456 E3**
Warranwood, VIC **151 G1**
Warrawagine, WA **398 D6**

Warrawee, NSW 47 G4
Warraweena, SA **347 F2**
Warrawong Sanctuary, SA 299, 303 F3
Warrayure, VIC 195 B6, 200 A1
Warreah, QLD **282 A2**
Warrell Creek, NSW 62 B6, **115 H5**
Warren, NSW **118 C2**
Warren, QLD **267 A4**
Warren Vale, QLD **278 D5**
Warrenbayne, VIC **208 D4**
Warriedar, WA **402 D1**
Warriewood, NSW 47 K3
Warrigal, NSW **118 B1**
Warrigal, QLD **281 J2**
Warrimoo, NSW 81 K5
Warrina (Ruin), SA **342 C4**
Warringa, TAS **480 B2**
Warrion, VIC 201 F3, **211 H3**
Warrnambool, VIC 198, 199, 200 B4, **210 E4**
Warrobil, NSW **118 E3**
Warrong, QLD **286 D2**
Warrong, VIC 200 A3, **210 E3**
Warroo, NSW **118 B4**
Warroora, WA **400 B2**
Warrow, SA **348 B1**
Warrumbungle, NSW **118 D1**
Warrumbungle NP, NSW 39, **114 B6**
Warruwi, NT **433 G2**
Wartaka, SA **346 D4**
Wartook, VIC 195 B2, **206 E5**
Warumbul, NSW 49 G5
Warwick, QLD 235 A2, 271 D6, 273, **287 H5**
Warwick, WA **362 D1**
Warwick Farm, NSW 48 D2
Washpool NP, NSW **115 G3**
Watagans NP, NSW **119 H4**
Watalgan, QLD **287 H2**
Watarrka NP, NT **442 B3**
Watchem, VIC **207 F3**
Watchupga, VIC **207 F2**
Waterbag, NSW **116 C1**
Waterbank, WA **398 E4**
Waterfall, NSW 48 E6, 107 D1
Waterfall Gully, SA 302 E2
Waterford, VIC 177 A1, **213 G1**
Waterford, WA 362 E4
Waterloo, NSW 49 H2
Waterloo, NT **435 B3**
Waterloo, SA **347 F6**
Waterloo, TAS **484 E4**
Waterloo, VIC 159 B3, **211 G1**
Waterloo Corner, SA **300 C3**
Waterman, WA 362 C1
Watersmeet, TAS 473 E6
Watervale, SA **347 F6**
Waterwitch, 1854, TAS **478 A2**
Watgania, VIC 195 D5
Wathana, QLD **282 D2**
Watheroo, WA **402 C3**
Watheroo NP, WA **402 B3**
Wathumba Creek, QLD 259 D2
Watson, ACT **135 C2**
Watsons Bay, NSW 45, 47 K6, 49 K1
Watsons Creek, NSW **114 E5**
Wattamolla, NSW 49 G6
Watten, QLD **281 H3**
Wattle Creek, VIC **207 G5**
Wattle Flat, NSW **118 E4**
Wattle Flat, SA 337 C1
Wattle Grove, WA 363 G4
Wattle Hill, TAS 469 B3, **485 G3**
Wattle Hill, VIC 200 E5, **211 G5**
Wattle Park, SA 302 E1
Wattle Vale, NSW **112 B4**
Wattleup, WA 364 C3
Waubedebars Grave, TAS **481 K5**
Waubra, VIC 159 C3, **211 H1**
Wauchope, NSW 104, **119 K1**
Wauchope Roadhouse, NT **439 H3**
Waukaringa (Ruin), SA **347 G4**
Wave Hill, NSW **116 E2**
Wave Hill, NT **435 D4**
Wave Rock, WA **405 G1**

Wavell Heights, QLD 229 F6, 231 F1
Waverley, NSW 45, 49 J2
Waverley, QLD **286 C2**
Waverley Downs, NSW **112 C2**
Waverney, QLD **284 E2**
Waverton, NSW 47 H6, 49 H1
Wayatinah, TAS **484 D1**
Waygara, VIC 177 E2
Wayville, SA 297 C5, 299, 302 D1
Weabonga, NSW **114 E6**
Wearne, NSW **114 D2**
Webbs, NSW **118 C3**
Wedderburn, NSW 48 C6
Wedderburn, VIC **207 H3**
Wedderburn Junction, VIC **207 H3**
Weddin NP, NSW **118 C5**
Wee Elwah, NSW **117 H4**
Wee Georgie Wood Railway, TAS **479 E6**
Wee Jasper, NSW 122 B2, **137 A1**
Wee Waa, NSW **114 C4**
Weebo, WA **401 G5**
Weedallion, NSW **118 C6**
Weegena, TAS **480 C3**
Weelamurra, QLD **286 B5**
Weelarrana, WA **401 F3**
Weemelah, NSW **114 B2**
Weeragua, VIC **214 B4**
Weerangourt, VIC **210 D3**
Weerite, VIC 200 E3, **211 G3**
Weetah, TAS **480 D3**
Weetaliba, NSW **114 C6**
Weetangera, ACT **135 B2**
Weethalle, NSW **118 A5**
Weetulta, SA **348 E1**
Wee-Wee-Rup, VIC **207 J2**
Wehla, VIC **207 H4**
Weilmoringle, NSW **113 H2**
Weipa, QLD **277 B4**
Weja, NSW 117 K5, **118 A5**
Welaregang, NSW **122 C4**
Welbourne Hill, SA **341 J3**
Welbungin, WA **402 E4**
Weldborough, TAS **481 H2**
Welford NP, QLD **285 G2**
Wellard, WA **364 D4**
Wellclose, QLD **285 J2**
Wellers Hill, QLD 231 F3
Wellingrove, NSW **115 F3**
Wellington, NSW 104–5, **118 D3**
Wellington, SA **349 G2**
Wellington Mill, WA 375 D5
Wellington Point, QLD 231 J3
Wellshot, QLD **281 H5**
Wellstead, WA **405 F4**
Welltown, QLD **287 F5**
Welltree, NT 425 A2, **432 C4**
Welshmans Reef, VIC **207 J5**
Welshpool, VIC **212 E4**
Welshpool, WA 362 E4
Wembley, WA 362 C3
Wembley Downs, WA 362 C2
Wemen, VIC **204 E4**
Wenglepong, QLD 247 A4
Wenlock (Ruin), QLD **277 C4**
Wentworth, NSW **116 C6**
Wentworth Falls, NSW 81 F4, **119 F5**
Wentworthville, NSW 46 E6, 48 E1
Wepar, SA 323 E5, **349 H6**
Weranga, QLD **287 G4**
Werna, QLD **281 F3**
Wernadinga, QLD **278 C4**
Werneth, VIC 201 F2, **211 H3**
Werribee, NSW 47 H6, **212 A2**
Werribee South, VIC 201 K2, **212 A3**
Werrikimbe NP, NSW **115 G6**
Werrimull, VIC **204 C3**
Werrington, NSW 46 A5
Werrington County, NSW 46 A4
Werrington Downs, NSW 46 A4
Werris Creek, NSW **119 G1**
Wertaloona, SA **347 G4**
Wesley Vale, TAS **480 C2**
West Beach, SA 299, 302 B1
West Cape Howe NP, WA **404 E5**

West Croydon, SA **300 C6**
West End, QLD 225 A6, 230 E3
West Frankford, TAS **480 D2**
West Hill NP, QLD **283 F4**
West Hobart, TAS 453 A3, 456 C4
West Hoxton, NSW 48 C3
West Kentish, TAS **480 B3**
West Lakes, SA **300 B6**
West Lakes Shore, SA 300 A6
West Leichhardt, QLD **280 C2**
West Lindfield, NSW 47 H5
West Lynne, NSW 77 C6
West MacDonnell NP, NT **442 C2**
West Melbourne, VIC 147 A2, 150 C2
West Montagu, TAS **479 B2**
West Moonah, TAS 456 C3
West Pennant Hills, NSW 47 F4
West Perth, WA 362 D3
West Pine, TAS **480 A2**
West Pinjarra, WA 387 D3
West Pymble, NSW 47 G5
West Richmond, SA 302 C1
West Ridgley, TAS **479 E4**
West Ryde, NSW 47 G5
West Scottsdale, TAS **481 F2**
West Swan, WA 363 F1
West Wyalong, NSW 105, **118 B5**
Westbourne Park, SA 302 D2
Westbury, TAS 476, **480 D3**
Westby, NSW **121 K3**
Westby, VIC **207 J1**
Westdale, NSW **114 E6**
Westdale, WA **404 C1**
Western Australia 350–407
Western Australian Museum, Perth, WA 359 C3, 360
Western Creek, NT **436 C2**
Western Creek, TAS **480 C4**
Western Flat, SA 323 E1, **349 H4**
Western Junction, TAS **481 F3**
Western Plains Zoo, Dubbo, NSW 66, **118 D2**
Westerton, QLD **281 F6**
Westerway, TAS **484 E2**
Westfield, WA 363 G6
Westgate, QLD **286 B3**
Westgrove, QLD **286 E3**
Westlake, QLD 230 C4
Westland, QLD **281 G5**
Westleigh, NSW 47 F4
Westmar, QLD **287 F5**
Westmead, NSW 46 E5
Westmere, VIC 200 D1, **211 F2**
Westminster, WA 362 D2
Westmoreland, QLD **278 A4**
Weston, ACT **135 B4**
Weston Creek, ACT 135 B4, **137 C2**
Westonia, WA **403 F4**
Westward Ho, QLD **280 D5**
Westwood, QLD 267 A5, **283 F5**
Westwood, TAS **480 E3**
Wetherby, QLD **281 F3**
Wetherill Park, NSW 46 D6, 48 D1
Wet'n'Wild Water World, Gold Coast, QLD 246, 247 B3
Whalan, NSW 46 B5
Whale Beach, NSW 47 K2, 71 B6
Whale World, Albany, WA 366, 369 D3
Wharminda, SA **346 C6**
Wharparilla, VIC **208 A2**
Wheeler Heights, NSW 47 K4
Wheelers Hill, VIC **151 G3**
Wheeo, NSW **122 C1**
Whetstone, QLD **287 G6**
Whian Whian, NSW 84 B1
Whim Creek, WA **398 B6**
Whiporie, NSW **115 H3**
Whipstick NP, VIC **207 J4**
Whirily, VIC **207 F2**
Whistler, 1855, TAS **478 A1**
Whitby, WA 365 G4
White Beach, TAS 469 C5, **485 H4**
White Cliffs, NSW **112 B5**
White Cliffs, WA **401 H6**

Woorim, QLD 229 J1, 255 D6
Woorinen, VIC 205 G5
Woorlba, WA **407 B4**
Woorndoo, VIC **211 F2**
Wooroloo, WA **402 C5**
Wooroona, QLD **280 B2**
Wooroonook, VIC **207 G3**
Wooroonooran NP, QLD 238, **279 J4**
Woosang, VIC **207 G3**
Wootaroo (St Helens), QLD 263 B5
Wootha, QLD 255 B5
Wootton, VIC **119 J3**
Woronora, NSW 49 F4
Woronora Heights, NSW 49 F4
Worrigee, NSW 97 C2
Worsley Refinery, WA **404 C3**
Wotonga, QLD 282 D4
Wowan, QLD 267 A5, **287 F1**
Woy Woy, NSW 71 B5, 108, **119 H5**
Wrattonbully, SA 323 E3, **349 H5**
Wreck Bay, NSW 97 C5
Wrest Point, TAS 453 D6, 455
Wright Bay, SA 323 B3
Wrightley, VIC **208 D4**
Wrotham Park, QLD **279 G3**
Wubin, WA **402 C3**
Wudinna, SA **346 B5**
Wujal Wujal, QLD **279 H2**
Wuk Wuk, VIC 177 B2, **213 G2**
Wulagi, NT 418 D2
Wulgulmerang, VIC **209 J5**
Wumalgi, QLD **283 F4**
Wunara Store, NT **440 C2**
Wundowie, WA **402 C5**
Wunghnu, VIC **208 C3**
Wungong, WA 365 G3
Wunkar, SA 333 B3, **349 H1**
Wurankuwu, NT **432 C2**
Wurruk, VIC 177 A3, **213 F3**
Wurtulla, QLD 255 D5
Wuttagoona, NSW **117 H1**
Wutul, QLD **287 H4**
Wyaga, QLD **287 F5**
Wyalkatchem, WA **402 D4**
Wyalong, NSW **118 B5**
Wyan, NSW **115 H2**
Wyanbene Caves, NSW **122 C3**
Wyandotte, QLD **279 H5**
Wyandra, QLD **286 B4**
Wyanga, NSW **118 C3**
Wyangala, NSW **118 D5**
Wybalenna, TAS **482 C2**
Wybong, NSW 91 C1
Wycarbah, QLD 267 A4, **283 F5**
Wycheproof, VIC **207 G2**
Wychitella, VIC **207 H3**
Wycliffe Well Roadhouse, NT **439 H3**
Wydgee, WA **402 E1**
Wye River, VIC 201 G5, **211 J4**
Wyee, NSW 71 C2, **119 H4**
Wyeebo, VIC 187 D1, **209 G3**
Wyelangta, VIC 201 F5, **211 H4**
Wyerba, QLD **287 H6**
Wyloo, WA **400 C2**
Wyloona, NSW **112 C6**
Wymah, NSW **121 K4**
Wyndham, NSW **122 C5**
Wyndham, WA 396, **399 K2**
Wynn Vale, SA **300 E5**
Wynnum, QLD 227, **231 H2**
Wynyangoo, WA **400 E5**
Wynyard, NSW 43 C3
Wynyard, TAS 476, **479 E3**
Wyomi, SA 323 B2
Wyoming, NSW **117 G6**
Wyong, NSW 71 C3, 108, **119 H4**
Wyong Creek, NSW 71 C3
Wyperfeld NP, VIC **204 C6**
Wyreema, QLD 271 D4
Wyrra, NSW **118 B5**
Wyrrabalong NP, NSW **119 H4**
Wyseby, QLD **286 E2**
Wyuna, VIC **208 B3**

Y

Yaamba, QLD 267 A3, **283 G5**

Yaapeet, VIC **206 D2**
Yabba, QLD 255 A4
Yabba North, VIC **208 C3**
Yabba Vale, QLD 255 B3
Yabbra NP, NSW **115 G2**
Yaboroo, QLD **282 E3**
Yabulu, QLD **279 K6**
Yacka, SA **347 F6**
Yackandandah, VIC 187 B1, **209 F3**
Yadlamulka, SA **346 E4**
Yagoona, NSW 49 F2
Yahl, SA 323 E6
Yakabindie, WA **401 F5**
Yakara, QLD **285 G5**
Yakka Munga, WA **399 F4**
Yalamurra, QLD **285 J3**
Yalardy, WA **400 C4**
Yalata, SA **345 F3**
Yalata Roadhouse, SA **345 F3**
Yalbalgo, WA **400 C4**
Yalboroo, QLD 263 A5
Yalbra, WA **400 D4**
Yalgogrin, NSW **118 A5**
Yalgorup NP, WA 386, **404 B2**
Yallakool, NSW **121 A3**
Yallalong, WA **400 C5**
Yallaroi, NSW **114 D2**
Yalleroi, QLD **282 B6**
Yallingup, NSW 371 B1, **404 B3**
Yalloch, NSW **117 G3**
Yallook, VIC **207 J3**
Yallourn North, VIC **212 E3**
Yallunda Flat, SA **348 B1**
Yalpara, SA **347 F4**
Yalwal, NSW 107 A4, **122 E2**
Yalymboo, SA **346 D3**
Yamala, QLD **282 E5**
Yamanto, QLD 230 A6
Yamarna, WA **401 J5**
Yamba, NSW 109, **115 J3**
Yamba, NSW **112 B3**
Yambacoona, TAS **478 A1**
Yambah, NT **442 D1**
Yamboyna, QLD **282 D5**
Yambuk, VIC **210 D4**
Yambutta, QLD **285 G3**
Yan Yan, QLD **282 E5**
Yan Yean, VIC **212 B1**
Yanac, VIC **206 C3**
Yanakie, VIC 179 A2, **212 E5**
Yancannia, NSW **112 A4**
Yanchep, WA **402 B5**
Yanchep NP, WA **402 B5**
Yanco, NSW **121 J1**
Yanco Glen, NSW **116 B2**
Yandal, WA **401 G5**
Yandamindra, WA **401 H6**
Yandanooka, WA **402 B2**
Yandaran, QLD **287 H2**
Yandeyarra, WA **398 C6**
Yandil, WA **401 F4**
Yandilla, NSW **113 F5**
Yandilla, QLD 271 B5
Yandina, QLD 255 C4, 274, **287 J4**
Yandina Creek, QLD 255 C4
Yando, VIC **207 H2**
Yandoit, VIC 159 D2, 167 A1, **207 J5**
Yanerbie Beach, SA **345 J5**
Yanergee, NSW **114 C6**
Yangalake, NSW **120 E2**
Yangan, QLD 271 E6, **287 H5**
Yangebup, WA 362 D6
Yaninee, SA **346 B5**
Yankalilla, SA 337 B2, **348 E3**
Yankaninna, SA **347 G1**
Yanna, QLD **286 B4**
Yannathan, VIC **212 C3**
Yanrey, WA **400 C2**
Yantabulla, NSW **112 E3**
Yantanabie, SA **345 J4**
Yaouk, NSW 77 D2, **137 A5**
Yappala, SA **313 B3**
Yara, NSW **117 J4**
Yaraka, QLD **285 H2**
Yarck, VIC **208 C5**
Yardea, SA **346 B4**
Yarding, WA **402 E5**

Yaringa, WA **400 B4**
Yarlarweeior, WA **400 E4**
Yarloop, WA 375 D2, **404 C2**
Yarmawl, NSW **121 J1**
Yaroomba, QLD 255 C4
Yarra Creek, TAS **478 B2**
Yarra Glen, VIC **212 C2**
Yarra Junction, VIC **212 C2**
Yarra Ranges NP, VIC 143, **212 C2**
Yarra River, Melbourne, VIC 146, 147, 148
Yarrabah, QLD **279 J3**
Yarrabandai, NSW **118 B4**
Yarraberb, VIC **207 J4**
Yarrabubba, WA **400 E5**
Yarraby, VIC **205 G5**
Yarraden, QLD **277 C6**
Yarragon, VIC **212 D3**
Yarralin, NT **435 D3**
Yarraloola, WA **400 C1**
Yarralumla, ACT 129 B4, 132, 135 B3
Yarram, VIC 202, **213 F4**
Yarram Park, VIC **195 D5**
Yarrama, NSW **117 J2**
Yarramalong, NSW 71 B3, **119 H4**
Yarraman, NSW **119 F2**
Yarraman, QLD 271 D2, **287 H4**
Yarramba, SA **347 J3**
Yarrangobilly Caves, NSW 76
Yarrangobilly Caves, NSW 76, 77 C2
Yarranlea, QLD 271 C4
Yarrara, VIC **204 B3**
Yarras, NSW **115 G6**
Yarraville, VIC 150 C2
Yarrawalla, VIC **207 J2**
Yarrawalla South, VIC **207 J3**
Yarrawarrah, NSW 49 F5
Yarrawin, NSW **113 H4**
Yarrawonga, NT 419 G5
Yarrawonga, QLD **286 B3**
Yarrawonga, VIC 202, **208 D2**
Yarromere, QLD **282 B3**
Yarrongobilly Caves, NSW **122 B3**
Yarronvale, QLD **285 J4**
Yarroweyah, VIC **208 C2**
Yarroweyah South, VIC **208 C2**
Yarrowitch, NSW **119 J1**
Yarrowyck, NSW **114 E5**
Yarwun, QLD 267 D5, **287 G1**
Yass, NSW 109, **122 B2**
Yatala, QLD **247 A2**
Yatala Vale, SA **301 F4**
Yatchaw, VIC **210 D2**
Yatee, QLD **239 C4**
Yathong, NSW **117 H3**
Yathonga, NSW **112 D5**
Yatpool, VIC **204 D3**
Yattalunga, SA **301 G2**
Yatteyattah, NSW 97 A6, 107 B5
Yea, VIC **208 C5**
Yealering, WA **404 E2**
Yearinan, NSW **114 B6**
Yearinga, VIC **206 B3**
Yednalue, SA **347 F4**
Yednia, QLD 255 A5
Yeeda, WA **399 F3**
Yeelanna, SA **348 B1**
Yeelirrie, WA **401 F5**
Yeerip, VIC **208 D3**
Yeerongpilly, QLD 230 E3
Yelarbon, QLD **287 G6**
Yelbeni, WA **402 E4**
Yellow Rock, NSW 81 K4
Yellowdine, WA **403 G4**
Yellow Water (Kakadu NP), NT 412, 427 C3
Yelta, NSW **117 F2**
Yeltacowie, SA **346 D3**
Yelvertoft, QLD **280 B2**
Yelverton, WA 371 C2
Yenda, NSW **121 H1**
Yengarie, QLD 259 B4
Yengo NP, NSW **119 G4**
Yenloora, QLD **285 H5**
Yennora, NSW 46 E6, 48 E1
Yeo Yeo, NSW **122 A1**
Yeodene, VIC 201 G4, **211 H4**
Yeoval, NSW **118 D3**

Yeppen, QLD **267 B4**
Yeppoon, QLD 267 B3, 275, **283 G5**
Yerecoin, WA **402 C4**
Yerelina, SA **347 G1**
Yerilla, WA **403 K2**
Yerong Creek, NSW **121 K3**
Yeronga, QLD 230 E3
Yerra, QLD 259 A4
Yerranderie, NSW 107 A1
Yerrinbool, NSW 107 B2, **119 F6**
Yerrinbool, NSW **121 F1**
Yethera, NSW **118 B3**
Yetman, NSW **114 E2**
Yeungroon, VIC **207 G3**
Yiddah, NSW **118 B5**
Yidney Scrub, QLD 259 D3
Yiki, SA **337 D2**
Yilliminnung, WA **404 D2**
Yin Barun, VIC **208 D4**
Yindi, WA **407 A3**
Yinkanie, SA **333 B2**
Yinnar, VIC **212 E3**
Yinnetharra, WA **400 D3**
Yirrkala, NT **434 D2**
Yiyili, WA **399 J4**
Yokine, WA 362 D2
Yolla, TAS **479 E4**
Yongala, SA **347 F5**
Yoogali, NSW **121 H1**
Yoongarillup, WA 371 D2
Yoorigan NP, NSW **119 K2**
York, WA 396, **402 D5**
York Plains, TAS **485 G1**
Yorketown, SA 338, **348 E2**
Yorkeys Knob, QLD **239 C3**
Yorkrakine, WA **402 E4**
Yorktown, TAS **480 D2**
Yornaning, WA **404 D2**
Yornup, WA **404 C4**
Yoting, WA **402 E5**
Youangarra, WA **403 F1**
Youanmi Downs, WA **403 F1**
Youanmite, VIC **208 C3**
Young, NSW 109, **122 B1**
Youngareen, NSW **118 A5**
Youngerina, NSW **112 E3**
Youngs, WA 369 B3, **404 E5**
Yowah, QLD **285 H5**
Yowergabbie, WA **400 E5**
Yowie Bay, NSW 49 G4
Yudnapinna, SA **346 D4**
Yuelamu, NT **439 F5**
Yuendumu (Police Stn), NT **438 E5**
Yugar, QLD 228 C6
Yuimmery, WA **401 F6**
Yuin, WA **400 D5**
Yukan, QLD **283 F3**
Yulara (Ayers Rock Resort), NT 422,
    423 A3, 430, **441 D4**
Yulcarley, NSW **112 E3**
Yuleba, QLD **286 E4**
Yullundry, NSW **118 D4**
Yuluma, NSW **121 J2**
Yumali, SA **349 G3**
Yuna, WA **400 C6**
Yundi, SA **337 D1**
Yungaburra, QLD 239 B5, 275, **279 J4**
Yungera, VIC **205 G4**
Yungundi, NSW **118 C2**
Yunnerman, QLD **286 C5**
Yunta, SA **347 G4**
Yuraraba, QLD **287 G5**
Yuraygir NP, NSW **115 J4**
Yuruga, QLD **279 J5**
Yuulong, VIC 200 E5, **211 G5**

Z

Zamia, QLD **282 D6**
Zanthus, WA **407 B3**
Zeehan, TAS 476, **483 B1**
Zenoni, QLD **285 G5**
Zetland NSW 49 H2
Zig Zag Railway, NSW 79, 80 D1
Zillmere, QLD **229 F6**
Zumstein, VIC 195 C2, **206 E5**

ACKNOWLEDGMENTS

This atlas was produced with the help of hundreds of regional and local tourist officers throughout Australia, whose kind assistance is gratefully acknowledged. The publisher would also like to thank the following organisations for their assistance:

Canberra Tourism and Events Corporation; Central Australian Tourism Industry Association; Department of Conservation and Land Management, Western Australia; Department of Indigenous Affairs, Western Australia; Environment Australia; National Parks and Wildlife, South Australia; New South Wales National Parks and Wildlife Service; Northern Land Council; Northern Territory Tourist Commission; Parks and Wildlife Commission of the Northern Territory; Parks Victoria; Queensland Parks and Wildlife Service; St John Ambulance Australia; South Australian Tourism Commission; Tasmanian Parks and Wildlife Service; Tourism New South Wales; Tourism Queensland; Tourism Tasmania; Tourism Top End; Tourism Victoria; Western Australian Tourism Commission

The publisher would like to thank the following individuals and organisations for their generosity in supplying photographs and images, and for their permission to reproduce photographic material used in this book.

Joe Armao/The Age: p.149 (T)
Bill Belson/Lochman Transparencies: p.367
Peter Brennan: p.106 (T)
W E Brown: p.450 (T)
Canberra Tourism and Events Corporation: pp.126 (T), 127 (T and B), 131, 136
Coolangatta Estate: p.96 (T)
Gregory's Automotive Products: pp.20 (B), 21 (T)
Geoff Higgins/Photography E-Biz: pp.4 (1,2), 5 (2,3,4,5), 6 (1,2), 10 (T and B), 11 (T), 12 (B), 13 (B), 14 (B), 15 (T), 19, 20 (T), 21 (B), 22, 23, 25 (T and B), 28 (T and B), 29 (B), 32 (T and B), 34-35, 36 (T and B), 38, 39, 42 (T and B), 51, 55, 57, 61, 63, 65, 67, 69, 70 (T and B), 72, 74, 79 (T), 83, 85, 92, 93, 98, 101, 102, 106 (B), 123, 124-125, 126 (B), 128 (B), 130, 133, 134 (T and B), 140 (T and B), 141, 143, 146 (B), 155, 158 (T), 159, 160, 161, 166, 180, 184, 189, 190, 196, 198, 199 (B), 202, 215, 219, 221 (B), 240, 245, 251, 252, 256, 257, 264, 266 (T and B), 268, 274, 288-289, 290 (T and B), 291, 292, 293 (T), 295, 296 (B), 298, 299, 305, 306, 307, 308, 309, 310, 311, 312, 315, 316, 320, 322, 324, 325, 326 (T and B), 328, 329, 330, 331, 332, 334, 335, 336, 338, 339, 350-351, 352 (T and B), 353, 355 (T), 356 (T and B), 358 (T and B), 360, 361, 366, 368, 369, 370 (T and B), 372, 373, 376, 377, 378, 380, 381, 382, 383, 384, 388, 389, 390, 391, 392, 396, 397, 408-409, 410 (T), 411, 412, 413, 416 (T and B), 420, 422 (T and B), 423, 426, 428, 430, 431, 444-445, 446 (T and B), 447, 448, 449, 452 (T and B), 454, 458, 459, 461, 462, 463, 464, 465, 466, 467, 468 (T and B), 470, 471, 472 (T), 474, 475, 476, 477
Houghton Winery: p.357
Wade Hughes/Lochman Transparencies: p.374 (T)
Hunter Regional Tourism Organisation: pp.40, 58 (B), 90 (T), 94
Darran Leal Publishing and Photography Pty Ltd: pp.14 (T), 142, 220, 223 (T), 234 (T), 293 (B), 319, 354, 355 (B),
Jiri Lochman/Lochman Transparencies: p.374 (B)
Steve Lovegrove/Tasmanian Photo Library: pp.451, 460 (B)
Melbourne Aquarium: p.148
Grant Nichol: pp.15 (B), 33 (T), 45, 50, 52, 58 (T), 60, 64, 66, 68, 73, 75, 76 (B), 79 (B), 84, 86, 87, 88, 90 (B), 91, 96 (B), 99, 100, 103, 104, 108, 109, 132, 157, 163, 164 (B), 175, 178 (T), 188, 192, 197, 237, 254 (B), 261, 270 (T), 296 (T), 321, 386, 393, 394, 424, 472 (B)
Northern Territory Tourist Commission: pp.13 (T), 29 (T), 30 (T and B), 414 (T and B), 415 (T and B)
Orlando Wines: p.294
Dennis Sarson/Lochman Transparencies: p.385
Barry Silkstone/South Australian Tourism Commission: p.304
South Australian Tourism Commission: pp.314, 318, 333
Len Stewart/Lochman Transparencies: p.387
The Mercury, Hobart: p.455
Tourism New South Wales: pp.37, 41, 53, 54, 56, 76 (T), 78, 89, 105
Tourism Queensland: pp.3, 5 (1), 6 (3), 11 (B), 24, 31, 33 (B), 216-217, 218 (T and B), 221 (T), 222, 223 (B), 224 (T and B), 226, 227, 232, 233, 234 (B), 235, 236, 238, 241, 242, 243, 244, 246 (T and B), 248, 249, 250, 253, 254(T), 258 (T and B), 260, 262 (T and B), 265, 269, 270 (B), 272, 273, 275
Tourism Victoria: pp.4 (3), 12 (T), 138-139, 144, 145, 149 (B), 154, 156, 158 (B), 162, 164 (T), 167, 168, 169, 170 (T and B), 172, 173, 174, 176 (T and B), 177, 178 (B), 181, 182, 183, 185, 186 (T and B), 191, 193, 194 (T and B), 199 (T),
Victorian Arts Centre: p.146 (T)
Viewfinder Library: pp.44, 82
Dave Watts: pp.16 (T and B), 450 (B), 460 (T)
Dave Watts/Nature Focus: p.17

Cover Pics
Front Cover: Red sand dune, Outback Queensland **(Tourism Queensland)**
Back Cover: Scuba diving, Great Barrier Reef, Queensland **(Tourism Queensland)**
Title Page: Four wheel driving, Cape Tribulation NP, Tropical North Queensland **(Tourism Queensland)**